The Five Basic Human Sexual Needs

- **Physical Needs**
  The biological aspects of human sexuality, including anatomy and physiology, sexual arousal and response, sexual health, conception, pregnancy, and birth

- **Social Needs**
  The social aspects of human sexuality, including social control of sexuality, sexual behavior across the life span, sex and gender, sexual orientation, consensual sexual behavior, sexual coercion, and commercialization

- **Emotional Needs**
  The feelings associated with sex and love: joy, anxiety, anger, and sadness

- **Spiritual Needs**
  The relationships among sexuality, spirituality, and religion and the effects on sexual attitudes and behaviors

- **Cognitive Needs**
  The ways in which you and others think about sexual identity and behavior, including coverage of sexual politics, and legal issues

Each of the five basic needs will be highlighted by a specific color so that the reader will know which need is being emphasized in a respective chapter.

Human Sexuality

MEETING YOUR BASIC NEEDS

TINA S. MIRACLE **ANDREW W. MIRACLE** **ROY F. BAUMEISTER**

Prentice
Hall

Upper Saddle River, New Jersey 07458

Library of Congress Cataloging–in–Publication Data

Miracle, Tina S.
    Human sexuality: meeting your basic needs / Tina S. Miracle, Andrew W. Miracle, Roy F. Baumeister.
        p. cm.
    Includes bibliographical references.
    ISBN 0-13-032658-5
    1. Sex instruction. 2. Sex. 3. Sex (Psychology) 4. Hygiene, Sexual. 5. Birth control. 6. Sexual disorders.
    I. Miracle, Andrew W. II. Baumeister, Roy F. III. Title.

HQ31 .M655 2002
306.7—dc21   2001060266

Senior Acquisitions Editor: Jayme Heffler
Associate Editor in Chief, Development:
    Rochelle Diogenes
Development Editor: Karen Trost
VP/Director of Production
    and Manufacturing: Barbara Kittle
Senior Managing Editor: Mary Rottino
Production Editor: Kathleen Sleys
Production Assistant: Elizabeth Best
Prepress and Manufacturing Manager:
    Nick Sklitsis
Prepress and Manufacturing Buyer: Tricia Kenny
AVP/Director of Marketing: Beth Mejia
Executive Marketing Manager: Sheryl Adams
Marketing Manager: Jeff Hester
Marketing Assistant: Ron Fox

Creative Design Director: Leslie Osher
Art Director: Nancy Wells
Interior Designer and Cover Designer:
    Laura Gardner
Director, Image Resource Center: Melinda Reo
Image Specialist: Beth Boyd
Manager, Rights and Permission: Kay Dellosa
Image Permissions Coordinator:
    Michelina Viscusi
Photo Researcher: Diana Gongora
Line Art Manager: Guy Ruggiero
Illustrations: Mirella Signoretto; Precision
    Graphics; Medical and Scientific
    Illustration; Steve Mannion
Permissions Researcher: Lisa Black

This book was set in 10/12 Janson Text by TSI Graphics
and was printed and bound by R. R. Donnelley and Sons / Willard
Covers were printed by Phoenix Color Corp.

For permission to use copyrighted material, grateful
acknowledgment is made to the copyright holders listed
on page 649, which is considered an extension of this
copyright page.

© 2003 by Pearson Education, Inc.
Upper Saddle River, New Jersey 07458

Printed in the United States of America
10 9 8 7 6 5 4 3 2 1

ISBN 0-13-032658-5

Pearson Education LTD., *London*
Pearson Education Australia Pty. Limited, *Sydney*
Pearson Education Pte. Ltd., *Singapore*
Pearson Education North Asia Pte. Ltd., *Hong Kong*
Pearson Education Canada Inc., *Toronto*
Pearson Education de Mexico, S.A. de C.V.
Pearson Education—Japan, Inc. *Tokyo*
Pearson Education Malaysia, Pte. Ltd
Pearson Education, Upper Saddle River, New Jersey

*To our children, Rebekah Miracle,
Jed Miracle and Athena Baumeister*

Brief Contents

Chapter

Contents

Chapter 6

Contraception and Abortion 166

Chapter 14

Chapter 15

Box Contents

Preface

We all know that the Human Sexuality course is one of the most popular courses on campus. Why? Let's face it, most people have an interest in sex and want to know what this course is all about. When you think of human sexuality, what comes to mind? You might think about the physical act of sex, romance, relationships, childrearing, contraception, or love, just to name a few. We hope to demonstrate that human sexuality encompasses a wide range of feelings, behaviors, attitudes and thought-processes. Human sexuality consists of far more than the obvious **physical** responses involved. **Social** interaction, **emotional** commitment, **spiritual** contemplation, and **cognitive** decision-making are all involved. Our goal in writing *Human Sexuality: Meeting Your Basic Needs* is to provide the student with information concerning these five human needs in a style that is clear, readable and useful, both for their present studies and as a foundation for future decision-making. Organizing the information in this way helps readers gain a greater understanding of the subject matter as well as take a more proactive approach to their sexuality.

As you embark upon your journey through *Human Sexuality: Meeting Your Basic Needs,* you will see how we consistently emphasize the connections among these five dimensions of sexuality. Our goal in creating this organization, is to ensure that the reader gain the greatest understanding of sexuality and have the ability to apply it to his or her own personal life. While most students have an intrinsic interest in sex, this interest may not survive a dull recitation of data and statistics. Our conceptual framework personalizes the subject matter and makes it more compelling, meeting the challenge of presenting information in a way that is neither too simplified and patronizing, nor overly technical and inaccessible. This style of presentation provides instructors maximum flexibility in promoting student curiosity and imagination. We challenge students' preconceptions, stimulate their intellects, and promote responsible sexual decision-making.

DIVERSITY

Throughout the text we have maintained a nonjudgmental perspective sensitive to the wide range of cultures, beliefs, values, and attitudes that exist in the world today. Gay, lesbian, and bisexual issues are discussed in Chapter 11, "Sexual Orientation," and are also integrated throughout the text. Abstinence is presented as a viable option in the discussion of sexual behaviors and sexual decision making. Sexuality is considered from a multicultural perspective. The text also reflects the diversity of ethnic backgrounds, socioeconomic status, and spiritual beliefs of its readers and the societies in which they live.

COMMUNICATION

Because communication is such an essential aspect of human sexuality, we have included this topic in appropriate areas throughout the text. In Chapter 2, for example, a box entitled "There Are No Stupid Questions" describes how to talk with your physician about cancer care. Chapter 7 includes a figure entitled "How We Talk About AIDS." Chapter 10 discusses gender differences in communication and online gender identity. Chapter 13 emphasizes communication as a tool for avoiding unwanted sexual advances. Chapter 15 features a section on intimacy, love, and sexual communication that covers both verbal and nonverbal communication. Chapter 19 includes a box on talking to your children about sex.

THE IMPACT OF TECHNOLOGY

Throughout history, but especially in the past several decades, advances in technology have had a major impact on all areas of life, including sexuality. The text addresses the growing importance of the global virtual society created by the Internet in features entitled "Exploring Sexuality Online." In addition, suggested Web sites related to the content of each chapter are included on the Web site for this text, www.prenhall.com/miracle.

SEXUAL HEALTH

Human Sexuality: Meeting Your Basic Needs emphasizes the importance of a proactive approach to sexual health in today's world. We intend to provide students with the best, most comprehensive information to help them safeguard their sexual and reproductive health. There is extensive discussion of health-related topics, including HIV/AIDS and other sexually transmitted infections (STIs), the various forms of contraception, sexuality and disabilities, and disorders of the reproductive tract. The discussion on contraceptives cover their effectiveness (including protection against STIs), advantages, disadvantages, and the cost concerns for each type. You will find *"Sexual Health and You"* boxes throughout the text.

THE EVOLUTIONARY PERSPECTIVE

The evolutionary perspective, drawn from Charles Darwin's theory of evolution, has become increasingly important in recent decades in explaining sexuality and sexual behavior. We integrate this important view throughout the text to explain various aspects of human sexuality and sexual behavior. In Chapter 1, the ability of species to adapt to their environment is used to explain why sex exists and why there are two human sexes (rather than one or ten). In Chapter 3, we use this perspective to explain the continuous nature of the female sexual response and the existence of female orgasm. In Chapter 8, the evolutionary perspective helps explain the cultural suppression of female sexuality and why society restricts sex between close relatives. Chapter 10 cites the evolutionary perspective in discussing physical differences between men and women and gender differences in promiscuity. In Chapters 11, 13, 14, and 16 the evolutionary perspective is one of several used to describe the basis of sexual orientation, sexual coercion, prostitution, and jealousy, respectively. Chapter 15 relates the evolutionary adaptiveness of our species to sexual attraction, female beauty as an external cue of childbearing ability, advantages of committed relationships, and gender differences in love.

CONTENTS

Text is organized around the five categories of human needs: physical, social, emotional, spiritual, and cognitive.

Chapter 1 provides an overview of human sexuality as well as an introduction to the five basic needs. Descriptions of different types of sex research are accompanied by real examples, along with information on how to evaluate research studies. This chapter also introduces the various theoretical perspectives on human sexuality, including psychoanalytic theory, social constructionism, feminist theory, the evolutionary theory,

and social exchange theory. We return to these perspectives throughout the text to help students understand the topics presented.

Chapters 2 through 7 provide students with a solid foundation for understanding their *physical* needs. The biological factors affecting human sexuality are presented, including anatomy and physiology, sexual arousal and response, sexual dysfunctions, and conception, pregnancy, and birth. Practical information concerning birth control and sexually transmitted infections is also provided.

Building on an understanding of the biological aspects of sexuality, Chapters 8 through 14 explore its *social* aspects. Social control of sexuality, sexual behavior across the life span, sex and gender, sexual orientation, consensual sexual behavior, sexual coercion, and the commercialization of sex are the subjects of these chapters. Topics of concern to many students, including sexual harassment, date rape, and atypical sexuality, are discussed in depth.

The feelings of joy, sadness, anger, and anxiety that can be associated with sex and love are examined in Chapters 15 and 16. The topics sexual attraction, romance, passion, jealousy, and intimate relationships allow students to explore the *emotional* aspects of sexuality.

The effect of *spirituality* on sexual attitudes and behaviors is examined in Chapter 17, which describes the relationships among sexuality, spirituality, and religion. The chapter also reviews the attitudes of a number of world religions toward sexuality and sexual behavior.

The final section of the text addresses the *cognitive* aspect of sexuality. Chapter 18 offers comprehensive coverage of sexual politics and legal issues, including the controversial subject of abortion. Chapter 19 describes how, when, and by whom sexuality is taught to our children. Chapter 20 helps students navigate the ethical decision-making process and make sexual choices.

SPECIAL FEATURES

Every chapter contains features to highlight important issues in sexuality.

Considerations

This feature encourages further student thought and discussion on complex and controversial issues such as sexual harassment, female genital mutilation, human cloning, and abortion. Each box includes one or more critical thinking questions designed to encourage students to form their own conclusions.

Cross-Cultural Perspectives

Cultural and ethnic variations that reflect the diversity of human sexual behavior are highlighted here. Topics include folk remedies for sexually transmitted infections, cross-cultural variations in scent preferences and standards of beauty, and cultural variations in the frequency and duration of noncoital sexual activity (foreplay).

Sexual Health and You

The ways in which students can ensure their sexual health, including breast and testicular self-examinations, gynecological and rectal exams, and knowing what to do if they've been raped are highlighted here.

Exploring Sexuality Online

This feature investigates the impact of computers and the Internet on issues related to sexuality, such as online sexual therapy, cyberromance, online pornography, and Internet pedophiles.

Ask Yourself

The *Ask Yourself* feature is a self-assessment inventory included in pertinent chapters so students can evaluate and reflect on their own beliefs and experiences. *Ask Yourself* in Chapter 1 tests students on what they think they already know about sexuality. Topics in later chapters include abortion and sexual values.

Frequently Asked Questions (FAQs)

Frequently asked questions (FAQs) are scattered throughout the text to catch the students' eye and pique their interest in what they are about to learn. These offer an active learning experience by maintaining a continuing dialogue with the student.

Marginal Quotations

Quotations from academic sources (for example, Sigmund Freud) and nonacademic sources (for example, Robin Williams, Bill Clinton, Shakespeare) are included in the margins to reinforce the information presented in the text.

Campus Confidential

Another marginal feature, *Campus Confidential*, consists of students' personal reflections. These are taken from the authors' files, with minor revisions to preserve anonymity. Topics include the decision to remain a virgin, sexual attraction as a basis for a relationship, and the revelation that a close friend is gay.

SUPPLEMENT PROGRAM
Companion Website

An extensive, dynamic Web site has been created by Sandra Caron, the University of Maine at Orono, to provide ongoing, up-to-date support for this textbook. Log on to www.prenhall.com/miracle and explore a wealth of web resources to increase your understanding of issues related to sexuality and healthy decision making. Students have access to the free online study guide, which includes outlines for each chapter; labeling exercises; and multiple choice, fill-in-the-blank, and essay questions for each chapter. Students will have access to information on sexual health and issues relating to sexuality on the world wide web. An Interactive Student Survey Module enables students to learn more about their personal views and attitudes.

INSTRUCTOR SUPPLEMENTS
Instructor's Manual

Prepared by Stephanie Chisolm, James Madison University, this supplement provides resources for each chapter of the text: summary, review of major concepts, lecture

suggestions and topic outlines, suggestions for classroom discussions, and additional resource materials.

Test Item File

Prepared by Carol Galletly, Ohio State University. This test item file contains over 2,000 questions in multiple choice, true/false, and essay format, covering factual, conceptual, and applied material from the text.

Prentice Hall Custom Test

This computerized version of the test item file, available in both IBM and Macintosh formats, allows full editing of questions and the addition of instructor-generated items. Other special features include random generation, scrambling question order, and test preview before printing.

Power Point Presentation Slides

The power points available for this text include charts and graphs from the text, along with lecture outlines tied to each chapter. They are available on the Web site, www.prenhall.com/miracle.

Distance Learning Solutions

For instructors interested in distance learning, Prentice Hall offers courses in Blackboard. See your local Prentice Hall representative or visit our special demonstration at *www.prenhall.com* for more information.

Films for the Arts and Humanities

With a qualifying order, films in the discipline of psychology are available. Please contact your local representative for a complete listing.

ACKNOWLEDGMENTS

We would like to express our thanks to the Prentice Hall editorial team, including Laura Pearson, Vice President and Editorial Director, and Jayme Heffler, Senior Acquisitions Editor, for their continuing enthusiasm and support for our pursuit of innovation and excellence in this project. Special thanks to Jayme for putting Roy together with Tina and Andy and creating a highly effective team of authors. We also appreciate the early support of Paige Atkins, the sales representative who encouraged us to talk with the Prentice Hall team.

The authors and the production team have shared day-to-day work on the book, especially in the latter stages. Karen Trost, Development Editor, helped to weave three voices into one. Production editor Kathy Sleys worked closely with us through the entire production process and pushed us to insure that the book met the tight production schedule. Mary Rottino, Managing Editor supervised the production process. Theresa Herbst was responsible for getting the virtual tour of the book up and running on the Web site. Many thanks to the extremely capable marketing team that

includes Sheryl Adams, Executive Marketing Manager, Jeff Hester, Marketing Manager, and Ron Fox, Marketing Assistant.

We are most appreciative for the fabulous design of this text. The design team included Laura Gardner, Designer, Nancy Wells, Design Director, and Guy Ruggiero, Line Are Manager.

The authors also wish to thank our colleagues who made *Human Sexuality* pedagogically complete. Sandra Caron has produced a great Web site that will assist students and instructors. Stephanie Chisolm has created an Instructors Manual that will facilitate learning as well as classroom instruction. And, Carol Galletly has developed a helpful test bank.

Finally, we wish to thank all of the reviewers—whose suggestions of draft chapters contributed substantially to the final product.

Judi Addelston	Valencia Community College
Sandra L. Caron	University of Maine
Stephanie Chisolm	James Madison University
Steve L. Ellyson	Youngstown State University
Patricia Fetter	Northeastern University
Suzanne G. Frayser	Colorado College
Carol Galletly	Ohio State University
Scott Hershberger	California State University at Long Beach
Larry Lance	The University of North Carolina at Charlotte
Donald Maltosz	California State University at Fresno
Frank Muscarella	Barry University
Paul Sargent	San Diego State University
John W. Sherman	Erie Community College North
K. David Skinner	Barry University
S. Lee Spencer	Arizona State University
Ellen Williams	Mesa Community College

We hope that you will find the textbook, Web site, and supplementary materials useful. Our fervent goal is to provide the best, most up-to-date information to teach students about sexuality and fulfill their individual needs. We welcome your comments and suggestions. Please contact us via e-mail.

Tina S. Miracle
University of Miami
School of Medicine
tmiracle@med.miami.edu

Andrew W. Miracle
Florida International University
miraclea@fiu.edu

Roy F. Baumeister
Case Western Reserve University
Rfb2@cwru.edu

TINA AND ANDY MIRACLE   Had we read the research in Chapter 15 before we got married more than three decades ago, this book might not have been written. We got engaged after two dates, and did not have proximity, familiarity, or similarity going for us; luckily, there was plenty of readiness and reciprocity.

Proximity was a definite problem since Andy spent most of our year-long engagement period living in Tarija, Bolivia doing community development work, while Tina was going to school and working in New York. Two dates is hardly adequate time for much familiarity, and dissimilarities abounded given our different religious and cultural backgrounds. However, over the years we have each learned to compromise and to trust one another. The result is that as individuals we both feel that the costs of occasional inconveniences are greatly outweighed by the continuing benefits of the relationship (see social exchange theory in Chapter 1). In non-scientific terms, after more than 30 years of marriage we still love each other and while sometimes we're not sure we want to spend the next hour together, we know we want to spend the rest of our lives together.

Over the years, we have heard every possible comment on our last name, and also managed successfully to merge our personal and professional lives. Tina began her undergraduate degree in English at Chatham College, and completed her B.A. as well as her master's and a specialist's degree (Ed.S.) in counseling at the University of Florida. An undergraduate religion major at Princeton University, Andy received a master's degree in Latin American Studies and his Ph.D. in Anthropology at the University of Florida. With then three-year-old daughter Rebekah and newborn son Jed, we spent a year in La Paz, Bolivia while Andy completed his dissertation research among the Bolivian Aymara with the assistance of a Fulbright-Hays award and a grant from the National Institute of Mental Health.

As a cultural anthropologist, Andy not only enjoys teaching but he has published extensively, including ten books in the fields of anthropology and education, sports sociology, culture and health, and human sexuality. He began his academic career at Texas Christian University in 1976, was chair of the Department of Health Sciences at Cleveland State University for four years, and currently is Associate dean of the College of Health and Urban Affairs and Professor of Public Health at Florida International University. Andy is past president of both the Southern Anthropological Society and The Association for the Study of Play.

For the first twenty years of Tina's career as a psychotherapist, she worked primarily with survivors of sexual abuse and assault as clinical director at a residential treatment center for emotionally disturbed children, in private practice, and at a rape crisis center. She is a licensed professional clinical counselor and a member of the American Association of Sex Educators, Counselors and Therapists. When a retinal disease resulted in Tina becoming severely visually impaired, she began working with blind and visually impaired children and their families at the Cleveland Sight Center, and currently she is a research and clinic coordinator at the Bascom Palmer Eye Institute at the University of Miami School of Medicine.

Together, Tina and Andy frequently give lectures and workshops on issues related to human sexuality.

ROY F. BAUMEISTER

You might think that no one would have to explain how he or she became interested in sex. After all, everyone is interested in sex, right? And yet relatively few people in my field of social psychology actually study sex.

When I finished high school, I chose to attend Princeton because it was reputed to have the best mathematics department in the country, and I intended to become a mathematician. A couple semesters of higher mathematics soon persuaded me, however, that I wanted something with more intrinsic interest and more relevance to the central aspects of human life. My next choice was philosophy, because I thought it would enable me to grapple with the grand, ultimate questions about the human condition. Unfortunately, most philosphers these days have to choose narrow rather than grand questions, and moreover there are not many jobs for them. While reading moral philosophy, I came across some of Freud's writings and was struck by one astonishing fact: He was trying to decide which ideas were right by using scientific observations. I began to realize that psychologists could tackle great questions and they even had the scientific method to help them find the right answers.

In graduate school at Duke and again at Princeton, I learned how to conduct laboratory experiments. Issues of self and identity were first gaining recognition as important keys to life, and so my early work explored issues of self-esteem, public constraints on identity, and what happens when people focus attention on themselves. Although I continue to find such work satisfying, I became chagrined at the narrow focus that one had to keep.

A crucial step in my career occurred when I found that one could tackle broad questions by pulling together the results of many different studies. A single experiment had to focus on something narrow, but by combining many different findings one could begin to see the big picture. To me, this was the key for how to go back to addressing the broad philosophical questions that fascinated me. Some of my book titles reflect these efforts: *Meanings of Life, Evil:Inside Human Violence and Cruelty, Identity: Cultural Change and the Struggle for Self.*

To me, sex is another one of the grand mysteries of life, and so it was a natural topic to pick up when I had finished my work on evil and violence and was looking for something new and interesting. For the book on evil, I had had to immerse myself in reading about a great many terrible things that people have done to one another, and the idea of moving on to study sex was appealing because it promised a chance to focus on a more pleasant, positive aspect of human nature.

Roy F. Baumeister received his Ph.D. in social psychology from Princeton University and had a postdoctoral fellowship in sociology at the University of California at Berkeley. In 1979 he joined the faculty of Case Western Reserve University as an assistant professor and rose through the ranks, becoming at one point the youngest full professor at the university. He now holds the E.B. Smith Professorship in the Liberal Arts there. He has also taught and done research at the University of Virginia, the University of Texas, the Max-Planck-Institute in Munich, Germany, and at the Center for Advanced Study in the Behavioral Sciences at Stanford University. He has published nearly 250 scientific works including 14 books.

Human Sexuality

CHAPTER 1

Finding Your Way in a Diverse World

- **Human Sexuality and Basic Needs**
  Your basic sexual needs can be classified as physical, social, emotional, spiritual, and cognitive.

- **Meeting Your Needs**
  Understanding sexuality is essential to the individual, personal process of meeting your needs.

- **Sexuality and Human Diversity**
  We can increase our understanding of others by learning about how people relate to each other sexually in other cultures and within our own increasingly diverse society.

- **Sex Research**
  Knowledge about research on the physiology and psychology of sexuality can be a foundation for personal decision making.

- **Theoretical Perspectives on Sexuality**
  Some of the various perspectives on sexuality include the psychoanalytic, social, constructionist, feminist, evolutionary, and social exchange theories.

PHYSICAL

SOCIAL

EMOTIONAL

SPIRITUAL

COGNITIVE

HUMAN SEXUALITY AND BASIC NEEDS

Sex. Quickly jot down some of the feelings, thoughts, and images this word evokes for you. Is it the memory of a past experience, thoughts of a current relationship, or fantasies about future encounters? The responses by you and your classmates will more than likely vary widely, but rarely do we draw a blank on this subject. Whether your reaction is excitement, concern, or moral outrage, few of us are neutral about the topic of sex, the biology of maleness and femaleness, and the ability to experience and express sexual feelings.

Unfortunately, much of what we read and hear about sexuality today is sobering or frightening. The devastation of AIDS, the abortion battlefield, adolescent pregnancies, child sexual abuse, rape, and hate crimes against those who are sexually different may make sex seem more risky than joyful. While these problems are real and should not be ignored, the pleasures and benefits of sexuality also should be appreciated as a natural extension of other aspects of our lives. It is as important to be knowledgeable about sexual risks as it is to be knowledgeable about ways to enhance your sexual pleasure.

People express their sexuality in many different ways. We have the capacity for reproduction, the potential for erotic experiences, and the need for love and personal fulfillment. In this text, we have chosen to explore the complexity of human sexuality in relation to basic human needs in five different categories:

- Physical Needs: anatomy and physiology of your sexual organs (Part One)
- Social Needs: your sexual interactions with others (Part Two)
- Emotional Needs: your personal responses to sexual experiences (Part Three)
- Spiritual Needs: the meaning that sexuality imparts to your life (Part Four)
- Cognitive Needs: the ways in which you and others think about sexual identity and behavior (Part Five)

If you are sexually active, is it principally to answer the physical urge to procreate, to solidify a social relationship, to meet an emotional need to feel desirable, to experience spiritual fulfillment, or to cognitively explore your sexuality? If you are not sexually active, is it primarily because of the physical concern that you might contract a disease? Are your social and emotional needs met without sex? Do your personal values and ethics prohibit a sexual relationship at this time in your life? Have you consciously considered whether abstinence meets your sexual needs? These questions illustrate some of the ways that these five basic human needs, the organizing principle of this text, influence individual sexual behavior (see CONSIDERATIONS Box).

As you will learn, there is tremendous overlap in these categories (Figure 1.1). For example, the physical act of **conception** also involves society's need to have cohesive family units, religious beliefs about **procreation,** and an emotional need for **intimacy.** A sexual problem may have a physical basis, be part of a couple's relationship conflict,

> **❝**[D]anger and fear, exultation and ecstasy, [and] good and evil . . . converge within the sexual arena: they comprise a small sample of the meaning with which humans endow their sexual experiences **❞**
>
> (FRAYSER, 1985, P. 1).

Conception: the union of sperm and ovum

Procreation: the act of reproduction

Intimacy: a close, affectionate, usually loving relationship

3

Which Need Is Being Met?

CONSIDERATIONS

In the movie *Indecent Proposal*, Demi Moore's character, Diana, is a young, happily married yet financially strapped woman who is offered a million dollars in exchange for one night of sex with a stranger. Diana says to her husband, "This is my body, not my mind, not my heart."

 When Diana decides to go ahead with the deal, which of the needs we have described is she expecting to meet?

—*Do you think it is possible to separate your body from your heart, or your mind?*
—*Would you do what Diana did? Why or why not?*

and/or be a sign of an individual's psychological distress. Sexual orientation may be influenced by biology as well as be an important part of one's social identity, meet emotional and spiritual needs, and have legal and political ramifications. Abortion is a physical procedure that can have tremendous social, emotional, spiritual, and cognitive consequences. It is in exploring the interactions of these needs that you may gain the greatest understanding of human sexual behavior.

The predominance of sexual reproduction in the reproductive world is especially remarkable when you consider the costs of sex. The biological costs of sexual reproduction include the expenditure of energy and the mixing of one's **genes,** hereditary information that is transferred from cell to cell, with those of another organism (who might not be as well endowed genetically). Social costs include wasted resources and social conflict as well as the difficulty in finding the right person with whom to mate. Emotionally, sex can cost us as we deal with our sexual fears, anxieties, and worries. Sex can take a spiritual toll as we attempt to reconcile our behavior with our values. And the cognitive costs of sexual decision-making occupy a great deal of our political, legal, educational, and personal agendas.

In theory, human beings might have evolved so that each adult could simply clone itself to produce a baby, without involving another person. At the opposite extreme, we might have evolved so that seven or eight different sex categories were required for the process of sexual reproduction. Why did our species (and so many others) settle on sexual reproduction that involves two sexes?

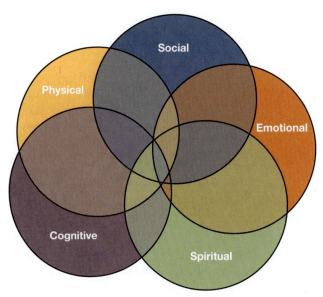

FIGURE 1.1 Five Categories of Sexual Need.

From an evolutionary perspective, the answer to this paradox is that sex makes reproduction a dynamic process that greatly increases the ability of a species to adapt to new and different surroundings. Asexual reproduction produces an identical copy of an organism, and so generation after generation has exactly the same genetic blueprint. The organism may be well suited to the present environment, but if the environment changes or a new one is encountered, the asexual species cannot change to adapt to it, whereas sexual species can easily change. Nearly all species that use asexual reproduction (like the well-manicured suburban lawn in our earlier example) are relatively recent arrivals on the planet; sexual species go back much farther (Gould & Gould, 1997). Scientists speculate that asexual species have emerged throughout the history of the earth, only to die out when conditions such as climate underwent dramatic change.

What accounts for this superior ability to withstand change? Each baby produced by sexual reproduction is a unique mixture of the genes of the two parents. Even if a man and woman have a dozen children, each child will be slightly different from the others in its genetic makeup (except for identical twins, of course). If war or famine forces the family to move to a new environment with a different climate, one child will likely possess a combination of genes that will be better suited to the new environment than the others. For example, the parents might produce one child whose body sheds heat easily and another child that retains heat for a long time. If they move to a hot climate, the first one will do better, but the second one will be better suited to a colder climate.

Biologists have less to say about the possibility of multiple sex categories. Although the greater genetic variability may appear to be an advantage, it may simply be that the various costs and obstacles rise exponentially with each new partner required. In plainer terms, it is hard enough for one man and one woman to come to an understanding that will allow them to create and raise babies—you can imagine that it might be almost impossible among six different kinds of adults! The greater the number of obstacles to reproduction, the less likely it is that the species will reproduce.

Sexual reproduction involving two sexes may be a kind of compromise between the efficiency of asexual reproduction and the genetic flexibility of a multiple-gender arrangement. Two are enough to create diversity but not so many that the process becomes prohibitively inefficient.

Physical Aspects of Human Sexuality

Sex may not be the most important thing in life, but since it is our means of reproducing, it is certainly the most important thing to life. The physical realm of sexuality includes the sexual organs of the human body (Figure 1.2) and the act of sexual reproduction that can create a new human life. Although sexuality involves far more than the "plumbing," biological and physical needs exert great influence on our lives.

Understanding the biology of human sexuality has both immediate and long-term benefits. For example, learning about your sexual organs and how they work, will help you to recognize any personal sexual dysfunction or problem. Information about the physical aspects of sex also can assist you in protecting your health against sexually transmitted infections (STIs) such as the human immunodeficiency virus (HIV) that causes acquired immunodeficiency syndrome (AIDS). Understanding the biology of conception is equally important to those who want to get pregnant and those who do not. Finally, by understanding the biological bases of sexual arousal, you can give and receive greater pleasure.

Social Aspects of Human Sexuality

To be human is to be social. Most of us live with, depend on, and care for other people throughout our lives. As you develop relationships you will find (or may already have found) that other people's desires and needs impact your own. A behavior that occurs with such frequency, one that has occurred throughout history and in all cultures, would be significant even if it were not responsible for maintaining the existence of the human race.

FAQ:

Why Does Sex Exist?

At first glance the answer to this question might seem obvious—"Sex is needed to produce babies." However, **sexual reproduction,** the process of creating new organisms by combining the genetic material of two or more parents, is not the only means of reproduction. Some species reproduce by **asexual reproduction,** a splitting into two equal halves or creating buds that develop into separate organisms.

It is even possible for sexual and asexual reproduction to exist side-by-side in the same species. The grass that grows in a typical suburban lawn or city park is a good example. Grass can reproduce sexually, but to do this it has to grow very long and create seeds (fertilized by contact with other grasses), which are then scattered by the wind and start new plants in the soil. Most grass is kept mowed and never grows long enough to produce seeds. So how does grass fill in bare spots in a lawn? The existing plants send out underground runners by asexual reproduction that produce new shoots.

Sexual Reproduction: the production of offspring from the union of two different organisms or parents

Asexual Reproduction: the production of offspring by a single organism or parent

Genes: the basic units of heredity that carry information about traits passed on from parent to offspring

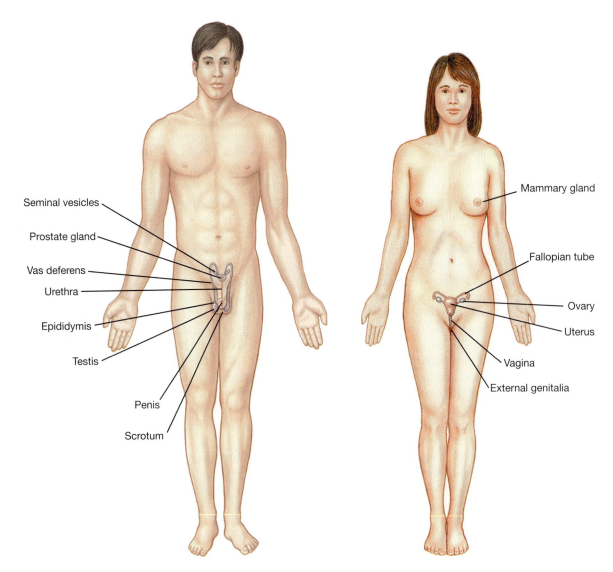

Seminal vesicles

Prostate gland

Vas deferens

Urethra

Epididymis

Testis

Penis

Scrotum

Mammary gland

Fallopian tube

Ovary

Uterus

Vagina

External genitalia

FIGURE 1.2 The Male and Female Reproductive Systems.

Despite the fact that the biology of sexuality is essentially the same for all human beings, as social creatures we each experience sexuality in our own way.

Society plays a significant role in shaping the sexuality of individuals. The study of different societies reveals that people experience sexuality in various ways despite the fact that the biology of sexuality is essentially the same for all human beings. In other words, although all humans share the same basic sexual organs, we don't respond to sexual stimuli in the same ways, and these responses are shaped by the society in which we live.

Some aspects of social knowledge influence the sexuality of an entire group, while other aspects have more limited effects. Gender identity, gender roles, the choice of sexual partners, and the power to enjoy or to misuse and abuse sex are important social factors that are perceived in different ways by different groups. Balancing individual rights with the rights of society is a constant and crucial challenge.

Emotional Aspects of Human Sexuality

Physical comfort alone is not sufficient to guarantee happiness; most of us require some degree of social interaction to feel emotionally fulfilled. Sex and sexual relationships can have a significant impact. Sexual relationships can make you glad, sad, mad, or scared—sometimes all at the same time. Experimenting with a new sexual behavior can result in feelings of excitement, fear, and/or guilt. Rejection by a sexual partner can lead to anger, sadness, and frustration.

Sex is associated with the full range of emotional responses. Knowing more about sexuality can improve your ability to deal with your own emotional responses and affect your ability to enjoy your sexuality. Developing an understanding of the emotional impact of sexuality can help you make decisions that can increase your personal happiness. For example, the belief that it is important to love the person you have sex with will influence your decision about when in a relationship to have sex. If you know that having sex is likely to make you feel guilty or anxious, you may choose to abstain from sexual activity. If you believe that sex is an important part of emotional intimacy, you may choose to have sex with a person who meets this emotional need rather than someone to whom you have a strong, strictly physical attraction.

Sex is associated with the full range of emotional responses.

Spiritual Aspects of Human Sexuality

The concept of spirituality is often associated with organized religion. However, in a broader sense, spirituality encompasses our values, ethics, and morality, as well as the personal qualities, ideas, and traditions that help give meaning to our lives. Regardless of the basis of your spirituality, understanding human sexuality will allow you to explore your values and priorities.

Nearly all religions have supported some set of moral rules about sex. A few religions, such as followers of Tantric practices, hold sex in such high esteem that they incorporate sexual practices into their sacred rituals. Other religions regard sex as a necessary evil and seek to stifle its expression as much as possible without preventing reproduction. The Shakers, a religious sect that emigrated to the United States in 1774, were so named because of the group's ecstatic form of worship. The Shakers emphasized simplicity and celibacy. The members lived in gender-segregated dormitory-like housing, and while they came together to work and to pray, celibacy was vital to their idea of a truly selfless and spiritual community (Horgan, 1982). Without children brought up in the faith, the Shakers could only survive as long as there was a steady stream of converts; needless to say, this religion has died out. Unfortunately, in various religions there have been many cases in which individuals have exploited their official positions to obtain sex from religious novices who trust them. For example, several Catholic priests have been convicted of child sexual abuse; and it has been reported that David Koresh, leader of the Branch Davidians, the religious sect that battled with the government in Waco, Texas, in 1993, had sexual relations with many of his followers.

Homo sapiens: the species of primates to which modern humans belong

Cognitive Aspects of Human Sexuality

Cognition is defined as the act or process of knowing. In other words, cognition is thinking. And which of your organs do you use to undergo this important task? Your brain! The brain/body ratio is larger in **Homo sapiens** than in any other species (Wallace, Sanders, & Ferl, 1996). We use our large brains to investigate, categorize, label, talk, and form ideas about all aspects of our lives and our environment, including sexuality. The more you know about sexuality, the better your understanding of the sexual issues that affect you as an individual and as a member of society. Accurate information is as essential in developing opinions on issues such as sex education, laws regarding sexuality, and the ongoing political debate about sexual issues as it is to your personal decisions about sex.

Regardless of your spiritual beliefs, understanding sexuality allows you to explore your values and priorities.

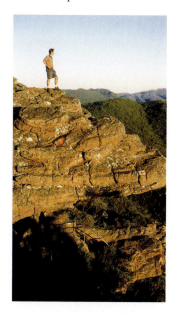

MEETING YOUR NEEDS

Because sexuality is a universal concern, you will be able to relate closely the information presented in this text to your personal experiences. Your specific needs are not exactly the same as anyone else's (see CAMPUS CONFIDENTIAL box); to complicate matters, your own needs change over the course of your lifetime. Physical needs may change because of health problems, aging, or the desire to have (or not have) children.

The more you know about sexuality, the better your cognitive understanding of the sexual issues.

Some of us need a great deal of social interaction, while others are content to spend much of their time alone. Emotional needs are in a constant state of flux. No two individuals will have the same exact emotional response to a given situation, and the same individual may react differently to a given situation at different times. People also have different spiritual and cognitive needs and different ways of fulfilling them.

We all have different sexual needs and different ways of getting these needs met. For example, a physical need for sexual release may be met by **masturbation, heterosexual** or **homosexual activity,** or taking the proverbial cold shower. Your ideal social life might include partying every night with a different person, or developing an intimate relationship with one individual. Perhaps your emotional needs are met by your relationships with your friends, your closeness to your family, or sexual intimacy with your partner. Your spiritual needs might best be met by lifelong celibacy, postponing sexual relationships until marriage, or the ecstatic pleasure of sex with a loving partner. Cognitive sexual needs might be fulfilled by increasing your knowledge about sexual issues, becoming politically active, or making thoughtful intuitive decisions about your sexuality. Only you can determine how to express and satisfy your various sexual needs. Inevitably you will be faced with new choices and opportunities. This text will help you to foresee the consequences and responsibilities that result from the decisions you make.

SEXUALITY AND HUMAN DIVERSITY

Cross-Cultural Perspectives

To distinguish the biological influences on sexuality from the cultural influences, we must analyze a culturally varied sample of peoples, not just Americans or Western Europeans. All peoples have sex but not always in the same ways, with the same beliefs, or for the same reasons. Keep in mind that while you may find the sexual beliefs and behaviors of some cultures to be bizarre, people in other cultures could be thinking the same thing about yours. Cross-cultural understanding can break through stereotypes and help us to appreciate sexual practices and attitudes that are outside our own experience.

Although we are all members of the same species, we speak different languages, live in different communities, and have different values. The widely held belief that "people are pretty much the same all over the world" ignores the influence of culture on our biology and promotes the erroneous notion that people throughout the world share the same sexual desires, values, and goals. In order to appreciate what we have in common with other cultures it is important to recognize and respect our differences.

Despite the occasional culture with highly unusual sexual practices, the sexual practices of most cultures are similar in many respects. You should certainly not expect to have a bizarre or wildly different experience simply because you go to bed with someone from a different cultural background. Knowledge of the similarities and the differences among cultures is a powerful tool in our quest to understand human sexuality. To help you gain this knowledge, throughout the text we have included boxes entitled "Cross-Cultural Perspectives," which include material that reflects the diversity of human sexual attitudes and behavior.

The Challenge of Diversity

There is no such thing as The American Way. The United States is an extremely diverse, multicultural society. Our members include the very rich, the very poor, and those with sufficient incomes. We live in urban, rural, and suburban environments. We speak many languages and have a wide range of traditions, racial backgrounds, and philosophical, religious, social, and political views. Our attitudes and beliefs about sexuality are just as diverse.

Masturbation: stimulation of the genitals for sexual pleasure by manual contact or means other than sexual intercourse

Heterosexual Activity: sexual relations with the opposite sex

Homosexual Activity: sexual relations with the same sex

Sexologist: sex researcher

Within U.S. society there are numerous identifiable subgroups. It is important to resist the temptation to make generalizations about the homogeneity of their sexual attitudes and beliefs as well. For example, it is unlikely that any two urban, middle-class, African American, college-educated, Protestant males will hold identical beliefs about sexuality. The same goes for any two suburban, upper-class, white, high-school-educated, Catholic females.

Paradoxically, diversity can be both a strength and a weakness. It can promote mutual tolerance and appreciation, but it can also create conflict and mistrust. An understanding of our differences can increase our tolerance of those with different beliefs and decrease our tendency to judge them as "right" or "wrong," "good" or "bad."

SEX RESEARCH

As you explore the path of risks and rewards related to your sexuality, accurate information is essential. There is an abundance of information and a wide variety of perspectives available; an understanding of current scientific research can provide useful guidelines for sexual decision making. Have you ever heard the myth that you can't get pregnant the first time you have intercourse? Imagine the consequences if you believed this to be true and acted on that belief! Most research that reaches the general public is reported in sound bytes or filtered by spin doctors. It is critical to examine the big picture before accepting information as truth.

Different studies on the same topic may come to different conclusions. You need to be able to discriminate between competing messages. For example, if one recent study concluded that sexual orientation results solely from environmental factors and socialization while another study found that sexual orientation is caused by biological factors alone, to compare these findings you would need to have an understanding of the research practices and methods used in each study.

Although different studies and different findings may be confusing, there really has been enormous progress toward a complete and accurate understanding of sexuality. Scientists make mistakes, but in the long run other scientists correct their mistakes. However, even as our understanding of human sexuality is enhanced, we need to remember that there are still errors and gaps remaining. Researchers are always looking to correct those errors and close those gaps with new studies. Researchers further scientific understanding by making a series of small contributions to advance the total amount of knowledge.

Sex research is important on a social level as well as a personal level. Human sexuality is inherently linked to many of the most important social concerns in the world today. Many public health crises, including sexually transmitted infections, family planning, sexual assault, and adolescent pregnancy, are related to human sexuality and how sexual attitudes, beliefs, and values contribute to these problems. Research can provide the basis for improved health care, effective social policies, and improvements in public perception. For example, research that increased awareness that HIV/AIDS is a disease with the potential to affect the general population resulted in a change in society-wide perceptions about AIDS being a "homosexual disease." Increased political activity to change health-care practices and legislation in turn increased funding for AIDS research.

There are those who look on sex research as a semirespectable form of pornography and think of **sexologists,** scientists who study human sexuality, as voyeurs. Sex research, which must compete with other scientific disciplines for funding, has become a political football, and some researchers prefer to avoid potentially controversial subjects. As a result "whole areas of study are left to marginal and politically invested researchers" (Tiefer, 1995, p. 179). However, we are slowly making progress. Gradually, over the past 50 years, there has been an increase in scholarly research resulting in a growing body of knowledge about human sexuality, reflecting the view that it is nearly always better for science to pursue the truth than to leave important areas of life shrouded in ignorance, superstition, and rumor. In the words of Paul Abramson, who

CAMPUS CONFIDENTIAL

"I guess I'm part of a silent minority—the college-aged virgin. Sean and I care about and are attracted to each other. We've come close, but haven't had intercourse and it's getting frustrating for both of us. If we don't have sex, I'm not sure that the relationship will go much further. But, if we do have sex, I'm worried about the possibility of diseases or pregnancy. It would be embarrassing to ask Sean about previous sexual partners and stuff. How would I know if he's telling me the truth anyway? If I bring a condom, will he think I do this all the time, or that I'm well prepared? What if he doesn't want to use it? Should I make him or just forget it? What if it hurts? Or I don't like it? Or I'm not good in bed? I have no idea what I'm doing. I've browsed through a few sex manuals—but some of the positions look like things only Olympic gymnasts could do; the rest just look silly. The missionary position looks easy—but do I really want the missionary seal of approval on my sex life? The idea of Sean seeing me naked really freaks me out . . . I don't know which I need more—to lose 10 pounds, or read the *Kama Sutra.*

I don't know why I'm making such a big deal out of this. Most of my friends are having sex and don't seem to regret it. But it is a big deal to me. I'm so confused. I don't know what to do." ●

The diversity of cultures within the United States makes it impossible to generalize about the sexual behavior, attitudes or beliefs.

served as editor of the *Journal of Sex Research* for many years, "future generations will find it incomprehensible—and perhaps unconscionably negligent—that so little effort was marshaled to obtain data on and establish a science of human sexual behavior" (1990, p. 162).

Ethical Concerns of Sex Research

Whatever the field of study, the **scientific method** of investigation involves (1) formulating a research question and (2) putting that question into the form of a hypothesis, a prediction about the expected research results. Then, the researchers (3) test the hypothesis and (4) draw conclusions about it based on an analysis of the results. Like all scientists, sex researchers are expected to question, predict, observe, describe, and explain the events being studied.

Because scientists are human, and thus subject to social and cultural influences, their personal values, attitudes, and assumptions about human sexuality must be considered to ensure that their conclusions are not distorted. Great care must be taken in formulating the questions asked to avoid biased results that favor one side, group, or person, rather than another, thereby inhibiting impartial judgment.

Generally the first rule for any research involving human subjects is to do no harm. Sexuality researchers must consider the protection of their subjects' rights to privacy, as well as their physical and psychological welfare. Researchers are obligated to demonstrate that the potential benefits of the proposed study outweigh possible risks to the participants. Because embarrassment can be interpreted as a form of psychological harm, there can be serious constraints on sex research.

Researchers are obligated to receive informed consent from their subjects before a study begins. **Informed consent** means that a researcher provides sufficient information about the proposed research for the potential subject to make an informed decision about whether or not to participate. Such information includes the nature and length of the study, how the results will be used, and how personal information will be protected. However, informed consent can be especially problematic in studies in which it is necessary to deceive subjects. For example, if subjects knew before a study began that it involved perceptions of physical attractiveness their responses might be influenced. In such cases the study may proceed if it is determined that the deception is necessary and unlikely to cause significant harm to participants. At the end of the experimental session, the researcher debriefs the participant, that is, explains to him or her the goals of the study and why the specific procedures were used. Any deceptions are normally explained at this time, so that no one leaves the experiment with a false idea about what transpired.

Confidentiality, keeping the identity and responses of a research study private, should be given top priority in sex research. No information should be released that identifies a study's participants. While it is sometimes necessary for a researcher to know a subject's name or other personal data, it is essential to prevent the inappropriate release of this information.

Research Methods

Sampling Techniques   No researcher can possibly survey, observe, or conduct laboratory experiments on the entire population. If you are conducting a study of adult female masturbation, obviously you could not individually question each and every woman in the world or even in your city. The size of the sample would be so large that the time and money required would make it impossible to collect and analyze the data. In addition, it is unlikely that you could get everyone to agree to take the survey or to give honest responses.

In order to deal with this problem, researchers select a **sample,** that is, a group from which results may be generalized to a larger population, called the **target popu-**

Scientific Method: a set of rules and procedures on how to study, observe, or conduct experiments

Informed Consent: agreement of participants in a research study that they understand the purpose, risks, and benefits of the study

Confidentiality: keeping the identity and responses of a research study private

Sample: the portion of a population selected for a study and from which research results may be generalized

Target Population: the larger population being studied, which the sample should represent

lation. The larger the sample the more likely it will represent characteristics of the target population. In order to be representative, a sample should closely match demographic variables, such as the age, sex, religion, education, ethnicity, and income level of the target population being studied.

In a **random sample,** everyone in the target population has an equal chance of being selected to participate in the study. In this approach, the resulting sample may or may not be representative of the larger population. For example, consider a carefully constructed national survey; one thousand or two thousand people are contacted and asked which candidate they favor in an upcoming presidential race. The pollsters hope to use the results of these few thousand individuals to predict the outcome of an election in which many millions of people will vote—and normally the polls are quite accurate. Calling every fifth phone number in your local telephone directory to ask their opinion on a topic would give you a random sample of people in your community who have listed telephone numbers but it excludes those who do not have telephones and those with unlisted numbers.

Sometimes researchers will choose to use a **stratified sample** in order to compare specific segments of the population. For example, if you wished to compare generational attitudes in the United States toward male and female masturbation, you would need a sufficient number of respondents in each of the designated age categories. Thus you might decide to stratify the sample to ensure the necessary age distribution so you could do the analysis with a high degree of confidence. You also might want to stratify by sex, race/ethnicity, educational level, religiosity, or some other variable. Using stratified sampling, you would interview only those individuals, selected at random, who met your criteria of inclusion. The percentage of respondents in each of these categories might not approximate the corresponding percentage of the U.S. population. However, the purpose of your study is to address generational differences, not the attitudes of the U.S. population as a whole, and your sample should be representative of the generations as you defined them.

Samples that are not representative of the larger group are known as **biased samples.** For example, if you were studying college students' attitudes toward lesbians it would be legitimate to select a sample from various college campuses. However, using this same sample to generalize about the attitudes of all Americans would be biased.

Interviews and Surveys Surveys are the most popular way to obtain research data about sexual attitudes and behaviors. A **survey** questioning a sample population about their behaviors or attitudes can be conducted face-to-face, by telephone, on the Internet, or by completing a pencil-and-paper questionnaire. A face-to-face personal **interview** involves more than just asking people questions about their sex lives. Interviewers are usually trained to explain the purpose of the research, to clarify questions, and to report accurately the participants' answers. One consideration that must be taken into account when designing a personal interview is possible interviewer or subject embarrassment about discussing sexual subjects face-to-face. The willingness to participate may be a source of sample bias, that is, the volunteers who agree to be interviewed may be more confident or open in dealing with sexuality than those who refuse to participate.

Because fewer people are needed, written surveys, or **questionnaires,** are more economical to conduct than interviews. Questionnaires may be sent through the mail or given directly to the subjects; in the latter case the study can be set up so that the subjects complete the questionnaire in the presence of the interviewer or in a location of the subject's choosing during a specified time period. The greater privacy and anonymity afforded by questionnaires may result in people answering the questions more honestly (Clement, 1990). However, as with the interview format, this research instrument depends upon accurate recall as well as honesty regarding sexual behavior. To complicate matters further, because sex is such a value-laden issue, some people may adjust their answers to appear more or less sexually experienced or knowledgeable. For example, in American society, men tend to exaggerate their sexual experience and

Random Sample: a sample drawn without bias from a population so that each individual has an equal chance of being selected

Stratified Sample: a sample drawn to ensure that specific subgroups of a population are adequately represented

Biased Sample: a sample that is not representative of the larger group

Survey: a research method in which subjects are interviewed or complete a questionnaire

Interview: a research method in which subjects are asked questions by an interviewer

Questionnaire: a method of research in which subjects are asked to respond to a list of written questions

Alfred Kinsey and his team of researchers used surveys in their pioneering research on human sexuality.

women to minimize their sexual activity (Havemann & Lehtinen, 1990). Other subjects may give the answers they think are expected, or may be reluctant to admit ignorance of terms used in a questionnaire. For example, a subject might not be familiar with the term *fellatio* and be reluctant to admit this. Questions must be phrased carefully and simply; different individuals can interpret a question such as "Are you sexually satisfied?" very differently. Questionnaire results included in magazines and on Internet sites often are reported without their inherent bias identified.

The Work of Alfred Kinsey. Alfred Kinsey (1894–1956), an insect biologist who spent most of his career studying wasps, used interviews to conduct some of the most significant early sex research. Almost by chance Kinsey was assigned to teach a course on marriage and sexuality at Indiana University, and when he went to prepare his lectures he was shocked and dismayed at the lack of solid scientific information available on the topic. Kinsey began to interview his students about their sex lives and experiences, and the surprising results made him recognize that important, groundbreaking work was needed.

Kinsey founded and directed the Institute for Sex Research at Indiana University, which today (as the Kinsey Institute for Research in Sex, Gender, and Reproduction) remains one of the world's foremost centers for the study of sexuality. Kinsey compiled the results of his interviews with men into a book entitled *Sexual Behavior in the Human Male* (1948), often referred to simply as The Kinsey Report, which surprised many by becoming a runaway bestseller. The second report, *Sexual Behavior in the Human Female*, was eagerly anticipated and its publication in 1953 was treated as a major news event.

Kinsey pioneered a purely scientific approach to sex, removing it from its traditional moralistic and theological context. In his view, scientists should concentrate on an objective collection of facts without making value judgments. This approach, and the commercial success of Kinsey's work, brought a new awareness about the diversity of human sexual behavior. Kinsey's findings have been brought into question in recent years because, despite its large size, the sample in his studies did not reflect an accurate representation of the U.S. population. Further criticism of his work surfaced when a director of the Kinsey Institute stated that Kinsey based many of his findings about childhood sexual activity on the diaries of an anonymous child molester (Leland, 1995). Other detractors claimed that Kinsey was a secret masochist and homosexual whose real agenda was to promote the acceptance of homosexuality (Jones, 1997). Congress investigated whether he was a Communist, his sources of funding were pressured into cutting him off, and postal officials held up shipments of his books on the grounds that they violated obscenity laws. Today's sex researchers acknowledge an immense debt to this remarkable pioneer, but Kinsey died, "an exhausted and broken man" (Petersen, 1999, p. 228) before he received recognition for his accomplishments.

The National Health and Social Life Survey. Conceived in 1987 as a response to the AIDS crisis, the National Health and Social Life Survey (NHSLS) examined sexual practices and attitudes throughout the United States. Although originally funded by the federal government, in 1991 the U.S. Senate passed an amendment prohibiting the government from funding the study, due to the fears and concerns of some officials. Private foundations stepped in and provided the necessary financial support to complete the research, and in 1992, the National Opinion Research Center at the University of Chicago began the most comprehensive survey of American sexuality ever undertaken.

Unlike previous studies that relied on volunteer participants, this NHSLS study was the first to use a randomly selected representative sample. The study dispelled many of our most sacred myths about sexual behavior. John Gagnon, a coauthor of the survey, stated: "We have had the myth that everybody was out there having lots of sex of all kinds. That's had two consequences. It has enraged the conservatives. And it has cre-

"These social scientists are pleased to report that of the 4,369 random Americans they chose to survey, only 20 percent refused to participate. Well, that's 20 percent right there who are up to something. And you know good and well that some percent of the others are lying like dogs."

HUMORIST ROY BLOUNT JR. (1995)

ated anxiety and unhappiness among those who weren't having it, who thought 'If I'm not getting any, I must be a defective person'" (Lewin, 1994, p. A1). The NHSLS survey results were published in two books. The first was a detailed and scholarly description of the research entitled *The Social Organization of Sexuality* (Laumann et al., 1994). The second, *Sex in America: A Definitive Study* (Michael et al., 1994), was published as a trade book. The data from this research are considered to be the best currently available.

Other well-known sex surveys include the Hunt Report (1974), the Hite Reports (1976, 1981), and the Janus Report (1993). Much of the research reported in popular magazines such as *Cosmopolitan* or *Playboy* is also based on survey data.

Observational Research   As its name implies, **observational research** entails observing, studying, and recording a subject's behavior, either in a laboratory or in the *field*, the setting in which the behavior naturally occurs. Use of the observational method reduces the incidence of the problems encountered in the use of interviews and surveys, that is, having to rely on a subject's memory, honesty, or understanding of the research questions. However, only small populations can be studied using this method. The laboratory is used when it is impractical to study a subject in its natural setting. Given their use of monitoring equipment and the extent of personal intrusion required, it is unlikely that Masters and Johnson could have conducted their research regarding the human sexual response in their subjects' bedrooms (see "Laboratory Research," later in this section).

Anthropologist Margaret Mead used observational research in a field study of the sexual attitudes and behaviors of Pacific islanders.

Field Research.   Anthropologists traditionally gather data by living among the people they study and unobtrusively observing their subjects. By both observing and participating in a field study, a researcher can obtain a unique understanding of values, rituals, behaviors, and beliefs. Because sex is such a personal matter, there are obvious limitations on this type of research, but psychologists may use this method to observe patterns of the more public aspects of sexual behavior, such as the courtship routines of college students in a local singles' bar.

Anthropologist Margaret Mead (1901–1978) collected data on sexual behavior in several primitive cultures. Her work, which focused on childhood and adolescence in the Pacific islands, helped promote a cross-cultural approach to sex research. Mead's *Coming of Age in Samoa* (1928) hypothesized that the psychological changes associated with puberty are culturally, not biologically, based. Adolescence in Samoa was described as being a relatively easy period without the sexual frustrations and stress that characterize American teens.

Ethnographer bias and cultural variation within a society may lead to widely different views of any given culture. Mead's work challenged stereotypes about sex roles and explained how men and women learn to behave in the expected ways of their own culture. Although some of her conclusions have been questioned (later researchers in other Samoan villages reached very different conclusions [Freeman, 1983]), Mead's *Sex and Temperament in Three Primitive Societies* (1936) has heightened the awareness of current sex researchers to *ethnocentrism*, the assumption that the ideas of one's own ethnic group, nation, or culture are superior to others.

Laboratory Research.   William Masters and Virginia Johnson were the first researchers to use the technique of direct observation in a laboratory setting to study physiological changes during sexual arousal. Masters, a gynecologist, and Johnson, a nurse, observed men and women engaged in a variety of sexual activities. Physiological responses were measured by electronic sensors, recorded on specially designed photographic equipment, and directly observed by the researchers. Afterward, the subjects were interviewed in detail about their experiences. Following the publication of this research in *Human Sexual Response* (1966), Masters and Johnson began to focus their studies on sexual problems and the treatment of sexual disorders. Criticism of Masters and Johnson's work has included comments that the unnatural laboratory setting distorted their findings, and that by selecting only subjects who had a history of positive

Observational Research: a method of research in which subjects are watched and studied in a laboratory or natural setting

orgasmic experience they biased their conclusions (Tiefer, 1995). However, the work of the institute founded by Masters and Johnson continues to make valuable contributions to sex research.

Case Studies   A **case study,** or detailed in-depth study of a single individual or a small number of subjects, is often used to investigate rare or highly unusual aspects of sexuality. Because of the small number of subjects involved, case studies allow for greater flexibility and can cover a longer time period than other research methods. A case study can be done with a living subject or by using historical research data. Because case studies are so limited in scope, it is not possible to generalize any findings to the rest of the population.

Sigmund Freud (1856–1939) was an Austrian physician who developed an interest in understanding the emotional roots of physical illnesses. Although middle-class Victorian society regarded sex as a minor and mildly disgusting part of life, unsuitable for serious inquiry or even conversation, Freud came to think that sexual desire was one of the most powerful forces in the psyche, and that it was necessary to understand sex in order to understand human nature. Throughout his life, Freud developed and refined a series of controversial theories about human sexuality based on case studies of his own patients and of historical figures. These formed some of the core ideas of the theory of psychoanalysis, a powerfully influential theory of psychology as well as the basis for clinical treatment of many mental illnesses (see "Psychoanalytic Theory" later in this chapter for more on Freud's perspective).

One of the best-known examples of the historical case study approach is Freud's (1943) study of Leonardo da Vinci. Using historical records, Freud concluded that the Renaissance inventor and artist exhibited repressed homosexual impulses.

Experimental Research   In **experimental research,** behavior is studied under controlled conditions, usually in a laboratory setting. Proper experimentation is a challenging procedure subject to many rules and guidelines, and many universities offer entire courses devoted to teaching experimental methods. The essence of experimental research is the controlled creation of particular conditions so as to be able to study the results and make conclusions about what causes what. Often these conclusions require comparing treatment groups to control groups. Subjects are presented with stimuli under managed conditions that allow for reliable measurement of their reactions. This method is often used to match or compare the behavior or responses of two different groups. For example, in one study, college men were randomly assigned to view five feature-length films over a 2-week period. One group saw X-rated nonviolent films; another group watched R-rated "slasher" films; (like *Friday the 13th*); and a third group saw other R-rated films. Afterward, the subjects looked at a videotaped reenactment of a rape trial. The researchers found that men who had watched the R-rated slasher films showed less sensitivity toward the alleged rape victim than did those who had seen the R- or X-rated films (Linz et al., 1988).

Although experimental research allows for the control and manipulation of variables, the artificial laboratory environment sometimes can distort results. For example, the degree of arousal caused by viewing sexually explicit materials may be different in the laboratory setting because the subjects are aware they are being monitored. Table 1.1 summarizes the research methods described in this textbook.

Quantification, Classification, and Interpretation of Research Data

Now that you have hundreds of responses to your survey in front of you, you need to quantify, or count, the responses, and classify them, that is, break them down into categories. For example, depending upon your hypothesis, you count the number of subjects who performed a certain behavior and/or count how many times one subject performed the behavior. You must then carefully devise categories in which to group

Case Study: an in-depth study of an individual or a small group of individuals

Experimental Research: a method in which researchers restrict, change, or manipulate a subject's experience and assess the effects on the subject

TABLE 1.1

Sex Research

	Description	Examples	Advantages	Disadvantages
Interviews and Surveys	Data is obtained by asking subjects to answer written or oral questions	Kinsey (1948, 1953); NHSLS (1994); Janus (1993); Hunt (1974)	Relatively efficient, inexpensive, and quick method of obtaining data from a large numbers of subjects	Problems of demographic and volunteer bias. Information may be inaccurate due to social desirability bias, exaggeration, denial, or differences in understanding terms
Observational Research	Direct observation of subjects, either in their natural environment or in a laboratory	Mead (1928); Masters and Johnson (1966)	Minimizes possibility of data falsification	Observer effect may influence subjects or distort researchers' perceptions; volunteer bias and artificial setting of laboratory research
Case Studies	An in-depth study of a single subject or small group of subjects in which information is obtained through interviews, questionnaires, or historical records	Freud (1943)	Provides in-depth understanding of subjects	Potential for observer bias and inaccurate data; limited generalization of findings
Experimental Research	Seeks to confirm cause-and-effect relationships by observing and recording subjects' reactions to manipulated variables	Linz et al. (1988)	Provides the strongest evidence of cause-and-effect relationships; provides a controlled environment for manipulating variables	Limitations of variables that researchers can ethically manipulate; artificiality of setting may influence subjects' responses

these data. One example of a category is "Japanese American males between the ages of 18 and 24 who masturbate weekly."

Statistics can be used in many different ways. As the term suggests, **descriptive statistics** simply describe the data. One example of a descriptive statistic is "42 percent of people learn about sex from a friend." **Inferential statistics** allow for making predictions based on probability statements. For example, one such prediction is "because a high percentage of people learn about sex from friends, a high percentage of people probably have inaccurate sexual knowledge."

Correlation is a term used to describe the degree to which any two or more variables are related to each other. Correlation can be positive or negative. An example of positive correlation is that an exclusive primary sex partner is associated with the highest rates of positive feelings about sex (Laumann et al., 1994). An example of negative correlation is the *decrease* in the incidence of sexually transmitted infections with *increased* use of condoms. Correlation should not be confused with **causation,** which means that one variable causes another to occur; this is sometimes referred to as a cause-and-effect relationship. There is no causation between the variables in our previous example, condoms and sexually transmitted infections (decreased use of condoms does not *cause* sexually transmitted infections). However, there is a direct causative relationship between human papilloma virus and genital warts.

Descriptive Statistics: numbers used to present a collection of data in a brief yet meaningful form

Inferential Statistics: a set of procedures for determining what conclusions can be legitimately inferred from a set of data

Correlation: a statistical measure of the linkage or relationship between two or more variables

Causation: the act or agency that produces an effect

"Research will never transform women into starry skies and morning light. Science offers a different kind of beauty. It opens the worlds within worlds."

(BLUM, 1997, P. 91)

Researchers must be careful to differentiate between describing the occurrence of an event and making conclusions about that event. For example, your study might show that less than 1/10 of 1 percent of your subjects engaged in oral-genital sex. However, you cannot conclude that this act is deviant or abnormal simply because the majority of individuals in the group did not engage in this behavior.

Evaluating the consistency or accuracy of the instrument or technique that was used in the research study tests the **reliability** of data; that is, would a repeat of the study produce the same or similar results in different clinical experiments or statistical trials. Kinsey, for example, checked the reliability of his data by reexamining participants after at least 18 months. In addition, **validity** assesses the extent to which research is measuring what the researcher intends.

Evaluating Sex Research

To help you differentiate legitimate, scholarly research from an unscientific opinion poll, you need to examine a study carefully. A first step is to look at the researcher's credentials and affiliations. Researchers attached to an academic institution or a government research center generally will have greater credibility than those who are not professionally trained or those connected to a special interest group. Next, evaluate the research methods used, the makeup of the sample population, and any research preconceptions and biases. For example, the results of a study of feelings of guilt associated with premarital intercourse using a sample drawn from a conservative church-related school might be very different from a sample drawn from a large public university.

Also consider where the findings are published. Research published in a reputable scholarly journal in which articles undergo peer review must be viewed differently from magazine articles in which results may be simplified or sensationalized to entertain readers. There are a number of journals and newsletters exclusively devoted to the topic of sex research. These include: *Annals of Sex Research* (quarterly), *Annual Review of Sex Research* (annually), *Archives of Sexual Behavior* (bimonthly), *Contemporary Sexuality* (monthly newsletter), *Journal of Sex Research* (quarterly), *Sex Roles: A Journal of Research* (monthly), and *Journal of Sex Education and Therapy* (quarterly). When possible, it is

WWW EXPLORING SEXUALITY ONLINE

Sex Research Online

The World Wide Web is an increasingly popular, efficient, and practical way to gather information and share resources. It operates much the same as a research paper in which each footnote takes you to the original source.

With the growth of information available on the Internet and the development of more and better search tools, the Internet has become an important venue for publishing research. However, advanced technology does not ensure advanced quality or accuracy of information.

You need to examine online research even more carefully than traditionally published studies. Journals and even magazines do a lot of the work for you to maintain their credibility, but just about anyone can publish just about anything on the Internet. To critically evaluate the usefulness of the information you find on the Net, ask the following questions: Who authored the study? What are the author's credentials? Does he or she have any academic or professional affiliations? Does the Web site just serve as the author's virtual soapbox? Was the information reviewed by anyone? If so, who are the reviewers, and what are their affiliations and credentials? How often is the information updated? Who sponsors the Web site? Is the information commercially biased to help sell a product or service?

Reliability: the consistency or accuracy of a research measure

Validity: the extent to which research measures what the researcher intends

best to go to the original source to find out what the study really reported. Finally, look at other studies on the topic to compare findings. A good research study can be *replicated*, or repeated with the same results, by someone else. If the results differ, alternative explanations for the findings should be explored. Research can provide useful knowledge and information; understanding what is presented is up to you.

THEORETICAL PERSPECTIVES ON SEXUALITY

Progress in research requires both methods and ideas. While everyone seems to have ideas about sex, sex researchers have had difficulty coming up with anything approaching a consensus on which perspective offers the best insights or which methods are the best way to conduct research. Several major theoretical perspectives are identified in the following sections; as you read them, you may want to identify the theoretical perspective that most closely matches your own views.

Theories are not meaningless abstractions but practical, even necessary, approaches to human problem solving. A good theory is one that can explain and predict. A theory is a way of looking at events, a way of organizing data, a way of understanding human behavior. Human beings are theoretical by nature. Whenever you approach a problem you already have a set of assumptions, about the world in general and about the specific category of phenomena into which the problem falls, to guide your actions. Moreover, all theoretical models are influenced by history, the cultural setting at the time of their development, happenings in other disciplines or world affairs, and intellectual understandings and social needs of the time.

During the first half of the 20th century, when Freud's psychoanalytic theories dominated much of social science, there was a great deal of reluctance even to discuss the biology of human social behavior. The focus was on the social environment—primarily through the mechanisms of socialization—to explain human behavior, including its variations. Over the past few decades researchers have begun using sophisticated equipment to explore the brain and responses to various sexual stimuli, new techniques have been developed to evaluate fetuses in utero, the study of the human genome has opened new possibilities for addressing genetic diseases, and the cloning of humans is rapidly becoming a possibility. It is hardly coincidental that during the same period, many social scientists have begun leaning toward biological or evolutionary theories in attempts to explain any number of human phenomena, including behaviors related to sexuality.

Most social scientists—ourselves included—believe that no single paradigm ultimately will be shown to explain sexual behaviors. The environment and biology are undoubtedly interactive in ways that are still not understood. The current lack of consensus among social scientists has resulted in a theoretical richness that provokes debate, periodically yields insight, and contributes generally to the advancement of knowledge. With this in mind, we have presented data based on studies from a variety of theoretical perspectives. As you read this textbook, keep the various theoretical models in mind, and ask yourself which theories seem to explain known reality best for you.

Psychoanalytic Theory　**Psychoanalytic theory** is an approach to understanding behavior that focuses on how hidden or unconscious feelings and fears influence motivation, thoughts, and behaviors, as well as the development of personality traits and psychological problems. This approach is based on the work of Sigmund Freud, who we introduced to you in the section of this chapter on the case study approach. Freud came to believe that the *sex drive* (defined broadly as the quest for pleasure and satisfaction of any sort) and aggression are two of the most powerful motivations in the human psyche. This idea was radical for his time, although today many have come to agree that sexual and aggressive motivations have an innate or biological basis. If the entertainment industry were viewed as a reflection of society, the sex and violence that are always on display would seem to support his view as well.

Psychoanalytic Theory: theory of personality originated by Sigmund Freud that is based on the belief that unconscious conflict can result in psychological or physical symptoms

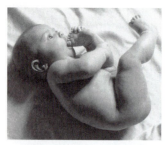

Based on the work of Sigmund Freud, psychoanalytic theory holds that the sex drive begins at birth and develops through several stages.

Psychoanalytic theory holds that the sex drive develops through several stages. Newborns enter an *oral stage*, in which pleasure is received through the mouth (which is convenient for suckling). Next comes the *anal stage*, in which the parental efforts at toilet training collide with the child's newfound pleasure in defecating. Then comes the *phallic stage*, with the sex drive focused on the genital area, although both boys and girls think of the penis as the principal organ. In this stage the *Oedipus complex* (named after the prince of Thebes who in Greek legend unknowingly murdered his father and married his mother) develops, in which the boy develops a romantic love for his mother and wants to marry her and replace his father. The parallel pattern for girls, the *Electra complex* (named for Electra, who in Greek legend avenged the death of her father by murdering her mother and the mother's lover) involves the desire to replace the mother and marry the father. When the child recognizes the impossibility of this love, he or she represses all sexual desire, and the sex drive remains latent (undeveloped) until puberty, whereupon it emerges with new force and pushes toward adult sexuality. In Freud's view a person can become stuck, or fixated, at any stage. A **fixation** was understood as a pattern in which a person remains tied to a way of thinking, feeling, or acting that was characteristic of an earlier stage in life. Freud did not have a clear theory about how this happened, but he was firm in his belief that what happens at one point in life can remain powerful and influential over one's psychological processes for years afterward. For example, a person with an *oral fixation* may continue to seek pleasure through the mouth even into adulthood. The oral fixation may take various forms, such as a constant desire to eat, a passion for playing the clarinet, or a preference for performing oral sex.

Freud's theories also emphasized *defense mechanisms* as ways of avoiding unpleasant facts and unacceptable desires about oneself. For example, if you felt sexual attraction toward a member of your own sex but regarded homosexuality as unacceptable, you would engage in defense mechanisms to conceal your feelings from yourself. *Projection*, the belief that certain feelings are not one's own but rather other people's feelings ("I'm not hostile, you are!"), is an important defense mechanism in Freud's theories. Someone who believes that everyone else is gay might simply be trying to avoid facing up to his or her homosexual feelings. Another defense mechanism, *reaction formation*, involves converting one's feelings into an opposing emotion. Freud suggested that people who are fighting to hide homosexual feelings might become outspoken critics of homosexuality or even antigay bigots who engage in violent behavior toward gays.

Freud's contemporaries were shocked by some of his conclusions, particularly his work with children. Freud concluded that children do have sexual feelings and interests, even though they may not be ready to engage in coitus. He observed that children are quite curious about the difference between male and female genital organs and about where babies come from, and they often develop elaborate, fantastic theories about sex and reproduction.

Freud observed that little girls sometimes were dismayed to discover that boys had something (a penis) that they did not, and he elaborated this into the controversial hypothesis that women generally suffer from *penis envy*. According to Freud, each human being starts life as both male and female psychologically. The process of being socialized into either a male or a female role is viewed as a loss, not a gain, as children have an instinctive horror of losing half of themselves in this process. According to this theory, the process of socialization is faced earlier in life by girls and is more traumatic for girls than for boys, because the missing part is more obvious. Little boys can believe they will grow up to become mothers or fathers, but little girls cannot avoid the recognition that they will not be able to assume the father role. Freud proposed that men later develop some envy of women's ability to have babies, and adult men's efforts to be creative in cultural or artistic spheres could spring from this envy of natural female creativity. In adult women, penis envy was seen as the reason to seek a penis in sexual intercourse or to have a baby (a penis substitute).

Freud's views that people are often not fully conscious of their motives or reasons, that sex and aggression are powerful motivations, that people sometimes project their feelings and thoughts onto others, and that many aspects of personality and behavior are designed to help the person avoid anxiety, continue to be major forces in psychological theory and practice. Other concepts, such as penis envy and the Oedipus and Electra complexes, are no longer in favor.

Social Constructionism In 1967, Berger and Luckmann published *The Social Construction of Reality*. This text became an influential articulation of the view that reality is composed of more than atoms, molecules, and other physical entities. Crucial to their argument is the premise that groups of people share understandings of certain common phenomena and that these have a profound influence on human behavior. This theory, called **social constructionism**, has had an important influence on many areas of research, including sexuality.

Social constructionism recognizes the importance of **socialization**—the process of learning how to think, act, and feel the way other members of a particular culture or society do. Instead of thinking of human beings as biological entities with actions driven by innate drives, social constructionists emphasize the diversity and flexibility of human behavior. In their view, people can be socialized to act and feel in a wide variety of ways. The same sex act might evoke pleasure in one person, guilt in another, love in a third, and pride in a fourth, depending on their upbringing and the broader context of the experience.

It probably is no coincidence that social constructionism burst on the intellectual scene when it did. The Sexual Revolution of the 1960s was part of an era of rapid social change, partly in rebellion against the stable, traditional relationships and values of the 1950s. Previously, many Americans had accepted as a given that premarital sex was wrong and that marriage was the only proper context for sexual intercourse. The Sexual Revolution brought radical changes in how people thought about their bodies and made their sexual decisions, confronting people with other possible sets of values. These rapid changes in sexuality highlighted how much sex depended on socialization and cultural norms, and showed that sexual morals were not written in stone but were susceptible to change.

The 1960s were also a watershed in the women's movement. Many women rejected the stereotyped gender roles of previous decades in favor of a broader range of opportunities to participate in society. The feminist movement embraced social constructionism for a variety of reasons. Opponents of feminism claimed that it was "natural" for women to stay at home as wives and mothers. Social constructionism offered powerful intellectual ammunition to reject such views. From a social constructionist perspective, women are not innately destined for a "natural" role as wife and mother. Rather, such roles are seen as social constructions shaped by political ideologies, religious dogmas, and historical traditions.

Feminist Theory **Feminist theory**, sometimes referred to simply as feminism, is a set of ideas developed in connection with the women's movement of the 1970s and 1980s. Some critics believe that feminist theory emphasizes male oppression and female victimization, and others believe that feminism promotes women as being superior to men. However, the primary focus of feminism is an acknowledgment of the innate differences between men and women and a simultaneous celebration of their inherent equality.

Feminism covers a broad range of ideas, and conflicting opinions have emerged on a variety of issues, including sexuality. Although there is no single feminist perspective on sexuality, most feminists would agree that in the past the woman's point of view often was missing from sex research and that white, middle-class, heterosexual males dominated the field. Feminist scholars argue that this emphasis on male sexuality promotes a narrow view of sex that is centered on the genitals rather than on relationships.

According to some feminist theorists, patriarchy, a social system in which men are the head of household and have authority over women and children, has worked to stifle women's sexuality, perhaps so that women will serve men's pleasure instead of seeking their own. Proponents of this view insist that women have as much right as

Social Constructionism: theory that emphasizes the importance of social learning on how we evaluate and apply socialization and information to our lives

Socialization: the process of learning how to think, act, and feel the way other members of a particular culture or society do

Feminist Theory: theoretical views that emphasize the need to include the female experience and perspective in research

Feminist theory promotes women's rights and argues that the emphasis on male sexuality promotes a narrow view of sex that is centered on the genitals rather than on relationships.

men to engage in premarital sex with multiple partners and to experiment with ways of finding pleasure. Another line of thought focuses more heavily on men as oppressors and exploiters; sexual intercourse is seen as a means to keep women in a socially inferior position. Having sex with a variety of different partners can be seen as a way of rebelling against male domination. Some extremists encourage women to seek liberation by rejecting men as sexual partners, and they promote lesbianism and masturbation as the only "politically correct" forms of female sexuality. Despite the conflicting opinions, feminists generally agree that women should be encouraged to learn about their own bodies and explore their sexuality.

Feminist theorists are especially sensitive to sexual patterns that exploit women. For example, rape, that is, the use or threat of force to obtain sex (see Chapter 13), is interpreted as a political act rather than as an illicit attempt to obtain sex. According to many feminist writings (most notably Brownmiller's 1975 book *Against Our Will: Men, Women, and Rape*), rape occurs as part of a conspiracy by all men to intimidate all women. Even men who do not rape are seen as supporting and benefiting from rape because the very possibility of rape keeps women in a state of fear and prevents them from entering fully into society. For example, fear of being raped might prevent a woman from going out late at night to close a business deal, thus keeping her from competing equally with a man.

Some feminists regard pornography, sexual harassment, prostitution, and rape as related manifestations of the way that male-dominated society oppresses and suppresses women. Pornography is regarded by some feminists as part of patriarchy's system for exploiting women, reducing women to "sex objects" valued solely for their sexual attributes. Prostitution also is often regarded as a form of male exploitation of women, and some feminists regard prostitutes themselves as unfortunate women who are forced into serving men.

Evolutionary Theory **Evolutionary theory** is another important theoretical perspective on sexuality. It is based on the idea that species developed to their present state by adapting to their environment. Although the ideas of Charles Darwin (1809–1882), the founder of evolutionary theory, predate Freudian and feminist views, their relevance to sexuality has been a major theme of the last three decades. Several excellent works have provided thorough treatments of the evolutionary approach to sex (for example, Buss, 1994; Ridley, 1994; Symons, 1979).

Evolutionary theory is based on the idea of **natural selection,** the process by which nature determines which individuals survive and reproduce (Wallace et al., 1996). Natural selection is like a game: Each member of the species competes against the others, with the rules set by the environment. Because sexual reproduction involves genetic recombination (see Chapter 5), the offspring have new combinations of genes. According to the process of natural selection, the offspring with the gene combination that enables it to live most effectively in the environment will predominate. For example, if the environment is cold, those offspring with the genes that enable them to cope well with the cold will do better than those better adapted to warmer temperatures.

The philosopher Herbert Spencer (1820–1903) coined the phrase "survival of the fittest" to describe the competition that occurs in evolution. While this phrase has remained popular and influential, in recent years there has been a subtle yet crucial shift in evolutionary thinking from survival to reproduction. The ultimate test of the survival of the species is the ability to pass on genes to future generations. Regardless of how long you live, you must reproduce in order to pass on your genes. The increased emphasis on reproduction means that sex has come to figure ever more prominently in evolutionary thinking.

Strictly speaking, even reproducing is not enough to ensure success. If you produce many offspring but none survive—like the oak tree that creates thousands of acorns that rot or are eaten by squirrels—you still have not succeeded at your evolutionary task. It is necessary to produce offspring that can survive long enough to reproduce in their turn. Put more simply, grandchildren are the mark of evolutionary success.

Evolutionary Theory: theory that emphasizes the gradual process of development of species through biological adaptation

Natural Selection: the process by which forms of life having traits that better enable them to adapt to specific environmental pressures will tend to survive and reproduce in greater numbers

There are two basic biological strategies for successful reproduction. One is to produce as many offspring as possible to maximize the chances that some will survive (the **"r" strategy**). For example, the sea star releases 2.5 million eggs in one spawning (Wallace et al., 1996). The other is to produce relatively few offspring but invest a great deal of care in each one, to maximize each one's prospects of growing up and reproducing in turn (the **"K" strategy**).

The human race employs many variations of the "K" strategy. In recent years, one line of thought among evolutionary theorists has been the consideration of gender differences in the quality versus quantity approach, which has important implications for the study of promiscuity, mate selection strategies, and the nature of sex appeal. The minimum effort a person must expend in order to produce a child varies tremendously with gender. For the male, sexual reproduction can theoretically be accomplished by having intercourse one time. After those few minutes of pleasure, the man might never have any more involvement in the process. The female's involvement goes far beyond intercourse to include 9 months of pregnancy plus the sometimes-dangerous process of giving birth.

The number of possible offspring also varies greatly with gender. In principle, a man can impregnate three different women during his lunch hour. Once a woman becomes pregnant, she cannot conceive again until the baby is born, or longer if she breast-feeds the baby and ovulation does not resume. In other words, whereas a man can make several babies in a single day, a woman can normally produce about one per year.

Sexual desires, feelings, and behavior are considered by evolutionary theorists to be strongly shaped by gender differences, because the men and women who adapted best to their environment passed along the most offspring. From an evolutionary standpoint, men have evolved to be less selective about their mates than women. If a man copulates with a woman with less-than-ideal genes, he has not lost anything more than a few minutes of physical activity and an easily replaceable load of sperm. He can quickly move on and mate with a more suitable partner. In contrast, if a woman creates a baby with an unfit partner, she cannot mate with a new partner for nearly a year. The biological costs of having sex with the wrong person are much greater for women than men. As a result, women have evolved to be more cautious and patient sexual decision makers than men.

Differences in promiscuity follow the same evolutionary logic. Men can produce the most offspring by having sex with the most partners. There are reports of certain kings and emperors who produced hundreds of children, because the man copulated with many wives, mistresses, and concubines. No single woman can produce hundreds of offspring; indeed, it is the rare woman who manages to produce even a dozen children. Regardless of whether she has sex with one man or a hundred men, a woman can produce only about one child per year. The man who has sex with a hundred women is almost certain to make more babies than the man who has sex with only one woman. Thus promiscuity may be a more viable reproductive strategy for men than for women.

Some evolutionary theorists extend the argument to suggest that monogamy is better than promiscuity for women. Historically, the father's presence helped ward off danger and increase the children's chances of survival. A woman who mated with one man, kept him in love with her, and enlisted his support for herself and her children probably had a better chance of having her children survive than the promiscuous woman without a permanent partner. For this reason, women may have been shaped by evolution to seek long-term monogamous relationships with their sex partners.

Social Exchange Theory **Social exchange theory** has its roots in sociological analyses such as those of George Homans (1950, 1951) and Peter Blau (1964). In essence, social interactions are analyzed in terms of costs and rewards, just as an economist might describe financial transactions, except that the range of costs and rewards extends beyond money. For example, the rewards or benefits of sex might include pleasure,

"r" Strategy: a biological strategy for successful reproduction that emphasizes producing as many offspring as possible

"K" Strategy: a biological strategy for successful reproduction that emphasizes producing fewer offspring and investing a great deal of care in each offspring

Social Exchange Theory: theory in which social interactions are analyzed in terms of costs and rewards

pride and status, or feeling loved. The costs might involve the risk of rejection, performance anxiety, feelings of guilt, an unwanted pregnancy, or sexually transmitted infection. When people engage in social interactions, they trade benefits, so everyone gets something that he or she wants.

Waller and Hill (1951) applied social exchange theory to their *principle of least interest:* Whoever loves less has more power in the relationship. If you have ever been in a relationship in which you loved the other person more than that person loved you, you can probably recall the relatively powerless feeling that accompanies that situation. You might have felt that you would be willing to do anything for that person, whereas the other person was unwilling to do what you wanted. You were the one waiting for the phone to ring. Whenever the two of you had different preferences, you were probably the one to give in. As developed by Baumeister and Tice (2001) and applied to sex, the principle of least interest suggests an important gender difference: Men usually want sex more than women do. By the principle of least interest, this gives women a power advantage in negotiating the relationship. Thus, from this perspective, sex is a female resource: Sex is something that women give to men, and so men must give women other things in return in order for the social exchange to succeed.

The most obvious instance of social exchange of sex involves prostitution. The usual pattern in prostitution is that men give women money in exchange for sex. This pattern has been observed throughout history and in cultures all over the world. The opposite pattern—women giving money to men in order to obtain sex—has been much rarer, perhaps in part because women tend to have fewer financial resources than men, and is consistent with the social exchange notion of sex as a female resource.

There are many other ways in which sex operates as a female resource. In courtship, the man traditionally pays for dinner and dates. Social exchange theory sees this as a kind of "trade" in which the man contributes these material resources and the woman contributes sex. A woman may feel cheated if she has sex with a man who never takes her out on the town, or a man may complain about the amount of money he spent on a woman without "getting lucky."

Commitment is another important resource that men may offer in exchange for sex. In many societies, premarital and extramarital sex is relatively scarce, and marriage is the main opportunity to obtain sex. Young men find they must make the commitment to marriage—in effect promising to provide for a woman and be faithful to her for many years—in order to have sex. Older women in such societies advise their daughters, "Why should a man buy the cow if he can get the milk for free?" In other words, they should avoid premarital sex, not necessarily because of the dangers of pregnancy and disease, but in order to obtain male commitment.

ASK YOURSELF

It will be interesting to find out how much you really know about sexuality before you go on to study the subject in some detail. The following true/false statements may help you discover the areas you need to attend to most closely. (The answers are given at the end of the chapter.)

1. Romance serves an evolutionary purpose by joining males and females in long-term partnerships.

2. A female is born with all the eggs her ovaries will ever produce.

3. It is important for couples to have simultaneous orgasms.

4. There is a right way and a wrong way to have sexual intercourse.

5. After a year of unprotected intercourse, 80 percent of women will become pregnant.

6. Before or during menstruation, nearly all women are very irritable and depressed.

7. A condom is an excellent form of contraception when it is used correctly and with spermicidal foam.

8. Females rarely masturbate.

9. Masturbation causes a variety of physical and psychological problems.

10. There are several widely available aphrodisiacs that can create sexual desire in an otherwise unwilling partner.

11. In the United States, there are more new cases of chlamydia each year than any other sexually transmitted infection.

12. If you contract a sexually transmitted infection once, you can't get it again.

13. If you are sexually active, the most effective protection against sexually transmitted HIV/AIDS is a correctly used condom.

14. If a pregnant woman is HIV positive, it is likely that her fetus also will be infected with HIV.

15. A man's inability to have an erection is almost always caused by hidden psychological problems.

16. Taking anabolic steroids may result in permanent sterility and an inability to have an erection.

17. Every individual is either homosexual or heterosexual.

18. Homosexual women and men are considered mentally ill by psychiatrists.

19. About one out of five young men has had at least one homosexual experience.

20. In some societies, every young adolescent boy is expected to perform oral sex on older boys.

21. New lovers' bodies produce a natural chemical similar to amphetamines.

22. People who live together for a few years before they marry increase their chances of having a long and happy marriage.

23. It is abnormal for a married adult to masturbate.

24. A woman's sex life ends with menopause.

25. After age 40, men become increasingly concerned with emotional intimacy.

26. Transvestites and transsexuals are usually homosexuals.

27. The degree of a person's masculinity or femininity can be accurately determined from his or her appearance.

28. Most religions teach social and personal control of sexuality.

29. Men who reveal their genitals in public usually become rapists.

30. Exposure to pornographic materials always leads to a desire for more pornography.

31. Rapists usually attack strangers.

32. Some cultures have a high incidence of rape and in other cultures rape is unknown.

33. Recent research has found that some antidepressants can markedly reduce symptoms of both PMS and sexual compulsion.

34. The professional practices of sex counselors and therapists are closely monitored by consumer groups.

35. Nearly all women who have an abortion become seriously depressed.

■ R E V I E W

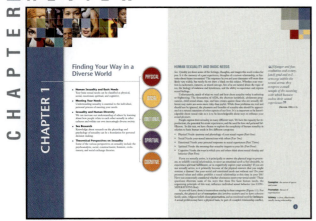

The authors suggest there are five basic human needs that can be applied to human sexuality. These are **1**_____, _____, _____, _____, and _____ needs.

The physical realm of sexuality includes the sexual organs of the human body and the act of sexual reproduction. Information about the physical aspects of sex can assist you in protecting your health against sexually transmitted infections. Moreover, understanding the biology of conception is important to those who want to get pregnant and to those who do not. Further, understanding the biological bases of sexual arousal allows you to give and receive greater pleasure.

Society plays a significant role in shaping the sexuality of individuals. Although all humans share the same basic sexual organs, we don't respond to sexual stimuli in the same ways, and these responses are shaped by the society in which we live.

Sex is associated with the full range of emotional responses. Knowing more about sexuality can improve your ability to deal with your own emotional responses and affect your ability to enjoy your sexuality.

The concept of spirituality is often associated with organized religion. However, in a broader sense, spirituality encompasses our values, ethics, and morality, as well as the personal qualities, ideas, and traditions that help give meaning to our lives.

2_____ is the act or process of knowing, and the more you know about sexuality, the better your understanding of the sexual issues that affect you as an individual and as a member of society.

3_____ are scientists who study human sexuality.

The **4**_____ of investigation involves formulating a research question, and putting that question into the form of a **5**_____, a prediction about the expected research results. Then the researchers test the hypothesis and draw conclusions about it based on an analysis of the results.

Research issues include obtaining **6**_____, which means that a researcher provides sufficient information about the proposed research for the potential subject to make an informed decision about whether or not to participate. **7**_____ involves keeping the identity and responses of a research study private.

Researchers often select a **8**_____, that is a group from which results may be generalized to a larger population. In a **9**_____ sample, everyone in the target population has an equal chance of being selected to participate in the study. Written surveys, or **10**_____, are more economical to conduct than interviews.

11_____ founded the Institute for Sex Research at Indiana University. Data from the **12**_____ are considered the best currently available on human sexuality in the United States. William **13**_____ and Virginia **14**_____ were the first researchers to use the technique of direct observation in a laboratory setting to study physiological changes during sexual arousal.

15_____ statistics describe the data; **16**_____ statistics allow one to make predictions based on probability statements. **17**_____ is a term used to describe the degree to which any two variables are related to each other—either positively or negatively.

18_____ is a measure of consistency, or the likelihood that a repeat of the study would produce the same or similar results. **19**_____ assesses the extent to which research is measuring what the researcher intends.

A theory is a way of looking at events, a way of organizing data, a way of understanding human behavior. A good theory is one that can explain and predict. Several theories are described in this textbook. For example, **20**_____ theory is an approach to understanding behavior that focuses on how hidden or unconscious feelings and fears influence motivation, thoughts, and behaviors, as well as the development of personality traits and psychological problems. This theory is based on the work of **21**_____.

The theory of **22**_____ is based on the premise that groups of people share understandings of certain common phenomena and that these have a profound influence on human behavior. **23**_____ is the process of learning how to think, act, and feel the way other members of a particular culture or society do.

The primary focus of **24**_____ theory is an acknowledgement of the innate differences between men and women and a simultaneous celebration of their inherent equality. Feminist scholars argue that an emphasis on male sexuality promotes a narrow view of sex that is centered on the genitals rather than on relationships. Feminist theorists are especially sensitive to sexual patterns that exploit women.

25_____ theory is based on the idea that species developed to their present state by adapting to their environment. This theory is based on the concept of **26**_____, the process by which nature determines which individuals survive and reproduce.

27_____ theory analyzes social interactions in terms of costs and rewards.

SUGGESTED READINGS

Bancroft, J. (Ed.). (2000). *The Role of Theory in Sex Research.* Bloomington: University of Indiana Press.
   A collection of essays by scholars representing a range of viewpoints and contrasting theoretical approaches on sexuality and sex research.

Brannigan, G. G., Allgeier, E. R., & Allgeier, G. (Eds.). (1997). *The Sex Scientists.* Reading, MA: Addison-Wesley.
   A collection of 15 unique research stories by leading researchers in human sexuality.

Bullough, V. L. (1994). *Science in the Bedroom: A History of Sex Research.* New York: Basic Books.
   Summarizes the history of modern sex research and evaluates hundreds of specific studies.

Diamond, J. M. (1998). *Why Is Sex Fun? The Evolution of Human Sexuality.* New York: Basic Books.
Written by an evolutionary biologist, this book explores the question of why people care so much about sex and how human sexuality differs from that of other species.

Money, J. (1998). *Sin, Science, and the Sex Police: Essays on Sexology and Sexosophy.* Amherst, NY: Prometheus Books.
   This is the latest in a series of writings by one of the 20th century's foremost theoreticians of human sexual relations.

Suggs, D. N., & Miracle, A. W. (Eds.). (1999). *Culture, Biology, and Sexuality.* Athens: University of Georgia Press.
   This book is a collection of articles by cultural and physical anthropologists on the biological and cultural interface of sexuality.

ANSWERS TO "ASK YOURSELF"

1, 2, 5, 7, 11, 13, 16, 19, 20, 21, 25, 28, 32, and 33 are True.

3, 4, 6, 8, 9, 10, 12, 14, 15, 17, 18, 22, 23, 24, 26, 27, 29, 30, 31, 34, and 35 are False.

ANSWERS TO CHAPTER REVIEW

1. physical, social, emotional, spiritual, cognitive; **2.** Cognition; **3.** Sexologists; **4.** scientific method; **5.** hypothesis; **6.** informed consent; **7.** Confidentiality; **8.** sample; **9.** random; **10.** questionnaires; **11.** Alfred Kinsey; **12.** National Health and Social Life Survey; **13.** Masters; **14.** Johnson; **15.** Descriptive; **16.** inferential; **17.** Correlation; **18.** Reliability; **19.** Validity; **20.** psychoanalytic; **21.** Sigmund Freud; **22.** social constructionism; **23.** Socialization; **24.** feminist; **25.** Evolutionary; **26.** natural selection; **27.** Social exchange.

CHAPTER 2

Human Sexual Anatomy and Physiology

PHYSICAL

SOCIAL

EMOTIONAL

SPIRITUAL

COGNITIVE

Female Sexual Anatomy and Physiology

- **Female Internal Sexual Organs**
  The internal sexual organs of the human female include the ovaries, fallopian tubes, uterus, and vagina.

- **Female External Sexual Organs**
  The external sexual organs of the human female include all of the parts of the vulva: the mons veneris, the labia, the vestibule, and the clitoris.

- **The Menstrual Cycle**
  The menstrual cycle, the preparation of the female reproductive system for pregnancy, occurs in women between puberty and menopause.

- **Menopause**
  Menopause, the permanent cessation of ovulation, is a life transition marked by a number of physiological changes.

- **Disorders of the Female Sexual Organs**
  The female sexual organs are subject to a number of disorders, including endometriosis, fibroids, cervical and ovarian cancers, ovarian cysts, and vaginitis.

- **Breasts**
  The primary function of female breasts is the production of milk. The most serious disease of the breast is breast cancer.

- **Diseases of the Breast**
  Both noncancerous and cancerous lumps may occur in the female breast. Breast self-examinations and mammograms are important in the early detection of breast cancer. Men also may develop breast cancer, though much less frequently than women.

Male Sexual Anatomy and Physiology

- **Male Internal Sexual Organs**
  The internal sexual organs of the human male include the seminiferous tubules, epididymis, vas deferens, seminal vesicles, prostate gland, and Cowper's glands.

- **Male External Sexual Organs**
  The external sexual organs of the human male include the scrotum, testes, and penis.

- **Disorders of the Male Sexual Organs**
  The male sexual organs are subject to a number of disorders, including prostate and testicular cancers, testicular torsion, epididymitis, and Peyronie's disease.

As you learned in Chapter 1, human sexual anatomy and physiology evolved to enhance reproduction and promote the survival of the species. To ensure the successful adaptation and reproduction of the species, three objectives must be accomplished: fertilization of an egg by a sperm; successful development of a fetus resulting in live birth of a healthy individual; and survival of the offspring until physical maturity to reproduce another generation.

Our social interactions, emotional responses, and even our cultural institutions and values are inextricably linked to our physical sexual needs. Increased knowledge of the structure and function of your reproductive organs can improve your sexual health, increase your sexual pleasure, and cause you to be more responsible in your sexual behavior.

Although men and women sometimes glorify, vilify, or are mystified by one another's bodies, when you take a close look, they are remarkably similar. Female sexual organs and male sexual organs develop from similar tissue before birth. In Chapter 10 you will learn more about the **homologous,** or corresponding, nature of the male and female bodies and the amazing synchrony that is necessary for fertilization and the reproductive success of our species.

This chapter provides descriptions of both the structure (*anatomy*) and function (*physiology*) of the sexual organs of the human male and female bodies. Even when we are aware of our exteriors, most of us have no idea what our interior bodies are doing from one moment to the next. In this chapter you will gain a clearer understanding of the **genitals** (the external sexual organs) and the internal sex organs that make this "plumbing" work.

Female Sexual Anatomy and Physiology

Understanding the purpose and function of the parts of the body involved in female sexuality and reproduction is critical to maintaining sexual satisfaction and reproductive health. Not knowing the location and function of the clitoris, for example, may diminish sexual pleasure. Or, if a woman doesn't know the importance of regular pelvic exams and Pap tests, she may compromise her health.

Homologous: having the same basic structure

Anatomy: the form and structure of an organism

Physiology: the vital processes or normal functions in a living organism

Genitals: male and female sexual organs

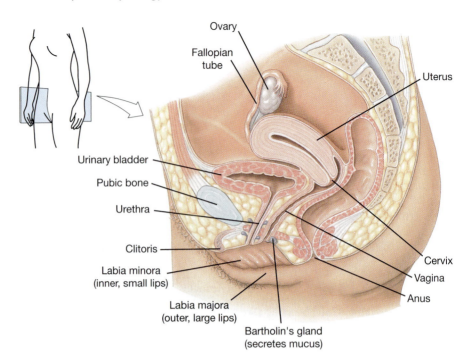

FIGURE 2.1 **The Female Internal Sexual Organs.** The internal sexual organs of the human female include the ovaries, fallopian tubes, uterus, and vagina.

FEMALE INTERNAL SEXUAL ORGANS

The internal sexual organs of the human female consist of the ovaries, fallopian tubes, uterus, and vagina (Figure 2.1). We will explain the functions of these various organs by tracing the pathway of an unfertilized egg from an ovary out of the body.

Ovaries

Ovaries: female gonads that produce ova and sex hormones

Gonads: organs that produce the sex cells and sex hormones; testicles in males and ovaries in females

Estrogen: a hormone secreted by the ovary and responsible for typical female sex characteristics

Progesterone: a hormone produced in the ovary that prepares and maintains the uterus for pregnancy

Ova: egg cells

Ovulation: the discharge of a mature ovum from the ovary

Fertilize: to join male and female cells, sperm and ova, so that offspring develop

Fallopian Tubes: ducts that connect the ovaries to the uterus; oviducts

Oviducts: fallopian tubes

Fimbriae: the fingerlike projections at the end of the fallopian tube nearest the ovary that capture the egg and deliver it into the tube

Each human female has two **ovaries** (Figure 2.2) about the size, shape, and texture of an irregular unshelled almond (though not almond-colored; the ovaries are a dull gray). Located at the ends of the fallopian tubes, one on each side of the uterus, the ovaries are attached to the uterus by ovarian ligaments, a type of connective tissue. The ovaries are **gonads** that perform two primary functions: the production of the female sex hormones **estrogen** and **progesterone,** and the production of mature **ova,** or egg cells. At birth, a female infant's ovaries contain about 400,000 immature ova, all of the eggs she will ever have. This is far more eggs than a woman will ever need; during her reproductive years only about four to five hundred ripened eggs will be released for possible fertilization. The *ovarian follicles* are small sacs containing ova. After maturing in the ovarian follicles, eggs are released (usually one at a time) during the process of **ovulation.** The released egg is gently drawn from the surface of the ovary into the fallopian tubes (the topic of the next section). This journey, which typically takes 3 or 4 days, is the period during which a woman is *fertile*, that is, the time when pregnancy may occur. If the egg is not **fertilized** during this time, it is expelled during menstruation.

Fallopian Tubes

The twin **fallopian tubes,** or **oviducts,** are hollow, muscular tubes approximately 10 centimeters or 4 inches long, attached one on each side of the uterus (see Figure 2.1). They extend outward from the uterus toward, but are not attached directly to, the ovaries. Each funnel-shaped fallopian tube fans out into fingerlike extensions called **fimbriae,** which drape over the ovary, but may not actually touch it. Hairlike cilia on the fimbriae become active during ovulation, coaxing the egg from the ovary and propelling it down the length of the tube toward the uterus. If sperm are present, the egg

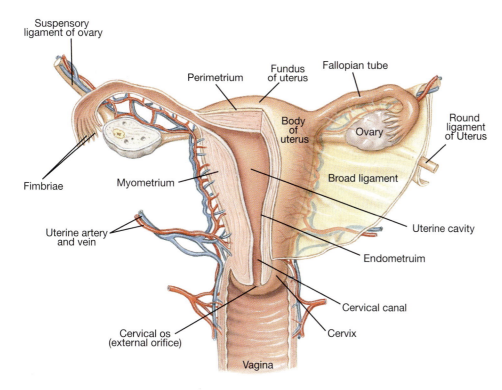

Suspensory
ligament of ovary

Perimetrium

Fundus
of uterus

Fallopian tube

Body
of
uterus

Ovary

Round
ligament
of Uterus

Fimbriae

Myometrium

Broad ligament

Uterine cavity

Uterine artery
and vein

Endometruim

Cervical canal

Cervical os
(external orifice)

Cervix

Vagina

FIGURE 2.2 The Ovaries
and Uterus. Source: Martini, 2001.

may be fertilized while in the upper portion of the fallopian tube. If the fertilized egg does not precede all of the way to the uterus, an aptly named *tubal pregnancy* may result. (See Chapter 5 for more on this potentially dangerous condition.)

Uterus

The **uterus,** or **womb,** is a hollow, muscular organ shaped like an upside-down pear (see Figure 2.2) in which a fertilized egg implants and develops into a fetus. The uterus is suspended in the pelvic cavity by a number of flexible ligaments. Usually the uterus is positioned so that the top slants forward toward the abdomen (*antroverted*), although in about 10 percent of women the uterus tips backward toward the spine (*retroverted*). A retroverted uterus generally becomes antroverted spontaneously during the third month of pregnancy (Martini, 2001). If a woman has not given birth, the uterus is about 3 inches long, 3 inches wide, about an inch thick near the top, and weighs about 2 ounces. No organ undergoes the same kind of dramatic change in adulthood as the uterus. It grows to 2 pounds by the end of pregnancy, independent of the weight of the fetus or placenta, and then after pregnancy shrinks back almost (but not quite!) to its original size.

Nature seems to like to do things in groups of three. The uterus is divided into three major parts. The uppermost part of the uterus (the bottom of the pear) is the **fundus.** The central region of the uterus in which the fetus develops is called the **uterine body.** The **cervix,** the lower part of the uterus, projects down into the vagina and opens slightly for the release of menstrual blood and even more so for the birth of a baby. Viewed through the vagina, the cervix of a woman who has never been pregnant appears like a smooth, pink disk with a small hole, called the **os,** in the middle—some have described it as looking something like a glazed doughnut.

The uterine wall is composed of three layers. The innermost layer, the **endometrium,** is richly supplied with blood vessels and glands. It is the endometrial tissue that is expelled through the cervix and vagina during menstruation (see page 34). The middle, muscular layer, the **myometrium,** gives the uterus strength and flexibility and is the source of the contractions necessary for childbirth. The outermost layer, the **perimetrium,** provides an external cover for the uterus.

Uterus: hollow, muscular internal female organ in which the fertilized egg develops until birth

Womb: the uterus

Fundus: the uppermost part of the uterus

Uterine body: the central region of the uterus in which a fetus may develop

Cervix: small, lower end of the uterus that protrudes into the vagina

Os: opening in the middle of the cervix that leads to the interior of the uterus

Endometrium: tissue that lines the inside of the uterine walls

Myometrium: the smooth muscle layer of the uterine wall

Perimetrium: the thin membrane covering the outside of the uterus

What is the G Spot?

Ancient Indian texts from the 11th century refer to an area in the front part of the vagina that was later named after German gynecologist Ernest Gräfenberg, who described this sexually arousable spot in an article published in 1950. The **Gräfenberg spot,** sometimes referred to as the *G spot*, usually is described as a mass of tissue about the size of a bean that is located on the front wall of the vagina midway between the pubic bone and the cervix. See Figure 2.3. It has been reported that some women experience sexual arousal, orgasm, and even "ejaculation" when the G spot is stimulated (Darling, 1990; Davidson et al., 1989; Zaviacic & Whipple, 1993). There are those who think that the G spot is not a spot that can be touched with a finger but more accurately should be called the G zone to describe a fairly large area composed of the lower anterior wall of the vagina and the underlying urethra and surrounding glands (Alzate & Lodano, 1984; Heath, 1984).

If you can't find your G spot, don't be alarmed; one study reported that a tissue mass corresponding to the G spot was found in less than 10 percent of women examined (Masters, Johnson, & Kolodny, 1992). Other investigators have found no evidence for the existence of this area of heightened sensitivity (Goldberg et. al., 1983), or think it may be nothing more than a spot where the roots of the clitoris run deep into the vaginal wall (Angier, 1999).

FIGURE 2.3 How to Find the Grafenberg Spot. To locate the Grafenberg spot, use two fingers and press deeply into the anterior wall of the vagina.

Vagina

The **vagina** is an elastic, muscular tube that extends back and upward from the external vaginal opening to the cervix (see Figure 2.2). The vagina has three major functions: the receptacle for the penis during sexual intercourse, the passageway for menstrual flow, and the birth canal through which a **fetus** becomes a baby during childbirth. The vagina is a 3- to 5-inch-long passageway built of skin, muscle, and fibrous tissue that extend at a 45-degree angle from the labia to the cervix. You might think of the vagina as being something like a turtleneck sweater (see CROSS-CULTURAL PERSPECTIVES for other views of the vagina). At rest, the walls of the vagina lie against one another. During sexual arousal, the cervix lifts upward and the vagina expands in length to receive the penis. The width of the vagina is similarly flexible, to accommodate many dimensions, from an incoming penis or tampon to an outgoing baby.

CROSS-CULTURAL PERSPECTIVES

Genital Mythology

Many societies throughout the world have folklore about dangerous genitalia. Myths about vagina dentata, *vaginas with teeth that can kill men during intercourse, occur among American Indian groups north of Mexico as well as in* South America, India, Siberia, Greenland, and the Pacific islands. *Penis dentatus, the penis with teeth, is believed to be so powerful that it can eat, drink, and even cut down trees (Gregersen, 1994).*

The walls of the vagina consist of three layers. The inner lining, or *vaginal mucosa*, is a mucous membrane that is similar to the inside of the mouth. The cells of the vaginal mucosa are the source of vaginal lubrication that facilitates the insertion of a penis into the vagina during intercourse. As its name suggests, the *muscularis*, the middle

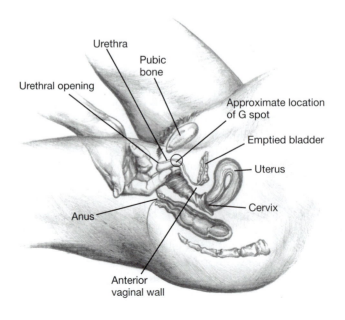

Urethra

Pubic bone

Urethral opening

Approximate location of G spot

Emptied bladder

Uterus

Cervix

Anus

Anterior vaginal wall

layer of the vaginal walls, is muscular; it is these muscles that contract during orgasm. The outer, fibrous layer connects the vagina to other pelvic structures. The vaginal walls are richly supplied with blood vessels throughout, but the sensory nerve endings are concentrated in the lower third of the vagina nearest the vaginal entrance.

FEMALE EXTERNAL SEXUAL ORGANS

The external sexual organs of the human female include all the parts of the vulva: the mons veneris, labia, vestibule, urethral opening, introitus, hymen, and clitoris (Figure 2.4).

Vulva

The external portion of the female reproductive system is collectively referred to as the **vulva.** The vulva includes the mons veneris, the labia, the urinary and vaginal openings, and the clitoris. The functions of the vulva are to protect the woman's internal sexual organs, to act as a source of her sexual pleasure, and to enhance the arousal of her partner. Beneath the hair, skin, and fatty pads of the vulva are a vast network of tissues and vessels that underlie the external sex organs. Two bundles of erectile tissue wrapped in muscle, the **vestibular bulbs,** are attached to the clitoris at the top and extend downward along the sides of the vaginal opening. During sexual arousal, the vestibular bulbs become engorged with blood, inflating the size of the clitoris and lengthening the vagina.

Mons Veneris

The **mons veneris** (Latin for "mound of Venus," named for the Roman goddess of love), also called the mons pubis, is the pad of fatty tissue that cushions the *pubic symphysis,* the slightly movable joint between the left and right pubic bones (see Figure 2.1). The pubic symphysis is relatively delicate and could be bruised by the impact of sexual intercourse (or riding a bicycle). The mons is supplied with a large number of nerve endings, and some women find manual stimulation of the mons to be pleasurable.

Vagina: the stretchable canal that extends from the external genital opening to the cervix

Fetus: the developing human organism from about 8 weeks after conception until birth

Gräfenberg Spot: a mass of tissue in the front wall of the vagina, claimed by some women to produce sexual arousal, orgasm, and an ejaculation of fluids when stimulated; also called **G spot**

Vulva: the external female genitals

Vestibular Bulbs: structures on each side of the vaginal opening that engorge with blood and swell during sexual arousal

Mons Veneris: mound of fatty tissue over the pubic bone above the vagina

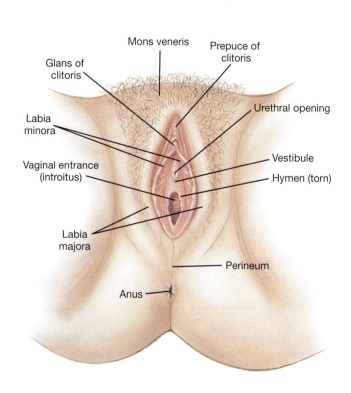

FIGURE 2.4 The Female External Sexual Organs.
Source: Martini, 2001.

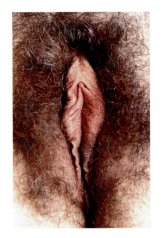

The appearance of external female genitalia vary considerably, as these three examples show.

Labia

Extending down from the mons, the vulva includes two prominent sets of skin folds, collectively referred to as the labia (Latin for "lips"): the **labia majora** (the big or outer lips) and the **labia minora** (the little or inner lips) (see Figure 2.4). With their vast network of nerve endings, the labia are an important source of sexual sensations for most women.

Beneath the outer folds of skin of the labia majora is a network of connective tissue and fat. Under the fat is erectile tissue that engorges with blood during sexual arousal. When they are not stimulated, the labia majora usually are folded together, to protect the urinary and vaginal openings. The fat of the labia, like that of the female breasts and hips, is sensitive to estrogen, the hormone of sexual maturity that will be discussed in more detail in Chapter 3. When estrogen surges through the female body during puberty, fatty deposits cause the labia to increase in size. Also during puberty, pubic hair grows on the outer sides of the labia majora. The skin of the outer sides of the labia majora usually is darker than the skin color of the thighs. The inner surfaces of the labia majora are hairless and lighter in color. The appearance of the labia majora can vary from thick and bulging to thin and flat. Within the tissue of the labia majora are smooth muscles, oil and fat glands, and nerve endings similar to those in the mons.

The labia minora, or inner lips, are the hairless inner folds of skin located within the labia majora that enfold and protect the vagina and nearby urethral opening. The labia minora contain oil glands (which can be felt through the thin skin as tiny bumps) and many nerve endings, so they are very sensitive to stimulation. Within the labia minora are small glands called **Bartholin's glands.** The function of these glands is something of a mystery. The few drops of fluid that they secrete during sexual arousal are not enough to effectively lubricate the vagina, though they may slightly moisten the labia. Additional functions of these glands are unknown. The labia minora are among the most variable part of female genitalia. They vary in size from one woman to another; in addition, the two may not be exactly symmetrical in the same woman, a cosmetic variation that is a cause for concern among some women (see CONSIDERATIONS box).

In some women the labia minora are hidden between the labia majora; in others, they may protrude. Like the labia majora, the labia minora swell with blood during sexual arousal, even doubling or tripling in size at peak arousal.

Vestibule

The area of the vulva inside the labia minora, the **vestibule** ("entranceway"), is rich in blood vessels and nerve endings, making it even more sensitive to the touch than the labia minora. At the front of the vestibule (toward the abdomen), the labia minora meet

Labia Majora: large folds of skin that form the outer lips of the vulva

Labia Minora: folds of skin located within the labia majora that form the inner lips of the vulva

Bartholin's Glands: small glands inside the vaginal opening that secrete a few drops of fluid during sexual arousal

Vestibule: the area of the vulva inside the labia minora

to form a fold or small hood of skin called the **prepuce,** or clitoral hood. Beneath the prepuce lies the clitoris. When the clitoris is erect and the labia minora spread, the vestibule become visible (see Figure 2.4).

Urethral Opening

The **urethral opening** is located below the clitoral glans and above the vaginal opening. Urine collected in the bladder passes through the **urethra,** a short tube connected to the bladder, and is excreted through the urethral opening. The urethral opening is not a reproductive organ. Although urine and semen both pass through the male penis, for women, urination and **coitus** do not occur through the same bodily opening.

Introitus and Hymen

The opening of the vagina, called the **introitus,** is located between the urethral opening and the **anus.** Partially covering the introitus is a fold of connective tissue called the **hymen,** a thin membrane containing a large number of blood vessels. The hymen may vary in shape and size (Figure 2.5) and may surround the vaginal opening (an annular hymen), form a bridge over it (a septate hymen), or appear as a sievelike covering (a cribriform hymen). Normally the hymen has an opening large enough to permit menstrual flow or the insertion of a tampon, but too small to permit entry of an erect penis without tearing.

Although the function of the hymen is unknown, it has a great deal of cultural significance. In many societies, the presence of an intact hymen was historically considered proof that a woman had never had intercourse. But an intact hymen is not proof of virginity. Some girls are born with minimal or incomplete hymens; the hymen can also be ruptured by accident or by normal exercise. When an intact hymen is ruptured there may be no discomfort and only minimal bleeding. Although pain and bleeding can occur the first time a woman has intercourse, it may be related to muscular tension due to anxiety and not associated with the rupture of the hymen.

Clitoris

The **clitoris,** located in the vestibule at the top of the labia minora under the prepuce (see Figure 2.5), is a small body of spongy tissue that is highly sexually sensitive. The clitoris is a three-sectioned cylindrical structure. The head or **clitoral glans** (a glans is a small, round mass or tissue that can swell and harden) is the most visible external part of the clitoris. The glans is located at the top of the clitoral shaft, or body, which is partly visible, and then extends under the muscle tissue of the vulva and up toward the joint where the plates of the pubic bone meet. The clitoral shaft is surrounded by a capsule of *fibroelastic* tissue (the tube that you feel

FIGURE 2.5 Annular, Septate, and Cribriform Hymens.

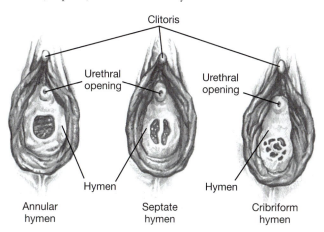

Annular hymen

Septate hymen

Cribriform hymen

Clitoris

Urethral opening

Urethral opening

Hymen

Hymen

FAQ:

Are the clitoris and penis pretty much the same?

Although the clitoris and the penis are derived from the same embryonic tissue, they are not literal counterparts. An aroused clitoris is swollen but not rigid like an erect penis. Although it is usually much smaller than a penis, the clitoral glans has 8,000 nerve fibers, almost twice as many as the penis. In fact, the clitoris has the highest concentration of nerve fibers in the body. Unlike the penis, as a rule the clitoris of the female mammal has no secretory or excretory functions (the exception is the spotted hyena of Africa whose vagina and clitoris are one organ). The clitoris is the only sexual organ whose only purpose is pure pleasure.

Prepuce: a covering fold of skin

Urethral Opening: the duct through which urine is discharged from the bladder

Urethra: the tube through which urine from the bladder is expelled

Coitus: sexual intercourse

Introitus: the opening of the vagina

Anus: the opening through which solid waste is eliminated from the body

Hymen: membrane that partially covers the vaginal opening

Clitoris: highly sensitive female organ located above the urethral opening that's only known function is sexual pleasure

Clitoral Glans: the head of the clitoris, which has a large number of nerve endings

CONSIDERATIONS

Private Proportions

Women's genitals vary in size, shape, and color. Just as women may be dissatisfied with the appearance of their noses, thighs, or breasts, there are those who are unhappy with the appearance of their genitals. Although it is less common than other types of plastic surgery, every year a few women undergo surgery to change the appearance of their genitals for aesthetic reasons or in hopes of improving their sex life. Although there are no precise statistics on the number of cosmetic procedures performed on female genitalia, the president of the American Society of Plastic and Reconstructive Surgery estimates that it is extremely rare (Schnur, 2000).

Labiaplasty is perhaps the most common female genital cosmetic procedure. In this procedure large, long, or asymmetrical labia minora are reconstructed by the surgical removal of excess skin. *Liposuction* can be used either to remove unwanted fat deposits from the mons, or to plump up or reshape the labia. Vaginal tightening and *clitoroplasty*, removal of the clitoral shaft, purportedly result in heightened sensitivity. These surgeries are expensive and, because they are cosmetic, are generally not covered by insurance. Like all surgeries, there are risks, including infection, scarring, and excessive bleeding. There is no evidence that any of these procedures improve sexual satisfaction.

 Can you think of a good reason to undergo this type of cosmetic surgery?

—*What type of research (experimental, case study, interview, etc.) would you do to discover whether the sexual satisfaction of women who undergo these procedures is improved?*

—*Prepare an outline of your experimental procedure.*

---

under the flesh) and is attached to twin **crura,** or roots, internal wing-shaped structures that branch inward from each side of the clitoral shaft and attach to the pelvic bone. Unlike the clitoral glans, the shaft has relatively few nerves. It is threaded through with thousands of blood vessels, allowing it to swell during arousal and push the glans upward.

Because so much of the clitoris is beneath the skin, it's hard to get an accurate measurement. Most measurements of clitoral size concern the clitoral glans and shaft. The average size of the adult clitoris from base to glans is about 16 millimeters, approximately the diameter of a dime (Verkauf et al., 1992). Like all body parts, there is considerable individual variation in size and shape (see CONSIDERATIONS box).

THE MENSTRUAL CYCLE

The sexual and reproductive lives of a woman are interwoven with **menstruation,** the sloughing off of uterine lining that takes place if conception has not occurred. But menstruation is only one part of the **menstrual cycle,** the series of events that occurs each month during a woman's reproductive years. The words *menstruation* and *menstrual* are derived from the Latin *mensis,* "month," because the human menstrual cycle averages 28 days, or about a month. Every month from her first menstrual cycle (**menarche**) as a preteen or teenager to her last (**menopause**) in her 40s or 50s, a woman's uterine lining prepares for the fertilization of an egg cell. A woman who has two pregnancies will average about 500 menstrual cycles in her lifetime. Although usually referred to as blood, menstrual fluid is actually a mix of blood, mucus, and cells from the endometrium, the lining of the uterus. If fertilization does not occur, the uterine lining sheds or sloughs off and is discharged as menstrual flow.

Menarche

The first menstrual cycle, which signals the start of puberty in young women, is called menarche. In the United States the average age at menarche is about 12 years (Herman-Giddens et al., 1997). The average age at first menstruation has decreased by 4 months every decade since 1830 (Welch, 1992) but has remained fairly stable for the last 30 years (Dann, 1996). One hundred years ago, the average age of menarche was 16 years. As we will discuss in Chapter 9, scientists have offered several possible explanations for

Crura: two trunks of the clitoris that separate and join at the pubic arch and attach the clitoris to the pubic bone

Menstruation: the sloughing off of built-up uterine lining that recurs in nonpregnant women from menarche to menopause

Menstrual Cycle: the time from the beginning of one menstrual period to the beginning of the next; typically 28 days

Menarche: the initial onset of menstruation in life

Menopause: the cessation of menstruation in life

this change. There is a wide variation in the age of onset of menstruation. Numerous factors are involved in the timing of the first menstrual period, including genetics, diet, climate, stress, and emotional interaction (Frayser, 1985). In some societies menarche is celebrated as the time when a girl becomes a woman. We will discuss the social implications of menarche and menstruation in more detail in Chapter 8.

Length and Frequency of the Menstrual Cycle

The menstrual cycle is measured from the first day of menstrual flow to the day before the next flow begins. The length of the menstrual cycle ranges from 24 to 42 days (Belsey & Pinol, 1997), with an average length of 28 days. Some women's cycles are as regular as clockwork, while for others the lengths of the cycles vary widely. A woman's period may arrive a few days earlier or later than usual for a number of reasons. Travel to a different time zone, sleep deprivation, stress, or changes in diet and exercise can delay or accelerate menstruation. There can also be variations in the amount of flow; sometimes the menstrual flow is heavy and other times it is light. A single absent or particularly heavy period is no reason to panic, but significant changes in your period can be an early-warning sign of a possible health problem (see "Menstrual Problems" later in this chapter).

Hormonal Regulation of the Menstrual Cycle

Have you ever heard the expression "raging hormones"? This phrase is commonly used to describe feelings experienced during the menstrual cycle, although it can also be used to refer to teenagers undergoing the dramatic changes of puberty. Biologically, **hormones** are chemicals that are released at one location in the body and sent to act on another. A number of different organs distributed throughout your body, collectively called the **endocrine system,** act together to regulate hormone levels. The endocrine system is a form of chemical communication. The chemical messengers sent on these errands are the hormones, and the circulatory system (the blood) is the path they take to accomplish their mission, whether it is sexual arousal, initiating the changes of puberty, or delivering a baby.

The **hypothalamus** and **pituitary gland** in the brain, various endocrine glands, and activity of the ovaries and uterus all play roles in the regulation of the menstrual cycle (Figure 2.6). The hypothalamus, sometimes called the "master gland," oversees this process via a mechanism called *negative feedback.* When the hypothalamus detects decreased hormone levels in the bloodstream, it stimulates the other players to increase the levels of these hormones. Once hormones reach a certain level, the hypothalamus orders a decrease in hormone production. More details about the raging of the hormones appear in the following discussion of the phases of the menstrual cycle.

Phases of the Menstrual Cycle

While several models of the menstrual cycle have been suggested, the menstrual cycle is most easily understood as consisting of three phases: *menstrual, proliferative,* and *luteal.* Complex ovary and uterine changes characterize each of these phases (see Figure 2.6).

The Menstrual Phase   While the **menstrual phase** actually signifies the end of the cycle (if a cycle can be said to have a beginning and an end!), it is the easiest place to begin since it is marked by the onset of menstruation, the only visible sign of the menstrual cycle. As you have already learned, the menstrual phase consists of the sloughing off and discharge of the endometrium, the inner lining of the uterus. This process may take 3 to 6 days. Menstruation is the result of falling levels of estrogen and progesterone in the blood (see the "Luteal Phase" later). Without these hormones to sustain it, the endometrium disintegrates, and the dead cells along with small amounts of blood are discharged through the cervix and vagina. Typically 1 to 2 fluid ounces (i.e., 2–3 Tbs) of menstrual flow occur with each menstrual period.

"[W]e bleed to rid the uterus of potentially dangerous pathogens that might have hitched a ride inside on the backs of sperm. Think of it. The uterus is a luxurious city just waiting to be sacked, and sperm are the ideal Trojan horse."

(ANGIER, 1999, P. 116)

Hormones: chemicals produced by one tissue and conveyed by the bloodstream to another to effect physiological activity

Endocrine System: the body system of ductless glands that produce and secrete hormones directly into the bloodstream

Hypothalamus: brain structure that plays a major role in controlling the production of sex hormones and regulates many sexual responses

Pituitary Gland: small gland in the base of the brain that receives instructions from the hypothalamus and secretes hormones

Menstrual Phase: the phase of the menstrual cycle during which the lining of the uterus is shed

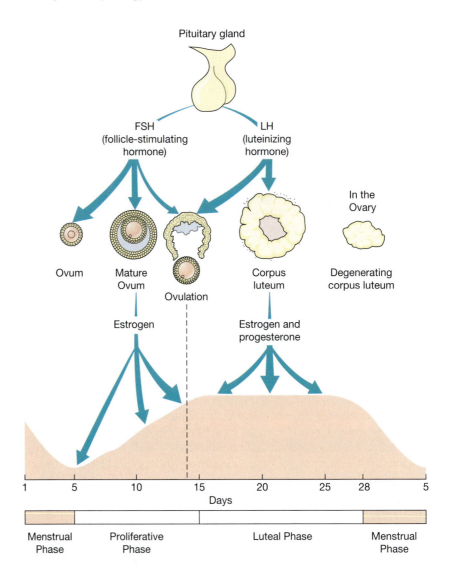

FIGURE 2.6 The Menstrual Cycle.

Proliferative Phase: the phase of the menstrual cycle in which the ovarian follicles mature

Gonadotropins: hormones that stimulate the activity of the function of the gonads (ovaries and testicles)

Gonadotropin-Releasing Hormone (Gn-RH): hormone produced and released in a pulsating manner by the hypothalamus; controls the pituitary gland's production and release of gonadotropins

Follicle-Stimulating Hormone (FSH): pituitary hormone that stimulates the development of the ovarian follicles (eggs) and the release of estrogen in women

The Proliferative Phase During the **proliferative phase**, the lining of the uterus proliferates or expands as the pituitary gland increases production of **gonadotropins**, hormones that stimulate activity in the ovaries (and in testes, which we will discuss later in this chapter). The low level of estrogen at menstruation signals the hypothalamus to release a hormone called **gonadotropin-releasing hormone (Gn-RH)**, which then stimulates the pituitary to produce two other hormones, **follicle-stimulating hormone (FSH)** and **luteinizing hormone (LH)**. FSH causes the ovaries to increase secretion of estrogen, which initiates a new proliferative phase. LH causes the ovary to release a mature ovum and stimulates the development of the **corpus luteum,** the mass of cells left in the ovary after the follicle ruptures and an egg is released.

During the proliferative phase, ovarian **follicles** mature as the ovaries prepare for ovulation, and the endometrium changes in order to allow a fertilized ovum to implant. Midway through the proliferative phase, estrogen production by the ovaries increases. The estrogen and other hormones prepare the developing follicle for ovulation. When the estrogen level peaks, the pituitary gland decreases the release of FSH and stimulates LH production. In response to the increased levels of LH in the bloodstream, the mature follicle ruptures and releases an ovum.

Ovulation, the release of the mature ovum from the ovary, marks the transition from the proliferative phase to the luteal phase. Immediately following ovulation is the time during the cycle when a woman is most likely to become pregnant. As many as 10

or 20 ova (eggs) may begin to ripen, but usually a single ovum is released from the surface of the ovary; the other ova degenerate. Ovulation typically occurs at midcycle, approximately day 14 of a typical 28-day menstrual cycle. However, it may occur from day 9 to day 19, and in some cycles there may be no ovulation (Masters & Johnson, 1966; Masters, Johnson, & Kolodny, 1992). **Anovulatory cycles,** cycles during which no egg is released, occur most frequently in the years just after menarche.

At ovulation, increases in estrogen cause the endometrium to thicken, due to the growth of tissue and blood vessels. As endometrial cells grow, the uterine lining expands up to 10 times its normal thickness. Increases in estrogen also cause cervical mucus secretions to increase. The mucus changes consistency, becoming clear, slippery, and stretchy. The pH of the mucus also becomes more alkaline, which contributes to sperm motility and longevity.

A woman's *basal body temperature* drops slightly at ovulation and then rises about 1 degree Fahrenheit the following day. A woman who wishes to become or not to become pregnant may use this information to help her determine the day of ovulation. However, changes in body temperature also may result from factors unrelated to ovulation so, as we discuss in Chapter 6, this may not be a reliable method of birth control. Some women experience cramping during ovulation called *mittelschmerz* (German for "middle pain," reflecting the fact that it occurs in the middle of menstrual cycles). The pain occurs on the same side of the abdomen as the ovary releasing an ovum.

The Luteal Phase   The **luteal phase** (also referred to as the postovulatory or secretory phase) begins immediately after ovulation and lasts until menstrual flow begins again. Luteal refers to the *corpus luteum*, which is formed during this phase. The corpus luteum produces large amounts of progesterone. Progesterone, along with estrogen produced by the ovaries, causes the uterus to prepare for the possible implantation of a fertilized egg and serves to regulate the production and release of other hormones in the woman's body.

If **implantation** of a fertilized ovum does not occur, the pituitary gland responds to high estrogen and progesterone levels by decreasing production of LH and FSH; this causes the corpus luteum to degenerate (10 to 12 days after ovulation) and estrogen and progesterone production to drop abruptly. The reduction of hormone levels causes endometrial cells to die, initiating the menstrual phase (Masters, Johnson, & Kolodny, 1992). So we're back to the "beginning" of the cycle.

Menstrual Synchrony

In 1971 biologist Martha McClintock presented data on **menstrual synchrony** after looking at the menstrual cycles of several groups of college roommates. The roommates began the semester with menstrual cycles randomly distributed throughout the month. Over the course of the school year, the roommates' cycles gradually converged until after 7 months the dates of onset of menstruation among the roommates were 33 percent closer than they had been at the beginning of the school year. Among a control group of women who did not share a room, there were no signs of menstrual synchrony. However, in a review of the menstrual synchrony studies published over the past 25 years, 16 were found to have statistically significant evidence of synchrony and 10 had no evidence of statistically meaningful patterns. A few studies have found evidence of asynchrony—as the months passed women who lived together became less harmonized in their periods rather than more (Weller & Weller, 1993). Menstrual synchrony was not found for 30 cohabiting lesbian couples (living together an average of 35 months) from whom 3 months of menstrual data were collected (Weller & Weller, 1998).

There is evidence that menstrual synchrony is affected by the release of **pheromones,** airborne chemicals released into the environment by certain animals, which affect the behavior of other animals of the same species. The pheromones affecting the length of the human menstrual cycle may be detected by the sense of smell,

Luteinizing Hormone (LH): hormone secreted by the pituitary gland that triggers ovulation and helps prepare the uterine lining for implantation

Corpus Luteum: the mass of cells left in the ovary by the ruptured follicle during ovulation, releasing an egg; subsequently it produces progesterone and estrogen

Follicle: small sac in the ovary that contains a developing egg

Anovulatory Cycles: cycles without ovulation

Luteal Phase: phase of the menstrual cycle in which the corpus luteum is formed and the uterus is prepared to nourish a fertilized egg

Implantation: attachment of the fertilized egg to the uterine lining

Menstrual Synchrony: the development of congruent menstrual cycles that sometimes occur among women who live together

Pheromones: airborne chemical substances secreted externally by some animals that convey information or produce specific responses in other members of the same species

Pads or tampons?

Dealing with menstrual discharge has been a concern for thousands of years. The women of ancient Egypt fashioned tampons from rolls of softened papyrus leaves. The ancient Japanese used paper, and Romans used wads of wool. The first disposable sanitary napkin was marketed in the late 1800s, but sanitary napkins did not become popular until after World War II. In 1933 Dr. Earle Cleveland Haas patented the internally worn tampon.

Today sanitary napkins (pads) and tampons are the most popular products. However, the federal Food and Drug Administration (FDA) has approved a number of new products in recent years. A product called Instead, a disposable cup, is inserted into the upper vagina, under the cervix; it rests against the rear wall of the vagina and behind the pubic pone. Instead, which is made of flexible, medical-grade plastic, softens with body heat to mold to a woman's individual anatomy. It collects, not absorbs, menstrual flow and can be worn about twice as long as a tampon. The Keeper, a reusable cup, also is worn internally. This soft rubber cup is inserted into the lower vagina to collect menstrual flow. The device is held in place by suction and, unlike Instead, The Keeper can be reused each month for up to 10 years.

but at such low levels that they cannot be consciously detected. The phases of the woman's cycle are either lengthened or shortened, depending on which phase of the menstrual cycle she was in when she was exposed to the pheromones. Pheromones from women in the menstrual phase tend to shorten the cycle of women exposed to them, while pheromones from women in the proliferative phase lengthen the recipient's menstrual cycle. Secretions taken from women during the luteal phase of the cycle have no detectable impact on the timing of other women's periods (Stern & McClintock, 1996).

Sexual Activity and the Menstrual Cycle

In most animal species females are more interested in sex around the time of ovulation, which as you have already learned is when fertilization is most likely to occur. Although human females can engage in sexual behavior any time during the menstrual cycle, a number of studies have investigated the possibility that female sexual desire is linked to the hormonal changes associated with the phases of the menstrual cycle. While some research suggests that women tend to have more erotic interests around the time of ovulation (Dennerstein et al., 1994, Regan, 1996), other studies have found little or no difference in arousability at the different phases of the menstrual cycle (Morrell et al., 1984; Meuwissen & Over, 1992). The effect of hormones on sexual desire will be discussed more thoroughly in Chapter 3.

While there is no medical reason to avoid intercourse during the menstrual phase, some couples prefer to abstain from coitus during this time (Barnhart et al., 1995). One reason for avoiding intercourse is the reduction in the woman's sexual desire due to uncomfortable symptoms of menstruation (see "Dysmenorrhea" in the next section). However, sexual activity (orgasm) may actually help relieve these symptoms (Choi, 1992). People may also avoid sex during menstruation because of religious beliefs, cultural taboos (see CROSS-CULTURAL PERSPECTIVES box), or a dislike of messiness. As we will discuss in Chapter 6, having intercourse during a woman's menstrual period is not a reliable form of birth control.

Menstrual Problems

While many women have some physical or mood changes during the menstrual cycles (McFarlane & Williams, 1994), several conditions associated with menstruation require special attention. See Table 2.1 for a summary of symptoms and possible causes.

Dysmenorrhea Dysmenorrhea is the medical term for painful menstruation. Symptoms may include pelvic or lower abdominal cramping, backache, and a feeling of being bloated, sometimes accompanied by diarrhea, nausea, or vomiting. Most women have experienced some degree of dysmenorrhea at one time or another. Symptoms usually begin approximately 24 hours before menstrual flow starts and continue for 2 to 3 days.

Dysmenorrhea is classified into two types, depending upon the onset and cause of the discomfort. If no pelvic abnormalities are present or the condition is present from the onset of menses, the condition is called *primary dysmenorrhea*. Primary dysmenorrhea is caused by an excessive release of *prostaglandin*, a hormonelike substance produced by many tissues of the body, including the lining of the uterus. Various medications, such as aspirin, naproxen sodium, and ibuprofen can provide symptom relief. Birth control pills are 90 percent effective in relieving the discomfort of dysmenorrhea. As we have already noted, being orgasmic also may reduce the symptoms (Masters & Johnson, 1966). *Secondary*

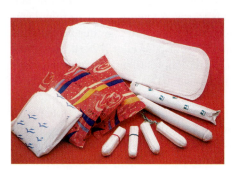

Various methods of dealing with menstrual discharge include the use of sanitary napkins (pads), tampons, Instead, and The Keeper.

Curses

The idea that menstrual blood is toxic is found in many cultures. Menstruating women have been said to make meat go bad, wine turn sour, bread dough fall, mirrors darken, and knives become dull. Some anthropologists have suggested that hunting societies have been particularly stringent in keeping women quarantined when they are menstruating, in part because of fears that menstrual odor attracts animals (Angier, 1999). Many societies that associate menstruation with impurity or regard the menstrual flow as dangerous to others isolate menstruating women to protect the community. Magical precautions and purification rites are also undertaken in a vast number of cultures. In many New Guinea societies men consider menstrual blood so poisonous that they take extraordinary measures to avoid coming into contact with it (Meigs, 1984).

There are at least 12 societies in the world where people believe menstruation is caused by sexual intercourse. This belief might be explained by the fact that most girls in these societies either marry or are allowed to have sex before puberty (Gregersen, 1994). Other cultures be-

In many indigenous societies in North and South America, as well as other areas of the world, menstruating women were segregated in special living quarters.

lieve that menstrual blood is therapeutic or endows special powers on women. Moroccans have used menstrual blood in dressings for sores and wounds, while among the Yurok of northern California, women traditionally believed that a menstruating woman should isolate herself because this is the time when she is at the height of her powers. Thus, her time should not be wasted on mundane tasks or social distractions, nor should her concentration be broken by concerns with the opposite sex. Rather, all of her energies should be applied in concentrated meditation on her life. The menstrual shelter, or room, was seen as a place where women go to make themselves stronger (Buckley, 1982).

dysmenorrhea is diagnosed when a specific physical condition, for example, endometriosis, pelvic inflammatory disease, ovarian **cysts,** or **tumors,** accompanies the menstrual pain. To obtain relief from secondary dysmenorrhea the underlying condition must be treated.

Menorrhagia   If a woman experiences excessively heavy or prolonged menstrual bleeding (soaking through at least one pad or tampon every hour for several consecutive hours), she may have **menorrhagia.** Hormone imbalances or a variety of medical disorders may cause this abnormal uterine bleeding.

In a normal menstrual cycle there is a balance between estrogen and progesterone. If this balance is disrupted, the endometrium continues to build up during the proliferative phase. When it sheds during the menstrual phase, heavy bleeding results. If a hormone imbalance is responsible for menorrhagia, *hormone therapy,* treatment that prevents cancer cells from getting the hormones they need to grow, may be recommended. Another common cause of menorrhagia is the presence of uterine **fibroids** (discussed in "Disorders of the Female Sexual Organs"). In some cases endometrial **cancer** (cancer of the lining of the uterus), inflammation or infection of a reproductive organ, polyps, thyroid conditions, or other diseases may be responsible for the excessive bleeding. In order to alleviate menorrhagia in such cases, the underlying medical condition must be treated.

Dysmenorrhea: pain or discomfort before or during menstruation

Cyst: membranous sac containing a gaseous, liquid, or semisolid substance

Tumor: an abnormal mass of tissue

Menorrhagia: excessive menstrual discharge

Fibroids: benign smooth muscle tumors of the uterus that may cause pain, irregular bleeding, and an enlarged uterus

Cancer: disease in which cells in body grow without control

TABLE 2.1	
Menstrual Problems	
Problem	**Possible Cause**
Absent or Infrequent Periods	Pregnancy
	Menopause
	Hormone imbalance
	Low body fat
	Stress
Spotting	Ovulation
	Breakthrough bleeding
	Thyroid imbalance
	Cervical polyps
	Cervical cancer
	Drug reaction
	Infection
Prolonged and Heavy Periods	Fibroids
	Endometrial polyps
	Perimenopause
Short and Light Periods	Hormonal imbalance

Amenorrhea   **Amenorrhea** is the complete absence of menses for more than 6 months. *Primary amenorrhea* is the failure to begin to menstruate at puberty. This may be caused by problems with the reproductive organs, hormonal imbalances, or poor health. *Secondary amenorrhea* is the absence of menstrual periods in women who have had regular periods in the past. There are a number of causes of secondary amenorrhea. For most sexually active women in their reproductive years, amenorrhea is a signal of possible pregnancy. In older women, it may mean that menopause is approaching. In both cases, amenorrhea is perfectly normal. However, for nonpregnant women in their reproductive years, amenorrhea is usually a sign of a disturbance in the secretion of ovarian hormones. Other causes include defects in or absence of the uterus or vagina (see CONSIDERATIONS box for another cause).

When body fat falls below 5 percent, the body stops producing estrogen and ovulation ceases. Women with eating disorders such as *anorexia nervosa* and *bulimia* (Schweiger, 1991), as well as female athletes such as long-distance runners, can experience estrogen shutdown (Prior & Vigna, 1991; Shangold, 1985). When these women gain some body fat, they usually resume normal menstrual cycles.

Amenorrhea: the absence of menstruation for more than 6 months

Eliminating "The Curse"

CONSIDERATIONS

Since some hormone-based contraceptives, especially Depo-Provera, make it simple, safe, and relatively inexpensive to eliminate menstruation, having a period can be optional. Certainly some women consider menstruating a pain—both in terms of the physical discomfort and the nuisance factor. Some might view menstruation as unnecessary and even dangerous since it is the cause of so many health problems for women. Others feel that no matter how inconvenient it may be menstruation is an essential part of being a woman.

 If you had the opportunity, would you eliminate menstruation? Why or why not?

Toxic Shock Syndrome   **Toxic shock syndrome** is a rare but sometimes fatal bacterial disease among menstruating women that was first recognized in the late 1970s. The toxin-secreting bacteria (certain strains of staphylococcus aureus and group 4 streptococci) that cause toxic shock are usually already present in the body in harmless numbers. If these bacteria proliferate in the vagina, the toxins may cause high fever, a rapid drop of blood pressure, a rash followed by peeling skin on the palms of the hands and the soles of the feet, nausea, vomiting, diarrhea, and aching muscles (Vastag, 2001).

Toxic shock syndrome appears to be linked to tampon use, particularly the use of superabsorbent tampons. Tampons left in the vagina for 6 hours or more may provide an environment conducive to overgrowth of toxin-producing bacteria. As a precaution, it is recommended that a woman use the least absorbent tampon needed for her flow; she should also change tampons every 2 to 4 hours, and use sanitary pads during the night.

Premenstrual Syndrome (PMS)   **Premenstrual syndrome (PMS)** usually is defined by a set of symptoms including tension, irritability, sluggishness, impatience, dizziness, nervousness, depression, indecisiveness, breast tenderness, constipation, headache, or a bloated feeling that appear beginning 2 or 3 days before the onset of menstrual flow (Stewart & Tooley, 1992) (see CAMPUS CONFIDENTIAL box). One study found that approximately half of the 40 to 50 percent of North American women who crave chocolate or sweets do so principally in the premenstrual part of their cycle (Michene et al., 1999). Severe PMS symptoms may afflict 10 to 20 percent of women of childbearing age (Woods et al., 1987) and can interfere with the ability to function socially or at work (Mortola, 1998). Women diagnosed with PMS do not necessarily have all of these symptoms, and it is not clear how many women actually suffer from some degree of PMS. Premenstrual syndrome should not be confused with *Premenstrual Dysphoric Disorder (PMDD)*, a psychiatric disorder characterized by more severe mood changes that interfere with normal activities and relationships in the luteal phase of the menstrual cycle (APA, 1994). Advertisements for antidepressant medication to treat PMDD may lead to greater recognition and improved treatment of PMDD, but also may lead to greater confusion and concern.

The cause or causes of PMS are not known, and it remains a controversial diagnosis (Olasov & Jackson, 1987; Robinson, 1989). According to one study, a majority of the women who report symptoms of PMS to their physicians have other medical or psychiatric disorders (Korzekwa & Steiner, 1999). Women seeking help for PMS have been reported to have significantly higher levels of depression and anxiety (Hunter et al., 1995). In addition, there is some evidence that attitudes toward menstruation and premenstrual experience are associated with exposure to messages about menstruation during adolescence (Anson, 1999): negative messages may result in negative experiences. Not everyone agrees that symptoms of PMS are necessarily negative. There is other research that suggests that the premenstrual phase of the cycle is accompanied by heightened activity, intellectual clarity, and feelings of well-being, happiness, and sexual desire (Nicholson, 1995).

Rather than being a matter of "raging hormones," that is, excess or deficiencies of hormones, in one study women with severe PMS were found to respond differently to normal hormone levels (Schmidt et al., 1998). In other words, they were more sensitive to the normal hormone fluctuations of the menstrual cycle. PMS is most likely the result of a complex interaction between ovarian hormones and central nervous system neurotransmitters such as serotonin (Mortola, 1998).

Many of the symptoms of PMS can be minimized by lifestyle adjustments. Simple measures that can reduce PMS symptoms include a well-balanced diet, not smoking, aerobic exercise, and relaxation techniques (Frackiewicz & Shiovitz, 2001). Limiting caffeine intake may also help. For more severe cases, drugs that have been shown to be effective include the antidepressant medications Prozac and Zoloft, which belong to a class of medications known as selective serotonin reuptake inhibitors (SSRIs).

CAMPUS CONFIDENTIAL

"For about 5 days every month, I have raging PMS. Irritable doesn't even begin to describe my mood. It's way beyond irritable to have a major temper tantrum because someone moved my stapler. And talk about moody . . . a soppy TV commercial can make me bawl like a baby.

"I know my irrational behavior affects my relationships, but when I'm PMS-ing I don't really care. What I really hate is when someone tells me that PMS is all in my head. I don't think I have any abnormal hang-ups about being a woman or think of my period as a "curse." But no matter how hard I try, right before my period I get bloated and achy, I have difficulty concentrating, and the smallest thing can set me off. Hormones are real, menstruation is real, and PMS is real, too." ●

Toxic Shock Syndrome: disease that occurs most often in menstruating females using tampons in which an overgrowth of bacteria may cause fever, vomiting, diarrhea, and often shock

Premenstrual Syndrome (PMS): physical and emotional symptoms of discomfort that occur in some women prior to menstruation

FAQ:

Is There a Male Menopause?

Since men do not have a menstrual cycle, strictly speaking they cannot undergo menopause. A sudden arrest of gonadal functions and fertility does not occur in middle-aged men as it does in middle-aged women. However, there are some who believe that male menopause (sometimes referred to as **viropause** or **andropause**) does exist. Proponents of this view claim that male menopause affects men ages 45 to 60 and causes symptoms including irritability, depression, indecisiveness, memory loss, weight gain, reduced endurance, a lower sex drive, and increased difficulty with **erections**. As they age, men typically produce less testosterone, the hormone primarily responsible for characteristics such as hair growth and sex drive. However, the decline in testosterone production is not great. Two thirds of men over age 65 produce as much or more testosterone than healthy 20-year-olds. Health problems such as cancer, heart disease, and diabetes, as well as drinking and smoking, can lower testosterone levels. For some men, testosterone pills, injections, or patches can be helpful, although there may be risk factors including prostate enlargement and prostate cancer.

Viropause/Andropause: male menopause; period when testosterone levels may decrease

Erection: firm and enlarged condition of a body organ or part when surrounding erectile tissue becomes engorged with blood; especially such a condition of the penis or clitoris

MENOPAUSE

Some young women look forward to their first menstrual period and others dread it. Similarly, some women think that menopause, sometimes referred to as "the change of life" or simply "the change," means the loss of their youth, attractiveness, and femininity while others eagerly anticipate a new lease on life—physically, emotionally, sexually, and spiritually.

Menopause, the permanent cessation of menstruation, is a life transition, not a disease. It is one of the physiological changes of the *climacteric*, the time period of a woman's natural transition from fertility to infertility. The climacteric generally lasts for about 15 years, approximately from age 45 to 60. The cessation of menstruation is about a 2-year process beginning at around age 50.

Until the last 200 years or so, most women never experienced menopause because they didn't live that long. Today, the average life expectancy for a woman in Western societies is approaching 80 years. This means that the average woman can expect to live about one third to half of her adult life after menopause (Beck, 1992).

The period before menstruation completely stops is called **perimenopause**. Beginning about age 35, the menstrual cycles of many women begin to shorten, to about 23 days on average by the mid-40s (Whitbourne, 1985). By her late 40s, a woman's cycles often become erratic. Another early sign of menopause is "gushing," the sudden heavy flow of menstrual blood that may be dark or clotted, and may seep through the normal tampon or sanitary napkin protection. Surgical menopause occurs if the ovaries are removed, or damaged so that they no longer produce hormones. In such cases menopause begins immediately with no perimenopausal period.

As a woman approaches age 50, the ovaries gradually stop producing progesterone and estrogen, so egg cells will no longer ripen. A decrease in progesterone lessens the possibility of embryo implantation in the uterus. The lowered levels of estrogen may result in unpleasant physical sensations such as night sweats, hot flashes, and alternating cold sweats. All of these symptoms result from the body's inability to dilate (expand) or to constrict (squeeze) blood vessels and thus to maintain an even body temperature. Other signs of estrogen deficiency include dizziness, headaches, joint pains, heart palpitations, difficulty sleeping, tingling, and burning or itchy skin. With less estrogen and elevated FSH levels, bones can become brittle (a condition known as *osteoporosis*), rates of heart disease can increase, the vagina becomes less moist, and the skin generally becomes dry and thin.

Some 10 to 15 percent of North American women experience no problems during menopause, while another 10 to 15 percent have severe symptoms. The remaining 70 to 80 percent have some symptoms that come and go over a period of years (Sheehy, 1992). Cross-cultural data indicate that while women in all societies experience some of the same symptoms, relatively few women have severe problems. Women in some non-Western societies report less severe symptoms than menopausal women in the West do (Sixth International Congress on the Menopause, Bangkok, 1990, in Sheehy, 1992).

While most women do not experience a loss of sex drive during or after menopause, perhaps as many as 30 percent do (Sheehy, 1992). However, as we shall discuss more fully in Chapter 9, a woman's sexual life does not end when menopause begins. Some women even report an increased sex drive after menopause often attributed to no longer worrying about unintended pregnancy. Four or 5 years after menopause, some women experience a decrease in the levels of testosterone, the most important hormone in the sexual function of men and women. Decreased testosterone is often correlated with a decrease in sexual appetite in both men and women. Vaginal dryness and the thinning of vaginal tissue can lead to discomfort during sexual intercourse and masturbation for some women.

Treatment Alternatives

As we have already stated, menopause is not a disease, it is a naturally occurring life transition. For some women the symptoms of menopause may be disruptive, but they are not dangerous. Some women find that a healthy diet, regular exercise, moderate alcohol use, not smoking, and stress-reduction provide all the help they need. Other women find alternative therapies, such as acupuncture, to be helpful. However, about 10 million women, approximately 20 percent of menopausal American women (Love, 1998), rely on **hormone replacement therapy (HRT),** including estrogen, **progestin,** and sometimes testosterone, to counter the estrogen deficiency that occurs in post-menopausal years.

In addition to being one of the most widely prescribed treatments in the United States, HRT is also one of the most controversial. You have already learned about estrogen's role in the menstrual cycle. Estrogen, which will be discussed more fully in the next chapter, also affects tissues throughout the body. This makes the decision of whether or not to use estrogen or any type of HRT a complicated one. Some research has shown that postmenopausal estrogens can reduce the risk of osteoporotic fractures (Willett et al., 2000). On the other hand, a recent study cautions that women should not decide to go on hormone replacement therapy because they think it will protect them against heart disease, as widely used HRT guidelines were developed before the results of randomized trials become available or the results are inconsistent and unclear (Manson & Martin, 2001). Furthermore, the long-term use of unopposed estrogen (estrogen used alone) may sharply increase a woman's risk of two deadly diseases, endometrial cancer and breast cancer (Grodstein et al., 1997).

DISORDERS OF THE FEMALE SEXUAL ORGANS

Endometriosis

Endometriosis is a non-life-threatening condition in which the tissue that normally lines the uterus grows in other areas of the body, causing pain, irregular bleeding, and sometimes infertility. Typically the tissue growth occurs in the pelvic area, on the outside of the ovaries, uterus, bowels, rectum, or bladder, or invading the delicate lining of the pelvis, but it can occur in other areas of the body as well.

What's Your Risk?   Endometriosis occurs in an estimated 10 to 20 percent of women during their reproductive years. The prevalence may be as high as 15 to 50 percent among infertile women. It is still not clear why endometriosis occurs. Some experts believe menstrual blood flows backward through the fallopian tubes, and then enters and become implanted on other parts of the body. Others believe that the lymph or blood systems carry endometrial tissue to different parts of the body. Although typically diagnosed in women between the ages of 25 and 35, endometriosis probably starts to develop about the time that regular menstrual periods begin. Genetics appears to play a role, as the risk for a woman who has a mother or sister with endometriosis is six times greater than that of the general population. Other risk factors include a menstrual cycle length of 27 days or less, early onset of menstruation, and periods lasting 7 or more days.

How Is It Detected?   Pain is the most common symptom of endometriosis, and can occur during menstruation, ovulation, or intercourse. Back pain and painful bowel movements also affect some women. The severity of the pain and the extent of the tissue invasion are not linked. Women with mild endometriosis may experience severe pain, while those with severe endometriosis may have little or no pain.

Women with endometriosis are likely to menstruate heavily, have *spotting* (bleeding between periods), and have irregular periods. A pelvic exam may reveal the presence of tender nodules with a lumpy consistency in the posterior vaginal wall or near the ovaries. In addition, the uterus may be fixed or retroverted, or there may be pain when the uterus is palpated. It can be difficult to diagnose endometriosis during a pelvic exam; *laparoscopy,* a procedure in which a long, narrow tube (a laparoscope) is inserted through an incision in the navel, permitting the visual inspection of organs in the pelvic cavity, may be required for a definitive diagnosis.

Perimenopause: period before menstruation completely stops at menopause

Hormone Replacement Therapy (HRT): use of synthetic hormones to replace estrogen no longer produced by the ovaries in postmenopausal years

Progestin: hormone of the corpus luteum from which progesterone can be isolated in pure form

Endometriosis: condition in which endometrial tissue grows in pelvic regions outside the uterus

Hysterectomy: surgical removal of the uterus

Gynecology: branch of medicine that deals with women's health, especially the diagnosis and treatment of disorders affecting the reproductive organs

How Is It Treated?   Treatment usually depends on the extent of the disease, the woman's desire for childbearing, and the severity of the symptoms. If there are few, mild symptoms, "watchful waiting," or monitoring of the condition without intervention, may be recommended. Hormone therapy may be used to prevent ovulation or to interfere with the production of hormones. Surgical options include surgical removal of glandular tissue or scar tissue. In the most severe cases, **hysterectomy,** the surgical removal of the uterus, or *oophorectomy*, removal of the ovaries, may be advised.

WWW SEXUAL HEALTH AND YOU

The Gynecological Exam

A pelvic exam is a visual and manual medical evaluation of a woman's reproductive system. The external genitals are examined first to determine if there is any swelling, irritation, discoloration, or abnormal discharge. Then there is a visual internal examination. The examiner inserts a *speculum* to spread the vaginal walls in order to check for cervical abnormalities. A Pap test (see text discussion) is performed, and the examiner then conducts a bimanual internal examination by inserting two gloved fingers into the vagina while pressing the other hand on the lower abdomen to check the uterus, ovaries, and fallopian tubes. Finally, a rectovaginal exam is performed in which a finger is inserted in the rectum and two fingers are inserted into the vagina for further examination of the internal pelvic organs and the rectum.

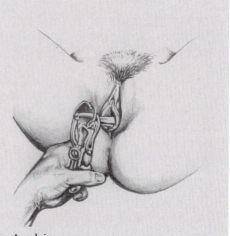

A pelvic exam.

Pelvic exams can be the cause of much anxiety for some women. Females in our society are socialized to keep their pubic area covered, and even women who may feel comfortable with exposing their genitalia to their sexual partners can find a vaginal examination to be uncomfortable or even highly stressful.

A sociological study described the woman's transition from a person to a "pelvic" during a vaginal exam. The authors of the study note that the vagina is conceptualized as a sacred object. The following routines adopted by the mostly male medical profession are designed to ensure the continued sacredness of the vagina and avoid any hint of personal violation (Henslin & Biggs, 1978):

The doctor is not present while the woman removes her clothing, which prohibits any suggestion of a striptease. The drape sheet placed over the patient keeps her genital area exposed, allowing that area to become an object separate from the rest of the woman's body. The drape sheet also keeps the woman from seeing her exposed genitals and the doctor's examination. A female nurse is present during the exam to act as a chaperon and to give assurance that no sexual acts will take place. After the exam, the doctor leaves the room so that the woman can dress in private. "[P]atients who have just had their genital area thoroughly examined both visually and tactilely by the doctor are concerned that the same man will see them in their underclothing" (Henslin & Biggs, 1978, p. 166).

Endometrial Cancer

Cancer originating in the lining of the uterus is called *endometrial cancer*. Nearly all of these life-threatening cancers occur in the form of adenocarcinomas (tumors of glandular cells). Endometrial cancer is the most common malignancy of the female reproductive organs.

What's Your Risk?   In the United States, white women are four times as likely to get endometrial cancer as African American women. The disease most often occurs in women between the ages of 55 and 75 (Miller et al., 1996). Women who develop endometrial cancer before age 45 usually have a history of infrequent or absent menstrual periods.

Estrogen is the major risk factor for the most common type of endometrial cancer. Estrogen-related exposures that have been shown to increase the risk include estrogen replacement therapy for treatment of menopausal symptoms (discussed earlier), use of Tamoxifen (a drug used in the treatment of breast cancer), early menarche (before age 12), late menopause (after age 52), never having been pregnant, and a history of failure to ovulate. Research has not implicated estrogen exposure in the development of other, more aggressive types of endometrial cancer, which have a poorer prognosis. The use of progesterone plus estrogen rather than the exclusive use of estrogen is believed to offset the increased risk associated with estrogen replacement therapy. Other risk factors include infertility, diabetes, gallbladder disease, hypertension, obesity, family history, previous breast or ovarian cancer, and prior pelvic radiotherapy. Pregnancy and the use of oral contraceptives appear to provide protection against endometrial cancer.

How Is It Detected?   Abnormal bleeding from the uterus is the primary symptom of endometrial cancer. About 90 percent of patients diagnosed with endometrial cancer complain of post-menopausal bleeding or irregular vaginal bleeding. In about 10 percent of cases, the discharge associated with endometrial cancer is white rather than blood-tinged. In later stages of the disease women may experience pelvic pain, a pelvic mass, or weight loss. At this time there is no recommended screening test or examination that can reliably detect most endometrial cancers in asymptomatic women. Endometrial biopsy is sometimes recommended at menopause and periodically thereafter for women at very high risk of developing this type of cancer (American Cancer Society, 2001).

How Is It Treated?   There are four basic types of treatment for women with endometrial cancer. Treatment of endometrial cancer is usually twofold. In most cases a hysterectomy is performed immediately. Due to the danger of *metastasis*, the spread of cancer cells to other areas of the body, surgery may be followed by a course of *radiation* (the use of high-energy rays to kill cancer cells and stop them from growing), *hormonal therapy* to keep cancer cells from getting the hormones they need to grow, or *chemotherapy*, the use of drugs to kill cancer cells. The 1-year survival rate for endometrial cancer is 93 percent. If the cancer is detected at an early stage, the 5-year survival rate is 95 percent; this drops to 64 percent if it is not diagnosed until a later stage.

Uterine Fibroids

Fibroids are balls of solid tissue that can grow inside the uterus, within the uterine wall, or outside the uterine wall. Fibroids can range in size from a grain of rice to a basketball. Fibroids frequently occur in groups or clumps, which tend to enlarge and distort the uterus. Fibroids are almost always **benign,** becoming cancerous in less than 1 percent of cases.

What's Your Risk?   Fibroid tumors are very common, affecting up to 25 percent of women over age 30, and 20 to 40 percent of all women of reproductive age. African American women are three to nine times more likely to be affected by uterine fibroids

Benign: noncancerous; does not invade nearby tissue or spread to other parts of the body

than white women. Sometimes fibroids worsen during pregnancy, when larger amounts of estrogen are produced, or in menopausal women using hormone replacement therapy. Fibroids are often found in women with endometriosis.

How Is It Detected?   The majority of women with uterine fibroids have no symptoms. However, some women have excessive menstrual bleeding, longer menstrual periods, spotting, menstrual pain, pain in the abdomen or lower back, constipation, and frequent or difficult urination. Fibroids are usually discovered during a pelvic exam. Sometimes diagnosis is difficult, especially in obese women. Fibroid tumors have been mistaken for ovarian tumors, pelvic inflammatory disease, and pregnancy. A transvaginal or pelvic ultrasound may be used to confirm the diagnosis. Dilation and curettage (D and C), a procedure in which the cervix is widened and the uterine lining scraped, may be necessary to rule out other potentially **malignant** conditions.

How Is It Treated?   The method of treatment of uterine fibroids depends on the severity of symptoms, age, pregnancy status, desire for future pregnancies, general health, and characteristics of the fibroids. If fibroids are not causing pain, bleeding, or discomfort, many physicians recommend leaving them alone and monitoring them for growth and complications. The decrease in estrogen levels at menopause may lead to shrinkage of fibroids and relief of symptoms.

If fibroids are large or are causing symptoms, there are a number of treatment options. *Endometrial ablation*, "washing" the uterine lining, does not treat the fibroids themselves, but alleviates the symptom of heavy bleeding. Ablation is used to treat excessive bleeding from other noncancerous conditions and is not the preferred option for women who want to have children. In a new version of this procedure a balloon is placed in the uterine cavity via a catheter, and then inflated with a hot liquid. Hormone therapy may be used alone, or in conjunction with surgery, to shrink fibroids. The surgical options include one of three types of *myomectomy*, a procedure that removes the fibroids but leaves the uterus intact.

In a new, less invasive technique called *fibroid embolization*, a catheter is inserted through a tiny incision in the groin into the femoral artery and then fed into the uterine artery. The catheter is used to inject tiny plastic particles that block the blood vessels feeding the fibroids, causing them to shrink. Because of the risk of damage to the ovaries, embolization is usually restricted to women who are not planning a pregnancy.

Cervical Cancer

Cervical cancer, cancer of the lower portion of the uterus, begins in the lining of the cervix and does not form suddenly. There is a gradual change from a normal cervix to precancer to cancer. Some women with *precancerous* changes of the cervix will develop *malignant* cancer. This usually takes several years, but sometimes can happen more rapidly.

What's Your Risk?   The risk of cervical cancer is very low among girls in their early teen years; the risk increases between the ages of 15 and 35. Although the risk of cervical cancer does not increase significantly after age 50, the average age of women newly diagnosed with cervical cancer is between 50 and 55 years. The risk of cervical cancer is closely linked to sexual behavior and to infection with certain types of **human papilloma virus (HPV),** a sexually transmitted infection we will discuss in Chapter 7. Most of the more than 80 types of HPV are benign and cause genital warts at worst. But persistent infection with any one of 13 types of HPV is responsible for at least 95 percent of cervical cancer (American Cancer Society, 2000b).

How Is It Detected?   Women with cervical precancers and early cancers are usually symptom-free; typically it is only in later stages, after the disease becomes invasive, that symptoms develop. Unusual vaginal discharge, abnormal vaginal bleeding, and spotting are

Malignant: cancerous; a growth that invades nearby tissue or spreads to other parts of the body

Human Papilloma Virus (HPV): a sexually transmitted infection that causes genital warts

some of the symptoms of advanced cervical cancer. Pain during intercourse or bleeding following intercourse is also common. However, each of these signs may be caused by other conditions; professional medical testing is the only way to ensure an accurate diagnosis.

Cancer of the cervix can usually be found early by having a Pap test as part of the pelvic exam (see SEXUAL HEALTH AND YOU box). The Pap test is a simple procedure in which a small sample of cells is swabbed from the cervix, transferred to a slide, and examined under a microscope. It is currently the only screening test that can be used to prevent cancer, by picking up cellular changes before they become cancerous. The American Cancer Society recommends that all women begin yearly Pap tests at age 18 or when they first become sexually active. However, more than half of the women diagnosed as having cervical cancer in the United States have not been screened with a Pap test within the past 3 years, and many women in developing countries are unable to get the test. Studies show that a new test that can be done by doctors or by women themselves could greatly increase the number of women who can be tested worldwide. The test, a vaginal swab for HPV/DNA, is just as sensitive as a Pap smear for detecting cervical cancer and precancerous changes; scientists predict that eventually it will become a primary screening test (Schiffman et al., 2000; Wright et al., 2000).

It is important to note that the Pap test is a screening test, not a diagnostic test. While the Pap test rarely fails to detect full-blown cervical cancer, as many as 20 percent of precancerous conditions may be missed. Women who have abnormal Pap test results usually will undergo a *colposcopy*, a procedure in which the cervix is viewed through an instrument with magnifying lenses that makes it possible to see the surface of the cervix closely and clearly. If an abnormal area is seen, a *biopsy*, the removal of a sample of tissue to check for cancer cells, is the only way to determine if the cells are precancerous or cancerous.

How Is It Treated?   Treatment options largely depend on the stage of the disease. If an area of abnormal cells is detected during colposcopy or upon biopsy, the abnormal tissue can be removed using LEEP (loop electrosurgical excision procedure), in which tissue is removed with a wire that is heated by electrical currents, or the cold knife cone biopsy, which uses a surgical scalpel rather than a heated wire to remove tissue. Other techniques for tissue removal include cryosurgery or laser surgery. During cryosurgery

www S EXUAL HEALTH AND YOU

There Are No Stupid Questions

It is important to be able to talk with your physician about cancer care. No question is too trivial. In addition, if you are unsure about your doctor's recommendations, you should not be afraid to get a second opinion. Some questions to consider:

- What type of cancer do I have?
- Has the cancer spread to lymph nodes or internal organs?
- What is the stage of my cancer and how does it affect treatment options and prognosis?

- What treatments are appropriate for me, what do you recommend and why?
- What are the risks and side effects that I should expect? If I want children, will the treatment affect my fertility?
- What should I do to get ready for treatment?
- What are the chances for recurrence?

a metal probe cooled with liquid nitrogen is used to kill the abnormal cells by freezing them. Laser surgery uses a focused beam of high-energy light to vaporize the abnormal tissue. Other surgical options include a simple hysterectomy (removal of the uterus) or a radical hysterectomy and pelvic lymph node dissection (removal of the uterus, tissues next to the uterus, and lymph nodes from the pelvis). In the most severe cases, a pelvic exenteration (removal of uterus, tissues next to the uterus, pelvic lymph nodes, the bladder, vagina, rectum, and part of the colon) may be necessary. Radiation or chemotherapy may be recommended in addition to surgery.

Eighty-nine percent of cervical cancer patients survive 1 year after diagnosis and 70 percent survive 5 years. When detected at an early stage, invasive cervical cancer is one of the most successfully treatable cancers with a 5-year survival rate of 91 percent for localized cancers.

Ovarian Cysts

Ovarian cysts are balloonlike swellings of fluid contained within an envelope of ovarian tissue. Most types of ovarian cysts are harmless and will go away without any treatment. The most common type of ovarian cyst is called a *functional ovarian cyst.* Recall that, during ovulation, a follicle forms inside the ovary and ruptures when an egg is released. If pregnancy does not occur, the empty follicle usually dissolves and is reabsorbed. Sometimes the follicle does not dissolve, but instead becomes a fluid-filled cyst. Functional ovarian cysts may occur as the result of abnormal hormonal signals, stress, or illness, or simply because the surface of the ovary tends to become thickened and scarred after years of ovulation. These cysts will often shrink and disappear within two or three menstrual cycles.

There are several types of *nonfunctional ovarian cysts.* For example, endometrioma can form when tissue from the uterine lining becomes attached to an ovary in women with endometriosis. Cystadenomas develop from ovarian tissue; some are filled with watery fluid and others with a gelatin-like material. Dermoid cysts contain skin and other tissue such as hair, bone, or even teeth; these cysts develop from ovarian germ cells—the cells that produce human eggs.

What's Your Risk?   Any woman who ovulates may develop an ovarian cyst, and women who have had one cyst are at an increased risk for additional cysts. About 20 percent of women have a condition called *polycystic ovary syndrome (PCOS)* that causes many tiny, harmless cysts to form on the ovaries. Women taking fertility drugs and women with higher-than-normal levels of testosterone are especially at risk for developing this condition.

How Is It Detected?   The majority of ovarian cysts don't cause any symptoms. Some women experience low levels of pain or pressure in the lower abdomen. Intense pain and nausea can occur if cysts become twisted or rupture. Pain during intercourse, constipation, and a need to urinate frequently are additional signs of ovarian cysts. Ovarian cysts can be discovered during a pelvic exam.

How Is It Treated?   If there are no symptoms or if the cysts are small, the doctor may recommend that the cysts be monitored for two or three menstrual cycles without treatment. Birth control pills are sometimes used to prevent ovulation in women with functional cysts, causing the cysts to shrink and fewer new cysts to form. Surgical treatment may be required for cysts in women past menopause, for very large cysts, or for cysts accompanied by severe symptoms. The type of operation will depend on how early the cyst is found, its size, the type of cyst, and the age of the woman. Laparoscopy, removal of an ovary, or removal of both ovaries and the uterus are possible types of surgery.

Ovarian Cancer

The most common *ovarian cancer* in women age 55 to 80 is *adenocarcinoma*, cancer that develops in the lining of the inner surface. Malignant ovarian tumors in women under age 30 will usually be germ cell tumors, which can be some of the most aggressive cancers known.

What's Your Risk?   Each year more than 26,000 women in the United States are diagnosed with ovarian cancer; approximately 1 in 70 women will develop the disease (American Cancer Society, 2000c). While ovarian cancer ranks fifth in cancer incidence among women, it causes more deaths than any other cancer of the female reproductive system. Overall incidence rates are highest among Native American women, followed by whites, Vietnamese, Hispanic, and Native Hawaiian women. Rates are lowest among Korean, Chinese, and Native Alaskan women. Mortality patterns differ from the incidence rates of ovarian cancer; white women have the highest mortality rates in each age group (Miller et al., 1996).

The risk of ovarian cancer increases with age and is highest among women over 60. Women who have never had children are twice as likely to develop ovarian cancer as women who have had children; women who have previously been diagnosed with breast, intestinal, or rectal cancer are also twice as likely to develop the disease (American Cancer Society, 2000c). The most important risk factor for ovarian cancer is a family history of a first-degree relative (mother, daughter, or sister) with the disease. Women with two or more first-degree relatives who have had ovarian cancer are at the highest risk (Piver et al., 1996).

How Is It Detected?   Often there are no symptoms in the early stages of ovarian cancer. The cancer may grow for some time before it causes pressure, pain, or other problems; even when symptoms do appear, they may be so vague that they are ignored. As an ovarian tumor grows, it can cause fluid to build up in the abdomen, resulting in swelling, bloating, or general discomfort. Loss of appetite, indigestion, nausea, and weight loss are other possible symptoms. In addition to the fluid buildup in the abdomen, in some cases fluid may also collect around the lungs, causing shortness of breath. Some women with the disease may experience vaginal bleeding, and as the tumor grows it may press on the bowels or bladder, causing diarrhea, constipation, or frequent urination.

A thorough pelvic examination is essential to the detection of ovarian cancer. If the physician discovers irregularities, a transvaginal ultrasound, CT (or CAT) scan, or X-ray exam may be able to differentiate healthy tissue, fluid-filled cysts, and tumors. Although an ovarian cancer blood antigen, CA-125, has been identified, it is not always present in women who have early-stage ovarian cancer and may be found in some women with benign gynecologic diseases. Research data suggest that a small extracellular phospholipid (lyphosphatidic acid or LPA) may be a more sensitive marker for ovarian cancer than CA-125 (Xu et al., 1998). However, at the present time, the only sure way to diagnose the disease is to have a biopsy examined by a pathologist.

How Is It Treated?   Treatment for ovarian cancer depends on a number of individual factors, including the stage of the disease, the woman's age, and her general health. Surgical intervention is the initial treatment in the majority of cases. Usually the surgeon will perform a hysterectomy with bilateral salpingo-oophorectomy. This impressive-sounding procedure involves the removal of the ovaries, the uterus, and the fallopian tubes. If the cancer is detected early, especially in younger women, it is possible to limit surgery to the cancerous ovary. Surgery may be followed by chemotherapy, or less often by radiation therapy, to kill any remaining cancer cells, or to prevent recurrence.

When detected in its early stages, the 5-year survival rate for ovarian cancer is 93 percent. However, only about 24 percent of all ovarian cancers are identified at this stage (Friedrich, 1999). Because of the absence of symptoms or reluctance to obtain treatment, women are not usually diagnosed until the cancer has spread, causing the overall 5-year survival rate to plunge to 46 percent.

Vulvar Cancer

Cancer of the vulva, or *vulvar cancer*, is a malignancy that can occur on any part of the female external reproductive system but most often affects the inner edges of the labia majora or the labia minora. Less often, vulvar cancer occurs on the clitoris or the Bartholin's glands. Over 90 percent of cancers of the vulva are *squamous* cell carcinomas, a type of skin cancer that occurs in squamous cells, the main cell type of the skin. The second most common type of vulvar cancer (about 4 percent) is melanoma, the deadliest type of skin cancer.

What's Your Risk? In the United States, vulvar cancer accounts for 4 percent of all cancers of the female reproductive organs and $\frac{1}{2}$ percent of all cancers in women. The American Cancer Society (2000f) estimates that about 3,200 cancers of the vulva will be diagnosed each year.

Age is an important risk factor. Of the women who develop vulvar cancer, 75 percent are over age 50 and two thirds are over 70. However, the number of vulvar cancer patients under age 40 is increasing.

Infection by HPV is thought to be responsible for about 30 to 50 percent of vulvar cancers. Of the more than 80 types of HPV that have been identified, some, including HPV 16, 19, and 31, are considered "high-risk" types. Smoking, other genital cancers, and chronic vulvar inflammation caused by infections and poor hygiene have also been suggested as risk factors for vulvar cancer.

How Is It Detected? The most common early symptom of cancer of the vulva is persistent itching that does not improve. Because several less serious conditions, such as a yeast infection (see the upcoming discussion of vaginitis), can cause this symptom, many women fail to recognize the potential seriousness of their problem. As the disease progresses, a distinct tumor may emerge in the form of a red, pink, or white bump or bumps with a wartlike or raw surface. An area of the vulva may appear white and feel tough. Some women complain of pain, burning, painful urination, bleeding, and discharge. The appearance of a darkly pigmented lesion or a change in a mole that has been present for many years may indicate vulvar melanoma.

Clinical Trials

To learn more about promising new and experimental types of treatment, researchers conduct studies known as clinical trials. The researchers use these trials to answer the following questions: Is the proposed treatment effective? Does it work better than existing treatments? What are the side effects? Do the benefits of the treatment outweigh the risks involved? Which patients is the treatment most likely to help? Most clinical trials involve a control group given a **placebo,** a "sugar pill" or dummy medication, so the researchers can compare the progress of the treated group with that of the untreated group. In most cases, patients do not know whether they are taking the experimental treatment or the placebo.

If your physician discusses the possibility of enrolling you in a clinical trial, you should be well informed about the proposed course of treatment. Enrollment in a clinical trial is strictly voluntary. Before agreeing to participate in a clinical trial you should find out what side effects you might expect, how long the study will last, what will happen if you are harmed by the research, and what type of long-term follow-up care is part of the study.

Would you enroll in a clinical trial?

—*What if you found out you were a member of the control group?*

—*Should clinical trials of treatment for a life-threatening illness such as ovarian cancer be conducted with or without a control group?*

If vulvar cancer is suspected, a physician will usually conduct a visual and manual inspection. To make a final diagnosis, a biopsy is performed.

How Is It Treated? As with other cancers, options for treating vulvar cancer depend on the stage of the disease and include surgery, radiation, and chemotherapy. Laser surgery to vaporize the layer of skin containing abnormal cells is not used for treating invasive cancer. Excision involves removing the cancer and about $\frac{1}{2}$ inch of the surrounding skin. In a complete radical vulvectomy, the entire vulva along with deep tissues including the clitoris is removed. When vulvar cancer is detected early it is highly curable. The overall 5-year survival rate when the lymph nodes are not involved is 90 percent. However, when cancer has spread to the lymph nodes the 5-year survival rate drops to 50 to 60 percent.

Vaginitis

Vaginitis is an inflammation of a woman's vagina that may be due to infection by bacteria, fungi, viruses, or parasites, a lack of estrogen, or a chemical imbalance. The vulval area secretes sebum, a blend of oils, waxes, fats, cholesterol, and cellular debris that serves as a waterproofing against bacteria that might otherwise be harmful. When conditions are healthy, the bacteria in the vagina aren't harmful. Each vaginal cell contains large quantities of glycogen, a stored sugar molecule. Protective bacteria use glycogen as their energy source. The slightly acidic environment of the vagina helps foster the growth of these bacteria. When the pH balance of the vagina is disrupted, one or more types of organisms can begin to thrive, resulting in vaginitis.

There are three primary types of vaginitis. The two that are spread by sexual contact, bacterial vaginosis and trichomoniasis, will be discussed in Chapter 7. The most common type of non-sexually contracted vaginitis is a yeast infection caused by *Candida albicans*, a fungus that regularly exists harmlessly on the vagina, the mouth, and the digestive tract. As described previously, a yeast infection develops when the pH of the vagina is altered, causing it to become less acidic. The decreased acidity results in an overgrowth of Candida organisms, causing the uncomfortable symptoms of a yeast infection.

What's Your Risk? Diabetes and hormone imbalance are two causes of the overgrowth of the Candida fungus. Hormonal fluctuations that occur during pregnancy, at various times during the menstrual cycle, or with the use of oral contraceptives can all upset the vaginal environment. Prolonged use of antibiotics, or use of a strong antibiotic, can also upset the balance of vaginal flora; if a woman eats yogurt or takes acidophilis when on antibiotics, the risk of a yeast infection is reduced.

How Is It Detected? The most common symptoms of a yeast infection are itching, burning, and redness in the vagina and the vulva. Some women also experience vaginal discharge, pain, and/or a burning sensation during intercourse. The vaginal discharge, which is generally white, may have a faint, sweet, yeasty smell and a texture resembling cottage cheese.

The symptoms overlap with those of a number of other disorders, so accurate diagnosis requires an examination by a health-care practitioner, particularly for a first bout of the problem. The National Vaginitis Association (2001) recommends testing a sample of vaginal discharge in addition to having a visual pelvic examination.

How Is It Treated? The usual treatment for yeast infections is nonprescription antifungal creams or suppositories. Treatment with a nonprescription medication is recommended only for those who are sure they have a yeast infection and not some other type of vaginitis or sexually transmitted infection. Chronic yeast infections may require treatment with a prescription antifungal medication.

FAQ:

Can snug-fitting jeans cause a yeast infection?

Studies have shown no evidence supporting the myths that tight pants or nylon underwear promote yeast infections. Yeast infections are not a health risk in and of themselves, though recurring infections may be an indication of an immune problem and should be brought to the attention of a doctor or other health-care professional.

Placebo: an inactive substance or preparation given to reinforce a patient's expectation to get well, as a control in an experiment, or to test the effectiveness of a medicine

Vaginitis: inflammation of the vagina, typically caused by bacteria or yeast infection

Secondary Sex Characteristics: physical characteristics, other than the genitals, that indicate sexual maturity and distinguish males from females

Mammary Glands: glands found in female mammals that produce milk

Nipple: protuberance through which milk is drawn from the breast

Areola: area of dark-colored skin on the breast that surrounds the nipple

BREASTS

Breasts are one of a number of human **secondary sex characteristics,** traits other than the genitals that distinguish males from females and indicate sexual maturity. Unlike the internal and external sex organs you have just learned about (the primary sex characteristics), secondary sex characteristics play no direct role in reproduction. Other secondary sex characteristics include the distribution of body hair and fat, body size and muscle mass, and the deepening of the male voice. While both males and females have breasts, the structure and size of the breasts tends to distinguish males and females.

In a physically mature female, each breast consists of 15 to 20 subdivided lobes of glandular tissue called mammary or milk glands surrounded by fatty and fibrous tissue (Figure 2.7). While the popular media and adolescent bathroom discussion may suggest otherwise, the primary function of female breasts is to produce milk for infants. The **mammary glands** secrete milk that a new mother can use to nurse her infant. A milk duct that opens on the surface of the **nipple** drains each lobe in response to the sucking of an infant. Breast size is determined by the amount of fatty tissue in the breast; there is little variation among women in the amount of glandular tissue present. Thus the size of a woman's breasts has no bearing on the amount of milk produced after childbirth.

The nipple of the breast consists mostly of smooth muscle fibers along with many nerve endings. The dark textured skin of the nipple extends 1 or 2 centimeters onto the surface of the breast to form a circular patch called the **areola.** The areola is permeated by a set of modified sweat glands, the little "goosebumps," called *Montgomery's glands.* The nipple and areola are highly sensitive to touch and temperature. The nerve and muscle fibers of the areola can cause the nipple to stiffen and become erect in response to direct or indirect stimulation. Not all women have sensitive breasts, nor do they all enjoy having their breasts fondled. Although generally less sensitive to touch than the female breast (Robinson & Short, 1977), many men have sensitive nipples and obtain sexual pleasure when their breasts are stroked or licked.

FIGURE 2.7   The Structure of the Female Breast. SOURCE: Martini, 2001.

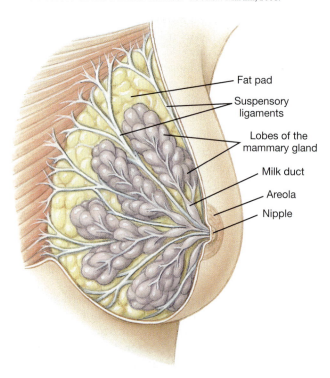

- Fat pad
- Suspensory ligaments
- Lobes of the mammary gland
- Milk duct
- Areola
- Nipple

"These protuberances around the mammary glands seem poorly placed. They bobble painfully when a woman runs. They flop forward to block vision when she leans over to collect food. And they can suffocate a suckling child. Moreover, breasts (of any size) are sensitive to touch. Why?"

(FISHER, 1992, P. 180)

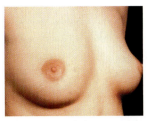 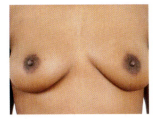 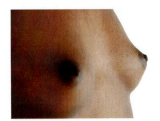

Breast size and shape vary in adult women.

FAQ:

Why is there such a variation in the size of women's breasts?

We don't know why there is such a wide variety of breast sizes, or what exactly controls the growth of the breast, particularly the fatty tissue that give the human breast its bulk. Breast size says little or nothing about a woman's health, fertility, or ability to breastfeed. As we stated earlier, breast size is primarily due to the amount of fatty tissue that is distributed around the glands. Breasts represent only a small fraction of the body's total fat mass, about 4 percent on average, and their size generally changes less in proportion to a woman's weight gain or loss than other body fat. Common variations in breasts include having one breast larger than the other (usually the left), an inverted nipple (a congenital condition in which the nipple does not protrude), and extra or false (nonfunctional) nipples. None of these is a health issue, although inverted nipples may make it more difficult to breastfeed an infant. Among adult females there is considerable variation in breast shape and size. There is no relationship between breast size and sexual responsiveness.

Male breasts differ from female breasts principally in having little glandular or fatty tissues. Lack of glandular tissue means male breasts cannot produce milk. Sometimes males' breasts can become enlarged, a condition known as *gynecomastia*. A significant number of adolescent boys (40 to 60 percent) are troubled by gynecomastia; during puberty, as they begin to develop an increase in the amount of glandular tissue around their breasts, breast size may increase as a result of a surge in estrogen. Although it may be a symptom of liver or thyroid disease or a sign of drug use, for the most part it is just a variation of male adolescent development that usually resolves itself within a year or two.

DISEASES OF THE BREAST

Three types of lumps can occur in the breasts. The most common of these are *cysts*, fluid-filled sacs, and *fibroadenomas*, solid rounded tumors. Both of these types of lumps are noncancerous and easily treated, and together account for 80 percent of breast lumps. The third type of lump is a sign of the most common form of cancer among women in the United States: breast cancer.

Breast Cancer

The rates of breast cancer in the United States have remained stable for decades (Kolata, 1993). However, increased awareness and advances in detection and treatment have led to increased rates of survival. Indeed, early detection and treatment are essential to preventing the spread of the cancer to other parts of the body where it may become deadly.

What's Your Risk?   Breast cancer represents 30 percent of all female cancers, affecting approximately 110 women per 100,000. It is not the cancer of the breast that is fatal. If untreated, the cancer may metastasize or spread to other vital body parts such as the brain, bone, or lungs.

In the United States the odds for a woman to develop breast cancer by age 85 are not insignificant. For younger women the chance is much smaller, however, the cumulative risk for all women is estimated at one in eight. (See Table 2.2.)

No specific cause of breast cancer is known. However certain risk factors that predispose a woman to breast cancer have been identified. Some risk factors can't be changed. Simply being a woman is the main risk factor for developing breast cancer. Genetic factors, a mother or sister with breast cancer history, aging, early menarche, and the late onset of menopause are known risk factors.

Lifestyle-related risk factors include smoking, alcohol consumption, not breastfeeding, never bearing children, or bearing a first child at a late age. Diet-related factors, especially fat intake, have been correlated with breast cancer rates on an international level, but a causal link has not been firmly established. Possible additional factors currently being studied include the use of oral contraceptives, exposure to toxic chemicals, and physical inactivity (American Cancer Society, 2000a).

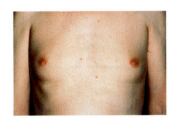

Gynecomastia.

TABLE 2.2

Odds for Developing Breast Cancer by Age

Problem	Possible Cause
From age 30 to age 40	1 out of 257
From age 40 to age 50	1 out of 67
From age 50 to age 60	1 out of 36
From age 60 to age 70	1 out of 28
From age 70 to age 80	1 out of 24
Ever	1 out of 8

SOURCE: American Cancer Society, 2001

Mammogram: X-ray exam of the breast to detect cancerous tumors

One study found that 75 percent of women who develop breast cancer have no identifiable risk factor other than gender and age (Hortobagvi, McClelland, & Reed, 1990). Breast size and cancer risk are not directly related, although large breasts can make discovery of small lumps more difficult. No evidence has been found that breast implants cause breast cancer.

How Is It Detected? Breast changes such as a lump, thickening, swelling, dimpling, tenderness of the nipple, and nipple discharge are among the symptoms of breast cancer in both men and women. However there are often no symptoms, particularly during the early stages of the disease, a fact that underscores the importance of early detection by self-examination and mammography. The most important factor in survival is early detection; 90 percent of cancerous lumps are first discovered by breast self-examination (see SEXUAL HEALTH AND YOU box).

Mammograms. A screening **mammogram** is the best tool currently available for finding breast cancer before a tumor is large enough to be felt in a BSE. The procedure consists of an X-ray of each breast while compressed in a device that flattens the breast so accurate pictures can be taken. The benefits of mammography greatly outweigh any potential risk from the low dose of radiation used. Most women report little or no discomfort with the procedure. To assure less discomfort, schedule a mammogram right after a menstrual period when the breasts are less sensitive.

Although mammograms are the best way to find breast cancer early, they do have some limitations. A mammogram may miss some cancers that are present (false negative) or may find things that turn out not be cancerous (false positive). Approximately 10 to 15 percent of tumors don't show up on a mammogram. Mammography is considered to be even less reliable with younger women who have denser breast tissue; the error rate is approximately 40 percent in women younger than 40 years.

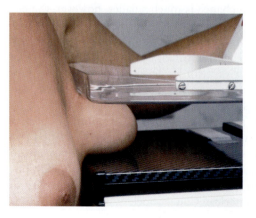

A mammogram is key to early detection of breast cancer.

Another procedure that is used to detect breast cancer is magnetic resonance imaging (MRI). This procedure is thought to be better at early detection of a tumor, but is considerably more expensive than a mammogram. Digital mammograms, computerized breast X-rays, were approved by the FDA in 2000. While sonograms and digital mammograms appear to be no better than regular mammograms in detecting breast cancer, the new technology does away with film exposure problems, as well as storage and loss issues.

SEXUAL HEALTH AND YOU

Breast Self-Examination

All women are advised to examine their breasts for unusual lumps every month. In that way they can become familiar with what is normal for their own breasts and increase the chances of early detection. Many women don't do regular breast self-examinations (BSE). They may forget, not think they're at risk, or be afraid of what they might find. Be afraid of *not* doing a BSE. If you do discover a lump, don't panic! Most lumps are not cancerous: For every malignant lump found in young women, 12 benign lumps are detected.

The best time to do a BSE is about a week after your menstrual period ends, when your breasts are less likely to be tender or swollen and least influenced by hormones. For those women who don't have regular periods, it's helpful to do a BSE about the same time every month. Regular inspection will give you confidence in what is normal for you and alert you to any changes.

There are three parts to a thorough BSE:

1. Examine your breasts in the shower or bath. Keeping your fingers flat and gently move the finger pads over every part of each breast, checking for any lumps, hard knots, or thickening. Use your right hand to examine your left breast and reverse the procedure to examine your right breast.

2. Inspect your breast before a mirror with your arms at your sides. Next, raise your arms overhead looking for changes in the contour of each breast, a swelling, dimpling of skin, or changes in the nipple. Then rest your palms on your hips and press down firmly to flex your chest muscles.

3. Lying down, put a pillow or folded towel under your right shoulder to examine your right breast (Figure 2.8). Place your right hand behind your head to distribute breast tissue more evenly on the chest. Use your left hand with fingers flat to press gently in small circular motions around an imaginary clock face. Begin at 12 o'clock, the outermost top of your right breast, and so on around the circle back to 12. A ridge of firm tissue in the lower curve of the breast is normal. Then move in an inch toward the nipple. Keep circling to examine every part of your breast, including the nipple. Then slowly repeat the procedure by placing the pillow under your left shoulder, raising the left arm and using the fingers on your right hand to examine your left breast. Finally, gently squeeze the nipple of each breast to check for discharge.

FAQ:

Can men get breast cancer?

Although breast cancer is 100 times more common among women, the American Cancer Society (2000a) estimates some 1,600 new cases of invasive breast cancer will be diagnosed among men in the United States each year. The average male breast cancer patient is 59 years old. Because the disease is so rarely found in men there have been few studies of the risk factors. It is thought that hormones and the environment play a role; however, about half of men who get breast cancer have no known risk factors. One reason that men have few breast cancers is simply that they have less breast tissue. In men, the only tissue that resembles the milk ducts in women is located directly beneath the nipple—and that is where most male breast cancers occur.

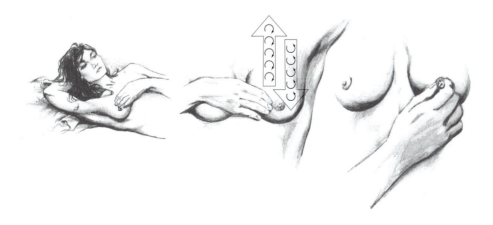

FIGURE 2.8   Breast Self-Examination.

Lumpectomy: surgery to remove a breast tumor and a small amount of tissue surrounding the tumor

Mastectomy: surgical removal of the breast

The American Cancer Society recommends that beginning at age 40 women should have an annual mammogram. Women who have a first-degree relative with the disease (mother, sister, or daughter) should have their first mammogram 10 years before the age at which the relative was diagnosed; for example, if your mother was 42 when she was diagnosed, you should have your first mammogram at age 32. If a suspicious lump is found, diagnosis is made by a biopsy, i.e., removal and examination of a small amount of tissue from the suspected area or the surgical removal of all or part of the area in question.

How Is It Treated?   Treatment choices for breast cancer are complex and depend on a number of factors including age, general health, and the size, location, stage, and features of the tumor. Treatment options include surgery, radiation therapy, hormone therapy, and chemotherapy. Two or more methods may be used in conjunction.

There are several types of surgery used to treat breast cancer. In a **lumpectomy** only the lump in the breast is removed, although some surgeons also take out some of the lymph nodes under the arm. In a *segmental mastectomy* the cancer and a larger area of breast tissue are removed, occasionally including some of the lining over the chest muscles below the tumor, and possibly some lymph nodes under the arm. A total **mastectomy,** sometimes called a *simple mastectomy,* involves the surgical removal of the whole breast, and possibly some lymph nodes under the arm. A *modified radical mastectomy* involves the removal of the breast, most of the lymph nodes under the arm, and often the lining over the chest muscles; the smaller of the two chest muscles also is taken out to aid in the removal of the lymph nodes. In a *radical mastectomy,* the breast, the chest muscles, all of the lymph nodes under the arm, and some additional fat and skin are removed.

For many years the radical mastectomy was the operation of choice. Now it is used mainly when the tumor has spread to the chest muscles. Numerous studies have shown that for early-stage disease, long-term survival rates after lumpectomy followed by radiation therapy are similar to the survival rates for modified radical mastectomies. Lumpectomies leave the breast intact. When the breast is removed through a mastectomy, reconstruction is often an option either at the same time as the surgery or at a later date.

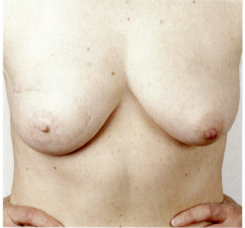

(a) A woman after a mastectomy without reconstructive surgery. (b) A woman with a reconstructed breast following a mastectomy.

Chemotherapy may be given orally or by injection in cycles, with each treatment period followed by a recovery period. Usually chemotherapy is administered on an outpatient basis. Another treatment option is hormonal therapy, which is used to keep cancer cells from getting the hormones they need to grow. This treatment may require the use of drugs, or surgery to remove the ovaries, which produce the majority of female hormones. Like chemotherapy, hormonal therapy is a systemic treatment affecting cells throughout the body.

Ninety-six percent of women with localized breast cancer survive at least 5 years after diagnosis. If the cancer has spread, the survival rate is about 75 percent. An increase in the survival rate is probably due to better and earlier detection, increased use of chemotherapy and radiation along with surgery, and better techniques for discovering metastases.

Semen: fluid containing sperm and secretions from the testicles, prostate, and seminal vesicles that is expelled from the penis during ejaculation; ejaculate

Ejaculate: semen

Sperm: male reproductive cell

Seminal Fluid: fluid from the prostate and other sex glands that helps transport semen out of a man's body during ejaculation

Spermatogenesis: the production of sperm cells

Male Sexual Anatomy and Physiology

Like the female sexual anatomy, the function of the male sexual organs is to ensure sexual arousal and reproduction. The penis and scrotum, which contains the testes, are the most observable parts of a man's sexual anatomy. However, the internal organs are essential to ensure that sexual functions, including erection, ejaculation, and fertilization (which will be discussed in Chapters 3 and 5) are possible. The male reproductive system is best understood by following the pathway of sperm from the site of production in the seminiferous tubules of the testes to ejaculation out the urethral meatus (or opening) of the penis.

MALE INTERNAL SEXUAL ORGANS

The primary function of the internal sexual organs of the human male (Figure 2.9) is the production of **semen.** Semen, sometimes referred to in clinical terms as **ejaculate,** is the **sperm**-containing **seminal fluid** ejaculated through the opening of the penis. A teaspoon

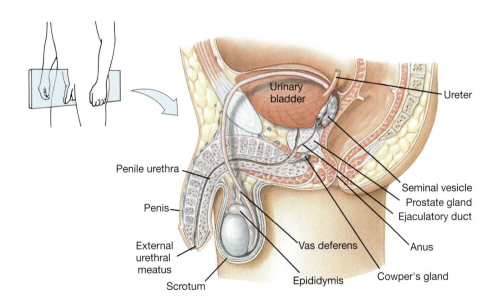

FIGURE 2.9   The Male Internal Sexual Organs. Source: Martini, 2001.

FAQ:

Why is it difficult for men to urinate when they have an erection?

When a man has an erection, the prostate gland squeezes shut the urethral duct to the bladder. This prevents urine from flowing down the urethra (and prevents semen from going up into the bladder). Thus normally, before a man with an erection can urinate, the pressure on the urethral duct must be released to allow passage of the urine down the urethra. Once this happens a man may urinate even though he may still have a partial erection. This is a common occurrence when a man awakens with a morning erection. (Contrary to popular opinion, the erection is caused by sexual arousal during the REM phase of sleep, not the need to urinate.) Usually by the time the bladder has been voided, the corpora cavernosa (see section on the penis) have disgorged the excess blood, leaving a flaccid or near flaccid penis.

of semen typically may contain between 200 and 500 million sperm, but a single sperm is all that is needed to fertilize an egg. Sperm are so small that they constitute only about 1 percent of the total volume of semen. The rest of the fluid is composed of ascorbic and citric acids, enzymes, fructose, water, and other substances. The amount of semen ejaculated by a male varies but averages roughly a teaspoonful. The volume of semen is also influenced by the length of time since the last ejaculation, the duration of arousal prior to ejaculation, and age (a man tends to produce less ejaculate as he gets older).

Seminiferous Tubules

Sometime after the onset of puberty, sperm production, called **spermatogenesis** (*genesis* = birth), takes place within the **seminiferous tubules.** Located within the testes (Figure 2.10) these thin, densely coiled sperm-bearing tubes are located inside the approximately 250 cone-shaped lobes of the interior of each testicle. Placed end to end, these tiny tubules would span the length of several football fields. Leydig's cells or interstitial cells, found between the seminiferous tubules, produce **androgens,** the hormones that promote the development of male genitals and secondary sex characteristics. The most important androgen is testosterone. (See Chapter 3 for a discussion of testosterone's role in sexual arousal.) The close proximity of Leydig's cells to blood vessels allows direct secretion of androgens into the bloodstream.

Epididymis

Sperm produced by the seminiferous tubules mature during storage in the C-shaped **epididymis** that is attached to the back and top surface of each testis (see Figures 2.9 and 2.10). Sperm may be stored in the epididymis for a period of several weeks. During this time the sperm cells continue to mature but are completely inactive.

Vas Deferens

Eventually the sperm stored in the epididymis move into the **vas deferens,** twin tubes that begin at each testis (see Figure 2.10). The vas deferens carries sperm up into the body cavity, where at the base of the bladder they form the ejaculatory ducts. The two

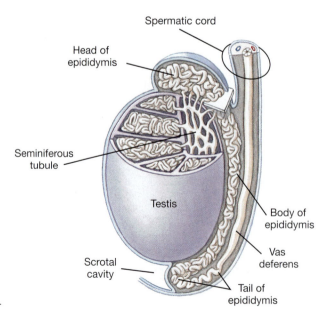

FIGURE 2.10 The Testes. Source: Martini, 2001.

ejaculatory ducts run through the prostate gland and connect to the urethra. The urethra is the common duct that also carries urine from the bladder to the opening of the penis where it is expelled from the body.

Seminal Vesicles

The **seminal vesicles** are two small glands located next to the ends of the vas deferens (see Figure 2.9). The excretory ducts of the seminal vesicles join the vas deferens to form the ejaculatory ducts. The seminal vesicles contribute to the production of seminal fluid, the viscous fluid ejaculated through the penis. The secretion of the seminal vesicles is high in fructose, a form of sugar. This sugar serves as a nutrient for the sperm, which require energy to make it to their destination. Once enriched by the secretions of the seminal vesicles, the sperm begin to propel themselves by the whiplike action of their tails.

Prostate Gland

Like the seminal vesicles, the **prostate gland** contributes ingredients to the seminal fluid soup. Secretions of the prostate gland constitute about 30 percent of the seminal fluid released during ejaculation; the other 70 percent is produced by the seminal vesicles. Both the ejaculatory ducts and the urethra pass through this gland, located at the base of the bladder and normally about the size and shape of a walnut (see Figure 2.9). It is composed of muscle as well as glandular tissue. During arousal, the muscular tissue of the prostate gland squeezes shut the urethral duct to the bladder, thus preventing urine from mixing with the semen and disturbing the chemical balance required by sperm. If the prostate gland becomes enlarged, as it often does as men age, the swelling can close off the ejaculatory ducts and urethra, making urination difficult and painful.

Seminiferous Tubules: thin coiled tubes located in the testicles in which sperm are produced

Androgens: hormones that promote the development of male sex characteristics

Epididymis: tightly coiled thin-walled tube where sperm maturation is completed

Vas Deferens: tubes that convey sperm from the testes to the ejaculatory duct of the penis

Seminal Vesicles: small glands that lie behind the bladder and secrete fluid that combines with sperm in the ejaculatory ducts

Prostate Gland: gland, which lies just below the bladder and surrounds the urethra, that produces about 30 percent of the seminal fluid released during ejaculation

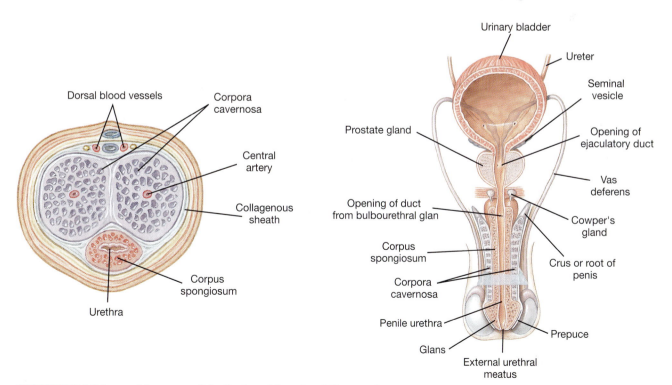

FIGURE 2.11 Internal Structure of the Penis and Associated Organs. Source: Martini, 2001.

Cowper's Glands: glands located beneath the prostate that produce a clear, colorless liquid before ejaculation that neutralizes acid to prevent damage to the sperm

Scrotum: the external pouch of skin beneath the penis that contains the testicles

Testes: the male reproductive organs within the scrotum that produce sperm and are the primary source of testosterone; testicles

Testicles: testes

Spermatic Cord: cord that suspends the testes within the scrotum

Penis: the male sexual organ

Foreskin: covering of skin over the penile glans; prepuce

Prepuce: foreskin

Corpus Spongiosum: structure at the base of the penis that extends up into the shaft and forms the penile glans

Corpora Cavernosa: structures in the shaft of the penis that engorge with blood during sexual arousal

Circumcision: surgical removal of the foreskin

Cowper's Glands

The **Cowper's glands,** also called the bulbourethral glands, are two small structures about the size of a pea located one on each side of the urethra just below the prostate gland (see Figure 2.11a). When a man is sexually aroused these glands may produce a fluid secretion called pre-ejaculate. Tiny ducts carry this secretion from the Cowper's glands to the urethra. It neutralizes the acidity of the urethra and also may help to lubricate the urethra and thus increase the flow of seminal fluid.

Some men notice the secretion of the Cowper's glands as soon as they get an erection; others rarely or never produce these droplets. For many men, however, this secretion appears just prior to ejaculation. While this fluid is not semen, it may contain healthy sperm if the man has not urinated since the last ejaculation. This is one reason why the withdrawal method of birth control (withdrawal of the penis from the vagina prior to ejaculation) is not highly effective.

MALE EXTERNAL SEXUAL ORGANS

The external sexual organs of the human male include the scrotum, testes, and penis (Figure 2.12).

Scrotum

The **scrotum** is a pouch of skin that normally hangs loosely from a man's abdominal wall directly beneath the penis (see Figures 2.9 and 2.12). This organ is also called the scrotal sac, reflecting its role in containing the **testes** or **testicles.** The scrotal sac consists of two layers. The outermost layer is a covering of thin skin that usually is a darker color than other body skin and becomes sparsely covered with pubic hair during adolescence. The second layer is composed of smooth muscle fibers and connective tissue. The scrotum's primary function is to maintain the temperature at which the testes most effectively produce sperm. The average scrotal temperature is lower than body temperature by approximately 3.1 degrees Centigrade (5.6 degrees Fahrenheit). Hanging the testes outside the body cavity is thus a way to keep them cool and to assure maximum sperm production. As the temperature of the testes rises, sperm production is reduced and may even cease. This is the reason that men are advised to wear

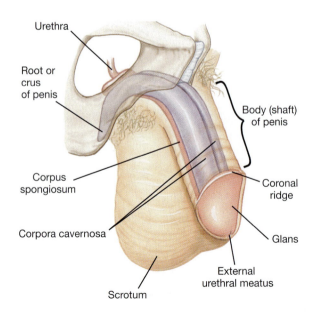

FIGURE 2.12 The Male External Sexual Organs.
SOURCE: Martini, 2001.

boxer shorts and loose clothing if they are having trouble conceiving a baby. There are relatively few nerve endings in the scrotum, so it is not highly sensitive, although some men find scrotal stimulation highly arousing. When a male is "kicked in the balls," the pain results from damage to the testes, not the scrotum.

Testes

Within the scrotal sac are two separate compartments or cavities, each of which houses a single testicle or *testis* (plural, testes). Each testis is suspended within the scrotum by the **spermatic cord** (see Figure 2.10). The spermatic cord contains the vas deferens (see section on Male Internal Sexual Organs), blood vessels, nerves, and fibers of the *cremasteric muscles.* The cremasteric muscles influence the position of the testicle in the scrotal sac and are affected by temperature and sexual stimulation; they can also be contracted voluntarily (try it!). Supposedly, some practitioners of Asian martial arts learn to retract the testes fully into the body cavity to protect them during combat.

The testes have two major functions: the secretion of sex hormones and the production of sperm. In most men the testes are asymmetrical, that is, they are not the exact same size and shape. The left testicle often hangs lower than the right since the left spermatic cord is longer than the right.

Penis

The **penis** has two functions: the passage of urine from the bladder to the exterior, and the passage of sperm from the testes to the exterior. It is divided into three major areas: the tip of the penis is called the *glans*, the body of the penis is called the *shaft*, and the portion of the shaft that extends internally and is attached to the pelvic bones is called the *root* (see Figure 2.12). The skin that covers the glans of an uncircumcised penis is the **prepuce** or **foreskin** (see Figure 2.11a). The shaft of the penis contains nerves, blood vessels, fibrous tissue, and three parallel cylinders of spongy tissue (Figure 2.11b). The cylinder on the underside of the shaft, which extends into the glans, is the **corpus spongiosum** (spongy body). The urethra runs through the middle of the corpus spongiosum. Urine and sperm pass through the urethra and exit at the *urethral meatus*, the urinary opening in the glans. Two cylindrical bodies called **corpora cavernosa** (cavernous bodies) run along the top of the shaft. To accomplish its second function, the penis must stiffen, or become erect. This is accomplished by a sudden influx of blood into the corpus spongiosum and the corpora cavernosa. At the root of the penis, the corpora cavernosa branch into tips called crura that are attached to the pelvic bones. Although an erect penis is sometimes referred to as a "boner," there are no bones in the human penis (but the walrus and other mammals do have penis bones that are associated with erections). There is an extensive network of muscles at the base of the penis, but the penis itself does not contain much muscle tissue.

Circumcision   Circumcision, the surgical removal of the prepuce or foreskin of the penis, is one of the oldest surgical procedures known to humans. For more than 3,000 years, Jewish families have been circumcising their newborn males on the eighth day after birth as a sign of their covenant with God. Most Jewish and Muslim families routinely choose to have their sons circumcised. You may have heard the term *female circumcision* used to refer to the ritual excision of the vulva, but this is a misnomer, as the vulva is not a foreskin (this topic, more correctly referred to as female genital mutilation, will be explored in detail in Chapter 8).

The National Center for Health Statistics estimates that about 60 percent of all male infants born in the United States are circumcised (Figure 2.13). This is in sharp contrast with other Western societies, in which circumcision is much less common. The medical value of neonatal circumcision is a subject of heated debate. The American Academy of Pediatrics has issued new circumcision policies three times in as many decades. In the 1970s, the academy's position was that there was no medical reason for circumcision, but in the 1980s it reported potential medical benefits.

FAQ:

Why should men wear an athletic supporter?

Only 1 in 10 adult men engaging in recreational contact sports bothers to wear an athletic cup or supporter, risking injury and permanent infertility (Gerací et al., 1998). Whenever men participate in an activity that involves contact they are advised to choose their support wisely. Hard plastic cups, the kind that ice hockey goalies are required to wear, offer the most protection. Since most men who are injured while bicycling do so while going down steps (yes—steps!), standing up on the pedals when riding over extremely bumpy surfaces is recommended to keep the vibrations from damaging the groin area. A man who has experienced an injury to the testicles should lie down, apply an ice pack to the affected area, and take a pain reliever such as ibuprofen or acetaminophen. If the testicles become swollen, black and blue, or if extreme pain persists for more than several minutes, a doctor should be seen immediately and the patient should request a scrotal ultrasound exam.

 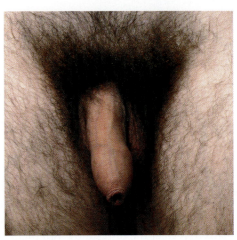

(a) A man with a circumcised penis. (b) A man with an uncircumcised penis, showing the prepuce, or foreskin.

FAQ:

What is the most sensitive area of the penis?

While the entire penis has many nerve endings, making it highly sensitive to touch, pressure, and temperature, the glans has the highest concentration of nerve endings. The *coronal ridge*, the aptly named ridge of tissue that rings the glans and forms the border between it and the shaft (*coronal* = crown; see Figure 2.12), is a particularly sensitive area. Another area that is highly responsive to manual and oral stimulation is the *frenulum*, a thin strip of skin on the underside of the penis that attaches the glans to the shaft.

In 1999 the Academy concluded that although there are potential benefits, the data are not significant enough to recommend routine circumcision (American Academy of Pediatrics, 1999). Although uncircumcised boys have four times the risk of getting urinary tract infections in their first year, the risk is still only 1 in 100 (Fergusson, Lawton, & Shannon, 1988; Herzog, 1989; Roberts, 1990). And, while uncircumcised men, particularly those with *phimosis* (the inability to retract the foreskin), have three times the risk of developing penile cancer, the risk is extremely low. Only nine out of a million American men are diagnosed with the disease annually (Harahap and Siregar, 1988; McAninch, 1990; Rotolo & Lynch, 1991). While there have been some claims that cervical cancer is more frequent in women who have sexual relations with uncircumcised partners, research has not supported this assertion (Brinton et al., 1989; Snyder, 1991; Wallerstein, 1980). Moreover, while some studies suggest that circumcised men have a reduced risk of contracting HIV, behavioral factors are more important risk factors than circumcision (Halperin & Bailey, 1999).

Although some of those opposed to circumcision claim that removal of the foreskin may reduce sexual pleasure, other reports indicate that circumcised men suffer less sexual dysfunction, especially those over age 45. The National Health and Social Life Survey asked men about their circumcision status, history of sexually transmitted infections, and experience of sexual dysfunction. There were no significant differences between circumcised and uncircumcised men in the contraction of sexually transmitted infections, but uncircumcised men were slightly more likely to experience sexual dysfunction, especially in later life (Laumann et al., 1997).

There are those who argue against routine circumcision, stating that the foreskin may serve an important but as yet un-

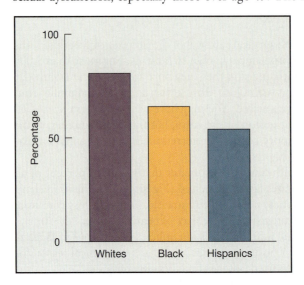

FIGURE 2.13 Who Gets Circumcised?
SOURCE: Data from Laumann, et al., 1994

known function. Others oppose what they see as an unnecessary, traumatic surgical procedure that poses possible complications including hemorrhage, infections, mutilation, shock, psychological trauma, and even death in rare cases (Chessare, 1992; Thompson, 1990).

Historically, circumcision is the only surgical procedure that is routinely performed without first administering analgesia or anesthesia (Wiswell, 1998). It was thought that newborns did not feel pain and that the risks involved in using anesthesia on infants were too high to justify its use. However, during circumcision boys were noted to be agitated, cry intensely, and have changes in facial expression indicating that the procedure was indeed painful (Williamson, 1997; Wiswell, 1998). Many physicians now use a local analgesic or a dorsal penile nerve block, a form of local anesthesia, to reduce circumcision pain and stress response (Holliday et al., 1999).

There is as much variation in the appearance of the external male genitalia as in the female vulva. Male genitalia reach adult proportions at approximately 15 years of age. Some people believe that you can predict penis length by a man's height or shoe size. Believe it or not, this idea has been researched, and it was found that neither body height nor foot size serve as practical estimators of penis length (Siminoski & Jerald, 1993). Compared to other species, the human penis is relatively large. A gorilla's erection might measure only 3 inches—though that of the blue whale, the world's largest mammal, may be 10 feet. Although the size of the male external sexual organs has been a source of pride (and concern) throughout history, these private proportions have little to do with sexual performance or satisfaction of either the male or the female partner (see CONSIDERATIONS box).

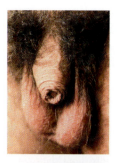

Natural variations in penis size and shape.

DISORDERS OF THE MALE SEXUAL ORGANS

Prostate Cancer

Prostate cancer, cancer of the prostate gland, is second only to skin cancer as a leading cancer killer among American men. Although it is estimated that over 180,000 new cases of prostate cancer are diagnosed annually in the United States and that one in six

How Big Is Big Enough?

Cosmetic surgery to enlarge the penis, called *phalloplasty*, may not be as popular as breast augmentation, but in the past few years it has become increasingly popular. In 1996 men spent about $12 million on penile enlargements. Introduced in the United States in 1991, one penis-lengthening procedure involves severing the crura, the ligament that attaches the penis to the pubic bone; this allows the internal portion of the penis to drop down to the exterior. Another method combines this surgery with stretcher devices, specially designed weights that stretch the penis to prevent reabsorption of the internal portion into the abdomen. There have been no clinical studies of the results of penile augmentation. Individual surgeons claim the procedure may add ¹/₂ to 3 inches in length, though less than an inch seems to be common.

Thickening the penis (increasing its circumference) involves tissue grafts or injections of fat (extracted from the abdomen or other parts of the body) into the penis. Postsurgery increases of 1.1 to 2.1 centimeters (or approximately ¹/₂ to ³/₄ inches) in circumference have been

reported, though there are claims of increases of 1 to 1¹/₂ inches in girth (Austoni & Guarneri, 1999).

If a man is born with an extremely small penis, penile enlargement may be a psychological if not medical necessity. However, most men who choose to undergo penile enlargement do not necessarily have smaller-than-average penises (Alexander, 1994). As with any surgery, there are potential risks. And many plastic surgeons report that the results are rarely impressive and can be disfiguring or even dangerous (Resnick, 1999).

Fat injection techniques may result in lumps, and because the body rejects a significant portion of the fat injection, the procedure may need to be repeated several times for a satisfactory result. Surgical techniques may result in scarring, loss of sensation, and other problems, including impotence. None of these penile augmentation procedures are endorsed by the American Urological Association or the American Society of Plastic and Reconstructive Surgeons.

 In what cases do you think the benefits of penile enlargement might outweigh the risks?

FAQ:

Can a man be "uncircumcised"?

Most men who seek to have their foreskin restored cite one of two reasons. The first is that they want to "regain . . . something taken from them without their consent" (Toppo, 1996, p. 21). The second reason is that some believe that restoration of the skin over the head of the penis restores a large amount of sensation, making for greater sexual pleasure. Surgical restoration of the foreskin is possible using skin grafts. Some men choose circumcision reversal without medical or surgical intervention. The process is time consuming, taking from 1 to 5 years of constant attention and care. Using stretching methods similar to those used to grow skin for skin grafts, some men use techniques that they claim eventually will permanently extend skin from the penile shaft over the penile glans.

American men will develop prostate cancer in his lifetime, many men have limited awareness of the symptoms, treatment, and consequences of the disease. Prostate cancer is curable if detected early. The 5-year survival rate for men whose tumors are diagnosed in the local and regional stages of the disease is 100 percent (American Cancer Society, 2000d).

What's Your Risk?   More than 80 percent of men with prostate cancer are over age 65; the median age is 72. Since 1970 the incidence of prostate cancer in the United States has risen 50 percent and deaths have risen 40 percent. The risk of prostate cancer increases as men age. As the life span of Americans increases, more and more men live to an age at which they are at high risk.

Men with high levels of the hormone insulin-like growth factor-1 (IGF-1) have four times the risk of prostate cancer as men with lower levels, though high levels do not mean that men are certain to develop the disease (Pollak, 1998). A high-fat diet is an environmental factor that has also been identified. In countries with a traditional low-fat diet, such as China and Japan, the incidence of prostate cancer is extremely low. Reflecting the flaws in the traditional American diet, prostate cancer rates for first- and second-generation Japanese Americans are considerably higher than those of their relatives in Japan. A large study found that men who consumed at least 2.5 servings of dairy products daily (not unusual in the traditional American diet) were about 30 percent more likely to develop prostate cancer than those who averaged less than half a serving a day (Chan et al., 1998).

How Is It Detected?   The average case of prostate cancer takes as long as a decade to develop. In its early stages, there are often no apparent symptoms. Later signs include urinary difficulties, blood in the urine, painful ejaculation, fatigue, weight loss, and bone pain in the lower back, hips, or pelvis. These symptoms may be attributed to other less serious health problems.

Exams and tests for prostate cancer include a digital rectal exam (see SEXUAL HEALTH AND YOU box later in this chapter), blood tests, a urine test, ultrasound, and X-rays. A physician may also perform a *cystoscopy*, a procedure in which the doctor looks into the urethra and bladder though a thin, lighted tube. If test results suggest that cancer may be present, the physician will perform a biopsy on the prostate tissue.

About 75 percent of men with prostate cancer have elevated levels of a protein called prostate-specific antigen (PSA). Testing blood for PSA has been a standard screening method for older men since about 1990. However other conditions, such as noncancerous prostate enlargement (see section on Prostatitis), can also elevate PSA levels, so doctors must perform needle biopsies, removing a sample of tissue with a needle, in order to determine whether or not the condition is malignant.

A blood test, approved by the FDA in 1998, has eliminated the need for many biopsies. While the traditional PSA test measures levels of PSA chemically bound to other proteins, the newer, free PSA test measures blood levels of "free" or unbound PSA in the blood serum. The newer test does not replace traditional PSA testing but is given as a follow-up when the traditional test yields uncertain results. A new urine test to detect prostate cancer in its earliest stages (years before it is clinically detectable) shows promise (Voeker, 2000).

Used routinely, traditional PSA testing alone could reduce deaths from prostate cancer by more than 66 percent. Researchers at the National Cancer Institute reported that in 1997 the prostate cancer death rate for white men under age 85 in the United States had fallen below what it had been in 1986, the first year the PSA test was used for screening. In men ages 60 to 79, the 1997 death rate was lower than any year since 1950. Yet none of these current research findings are proof that the PSA tests save lives. Many medical organizations and experts on prostate cancer don't agree about when or even if PSA screening should be done. The disagreement about whether the test is worthwhile stems from the age of the affected population; because of the long, slow progress of the disease, older men with prostate cancer are more likely to die from other, unrelated illnesses, and treatment can produce serious, debilitating side effects such as impotence and incontinence (Sung, Kabalin, & Terris, 2000). More definitive answers must await studies currently underway that compare the survival rates of men who get the blood tests and those who do not.

How Is It Treated?   The recommended treatments for prostate cancer include watchful waiting, surgical intervention, radiation, and hormone therapy (Table 2.3).

Watchful Waiting.   For those men whose prostate cancer is slow growing and found at an early stage, "watchful waiting" rather than treatment may be recommended, especially for older men and those with other serious medical problems, since the side effects of treatment might outweigh the possible benefits.

Surgical Intervention.   A standard early stage treatment is radical *prostatectomy*. This involves the surgical removal of the prostate without affecting the nerves essential for an erection. In *retropubic prostatectomy*, the prostate and nearby lymph nodes are removed through an incision in the abdomen. In *perineal prostatectomy*, the prostate is removed through an incision between the scrotum and the anus.

Radiation.   Another common treatment for prostate cancer is radiation therapy. In early-stage cancer, radiation can be used instead of surgery or it may be used after surgery to destroy any cancer cells that may have been missed.

Hormone Therapy.   Hormone therapy prevents the prostate cancer cells from receiving testosterone, the hormone they need for growth. There are several forms of hormone therapy. Because the testicles are the source of testosterone, one option is an *orchiectomy*, surgical removal of the testicles. One alternative to surgery is the use of a luteinizing hormone-releasing hormone (LH-RH) agonist to prevent the testicles from producing testosterone. Patients may also take the female hormone estrogen to prohibit testosterone production.

A study recently published in the *Journal of the American Medical Association* found that 60 percent of men who had their prostate gland removed suffered from erectile dysfunction (the inability to have an erection) and had some decline in urinary function 18 months after the surgery. Yet the researchers found that nearly 75 percent

---

TABLE 2.3

Treatment Options for Prostate Cancer

Treatment	Advantages	Disadvantages
Prostatectomy	100% cure rate for cancer limited to the prostate	Hospital stay and recovery Risk of erectile dysfunction and incontinence
Radiation Therapy (internal or external)	Can eliminate the need for surgery Outpatient procedure	Recurrence of cancer May be some pain at site of radiation Not appropriate for cancer that has spread beyond the prostate gland
Hormone Therapy	Outpatient procedure Temporary tumor shrinkage	Recurrence of cancer Sexual dysfunction
Watchful Waiting	No side effects or treatment risks	Risks the spread of cancer cells to other organs and tissue

said they were satisfied with the results (Stanford et al., 2000). Radical prostatectomy and external radiation patients showed comparable rates of improvement in sexual function during the first year after treatment. However, in the second year, the sexual function of radiation patients began to decline, while that of the surgery patients did not. After two years, men in each group had similar rates of erectile dysfunction (Litwin et al., 1999).

Prostate Cancer Vaccine. Researchers have recently developed a vaccine that helps strengthen the body's immune system against prostate cancer. The vaccine uses the patient's own cells, grown in his own plasma, to trigger the immune system to attack cancerous cells in the prostate. The results of the first human trials showed that the vaccine could trigger the immune system to fight cancer in the same way that it fights infection. While the researchers found the results to be promising, more research will be necessary to determine the effectiveness and safety of this approach before it becomes available to the general public (Simons et al., 2000).

Prostatitis

Prostatitis, inflammation of the prostate gland, is a common disorder that may occur in men of any age. There are two types of prostatitis: bacterial and nonbacterial. *Bacterial prostatitis* may occur as either an acute or chronic disorder. Acute cases often occur only once and respond to medical treatment. Chronic bacterial prostatitis is associated with an underlying defect in the prostate that becomes a focal point for the persistence of bacterial infection in the urinary tract; it is more difficult to treat than acute cases. Bacterial prostatitis causes fever and chills, pain in the lower back and genital area, body aches, painful urination, and the frequent and urgent need to urinate. *Nonbacterial prostatitis* has the symptoms of bacterial prostatitis but no evidence of a known infecting organism. *Prostatodynia* is a condition in which the symptoms and signs of prostatitis are present, without evidence of inflammation of the prostate or bacterial causes (Vastag, 2001).

What's Your Risk? Prostatitis accounts for up to 25 percent of all medical office visits by young and middle-aged men with genital and urinary symptoms. Nonbacterial prostatitis is eight times more common than bacterial prostatitis (MedicineNet.com, 2001).

How Is It Detected? Prostatitis is indicated by the presentation of symptoms mentioned earlier (fever and chills, pain, body aches, and painful or frequent urination). The evidence of white blood cells and bacteria in the urine can confirm bacterial prostatitis. The lack of bacteria in the urine indicates nonbacterial prostatitis.

How Is It Treated? Bacterial prostatitis is treated with antibiotics (Roberts et al., 1997). Chronic bacterial prostatitis may require 4 to 6 weeks of treatment due to the poor penetration of antibiotics into the prostate. Though nonbacterial prostatitis is the most common form, it also is the least understood. There is no treatment for nonbacterial prostatitis; symptoms may go away and then return without warning.

Benign Prostatic Hyperplasia (BPH)

It is not uncommon for the prostate gland to become enlarged as a man ages. *Benign prostatic hyperplasia (BPH)* is a noncancerous enlargement of the prostate. Though the prostate continues to grow during most of a man's life, enlargement does not usually cause problems until later in his life. As the prostate enlarges, the surrounding capsule (see Figure 2.11a) stops it from expanding, causing the gland to press against the urethra. In response to this pressure, the bladder wall becomes thicker; it also becomes irritable, or more easily stimulated, so the bladder begins to contract even when it contains small amounts of urine, causing more frequent urination. As the bladder weakens, it loses the ability to empty itself completely.

What's Your Risk?   By 60 years of age, 80 percent of men have an enlarged prostate and suffer some degree of urinary difficulty. This condition is considered a natural result of aging. The cause of BPH is not well understood. Studies done with animals have suggested that the increasing amounts of estrogen within the gland as a man ages intensify the activity of substances that promote cell growth.

How Is It Detected?   Many of the symptoms of BPH occur when the swollen prostate squeezes the urethra and blocks normal urine flow. The most common symptoms are a weak or hard to start urine stream, a feeling of incomplete bladder emptying, and waking during the night several times to urinate. BPH does not necessarily lead to cancer or impaired sexual functioning. In a small percentage of men there may be some damage to the bladder or kidneys. Diagnosis may be aided by a digital rectal exam, ultrasound, a urine flow study, or other tests. A check for BPH should be part of a regular physical examination for men over age 50.

How Is It Treated?   About one third of those afflicted with BPH opt for surgery, usually in cases of severe prostate enlargement. Men are often counseled to consider treatments other than surgery to relieve their symptoms, including, in some cases, no treatment at all. The standard surgical procedure for BPH is a *transurethral resection of the prostate (TURP)*. A tiny looped wire is inserted through the urethra and excess prostate tissue is trimmed away. Balloon dilation is another option; a balloon is inserted through the urethra and expanded to push back prostate tissue and widen the urinary path. Drugs, such as finasteride, may be used to shrink the prostate. In 1997 the FDA approved the use of the Prostatron, a computer-controlled device that shrinks the prostate through the use of heat. The Prostatron procedure takes about an hour and can be done on an outpatient basis with local anesthetic.

Testicular Cancer

Cancer of a testis usually can be discovered as a small lump before the cancer spreads to other parts of the body. However, relatively few men routinely perform a self-examination. (See SEXUAL HEALTH AND YOU box.)

What's Your Risk?   *Testicular cancer*, cancer of the testicles, comprises only 1 percent of all cancers in American males but is the most common malignancy in men ages 15 to 35 and is the second most common form of cancer among men under age 40. About 7,600 new cases occur in the United States each year. The incidence of testicular

SEXUAL HEALTH AND YOU

Digital Rectal Exam

Because of the proximity of the prostate gland to the rectum (see Figure 2.9), the digital rectal examination is the best way to detect changes that might indicate prostate cancer. To perform a digital rectal exam, the physician inserts a lubricated, gloved finger into the rectum. During the exam the patient bends forward over an examination table or lies on his side with legs bent while the physician feels the size, shape, and texture of the prostate gland. Some men may feel as though they have to urinate or defecate during the exam, or the probing may cause them to have an erection. This should not prevent men from undergoing this important procedure. If a hardened area, lump, or other irregularity is found, X-ray, biopsy, or other tests for cancer may be performed.

Going Nuts

Figure skater Scott Hamilton, Tour de France champion cyclist Lance Armstrong, and comedian and MTV host Tom Green might not seem to have much in common, but all three men are survivors of testicular cancer, a malignancy that can affect the tissue in one or both testicles. When Tom Green was diagnosed with testicular cancer at age 28, he found that laughter was still his best medicine. Green had TV cameras in the hospital when he underwent two surgeries, one to remove his right testicle and the second to take out the surrounding lymph nodes. Green created a charity, "Tom Green's Nuts Cancer Fund," and a theme song: "Hey, kids, feel your balls so you don't get cancer."

 Do you think that you would be able to keep as positive an attitude as Tom Green has?

—*Do you think that his attitude helped him beat his cancer?*

cancer has increased 56 percent in the United States since 1973. For unknown reasons, no rise in incidence has occurred among African American men, who account for only 5 percent of all cases in the United States (American Cancer Society, 2000e).

While the causes of testicular cancer are not known, studies show that several factors increase the likelihood of a man developing the disease. Men who have an undescended testicle are at higher risk of developing testicular cancer. There is some evidence that men whose mothers took DES (diethylstilbestrol) medication to prevent spontaneous abortion during pregnancy are at higher risk for reproductive tract abnormalities (Vastag, 2001). DES is no longer administered to pregnant women. Contrary to popular myth, there is no evidence that masturbation or other sexual activity increases the risk of testicular cancer. Sports activities do not appear to be related, despite the publicity given to the diagnoses of skater Scott Hamilton and cyclist Lance Armstrong.

How Is It Detected?   Only half of those with testicular cancer report any pain in the early stages of illness. Men discover most cases of the disease during self-examination. It is critical for men, especially those ages 15 to 35, to perform regular testicular self-examinations to detect the presence of a tumor (see SEXUAL HEALTH AND YOU box). Men should seek medical care if they notice any of the following symptoms: a painless lump or swelling in either testicle, any enlargement of a testicle or change in the way it feels, a feeling of heaviness in the scrotum, a dull ache in the lower abdomen or groin, a sudden collection of fluid in the scrotum, or pain or discomfort in a testicle or in the scrotum.

To help find the cause of symptoms, a physician will perform a visual and manual examination of the testes and scrotum and may order an ultrasound or blood tests that measure the levels of substances that serve as tumor markers, such as alpha-fetoprotein (AFP), human chorionic gonadotropin (HCG), and lactase dehydrogenase (LDH). However, a biopsy of testicular tissue is the only sure way to know whether cancer is present.

How Is It Treated?   The survival rate for testicular cancer detected in the early stages is about 96 percent. There are four types of treatment: surgery, radiation, chemotherapy, and bone marrow transplantation. Surgery to remove the testicle is a common treatment for most stages of testicular cancer. If only one testis is removed, the remaining testis will supply adequate amounts of hormones. If both testes must be removed, testosterone may be given to compensate for hormone loss; artificial testes implants are available for cosmetic purposes.

Testicular Torsion

Testicular torsion occurs when a testis is rotated, twisting the spermatic cord. This may cut off blood flow to the testicles and surrounding structures within the scrotum, resulting in permanent damage to the affected testis.

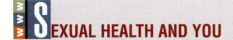

SEXUAL HEALTH AND YOU

Testicular Self-Exam

Isolate a testis and pull the skin of the scrotum tightly around it. Look for a pea-sized lump. Then carefully roll the testis between the thumb and fingers, feeling for any lumps. Repeat this process with the other testis.

The presence of a lump is not necessarily an indication of cancer, but you should seek a physician's examination immediately.

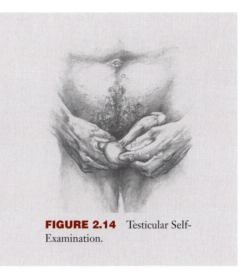

FIGURE 2.14   Testicular Self-Examination.

What's Your Risk?   Incidence of testicular torsion in males under age 25 is approximately 1 in 4,000. It is believed that some men may be predisposed to testicular torsion as a result of a lack of support, that is, inadequate connective tissue within the scrotum. However, the condition also can result from trauma or injury to the scrotum. Wearing an athletic supporter or cup when participating in contact sports may help to reduce injuries to the testes, including testicular torsion. Testicular torsion also may occur after strenuous exercise, or there may be no obvious cause. However, the incidence is higher during infancy and between the ages of 12 and 18 years when the testicles are growing most rapidly.

How Is It Detected?   Symptoms of testicular torsion include the sudden onset of severe pain in a testicle along with scrotal swelling and elevation of the affected testis. Additional symptoms are the presence of a testicular lump and blood in the semen.

How Is It Treated?   Any acute scrotal pain should be evaluated immediately. Testicular torsion is considered a surgical emergency. Surgery to untangle the twisted spermatic cord involves an incision in the scrotum. The testicle is uncoiled and sutures are used to secure the testis and prevent it from rotating again. The unaffected testicle is secured by suture at the same time, because the unaffected testicle is at increased risk for torsion at a later date. In one study of emergency room patients of ages 4 months to 47 years, surgical intervention undertaken within 4 hours of symptom onset salvaged the testicle in 100 percent of the cases. The salvage rate dropped to 75 percent when surgery took place within 8 to 16 hours, and to 25 percent beyond 16 hours (Watkin et al., 1996).

Epididymitis

Recall that the epididymis is the C-shaped organ extending along the top of each testis that is responsible for storage of sperm produced by the seminiferous tubules (see Figures 2.9 and 2.10). When a man is experiencing scrotal pain, *epididymitis*, an inflammation of the epididymis, is by far the most common diagnosis. Although it was once widely believed that straining of the groin area was a contributing factor, infection is now considered the most common cause of this condition. Infection may become so severe that it spreads to the adjacent testicle. Such cases may cause fever and, rarely, abscess formation.

What's Your Risk?   Bacterial organisms associated with urinary tract infections, sexually transmitted infections, and infection of the prostate, or surgical removal of the prostate typically causes epididymitis. Sexually active men who are not monogamous and do not use condoms are at increased risk. Men who have recently had prostate surgery or have a history of genitourinary tract problems also have higher-than-average incidence rates.

How Is It Detected?   The primary symptoms of epididymitis are scrotal pain and swelling. The pain or swelling may be mild or severe. At times the epididymis may become so inflamed that the patient is not able to walk. Tenderness is usually localized to a small area of the testicle where the epididymis is attached. Enlarged lymph nodes in the groin area and a discharge from the penis are additional symptoms; a rectal exam may reveal an enlarged prostate. Urinalysis and blood tests may be performed to screen for bacteria.

How Is It Treated?   For acute epididymitis, treatment with antibiotics, bed rest, scrotal support, and oral anti-inflammatory medication are effective. In chronic epididymitis, symptoms seem to persist even after the initial treatment. In these cases a second round of therapy may be helpful. Longer-term use of anti-inflammatory medication may be recommended. Surgical treatment is an uncommon last resort.

Penile Cancer

In *penile cancer*, cancer cells are found on the skin and in the tissues of the penis. This rare form of cancer accounts for less than $\frac{1}{2}$ percent of all malignancies in the United States. Most cases occur in men over 50 years of age.

What's Your Risk?   Although the definitive causes of penile cancer are not known, researchers have identified certain risk factors. The typical man diagnosed with cancer of the penis is over age 50, has had multiple sexual partners, and has had a sexually transmitted infection, especially HPV (genital warts). A long history of smoking increases a man's risk of developing penile cancer from 1 in 100,000 to 1 in 600 (Fair, Fuks, & Scher, 1993). Additional risk factors include not being circumcised. The risk of penile cancer is 3.2 times higher for uncircumcised men than for circumcised men. Researchers speculate that it takes more effort to keep an uncircumcised penis clean and free of *smegma*, a thick, cheeselike sebaceous secretion that collects beneath the foreskin, especially if the foreskin is difficult to pull back entirely (American Cancer Society, 1999).

How Is It Detected?   The cancer usually begins as a small, painless sore on the glans or the foreskin that won't heal. Symptoms like this are sometimes mistaken for a sexually transmitted infection. Tissue biopsy is the only way to make a definitive diagnosis.

How Is It Treated?   As with other cancers, surgery, radiation, and chemotherapy are standard methods of treating penile cancer. Surgical possibilities range from excision of the cancer and as little normal tissue as possible to a total *penectomy* (amputation of the entire penis). Usually only about one fourth of the length of the penis is amputated so the man may still be capable of orgasm and ejaculation. Although it is rare, penile cancer is deadly. Of the 1,300 men in the United States who develop penile cancer this year, only half will be alive 5 years from now. Early intervention is essential to survival. If the cancer is caught early and there is no lymph node involvement, the 5-year survival rate increases to nearly 90 percent.

Peyronie's Disease

Usually, a man's erect penis is straight. *Peyronie's disease* is a condition characterized by a bending or curving of the erect penis. The cause of Peyronie's disease is uncertain. However, many researchers believe it is caused by damage to the erectile bodies, the two long chambers within the penis that inflate with blood to cause an erection. When one of these bodies is stretched or bent during an erection, the damage can result in a thickened, inelastic scar on the outside of the erectile tissue, usually on the topside of the penis. It is the presence of this scar that causes the bending of the penis. Think of a long, thin balloon (the penis) with a piece of duct tape (the scar) stuck on one side. When you blow up the balloon, the duct tape prevents the area it covers from expanding properly, causing the inflated balloon to bend toward that side. A scar on the top of the penile shaft causes the penis to bend upward; a scar on the underside causes it to bend downward. In some cases, scars develop on both top and bottom, leading to indentation and shortening of the penis.

What's Your Risk?   When the distortion of the penis is severe, it may cause erectile dysfunction or pain during sexual intercourse (Vastag, 2001). While there are no precise figures, urologists who treat erection problems estimate it affects about 1 in 100 patients (National Institute of Health, 1995). Although it usually afflicts men in their 40s or 50s, both younger and older men can acquire this condition. As a result of aging, diminished elasticity near the point of attachment of connecting tissue might increase the chances of injury. Trauma explains some cases of Peyronie's disease, but most develop slowly and with no apparent traumatic event.

How Is It Detected?   We have already described the obvious structural symptoms of Peyronie's disease. These may occur without pain. Alternatively, intercourse may be painful and in severe cases, impossible. A physician should check any significant curve, bend, or unusual narrowing along the shaft of the penis, especially if it's accompanied by pain.

How Is It Treated?   Because the scar often shrinks or disappears without treatment, most medical experts suggest waiting 1 to 2 years or longer before attempting corrective surgery. There are two surgical options available. In the least intrusive, the Nesbit procedure, a small incision is made into the skin on the outside of the curve. The skin is then tightened on that side, counteracting the pull of the scar tissue and leaving the penis straighter. This procedure may shorten the penis a fraction of an inch or more. The second type of surgery involves removal of all or part of the scar tissue itself. Because the scar is located on the outside of the erectile tissue, any type of incision at that point may hinder erections. New treatments with less severe side effects are currently in development. These include laser surgery techniques and a calcium-blocker medication that may prevent the hardening of the scar. Table 2.4 provides information on other penile conditions.

TABLE 2.4			
Other Penile Conditions			
Condition	**Cause**	**Symptoms**	**Treatment**
Sclerosing Lymphangitis	Thrombotic vein probably due to trauma during intercourse	A hard, ropelike thickening that encircles the penile shaft	Will usually subside without treatment
Pearly Penile Papules	Common benign skin growths	Skin condition that looks like grains of sand dotting the corona	No treatment necessary
Fixed Drug Reaction	Rare localized allergy to a medication, often an oral antibiotic	Red, weeping rash the size of a quarter on the head of the penis	Medication change

■ R E V I E W

Human sexual anatomy and physiology evolved to enhance reproduction and promote survival of the species.

There are four female internal sexual organs. Eggs are produced by **1**_____ and carried down the **2**_____ (also called the oviducts) to the **3**_____. The lower end of the uterus extending into the vagina is the **4**_____. The wall of the uterus consists of three layers called the **5**_____, _____, and _____. A mature ovum may be fertilized by a sperm in the upper portion of a fallopian tube, but it should then become implanted in the lining of the **6**_____. The **7**_____ is the soft, muscular organ that leads from the uterus to the external surface of the female body. The hymen is a thin membrane stretched across the **8**_____ or opening at the lower end of the vagina.

The **9**_____ consists of the external female sex organs. The **10**_____ is the area over the pubic bone. The **11**_____ are the outer folds of skin that provide protection for the urethral opening and the introitus. The **12**_____ are the inner folds of skin at the front of the vestibule that form the prepuce or clitoral hood. The **13**_____ is the most sensitive area of female genitalia.

A female's first menses is called **14**_____. During the **15**_____ phase of the menstrual cycle, dead cells sloughed off the endometrium combined with small amounts of blood pass through the vagina, constituting the menstrual flow. **16**_____ is the release of an ovum from the ovary. The **17**_____ phase of the menstrual cycle begins immediately after ovulation and lasts until menstrual flow begins again.

18_____ is painful menstruation. **19**_____ is the absence of menstruation. Menopause is the permanent cessation of menstruation, part of the larger process of gradual decline in the reproductive capacity of the ovaries known as **20**_____.

21_____ cancer is the most common malignancy of the female reproductive organs. Uterine **22**_____ are balls of solid tissue that grow inside the uterus. A **23**_____ test can detect cervical caner, and should be performed annually. **24**_____ is an inflammation of the vagina that may be due to a number of causes, including bacteria, fungi, and viruses.

Breasts and pubic hair are examples of secondary sex characteristics. The human breasts are modified sweat glands called **25**_____ glands. The dark, sensitive skin surrounding the nipple is the **26**_____. Breast cancer is the most common form of cancer among women in the United States. Breast self-exams and **27**_____ are important in the early detection of breast cancers.

The **28**_____ or scrotal sac is the pouch that contains the testes. The testes produce **29**_____ and male sex hormones or **30**_____, the most important of which is testosterone. Developed sperm are moved from the seminiferous tubules in the testes to the **31**_____ and then into the vas deferens. A vas deferens joins the excretory duct of a seminal vesicle to form an ejaculatory duct. The two ejaculatory ducts, one from the vas deferens leading from each testis, run through the **32**_____ gland and connect to the urethra. The seminal vesicles contribute to the production of **33**_____ fluid. **34**_____ is the sperm-containing seminal fluid ejaculated through the urethral **35**_____ or opening of the penis. The tip of the penis is called the **36**_____, and the skin which covers it in an uncircumcised male is the **37**_____ or foreskin.

38_____ cancer is second only to skin cancer as a leading cancer killer among men in the United States. However, **39**_____ cancer is the most common malignancy in men ages 15 to 35.

SUGGESTED READINGS

Angier, N. (1999). *Woman: An Intimate Geography.* Boston: Houghton-Mifflin.

Angier, who calls her book "a celebration of the female body," describes the hormonal and neural underpinnings of sexual desire and challenges the insistence of evolutionary psychologists on the innate discordance between the strength of the male and female sex drives.

Barbach, L. (2000). *The Pause: Positive Approaches to Perimenopause and Menopause* (2nd Ed.). New York: Plume.

Dr. Barbach discusses the various natural physical and emotional changes that occur during menopause and presents traditional and alternative treatment approaches.

Ensler, E. (1998). *The Vagina Monologues.* New York: Villard Books.

Based on the play, *The Vagina Monologues,* this book contains meditations involving personal reminiscences and interviews with dozens of women whose attitudes range from fear to fascination.

Love, S. M., & Lindsey, K. (1995). *Dr. Susan Love's Breast Book.* New York: Addison-Wesley.

A breast surgeon and women's health advocate gives straightforward information about diseases of the breast and treatment options.

Paola, A. S. (1999). *Under the Fig Leaf: A Comprehensive Guide to the Care and Maintenance of the Penis, Prostate, and Related Organs.* Los Angeles: Health Information Press.

A comprehensive guide to men's health for consumers, this book covers prostate cancer, Viagra, circumcision, scrotal masses, and more.

Schulen, C. D. (2000). *The Change'll Do You Good: The Baby Boomer's Guide to Menopause.* Chicago: DCS Publishing.

The author dispels the common myths surrounding menopause and provides clear information to help understand what is happening to a woman's body during this time.

ANSWERS TO CHAPTER REVIEW:

1. ovaries; **2.** fallopian tubes; **3.** uterus; **4.** cervix; **5.** endometrium, myometrium, perimetrium; **6.** uterus; **7.** vagina; **8.** introitus; **9.** vulva; **10.** mons veneris; **11.** labia majora; **12.** labia minora; **13.** clitoris; **14.** menarche; **15.** menstrual; **16.** Ovulation; **17.** luteal; **18.** Dysmenorrhea; **19.** Amenorrhea; **20.** climacteric; **21.** Endometrial; **22.** fibroids; **23.** Pap; **24.** Vaginitis; **25.** mammary; **26.** areola; **27.** mammograms; **28.** scrotum; **29.** sperm; **30.** androgens; **31.** epididymis; **32.** prostate; **33.** seminal; **34.** Semen; **35.** meatus; **36.** glans; **37.** prepuce; **38.** Prostate; **39.** testicular;

Sexual Arousal and Response

PHYSICAL

SOCIAL

EMOTIONAL

SPIRITUAL

COGNITIVE

■ **One Advantage of Being *Homo sapiens***
Unlike other mammals, human females are continuously responsive to and available for sexual activity, independent of ovulation.

■ **Biological Foundations for Sexual Arousal and Response**
The brain and central nervous system, including the five senses, play roles of varying importance in human sexual arousal and response.

■ **Sex Hormones**
The sex hormones, including testosterone, the estrogens, progesterone, oxytocin, and vasopressin, play crucial roles in regulating sexuality.

■ **The Sexual Response Cycle**
There are a number of theories regarding the events of sexual arousal and response, including Masters and Johnson's EPOR model; Kaplan's model of desire, excitement, and orgasm; and Reed's ESP model.

■ **Orgasm**
Men and women experience orgasm, the peak of sexual arousal, somewhat differently. The events and frequency of female orgasm vary more than those of male orgasm.

■ **Sexuality and Disabilities**
Although they may interfere with sexual arousal and response, physical and psychological disabilities don't necessarily preclude sexual expression.

Sexual arousal, a heightened state of sexual interest and excitement, has both psychological and physical bases. There is much more to sex than the physical process of intercourse. Without the subjective feeling of pleasure, physiological arousal will not occur. However, knowledge of the physical changes that occur during sexual arousal is essential to a complete understanding of human sexuality. Sexual arousal and response are influenced by a number of factors. Of course, what one person finds sexually arousing, another might not. The patterns we will describe in the following pages can vary from person to person, and even from experience to experience.

Other biological factors and sensory processes also play significant roles in the **sexual response cycle,** the series of physiological processes and events that occur during sexual activity. In this chapter we focus primarily on the biology of sexual response. Later chapters will describe the influences of our emotional, social, and cultural needs on our sexual experiences.

ONE ADVANTAGE OF BEING HOMO SAPIENS

Unlike most species, humans engage in a great deal of sexual behavior that is not reproductive. But how much of our sexual response is preprogrammed, or biological, and how much is learned, either through personal experience or cultural expectations? This question has particular significance in the discussion of individual variations in sexual arousal as well as the differences between males and females.

Is mating, even among animals other than humans, just about reproduction? The **estrous** cycle, sometimes referred to simply as *estrus*, is the periodic state of sexual excitement in the female of most mammals, excluding humans, that immediately precedes ovulation and during which the female is most receptive to mating.

The cycle may range in length from 18 to 35 days (Jolly, 1972), a period that is much longer than necessary simply for fertilization. It is unlikely that all of the behavior that occurs during this time is for the purpose of reproduction. For example, females mate with many more males than is necessary for fertilization (Hrdy, 1981). Furthermore, although estrus is usually absent during pregnancy, some mammals may continue sexual activity during this time.

We can be certain that no member of the genus *Homo* ever experienced estrus. However, we can only guess at whether any of our pre-*Homo* ancestors were ever "in heat." One sure sign that evolution is progress is the unique capability of human females for continuous response to and availability for sexual activity, independent of ovulation (see CONSIDERATIONS box).

BIOLOGICAL FOUNDATIONS FOR SEXUAL AROUSAL AND RESPONSE

Which body parts do you most closely associate with sex? Although vaginal lubrication and an erect penis are more obvious physical signs of sexual arousal, it is important to remember that the genitals are not the only organs involved in sexual arousal and response; many body systems contribute to this process.

Sexual Arousal: heightened state of sexual interest and excitement

Sexual Response Cycle: physiological processes and events that occur during sexual activity

Estrous: the cycle of most female nonprimate mammals when they are most sexually receptive to males

Prime Mates

Because *Homo sapiens* share about 98 percent of their genetic material with both chimpanzees and bonobos, studying these evolutionary relatives can be useful in our understanding of human behavior.

The bonobos were described by Frans de Waal in his 1997 book *Bonobo: The Forgotten Ape.* Unlike their chimpanzee cousins, who are known for violence, male domination, and sexual efficiency, bonobos are peaceful, egalitarian, and lead sex-filled lives in the tropical forests of the Republic of Congo in Central Africa. According to de Waal, bonobos, not humans, appear to be the most sexual primates. They are constantly having sex of every variety, both heterosexual and homosexual, and with partners of all ages.

Adult male bonobos grab and mouth each other's genitals. Females regularly have sex with each other by placing their pelvises together, either face-to-face or rear-to-rear, and rubbing each other rapidly. Juvenile male bonobos suck on each other's penises and allow adult males to fondle them. They also participate whenever adults have sex by poking fingers and toes into the adults' body parts. Male and female bonobos copulate in both the typical mammalian back-to-front position and the face-to-face position, either standing or lying down with either the male or female on top. Furthermore, bonobos manually stimulate themselves and each other.

What makes bonobo sexuality of interest to researchers is that they use sex not only for reproduction but also just for the fun of it. Bonobos suggest that our idealization of private, monogamous sexual behavior might be a relatively recent deviation from our evolutionary heritage. Like bonobos, our ancestors may have used sex on a daily basis to form alliances, trade goods and favors, establish friendships, and keep the peace (Small, 1995).

According to Frans de Waal, bonobos, not humans, appear to be the most sexual primates. They are constantly having sex of every variety, both heterosexual and homosexual, and with partners of all ages.

? *Why should we be interested in bonobo sexuality?*

—Do you think that studying bonobos adds to our knowledge of human sexual behavior?

—Do you think that primates and humans are too different for us to learn much from them?

The Brain

Orgasm: the peak state of sexual excitement; it is marked by rhythmic contractions of the pelvic floor muscles

Cerebral Cortex: thin outer layer of the brain's cerebrum that is responsible for higher mental processes including perception, thought, and memory

Limbic System: a group of interconnected deep brain structures that especially influence motivation and emotion

We may talk about following our hearts, but it is actually our brains that direct a great deal of our sexual behavior. The male erection and female vaginal lubrication may be triggered by direct stimulation, but it is the brain that interprets the stimulation and begins the process of sexual arousal and response. Motivation, desire, and behavior also are part of the thinking brain, the "executive function" that exercises volition, choice, and self-control. Even when we think we're "behaving like animals," very little of our conduct is really automatic.

Fisher and Byrne (1978) tested the arousal value of sex films on both male and female participants. Half the viewers in their study saw soft-core films in which the actors and actresses kept their underwear on, while the rest saw hard-core films with full nudity and explicit sex. To the researchers' surprise, the participants were equally aroused regardless of how explicit the film was. In this same study, the researchers tested the role of the thought process in sexual arousal. Prior to viewing the film, viewers were given different story lines for the sex scenes they watched. Some were told that the people on the screen were newlyweds. Others were told they were a prostitute and a client. Still others were told the scene involved a young man and woman who had just met each other at a dance. The context had a great degree of influence on how aroused the subjects became. Both male and female viewers were more aroused when they thought they were watching sex between two people who had just met. The prostitution and newly-wed themes elicited lower levels of arousal (on both self-report and physiological measures), even though viewers were seeing exactly the same video clip. In other words, arousal depended less on what people actually saw than on what they thought it meant.

While various parts of the brain are involved in sexual response and behavior, the two most important are the **cerebral cortex** and the **limbic system** (Figure 3.1). The upper part of the brain, the cerebral cortex, is the "thinking center" of the brain, and is the area of the brain responsible for sexual fantasies, desires, thoughts, and images (it is also responsible for nonsexual thought processes). When the brain receives arousing messages, the cerebral cortex interprets this sensory information and transmits messages through the spinal cord causing an increase in heartbeat and respiration (breathing), which can alter muscle tension (or myotonia), send blood to the genitals, and increase skin sensitivity. Your ability to consciously identify these physical changes can actually contribute to your sexual arousal.

The limbic system, located within the cerebrum in the area below the cortex, consists of the *thalamus*, the *hypothalamus*, and other structures important to sexual arousal. This complex group of structures controls our emotions, motivations, memories, and behavioral drives (Everitt, 1990). In 1939, Heinrich Klüver and Paul Buey first demonstrated the importance of the limbic system in regulating sexual behavior in animals. When they destroyed certain areas of the limbic system, it tamed wild monkeys, but also triggered an increase in the frequency, intensity, and ability to perform sexual behaviors.

Sex and the Senses

The five human senses—*touch*, *sight*, *smell*, *hearing*, and *taste*—all contribute to sexual arousal and to the sexual response cycle. However, the same sensory stimulation can evoke different responses in different people. In one study (Herz & Cahill, 1997), researchers asked men and women to rate the importance of olfactory (smell), visual (sight), auditory (sound), and tactile (touch) information on their sexual response. Males rated visual and olfactory information as equally important in the selection of a

FAQ:

Can you have an orgasm just by thinking about sex?

The brain has been called our most important sexual organ. Sexual sensations, including **orgasm,** may be triggered by sexual stimulation that originates in the brain in the form of thoughts, fantasies, or memories. We can become aroused by images, words, aromas, and sounds, or without any outside sensory stimulation whatsoever in the form of thoughts, fantasies, or memories. Your brain, glands, nervous system, circulatory system, and reproductive system are all involved in your sexual fantasies. The fact that many people become sexually aroused during sleep, sometimes even to the point of orgasm, is one important sign that the brain contains all the information necessary to produce sexual arousal (at least sometimes).

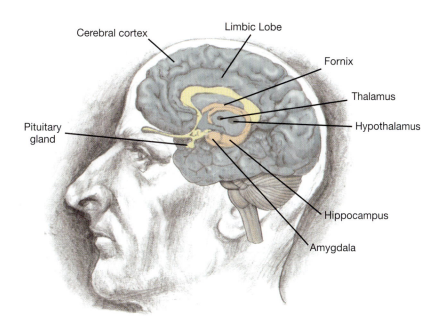

Cerebral cortex
Limbic Lobe
Fornix
Thalamus
Hypothalamus
Pituitary gland
Hippocampus
Amygdala

FIGURE 3.1 The limbic system of the brain, associated with emotion and motivation, is important in human sexual function.

What are erogenous zones?

Nerve endings are unevenly distributed throughout the body, causing some areas to be more sensitive to touch than others. Those body areas most sensitive to tactile stimulation are sometimes referred to as **erogenous zones.** The erogenous zones of the human body include the genitals, buttocks, anus, perineum, breasts, and inner surfaces of the thighs, neck, ears, navel, armpits, and mouth. As you have already learned, areas that may be extremely sensitive in one person may provoke no reaction, or even a negative reaction, in another. The only way to determine the location of your partner's erogenous zones is through experimentation.

Erogenous Zones: parts of the body that are especially sensitive to stimulation

Touch is probably the most frequent method of sexual arousal and has the most direct effect on sexual response.

lover, while females considered olfactory information to be the single most important variable; in the words of an old television commercial, "If he stinks, forget it!" (The ad was for deodorant, of course!) When considering what sense had the most negative effect on sexual desire, females rated body odor highest; males regarded smells as being much more neutral stimuli for sexual arousal (Herz & Cahill, 1997).

Touch   The skin is the largest organ in the human body. Stimulating an area of the body by touch is probably the most frequent method of sexual arousal and has the most direct effect on sexual response. A soft kiss on the lips, a tender touch on the arm, or a gentle lick on the ear all can be highly arousing, as can stroking a penis or the brushing of lips across a nipple.

Sight   Visual information plays a major role in sexual arousal. The fashion, diet, and cosmetic industries, as well as the market for erotic photographs and movies, reflect the emphasis our society places on visual arousal. Animals other than humans also use visual cues to signal sexual attraction. The peacock's plumage and the lion's mane may be the animal kingdom's version of a low-cut blouse or skin-tight jeans.

Studies show that men and women respond differently to visual stimulation. In one study, 54 percent of the men but only 12 percent of women became erotically aroused when they were shown photos and drawings of nudes (Reinisch, 1991).

Smell   Recent research indicates that the sense of smell may control human sexual activity, compatibility, group behavior, and other social activity, just as it does in animals (Stern & McClintock 1998). In Chapter 2 we introduced pheromones, naturally produced chemicals that affect behavior through the sense of smell. The pheromones produced by a queen bee inhibit the sexual development in other females, who then become workers. Male mice use pheromones to promote the sexual development of nearby females, and if a sow or a cow in heat smells the pheromones contained in male urine she will take a mating stance (see CROSS-CULTURAL PERSPECTIVES box).

Only recently has the presence of human pheromones been confirmed. One study evaluated the effect of synthesized male pheromones placed in an aftershave lotion on six behaviors in men: petting, formal dates, informal dates, sleeping next to a romantic partner, sexual intercourse, and masturbation. Pheromone users had increased rates of intercourse, sleeping with romantic partners, petting, and informal dates; there was no effect on masturbation or formal dates (Cutler et al., 1998). Although the full extent to which pheromones influence human sexual behavior is unknown, researchers suspect that different pheromones may control different activities.

CROSS-CULTURAL PERSPECTIVES

Sex Scents

Olfactory preferences are determined in large part by culture. Women in some societies use their vaginal secretions as a perfume, rubbing some behind the ear or on the neck to attract and arouse sexual partners. Sweat is an almost universal ingredient in love potions throughout the world. In parts of the Balkans and Greece some *men carry handkerchiefs in their armpits during festivals and offer these as tokens to women they invite to dance. In contrast, in America, most people think that the smell of a moist vagina or sweaty armpit would not be appealing, and indeed many people regularly use deodorants to conceal these odors from a dating partner.*

Visual cues play a major role in sexual arousal.

Our sense of hearing influences sexual arousal and response. Sex and love have been the inspiration for music and music is often used to set a romantic mood.

What smells arouse men the most? What do women like best?

A research study measured changes in penile response and vaginal blood flow in response to different odors (Hirsch, 1998). In contrast to what the floral and perfume industries would have us believe, the study reported that the odors found most arousing were not flowers or cologne. The aromas that evoked the greatest response in men were pumpkin pie and lavender, while women were most stimulated by the smell of licorice coated candy (Good & Plenty), cucumbers, and baby powder. None of the odors tested was found to inhibit the sexual desire of men. However, smells that inhibited vaginal blood flow in women included cherries, charcoal-barbecued meat, and men's colognes. This same researcher theorized that odors might act directly on the link between the olfactory sense and the brain's limbic system (Hirsch, 1998).

Hearing   Our sense of hearing also influences sexual arousal and response. For some, romantic music may set the mood (see CONSIDERATIONS box). Others may be sexually aroused when their lovers "talk dirty" or moan during lovemaking.

Tiny hair cells in the inner ear vibrate to transmit sounds. By examining these cells, researchers have found women's ears to be more sensitive than men's. Females hear high-pitched sounds better than males while men are more comfortable with louder sounds than women (Bloom, 1998).

In one study, male college students were shown 60-second erotic videos both with and without the accompanying audio. There was a significant positive correlation between male sexual arousal and sound, as measured by penile plethysmograph and self-report (Gaith & Plaud, 1997).

Another study found that a male partner's silence during lovemaking inhibited the female partner's sexual response (DeMartino, 1990). However, silence might be preferable to some other sounds, such as your partner burping during an embrace or the ringing of the phone. Many people find the sound of the words "I love you" to be the most arousing of all.

Taste   The role of taste in human sexual arousal has not been fully investigated. Some individuals may be sexually aroused by the taste of vaginal secretions or seminal fluid. It is possible that genital secretions contain chemicals that have an arousing effect, or it may be the psychological association of the flavors with past sexual pleasure that cause the excitement.

Aural Sex

Whether it is Ravel's "Bolero" or Barry White, music can simulate or stimulate sexual activity. Sounds of ecstasy have been a staple of pop music since the 1960s. Songs that contain sounds of female orgasm include: Marvin Gaye's "You Sure Love to Ball" (1973), Donna Summer's "Love to Love You Baby" (1975), Duran Duran's "Hungry Like the Wolf" (1982), Prince's "If The Kid Can't Make You Come" (1984), and Prince's "Orgasm" (1995). Sounds of male sexual pleasure are rarely heard in music. Perhaps this is because sound may be the only indication that some men have of women's orgasm, whereas women have more obvious physical evidence of a male partner's climax (Corbett & Kapsalis, 1996). The disembodied female vocalist

"oohing" and "aahing" herself into the throes of ecstasy "may stand as the most prominent signifier of female pleasure in the absence of other more visual assurances. Sounds of pleasure . . . seem almost to flout the realist function of anchoring body to image, halfway becoming aural fetishes of the female pleasures we cannot see" (Wiliams, 1989, pp. 122–123).

 Is there a song that almost always puts you in the mood for love?

—*What sounds, or words, do you like most, and least, to hear when making love?*

—*Can you think of a sound that would be an absolute turnoff?*

Chocolate, which contains phenylethylamine (PEA), a chemical believed to produce a lovelike sensation, is a very appropriate Valentine's Day gift.

In a 1980 study, Farb and Armelagos noted that the tradition of giving a box of chocolates on Valentine's Day might have arisen because chocolate contains phenylethylamine (PEA), a chemical believed to produce a lovelike sensation. Then again, foods such as salami and cheddar cheese have even higher levels of PEA—although few people would consider a deli sandwich an appropriate romantic gift. Chocolate also contains cannabinoids, the compound responsible for marijuana's high, although the amount isn't remotely close to that found in marijuana. In addition, the stimulants caffeine and theobromine are hidden in those delicious chocolate bars. The fat and sugar in chocolate candies are also likely to increase the volume of the brain chemical serotonin, which among other functions is responsible for making us feel good.

SEX HORMONES

The word *hormone* comes from the Greek *horman*, which means to arouse, to excite, to urge—which is exactly what our hormones do. Hormones, chemical substances secreted by your endocrine system (Table 3.1) arouse, excite, and influence your sexuality throughout your life. The endocrine system is a separate control system for the body, apart from the nervous system, and is comprised of ductless glands that release secretions directly into the bloodstream. There are several different types of hormones. For example, if you are in a stressful situation, hormones are deposited into the bloodstream by the adrenal, pituitary, thyroid, and other glands, resulting in an increase in heart rate, muscle tension, blood pressure, and perspiration. Sexual arousal works in a similar way. When you are aroused by a sexual stimulus, your endocrine system is activated, hormones are secreted, and changes occur in your body. Although androgens (from the Greek *andros*, for male) are commonly referred to as male sex hormones and estrogen (from the Greek *oistros*, for gadfly or frenzy) as the female sex hormone, neither hormone is gender exclusive. The difference is how much hormone circulates in the bloodstream.

Testosterone

Testosterone, the most important androgen, is secreted in small amounts by the adrenal glands in both males and females and in much larger amounts by the testes (Figure 3.2 on page 82). On average, men have at least 10 times more testosterone than women do (Worthman, 1999). Women produce testosterone in their ovaries and adrenal glands. The brain can convert testosterone into estradiol (a form of estrogen) so that the so-called male hormone becomes the so-called female hormone. In women, testosterone increases the flow of estrogen to the center of the brain that controls sexual motivation and drive. Each of us inherits a certain baseline level of testosterone, but testosterone levels are not constant; they fluctuate on a daily cycle and in response to daily events. Research has shown that testosterone levels change in response to physical, emotional, and intellectual challenges (Booth et al., 1992; Booth et al., 1995). On average, testosterone levels of U.S. males tend to go into a steady decline after age 20; the hormone's concentration in the blood decreases by about 30 percent by the time a male reaches 80.

In the developing human fetus, testosterone provides the early signal for the development of a male body, and it is responsible for the primary differences in male and female appearance. Even in adults, an imbalance in testosterone levels can alter body shape. It is clear that testosterone interacts with the nerve cells that make up the brain. We are not certain, however, what role the hormone plays in the development of personality and behavior (Blum, 1997).

A decrease in testosterone often is associated with a decline in male sexuality. In an attempt to restore their virility, in the 1920s physicians actually grafted monkey testes onto aging men (Blum, 1997). However, this pattern of hormone decline with aging is not universal. A cross-cultural study (Worthman, Beall, & Stallings, 1997) indicated that male subjects in Bolivia had a modest decrease in testosterone levels after

TABLE 3.1

Hormones of the Reproductive System

Hormone	Source	Regulation of secretion	Primary effects
Gonadotropin-releasing hormone (GnRH)	Hypothalamus	Males: inhibited by testosterone and possibly by inhibin. Females: GnRH pulse frequency increased by estrogens, decreased by progestins	Stimulates FSH secretion, LH synthesis
Follicle-stimulating hormone (FSH)	Anterior pituitary	Males: stimulated by GnRH, inhibited by inhibin. Females: stimulated by GnRH, inhibited by inhibin	Males: stimulates spermatogenesis through effects on sustentacular cells Females: stimulates follicle development, estrogen production, and oocyte maturation
Luteinizing hormone (LH)	Anterior pituitary	Males: stimulated by GnRH. Females: production stimulated by GnRH, secretion by the combination of high GnRH pulse frequencies and high estrogen levels	Males: stimulates interstitial cells to secrete testosterone Females: stimulates ovulation, formation of corpus luteum, and progestin secretion
Androgens (primarily testosterone and dihydrotestosterone)	Interstitial cells of testes	Stimulated by LH	Establish and maintain secondary sex characteristics and sexual behavior; promote maturation of spermatozoa; inhibit GnRH secretion
Estrogens (primarily estradiol)	Granulosa and thecal cells of developing follicles; corpus luteum	Stimulated by FSH	Stimulate LH secretion (at high levels); establish and maintain secondary sex characteristics and sexual behavior; stimulate repair and growth of endometrium; increase frequency of GnRH pulses
Progestins (primarily progesterone)	Granulosa cells from midcycle through functional life of corpus luteum	Stimulated by LH	Stimulate endometrial growth and glandular secretion; reduce frequency of GnRH pulses
Inhibin	Sustentacular cells of testes and granulosa cells of ovaries	Males: stimulated by factors released by developing spermatozoa. Females: stimulated by developing follicles	Inhibits secretion of FSH and possibly of GnRH

SOURCE: Martini, 2000, p. 1057.

age 30, with hormone levels remaining relatively stable after that time. On the other hand, testosterone levels in Tibetan males do not peak until the late 50s and then fall precipitously during the 60s and 70s. Neither the cause nor the possible significance of these variations is known.

There is as much controversy about the connection between blood levels of testosterone and measures of sexual desire, or **libido,** as there is about the connection

Libido: sexual desire

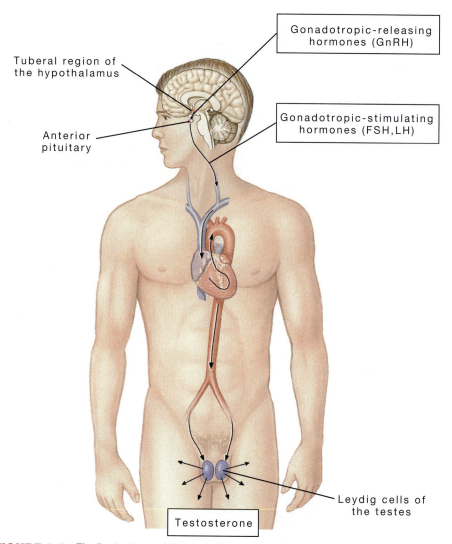

Tuberal region of
the hypothalamus

Anterior
pituitary

Gonadotropic-releasing
hormones (GnRH)

Gonadotropic-stimulating
hormones (FSH, LH)

Leydig cells of
the testes

Testosterone

FIGURE 3.2 **The Production and Release of Testosterone in Males.** Stimulation of the tuberal region of the hypothalamus causes the release of gonadotropic-releasing factor, which causes the anterior pituitary to secrete luteinizing hormone (LH). LH then travels through the bloodstream to stimulate the Leydig cells of the testes to manufacture and release testosterone.

between testosterone and aggression (see CONSIDERATIONS box). Researchers at the Yerkes Primate Research Center at Emory University found that when male monkeys win a contest their T-levels increase for about 24 hours; the T-levels of the losers remain lower for even longer than a day. However, if the loser simply sees a sexually receptive female, his testosterone level shoots back up. "So now you know [what accounts for] the popularity of strip bars: they're where male losers go to get their T back up," claimed one of the Yerkes researchers (Wallen, 1997 quoted in Tierney, 1998, p. B1).

One of the best overviews of research on testosterone, *Heroes, Rogues, and Lovers* (Dabbs, 2000), portrays testosterone as a mixed blessing, with both good and bad features. According to Dabbs, high levels of testosterone (in both men and women) lead to more sexual activity, which of course helps make more babies. But it also leads people to become more fickle and restless, so they are less likely to stay around to nurture and support the children. Remarkably, nature seems to have instilled some mechanisms to make parents stick around. Dabbs reports that testosterone levels are high in single men, drop when the men get married, and drop even more when their wives

"Roid" Rage

When most people hear the word *steroid* they think of **anabolic steroids,** the drugs that bodybuilders and other athletes take in an effort to inflate their strength and bulk. These drugs usually are a synthetic version of testosterone. When scientists first created synthetic testosterone it was thought to be a "wonder drug" that would keep men young and strong well into old age. We now know better.

People, usually athletes, take anabolic steroids to improve their physical appearance and their performance. Steroids can also cause heart attacks, strokes, liver injury, damage to the reproductive system, and personality changes (Todd, 1987). It has been reported that steroid use in adolescents causes premature closing of the epiphyseal growth plates in the skeletal system, leading to shorter stature (Yesalis, Wright, & Bahrke, 1989).

Steroids also have a reputation for making men violent and aggressive. Violent criminals tend to have higher-than-average levels of testosterone. Separate studies in men's and women's prisons have found that murderers have higher levels of testosterone than other convicts, and, more generally, violent criminals have higher testosterone levels than nonviolent convicts. Although several studies have linked high testosterone levels (T-levels) to aggressive behavior in both animals and humans, others question the link between testosterone and aggression. Only three studies have reported a link between aggression or adverse overt behavior and anabolic steroid use (Bahrke, Yesalis, & Wright, 1997). Studies administering moderate doses of testosterone for clinical purposes reveal essentially no adverse effects on male sexual and aggressive behavior (Ibid., 1997).

Anabolic steroids, taken by some men to improve their physical appearance and performance, can cause heart attacks, strokes, liver injury, damage to the reproductive system, and personality changes.

Other studies look to psychosocial factors that may bring about the aggression attributed to steroids (Sharp & Collins, 1998). For example, the effects of previous psychiatric history, environmental and peer influence, and individual expectations remain unclear. One researcher hypothesizes that behavior we sometimes attribute to steroid abuse is actually the "nasty personality of some athletes reinforced by a sports culture that glorifies the physical response" (Yesalis, 1997).

? ***Do you know anyone who uses anabolic steroids?***

—Have you ever used or considered using steroids?

---

have babies. In one study, expectant fathers who held a baby doll wrapped in a blanket experienced a statistically significant drop in testosterone within just half an hour (Storey et al., 2000). Men who remain single throughout life have high testosterone levels (but not as high as those who marry and then divorce). In general, men with high levels of testosterone are more likely to seek out sex and aggression, but are less reliable providers for their wives and children. In numerous species (including our own), males with low testosterone levels live longer (Worthman, 1999). Testosterone level also affects the workplace—or is it the other way around? (See CONSIDERATIONS box).

There may also be a link between T-levels and libido in women (Crenshaw, 1996; Hutchinson, 1995; Rako, 1996). At the onset of menopause, a woman's ovaries and adrenal glands begin to produce less testosterone and other androgens. As a result, the amount of testosterone circulating in the body is reduced by at least half. While some women may react to this change by experiencing a noticeable drop in sexual desire, others may not notice any difference. One study showed a decrease in sexual desire among premenopausal women whose ovaries were surgically removed

Anabolic Steroids: synthetic derivative of testosterone

High "T"

In a survey of various occupations, Dabbs found that testosterone levels varied widely. Comparing T-levels of nonlawyers, attorneys, and trial lawyers, Dabbs (1998) found that although the testosterone levels of attorneys matched those of doctors and similar professionals, they lagged behind those of construction workers and others in blue-collar jobs. However, trial lawyers had testosterone levels that were about 30 percent higher than other lawyers. And it wasn't just the men. Female trial attorneys had higher testosterone levels than those who didn't go to court. Farmers and white-collar workers such as office workers had low levels of testosterone, and ministers had the lowest of all occupations tested. Blue-collar workers had high levels of testosterone, and actors—especially ones favoring outrageous roles—had the highest, outranking even professional football players on the testosterone scale.

One study (Urdy, Morris, & Kovonock, 1995) found that women who choose a professional career tended to have higher T-levels than women who stayed home to raise their children. The high-T women were less likely to have children and less interested in becoming parents. When they did have children, their daughters also tended to have high testosterone levels. It is unknown if these results reflect a genetic predisposition for high testosterone, or if the high-testosterone mothers treated their daughters differently than mothers with lower T-levels.

Dabbs (2000) found that testosterone levels were high among the chronically unemployed, probably because their inclination to adventure made them poor prospects for steady work. On the other hand, losing a job may cause a decrease in testosterone, because many men experience that as a blow to their masculinity. People with low testosterone tend to get better grades in school, and enter into higher-status occupations (although within many competitive areas, high-testosterone people seem more likely to fight their way to the top). Low-testosterone men have happier

Both the male and female trial attorneys on *Ally McBeal* might be expected to have high testosterone levels.

marriages, feel closer to their friends and families, and smile more genuinely than high-testosterone men. Dabbs quoted various observers about the smiles of men with high testosterone. One described that smile as "wolfish," having a kind of dangerous or predatory aspect. Another, the political observer Myra MacPherson, said the high-testosterone smile is "a politician's smile—the kind that never reaches the eyes" (Dabbs, 2000, p. 156).

? ***What other professions do you think might have high testosterone levels?***

—*What professions do you think might have low testosterone levels?*
—*Do you think that that a male with a low-T-level job is less masculine or a woman in a high-T-level job is less feminine?*

during a hysterectomy. When these women received estrogen and testosterone therapy, there was a significant increase in libido (Sherwin, 1996). However, there is more to libido than hormones. As we will discuss in Chapter 4, a lack of sexual desire may have a number of causes.

Estrogens

Estrogens are present in both men and women, but they circulate at the highest levels in women. The male testes and the female ovaries produce the estrogens. Men make estradiol while women make other estrogens as well. Early in female adolescence, the brain begins secreting regular bursts of hormones that stimulate the

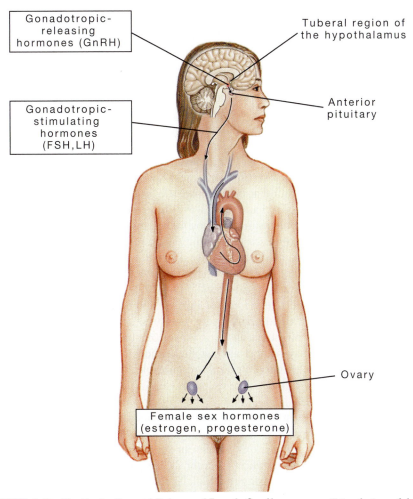

Gonadotropic-
releasing
hormones (GnRH)

Tuberal region of
the hypothalamus

Gonadotropic-
stimulating
hormones
(FSH,LH)

Anterior
pituitary

Ovary

Female sex hormones
(estrogen, progesterone)

FIGURE 3.3   The Production and Release of Female Sex Hormones.   Stimulation of the tuberal region of the hypothalamus causes the release of gonadotropic-releasing factor, which causes the anterior pituitary to secrete gonadotropic-stimulating hormones. The gonadotropic-stimulating hormones then travel through the bloodstream to the ovaries, stimulating the production and release of the female sex hormones.

ovaries (Figure 3.3). The ovaries in turn discharge estrogen, which encourages the development of the adult female body and regulates the menstrual cycle. At one time it was believed that the ovaries were a source of female weakness; one historical treatment for moodiness was removal of a woman's ovaries (Blum, 1997). Today it is known that, rather than a source of problems, the estrogens have beneficial effects in both men and women. As a matter of fact, the estrogens, especially estradiol, appear more directly necessary to survival than the androgens.

To make estrogen, the body needs an enzyme called **aromatase.** With aromatase, a tissue of the body can transform a precursor hormone into estrogen. The precursor may be testosterone (which women make in their ovaries, adrenal glands, and possibly in the uterus and the brain) or another androgen. The ovaries produce aromatase as well as testosterone, so the androgen can instantly be converted into estrogen. Other tissues that contain aromatase include fat, bones, muscle, blood vessels, and the brain. Give any of these tissues a bit of precursor hormone, and they'll convert it to estrogen.

There are at least 60 forms of estrogen in the body, the most important of which are *estradiol, estriol,* and *estrone.* Generally, different tissues of the body produce

Aromatase: an enzyme that converts androgen to estrogen

"The difficulties of correlating estrogen to human sexual behavior are considerable. What sort of behavior are you looking at? What are the relevant data points? Frequency of intercourse? Frequency of orgasm? Frequency of masturbation or sexual fantasy? The sudden urge to buy Cosmopolitan?"

(ANGIER, 1999, P. 217)

the different estrogens, though there is a lot of overlap, redundancy, and unknowns. **Estradiol,** the principal estrogen of women's reproductive years, is the product of the ovaries. It flows out of the cells of the follicles and from the corpus luteum. In men, the testes produce estradiol. Estradiol is considered the most potent of the three estrogens. Estradiol production in girls begins to rise slowly at about age 8 and continues its ascent until the onset of puberty, at which point it levels off. It remains dominant until menopause, except during pregnancy when estradiol production shuts down. **Estriol** is generated by the placenta, and, to a lesser extent, by the liver. It is the major "pregnancy estrogen," the source of many of the symptoms of gestation such as morning sickness. Estriol levels remain high until after childbirth, when estradiol kicks back in. **Estrone** is the primary estrogen of menopause. As the ovaries stop producing estradiol at menopause, the fat cells start making estrone. As we discussed in the previous chapter, it is the decreased level of estrogen that is thought to cause health problems in some postmenopausal women.

Estradiol appears to stimulate the immune system and direct the immune response to where it is needed (Morrell, 1995). Estradiol is also essential to a healthy heart. It seems to make blood platelets slightly less active, which makes them less prone to clumping and clotting the arteries (USDA, 1995). Researchers at Johns Hopkins University have found that a form of estrogen compound increased the blood flow to the heart in men with coronary artery disease by nearly one third (Blumenthal et al., 1997). Researchers investigating estradiol's effects on brain function have found evidence that estradiol may protect against Alzheimer's disease. The discovery of a specific structure on the estrogen molecule responsible for estrogen's ability to protect nerve cells from death may prove useful in treating and preventing Alzheimer's disease (Gordon et al., 1997).

While estrogen performs many valuable functions, there can be too much of a good thing. Excess estrogen in men can result in erectile difficulties and enlargement of the breasts. Hormonal fluctuations, which can aggravate endometriosis and uterine fibroid tumors (disorders discussed in Chapter 2), can increase with excess estrogen. In addition, evidence is accumulating that high levels of estrogen may increase the risk of breast cancer.

The Link Between Estrogen and Female Sex Drive A female mouse can't mate if she is not in estrus. Unless she is in estrus, her ovaries do not secrete estrogen and progesterone, and without hormonal stimulation, the mouse can't assume the mating position (lordosis) in which she arches her back and flicks aside her tail, which makes her vagina accessible to the male mouse's penis. But, as you learned in Chapter 2, human females, and other female primates, have been freed from hormonal control and can have sex throughout the menstrual cycle. Researchers have long wondered whether the hormonal process that regulates the menstrual cycle affects female sexual behavior as the estrus cycle affects the behavior of other mammals.

Stanislaw and Rice (1988) found that in any given menstrual cycle, sexual desire was usually first experienced a few days before the basal body temperature (BBT) shift, around the date of expected ovulation. These events are correlated with changing hormone levels. While these results suggested that hormonal factors do in fact contribute to sexual desire, other studies have found no association between rates of intercourse and where a woman is in her ovulatory cycle (Wilcox et al., 1995).

The endocrine system plays an important role in human sexual behavior, but the effects of hormones and their relationship to the various sexual behaviors is not yet fully understood. We do know that hormones are necessary to maintain a satisfying human libido, but we also know that hormones alone are not enough. In women, estrogens prime the central nervous system and sensory organs for sex (Graziottin, 1998), but there are other as yet unknown factors that contribute to the female libido as well.

Estradiol: principal estrogen produced by the ovary during a woman's reproductive years

Estriol: an estrogen hormone found in the urine during pregnancy

Estrone: a weaker estrogen found in urine and placental tissues during pregnancy

Progesterone

Estrogens tend to work in concert with another set of hormones, the **progestins.** These hormones essentially wait to perform their function until pregnancy, when they are responsible for all kinds of managerial functions. The best-known progestin is **progesterone,** the so-called hormone of pregnancy that prepares the endometrium for implantation of the fertilized ovum; and later is used by the placenta to prevent rejection of the developing embryo and fetus. Progesterone promotes weight gain and nutrition storage and helps stimulate the breasts for milk production. By inducing the growth of muscle cells around capillaries in the uterus they protect women from the dangers of hemorrhage when pregnancy does not occur and the fertilized egg is washed away in the menstrual cycle. It is the progestins that are responsible for the complaints of swollen ankles and puffiness; inducing fluid retention increases the volume of blood circulating in the body to ensure that mother and baby both get enough blood and oxygen.

Oxytocin and Vasopressin

When you think of sexual behavior, romantic love and parental love, the first words you think of are probably *not* **oxytocin** and **vasopressin.** But scientists believe that these sex hormones have a great deal of influence on our sexual and romantic experiences. Both males and females possess these "love hormones," but oxytocin plays a stronger role in females and vasopressin has more influence in males. It is unknown why the sexes might need two different hormones to achieve the same purpose. Oxytocin and vasopressin are both produced in the hypothalamus and are **peptide hormones,** as opposed to **steroid hormones** like estrogen or testosterone. Steroid hormones slip back and forth from the brain to the bloodstream and back to the brain, but peptide hormones move only from brain to blood. We do not understand the roles of oxytocin and vasopressin completely, partly because each of them serves a number of different functions.

Oxytocin has been found to cause uterine contractions during orgasm and labor, increase sexual receptivity, speed ejaculation, and increase penile sensitivity (Newton, 1978; Pedersen, 1992). Oxytocin is released by the pituitary gland, and is present in a range of nerve cells throughout the brain. The concentration of oxytocin is highest in the limbic system but it is also found in the brain stem and spinal cord. Through its association with the sense of smell, oxytocin also orchestrates the body's response to pheromones.

In mammals, oxytocin in combination with estrogen increases sensitivity to touch and encourages mating, grooming, and cuddling in both sexes. Infusing oxytocin into the brains of nonpregnant female rats rapidly induced maternal behavior toward young pups (Pedersen et al., 1992). Similar findings have been reported in ewes, which usually are hostile to offspring other than their own (Kendrick et al., 1987). Furthermore, it appears that oxytocin not only fosters the bond between mothers and children, but it may also increase sexual activity. When oxytocin was infused into the brains of female rats, which are not very sexually receptive when not in estrus, their sexual activity increased considerably (Caldwell et al., 1984). It has been suggested that oxytocin can stimulate sexual behavior in humans (Anderson-Hunt & Dennerstein, 1994). In one study, women were asked to masturbate to climax, and their blood levels of oxytocin were measured before and after orgasm. The concentration of oxytocin climbed slightly, but measurably, with climax, and the greater the increase, the more pleasurable the women reported their orgasm to be (Pedersen et al., 1992).

Vasopressin is secreted from the brain's posterior pituitary and causes the contraction of vascular and other smooth muscles. While vasopressin resembles oxytocin in its chemical structure, in most respects it opposes the influence of oxytocin. Vasopressin acts as an antidiuretic, which prevents water and salt depletion, stimulates

Progestin: generic term for any substance, natural or synthetic, that effects some or all of the biological changes produced by progesterone

Progesterone: an antiestrogenic steroid produced by the corpus luteum and placenta or prepared synthetically that stimulates proliferation of the endometrium and is involved in the regulation of the menstrual cycle

Oxytocin: pituitary hormone that stimulates uterine contractions during labor and facilitates the secretion of milk during nursing

Vasopressin: a pituitary hormone that causes blood vessels and smooth muscles to contract

Peptide Hormones: group of hormones such as oxytocin and vasopressin that are produced in the hypothalamus

Steroid Hormones: group of hormones that include estrogen and testosterone

Excitement Phase: first stage of Masters and Johnson's sexual response cycle; characterized by erection in the male and vaginal lubrication in the female

Myotonia: muscle tension

Vasocongestin: engorgement of blood vessels in response to sexual arousal

blood vessel constriction, and helps control blood pressure. In men, vasopressin levels increase when arousal occurs. Some researchers believe that vasopressin enhances mental alertness and moderates emotional response, allowing us to notice and respond to subtle sexual cues such as a glance or a gesture (Beckwith et al., 1990; deWied et al., 1989).

THE SEXUAL RESPONSE CYCLE

The cycle of human sexual response, the series of physiological processes and events that occur during sexual activity, is as complex and varied as the people who participate. However, it is useful to have models that describe common physiological changes and patterns in order to determine whether our experiences fall within the expected range (not to worry—almost everyone's do). Through their research, Masters and Johnson (1966), Helen Singer Kaplan (1979), and David Reed (1998) have come up with three ways of describing the events that occur during a sexual encounter.

Masters and Johnson's EPOR Model

Masters and Johnson recorded more than 10,000 cycles of sexual arousal and orgasm over a period of 12 years to arrive at a model of sexual arousal and response. There are four successive physiological phases to the sexual response cycle in their model: excitement, plateau, orgasm, and resolution (EPOR) (Figure 3.4).

The **excitement phase** is the first phase of the EPOR model. Both males and females may experience erection of the nipples, and increases in **myotonia** (muscle tension, spasm, or rigidity), heart rate, and blood pressure. In males, the excitement phase also produces penile erection because of the increased flow of blood to the erectile tissues. The time between the onset of stimulation and erection may be much shorter in young males than in older men. Also during this phase, the skin of the scrotum thickens, the testes increase in size, and the testes and scrotum are pulled up next to the man's body. In females, vaginal lubrication may begin within 10 to 30 seconds after the onset of sexual stimulation. **Vasocongestion,** the engorgement of blood vessels in response to sexual arousal, swells the clitoris and the labia majora, causing the labia to spread apart. The labia minora also increase in size, and the walls of the inner two thirds of the vagina expand. As the vaginal walls thicken, the increase in blood flow causes the normally pink tissue to darken. The uterus also becomes engorged with blood and is elevated further up into the body cavity. The breasts enlarge and blood vessels near the skin's surface may become more pronounced.

FIGURE 3.4 Masters and Johnson's four phases of the human sexual response. (a) Male sexual response; (b) two patterns seen in females; in pattern 1, the female experiences one or more orgasms, and in pattern 2, she does not experience an orgasm.

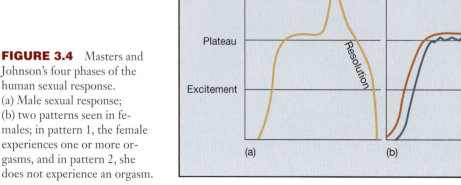

The **plateau phase** is an advanced state of arousal that precedes orgasm. By this phase a reddish rash called the **sex flush** may appear on the chest or breasts in about one fourth of males and three fourths of females. Myotonia may cause spasms in the hands and feet, as well as facial grimaces. Breathing becomes rapid, and the heart rate and blood pressure continue to rise. Males show a slight increase in the circumference of the coronal ridge of the penis and the glans turns purplish as a result of vasocongestion. The testes are pulled further in toward the man's body and may swell to 1½ times their previous size. At this time a few drops of fluid from the Cowper's glands may appear at the tip of the penis. Vasocongestion swells the outer third of the female's vagina, producing the **orgasmic platform.** The inner part of the vagina expands fully and the uterus becomes fully elevated. The clitoris shortens and withdraws beneath the clitoral hood. The labia minora become redder; this is sometimes referred to as the **sex skin.** The areolas become so engorged with blood they may swell around the nipples. A mucuslike fluid is secreted from the Bartholin's glands on either side of the vaginal opening.

If an individual does not reach orgasm, myotonia and vasocongestion may take an hour or more to disappear. Continuing vasocongestion may cause a feeling of pelvic discomfort or fullness known as "blue balls" in males, a harmless condition that can be relieved by masturbation or by the passage of time (but time may appear to move very slowly to someone who is experiencing this condition). A woman who becomes highly stimulated but does not get sexual release may experience similar sensations, which can also be relieved by masturbation or the passage of time (Barbach, 1975).

In the **orgasmic phase,** rhythmic muscle contractions begin throughout the body in both males and females, while blood pressure, respiration, and heart rate continue to increase. The man experiences two stages of muscle contractions, sometimes referred to as the emission expulsion stage. In the first, the vas deferens, the seminal vesicles, the ejaculatory duct, and the prostate gland cause seminal fluid to collect in the urethral bulb, which expands to accommodate the fluid. The internal sphincter muscle of the bladder contracts to prevent seminal fluid from entering the bladder and urine from being ejaculated with the semen; if this muscle malfunctions, seminal fluid may enter the bladder rather than be ejaculated, an uncommon but harmless event called a *retrograde ejaculation.* At this time the man may experience a subjective feeling of impending ejaculation. In the second stage of the male orgasmic phase the external sphincter muscle of the bladder relaxes to allow the passage of semen. The muscles surrounding the urethra, the urethral bulb, and the base of the penis then contract rhythmically to propel the ejaculate out of the body and produce the pleasurable sensations associated with orgasm.

Female orgasm is marked by contractions of the pelvic muscles surrounding the vagina and release of vasocongestion that alleviates the muscle tension built up during the previous phases and produces a subjective feeling of release. Females also experience rhythmic contractions of the uterus and the anal sphincter during this phase. However, it should be noted that not all females enjoy orgasm with every experience of coitus.

The **resolution phase** follows orgasm. During this phase the body returns to its prearousal state. In both males and females myotonia decreases within a few minutes after orgasm, and blood pressure, heart rate, and respiration return to normal levels. Many individuals find their bodies covered in sweat and experience a general feeling of relaxation and satisfaction.

After ejaculation a male loses his erection in two stages. Within a minute, half the size of the erection is lost as blood from the corpora cavernosa, the tissues that engorge with blood, recedes. Then the remaining swelling subsides as the blood in the corpus spongiosum, a chamber on the underside of the penis, decreases. At this point the testes and scrotum return to their relaxed forms and positions. In females, swelling of the areolas and nipples decrease, and the sex flush rapidly disappears. The clitoris, vagina, uterus, and labia return to their relaxed states, and the "sex skin" returns to its prearousal coloration.

Plateau Phase: the second phase of Masters and Johnson's sexual response cycle in which muscle tension, heart rate, and vasocongestion increase

Sex Flush: rash that appears on the chest or breasts of some individuals during the sexual response cycle

Orgasmic Platform: the thickening of the walls of the outer third of the vagina that occurs during the plateau phase due to vasocongestion

Sex Skin: reddening of the labia minora that occurs during the plateau phase

Orgasmic Phase: the third phase of Masters and Johnson's sexual response cycle in which orgasm occurs

Resolution Phase: the fourth phase of Masters and Johnson's sexual response cycle during which the body gradually returns to its prearoused state

Refractory Period: period of time following orgasm during which a male is no longer responsive to stimulation

After resolution males enter what Masters and Johnson call a **refractory period** during which they are physiologically incapable of another orgasm or ejaculation. This period may last from a few minutes in adolescent males to a much longer period for older men. Females do not experience a refractory period. They may be restimulated quickly to the orgasmic phase.

Kaplan's Model of Sexual Response

In contrast to the four phases in the Masters and Johnson model, over many years of research sex therapist Helen Singer Kaplan (1974, 1979, 1987) developed a model of sexual response consisting of three independent components: desire, excitement and orgasm (Figure 3.5).

Desire is the most important element of Kaplan's model; it demonstrates the role of psychological and cognitive needs in the human sexual response cycle. Excitement and orgasm are described as primarily physiological components. The *excitement* phase consists of initial vasocongestion of the genitals, resulting in erection in the male and vaginal lubrication in the female. The *orgasm* phase is marked by pelvic muscle contractions in males and females, and ejaculation in males. In Kaplan's model, these three components are independent and not entirely sequential. For example, an individual might experience sexual excitement and perhaps orgasm without much desire. Other individuals may find that excitement stimulates sexual desire.

This model is useful for therapists precisely because it distinguishes desire as an independent component of the sexual response cycle, and, as you will discover in Chapter 4, lack of sexual desire is the most common problem clients bring to sex therapists. As we will discuss more fully in Chapter 4, an individual who lacks desire may not seek sexual stimulation or be able to respond when it is present.

Reed's ESP Model

David Reed's *Erotic Stimulus Pathway (ESP)* theory (1998) divides the sexual response cycle into four phases that contain elements of both Kaplan's and Masters and Johnson's models (Figure 3.6) as well as elements of the five basic needs discussed in Chapter 1. The first phase of Reed's model is *seduction*, the phase when an individual learns how to attract someone sexually. A seduction translates into memories and rituals. As a teenager you might have gone through a series of grooming rituals before going on a date. These rituals may have helped you feel you look good, which can translate into feeling good about yourself. The better you feel about yourself, the better you are at attracting others. These positive feelings are translated into sexual desire and arousal; the seductive techniques are stored in memory and can be activated at a later time.

In the *sensation phase*, the senses enhance sexual excitement extending it into a plateau phase, which makes us want to continue the pleasurable moment over a longer period of time. According to Reed, these seduction and sensation experiences are the psychological input to the physiology of sexual response.

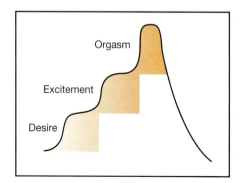

FIGURE 3.5 Kaplan's three-stage model of the sexual response cycle. This model is distinguished by its identification of desire as a prelude to sexual response.

In the *surrender phase*, orgasm occurs. Reed's theory purports that people with orgasmic dysfunction (which will be discussed in Chapter 4) may be in a power struggle with themselves or with their partners or with the messages received from society about sex. Overcontrol or undercontrol can affect orgasmic potential and the ability to allow all of our passion to be expressed.

The final phase of Reed's model is the *reflection phase* where meaning is brought

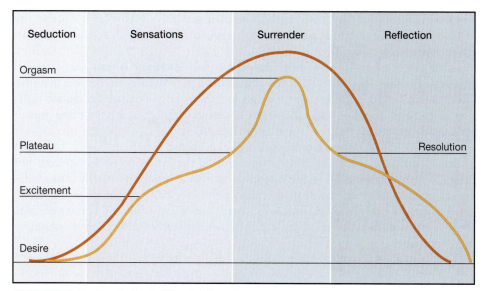

FIGURE 3.6 Reed's Erotic Stimulus Pathway.

to a sexual experience. Whether the experience is interpreted as positive or negative may determine the desire for subsequent sexual activity or under the same specific circumstances.

ORGASM

Why does the psychobiological experience of orgasm warrant so much attention? Our view is that orgasm is a complex response to a wide variety of social, physical, and mental stimuli. The differences in the behavioral expression of orgasm and the reported changes in consciousness and involuntary movements associated with orgasm in some individuals once led people to worry about its potential for harm both morally and biologically. During the 19th century, some medical professionals were so worried about the "dangers" of orgasm that they debated who should have orgasms and how often (Laumann et al., 1994).

The roots of the word *orgasm* include the Greek word *orgasmos*, meaning to grow ripe, swell, and be lustful, and the Sanskrit *urja*, meaning nourishment and power. From an evolutionary perspective, the importance of sex is reproduction, and while male orgasm is inextricably linked to reproduction, females don't have to have an orgasm to procreate. If you're trying to have a baby, male orgasm may be important to you, but for most of us, the importance of orgasm is pleasure, not procreation.

Studies comparing the orgasms of males and females indicate that they are more similar than you would think; there is more variation among individuals than between males and females (Proctor, Wagner, & Butler, 1974; Vance & Wagner, 1976; Wiest, 1987). Both women and men experience pleasurable sensations—orgasms "feel good." Both men and women describe the approach to a level of excitement beyond which it becomes progressively difficult to maintain voluntary control—the "point of no return." Other sensory perceptions may fade in the heat of the moment; people may experience some numbness in their senses and may not be very sensitive to painful stimuli (Katchadourian & Lunde, 1975).

Young men in adolescence and their early 20s report more frequent orgasms than older men do, while women generally experience their highest number of orgasms from their mid-20s to their mid-40s. However, these statistics do not reflect how often a man or woman would like to have sex or how much they are enjoying it. One reason for this possible orgasmic difference between men and women is that as

CAMPUS CONFIDENTIAL

"All orgasms are not created equal. Some are like a whisper . . . gentle and soft, others are more like a raging scream . . . intense and dramatic. I don't really care if my orgasm is clitoral or vaginal, as long as it feels good." ●

women become older they learn more about their sexuality and may feel more secure in their relationships, but as men age the lengths of their arousal, response, and refractory periods increase (Reinisch, 1991).

Biologist Stephen Jay Gould has argued that female orgasm is simply a byproduct of human development. Recall that the clitoris develops from the same tissue that produces the penis. Gould argues that the female orgasm exists because the clitoris is the homologue of the penis—"the same organ, endowed with the same anatomical organization and capacity of response" (Gould, 1987, p. 16).

Anthropologist Melvin Konner (1990) believes that female orgasm is the result of gender differences in selective pressures during the evolution of our species. For males in many mammalian species, reproduction is as simple as inseminating a female. For most females, mammalian reproduction inevitably entails gestation, labor, and nursing. Thus, in an evolutionary sense, males are rewarded for copulation, while females do best by choosing carefully among suitors and trying to sustain a bond with one.

Anthropologist Helen Fisher believes that human female orgasm does have a reproductive purpose. "I think female orgasm evolved for genuine purposes: to encourage females to seek sex, to make an intimate connection with a reproductive mate or extra lover, to signal enjoyment to this partner, and to aid fertilization" (Fisher, 1992, p. 183). There is some common-sense appeal to the notion that females who enjoy sex will be more likely to do it, and hence more likely to reproduce, than other females.

Sarah Hrdy (1996) proposes that while the female orgasm is not currently adaptive, it might have provided motivation for our female primate ancestors to mate with a range of partners. Such behavior would confuse the issue of paternity and increase the likelihood that a female could extract food and protection for her offspring from a number of different males. Hrdy raises the depressing possibility that, because the female orgasm is no longer functional, it is on its way out in an evolutionary sense; if she's right, our descendants may never share this glorious experience!

Randy Thornhill and Steven W. Gangestad (1996) speculate that female orgasm is an *atavism*, a trait that occurs in an individual because it occurred in an ancient ancestor. However, these University of New Mexico scientists also have proposed a theory with a rather unscientific name, the "upsuck theory," that the muscle contractions of female orgasm help suck the sperm into the fallopian tubes. Popular wisdom has sometimes upheld the belief that a woman cannot get pregnant unless she has an orgasm—wrong! But it is plausible than an orgasm might facilitate the process of getting pregnant in some way.

Men rarely wonder whether or not they have had an orgasm because of the obvious physical signs of ejaculation. Although the terms are often used interchangeably, *ejaculation* and *male orgasm* are not synonyms, but related physical events. A man cannot ejaculate without experiencing an orgasm, but it is possible for him to have an orgasm without ejaculating, for example in men with disease of the prostate, those practicing Tantric sex, or in prepubescent boys.

The physical signs of orgasm are not as obvious in women, and vary to a much greater extent, so a woman (and/or her partner) may not even know whether she has experienced an orgasm (see CONSIDERATIONS box).

Variation in Female Orgasm

Female orgasm has assumed a more convoluted role in the scientific understanding of sexuality. In the early 1900s, Sigmund Freud (1905) theorized that there were two distinct types of orgasm, vaginal orgasm and clitoral orgasm. Moreover, he took what appeared to be the anatomical locus of an orgasm to be a measure of developmental maturity. According to Freud, orgasms caused by clitoral stimulation were immature; by the time a woman entered puberty and was physically ready to have intercourse with a man, her center of orgasm should be transferred to the vagina (see CAMPUS CONFIDENTIAL feature for one woman's perspective). This theory influenced

Faking It

The psychological goal of orgasm that is so pervasive in many cultures may pressure some people, almost always women, to pretend they are having an orgasm. One study (Elliott & Brantley, 1997) of college students found that 60 percent of heterosexual college women and 71 percent of lesbian or bisexual women had faked having an orgasm, while only 17 percent of heterosexual college men and 27 percent of gay or bisexual men had faked it.

The most common reason given by women for faking an orgasm was to avoid disappointing or hurting their partners (Darling & Davidson, 1986). Other factors related to faking orgasm may include poor communication, limited knowledge of sexual techniques, a need for partner approval, an attempt to conceal a deteriorating relationship, protection of a partner's ego, or having given up hope of changing the partner's behavior (Lauersen & Graes, 1984).

If you usually climax when you're with your partner, but every now and then for some reason it's just not happening and what you really want to do is go to sleep, occasionally faking an orgasm might not be a big deal. But feigning orgasm most or all of the time can be far more problematic. It is hard to tell your partner that you have been faking enjoyment, but your partner deserves to know what is really going on.

As anyone who has seen the 1989 movie *When Harry Met Sally* knows, some women can do a very effective job of faking orgasm.

 Can you think of a good reason why someone might want to continue faking orgasms?

—*Can you always tell if a partner is faking?*
—*What are other reasons why someone might fake orgasms?*
—*What are some ways that you might approach talking with your partner about this problem?*

---

thought on female sexual response for decades. Women who did not reach orgasm by the movements of the penis in their vagina were considered physically or psychologically inferior or abnormal.

The research of Masters and Johnson (1966) was crucial in dispelling Freud's theory by showing that there is no measurable physiological difference between female orgasms resulting from clitoral stimulation and those from vaginal stimulation. It is now widely thought that all female orgasms are the result of direct or indirect clitoral stimulation. The clitoris can be directly stimulated by hand, mouth, or vibrator, or indirectly during certain positions of intercourse. However the clitoris is stimulated, the center of the orgasmic response is around the vagina or around the uterus. In other words, all female orgasms "are triggered by stimulation of the clitoris and expressed by vaginal contractions" (Kaplan, 1974, p. 31). As you learned in Chapter 2, the clitoris is not necessary for reproduction and is thus the only human organ with the sole purpose of providing pleasure.

Josephine and Irving Singer (1972) postulated that in addition to noting observable physiological changes, emotional satisfaction is an important factor in the female orgasmic response. The Singers describe three types of female orgasm: vulval, uterine, and blended. According to their theory, a vulval orgasm may result from either manual stimulation or coitus. The vulval orgasm is accompanied by contraction of the orgasmic platform and is not followed by a refractory period. A uterine orgasm occurs only as a result of intercourse and is typically characterized by a woman holding her breath and then explosively exhaling at orgasm. This type of orgasm is said to produce a great deal of relaxation and satisfaction and is followed by a refractory period. The blended orgasm is a combination of vulval and uterine orgasms.

> *[Some women] never bought Freud's idea of penis envy; who would want a shotgun when you can have a semiautomatic?*
>
> (ANGIER, 1999, P. 63)

FAQ:

Are men as capable of having multiple orgasms as women?

It is not uncommon for a woman to have several sequential orgasms, separated in time by only a brief interval, while the spacing of male orgasms typically is more protracted. There is evidence that some men are capable of teaching themselves to be multiply orgasmic (Comfort, 1972; Robbins & Jensen, 1978). Researchers found one man who experienced six orgasms in the laboratory, with an interval of 36 minutes between the first and the last orgasm, and who maintained an erection during the entire period (Whipple & Myers, 1998). Other researchers (e.g., Dunn & Trost, 1989) report that some men are able to have multiple orgasms, delaying ejaculation until their final climax.

EXPLORING SEXUALITY ONLINE

Virtual Orgasm

Technology is a wonderful thing. A new form of sexual experience is being developed as an offshoot of virtual reality. Virtual reality is envisioned as a way to enhance the pleasure of viewing an erotic scene or activity. Instead of watching others perform, the person participates, providing a much more satisfying experience. The viewer puts on a helmet or enters a virtual reality room and participates in a realistic sexual experience of his or her choice without fear of disease, rejection, or embarrassment. Visual imagery can be enhanced with electronically simulated sensations such as odors, tastes, touch, and pressure. Virtual sex has the potential not only to enhance normal sensations but also to create sensations never before experienced. Visionaries predict that virtual sex programs will not only be available for solo use, but for experiences in which the participant can select one or more partners from a wide range of choices. Couples would be able to use virtual sex to enhance their sensations and explore alternate styles and preferences (Maxwell, 1997).

For most women, penile thrusting is less efficient in causing female orgasm than direct clitoral stimulation. In a famous study by Sheri Hite (1976), for example, only about 30 percent of the women could reach orgasm regularly from intercourse without more direct manual clitoral stimulation. However, approximately 44 percent of those tested experienced regular orgasm from manual stimulation of the clitoris (as "foreplay"), either by a partner or through self-stimulation, and 42 percent experienced regular orgasm during oral stimulation of the clitoris. By comparison, 99.5 percent of women were able to experience orgasm during masturbation.

Multiple and Simultaneous Orgasms

The much-sought-after phenomenon of **multiple orgasms** occurs when one orgasm quickly (although no one has ever defined just how "quickly") follows another. Women are biologically far more likely to have multiple orgasms than men, because of the refractory period that men experience. Some women are able to have several orgasms only seconds apart; men usually need much more time. Although only a small portion of the female population experiences them, Masters and Johnson (1966) and Fisher (1992) suggest that nearly all women are physically capable of multiple orgasm. Many factors could account for the discrepancy between experience and capability, but the most likely is that, once orgasm is reached, stimulation usually stops.

Some couples think that having **simultaneous orgasms** is the ultimate sexual experience. Others believe that while climaxing together might be nice, if and when it occurs, having simultaneous orgasms is no more satisfying than sequential orgasms. The Janus Report (1993) found that the vast majority of men and women surveyed did not feel that simultaneous orgasm is necessary for gratifying sex. It's difficult for two people to "choreograph" the coordination of their orgasms. To do so, you and your partner must time your response cycles so that you know approximately how long it takes for each of you to reach orgasm during a typical sexual experience. As we have discussed, the sexual response cycle varies widely from experience to experience, and the stress of "timing it just right" may very well defeat the purpose. It is more important that partners enjoy one another. Another disadvantage of simultaneous orgasm is that the partners are so wrapped up in their own responses they cannot enjoy each other's orgasms.

Multiple Orgasms: experiencing one or more additional orgasms within a short time following the first

Simultaneous Orgasm: partners experience orgasm at the same time

Rx: More Orgasms

A statistical study in the *British Medical Journal* found that men who have more orgasms live longer. According to the analysis, having regular sex reduces the risk of death by about half. Men who said they had sex twice a week had a risk of dying half that of those reporting they had sex only once a month. The authors of the study said they had tried to adjust the study's design to account for other factors that might explain their findings, for example, that healthier, fitter men generally engaged in sex more often. Even with this adjustment, the differences in risk could not be explained. Hormonal effects on the body resulting from more frequent sexual activity could be one possible explanation of this phenomenon (Davey-Smith et al., 1997). Until a more complete explanation is found, go ahead and improve your health!

SEXUALITY AND DISABILITIES

In a society where "sexy" is often equated with "healthy," we tend to desexualize the disabled, preferring not to think about their sexual needs and potentials. Those who are physically dependent to any extent are seen as being childlike; because of this, involvement in sexual relationships is considered inappropriate. Many individuals make the assumption that the chronically ill or disabled are unable to have erections, reach orgasm, or enjoy sexual pleasures. These are myths that we hope to dispel in this section.

Arthritis

Rheumatoid arthritis is a chronic multisystem disease characterized by a persistent inflammation of peripheral joints. Inflammation of the joints can interfere with sexual activity. Several small clinical studies have shown that approximately half of arthritic men and women experience sexual problems including fatigue, weakness, pain, and limited movement in joints. Pain and stiffness of the hip joints are the main causes of sexual difficulty for arthritis sufferers, though some report a loss of libido or sex drive. Moreover, some arthritis drugs, especially corticosteroids, have been shown to reduce sex drive (Reinisch, 1991).

Sexual dysfunction in arthritic patients may be difficult to manage for several reasons. The nature of the problem may be difficult to diagnose because it often is complicated by the underlying medical condition. In addition, chronic illness places a great deal of stress on patients and their relationships (Nadler, 1997). Those suffering from arthritis, need to experiment to find one or more positions that avoid or reduce pain and pressure on the affected joints.

Cardiovascular Disease

In the United States 68 million individuals have some form of *cardiovascular disease*, heart-related disorders including coronary artery disease and *arteriosclerosis* or hardening of the arteries. Sexual problems following a heart attack are common. Although researchers have generally agreed that sexual activity initially tends to decline after an acute cardiac event, there usually is an eventual return to the previous level of sexual activity (Stitik & Benevento, 1997). Sexual problems following cardiovascular disease often are due to anxiety or lack of information. While blood pressure does increase during sexual activity, sex is not hazardous to people with high blood pressure if the condition is under control. Most physicians prohibit sexual activity only in severe cases. However, anyone suffering a heart attack should consult a physician before resuming sexual activity.

Arteriosclerosis is among the more common causes of erection problems in older men. This disease can result in a reduction of blood supply to the penis. Erectile problems may be an early symptom of arteriosclerosis. Although common, this problem often responds to treatment.

Cerebral Palsy

A mild to severe loss of muscle control, which may disrupt speech, facial expression, balance, and body movements, characterizes *cerebral palsy,* a chronic condition most often caused by damage to the brain during or before birth. Genital sensation is not disturbed by cerebral palsy; sexual interest, the capacity to have orgasm, and fertility are similarly unimpaired. There may be limitations to some sexual activities; for example, certain positions for intercourse may be difficult or impossible, depending on the nature and degree of muscle spasticity. Partners can adjust positions and find alternative ways of pleasuring one another.

Cerebrovascular Accidents

Although *cerebrovascular accidents (CVA),* more commonly known as *strokes,* are the third leading cause of death in North America, little is known regarding sexual problems and sexual expression and adjustment following CVA. Overall, stroke may affect both physical and psychosocial aspects of sexuality. Common physical problems include erectile dysfunction in men and poor vaginal lubrication in women (Monga, 1993; Monga & Osterman, 1995). In addition, *aphasia* (the absence or impairment of the ability to communicate, which can be caused by stroke) and other impairments of language skills can affect sexual relationships (Kinsella & Duffy, 1979). Alternate positioning and means of sexual expression can be helpful for many stroke victims.

Diabetes

Approximately 16 million Americans have *diabetes,* a complex disorder that affects the ability of the body to produce or properly respond to insulin. Sexual problems may result from nerve damage, a routine complication of diabetes (Masters et al., 1992). In a small number of cases, sexual dysfunction may be due to circulatory problems related to the disease. Both the nerve damage and the circulatory problems tend to be permanent and untreatable. Diabetes is the leading organic cause of erectile problems in men. Half of all men with adult-onset diabetes report difficulty or inability to attain or maintain an erection. The use of medications such as Viagra or penile implants are common treatments. Women with adult-onset diabetes are more susceptible to vaginal infections, which can result in decreased vaginal lubrication.

Multiple Sclerosis

Multiple sclerosis (MS), a neurological disease of the brain and spinal cord characterized by degeneration of the protective covering of the nerves, is the most common disabling neurological disease of young adults, affecting approximately 350,000 people in the United States each year (Anderson et al., 1992). Complications of the disease include cognitive, sensory, and motor dysfunction. Effects on sexual functioning depend on which areas of the brain or spinal cord are involved. The level of disease activity, the duration of the disease, and the degree of fatigue, depression, spasticity, and bowel and bladder problems also affect sexual functioning. Many men with MS have difficulty achieving and maintaining erections. In women, numbness and tingling in the vaginal area and difficulty in lubrication are common. In one study, 63 percent of people with MS reported their sexual activity had declined since their diagnosis; other surveys suggest that as many as 91 percent of men and 72 percent of women with MS may be affected by sexual problems (Hendley, 1996). Medications for spasms and pain may be helpful. For problems with fatigue, positions that require less exertion can be used. Other options include medication, penile implants, and lubricants.

Psychiatric Illness

Decreased libido is one of the symptoms of depression, the most frequently diagnosed psychiatric disorder in the United States. *Depression,* the most common form of mood disorder, is characterized by problems with appetite, sleeping, loss of energy, lack of interest and pleasure in usual activities (including sex), depressed or sad mood, and negative self-concept. Unfortunately, many antidepressants prescribed to treat depression have the side effect of decreased sexual desire. Other psychiatric illnesses, such as *bipolar disorder* (formerly called manic-depressive illness, which includes periods of depression that may suddenly lift and are followed immediately by periods of mania in which the person exhibits exaggerated energy and elation) or *schizophrenia* (a serious mental illness characterized by a loss of contact with reality, problems with incoherent thought patterns, and attention, motor, and perceptual problems), also may affect sexual desire and behavior.

There are many misconceptions about sexuality and the mentally disabled. Although many believe otherwise, the "mentally handicapped are more likely to be victims than perpetrators of sexual exploitation" (Reinisch, 1991, p. 283). While research has shown that the sexual development and behavior of the mentally and intellectually disabled is similar to the nondisabled, the physical and emotional changes of puberty may be difficult for them to handle. "Without special education programs to help them learn about physical changes and our society's rules for handling sexual feelings, some inadvertently behave in socially unacceptable ways" (Reinisch, 1991, pp. 283–284). Treatment of any mental illness should include counseling regarding appropriate sexual expression.

Despite his spinal cord injury, Christopher Reeve and his wife Dana maintain a sexual relationship.

Sensory Impairment

Impairment of one of the senses, such as vision, hearing, or speech, does not directly affect genital responsiveness. For example, the 1991 Kinsey Report notes, "Some research on the sexual behavior of visually impaired people has established that their feelings, attitudes, and behavior are similar to those of sighted people" (Reinisch, 1991, p. 284). Sexual difficulties may be related to a lack of sex education or decreased self-confidence resulting from the impairment. Psychological problems associated with the impairment are far more likely to interfere with a sexual relationship than the impairment itself. Deafness or blindness, particularly if it occurs in adolescence or adulthood, may cause depression, social withdrawal, distorted body image, and/or fear of rejection. These emotions can have an adverse affect on anyone's sexuality. Counseling may be appropriate for anyone with sensory impairment.

Spinal Cord Injuries

Spinal cord injuries (SCI), injuries to the spinal cord from events such as automobile accidents, serious falls, or diving accidents, affect approximately 200,000 Americans. *Spinal cord disease* may affect an additional 300,000 (Sipski, 1997). Such events may cause *paraplegia* (paralysis of the legs) or *quadriplegia* (paralysis of all four limbs) and loss of all sensations below the level of the injury or disease. Normal bladder and bowel function usually is lost, and the individual is apt to have significant loss of sexual function.

You can have sex in a wheelchair, while suffering from arthritis, or after heart surgery. Although there may be difficulties due to physical limitations, the individual's adjustment to the disability, or the availability of partners, individuals with disabilities have the same sexual needs and feelings as anyone else. In any person, able or disabled, a healthy attitude is the most important factor in achieving a healthy sex life.

If a disability occurs early in life it may affect socialization; a smaller social circle limits the opportunity for sexual learning and the availability of sexual partners. A condition can cause direct or indirect effects on sexual functioning. A direct effect is any difference in function of your genitals or another body system that specifically affects sexual response. For example, erectile dysfunction can be a direct effect of prostate cancer. An indirect effect can be symptoms such as pain or fatigue caused by the condi-

CONSIDERATIONS

The Orgasm Pill

Researchers Barry Komisaruk and Beverly Whipple (1997) believe that they have isolated a chemical that produces orgasms in women, even those who have suffered spinal cord injuries. Through experiments with rats, researchers isolated the neurotransmitter that is believed to cause the sensation of orgasm in the brain. These findings might one day lead to a pill that would give the same sensation as an orgasm.

? Aside from its obvious use, can you think of any potential abuse for such a pill?

—If a pill were available that would provide you with the sensations of orgasm, would you be interested?

—Do you think such a pill might replace your desire and need for coitus?

—What might be the long-term social implications of such a pill?

tion that diminishes your ability for and/or interest in sexual activities. For example, those suffering from severe arthritis may have such extreme discomfort that sexual activity becomes undesirable.

Medical treatments can interfere with sexual responses, as can the psychological effects of being sick, injured, or disabled. A belief that you are less attractive or less sexually desirable because of your condition can reduce your willingness to pursue sexual relationships. Your partners' reactions also have an impact. For example, a sexual partner may be afraid that sexual activity will hurt you or worsen your condition. As indicated above, a positive attitude on the part of the disabled person and his or her partner can make all of the difference in the expression of their sexuality.

CHAPTER 3 ■ R E V I E W

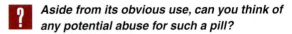

Most female primates undergo an **1**_____ cycle that includes a period of sexual receptivity followed by ovulation. However, human females are capable of being continuously receptive to and available for sexual activity independent of ovulation. While the physical responses to sexual arousal vary with the individual, the most obvious physical signs of sexual arousal are vaginal **2**_____ for females and penile **3**_____ for males.

The brain may be the most important human sexual organ since it processes emotions, thoughts, fantasies, and desires. Some typical correlates of sexual excitement are increases in heartbeat, blood to the genitals, **4**_____ (or breathing), and skin sensitivity. In addition, the body may experience **5**_____ (or muscle tension) and engorgement of blood in the genitals.

All five human senses may contribute to sexual arousal. For example, touch or tactile stimulation and smell or olfactory stimulation can increase sexual arousal. **6**_____ are naturally produced chemicals that affect behavior through the sense of smell.

7_____ are chemical substances secreted by the endocrine system. There are three primary categories of sex hormones: **8**_____, _____, and _____. All three are present in varying amounts in males and females. The most important androgen is **9**_____, which is produced by the testes, ovaries, and adrenal glands.

The endocrine system plays an important role in sexual behavior. The hypothalamus regulates the production of sex hormones and sends signals to the pituitary gland that in turn directs the production of androgens in males and estrogens in females. The feedback loop is completed when the testes or ovaries send hormonal signals to the hypothalamus and the pituitary to help self-regulate the system. The chemicals **10**_____ and _____, produced by the pituitary, also can be triggered by sex and desire.

Masters and Johnson have proposed the EPOR model of sexual response for males and females. The four phases of this model are: **11**_____, _____, _____, and _____. Helen Kaplan has proposed a model of sexual response consisting of three independent components: **12**_____, _____, and _____. David Reed's ESP model has four phases: **13**_____, _____, _____, and _____.

Studies indicate that the orgasms of males and females feel similar, and that there is more variation among individuals than between males and females. However, females are much more likely than males to experience more than one orgasm, or **14**_____. Since the female orgasm is not necessary for human reproduction, much debate continues regarding its evolutionary significance.

A healthy body is not a prerequisite for a healthy sex life. A healthy attitude about your sexuality and yourself is the most important factor. The specific impact of illness or disability on sexual function depends on: (1) the severity of the impairment; (2) personal factors, such as age; (3) partner factors, including sexual history and the nature of past relationships. While it is common to de-sexualize the disabled, individuals with disabilities can have the same sexual needs and feelings as anyone else.

Cerebral palsy affects muscle control but it does not affect genital sensation, sexual interest, the capacity to have orgasm, or fertility. Multiple sclerosis is the most common neurological disease of young adults in the United States. **15**_____, or hardening of the arteries, and diabetes are common causes of erectile problems. Decreased libido may result from depression; moreover, medications prescribed to treat depression also may decrease sexual desire.

Injuries of the **16**_____ may cause paraplegia, paralysis of **17**_____, or quadriplegia, paralysis of all four limbs. When all sensations are lost below the level of the injury, normal bladder and bowel functions and significant sexual function may be affected, although sexuality can be expressed in alternative ways.

SUGGESTED READINGS

Blum, D. (1998). *Sex on the Brain: The Biological Differences Between Men and Women.* New York: Penguin USA.
Blum examines the structure and function of the male and female brains.

Crenshaw, T. (1997). *The Alchemy of Love and Lust: How Our Sex Hormones Influence Our Relationships.* New York: Pocket Books.
Crenshaw, a sex therapist, discusses the role of hormones in the different sexual stages and how hormones determine the course of human relationships.

Love, S. (1997). *Dr. Susan Love's Hormone Book.* New York: Random House.
This book offers information about hormones and hormone replacement therapy. The emphasis is that menopause is not a disease that needs to be cured but a natural stage of life.

Masters, W., & Johnson, V. (1966). *Human Sexual Response.* Boston: Little Brown & Company.
This is the classic text on the biological patterns of human sexual response.

Sipski, M. L., & Alexander, C. (Eds.). (1997). *Sexual Function in People with Disability and Chronic Illness.* Gaithersburg, MD: Aspen Publications.
This collection offers a comprehensive overview of how various illnesses and disabilities affect sexual function, along with treatment options.

ANSWERS TO CHAPTER REVIEW

1. estrous; **2.** lubrication; **3.** erection; **4.** respiration; **5.** myotonia; **6.** Pheromones; **7.** Hormones; **8.** androgens, estrogens, progesterones; **9.** testosterone; **10.** oxytocin, vasopressin; **11.** excitement, plateau, orgasmic, resolution; **12.** desire, excitement, orgasm; **13.** seduction, sensation, surrender, reflection; **14.** multiple orgasms; **15.** Arteriosclerosis; **16.** spinal cord; **17.** the legs

CHAPTER 4

Sexual Dysfunctions and Therapies

PHYSICAL

SOCIAL

EMOTIONAL

SPIRITUAL

COGNITIVE

- ■ **Disorders of Sexual Desire**
  Problems with sexual desire are the most common complaints of couples seeking sexual therapy. The cause of desire disorders may be physical, psychological, or a combination of these factors.

- ■ **Disorders of Sexual Arousal**
  The most common sexual arousal problem in men is erectile dysfunction; women often have difficulty with vaginal lubrication.

- ■ **Orgasmic Disorders**
  Males may suffer from premature ejaculation, and females from anorgasmia, that is, the inability to have an orgasm.

- ■ **Sexual Pain Disorders**
  Pain experienced during sexual arousal or intercourse can be caused by priapism, dyspareunia, or vaginismus.

- ■ **Effects of Drugs and Alcohol on Sexual Function**
  Despite their popular image, drugs and alcohol have a number of adverse effects on sexual function.

- ■ **Sexual Therapy**
  Sexual therapy, the treatment of sexual dysfunctions and the enhancement of sexual satisfaction and desire, may involve medical intervention and/or psychological counseling.

Popular culture leads us to believe that everyone is always ready, willing, and able to have sex; however, at any time throughout our lives the sexual fires may be slow to ignite. Your sexual well-being is intimately connected to your emotional and physical health. **Sexual dysfunction,** a problem with sexual desire, arousal, or satisfaction, often coincides with other health problems. Without an understanding of the cause of a sexual problem it is difficult to provide effective treatment. Sexual dysfunction can contribute to personal and interpersonal stress; treatment is essential to identifying (or ruling out) significant medical or psychological problems. A disorder caused by an organic disease requires different treatment than a sexual problem resulting from relationship conflict.

While it is difficult to separate cause and effect, sexual health and overall happiness are closely linked. A recent report in the *Journal of the American Medical Association* found that 43 percent of American women and 31 percent of men ages 18 to 59 said they suffered from one or more sexual problems (Laumann, Paik, & Rosen, 1999) (Table 4.1). Men with erectile dysfunction were more than four times as likely to be unhappy than men without this problem, while women who had difficulty becoming sexually aroused were five times more likely to be dissatisfied with their lives than other women (Laumann, Paik, & Rosen, 1999). In contrast to what the clothing industry would have us believe, sex is not an alluring undergarment that can be put on and taken off; it is an integral part of life as a whole.

The American Psychiatric Association (1994) places sexual disorders into four categories: disorders of sexual desire, disorders of sexual arousal, orgasmic disorders, and sexual pain disorders. But don't put yourself into one of these boxes just yet. Anyone can experience any of these on occasion. It is important to distinguish between a rare or occasional problem, which is normal, and a frequent or chronic problem, one that occurs consistently over a long time period. Who hasn't had a time when you (or your partner) would really just as soon watch television as have sex? Not every sexual experience is worthy of poetic rapture. In order to be considered a sexual dysfunction, the symptoms must be persistent and pervasive and the problem must cause the individual personal distress. If your partner is unhappy with the frequency of sex in your relationship but you are not, by definition you do not have a sexual dysfunction.

There are two types of dysfunctions: primary and secondary. A person who has never had satisfactory sexual relations suffers from *primary sexual dysfunction*, while one who has had successful sexual relations at some time but is currently having chronic difficulty suffers from *secondary sexual dysfunction*. It is not always easy to distinguish those who have a sexual dysfunction from those who don't. As one researcher states, "Just as everyone able to complete the sexual response cycle isn't having great sex, everyone with a sexual dysfunction isn't having lousy sex" (Schnarch, 1991, p. xiv). Another way of categorizing sexual dysfunction is as lifelong, acquired, situational, or generalized (Table 4.2).

Sexual Dysfunction: a persistent sexual disorder or impairment that interferes with sexual desire, arousal, or satisfaction

TABLE 4.1

	Lack of Interest in Sex		Can't Achieve Orgasm		Erectile Dysfunction	Pain During Sex	Climax Too Early
	Women	Men	Women	Men	Men	Women	Men
AGE							
18–29	32%	14%	26%	7%	7%	21%	30%
30–39	32	13	28	7	9	15	32
40–49	30	15	22	9	11	13	28
50–59	27	17	23	9	18	8	31
EDUCATION							
Less than high school	42	19	34	11	13	18	38
High-school grad	33	12	29	7	9	17	35
Some college	30	16	24	8	10	16	26
College grad	24	14	18	7	10	10	27
MARITAL STATUS							
Married	29	11	22	7	9	14	30
Never married	35	19	30	9	10	17	29
Separated/ divorced/ widowed	34	18	32	9	14	16	32
RACE/ETHNICITY							
White	29	14	24	7	10	16	20
Black	44	19	32	9	13	13	34
Hispanic	30	13	22	9	5	14	27

Sexual Problems in Americans

SOURCE: Laumann, Paik, & Rosen, 1999.

At one time it was thought that most sexual disorders resulted from psychological problems. There has been a general trend in Western culture to blame psychosocial factors for sexual problems, especially those experienced by women (Davis, 1998). We now know that sexual dysfunction may have any of a number of causes: biological, interpersonal, emotional, cultural, or any combination of these. Researchers in England recently investigated the association of sexual problems with social, physiological, and psychological problems in 789 men and 979 women ages 18 to 75 years (Dunn, Croft, & Hackett, 1999). Results indicated that sexual problems were most commonly associated with self-reported physical problems in men and with psychological and social problems in women. The difference between the genders is no accident. As we discuss throughout this book, many theorists believe that male sexuality tends to be more closely linked to biological factors, and female sexuality depends more on the social and interpersonal context.

TABLE 4.2

Classifications of Sexual Dysfunction

Lifelong	The dysfunction has always been present
Acquired	At some point the person was able to function without the problem
Situational	The dysfunction occurs in some situations but not in others
Generalized	The problem occurs regardless of the situation

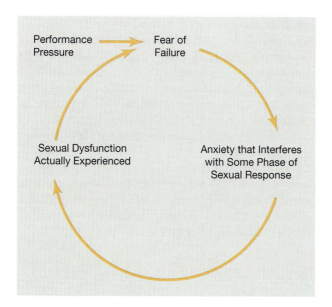

FIGURE 4.1 The Cycle of Sexual Dysfunction. Social pressure to perform in an idealized manner may result in a heightened fear of being unable to perform adequately. This may interfere with sexual response, and the resulting experience of sexual dysfunction may lead to increased fear of failure in the future.

Treatment for sexual dysfunction may be medical, psychological, or a combination of the two. Medical therapies include various approaches such as hormone therapy, prescription medication, and surgery. Psychological treatment includes behavioral models as well as psychodynamic or talk therapy. A review of four professional journals (the *Journal of Sex Education and Therapy*, the *Journal of Sex & Marital Therapy*, the *Journal of Sex Research*, and *Archives of Sexual Behavior*) found that the medical model has become the dominant treatment for male sexual dysfunctions (Winton, 2001).

You might be wondering why this chapter is included in the section of our text on physical needs rather than under social or emotional needs. As with most aspects of our sexuality, there are multiple dimensions to any sexual disorder. Sometimes the problem is purely a medical one, or it might be solely a relationship problem or only related to an individual's emotional distress. Sometimes the problem might be related to all of your basic needs. You might have a health problem and at the same time feel unfulfilled in your relationship because it conflicts with your sexual values and cognitive beliefs. Some people may feel societal pressure to perform sexually. These real or imagined pressures may result in a fear of performing that ultimately produces a sexual dysfunction (Figure 4.1). We include sexual dysfunction as a physical need, because that is where most therapists start when evaluating a client; any underlying physical problem is ruled out before exploring other possibilities.

DISORDERS OF SEXUAL DESIRE

Sexual desire, or libido, runs along a continuum. For some, having sex once a day is not enough; for others, sex once a year is too often. Sexual desire in the same individual can also vary, from day to day or over the years. It's not unusual for us to compare ourselves to others to see how our sex lives measure up. But little is known about what constitutes normal sexual desire or how sexual desire may differ between men and women. Moreover, there are no established criteria by which to measure sexual desire. Since we lack scientific data, we must rely on information from clinical observation and statistical surveys. "Normal" may simply be what is usual or typical for you. Stress, fatigue, and general health can affect your level of sexual desire, as can more serious medical conditions, relationship problems, and emotional difficulties. Being too tired one night is not a problem; the problem occurs when there is an unsatisfactory change in the overall pattern of sexual desire.

Sexual desire disorders are the most common reason couples seek sex therapy. However, those seeking help often mistake a lack of sexual desire for a problem of sexual arousal, such as erectile dysfunction, or an orgasmic disorder. Sex therapists report that nearly half of all clients are diagnosed with sexual desire disorders (Reinisch, 1991).

The most common health-related causes of decreased sexual desire are depression, stress, side effects of drugs, and changes in hormonal levels, especially testosterone. Any disruption of the brain or central nervous system, such as that experienced in a stroke, can affect the biological mechanisms necessary for experiencing sexual desire (Reinisch, 1991).

In the past, disorders of sexual desire were considered to belong to psychology, not medicine. Although we are learning that endocrine fluctuations and neural activity of the brain affect sexual desire, the influence these neurological and biochemical systems exert is uncertain. Today you are as likely to be treated for a sexual desire disorder by your physician as by a mental-health professional.

Hypoactive Sexual Desire

Hypoactive sexual desire is the technical term for a lack of interest in sex (APA, 1994). It may include an absence of sexual fantasies or thoughts as well as a lack of interest in sexual activity. Women with hypoactive sexual desire are sometimes referred to as being "frigid." This pejorative term, rarely used to describe men with low libido, places blame squarely on the woman rather than exploring the sociocultural, emotional, and physical factors that might contribute to her low libido.

Almost everyone has periods in life when they have little or no interest in sex. As with other sexual difficulties, hypoactive sexual desire can be a chronic or episodic problem. For some people, a low level of desire affects all sexual interactions; in others, it is specific to one partner, situation, or sexual activity. A temporary change in sexual desire is usually due to a specific stressor and generally is not considered to be a serious sexual problem.

There are different degrees of hypoactive sexual desire. Some individuals may not initiate sex, but they enjoy sexual relations when their partners come on to them. Others may avoid genital sex but enjoy other types of physical affection. And there are those individuals whose loss of sexual interest is so pervasive that any form of physical affection is repellent.

Biological factors such as the changes associated with menopause, nerve damage, diabetes, heart disease, smoking, and obesity are all possible roots of a problem with sexual desire. Reduced or deficient ovarian function resulting in decreased androgen levels may also affect libido. Medications, including antidepressants and certain drugs for birth control, baldness, and high blood pressure, can inhibit libido. Hormones have a significant effect on our sexual desire; the normal hormonal fluctuations that occur with aging (a decrease in estrogen and testosterone) can result in decreased sex drive.

Psychological factors have a tremendous effect on libido. These include stress, depression, past sexual abuse, poor body image, and a history of unsatisfactory relationships. Hypoactive sexual desire can be related to conscious or unconscious negative thoughts and feelings about sex formed by cultural upbringing or past sexual abuse. When activated by sexual thoughts, fantasies, or emotions, the sexual pleasure centers of the brain create physical sexual excitement. However, the process cannot occur if sexual desire messages are overridden by other emotions or shut down by other brain centers. For example, if a person associates pain with sexual intercourse, the need to avoid pain takes priority over seeking pleasure. Individuals with sexual desire problems often perceive danger where there is none and shut down sexual feelings in situations that are, in reality, safe (Knopf & Seiler, 1990). While individuals may be fully aware of this process and able to identify the source of their difficulties, more commonly, these desires are unconsciously suppressed.

Depression and sexual desire problems often coexist. To complicate things further, as you just learned in Chapter 3, antidepressant medications can induce sexual problems

Sexual Desire Disorders: sexual dysfunctions in which people have a persistent or recurrent lack of desire for sex

Hypoactive Sexual Desire: having little or no interest in sex

or make them worse, creating a vicious circle. Your attitude toward sex can also be a physical expression of problems in the relationship. If you're angry, hurt or bored with your partner, it is likely to spill over into the bedroom. It is sometimes difficult to determine which comes first, a bad relationship or a bad sex life.

As indicated earlier, hypoactive sexual desire, like all sexual dysfunctions, is diagnosed only if it is a problem for the individual, not if it only upsets the individual's partner. Differences in sexual desire between the partners in a relationship are not uncommon. Because one partner doesn't want sex as often or at the same time as his or her partner doesn't necessarily mean that the less-interested partner has a hypoactive sexual desire disorder. Some people are content with a low libido and others only have sex "to pacify or silence the complaints of their disgruntled partners" (Schover & Leiblum, 1994, p.18). However, most of those who have hypoactive sexual desire want to enjoy sexual feelings but find that they are unable to do so. The desire to enjoy sex is key to treatment of hypoactive sexual desire, the topic of the next section.

Treatment for Hypoactive Sexual Desire

Once dismissed as an intractable psychological problem or an inevitable result of menopause, hypoactive sexual desire is now getting increased attention from researchers and the medical establishment. However, barring any biological cause, sexual desire disorders may be the category of sexual problem that is most difficult to treat (Hawton, Catalan, & Fagg, 1991; LoPiccolo & Friedman, 1988).

Insight-oriented **psychotherapy,** in which a client talks with a therapist to heighten self-awareness, can help reveal and resolve deep-seated psychological conflicts that inhibit sexual desire. Some therapists believe this type of psychotherapy to be especially helpful in the treatment of low sexual desire. **Behavior therapy,** which focuses on modifying behavior and may include self-stimulation exercises combined with erotic fantasies, may sometimes be recommended for clients experiencing hypoactive sexual desire (LoPiccolo & Friedman, 1988).

When low sexual desire is linked to depression, treatment with antidepressant medication or psychotherapy may be helpful. However, as already noted, antidepressants themselves have the potential to cause sexual dysfunction; as a matter of fact, nearly all antidepressants approved for use in the United States have a negative effect on sexual function (Sussman, 1999). Some studies have reported that between 35 and 75 percent of patients taking selective serotonin reuptake inhibitors (SSRIs), such as Prozac and Zoloft, reported sexual dysfunction as a side effect. The most frequent sexual side effects reported are delayed ejaculation, absent or delayed orgasm, and sexual desire and arousal problems (Rosen, Lane, & Menza, 1999). Another study suggests that sildenafil citrate (marketed as Viagra, which we will discuss more fully later) can help both women and men taking antidepressants restore sexual desire (Nurmberg, Lodillo, & Hensly, 1999). A large research study is currently underway (Berman & Berman, 2001) that could lead to FDA approval of Viagra for women.

Many women who choose hormone replacement therapy during and after menopause receive only estrogen. However, as you learned in Chapter 2, the levels of testosterone and other androgens also diminish in menopausal women. Although it is known that testosterone plays a key role in sexual desire for both men and women, it is not routinely included in hormone replacement regimes. Studies have shown that women who received estrogen and testosterone feel much better sexually than those who receive only estrogen (Kauntitz, 1997; Sherwin, 1997). A study published in the *New England Journal of Medicine* (Shifren et al., 2000) found that the use of an experimental testosterone skin patch could improve sexual well-being in women who have had a hysterectomy, so-called surgically menopausal women. However, testosterone is still controversial and some health-care professionals are reluctant to prescribe it because of earlier studies showing that, in high doses, testosterone has masculinizing side effects like increased hair growth and deepening of the voice. It also can cause weight gain and acne. More serious side effects of high doses include increased cholesterol levels and

Psychotherapy: treatment of emotional problems primarily through verbal and nonverbal communication and interventions rather than other treatments such as medications

Behavior Therapy: therapy that seeks to modify undesirable behaviors using learning techniques

Aphrodisiac: a substance that increases or is believed to increase sexual desire or capability

Sexual Aversion: an extreme and irrational fear of sex

the risk of liver and heart disease. However, the doses currently recommended are so low that side effects are virtually nonexistent. Testosterone also may be given to younger women who take birth control pills or who have other conditions leading to a lower-than-normal testosterone level (Warnock et al., 1997).

Because low sexual desire has both physical and psychological causes, it only makes sense that a mind-body approach would provide optimal treatment possibilities. Medications or hormone treatment might be supplemented and complemented by psychotherapy that may specifically focus on sexual problems or more generally on emotions and relationship problems.

Sexual Aversion

Low sexual desire that includes fear, disgust, and avoidance of sexual activity is considered **sexual aversion** (Kaplan, 1987, 1995). Even the thought of sexual contact may result in extreme anxiety and include physiological symptoms such a rapid heartbeat, nausea, dizziness, and trembling. Those who develop fearful reactions to sex may have a history of physical or sexual abuse or a severely rigid or punitive upbringing. Others may have health concerns, real or imagined, resulting in an aversion to sexual intimacy.

CONSIDERATIONS

Love Potion #9: Aphrodisiacs

For centuries humans have searched for **aphrodisiacs,** food, drinks, drugs, scents, or devices that can increase sexual desire or enhance sexual performance. Historically, the most popular aphrodisiacs have been foods or love potions. Despite thousands of years of tradition and belief, the Food and Drug Administration (1989) has found no scientific evidence that any so-called aphrodisiac works to treat sexual dysfunction. However, it can be difficult to separate folktale from fact when discussing aphrodisiacs. The strong belief that a food can increase sex drive or enhance sexual performance may be enough.

Other passion foods and potions include oysters, ginseng root, powdered rhinoceros horn, turtle eggs, and animal testicles ("prairie oysters"). It's easy to see how animal sexual organs acquired this reputation; in other cases a food's resemblance to sexual organs sparked interest in their sexual powers. For example, the rhinoceros horn resembles the penis or oysters might be reminiscent of testicles.

Chilies, curries, and hot peppers are believed to be aphrodisiacs in many cultures. In fact, these spicy foods do raise heart rate and sometimes increase sweating, two physiological changes that are similar to the reactions experienced during sex. Cantharides (Spanish flies) comes from the dried remains of a southern European beetle. Its reputation comes from the swelling of blood vessels that can produce genital stimulation and might be interpreted as sexual desire. However, when taken internally the powder can cause burning of the mouth and throat and swelling of the bladder and urethra, and if taken in excess can cause violent illness and even death.

The belief that some foods, like oysters, have aphrodisiac powers may be due to their resemblance to sexual organs.

Yohimbine, a substance derived from the bark of the African yohimbe tree, has become increasingly popular as an aphrodisiac over the past few years. Although one study (Mann et al., 1996) found that men with erectile dysfunction improved when treated with yohimbine and there are a lot of anecdotal reports of its powers, follow-up studies have been inconclusive.

 Is there a particular food, drink, or scent that "puts you in the mood"?

 —*Do you think it enhances your performance, or do you associate it with past pleasurable encounters?*

Treatment for Sexual Aversion

According to Masters and Johnson, the key to treating sexual aversion is empowerment. The person experiencing sexual aversion is temporarily put in control of any situation involving physical intimacy (Masters et al., 1987). A series of sensate focus exercises (see SEXUAL HEALTH AND YOU box) is used to allow the person to develop comfort with his or her own body, tolerate mild anxiety, and gradually increase the level of sexual contact. See the section of this chapter on Sex Therapy for more on how sensate focus exercises are used to treat sexual disorders.

Sensate Focus Exercises: form of therapy designed by Masters and Johnson to treat a variety of sexual problems without the pressure to "perform"

SEXUAL HEALTH AND YOU

Sensate Focus Exercises

Sensate focus exercises are a form of therapy designed to help couples respond erotically with all areas of the body without the pressure to "perform." Masters and Johnson developed the concept in 1970. Although the technique was created to treat a variety of sexual problems, couples not experiencing problems can also use sensate focus exercises to enhance their sexual relationships. The original Masters and Johnson techniques were developed for couples who were willing to devote 2 weeks to an intensive daily sexual therapy program. While there is more flexibility for therapists using this therapy today, certain ground rules are fundamental. Couples must agree to establish a moratorium on sexual intercourse during the treatment period. They must have no extramarital affairs during the course of therapy and the use of alcohol, mood-altering drugs, or nonprescription medications is prohibited. Both partners must agree to set apart a specific time of the day to do individual homework assignments. The couple must agree to set aside any disagreements or grievances, and they must be explicit in telling each other what does and does not stimulate them.

In the first sensate focus exercise, which consists solely of touching, partners take turns exploring one another's bodies (Figure 4.2) while following some essential guidelines. The person who will be doing the touching takes some time to create a comfortable atmosphere—perhaps turning off the phone, lighting candles, and playing soft music. The couple disrobes and the toucher begins to explore his or her partner's body in a nonsexual way, without the goal of pleasing or arousing the partner (although that may well happen). Intercourse and the touching of breasts and genitals are prohibited. Instead, the toucher focuses on his or her own pleasure by experiencing the texture, form, and temperature of the partner's body. The person being touched remains quiet except when any touch is uncomfortable. Next, the partners switch roles, following the same guidelines.

In Step 2 the couple explores all parts of the body manually or orally, but exclude the breasts and genitals. The partners are encouraged to take turns so that both can find ways to relax and arouse each other. Manual or oral stimulation of the breasts is allowed in Step 3, and in Step 4 the women is encourage to caress the man's penis and scrotum. The goal is not to achieve erection or orgasm but to create an atmosphere for a pleasurable experience.

Step 5 is the manual caressing of the genitals to bring both partners to orgasm. During this step, if there is concern about premature ejaculation, the woman is instructed in the "squeeze" or "start-stop" exercise (described later in this chapter) to delay ejaculation. Intercourse is allowed in Step 6, but the goal is simply vaginal penetration. Only a minimum amount of thrusting is permitted, and it is advised that the man lie on his back with the woman on top. Step 7 is an extension of Step 6, with prolonged thrusting to orgasm with the woman on top. Step 8 allows intercourse with the man on top.

FIGURE 4.2 In sensate focus, partners sensually explore each other's bodies. This can contribute to the mutual enhancement of a couple's sexual enjoyment.

Compulsive Sexual Behavior

So far we have discussed problems with inadequate sexual desire. There is also a disorder involving excessive sexual desire or behavior, called **compulsive sexual behavior.** The problem is, who decides what is excessive and how much sex is too much? There is no agreement among professionals about the definition, diagnosis, treatment, or even the terminology to describe this behavior, and the American Psychiatric Association does not recognize it as a legitimate psychiatric disorder. Although it is not a medically recognized sexual disorder, because of the widespread interest and concern with compulsive sexual behavior, we feel it is important to include a discussion of it in this section. The various terms used reflect not only the confusion about this problem but also different values, attitudes, and theoretical orientations. In the past, the pejorative term *nymphomania* was used to describe women with a higher level of sexual desire than was deemed to be appropriate, and *satyriasis* was used for men. These terms have since been discarded, but there is still no consensus regarding a label; you may also hear the terms *sexual addiction, hypersexuality, sexual impulsivity,* and *sexual dependence* used to describe this disorder.

The term *sexual addiction* first became popularized in 1983 with the publication of Patrick Carnes' book *Out of the Shadows: Understanding Sexual Addiction.* Carnes argued that there are a large number of people whose craving for the "high" of sex is out of control to the degree that it can legitimately be considered a true addiction. Rather than enjoying sex as a pleasurable activity, the sex addict relies on sex for comfort, nurturing, or stress relief. See Table 4.3 for symptoms associated with compulsive sexual behavior, and Table 4.4 for profiles of the various types of sex addicts. Please note that having one or two of these patterns does not make you a sex addict! Persons suffering from compulsive sexual behavior exhibit *seven or more* of these symptoms.

Several researchers believe that compulsive sexual behavior is a valid and serious sexual disorder in which obsessive sex can lead to a dependency similar to that caused by alcohol and drugs. Others think that the problem has more in common with compulsive behaviors such as eating or gambling or impulse disorders such as kleptomania. Some see the label of sexual addiction as a means of pathologizing illegal sexual behavior (Rinehart & McCabe, 1998), for example, using sexual addiction as an explanation for rape. Others think that it is simply an excuse for being irresponsible.

Sexual addiction may be related to a biochemical abnormality. Individuals become hooked on the pleasurable neurochemical changes that take place in the body during sexual behavior. Liebowitz (1983) has found that many so-called "relationship-junkies" (those who go from one sexual relationship to the next) suffer from a craving for the brain chemical PEA. In an experimental study, subjects were given antidepressants to

Compulsive Sexual Behavior: excessive sexual desire and behavior

TABLE 4.3

Symptoms Associated with Compulsive Sexual Behavior

BEHAVIORAL SYMPTOMS:
  Frequent sexual encounters
  Compulsive masturbation
  Seeking new sexual encounters out of boredom
  Repeated unsuccessful attempts to stop or reduce excessive behaviors
  Engaging in sexual activities without physiological arousal
  Legal involvement resulting from elicit sexual behavior
  Frequent use of pornography
COGNITIVE AND EMOTIONAL SYMPTOMS:
  Obsessive thoughts about sex
  Rationalization for continuing sexual behavior
  Guilt resulting from excessive or problematic sexual behavior
  Loneliness, boredom, and rage
  Depression, low self-esteem
  Shame and secrecy regarding sexual behavior
  Indifference to usual sexual partner
  Lack of control in many aspects of life
  Desire to escape from or suppress unpleasant emotions
  Preference for anonymous sex
  Experientially disconnecting intimacy from sex

SOURCE: Adapted from Gold & Heffner, 1998.

boost levels of PEA and other natural amphetamines. After this treatment, they no longer craved the PEA high and could make more considered choices in sexual activity. Sabelli, Carlson-Sabelli, and Javaid (1990) reached similar conclusions in their study: 33 happily attached people were all found to have high levels of PEA, while a couple going through a divorce had low PEA levels. Other researchers have also concluded that those who have low levels of PEA are more likely to pursue sexual variety and excitement (Sostek & Wyatt, 1981; Weiss, 1987).

Those who do not believe that compulsive sexual behavior is a disorder criticize it as a fad diagnosis with no scientific basis. Calling conventional sexual behaviors taken to an extreme an addiction negates personal responsibility for behavior; so-called addicts may seek to excuse their behavior behind the shield of an uncontrollable disease (Konner, 1990). Historically there is a long tradition of pathologizing behavior that some might find distasteful; these behaviors have included masturbation, oral sex, homosexuality, and extramarital sex. Behaviors that conflict with your value system may be problematic, but that does not mean that the person is "sick."

TABLE 4.4

Six Scenarios of Sex Addicts

Hitters	experts at one-night stands
Drifters	wander from one sexual encounter to another
Romantics	intensely seductive
Nesters	both yearn for and flee from domesticity
Tomcats	married but nevertheless they are constantly on the prowl
Jugglers	try to manage a number of simultaneous relationships.

SOURCE: Adapted from Trachtenberg, 1988.

Sexual Arousal Disorder: sexual dysfunctions in which there is a persistent or recurrent failure to become adequately sexually aroused to engage in or sustain sexual intercourse

EXPLORING SEXUALITY ONLINE

Can You Become Addicted to Online Sex?

Most people log onto sexually oriented Internet sites without any negative impact. However, like any sexual behavior, online sex is different for each person, ranging from recreational to pathological. Enjoying an occasional stroll through sexual cyberland is one thing; using cybersex to the exclusion of other relationships, or going broke from visits to porn.com sites is quite another. According to a study published in *Professional Psychology: Research and Practice* (Cooper et al., 1999), about 15 percent of the 57 million Internet users in the United States visit sexually oriented sites. Of those, 8 percent spend more than 11 hours a week at such sites and run a risk of having a compulsive sexual problem. This compares to the estimated 5 percent of the general population who deal with issues of sexual compulsivity.

Treatment for Compulsive Sexual Behavior

Since sexual addiction is not a medically recognized diagnosis, there is no standard treatment protocol and few empirical evaluations of the efficacy of treatment (Gold & Heffner, 1999). Typically treatment may include the combination of drugs used for other compulsive disorders or antidepressant medications, a 12-step program such as Sex Addicts Anonymous, behavior therapy to control compulsivity, or treatment of underlying emotional problems such as depression or anxiety.

DISORDERS OF SEXUAL AROUSAL

Sexual dysfunction may occur at any point of the sexual response cycle, but most typically it involves difficulties related to sexual arousal or orgasm, thus the term **sexual arousal disorder.**

CONSIDERATIONS

A President: Sex Addict or Philanderer?

Former president Bill Clinton has finally admitted that he has had numerous extramarital affairs, including the famous encounters with Monica Lewinsky. Some experts have stated that he suffers from sexual addiction. Others consider him an opportunistic philanderer who used his power to cheat on his wife.

From what you have read about Bill Clinton, and what you have learned here, do you think that he suffers from compulsive sexual behavior? Do you think that any, all, or some sexually compulsive or irresponsible behavior is an addiction?

When Congress impeached former President Bill Clinton for lying about his affair with White House intern Monica Lewinsky, some people speculated that Clinton might be a sex addict.

Erectile Dysfunction

Erectile dysfunction (ED) is a persistent inability to sustain an erection sufficient to complete sexual activity (APA, 1994). Difficulty in becoming erect or maintaining an erection is caused by a failure of the blood to flow into and engorge the erectile tissues of the penis to make it firm and erect. You may have heard this condition referred to as *impotence*. Because this term is imprecise and implies personal failure or a challenge to masculinity, experts prefer to use the term *erectile dysfunction*. This emphasizes the medical aspect of the problem and more clearly defines its role in male sexual function. **Erectile dysfunction** can be classified into one of two categories. Men with *life-long erectile dysfunction* have had this disorder throughout their lives. As implied by its name, *acquired erectile dysfunction* occurs after a period of normal functioning. (Compare these terms to primary sexual dysfunction and secondary sexual dysfunction described at the beginning of this chapter.)

It is not uncommon for a healthy man of any age occasionally to experience erectile problems. This occasional problem may be caused by a number of factors, including fatigue, stress, alcohol consumption, or a short-term illness. However, chronic erectile dysfunction should be evaluated and treated quickly. More than 50 percent of men ages 40 to 70 (that's 10 to 30 million in the U.S. alone!) experience some degree of erectile dysfunction, and the prevalence increases dramatically with age. Contrary to popular belief, most chronic problems are not psychological; rather they are indicators of a physical problem that requires prompt medical attention.

Physical factors that can affect a man's ability to have and sustain an erection include diabetes, vascular disease, high blood pressure, and various neurological disorders (Table 4.5). It is thought that about 25 percent of all erection problems are caused by alcohol, illicit drugs, or prescription drugs given to treat other conditions (Leary, 1992).

It is believed that a lack of the chemical *nitric oxide* may play an important role in many cases of erectile dysfunction. When the penis is flaccid, the arteries that carry blood to the penis are clamped tightly so they carry little oxygenated blood. As a matter of fact, the relaxed penis contains less oxygen than any other organ of the human body. During sexual stimulation, the brain sends a signal to nerves in the smooth muscles of the penile arteries to produce nitric oxide. The nitric oxide relaxes the clamped arterial muscles and allows blood to flow into the penis. Anything that deprives the penis of oxygen—vascular disease, lack of exercise, sleep deprivation, smoking, diabetes, sexual abstinence, or physical injuries—can contribute to erection difficulties (Blakeslee, 1993).

Men who have vascular problems may not get enough blood flowing to the penis. In such cases the nerves that make nitric oxide are malnourished and erections are either absent or partial. Erectile problems occur in 50 percent of men who have undergone

TABLE 4.5
Causes of Erectile Dysfunction
Diabetes mellitus
Hypertension (high blood pressure)
Arteriosclerosis
Renal failure
Heart disease
Neurological disorders
Injury to the pelvic or perineal area
Surgery to the bowel, bladder, rectoperitoneum, spine, urethra, prostate, etc.
Psychological reasons
Prescription medications
Vascular disease
Alcohol and illicit drugs

Erectile Dysfunction: the inability to have or maintain an erection firm enough for coitus

Honey, I Shrunk My Genitals

Koro, a syndrome characterized by an acute panic that the genitals are shrinking and retracting into the body and the fear of impending death, is found primarily in China, India, and Southeast Asia. Koro is usually considered to be a culturebound psychiatric syndrome. The syndrome is maintained by cultural beliefs that affect the entire community, not just those who are diagnosed with it (Sheung-Tak, 1996). Research has found that one factor associated with male koro is penile shortening in situations of fear or anxiety-arousing situations (Chowdbury, 1997). Although it is less frequent, women also may report koro symptoms. In women, fear of breast damage was the most prevalent symptom of koro anxiety (Chowdbury, 1994).

Men in some New Guinea societies fear sexual contact with women because of a belief that the act of sexual intercourse increases a man's chances of being contaminated. "Men believe the vital fluid

residing in a man's skin makes it sound and handsome, a condition that determines and reflects his mental vigor and self-confidence. . . . Hence, every ejaculation depletes his vitality and overindulgence must dull his mind and leave his body permanently exhausted and withered" (Meggitt, 1965, p. 210).

One cross-cultural study found that restrictive attitudes about sex were related to incidence of erectile dysfunction. Those cultures that had more restrictive attitudes toward female premarital sex, marital sex, and extramarital sex reported a higher prevalence of men with erectile problems (Welch & Kartub, 1978). Broude and Green (1976) found evidence of erectile dysfunction in 80 percent of the societies they studied. In some of these cultures, the wearing of charms and other forms of magical cures were used to ward off erectile problems.

coronary bypass surgery. Many drugs that are used to treat heart disease interfere with blood flow, with similar effects. Nerve damage resulting from prostate surgery or some hormone imbalances can also cause erectile dysfunction (Blakeslee, 1993). Diabetes can damage blood vessels and nerves needed for erections; in more than 50 percent of men diagnosed with diabetes, the first signs of the illness are decreasing firmness of erections (Reinisch, 1991). Men with heart disease who smoke have a *sevenfold* increase in erectile dysfunction (Manning, 1993b).

Treatment for Erectile Dysfunction

Treatment for erectile dysfunction differs based on whether the disorder has a physical or psychological basis. Physically sound men usually have erections for approximately 3 hours each night during rapid eye movement (REM) sleep. If a man's erectile dysfunction has a physical cause, he will not have these overnight erections. The *nocturnal penile tumescence (NPT)* test can be performed in a sleep laboratory to measure erection patterns during sleep. A device something like a blood pressure cuff is placed around the man's penis before he falls asleep. As an erection develops, the swelling and enlargement of the penis create pressure, which is recorded to identify when erections occur. This information is compared to the man's simultaneous brain wave pattern to see if erections occur when a man is experiencing REM sleep.

A cheap and easy substitute for the NPT test can be performed at home with postage stamps (that's right, postage stamps!). Before going to sleep, the man attaches postage stamps from a perforated roll to his penis by moistening them and pressing them in a snug circle around the base. (Leave them attached to each other in the perforated roll.) If his penis becomes erect during the night, the increased size of the penis will separate the stamps at the perforations and detach them from his penis, indicating that the physical functioning of the penis is still intact and pointing to a psychological source of the erectile difficulty. In contrast, if the penis does not have the normal erections during sleep, the roll of stamps will remain snug around the penis. (Please note that this test does not work with the new self-adhesive rolls of stamps issued by the Post Office, which are not connected to each other like those on a traditional perforated roll.)

Another diagnostic tool is the snap gauge, a device equipped with three bands that is fitted around the shaft of a man's penis at bedtime. Each band is of a different tensile strength so that an increased degree of penile enlargement is required to break each ring. Minor swelling will break only the first ring, further swelling will break the second ring, but only a fully rigid erection will rupture the third ring. The snap gauge has the advantage of being relatively inexpensive and does provide limited information about erective capability. It does not, however, provide any information on the nature and extent of REM sleep or the frequency and duration of nocturnal erections. A single, brief erection would break all three rings, but might not be adequate for intercourse.

The Rigi-Scan is a newer device calibrated to provide information on penile rigidity as well as tumescence (swelling). The Rigi-Scan is actually a small computer that can be easily slipped into a pocket in a Velcro cuff that fits easily around a man's thigh. Connected to the computer are flexible wires linked with two soft cloth-covered loops. One loop is affixed to the tip of the penis and the other to the base. During the night, the Rigi-Scan computer records the number and vigor of the man's erections. He returns the device to his doctor, who gets a computer printout for analysis.

Although many physicians still rely on these tests, especially the NPT, others question whether involuntary erections at night are related to the waking erections of sexual intercourse. Another approach requires a two-stage study (Wincze et al., 1988). The standard NPT test is done and, on another day, penile tumescence is measured as the man views a series of videotapes depicting oral and genital sex followed by a sexually neutral file, usually a travelogue. In addition to the measurement of penile tumescence, subjects are asked to indicate how aroused they were by either film. A substantial number of men who had spontaneous nocturnal erections and described the erotic tapes as arousing did not have an erection when viewing the tape. Possibly these men have a subtle malfunction in the system responsible for activating erections.

Once the basis for erectile dysfunction has been established, a course of treatment must be selected. Probably no medication since the birth control pill has generated more publicity than sildenafil citrate, known better by the trade name given to it by the Pfizer Corporation, *Viagra*. Since its approval by the FDA in 1998, the demand for Viagra has been unprecedented. It was estimated that as many as 10,000 prescriptions per day were being written shortly after it became available (Handy, 1998).

As you learned in the previous section, when a man is sexually stimulated, his brain sends signals to the nerves surrounding the penis that release nitric oxide. The release of nitric oxide causes the penis to make the chemical *cyclic guanosine monophosphate (cyclic GMP)*. Cyclic GMP is the gatekeeper that widens blood vessels in the penis, allowing blood to gush in and causing the penis to become erect. In order to avoid potential embarrassment, another chemical in the body, *phosphodiesterase type 5 (PDE5)*, destroys cyclic GMP once the fun is over. While PDE5 is always present in the penis, cyclic GMP is produced only during arousal. Men with erectile dysfunction may not produce enough cyclic GMP to overtake the PDE5. Viagra works by blocking PDE5 and boosts the effect of cyclic GMP in the penis by slowing down its chemical degradation, allowing cyclic GMP to overtake PDE5 and causing an erection.

In clinical trials Pfizer reported that Viagra had the remarkable success rate of 60 to 80 percent depending on the dosage. A 1998 report in the *New England Journal of Medicine* concluded that Viagra is an effective and well-tolerated treatment for men with erectile dysfunction (Goldstein et al., 1998). However, don't rush out to buy it just yet. The erectile tissue in the penis has a finite number of receptors for cyclic GMP.

"There are two events . . . I regret missing: Woodstock and buying Pfizer at $48."

JIM PETERSEN,
PLAYBOY SENIOR EDITOR

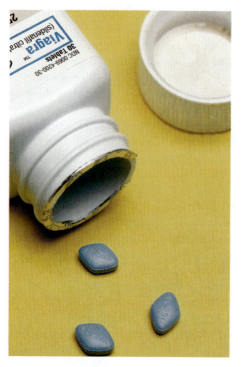

The "little blue pill," Viagra, is believed to be an effective treatment for erectile dysfunction although some men may have serious side effects. The effectiveness of Viagra for women with sexual arousal disorders is being studied.

This means that men with adequate levels of cyclic GMP have their receptors filled already and won't experience any response to the drug. In other words, men who can have an erection naturally probably won't benefit from Viagra.

Viagra is effective, but it isn't a magic cure; some patience is required. Physicians recommend taking Viagra an hour before having sex. After the hour, don't expect an instant reaction; desire, attraction, or stimulation are still required to achieve erection. As with any medication, there are possible side effects. Patients with heart conditions such as clogging of the arteries, and especially those taking blood-pressure-lowering nitrate drugs cannot safely take Viagra. The FDA has reported over 100 deaths of men taking Viagra, of whom 70 percent had risk factors for cardiovascular or cerebrovascular disease. About a third of men experience one or more side effects, including headaches, flushing, indigestion, stuffy nose, and temporary changes in visual perception of color (seeing blue) or brightness (Arora & Melilli, 1999).

Viagra has had some unexpected effects on some relationships. There are reports that some women are less than thrilled when their partners' sexual functioning is restored (Nordheimer, 1998). Women who have their own medical problems or are content with a relationship that does not include sexual intercourse may be disturbed by living with a mate who is suddenly sexually active. This may contribute to another difficulty—infidelity. One woman sued Pfizer, claiming her 10-year common law marriage fell apart after her 70-year-old partner began taking Viagra. She claimed that the company should warn consumers that the drug could be hazardous to marriages.

Recall that Pfizer reported the success rate for Viagra at 60 to 80 percent; this means that it does not work for everyone. The highest failure rate is among men who have had radical prostate surgery and those with long-standing insulin-dependent diabetes. There are a number of other treatments available to treat erectile dysfunction. Among these are *penile injections*, which involve injecting one's penis with a hypodermic needle, a treatment obviously not for the squeamish. Phentolamine (an alpha-blocker), papaverine (a smooth-muscle relaxer), and alprostadil (a prostaglandin) are all effective chemical injections. These chemicals overcome neurologic signals that normally keep the penis flaccid and help encourage the release of intrapenile chemicals like nitric oxide to increase blood flow into the corpora cavernosa. A noninvasive alternative is a *vacuum constriction device* that helps men achieve erection through vacuum pressure. A cylinder is held over the penis and connected to a hand operated vacuum pump. The vacuum increases the flow of blood into the penis, inducing an erection.

If none of these methods is effective, some physicians may recommend a *penile implant*, a prosthetic device to restore erectile capability. There are a number of different types of implants available today. The Scott prosthesis, a multicomponent silicone inflatable penile prosthesis (IPP) was first used in 1973. A tube from a fluid reservoir implanted in the lower abdomen is connected to a bulb in the scrotum. The penis remains in a normal flaccid state until intercourse is desired. Pumping the scrotal bulb to transfer the fluid from the reservoir to the penile implant creates the erection. Another type of implant, the Small-Carrion prosthesis, is inserted in the penile corpora cavernosa and provides a perpetual erection. The Jonas prosthesis is a semimalleable device that depends on a network of internal silver wires to allow for some degree of flexibility. The

OmniPhase and DuraPhase implants have internal cables that allow the device to bend to a flaccid state when not in use. The Finney prosthesis is hinged and converts from flaccid to rigid sate by locking the hinge in place. The newer Hydroflex and FlexiElate, which have internal fluid systems and are designed as self-contained penile prostheses, transform a flaccid penis to an erect state by manipulation of a valve implanted in the tip of the penis.

In 1989 (the pre-Viagra days), an estimated 27,400 penile implants were performed (Spark, 2000). Surgical implants have become less popular, not only because of the success of Viagra, but also because of the cost, surgical complications, mechanical malfunctions, and fears that the silicone material could be harmful (Blakeslee, 1993). Because any existing natural erectile capacity is destroyed by implant surgery, it is recommended for use only in cases where all other treatment possibilities have been unsuccessful.

Counseling and sex therapy are sometimes effective in helping men with erectile dysfunction, especially if there are psychological factors involved. Sex therapy promotes education and symptom relief as well as personal and couples counseling to explore interpersonal and relationship issues that can contribute to sexual dysfunction. Sexual arousal disorders in males and females may owe to any of a number of causes. See Table 4.6.

Female Sexual Arousal Disorder

Female sexual arousal disorder occurs when a woman is unable to attain or maintain adequate vaginal lubrication until completion of sexual activity (APA, 1994). Disorders of female sexual arousal often accompany other sexual disorders such as orgasmic disorders (see following section) and hypoactive sexual desire disorders (Segraves & Segraves, 1993). Symptoms include a lack of vaginal lubrication; decreased clitoral and labial sensation; decreased clitoral and labial engorgement; or a lack of vaginal lengthening, dilation, and arousal. Unfortunately, there has been very little research involving problems of female sexual arousal. However, some of the knowledge gained from studies of male physiology may be applicable to women. Oxygen deprivation of the clitoris may result in sexual problems in women, just as oxygen deprivation of the penis causes dysfunction in men.

Adequate arousal in females depends on both physical and psychological factors. Reduced vaginal lubrication may be due to a low level of estrogen, certain vaginal infections, diseases, medications, drugs, or alcohol. A subjective feeling of arousal may occur

TABLE 4.6
Illnesses That May Interfere with Sexual Arousal or Desire
Testosterone deficiency caused by aging
Disease of the testicles, surgery, or injury to the testicles
Diseases of the pituitary gland
Diabetes
Surgical removal of adrenals or ovaries
Cardiac disease, including coronary artery disease, postcoronary recovery, high blood pressure
Liver problems including hepatitis and cirrhosis
Kidney problems including nephritis, renal failure, dialysis
Pulmonary diseases
Degenerative diseases
Thyroid diseases
Head injuries
Psychomotor epilepsy
Hypothalamic lesions
Pituitary gland tumors
Advanced malignancies

Female Sexual Arousal Disorder: sexual dysfunction in which there is persistent or recurrent inadequate vaginal lubrication for coitus

without lubrication and vaginal expansion in postmenopausal women (Leiblum et al., 1983), nursing women, or those who have undergone treatment for pelvic cancer (Schover, Evans, & Von Eschenbach, 1987). The more common psychological bases of female sexual arousal disorder include feelings of guilt, a deep-seated anger toward a partner, a history of sexual trauma, anxiety, and ineffective stimulation by the partner (Morokoff, 1993).

Treatment for Female Sexual Arousal Disorder

The medical and financial success of Viagra has led researchers to investigate the possibility that the drug might also be helpful to women with sexual arousal disorders. Like the penis, the clitoris becomes engorged with blood during sexual arousal. Viagra appears to work the same way in women as it does in men, leading to increased blood flow to the vagina, clitoris, and labia causing engorgement of these tissues, enhanced sensation and increased vaginal lubrication. However, Viagra will not be approved for women until the completion of clinical trials, which are now ongoing in the United States. Researchers caution that while it may work for some women, women who have the combined problems of sexual desire disorder and sexual arousal disorder would most likely not benefit from Viagra.

Any treatment for a sexual dysfunction in women or men should begin with a medical examination to rule out the contribution of medical problems to the difficulty. Once physical problems have been ruled out, treatment focuses on reducing and eliminating any anxiety that inhibits the natural reflexes involved in the arousal process. In therapy, clients learn that they cannot will themselves to an aroused state and that they do not need to perform to become sexually aroused.

ORGASMIC DISORDERS

Orgasmic disorders include difficulty or inability to reach orgasm after sufficient sexual stimulation and arousal, or any difficulty or delay in the timing of orgasm. The former are more common in women, and the latter are more common in men. Who determines whether a man ejaculates prematurely? How fast is too fast? Must a woman experience an orgasm during every sexual encounter? Perhaps the best way to approach this issue is consensus; if neither partner is dissatisfied then there probably isn't a problem.

Premature Ejaculation

There is as much disagreement among the experts as to what constitutes premature ejaculation as there is among the parties involved. Masters, Johnson, and Kolodny (1994) state that a man ejaculates prematurely if his partner isn't orgasmic in at least half of their coital episodes, while Kaplan (1974) suggests that it occurs when a man does not have voluntary control over when he ejaculates. The American Psychiatric Association (1994) defines premature ejaculation as "persistent or recurrent ejaculation with minimal sexual stimulation before or shortly after penetration and before the person wishes it" (p. 511). Certainly, ejaculation can be considered premature if it occurs prior to penetration. In this text we define **premature ejaculation** as a sexual dysfunction in which ejaculation occurs so rapidly that it interferes with the couple's sexual satisfaction.

Some therapists prefer the term *rapid* or *early ejaculation* because of the implication that the term *premature* connotes. Men with this problem are not underdeveloped, immature, or any less masculine than other men. While the condition is sometimes associated with young, sexually inexperienced men, it can occur in men of all ages and backgrounds.

There is no definitive physical or psychological explanation for premature ejaculation. Medical problems such as abnormalities of the prostate gland or inflammation of the genitals rarely are involved although occasionally unusually high nerve sensitivity

Orgasmic Disorders: Sexual dysfunctions in which despite sufficient sexual stimulation an individual is persistently or recurrently unable to reach orgasm

Premature Ejaculation: sexual dysfunction in which ejaculation occurs so rapidly as to interfere with the couple's sexual satisfaction

around the opening of the penile glands and frenulum can lead to premature ejaculation. There *is* a physiological point of no return; recall from Chapter 3 that in the second stage of the male orgasmic phase, once the external sphincter muscle relaxes to allow the passage of semen into the penis, ejaculation will occur automatically (see section on Masters and Johnson EPOR Model in Chapter 3).

Contrary to popular myth, premature ejaculation is not caused by excessive masturbation. Inattention to the sensory signals that indicate ejaculation is about to occur is the most common cause of premature ejaculation. Since most boys have their first ejaculatory experience as a result of either a wet dream or masturbation (which we will discuss in Chapter 12) it is not surprising that they have no reason to adjust the tempo of their earliest sexual encounters in order to accommodate a partner. This conditioning of rapid ejaculation is fostered by both private masturbatory experiences (in which speedy responsiveness may be a necessity in order not to be caught in the act by family members) and early sexual encounters in which noncoital sex play also places a premium on swift ejaculation where discovery also may be an issue (Master, Johnson, & Kolodny, 1994) (see CAMPUS CONFIDENTIAL box). One study indicated that a long history of using withdrawal as a method of contraception might condition rapid responsiveness (Pierson & D'Antonio, 1974).

Anxiety can play a role in rapid ejaculation, although it may be unclear whether this is the cause or an effect of the problem. Anxiety triggers electrical and chemical changes in the nervous system that may accelerate the ejaculatory reflex; at the same time, performance anxiety (which will be discussed in Chapter 16) may heighten the loss of ejaculatory control. A vicious cycle can develop; the more anxious a man becomes, the less ejaculatory control he may have.

Treatment for Premature Ejaculation

The basis of current therapy for rapid ejaculation is to enable men to tolerate progressively more intense sexual stimulation, to alleviate their concerns about sexual performance, and to help them concentrate on pleasure rather than ejaculatory control (Levine, 1992). There are various techniques to help a man focus his attention on the buildup of erotic sensation in his body as he approaches orgasm.

The Stop-Start Technique   A therapy often recommended for men troubled by premature ejaculation is based on the *stop-start technique* first developed by urologist James Semans (1956). The stop-start technique is designed to prolong sensations before orgasm, thereby giving the man the chance to experience and control his ejaculatory reflex (Figure 4.3).

The man's partner is instructed to stimulate his penis orally or manually until he feels he is about to have an orgasm. Stimulation is then stopped until the pre-ejaculatory sensations subside. During each session the couple repeats the stop-start procedure several times and then allows ejaculation to occur on the last cycle. This exercise is repeated once a day for 15 to 30 minutes. As the man's ejaculatory control improves, the couple progresses to genital-to-genital contact with the man's partner sitting astride him so that the man can relax his body. The man puts his penis in his partner's vagina and lies quietly for a few moments before beginning slow movements. Couples are encouraged not to think of this as intercourse but instead to look at it as an extension of the touching that has occurred during previous sessions. When the man begins to feel close to orgasm, they stop and relax. The stop-start technique is continued as the man progressively increases ejaculatory control.

The Squeeze Technique   The *squeeze technique* is another method of treating premature ejaculation. When the man feels that ejaculation is about to occur, his partner places the middle and index fingers on the front of the penis, below the head of the penis or at the base, with the thumb on the back side, and squeezes his penis for about 4 seconds (Figure 4.4). Considerable pressure can be applied without causing pain on the

CAMPUS CONFIDENTIAL

"It wasn't a big deal in high school when it seemed like sex always had to be in a hurry. I mean, how much time can a guy spend in the bathroom without someone pounding on the door asking if you're all right? And parents' couches and cars aren't exactly ideal places for doing it. Back then, sex always had to be hurried up. But now that I'm a little older, have a serious girlfriend, and my own apartment, it's different. I really want to be able to take my time and enjoy it, but it seems like as soon as I start getting excited I come. My girlfriend doesn't complain, but I know it must be frustrating for her, too." ●

FIGURE 4.3 The Stop-Start Technique. The woman repeatedly provokes an erection and then allows it to subside. This avoids the promotion of performance anxiety because there is no demand for coitus. By experiencing repeated erections, the man loses any fear that loss of an erection means it will not return.

erect penis. While some men may ejaculate while their partner is applying the squeeze technique or shortly after, this usually does not happen after a few sessions.

The couple is instructed to use the technique during a minimum of three different sessions within a day or two of each other. Eventually, continuing to use the squeeze technique, the couple proceeds to the female superior position, with insertion of the penis in the vagina and slow thrusting. The woman dismounts and squeezes every 1 to 2 minutes before the couple moves on to more vigorous thrusting and ejaculation. Masters, Johnson, and Kolodny (1994) claim that a 5-year follow-up of 196 couples who came to their institute for 2 weeks of treatment for premature ejaculation demonstrated a 98 percent success rate using the squeeze technique. The man can use both the stop-start technique and the squeeze technique alone during masturbation; the gains made can then be transferred to sexual activity with a partner.

Drug Treatment Some researchers have reported successful treatment for premature ejaculation using small doses of drugs normally prescribed for depression or obsessive behavior (Waldinger et al., 1998). In several cases, men who had ejaculated within seconds to a minute or two of beginning intercourse were able to delay ejaculation for 20 minutes or longer (Petit, 1994). In one study, men receiving clomipramine reported a significantly greater sense of control over their orgasm while on the drug (Strassberg et al., 1999).

FIGURE 4.4 The Squeeze Technique. The man or his partner applies firm pressure for several seconds below the glans or at the base of the penis (front and back, not sides).

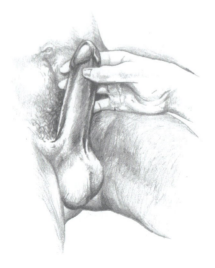
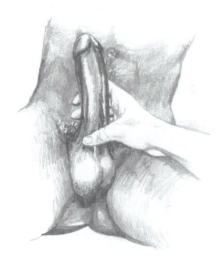

Male Orgasmic Disorder

For some men the problem is not that they ejaculate too soon, but that they are not able to ejaculate at all. Men who are able to have erections but cannot ejaculate may suffer from **male orgasmic disorder,** a condition also known as ejaculatory incompetence, or delayed, inhibited, or retarded ejaculation. Approximately 4 to 9 percent of men suffer from an inability to ejaculate during sexual intercourse (Spector & Carey, 1990). Some may be able to ejaculate by masturbating or by oral sex, but cannot climax during coital activity (Munjack & Kanno, 1979). A related disorder, in which there is seepage of semen without orgasmic sensations, is known as *partial ejaculatory incompetence* (Kaplan, 1974).

Treatment for Male Orgasmic Disorder

Physical causes of ejaculatory incompetence include multiple sclerosis, neurological damage that interferes with neural control of ejaculation, and drug side effects. Helen Singer Kaplan (1974) suggests a psychological cause: Some men with this disorder may be unconsciously "holding back" their ejaculate from their partners because of underlying hostility or resentment. Masters and Johnson (1970) discovered a possible cultural basis; they found that men with delayed ejaculation frequently had strict religious backgrounds that may have left a residue of unresolved guilt about sex. Emotional factors, such as fear of pregnancy, may also play a role. As with other sexual dysfunctions, men with retarded ejaculation often attempt to resolve the problem by "trying harder," which as you might guess only compounds the problem. Once medical causes have been ruled out, treatment of underlying psychological factors is undertaken.

Female Orgasmic Disorder

The terms **anorgasmia** and **female orgasmic disorder** refer to the inability of women to experience orgasm. According to the American Psychiatric Association (1994), the condition is diagnosed when there is a persistent or recurrent delay in, or absence of, orgasm following a normal sexual excitement phase. The prevalence of women who suffer from orgasmic dysfunction is estimated to be 5 to 10 percent (Spector & Carey, 1990). Some women who are anorgasmic may be extremely dissatisfied and depressed about the absence of orgasms during sexual activity. Others may experience arousal and lubrication, and enjoy their sexual relationships, in which case there is no cause for concern.

CROSS-CULTURAL PERSPECTIVES

Mangaia

From an early age boys and girls on Mangaia, a Polynesian island, are encouraged to explore their sexuality through sexual play and masturbation. Parents don't just condone childhood sexual behaviors; they encourage their children to develop their sexuality. Although they might pretend to be asleep when a boy came to visit their daughter in the family hut, parents listen for the sounds that would tell the couple had reached orgasm. Mangaians don't value virginity because virgins don't know how to provide sexual pleasure. Mangaian males are instructed about the benefits of bringing their female partners to multiple orgasms before ejaculating and they practice these techniques as often as possible. Girls also are encouraged to express their sexuality and all Mangaian females are reported to experience orgasm (Marshall, 1971).

Male Orgasmic Disorder: sexual dysfunction in which a male is unable to ejaculate during coitus

Female Orgasmic Disorder: sexual dysfunction in which a woman is unable to achieve orgasm during sexual activity

Anorgasmia: failure to experience orgasm

Inis Beag

On the Irish island of Inis Beag, it was thought to be abnormal for women to experience orgasm. Premarital sex was all but unknown on the island. Couples married at a relatively late age, usually in the late 30s for men and middle 20s for women, and before marriage men and women socialized separately. Anthropologist John Messenger (1971) reports that any woman who found pleasure in sex, and especially one who experienced orgasm, was considered to be deviant.

Mothers taught their daughters that they would have to submit to their husband's animal cravings and that the husband was always the initiator of sex. When a man and wife did have intercourse, because of taboos against nudity they did so with their clothes on, with only brief foreplay and the man ejaculated as rapidly as he could. Men of Inis Beag believed that sexual activity would drain their strength, so they avoided sex before sporting activities or strenuous work.

About 5 percent of the cases of orgasmic dysfunction in women are the result of organic causes (Masters, Johnson, & Kolodny, 1985). Such causes include chronic illnesses such as diabetes, hormone deficiencies, alcoholism, pelvic infections, or other conditions that cause damage to the pelvic nerves.

Anorgasmia can also have a psychological basis. One is a psychological link between sex and problematic past experiences. Anorgasmia can also serve as a defense against an anxiety-producing situation (Levine, 1992). However, the most common cause of female orgasmic disorder may be the persistent belief that sex equals intercourse. As discussed in Chapter 3, most women do not experience orgasm without adequate stimulation of the clitoris.

It is extremely rare for women to experience *rapid female orgasm*, the female equivalent of premature ejaculation. Some women do report that they have orgasms too quickly before their partners and then are not interested in further stimulation. However, since women are more capable of having multiple orgasms, rapid orgasm may not necessarily be a problem for the individual or the couple.

Treatment for Female Orgasmic Disorder

During the Victorian era, physicians diagnosed a broad range of women's problems as due to hysteria, an affliction that was thought to be linked to the female sex organs. To treat hysteria, physicians routinely used "pelvic massage," essentially manually stimulating the women to orgasm. Given the Victorian reticence about sexuality, it is quite plausible that these visits constituted the only source of orgasms for some Victorian women. Such treatments may have encouraged women to make and keep regular appointments with their physicians, but the physicians themselves did not seem to have been fond of this part of their duties. To spare their own fingers the exertions of pelvic massage, physicians eagerly adopted the **vibrator** when it was invented in 1883, and it became one of the standard medical tools for several decades (Maines, 2000). Today vibrators usually are battery operated but early models were steam powered. Neither the diagnosis of hysteria nor the treatment of female patients with vibrator-induced orgasms is part of mainstream medical practice today.

Anorgasmic women need to be reassured that orgasm is possible but that it is not always essential to a satisfying sex life. They must also become comfortable with the idea that they are responsible for their own orgasms and accept the clitoris as a sexual organ. A willingness to learn to stimulate themselves or teach their partners to stimulate them is also essential to successful treatment. With knowledge of and comfort with clitoral stimulation, it is highly likely that anorgasmic women will respond to treatment.

Vibrator: a mechanical device that shakes slightly and quickly, which is held against the body to achieve sexual pleasure

Some couples find that the coital alignment technique (sometimes called "the new and improved missionary position," see Chapter 12 for a description of the missionary position) is most effective for female orgasm. More than a position, the coital alignment technique is a coordinated movement in which the male lies on top of his partner with his head next to hers. The woman wraps her legs around her partner with her feet resting on his calves. The man positions himself so that the base of his erect penis pushes up against his partner's clitoris and begins a subtle, rocking movement. As the woman pushes up on the top of her partner's penile shaft, he resists with less force than she pushes. Then, as he pushes down against her clitoris, she resists with less force than he pushes. The rocking, vibrating movement of this technique (rather than the standard friction of thrusting in other coital positions) may stimulate female orgasm.

Many therapists recommend learning to masturbate to orgasm as one of the most effective techniques for treating anorgasmia. Masturbation increases body awareness through self-exploration and self-stimulation. Therapists also may recommend sensate focus exercises or have more general suggestions for increasing comfort with one's own body and learning what kinds of thoughts, touches, and sensations are most stimulating and pleasurable.

In May 2000 the Eros-CTD (clitoral therapy device) became the first treatment for female orgasmic disorder approved by the FDA. In essence the clitoral therapy device is a small pump with a tiny plastic cup attachment that fits over the clitoris and surrounding tissue. It provides gentle suction, simulating the sucking effect of oral sex and stimulating blood flow to the vaginal area.

After a woman is able to experience orgasms through mechanical or self-stimulation, she may proceed to experiencing orgasm with her partner. A variety of activities may be recommended, including masturbating in the presence of a partner and placing her hand over her partner's hand when the partner stimulates her manually. Figure 4.5 shows a recommended position for engaging in the latter activity.

Once the couple proceeds to intercourse, many women find that they must experiment with positions to find those that provide the most effective clitoral stimulation. The female superior position is often suggested because it allows the woman

FIGURE 4.5 A position used in treating female sexual disorders.

FIGURE 4.6 Coitus in the Female-Superior Position. This position is suggested for female orgasmic disorder because it allows the woman freedom of movement and control of her genital sensations.

freedom of movement and control of her genital sensations (Figure 4.6). Using this position the woman is better able to experience the most pleasurable sensations, and to sustain them longer through deliberately slow thrusting, thus avoiding rapid orgasm by the male.

As we have stated previously, some women may be unable to climax through intercourse alone. Oral or manual stimulation prior to intercourse, manual stimulation during intercourse by the woman or her partner, or the use of a vibrator during intercourse are options that can allow a woman to experience orgasm during intercourse.

SEXUAL PAIN DISORDERS

Sometimes sex is not just unsatisfying, it is actually painful. Although sexual stimulation triggers the pain, the primary cause of **sexual pain disorders** can be physically or psychologically based.

Priapism

Priapism refers to a condition in which a man experiences a continued erection that will not subside. This can be extremely painful. Because priapism can lead to damage of the penis's vascular system to the point where erectile ability is permanently destroyed, the man must seek immediate medical assistance. Priapism is a potential negative side effect of several commonly prescribed medications, and drug-related causes are implicated in 15 to 36 percent of cases (Weiner & Lowe, 1998). Typically, priapism is due to a failure in the mechanism that frees the blood trapped in an erect penis. It also can be the symptom of a severe physiological problem such as spinal cord disease or leukemia.

Treatment for Priapism

Priapism is a medical emergency and requires immediate intervention. An erection that persists beyond 6 hours deprives the penis of adequate oxygen. Treatment of priapism

Sexual Pain Disorders: Sexual dysfunctions in which persistent or recurrent pain is experienced during sexual intercourse

Priapism: a condition characterized by persistent erection of the penis

usually requires the infusion of chemicals. Often this treatment alone allows blood to drain from the penis. For those men whose priapism remains even after medical treatment, surgery is required.

Dyspareunia

Dyspareunia, genital pain during intercourse, is classified as a sexual dysfunction. However, since sexual and urological functions are closely related anatomically, hormonally, and psychologically, some scientists argue that it would be more accurate to describe dyspareunia as a pain syndrome (Meana et al., 1997).

Dyspareunia is more commonly diagnosed in women, but some men also suffer from this disorder. The foreskin of uncircumcised men may be so tight that sexual arousal is painful. Inadequate hygiene of the foreskin may result in infection that can cause irritation of the glans. Infections of the penis, foreskin, testes, urethra, or the prostate can cause men discomfort or extreme pain during sexual activity. Other possible causes are an allergic reaction to a spermicidal cream, foam, condom, or diaphragm.

Anything that disrupts the secretion of vaginal lubrication during sexual arousal can result in vaginal dryness, the most common cause of female pain during intercourse. There are many factors that can cause insufficient lubrication, including inadequate stimulation prior to intercourse, changes in a woman's hormone levels caused by menopause or breast-feeding, and medications such as antihistamines. Some women find that using a lubricated condom or water-soluble lubricant is helpful. Postmenopausal women may consider hormone replacement therapy to alleviate vaginal dryness.

Treatment for Dyspareunia

Pain felt at or near the entrance to the vagina may be the result of a vaginal or urinary tract infection or can be related to scarring from an episiotomy during childbirth. Spermicides, feminine hygiene products, and tight clothing also can create soreness. Feeling pain deep inside the vagina or in the lower abdomen during intercourse may be a sign of endometriosis, pelvic inflammatory disease, or other reproductive tract disorders.

Medical research has found that some women are allergic to their partners' seminal fluid. Known by the two-dollar term *human seminal plasma hypersensitivity*, the condition was first described in 1958. A 1997 study found that 12 percent of patients examined by allergists met the diagnostic criteria for an allergy to seminal fluid (Bernstein et al., 1997). Symptoms include wheezing, itching and hives all over the body, chest tightness, vomiting, or diarrhea. Severe reactions include loss of consciousness or complete circulatory collapse.

Nearly all the research on dyspareunia concerns vaginal intercourse but some investigators are examining the frequency and severity of *anodyspareunia*, pain in same-sex anal intercourse. One study found that approximately 12 percent of gay men found anal sex too painful to continue. Factors associated with a greater amount of pain were anxiety, depth and rate of thrusting, and discomfort with their homosexuality (Rosser et al., 1998).

Vaginismus

Vaginismus is the recurrent or persistent involuntary contraction of the muscles surrounding the outer third of the vagina when vaginal penetration is attempted. The vaginal muscles clamp down, making penetration painful and sometimes even impossible. A woman may suffer from this disorder throughout her life or suddenly develop vaginismus in response to a sexual trauma or a medical condition. Some researchers question if the diagnostic emphasis should be placed on fear or resistance to penetration rather than on pain or distress (Ng, 1999; Reissing et al., 1999).

Dyspareunia: sexual dysfunction in which there is a persistent or recurrent pain or discomfort during coitus

Vaginismus: a sexual dysfunction characterized by involuntary spasmodic contractions of the vaginal muscles that prevent penetration or make coitus painful

Treatment for Vaginismus

Once a medical problem is ruled out, treatment typically takes a behavioral approach. Relaxation and body awareness exercises such as sensate focus exercises are often recommended. Once a woman becomes more relaxed, the next step is insertion of her finger or a narrow vaginal dilator. After relaxing her vagina with a finger or dilator inside, she is instructed to consciously contract and relax the vaginal muscles. The woman controls the pace of treatment at all times. She progresses to wider dilators or more fingers. When the woman is able to tolerate insertion and containment of a dilator or number of fingers approximately equivalent in diameter to a penis, her partner may then join her. Her partner begins by inserting a finger into her vagina. After her partner can insert several fingers without the woman experiencing an involuntary vaginal muscle spasm, the couple may then attempt relaxed, nondemand coitus at the woman's pace (LoPiccolo & Stock, 1986).

EFFECTS OF DRUGS AND ALCOHOL ON SEXUAL FUNCTION

Sex, drugs, and rock-and-roll. At least two of these things do *not* go together! Although some people report that the use of drugs and alcohol make them feel less inhibited and freer to enjoy sex, acute or chronic use of alcohol, recreational and many prescription drugs can produce sexual dysfunction in both men and women. In addition to the physical problems related to drug and alcohol use and abuse, substance abuse may affect emotions and strain relationships, further contributing to sexual problems.

Alcohol and many other substances exert their primary effects on the brain: the cerebral cortex, autonomic nervous system, and the limbic system ("pleasure center"). Impairment of the cerebral cortex and the limbic system interferes with motivation, judgment, and emotionality. Alcohol and other drugs also can interfere with the functioning of the endocrine system.

Alcohol, barbiturates, and other depressants decrease spinal reflexes and transmission in peripheral nerves. In women, vaginal secretions, vaginal blood volume, arousal, and orgasm are reduced as alcohol levels increase. In men, depressants can inhibit sexual arousal, reduce erectile capacity, and slow or eliminate ejaculation and orgasm (Gilman, 1985; Smith, 1977).

In moderate to high doses, and especially with chronic use, alcohol can result in inhibited spinal reflexes, and testicular and liver damage. Damage to the testicles decreases serum testosterone levels and increases estrogen levels. Increased estrogen can cause irreversible breast enlargement in men. The decreased testosterone levels lower sperm counts, and it is possible that permanent sterility and testicular atrophy may result from long-term excessive drinking. Effects on women who drink regularly and for a prolonged period include atrophy of the ovaries, menstrual difficulties, and infertility (Reinisch, 1991). Women who drink while they are pregnant increase their risk of miscarriages and fetal abnormalities.

One drug that is commonly abused because it is believed to intensify or prolong the sensation of orgasm is amyl nitrate (snappers or poppers). Some people report that inhaling the drug at the instant of orgasm enhances their pleasure. However, valid scientific data of the effectiveness of amyl nitrate is lacking; its side effects, including dizziness, headaches, and fainting, can be dangerous.

Although cigarette advertisers often use sexual messages to sell their products, cigarette smoking can cause diminished sexual response. Smoking causes the blood vessels to constrict, reducing the flow of blood to the heart, lower extremities, and the pelvic area—including the penis, thereby decreasing the frequency and duration of erections (Mohr & Beutler, 1990). Smoking also decreases the levels of estrogen.

There are some reports that in small doses stimulants such as amphetamines (speed, uppers) and cocaine may cause men to have a sustained erection and delay in orgasm. These drugs activate the central nervous system but are not known to have specific sexual effects. In moderate to high doses these drugs can result in erectile and orgasmic

TABLE 4.7

Prescription Medications and Sexual Problems

Type of Drug	Some Brand Names	Potential Problems
Tranquilizers; antianxiety drugs	Valium, Xanax, Ativan	Changes in libido; erection problems; delayed orgasm/ejaculation
Antidepressants	Prozac, Zoloft, Paxil, Effexor	Changes in libido; delayed orgasm/ejaculation
Ulcer medication	Tagamet	Decreased libido; erectile dysfunction
Some birth control pills	Ortho-Novum, Loestrin, Ovcon 35 and 50	Lubrication changes

dysfunction. Heroin also produces decreased erection and orgasm in moderate to high doses, especially with chronic use.

Oftentimes patients taking prescription medications are surprised to learn that a drug they are taking to treat one problem is causing another. Many commonly prescribed medications have side effects affecting sexual desire, arousal, or functioning. It is wise to consult your doctor about the side effects of any medication that you will be taking on a long-term basis (Table 4.7).

Common sense would indicate that the best course of treatment for sexual problems caused by substance abuse is to stop the abuse. But quitting can cause its own problems. Usually sexual functioning returns to normal with abstinence from drugs or alcohol or the discontinuation of problem-causing medications. However, withdrawal from alcohol and other drugs, especially depressants, may result in problems with premature ejaculation.

SEXUAL THERAPY

Many people suffer in silence when they have a sexual problem. Some may not seek help because they are embarrassed about the problem. However, it is not necessarily their own embarrassment that they are worried about. A study conducted for the Partnership for Women's Health at Columbia University (1999) found that 68 percent of people with sexual problems were reluctant to mention them to their health-care provider because they were afraid that the discussion would embarrass their physicians! And they might not be completely wrong—many health-care professionals, including physicians, receive no specific training in treating sexual disorders.

The success and social acceptance of Viagra has opened the door for many patients seeking help for sexual problems. Many are further encouraged by the fact that other drugs, including neurotransmitters such as dopamine and neuropeptides like oxytocin, show early evidence of effectively treating arousal and orgasm disorders in both men and women. As you have already learned, factors other than biology, including depression, stress, a history of sexual or emotional abuse, body image and self-esteem problems, and relationship difficulties, also may contribute to sexual dysfunction. Some sex therapists have been concerned about the growing medicalization, or "viagratization," of treatment for sexual dysfunction, while others call upon sex therapists to join physicians and realize that "it is not about whose approach is better; it is about determining the best approach for each individual patient and sharing in this new era of opportunities" (Berman & Berman, 2001, p. xvi).

There are many options for those seeking sexual therapy. Among those we shall discuss are psychotherapy, online sex therapy (see EXPLORING SEXUALITY ONLINE box), the PLISSIT model, psychoanalytic and behavioral treatment approaches, and psychosexual therapy.

Psychotherapy

Psychotherapy, often referred to as *talk therapy*, focuses on understanding emotions and resolving relationship problems. While there are a variety of psychological methods and techniques designed to treat sexual disorders, no one therapeutic approach has proven to be superior to others (Hubble, Duncan, & Miller, 1999; Norcross & Newman, 1992). Extensive reviews of studies documenting the use of psychotherapy for sexual dysfunction (O'Donohue, Dopke & Swingen, 1997; O'Donahue, Swingen, Dopke & Regev, 1999) found that most of the studies had serious flaws. While there has been a proliferation of models and techniques claiming high success, there is "a paucity of controlled outcome research or studies of treatment process variables in sex therapy" (Rosen & Leiblum, 1995, p. 87).

Although the authors of these studies concluded there are no well-established psychological treatments for sexual problems, many people find psychotherapy to be extremely helpful. It is suggested that "successful sex therapy is more about therapy with people who happen to be experiencing sexual difficulties than about the application of a unique therapeutic modality or treatment techniques" (Donahey & Miller, 2001, p. 222).

 EXPLORING SEXUALITY ONLINE

Online Sexual Therapy

The Internet is a wonderful tool for obtaining information about sexual problems, but it may not be the best place to seek treatment for those problems. Clinicians currently are offering e-mail therapy addressing a number of problems, including sexual dysfunction.

Potential advantages of online therapy include affordability, convenience, and anonymity. While it may be easier to share your sexual problems on the small screen, it is critical that you take any advice given online with a grain of salt, and not put your life and well-being into a stranger's hands. While some groups, like the American Counseling Association, have issued guidelines for practicing psychotherapy on the Internet, just because someone has a Web site doesn't mean that person has the credentials or expertise to help you. Therapy relies heavily on the relationship between the client and therapist and, in the case of group therapy, the client and the other members of the group. Therapists listen not only to what is said and how it's said, but what is not said. These relationships can't be replicated online. In addition, privacy should not be mistaken for confidentiality. It may be difficult to know who has access to your online descriptions of your sexual problems.

The use of the Internet for prescribing and dispensing medication has also become increasingly prevalent in recent years. Many patients are receiving Viagra from an Internet physician. The American Medical Association believes that certain guidelines must be followed before prescribing any medication: a medical history is obtained or readily available; information about the benefits and risks of the prescribed medication is given to the patient; an examination of the patient is undertaken to determine a specific diagnosis and whether there is a medical problem; additional interventions and follow-up care are initiated if necessary, especially for drugs such as Viagra that may have serious side effects (see page 114). Adhering to these guidelines is impossible in an online physician/patient relationship.

PLISSIT

No, not "pssst!"—PLISSIT! The acronym PLISSIT stands for Permission, Limited Information, Specific Suggestion, and Intensive Therapy. Determining whether you need expert help with a sexual problem, and what kind of therapy might be right for you, is made easier by the PLISSIT model developed by Jack Annon in 1974. PLISSIT consists of four sequential therapeutic levels, each of which provides increasingly intensive and in-depth therapy (Figure 4.7).

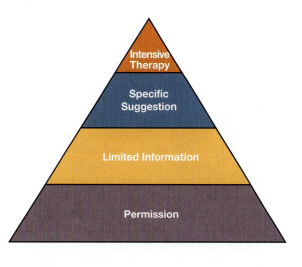

FIGURE 4.7 The PLISSIT Model of Sex Therapy. Some sex problems are resolved at each step so fewer people progress to the next step.

Many of those with a sexual problem only need *Permission* to talk about their sexual concerns in a nonjudgmental and supportive environment. The process of open communication about sexual matters is sometimes sufficient to resolve a problem. Others may need *Limited Information* to increase their general knowledge and understanding about sexuality or about a specific sexual concern. There is a great deal of misinformation about sex in locker rooms and bedrooms across the country (and throughout the world); receiving accurate information may alleviate the individual's concerns enough to eliminate the difficulty. *Specific Suggestions* made by the therapist regarding sexual behaviors, attitudes, or techniques may resolve sexual conflicts for those who are comfortable discussing sexual concerns and have adequate information but are in need of assistance with a particular situation. Activities such as sensate focus exercises may be recommended to reduce anxiety or enhance sexual pleasure. Most of those with sexual concerns may need only steps 1, 2, and/or 3 and a few brief sessions to resolve their problems. Others may have significant emotional difficulties or relationship problems that require *Intensive Therapy*. Intensive therapy consists of psychotherapy combining behavioral techniques with insight-oriented therapy, that is, the exploration of emotions and experiences that have contributed to sexual expression.

Psychoanalytic Treatment Approach

Psychoanalysts generally hold the view that sexual disturbances are symptoms of emotional conflicts arising in childhood. The disturbances are likely to persist unless the underlying unconscious conflict is resolved. Traditional psychoanalytic therapies are not intended to reduce symptoms, and are thus not specific treatments for sexual disorders. Rather, psychoanalysis is an attempt to understand the underlying meaning of these symptoms in the context of the patient's life experience. This analytic approach provides the patient the opportunity to rework developmental issues and to restructure personality, eliminating the sexual conflict (Meissner, 1980). However, psychoanalysis is not for everyone. It is an expensive, long-term commitment, and if it turns out that the disorder has no deep-rooted cause, it may not work (Adams, 1980).

The crucial difference between the psychoanalytic approach and the behavioral approach (discussed next) is that psychoanalytic treatment regards the sexual problem as a symptom of a deeper, more important problem, whereas the behaviorist regards the sexual problem as the primary problem to be solved. To a psychoanalyst, merely fixing the symptom so that the person can have sex is not a cure. The behaviorist focuses exclusively on curing the sexual problem. Many sexual problems are indeed specific to sex, and so the behaviorist's narrow focus is often justified (and quite enough to satisfy the patient!). In other cases, sexual problems may well be linked to broader emotional problems or to mental illness; in such cases focusing narrowly on the sexual aspect of the problem will not be effective.

Behavioral Treatment Approach

Behavioral therapy is geared directly to changing behaviors. In a behavioral approach, "the consideration of intrapsychic dynamics [the underlying conflict in the psychoanalytic approach] may often be irrelevant, a waste of time and distract from an efficient course of treatment" (Fensterheim & Kantor, 1980, p. 314). From a behavioral perspective, a person can be emotionally healthy yet still have sexual difficulties. These problems will respond to conditioning techniques designed to eliminate any anxiety associated with sexual activity, such as the treatments described earlier for premature ejaculation. Behavioral models of sex therapy usually are short-term and attempt to modify the dysfunctional behavior directly, as opposed to the long view taken by psychoanalytic therapy.

Many sex therapists use, or are influenced by, the behavioral techniques developed by the Masters and Johnson Institute in St. Louis, Missouri. The Institute offers an intensive treatment format in which the couple meets with a male and female cotherapist team over a 10-day period. Couples are encouraged to focus strictly on their relationship with a minimum of external distractions or competing responsibilities as they deepen their emotional and physical intimacy. Therapy begins with an initial evaluation interview with both partners. Psychological and physical contributions to the problem are explored. If a physical problem is suspected, a specialist is consulted. The Masters and Johnson Institute claims a high success rate in the use of its behavioral approach to treat primary and secondary orgasmic dysfunction, vaginismus, erectile dysfunction, premature ejaculation, and ejaculatory incompetence. However, therapists outside the Masters and Johnson Institute have used their methods with mixed results.

Some research evidence suggests that a single therapist is about as effective as the male-female team used at the Institute (Arentewicz & Schmidtt, 1983; Libman, Fitchen, & Brender, 1985; LoPiccolo & Stock, 1986). Others have found that treatment benefits do not seem to depend on whether the sessions are conducted within a short time period, as in the Masters and Johnson method, or spaced over time (Libman, Fitchen, & Brender, 1985). Individual therapy with preorgasmic women and group treatment programs also have been successful in treating women experiencing orgasmic dysfunction (Cotten-Huston & Wheeler, 1983; Kilmann et al., 1987). In addition, critics have noted that Masters and Johnson followed up on a relatively small number of patients and therefore may have seriously underestimated the actual number of treatment reversals (failures) (Adams, 1980; Zilbergeld & Evans, 1980). Still, given the drawbacks of psychoanalysis mentioned earlier, it seems appropriate to try the behaviorist approaches first when dealing with the majority of sexual problems.

Psychosexual Therapy

Treatment techniques developed by psychiatrist Helen Singer Kaplan (1974, 1979, 1983) combine the behavioral approach with psychoanalytic methods. She called her approach **psychosexual therapy.** Kaplan viewed sexual problems as having both immediate and remote causes. Unlike Masters and Johnson, Kaplan's treatment method does not require that the couple come to a specific location. Instead, they practice the assigned exercises in their own homes and see a single therapist, rather than the cotherapists of opposite sexes in the Masters and Johnson approach. Therapists using Kaplan's method first approach the problem with behavioral therapy. Sessions focus on improving communication, eliminating anxiety, increasing sexual knowledge, and improving sexual skills. (Do you recognize any similarities to PLISSIT here?) Only in severe cases is more prolonged psychoanalytic treatment required to probe deeply into the client's personality. An initial evaluation interview includes a medical, psychiatric, and sexual history. The typical course of treatment, which lasts between 6 and 16 weeks, consists of sexual tasks designed specifically for each couple combined with weekly or twice weekly sessions with the therapist to report the success of the exercises and explore feelings the couple experienced while doing their homework.

Psychosexual Therapy: treatment approach developed by Helen Singer Kaplan that combines behavioral and psychoanalytic techniques

Sex Surrogates or Hookers?

Some therapists, including Masters and Johnson, have used a substitute sex partner, or sex surrogate, to treat sexual problems. The surrogate, working under the close supervision of a therapist, is a trained, experienced professional who can teach effective sexual arousal techniques. The surrogates used by Masters and Johnson were unpaid volunteers. Since there is no emotional relationship, it is thought that a surrogate can be a non-threatening sex partner with whom the client can practice and from whom the client can receive useful feedback. Although the Masters and Johnson Institute claimed that therapy with surrogates helped 32 of 41 clients reverse a sexual dysfunction, because of adverse publicity they discontinued the use of partner surrogates in their programs.

Some of those opposed to the use of surrogates base their arguments on moral premises. They believe that surrogates are little more than prostitutes and that it is wrong to condone sex between unmarried persons. Others may object to surrogates for therapeutic reasons, since the ability to have satisfactory sexual relations with a surrogate does not ensure the ability to function with one's own sex partner. Some programs continue to use sexual surrogates, particularly for clients who do not have a partner.

 In what cases do you think the use of sexual surrogates is justified?

—Should the client's partner be involved in deciding whether or not to use a sexual surrogate in therapy? Why or why not?

Choosing a Sex Therapist

Many different types of mental health professionals provide sexual therapy and treatment. Psychiatrists are medical doctors (M.D. or D.O.) who spend 1 to 2 years after their medical training in a psychiatric residency, which includes neurology, psychopharmacology, and diagnosis. Some programs include extensive training in therapy, while others emphasize medications. In most states, psychiatrists are the only mental-health professionals who can prescribe medicines or admit patients to hospitals. Psychologists usually have a doctoral degree (Ph.D., Psy.D., or Ed.D.) and have postgraduate training in research, behavioral studies, developmental stages, psychological testing, diagnosis, and psychotherapy. Social workers have a master's degree (M.S.W.) with training that usually emphasizes family systems and practical experience. Marriage and family therapists (M.F.T., M.A., or M.Ed. degrees) also have training in family and relationship problems.

Unless a therapist is well trained with a basic knowledge and understanding of sexual anatomy and physiology, as well as an awareness of psychological factors, the therapist may do more harm than good (Waggoner, 1980). Unfortunately, most states do not require licensing for sex therapists. Almost anyone can open an office and offer advice. You don't need academic coursework, degrees, clinical supervision, or other training in human sexuality to practice sex therapy in most places. However, the Society for Sex Therapy and Research (SSTR) and the American Association of Sex Educators, Counselors, and Therapists (AASECT) does train and certify sex therapists in North America and publishes national directories of therapists certified by their agencies. In addition, the American Psychological Association, the American Psychiatric Association, and the American Association of Marriage and Family Therapy are involved in certification-granting programs related to sex therapy. That said, certification does not guarantee effective therapy. Despite the claims of some therapists, we continue to have "a poor understanding of why such therapies are relatively successful in some cases yet seem to fail over the long run with many" (Meissner, 1980, p. 307).

Don't be afraid to ask the therapist anything and everything that you believe might be relevant to your treatment. Question the therapist about his or her education, training, credentials, and experience. If the therapist has not already informed you, ask how long therapy is expected to take, the number of sessions per week, how much it will cost, and what will be expected of you during and between therapy sessions.

Therapy is an intimate experience. Often a patient will experience **transference,** feelings of attachment or attraction to a therapist. This is especially problematic in sexual therapy, where the patient is revealing very intimate details. However, it is the therapist's job to recognize this process and not to act on these feelings. All professional

Transference: the projection of feelings, thoughts, and wishes onto the therapist, such as feelings of attachment or attraction to a therapist

associations strictly forbid sexual relations between therapists and patients. Unfortunately, some renowned therapists have provided poor examples. Movies have reinforced a romanticized image of a therapist having sex with a patient. Ingrid Bergman in *Spellbound*, Barbara Streisand in *Prince of Tides*, Jeanne Tripplehorn in *Basic Instinct*, and Lena Olin in *Mr. Jones* all had sexual relationships with patients. While these movies depicted female therapists having sex with a male patient, it is more likely that male therapists will have sexual relations with a patient. A nationwide anonymous survey in 1986 found that 7 percent of male psychiatrists and 3 percent of female psychiatrists admitted they had been sexually involved with a patient (Gartrell et al., 1986). Perhaps even more alarming is that while 65 percent of psychiatrists said that they had treated patients who were sexually involved with their previous therapists, they only reported 8 percent of these cases to authorities (Gartrell et al., 1987).

California's guide, *Professional Therapy Never Includes Sex* (1989), provides some warning signs that a therapist may be serving his or her own needs and not yours. If the therapist is spending more time discussing his or her own problems than yours, suggests that you meet at a nonprofessional location or after hours, makes sexual innuendoes or jokes, or makes physical contact, you should terminate therapy immediately and consult another professional, making sure to notify the new therapist of the inappropriate conduct so that he or she can help repair any damage it may have caused to your treatment.

Some individuals prefer to see a therapist for individual therapy because they are not in a relationship or because their partners refuse to attend therapy. Others find that couples therapy best meets their needs. Some feel more comfortable with a therapist of the same sex or have a preference for a particular therapeutic approach. Another option is group therapy with other individuals or couples who are experiencing similar problems. These groups may be all male or all female, or they may include both men and women; the group may deal with specific sexual issues, or with a range of sexual and relational topics. The most important thing is that you are comfortable with the arrangement you select.

■ R E V I E W

There are four basic categories of sexual problems that people may experience: disorders of sexual desire, disorders of sexual arousal, orgasmic disorders, and sexual **1**_____ disorders. Sexual therapy involves the treatment of sexual dysfunction as well as improving and enhancing sexual satisfaction and desire. Therapy may involve medical intervention, medication, and/or psychological counseling.

2_____ is an absence or low level of sexual desire. Compulsive sexual behavior is a condition in which an insatiable need for sex interferes with daily functioning. Compulsive sexual behavior might qualify as an addiction since it can function both to produce pleasure and to provide escape from internal discomfort, and it may be accompanied by a recurrent failure to control the behavior and a continuation of the behavior despite significant harmful consequences. While many therapists believe this is a fad diagnosis, it nevertheless is true that there are people who either cannot or do not control their sexual desires or behavior.

Sexual dysfunction may occur at any point of the sexual response cycle, but most typically it involves difficulties related to sexual arousal or to orgasm. **3**_____ is a condition that prevents the achievement of an erection or the ability to maintain it during coitus. As many as 30 million American men have erection problems; older men are more likely to be affected than younger men. Two treatments for premature ejaculation are the **4**_____ and _____ techniques. **5**_____ is a condition in which a man experiences a continued erection that will not go down. The inability to ejaculate during sexual intercourse is **6**_____; it is also known as ejaculatory incompetence, or delayed, inhibited, or retarded ejaculation.

   7_____ is a condition of women who are not able to experience orgasm.

   8_____ is genital pain or pain during intercourse, which may be experienced by men or women. Moderate to high levels of alcohol and drug use, including tobacco use, can adversely affect sexual satisfaction.

9_____ involves an involuntary contraction of the muscles surrounding the opening of the vagina that can prevent pleasurable coitus.

   Sexual problems can be treated through the use of medication or by various forms of therapy. The psychoanalytic approach attempts to probe the patient's psyche to find an underlying cause of the disorder. The behavioral approach is aimed at changing the disturbed behaviors directly, through the use of behavior modification.

   An effective therapist is an advocate for effective change. Therapy is an intimate experience and **10**_____, or feelings of attachment or attraction to a therapist, is often part of the course of psychotherapy. However, no ethical therapist will take advantage of those feelings. If a therapist makes sexual innuendoes or physical contact, the patient should terminate therapy and consult another professional.

SUGGESTED READINGS

Berman, J., & Berman, L. (2001). *For Women Only: A Revolutionary Guide to Overcoming Sexual Dysfunction and Reclaiming Your Sex Life.* New York: Henry Holt.
   Written by a urologist and her sister, a sex therapist, this comprehensive handbook examines women's sexual health and discusses a full spectrum of treatment options.

Goodman, A. (1999). *Sexual Addiction: An Integrated Approach.* Madison, CT: International Universities Press.
   This book describes the biological, sociocultural, and psychoanalytic theories of sexual addiction and integrates them into a coherent approach. Goodman discusses diagnostic criteria, differential diagnosis, relevant epidemiological data, and treatment modalities.

Milstein, R., & Slowinski, J. (1999). *The Sexual Male: Problems and Solutions.* New York: W.W. Norton.
   The authors provide advice for dealing with male sexual problems.

Newman, A. J. (1999). *Beyond Viagra: Plain Talk About Treating Male and Female Sexual Dysfunction.* Montgomery, AL: Starrhill Press.
   Newman, a urologist, reviews the causes of sexual dysfunction and the treatment options.

Reichman, J. (1998). *I'm Not in the Mood: What Every Woman Should Know About Improving Her Libido.* New York: William Morrow.
   This book looks at the role of testosterone in stimulating sexual interest. While the emphasis is on hormones, Reichman also describes psychological concerns, relationship issues, medications, disease, surgery, and other problems that interfere with sexual satisfaction.

Spark, R. F. (2000). *Sexual Health for Men: The Complete Guide.* New York: Perseus.
   Despite using the term *impotence* instead of *erectile dysfunction*, the author, a Harvard Medical School physician, offers a compassionate and comprehensive guide to risks and benefits of various treatments, including alternative medicine options.

ANSWERS TO CHAPTER REVIEW

1. pain; **2.** Hypoactive sexual desire; **3.** Erectile dysfunction; **4.** start-stop, squeeze; **5.** Priapism; **6.** Male orgasmic disorder; **7.** Anorgasmia; **8.** Dyspareunia; **9.** Vaginismus; **10.** transference.

CHAPTER 5

Conception, Pregnancy, and Birth

PHYSICAL

SOCIAL

EMOTIONAL

SPIRITUAL

COGNITIVE

- ### Conception
  The union of egg and sperm may require 24 hours or more and typically occurs in one of the Fallopian tubes.

- ### Fetal Development
  Nine weeks after conception, when all the major organs have been formed, the embryo is called a fetus. It is at this stage that genitalia are distinguishable.

- ### Pregnancy Detection
  Pregnancy can be detected by a chemical test to detect human chorionic gonadotropin (HCG) or through a pelvic examination.

- ### Pregnancy
  The 9 months of pregnancy can be divided into three segments, called trimesters, of approximately 3 months each.

- ### The Responsibilities of Pregnancy
  Responsible prenatal care includes exercise, good nutrition, and avoidance of all drugs and alcohol.

- ### Problems in Pregnancy
  Environmental, genetic, or organic factors may end a pregnancy, threaten the life of the mother, and/or result in birth defects.

- ### Expectant Fathers
  The effects of a woman's pregnancy on the father, which include emotional and biological changes, can be significant.

- ### The Birth Experience
  Labor consists of three stages: strong contractions of the uterus, the birth of the baby, and delivery of the placenta and membranes. Most deliveries in our society occur in a hospital or specialized birth setting.

- **Postpartum**

  The postpartum experience is marked by significant physiological and psychological changes. Decisions about breast-feeding may add to postpartum stresses.

- **Infertility**

  A woman may not become pregnant for a number of reasons, and a man will have difficulty impregnating his partner if he does not produce a sufficient number of sperm. In addition to adoption, there are a number of procedures that may be effective for infertile couples.

Sexual reproduction is the story of the creation of a human being from the moment of conception through the development and birth of a newborn baby. Every act of intercourse brings with it the possibility of creating a new life. In this chapter we explore the relationship of sexual activity to reproduction and describe the series of events from the union of egg and sperm to the announcement "It's a boy!" or "It's a girl!"

Conception occurs when an ovum is penetrated by and united with a sperm cell. Usually this process, also known as **fertilization,** takes place in the upper portion of a woman's fallopian tube (see Figure 2.1 in Chapter 2). The fertilized egg eventually makes its way into the uterus where it is implanted in the endometrium and develops into a fetus during the 9-month gestation period known as **pregnancy. Birth** is the expulsion of the fetus from the uterus through the birth canal and vaginal opening into the wide, wide world.

CONCEPTION

As you learned in Chapter 2, a male produces sperm throughout his adult life, while a female is born with all the ova she will ever have. A female fetus contains approximately 6 to 7 million ova, most of which will degenerate before birth. At birth, a woman's ovaries contain approximately 400,000 eggs; typically less than 500 of these will be ovulated during a female's reproductive years. The sperm is one of the tiniest cells in the human body. The total length of a sperm is only about 2/500 of an inch. The ovum, measuring about 1/175 of an inch, is the largest.

Because of their special role in delivering the genetic material of the parents, eggs and sperm are formed by a specialized process called **meiosis** (Figure 5.1a). Unlike the cells in the rest of your body, which have 23 *pairs* of chromosomes (a total of 46), the nuclei of eggs and sperm contain a *single copy* of each chromosome (a total of 23). When a sperm and an ovum are merged during fertilization, the fertilized egg ends up with 23 pairs of chromosomes. All other human cells are produced through **mitosis,** a process in which the genetic material in the nucleus doubles prior to cell division (Figure 5.1b), so that the two new cells end up with a full set of 23 pairs of chromosomes.

Sexual reproduction: the process in which two cells fuse to form one fertilized cell with a new genome that is different than that of either parent

Conception: fertilization of an ovum by a sperm to form a viable zygote

Fertilization: conception

Pregnancy: the period between conception and birth during which offspring develop in the womb

Birth: the act or process of bearing children

Meiosis: cell division that produces reproductive cells in sexually reproducing organisms in which the nucleus divides into four nuclei each containing half the chromosome number

Mitosis: cell division in which the nucleus divides into nuclei containing the same number of chromosomes

Germ cell: an ovum or sperm cell or one of its developmental precursors

Primary Oocyte: the enlarging ovum before maturity is reached

Secondary Oocyte: an oocyte that arises from the primary oocyte after it completes the first meiotic division

Polar Body: the smaller of two cells produced during meiotic division

Primary Spermatocyte: early stage in the development of sperm cells before maturity is reached

Secondary Spermatocyte: a spermatocyte that arises from the primary oocyte after it completes the first meiotic division

Spermatids: cells produced through meiosis in males that mature into sperm cells

Sperm Cells: mature male reproductive cells

Spermatozoa: sperm cells; spermatozoon, sing.

Meiosis of the female **germ cell** or ovum occurs early in the menstrual cycle. First the chromosomes in the nucleus of an immature egg, called a **primary oocyte,** divide into a **secondary oocyte** and a **polar body** (see Figure 5.1a). Because the chromosomes are not duplicated prior to this event, each of these cells contains only half the genetic material of the original cell. Then in preparation for another round of cell division the chromosomes in the nuclei of the secondary oocyte and polar body double. The secondary oocyte divides into another polar body and a cell that will become a mature ovum. The polar body produced by the first division of the primary oocyte divides into two new polar bodies. The mature ovum is ready for fertilization, but the polar bodies are incapable of any further development and degenerate.

The genetic material inside a sperm is produced via a similar process. A primitive germ cell called a **primary spermatocyte** divides into two new cells, each with half the genetic material of the primary spermatocyte. Each of these new cells, called **secondary spermatocytes,** contains either an X chromosome or a Y chromosome (not both, like the primary spermatocyte). Each secondary spermatocyte replicates the chromosomes in its nucleus and divides into two new cells called **spermatids.** Each primary spermatocyte thus produces four spermatids, half containing X chromosomes and half containing Y chromosomes. The spermatids mature into **sperm cells,** which are ready to pair their genetic material with the 23 chromosomes carried by an ovum. Mature sperm cells, also called **spermatozoa,** have a *head*, a cone-shaped *midpiece* and a *tail* (Figure 5.2). The head contains the nucleus with the genetic material, the midpiece provides energy for swimming, and the tail lashes back and forth to propel the sperm on its journey.

When a woman ovulates at about day 14 of the average menstrual cycle, an egg is drawn into the fimbria, the long fingerlike structures at the end of one of the fallopian tubes; the cilia, hairlike structures that line the fallopian tube, push the egg toward the uterus. If fertilization does not occur, the egg disintegrates.

Recall that sperm are manufactured in the seminiferous tubules of the male's testes. Sperm have a longer, more complicated journey than eggs. After they are collected and stored in the epididymis, they move up and over the top of the bladder in the vas deferens, and then down through the ejaculatory duct where they mix with seminal fluid.

FIGURE 5.1 Steps in Meiosis and Mitosis. Source: Martini, 2001.

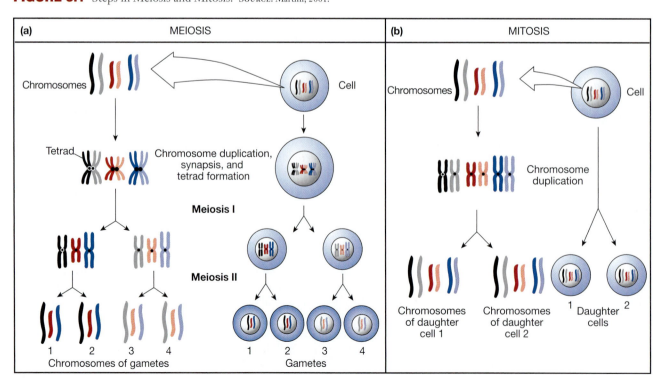

During intercourse, if the man ejaculates into the vagina, the sperm enter the woman's uterus through the cervix. Once inside the uterus the sperm are propelled toward the fallopian tubes by **motility,** the whiplike action of the tail of the sperm. If a sperm encounters the egg and is able to unite with it, fertilization occurs (Figure 5.3). After ejaculation, sperm typically survive about 48 hours within the female body but are capable of living as long as 8 days.

Of the 200 to 400 million sperm that are ejaculated into the vagina only about 1 in 1,000 will ever arrive in the vicinity of an ovum. Some become immobilized because they clump together, and the acidic environment of the vagina kills some. Gravity also plays a role; unless the woman remains prone, most sperm spill out of the vagina. Of those sperm that enter the uterus through the cervix, only a few thousand are likely to reach the fallopian tubes. Of those that make it as far as the fallopian tubes, some will pick the wrong one (ovulation usually occurs in one of the two tubes during each menstrual cycle). Perhaps 200 to 300 sperm actually get near the egg. Although the speediest sperm may arrive at the egg within an hour after ejaculation, typically they move about 1 to 3 centimeters, or about 1 inch, per hour. This long and difficult journey helps to ensure that only the healthiest sperm have an opportunity to fertilize the egg, thus reducing the potential for birth defects.

Once inside the female's body, how do the sperm know where to go? It has been known for some time that fish sperm find fish eggs in millions of gallons of seawater because fish eggs emit "smelling" chemicals (the *pheromones* described in Chapters 2 and 3). The receptors that your nose uses to pick up the scent of cologne have recently been found on human sperm (Walensksy et al., 1997), suggesting a microscopic courtship between sperm and eggs. Now that they have found the receptors, researchers are looking for the pheromones emitted by the eggs.

Typically conception occurs in the outer third of the fallopian tube, where the sperm undergo a process known as capacitation. **Capacitation** is a change in the sperm that gives it the ability, or *capacity*, to penetrate the egg. It is only after capacitation that sperm are able to secrete an enzyme called **hyaluronidase** that eats away at the **zona pellucida,** a jellylike protective coating around the egg. Typically, 3 or 4 dozen capacitated sperm cluster around the egg, attempting to fertilize it (see Figure 5.3). It requires the combined enzymes from numerous sperm to break down the zona pellucida enough so that a single lucky sperm can enter the egg.

The egg extends tiny growths called microvilli outward from its surface to capture this lucky sperm. While the microvilli hold the single sperm down on the egg membrane,

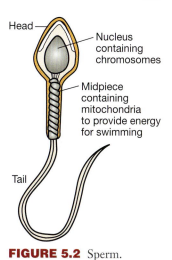

FIGURE 5.2 Sperm.
SOURCE: Hyde and Delameter, 1999.

Motility: spontaneous movement

Capacitation: the changes that a sperm goes through to be capable of penetrating the layers covering the egg

Hyaluronidase: enzyme found in the testes that degrades hyaluronic acid in the body thereby increasing tissue penetrability to fluids

Zona Pellucida: A translucent, elastic, noncellular layer surrounding the ovum of many mammals.

FIGURE 5.3 Fertilization, the Union of Sperm and Egg. SOURCE: McCammon, Knox and Schacht, 1998.

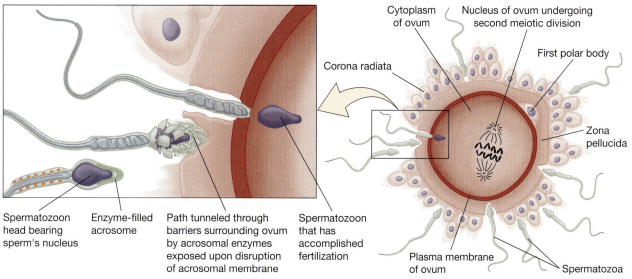

Spermatozoon head bearing sperm's nucleus

Enzyme-filled acrosome

Path tunneled through barriers surrounding ovum by acrosomal enzymes exposed upon disruption of acrosomal membrane

Spermatozoon that has accomplished fertilization

Cytoplasm of ovum

Nucleus of ovum undergoing second meiotic division

First polar body

Corona radiata

Zona pellucida

Plasma membrane of ovum

Spermatozoa

FAQ:

Which parent determines the sex of the child?

Chromosomes determine gender, which will be discussed in detail in Chapter 10. Women have two X chromosomes (XX) and men have one X and a Y chromosome. Because females are XX, all of their eggs carry a single X chromosome. Because males are XY, half of their sperm carry a Y chromosome, and the other half carry an X chromosome. A zygote with two X-chromosomes develops into a female. A zygote with one X and one Y chromosome develops into a male. Thus it is the man's sperm that determines the sex of the offspring.

King Henry VIII of England is famous for divorcing and beheading wives because they failed to give him a son to be heir to his throne. If Henry had had the benefits of genetic counseling, he would have known that it was his own chromosomal contribution that determined the gender of his progeny. Then again, Henry probably would have just found another excuse to remove and replace his spouses.

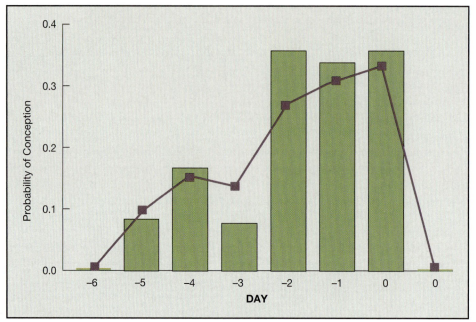

FIGURE 5.4 **Probability of Conception on Specific Days near the Day of Ovulation.** The bars represent probabilities calculated from data on 129 menstrual cycles in which sexual intercourse was recorded to have occurred on only a single day during the six-day interval ending on the day of ovulation (day 0). The solid line shows daily probabilities based on all 625 cycles, as estimated by the statistical model. SOURCE: Massachusetts Medical Society, 1995.

the egg produces a brief electrical block on its surface and secretes a hard outer coat consisting of protein that makes the zona pellucida impenetrable to all other sperm. Then the egg pulls the sperm inside and moves its nucleus to meet that of the sperm.

Fertilization begins when the sperm contacts the zona pellucida and ends when genetic material from the sperm and egg combine. This complex process may require 24 hours or longer to complete. The window of fertility during the menstrual cycle is only 6 days: the day of ovulation and the 6 days leading up to it. Among healthy women trying to conceive, nearly all pregnancies occur during a 6-day period ending on the day of ovulation (Wilcox et al., 1995) (Figure 5.4).

FETAL DEVELOPMENT

The union of egg and sperm is only the beginning. Successful reproduction happens only as a result of millions of individual events, from cell division and multiplication to the coordination of chemical production within the fetus and the mother's body. These events also determine the many visible and not so visible characteristics of the fetus, including its gender.

About 30 hours after fertilization, the fertilized egg, called the **zygote,** starts its journey down the fallopian tube and begins the process of cell division. The single-celled zygote splits into two cells; each of those two then divides again to produce four cells, which then become 8, 16, then 32, 64, 128 and so on. The ensuing collection of cells is called a **morula** (from the Latin word for mulberry) because it resembles a mulberry. As the division process continues, each cell becomes progressively smaller. Through mitosis (see Figure 5.1b) the genetic material in each cell is duplicated prior to cell division, ensuring that each cell in the body—whether a bone cell, nerve cell, skin cell, or some other—has the same genetic code.

It takes 3 or 4 days for the morula to travel down the fallopian tube, from the site of fertilization, to the uterine cavity. By this time the morula has developed a hollow inner portion containing fluid and is called a **blastula** (Figure 5.5). The blastula continues to grow inside the uterus, obtaining oxygen and nourishment from secretions of

Zygote: an egg that has been fertilized but not yet divided

Morula: the mass of cells resulting from the cleavage of the ovum before the formation of a blastula.

Blastula: the early developmental stage of an animal, following the morula stage and consisting of a single, spherical layer of cells enclosing a hollow, central cavity

Double Duty

Identical twins are the result of a single fertilized egg that for some unknown reason subdivides into two parts. Identical twins share a single placenta and are virtually identical in every respect, from body type to genetic material. Because they share identical genetic material, identical twins are either both boys or both girls. Fraternal twins are produced when two sperm fertilize two separate eggs simultaneously. Fraternal twins have separate placentas; because the genetic material is completely separate, they can be as alike or as different from one another as siblings born at different times, and can be boy/boy, girl/girl, or boy/girl.

There are a few reported cases of women who conceived naturally during two different menstrual cycles: twins conceived a month apart. In some instances the babies were conceived by different fathers, making the "twins" half-siblings. This extremely rare occurrence results when hormones produced by the first pregnancy are not strong enough to suppress the action of the pituitary gland that normally tells the ovaries to shut down.

 How can you tell if twins are identical or fraternal?

—How could you tell if different fathers conceived "twins"?

---

the endometrium. After a few days of continued growth, the blastula has become a **blastocyst** with one group of cells that will become the fetus and another group that will become the placenta. The blastocyst then implants itself into the endometrium. The endometrium has been preparing for this possibility since hormone secretions were triggered in the second half of the menstrual cycle. Implantation is completed about 10 to 12 days after fertilization. For a summary of this process, see Figure 5.6.

In some women implantation is accompanied by "spotting" or light bleeding, which can be confused with menstruation. This may cause the woman to miscalculate when pregnancy actually began and lead to an incorrect estimation of the expected date of delivery.

Blastocyst: an embryo composed of two groups of cells. One group will develop into the fetus and the other will become the placenta

PREGNANCY DETECTION

As we discussed in Chapter 2, missing a menstrual period is not necessarily a sign of pregnancy. Most women have irregular periods once in a while; some can never predict them. As stated previously, because of spotting on implantation, the presence or absence of blood is not an accurate indicator of pregnancy. The detection of a fetal heartbeat is the only true sign of pregnancy.

Chemical tests for pregnancy are based on the fact that the placenta produces human chorionic gonadotropin (HCG), a hormone that can be detected in a woman's blood or urine. Most home pregnancy tests can detect elevated HCG levels as early as 3 to 4 days after implantation or approximately 10 to 12 days after conception.

One such chemical test, the home pregnancy test, is a relatively inexpensive way to determine whether a woman is pregnant. Some home tests work by holding a stick in the stream of urine. Others involve dipping a diagnostic strip in a container of collected urine. Results show up differently with different products; a "yes"

FIGURE 5.5 A fertilized egg or zygote develops into a morula and after 3 or 4 days into a blastula (a). After a few more days inside the uterus, it becomes a blastocyst (b and c) and implants itself into the endometrium.

(a)

(b)

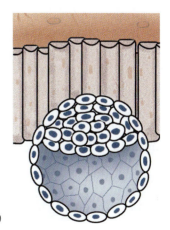

(c)

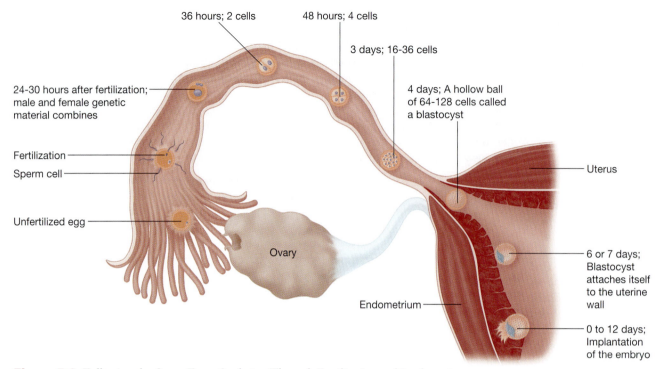

24-30 hours after fertilization; male and female genetic material combines

36 hours; 2 cells

48 hours; 4 cells

3 days; 16-36 cells

4 days; A hollow ball of 64-128 cells called a blastocyst

Fertilization

Sperm cell

Unfertilized egg

Ovary

Uterus

Endometrium

6 or 7 days; Blastocyst attaches itself to the uterine wall

0 to 12 days; Implantation of the embryo

Figure 5.6 Following the Ovum From Ovulation Through Fertilization and Implantation.

can be a colored line or a symbol in a test window. Results of the test should be read as soon as possible after the timed reaction period. With some of the tests, a delay of as little as 10 to 20 minutes can turn a negative result to a positive one. While manufacturers may claim high accuracy rates for their products, independent studies have found that the diagnostic efficiency of a home pregnancy test is greatly affected by how carefully it is used (Bastien et al., 1998).

Home pregnancy test kits may be more sensitive than many pregnancy kits used in laboratories or health centers (Wheeler, 1999), but they are not as accurate. When in doubt, consult a health-care practitioner about an in-office test. A skilled health-care practitioner can also detect pregnancy through a pelvic exam. About a month after conception, **Hegar's sign,** a soft spot between the uterine body and the cervix can be detected by placing one hand on the abdomen and two fingers in the vagina.

Hegar's Sign: changes in the size, shape, and consistency of the uterus (uterus becomes softened or "doughy") between the uterine body and the cervix

PREGNANCY

So you (or your partner) are pregnant! What happens next? The physical, social, emotional, spiritual, and cognitive effects of pregnancy certainly can be overwhelming for the expectant mother and father. Societies often treat pregnant women as having special status, sometimes with special laws and privileges (like Stork Parking, designated parking spots at the mall). Pregnant women may find themselves to be the welcome or unwelcome center of attention from friends and family. Expectant parents are likely to experience a range of emotions including great elation (joyously announcing, "We're pregnant!") and massive anxiety ("Are we ready to be parents?" "Will our baby be normal?"). Those who are ambivalent about pregnancy may experience confusion or depression. Creating a new life can have tremendous spiritual meaning as a source of personal fulfillment and a connection to nature or the Creator.

Home pregnancy tests.

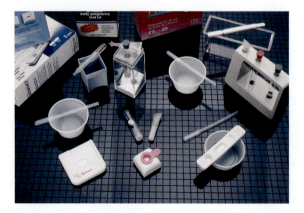

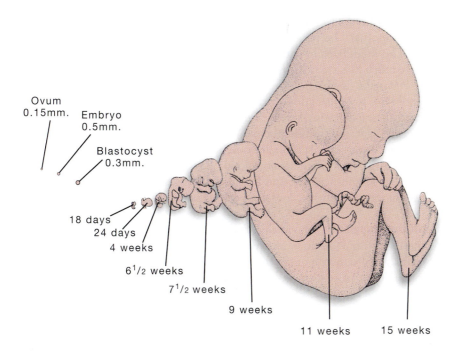

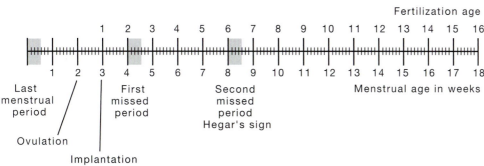

FIGURE 5.7 Growth of the Embryo and Fetus From Conception Through the First 15 Weeks. As indicated on the figure, the ovum and blastula are enlarged; all other stages are shown at their actual sizes.

Although it may seem like your pregnancy lasts forever, the average pregnancy lasts for 266 days, which translates to 38 weeks, or almost 9 months. Few babies are born exactly on their "due date," but the great majority are delivered within 10 days before or after the date. Pregnancy is divided into three 3-month periods called trimesters. Thus the **first trimester** is the first 3 months after fertilization. The **second trimester** consists of the fourth through sixth months of a pregnancy. The **third trimester** begins with the seventh month of pregnancy and ends with delivery (Figure 5.7).

The First Trimester

The Embryonic Stage   The first 8 weeks after fertilization are collectively called the **embryonic stage.** After implantation, parts of the blastocyst develop into the placenta and the fetal membranes including the amniotic sac. The **placenta** is the organ surrounding the embryo through which it obtains nourishment and oxygen from the mother's blood. The circulatory systems of the mother and embryo do not mix. The fetal membrane of the placenta permits only certain substances to pass through. For example, oxygen is permitted to pass from the mother to the embryo and carbon dioxide and other wastes pass from the embryo to the mother and are eliminated by the mother's lungs and kidneys.

First Trimester: first 3 months of pregnancy

Second Trimester: the fourth, fifth and sixth months of pregnancy

Third Trimester: the last 3 months of pregnancy

Embryonic Stage: the stage of prenatal development that lasts from implantation through the first 8 weeks and is characterized by the differentiation of the major organ systems

Placenta: the organ in most mammals, formed in the lining of the uterus by the union of the uterine mucous membrane with the membranes of the fetus, that provides for the nourishment of the fetus and the elimination of its waste products.

Amniotic Sac: the sac containing the developing fetus

Amniotic Fluid: fluid within the amniotic sac that suspends and protects the fetus

Umbilical cord: tube that connects the fetus to the placenta

Fetus: in humans the product of conception from the beginning of the ninth week until birth

The embryo develops within the **amniotic sac,** a protective environment in the mother's uterus. The embryo is suspended within this clear membrane in **amniotic fluid.** The fluid helps maintain a steady temperature and cushions the embryo from damage much like a shock absorber.

During the first month, the embryo grows rapidly in size and complexity. Most of the embryo's systems and body parts begin to form. After 4 weeks the embryo has a primitive heart, digestive system, and central nervous system. During the second month of development, the **umbilical cord,** which contains two arteries and a vein connecting the embryo to the placenta, becomes distinct. Facial features, hands, feet and bony tissue all form, as do all the major blood vessels. In males, the development of testicular tissue distinguishes male and female embryos for the first time. The formation of ovaries in female embryos does not begin for another few weeks.

Fetal Development The fetal period of development begins in the ninth week after fertilization. From this point until delivery, the developing child is referred to as a **fetus.** During the third month of development, the fetus becomes increasingly human in appearance. Fingernails, toenails, hair follicles, and eyelids appear. Limbs become more proportionate and both male and female genitalia are distinguishable. There is some evidence of a correlation between first trimester size and birth weight (Gordon et al., 1998).

Effects on the Expectant Mother During the first trimester of pregnancy the placenta produces increased levels of hormones, especially estrogen and progesterone. Increased hormonal levels cause many of the physical symptoms that women may experience during the first trimester of pregnancy.

Within the first weeks of pregnancy some women experience tenderness, a tingling sensation or fullness of the breasts due to hormonal stimulation of the mammary glands. Some women also notice nausea, fatigue, or a change in appetite (see CONSIDERATIONS box). Foods that may have been favorites prior to pregnancy now may have no appeal, and she may crave others, which she never liked before. Some women experience frequent urination, irregular bowel movements, and increased vaginal secretions.

The Second Trimester

Fetal Development The greatest amount of fetal growth occurs during the fourth month of pregnancy, the first month of the second trimester. Late in the fourth month, fetal movement, sometimes referred to as *quickening*, will probably be noticeable. During the fifth month, the fetal heartbeat becomes strong and can be heard with a stethoscope or by placing an ear on the woman's abdomen.

(a)

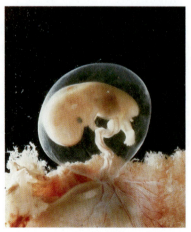
(b)

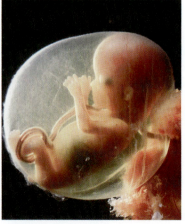
(c)

(a) The embryo at about 4 weeks of development. The major organs are forming and you can see the bright red blood-filled heart.
(b) The fetus at 9 weeks of development. (c) By 16 weeks all internal organs are formed but not yet fully functional.

CONSIDERATIONS

Morning Sickness: It's Not a Sickness and It Doesn't Just Happen in the Morning

During the first few months of pregnancy, about half of all pregnant women experience **morning sickness,** which is a misnomer since nausea, vomiting, and food aversions can occur at any time during the day (Thompson, 1993). After examining the results of nearly 80,000 successful and unsuccessful pregnancies, researchers at Cornell University found that morning sickness plays a role in the survival of both the fetus and the mother. The nausea and vomiting that occur during the first trimester may help to protect both mother and fetus from exposure to infectious organisms and toxic chemicals that could result in damage, miscarriage, or even maternal death.

The three top food aversions that develop during pregnancy are to (1) meat, (2) nonalcoholic beverages like coffee, and (3) vegetables. The highest frequency of morning sickness was found in Japan, where 84 percent of pregnant women reported experiencing nausea and

vomiting. Raw fish, a food frequently enjoyed in Japan, can carry parasites that can be harmful to the developing fetus and make the pregnant woman quite ill. The researchers theorize that nauseous women are less likely to consume certain foods that may be damaging to the fetus at a time when its major organ systems are developing (Flaxman & Sherman, 2000). The Cornell biologists who conducted the study do not dispute the role that hormones play in morning sickness. Rather, they believe that there is a reason that hormones cause this discomfort.

 What do you think of this explanation for morning sickness?

—Aside from protection of the mother and the fetus, come up with another plausible explanation for morning sickness.

In the sixth month the fetus opens its eyes, and by the 24th week it is sensitive to light and can hear sounds in utero. While it may begin to resemble a small human in form during the second trimester, the fetus usually is not sufficiently developed at this point to survive outside the mother's body. Its immature lungs cannot supply the required oxygen for survival outside the womb at this stage.

Effects on the Expectant Mother During the second trimester, a woman may be more physically aware of her pregnancy as she experiences fetal movement and a rapidly expanding waistline. While morning sickness and other symptoms of the first trimester may disappear, some women begin to experience indigestion and constipation as the fetus grows larger and compresses the internal organs. The skin over the abdomen must stretch a great deal to accommodate the enlarged fetus, and iridescent stretch marks may appear in this area. Also during the second trimester, the placenta begins to produce hormones to prepare the breasts for milk production. In response the breasts and areolae enlarge, and the nipples and areolae darken. **Colostrum,** a thin yellowish fluid that is a precursor to breast milk, may leak out of the nipples. Colostrum does not usually begin to flow with any regularity until after the baby begins to suckle.

The Third Trimester

Fetal Development During the seventh month the development of the brain and nervous system is completed. At the beginning of the third trimester, the skin of the fetus is wrinkled and covered with downlike hair that generally is lost by the end of the eighth month. Most of the third trimester is spent increasing body weight to improve the fetus's chances of survival at delivery. At the end of the eighth month the average weight of a fetus is 2,500 grams (5 pounds 9 ounces); the average at full term, a few weeks later, is 3,300 grams (7 pounds 6 ounces). The fetus gains weight most rapidly during the third trimester and acquires antibodies from the mother for protection against infection during early infancy. There is also a lot of movement going on. In preparation for birth, the fetus usually turns so that its head is pointed down toward the birth canal, if it is not already in this position.

Morning Sickness: symptoms of pregnancy including nausea, vomiting, and food aversions experienced by some women

Colostrum: thin yellowish fluid secreted by the mammary glands at the time of parturition that is rich in antibodies and minerals. It precedes the production of true milk

Edema: excessive accumulation of fluid resulting in swelling

Braxton-Hicks Contractions: "false labor"; intermittent, painless contractions that may occur every 10 to 20 minutes after the first trimester of pregnancy.

Effects on the Expectant Mother   During the third trimester the added weight of the fetus will cause a shift in a pregnant woman's center of gravity. Some women feel awkward and unconsciously alter the way they walk, which can result in backache. Other typical symptoms of the third trimester include leg cramps, a need to urinate frequently, and shortness of breath. The latter two symptoms result from the pressure of the enlarged uterus downward on the bladder and upward on the lungs (Figure 5.8). Pressure from the enlarged fetus can cause problems with varicose veins in the rectum (hemorrhoids) or legs, and nosebleeds may occur as a result of increased blood volume. Fluid retention can cause **edema,** or swelling, in the hands or feet.

Also in the last months many women experience **Braxton-Hicks contractions.** These brief sensations of muscles tightening are not a sign of labor, but may become more frequent as labor approaches. Finally, the combination of strong fetal kicks, the need to urinate frequently, and the difficulty of finding a comfortable position may interfere with getting a restful night's sleep. The typical weight gain during pregnancy is 20 pounds (Table 5.1), although some women gain considerably more weight.

One study that examined changes in the health of women during a normal pregnancy found that their physical functioning, role limitation due to physical problems, and pain scales all decreased as pregnancy progressed. The researchers found that sociodemographic factors such as employment, level of income, and presence of a spouse or support partner had only a small influence on *functional status*, the routine daily lives, of pregnant women (Hueston & Kasik-Miller, 1999).

FIGURE 5.8 The Ninth Month of Pregnancy. (a) In the ninth month of pregnancy the uterus and abdomen increase in size to accommodate the full-term fetus. (b) This photograph of actress Demi Moore, which appeared on the cover of *Vanity Fair* magazine, helped project a more positive image of the sexuality of the pregnant woman.

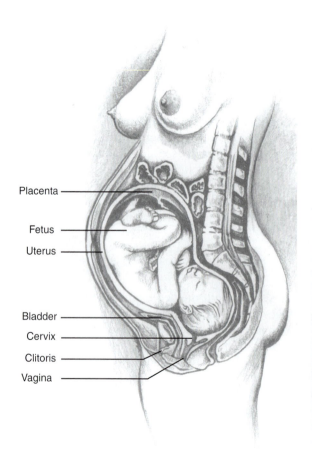

Placenta

Fetus

Uterus

Bladder

Cervix

Clitoris

Vagina

TABLE 5.1

Typical Weight Gain During Pregnancy

$7\frac{1}{2}$ pounds to the baby
$3\frac{1}{2}$ pounds to the placenta, membranes, and amniotic fluid
$2\frac{1}{2}$ pounds to the increase in size of the uterus
$3\frac{1}{2}$ pounds of additional blood
1 more pound of breast
2 to 3 pounds due to normal fluid retention

Total weight gain: about 20 pounds

THE RESPONSIBILITIES OF PREGNANCY

Prenatal Medical Care

Good **prenatal** care protects the health and well being of both the fetus and the expectant mother. Most of the time pregnancies and births go smoothly but problems can occur. It is the responsibility of the expectant parents to be informed and to take every possible step to ensure the birth of a healthy baby. This includes engaging in health-promoting practices, as well as seeking the care of a professional health-care practitioner as soon as a pregnancy is suspected. Prenatal care serves two purposes: (1) it prevents problems, and (2) it promptly detects and minimizes the effects of complications encountered during pregnancy.

Exercise and Physical Activity

Pregnancy is not an illness, disease, or disabling condition. Maintaining normal physical activity during pregnancy benefits the health of both the pregnant woman and the fetus. Only in exceptional cases should a woman stop work, sports, and recreational activities, and most physicians recommend regular physical exercise. If particular activities become difficult due to fatigue or discomfort, the mother can substitute less strenuous activities.

Diet and Nutrition

As the source of nutrition for the developing fetus, the pregnant woman must maintain a healthy, well-balanced diet. She needs extra protein and a variety of minerals and vitamins to ensure proper fetal development. Poor nutrition can result in premature delivery and low birth weight, the leading causes of infant mortality. Malnourished babies can also suffer brain damage and other lifelong deficiencies. Certain nutrients are essential early on in pregnancy, perhaps even before a woman is aware she is pregnant. For example, folic acid is highly recommended for all pregnant women. Daily doses of folic acid as small as 100 micrograms have been shown to reduce the number of brain and spinal cord birth defects by about 22 percent; dosages of 200 micrograms lower the birth defect rate by 47 percent (Mills & England, 2001). If you are planning to conceive, check your vitamins; many multivitamins already contain folic acid.

Certain foods should be avoided during pregnancy. For example, you may have to give up sushi and your morning coffee, at least the caffeinated variety. Six or more cups of coffee a day can double a pregnant woman's risk of miscarriage (Klebanoff et al., 1999). As we have already discussed, raw fish and other uncooked seafood can pose a health risk to a pregnant mother and her fetus.

Prenatal: existing or occurring before birth

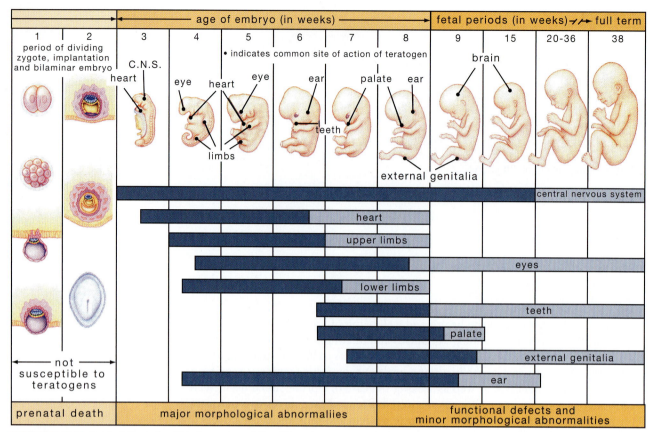

FIGURE 5.9   Critical Periods of Embryonic and Fetal Development. Light blue indicates the period during which organs are most susceptible to alcohol, drugs, or viral infection. SOURCE: Starr and McMillan, 1997.

The Effects of Drugs and Alcohol

Although the circulatory systems of the mother and fetus are separate, almost any drug a pregnant woman uses will cross the placenta and affect the fetus. Even drugs that seem safe for the mother may have disastrous effects on the unborn child. Sometimes the specific effect of a toxic drug depends upon when during the pregnancy it is used. For example, some drugs are especially dangerous if used early in the pregnancy since they can affect the formation of a particular organ. Such a drug if used later in the pregnancy, after formation of the organs, might have little or no effect on the fetus.

Any drug, legal or illegal, that can cause a malformation or birth defect in the embryo or fetus is called a **teratogen.** See Figure 5.9 for an outline of the critical periods of development and the susceptibility of various organs to teratogens. A wide variety of medications and other substances can adversely affect a developing fetus. Aspirin, for example, can cause the rupture of fetal blood vessels, especially if taken with caffeine and phenacetin, a drug common in headache medications. The results can be deadly (Collins & Turner, 1975). Accutane (or isoretinoin), an acne medication, can cause spontaneous abortion of the fetus or major birth defects (Lammer et al., 1985). Antibiotics, anticancer drugs, anticoagulants, lithium, quinine, and many other medications are known teratogens.

Tranquilizers, such as Valium, Librium, and Equanil can cause fetal malformations. Anticonvulsants, such as those used to control epilepsy, and many hormones can also cause birth defects. The safest practice is to avoid all potential teratogens during pregnancy. When in doubt, consult a health-care practitioner for advice on the safest medications to take.

Teratogen: a drug or other substance capable of interfering with the development of a fetus, causing birth defects

Fetal Alcohol Syndrome (FAS): cluster of symptoms caused by maternal alcohol use in which a child has developmental delays and characteristic facial features

Illicit drugs such as cocaine, heroin, barbiturates, ecstasy, and amphetamines also cause problems for the fetus, including low birth weight and premature birth that can result in severe health problems and developmental delays. If the fetus becomes addicted to the drug, he or she is subjected to the pain of withdrawal in the first days after birth, as well as immeasurable risks for future emotional and physical well-being. Responsibility does not end with the child's birth. Some drugs, such as alcohol and marijuana, are transmitted to the infant through a nursing mother's milk.

Smoking during pregnancy is associated with lower birth weights, spontaneous abortions, and a variety of complications during pregnancy and labor. In-utero exposure to cigarette smoke is associated with persistent breathing problems. Researchers suspect that cigarette smoke damages the lungs of the fetus at critical points in their development or that exposure to smoke makes babies more susceptible to early respiratory infections that may damage the lungs (Gilliland et al., 2000). Secondhand smoke should also be avoided, as it may also harm the fetus.

Alcohol consumed in any amount is known to cause damage to a developing fetus; the damage can be considerable if the mother-to-be drinks heavily. Children born to heavy drinkers suffer a complex of symptoms known as **fetal alcohol syndrome (FAS).** Although the incidence of alcohol consumption during pregnancy declined in the late 1980s, according to the Centers for Disease Control there's been a sixfold increase in the number of FAS babies born in the United States over the last 15 years. FAS infants experience growth deficiencies, brain and nervous system damage, and facial abnormalities, especially certain eye defects (Clarren & Smith, 1978; Dorris, 1989; Ouellette et al., 1977). There also are long-term behavioral consequences such as hyperactivity (Coles et al., 1997; Streissguth, Sampson, & Barr, 1989).

How much alcohol is too much when a woman is pregnant? No one knows. Even moderate drinking, as little as one drink a day, has been shown to increase the risk of a growth-retarded infant substantially (Mills & England, 2001). It appears that even a single drinking binge by a pregnant woman can be enough to permanently damage the brain of her unborn child, causing learning disabilities and other neurological disorders (Konomidour et al., 1999). The numbers of infants affected by maternal drug use is staggering. Silverman (1989) reports that 375,000 infants may be affected each year by their mothers' drug use during pregnancy. Another study has found that 15 percent of pregnant women in the United States tested positive for substance abuse (Chasnoff, Landress, & Barrett, 1990). Women who already have healthy children appear to see less harm in drinking alcohol during pregnancy than do women with no children (Coles et al., 1997). The conclusions are obvious. Unless medications are prescribed by a physician, a pregnant or nursing woman should use no drugs of any kind, including alcohol and tobacco. For a summary of responsible prenatal health practices, see Table 5.2.

Sex During Pregnancy

For most women there is no need to change or reduce sexual activity during pregnancy. There seems to be great variation in women's sexual feelings during pregnancy, especially during the first trimester. Some women report increased sexual awareness and pleasure, while others do not, perhaps because of the discomfort of morning sickness. Masters and Johnson (1966) found that 80 percent of women had heightened sexual desire and physical response in the second trimester. Late in the pregnancy, because of the woman's physical changes, it may be convenient to adjust sexual positions or rely more on noncoital sex play. Many couples find such experimentation exciting as well as rewarding. However, unless it is an unusual pregnancy, sexual intercourse poses no danger to the mother or the fetus. Very late in pregnancy, after the membranes have ruptured, the woman should abstain from vaginal intercourse and oral stimulation of the vulva or clitoris because of the danger of fetal infection. A woman in danger of miscarriage should abstain from any sexual activity that might result in female orgasm, since the accompanying contractions of the uterus could trigger early labor.

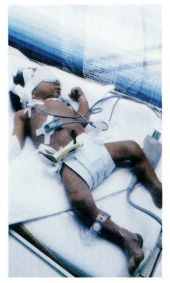

A so-called crack baby, an infant whose mother used crack cocaine during pregnancy. Babies born to cocaine-using mothers may be born with an addiction to cocaine themselves and be subjected to health risks, even death.

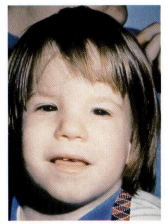

A child with fetal alcohol syndrome (FAS). Superficial physical symptoms include narrow eye openings, small head, low and prominent ears, flattened midface, and a long, smooth upper lip. The more serious effects include growth deficiencies, brain and nervous system damage, hyperactivity, and other behavioral problems.

TABLE 5.2

Responsible Prenatal Health Practices

1. As soon as you suspect you are pregnant, seek professional health care.
2. A healthy mother increases the odds for a healthy baby. Take care of yourself and eat a well-balanced, healthy diet.
3. Exercise is essential to good health. Engage in moderate exercise.
4. A happy woman increases the odds for a physically and emotionally healthy baby. Maintain good personal relationships with friends and family.
5. Avoid activities that might be physically dangerous to the fetus, such as those that might subject it to violent blows or the trauma of a fall (no skydiving or downhill skiing!). If you are suffering any physical abuse, seek shelter for your baby's safety as well as your own.
6. Take no drugs unless prescribed by a physician. Abstain from tobacco and alcohol use. Continue this pattern while nursing your new baby.
7. Expectant fathers—provide active emotional and physical support for the expectant mother. This includes encouraging healthy behaviors and providing a nurturing environment.

SOURCE: Buss, 1988.

PROBLEMS IN PREGNANCY

Maternal Risks

Significant advances in health care and in medical technology allow the majority of women to give birth safely. However, under any conditions, childbirth is not totally free of pain or risk. Today, pregnancy death rates vary considerably throughout the world. Mortality rates tend to be much higher in developing areas of the world and much lower in the fully industrialized countries of Western Europe and North America. Globally, nearly 600,000 women die in pregnancy and childbirth every year; for every woman who dies, another 30 suffer serious pregnancy-related injury. Nearly 8 million babies are stillborn or die within the first week of their lives. According to the World Health Organization (WHO, 1998), 90 percent of the pregnancy-related deaths occur in sub-Saharan Africa and Asia. In Africa, 1 out of every 15 women faces a lifetime risk of maternal death, compared with 1 in 65 in Asia, 1 in 130 in Latin America, 1 in 1,400 in Europe, and 1 in 3,700 in North America.

Birth Defects

Mothers are not the only ones at risk. Birth defects, abnormalities in physical or mental structure or function present at birth, range from minor to life threatening. A major birth defect of some type occurs in approximately 3 percent of all live births. These birth defects may be genetic in origin (as in Down syndrome, Tay-Sachs disease, hemophilia, and sickle cell disease) may be the result of an infection (such as rubella and sexually transmitted infections) or maternal illness (such as diabetes), or can be caused by a teratogenic agent (see earlier discussion). Another possible source of birth defects may be environmental chemicals. Pregnant women who were exposed occupationally to organic solvents during their first trimester of pregnancy had significantly more malformed fetuses than the control group (Khattak et al., 1999). This illustrates the fact that external influences, even ones that are not disastrous for the adult, may have serious negative consequences for the fetus.

Down Syndrome An increasing number of women are delaying a first pregnancy for career, financial, or other reasons (Harker & Thorpe, 1992; Nachtigall, 1991). There is some risk that an older woman may have difficulty getting pregnant since fertility decreases with age, but the most significant risk is chromosomal abnormality; as women age, their eggs also age, and there is an increased chance of having a baby with a chromosomal defect. The most common such chromosomal abnormality is an extra (third) copy of chromosome 21, which produces **Down syndrome.** The symptoms of Down syndrome include mental retardation and altered facial features. While the estimated rate of Down syndrome per 1,000 women at age 30 is 2.6, it increases to 5.6 at age 35, 15.8 at age 40, and 53.7 at age 45 (Hook, Cross, & Schreinemachers, 1983). However, it should be noted that more than 90 percent of all children and 70 to 80 percent of children with Down syndrome are born to women younger than 35 (Pauker & Pauker,1994).

Prenatal Testing   Today there are several means of detecting birth defects early in a pregnancy (another important reason to seek prenatal medical care!). **Amniocentesis** involves withdrawing amniotic fluid by inserting a needle through the woman's abdomen and into the uterus (Figure 5.10). Analysis of the fluid can lead to detection of Down syndrome and other genetic conditions; because it involves examination of the fetal chromosomes, it can also reveal the sex of the fetus (if you do not want to know, make sure you say so!). Amniocentesis can be performed after the 16th week of pregnancy. It takes approximately 3 to 4 weeks to obtain the results of the test.

Chorionic villus sampling (CVS) involves the insertion of a thin catheter through the cervix and into the uterus to obtain a small sample of chorionic villi (singular, villus) (Figure 5.11). The villi are small hairlike protrusions on the chorion, the membrane that surrounds the fetus. CVS can be done by the eighth week of pregnancy. Analysis, similar to that conducted on the amniotic fluid, takes only a couple of days, and can detect genetic abnormalities. In a study comparing CVS with amniocentesis, it was concluded that CVS is a safe and effective means for early diagnosis of genetic defects, although it does carry a slightly higher risk of miscarriage than amniocentesis (Hines, 1999).

An **ultrasound examination** also can detect many birth defects, although the analysis is not as detailed or as accurate as amniocentesis and CVS. In this procedure ultrasound waves are used to form a picture of the fetus in utero, called a **sonogram.** A trained technician uses a transmitter contacting the skin of the woman's abdomen, which broadcasts a brief, narrow burst of high-frequency sound; the resulting echo from the fetus produces the picture. Obviously, ultrasound can only detect the physical manifestations of any genetic defects. Ultrasound is also useful in monitoring the

Down Syndrome: a genetic disorder, associated with the presence of an extra chromosome 21, characterized by mild to severe mental retardation, a low nasal bridge, and epicanthic folds at the eyelids

Amniocentesis: test performed during the 16th to 18th week of pregnancy in order to determine the presence of birth defects in the developing fetus

Chorionic Villus Sampling (CVS): a test that is done early during pregnancy to check for the presence of genetic disorders. It involves obtaining a biopsy of the placenta, usually between the 10th and 13th weeks of pregnancy

Ultrasound Examination: the use of high frequency sound waves to locate body tissue and form a picture of the fetus in utero

Sonogram: the visual pattern or picture resulting from an ultrasound examination

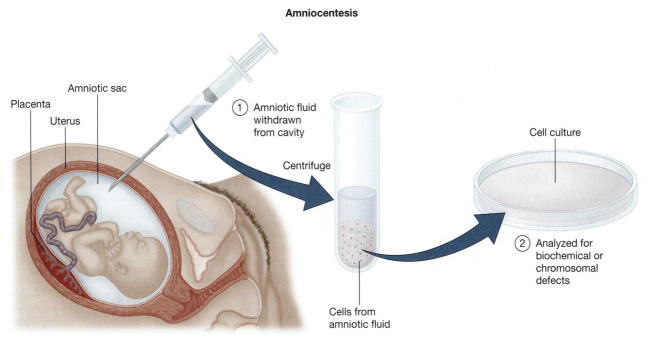

FIGURE 5.10 Amniocentesis.

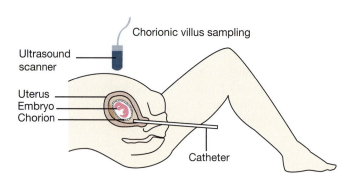

FIGURE 5.11 Chorionic Villus Sampling.

Rh Incompatibility: a condition in which antibodies produced by a pregnant woman are transmitted to the fetus and may cause brain damage or death

Toxemia: an abnormal condition associated with the presence of toxic substances in the blood

Preeclampsia: symptoms that are a precursor of eclampsia, a serious condition affecting pregnant women in which the entire body is affected by convulsions and the patient eventually passes into a coma

An ultrasound image (sonogram).

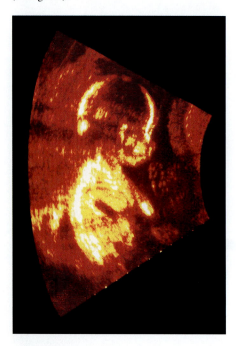

growth of the fetus, detecting twins, and aiding in the diagnosis of certain medical problems. Because it is not as invasive as CVS and amniocentesis, the risk to the fetus is believed to be much lower.

Rh Incompatibility

The Rh factor is a substance in the blood that is either present (Rh positive) or absent (Rh negative). **Rh incompatibility** is a condition in which antibodies from the pregnant woman's blood destroy red blood cells in the fetus. This can occur when Rh-positive blood mixes with Rh-negative blood, and in reaction the Rh-negative blood forms antibodies. While there usually is little interchange between the pregnant woman's blood and the fetus's (recall that the two have separate circulatory systems), exchange of blood can occur during delivery. Rh incompatibility can cause fetal anemia, mental retardation, or death.

This problem can occur only when an Rh-negative woman is pregnant with an Rh-positive fetus. There is generally no problem with the first such pregnancy, since the antibodies form after delivery. The development of Rh sensitivity and risk to subsequent children can usually be prevented if the mother is given medication within 72 hours after delivery or through abortion of an Rh-positive fetus to prevent formation of the antibodies.

Toxemia

Toxemia, a condition that occurs infrequently in expectant mothers, is characterized by high blood pressure, severe swelling, and protein in the urine. Toxemia appears in about 6 percent of pregnant women, usually in first pregnancies of very young women or those over age 35. Its cause is unknown. Left untreated, toxemia can progress to convulsions, coma, and even death of the mother or the fetus. Toxemia underscores the need for prenatal medical care, since it can be difficult to self-diagnose in the early stages.

Pregnancy-Induced Hypertension

As its name implies, pregnancy-induced hypertension is high blood pressure brought on by pregnancy. If left untreated, elevated blood pressure levels can also lead to preeclampsia or eclampsia. In **preeclampsia,** elevated blood pressure is accompanied by generalized edema (fluid retention) and protein-uria (protein in the urine), and is associated with an increased risk of fetal death. In severe cases, women with preeclampsia may experience vision problems, severe headaches, and abdominal pain. If preeclampsia progresses to eclampsia, a potentially fatal condition, the woman may have convulsions and go into a coma.

Ectopic Pregnancies

An **ectopic pregnancy** occurs when a fertilized egg implants somewhere other than the inner lining of the uterus. An ectopic pregnancy occurs in about 2 of 60 pregnancies. Most are due to an inability of the fertilized egg to make its way through a fallopian tube into the uterus. The large majority (95 percent) of ectopic pregnancies occur in the fallopian tubes (also referred to as a tubal pregnancy), but in rare cases implantation may occur in the abdominal cavity, on the cervix, or on an ovary.

The fertilized egg begins to develop, forming a placenta and producing the hormones and symptoms of pregnancy. The embryo may spontaneously abort and be released into the abdominal cavity, or it may continue to grow, stretching the tube until it ruptures. Sharp abdominal pain, cramping, and vaginal bleeding are all symptoms of a tubal rupture. Ectopic pregnancies cannot be carried to term, and may require surgical intervention.

Miscarriage

A spontaneous abortion that occurs in the first 20 weeks of pregnancy is called a **miscarriage.** While some women miscarry without knowing they are pregnant or realizing what has happened, 20 percent of pregnancies terminate in known miscarriages (see CAMPUS CONFIDENTIAL box). Early miscarriages may appear as heavy menstrual flow, while later ones may involve bad cramps, heavy bleeding, and/or recognizable uterine contents such as an embryo, amniotic sac, and placenta. Most miscarriages occur because of a defect in the embryo. About 60 percent of spontaneously aborted fetuses showed an abnormality incompatible with survival (Singer, 1995). A miscarriage does not mean that a woman will be unable to have a full-term pregnancy in the future.

Preterm Birth

When a child is born before the normal gestation period (term) is completed, his or her birth is considered to be preterm (pre = before). However, because the date of conception cannot always be determined, **premature birth** or **preterm birth** often is defined in terms of birth weight rather than weeks of gestation. Infants weighing less than 2,500 grams (5 pounds 9 ounces) are considered to be preterm, or "preemies." It is estimated that 7 percent of babies born in the United States are premature.

Preterm births are caused by many social and physical factors. Maternal factors such as age (younger than 16 or over 40), poor nutrition, heavy smoking, and syphilis are associated with prematurity. However, in over half the cases the cause of prematurity is unknown (Pritchard et al, 1985); it appears that no single factor may be responsible (Iams et al., 1998).

Preterm birth is the leading cause of newborn and infant mortality in the United States. Eight to 10 percent of births occur before 37 weeks gestation; the 1 to 2 percent of births that occur before 32 weeks account for half of **perinatal** deaths (those around the time of birth; peri = around). Premature infants may have difficulty swallowing and digesting food, and may require special intravenous feedings. Because the respiratory system may be underdeveloped, the baby may have difficulty breathing and moving air through the respiratory tract. Because of the immaturity of the lungs, the lung surfaces may be unable to absorb the amount of oxygen necessary for survival. Preterm infants are often placed in **incubators,** special cribs with controls to constantly monitor temperature and oxygen levels.

EXPECTANT FATHERS

When an expectant father places his hands on his partner's pregnant belly to feel a fetal foot pushing against the uterine wall, or hears the fetal heartbeat for the first time, the joy he experiences may make a positive contribution to the current and future health

CAMPUS CONFIDENTIAL

"I miscarried early in my pregnancy, probably during my second month. It was really weird because I had only just suspected I was pregnant. I wasn't even sure I was pregnant when I miscarried. I'd missed a couple of periods and was trying to work up the nerve to do a home pregnancy test when I started having really bad cramps. At first I thought I was constipated or getting my period, but the cramps kept getting worse. I went into the bathroom and suddenly realized that it wasn't a bowel movement I was pushing out. I started shaking and crying and didn't want to look in the toilet. I finally got myself together and went to the health center and they confirmed that I'd had a miscarriage.

"I guess it wasn't really a baby yet, or really even a pregnancy . . . but for some reason I still felt unbelievably sad. I was really nervous throughout my next pregnancy, even though my doctor kept reassuring me that everything was going well. And she was right. Our son was full term, perfectly healthy, and a total joy!" ●

Ectopic Pregnancy: pregnancy in which the fertilized ovum become implanted some place other than the uterus

Miscarriage: spontaneous abortion; spontaneous expulsion of a human fetus before it is viable and especially during the first 20 weeks of gestation

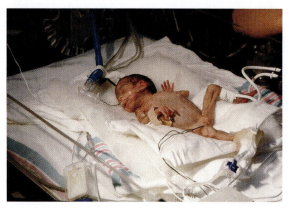

Preterm infant in an incubator.

of the fetus. There are those who believe that the developing fetus is affected by both its physical and emotional environments. So a man's contribution to parenting does not cease between conception and childbirth. A Swedish study found that fathers' negative experiences during childbirth were correlated with the amount of crying in their child during the first months after birth (Wikander & Theorell, 1997).

Men respond differently to the changed shape of a pregnant woman. Some men believe that their partners are never so sexy as when they are pregnant. Others find the changes unappealing, especially in the third trimester, and an increase in the woman's self-absorption and physical fatigue may contribute to a widening gulf in personal relations.

CROSS-CULTURAL PERSPECTIVES

Expectant Fathers

In some societies men are expected to experience physical symptoms of pregnancy. This condition is called **couvade syndrome.** *For example, among Australian aborigines, men get morning sickness. In fact the man's nausea may be the first evidence that his spouse is pregnant. With this realization the man will abstain from eating certain foods believed to be harmful to the developing fetus. Later, when it is time for the birth, the man may complain* *of abdominal pains and take to his bed. Only after the actual birth will the man, exhausted from his labor, feel well enough to return to his normal routines.*

While there is less societal support for such symptoms among pregnant fathers in our culture, couvade syndrome is not uncommon. It has been reported that some such sympathetic symptoms were experienced by 23 percent of a group of American expectant fathers (Lipkin & Lamb, 1982).

Commitment and sharing can be promoted in other ways besides sexual activity. Participating as a couple in as many of the pregnancy activities as possible, from routine checkups to birthing classes, can reinforce a couple's commitment to one another and to the upcoming addition to their family. The recent passage of family leave legislation allows many new fathers to take paternity leave from their jobs so that they can be there to support their partners after the child is born.

THE BIRTH EXPERIENCE

Labor

The trimesters of pregnancy culminate in three stages of **labor,** the rhythmic contractions of the uterus that expel the fetus, placenta, and membranes from the woman's body. The length of each stage of labor may vary considerably from one woman to another and from one pregnancy to the next.

A few weeks before the onset of labor, both the woman and the fetus begin to prepare for the inevitable. The fetus turns so that the widest part of its head is positioned firmly against the woman's pelvic bones. This process is called **engagement** (it is also referred to as "dropping" or "lightening"). Eventually the woman's cervix begins to thin in preparation for the stretching required for passage of the baby; this process is called **effacement.** The mouth of the cervix also begins to **dilate,** or open.

Dilation may dislodge the mucous plug in the cervix, resulting in a discharge called "bloody show." This "show" is simply a small amount of blood resulting from broken

Premature Birth/Preterm Birth: child born prior to 37 weeks gestation, though often defined in terms of birth weight rather than gestation

Perinatal: phase surrounding the time of birth, from the 20th week of gestation to the 28th day of newborn life.

Incubator: an apparatus for maintaining an infant, especially a premature infant, in an environment of controlled temperature, humidity, and oxygen concentration

Couvade Syndrome: males having "sympathetic pregnancies" in which they experience a number of pregnancy symptoms

Labor: process by which childbirth occurs, beginning with contractions of the uterus and ending with the expulsion of the fetus or infant and the placenta

Engagement: process prior to childbirth during which the fetus turns so that the widest part of its head is positioned firmly against the woman's pelvic bones

Effacement: the thinning of the cervix, which occurs before and while it dilates

Dilate: to open or grow wider; expand

Pregnant Fathers?

In the 1994 movie *Junior*, Arnold Schwarzenegger played a scientist who has a fertilized egg implanted in his body, takes a "wonder drug," and becomes pregnant. Although the movie may seem like science fiction, the technology needed to make a man pregnant already exists. Hormones can be supplied by injection, and after in vitro fertilization of an egg, the embryo would be inserted into the male's abdominal cavity. A placenta would be implanted to absorb nutrients from the bloodstream. Delivery would be via laparotomy, similar to cesarean section. Abdominal pregnancies occur naturally in about 1 in every 10,000 pregnancies, some of which do result in live births (Teresi, 1994).

 What do you think about the possibility of men becoming pregnant?

> —*What would be some of the social ramifications of men bearing children?*
> —*How do you think it might change the relationships between men and women?*
> —*If male pregnancy were an option, is it something you would consider for yourself or your partner?*

---

capillaries at the surface of the ripening cervix. Mucous tissue that had plugged the cervix becomes dislodged resulting in a discharge of bloody mucus. In about 10 percent of women, the membranes of the amniotic sac rupture prematurely, releasing the amniotic fluid that has been protecting the fetus for almost 9 months. When her "water breaks," a woman will feel a flood of warm fluid; after this event, labor typically begins within a day.

In the last days of pregnancy, many women experience strong Braxton-Hicks contractions. Because such an event causes many anxious new parents to rush to the hospital, it is often referred to as false labor. It is difficult to distinguish false labor from the real thing, but Braxton-Hicks contractions tend to be more irregular than the true contractions of labor. Real labor contractions get longer, stronger, and closer together as birth approaches. In addition, the discomfort of false labor is usually in the lower abdomen and groin, while the pain of true labor is felt in the back and abdomen.

The First Stage of Labor   If the couple does end up at the hospital, a health-care professional can confirm whether the contractions are the real thing by an internal examination. False labor does not increase effacement or dilation; it is the strong uterine contractions of the first stage of labor that result in the flattening, thinning, and opening up of the cervix (Figure 5.12a). These changes must occur before delivery can occur. Measurement of the dilation of the cervix defines the boundaries between the early, active, and transition phases of first stage labor. During the early phase the cervix dilates up to 4 centimeters, from 4 to 8 centimeters in the active phase, and from 8 to 10 centimeters in the transition phase.

On average, the first stage of labor lasts 13 hours for a first labor and 8 hours for subsequent ones. However, there is great variation in the length of labor from woman to woman and from pregnancy to pregnancy. Early in labor the contractions are mild, lasting 20 to 40 seconds, and they may be 10 to 20 minutes apart. A woman may be able to walk around; in fact, walking makes many women feel more comfortable and may shorten the overall time of labor (Lupe & Gross, 1986). Contractions bring with them the urge to push the baby out; resisting this urge is perhaps the greatest challenge of the first stage of labor. Pain medications typically are not recommended at the early phases of the first stage of labor, since they may lessen the strength of the contractions, lengthening the time of labor. Later in the first stage, when the contractions become much stronger and are closer together, medication is available to help ease the pain and relax the mother-to-be. As you have already learned, any medications have potential risks for pregnant woman and the fetus. However, careful use under medical supervision can provide considerable pain relief with minimal risks. Childbirth medications will be discussed in the section on Childbirth Alternatives.

The Second Stage of Labor   The second stage of labor (Figure 5.12b) begins when the cervix is fully dilated to 10 centimeters, and ends with the birth of the baby. This

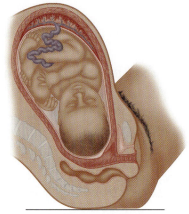

(a) In the first stage of labor, the cervix begins to dilate

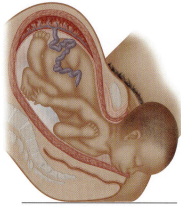

(b) The infant is delivered in the second stage

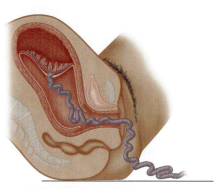

(c) Third stage is the delivery of the placenta

Figure 5.12 The Birth Process. (a) In the first stage of labor the cervix begins to dilate to allow the passage of the fetus through the birth canal. (b) The infant is delivered in the second stage. (c) The third stage is the delivery of the placenta.

stage lasts, on average, about 80 minutes for first pregnancies and 30 minutes for subsequent ones. This is often a more active and less stressful time for the woman; she is finally able to push during her contractions. In contrast, the fetus may experience increasing amounts of stress, and is carefully monitored during this stage. Throughout labor the fetus is constricted and pushed forcefully for hours on end, a great contrast to its previous existence of peaceful idyllic bliss in utero.

Once the head is delivered, blood and mucus are wiped away and the nose and mouth is suctioned to induce breathing. As the rest of the body is delivered, the umbilical cord is clamped and cut, leaving only a stub that will wither and fall off in a few days. With the baby's first breaths, the skin color changes from blue to a rosy pink. To prevent possible eye infections, drops are placed in the baby's eyes and he or she is given a shot of vitamin K to prevent possible bleeding. The baby undergoes a number of tests; the cumulative result of these tests is called the *Apgar score*. When the tests have been completed, the mother can nurse the baby if she so desires.

The Third Stage of Labor The third stage of labor, the delivery of the placenta and fetal membranes (Figure 5.12c), usually takes only 10 to 12 minutes. Typically, a few uterine contractions separate the placenta from the uterine wall and expel the afterbirth through the vagina without incident. However, the mother must be monitored closely in case any hemorrhaging results.

Childbirth Alternatives

Some pregnant women, realizing that it is time to deliver, stop hoeing, walk to the edge of a field, build a grass shade rest, lie down, give birth, clean the newborn, bury the placenta, and return to their hoeing. This is no more unusual than the custom of confining women to a hospital for up to a week with each delivery. While there is

So Smart It Hurts

CONSIDERATIONS

At some point in human evolution the brain became so large in proportion to the woman's birth canal that it became difficult for women to give birth. This tight squeeze is known as the *obstetrical dilemma* (Fisher, 1992). In addition to increased brain size, our distant ancestors began to walk upright so the pelvis bore more of the weight of pregnancy. As a result, the pelvis became shorter and the birth canal narrower (Konner, 1990). By the time of *Homo erectus*, hundreds of thousands of years ago, giving birth had become so difficult that women needed a helper to catch the baby; thus the tradition of the **midwife** began even before the evolution of Homo sapiens. (Fisher, 1992).

 What do you think of the obstetrical dilemma?

—Do you think that women who have relatively easy deliveries have babies who are less intelligent?

much cultural variation in the childbirth process, this most common experience for women has continued largely unchanged for thousands of years. In addition to the fields and the hospital, many women deliver at home assisted by family and a specialist called a midwife.

Birthplace Options Physicians, midwives, childbirth educators, and expectant parents have disagreed for centuries about whether childbirth should be treated as a medical emergency or a normal life event. Advocates of each view now seem to agree on one thing: women should have the widest possible range of choices in childbirth.

Today pregnant women in the United States have options about the location and nature of delivery that were unavailable to past generations of women. A hospital delivery provides backup technology in case a problem becomes evident during delivery. Although some women find the austere, bureaucratic environment of a hospital to be cold and impersonal, some hospitals have made drastic changes in recent years to be more accommodating to women and their families. Free-standing birthing centers and birthing rooms that create a homelike environment and permit the entire family to participate in the experience are becoming widely available. Some couples still find home to be a more comfortable, loving, and natural place to have a baby. Proponents of home birth believe that it gives the woman more control over the process, with greater support from family and friends than a hospital will allow.

Pain Relief Options Many mothers would probably agree that childbirth is a wondrous—and painful—experience. Much of the pain is caused by the strong rhythmic contractions of the uterus as it stretches the cervix wide enough to allow the baby through and into the birth canal. The pressure of the baby's head passing through the normally narrow birth canal adds to the discomfort. A woman's internal pelvic structure, the size of the baby, and the position of the baby's body also play a part in how difficult labor will be. There are several types of medications used to deal with the pain of labor. Each of these has potentially different effects on the woman and the fetus.

Debate about whether, or how, to ease the pain of childbirth is nothing new. In 1591 the Scottish midwife Agnes Sampson was burned as a witch for attempting to reduce the pain of a woman in labor. When physician Sir James Simpson introduced chloroform as a pain reliever in 1847, some people objected to its use in childbirth on the grounds that pain was a punishment from God. Only after Queen Victoria demanded chloroform for the birth of her eighth child in 1853 did the use of pain relief in childbirth become accepted.

In the early part of the 20th century hospitals began to administer "twilight sleep"—a dose of morphine at the onset of labor followed by a shot of a sedative then a whiff of chloroform. While this eased the pain of childbirth, heavy sedation prevented the mother from pushing the baby. This increased the need for forceps deliveries and Cesarean sections, which are more risky for mother and child.

Midwife: a person, usually a woman, who is trained to assist women in childbirth

Epidural Anesthesia: an injection through a catheter of a local anesthetic to relieve pain during labor, usually done at the lumbar level of the spine

Hydrotherapy: hot whirlpool baths used in birthing centers

Lamaze Method: method in which a woman and her coach (often the baby's father) learn about childbirth and how to relax and breathe in patterns that conserve energy and decrease pain

Obstetrician: a physician who specializes in pregnancy and childbirth

Doula: a woman who assists women during labor and after childbirth

Episiotomy: a surgical incision in the perineum that widens the birth canal to prevent tearing during childbirth

Epidural anesthesia, applied through the spinal cord, numbs a woman from the waist down but allows her to push. The epidural has grown in popularity since the 1970s. In the United States today, 80 percent of women in labor receive some form of pain medication; 33 percent of those use epidurals.

A new *"walking"* epidural, also called the *dual spinal-epidural* or *epidural light,* was first developed in England in 1987. This procedure relies on new technology (a smaller needle with a rounded tip that is less likely to damage spinal fibers) and new techniques (a two-phase system for delivering anesthetic continuously in doses many times lower than those commonly used a decade ago). The procedure appears to give good pain relief with fewer side effects. Some hospitals also use **hydrotherapy,** hot whirlpool baths or showers with massaging heads, in birthing centers with favorable results (Shute, 1997).

One study found that several factors predict the degree of pain a woman perceives during childbirth. The duration of labor, depression, and the expectancy that childbirth education would facilitate medication-free childbirth predicted less pain. A physician who anticipates complications, induced labor, and less motivation to be medication free, predicted greater pain intensity (Dannenbring, Stevens, & House, 1997).

Delivery Options There are several birthing alternatives that incorporate education, relaxation, and emotional support. Perhaps the best-known method of prepared childbirth is based on the philosophy of French obstetrician Fernand Lamaze. Although the **Lamaze method** and other prepared childbirth methods are sometimes referred to as "natural childbirth," most do not prohibit the use of anesthetics. Lamaze techniques consist of learning to relax abdominal and perineal muscles voluntarily and to use controlled breathing exercises to dissociate the involuntary labor contraction from pain sensations. An important component of the Lamaze method is that a coach accompanies the woman during classes, labor, and delivery. The Lamaze coach, often the woman's husband or partner, plays an integral role in the woman's learning and using the techniques during labor and delivery. The coach times contractions; helps the woman relax; provides feedback, encouragement, and moral support; and helps elevate her back as she pushes.

A number of studies indicate that childbirth training provides a number of benefits. These include a reduction in the length of labor, lowered incidence of birth complications, a decrease in the use of anesthetics, a more positive attitude toward childbirth, and an increased sense of being in control (Slade et al., 2000; Zax et al., 1975). Childbirth training also allows the expectant father to have an active, useful role in the birth experience.

A midwife (not necessarily but usually a woman) is a nonphysician trained to assist a woman during childbirth. Many midwives also provide prenatal care and birth education. Depending on local law, midwives may deliver babies in the mother's home, in a special birthing center or clinic, or in a hospital. Most midwives specialize in normal, uncomplicated deliveries, referring women with health problems that could require hospitalization during birth to a hospital-based **obstetrician,** a medical doctor with special training in labor and delivery. Other midwives work with physicians as part of a team.

Trained labor coaches known as **doulas** (from the Greek word meaning servant or handmaiden) are becoming increasingly popular. Doulas provide emotional and physical support during pregnancy, labor, and delivery. Research shows that the benefits of having a doula go beyond having shorter and less painful labors. In one study women were assigned a doula at random; those who had doulas during labor were found to be more sensitive, loving, and responsive to their infants 2 months after birth (Landry & Kennell, 1998).

Medical Intervention When a spontaneous vaginal delivery is not possible, medical intervention becomes necessary to the health of mother and baby. An **episiotomy** is a surgical incision in the woman's perineum

Prepared childbirth class.

(Figure 5.13) that gives the fetus's head more room to emerge. Most physicians perform episiotomies routinely at the time of *crowning*, when the baby's head first appears at the opening of the vagina.

The rationale is that by cutting this tissue and then suturing it closed after the delivery is complete, the force of the emerging newborn's head is less likely to tear the tissue. A clean-cut incision is easier to repair and is more likely to heal quickly and safely than ripped tissue. The episiotomy also is believed to reduce the pressure against the fetus's head, lessening the trauma of the birth experience, and to more readily permit the use of forceps or vacuum devices. Another reason sometimes given in support of episiotomy is maintenance of vaginal tightness for heightened sexual pleasure. Those who argue against routine episiotomies contend that the vaginal opening has a tremendous capacity to stretch and recover without tearing and routine episiotomies during uncomplicated labor present greater risks than benefits (Maier & Malony, 1997).

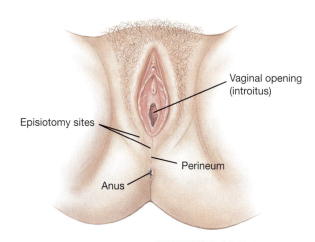

FIGURE 5.13 Episiotomy.

Forceps, a medical instrument that looks like tongs, are designed to clasp the infant's head and are sometimes used to assist the baby through the birth canal. Forceps deliveries are often used after medications have reduced the strength of uterine contractions or if the baby's head has not rotated into a face-down position. The use of forceps is not recommended for routine deliveries.

Vacuum extraction is sometimes used along with or instead of forceps in difficult deliveries. In 1998 the FDA issued a public health advisory, "Need for Caution When Using Vacuum Assisted Delivery Devices," to all practitioners delivering babies. A 1999 study (Towner et al.) suggested that a difficult labor posed as much risk as the selected method of delivery. The study found that the risks of brain injury and death were highest with combined methods of delivery (vacuum-assisted and forceps) and failed operative attempts at vaginal delivery. Use of forceps alone, use of vacuum devices alone, and cesarean section during labor were associated with an intermediate risk of injury. The risk was lowest with spontaneous vaginal delivery and cesarean section without labor.

Cesarean section, or *C-section*, is the removal of the fetus through an incision in the walls of the abdomen and uterus. This operation is performed when normal vaginal delivery threatens the well-being of the woman or the fetus. Nearly one of every five births in the United States is now by C-section (Gilbert, 1998). Two common causes of C-section include a pelvis too small to permit passage of the fetus's head through the birth canal, and a fetus that does not and cannot be turned for a head-first emergence.

Many expectant mothers report that medical intervention in pregnancy and childbirth results in feelings of alienation from their bodies and a lack of control over the childbirth experience. The use of medical technology can also impact the father's experience, causing him to feel less involved and to have decreased control over pregnancy and childbirth (Williams & Umberton, 1999). However, there are cases in which medical intervention is necessary; communication with your health-care professional regarding your options is essential to a positive birthing experience.

Forceps: an instrument resembling a pair of pincers or tongs, used for grasping, manipulating, or extracting the fetus from the uterus or vagina

Vacuum Extraction: removal of the fetus from the uterus or vagina at or near the end of pregnancy with a metal traction cup that is attached to the fetus's head. Negative pressure is applied and traction is made on a chain passed through the suction tube

Cesarean Section: method of childbirth in which the fetus is delivered through a surgical incision in the abdomen; C-section

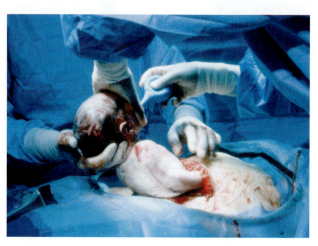

Cesarean section.

POSTPARTUM

Certainly no life event rivals the hormonal and psychosocial changes associated with pregnancy and childbirth. After the birth of her baby, the woman's body undergoes drastic physiological and psychological changes. When the placenta is expelled the levels of estrogen and progesterone

FAQ:

Once a cesarean, always a cesarean?

At one time it was thought that once you had a C-section, you could not deliver vaginally because of concern that uterine scars might rupture during labor. However, women who have had cesarean deliveries can indeed have subsequent safe vaginal deliveries (Kolata, 1980; McMahon et al., 1996; Notzon, Placek & Taffel, 1987; Weitz, 1985). This is called *vaginal birth after cesarean (VBAC)*.

drop sharply before gradually returning to normal levels over a period of a few weeks to a few months. In addition, labor and delivery are hard work and the woman may feel exhausted. Episiotomy can cause some discomfort, and there is additional recovery needed after delivery by cesarean section.

Postpartum Mood Disorders

The **postpartum** period is a time of high risk for the onset of mood disorders ranging from the "maternity blues" (feeling stressed) to a major depressive disorder (a marked clinical depression) and postpartum psychosis (including delusions and hallucinations) (Miller, 1999). Many factors may contribute to these mood disorders. There is the stress and exhaustion associated with caring for a newborn at a time when a woman's energy levels are already low. Because the infant may require feeding, changing, or other care several times during the night, sleep deprivation can be a problem for several weeks or several months. Plunging hormone levels may also affect the new mother's outlook.

Sex After Delivery

After delivery, physicians usually recommend that women abstain from coitus for a few weeks to allow the vagina and uterus to return to normal shape and size. Waiting also allows an episiotomy to heal. Noncoital sexual expression is one rewarding option during this waiting period. One study in Great Britain found that compared to before pregnancy, women reported a decrease in frequency and satisfaction with sexual intercourse. Vaginal pain and a loss of sexual desire were the most frequently cited problems (Barrett et al., 1999).

Breastfeeding

The vast majority of women throughout the world breast-feed their babies. However, for the past few decades most babies in the United States have been bottle-fed. Women's breasts prepare for **lactation,** milk production, within 2 or 3 days after delivery. For the few days prior to milk production the breasts secrete a thin fluid called **colostrum** that is high in protein and gives the newborn a temporary immunity to infectious diseases. Two hormones secreted by the pituitary, **prolactin** and oxytocin are involved in lactation. Prolactin is produced while the woman nurses her child and stimulates the production of milk. Oxytocin stimulates the breasts to eject milk in response to the baby's sucking.

Breast-feeding provides nutrition and keeps mother and baby together, thereby greatly enhancing the probability of survival of the infant. It is also a means of regulating birth spacing, albeit an imperfect one; a woman generally does not ovulate until she has stopped nursing her baby. However, as we mention in Chapter 6 (see the CROSS-CULTURAL PERSPECTIVES box, page 169), do not count on nursing as birth control! Remember, ovulation occurs *before* menstruation, so there's no way to tell! Mother's milk helps the baby fight infections, is instantly available, and does not require sterilization. Nursing may also provide psychological benefits for both mother and child, and helps shrink the uterus to its normal size after childbirth. A woman struggling with breast-feeding can contact a lactation consultant, a service available through many hospitals.

On the other hand, any drugs or medications taken by the mother are usually secreted in her milk where they can affect the infant (Platzker, Lew, & Stewart, 1980). Some women are physically unable to breast-feed. Others choose not to for a variety of reasons. Breast-feeding can be inconvenient for mothers who work outside the home. Even those who remain at home may not be comfortable nursing their children in public settings. Fathers and other caretakers can bottle-feed infants, help that new mothers appreciate at 4:00 A.M.

Breast-feeding.

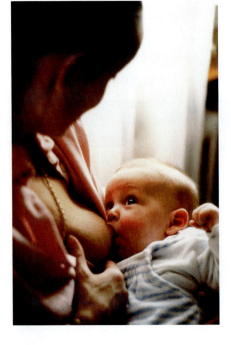

Mother Nature

Maternal instinct and good mothering go together like peanut butter and jelly. Or do they? According to Sarah Hrdy (2000), the good mother who unselfishly lives for her children is not only uninvolved in the feminist sense, but could not evolve in the anthropological sense. Hrdy uses literature, history, anthropology and evolutionary biology to support her theory that motherhood is neither instinctual nor automatic. A mother's decision to nurture or abandon a child is influenced by a multitude of selective forces that shape maternal behavior. Work by Harvard biologist David Haig (1993) suggests that this struggle begins early in pregnancy and that some complications of pregnancy result from a fetal demand for better nourishment that is detrimental to the mother's health. In Haig's view, maternal diabetes and pre-eclampsia reflect a conflict for survival between mother and fetus.

 What is your definition of a "good" mother?

—Are good mothers born that way or do they learn how to be good parents?

—What other explanation can you think of that explains maternal extinct?

—Do you think fathers have a paternal instinct?

A study of a group of urban multi-ethnic low-income mothers in the United States indicates that regardless of their feeding method, mothers tended to attribute higher health benefits to breast-feeding and perceived community norms as favoring breast-feeding. Those who chose not to breast-feed perceived social disapproval of breast-feeding in public, ridicule by friends, lack of support from some health providers, and difficulties associated with working (Guttman & Zimmerman, 2000).

Masters and Johnson (1966) found that women who nurse their babies have considerably higher sexual interest in the early months after giving birth than women who do not nurse. Women sometimes become sexually aroused while breast-feeding their infants, and some may even have orgasms while nursing. This in no way means that the woman is sexually attracted to her child. Arousal may be the result of the surges of hormones related to breast-feeding, or the mother may experience strong psychological effects from the tactile interactions with the infant.

The American Academy of Pediatrics (AAP, 1997) recommends that mothers breast-feed for at least 1 year. The AAP guidelines also urge employers to provide a place for women to nurse at work and recommend that insurance companies pay for services such as lactation counseling to teach new mothers the basics of nursing. In addition, it is recommended that mothers begin breast-feeding within the first hour of birth and feed newborns on demand as often as 12 times daily if needed; milk can be pumped and stored for later use when breast-feeding is not possible.

INFERTILITY

Infertility is often defined as the inability to conceive for 1 year or more. Approximately 5.3 million couples in the United States are said to be infertile. According to the National Center for Health Statistics (NCHS, 1995) the percentage of childless infertile couples increased from 14.4 percent in 1965 to 18.5 percent in 1995. Some of the increase is due to the fact that fertility decreases with age; there are a greater number of 30- and 40-year-olds attempting a first pregnancy. In addition, the greater the number of sexual partners, the greater the risk of a sexually transmitted infection that could impair fertility. In approximately 40 percent of couples it is the woman's infertility that prevents conception. In another 40 percent of cases the man is infertile. In 20 percent both partners are unable to conceive, or the cause is unknown.

Female Infertility

Female infertility affects approximately 1 in 12 women 15 to 44 years of age (NCHS, 2000). A woman may not become pregnant for a number of reasons. **Anovulation,** the failure to ovulate, is the most common fertility problem among women. Anovulation

Postpartum: period following childbirth

Lactation: production of milk by the mammary glands

Colostrum: a thin fluid secreted by the breasts at the termination of pregnancy before milk production begins; it is high in proteins and rich in antibodies that confer temporary immunity to the newborn

Prolactin: pituitary hormone that stimulates production of milk

Infertility: inability to conceive a child

Anovulation: the absence of ovulation

may result from hormonal irregularities, malnutrition, genetic factors, or stress. The latter includes the stress of prolonged strenuous physical activity such as regular long-distance running.

Blockage of the reproductive tract can prevent sperm from entering the uterus or fallopian tubes. Such a barrier may result from cervical mucus or scar tissue from infectious diseases. A common cause of scarring is **pelvic inflammatory disease (PID)** (see Chapter 7). Several types of bacteria and viruses may cause PID. Among women who have a single episode of PID, 20 percent will become infertile (Westrom, 1980).

Endometriosis is another common cause of infertility (see Chapter 2). When cells break away from the endometrium they may grow on the surface of the ovaries or fallopian tubes and block the passage of ova. It is estimated that 15 percent of female infertility is due to endometriosis.

The cervical mucus of some women may contain antibodies that attack the male's sperm, a condition called **cervical factor infertility.** In addition, infections and abnormalities of the cervix, vagina, uterus, fallopian tubes, or ovaries can destroy sperm or prevent them from reaching the ovum. Sexually transmitted infections cause about 20 percent of all female infertility (Office of Technology Assessment, 1988). Alcohol and drug use, including tobacco and marijuana, also are known to affect female fertility adversely.

Male Infertility

Infertility affects approximately 1 man in 25. In about 30 to 40 percent of affected men, the results of semen analyses are abnormal but no cause of the infertility can be found. A man will have difficulty impregnating his partner if he does not produce a sufficient number of sperm, if the sperm lack sufficient motility to reach the fallopian tubes, or if the sperm are malformed. By far the most common cause of male infertility is low sperm count. Normally a male produces 40 to 150 million sperm per milliliter of semen. A count (called the *sperm density*) of fewer than 20 million is considered low. There are several correctable causes of low sperm counts: frequent ejaculation, tight underwear, frequent hot baths, use of electric blankets, or anything that raises scrotal temperature by as little as 1 to 2 degrees Fahrenheit (Leary, 1990; Robinson & Rock, 1967); prolonged strenuous physical activity such as regular long-distance running can also play a role. Undescended testes that have not been surgically corrected also may result in a low sperm count, as can hormone deficiencies. A damaged or enlarged vein in the testes or vas deferens, called the varicocele, can cause infertility by raising the temperature in the scrotum (Schlegel, 1991). This condition is surgically correctable (Crocket, Takihara & Cosentino, 1984).

Ejaculated sperm normally should be able to swim for at least 2 hours. Low motility, or sluggishness, means that the sperm will not make it up the fallopian tube before it degenerates. Sperm motility can be affected by prostate or hormonal problems, scar tissue resulting from infection, or genetic predisposition.

Sperm with malformed heads or tails may be incapable of fertilization. There are several common causes of such malformation, including infectious diseases and trauma to the testes. Some men have an autoimmune response in which their own antibodies attack their sperm. The loss of a tiny piece of the male sex chromosome appears to cause the most severe form of male infertility. The loss of this piece causes the deletion of one or more genes in a small area of the Y chromosome. Some of the men with this defect can make immature sperm cells, but none produce mature sperm. Researchers believe that the genetic flaw arises spontaneously and is not inherited (Sun et al., 1995).

An analysis of data collected from 1938 to 1990 indicates that sperm densities in the United States have decreased an average of about 1.5 percent a year; those in European countries have declined about twice that rate—3.1 percent a year (Swan, Elkin, & Fenster, 1997). Some recent studies have suggested that environmental exposures may account for declining sperm counts. Environmental toxins, such as pollutants, radiation, alcohol, tobacco, and drugs, may produce low sperm counts and malformed sperm (Hurd et al., 1992; Sharpe & Skakkebaeck, 1993; Wiles & Campbell, 1993).

Pelvic Inflammatory Disease (PID): an inflammation of the female pelvic organs, most commonly the fallopian tubes, usually as a result of bacterial infection

Cervical Factor Infertility: condition in which the cervical mucus of some women contains antibodies that attack the male's sperm

Dealing With Infertility

Although a couple might be identified as infertile after a year of attempting pregnancy without success, in most cases couples are advised to wait at least 2 years before seeking treatment for infertility. Before taking any course of infertility treatment couples should be informed about their chances of conceiving spontaneously. Fertility and infertility are not an all-or-nothing diagnosis. Because a couple has not conceived after a year, or even several years, it does not mean that they will never be able to conceive. Treatment of infertility usually does not make the difference between conceiving and not conceiving; the difference is in conceiving sooner rather than later (Velde & Cohlen, 1999).

There are many pathways to becoming a parent. The choice of which path is taken appears to depend more on circumstance than inherent differences. However parenthood is achieved, parental concerns and enjoyment are similar.

There are several alternatives that couples may consider, depending on the cause of infertility and their personal needs. Some of these treatments are more invasive than other methods, and some have higher success rates than others. Seeking treatment for infertility is not something to be pursued casually. It requires commitment and cooperation, and in many cases a significant financial investment.

The Psychological Impact of Infertility   Infertility may have psychological origins as well as psychological effects. Using the Infertility Distress Scale, one researcher found that the perceived stress resulting from infertility is a risk factor for a decrease in sperm quality (Pook et al., 1999). Research results suggest that couples entering fertility programs are generally psychologically well adjusted. Both women and men experience waiting for the outcome of the treatment and unsuccessful treatments as most stressful; anxiety and depression are the most common reactions reported. After a successful treatment, formerly infertile couples experience more stress during pregnancy than do fertile couples. Factors including poor coping strategies, anxiety, and depression were shown to be associated with lower pregnancy rates following fertility procedures (Eugster & Vingerhoets, 1999). Mothers with children conceived by in vitro fertilization (discussed later) were found to express a higher quality of parent-child relationship than those with naturally conceived children (ibid). Fathers with a history of infertility appear to be more involved in interacting with their infants (Holditch-Davis et al., 1999)

Infertility is a stressor that affects both men and women and can impact a couple's relationship. Sexual dysfunction can both contribute to infertility and be a byproduct of the diagnosis. Men and women may experience infertility differently. Women use the coping strategies of social support, escape-avoidance, problem solving, and positive reappraisal to a greater degree than their partners. Findings suggest that coping at both the individual and the couple level should be considered when dealing with the emotional affects of infertility; infertile couples may want to consider counseling (Jordan & Revenson, 1999).

Surgical Procedures   When the cause of infertility is endometriosis, surgery is sometimes successful in removing tissue or adhesions that are preventing the fertilized embryo from implanting in the uterine wall. Laser surgery is becoming more common as a treatment for endometriosis, with subsequent pregnancy rates of about 40 to 65 percent (Berger, Goldstein, & Fuerst, 1989). Endometriosis can also be treated with drugs.

Superovulation   **Superovulation,** the production of mature ova at an accelerated rate or in large numbers at one time, is often the first option considered for anovulation. The drug clomiphene citrate (trade name Clomid) induces ovulation by stimulating the production of pituitary hormones. About 50 percent of the women treated with clomiphene become pregnant. Women who do not become pregnant with clomiphene may be given human menopausal gonadotropins (HMG), which stimulate the ovaries directly to produce eggs. HMG is effective in stimulating ovulation for 90 percent of women with functioning ovaries; 60 to 70 percent of these will become pregnant.

Superovulation: stimulation of multiple ovulation with fertility drugs

In Vitro Fertilization (IVF):
fertilization outside of the body in a laboratory

With both HMG and clomiphene there is an increased chance that the woman will have multiple births (see CONSIDERATIONS box). Multiple births occur in 1.2 percent of routine pregnancies. With clomiphene the risk increases to 8 percent, and 20 percent of pregnancies assisted by HMG lead to multiple births due to overstimulation of the ovaries. HMG also poses serious health risks for some women; fluid can leak into the abdomen, and the ovaries can become enlarged or even rupture.

In vitro fertilization When the reproductive tract is blocked, preventing an ovum from reaching the fallopian tube or uterus, there are two common means of treatment. If microsurgery is unsuccessful in removing scar tissue and repairing blocked fallopian tubes, women may be treated with **in vitro fertilization (IVF)** (in vitro is Latin for "in glass"). IVF involves removing mature eggs from a woman's ovary and fertilizing them with sperm in a laboratory before surgically implanting them in the woman's uterus (intrauterine implantation) or cervix (intracervical implantation). Intrauterine insemination in combination with superovulation is three times as likely to result in pregnancy as treatment with superovulation and intracervical insemination or intrauterine insemination alone (Guzick et al., 1999).

CONSIDERATIONS

Multiplying the Odds, Multiplying the Risks

The aggressive use of fertility drugs has resulted in a fourfold increase in the annual number of multiple births since 1970. Normally a woman will produce just one viable egg a month. By forcing the release of numerous eggs at once, fertility drugs raise the chance of multiple births. When supercharged with a drug, a woman's ovaries can release as many as 40 eggs in one cycle.

Though multiple births are rare under normal conditions, one third of all IVF pregnancies result in multiple births. The rate of multiple births during superovulation cycles is about 30 percent (Velde & Cohlen, 1999). The rate of triplet live births and the ratio of triplet births per 100,000 births rose 272 percent between1980 and 1995 (National Center for Health Statistics, 1997).

Unlike those of some other mammals, the human uterus is not designed for multiple births. Crowding can cause premature birth with severe consequences. On average, each additional fetus shortens the normal 40-week gestation period by about $3\frac{1}{2}$ weeks. Even if born alive, triplets, quadruplets, and quintuplets are 12 times more likely than other babies to die within a year. There are serious risks of respiratory, gastrointestinal, and neurological disorders, including blindness, cerebral palsy, and mental retardation. The American Society for Reproductive Medicine (ASRM, 1999) recommends that fertility specialists limit the number of viable embryos they place in a woman's womb. However, fertility clinics are not regulated, and some doctors are as eager to conceive as their patients.

Research shows that the risk of multiple births from fertility treatments varies by maternal age and the number of embryos transferred (Schieve et al., 1999). The American College of Obstetrics and Gynecologists addressed the issue of multiple embryo pregnancies in 1999 and recommended that fewer embryos be implanted during fertility treatment. The ASRM now proposes the implantation of only two embryos for women under 35 with excess healthy eggs and no more than three embryos for women under 35 with fewer healthy eggs. For women 35 to 40, no more than four implanted embryos are recommended and no more than five for women 41 and older (ASRM, 1999).

One alternative is multifetal pregnancy reduction (MFPR), techniques developed over the past 15 years to deal with the increase in multiple gestations resulting from infertility treatment. MFPR is a technique that reduces the number of fetuses in an effort to increase the likelihood that the pregnancy will continue. Consequently, the risks to the mother and remaining fetuses are reduced. This procedure is more likely to be performed when there are four or more fetuses present. The number of fetuses is often reduced to two, although in some circumstances they may be reduced to one. MFPR is usually performed between 9 and 12 weeks gestation, but has been performed as late as 24 weeks gestation (ASRM, 1999). There are many factors to consider when a woman is pregnant with three or more fetuses. Couples who have spent a great deal of energy, time, and money in pursuing pregnancy often are unprepared to deal with a decision to reduce the number of fetuses.

 Under what, if any, circumstances do you think it would be ethical to consider MFPR?

Gamete Intrafallopian Transfer Two procedures related to IVF have been proven especially helpful in some cases of infertility. One of these, **gamete intrafallopian transfer (GIFT),** involves the placement of a mixture of egg and sperm directly into a fallopian tube for fertilization. GIFT is possible only if a woman has at least one healthy fallopian tube. This procedure is useful in cases of severe endometriosis and cervical factor infertility.

Zygote Intrafallopian Transfer **Zygote intrafallopian transfer (ZIFT)** can be thought of as a combination of IVF and GIFT. The woman's eggs are fertilized by the man's sperm in vitro, and the fertilized egg is then transferred back to the woman's fallopian tube. A primary advantage of this procedure is that only fertilized eggs are placed in the fallopian tube.

For women who are anovulatory, egg donors may be used to supply an egg that can be fertilized by sperm and then placed in the infertile woman through intrauterine insemination or ZIFT procedures. Commonly a woman will choose a sister or close relative to donate the egg. However, some women use this procedure to avoid passing along a genetic disorder; in such cases they may choose to rely on a friend or stranger who does not possess that specific genetic material.

Artificial Insemination If a man's sperm count is low, but above 10 million per cubic centimeter, **artificial insemination,** insertion of his sperm directly into the vagina near the mouth of the cervix, may be successful. Artificial insemination has been around for hundreds of years. The first birth by artificial insemination in the United States occurred in the late 1800s, though it wasn't reported for another 25 years because of the religious and moral convictions of the day. The Roman Catholic Church still considers artificial insemination to be a sin.

> **Gamete Intrafallopian Transfer (GIFT):** a procedure where eggs are retrieved from the woman, placed together with sperm in a catheter, and transferred back into the woman's fallopian tubes to allow fertilization inside the woman's body
>
> **Zygote Intrafallopian Transfer (ZIFT):** fertilizing eggs and sperm outside of the body and immediately placing them in the fallopian tubes to enhance the chances of pregnancy
>
> **Artificial Insemination:** the process of depositing specially prepared sperm inside the woman's reproductive tract

Beating the Biological Clock

CONSIDERATIONS

From menarche to menopause, women have a relatively brief window of opportunity when they can become pregnant. Today's women are delaying childbearing as never before; the rate of first birth for women in their 30s and 40s has quadrupled since 1970. Times may have changed, but biology hasn't. As we have discussed, women are born with all the eggs they will ever have, but fertility decreases with age and by the age of 40 her eggs are virtually gone. As women age, their eggs become more susceptible to genetic errors that can compromise the success of fertilization. Despite technological advances, advancing age decreases a woman's ability to have children.

The biological clock can weigh heavily on women in their 20s and 30s who want to have children, but not right now. Although science has made enormous strides in treating infertility, there are still many obstacles to overcome. There has been some success with freezing a woman's eggs for later use. In 1986 a doctor in Australia documented the first known births from implanted frozen eggs, and in 1997 a Georgia woman gave birth to the first babies (twin boys) in the United States born from eggs that were frozen, and then thawed, before they were fertilized. However, there is concern that eggs tend to crystallize in subzero temperatures, disrupting their chromosomal integrity.

In 1999 researchers revealed that for the first time ovarian tissue worked normally after being removed from a woman, frozen, and returned to her body 2 years later (Oktay & Karlikaya, 2000). And a 35-year-old cervical cancer patient who had undergone sterilizing radiation treatment had part of her ovary transplanted under the skin of her forearm. Eventually, when she is ready, she can have her eggs taken from her arm for in vitro fertilization.

One procedure that holds promise, called "nuclear transfer," injects an older woman's DNA into a younger woman's egg before it is fertilized. In this procedure a healthy donor egg is harvested from a younger woman and the nucleus of the egg (which contains her DNA) is removed. An older woman's nucleus is transferred into the younger woman's egg and an electrical charge fuses the two components. The shell of the younger egg now contains the older woman's DNA. The new egg is then fertilized with sperm resulting in an embryo that is placed in the older woman's uterus.

? *If science can slow down a woman's biological clock, women may become new moms in their 60s and 70s. What are the social, emotional, and ethical implications of aging, or even aged, parents?*

Sperm Donor: male who gives his sperm for artificial insemination

Embryo transplant: the process of depositing fertilized eggs (or embryos) inside the uterus

EXPLORING SEXUALITY ONLINE

How Do You Want Your Eggs?

In 1999 a Web site was launched to auction the eggs of beautiful women to the highest bidder. Prices for eggs from one of "Ron's Angels" were reported to be as high as $150,000. The site features a color photo and profile highlighting the prospective donor's age, occupation, education, measurements, parents' ages, ethnic and religious background, and health history. As for the potential parents, the site only screens their financial status—can they pay their bill?

Artificial insemination means the sperm do not have to rely on their own powers to swim to their destination. The procedure concentrates the mass of sperm at the mouth of the cervix; during coitus, only small fractions of sperm get to this location. If the man's sperm are malformed, if the sperm count is less than 10 million per cubic centimeter, or if sperm motility is low, the most effective treatment may be artificial insemination by a donor. In the treatment of infertile couples, donor sperm also can be used in combination with in vitro fertilization, GIFT, and ZIFT procedures. In 1974, passage of the Uniform Parenting Act eliminated any doubt about the identity of the child's father in such cases; the legislation indicated that the husband of the woman bearing the child, not the sperm donor, is the natural father.

A sperm bank stores frozen sperm from men who are paid to masturbate to provide a sample of healthy semen. A donor is selected on the basis of health, intelligence, and a match of physical characteristics with the infertile father. One of the 150 sperm banks in the United States claims to reject nearly 95 percent of the men who apply to be donors (Eby, 2000). The pregnancy rate for artificial insemination using frozen sperm is about 60 percent.

Embryo Transplants **Embryo transplants** involve artificial insemination (usually with the sperm of the infertile woman's husband) of a third party, the removal 5 days later of the fertilized embryo from the donor's uterus, and implantation into the infer-

Getting by With a Little Help From Your Friends

CONSIDERATIONS

When filmmaker Julie Cypher and her former partner, singer Melissa Etheridge, decided to have a child, they chose artificial insemination with sperm donated by their friend, musician David Crosby. Crosby, who has a history of substance abuse and other health problems, might not have been everyone's genetic ideal or first choice as a *directed donor*, that is, a sperm donor who is known rather than anonymous.

While it might be fun to ponder the advantages of Bill Gates's sperm versus Michael Jordan's, the issues surrounding artificial insemination are less frivolous for many people—particularly single women and lesbians. Just how many single or gay women are being artificially inseminated is not known because of privacy issues.

However, the director of the world's largest sperm bank estimates that about 40 percent of his clients are single women.

Who do you think would be an ideal sperm donor?

—Who would be an ideal egg donor (see earlier EXPLORING SEXUALITY ONLINE box)?

—Would you consider being or using a directed sperm or egg donor?

—If you were a donor, would you want to meet your offspring one day?

—What would you tell a child born through these methods about his or her parentage?

tile woman's uterus. Key to success is synchronizing the menstrual cycles of the two women through the use of birth control pills. A potential problem is the ambiguous laws defining motherhood in such cases. Who is the biological mother—the one who carries the baby in her womb, or the one who shares her genes?

Surrogate Mothers   A nonsurgical means of dealing with infertility when a woman is unable to conceive is the hiring of a **surrogate mother.** The surrogate mother may be someone known to the infertile couple or a stranger who volunteers and may be paid a fee to be inseminated with the male partner's sperm. If a woman has functioning ovaries but does not have a suitable uterus, it is possible to have one of her eggs, fertilized by her husband's sperm, implanted in the surrogate mother. More commonly though, the surrogate mother's own eggs are used. In addition to the fees paid to the surrogate, usually in the range of $2,000 to $20,000, the couple can expect to pay additional legal fees. In several highly publicized cases, after agreeing to serve as a surrogate, the woman has changed her mind about surrendering the newborn after delivery.

In a 1997 report, the Centers for Disease Control (CDC) found that fertility treatments failed 70 to 80 percent of the time. After age 35, the likelihood of success decreases with the woman's age. The agency reported that in 1995 doctors initiated 59,142 treatments using **assisted reproductive technology (ART)** procedures. The treatments, called cycles, resulted in 11,315 live births. In 78 percent of the cycles fresh embryos from a couple's egg and sperm were used; most came from in vitro fertilization. In 14 percent frozen embryos were used and in 8 percent donated eggs were used. The statistics varied widely by clinic, with success rates ranging from 7 to more than 35 percent. Success rates of any given clinic depend in large part on the number of patients treated, their ages, and their diagnoses. Of the 78 percent of pregnancies that led to live births, 49.8 percent were single births, 23.8 percent had twins, and 4.5 percent had triplets or higher multiples.

Adoption   **Adoption** is another means of becoming a parent. It is the *only* means for couples in which both the man and woman are infertile. Adoption also has many advantages over some of the more invasive and risky techniques described previously. However, it can be expensive. According to the National Adoption Center, the average cost of an adoption is $12,000; adopting a healthy infant in the United States can cost up to $25,000. In addition, there may be a lengthy waiting period and requirements regarding age, marital status, or income.

Private adoptions through an agency or an intermediary, such as a lawyer, are usually the most expensive, but they may be less restrictive and have a shorter waiting period. Adopting a child through a state social service agency is usually the least expensive route. Unlike private placements, in which most parents expect to adopt a newborn, children available for adoption through public agencies have varying demographic profiles, and most are between ages 2 and 10. Since 1985, families in the United States have adopted more than 125,000 children from other countries. Most of these children had been in institutional care before adoption; it is now recognized that many of them require specialized attention for a variety of medical, emotional, and developmental difficulties (Miller, 1999).

Millions of couples are visiting the Internet to get adoption information. Today there are nearly 1,000 adoption Web sites, including 60 sites with photographs of children in the United States and foreign countries, according to the federally funded National Adoption Information Clearinghouse. The National Adoption Council's Web site has had about 25 million visitors since it started in October 1995. It features about 400 children each year and claims nearly 40 adoptions directly related to searches on its site. However, as a with any important decision, it is important to carefully investigate Internet adoption resources. A widely publicized 2001 case involved an adoption facilitator who promised the same set of twins to several couples, causing an international legal quagmire.

Surrogate Mother: a women who agrees to be impregnated through artificial insemination and then give the child to another woman who is incapable of becoming pregnant

Assisted Reproductive Technology (ART): a term used to describe medical procedures that enhance the opportunity for egg fertilization and pregnancy

Adoption: the process of taking a child into one's family through legal means and raising the child as one's own

Hello Dolly

When Dolly the lamb became the first animal cloned from an adult cell, it marked the beginning of new possibilities in fertility alternatives. A handful of fertility centers already are conducting experiments with human eggs that lay the foundation for human cloning. Ultimately scientists expect cloning to be combined with genetic enhancement, adding genes to give desired traits. Unlike human reproduction, cloning would involve taking a cell from a living person and slipping it into an egg cell that has had the genetic material removed. The genetic material of the adult cell would direct the development of a new embryo, then fetus, then person who is the identical twin of the person who provided the initial cell.

Some people want to enact laws that would make human cloning illegal. Opposition to human cloning comes from those who believe that the creation of human life is too important to entrust to scientists, and those who fear the consequences of producing an unlimited number of genetically perfect, identical individuals. Proponents of cloning argue that it is no worse than other fertility options and that, like in vitro fertilization, artificial insemination, and surrogate motherhood, cloning will slowly but steadily gain acceptance.

? **Do you think that human cloning should be allowed?**

—Would you do it? Why or why not?

REVIEW

CHAPTER 5

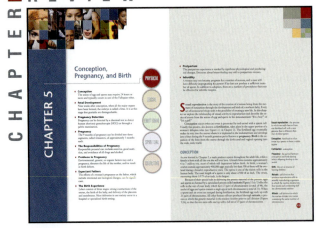

1_____ occurs when an egg released from a female's ovary is penetrated by a single male sperm. Fertilization usually occurs in the upper portion of a **2**_____. The fertilized egg makes its way into the **3**_____ where it becomes implanted in the lining of the uterine wall.

Egg and sperm cells are called germ cells. As a result of **4**_____, each gene cell contains a single set of chromosomes instead of the pairs of chromosomes contained by all other cells in the body.

Some sperm ejaculated into the vagina may pass through the cervix into the uterus and enter a fallopian tube containing an egg. **5**_____ is the process whereby sperm acquire the ability to penetrate the egg. Afterward the sperm secrete an enzyme to dissolve the **6**_____, the protective coating around the egg. Once a single sperm has penetrated the egg, the egg becomes impenetrable to other sperm.

As it develops for the first few days, the newly fertilized egg is called a **7**_____ (from the Latin word

for mulberry). Soon it has developed a hollow inner portion and then is known as a **8**_____. About 2 weeks after fertilization, the blastula develops a placenta and fetal membrane, and is then called an **9**_____. About the ninth week after fertilization, the developing embryo has formed the major organ systems and henceforth is called a **10**_____.

Good prenatal care is the responsibility of the expectant parents. Some of the basics of good prenatal care include good nutrition and avoidance of all drugs, including alcohol, tobacco, and over-the-counter medications such as aspirin. Any drug which can cause a birth defect is called a **11**_____.

Today there are several means of detecting certain types of birth defects. **12**_____ involves the analysis of amniotic fluid withdrawn by inserting a needle through the pregnant woman's abdomen and into the uterus. **13**_____ involves the insertion of a catheter through the cervix and into the uterus to obtain a sample of chorionic villi. An ultrasound examination also may detect some birth defects.

When males experience physical symptoms of pregnancy, this is called the **14**_____.

During the first stage of labor, the cervix begins to thin in preparation for stretching; this is called **15**_____. In addition, the mouth of the cervix also begins to **16**_____ or to open wider. The second stage of labor begins when the cervix is fully dilated and ends with the birth of the baby. The third stage of labor includes the delivery of the placenta and the membranes. Normally birth occurs as the fetus is expelled from the uterus through the **17**_____ and out the vaginal opening. An episiotomy is a surgical incision in the female's **18**_____. A **19**_____ is the removal of the fetus through an incision in the walls of the abdomen and uterus.

20_____ or milk production begins 2 or 3 days after delivery; prior to this the breasts will have produced only **21**_____. Breast-feeding not only provides nutrition and protection from disease for the infant, it also decreases the likelihood of another immediate **22**_____.

Female infertility may have several causes. Twenty percent of women who have suffered from an episode of pelvic inflammatory disease will become sterile. **23**_____, a condition in which uterine tissue grows on various parts of the abdominal cavity, is another common cause of infertility.

A man will have difficulty impregnating his partner if he does not produce a sufficient number of sperm, if the sperm lack sufficient motility to reach the fallopian tubes, or if the sperm are malformed. By far the most common cause of male infertility is low sperm count.

There are several procedures to help infertile women. **24**_____ includes the removal of mature eggs from a female's ovary and fertilizing them with sperm in a laboratory before surgically implanting them in the woman's uterus. **25**_____ involves the placement of a mixture of egg and sperm directly into a fallopian tube. **26**_____ involves the fertilization of eggs by sperm in vitro with the fertilized eggs then being transferred back to the female's fallopian tube. **27**_____ involve artificial insemination of another woman, usually with the sperm of the infertile woman's husband, and the subsequent removal and surgical implantation of the embryo into the infertile woman's uterus. All of these procedures are expensive and not always successful. Couples unable to have children also may use a surrogate mother or adopt a child.

SUGGESTED READINGS

Gollaher, D. L. (2000). *Circumcision: A History of the World's Most Controversial Surgery.* New York: Basic Books.
Gollaher offers an historical approach to the world's most widely practiced and perhaps least understood surgery.

Huggins, K. (1999). *The Nursing Mother's Companion.* (4th Ed.). Boston: Harvard Common Press.
This is a guide for women who want to nurse, with practical advice for common problems.

Iovine, V. (1999). *The Girlfriends' Guide to Pregnancy: Or Everything Your Doctor Won't Tell You.* New York: Pocket Books.
An irreverent and reassuring guide to pregnancy and childbirth.

Jansen, R., & DeCherney, A. (1998). *Overcoming Infertility: A Compassionate Resource for Getting Pregnant.* New York: W.H. Freeman.
This is a holistic examination of infertility, including the mechanisms of successful conception and the possible reasons for lack of success, testing methods, and the possible remedies.

Jones, C. (1999). *The Adoption Sourcebook: A Complete Guide to the Complex Legal, Financial and Emotional Maze of Adoption.* Los Angeles: Lowell House.
Jones has written a concise guide to the emotional and procedural aspects of adoption, with detailed information for those considering this means of building a family.

Mitford, J. (1992). *The American Way of Birth.* New York: Dutton.
This book traces the history of childbirth in America and assesses conventional and alternative birthing methods.

Sears, W., Sears, M., & Holt, L. H. (Contributor). (1997). *The Pregnancy Book.* Boston: Little, Brown.
This month-by-month guide describes what is happening each month of the pregnancy, and it provides information on a variety of topics of interest to an expecting couple.

Stoppard, M. (2000). *Conceptions, Pregnancy and Birth.* New York: Dorling Kindersley.
This is a comprehensive guide for pregnant women, with case studies and lots of photographs and illustrations.

ANSWERS TO CHAPTER REVIEW

1. Conception; **2.** fallopian tube; **3.** uterus; **4.** meiosis; **5.** Capacitation; **6.** zona pellucida; **7.** morula; **8.** blastula; **9.** embryo; **10.** fetus; **11.** teratogen; **12.** Amniocentesis; **13.** Chorionic villus sampling; **14.** couvade syndrome; **15.** effacement; **16.** dilate; **17.** birth canal; **18.** perineum; **19.** cesarean section; **20.** Lactation; **21.** colostrum; **22.** conception; **23.** Endometriosis; **24.** In vitro fertilization; **25.** Gamete intrafallopian transfer or GIFT; **26.** Zygote intrafallopian transfer or ZIFT; **27.** Embryo transplants.

CHAPTER 6

Contraception and Abortion

PHYSICAL

SOCIAL

EMOTIONAL

SPIRITUAL

COGNITIVE

- **A Brief History of Contraception and Abortion**
  People have been attempting to prevent pregnancy or to control the timing of births throughout recorded history.

- **An Overview of Birth Control Today**
  Modern medical technology has greatly improved contraceptive effectiveness.

- **Barrier Methods of Birth Control**
  The male condom, the female condom, the diaphragm, the cervical cap, and the vaginal sponge are all barrier methods of birth control.

- **Mechanical Methods of Birth Control**
  The intrauterine device (IUD) is the only mechanical method of birth control currently available.

- **Chemical Methods of Birth Control**
  There are a variety of spermicides available that serve as chemical methods of contraception.

- **Hormone-based Contraceptives**
  Oral contraceptives, injectable contraceptives, and implants all work by regulating a woman's hormone levels and inhibiting or preventing ovulation.

- **Surgical Methods of Birth Control**
  Vasectomy is the surgical procedure for sterilization of males. Tubal ligation is the most commonly used surgical procedure to sterilize females.

- **Fertility Awareness Methods**
  Natural contraceptive methods are based on determining a woman's ovulation and then avoiding intercourse on days when conception would be most likely.

- **Postcoital Contraception**
  Emergency contraception can be used within 72 hours if a woman thinks that her contraception has failed or if no other method of contraception was used.

■ **Abortion**
Abortion, the voluntary ending of a pregnancy, is not a method of contraception.

■ **New and Future Contraceptive Technology**
The future of contraception includes the development of oral contraceptives and implants for males, and numerous improvements for existing devices.

Y ou may not want to have children; or you may want to plan when to have a child. **Contraception,** also referred to as birth control, involves the physical methods of preventing pregnancy, but it has many dimensions—social responsibilities and constraints, emotional reactions, cognitive judgments, and spiritual values. Your choice among abstinence, a condom, fertility awareness, or some other method described in the following pages is influenced as much by your relationship with your partner, the values you share (or don't share) with your parents, your religious beliefs, your cultural background, and the legal system of the society in which you live as by the effectiveness and convenience of the various methods.

While population concerns may not be foremost in your mind when you are making contraceptive choices, birth control is vitally important for both yourself and the society you live in. Selection of a contraceptive method is an intensely personal, individual decision that affects the birth rate and population growth of the entire society. Therefore it is not surprising that attempts to control reproduction have characterized virtually every known society. As we will discuss in Chapter 18, many societies attempt to legislate access to contraception.

There are many ways to control fertility that may not involve a specific birth control method or device. For example, if a society could successfully limit sexual intercourse to married couples, the number of potential births would be substantially reduced. While limiting sexual partners may be the ideal for many people, it is seldom fully effective, since premarital, and extramarital sexual relationships exist almost everywhere.

Anything that prevents women from becoming or from staying pregnant will result in lowered birth rates and thus slow population growth (Harris & Ross, 1987). Conditions that demand men be away from their home communities for long periods of time, whether for work or for war, may result in a decreased number of pregnancies. Beliefs such as the **post partum taboo** that forbids coitus for a specified period of time after the birth of a child, also may result in more widely spaced births and therefore fewer children being born into a community.

Contraception: the deliberate prevention of conception or impregnation through the use of various devices, agents, drugs, sexual practices, or surgical procedures

Post Partum Taboo: cultural belief that forbids sexual intercourse for a specified period of time after the birth of a child

A BRIEF HISTORY OF CONTRACEPTION AND ABORTION

Contraceptive devices are nothing new. In ancient societies contraceptive methods ranged from the magical to the highly effective. Two thousand years ago the Chinese inserted oil-soaked paper into the vagina to cover the cervix. In Oceania, moss plugs were used for this purpose. Ancient Egyptians used a very appealing concoction of crocodile dung and honey. In ancient Athens, women rubbed their cervix with oil of cedar and an ointment of lead to prevent conception. A sixth century Greek physician recommended a cervical cap made by cutting a pomegranate in half, scooping out the flesh of the fruit and then inserting it into the vagina prior to intercourse. A contraceptive sponge in use in the 1800s was soaked in a solution of quinine prior to insertion and had a string attached for easy removal. The diaphragm, a popular form of contraception today, was invented back in 1842 by a German anatomy professor.

The ever-popular condom also has ancient origins. Roman soldiers reputedly made condoms from the muscles of dead enemies—very romantic! Other appealing sources of this type of protection included the small intestines of animals, fish bladders, and lambskins. The precursor of the modern condom was a linen sheath designed in 1564 by an anatomist for protection against venereal disease. After the invention of vulcanized rubber in the 1800s, the "rubber" was first introduced at the Philadelphia World Exposition in 1878.

Two other ancient and widespread forms of contraception that are still practiced today are **coitus interruptus,** the removal of the penis from the vagina prior to orgasm, and **interfemoral coitus,** rubbing the erect penis between the thighs of a woman without insertion into the vagina. Interfemoral coitus is not likely to result in conception, but it is possible that sperm deposited just outside the vagina could cause a pregnancy, and this method offers no protection against sexually transmitted infections. Coitus interruptus, on the other hand, is not very effective since men may fail to withdraw prior to orgasm, despite their best intentions. Moreover, secretions from the Cowper's glands sometimes carry live sperm into the vagina before orgasm and ejaculation. Even though this method is widely used today, aside from this brief mention you will not find coverage of coitus interruptus (also called withdrawal or the withdrawal method) in this chapter because it is a non–method of birth control.

There are many ways to control fertility that may not involve a specific method or device. Until the 19th century, the Cheyenne, a North American Indian people of the western plains, practiced birth control through abstinence in order to space the births of their children by as much as 7 years or more. They did this in order to devote their full attention to each child rather than to have many children making simultaneous demands upon them. While this custom was not intended for population control nevertheless it limited population growth, since this practice meant that most women would have only two or three children. The result was that the Cheyenne were better able to live in balance with their environment, since they did not have more children than the environment could support or more children than they could care for. When change was forced upon them by warfare and disease, they were forced to adopt new beliefs and practices in order to repopulate. For another widely used method of birth control, see the CROSS-CULTURAL PERSPECTIVES box.

Abortion methods have changed, but the termination of pregnancies is also an ancient practice. Historians report that the ancient Egyptians, Greeks, and Romans purposely limited population size using a variety of methods. Hippocrates recommended Queen Anne's lace (also known as wild carrot) to induce abortions. The use of the seeds of the herb for emergency contraception was reportedly widespread. In one of his plays Aristophanes mentioned pennyroyal, a plant that contains pulegone, a chemical that can terminate pregnancies (Riddle et al., 1994).

In early 19th century rural America, herbal and home remedies for terminating pregnancies were passed down through the generations by word of mouth. Native American healers and midwives prescribed herbs or roots thought to induce miscarriage. Midwestern pioneer women rubbed gunpowder on their breasts and drank tea made from boiling rusty nails. Information about elixirs and drugs that induced abortion

Coitus Interruptus: sexual intercourse deliberately interrupted by withdrawal of the penis from the vagina prior to ejaculation

Interfemoral Coitus: sexual activity in which the male rubs his erect penis between the thighs of a woman without insertion into the vagina

Abortion: induced expulsion of a human embryo or fetus

Birth Control and Breast-Feeding

Historically, perhaps the most important method of birth control has been breast-feeding (Harrell, 1981). Traditions of extended periods of breast-feeding may delay subsequent pregnancies since the chemical prolactin, which is produced during lactation, suppresses ovulation. Thus when a woman breast-feeds each child for 3 to 5 years, as they do in some cultures, it means that she is less likely to

have babies in close succession. Despite a widespread decline in breast-feeding, and this is by no means a totally reliable form of birth control, worldwide more births are still prevented by nursing than by any other means of contraception (Konner, 1990). (Note that a woman breast-feeding an infant can get pregnant, though statistically it lowers the odds a little.)

appeared in home medical manuals as well. The 1808 edition of *The Married Ladies Companion* recommended bleeding from the foot, hot baths, tea brewed from the tansy plant, jumping exercises, douching, and cathartics such as chamomile and aloe (D'Emilio & Freedman, 1988). Although a few individuals may still use these methods, none of these methods of terminating pregnancy are widely in use today.

AN OVERVIEW OF BIRTH CONTROL TODAY

"Will it work?" may be the most frequently asked question about any method of contraception (see Figures 6.1 and 6.2 for the contraceptive choices men and women make). How is the effectiveness of the various methods determined? No study can ascertain the proportion of women who would have become pregnant had they not used the contraceptive method under investigation, so it is impossible to measure effectiveness directly. Therefore we focus attention on pregnancy rates or probabilities of pregnancy during contraceptive use, which are directly measurable. For example, if 20 percent of women using a birth control method became pregnant accidentally in their first year of use, you might think it makes sense to say that the method is 80 percent effective. However, this is not the case because even if they relied solely on chance, 90 percent, not 100 percent of these women would have become pregnant. The method under consideration thus reduced the probability of pregnancy from 90 percent to 20 percent, a reduction of 78 percent. In this sense, the birth control method could be said to be 78 percent effective at reducing pregnancy in the first year of use (Trussell & Kowal, 1998).

Estimates of contraceptive efficacy often are described in terms of "typical use" versus "perfect use." Typical use statistics are derived from information from nationally representative samples of users. Pregnancy rates during typical use reflect how effective methods are for the average person who does not always use methods correctly or consistently. It is important to understand that typical use does not imply that a contraceptive method was actually used. In most clinical trials, which rely on self-reporting, a woman is "using" a contraceptive method if she considers herself to be using that method. For example, typical use of the condom could include actually using a condom only occasionally, and a woman could report she is "using" the pill even though her supplies ran out several months ago or if she skipped pills (Trussell & Kowal, 1998).

The decision to become sexually active brings with it the responsibility to avoid unwanted pregnancy (see CONSIDERATIONS box). Modern technology has brought great advances in contraceptive technology. Many forms of birth control are close to 100 percent effective. Correct and consistent use of most contraceptive methods results in a low risk of pregnancy. However, even a low annual risk of pregnancy implies a high

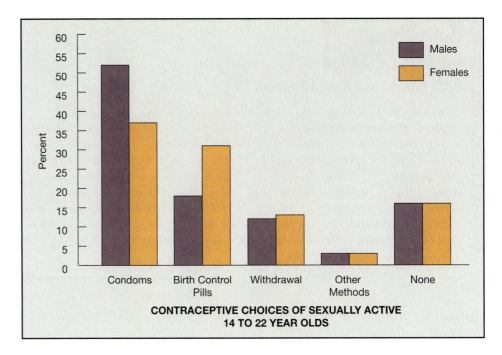

FIGURE 6.1 Contraceptive Choices of Sexually Active 14- to 22-Year-Olds.

cumulative risk of pregnancy during a lifetime of use. For example, an annual probability of pregnancy of 3 percent implies a 26 percent probability of pregnancy over 10 years (Trussell & Kowal, 1998).

Half of these unintended pregnancies occur in women using contraception in the month they conceived, and in the other 50 percent of cases the couple stopped contraceptive use because they found their method difficult or inconvenient (Trussell, Vaughan & Stanford, 1999). Although these statistics are alarming, the situation worldwide is improving (see CROSS-CULTURAL PERSPECTIVES box, "Worldwide Contraceptive Use").

A false sense of security may interfere with birth control decisions. In one study of sexually active female undergraduate students, it was found that those who perceived themselves as less likely than other women to get pregnant were also less likely to use effective contraception (Burger & Burns, 1988). Other researchers have found that sexual attitudes and feelings strongly influence contraceptive behavior. Negative attitudes toward sex, such as guilt and anxiety, are associated with a failure to use contraceptives (Byrne & Fisher, 1983).

CROSS-CULTURAL PERSPECTIVES

Worldwide Contraceptive Use

According to United Nations estimates, in 1965 only an estimated 8 percent of women in developing nations were using contraception. By 1991 more than 50 percent were using contraception. Some countries with a notable increase in contraceptive use were Thailand, Indonesia, Mexico, Colombia, Brazil, and Bangladesh. The World Bank estimates that third world countries spend a total of $3 billion a year on family planning. If United Nations estimates are correct, developing countries spend about $9 billion on contraceptives and need 44 billion condoms, 9 billion cycles of oral contraceptives, 150 million sterilizations, and 310 million IUDs or Norplant insertions (Sinding & Segal, 1991).

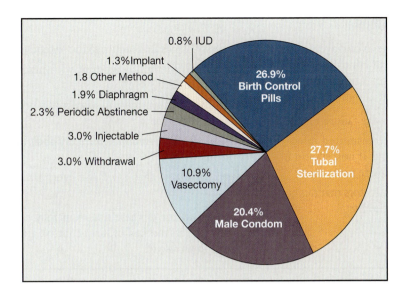

FIGURE 6.2 Contraceptive Choices for Sexually Active Women.

Women, especially those with negative feelings about sex, may fear that if they practice contraception or ask a man to use a condom, they will appear overly experienced and eager to have sexual relations (Marecek, 1987). Instead, they fail to use protection and place themselves and their partners at risk. A 1999 study, entitled "When You Carry a Condom All the Boys Think You Want It: Negotiating Competing Discourses About Safe Sex," found that though most students associated condoms with safe sex, many were ambivalent about using them. Reasons given for not using a condom included problems of negotiation (whether or not to use contraception) and limited availability, as well as the aforementioned risk of a damaged reputation (Hillier et al., 1999).

Contraceptive failure rates are highest among cohabiting and other unmarried women, those with an annual family income below the federal poverty level, African American and Hispanic women, adolescents, and women in their 20s. Limited access to birth control due to financial constraints and the other educational and medical disadvantages associated with poverty appear seriously to impede effective contraceptive practice in the United States (Fu et al., 1999).

The paragraph you just read cited studies of women. However, birth control is not just a woman's issue. Responsibility must be shared if contraception is to be effective. Couples need to discuss birth control before having intercourse; the heat of the moment is not the time to decide on a contraceptive method. Both men and women must be assertive in refusing to have intercourse if their partners object to their contraceptive requests. The descriptions on the following pages of the most common forms of birth control in our society are intended to supply you with information you can use to make informed decisions. Each of the methods of contraception described, including barrier methods, mechanical methods, chemical methods, permanent birth control, and natural birth control, requires communication between you and your partner(s), and consistent and correct use. Although it may not seem terribly romantic, contraceptive planning can enhance the sexual pleasure of heterosexual couples by eliminating the anxieties of a possible unwanted or unplanned pregnancy.

BARRIER METHODS OF BIRTH CONTROL

As we discussed in Chapter 5, conception occurs when a sperm fertilizes an ovum (egg). The fertilized egg, or embryo, then attaches to the wall of the uterus and develops into a viable fetus. There are two ways of preventing this event. The sperm are either blocked from reaching the egg, or any eggs that have been fertilized by sperm

CONSIDERATIONS

Deciding on a Contraceptive Method

Are you sexually active? If you are, then you have probably already chosen a method of birth control, or you should have! There are many factors to consider in choosing a contraceptive method that is right for you.

1. Is this method effective? What is the failure rate?

2. Does it protect against sexually transmitted infections as well as prevent pregnancy? If not, should I combine methods for more complete protection?

3. Is it safe to use? Do I have any risk factors that might cause problems in using this method?

4. Can I afford to use it regularly?

5. Is it easy and convenient to use?

6. Is it messy? Does that matter to me or to my partner?

7. Is using this method consistent with my religious and moral beliefs?

8. Is a method that has to be in place hours prior to intercourse practical for me?

9. Is my partner in agreement with my choice of birth control?

10. Is this a method that I will use every time I have sex?

"No" answers to any of these questions may cause you to avoid using your method of birth control, and it can't work if you don't use it!

Male Condom: a flexible sheath, usually made of thin rubber or latex, designed to cover the penis during sexual intercourse for contraceptive purposes or as a means of preventing sexually transmitted diseases

are prevented from developing further. As the name implies, barrier methods of contraception throw up a roadblock between the sperm and the ready-to-be-fertilized egg so that sperm are unable to reach the egg. Barrier methods include the male and female condoms, the diaphragm, the cervical cap, and the vaginal sponge.

The Male Condom

Also called a "rubber," "safety," or "prophylactic," the **male condom,** which until the introduction of the female condom was simply called a *condom,* is a balloonlike sheath of thin latex, plastic, or animal tissue worn over the erect penis. Usually packaged rolled up, condoms come in a variety of colors; some are prelubricated or coated with a spermicide. The condom collects ejaculated semen so that sperm can't enter the uterus. Condoms made from animal tissue, thus sometimes called "skins," protect against pregnancy but not against sexually transmitted infection because the pores in the tissue are large enough that microscopic organisms can pass through.

Most condoms sold in the United States today are made of latex. Polyurethane, or plastic, condoms are just as effective as latex condoms, although they cost somewhat more. Because polyurethane condoms are thinner than latex, some men report increased sensation during intercourse when using them. Table 6.1 provides a comparison of the characteristics of latex, natural, and plastic condoms.

Spermicidally lubricated condoms have been available in the United States since 1983; however, there is no evidence that these condoms are more effective than condoms without spermicide (CDC, 1993). Use of a separate vaginal spermicide is recommended

TABLE 6.1

Characteristics of Latex, Natural, and Plastic Condoms

	Latex	Natural	Polyurethane
Material	Natural rubber	Lamb cecum	Plastic
Lubricant use	Water-based only	Any	Any
Cost	Low	Moderate	Moderate/high
Prevention of pregnancy	Yes	Yes	Yes
Prevention of sexually transmitted infection	Yes	No	Likely

SOURCE: Modified from *Contraceptive Technology Update,* March 1995.

as a backup method superior to spermicide applied to the surface of the condom or use of a spermicidally lubricated condom. Applying spermicide vaginally guarantees its presence in the vaginal area should the condom break or fall off.

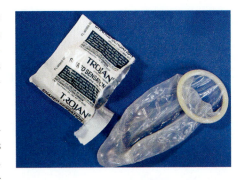

Male condoms.

Method of Use   The accompanying SEX- UAL HEALTH AND YOU box illustrates the correct method of using a male condom. First, check the expiration date on the package, and discard it if it is outdated. The condom must then be checked for tiny holes or tears. The condition of the condom must also be examined; if the rim is cracked or the condom is sticky, it is deteriorating and should be discarded. The condom is unrolled onto the erect penis before any contact between the vagina and penis. Some space should be left at the end of the condom to collect ejaculate (Figure 6.3a). It is important to roll the condom down to the base of the penis and to smooth out any air bubbles (Figure 6.3b&c). After ejaculation, but before the erection is lost, hold the rim of the condom while carefully withdrawing the penis, so that the condom does not slip off and spill ejaculate into the vagina (Figure 6.3d). The condom should then be discarded (don't flush it, or it could clog your plumbing). Condoms are designed for one-time use; if reused they may lose their elasticity and tear, permitting ejaculate to escape into the vagina.

Female Condom: a device consisting of a loose-fitting polyurethane sheath closed at one end, which is inserted intravaginally before sexual intercourse

Effectiveness   Used correctly, good quality condoms have a failure rate of about 2 to 3 percent. The failure rate in actual or typical practice is about 16 percent. The correct use of a good quality condom and a spermicide gives close to 100 percent protection.

Although users often fear the condom will break or fall off during use, studies indicate these events rarely occur with proper use (Warner & Hatcher, 1998). Defective condoms are rare and account for less than 2 percent of all condom failures. Most failures occur because of incorrect usage, such as failure to leave space at the tip to collect the sperm, contact between the penis and vagina prior to condom use, or the condom slipping off during sex. In a study of female sex workers in Nevada brothels, of 353 condoms used by the sex workers during the study, none broke and none fell off during intercourse and only two (0.6 percent) slipped off during withdrawal (Albert et al., 1995). Condoms will deteriorate if improperly stored, exposed to heat or sunlight, or brought into contact with oil-based lubricants or vaginal medications. Oil-based products such as Vaseline can corrode latex. Table 6.2 shows a number of safe and unsafe methods of condom lubrication. Condoms also deteriorate over time, and so they should not be used past the expiration date marked on the packaging.

TABLE 6.2

Condom Lubricants	
Safe	**Unsafe**
Egg whites	Baby oil
Glycerine	Cold cream
Spermicide (Nonoxynol-9)	Cooking oils (olive, peanut, corn, etc.)
Saliva	Hand or body lotion
Water	Massage oil
	Petroleum jelly
	Suntan oil
	Mineral oil

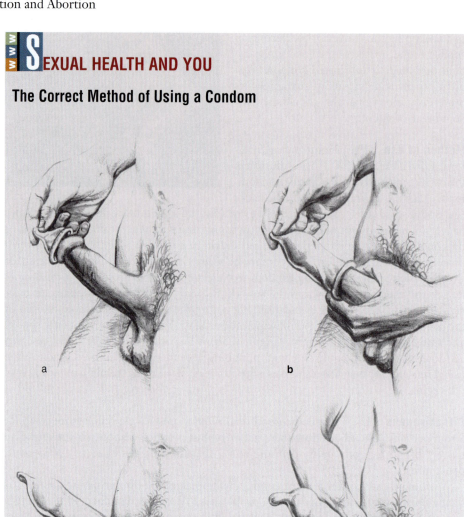

SEXUAL HEALTH AND YOU

The Correct Method of Using a Condom

FIGURE 6.3 **Using a Male Condom.** (a) Place the rolled condom on the erect penis. Squeeze any air out of the condom tip and leave about $\frac{1}{2}$ inch of space at the tip. (b) Roll the condom down, smoothing out any air bubbles. (c) Roll the condom to the base of the penis. (d) After ejaculation, hold the condom at the rim while removing it.

Cost and Availability   Condoms range in cost from approximately $6 to $10 a dozen, though many family planning clinics give them away for free. Condoms can be purchased without a prescription and are readily available at most drugstores, at many supermarkets, via the Internet (see EXPLORING SEXUALITY ONLINE box), on many college campuses, and at some high schools. Mail-order catalogues, specialty stores, and vending machines also sell a wide variety of condoms.

Advantages   Condom use offers several benefits. Latex or polyurethane condoms used with a spermicide offer the best protection against HIV and other STIs, in addition to being highly effective in preventing pregnancy. Condoms are portable, easy to

www EXPLORING SEXUALITY ONLINE

Online Condoms

For people too busy, or too embarrassed, to buy condoms at their local drugstore, they are now available over the Internet from several mail-order companies. Condomania (www.condomania.com), Condom USA (www.condomusa.com), Condoms Express (www.webcom.com/condom), and 10-10 Condoms (www.10-10condoms.com) are some of the Web sites that offer advice and a wide selection of styles that can be purchased directly and discreetly online.

CAMPUS CONFIDENTIAL

"I guess sexual spontaneity is something my generation will just have to learn to deal with. It's really a pain, but as a friend of mine says, 'No f— is worth dying for.' And it's not just AIDS I worry about; I'm definitely not ready to have a baby and I don't want to explain herpes to every guy I sleep with. A lot of guys say they don't like using a condom because just when things are getting hot you have to stop and put it on. But my boyfriend and I make it a part of sex play. The first few times we made love I was afraid to ask him to wear a condom. Then I finally got it through my head that if I don't know a guy well enough to ask him to use protection, I don't know him well enough to have sex with him. If he complains that the sex doesn't feel as good wearing a condom, I tell him that I enjoy sex a hell of a lot more if I don't have to worry about disease or pregnancy." ●

obtain, and relatively inexpensive. They do not affect hormone systems and have no adverse side effects. Condoms encourage male participation in contraception since they are currently the only temporary birth control measure available for men. There is some evidence that condoms can help men maintain their erections longer and prevent premature ejaculation (Warner & Hatcher, 1998). Postcoital leakage of semen from the vagina or anus is avoided by using condoms. Because condoms contain no hormones or chemicals, they cause few medical problems among users.

Disadvantages   Some men feel that using condoms lessens sexual sensations since there is no direct contact of the penis with vaginal or rectal walls. Some men cannot consistently maintain an erection during condom use. Condoms have to be used right at the time of intercourse, so their application may disrupt spontaneity. As described earlier, it is possible for condoms to slip off, tear, or deteriorate due to age. There are rare allergies to latex, and some people are allergic to certain spermicides used in lubricated condoms.

The Female Condom

The **female condom,** which was approved for use by the FDA in 1993, provides a physical barrier that lines the vagina entirely. It is a disposable 7-inch polyurethane pouch. Flexible rings anchor the pouch at both ends. The inside ring covers the cervix like a diaphragm (see SEXUAL HEALTH AND YOU); the outer ring extends outside the vagina and covers the labia. It is most effective when used with a lubricant and spermicide. Female condoms account for about 1 percent of the U.S. market for barrier contraceptives.

Method of Use   The accompanying SEXUAL HEALTH AND YOU box illustrates the correct method of using a female condom. You can insert the female condom immediately before intercourse or as long as 8 hours ahead of time. Before using the female condom, wash your hands with soap and water. Remove the condom from its package (see Figure 6.4a). Hold the pouch with the open end hanging down. Use the thumb and middle finger of one hand to squeeze the inner ring into a narrow oval for insertion; place your index finger between the thumb and middle finger to guide the condom during insertion. With your other hand, spread the lips of your vagina. Insert the inner ring and the pouch of the condom into the vaginal opening and with your index finger or the applicator, push the

The female condom.

inner ring with the pouch the rest of the way up into the vagina (Figure 6.4b). The out-side ring lies against the outer lips when the condom is in place; about 1 inch of the open end will stay outside the body (Figure 6.4c). Once the penis enters, the vagina will expand and the slack will decrease. Remove the condom immediately after inter-course, before you stand up. Squeeze and twist the outer ring to keep semen inside the pouch. Pull the condom out gently and discard it. Use a new female condom for each act of intercourse.

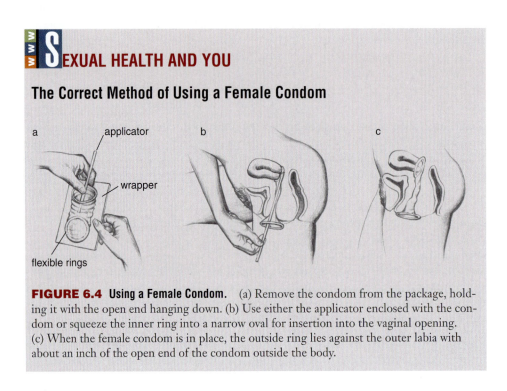

SEXUAL HEALTH AND YOU

The Correct Method of Using a Female Condom

a   applicator

wrapper

flexible rings

b

c

FIGURE 6.4 Using a Female Condom.   (a) Remove the condom from the package, hold-ing it with the open end hanging down. (b) Use either the applicator enclosed with the con-dom or squeeze the inner ring into a narrow oval for insertion into the vaginal opening. (c) When the female condom is in place, the outside ring lies against the outer labia with about an inch of the open end of the condom outside the body.

Effectiveness   Studies show the female condom to be almost as effective as the male condom; a 5 percent failure rate is reported with perfect usage. A 21 percent failure rate is experienced with average use. Most failures are due to incorrect insertion of the condom. It must be in the proper location in the vagina to be maximally effective.

Cost and Availability   Female condoms cost about $2.50 each—about three to five times as much as a male condom. The female condom is available in many clinics and drugstores. Female condoms are not as widely available, or as popular, as the male condom.

Advantages   With the female condom, women do not have to negotiate condom use with a male partner. Unlike the diaphragm and sponge, the female condom ensures that the penis never touches the woman's skin, so she is not exposed to semen and he is not exposed to vaginal secretions. Unless the female condom slips out of place or is torn, it should provide protection against STI exposure that is at least as good as that provided by latex male condoms. Some women who have used the female condom re-port that it is less disruptive to use than the male condom because it can be inserted before lovemaking and, unlike the male condom, its use doesn't have to be coordi-nated with an erection. Because the female condom is made of such thin polyurethane, many men report that it provides more sensitivity than use of a male condom.

Disadvantages   So far the female condom has not been popular with consumers; it may take a while for both men and women to get used to the appearance and use. Cor-rect insertion also takes some practice, as does applying the right amount of lubricant. The expense in comparison to the male condom may also be a big drawback.

Diaphragm

A **diaphragm** is a soft, shallow dome-shaped latex disk with a flexible spring rim, usually 2 to 4 inches in diameter. It covers the cervix in order to prevent sperm from entering the uterus. Because of the variations in cervical size and shape, the diaphragm must be fitted by a health-care professional. A diaphragm can be considered a combination between a barrier method and a chemical method of contraception; it is always used with a spermicide to kill the sperm that cross the barrier, that is, get inside the rim of the diaphragm.

The diaphragm.

Method of Use   The accompanying SEXUAL HEALTH AND YOU box illustrates the correct method for use of a diaphragm. The diaphragm may be inserted just before intercourse or up to 6 hours beforehand. It takes some practice to use a diaphragm correctly; it is highly recommended that you try it out once or twice before relying on it for contraception. Place about a tablespoon of spermicide into the shallow cup and spread it around (Figure 6.5a). Fold and squeeze the cup together in one hand; with the other hand spread apart the vaginal lips and push the diaphragm into the vagina with the spermicide facing up (Figure 6.5b). Push the lower rim with a finger until the diaphragm is positioned against the cervix (Figure 6.5c).

▪▪▪ S EXUAL HEALTH AND YOU

The Correct Method of Using a Diaphragm

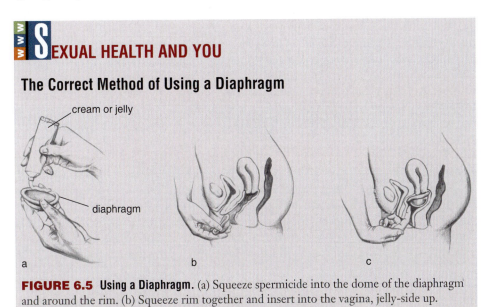

cream or jelly

diaphragm

a   b   c

FIGURE 6.5 Using a Diaphragm. (a) Squeeze spermicide into the dome of the diaphragm and around the rim. (b) Squeeze rim together and insert into the vagina, jelly-side up. (c) Check the placement to make sure the cervix is covered.

If you are going to have intercourse more than once, you can leave the diaphragm in place, but you must introduce more spermicide into the vagina with an applicator. The diaphragm must be left in place at least 6 hours after intercourse. Wearing it for more than 24 hours is not recommended because of the possible risk of toxic shock syndrome. To remove the diaphragm, locate the front rim with your finger. Hook your finger over the rim or behind it, and then pull the diaphragm down and out. Wash the diaphragm with plain soap and water and dry it. Do not use talcum powder or allow your diaphragm to have contact with oil-based products.

Effectiveness   Diaphragms have about a 6 percent failure rate when used consistently and correctly. However, with typical use their failure rate is about 18 percent. Failures may be due to the diaphragm becoming dislodged or fitting poorly. Failures also can be caused by removal of the diaphragm too soon after intercourse, inadequate amounts of spermicide, or use of a deteriorated diaphragm.

Diaphragm: device consisting of a thin flexible disk, usually made of rubber, that is designed to cover the cervix to prevent the entry of sperm during sexual intercourse

The cervical cap.

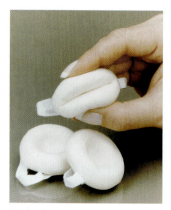

Vaginal sponge.

Cost and Availability   Diaphragms cost $13 to $25 plus fees for a medical examination and supplies of spermicidal jelly or cream. A diaphragm is available by prescription only. An internal pelvic examination to be measured and fitted for the proper size and type of diaphragm is necessary. Replacement is recommended every 2 years; the diaphragm must be refitted after a pregnancy.

Advantages   As with other barrier methods used with spermicides, the diaphragm offers some protection against STIs. Laboratory research shows nonoxynol-9 is lethal to the organisms that cause gonorrhea, genital herpes, trichomoniasis, syphilis, and HIV (see Chapter 7 for more on STIs). Although the effect of spermicides on STIs has not yet translated directly to effective protection in human studies, protection against spread of STIs potentially could be the most important noncontraceptive benefit of vaginal barrier use (Stewart, 1998). Side effects are very limited. Use of the diaphragm does not interfere with the woman's hormonal system. Cared for properly, it can last for several years. A diaphragm does not alter a woman's hormones and gives her control over contraception.

Disadvantages   Insertion of the diaphragm can interfere with spontaneity. It cannot be used if there is vaginal bleeding or infection. The discharge of spermicide can be messy, as can removal and cleanup of the diaphragm after sex. Some people feel the taste of the spermicide makes oral sex less enjoyable. Some people are allergic to or sensitive to spermicide; the most common problem associated with vaginal barrier methods used with spermicide is local skin irritation. Some women experience cramps, bladder pain, or rectal pain when wearing a diaphragm; a refitting with an alternative size or type may resolve the problem. The balance of vaginal flora is changed among women who use spermicide for prolonged periods; because of this, some women report having more urinary tract and yeast infections when using a diaphragm (Foxman, 1990; Hooten et al., 1991).

Cervical Cap

A **cervical cap** is a small, soft, thimble-shaped latex or plastic cup with a firm round rim that fits snugly over the entrance to the cervix to prevent sperm from entering the uterus. Widely used in Europe for years, the cervical cap has been approved for use in the United States since 1988. Like the diaphragm, because of individual variations in internal structure, the cervical cap must be fitted by a health-care professional.

Method of Use   The cervical cap can be inserted just before intercourse or ahead of time. Some experts recommend that you allow 30 minutes between insertion and intercourse, if possible, so a good suction develops (Stewart, 1998). The cap provides effective contraceptive protection for 48 hours, no matter how many times you have intercourse. Before insertion, fill the cap about one third full with spermicidal jelly or cream. Spread the cream around the inside of the cap but not onto the rim. Next, find your cervix (it feels something like a short, firm nose projecting into the vagina). Separate the lips of your vagina with one hand. With the other hand squeeze (fold) together the rim of the cap between your thumb and index finger. Slide the cap into your vagina and push it along the rear wall of the vagina as far as it will go. Using your finger to locate your cervix, press the rim of the cap around the cervix until it is completely covered (Figure 6.6). Finally, check the cap position by pressing the dome of the cap to make sure your cervix is covered. As you sweep your finger around the cap rim, the cervix should not be felt outside the cap. Use of additional spermicide for repeated intercourse with the cap is optional. To remove the cap, press on the cap rim until the seal against your cervix is broken, then tilt the cap off the cervix. Hook your finger around the rim and pull it sideways out of the vagina. Wash the cap with plain soap and water and pat dry.

Effectiveness   When used correctly, the cervical cap has a failure rate of about 6 percent. With typical use, it has a failure rate of about 18 percent. Most failures are due to the cap being dislodged, improperly inserted, or improperly fitted. The rubber can also deteriorate if it comes in contact with oil-based lubricants or vaginal medications.

Cost and Availability The cost ranges from about $30 to $40 for the cervical cap itself. The fee for the initial fitting by a health-care professional varies. It is available by prescription only. Replacement is recommended every year.

Advantages When used with a spermicide, the cervical cap offers protection against STIs similar to that of the diaphragm. Since it can be inserted long before intercourse it does not interfere with spontaneity. There are few adverse side effects and it does not interfere with hormonal systems. Due to its smaller size, it may be more comfortable for some women than a diaphragm.

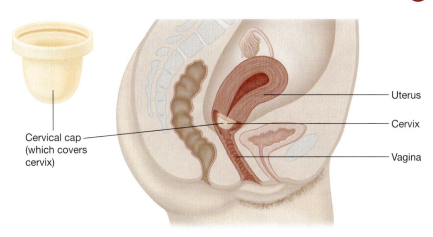

FIGURE 6.6 Placement of the Cervical Cap.

Disadvantages Some people are allergic to latex; in such cases, a plastic cap can be substituted. Others are sensitive to the spermicides used with the cap. Some women find the cervical cap uncomfortable, difficult to insert, or hard to remove. There is some increased risk of urinary tract infections and toxic shock syndrome with use of the cervical cap.

Vaginal Sponge

The **vaginal sponge** is a soft, disposable, 2-inch synthetic sponge containing spermicide. It is inserted into the vagina and expands to fit over the cervix. The sponge is another combination method; it helps prevent sperm from entering the uterus, and the spermicide kills or renders sperm inactive.

Method of Use A vaginal sponge can be inserted up to 18 hours before intercourse. After removing the sponge from its package, dampen it with a few tablespoons of water and squeeze it until foam appears to activate the spermicide. Insert the sponge into the vagina either by hand or with an applicator enclosed in the package. Slide the sponge along the back wall of the vagina until it rests against your cervix. The dimple side should face your cervix, with the loop away from your cervix. Check to be sure that the sponge covers your cervix. While the sponge is in place, a couple can have repeated intercourse without adding more spermicide. After intercourse, the sponge is left in place for at least 6 hours; it can be left in place for up to 24 hours. The sponge is removed by pulling on the attached tape or loops and is then discarded.

Effectiveness Vaginal sponges have an 8 percent failure rate with perfect use, and a 24 percent failure rate with typical use. Most failures are due to improper insertion. A small number of women expel the sponge, particularly during a bowel movement. There are also higher failure rates for women who have had children than for childless women.

Cost and Availability The cost is about $3 to $5 for a package of three sponges. In 1995 the sponge was taken off the market voluntarily by its original maker after an FDA inspection found bacterial contamination of water and other problems at a manufacturing plant. The FDA did not raise concerns about safety or effectiveness of the sponge and a new manufacturer bought the rights to the sponge in 1998, and reintroduced it the following year. Now that the sponge is back on the market in the United States, it is available without a prescription in most drug stores and is the most popular over-the-counter female contraceptive method in the United States.

Vaginal Sponge: a soft, disposable, synthetic sponge containing spermicide inserted into the vagina, which helps prevent sperm from entering the uterus and kills or makes sperm inactive

"Spongeworthy?"

In an episode of *Seinfeld*, Elaine Benes ran from pharmacy to pharmacy trying to corner the market on vaginal sponges after their sole manufacturer voluntarily suspended production, which actually did happen in 1995. In 1999 the Today sponge was reintroduced, making it possible for Elaine to once again have safer sex with a man she deemed to be "spongeworthy."

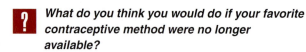

What do you think you would do if your favorite contraceptive method were no longer available?

—How big a role does convenience play in your contraceptive decision making?
—How do you decide which potential sex partners might be "spongeworthy"?

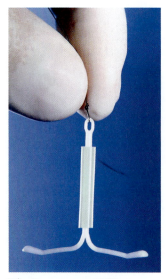

The Progestasert IUD.

Advantages The spermicide contained in the sponge provides some protection against STIs. Because it can be inserted up to 18 hours prior to intercourse, it does not interfere with spontaneity. It is inexpensive, no prescription is needed, and one size fits all. The sponge doesn't leak so it is not as messy as some other methods, and it is not necessary to apply more spermicide for additional acts of intercourse. It remains effective for up to 24 hours and does not interfere with the hormonal system.

Disadvantages Some women experience irritation or discomfort wearing the sponge. Others are allergic to the spermicides. Difficulty removing the sponge has also been reported. There is some increase in yeast infections reported, and a slightly increased risk of toxic shock syndrome. The vaginal sponge is not quite as effective a method of contraception as other barrier methods of birth control.

MECHANICAL METHODS OF BIRTH CONTROL

Intrauterine Device (IUD)

There is currently only one mechanical method of birth control available: the **intrauterine device (IUD),** a small plastic or copper device placed into the uterus. Although in the United States only about 1 percent of women use an IUD, worldwide, it is estimated that over 100 million women use an IUD, about 12 percent of married women of reproductive age (Treiman et al., 1995).

There are three types of IUDs available in the United States at this time, the Copper-T 380A (Copper T, marketed as Paragard), the levonorgestrel-releasing system (LNg 20, marketed as Mirena), and the Progesterone T (marketed as Progestasert). IUDs appears to work primarily by preventing sperm from fertilizing ova. IUDs do not cause abortions; they prevent fertilization. The Copper IUD causes an increase in uterine and tubal fluids containing copper ions, enzymes, prostaglandins, and white blood cells that alter tubal and uterine transport and affects the sperm and ovum so fertilization does not occur. Progestin IUDs (the LNg 20 and Progesterone T) primarily have a hormonal method of action.

Method of Use A full pelvic exam, Pap smear, pregnancy test, and tests for STIs are performed before insertion of an IUD (Figure 6.7). There is no scientific reason to support the common practice of insertion only during menstruation (WHO, 1987) except as an indicator that the woman is not pregnant. A health practitioner must insert and remove the IUD. Insertion may cause cramping or bleeding, which will subside after 10 to 15 minutes. The IUD has fine plastic threads that hang down into the vagina. These must be checked periodically to be sure the IUD is still in place. Most healthcare practitioners recommend a follow-up visit after the woman's next menstrual period (about 3 to 6 weeks after insertion) to check that the IUD is still in place and that no signs of infection have developed.

Intrauterine Device (IUD): a plastic or metal loop, ring, or spiral that is inserted into the uterus to prevent implantation

Effectiveness Among women who use the IUD perfectly (checking the strings regularly to detect expulsion), the probability of pregnancy during the first year of use is 0.6 percent for the Copper T, 1.5 percent for the Progesterone T, and 0.1 percent for the Levonorgestrel IUD. Among typical users, the corresponding probabilities of pregnancy are 0.8 percent for the Copper T, 2 percent for the Progesterone, and 0.1 percent for the Levonorgestrel. Over the long run, the Levonorgestrel IUD is the single most effective method of reversible contraception available today, followed closely by the Copper T.

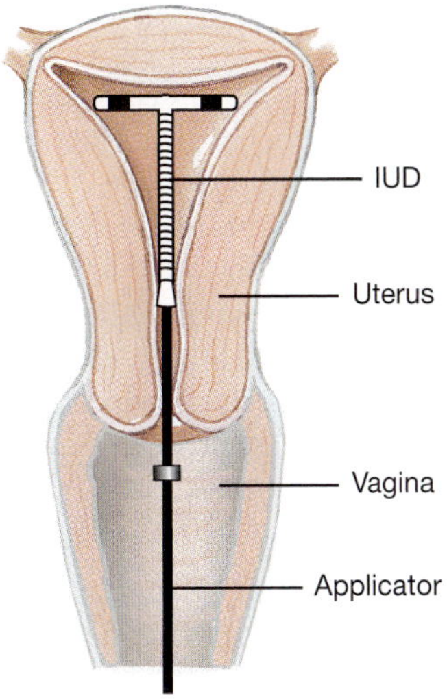

Cost and Availability Although the initial cost for an IUD and its insertion is high, the ongoing costs are minimal. IUDs cost $200 to $300 plus doctor's fees (about $150) for an initial exam, insertion, and removal of the IUD. The cost of an IUD insertion in a public family-planning clinic ranges from about $150 to $200. The Progesterone IUD must be replaced annually; the Copper T lasts up to 10 years, and the Levonorgestrel IUD 2 to 5 years.

FIGURE 6.7 Placement of the Intrauterine Device (IUD).

Advantages The IUD is a very effective means of preventing pregnancy. It doesn't interfere with spontaneity of sex and you don't have to worry about remembering to use it. As you just read, it may be left in place for 1 to 5 years, depending on the type. Women who cannot use hormonal methods can use the Copper T; the progesterone and LNg 20 have the additional benefits of decreasing menstrual blood loss and the incidence and intensity of dysmenorrhea. The LNg 20 also appears to reduce a woman's risk of developing pelvic inflammatory disease (see Chapter 7) (Toivonen, Luukkainen, & Allonen, 1991) and is an effective treatment of menorrhagia (Anderson & Rybo, 1990).

Disadvantages In the mid-1970s one IUD, the Dalkon Shield, was taken off the market after causing pelvic infections and infertility in thousands of American women. Since that time many women and physicians have viewed the IUD with suspicion. However, research has determined that the complications had to do primarily with the design of the Dalkon Shield; that design is no longer in use.

There is a small risk of developing pelvic inflammatory disease following insertion of the IUD. This risk is associated with exposure to an STI within 20 days after the IUD is inserted (Farley et al., 1992; Lee, Ribin, & Borucki, 1988). Between 2 and 10 percent of IUDs users spontaneously expel their IUD within the first year. If a woman becomes pregnant with an IUD in place the IUD should be removed immediately to prevent complications. Data suggest that about half of intrauterine pregnancies occurring with the IUD in place end in spontaneous abortion; about 5 percent of those becoming pregnant on the IUD will have an ectopic pregnancy (WHO, 1987).

The IUD gives no protection against STIs. Also there may be increased menstrual bleeding and cramps and there is a slight risk of the IUD puncturing the uterine wall. The string of the IUD irritates some partners during intercourse. This may be remedied having the length of the string trimmed by a health-care practitioner.

CHEMICAL METHODS OF BIRTH CONTROL

The spermicides used with the condom, diaphragm, and cervical cap, and those embedded in the sponge are the chemical methods of birth control available today.

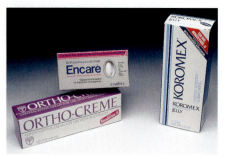

Various spermicides.

Spermicides

Vaginal spermicides contain an inactive chemical that kills sperm or renders them inactive. They come in various forms, including cream, jelly, film, foam, or suppository (see accompanying photographs). For some products, the formulation helps disperse the spermicide. In the case of gel and foam, the formulation itself may provide both lubrication and an additional barrier effect. Nonoxynol-9, the active chemical agent in spermicide products available in the United States, is a surfactant that destroys the sperm cell membrane. Other surfactant products, including octoxynol and benzalkonium chloride, are widely used in other parts of the world.

Method of Use   To be effective, spermicide must be placed in the vagina no longer than 1 hour before intercourse. The method of use varies depending on the product, so it is important to read the directions for the specific product in use. Another reason for close attention to the package directions is that some products are not immediately effective and you must wait 10 to 15 minutes for dissolution and dispersion prior to intercourse.

Spermicidal gels, creams, and foams are commonly marketed for use with a diaphragm, cervical cap, or condom, but they also can be used alone. Spermicidal foam, cream, or gel can be inserted directly into the vagina with a special plungerlike applicator that comes with the product. Insert the applicator as far as it will comfortably go. Then, holding the applicator still, push the plunger to release the gel, cream, or foam (Figure 6.8). The spermicide should be inserted deep in your vagina, close to the cervix. Suppositories are small, oval capsules manually inserted into the vagina at least 10 to 15 minutes before intercourse. The capsule dissolves when it comes in contact with vaginal secretions, activating the spermicide. When using spermicidal film, place one sheet of film on your fingertip and slide it in along the back wall of the vagina as far as you can so that the film rests on or near your cervix.

Effectiveness   When used alone, spermicides have a failure rate of 3 percent with perfect usage. Typical failure rates cover a wide range, from less than 5 percent to more than 50 percent. Spermicides are more effective when used in combination with other contraceptive methods, such as the aforementioned barrier methods (to compare failure rates, see earlier discussions of the condom, diaphragm, and cervical cap). For a spermicide to be effective, it must be placed correctly in the vagina no longer than 1 hour before intercourse. Most failures are due to improper usage.

Cost and Availability   Most spermicides cost less than $10. Single-use packets of gel or suppositories can cost less than $2.00. Spermicides are widely available without a prescription in most drugstores.

FIGURE 6.8 Application of Spermicides. Spermicidal gels and creams come in tubes, and foams come in a pressurized can. They are applied with plastic applicators that can be inserted deep into the vagina, close to the cervix.

Advantages   When used alone, spermicides may offer some protection from STIs. When used with a barrier method of birth control, spermicides are highly effective protection against HIV and other STIs. Spermicides can be purchased without a prescription, are inexpensive, and are readily available. They do not interfere with the hormonal system. Generally, they are free of negative side effects.

Disadvantages   Some people are allergic to or may be irritated by specific spermicides. Switching to another brand or type usually alleviates this problem. Some people dislike the additional discharge and find spermicides to be messy. Others find that the taste or smell of the spermicide interferes with the pleasures of oral-genital sex.

HORMONE-BASED CONTRACEPTIVES

Oral Contraceptives

Dr. Gregory Pincus and Dr. John Roack introduced **oral contraceptives,** also known as the **birth control pills** or simply "the Pill," in 1960. Dr. Roack, then a devout Roman Catholic, had hoped that his church would accept the pill as a "natural" method of birth control because no barriers to conception were involved. However, the Catholic Church didn't accept this explanation and does not approve of the oral contraceptives; in fact, the only forms of birth control approved by the Catholic Church are fertility awareness methods (discussed later) and abstinence.

There are two types of birth control pills. The more popular is the combination pill, which contains a synthetic estrogen and progestin. There are dozens of combination pills that contain varying amounts and ratios of these two hormones. There also is a progestin-only pill, also called the minipill. The progestin in the minipill causes cervical mucus to thicken and become more acidic, effectively blocking the passage of the sperm. Progestin also affects the uterine lining, preventing the implantation of fertilized eggs. In addition to the effects of progestin, the estrogen in combination pills prevents the maturation of ova, effectively stopping ovulation. The combined oral contraceptive pill is one of the most extensively studied medications ever prescribed.

Method of Use   A woman taking oral contraceptives should carefully follow the instructions that come with the medication and those given by her health-care practitioner. Combination pills contain 21 or 28 pill packets. The 28-pill packs contain seven pills that have no hormones but are included so the woman need not remember to stop taking her pills and then resume taking them again 7 days later as is required if using the 21-day packets. If a pill is forgotten one day, that pill should be taken immediately and the next pill taken as scheduled. If two or more pills are forgotten, a backup method of birth control should be used.

Effectiveness   With perfect usage the failure rate of oral contraceptives is only about 0.1 percent. With typical usage the failure rate is 6 percent. Most failures occur when women forget to take a pill, or don't take them at the same time every day, allowing hormone levels to rise enough to cause ovulation. Pregnancy may also occur when a woman discontinues taking the pill and fails to use another method of contraception.

Cost and Availability   Birth control pills are only available with a prescription. On an annual basis, generic oral contraceptives cost about $100 to $150. Clients at public clinics may pay as little as 30 cents to a dollar per month.

Advantages   When used correctly, oral contraceptives are a reversible, safe, and highly effective birth control method. An added benefit is that they regulate menstrual periods on a predictable 28-day cycle, often with a lighter menstrual flow. Some women find the Pill helps relieve premenstrual symptoms and helps clear up acne. The Pill may help reduce the risk of pelvic inflammatory disease, ovarian cysts, and fibrocystic

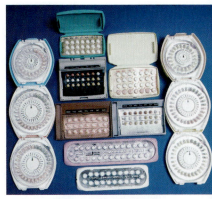

Different types of birth control pills.

Vaginal Spermicides: chemical agents that kill spermatozoa

Oral Contraceptives/ Birth Control Pills: pills, typically containing synthetic hormones, that inhibit ovulation and thereby prevent conception

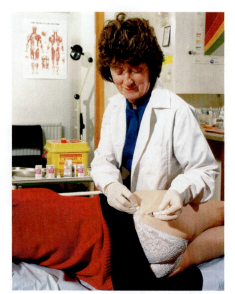

The injectable contraceptive Depo-Provera.

breasts. Studies have shown that women who use the combination Pill for at least a year have approximately half the risk of developing endometrial and ovarian cancer as those who have never used the Pill. The Pill does not interfere with spontaneity, as it doesn't have to be used at the time of intercourse. And, there is no mess.

Disadvantages   The Pill does not protect against STIs. Some women dislike having to take a pill every day, and the relatively high cost of oral contraceptives may be a problem for some women. Some women taking the combination pill report that they experience headaches, nausea, depression, bloating, skin problems, and weight gain. In some women, the Pill alters vaginal secretions and decreases levels of free testosterone, which may decrease libido (Graham et al., 1995). The Pill is not recommended for women who have circulatory problems, liver disease, history of blood clots, severe high blood pressure, breast or uterine cancer, sickle cell disease, diabetes, or are over 35 and smoke cigarettes. The relationship between oral contraceptives and breast cancer is unclear, but is currently being studied.

Injectable Contraceptives

The most commonly used **injectable contraceptive** is Depo-Provera. The active ingredient in Depo-Provera is medroxyprogesterone acetate, a progestin. Injection of this progestin, a long-acting synthetic hormone, every 3 months inhibits ovulation by suppressing levels of follicle stimulating hormone (FSH) and luteinizing hormone (LH) and by eliminating the LH surge (these hormones were discussed in Chapter 2). The pituitary glands of women taking Depo-Provera remain responsive to gonadotropin-releasing hormone (Gn-RH), which suggests that the site of action is the hypothalamus (Mishell, 1991). As do other progestins, Depo-Provera also alters the cervical mucus and prevents implantation in the uterine lining.

In October 2000, the Food and Drug Administration approved a monthly contraceptive injection for marketing in the United States under the brand name Lunelle. The shot contains a combination of estrogen and progestin, similar to that contained in combination pills. Compared with Depo-Provera, Lunelle is less likely to disrupt the menstrual cycle, and it does not cause as much weight gain; an added bonus is that, when desired, fertility resumes much more quickly than with Depo-Provera.

Method of Use   A health-care practitioner administers Depo-Provera injections every 3 months. The Depo-Provera is injected deeply into the deltoid (upper arm) or gluteus maximus (buttocks). Injection into the deltoid may be slightly more painful. Lunelle must be injected every 28–30 days, with the outside limit being 33 days.

Effectiveness   Depo-Provera is an extremely effective contraceptive option. The failure rate is 0.3 to 0.4 percent, making it one of the most effective contraceptives on the market. Failure can occur if a woman neglects to get her reinjection on schedule. Clinical trials indicate that Lunelle is highly effective (Shulman, 2000); there were no unintended pregnancies during the course of the U.S. trials. A definitive evaluation will require more lengthy studies.

Cost and Availability   Each injection of these contraceptives costs about $30 plus the doctor's fee. No laboratory tests are specifically indicated unless a woman is late for her shot; in such a case, she may need a pregnancy test before her practitioner agrees to reinjection. Injectable contraceptives are available by prescription only and must be done in a health-care facility.

Injectable Contraceptive:
injection of progestin to inhibit ovulation and prevent pregnancy

Advantages   A major advantage of injectable contraceptives is that no preparation is required prior to sexual intercourse, so spontaneity is uninterrupted. There is also no risk of forgetting to use birth control and the effects are reversible once the last injection wears off.

Although Depo-Provera does not cause long-term loss of fertility, ovulation may not return until 9 to 10 months after the last shot (Mishell, 1996). Depo-Provera is likely to cause amenorrhea (lack of menstruation), which some women consider an advantage. During the first year of Depo-Provera use, 30 to 40 percent of women do not have menstrual periods, and by the end of the fifth year, 90 percent are amenorrheic (Mishell et al., 1997).

With Lunelle, ovulation typically occurs within 60 days of the last injection. One small study found that 80 percent of the women became pregnant within a year after discontinuing use of Lunelle (National Women's Health Network, 2001).

Disadvantages   Injectable contraceptives do not provide any protection against STIs. Moreover, it is inconvenient to have to go to a health-care provider to get regular injections.

With Depo-Provera, some women experience severe weight gain, hair loss, headaches, fatigue, abdominal pain, acne, and severe depression; there is a possibility of increased risk for osteoporosis and breast cancer. Once a woman has gotten an injection, she cannot change her mind; the hormone will remain in her system for at least 3 months. It can take up to a year after Depo-Provera injections are stopped for fertility to return.

It is expected that Lunelle will produce more regular menstrual cycles than Depo-Provera. Nevertheless, at the end of the first year of use, more than 30 percent of Lunelle users reported irregular bleeding compared to 17 percent of pill users (National Women's Health Network, 2001). Amenorrhea is less common among Lunelle users than among Depo-Provera users. Weight gain for Lunelle users is less than it is for Depo-Provera users but more than for women taking the pill. Other side effects associated with Lunelle use seem comparable to those of the pill. However, since this is a relatively new drug, additional studies should produce more information about long-term use of the drug.

Implants

Birth control implants, such as Norplant, consist of two to six thin matchstick size rubber capsules inserted by a health-care professional under the skin in a woman's upper arm. Like injectable contraceptives, the Norplant capsules contain the synthetic hormone progestin, which thickens cervical mucus, blocking the passage of sperm into the uterus and prevents the implantation of fertilized eggs in the uterine lining. Although hard tubing was used in the past, Norplant implants currently are being produced only with soft tubing.

Method of Use   Norplant implants are inserted during a minor surgical procedure done under local anesthetic to numb a small area on the upper arm. A health-care practitioner makes small incisions about ⅛ inch long in a fanlike pattern; the capsules are inserted into these incisions. Insertion takes about 15 minutes. The capsules must be removed after 5 years, but they can be removed earlier. A new set can be implanted after removal of the old one.

Effectiveness   Because there is no possibility of user error, the typical use and perfect use estimates for Norplant are the same. The failure rate of implants is only 0.05 percent. Failure can occur if the implants are used beyond the 5-year period. Norplant is also less effective in women who weigh over 155 pounds. Failure rates increase in the sixth year of use so it is generally recommended that Norplant capsules be removed at the end of the fifth year.

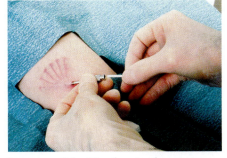
Insertion of the Norplant implant.

Birth Control Implants: rubber capsules containing progestin inserted under the skin in a woman's upper arm, which prevents ovulation and pregnancy

Cost and Availability   The cost of Norplant insertion ranges from $500 to $700 (this cost may include a physical exam and some laboratory tests). Removal may cost more because it takes more time. While the initial cost may be high, over 5 years' time this can be a cost-effective contraceptive method. Implants are available by prescription only and must be inserted and removed by a specially trained health-care practitioner.

Advantages   Implants are a highly effective and long-acting birth control. Implants don't interfere with spontaneity; you don't have to remember to do anything. Many women experience lighter menstrual periods with implants. Some women who are breast-feeding or otherwise cannot use the Pill can use implants such as Norplant.

Disadvantages   Implants provide no protection against STIs. There is a high initial cost and some women have reported that they suffered severe pain and scarring when their doctors removed Norplant capsules. Implants are not recommended for women with a history of blood-clotting problems, heart disease, stroke, liver disease, or breast cancer, or for women over age 35 who smoke cigarettes.

SURGICAL METHODS OF BIRTH CONTROL

Sterilization

One form of female **sterilization** is a **tubal ligation,** which literally means tying the fallopian tubes. However, this term is something of a misnomer. Most often the fallopian tubes are cut or clamped, not tied, to prevent the passage of eggs and sperm.

Men can be surgically sterilized through a procedure called a **vasectomy,** in which the vas deferens, the tube that delivers sperm from the testes, is cut or blocked, so that sperm cannot pass from the testes to the urethra (they are instead harmlessly reabsorbed by the body).

Method   Female sterilization involves ligation (tying off with a ligature), mechanical occlusion (closure or blockage of blood vessels) with clips or rings, or electrocoagulation (clotting of tissue using a high-frequency electrical current). Local anesthesia with light sedation is generally sufficient to minimize the pain caused by these sterilization procedures. Other methods of female surgical sterilization include *hysterectomy* (the removal of the uterus) and *oophorectomy* (the removal of the ovaries). These are major surgical procedures performed under general anesthesia. Unlike tubal ligation, hysterectomies and oophorectomies are almost always performed for reasons other than birth control, for example due to disease or serious infection.

The two major surgical procedures for tubal sterilization in the United States are the minilaparotomy and laparascopy. In the *minilaparotomy* a small incision is made just above the pubic hairline to provide access to the fallopian tubes. Through this incision, the surgeon grasps the tubes and occludes them with a clip or ring. The *laparoscopy* approach to sterilization involves making a small incision just below the navel and inserting an instrument to visualize the tubes so the surgeon can place rings, apply clips, or electrocoagulate the oviducts (Figure 6.9). Primarily because the incision is smaller, this method is less painful than minilaparotomy, has a lower rate of complications, a shorter recovery time, and leaves only a small scar. The oviducts also can be reached though an incision high in the vagina (called a *colpotomy*) behind the cervix. This allows direct visualization of the pelvic organs, and the oviducts can be directly sutured and cut.

A vasectomy is performed through two small incisions in the scrotum. The vas deferens is isolated and surgically divided. Some surgeons tie each end with a simple ligature while others cauterize the cut ends with a hot wire or needle electrode

Sterilization: the process of making a man or woman infertile

Tubal Ligation: surgical sterilization of a woman by obstructing or "tying" the fallopian tubes

Vasectomy: surgical sterilization of a man by cutting or blocking the vas deferens

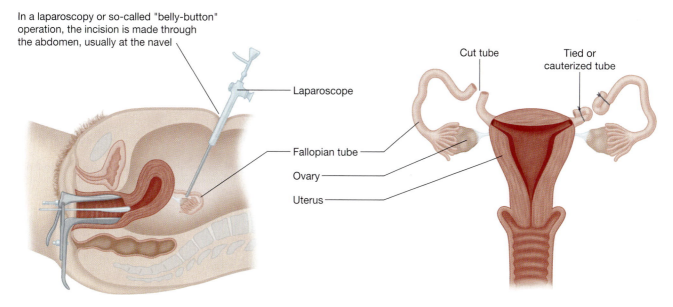

In a laparoscopy or so-called "belly-button" operation, the incision is made through the abdomen, usually at the navel

Laparoscope

Cut tube

Tied or cauterized tube

Fallopian tube

Ovary

Uterus

FIGURE 6.9 Laparoscopy. The surgeon approaches the fallopian tubes through a small incision in the abdomen just below the navel. A laparoscope is inserted through the incision, and a small section of each fallopian tube is cauterized, cut, or clamped to prevent ova from joining with sperm.

(Figure 6.10). A segment of the vas may be removed to obtain greater separation, although this procedure is not considered necessary. A "no-scalpel" procedure developed in China in 1974 is currently being used in many programs in the United States. In this approach the vas is reached through a puncture in the scrotum rather than through a scalpel incision. Thereafter the surgical procedure is the same as the scalpel method. Compared with the scalpel method, the no-scalpel method appears to have lower complication rates (Huber, 1985).

Effectiveness   Only about 0.5 percent of women experience an unintended pregnancy after female sterilization; 0.15 percent get pregnant following a male partner's sterilization. Approximately one third of pregnancies that occur after female surgical sterilization are ectopic. Women less than 35 years old and those who are not lactating (nursing) are more likely to conceive after sterilization. The tubes can rarely reopen after a tubal ligation. After a vasectomy it can take several months for the reproductive tract to be fully cleared of sperm. It is also possible for the cut ends of the vas deferens to heal together. For both of these reasons it is important to use additional contraception until a zero sperm count is confirmed.

Cost and Availability   The cost of sterilization procedures varies greatly. Prices range from $1,000 to $2,500 for a tubal ligation and from $250 to $500 for a vasectomy. Despite this high cost, of the contraceptive methods available in the United States, one study found vasectomy to be the most cost effective (Trussell et al., 1995). Sterilizations are surgical procedures that must be performed by physicians either in a hospital on an outpatient basis or a doctor's office.

Advantages   These are permanent, highly effective means of preventing pregnancy. Over the long term, sterilization is cost effective and there is nothing to buy or to remember to use. There is no need to interrupt lovemaking for contraception, which allows for complete spontaneity.

① Location of vas deferens

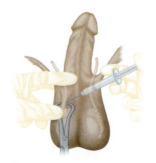
② Injection of local anesthetic

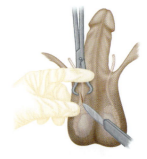
③ Incision over vas deferens

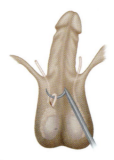
④ Isolation of vas from surrounding tissue

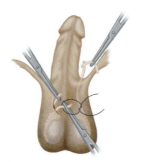
⑤ Removal of segment of vas; tying ends

⑥ Return of vas to position; incision is closed and process is repeated on the other side

FIGURE 6.10 Vasectomy.
This procedure is usually carried out in a doctor's office, using local anesthesia. Small incisions are made in the scrotum. Each vas deferens is cut, and the ends are tied off or cauterized to prevent sperm from reaching the urethra. After a vasectomy, the sperm continue to be produced by the testes but are harmlessly reabsorbed by the body.

Disadvantages   These procedures do not provide protection against STIs. Although recent advances in microsurgery have increased the possibility that some operations can be reversed, sterilization should be considered permanent. Other disadvantages is the need to undergo surgery and the expense at the time of the procedure.

FERTILITY AWARENESS METHODS

The methods described in the following sections involve **fertility awareness,** detailed knowledge and tracking of the female partner's menstrual cycle to identify when intercourse is most likely to result in a pregnancy. These birth control methods sometimes are referred to as *natural* methods of birth control. This term is not meant to imply that other contraceptive methods are unnatural, only that the natural signs and symptoms associated with the menstrual cycle are observed, recorded, and interpreted to identify when a woman is potentially fertile. To avoid pregnancy couples abstain from sexual intercourse during fertile times. Other couples combine fertility awareness methods or use a barrier method of birth control or withdrawal during potentially fertile days.

Cervical Mucus Monitoring

Using the **cervical mucus monitoring method,** women become alert to changes in the amount and texture of their cervical secretions. Near midcycle the pituitary gland releases luteinizing hormone (LH), which triggers ovulation and causes the follicle to transform in to the corpus luteum. The corpus luteum begins to produce progesterone while continuing to produce estrogen. Progesterone counteracts the effects of estrogen

Fertility Awareness: birth control methods that depend on detailed knowledge and tracking of the female partner's menstrual cycle to identify when intercourse is most likely to result in a pregnancy

Cervical Mucus Monitoring Method: a fertility awareness method of birth control in which women become alert to changes in the amount and texture of their cervical secretions and abstain from sexual intercourse during the period when ovulation is most likely to occur

and causes cervical secretions in the cervix to thicken and form a mucus plug that prevents sperm from traveling through the cervix.

Cervical mucus changes signal the beginning and the end of the fertile time, even among women who have irregular menstrual cycles. The fertility signs during the woman's menstrual cycles are caused by changes in circulating hormone levels, primarily estrogen and progesterone.

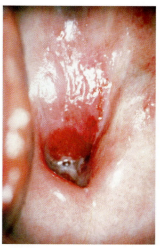

Cervical secretions.

Method of Use   Using this method of birth control requires a woman to observe the look, the touch, and the feel of her cervical secretions. Most women need help in the first few cycles to interpret their cervical secretion patterns and charts to determine the fertile time.

After menses, the cervical secretions are typically scant or absent. As the growing follicle releases more estrogen, cervical secretions appear. At first these secretions are sticky, thick, and cloudy. As estrogen levels peak at midcycle, the secretions become clear, stretchy, and slippery. The last day on which clear, stretchy, slippery secretions are observed is known as the peak day, the day on which conception is most likely. The fertile time begins when cervical secretions are first observed. The number of fertile days varies from about 6 to 12 days.

Effectiveness   The first year probability of pregnancy for methods based on using only cervical secretions to identify the beginning and end of the fertile time is about 3 percent among perfect users, and about 20 percent among typical users who abstain reliably during the fertile time (Trussell & Grummer-Strawn, 1990). Most failures are due to miscalculation of ovulation or to ovulation at an unexpected time in the cycle. Inadequate time devoted to charting the menstrual cycle or misunderstandings of the methods are also common.

Cost and Availability   This method is readily available and requires no special equipment. The only cost involved might be a nominal fee charged to train a woman in how to use the method correctly.

Advantages   There are no potentially adverse side effects, and this method does not interfere with sexual spontaneity. The cervical secretions method of fertility awareness increases a couple's knowledge of the female partner's reproductive potential and enhances self-reliance. Couples can calculate when ovulation occurs and use these methods if they are trying to conceive. Fertility awareness is acceptable to those religious groups that oppose other contraceptive methods, such as the Roman Catholic Church. Some individuals may be able to enjoy sex more if they don't feel the guilt they associate with the use of other contraceptives.

Disadvantages   This method offers no protection against sexually transmitted infections. Persistent reproductive tract infections may affect cervical secretions, thus making this method unreliable. The method requires regular observation and charting of cervical secretions to be effective, and abstinence or some other form of birth control on fertile days.

The Calendar Method

The **calendar method,** also called the **rhythm method,** is the oldest and most widely practiced of the fertility awareness–based methods of birth control (WHO, 1986). Fertile times are calculated using rules developed in the 1930s that are based upon three assumptions: (1) Ovulation occurs on day 14 (plus or minus 2 days) before the onset of the next menses; (2) sperm remain viable for about 4 days; and (3) the ovum survives for about 1 day. Typically a set number of days, usually a number between 18 and 21, are subtracted from the shortest cycle length in the past 5 to 12 cycles to identify the beginning and end of the woman's fertile time. Past cycle lengths give an estimate of the days the fertile time will occur (Figure 6.11).

Calendar Method/ Rhythm Method: a method of birth control in which the couple abstains from sexual intercourse during the period when ovulation is most likely to occur

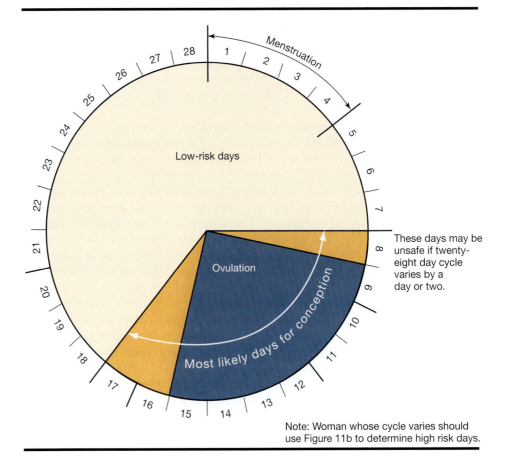

FIGURE 6.11 The Calendar or Rhythm Method. The calendar or rhythm method is based on avoiding intercourse when the sperm might meet the ovum. The darker shading shows the days on which the chances of conception are greater.

In the figure:
- Menstruation
- Low-risk days
- Ovulation
- Most likely days for conception
- These days may be unsafe if twenty-eight day cycle varies by a day or two.
- Note: Woman whose cycle varies should use Figure 11b to determine high risk days.

Method of Use   To use this method, keep a record of your past menstrual cycle length. A cycle begins on day 1 of menstrual bleeding and continues until the day before the next bleeding begins. To determine days to avoid coitus to prevent conception, subtract 18 from the number of days of the shortest menstrual cycle. For example, if your shortest cycle is 25 days, then day 7 would be the first high-risk day. To estimate when unprotected sex could resume, subtract 10 from the number of days in the longest cycle. For example, if your longest cycle is 30 days, you would be able to resume intercourse on day 20.

Effectiveness   Estimates of pregnancy rates for calendar calculations vary widely. This is due in part to the fact that many of the estimates come from flawed studies. One study estimated the probability of pregnancy during the first year of typical use to be about 13 percent (Kambic & Lamprecht, 1996).

Cost and Availability   This method is readily available. The only cost would be to obtain commercially prepared calendars for charting fertility. Some hospitals and clinics offer training in using the calendar method at no cost. Others may charge a nominal fee.

Advantages   As with other fertility awareness methods, the calendar method does not interfere with spontaneity. There are no side effects. Charting fertility signs can also be of help to couples wanting to conceive a child.

Disadvantages   The rhythm method provides no protection against STIs. Most failures are due to miscalculation of ovulation or to ovulation at an unexpected time in the cycle. Inadequate time devoted to charting the menstrual cycle or misunderstandings of the methods are also common. Some couples who do not choose to use an alternate method of birth control during fertile days may find it a disadvantage to abstain from sexual intercourse during peak days.

Length of Shortest Cycle (No. of Days)	First High Risk Day Is	Length of Longest Cycle (No. of Days)	Last High Risk Day Is
21 days	2nd day	21 days	10th day
22 days	3rd day	22 days	11th day
23 days	4th day	23 days	12th day
24 days	5th day	24 days	13th day
25 days	6th day	25 days	14th day
26 days	7th day	26 days	15th day
27 days	8th day	27 days	16th day
28 days	9th day	28 days	17th day
29 days	10th day	29 days	18th day
30 days	11th day	30 days	19th day
31 days	12th day	31 days	20th day
32 days	13th day	32 days	21th day
33 days	14th day	33 days	22nd day
34 days	15th day	34 days	23rd day
35 days	16th day	35 days	24th day

Note: Cycle begins on first day of menstruation

The Basal Body Temperature Method

With the **basal body temperature (BBT)** method, a resting body temperature is taken each morning and recorded for several months. The basal body temperature rises under the influence of progesterone. Most ovulatory cycles demonstrated a two-phase BBT pattern: lower in the first part of the menstrual cycle, rising to a higher level beginning around the time of ovulation, and remaining at the higher level for the rest of the cycle. By taking her temperature when she first wakes in the morning and recording it on a chart each day of her menstrual cycle, a woman can retrospectively identify when she may have ovulated.

Method of Use   To use the BBT method, take your temperature every morning at the same time before getting out of bed. Record the BBT on a chart (see Figure 6.12). Your temperature will probably rise about 0.4° to 0.8°F around the time of ovulation and remain elevated until the next menses begins. If you have 3 days of continuous temperature rise following six lower temperatures, you have ovulated and your postovulatory infertile time has begun. If you cannot detect a sustained rise in BBT, you may not have ovulated in that cycle. A true postovulatory BBT rise usually persists 10 days or longer. Some women notice a temperature drop about 12 to 24 hours prior to the rise caused by ovulation; others have no drop in temperature at all. A drop in your BBT probably means ovulation will occur the next day, so it is unsafe to have intercourse.

Effectiveness   Methods based on using BBT alone limit unprotected intercourse to the postovulatory infertile time. With perfect use, the first year probability of pregnancy is about 2 percent. With typical use, the probability of pregnancy increases to about 20 percent (Marshall, 1968).

Cost and Availability   The only costs are for a calendar and an accurate thermometer. (There are special thermometers, calibrated to $\frac{1}{10}$th of a degree, specifically for use in monitoring BBT.) This method is freely available. It requires no visits to a hospital, doctor, or pharmacy.

Advantages   As with other fertility awareness methods, there are no adverse side effects. And the BBT method does not interfere with sexual spontaneity. Couples also can

Basal Body Temperature (BBT): a fertility awareness method of birth control in which a woman takes her temperature when she first wakes in the morning and records it on a chart each day of her menstrual cycle to retrospectively identify when she may have ovulated in order to abstain from sexual intercourse when ovulation is most likely

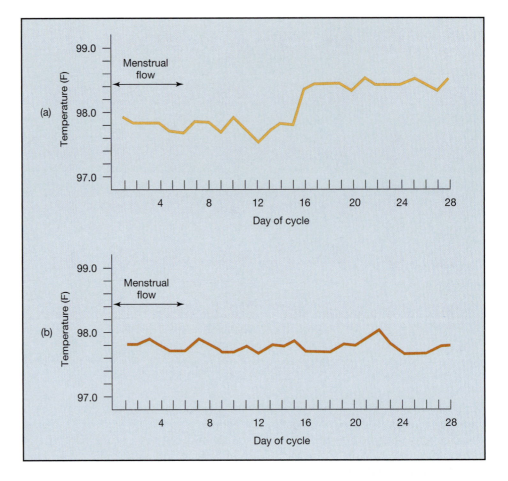

FIGURE 6.12 **A Basal Body Temperature (BBT) Chart.** Body temperature may dip slightly just prior to ovulation, followed by a rise of about 0.4 to 0.8 degrees that lasts throughout the rest of the cycle. (a) A cycle in which a sustained elevation in temperature occurred following ovulation on day 15. (b) No sustained temperature rise, which indicates that ovulation did not occur during this cycle.

use this method if they are trying to conceive. Fertility awareness is acceptable to those religious groups that oppose other contraceptive methods. For some individuals this may reduce the guilt they associate with the use of other contraceptives and allow them to enjoy sex more.

Disadvantages The BBT method offers no protection against STIs. The pressure to have intercourse only on "safe" days is difficult for some. There is a very long lead-time for the calendar and BBT methods, as accurate records are required for several months before starting to rely on them for contraception. Participants must be consistent and committed to careful observation and charting.

What Doesn't Work

CONSIDERATIONS

- **Douching,** the application of a stream of liquid to cleanse the vagina, does not provide protection against pregnancy; douching shortly after intercourse may even increase the likelihood of conception by flushing still-active sperm further up toward an egg.

- Taking a hot bath may make you feel cleaner, but it won't wash away any sperm.

- If you stand on your head, you might feel dizzy, but it won't prevent pregnancy.

- And jumping up and down to make the sperm fall out doesn't work either, as the sperm are supplied with enough energy to defy gravity.

? *What other myths about contraception have you heard?*

—*Where did you hear them?*
—*Did you believe them at the time?*

TABLE 6.3

Evaluating Contraceptive Methods

Most effective in preventing pregnancy	Implant Sterilization Injectable contraceptive IUD Birth control pill Condom
Most effective protection against STIs	Latex condom Diaphragm Cervical cap Sponge Spermicide
Least expensive	Fertility awareness–based methods Condom Sponge Diaphragm Cervical cap IUD
Fewest side effects	Fertility awareness–based methods Condom Sponge Diaphragm Cervical cap
Least effort required	Sterilization IUD Implant Injectable contraceptive

POSTCOITAL CONTRACEPTION

Emergency Contraception

Emergency contraceptives are methods for preventing pregnancy after unwanted or unprotected sexual intercourse. Although they have been available in other countries for about 25 years, it was not until February 1997 that the FDA approved their use in the United States. Emergency contraception is not an **abortifacient,** an agent that causes an abortion. Pills used for emergency contraception are sometimes confused with the "morning-after pill," which will be discussed under "Abortion," later in the chapter. Emergency contraception works in one of two ways: It blocks ovulation or it prevents the implantation of a fertilized egg. If implantation has already occurred, the pills will have no effect and the pregnancy will continue.

Method of Use There are several methods of emergency contraception. The most commonly used option is a regimen of combined oral contraceptive pills (the Yuzpe regimen, also called ECPs for emergency contraceptive pills) within 72 hours of unprotected intercourse. ECPs are for emergency use only. They are not recommended for routine use because they are less effective than regular contraceptives. Other options include the use of progestin-only minipills within 48 to 72 hours or insertion of a copper-releasing intrauterine device within 5 days to prevent implantation.

Effectiveness Because emergency contraception is used only once or infrequently, its effectiveness can only be estimated. After ECP treatment, pregnancy rates are typically in the range of 0.5 to 2.45 percent (Trussell, Ellertson, & Stewart, 1996). As we've

Douching: injecting a stream of water, often containing medicinal or cleansing agents, into the vagina for hygienic or therapeutic purposes

Emergency Contraceptives: methods of preventing pregnancy after unwanted or unprotected sexual intercourse

Abortifacient: a drug or device used to cause abortion

discussed previously, a treatment failure rate of 1.0 percent does not mean that the method was 99 percent effective, because most of the women treated would not have become pregnant even without treatment. A comparison of the expected pregnancy rate in women having unprotected sex and the pregnancy rate after treatment with ECPs found the effectiveness of postcoital contraceptives to be 87 percent, with no serious side effects (Espinos et al., 1999).

Cost and Availability　Emergency contraceptive pills are relatively inexpensive, as only a small number of pills are taken. Although in many states a physician must prescribe emergency contraception, information about self-administration is available on several Internet Web sites and through other media. A kit known as Plan B is now available in some states without a physician's prescription (see www.GoToPlanB.com). In addition, many common oral contraceptive pills can be used as emergency contraception. Although their manufacturers do not label the pills for this use, it is legal and commonplace for the medications to be used in this way. Currently, eleven brands of pills can be used as emergency contraceptive pills in the United States. One research study found that making emergency contraception more easily obtainable (without a prescription) does no harm and may reduce the rate of unwanted pregnancies (Glasier & Baird, 1998).

Advantages　Emergency contraceptives are the only methods a couple can use to prevent pregnancy after unprotected sexual intercourse or after a contraceptive "accident" (for example, if a condom broke or a diaphragm was inserted incorrectly). In addition, emergency contraceptives are the only contraceptive option available to rape victims. Because it can be used up to 5 days after intercourse, the IUD may be a useful option for women who present too late to take ECPs or for those women who want to continue using an IUD as a long-term method of contraception.

Disadvantages　Side effects of the use of emergency contraceptives are common. About half of women experience nausea and medication may be required to prevent vomiting. Less frequently, some women have temporary fluid retention, headaches, breast tenderness, or dizziness. ECPs change the amount, duration, and timing of the next menstrual period in about 10 to 15 percent of women. Side effects after postcoital insertion of an IUD are similar to those seen after routine insertion at other times and include abdominal discomfort and vaginal bleeding or spotting.

ABORTION

Abortion is a medical procedure that is performed in order to terminate a pregnancy. Until recently, the only option for women wanting to end a pregnancy was through use of a surgical technique. Today, medical abortifacients are also available that allow women to terminate unwanted pregnancies earlier and without surgical intervention.

There are several surgical and medical procedures currently used to terminate pregnancy. The selection of a procedure is usually dependent on availability and the time since the woman's last menstrual period. Legal abortions performed in a hygienic environment are relatively safe. Less than 1 percent of women who undergo legal abortion sustain a serious complication (AGI, 1998). The risk increases about 20 percent for each additional week of pregnancy past 8 weeks (Paul et al., 1999). Possible complications include infection, uterine or cervical perforation, and hemorrhage. This section provides simple descriptions of the various procedures used in performing an abortion; please see Chapter 18 for a discussion of the political and legal aspects of this controversial issue.

Surgical Methods

Vacuum Aspiration　**Vacuum aspiration** is the standard first-trimester surgical method of abortion. In this procedure the woman's cervix is dilated and a local anesthetic is applied;

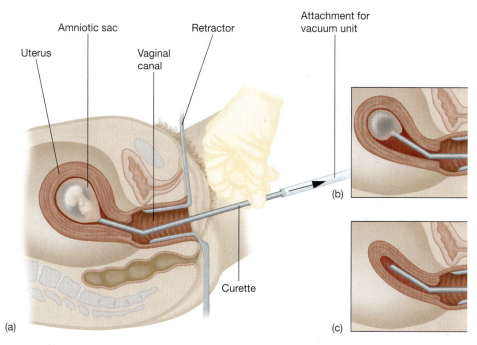

FIGURE 6.13 **Vacuum Aspiration.** (a) Removal of fetal material. (b and c) As fetal material is removed, the uterus contracts back to its original size.

the uterus is then emptied with a handheld syringe (Figure 6.13). This procedure can be done up to approximately 10 weeks past a woman's last menstrual period. It is usually performed in an outpatient clinic.

Suction Curettage   In **suction curettage,** the most frequently used abortion procedure in the United States, the cervix is gradually stretched using a series of increasingly thick rods or laminaria, dilators that absorb fluids from the cervical area and expand to stretch the opening of the cervix. Once the cervix is dilated, a small plastic tube is inserted through the cervical canal into the uterus. The tube is connected to the vacuum aspirator, a pump that uses gentle suction to evacuate the contents of the uterus. This method can be used from about 6 to 14 weeks after the last menstrual period. Usually performed with a local anesthetic on an outpatient basis, this procedure takes about 10 minutes.

Dilation and Curettage (D&C)   In **dilation and curettage (D&C),** a curette (a narrow metal loop) is used to gently scrape the walls of the uterus after the cervix is dilated (Figure 6.14). Now accounting for only a small number of abortion procedures, the D&C is typically performed at 18 to 20 weeks after the last menstrual period. This procedure is usually done in a hospital under general anesthesia.

Dilation and Evacuation (D&E)   After about 14 weeks from the last menstrual period, a **dilation and evacuation (D&E)** may be performed. Because the uterus is larger at this stage of pregnancy, the cervix must be dilated more carefully, using absorbent dilators that may be put into the cervix where they remain for several hours or sometimes overnight. After the cervix is sufficiently dilated, a local or general anesthetic is used and the dilators are removed. Surgical instruments and suction curettage are used to remove the contents of the uterus. The drug oxytocin is sometimes used to help the uterus contract and to slow bleeding. Usually performed in a doctor's office or clinic, a D&E procedure takes about 10 to 20 minutes.

Vacuum Aspiration/ Suction Curettage: abortion procedures performed during the first trimester of pregnancy, in which the contents of the uterus are withdrawn through a narrow tube

Dilation and Curettage (D&C): a surgical procedure in which the cervix is expanded using a dilator and the uterine lining scraped with a curette

Dilation and Evacuation (D&E): a surgical procedure in which the cervix is expanded using a dilator and then surgical instruments and suction curettage are used to remove the contents of the uterus

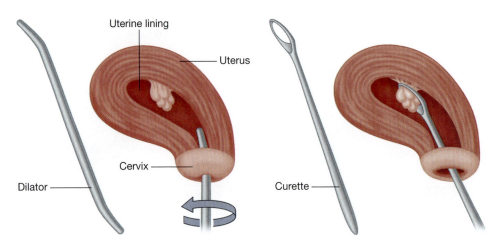

FIGURE 6.14 Dilation and Curettage (D&C). Side view showing the dilator opening the cervix through which a curette is inserted to scrape the uterine lining.

Hysterotomy A **hysterotomy** is a procedure similar to a cesarean section (see Chapter 5) in which the fetus and uterine contents are surgically removed through an incision in the abdomen and uterus. A hysterotomy is major surgery, performed under general anesthesia. This rarely used procedure is performed between 16 and 24 weeks after the last menstrual period.

Medical Methods

In the past few years, medical methods, or chemically induced abortions, have become options for women seeking an early abortion. In addition, some methods for later abortion are being refined.

Mifepristone Also known as RU-486 (the "morning-after" pill or the abortion pill), **mifepristone** is a form of nonsurgical abortion used to end pregnancy within 7 weeks of a woman's last menstrual cycle. Approved for use in the United States by the FDA in September 2000, mifepristone treatment includes a combination of two drugs administered during three visits to the doctor. After a physical exam, the woman takes three mifepristone tablets. Mifepristone is an antiprogesterone drug that blocks receptors of progesterone, a key hormone in the establishment and maintenance of pregnancy. Mifepristone softens and opens up the cervix. As a result, the fertilized egg is prevented from attaching to the uterine wall. Three days later the woman returns to the doctor's office to take two tablets of misoprostol, a hormonelike substance that is also used to treat ulcers. Misoprostol causes the uterus to contract and expel any remaining fetal tissue. About 2 weeks after initiating the abortion, the woman returns to the doctor a third time to be sure that she is no longer pregnant and that no fetal tissue remains in the uterus.

The drug combination causes bleeding and cramping that usually last 9 to 16 days but can continue for 30 days or more. About 50 percent of the women treated also report nausea and 25 to 33 percent experience headaches, vomiting, or diarrhea that last about 3 days. About 1 percent of women undergoing this type of abortion bleed severely, sometimes requiring blood transfusions. Mifepristone is effective in terminating 92 percent of pregnancies of up to 49 days (Spitz et al., 1998).

Hysterotomy: surgical removal of the fetus and uterine contents through an incision in the abdomen and uterus

Mifepristone: an abortion procedure, also known as RU-486, in which an antiprogesterone drug blocks receptors of progesterone and prevents the fertilized egg from attaching to the uterine wall

NEW AND FUTURE CONTRACEPTIVE TECHNOLOGY

It's an old, not so funny joke that if men got pregnant the perfect risk-free, fully reversible, completely effective means of birth control would have been invented years ago. We have made progress over the past 4,000 years. Men and women no longer have to abstain from sex or subject themselves to onerous, painful, and often ineffective procedures to prevent an unwanted pregnancy.

But for the most part the average American woman has the same contraceptive choices today she had 40 years ago. The sole exception is the transdermal patch, approved in 2001, that gradually releases a hormone into the body. This concept is similar to the nicotine patch currently in use for those wise people who wish to quit smoking. Women would only need to remember to replace the patch twice a month. Since the 1970s a combination of reduced government spending on research, fear of liability lawsuits, and abortion politics have slowed research into new methods of birth control.

The only contraceptive research and development being performed today is in the private sector. More than 100 experimental contraceptive methods are being studied around the world. It takes about 10 to 15 years and costs $20 to $70 million dollars to bring a new contraceptive method through research, development, and final approval for marketing by the U.S. Food and Drug Administration (Planned Parenthood, 1999).

The Contraceptive Future for Women

There are numerous contraceptives for women under development.

- A soft, doughnut shaped silicone contraceptive ring containing hormones is designed to be inserted into the vagina to fit around the cervix. Progestin-only and combination estrogen and progestin rings are being developed. The ring is intended to be removed during menstruation and is designed to be effective for 3 months to 1 year.

- An oral contraceptive that only needs to be taken once a month, called a menses inducer, is another method of birth control currently being studied. These pills are controversial, especially among antiabortion groups, since they could dislodge a fertilized egg after implantation.

- Implanon, a single-capsule implant, is designed to work for 2 or 3 years and is more potent than current implants such as Norplant.

- Biodegradable implants would gradually release hormones for 12 to 18 months before being absorbed harmlessly into the body.

- Microbiocides are one of the most exciting contraceptives of the future. They would form a chemical sheath that would kill sperm as well as bacteria and viruses, thus providing protection against both pregnancy and STIs, including HIV. About 60 different microbiocides are in development. The researchers' challenge is to develop a microbiocide that blocks STI transmission but is nontoxic and nonirritating when used repeatedly.

- Also under development are injectables that contain timed-release capsules so that women can choose how long they want to be protected.

- A gel designed to be absorbed through the skin prevents ovulation by releasing Nestorone, a synthetic progestin, through the skin.

- Several computer devices that predict "safe" days for sexual intercourse by measuring daily changes in body temperature and cervical mucus are currently being tested in the United States.

- Other devices measure two hormones in a woman's urine to determine when she is fertile and should abstain from sexual intercourse.

- Canada and the Netherlands have approved permanent nonsurgical tubal sterilization methods using chemicals very similar to Krazy Glue that are introduced into and seal the fallopian tubes.

- In a reversible, nonsurgical procedure that works like tubal sterilization, liquid silicone is injected into the fallopian tubes. The silicone hardens into a plug that blocks the tube. Unlike the chemical plugs, the silicone plugs are removable.

- Also under development are gonadotropin-releasing hormone (GnRH) agonists that can be used to prevent the release of FSH and LH from the pituitary gland. The release of FSH and LH triggers ovulation and spermatogenesis. Blocking the release of these hormones will temporarily suppress fertility for both men *and* women.

The Contraceptive Future for Men

There are also a number of contraceptive options currently being explored for men.

- Oral contraceptives for men would reduce sperm counts to levels that are unlikely to cause pregnancy without reducing testosterone levels.

- A weekly injection of synthetic testosterone could fool the body into shutting down real testosterone production in the testicles.

- A combination of synthetic testosterone and progestin similar to that used in Depo-Provera is being explored as an injectable for men that would suppress sperm production without diminishing sex drive.

- Battery-powered capsules implanted into each vas deferens emit low-level electrical currents to immobilize sperm as they flow by.

- Implants for men, similar to the Norplant implant now in use for women, involve two rods. One contains a synthetic version of gonadotropin-releasing hormone (GnRH), the other releases methyl-19-nortestosterone (MENT), a synthetic hormone that is 10 times stronger than natural testosterone.

- A birth control pill and implant combination for men consists of a two-part regimen. First a man would take a daily pill with synthetic progesterone. In order to counteract the side effects of progesterone, such as loss of libido, a small pellet of concentrated testosterone is implanted underneath the skin near the abdomen. The pellet would be replaced every 12 weeks.

- Silicone plugs, similar to the silicone plugs proposed for women, consist of tiny silicone cylinders inserted to block the vas deferens and prevent the passage of sperm.

- A reversible vasectomy that uses chemicals inserted into the vas deferens would temporarily block the movement of sperm.

■ **R E V I E W**

While individuals use birth control methods to control reproduction, they also affect the birth rate and population growth of a society. Anything that prevents just a small percentage of the fertile women in a society from becoming pregnant will slow population growth. Even the practice of extended periods of breast-feeding can delay subsequent pregnancies. This occurs because the chemical **1**_____, which is produced during lactation, suppresses ovulation.

Attempts at contraception are ancient and not all involve complex technology. For example, **2**_____ is the removal of the penis from the vagina prior to orgasm and **3**_____ involves rubbing the erect penis between the thighs of a woman without insertion into the vagina.

Condoms, diaphragms, cervical caps, and vaginal sponges are examples of the **4**_____ method of contraception because they rely on preventing sperm from reaching an egg. **5**_____ are chemicals that kill sperm in the vagina or render them inactive. IUDs are devices inserted into the **6**_____. Birth control pills contain synthetic **7**_____ that may affect the release of eggs from the ovaries, make implantation difficult, and thicken cervical mucus to block sperm activity. Depo-Provera is an injectable contraceptive that contains a progestin.

Males and females may choose to be sterilized surgically, thus preventing any future pregnancies. A **8**_____ involves cutting or clamping the fallopian tubes to prevent eggs and sperm from meeting. A

9_____ involves cutting or blocking the vas deferens to prevent sperm from leaving a man's body.

There are many factors to consider in selecting a contraceptive method. The most effective contraceptives are implants, injectables, the IUD, the Pill, sterilization, and the condom. The contraceptives offering the most protection against STIs are the barrier methods and **10**_____.

Abortion is a medical procedure performed to terminate pregnancy. The most frequently used abortion procedure in the United States is **11**_____.

SUGGESTED READINGS

Bullough, V. L., & Bullough, B. (1997). *Contraception: A Guide to Birth Control.* Amherst, NY: Prometheus Books.
  The Bulloughs evaluate birth control methods in terms of effectiveness and the advantages and disadvantages of the various methods.

Dierassi, C. (1998). *The Pill, Pygmy Chimps, and Degas' Horse: The Remarkable Autobiography of the Award-Winning Scientist Who Synthesized the Birth Control Pill.* New York: Basic Books.
  Dierassi describes the lucrative world of drug development and highlights the politics of contraception.

Hatcher, R. A. (1998). *Contraceptive Technology: 1990–1992.* (17th Ed.). New York: Irvington.
  Intended as a reference for health-care professionals, this volume includes comprehensive information on contraceptives, including emergency contraception, and treatment of sexually transmitted infections.

McLaren, A. (1990). *A History of Contraception.* Oxford, England: Basil Blackwell.
  Though the book is out of print, your library should have this well-researched study.

Petchesky, R. P. & Judd, K. (1998). *Negotiating Reproductive Rights: Women's Perspectives Across Countries and Cultures.* New York: Zed Books.
  The authors compare development and health policies in seven countries: Brazil, Egypt, Malaysia, Mexico, Nigeria, the Philippines, and the United States.

Riddle, J. M. (1997). *Eve's Herbs: A History of Contraception and Abortion in the West.* Cambridge, MA: Harvard University Press.
  Riddle shows that women from ancient Egypt to the 15th century relied on an extensive pharmacopeia of herbal abortifacients and contraceptives to regulate fertility. This knowledge was made inaccessible when the women were persecuted as witches and criminals.

ANSWERS TO CHAPTER REVIEW

1. prolactin; **2.** coitus interruptus; **3.** interfemoral coitus; **4.** barrier; **5.** Spermicides; **6.** uterus; **7.** hormones; **8.** tubal ligation; **9.** vasectomy; **10.** spermicides; **11.** suction curettage.

CHAPTER 7

Sexually Transmitted Infections

- **What Are Sexually Transmitted Infections (STIs)?**
  Sexually transmitted infections are infections spread, or transmitted, by sexual contact. The incidence of many of the more than 50 known STIs continues to increase.

- **Bacterial Infections**
  Sexually transmitted infections caused by bacteria include chlamydia, gonorrhea, syphilis, pelvic inflammatory disease (PID), and bacterial vaginosis.

- **Viral Infections**
  Viral infections spread by sexual contact include genital herpes, hepatitis, genital warts, and HIV and AIDS.

- **Parasitic Infections**
  Sexually transmitted infections caused by parasites include pubic lice, scabies, and trichomoniasis.

- **Ways to Avoid STIs**
  Prevention is the best way to control the spread of sexually transmitted infections. Practicing safer sex also lowers your risk.

- **What to Do if You Get an STI**
  If you are infected with an STI, it is critical to get medical attention as soon as possible to avoid further complications and to prevent infecting your sexual partner(s).

WHAT ARE SEXUALLY TRANSMITTED INFECTIONS (STIs)?

Sexually transmitted infections (STIs)—sometimes referred to as sexually transmitted diseases (STDs)—are infections that are passed from one person to another via sexual contact. They can cause debilitating or even fatal physical problems, affect your social life, produce emotional turmoil, change the way you think about sex, generate policy and legislation, and prompt moral or spiritual crises.

Some STIs may be spread by nonsexual as well as sexual contact. The more than 50 diseases identified as STIs vary in severity of symptoms, health risk, and degree of contagion. **Bacteria, viruses, protozoa, fungi,** or **parasites** may cause STIs (Figure 7.1). In fact, STIs have little in common other than the fact that they are transmitted by sexual contact.

You may have heard the term *venereal disease* used to refer to STIs. This term, today used only to refer to **gonorrhea, syphilis,** and **chancroid,** was named for Venus, the Roman goddess of love. Gonorrhea was first identified in the second century A.D., although it is believed to have existed long before that. The origin of syphilis continues to be a matter of debate. One widely held theory is that syphilis did not exist in Europe, Asia, or Africa until Columbus and his men brought back the disease from the New World in 1493. According to this New World theory, the disease spread to Asia by the crews of Vasco de Gama and other Portuguese navigators. No one seemed to want to claim ownership of this devastating illness. Columbus's men referred to it as "Indian measles." In China and Japan it was called "the Portuguese disease." The Turks referred to it as "the Christian disease." It is theorized that one effect of colonialism and conversion to Christianity was a breakdown of traditional social structure and morality (cf. Suggs, 1987). However, cultural change has not always resulted in traditional sexual codes being replaced with Christian ones, so syphilis and other STIs were able to proliferate (Gregersen, 1994).

Sexually transmitted infections are among the most common infections in the United States, yet most people dramatically underestimate their risk (Kaiser Family Foundation [KFF], 1998) for one of two main reasons. First, many of these infections are asymptomatic, so the affected individuals may not be aware of them. Second, the strong social stigma attached to those infected with STIs prevents open discussion (KFF, 1998).

Globally there are an estimated 333 million new cases of curable STIs among adults each year (World Health Organization, 1998). The United States has the highest rates of STIs in the industrialized world; the U.S. rate of infection is 50 to 100 times higher than that of other industrialized nations (Eng & Butler, 1997). An estimated 15.3 million new cases of sexually transmitted infections are reported in the United States annually; at least 25 percent of these occur among teenagers, and two thirds among those younger than 25 (KFF, 1998). Many adolescents at high risk for STIs have a self-reported history of sex with multiple partners, inconsistent use of condoms, and frequent substance abuse (Boyer et al., 1999).

Sexually Transmitted Infections (STIs): infections whose usual means of transmission is by sexual contact

Bacteria: plural of bacterium; a large group of single-cell microorganisms; some cause infections and disease in animals and humans

Viruses: a microscopic infectious organism that reproduces inside living cells

Protozoa: a family of unicellular organisms that are the simplest form of animal life

Fungi: plural of fungus; any organism that superficially resembles a plant but does not have leaves and roots, and lacks chlorophyll

Parasite: a plant or animal that for all or part of its life obtains food and physical protection from a living organism of another species (the host), which is usually damaged by and never benefits from its presence

Gonorrhea: a sexually transmitted infection caused by *Neisseria gonorrhoeae* bacteria that affects the mucous membrane chiefly of the genital and urinary tracts and is characterized by an acute purulent discharge and painful or difficult urination, though women often have no symptoms

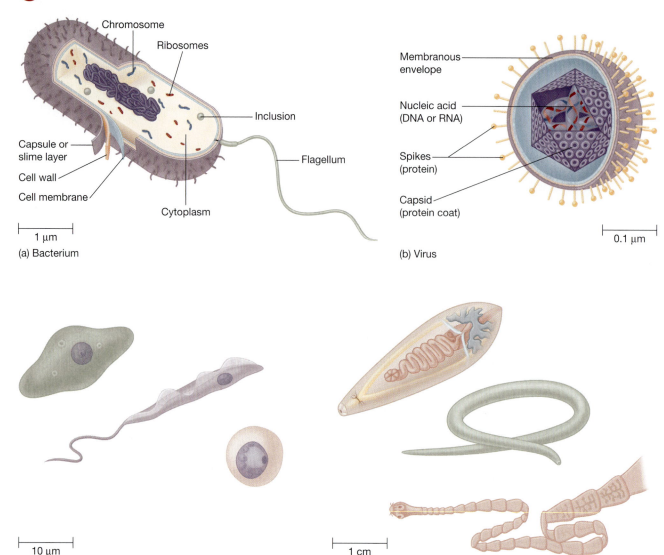

FIGURE 7.1 **Representative Pathogens.** (a) A bacterium. (b) A typical virus. Each virus has an inner chamber containing nucleic acid, surrounded by a protein shell and an outer membranous envelope. (c) Protozoan pathogens. (d) Multicellular parasites.

Syphilis: a sexually transmitted infection caused by the spirochete *Treponema pallidum* that may progress through several stages of development

Chancroid: a sexually transmitted infection caused by the bacteria *Hemophilus ducreyi* that causes multiple painful ulcers on the penis and the vulva

By age 24, one in three sexually active men and women in the United States will have contracted an STI (Boyer et al., 1999); at least one in four will contract an STI at some point in their lives (AGI, 1993). The National Health and Social Life Survey (NHSLS) found that 18 percent of women and 16 percent of men, or about one person in six, had been diagnosed by a physician as having had at least one STI at some point in their lives (Laumann et al., 1994). However, a 1994 survey of 450 physicians and 514 other health-care professionals found that 60 percent of the doctors and 51 percent of the other providers did not routinely evaluate their new patients for STIs (Institute of Medicine, 1994).

A number of factors may contribute to the rising incidence of STIs. An increasing tendency to have multiple sexual partners, increased sexual activity among adolescents, and the increased use of birth control pills rather than vaginal spermicides or the condom may facilitate the spread of STIs. Since many STIs have no obvious symptoms, an

CROSS-CULTURAL PERSPECTIVES

Folk Remedies

Folk remedies and beliefs about STIs vary considerably. At various times in Europe it was believed that having intercourse with a virgin was a cure for syphilis; this belief is apparently still held by some rural Serbians today. Among the Aymara of South America, an ancient treatment for syphilis is mercury mixed with animal fat. The Mangaians believe that a man will not contract gonorrhea from a woman with the disease if he does not ejaculate into her vagina. Mangaians also believe that copulating with a menstruating woman causes venereal diseases in men. In some Cuban cultures, Shango, the god of syphilis, is believed to inflict the disease, and the cure is exorcising his spirit (Gregersen, 1994).

infected individual may unknowingly transmit an STI to a partner (Bowie, Hammerschlag, & Martin, 1994). In addition, many people remain uneducated or uninterested in the causes and consequences of STIs.

Anyone who is sexually active with a partner can contract an STI. Unwashed, uneducated, and uninformed people are not the only ones at risk. The National Health and Social Life Survey confirmed that number of sexual partners, not race, educational level, or socioeconomic status, is the best predictor of STI risk (Laumann et al., 1994).

However, women, teenagers, the poor, and some ethnic groups do bear the brunt of STIs in the United States. Much of this is due to the lack of confidential, affordable health care. Moreover, due to the delicate lining and warm, moist environment of the vagina, it is twice as easy for a male to transmit an STI to a female as it is for a female to transmit a disease to a male (Laumann et al., 1994). For similar reasons, anal sex also increases the risk of contracting an STI. Moreover, there is a higher incidence of STIs among younger women than among older women. In adolescent girls and young women, the opening to the cervix is surrounded by the *ectropion*, a rim of red tissue composed of immature cervical cells. Sexually transmitted viruses and bacteria, especially chlamydia and the human papilloma virus, easily invade the ectropion. As a woman ages, these cells mature and the ring recedes into the cervical canal, making her less vulnerable to infection (Farley et al., 1997). Often lesbians are not screened for STIs because health-care professionals assume that lesbians have not been sexually active with men or they erroneously believe that women cannot transmit STIs to one another. However, it is important for health-care providers to know a patient's sexual history regardless of his or her reported sexual orientation (Diamant et al., 1999).

Some STIs, especially syphilis and gonorrhea, are far more common among African Americans and Hispanics than among whites. From 1996 to 1997, the rate of gonorrhea among African Americans was more than 30 times higher than among whites; the rate was two thirds higher among Hispanics than among whites (CDC, 2001a). In 1998, primary and secondary syphilis occurred 44 times more often among African Americans than among whites, and three times more often among Hispanics than among whites (CDC, 2001a) (see the CONSIDERATIONS box on the Tuskegee experiment).

No one can be completely safe from all STIs, some of which also may be contracted through nonsexual means. However, there are high-risk behaviors that increase the likelihood of contracting some STIs. See Table 7.1 for the level of risk associated with various sexual behaviors.

The financial costs of sexually transmitted infections to a nation are immense. The human costs of sexually transmitted infections to the infected individuals, their partners and families, and to society are of course incalculable.

CONSIDERATIONS

The Tuskegee Tragedy

The Tuskegee Study of Untreated Syphilis was a research program that was conducted by the U.S. Public Health Service from 1932 to 1972. In rural Alabama, 412 African American men with untreated syphilis were observed and compared to a group of 200 African American men without syphilis. The purpose of the study was to determine the practicability and effectiveness of measures for mass control of syphilis and the influence of environmental and social factors on the course of the disease.

Tuskegee was one of six rural areas in the South chosen for the study and the one that has been most controversial. Although there is no evidence that the government infected the men with syphilis in order to study them, the men were deliberately not told of their condition and left untreated so doctors could study the long-term effects of the disease, with devastating results. (For more on the effects of untreated syphilis, see the next section on Bacterial Infections.)

The Tuskegee study raises questions not only about the past but also about future research. In 1997 the editor of the *New England Journal of Medicine* argued that several U.S.-funded AIDS studies being conducted on pregnant women in Africa and Asia are unethical. The editor compared the research to the Tuskegee study because some women received a placebo rather than a drug that prevented HIV-positive mothers from infecting their babies (Angell, 1997).

The Tuskegee University National Center for Bioethics in Research and Health Care opened in 1999. The center educates and trains African Americans as bioethicists, focusing on medical issues for minorities. The program is partially funded by a $200,000 grant that President Clinton announced in 1997 when he formally apologized for the syphilis study on behalf of the U.S. government.

 In what cases do you think the experimental method should be compromised, that is, conducted without a control group?

BACTERIAL INFECTIONS

Bacteria differ from all other kinds of organisms in that they have no nuclei. Bacteria reproduce by **binary fission** (Figure 7.2), a cell division mechanism in which a parent cell divides into two genetically identical cells following the replication of its DNA. Because bacterial cells have only a single chromosome, a circular DNA molecule, bacterial reproduction generally occurs rapidly; under optimal circumstances some bacteria can divide every 20 minutes. Disease-causing bacteria secrete toxins that poison cells. If invading bacteria multiply too quickly for the immune system to contain them, large quantities of a toxin may enter the bloodstream or other tissue. Bacteria that

Binary Fission: a method of asexual reproduction that involves the splitting of a parent cell into two approximately equal parts

TABLE 7.1

Levels of Risk of Various Sexual Behaviors

High-Risk Sexual Behaviors	Moderate-Risk Sexual Behaviors	Low-Risk Sexual Behaviors
Oral-genital sex without a condom or dental dam	Oral-genital sex using a condom or dental dam	Body to body contact, embracing
Semen in the mouth	Kissing with no broken skin or mouth sores	Dry kissing
Vaginal intercourse without a condom	Vaginal intercourse using a latex condom	Massage
Anal intercourse without a condom	Anal intercourse using a latex condom	Mutual masturbation
Other oral or manual anal contact	External skin contact with semen, if break or sore on skin	Erotic books and movies, sharing sex toys

SOURCE: Hatcher et al., 1994.

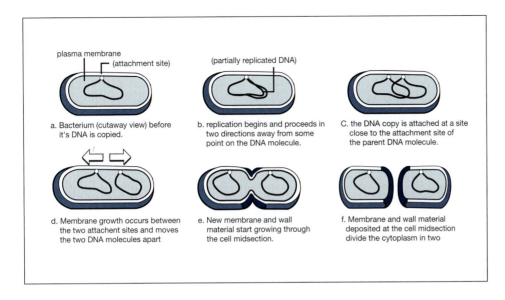

FIGURE 7.2 **Bacterial Reproduction by Binary Fission.** SOURCE: Starr & Wadsworth, 1995, p. 350.

release toxins into the bloodstream are especially dangerous because the toxin moves rapidly throughout the body and may affect the nervous system and other vital organs. The most common sexually transmitted infections caused by bacterial infection include chlamydia, gonorrhea, syphilis, pelvic inflammatory disease, and bacterial vaginosis.

Chlamydia

Chlamydial infection, or simply **chlamydia,** is not only the most common sexually transmitted infection, it is the most frequently reported infectious disease in the United States today. In 1998 the reported number of cases of chlamydia was 607,602, a rate of 236.6 per 100,000 persons. This increase reflects increased screening, recognition of asymptomatic infection, and improved reporting, as well as the continuing high incidence of the disease. The overall reported rate for women was nearly five times that for men (Centers for Disease Control [CDC], 2001b). However, the Centers for Disease Control (2001a) reports that chlamydia cases still are severely underreported, largely a result of substantial numbers of asymptomatic persons whose infections are not identified because screening is not available. The highest rates of infection are among 15- to 19-year-olds, regardless of demographics or location (NIAID, 2000a). In parts of the United States where large-scale chlamydia programs have been established, prevalence of the infection has generally declined (CDC, 2001b). Worldwide there are approximately 89 million people with chlamydial infections (WHO, 1996).

Cause and Transmission   Chlamydia is caused by an unusual bacterium, *Chlamydia trachomatis.* Why is this bacterium unusual? Although classified as a bacterium, this organism shares properties with both bacteria and viruses, and lives inside the cells that it infects.

Chlamydia is transmitted primarily by genital sexual contact though it may be spread by touch from one body part to another. If an infected person engages in penetrating anal sex, the bacterium that causes chlamydia can cause an inflamed rectum. The bacteria also have been found in the throat as a result of oral sexual contact with an infected partner. Secondary contact can transmit the disease as well. Fondling or foreplay may spread chlamydia from one part of the body to another if a person touches his or her eyes after touching infected genitalia, for example. In overcrowded, unsanitary conditions, insects or human waste also can spread chlamydia. Newborns passing through the birth canal may contract the disease from their mothers. When an infected mother gives birth there is a 60 to 70 percent chance that her baby will contract the disease.

Chlamydia: the most common sexually transmitted bacterium (*Chlamydia trachomatis*) that infects the reproductive system

Symptoms   As many as 24 percent of men and 70 percent of women may be asymptomatic and will not be identified without screening (Cates, 1999). If symptoms do occur, they usually appear within 1 to 3 weeks after exposure. Noticeable signs for males include a burning sensation when urinating, a slight penile discharge, or in later stages, swelling and discomfort in the testicles. Women may notice more frequent or painful urination, lower abdominal pain, or vaginal discharge. Later symptoms in women may include low abdominal pain, bleeding between menstrual periods, and low-grade fever. As previously indicated, rectal inflammation and conjunctivitis (inflammation of the lining of the eye) are also symptoms of chlamydial infection.

Diagnosis   Until recently the only reliable way to diagnose chlamydia was to test a sample of genital secretions. Several tests for diagnosing chlamydial infection use a dye to detect bacterial proteins. Although these tests are slightly less accurate than culturing secretions in the laboratory, the dye tests are less expensive, more rapid, and can be performed during a routine checkup (but chlamydia screening is not part of a routine gynecological exam, so if you are sexually active, you need to ask for this diagnostic test). The FDA has approved a test that uses a process called DNA amplification to detect chlamydia DNA. This test does not require a sample of genital secretions, and results are available in 24 hours.

Treatment   Once diagnosed, chlamydia is easily treated with antibiotics such as doxycycline, tetracycline, or erythromycin. A single dose of azithromycin is an alternative to the conventional 7-day regime of other antibiotics. If the symptoms do not disappear within 1 to 2 weeks after finishing the medication, a follow-up visit is indicated. Partners of infected persons also should be treated as a precaution and to prevent reinfection.

Possible Complications   Left untreated, chlamydia can spread to the female reproductive tract and cause pelvic inflammatory disease (PID). PID can cause infertility and chronic pelvic pain, and doubles the risk of ectopic pregnancy. Twenty to 40 percent of women with chlamydial infections develop PID (Howell, Kassler, & Haddix, 1997). Left untreated, the chlamydia organism is estimated to be the cause of approximately half the cases of epididymitis and nongonoccocal urethritis (NGU). Those infected with chlamydia have three to five times greater risk of being infected with HIV, possibly because the immune system is already weakened.

Research   In 1998 scientists were able to sequence the entire Chlamydia trachomatis genome, and based on these findings the National Institute of Allergy and Infectious Diseases (NIAID) is working on a microbicide as well as a vaccine to prevent chlamydial infection. Scientists also are looking for better ways to treat those infected with the disease and are developing simpler, less expensive diagnostic tests (described earlier). Other researchers are studying how the bacteria cause disease in the body and why some people suffer more severe complications than others.

Gonorrhea

Gonorrhea is a sexually transmitted infection sometimes referred to by the appealing names "the clap" or "the drip." The World Health Organization (1996) estimates that there are 62 million cases of gonorrhea worldwide. In 1998, 355,642 cases of gonorrhea were reported in the United States alone, suggesting that the downward trend since the advent of the national gonorrhea control program in the mid-1970s may be lessening (CDC, 2001c). Most of those infected with gonorrhea are between 20 and 24 years of age. The highest rate of infection is in females between the ages of 15 and 19.

Cause and Transmission   Gonorrhea is caused by a bacterium with the impressive-sounding name *Neisseria gonorrhoeae* (often abbreviated to gonococcus). This organism grows and multiplies quickly in warm damp places such as the vagina, urinary tract, cervix, mouth, and rectum.

Gonococci can be found on the tip of the penis or in the rectum, the vagina, or the throat of infected persons, so the disease is easily transmitted through oral, anal, or vaginal sex. It is also possible to contract gonorrhea by secondary contact if, for example, you touch your own or a partner's infected genitals and then put your hand in your mouth. The disease also can be transmitted from mother to newborn during childbirth. Gonorrhea is highly contagious. Women have approximately a 50 percent chance of infection after a single sexual encounter with an infected partner. Men have a 20 to 25 percent chance of contracting gonorrhea after a single exposure. If a man has sex three or more times with an infected partner, his chances of becoming infected increase to 60 to 80 percent.

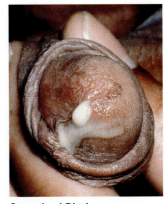

Gonorrheal Discharge.
Gonorrhea in the male often causes a thick, yellowish, puslike discharge from the penis.

Symptoms   The early symptoms of gonorrhea often are mild and affect men and women differently. In males, a clear penile discharge that later turns yellow to yellow-green and thickens, may appear 2 to 5 days after contact (see accompanying photograph). Men also may notice a burning sensation when urinating. Four of every five infected females have no symptoms in the early stages of gonorrhea. Later there may be increased vaginal discharge or burning during urination. Gonorrheal infection of the throat or rectum causes pain, itching, soreness, redness, and discharge.

Diagnosis   Three techniques are used to diagnose gonorrhea: gram stain (which is more accurate in men than women), detection of bacterial genes and DNA, and culture. The gram stain involves placing a sample of the discharge from the penis, cervix, or throat on a slide, staining it with a dye called gram stain, and examining the slide under a microscope. A urine test or cervical swab is used to detect the genes of the bacteria. The culture test involves placing samples of discharge onto a culture plate and incubating it up to 2 days to allow the bacteria to multiply. Many doctors prefer to use more than one method to increase the accuracy of diagnosis.

Treatment   Until recently, penicillin was highly effective in curing gonorrhea. Unfortunately, new penicillin-resistant strains of gonococcus have appeared. One of the most effective medications to treat gonorrhea today is the antibiotic ceftriaxone, which can be injected in a single dose. Since gonorrhea and chlamydia commonly occur together, many doctors prescribe a combination of antibiotics such as ceftriaxone and doxycycline or azithromycin. Single-dose oral therapy is available for those who do not like needles. All sexual partners of a person diagnosed with gonorrhea should be tested.

Possible Complications   Gonorrhea may spread to internal reproductive organs. The most common consequence of untreated gonorrhea is PID. An estimated 10 to 40 percent of women infected with gonorrhea develop PID if not adequately treated (Eng & Butler, 1997). Gonococcal PID often appears immediately after the menstrual period and can result in infertility in as many as 10 percent of affected women. Gonorrhea can also result in arthritis, heart problems, or severe eye infection. Because of the possibility of contracting gonorrheal eye infection (*ophthalmia neonatorum*) as they pass through the birth canal of an infected mother, all newborns are treated with silver nitrate drops to prevent blindness. Like chlamydia, infection with gonorrhea can increase a person's risk of contracting HIV because of the weakening of the immune system.

Research   Gonorrhea research is focused on prevention, diagnosis, and treatment of the infection. Because of the dramatic rise of antibiotic-resistant strains of gonococcus, developing an effective vaccine against gonorrhea remains a key research priority.

Syphilis

Syphilis is a sexually transmitted infection that may progress through several stages of development (see Symptoms section). Worldwide incidence of syphilis is estimated to be 12 million (WHO, 1998). In the United States, health officials reported over 35,600 cases of syphilis in 1999, including 6,650 cases of primary and secondary syphilis, a decline of 5.4 percent from 1998, and 556 cases of congenital syphilis (CDC, 2001c). However, it is estimated that few cases are reported; the true incidence of syphilis may be nearer to 70,000 (Kaiser Family Foundation, 1998). In 1999, syphilis occurred primarily in those aged 20 to 39. The reported rate in men was 1.5 times greater than the rate in women.

Cause and Transmission *Treponema pallidum*, a spiral-shaped bacterium called a spirochete, causes syphilis. The initial infection causes an ulcer at the site of infection. As the disease progresses, the bacteria move through the body, damaging many organs over time.

Syphilis can be contracted through oral, anal, or vaginal sex. The disease is described in four stages: primary, secondary, latent, and tertiary (see section on Symptoms). Syphilis is especially contagious in the first two stages, when sores are present. There is a one in three chance of contracting syphilis from a single sexual encounter with an infected partner. Syphilis is transmitted from the open sores of an infected individual to the mucous membranes or skin abrasions of sexual partners through vaginal or anal intercourse and oral-genital contact. In addition, syphilis can spread by touching an infected sore, or when the bacterium passes through the placental membrane to the fetus. The bacterium is also present in the bloodstream, and sharing needles with an infected person occasionally transmits syphilis. Secondary contact is unlikely. You cannot get syphilis from toilet seats, swimming pools, eating utensils, or shared clothing. In the late stages, once there are no longer open sores, syphilis is not contagious.

Symptoms The *incubation period*, the time between contracting the disease and the appearance of the first symptoms, can range from 10 to 90 days. In the *primary stage* of syphilis the only symptom may be the appearance on the genitals of a painless sore, or *chancre*, at the infection site (see accompanying photograph). It usually is found on the penis, the vulva, or the vagina, but can also develop on the cervix, tongue, lips, or other parts of the body. The chancre lasts from 1 to 5 weeks and will heal on its own with or without treatment. Because the chancre may be painless and may occur inside the body, it may go unnoticed.

There may be no further symptoms for up to 6 months. The *secondary stage* may bring a skin rash characterized by brown spots about the size of a penny that usually do not itch. The rash appears from 3 to 6 weeks after the chancre and can appear on any part of the body, though the palms of the hands and soles of the feet are almost always involved (see photograph). Other symptoms may occur including mouth sores, swollen joints, fatigue, patchy hair loss, headaches, or a mild fever. Even without treatment, these symptoms also will subside within a few weeks, and are often mistaken for a passing illness such as the flu.

The third stage of syphilis, referred to as the *latency stage*, begins when the secondary symptoms disappear. In this stage the infected person is symptom-free, but the bacteria remain in the body, where they can cause considerable damage. Approximately one third of those with latency stage syphilis go on to develop the complications of *tertiary syphilis*, including damage to the heart, eyes, brain and nervous system, bones, joints, or other parts of the body (see Possible Complications section). This stage can last for years or even decades.

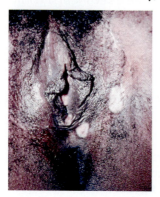 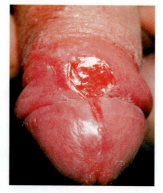

Syphilitic chancres on (a) the labia and (b) the penis.

Diagnosis   A physician may diagnose syphilis based on its signs and symptoms and/or the results of two types of tests: microscopic identification of the bacteria scraped from a chancre, and a blood test. A scraping from the surface of a chancre is examined under a special microscope for presence of the *Treponema pallidum* bacteria. Shortly after infection occurs, the body begins to produce antibodies to the syphilis bacteria that can be detected with a blood test. The blood screening tests most often used to detect syphilis are the venereal disease research laboratory (VDRL) test and the rapid plasma reagin (RPR) test. Because false positive results can occur in people with autoimmune disorders and certain viral infections, a blood test is usually administered to confirm positive initial test results.

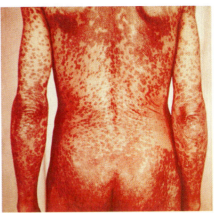

Syphilitic Rash.
In the secondary stage of syphilis a skin rash can appear on the body, including the back and the palms of the hands.

Treatment   In its first three stages, syphilis is usually treated with penicillin. Another antibiotic can be substituted if the affected individual is allergic to penicillin. Treatment is given intravenously or by daily injection for 10 to 21 days, depending on the stage of infection. Some people do not respond to the usual doses of penicillin; additional doses may be needed for those in later stages of the disease. It is important that those being treated for syphilis have periodic blood tests to check that the infectious agent has been completely destroyed. Sexual partners of infected persons must also receive immediate treatment. Those receiving treatment are advised to abstain from sexual contact until the syphilis sores are completely healed. There is no treatment or cure for tertiary syphilis.

Possible Complications   A person with tertiary syphilis may remain symptomless for years as bacteria continue to multiply in the circulatory system, brain, spinal cord, and bones. This silent invasion can result in brain damage, blindness, paralysis, and death. Physical malformations can appear as bacteria eat away at skin and bone. Syphilis sores can provide an entry site for HIV.

The effects of syphilis on a fetus are extremely serious. If untreated the risks of stillbirth or serious birth defects, including blindness, brain, and heart damage, are high. Between 40 and 70 percent of babies born to syphilis-infected mothers are infected with the disease. Some infants with congenital syphilis may have symptoms at birth, but most develop symptoms between 2 weeks and 3 months after birth. These symptoms may include skin sores, rashes, fever, hoarse crying, swollen liver and spleen, jaundice, anemia, and various deformities.

Research   The NIAID is working on developing new tests to more accurately diagnose syphilis and determine the stage of infection. In addition, a syphilis vaccine is in the works and may become available within the next decade. Development of a safe, effective, single-dose oral antibiotic for treatment of syphilis is also on the horizon.

Pelvic Inflammatory Disease

Each year in the United States more than a million women have an episode of acute **pelvic inflammatory disease (PID),** an inflammatory condition affecting a woman's reproductive system. Adolescents have the highest rate of infection. More than 100,000 women become infertile each year as a result of PID, and a large proportion of the 70,000 potentially dangerous ectopic pregnancies each year are the result of PID.

Cause and Transmission   Strictly speaking, PID is not a sexually transmitted infection; it is a complication that can occur when any of a number of disease-causing organisms migrates upward from the urethra and cervix into the upper genital tract (uterus, fallopian tubes, and ovaries). An overgrowth of bacteria normally present in small numbers in the vagina and cervix also may infect the upper genital tract.

It is believed that the bacterium that causes gonorrhea travels to the fallopian tubes, where it causes sloughing of some cells while it invades others. The bacteria

Pelvic Inflammatory Disease (PID): an inflammation of the female pelvic organs, most commonly the fallopian tubes, usually as a result of bacterial infection

multiply within and beneath these invaded cells, causing inflammation (swelling); if the infection spreads to other internal organs, more inflammation (and more pain) results. Chlamydia trachomatis and other bacteria are believed to act in a similar manner. Investigators do not know how other bacteria that normally inhabit the vagina gain entrance into the upper genital tract (National Institute of Allergy and Infectious Diseases [NIAID], 2000c).

PID may occur as a complication of a variety of infections, including gonorrhea, chlamydia, bacterial vaginosis (described next), and trichomoniasis (described under Parasitic Infections). Chlamydia is believed to account for approximately half of the recognized cases of PID in the United States. Recent data indicates that women who douche once or twice a month may be more likely to have PID than those who douche less than once a month. There are two possible reasons for the relationship between douching and PID. Douching may push bacteria into the upper genital tract, causing the infection. It may also ease discharge caused by an existing infection so the woman delays seeking treatment (Merchant, Oh, & Klerman, 1999).

Symptoms Some women may not have any symptoms. Others may first notice a vaginal discharge that can vary in color from white to yellow to greenish or brown. Menstrual periods may be disrupted; they may be longer or heavier than usual, or there may be spotting between periods. Pain during urination or sexual intercourse is a common symptom. Women with severe infections may experience pain around the liver, fever, nausea, or headaches.

Diagnosis PID can be difficult to diagnose because of the wide variation in signs and symptoms. It has been mistaken for appendicitis, endometriosis, an ovarian cyst, or ectopic pregnancy. The most accurate way to diagnose PID is to view the fallopian tubes with a laparoscope to see if they are inflamed or swollen with pus or if there is pus in the pelvis. Sonogram and biopsy of the uterine endometrium (endometrial biopsy) can be used to confirm the diagnosis.

Treatment Because multiple organisms may be responsible for a PID episode, a physician often prescribes at least two antibiotics that are effective against a wide range of infectious agents. Sometimes, the pockets of pus that form in the affected organs need to be surgically drained. In severe cases, surgery may be required to remove abscesses or scar tissue or to repair or remove affected organs (for example, the uterus, fallopian tubes, or ovaries).

Possible Complications PID is itself both a complication and a serious disease. Complications from PID can be even more serious. Women with recurrent episodes of PID are more likely to suffer scarring of the fallopian tubes that leads to infertility, tubal pregnancy, or chronic pelvic pain. Infertility occurs in approximately 20 percent of women who have had PID. A woman who has had PID is 6 to 10 times as likely to have a tubal pregnancy. Untreated PID causes chronic pelvic pain in about 20 percent of patients. It is common for women to have more than one occurrence of PID. As many as one third of women who contract PID will have the disease at least one more time, either because the infection was not fully eradicated or due to reinfection.

Research Scientists are currently studying the effects of antibiotics, hormones, and immune system boosters on PID. Ongoing research is also addressing the prevention of infertility and other complications. Clinical trials to test a suppository containing lactobacilli, bacteria normally present in the vagina, are in progress. These bacteria may decrease the risk of gonorrhea and bacterial vaginosis, both of which can cause PID. In addition, rapid, inexpensive, easy-to-use diagnostic tests are being developed to detect chlamydia and gonorrhea infection. Early screening and treatment of women with chlamydia reduces cases of PID by more than 50 percent (NIAID, 2000a).

Bacterial Vaginosis

Bacterial vaginosis (BV), once called nonspecific vaginitis or Gardnerella-associated vaginitis, is an inflammation of the vagina that may be caused by a variety of bacteria. It is the most common cause of *vaginitis*, which refers to any kind of vaginal infection or inflammation.

Cause and Transmission   Bacterial vaginosis is caused by an imbalance in the vaginal environment. This change occurs when the balance of the different types of bacteria normally present in the vagina is disrupted. Normally, lactobacillus is the most prevalent bacterium in the vagina. Women with BV have elevated numbers of organisms such as *Gardnerella vaginalis*, *Bacteroides mobiluncus*, and *Mycoplasm hominis*. An increased growth of Gardnerella combined with a decrease in lactobacilli results in BV.

Many cases of BV are transmitted via sexual contact. Many male partners of infected women also have the bacteria present in their urethra. However, the disease can also be caused by contamination of the vagina with fecal bacteria. It appears that douching and changing sexual partners may increase the risk of acquiring BV.

Symptoms   As with many other sexually transmitted infections, up to 40 percent of women infected with BV report no symptoms. In some cases there is a thin, odorous vaginal discharge, a burning sensation, or itching. The amount of discharge varies; it generally has the consistency of flour paste and is usually gray, but may be white, yellow, or green. The fishlike odor is noticeable, especially after sexual intercourse. Most men have no symptoms, but some may experience inflammation of the urethra or the penile glans.

Diagnosis   BV is diagnosed by examining a sample of vaginal discharge under a microscope, either stained or in special lighting. Diagnosis can be based on the absence of lactobacilli, the presence of numerous "clue cells" (cells from the vaginal lining coated with BV organisms), a fishy odor, and decreased acidity or change in the pH of vaginal fluid.

Treatment   BV can be treated with antibiotics such as metronidazole or clindamycin; however, women should not take metronidazole (Flagyl) during the first trimester of pregnancy. Sexual partners should be notified so they can be tested. Many women with symptoms of BV do not seek medical treatment and many asymptomatic women decline treatment (NIAID, 1998). It is questionable whether or not the male sex partners should be treated. Although the bacterium usually can be found in the male urethra, it generally does not cause symptoms in a man although he may unknowingly transmit the bacterium to others. However, there is no evidence that treating the male with metronidazole benefits either him or the female partner (Sobel, 1997).

Possible Complications   The bacteria associated with BV have been implicated in the development of PID. Left untreated, BV may become a factor in premature rupture of membranes during pregnancy and cause premature delivery. One study showed that pregnant women with BV in the 23rd to 26th weeks of pregnancy were 40 percent more likely to deliver a low birth weight baby. The CDC (1998) recommends that all pregnant women who previously have delivered a premature baby be checked for BV, regardless of the presence of symptoms. BV also may be associated with increased risk for other STIs and with abnormal tissue formation in the cervix.

Research   Researchers are focusing on the role that each microbe may play in causing BV. The role of sexual activity in the development of BV is poorly understood.

VIRAL INFECTIONS

A virus is a protein-coated package of genes that invades a healthy body cell, taking control of the cell's genetic machinery in order to reproduce itself. A virus operates something like a copying machine. After the virus inserts itself into a healthy body cell,

Bacterial Vaginosis (BV): vaginal infection resulting from a change in the balance of naturally occurring bacteria, allowing disease-causing bacteria, especially *Gardnerella vaginalis*, to predominate

EXPLORING SEXUALITY ONLINE

Computer Viruses

Obviously, you can't catch an STI online, even a virtual one. However, people who seek sex partners online are more likely to have had a sexually transmitted infection. In a study led by a researcher from the Centers for Disease Control, the online and sexual habits of 856 clients at a Denver HIV testing and counseling center were investigated. Of those surveyed, 15.8 percent reported using the Internet to find sex partners. Nearly one third of those online seekers said they had contracted a sexually transmitted infection and had been exposed to HIV-positive sex partners. In comparison, only one fifth of those who tried to find dates in more conventional ways had an STI and just 14 percent had been with an HIV-positive sex partner. The researchers concluded that those seeking sex partners on the Internet appear to be at greater risk for STIs than those who do not (McFarlane, Bull, & Rietmeijer, 2000).

Why do you think that people who seek out sex online are at greater risk for STIs?

Was this study biased because of the source of the data?

---

it uses that healthy cell's machinery to run off copies of itself. The virus can be considered the ultimate parasite. It cannot reproduce or survive on its own; it needs a **host** in order to replicate.

As a virus invades the host organism, the immune system responds, resulting in the death of either the virus or the host. Measles and influenza are classic examples of this type of *acute viral infection*. A different type of virus, a *slow virus*, was first identified in 1954 and describes diseases such as multiple sclerosis that progress slowly but steadily. A third type of virus is the *latent virus*. In cases such as infection with the herpes simplex virus, after the initial infection a latent virus causes occasional and varied symptoms over a relatively long period of time.

Genital Herpes

About one in four people in the United States over age 12—approximately 45 million individuals—is infected with HSV-2, the virus that causes **genital herpes** (CDC, 2001c), a sexually transmitted infection characterized by painful sores and blisters on the genitals. HSV-2 infection is more common in women than in men. This may be due to male-to-female transmission being more efficient than female-to-male transmission. Up to 1 million new HSV-2 infections may be transmitted each year in the United States (Kaiser Family Foundation, 1998).

Cause and Transmission   Two different but related forms of the herpes simplex virus cause genital herpes. Herpes simplex virus 1 (HSV-1) most often infects the lips, causing sores commonly known as fever blisters or cold sores, but it can also infect the genital area and produce sores there. In the United States only 10 to 20 percent of genital herpes is caused by HSV-1. Herpes simplex virus 2 (HSV-2) is the usual cause of genital herpes (80 to 90 percent), but also can infect the mouth during oral sex. It is not possible for HSV-1 herpes to mutate into HSV-2. However, there have been cases of mixed infections with both types of the herpes virus.

Both HSV-1 and HSV-2 are transmitted through direct contact. HSV-2 herpes is usually transmitted by oral, anal, or vaginal sex with an infected partner. The disease can also be transferred to a fetus during pregnancy. The herpes virus is of the latent variety described earlier. Most people get genital herpes by having sex with someone

Host: a plant or animal harboring another organism

Genital Herpes: a sexually transmitted infection caused by a herpes virus that results in the episodic outbreak of a painful skin eruption on the genitalia

having a herpes "outbreak" when the virus is active. During an outbreak, the virus usually causes visible sores that easily cast off or shed viruses. However, a person can also have an outbreak without visible sores (Wald et al., 2001). It is during these silent outbreaks that genital herpes is most often spread.

Symptoms   Symptoms of HSV-1 infection include small blisters on the lips, on the inside of the mouth, on the tongue, and/or in the throat. Affected individuals may also experience flulike symptoms such as muscle ache, headaches, fever, and swollen lymph glands. Herpes blisters usually crust over and heal within 10 to 16 days.

Symptoms of HSV-2 can differ from person to person. Early symptoms include an itching or burning feeling in the genital or anal area; pain in the legs, buttocks, or genitals; vaginal discharge; and a feeling of pressure in the abdomen. The most noticeable symptom is the sores, located where the virus entered the body, on the vagina, penis, anus, or mouth (see photographs). The sores, called papules, also can occur inside the vagina, on the cervix, or in the male or female urinary tract.

Symptoms usually appear within 2 to 10 days and last 2 to 3 weeks. However, symptoms have been known to develop as quickly as 24 hours after infection or as long as several years later. The papules turn into groups of small blisters filled with fluid that break open, becoming painful, shallow sores surrounded by a red ring. About 50 percent of infected individuals experience warning signs—tingling, tenderness, or itching sensations approximately 5 days prior to each herpes episode.

After the sores are gone, the virus enters its latent stage, remaining inside nerve cells at the end of the spine. Recurrences or flare-ups may be related to factors such as infections, stress, fatigue, or hormonal changes related to menstruation and pregnancy. The virus travels along the nerves to the skin near the site of the first infection, where new sores may appear. At these times small amounts of the virus may be shed in fluids from the mouth, penis, or vagina, or from barely noticeable sores. The infected person may or may not notice the shedding, as often it does not cause pain or discomfort.

The first outbreak is usually the worst. Subsequent outbreaks are usually mild and last only about a week. The frequency and severity of recurrent episodes vary greatly. Some people have only one or two outbreaks in a lifetime; others may have several outbreaks each year. The number and pattern of outbreaks often changes over time, further complicating efforts to manage the disease.

Results of several studies suggest that psychological stress and negative mood can trigger recurrences of genital herpes. A recent study found that persistent stressors and high levels of anxiety predicted genital herpes recurrence, whereas transient mood states, short-term stressors, and life change events did not (Cohen et al., 2000). Although some people report that outbreaks are brought on by another illness, exposure to sunlight, or having a menstrual period, in general outbreaks are unpredictable.

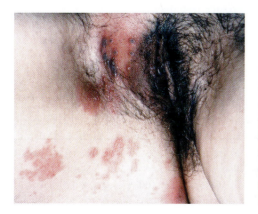
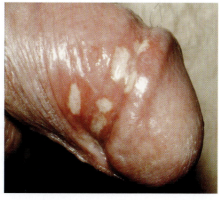

Genital herpes sores as they appear on (a) the labia and (b) the penis.

FAQ:

Is there a cure for herpes?

Unlike some sexual partners, herpes will stick around for the rest of your life. There is no cure. However, treatments are available that enable you to manage the disease and have a somewhat normal sex life. Physicians often prescribe antiviral medications that can prevent outbreaks and shorten those that do occur. The antiviral drug acyclovir (sold under the brand name Zovirax) may promote healing of sores and reduce the frequency of recurrence. Valacyclovir (Valtrex) treats later episodes of genital herpes. Famciclorvir (Famvir) is also used for this purpose and has the added benefit of helping to prevent future outbreaks. Treatment with Lysine, an amino acid, at the outbreak of HSV-1 can significantly reduce the duration of a herpes outbreak.

Diagnosis   Herpes is usually diagnosed by clinical examination of visible sores. In some cases, the sores are not visible to the naked eye and laboratory tests may be necessary before a diagnosis can be made. In the past, type-specific blood tests were not always accurate because they could not discriminate HSV-1, HSV-2, and other herpes virus antibodies (such as chicken pox and mononucleosis). New tests are extremely accurate and rarely confuse herpes simplex with other herpes viruses. The blood test cannot determine whether an infection is oral or genital. However, since most cases of genital herpes are HSV-2, a positive Type 2 test result most likely indicates a genital infection.

Possible Complications   If treated, genital herpes usually does not cause any major problems in healthy adults. However, untreated herpes may lead to complications, especially in women. (For treatment, see FAQ.) Women with untreated herpes have three times the risk of miscarriages, as well as an increased risk of cervical cancer. Herpes can be passed on to fetuses. The herpes virus may bypass the underdeveloped fetal immune system and infect cells of the nervous system; such infections can be fatal to infants. Women infected with herpes are advised to have cesarean deliveries to minimize this risk. Herpes sores can also provide an entry site for, and thus increase the risk of infection with, HIV.

Research   Because infection is currently a lifelong problem, researchers are focusing on the obvious—ways to prevent and to cure genital herpes. Scientists are also trying to determine what triggers outbreaks of the disease, and why some people have only one or two outbreaks in a lifetime while others may have several outbreaks each year.

Hepatitis

There are five forms of hepatitis, depending on the virus causing the disease (see Cause and Transmission section): hepatitis A, hepatitis B, hepatitis C, hepatitis D, and hepatitis E. Hepatitis A is the most common form of viral hepatitis in the United States, with an estimated 125,000 to 200,000 total infections each year; 33 percent of Americans have evidence of past infection. An additional 140,000 to 320,000 people are infected with hepatitis B annually in the United States, and an estimated 1 to 1.25 million Americans are chronically infected. An estimated 36,000 new cases of the third form of hepatitis, hepatitis C, are reported in the United States each year. Of the 3.9 million people infected with hepatitis C, 2.7 million are chronically infected. In general, the global pattern of hepatitis D, also called delta hepatitis, follows that of chronic hepatitis B infection, that is, the two viruses occur together. Hepatitis E occurs primarily in developing countries with inadequate environmental sanitation.

Cause and Transmission   **Hepatitis** is an inflammation of the liver; it can be caused by a number of viruses, and other factors such as alcohol abuse, some medications, and trauma can affect the onset and course of the disease. According to the National Institute of Allergy and Infectious Diseases, there are five major types of viral hepatitis. **Hepatitis A** was formerly called infectious hepatitis. **Hepatitis B,** formerly called serum hepatitis, is caused by infection with the Hepatitis B virus (HBV). Non-A, non-B hepatitis is caused by at least three different viruses: Hepatitis C, D, and E. Delta hepatitis, also known as hepatitis D, occurs only in people who already are infected with hepatitis B because it depends on HBV for replication.

Hepatitis A is sometimes spread through sexual acts involving oral/anal contact but is most commonly passed on by ingestion of contaminated food or water. Hepatitis B, C, and D can be found in the blood and, to a lesser extent in the saliva, urine, semen, breast milk, vaginal fluids, and sweat of an infected person. The disease is spread by direct contact with infected body fluids, usually by sexual contact (vaginal, oral, or anal), a needle-stick injury, or sharing a needle with an infected person. Newborns can contract the virus from an infected mother during childbirth. The virus also can be

Hepatitis A: inflammation of the liver caused by infection with the hepatitis A virus, which is spread by fecal-oral contact, including that of sex partners

Hepatitis B: inflammation of the liver caused by infection with the hepatitis B virus, which is most commonly passed on to a partner during intercourse, especially during anal sex, as well as through sharing of drug needles

passed by other intimate contact, including kissing. Drinking water contaminated by feces is the most commonly documented route of hepatitis E transmission. Hepatitis E is rarely transmitted sexually.

Symptoms   Some people infected with viral hepatitis have few or no symptoms. When and if symptoms do develop, they usually appear within 4 weeks but may take as long as 6 months to emerge. These symptoms, which range from mild to severe, include fatigue, headaches, poor appetite, abdominal pain, fever, vomiting, and (occasionally) joint pain, hives, or a rash. Urine may become darker in color. **Jaundice,** a yellowing of the skin and whites of the eyes, may develop. In later stages of infection the lymph nodes in the body swell and liver damage occurs.

About one third of those with HBV develop only mild flulike symptoms, without jaundice. About 15 to 20 percent of those infected with Hepatitis B develop short-term arthritic symptoms such as aching joints. Those with very severe HBV infection may experience personality changes and agitated behavior.

Some people may have no symptoms but are carriers of hepatitis B or C. There are an estimated 1.3 million HBV carriers in the United States and 300 million carriers worldwide. About 90 percent of babies who become infected with HBV at birth and up to half of youngsters who are infected before age 5, become chronic carriers. It is estimated that there are between 2 and 5 million chronic carriers of HCV.

Diagnosis   Hepatitis A is diagnosed with a blood test that detects **antigens** (in this case, proteins on the surface of the virus) in the blood. Several types of blood tests can detect signs of Hepatitis B even before symptoms develop. These tests measure liver function and identify HBV antigens or **antibodies** (proteins produced by the body in response to the HBV antigens) in the blood. A new test is now available to detect the antibodies present in more than 50 percent of those with acute hepatitis C and in almost all with all forms of chronic hepatitis. Until recently delta hepatitis could be diagnosed only by a *liver biopsy*, surgical removal of a tiny piece of the liver. A new procedure detects part of the genetic material of HDV in a patient's blood; a blood test also is available to detect the HDV antibody.

Treatment   A hepatitis A vaccine is available to prevent infection with the hepatitis A virus. Although data on long-term protection are limited, it is estimated that protection will last for at least 20 years. Those who travel or work in developing countries, children in communities that have high rates of hepatitis A outbreaks, sexually active homosexual men, drug users who share needles, and persons who have occupational risk factors (such as health-care workers), chronic liver disease, or clotting-factor disorders should be vaccinated against hepatitis A. Immune globulin provides effective protection against the hepatitis A virus for up to 3 months. Immune globulin also may be administered after exposure to the virus.

Vaccinations are also available to prevent hepatitis B. The American College Health Association recommends that all college students be vaccinated against hepatitis B. The U.S. Public Health Service recommends HBV vaccinations for sexually active people, health-care professionals, emergency workers, and people with an infected partner. It also recommends universal screening of pregnant women; immunizations for their newborns have become a routine part of regular medical checkups. All children up to age 12 should be vaccinated. The vaccine can fight off the HBV virus for at least 10 years. Hepatitis D can be prevented by vaccination against HBV.

High-risk behaviors that should be avoided to prevent hepatitis infection (as well as a number of other sexually transmitted infections) include sharing needles with an infected user, sexual contact with an infected partner, multiple sexual partners, and anal sex.

There is no cure for hepatitis, and no specific medication is prescribed for treatment. Treatment generally consists of bed rest, good nutrition, abstinence from alcohol, and administration of fluids to prevent dehydration. The FDA has approved alpha interferon for treatment of hepatitis B, but it has a number of drawbacks and is

Jaundice: a condition that turns the skin and the whites of the eyes a yellowish color, resulting from an excess of bilirubin in the blood, and often a symptom of liver disease.

Antigen: a substance that when introduced into the body stimulates the production of an antibody

Antibodies: any of a large variety of immunoglobulins normally present in the body or produced in response to an antigen that it neutralizes, thus producing an immune response

Human Papilloma Virus (HPV): genital warts; a sexually transmitted disease characterized by a soft wartlike growth on the genitalia

administered only to those with chronic conditions. For those who suffer severe liver deterioration, a liver transplant is sometimes an option. However, because the body can harbor the virus in the lymph nodes, spleen, skin, and other organs, the virus can infect a transplanted organ.

Possible Complications   Each year, 8,400 to 19,000 of those with symptomatic hepatitis B infections are hospitalized; an estimated 140 to 320 deaths are attributed to hepatitis B each year. Hepatitis C is the leading indicator of liver transplants in the United States; it causes chronic liver disease in 70 percent of infected persons and is responsible for 8,000 to 19,000 deaths from chronic liver disease each year.

Research   Researchers continue to search for new and improved preventative vaccines. In July 2001 a biotech company announced a $60 million 2-year research effort to develop therapeutic vaccines for hepatitis C, hepatitis B, and the virus that causes genital warts (see next section). Work is also focused on finding a cure.

Human Papilloma Virus (Genital Warts)

The virus that causes genital warts, **human papilloma virus (HPV),** is one of the most common causes of sexually transmitted infections in the world. An estimated 20 to 24 million people in the United States are infected with HPV. Each year 1 to 5 million new infections are diagnosed (Kaiser Family Foundation, 1998).

Cause and Transmission   HPV is not transmitted exclusively by sexual contact. Nearly 100 types of HPV have been identified. About half of these are spread via sexual contact and live only in genital tissue (Iwasawa et al., 1997; Vernon, 1997). Genital warts (condylomata acuminata) are caused by only a few of the many types of sexually transmitted HPV. Other common types of HPV, such as those that cause warts on the hands or feet, do not cause genital warts.

Genital warts are spread by sexual contact with an infected partner. They are extremely contagious. Approximately two thirds of those who have a single sexual contact with a partner infected with HPV will develop genital warts.

Symptoms   Almost half of women infected with HPV have no obvious symptoms (NIAID, 2000b). For others, the only symptoms may be warts around the genitals, anus, or (more rarely) in the throat, that appear 3 weeks to 18 months after being infected with the virus (see photographs). These warts may appear as low bumps with a flat hard center or as a bulging fleshy wart. Genital warts often occur in clusters; they can be very tiny or can spread into huge masses on genital tissue. Left untreated, the warts may take on a cauliflowerlike appearance and often itch. Untreated genital warts can grow to block the opening of the vagina, penis, anus, or throat and become quite uncomfortable. In women, genital warts grow more rapidly during pregnancy or when other vaginal infections are present.

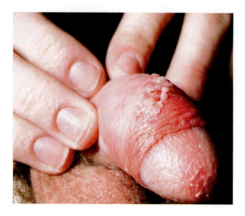
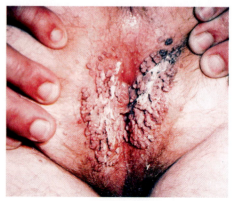

Genital warts (a) on the penis, and (b) on the vulva.

Diagnosis   Genital warts initially are diagnosed by clinical evaluation, that is, visual inspection of the genitals, during a physical or gynecological exam. The genital area may be swabbed with a solution that enhances the appearance of tiny warts. Diagnosis is confirmed by microscopic examination of tissue samples. There is no blood or swab test to diagnose HPV infection; however, a Pap smear may indicate the possible presence of cervical HPV infection.

Treatment   Treatment can eliminate the warts, but there is no cure for HPV. Thus the warts often reappear. Treatment may include cryosurgery (freezing the wart with liquid nitrogen), laser surgery, or application of a topical prescription medication such as podophyllin or imiquimod cream. Some doctors inject the antiviral drug alpha interferon directly into the warts. However, the drug is expensive and does not reduce the rate of recurrence.

Possible Complications   Infection with the HPV virus is associated with cervical, vulvar, anal, and penile cancers (Koutsky et al., 1992). Ninety percent of cases of cervical cancer are linked to certain strains of HPV (Cannistra & Niloff, 1996). Although most HPV infections do not progress to cancer, it is important for infected women to have regular Pap smears so that any potentially precancerous cervical disease can be treated.

Genital warts can enlarge during pregnancy making urination difficult. If the warts occur on the walls of the vagina, they can decrease elasticity and cause obstruction during childbirth. Rarely, infants born to women with genital warts develop laryngeal papillomatosis, potentially life-threatening warts in the throat.

Research   There are clinical trials for two types of HPV vaccines. One area of research is prevention of the disease itself. Another is the prevention of cervical cancers in individuals infected with HPV.

HIV and AIDS

At present the most deadly, though not the most prevalent, sexually transmitted infection is **acquired immunodeficiency syndrome (AIDS).** AIDS is a cluster of symptoms caused by the **human immunodeficiency virus (HIV).** Infection with HIV is not fatal. Rather, the virus disables the immune system, the body's usual defense against disease, leaving the infected person vulnerable to a variety of cancers and other infections to which the infected individual eventually succumbs (Figure 7.3).

A Brief History of AIDS   The first documented case of AIDS goes back to 1959 when a man living in Kinshasa, on the Congo River, died of the disease. Analysis of samples of his blood suggests that HIV evolved from a single introduction into this individual (Ho, 1998). The virus remained isolated for decades until war, drought, commerce, and urbanization shattered traditional African social institutions that may have contained its development and spread. After 1975, with increased global travel, HIV was able to circulate around the world. Changing social and sexual behaviors, the suppression of competing diseases, and modern medical practices such as blood transfusion, made many populations more susceptible to contracting the virus (Cowley, 1993).

In 1980 a technician at the Centers for Disease Control (CDC) noted that there were an unusual number of orders coming from New York City for a drug used to treat antibiotic-resistant cases of a severe form of pneumonia, *Pneumocystis carinii* pneumonia (PCP). By March 1981 at least eight cases of Kaposi's sarcoma (KS), a serious skin disease were identified, also in New York. All of these acutely malignant cases were in young homosexual men. A month later, Kaposi's sarcoma was diagnosed in a homosexual man from San Francisco who also had PCP and signs of immune depression dating back to 1978 (Shilts, 1987).

On June 5, 1981, the CDC issued a bulletin containing the first official announcement regarding the disease that became known as AIDS. The bulletin described

Acquired Immunodeficiency Syndrome (AIDS): a disease caused by infection with the human immunodeficiency virus (HIV-1, HIV-2), a retrovirus that causes immune system failure and debilitation

Human Immunodeficiency Virus (HIV): the virus that causes acquired immunodeficiency syndrome (AIDS)

FIGURE 7.3 From HIV to AIDS.

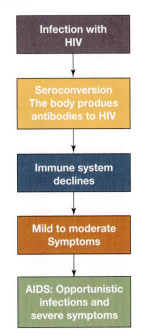

Immune System/Lymphatic System: the body's complicated natural defense against disruption caused by invading foreign agents

T-Cells: white blood cells, derived from the thymus gland, that participate in a variety of cell-mediated immune reactions

T-4 cells: antibody-triggered immune cells that seek and attack invading organisms; also called CD4+ or helper T-cells

Retrovirus: a type of virus that, when not infecting a cell, stores its genetic information on a single-stranded RNA molecule instead of the more usual double-stranded DNA

HIV-2: a virus closely related to HIV-1 that has also been found to cause AIDS. It was first isolated in West Africa. Although HIV-1 and HIV-2 are similar in their viral structure, modes of transmission, and resulting opportunistic infections, they have differed in their geographic patterns of infection.

five cases of a specific strain of severe pneumonia in young homosexual men in Los Angeles. A CDC report followed the next month advising physicians to be alert for Kaposi's sarcoma, *Pneumocystis carinii* pneumonia, and other infections associated with a suppressed immune system in homosexual men.

In 1981 more than two thirds of the then known AIDS patients lived in New York City, San Francisco, or Los Angeles. By the end of the year there were 180 registered or suspected cases of the disease in the United States (see Figure 7.4 for recent statistics), and the World Health organization counted 36 cases in Europe. Although the disease was no longer confined to homosexual populations, because of its origins this unusual cluster of illnesses was being called by some the "gay cancer" or "gay pneumonia." It was not until the summer of 1982 that the disease was officially given the name AIDS.

Cause Infection with the human immunodeficiency virus (see Figure 7.5) is almost universally accepted as the cause of AIDS; however, there are those that believe otherwise (see CONSIDERATIONS box). HIV probably existed long before the first report of infected human blood in 1959. Scientists have known for some time that a small African monkey, the sooty mangabey, is the natural reservoir of a virus that is very similar to HIV-2. The source of HIV-1, the dominant cause of the AIDS *pandemic* (worldwide epidemic), has remained elusive.

New evidence suggests that a chimp virus, simian immunodeficiency virus (SIV), mutated and crossed over to humans on at least three separate occasions, each time finding humans to be a more congenial host than other primates. The leap from chimps to humans could have occurred when hunters came in contact with infected blood while butchering chimps for food, a common practice in parts of Africa (Korber et al., 1999).

Like other viruses, HIV consists of genetic information surrounded by a protective outer shell of proteins and glycoproteins (Figure 7.5). How can such a simple organism wreak so much havoc? Because the virus uses the host cell's resources for reproduction, the genetic material is all that is needed. HIV selectively targets the **immune system,** also called the **lymphatic system,** which normally protects the body from infection. The specialized cells and proteins of the immune system present in the blood and other bodily fluids work together to eliminate bacteria, viruses, and fungi. One such specialized cell is the CD4+ T-lymphocyte or T-4 cell (also called the helper T-cell) that acts as a *host cell* for HIV. The virus anchors itself to a special protein (CD4)

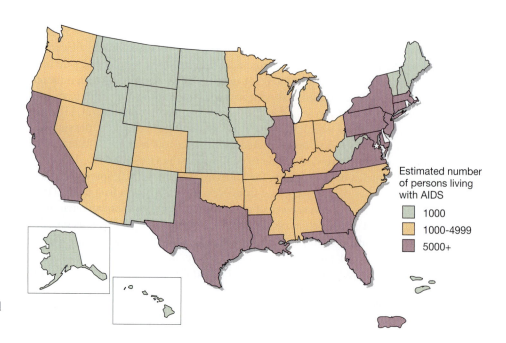

FIGURE 7.4 Map of estimated number of persons living with AIDS in the United States at the end of 1999.

Estimated number of persons living with AIDS
- 1000
- 1000–4999
- 5000+

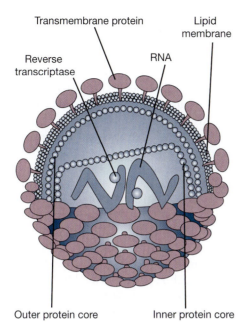

Transmembrane protein   Lipid membrane

Reverse transcriptase   RNA

Outer protein core   Inner protein core

FIGURE 7.5 **Human Immunodeficiency Virus (HIV), the Cause of AIDS.** This retrovirus has RNA as its genetic material. It has the ability to produce DNA from its RNA using the enzyme reverse transcriptase. The DNA is then incorporated into the chromosomes of the virus's human host cell.

T-cells are a type of lymphocyte (or white blood cell). They are an important part of the immune system. There are two main types of T-cells. **T-4 cells,** also called CD4+ cells, are "helper" cells. They lead the attack against infections. T-8 cells (or CD8+ cells) are "suppressor" cells that end the immune response. Researchers can distinguish T-cells by the specific proteins on the surface of the cells. These proteins are called "receptor sites" because they can lock onto particular molecules. Thus a T-4 cell is a T-cell with a CD4 receptor on its surface (New Mexico AIDS InfoNet, 1999).

on the surface of the helper T-cell. This causes the viral membrane to fuse with the host cell's membrane. In this way the genetic information gets inside the cell. Although the host cell's nucleus contains more than 1 million times as much genetic information as that stored under the protein shell of HIV, there is no way for the host cell to stop the virus once it has been invaded.

HIV belongs to a special group of viruses called a **retrovirus,** a virus that reverses the usual order of reproduction within the cells it invades (*retro* = backward). Once attached to the T-4 cell, HIV enters the cell and releases its RNA. The RNA is then converted to DNA by a process called reverse transcription, and it combines with the host cell's DNA. When the cell reproduces, it reproduces the virus. The infected cell produces viral particles that bud from the cell surface and infect other T-4 cells (Kleinsmith & Kish, 1995). In other words, HIV converts the cell that it has attacked into a copying machine to produce more and more HIV, destroying T-4 cells in the process. When T-4 cells multiply to fight an infection, they also make more copies of HIV. Because of the speed of this response, the destruction of the immune system is already underway half a day after infection.

The blood system normally contains about 1,000 T-4 helper cells per cubic millimeter. Following HIV infection the level of T-4 cells may remain normal for several years. There are usually no symptoms until the level of T-4 cells begins to fall. After the number of T-cells falls below 200 per cubic millimeter, the body's defenses weaken, leaving infected people extremely vulnerable to several opportunistic infections.

A second strain of the virus identified in 1986, **HIV-2,** is responsible for much of the current epidemic in West Africa. While HIV-1 is usually spread via male homosexual contact, HIV-2 is more commonly transmitted through heterosexual relations. HIV-1 and HIV-2 are similar in their viral structure, modes of transmission, and resulting opportunistic illnesses. However, they differ in their geographic patterns of infection. The virus has the capability to mutate and produce variants other than HIV-1 and HIV-2, even within the same individual.

HIV attacking a white blood cell.

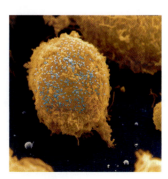

FAQ:

What is the importance of T-cell counts?

There are millions of different families of T-cells. Each family is designed to fight a specific type of infection. When someone is infected with HIV for a long time, the number of T-4 cells he or she has (T-cell count) goes down. This is a sign that the immune system is being weakened. The lower the T-cell count, the more vulnerable the person becomes to opportunistic infections, that is, the more likely it is that he or she will get sick.

T-cell tests are normally reported as the number of cells in a milliliter of blood. The normal range for T-4 cells is between 500 and 1,600, and T-8 cells are normally between 375 and 1,100. T-4 counts can drop dramatically in individuals with HIV, in some cases down to zero.

The T-cell value can vary considerably, even in healthy individuals. Time of day, fatigue, and stress can affect test results. Thus it is best to have blood drawn at the same time of day for each T-cell test and to use the same laboratory. Infections also can have a large impact on T-cell counts. When your body is fighting an infection, the number of white blood cells or lymphocytes (including T-4 and T-8 cells) goes up.

Incidence AIDS is not the first disease to devastate humankind, and it is probably not the last. While AIDS is not yet the mostly deadly plague humans have faced (that honor belongs to the bubonic plague, which killed as much as one third of Europe's population, at least 25 million people, between 1347 and 1351), it already has reached pandemic proportions. An estimated 21.8 million people have died from AIDS since the epidemic began, with 438,795 deaths occurring in the United States (CDC, 2001c).

A reported decline in AIDS deaths could reflect a drop in new HIV infections. It could also be the result of improved treatment of those already infected. Nationwide statistics are reported only when a person is diagnosed with full-blown AIDS. Newly developed medications called protease inhibitors prevent the virus from making copies of itself. As a result, HIV-infected people are less likely to progress to full-blown AIDS and show up in national reporting statistics (Table 7.2).

In the industrialized countries of North America, Western Europe, and the Pacific the availability of antiretroviral therapy such as protease inhibitors has continued to reduce the progression of HIV to AIDS. However, despite reduced media attention, AIDS is still an epidemic in much of the developing world (Figure 7.6).

There are 34 countries in which 91 percent of the AIDS victims have died; most of these are in Africa. Because of this devastating illness, the life expectancy in these countries is expected to decline by nearly 16 years to an average age of 47 by the year 2015. In Botswana, the country with the highest incidence of AIDS, one in every four adults is HIV-positive and life expectancy is expected to decline by 29 years over the next 5 years to an average of 41. By 2015, Botswana's population is expected to be reduced by 20 percent (WHO, 2000a).

AIDS is so widespread in some countries that U.S. officials worry that it could undermine economies, threaten military establishments and governments, and cause other regional problems. In seven countries in sub-Saharan Africa, 20 percent or more of adults are infected with HIV and could die within the next few years, orphaning some 40 million children. According to a United Nations report, infant mortality is expected to double and child mortality to triple throughout these areas (UNICEF, 2000).

Transmission Early in the AIDS epidemic, there were those who believed that the virus was primarily confined to certain groups of people. Some people disparagingly referred to these high-risk groups as the "Four-H Club": homosexuals, Haitians, heroin users, and hemophiliacs. Later, hookers became the fifth "H" (Grmek, 1990). The belief, or maybe the hope, was that "nice, normal" people didn't get AIDS; it was a

TABLE 7.2

Global Summary of AIDS Statistics

	Men	Women	Children under age 15	Total
People newly infected with HIV	2.5 million	2.2 million	600,000	5.3 million
Number of people living with HIV/AIDS	18.3 million	16.4 million	1.4 million	36.1 million
AIDS deaths in 2000	1.2 million	1.3 million	500,000	3 million
Total number of AIDS deaths since the beginning of the epidemic	8.5 million	9.0 million	4.3 million	21.8 million

SOURCE: UNAIDS/World Health Organization, 2000.

CONSIDERATIONS

A Controversial Approach to AIDS

It is estimated that 1 in 10 South Africans is HIV positive. In April 2000 President Thabo Mbeki of South Africa argued that his country had the right to deal with AIDS its own way, including consulting those who challenged the prevailing views on the cause and treatment of AIDS. Mr. Mbeki indicated that he gives equal weight to those who theorize that AIDS is caused by social factors such as drug use, poverty, malnutrition, and parasites rather than a virus. President Mbeki is the only African leader to question the theory that AIDS is caused by HIV, and the only one who has expressed doubts about the safety of the standard anti-AIDS drug AZT. In addition, Mbeki has been the only world leader to counsel an end to the "AIDS hysteria" by suspending "the dissemination of psychologically destructive and false message that HIV infection is invariably fatal" (McGreal, 2001, p. 14). For a while, the South African government declined to distribute AZT to pregnant women despite studies indicating its effectiveness in reducing the transmission of the virus from mother to child.

After an international panel failed to resolve the issue of the cause of AIDS, the health minister of South Africa subsequently moved to distribute some anti-AIDS drugs that President Mbeki had condemned as too toxic and ineffective. The South African government now argues that there is no ideological obstacle to the distribution of AIDS drugs, only financial constraints.

 Do you think that governments have the right to deny availability of medical treatments to their citizens?

—Do you think that other countries have a right to step in if a government's policies endanger its citizens?

disease "they" got, not "us." Even after 1983 when heterosexual transmission of HIV was demonstrated, many people still wanted to believe that they weren't at risk. We now know that it is not which group we belong to, but our actions that put us at risk.

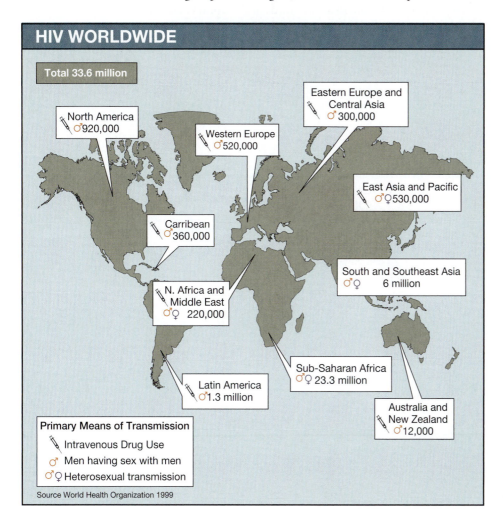

FIGURE 7.6 HIV/AIDS Map.
Source: Adapted from UNAIDS/ World Health Organization, 1999.

> *"With its links to sex, drugs, blood, and information, and with the sophistication of its evolution and of its strategy for spreading itself, AIDS expresses our era."*
>
> MIRKO D. GRMEK

Most scientists agree that HIV does not survive well in the environment, making the possibility of environmental transmission remote. In varying concentrations and amounts, HIV is found in blood, semen, vaginal fluid, breast milk, saliva, and tears. To be infected by HIV two conditions must be present: (1) the virus must be present in sufficient quantities—blood, semen, vaginal, and cervical secretions have the highest concentrations of the virus; and (2) the virus must penetrate a body membrane. The following paragraphs describe some of the actions that endanger you regardless of your age, gender, sexual orientation, ethnic group, religion, occupation, financial status, or educational level.

Blood Infection. Direct infection of the blood can occur by sharing infected hypodermic needles and syringes, a practice common among intravenous drug users. Blood from an infected person can be trapped in a needle or syringe and then injected directly into the bloodstream of the next person who uses the needle. The virus is transmitted by shared blood, not by the drugs or the needle itself. An infected tattoo or body-piercing needle is as dangerous as an infected needle used to shoot heroin or cocaine.

Transfusions of contaminated blood, blood products, or the transplants of infected organs, tissue, or semen transmit infection in a similar manner. Since 1985, donated blood and blood products in the United States have been screened for HIV antibodies. Tennis star Arthur Ashe contracted HIV from blood he received during a heart operation. Screening has substantially decreased the danger of receiving a contaminated transfusion, so the risk today is minimal. Hemophiliacs have been particularly hard hit because of the high number of blood transfusions they require. While the blood supply in the United States is considered to be safe, the World Health Organization (2000b) recently found that more than two thirds of the world's nations are failing to supply safe blood to their populations.

Puncture wounds to the skin caused by unsterile, contaminated, sharp objects can spread HIV. There have been a few cases of health-care workers being infected when they were accidentally pricked by a needle infected with an HIV patient's blood, or even more rarely, when infected blood contacts a health-care worker's open cut or splashes into a mucous membrane (Table 7.3).

TABLE 7.3		
Health-Care Workers With Documented and Possible Occupationally Acquired HIV/AIDS		
	Documented	**Possible**
Dental worker	0	6
Embalmer/morgue technician	1	2
Paramedic/EMT	0	12
Health aide/attendant	1	15
Housekeeper/maintenance	1	12
Laboratory technician, clinical	16	16
Laboratory technician, nonclinical	3	0
Nurse	23	34
Physician, nonsurgical	6	12
Physician, surgical	0	6
Respiratory technician	1	2
Dialysis technician	1	3
Surgical technician	2	2
Other health-care occupations	0	14
TOTAL	55	136

SOURCE: CDC, 1999.

Sexual Contact. The most common means of HIV infection is by sexual contact with an infected partner (Table 7.4). The virus can enter the body through the lining of the vagina, vulva, penis, rectum, or mouth. Sexual activity for those who are HIV-positive may pose a dilemma (Schiltz & Sandford, 2000). Some individuals hesitate to disclose their HIV status to potential sex partners. However, it may be difficult to protect sex partners fully against infection without informing them.

Both male-to-female and female-to-male transmission of HIV during heterosexual contact is possible. However, a woman is approximately 10 times more susceptible to contracting HIV during intercourse than a man. One reason is that there is a higher concentration of the virus in semen than in vaginal fluid. Common sense would also indicate that the infected semen is more likely to enter a woman's body through tiny cuts, tears, or sores in the labia or abrasions in the vagina than for vaginal fluid to enter a man's body. The number of women with HIV and AIDS in the United States is steadily rising. From 1985 to 1998 the reported AIDS cases in the United States occurring among women increased from 7 percent of the total number of cases to 23 percent. HIV infection is now the third leading cause of death among women ages 25 to 44 and the leading cause of death among African American women in this age group (NIAID, 1999).

Anal sex, whether homosexual or heterosexual, is an extremely risky practice because of the likelihood of minuscule tears in the anus that can provide an opening through which HIV can enter the bloodstream. The cells of the rectal membrane are particularly receptive to infection. Because of cultural taboos against acknowledging heterosexual anal intercourse, the health risks of this behavior appear to be severely underestimated. For example, seven times as many women engage in unprotected receptive anal intercourse as homosexual men (Halperin, 1999).

The evidence suggests that the risk of HIV transmission via oral-genital sex is substantially lower than that of vaginal or anal intercourse, but it is not risk free. Exposure to saliva presents a considerably lower risk than exposure to semen, as the number of viruses in saliva is much lower. However, oral trauma such as a cut or ulcerative conditions such as a cold sore or STI infection of the throat may increase the risk of HIV transmission (Scully & Porter, 2000).

Pregnancy, Childbirth, and Breast-Feeding. Approximately one quarter of untreated HIV-infected pregnant women pass along the virus to their babies (NIAID, 2000d). Most mother-to-infant transmission, an estimated 50 to 70 percent, probably occurs late in pregnancy or during birth. The exact ways that the virus is transmitted are not known, but scientists believe that infection occurs when mother's blood enters the fetal circulation or by exposure to the mother's infected mucous membranes during delivery. The risk of mother-to-child transmission is significantly increased if the mother has advanced HIV disease, large amounts of HIV in her bloodstream, or a lowered number of T-4 cells.

The baby of an HIV-infected mother initially will test positive for HIV as a result of receiving antibodies from the mother's bloodstream. However, as already stated, not all babies become infected. Current tests cannot differentiate between the mother's and the baby's infection, therefore it is necessary to wait a few months to determine whether the infant has been infected.

Mothers may also transmit HIV through their breast milk. Breast-feeding increases the risk of HIV transmission by about 14 percent. Data from a study that measured the frequency, timing, and risk factors of HIV transmission through breast-feeding suggest that the risk of HIV infection is highest in the early months of breast-feeding (Miotti et al., 1999). Infants of HIV-positive mothers should be bottle-fed.

Artificial Insemination. Prior to donor screening, a few cases of AIDS were attributed to artificial insemination with semen from an HIV-infected semen donor. At present the most likely source of risk of new infections associated with donor insemination is self-insemination instead of using semen that has been screened at medical clinic (Wortley, Hammond, & Fleming, 1998).

TABLE 7.4

AIDS Cases by Age Group, Exposure Category, and Sex Reported in the United States through June, 2000

Adult/Adolescent Exposure Category

	Percentage of males	Percentage of females	Percentage of total cases
Men who have sex with men	57%	—	48%
Injecting drug use	22	42	26
Men who have sex with men and inject drugs	8	—	6
Hemophilia/coagulation disorder	1	0	1
Heterosexual contact	4	40	10
Receipt of blood transfusion, blood components, or tissue	1	3	1
Other or risk not identified	7	15	9

Pediatric Exposure Category

	Percentage of cases
Hemophilia/coagulation disorder	3%
Mother with HIV infection	91
Receipt of blood transfusion, blood components, or tissue	4
Risk not reported or identified	2

SOURCE: CDC, 1999.

Nontransmission You have just learned how HIV can be transmitted. There are a number of myths and a great deal of misinformation about HIV transmission. According to the best possible information we have, the following routes do not transmit HIV:

1. *Insect bites.* Research conducted by the CDC (1997) and elsewhere has shown that mosquitoes, fleas, lice, and other bloodsucking or biting insects are not carriers of HIV. When an insect bites a person, it does not inject its own or a previously bitten person or animal's blood. Instead it injects its own saliva, which helps the insect feed efficiently. Yellow fever and malaria are transmitted in the saliva of certain mosquitoes. HIV, however, does not reproduce or survive in insects and is thus not present in insect saliva.

2. *Kissing.* Studies of people infected with HIV have found no evidence of the virus being spread by "social" close-mouthed kissing on the mouth or cheek. However, as you have learned, HIV is present in small numbers in the saliva of infected persons. The risk of infection from "deep" or "French" kissing involving the exchange of large amounts of saliva is unknown.

3. *Urine/feces.* Unless blood is present in an infected person's urine or feces, there is no danger of HIV transmission (Hatcher et al., 1990).

4. *Sweat/tears.* Sweat does not contain the virus. Only minuscule amounts of HIV, insufficient to cause infection, have been found in human tears (CDC, 1997).

5. *Sneezing/coughing.* Because HIV is not an airborne virus, being in close contact with an HIV-positive person who is sneezing or coughing poses no risk (CDC, 1997).

6. *Food.* Food prepared by an HIV-infected person carries no risk (CDC, 1997).

7. *Handshakes/hugs.* HIV cannot penetrate the epidermis (skin), only the more sensitive mucous membranes; therefore, there is no risk of transmission from handshakes or hugging (Hatcher et al., 1990).

8. *Swimming pools:* Should the semen, vaginal fluids, or blood of an HIV infected person be released in a pool, the chlorine used in most pools would quickly kill the virus (Hatcher et al., 1990).

9. *Toilet seats.* HIV dies quickly outside the body. Even if the virus were able to live on a toilet seat (which it cannot), it would not be able to enter the body of a person using the toilet, as it cannot penetrate the epidermis (Hatcher et al., 1990).

10. *Donating blood.* When donating blood, a needle is used only once and then thrown away; there is thus no risk of contact with another person's blood. Some people have confused the risk of *receiving* infected blood via a transfusion with a risk in *donating* blood.

11. *An uninfected partner.* If your sexual partner does not have HIV, there is no danger of infection. HIV is not caused by drug use or any specific sexual behavior. The problem is how to know who is infected and who isn't. Communication with your partner is essential to avoiding this and other sexually transmitted infections.

There have been no documented cases of HIV being spread through casual social or household contact (CDC, 1997). In 1993 there was one case of HIV spreading from an HIV-infected child to her foster sister. It was found that the child, who had been HIV-infected since birth, suffered bleeding gums and frequent nosebleeds; her foster sister had lesions on her arms from dermatitis. Additionally, sometimes the two girls shared a toothbrush. In another case, an HIV-infected hemophiliac teenager passed the virus to a younger brother through a shared razor that nicked both boys while shaving. These tragedies came not from casual contact but from known risk factors involving blood products (Cowley, 1993).

Symptoms   Many people have no symptoms when first infected with HIV. Others may notice flulike symptoms such as malaise, fever, headache, and enlarged lymph nodes within a month or two after being infected with the virus. Because these symptoms usually disappear within a week or two, the person often assumes it was just the flu.

More persistent and serious symptoms may surface within a few months, or infection may not develop for decades. During this highly variable asymptomatic period, the virus is actively infecting and killing cells of the immune system, and the infected person is highly contagious via the routes we have discussed. The effects of HIV are seen most obviously in the decline of T-cells—the immune system's key infection fighters—as the virus disables or destroys these cells without causing symptoms. During this stage the T-4 cell count drops below 500 (the normal level is between 500 and 1,600) but is still more than 200.

As the immune system deteriorates, a variety of complications begin to surface. One of the first symptoms experienced by many HIV-infected people is an enlargement of the lymph nodes for more than 3 months. Other symptoms include a lack of energy, weight loss, frequent fevers and night sweats, persistent oral or vaginal yeast infections, chronic rashes or flaky skin, pelvic inflammatory disease that does not respond to treatment, or short-term memory loss. Some people develop severe and frequent herpes sores in the mouth, genitals, or anus, or shingles, a painful nerve disease.

As noted earlier in the chapter, HIV depresses the function of T-4 cells and other cells of the immune system, opening the door to a wide variety of infections that the body could otherwise fight off. These aptly named **opportunistic infections** are caused by a wide range of microorganisms, many of which are normally present in the body or in the environment. The occurrence of opportunistic infections is one sign that the infection is progressing from HIV to full-blown AIDS.

Opportunistic Infections: illnesses caused by various organisms, some of which usually do not cause disease in persons with normal immune systems

Symptoms of opportunistic infections common in people with AIDS include the following: coughing, shortness of breath, seizures, lack of coordination, difficult or painful swallowing, confusion or forgetfulness, severe and persistent diarrhea, fever, vision loss, nausea and vomiting, weight loss, extreme fatigue, severe headaches, and coma. HIV-infected men are more likely to develop Kaposi's sarcoma, while women have higher rates of yeast infections of the windpipe, herpes simplex, and bacterial pneumonia (NIAID, 1999).

Diagnosis   HIV infection is usually diagnosed initially by testing a person's blood for the presence of antibodies to the virus. HIV antibodies generally do not reach detectable blood levels until 1 to 3 months following infection. It may take as long as 6 months for antibodies to reach levels high enough to show up in standard blood tests.

The **ELISA (enzyme-linked immunoabsorbent assay)** is the procedure used to detect the presence of HIV antibodies in the blood. Since 1986, there has been an ELISA test for HIV-2. While the ELISA is quite sensitive, it is not specific. The **Western Blot test,** which detects a specific pattern of protein bands linked to HIV, can be used to confirm the findings of a positive ELISA. The initial screening is done with ELISA, but no test is considered to be a true positive until the Western Blot has confirmed it. The combination of these two tests reduces the chance of a false positive finding to about 1 in 100,000. A finger-stick HIV rapid test is available, but it is less specific than traditional laboratory-based testing and results in more false positive results. Testing is free in most clinics.

An estimated 2 million people are tested anonymously each year. Of these, 700,000 never return for their test results. In 1996 the FDA approved home HIV tests that use the same ELISA/Western Blot methods used by doctors and clinics. The FDA-approved tests are more than 99 percent accurate beyond 6 months after possible exposure to the virus. The home tests cost from $30 to $50. Home tests can be purchased in some stores, over the phone, or on the Internet. Some are reluctant to order by phone or online, because of concerns about confidentiality. Be aware that some companies are selling unapproved tests whose accuracy is unknown; when purchasing a test, make sure it is FDA-approved.

A new HIV antibody test, OraSure, is referred to as a saliva test; however, it actually tests for antibodies in a fluid in the mouth called oral mucosal transudate. Like the more standard blood tests, you must wait 6 months after your last possible exposure to the virus for the most accurate test results. The saliva test is as accurate as blood testing but is more expensive.

HIV antibody testing is widely available at city, county, or state departments of health, and at clinics, hospitals, and doctor's offices. The National AIDS Hotline (1-800-342-AIDS) will give you the name of the nearest site that provides anonymous testing that is either free or low cost. It can take 2 to 4 weeks to receive test results.

Although the terms may seem synonymous, *confidential* and *anonymous* mean very different things in medical testing. **Confidential** test results are recorded in your medical record and may be accessible to your insurance company, and in some situations to your employer. This might jeopardize your health-care coverage or your job. When testing is **anonymous** you receive a code number and your name is never used.

A nonreactive, **seronegative** result means you have not developed antibodies to the virus. It does not always mean that you have not been infected, and it certainly does not mean that you are immune from contracting HIV. If you were infected recently, the test might not yet show the HIV antibodies and a follow-up test 4 to 8 weeks later is advisable. If you have engaged in any high-risk behaviors since you were tested, you need to be tested again.

A reactive, **seropositive** test means that you have developed HIV antibodies, not that you have AIDS. A positive test result cannot indicate when, or even if, you will develop AIDS. A positive test result does mean that you are infectious and can infect others with HIV if you exchange bodily fluids in any manner we have described earlier.

ELISA (Enzyme-Linked Immunoabsorbent Assay): a type of enzyme immunoassay to determine the presence of antibodies to HIV in the blood or oral fluids

Western Blot: a laboratory test for specific antibodies to confirm repeatedly reactive results on the ELISA test

Confidential: information that is communicated in confidence and cannot be disclosed without permission

Anonymous: information in which the party involved is not named or identified

Seronegative: showing no significant level of serum antibodies, or other immunologic marker in the serum, that would indicate previous exposure to the infectious agent being tested

Seropositive: showing a significant level of serum antibodies, or other immunologic marker in the serum, indicating previous exposure to the infectious agent being tested

If your HIV test is positive there are many things to consider. You will need to inform any sex or needle-sharing partners so they can get tested. In addition, it will be important for you to pay special attention to your own physical and mental health. You will need to decide which family members and friends you want to inform about your HIV status and the best way and time to tell them. (Figure 7.7 shows how difficult it is for many heterosexual college students to talk with their sexual partner about AIDS.) Health-care workers, including your dentist, also should be informed. You may want to get counseling or join a support group to help you deal with your feelings and to help answer your questions. If you are or continue to be sexually active, it is essential that you practice safer sex. Not only is there danger of infecting your partner(s), but you can also be reinfected, hastening the development of AIDS and further shortening your life.

Treatment   When AIDS first surfaced there were no medicines available to treat the underlying immune deficiency and few treatments for the opportunistic infections that resulted. Although some people still believe that a diagnosis of HIV is an immediate death sentence, over the past 10 years numerous anti-HIV drugs, as well as a number of other drugs to treat HIV-associated infections, have become available. These have greatly increased the life span of those living with HIV and AIDS.

The first drugs used to treat HIV infection are called **reverse transcriptase inhibitors.** These drugs stop the virus from making copies of itself at an early stage of HIV infection. This class of drugs includes AZT (zidovudine), ddC (zalcitabline), ddI (dideoxyinosine), d4T (stavudine), and 3TC (lamivudine). These drugs slow the spread of HIV in the body and delay the onset of opportunistic infections.

A second class of drugs has been approved to treat HIV infection. These **protease inhibitors** interrupt virus replications at a later stage in its life cycle. The include ritonavir (Norvir), saquinivir (Invirase), indinavir (Crixivan), amprenivir (Agenerase), and nelfinavir (Viracept). Because HIV can become resistant to both classes of drugs, combination treatment using both, the so-called AIDS cocktail, is necessary to effectively suppress the virus. Those newly infected with HIV as well as those with full-blown AIDS can benefit from combination therapy.

None of these drugs can cure HIV infection or AIDS. They all have potential side effects that can be severe, including depletion of red or white cells, inflammation of the pancreas, painful nerve damage, lactic acidosis, and a severely enlarged liver. The most common side effects associated with protease inhibitors include nausea, diarrhea, and other gastrointestinal symptoms. Researchers believe that highly active antiretroviral therapy (HAART) was a major contributor to the 47 percent reduction in deaths from AIDS in the United States between 1996 and 1997, but caution that HAART is not a cure and the long-term complications of anti-HIV therapy are unknown.

Possible Complications   People with AIDS are particularly prone to developing cancers such as Kaposi's sarcoma or lymphoma. These cancers usually are more aggressive and difficult to treat in people with AIDS. In light-skinned people, symptoms of Kaposi's sarcoma are round, brown, reddish, or purple spots that develop on the skin or mouth. In darker-skinned individuals the spots are more pigmented. Many people are so debilitated with the symptoms of AIDS that they are unable to maintain their usual routines; others may experience phases of severe illness followed by periods of normal functioning.

Questions about survival times past an AIDS diagnosis cannot be answered with any certainty. Until recently, the rate of long-term survival after diagnosis had been very low. Studies conducted on those diagnosed before 1986 showed a median survival time past an initial AIDS diagnosis of 10 to 13 months. The effects of the new combination therapies on survival time are just being felt.

Prevention   You have already learned the bad news: there is no HIV vaccine, and there is no cure. The good news is that the routes of HIV transmission are quite

Reverse Transcriptase Inhibitors: enzymes that convert the single-stranded viral RNA into DNA, the form in which the cell carries its genes

Protease Inhibitors: antiviral drugs that act by inhibiting the virus protease enzyme, thereby preventing viral replication

CAMPUS CONFIDENTIAL

"A few weeks ago I found out that one of my best friends is HIV positive. Of course I feel terrible about it, but I'm also confused and scared. I want to do something to help, but I have no idea what to do or what to say. It's too awful to talk about, and too important not to. When he told me about his test results I was so stunned that I didn't say much of anything. Just something lame like: "that really sucks." I feel badly because I've been avoiding him, but a part of me wishes that he would just disappear so I don't have to deal with this. I know that sounds terrible, but it makes me uncomfortable to be around him. I know that I won't catch AIDS by hanging out with him, but I'm not sure those scientists know everything or that they're telling us everything they do know." ●

limited, so there are several ways to decrease the chances of infection. Don't share needles or syringes *even once*. It doesn't matter if the needle is used to inject heroin or steroids or for tattooing or body piercing; sterile equipment is a must.

Abstain from engaging in sexual behavior that involves the exchange of semen or vaginal secretions. Latex condoms and a water-based lubricant should be used for all occasions of vaginal or anal intercourse. Knowing and limiting your sexual partners is a wise precaution, but does not guarantee your safety. One study found that most people know who infected them with HIV; often it was a long-term partner (Rosser, Gobby, & Carr, 1999).

It is extremely important to receive immediate treatment for any other sexually transmitted infection because of the important role that STIs play in increasing the risk of HIV infection. There are several ways that risk is increased. One is that inflammation increases the production of infection-fighting cells that can break through the mucous membranes in the genitals. Because these cells are also the key targets of HIV, their presence increases the pool of cells vulnerable to attack. Also, genital infections increase the levels of white blood cells in semen and vaginal secretions. Therefore, a person infected with both HIV and another STI carries even more infected cells and poses an even greater risk of infecting a partner. In addition, the genital lesions and sores caused by some other STIs can provide HIV easy access to the blood.

Pregnant women can reduce the risk of passing the virus to their babies by taking the drug AZT during pregnancy. A substantial decline in perinatal AIDS incidence is associated with an increase in AZT use (Lindegren et al., 1999). The Ghent International Working Group on Mother-to-Child Transmission of HIV recommends that pregnant women be tested for HIV infection and, if they are seropositive, that they undertake short-term AZT treatment and find alternatives to breast-feeding (Leroy et al., 1998).

Research New developments in AIDS research seem to crop up almost daily. Scientists continue to conduct research into the origin of HIV and to develop new drug therapies and test new vaccines. AIDS research has had benefits beyond treatment of those infected with HIV. Drugs developed to fight HIV have proved useful in treating several other viral diseases including hepatitis and influenza; retroviral vectors derived from HIV/AIDS research are being adapted for use in gene transfer therapy for cancer patients (NIAID, 1999). However, the ability of the AIDS virus to mutate and recombine in infected people and become resistant to drugs makes finding a cure or preventative vaccine extremely difficult.

Because HIV can rebound in patients who discontinue combination therapy, researchers are working to develop new ways to attack the disease. In 2000 the National Institutes of Health began its first full-scale tests of a vaccine for people already infected with HIV. It is hoped that adding injections of the vaccine, Remune, to standard combination drug therapy will keep the levels of HIV in the blood suppressed longer than anti-HIV drug therapy alone, and that it will thwart the progression of HIV infection to AIDS.

In September 2000, researchers at Massachusetts General Hospital reported their initial findings of a new strategy against HIV. The researchers theorized that combinations of powerful drugs started early might enable patients to mount a vigorous immune response to HIV. They reasoned that a well-controlled infection might function as a sort of vaccine. All of the study's eight participants were able to bolster their immune responses. Five of the eight have been off treatment for periods of 8 to 11 months, and their infections are still well under control. The study was small, and the results preliminary; no one knows how long the subjects will remain healthy. This approach is most likely to help people who have been infected for only a few months (Walker & Goulder, 2000).

Despite repeated exposure to HIV, some people remain uninfected because of a unique natural immune response. If it can be recreated, this natural immunity might serve as a model for a vaccine. A small number of female prostitutes in Africa seem resistant to HIV even though they often have sex with infected men. In one study of 1,900 Kenyan prostitutes, four became infected with HIV only after they stopped working as prostitutes or took breaks of 2 months or more (Altman, 2000).

TABLE 7.5

Among the Losses

Arthur Ashe: tennis player
Michael Bennett: director, choreographer, and co-producer of *A Chorus Line*
Amanda Blake: actress who portrayed "Miss Kitty" on TV's *Gunsmoke*
Brad Davis: film and stage actor, star of the film *Midnight Express*
Denholm Elliott: actor who appeared in *A Room With a View, Trading Places*
Perry Ellis: fashion designer
Keith Haring: artist
Rock Hudson: movie actor
Liberace: entertainer and pianist
Robert Mapplethorpe: photographer
Stewart McKinney: U.S. Congressman from Connecticut

Freddie Mercury: lead singer and lyricist for rock band "Queen"
Rudolf Nureyev: ballet dancer
Anthony Perkins: actor, star of *Psycho*
Robert Reed: television star; played the father in *The Brady Bunch*
Tony Richardson: Academy-award-winning director of *Tom Jones*
Randy Shilts: journalist and author
Jerry Smith: Washington Redskins tight end
Joseph Vasquez: director of *Hangin' With the Homeboys*
Ricky Wilson: guitar player for the "B-52s"
Eric "Eazy-E" Wright: rapper with NWA
And thousands of others loved and remembered by families and friends

Although scientists have so far been unable to find the source of their immunity, they are actively investigating this phenomenon as a potential basis for the development of an AIDS vaccine.

PARASITIC INFECTIONS

A **parasite** is an animal or plant that lives in or on a **host,** an organism of another species from which it obtains all or part of its sustenance. The host is typically, but not always, harmed by the presence of the parasite; it never benefits from its presence. **Ectoparasites** live externally on their hosts (*ecto* = outside). **Endoparasites** cause infection within the host (*endo* = within).

Pubic Lice

Pubic lice or **pediculosis** is infestation with a parasite more commonly known as "crabs." An estimated 3 million new cases of pubic lice are treated each year in the United States.

Cause and Transmission   Pubic lice are caused by *Phthirus pubis*, a tiny parasitic insect that invades the pubic region, grips a pubic hair with its claws, and sticks its head into the skin. It survives by feeding on human blood. Public lice are often referred to as crabs because under magnification they resemble a crab (see accompanying photograph).

Pubic lice are transmitted when they crawl from one infected person to another, often during sexual contact. The lice do not jump; in fact they move very slowly, only about 4 inches a day. Pubic lice live a maximum of 24 hours away from a human host, but the

Ectoparasite: a parasite that lives on the exterior of the host organism

Endoparasite: a parasite that lives within the host organism

Pubic Lice/ Pediculosis: infestation with lice of the family *Pediculidae pediculus*

A Pubic Louse.
Can you see why infection with this parasite is commonly known as "crabs"?

eggs may live up to 6 days. Skin-on-skin contact is not necessary for infection; nonsexual means of transmission can occur when a louse or its eggs drop off onto clothing or bedding. The lice may spread from the genitals to other hair-covered parts of the body.

Symptoms   Intense itching, produced by the lice piercing the skin to get blood, is often the first and most noticeable symptom of pubic lice. Some people may notice little blue marks on the skin where the lice have been feeding, or black dots of digested blood excreted by the lice on undergarments. Others may notice what at first appears to be a tiny freckle, until it moves!

Diagnosis   Pubic lice can be diagnosed by visual examination. Adult lice are about the size of the period at the end of this sentence. They are oval-shaped, and their color ranges from yellowish-gray to reddish-brown when full of blood. Nits, their tiny white eggs, are usually observed clinging to the base of pubic hair.

Treatment   Infection with pubic lice is completely curable with creams or shampoos available either by prescription or over-the-counter. Treatments containing lindane, a powerful pesticide, are most frequently prescribed. Pregnant women, infants, and young children may be advised not to use lindane. Treatments used for head lice, such as Kwell, A200, or RID also are effective against pubic lice. Repeated application is recommended in 5 to 7 days to kill any eggs that were incubating during the first treatment.

Possible Complications   Infection with pubic lice is not a disease. Untreated individuals don't get a fever, infection, have serious complications or long-term consequences. However, those infected with pubic lice may suffer severe, unrelenting itching. Scratching can cause bleeding and secondary infections.

Once an infected person has been treated for pubic lice it is important to wash all clothing and bedding in hot water and dry them on very high heat, or have them dry cleaned. It also is a good idea to vacuum living areas. All those who may have been exposed should be treated at the same time to avoid reinfection.

Scabies

Sarcoptes scabiei (usually referred to as **scabies**) is a common ectoparasitic infection found throughout the world. A more severe form of scabies, more common among people with compromised immune systems, is called Norwegian scabies; it is characterized by vesicles (a closed membrane cell) and formation of thick crusts over the skin, accompanied by abundant mites but only slight itching.

Cause and Transmission   Scabies is an infestation of the skin with *Sarcoptes scabiei*, a parasitic mite. Like pubic lice, the scabies mite attaches to the base of pubic hair. Unlike pubic lice, it burrows under the skin where it lays eggs and subsists for the rest of its 30-day life span. Scabies is highly contagious and can be contracted through sexual contact, or by using the clothing, bedding, or towels of an infected person. Scratching can transfer mites or eggs under fingernails from one body part to another. These tiny mites move much faster than pubic lice, covering about an inch a minute, looking for a spot to burrow under the skin and lay eggs. The mites live about 30 days and lay eggs at the rate of two or three a day. Eggs take 10 days to hatch. Scabies is not always sexually transmitted. Schoolchildren often pass it to one another.

Symptoms   Scabies causes intense itching, especially at night and frequently over much of the body, including areas where no mites are living. Reddish burrows, welts, or blisters may appear on the skin. A red, itchy rash appearing on the genitals, buttocks, feet, wrists, hands, armpits, scalp, or abdomen can cause a great deal of discomfort

Scabies: a contagious skin disease caused by a parasitic mite (see accompanying photograph). Symptoms may take 4 to 6 weeks to appear in a person who has not previously been infected. Those who have previously been infected with scabies may notice symptoms within a few days.

Diagnosis   Most diagnoses are made based upon the appearance and distribution of the rash and the presence of burrows. Scabies can be diagnosed through clinical inspection or scrapings of suspicious burrows. The mites are very small; about 1/10th the size of a pinhead, they can't be seen with the naked eye.

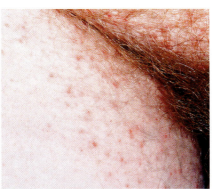

Scabies Rash.

Treatment   Several lotions used to treat pubic lice effectively treat scabies also. As with any medication, it is important to follow the direction of the prescribing physician or those on the label or package insert. Usually a second treatment of the lotion is necessary 7 to 10 days after the first to get rid of any new mites that may have hatched. Pregnant women, infants, and young children may be advised to use milder scabies medications.

Possible Complications   Scabies, like pubic lice, is not a disease. The primary complication is secondary infection caused by scratching. All clothes, bedding, and towels used by infested people in the 2 days before onset of the symptoms should be washed in hot water and dried in a hot dryer. Sexual partners and anyone else who has had close contact with a person infested with scabies should be treated at the same time to prevent reinfestation.

Trichomoniasis

Approximately 5 million cases of **trichomoniasis** occur annually in the United States (Kaiser Family Foundation, 1998); 170 million people worldwide acquire this sexually transmitted endoparasitic infection sometimes referred to as "trich" (WHO, 1998). Infection is more common in women who have had multiple sexual partners. About 20 percent of women experience one or more trichomoniasis infections at some time during their reproductive years (Sharts-Hopco, 1997).

Cause and Transmission   *Trichomonas vaginalis*, a one-celled protozoan causes trichomoniasis. Trichomoniasis primarily is contracted through sexual contact, usually by vaginal intercourse. The parasite does not flourish on the penis, mouth, or anus. It is theoretically possible, but unlikely, to catch trichomoniasis by sharing the damp towel, bathing suit, underwear, toilet seat, or other moist object of an infected person. Only rarely is trichomoniasis passed to babies at birth.

Symptoms   Most men and about one half of all infected women have no symptoms. Men may notice a slight penile discharge, the urge to urinate, or an irritated urethra. The most common symptoms noticed by women are burning, redness, and itching of the genitalia, and a whitish to yellowish-green foamy vaginal discharge with an unpleasant odor. Other symptoms include painful sexual intercourse, lower abdominal discomfort, and the urge to urinate.

Diagnosis   Trichomoniasis is diagnosed through a microscopic examination of vaginal secretions. It can be confirmed by growth of the parasite in laboratory culture. It is only found on urethral smears from men if a special wet-mount specimen is microscopically examined.

Treatment   Trichomoniasis is completely curable. Recommended treatments include the oral medications metronidazole and tinidazole. Metronidazole should not be taken during the first trimester of pregnancy. Partners of infected persons should be treated at the same time to avoid reinfection.

Trichomoniasis: an infection caused by a trichomonad (*Trichomonas vaginalis*) that results in vaginal discharge and itching and may also invade the male urethra and bladder

Possible Complications   Left untreated, trichomoniasis can cause pelvic inflammatory disease or can seriously infect other organs. It may cause infection and swelling of the lower reproductive tract, making intercourse painful. A person with trichomoniasis is at greater risk for cervical cancer. There is also an increased risk of HIV infection, possibly because the immune system is already weakened.

WAYS TO AVOID STIs

Ten Ways to Reduce the Risks of Contracting STIs

1. *Be abstinent.* If you have sexual relations with a partner you are at risk. Period. Masturbation and fantasy are risk-free.

2. *Use condoms.* Use, or have your partner use, a latex or polyurethane condom every time you have intercourse. And use it correctly (see Figure 6.3 in Chapter 6). Condoms don't do any good in your pocket, your wallet, or your handbag. Replace unused condoms that you've carried around for awhile. Heat and sweat can make it easier to tear a condom. Condoms must be used consistently. "Just this once" may be one time too many. If you don't carry a condom, you risk having your partner refuse or delay sexual activity and you increase your risk for contracting a sexually transmitted infection.

3. *Engage in safer sex.* Any behavior that involves the exchange of bodily fluids (semen, vaginal secretions, blood, or saliva) increases the risk of sexually transmitted infection. Avoid unprotected anal or vaginal intercourse, oral-anal or oral-genital contact. Anal intercourse is a particularly high-risk sexual behavior. Touching, massaging, rubbing, and kissing are all low-risk sexual behaviors.

4. *Get information and be observant.* Educate yourself about STI symptoms. Most people vastly underestimate the incidence of non-HIV sexually transmitted infections and their own risk of infection. However, being informed is not enough if you aren't able to negotiate safer sex with your partners. Examine yourself and your partner. Use your senses: vision, touch, and smell. Be aware of any discharge, lesions, or bumps.

5. *Be selective.* The fewer number of sexual partners you have, the lower your risk. If you are in a monogamous sexual relationship (one in which you and your partner only have sex with each other), your risk of infection is reduced. Be especially vigilant (see #2) with any partners who have engaged in high-risk behaviors.

6. *Communicate.* Ask potential partners about their health and behaviors that may put them at higher risk for STIs. Asking questions can begin a dialog about safer sex. However, since some potential partners may not know they are infected, and others may lie, never rely on communication alone.

7. *Be assertive.* Learn self-protection skills, how to negotiate safer sex, and how to say no. Be clear about your sexual limits, your sexual needs, and your desires. Ask your friends what "opening lines" they find effective and adapt an approach that works for you.

8. *Be honest.* Be honest with yourself and your partners. As difficult as it may be, you must tell any sexual partner(s) if you have a sexually transmitted infection. Revealing your infection may threaten your relationship, but not telling may threaten your health, or that of your partner. The failure to inform a sexual partner that you have a STI can also result in criminal prosecution or civil litigation based on sexual fraud. Denial can be suicide, and lying can be murder. Be as clear and calm as you can be. Blaming a partner for your infection generally is nonproductive, though, depending on the circumstances, you may want to reevaluate your relationship. Be prepared for reactions of anger and anxiety, and try not to get defensive.

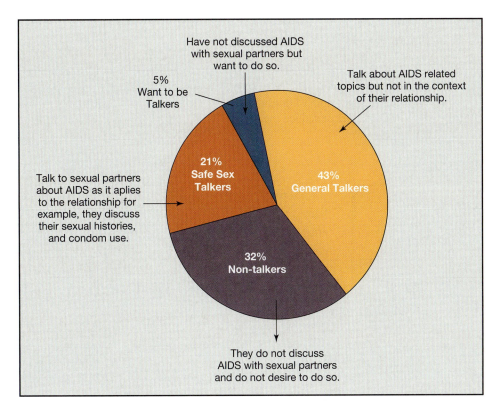

Have not discussed AIDS with sexual partners but want to do so.

5% Want to be Talkers

Talk about AIDS related topics but not in the context of their relationship.

Talk to sexual partners about AIDS as it aplies to the relationship for example, they discuss their sexual histories, and condom use.

21% Safe Sex Talkers

43% General Talkers

32% Non-talkers

They do not discuss AIDS with sexual partners and do not desire to do so.

FIGURE 7.7 **How We Talk About AIDS.**
SOURCE: Cline, Johnson, & Freeman, 1992.

9. *Stay sober.* Don't use substances that impair your judgment. Similarly, don't take advantage of someone whose judgment is impaired. If your date is too drunk to tell you he or she is infected, you may find out for yourself after it's too late.

10. *Get regular checkups.* If you are sexually active, have regular checkups for STIs, even if you are symptom-free. Have your partner undergo testing as well. If you suspect you have an STI, get tested and treated as soon as possible.

WHAT TO DO IF YOU GET AN STI

You've just noticed a peculiar bump on your penis or vagina or on your partner's genitals. You think maybe you should get tested for an STI, but you don't seek medical attention.

Don't let shame, embarrassment, fear, guilt, or denial keep you from consulting a physician as soon as possible. Many STIs can be detected in the early stages of development and can be successfully treated. Early treatment often can forestall complications of the STI. For example, if you are infected with HIV, there is some chance at keeping the virus levels low so that you will not develop full-blown AIDS. It is imperative that you see a physician, ask any questions you may have, and follow treatment instructions exactly.

Some people don't seek medical help because they can't afford to see a private physician, don't know where to go, or don't want an STI infection in their medical record. Fortunately diagnosis and treatment of STIs is provided at public health clinics throughout the United States at little or no cost. After taking a medical history and doing any necessary testing, a health-care practitioner will discuss your diagnosis with you. In some cases treatment will be started right away, while in other cases you may have to wait for laboratory test results.

If you are diagnosed with an STI you must inform your sexual partner(s) immediately so they can be tested and treated promptly. There are many reasons why people diagnosed with an STI don't inform their partners. For example, they may be embarrassed, or they may be married or in a committed relationship and have contracted the STI outside the relationship. As we have discussed, many STIs are asymptomatic, especially in the early stages, so you can't assume that because your partner doesn't have any symptoms yet that you're off the hook. Not informing partners may put them at risk for severe complications of the disease, and they may infect others or even reinfect you. Most STIs are not like the measles; having had an STI doesn't mean you can't get it again. You can. Be sure to use prevention strategies to reduce the likelihood of reinfection.

▋R E V I E W

Sexually transmitted infections (STIs) are diseases that may be contracted through sexual contact, such as vaginal or anal intercourse and oral sex. Women are more easily infected with STIs than men, though women are generally less likely to have symptoms. Some STIs put you at greater risk for contracting HIV/AIDS. Of the 50 or so STIs, the most common STI in the United States is **1**_____.

Chlamydia, syphilis, and gonorrhea are caused by different kinds of **2**_____. Bacterial vaginosis results from an overgrowth of organisms in the **3**_____. You need not be sexually active to have this infection.

4_____ is an inflammation of the uterine lining and fallopian tubes. It can be caused by a variety of infections including chlamydia, gonorrhea, and trichomoniasis. PID is best diagnosed with a **5**_____ and treated with antibiotics. Failure to treat PID may result in sterility.

Genital herpes may be caused by either of two viruses: herpes simplex 1 (HSV-1) or herpes simplex 2 (HSV-2). HSV-1 causes **6**_____ around the mouth, but also may be spread to genitalia during oral sex. HSV-2 causes 80 to 90 percent of all genital herpes in the United States, but it also may spread to the mouth during oral sex. These viruses cannot be cured. They are extremely contagious during an outbreak.

Hepatitis is caused by a **7**_____ which inflames the **8**_____. Hepatitis, especially hepatitis B, the most common form, may be spread by sexual contact. Human papilloma virus causes **9**_____. HPV has been linked to cervical and penile cancers. Once you have contracted the virus you cannot be cured. If removed, the warts may recur.

AIDS is the abbreviation for **10**_____, a cluster of symptoms caused by the **11**_____ virus or HIV. This virus disables the body's immune system, the usual defense against disease. In this vulnerable state, the body becomes susceptible to a number of rare cancers and infections to which it otherwise would be resistant. Two of these **12**_____ diseases are *Pneumocystis carinii* pneumonia or PCP and Kaposi's sarcoma.

HIV can spread from one host to another only through the exchange of white blood cells which are present in bodily fluids: blood, semen, vaginal and cervical secretions, and breast milk. HIV cannot live outside a live host, and it cannot be spread through the air. Thus casual contact with an HIV-infected person—including touching, kissing, and sharing clothes—cannot infect you. HIV can be contracted from sexual contact, blood transfusions, and the exchange of blood via a dirty needle. Approximately **13**_____ percent of pregnant HIV-positive women infect their babies, and a nursing mother can pass HIV though her breast milk to her child.

HIV cannot be transmitted by insects, saliva, urine, feces, sweat, tears, sneezing, coughing, food, handshakes, hugs, swimming pools, toilet seats, or by donating blood or having sex with an uninfected partner.

HIV attacks the human immune system by attaching itself to T-4 helper cells, a type of **14**_____ blood cell. Once inside these cells, the HIV uses the host's DNA to make copies of itself. As the number of T-4 cells falls below **15**_____ per cubic millimeter, the body's defenses weaken, impairing the body's capacity to resist disease.

The test for HIV consists of two procedures, the **16**_____ and the _____. A **17**_____ result means that your body has not produced antibodies to fight the virus. A **18**_____ result means that you have contracted HIV.

Medical treatments can allow HIV-infected individuals to live longer and to enjoy a better quality of life than they might without treatment. As yet there is no cure for HIV/AIDS, neither is there a preventative vaccine for the virus.

To decrease your chance of contracting HIV take the following steps: Practice safer sex. Don't share needles. Get treatment for other STIs that can greatly increase your chances of contracting HIV.

Pubic lice and scabies are parasites that cause intense itching. These parasites are spread by sexual and nonsexual contact. Topical treatments are effective, but clothing, towels, and bed linens should be washed in hot water to prevent reinfection. Also, sexual partners and others in close contact with the infected person should be treated.

Trichomoniasis or "trich" is caused by a **19**_____, a one-celled microorganism. Trichomoniasis can lead to pelvic inflammatory disease or PID.

If you think you might have an STI, see a physician immediately. Quick action may avoid more serious consequences. Inform your partners and abstain from sex while your infection is still active and contagious. If you have a recurring STI such as herpes, inform all your future partners. To reduce the risks of contracting STIs, abstain from sexual relations or engage in safer sex, be assertive in saying no, and stay sober.

SUGGESTED READINGS

Allen, P. L. (2000). *The Wages of Sin: Sex and Disease, Past and Present.* Chicago: University of Chicago Press.
> Lewis offers an exploration of the conflict between religious and medical theories of illness especially sexually related diseases from the late classical era to the present.

Bartlett, J. G. & Finkbeiner, A. K. (1998). *The Guide to Living with HIV Infection.* Baltimore: Johns Hopkins University Press.
> The Johns Hopkins University AIDS Clinic developed this guide.

Eng, T. R. & Butler, W. T. (Eds.) (1997). *The Hidden Epidemic: Confronting Sexually Transmitted Infections.* Washington, DC: National Academy Press.
> This volume provides the results of an investigation by the U.S. Committee on Prevention and Control of Sexually Transmitted Infections surveying the scope and impact of STIs.

Hooper, E. & Hamilton, B. (1999). *The River: A Journey to the Source of HIV and AIDS.* Little Brown and Co.
> The authors offer a comprehensive and controversial argument that HIV made the jump from simians to humans after the administration of oral polio vaccine in Africa in the 1950s.

ANSWERS TO CHAPTER REVIEW

1. chlamydia; **2.** bacteria; **3.** vagina; **4.** pelvic inflammatory disease; **5.** laparoscope; **6.** cold sores (or fever blisters); **7.** virus; **8.** liver; **9.** genital warts; **10.** acquired immunodeficiency syndrome; **11.** human immunodeficiency; **12.** opportunistic; **13.** 25; **14.** white; **15.** 200; **16.** ELISA, Western Bloc; **17.** seronegative; **18.** seropositive; **19.** protozoan.

CHAPTER 8

Social Control of Sexuality

PHYSICAL

SOCIAL

EMOTIONAL

SPIRITUAL

COGNITIVE

- **Who? Social Control and the Selection of a Sexual Partner**
  Your selection of a sexual partner may be influenced by a variety of social pressures and influences, some of which are outside your awareness.

- **When? Social Control and the Timing of Sexual Relations**
  The timing of sexual relations is regulated by cultural restrictions, such as the age when sexual activities are deemed appropriate and the accepted frequency of sexual activity.

- **Where? How Society Influences the Location of Sexual Activity**
  The location of sexual relations is limited in every society through the setting of standards for modesty in behavior and clothing.

- **How? Social Regulation of Sexual Behavior**
  Societies may control sexual behavior through language restrictions and direct regulation of female and male sexuality; regulation may involve various forms of social pressure and informal sanctions, formal laws, and even surgical means.

- **Why? Reasons for Social Control of Sexuality**
  Societies attempt to control sex in order to regulate population growth, reduce conflict, control disease, protect individuals from harm, or to resolve issues of paternity and inheritance.

- **The Double Standard and Suppression of Female Sexuality**
  In many societies, including our own, there is a sexual double standard—a pattern of sexual morality that permits a variety of sexual activities to males but denies them to females.

n Part One, we concentrated on the biological factors affecting your sexuality. The nature of sexual interaction between men and women depends partly on the biology of fertilization. But these biological processes are expressed according to our social environment and cultural beliefs. "Among human beings, nowhere has sex remained merely a physical act to relieve certain bodily tensions. It has been transformed within human societies to become a basic area for morality and the organization of society" (Gregersen, 1994, p. 1).

Your sexual thoughts, feelings, and behavior may be an individual experience, but they occur within a social context. No one else grew up in your family at the same time you did, with the same friends, in your neighborhood or hometown. All of these elements of your upbringing have specific influences on your life. The who, what, when, where, and why of your sexual attitudes are all influenced by the society in which you live.

Although the ways we behave may seem to be a matter of personal choice, social science research has shown us that they are actually quite predictable. Social influences may be as obvious as laws regarding the age at which two people can marry, or as subtle as our interpretation of body language. Every society regulates the ways in which sexuality is channeled into acceptable behaviors (Table 8.1). In that way, sexual behavior is very much like any other social behavior: "without consciously thinking about it, we play by the rules when we choose someone to have sex with" (Michael et al., 1994, p. 44).

Some societies insist on a very limited range of erotic acts. Others revel in erotic riches. However, no society encourages its members to have completely unrestricted sexual relationships. Thus, all societies exert control over sexuality. This tension between the individual and society is incredibly complex. As individuals we may want to chart our own course, do our own thing. However, other individuals doing their own things may interfere with our sense of individualism and our personal rights. Society comprises individuals. And, collectively, those individuals have a stake in the cumulative outcomes of individuals' sexual behaviors. However, it is individuals who make the behavioral decisions, experience the emotions, and live most directly with the consequences of those behaviors.

When studying the mechanisms of social control, you need to be careful to differentiate what anthropologist Gary Ferraro (1995) labels functions (the part something plays as perceived by the scientific observer) and motives (the actual intentions of members of the group):

> To suggest, for example, that a rain dance functions to build social cohesion among group members does not prove that this was in fact the intention of the people themselves. It may well be that the people themselves were conducting a rain dance for the rather straightforward purpose of causing rain. At the same time, it may also be true that one of the objective consequences of the rain dance is that it does in fact promote social cohesion. (Ferraro, 1995, p. 67)

Sociologist Robert Merton (1957) used the terms *manifest function* and *latent function* in a similar fashion to distinguish the reasons people generally acknowledge for a social rule or practice and outcomes from those rules or practices that may not be

TABLE 8.1

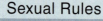

Sexual Rules

The Middle Ages:
Knight Moves

Rule 1. Suffer for Love. Worship Until It Hurts

Rule 2. Marriage Is No Excuse for Not Loving Someone Else

Rule 3. Never Hesitate to Grovel Sorrowfully in Song

Rule 4. Thou Shalt Always Be Courteous

Rule 5. Love Made Public Rarely Endures

The Victorian Era:
Ladies And Gentlemen

Rule 1. Write Love Letters That Bare Your Soul

Rule 2. Courtship Has Rules That You Must Never Break

Rule 3. Men Will Be Men and It Is the Job of Women to Curb Them

Rule 4. Women Must Repress, Repress, Repress

Rule 5. It Is a Woman's Job to Be a Perfect Wife in a Perfect Home

The Roaring Twenties:
Let The Good Times Roll

Rule 1. Dating Is a Show So Be a Star

Rule 2. Looks Aren't Everything but They Make the Phone Ring

Rule 3. To Get to First Base, Get a Car

Rule 4. Petting: Don't Ask, Don't Tell

Rule 5. Love Is a Game So You Better Have a Plan

The Fifties:
Happy Days

Rule 1. Be Ready to Get a Steady

Rule 2. You've Got to Be in Shape if You're Going to Attract a Mate

Rule 3. You Too Can Be a Sex Object

Rule 4. Men Are Men and Women Are Women. Don't Mix Things Up.

Rule 5. Explore Sex. Then Again, Maybe Not.

The Sixties:
The Sexual Revolution

Rule 1. If It Feels Good, Do It

Rule 2. If You Can't Be With the One You Love, Love the One You're With

Rule 3. One Pill Makes You Larger and One Pill Makes You Smaller and One Pill Keeps You From Having a Baby

Rule 4. Don't Rush Into Marriage: Live Together

Rule 5. Be a Swinging Single

The 21st Century:
Virtual Romance

Rule 1. Be Careful. It's a Jungle out There.

Rule 2. Connect the Computer—and Lower Your Expectations

Rule 3. What You See Isn't Always What You Get

Rule 4. Romance Gets No Respect

Rule 5. Rules Are Made to Be Broken

SOURCE: Adapted from Discovery Online.

obvious to the members of a society. The manifest reason for a rain dance is obvious to most participants—it is what motivates them; the latent (or hidden) functions may not be obvious at all, and they may be irrelevant to the participants.

For example, a society may condemn masturbation or oral sex, alleging that these practices are sinful or harmful in some way. However, a latent function of discouraging masturbation or oral sex is an increased likelihood of male-female coitus and thus the promotion of reproduction. (Note that pregnancies never result from masturbation or oral sex; yet if individuals just say "no" to these practices, there is an increased likelihood they will say "yes" to coitus.)

This is the mechanism of social control. We are motivated by certain beliefs or standards of "appropriate" conduct, and quite out of our awareness, through our behavioral decisions, we (along with almost all other members of society) will effectively give force to a significant social effect. In this chapter we shall examine some of the ways societies have controlled individuals' sexuality, and then turn to the why, their purpose for doing so.

WHO? SOCIAL CONTROL AND THE SELECTION OF A SEXUAL PARTNER

Society has a vested interest in mating. To some degree, every society limits its members' rights to choose sexual partners. The survival of the species is dependent on successful reproduction. A society that encouraged sexual relations with close genetic relatives (which does not produce the best offspring) or one in which homosexual relationships were the norm could not thrive. Forbidding sex with family members, restricting sexual relationships before or outside of marriage, and prohibiting homosexuality are examples of ways in which societies attempt to regulate sexual partnerships. Some societies try to maintain the social order by dictating who can sleep with whom. For example, as recently as the 1960s, there were laws on the books in many American states forbidding intercourse between black people and white people.

Anthropologist Suzanne Frayser (1985) conducted research on 62 cultures throughout the world. All of the cultures she investigated had specific rules and procedures that defined acceptable forms of reproductive and sexual relationships. Frayser defined a **reproductive relationship** as one in which reproduction is both expected and socially approved. According to Frayser, **sexual relationships,** in which reproduction is neither expected nor socially approved, are to be avoided. Whether or not a pregnancy or child results from a marital relationship, **marriage** is considered to be a reproductive relationship because procreation is both expected and socially approved. Incest, though variously defined, is a sexual relationship prohibited and punished in all the societies she surveyed. Extramarital relationships were forbidden in most (but not all) societies. Of all **nonmarital relationships**, **premarital relationships** were most likely to receive social approval. Of course, despite society's prohibitions, homosexual, **incestuous**, premarital, and **extramarital relationships** exist to some extent in all societies.

All societies have some form of marriage, a relationship in which sex and the birth of children are socially approved. It is not pure chance that marriage is a cultural universal. Marriage exists in some form in every society in the world because it promotes social stability, fosters economic sustenance, and ensures that children will be nurtured so that one day they will be productive and reproductive adults. Marriage also can be a source of emotional comfort, companionship and security—all of which contribute to social stability.

Because this relationship is so important to their survival, societies have lots of rules to follow when you are selecting a husband or wife. Some may dictate the acceptable number and length of reproductive relationships, restrict marriage to members of one's own community, set the age at which couples are expected to marry, determine who chooses the marriage partner, and restrict the grounds for the termination of a reproductive relationship.

Reproductive Relationship: a relationship in which reproduction is both expected and socially approved

Sexual Relationship: a relationship in which reproduction is neither expected nor socially approved

Marriage: the legal union of a man and woman as husband and wife

Nonmarital Relationship: a sexual relationship between nonmarried individuals

Premarital Relationship: a sexual relationship that takes place prior to marriage

Incestuous Relationship: a sexual relationship between persons so closely related that law forbids them to marry

Extramarital Relationship: a sexual relationship with someone other than one's spouse

Different societies have different traditions regarding the choice of a marriage partner (Table 8.2). In most traditional societies, parents arrange the first marriage of a son or daughter (Frayser, 1985) in order to forge alliances with another family. In some societies the couple might not meet until the wedding night, but in the vast majority of cultures, the prospective bride and groom do have some influence over the marriage transaction (Fisher, 1992). After all, marriage in any society concerns not only the prospective bride and groom but the families of the bride and groom and their communities as well.

If you are like most other people in Western society, you probably scoff at the notion of **arranged marriages,** those in which the selection of a spouse is outside the control of the bride or groom, and have the romantic notion that you will choose (or have chosen) your spouse without any such outside influence or interference. But society influences our choice of partners in many subtle ways. When researchers examined unmarried American couples they found that dating couples are about as alike as those who are married. Over 90 percent of couples are of the same race or ethnicity, more than 80 percent are in the same age group and have similar levels of education, and 60 percent share the same religion (Michael et al. 1994). In North America, informal social networks play a strong role in dictating the course of attraction and mating. Laumann et al. (1994) found that other people, such as friends, coworkers, and family, introduce most individuals to their future sex partners. Some couples do start off by one person introducing himself or herself to the other; statistically, such self-introductions more commonly lead to short-term sexual affairs than to lasting relationships and marriage (ibid).

TABLE 8.2

Type of Marriage Arrangement in 86 Cultures

The individual selects and/or courts a partner autonomously; approval by parent or by others is unnecessary.
Males   30.6%
Females   7.5%

The individual selects and/or courts a partner autonomously; approval by parents, kin or the community is necessary or highly desirable.
Males   19.1%
Females   28.5%

The individual suggests a partner to parents or others and arrangements for courtship or marriage proceed if the choice is approved. Or parents ask approval of individual to initiate a match. Or parents approach the individual or others on behalf of a suitor and can accept or reject the match.
Males   3.2%
Females   2.5%

Both individual choice and arranged marriages are possible.
Males   17.8%
Females   17.4%

Parents choose a marriage partner but the individual can object.
Males   16.6%
Females   23.0%

Parents choose a marriage partner; individuals cannot easily object or rarely object.
Males   12.7%
Females   21.1%

SOURCE: Adapted from Broude & Green, 1976.

Arranged Marriage: any marriage in which the selection of a spouse is outside the control of the bride and groom

The places people meet their sex partners also reveal the more subtle aspects of social control. Laumann et al. (1994) divided meeting places into two categories: those anyone could enter (such as a public bar or beach) and "preselected" locales that allowed only certain people to be present (such as a classroom or private party). The preselected meeting places were much more effective locations in which to meet sex partners. Moreover, the sexual relationships were more likely to be long-term relationships (as opposed to temporary flings) if they started in preselected places.

Opportunities to establish romantic relationships with those who are different from us are limited. We reside in neighborhoods and attend schools and churches that largely are segregated by social class and race or ethnicity. At the age society expects serious premarital relationships to form, many Americans are in schools or colleges where courtship options are largely restricted to other students similar in social class, educational status, and occupational mobility. Other places you might meet a potential mate, such as fraternities and sororities, clubs and churches, are also socially homogeneous. Is it any wonder that most of us find ourselves in lifelong relationships with others much like ourselves?

Several hypotheses have been suggested on the causes of **endogamy** (marrying within one's own group): the preferences of marriage candidates for certain characteristics in a spouse, the interference of third parties in the selection process, and the constraints of the marriage market in which candidates are searching for a spouse. **Social dominance theory** asserts that those with high status have nothing to gain by intermarriage, and those with low status have nothing to lose. An investigation of attitudes toward interethnic or interracial dating by whites, blacks, Hispanics, and Asian Americans strongly supported this theory. Groups of higher status were significantly less positive about interracial or interethnic marriage than those within a lower status group (Fang et al., 1998).

However, dating patterns cannot be explained completely by social dominance theory. The National Health and Society Life Survey (NHSLS) (Laumann et al., 1994) found that African American women were least likely to have a spouse or sex partner from another race. Black men courted white, Asian American, Hispanic, and other women much more often than black women associated with men from those other ethnic groups. The reasons for this especially high rate of endogamy among black women are a matter of current debate among experts; additional data are needed on this topic.

WHEN? SOCIAL CONTROL AND THE TIMING OF SEXUAL RELATIONS

Societies have great influence over the timing of sexual relations; many have stiff regulations regarding the age at which it is appropriate to start having sex, and they less directly influence the age at which sexual activity should end. Age restrictions vary widely, and the rules for boys and girls may differ (this sexual double standard is discussed later in this chapter). The rules may also vary depending on whether the young person is married or single. The vast majority of sexually experienced 15- to 19-year-old males are unmarried, while two thirds or more of sexually experienced young women are married (Singh et al., 2000).

When to Start

As a child approaches physical maturity, there is a need for society to control sexual behavior because of the possibility of pregnancy (Barry & Schlegel, 1984). In some cultures, a female becomes a potential sexual partner upon her first menses; sexual relations with a premenarche child are generally forbidden. Historically, Western cultures have generally expected women to refrain from premarital sexual intercourse, while sometimes tolerating sexual experimentation by men. In a study of 114 societies, Broude and Greene (1976) found that 55 percent either disapproved of or disallowed

Endogamy: marriage within one's own group in accordance with custom or law

Social Dominance Theory: complex societies are group-based hierarchies in which the dominant group is characterized by possession and control over a disproportionately large share of the material and symbolic goods people desire; most forms of group conflict and oppression are manifestations of humans' predisposition toward these social hierarchies

Although child weddings are illegal in India, marriage laws are difficult to enforce in remote rural areas and thousands of traditional child marriage ceremonies occur each year.

premarital sex for females, 24 percent approved of female premarital sex, and 21 percent of the societies tolerated premarital sexual behavior if the female was discreet. Cross-culturally, males usually are expected to have had some sexual experience prior to marriage (Gregersen, 1994).

In some societies any type of sexual behavior (not just intercourse) is strongly discouraged from the time of infancy. Recall from Chapter 4 the Irish island of Inis Beag—in this culture mothers avoided breast-feeding, parents showed little physical affection to their children, nudity was considered disgusting, masturbation was frowned upon, and premarital sex was forbidden. At the other end of the spectrum, childhood sexual behavior was accepted as natural in the Trobriand Islands off the coast of New Guinea and among the Hopi of the American Southwest. Older Trobriand children and adolescents slept unsupervised in "bachelor" huts where intercourse was an expected activity (Malinowski, 1927). And, traditionally, Siriono children of lowland Bolivia were allowed to masturbate openly, and among the Alorese of Indonesia nursing mothers masturbated their infants in order to provide them pleasure (Ford & Beach, 1951).

Another culture with a more liberal attitude toward childhood sexuality was the Polynesian society of Mangaia (Marshall, 1971). As you learned in Chapter 4, Mangaians viewed sexuality as completely natural, and children were told folktales with detailed descriptions of sexual acts. During puberty, adolescents received detailed instructions in sexual technique; a high rate of sexual activity was encouraged both before and after marriage. Part of the rite of passage into manhood for a Mangaian boy was receiving instruction in sexual techniques from an older woman so that he learned to provide maximum pleasure to his partners.

The Sex in America survey found that most adolescents reported having intercourse, although sex tended to be sporadic during the teenage years (Michael et al., 1994). The survey found that men reported having lost their virginity at a younger age than women and blacks at a younger age than whites. The age at which 50 percent of those surveyed had intercourse was 15 for black men, 16 for Hispanic men, and 17 for white men. Among women, 50 percent of black women waited until they were nearly 17, and 50 percent of white women and Hispanic women waited until they were nearly 18. About 90 percent of the members of each group had intercourse by age 22 (Figure 8.1).

When to Stop

As mentioned earlier, a society also may influence the age at which it is considered appropriate to terminate sexual behavior. Typically our society associates sexuality with youth. Older people are often perceived as asexual. However, these perceptions are

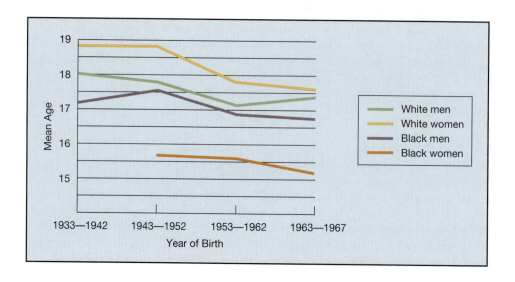

FIGURE 8.1 **Mean Age at First Intercourse.**

SOURCE: Adapted from Michael et al., 1994, p. 90.

changing (Miracle and Miracle, 2001). Winn and Newton (1982) found that 70 percent of the societies they studied had expectations of continued sexual activity for aging males. Similar reports about the continued sexual activity of aging women were found in 84 percent of the societies for which data were available. The cultural stereotype that sex is inappropriate for the elderly affects the sexuality of older adults more than any other factor. This stereotype affects the attitudes of younger people toward their elders as well as the way that older people think about themselves. The beliefs that older people shouldn't have sexual feelings or have diminished sexual capacity, can affect your own sexuality as you get older.

Age is only one way society influences the timing of sex. Societies can also establish preferences for the time of day or place certain days off limits. As we discussed in Chapter 2, in some cultures women are considered unfit for sexual relations during their menstrual flow. Men also may be banned from engaging in sexual relations with a woman who has recently given birth. This ban may extend for a fixed period of time, such as a year, or the woman may be forbidden sexual relations as long as she is nursing—which may continue for several years.

The myth that sex is inappropriate for older couples affects their sexuality.

Sexual Frequency

How often do you think Americans have sex? Despite the media images that bombard us, maybe not as often as you might think. Sex with a spouse on Saturday night might be the norm for some people. Others may have sexual relations daily, still others only a few times a year. Who has the most sex? Perhaps surprisingly, it is not single people but those who are married or living together. See Table 8.3 for information on who is doing it, and how often.

The data presented in Table 8.3 suggest how strongly social arrangements affect the frequency of sex. Those in socially structured relationships such as marriage or **cohabitation** ("living together") have the most frequent sex. Those looking for a partner, partners without easy access to a place to have sex, or those in relationships without a routine in which sex is expected or is legitimate are less likely to have sex. "They may have more partners, but they will have less sex" (Michael et al., 1994, p. 119).

When in a Relationship Should Sex Occur?

Try to guess the answer to the following two questions before reading further. What percent of married couples in modern America had sex within 2 days (48 hours) after they first met? And, what percent knew each other for more than a year before they

Cohabitation: to live together in a sexual relationship, especially when not legally married

---

TABLE 8.3

	Frequency of Sex in the Past 12 Months					
	Married Men	**Married Women**	**Cohabiting Men/ Never married**	**Cohabiting Women/ Never married**	**Non- cohabiting Men/ Never married**	**Non- cohabiting Women/ Never married**
Never	1%	3%	0%	1%	22%	30%
A few times a year	13	12	9	7	26	24
A few times a month	43	47	36	32	25	26
2-3 times a week	36	32	37	43	19	13
4 or more times a week	7	7	19	17	8	7

SOURCE: Adapted from Michael et al., 1992, p. 116.

first had sex? Most long-term romantic relationships eventually involve some sexual activity. But when should sex start? The norms differ widely among cultures, communities, and historical periods.

People tend to be misled about what other people are doing. Cohen and Shotland (1996) asked college students how many dates they thought other men or women would have before they had sex, and how long they would wait. The men said that they themselves expected to have sex after about 11 dates, but they thought the "average man" would expect to have sex after 3 or 4 dates. A similar discrepancy was found among the women. On average, the women said they would probably have sex after about 18 dates, but they thought the "average woman" would have sex after 13 or 14.

Thus, most people seem to overestimate how fast other people are leaping into bed with each other. And most people think their own practices are slower than average. It seems likely that the mass media have contributed to this pattern of *pluralistic ignorance*, a term coined in 1996 by two sex researchers (Cohen and Shotland, 1996). In the movies, people meet and quickly begin to have great sex. In normal life, however, people proceed much more slowly.

Finally, here's the answer you've been waiting for. The NHSLS (Laumann et al., 1994) concluded that only 1.4 percent of marriages consisted of people who had sex within 2 days after meeting. (Love at first sight is thus not as common a pattern as the movies would lead you to believe!) Moreover, almost half the couples surveyed (47%) knew each other for a year before they started having sex. Although the couple might have known each other at work or in school or in other ways for a long time before they expressed any romantic interest, getting to know your partner first seems to be a much more common pathway into marriage than love at first sight.

Is the situation different in short-term sexual affairs compared to long-term married relationships? Yes—but not all that much. In sexual affairs that lasted a very short time, from one-night stands to a week or two, again more couples (25%) knew each other for a year or more before they had sex; only 14 percent had sex within 48 hours after meeting for the first time (Laumann et al., 1994). Even one-night stands are more common between people who have known each other a long time than between people who have just met.

WHERE? HOW SOCIETY INFLUENCES THE LOCATION OF SEXUAL ACTIVITY

Most animals will have sex just about anywhere. Privacy and modesty regarding sexual behavior are distinctively human concerns (Fisher, 1992; Friedl, 1995). For many reasons, society limits public sexual expression. And it exerts its effects on private sexual activity as well. In the privacy of your own home, do you limit sexual behavior to certain rooms? For some, "proper" sexual activity takes place only in the bedroom. What do you think about sex in the kitchen?

Privacy

While Colonial Americans equated nudity and sexual behavior with sin, the small size of Colonial dwellings often interfered with privacy and allowed children to hear or see sexual activity among adults. Frequently family members all slept in the same room with only curtains dividing the beds; in some cases, whole families had to share a bed. Even those couples who escaped their children's eyes and ears found it difficult to avoid those of their neighbors in the loosely constructed houses of the era; people had little privacy (D'Emilio & Freedman, 1988).

In the not too distant past, neighbors did not discuss the physical details of what they did in bed. The rules were unspoken but clearly understood. If you talked about sex (and it really was better not to), then you could use vague terms or tell a sexual joke among gender peers, but you could never admit to having any personal problems or sexual concerns (Levine, 1992). Today the boundaries are not quite so clear. It is not terribly unusual for people to discuss their sex lives with close friends or, as anyone who watches daytime television knows, to discuss their sexual activities in explicit detail with millions of strangers.

Modesty

Sexual modesty and dress codes have existed since our Cro-Magnon ancestors fashioned leather tunics to cover their naked bodies (Fisher, 1992). Socially approved body coverings may vary widely (see CROSS-CULTURAL PERSPECTIVES box), but each society has restrictions on what body parts may be exposed to the public. We can learn a lot about a society's views of sexuality by examining its use of fashion to control nudity. The body parts that are concealed, revealed, emphasized, or enhanced reflect which body parts or physical features are considered attractive by a particular society.

In many cultures, nudity and sexual lust are symbolically linked. Christian missionaries to the Hawaiian Islands helped invent the muumuu to cover the breasts of native women because of their belief that nudity and sexuality were associated with sin. In many

CROSS-CULTURAL PERSPECTIVES

Of Penis Sheaths and Foreskin Ties

Generally, Western cultures equate nudity with exposure of the genitals or breasts, but in other cultures there is great variation in appropriate, modest attire. For example, many tropical societies—from New Guinea to the South American Amazon—consider an adult male sufficiently clothed as long as the glans of his penis does not show. In these societies men wear nothing more than a gourd or grass **penis sheath** *tied around the foreskin to prevent the glans from showing should a man have an erection. The shaft of the penis and the scrotum are of no concern and require no more covering than breasts—male or female.*

In the Amazon, the Tapirape culture displayed a variation of the penis sheath covering. Adult Tapirape males pulled the foreskin forward and tied it tightly with a twine to prevent the glans from ever showing in public (Wagley, 1977). This grass string was all the clothing that was required. However, with the foreskin tied shut, a man could not urinate in a stream, so he squatted, like women do.

Men and women of the Amazonian Yanomamo, who live along the border of Brazil and Venezuela, might appear to be naked to an outsider, but if you asked a Yanomamo woman to remove the thin

Mek warrier wearing a penis sheath

cord belt around her waist, she would respond in much the same way a North American woman would if you asked her to remove her blouse.

A Yanomamo man wears a string around his abdomen into which he tucks the foreskin of his penis so that his genitals lie closely against his stomach. Should a Yanomamo man's penis slip from place, he would likely react very similarly to a North American man discovering that his fly was open in public (Fisher, 1992).

As Western style clothing spreads throughout the world, more and more men wear trousers. The wearing of a penis sheath or foreskin tie is less obvious, but it has not disappeared altogether. Many traditional men continue to wear them underneath their trousers.

Penis Sheath: object or material that is tied around the foreskin to prevent the glans from showing should a man have an erection

Christian missionaries often covered the breasts of native women because of their beliefs that nudity was associated with sin.

Middle- and upper-class Victorian women were careful not to dress in a provocative or revealing manner. They bound their curves in corsets and wore long-sleeved dresses that hung an inch off the ground.

Islamic cultures women must be veiled from head to toe because of the belief that women are highly seductive. Faithful Mormons are required to wear a sacred garment at all times, even when having intercourse.

The Puritans dictated that clothing have no color or decoration that might distract them from their devotion to God. In the Victorian era, women were covered in high-necked dresses that went to the ground, with bloomers and crinolines underneath. In the 19th century, class strictures in Western societies were different for women than for men. The tightly corseted clothing for fashionable women in the 1800s "had elements of social control since it exemplified the dominant and very restrictive conception of women's roles" (Crane, 2000, p. 16). The bustles and tightly laced corsets of the turn of the century emphasized the breasts and hips while the flapper ideal of the 1920s required bound breasts to appear flat and straight. With the greater freedom after World War II came lower-cut and tighter women's clothing. The sexual revolution of the 1960s spawned miniskirts and hot pants (Glynn, 1982; Steele, 1985).

Although the *codpiece*, worn by European males during the 14th to 16th centuries (Figure 8.2), not only protected the penis but exaggerated its dimensions, the expression of sexuality in men's clothes was largely taboo in Western society until the 1970s when tight blue jeans became fashionable. Gender-bending fashion of the '70s, as personified by musicians such as Boy George, produced a "radical attack on the way in which dress encodes and prescribes gender" (Evans & Thornton, 1989, p. 7).

Today's fashion magazines are filled with breasts, buttocks, and midriffs, and transparent materials often reveal as much as they conceal. While in the past, female nudity may have evoked powerlessness and subordination, some contemporary clothing

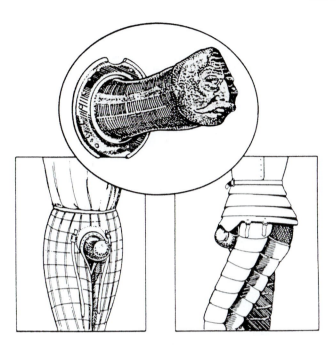

FIGURE 8.2   Codpieces.

CAMPUS CONFIDENTIAL

"I went to a nude beach for the first time when I was on vacation last year. I was pretty nervous. I don't think of myself as being a prude, but I'm not an exhibitionist either and I'm not used to parading naked in front of strangers. Naturally I worried about how my body looks. I'm not a total slob, but I'm not in the greatest shape these days. No one would rate me a perfect '10' but there really weren't any '10s' on the beach that day. Believe me, I looked and there was lots of jiggling flesh and bobbing body parts. I didn't want to be rude or crude looking at people, and, while there was a lot of looking going on, to my surprise, very little leering. People seemed to be comfortable with their nudity and, after a while, I became pretty comfortable too and just enjoyed a day at the beach. The best thing about a nude beach? No tan lines and no expensive bathing suit. The worst thing? Getting sunburned in very sensitive places."

designers interpret sexuality as a form of female power and control. Underwear as outerwear, body piercing, and leather items that were once viewed as fetishistic are now incorporated into mainstream fashion. Perhaps no item of clothing has changed as much as the bathing suit, which has gone from full-body covering attire to thong bikinis to nothing at all (see CAMPUS CONFIDENTIAL box). You may be surprised to learn that in the early years of the 20th century, men could be arrested on beaches if their bathing suits did not cover their chests (Capuzzo, 2001).

Clothing is a form of symbolic communication that can convey many different social and sexual messages. Some suggest that economics has an influence on how we dress (see CONSIDERATIONS box). Although clothing conveys both accurate and inaccurate messages about the wearer, the legal community often assumes that dress is an indication of the wearer's attitude or intent (Lennon et al., 1999). For example, if a woman was wearing a low-cut blouse when she was raped, it might be assumed that she was "asking for it," making prosecution more difficult. Fashionable clothing is also used to make statements about social class and social identity, but among these statements are important messages about the ways in which women and men perceive their gender roles (cf. Schwartz & Rutter, 1998).

CONSIDERATIONS

Skirt Lengths Go Up as the Stock Market Goes Down

Data from three studies of clothing fashion from 1885 to 1976 were used to establish a link between women's dress styles and the state of the economy. According to the findings, when the economy is bad, short skirts, narrow waists, and low necklines are popular, suggesting that women use these styles to signal their reproductive value. In other words, when the economy is bad, women are more likely to use clothing to advertise their availability (Barber, 1999).

?

What type of economic forecast and social message would maxiskirts and turtlenecks send?

—*Do you think women consciously use fashion to meet their economic needs?*

—*Do you think fashion is a reliable economic indicator?*

HOW? SOCIAL REGULATION OF SEXUAL BEHAVIOR

We have already seen some of the ways in which societies regulate sexuality. Other controls include restrictions on the use of sexual language and other overt and covert restraints on male and female sexuality.

Sexual Language

Language restrictions and prohibitions are a subtle yet effective way that societies control sexuality. Such rules originated in the belief that if people didn't have the vocabulary, they wouldn't talk about sex or do it (Wilson, 1972). From the time of the Puritans until very recently, an entire vocabulary of sexual terms has been banned in Anglo-American culture. The noted sexologist John Money says that the notorious word "f—" was originally a quite respectable word in the English language that could be used as freely as any other, then it became "an unspeakable, unprintable outcast," (Money, 1985, p. 15), and is only now slowly returning to more widespread usage.

Our lack of a sexual vocabulary has its roots in childhood. Children are routinely taught to name their body parts: "This is your nose; these are your toes; this is your elbow and this is your peepee." Only the sexual body parts are not given their correct names. How many mothers teach their daughters the word clitoris? How many fathers use the word testes or testicles when talking to their sons? In a study of 90 children ages 2 to 16 years, there were 37 different words and phrases used to describe genitalia. More than a third of the children used the term *private* to represent vagina, breasts, penis or anus (Cheung, 1999). School dictionaries and library books often contain no words for sexual anatomy or sexual practices. As we become adults, we may learn the correct terminology but often continue to have two separate sexual vocabularies. On formal occasions, the anatomically correct terms are used, but in informal conversations among friends or during sexual encounters "dirty" words are prevalent (Levine, 1992).

Seven Dirty Words

CONSIDERATIONS

Comedian George Carlin's (1999) monologue "Seven Dirty Words You Can Never Say on Television" was the subject of a 1974 Supreme Court decision that established indecency regulation in broadcasting for over two decades. As Carlin said in his monologue: "There are some people who would have you not use certain words. Yeah, there are 400,000 words in the English language and there are seven of them that you can't say on television . . . they must really be bad. They'd have to be outrageous to be separated from a group that large. There are no bad words. Bad thoughts. Bad intentions."

The authors of this text considered including a list of slang terms for sexual organs and sexual acts in order to demonstrate how the use of language is constrained by society—such as Carlin's seven words (most of which are used freely on television today) and other phrases that everyone knows and uses frequently but that are considered "dirty." However, it was decided that this list of terms would not be included in the textbook because it might be construed as offensive to some readers.

This is an example of social control. Social control is effective because it calls everything but the "mainstream" into question; it makes you hesitate as an individual because an unidentified "someone" or nonspecific "others" might object. George Carlin had to deal with television censors, but social control does not require actual threat of sanctions to coerce you into curbing your behaviors and aligning them with the perceived way of doing things.

Of course, large and powerful institutions in society—government, large businesses, and social organizations of all kinds—have the most influence in social control. Most of us conform rather than risk embarrassment, ostracism, or loss of opportunity or income. Social control is extremely effective because humans are social animals who seek the benefits of society and social interaction. Most of us are willing to trade some individual expression, or even a sense of moral authority, for the possible benefits of conforming—at least to a limited extent.

 Can you identify areas in which you have curbed your behavior or limited your individual expression recently rather than risk what you perceived might be negative social opinion?

—Have you ever restrained or modified your sexual expression because of social controls or sanctions?

—Was it worth it? How do you know?

Controlling Female Sexuality

As you learned earlier, the majority of a society's efforts to stifle sexuality have been directed toward women. The methods and techniques used to enforce these efforts vary widely. Many rely on informal social pressures. In Western culture, the fear of getting a bad reputation and being ostracized by peers has been one major way that girls have been influenced to restrain their sexual desires. In his classic study of American high-school life during the late 1950s, Coleman (1961) found that girls (much more than boys) regarded "having a good reputation" as crucial for being accepted in the elite cliques and circles in the teenage social scene. Girls spent a great deal of time discussing the social and sexual activities of other girls, and they would refuse to socialize with a girl who was perceived as having "gone too far." Despite the activities of the Sexual Revolution, in the 1960s American women still upheld the ideal of remaining a virgin until they married; a woman who lost her virginity was typically reluctant to tell her friends and anticipated that they would disapprove (Carns, 1973).

In some cultures, more extreme practices are used to curtail female sexuality. One of the most extreme is **female genital mutilation,** a series of procedures in which all or a portion of the external female genitalia is removed for cultural, religious, or other nontherapeutic reasons. The World Health Organization (2000) has identified four types of female genital mutilation that are practiced worldwide today. All of these are usually performed by a nonmedical practitioner without anesthesia and in unhygienic conditions on girls at an early age, before they can make an informed decision. The procedure is irreversible. Type I, incorrectly referred to as **female circumcision,** involves the excision of the clitoral hood, with or without excision of part or all of the clitoris. Type II, **clitoridectomy,** is the excision of the clitoris with partial or total excision of the labia minora. This is the most common type of procedure, accounting for up to 80 percent of all cases. Type III, **infibulation,** is the excision of part or all of the external genitalia and stitching or narrowing of the vaginal opening. This is considered to be the most extreme form of female genital mutilation and accounts for about 15 percent of all procedures. Type IV may involve pricking, piercing, or incising of the clitoris or the labia; stretching of the clitoris or labia; cauterization by burning of the clitoris and surrounding tissue; scraping of tissue surrounding the vagina (angurya cuts) or cutting of the vagina (gishiri cuts); or introduction of corrosive substances or herbs into the vagina to cause bleeding for the purpose of tightening or narrowing it. After marriage the vulva is cut open to allow for coitus with the woman's husband. All of these procedures decrease the pleasure women receive during sex, and they may even make it painful to have intercourse.

It is estimated that nearly 100 million women, mostly Muslims, have undergone some form of clitoridectomy, mostly in Africa, Asia and the Middle East. With increased emigration, clitoridectomies are now performed in Europe, Australia, and North America (World Health Organization, 2000), despite strict laws against it in many of these places.

Sociological reasons for female genital mutilation include identification with one's cultural heritage, participation in an initiation rite into womanhood, social integration, and the maintenance of social cohesion. Psychosexual reasons to attenuate female sexual desire include maintenance of chastity and virginity before marriage and fidelity during marriage, and to increase male sexual pleasure by tightening the vagina. In particular, girls are sometimes told that no man will marry them unless they have had this operation, although the available evidence suggests that men are willing to marry women with intact genitals and even prefer them. Shandall (1967, 1979) surveyed a large sample of Sudanese men, all of who had both a genitally intact wife and a genitally mutilated wife, and he found that the men nearly unanimously preferred the intact wife. It is perhaps not surprising that men prefer to make love to a partner who can enjoy sex herself, rather than one who finds it painful and unrewarding. Along the same lines, Lightfoot-Klein (1989) observed that Muslim men in nations where female genital surgery was performed routinely expressed a widespread preference for European women (who had not had the surgery), because they were more likely to enjoy sex.

"Most of the world's women do not control when, with whom, and with what protection, if any, they have sexual relations"

(WORLD HEALTH ORGANIZATION, 2000).

Female Genital Mutilation: surgical procedures in which all or a portion of the external female genitalia is removed for cultural, religious, or other nontherapeutic reasons

Female Circumcision: surgical removal of the prepuce, with or without excision of part or the entire clitoris

Clitoridectomy: surgical removal of the clitoris

Infibulation: surgical removal of part or all of the external genitalia and stitching or narrowing of the vaginal opening

CONSIDERATIONS

Mutilation of Women by Women

The social influences restraining female sexuality generally come from the community of women. Female genital surgery is no exception. When over 5,800 Sudanese women were asked about their own circumcisions as well as those done or planned for their daughters, close to 90 percent either had circumcised or planned to circumcise all of their daughters. Roughly half of those women reported favoring the most severe procedures, and many said they would do so even if the father was opposed to the practice (Williams & Sobieszczyk, 1997).

The decision about whether and when a particular girl will receive the operation is usually made by her mother or grandmother (Hicks, 1996; Lighfoot-Klein, 1989). Girls who have not yet had it are sometimes teased or put down by their female peers; having the operation confers higher status in the female adolescent peer group (Lightfoot-Klein, 1989). A woman such as a midwife, with only other women in attendance, nearly always performs the operation itself. In some cultures men are completely excluded according to one work on the topic (Boddy, 1989). The practices are defended and supported by women, while the men generally claim to be indifferent or even opposed to the practice (Boddy, 1989, 1998; Lightfoot-Klein, 1989; Williams & Sobieszczyk, 1997).

Many Western feminists and human rights activists have sought a worldwide ban on clitoridectomy. Critics believe that Westerners are intruding on what should be autonomous cultural traditions and beliefs, and that outsiders should not meddle in another society's affairs. Alice Walker (1993), among others, responds that "torture is not culture" and that subjecting females to a life with pain, increased risk for AIDS, infection, and possible death, and bereft of sexual pleasure, is unconscionable. In contrast, Germaine Greer (1999) has emphasized that female genital surgery is rooted in the community of women and is supported and carried out by women. She argues that Western feminists should respect the rights and values of female communities in other parts of the world and understand that these women may have important reasons for continuing these practices.

It is probably no coincidence that female genital surgery is practiced most in cultures where women face severe, pervasive disadvantages and lack legal, financial, occupational, and other rights. In such cultures, sex is the main asset a woman has, and female genital surgery may improve the value of that asset. If clitoridectomy were banned without making other improvements in women's opportunities, women in these cultures might be even worse off than they are now.

 Does its value in strengthening the position of women justify the practice of clitoridectomy?

Controlling Male Sexuality

Although some cultures practice rituals similar to clitoridectomy on males, control of male sexuality usually is handled formally by means of explicit laws, as well as by peer pressure. According to statistics from the Federal Bureau of Investigation (FBI, 1998), men account for 99 percent of the arrests for rape, 40 percent of the arrests for prostitution and commercial sex, and 93 percent of arrests for all other sex crimes. Men have historically dominated the arenas of politics and legislation, which reveals an interesting parallel in terms of same-gender control of sexuality. Men make laws that mainly restrict the sexual behavior of men, while women exert the social pressures that restrict the sexual behavior of women.

WHY? REASONS FOR SOCIAL CONTROL OF SEXUALITY

Unlike most other species, humans regularly engage in nonreproductive sexual behavior—sex for the fun of it. Consequently we have developed rules and regulations to govern individual sexual relationships. There are many practical reasons for societies' attempts to control sex, including population control, reducing conflict, economic production, disease control, the protection of individuals from sexual harm, and the determination of paternity. Societies also may want to restrict sex in order to prevent social disorder. One study found that the increased incidence of multiple sexual partners is correlated with increases in the rates of out-of-wedlock pregnancy,

Overpopulation: having too many people for the amount of food, materials, and space available

Underpopulation: having too few people to provide protection and other resources for a community

CROSS-CULTURAL PERSPECTIVES

Male Genital Mutilation

In an extreme form of male circumcision practiced by the Dowayo of West Africa, the entire shaft of the penis is peeled. Among certain Arab groups, the penis, scrotum, inner legs, and belly below the navel are cut without the use of an anesthetic. The brides-to-be of the young men are present at the ceremony and may refuse to marry if he so much as flinches during the cutting ceremony. (This contrasts with the surgeries on girls, which

men are not generally permitted to attend.) In some Polynesian societies the foreskin is not totally removed but the penis is slit lengthwise down to the urethra.

Only four societies are known to practice, or have practiced, removal of a testicle. The reasons for this ritual are not entirely clear, but to perform the operation on oneself seems to have been considered especially brave (Gregersen, 1994).

infant mortality, violent crimes, and poor educational achievement (Immerman & Mackey, 1999). All of these outcomes may create problems for society, so it is understandable that societies may sometimes try to influence sexual attitudes and behaviors.

Population Control

Heterosexual intercourse leads to babies. Too many or too few babies can create social problems. **Overpopulation,** having too many people for the amount of food, materials, and space available, can lead to mass starvation if the society cannot produce enough food for everyone. Societies facing overpopulation may try to restrict sex to prevent too many babies from being born. **Underpopulation,** the lack of population density, can leave a community at the mercy of its enemies, either through political pressure or warfare. For example, in a society in which population determines political representation,

Bad To The Bone

CONSIDERATIONS

Status as well as gender can determine social control of sexual behavior. Traditionally, in cases involving sexual misconduct, the higher the status of the accused, the lighter the punishment. Historically, punishment for rape cases heavily depended on the social standing, class, and race of both the assailant and the victim. Men of high social standing were unlikely to be brought to trial or convicted. The harshest penalties—castration and lynching—were applied to black men who sexually attacked, or in some cases were simply thought to desire, white women. Some believe that, in some ways, things may not have changed much from Colonial times to the present; the poor are still likely to suffer harsher forms of justice in such matters (D'Emilio & Freedman, 1988).

The opposite point of view is that the upper socioeconomic classes are subjected to *more* scrutiny and *higher* standards than the lower classes. In the United States, for example, premarital sex and out-of-wedlock babies became widespread and accepted in the poor

black community at a time when such acts were highly stigmatized in the more affluent white community. In the 1990s, the most powerful man in the world—President Clinton—was humiliated publicly (with worldwide news coverage) and nearly removed from his job as a result of having consensual oral sex with a young woman on his staff. Millions of poor and unknown men have done similar things with no apparent penalty.

 Why do you think the revelation that Jesse Jackson had a child out of wedlock received relatively little attention in the national media?

—*Who do you think has the most active sex lives— the rich, the poor, or the middle class?*

—*Who is most affected by messages of sexual restraint?*

—*At what level of society is sexual prudery most powerful?*

a decrease in numbers can mean a decrease in the number of politicians representing the community's interests. A society in such a predicament might prohibit birth control in order to increase the number of babies that each couple produces.

Consider the case of the Northern Cheyenne (see CROSS-CULTURAL PERSPECTIVES box for more on the Cheyenne). As hunter-gatherers on the Great Plains of North America during the 18th and early 19th centuries they needed to limit population growth because of the limited availability of food. This was accomplished through a complex system of values and behaviors. The Cheyenne had a policy of strict lifelong monogamy and they highly valued the parental role. It was believed that each child was special and deserved the full, undivided attention of the parents. After the birth of a son, a man might make a vow of celibacy so that he would not be distracted from the instruction of his child for several years. The result was a stable population that closely approximated zero population growth.

However, after decades of warfare with the U.S. Army in the later half of the 19th century, the reproductive needs of the Cheyenne changed drastically. When the remnant bands were herded onto reservations in the 1880s, the Cheyenne realized that

CROSS-CULTURAL PERSPECTIVES

The Sun Dance of the Cheyenne in the 19th Century

The focusing theme of the Sun Dance is world renewal; the purpose of the ceremony is to make the whole world over again. Prayers associated with the Sun Dance ask for growth of the world and its animals, birds, and people, and for blessing of stones, trees, grass, sunshine, and rainfall. As a result of this religious ceremony, the earth blesses the Cheyenne with abundance and they rejoice.

A pledger makes a vow to the supernatural forces to organize the Sun Dance; with the help of his extended family he accumulates the necessary food and gifts to sponsor the event. During the ceremony and the preparatory acts leading up to it, the pledger is called "The Reproducer" or "Multiplier," because through his initiative and sacrifice the tribe is reborn and will increase in numbers. However, from the moment of making the vow until the completion of the dance, the pledger and his wife must express no sexual desire; it is believed that sexual intercourse during this period would cause them to die.

At the designated time and place, a lodge is built around a tall center pole topped by a phallic rawhide effigy. Upon its completion the tribal priests consecrate the Sun Dance Lodge. Then the high

priest and the pledger's wife, wrapped in a buffalo robe, have sexual intercourse so that all that lives may be born. Any child resulting from this sexual act is considered very special. This act is the most solemn part of the ceremony; it is followed by four days of continuous dancing.

Following the dance, men who have taken a vow participate in self-torture as a form of religious sacrifice. The sacrifice involves the insertion of skewers through one's skin and then pulling against the skewers until they are ripped or cut free. The sacrifice is made as a result of a voluntary vow in the hopes of obtaining the "pity" of supernatural spirits, and thus achieving good fortune—perhaps the restoration of health to a loved one. Participation also brings public approval and social prestige. Such self-sacrifice does not contribute to the earth-renewal purposes of the Sun Dance, nor is it done on behalf of the tribe as a whole.

Though some elements have changed, today the Sun Dance is often celebrated on July 4th, thus linking the Cheyenne's revitalization of the world to the celebration of the birth of the nation (Adapted from Hoebel, 1978).

they needed to promote population growth if their society was to have any chance for survival. At that time, the population consisted largely of women, children, and the elderly. There were not enough men to serve as husbands for all the marriageable women, many of whom were war widows. Yet every fertile woman needed to have as many children as possible if a viable population base was to be restored. So, the traditional beliefs in strict monogamy and celibacy changed as women began having children outside marriage. This change in values was reflected in the increased emphasis on the Sun Dance, a fertility ceremony that the Cheyenne adopted at about the same time warfare began to deplete the male population (Hoebel, 1978).

A society's population depends most directly on its number of young women, because of the 9-month gestation period required for the birth of a child. To keep the population down, societies may try to regulate the number of women. Female infanticide is an extreme strategy that has been adopted at various times and places—from New Guinea to the Amazon Basin (Harris, 1975). Female infants are put to death (or allowed to die through benign neglect) while male infants are kept and nurtured. For example, among the Yanomamo of lowland South America, men demand that their firstborn child be male; thus women kill their infant daughters until they can present a male baby (Chagnon, 1968). In other societies, such as among traditional Tapirapé in Brazil, infanticide was practiced to control family size because there was no effective birth control available (Wagley, 1977). Based on fieldwork conducted from 1939 to 1940, Charles Wagley reported "an ironclad rule" that no woman should have more than three living children, and no more than two could be of the same sex (Ibid, p. 135). The motivation or rationale for this practice was to avoid hunger. However, it offered the latent functions of maintaining zero population growth and a balanced male:female ratio in society.

Female infanticide is not condoned in any present-day nation, but modern practices sometimes lead to an artificial imbalance in the sex ratio. For example, a traditional preference for sons in India led to the use of ultrasound and amniocentesis to determine the sex of fetuses so that females could be aborted—a practice the government has tried to combat. Similarly, male children are preferred in Chinese society, and a byproduct of China's one-child rule has been an increase in the rate of abortions of female fetuses.

The Reproduction/Production Relationship   The link between food supply and sexual rules is called the **reproduction/production relationship.** All societies are concerned with having enough food and resources for their present and future members. Food production is closely related to the resources of the environment in which the society is located and the technology available to exploit those resources. The mix of these environmental and technological variables changes over time, whether through the development of new farming tools, a disastrous drought, or a sudden influx of new neighbors. When a society has no effective means of increasing food production, it usually discourages births; when a society perceives resources as plentiful, it may change that policy. Religion, social prestige, status rewards, and even material rewards all have been used by societies to encourage conformity to social ideals, whether that means having large families or small ones.

For example, China has enforced its one-child policy chiefly by means of material benefits: Families that have extra children are penalized financially. In contrast, the United States seeks to encourage people to have children: the government provides tax deductions to parents for each child, even though one might argue that parents ought to pay extra taxes (because they require more government services, such as public schools). Some European countries (notably Germany) are quite concerned about low birth rates and have steadily increased the material incentives for parents, such as paying parents a substantial amount of money for having a child and guaranteeing all parents several years of leave from their jobs each time they have a child. In 2001, the German government paid all parents $122 per month tax-free for their first child, from birth until the age of 18 (longer if the child goes to a university). The second child

Reproduction/Production Relationship: the link between sex and a community having enough food and resources for their present and future members

brings another allowance of the same size, and additional children bring even larger monthly checks. A family with five children automatically receives about $700 every month and is eligible for additional government grants.

Conflict Reduction

Another reason that societies regulate sex is to reduce conflict. According to the eminent sexologist Ira Reiss (1986), some form of sexual possessiveness and jealousy is found in every known society. There is no disputing the fact that sexual jealousies and rivalries produce considerable anguish and conflict—and in countless cases, dangerous outbursts of violence. Jealousy is a leading cause of violent behavior between partners. Men and (less often) women have been known to attack and even murder someone who is having sex with their partner. Even collective violence, ranging from the Trojan War in antiquity (which was set off when the Trojan prince stole the beautiful Helen from her husband, the king of Sparta) to gang wars in modern urban ghettoes, has been stimulated by romantic rivalries. By regulating sexual behavior, a society may hope to reduce the violence that can arise from sexual competition. For example, legal penalties could offer jealous partners a way to get satisfaction without having to resort to violence.

Disease Control

Some societies may try to restrict sexuality in order to limit the spread of sexually transmitted disease, which has been a problem throughout history. In the 1970s, when the Sexual Revolution was at its peak, many people engaged in premarital and extramarital sex and experimented with multiple partners. One consequence was that many sexually transmitted infections spread rapidly, ranging from the familiar ones such as gonorrhea and syphilis to the newer threats of herpes and HIV/AIDS (see Chapter 7 for more on this). As a result, in the 1980s and 1990s there was a shift toward a less promiscuous and more restricted pattern of sexual behavior.

Although the Sexual Revolution and its backlash may have been extreme in a historical sense, this pattern is not unique. Following a period of limited sexual behavior, sexually transmitted infections become relatively scarce. People then begin to have sex more frequently and with more partners without much danger. But the increased sexual activity is gradually followed by the spread of diseases. As the danger of disease and evidence of its effects becomes apparent, people begin to perceive promiscuity as dangerous, causing them to change their own behavior and put pressure on their children to restrict sexual behavior. Because the diseases cannot flourish when sexual behavior is restricted, they die down, thereby paving the way for another cycle.

CROSS-CULTURAL PERSPECTIVES

Just Say No

Although an estimated 700 Kenyans die every day from AIDS and despite public service jingles that encourage "Sema Nami" ("Let's Talk" about AIDS), most obituaries refer only to a "mysterious" illness as the cause of AIDS-related deaths. Kenya's president Daniel arap Moi admitted that he is embarrassed to talk about condoms. In 2000 a German-based condom manufacturer planned to build a factory in Kenya that could have produced millions of condoms, but was so discouraged by government red tape and a lack of responsiveness that it moved its project to South Africa. Although in 2001 Moi's government arranged to import 300 million condoms as part of a campaign to control the rapid increase in AIDS, the President advised citizens to avoid sex rather than encourage condom use and urged all Kenyans to go without sex for 2 years.

Bailey and Aunger (1995) provided a revealing portrait of the costs of sexual permissiveness in a study of several societies in central Africa. In these cultures, there was little pressure to restrict sexual behavior. Women were not expected to remain virgins until they married, and extramarital sexual affairs were common and reasonably well accepted. Young unmarried men claimed to have an average of five different partners per year, and men in their 30s and 40s typically reported having two or three extramarital sex partners each year. Sound appealing? The costs, particularly the incidence of sexually transmitted infections, were tremendous. Nine out of every 10 men had contracted gonorrhea. In each of the tribal groups in the study, over one third of the women remained childless throughout life, not usually by choice. Most women wanted children and indeed a large family was regarded as a wonderful thing to have, but as you learned in Chapter 7, many sexually transmitted infections can destroy a woman's ability to have children. Bailey and Aunger found that most people seemed to understand that having sex with many partners led to these results, but the regret over these tragic outcomes had not yet resulted in widespread changes in sexual attitudes and practices.

Protection From Harm

Some societies seek to regulate sex because they believe that sex, or at least certain kinds of sex, can be harmful. This belief is not necessarily related to the consequences of sex, such as pregnancy or disease. In some cases sex becomes the focus of moral and religious concerns. Other societies may make legislative efforts to prevent unwanted sex acts from occurring. In such processes, the opinions of politically dominant groups may become law, even if no immediate practical reason can be cited.

One example of such a law concerns oral sex. Laws prohibiting oral sex, which exist in some states, do not accomplish any discernible goal—they do not control the population or prevent any diseases not already spread by genital intercourse. Instead, the religious leaders who established many American communities decades or even centuries ago regarded these sex acts as sinful, and the prohibitions remain on the books today.

Laws forbidding sex between adults and children are particularly strict. Many societies believe that sex can be harmful to children so they have made great efforts to shield children from exposure to information about sex. Although many of the bans on selling pornographic and erotic materials have been lifted in the United States in response to concerns about freedom of expression, the sale of such material to children continues to be forbidden. The entertainment industry is constantly under pressure to prevent children from seeing sexually explicit material.

Most societies have rules to prohibit rape and punish rapists. By and large, these laws focus on men forcing women to have sex against their will, although occasionally there are efforts to prosecute women who force themselves on men or people who commit homosexual rape. In any case, most societies seem to recognize that certain acts of sex are inherently wrong and therefore ought to be forbidden. Would you want to live in a society that failed to censor rape by imposing negative sanctions on those who commit rape?

Paternity Uncertainty and Inheritance

Violence is not the only social problem that accompanies unrestricted sex. Until the recent advent of DNA testing, there was no scientific way to know for certain the identity of the father of a particular child. If a woman had sex with several different men in the same time period, her child might be descended from any of them.

Since a baby emerges directly from the woman's body, maternity is less ambiguous. This imbalance creates more social pressure on women to be faithful. Certainly most societies have had stricter rules and more severe punishments for female infidelity than for male infidelity.

Theoretically, if men did not worry about whether the children were biologically their descendents, restrictions on female sexual behavior would be less important. For example, if a society existed in a setting where possessions were few or transient and money was unknown or unimportant, paternity might be relatively unimportant. In hunting and gathering societies such as the Mbuti in the Congo (Turnbull, 1968), children are taught to call all women of the mother's generation "mother" and men of that same generation "father." However, once people start accumulating possessions (including land or housing) and money, fathers want to provide only for their own children. The result is that sexual morality, at least with regard to prohibiting female **adultery,** becomes stricter as a society accumulates wealth and individuals face the generational redistribution of that wealth through rules of inheritance.

EXPLORING SEXUALITY ONLINE

A Society Without Control?

The developing society of cyberculture crosses geographic, ethnic, religious, and sexual boundaries. Like other cultures, it has its own language, history, philosophy, and a growing number of zealous believers who gather in virtual hangouts. Some cyberpunks, the founding parents of this new culture, consider William Gibson's 1984 novel *Necromancer* to be their "bible." Cyberpoets are using words and symbols to create new forms of literary expression. Cyberartists use fractals and computer-generated pictures and music to expand artistic expression. Cyberlovers may meet, date, and even have virtual sex without ever sharing physical contact with their significant others. Society is struggling with its role in this new culture as it continues to evolve. The Electronic Frontier Foundation, founded by musicians Mitch Kapor of Lotus and John Perry Barlow of the Grateful Dead, is one of a number of groups lobbying Washington to establish laws to regulate the virtual community.

 Do you think that the government should regulate what goes on in cyberspace? Why or why not?

THE DOUBLE STANDARD AND SUPPRESSION OF FEMALE SEXUALITY

The Sexual Double Standard

In many societies, including our own, there appears to be a sexual **double standard**— a pattern of sexual morality that permits a variety of sexual activities to males but denies them to females. The term has traditionally been used in connection with premarital sex in particular, to refer to the belief that it is acceptable for a man, but not for a woman, to have sex prior to marriage. Many use it more broadly to refer to any sort of behavior that is acceptable for one gender but not for another.

While many sources treat the sexual double standard as if it were common knowledge, evidence supporting it is mixed at best. Studies by Sprecher and her colleagues have failed to find any evidence of an imbalance in attitudes (e.g., Sprecher, 1989; Sprecher et al., 1997), and some studies even point toward a "reverse double standard" that condemns men more harshly than women for sexual misconduct (Milhausen & Herold, 1999; Sprecher, McKinney, & Orbuch, 1991). There has been a general decline in the double standard in recent decades. Combining the results from many studies, Oliver and Hyde (1993) found that support for the double standard was strongest and clearest in older studies, whereas by the 1980s it had lost much (though not all) of its power. Despite this decline, people continue to perceive that it exists today. For example, in a sample of university women students,

Adultery: extramarital relationship; sexual intercourse between a married person and a partner other than the lawful spouse

Double Standard: set of principles permitting greater opportunity or liberty to one group than to another, especially the granting of greater sexual freedom to men than to women

The Single Standard

In a cross-cultural study of 114 societies, Broude and Greene (1976) reported that about a third (34.5 percent) had a single standard for males and females in terms of attitudes toward extramarital sex. In these societies, extramarital sex was either allowed for both males and females or condemned for both.

In 43.1 percent of the societies premarital sex was allowed for husbands but not for wives. In an additional 22.4 percent of societies, extramarital sex was condemned for both husbands and wives, but wives were punished more severely for any infraction (Table 8.4).

Milhausen and Herold (1999) found that hardly anyone endorsed the double standard—but most of them believed that it existed. In other words, the women said they did not subscribe to it themselves, but they perceived pressure coming from others to conform to the double standard.

Why do people continue to believe in the widespread existence of a double standard even though researchers can find only weak and inconsistent evidence of it? One answer is that belief in the double standard may be partly an illusion created by the fact that women are generally less permissive than men toward sexual matters. On nearly all polls, including those cited by Smith (1994) as well as recent studies of supposedly liberated college students (Oliver & Hyde, 1993), women are less tolerant than men of a wide range of sexual activity. Thus, women are more likely than men to label some sexual activity as immoral. Women tend to say a particular act is wrong for both men and women, and men tend to say it is acceptable for both, leading to the illusion of a double standard.

Women who engage in premarital sex are considered by some to be "bad girls," while men doing the same thing are considered "studs." The pressure on the woman to ignore her sexual needs may be strong enough to reduce her experience of sexual desire and enjoyment, and it might in some cases result in sexual dysfunction.

The double standard has been one important form of the control of sexuality. It has put pressure on women to refrain from sexual behavior. The focus on women brings up a broader issue, namely the cultural suppression of female sexuality.

TABLE 8.4

Societal Standards for Male and Female Premarital Sex	
	Percent of 114 Societies
Single Standard: allowed for both	11.2%
Single Standard: condemned for both	23.3%
Single Standard Total	34.5%
Double Standard: allowed for husbands	43.1%
Double Standard: condemned for both, wife punished more severely	22.4%
Double Standard Total	65.5%

SOURCE: Adapted from Broude & Greene, 1976.

Wealthy Chinese women with bound feet.

Suppression of Female Sexuality

One important mechanism of the social control of sexuality involves the attempt to stifle female sexuality. In many societies, young women are pressured to refrain from sexual activity; these pressures may be strong enough to alienate the woman from her sexuality and reduce her experience of sexual desire and enjoyment. These pressure range from derogatory terms and bad reputations for young women who have more sex than is considered appropriate, to extreme practices such as genital surgery and foot binding.

The very suppression of female sexuality may seem paradoxical. It might seem logical that there are advantages to society when female sexuality is enhanced rather than suppressed. If each partner is provided at least the possibility of a satisfying and pleasurable sexual relationship within the marriage, it should reduce the attractiveness of extramarital partners. Also, if women enjoy sex, they are more likely to engage in sexual behavior and therefore increase the opportunities for reproduction (Tiger, 1992). Yet, in direct opposition to this seemingly sensible logic, some societies purposefully seek to stifle female sexual pleasure.

Written evidence of women's subjugation dates from about 1100 B.C. The law codes of ancient Mesopotamia describe women as possessions who could be killed for fornicating; however, husbands were permitted to copulate outside of wedlock, and if a woman didn't produce children, she could be divorced (Bullough, 1976). In traditional Indian families an honorable wife was expected to practice *suttee*, to throw herself on the funeral pyre of her deceased husband. In China, upper-class females had their toes curled underneath their feet and tightly bound, making it painful to walk and impossible to run away from home.

The different theoretical perspectives offer different reasons for the cultural suppression of female sexuality. Evolutionary theories emphasize the desire of men to prevent their mates from straying (and hence possibly becoming pregnant by another man); for this reason men might prefer women who lack sexual desire, as they would be more likely to remain faithful. Feminist theory has emphasized that stifling female sexuality may be part and parcel of the general efforts of men to oppress women.

Social exchange theory suggests that women might work together to regulate female sexuality. Because men have to give women resources in exchange for sex, sex itself becomes subject to the laws of supply and demand. If women restrict the supply, the price goes up. For example, a man will offer to marry a woman with no divorce option and to forego other women for life, in order to have exclusive sex with her. According to this theory women benefit by making it hard for men to obtain sex, because men have to offer women more.

Most of the research findings suggest that women in fact usually carry out the suppression of female sexuality. The sexual behavior and attitudes of teenage girls are affected by their mothers more than their fathers (Du Bois-Reymond & Ravesloot, 1996; Kahn, 1994; Libby, Gray, & White, 1978; Werner-Wilson, 1998). The influence of the mother is mainly toward restraining sexual activity (Lewis, 1973). Girls are influenced by the female peer group more than by the male peer group or by male platonic friends (Du Bois-Reymond & Ravesloot, 1996; Rodgers & Rowe, 1990). The female peer group is the main place where gossip and a "bad reputation" punish girls who are regarded as going beyond the norms of proper sexual behavior. Often the boys seem to like the girls with the so-called bad reputations, both as dating partners and as friends with whom one can trade jokes that most women don't like. Boyfriends do have some influence over teenage girls' sexuality, but generally this influence is directed toward increasing sexual activity rather than stifling it.

Other women also restrain the sexual behavior of adult women. A **meta-analysis** by Oliver and Hyde (1993) found that every single study on the sexual double standard showed that women supported it more strongly than men. More recent work has found that even among women who do not support the double standard, most believe that it still exists—and that it is mainly enforced by women. Milhausen and Herold (1999, p. 363) asked female college students "Who judges women who have had sex with many partners more harshly?" Four times as many said that women, not men were the harsher judges.

As was discussed earlier, in some cultures female sexuality is regulated by female genital mutilation. The available evidence indicates that, once again, mainly women support these practices. Women make the decision about whether a young girl should have the surgery; women carry out the surgery; women defend and support the surgical practices more strongly than men and sometimes even in the face of male opposition; and female peer groups recognize the surgery as a mark of status, so that girls who have not had the surgery are mocked and derogated (e.g., Boddy, 1989, 1998; Hicks, 1996; Lightfoot-Klein, 1989; Williams & Sobieszczyk, 1997).

These and other findings indicate that women mainly carry out the cultural control of female sexuality. When men do have direct influence over female sexuality, they usually use that influence to try to increase female sexuality rather than stifle it. Still, one should not assume that men have played no role in the suppression of female sexuality. In particular, the need for women to get a "high price" for sex is in part a response to their weak and vulnerable position in society. Throughout much of history, women did not have the same legal, financial, educational, political, and professional rights and opportunities as men. Sex was the only ticket that many women had for securing a good life, providing she made sure that in exchange for a sexual relationship a man would offer her a safe and secure position in the world (usually as his wife). Reiss (1986) combined data from nearly 200 different cultures and found that the less power and equality women had, the more extreme and powerful was the cultural suppression of female sexuality. In American history, the Sexual Revolution was perhaps only possible because women had finally gained many rights and opportunities to support themselves, and as a result it was no longer necessary for them to restrict the supply of sex.

Meta-analysis: the process or technique of synthesizing research results by using various statistical methods to retrieve, select, and combine results from previous separate but similar studies

■ R E V I E W

The biological processes of human sexuality are translated through our social and cultural traditions and beliefs. Social definitions of sex are different in different societies and change over time.

All societies influence the selection of sexual partners—some through arranged marriages, most by structuring the opportunities for meeting potential partners. Generally societies distinguish between reproductive and sexual relationships. A **1**_____ relationship is one in which reproduction is both expected and socially approved. A **2**_____ relationship is one in which reproduction is not expected nor socially approved and thus, in many societies, is to be avoided.

Societies have great influence over the timing of sexual relations; many have stiff regulations regarding the age at which it is appropriate to start, and less directly influence the age at which sexual relations should end. In the United States, married and cohabiting adults have more frequent sex than single adults or adolescents do.

Humans everywhere are concerned with privacy and modesty, though the culturally specific meanings of privacy and modesty vary considerably. Clothing often conveys a symbolic message, and is thus frequently an object of social control. Similarly, societies exert control over sexuality by attempting to control the use of language.

A more direct and severe method of controlling female sexuality is the practice of female genital mutilation. Female **3**_____ involves the removal of the clitoral hood. **4**_____ is the removal of the clitoris and all or part of the **5**_____. **6**_____ involves the removal of the clitoris, the labia minora, much of the labia majora and stitching or narrowing the vaginal opening.

Criminalizing some behaviors also may regulate male sexual behavior. Oftentimes, however, members of elite social groups are not punished or are not punished as severely as the poor for crimes such as rape.

Societies may regulate sexuality in an effort to reduce conflict, to control sexually transmitted infections, or to insure appropriate inheritance rights. Primarily, however, societies seem to regulate sexuality in order to control their **7**_____. In an effort to guarantee its long-term future, a society may regulate sexuality in order to increase **8**_____ growth or to limit it. All cultural beliefs and practices are tied to the needs and potentials of a society's environmental resources and the **9**_____ available to exploit those resources. In all societies, fertile **10**_____ are the key to reproduction and thus to population growth.

The belief that it is acceptable for a man but not for a woman to have sex prior to marriage is an example of the **11**_____ standard, one mechanism by which societies suppress female sexuality.

SUGGESTED READINGS

Crane, D. (2000). *Fashion and Its Social Agendas: Class, Gender, and Identity in Clothing.* Chicago: University of Chicago Press.

An exploration of fashion trends from 19th century France to modern America, drawing important links between style and social change.

Entwistle, J. (2000). *Fashioned Body: Fashion, Dress and Modern Social Theory.* Malden, MA: Blackwell.

A summary of the theories surrounding the role and function of fashion in modern society, and how fashion plays a crucial role in the formation of modern identity through its articulation of the body, gender, and sexuality.

Hodes, M. (Ed.). (1999). *Sex, Love, Race: Crossing Boundaries in North American History.* New York: New York University Press.

This volume contains chapters describing 400 years of interracial sexual relations in America, from French Louisiana to New England to territorial New Mexico to more recent experiences of Peace Corps volunteers in Africa. Most of the chapters focus on African American and Native American experiences with Americans of European descent.

Jackson, B. (1998). *Splendid Slippers: A Thousand Years of an Erotic Tradition.* Berkeley, CA: Ten Speed Press.

An exploration of the former practice of footbinding in China, the lore (erotic and otherwise) of this 1,000-year-old tradition, and a comparison with practices in other cultures.

Kassindja, F. & Miller-Bashir, L. (1999). *Do They Hear You When You Cry?* New York: Delta Publishers.

The author describes her life in West Africa and her decision to flee her country just hours before her own circumcision, eventually arriving in the United States, where she faced an immigration nightmare.

Low, B. S. (2000). *Why Sex Matters: A Darwinian Look at Human Behavior.* Princeton, NJ: Princeton University Press.

A survey of what is known about behavioral sex differences in animals and humans, covering biology, anthropology, sociology, and history.

ANSWERS TO CHAPTER REVIEW

1. reproductive; **2.** sexual; **3.** circumcision; **4.** Clitoridectomy; **5.** labia minora; **6.** Infibulation; **7.** reproduction; **8.** population; **9.** technology; **10.** females; **11.** double.

CHAPTER 9

Sex Across the Life Span

■ **Birth and Childhood**
Sexuality is experienced as early as the fetal stage. Infancy and childhood are times of sexual curiosity, exploration, and gender role imitation.

■ **Adolescence: The Transition to Adulthood**
Adolescence marks the onset of many changes, including the development of secondary sex characteristics, initiation of courtship and dating, sexual experimentation, and the construction of a personal identity.

■ **Adulthood: The Transition to Maturity**
During adulthood, we experience many types of relationships that impact sexuality. Singlehood, postponement of marriage, cohabitation, and marriage with or without children are all viable options. Divorce has become increasingly common in our society.

■ **Aging: The Final Transition**
Although there is no need for any healthy adult to ever stop being sexually active, many adults face changes and new challenges in their sexual lives as they age.

PHYSICAL

SOCIAL

EMOTIONAL

SPIRITUAL

COGNITIVE

Human sexuality does not begin with your first kiss in junior high and end at your graduation from college. Sexuality is a presence in our lives from the cradle to the grave—it is an essential part of our lives from the time we are born until the day we die. There are physical, emotional, spiritual, cognitive, and social dimensions to our sexuality at each life stage. Common biological patterns in sexual development as well as shared experiences among members of a society help to bind a culture together and set expectations about sexuality during each stage of life.

Anthropologists identify four universal life stages: birth, maturation, marriage, and death. Cultures use rites of passage to mark the transitions between stages. These rituals help an individual with the transition by publicly providing a new identity—announcing to his or her world that this person has a new status, new social roles, and new responsibilities. Each interval corresponds to a different stage of sexual development. The ways in which you physically, socially, emotionally, spiritually, and cognitively experience and express your sexuality at each point in the life cycle influence your experiences in each subsequent stage. Exploring your sexuality is a lifelong task, since your personality, your knowledge of yourself and others, your desires, and your needs change as you move through life.

BIRTH AND CHILDHOOD

Infancy

Even before you were born you were a sexual being with the capacity for sexual pleasure and response. Prenatal ultrasound pictures show that male fetuses have periodic erections for several months before birth (Calderone, 1983). Although it is more difficult to detect the sexual response of a female fetus, it is likely that females also have sexual responses in utero; evidence of lubrication and genital swelling have been reported (Martinson, 1976).

Within a day or two of birth, levels of testosterone and estrogen drop dramatically. In infant boys the testosterone level rises about a month later and then drops again to the lower level that both boys and girls maintain until puberty. Baby boys can have erections in the first few minutes after birth and newborn baby girls can have vaginal lubrication and clitoral erections within the first 24 hours after birth (Langfeldt, 1981).

Infancy is filled with sensual experiences. Much of the interaction between adults and infants—holding, cuddling, bathing and dressing—is sensuous in nature; infants may have a genital response to these pleasurable experiences. Research indicates that a child who is deprived of physical closeness during infancy may be more likely to experience difficulties forming intimate relationships later in life (Ainsworth, 1962; Harlow & Harlow, 1962; Money, 1980; Trause, Kennell & Klaus, 1977). In the last three decades, investigators have documented an increasing array of problems in children institutionalized during infancy, including delays in emotional, motor, social, speech, and physical development; interruptions in normal adult-child bonding, and risk of attachment disorders; severe emotional and behavior problems; and learning problems (Johnson, 2000).

Children are naturally curious about their own bodies and those of others.

The intimate contact of breast-feeding can cause an infant to have a physical, sexual response. Baby boys commonly experience erections and baby girls experience vaginal lubrication and clitoral erections while nursing. However, the physical, sexual reflexes of an infant should not be interpreted as erotic awareness (Martinson, 1981). As we discussed in Chapter 6, mothers also may experience sexual feelings while nursing.

As they gain control of hand movements and begin to explore their bodies, infants and young children quickly learn that self-stimulation is pleasurable and may repeat self-stimulating behaviors many times during the day (Bakwin, 1973). By the time a baby is 3 or 4 months old, genital stimulation is accompanied by smiling and cooing (Martinson, 1980), and babies show extreme annoyance if their self-stimulation is interrupted (Bakwin, 1974). Although infants are capable of having orgasms, deliberate masturbation to orgasm rarely occurs before age 1 or 2 (Reinish, 1990).

In the past, most people assumed that children neither knew nor cared about sexual things. Freud's psychoanalytic theory (discussed in Chapter 1) became controversial for its suggestion that children do have significant interest in sexual matters. Freud proposed a concept he called **polymorphous perversity:** the capacity to receive a form of sexual pleasure from stimulation of any part of the body. According to this view, the adult tendency to equate sexual pleasure with the genitals is a restricted form of sex. As you learned in Chapter 1, Freud thought that children develop an emotional attachment to the opposite-sex parent with a sexual dimension (the Oedipus and Electra complexes), and that the impossibility of fulfilling that relationship causes childhood sexuality (and polymorphous perversity) to be suppressed. This suppression is more severe among boys; as a result, adult women retain a greater degree of polymorphous perversity than adult men. Polymorphous perversity offers one explanation for why many people sexually enjoy stimulation of parts of the body other than the genitals and may even find such sex play essential to reaching full sexual arousal.

Childhood

Although children develop and express their sexuality in many different ways, certain patterns emerge. Adults may be concerned, alarmed, or embarrassed by a child's expressions of sexuality. Moreover, it can be difficult for parents, teachers, and even professionals to discern what is "normal." William Friedrich and his colleagues set out to define the boundaries of normal childhood sexual behavior in what became the largest, most comprehensive study of the topic to date (Friedrich et al., 1998).

In this study, researchers asked the mothers of children ages 2 to 12 years old who had no history of sexual abuse how often their children had displayed one of 38 types of sexual behavior in the previous 6 months. Behaviors that were reported by a significant number of mothers—20 percent or more—were deemed normal. By this standard, all of the behaviors listed in Table 9.1 are considered normal. Sexual behavior showed an inverse relationship with age; observed sexual behavior was most prevalent among the youngest children, ages 2 to 5. The behaviors that were observed most often were masturbation, touching the mother's or other women's breasts, and attempts to see adults and other children nude or undressing. These behaviors are attributed to children's natural curiosity about the body at a time when they are becoming interested in their own sex and developing an awareness of the differences between boys and girls (Friedrich et al., 1998).

By age 5, sexual behaviors reportedly decreased; at that age children become more modest and develop better self-control. Among children ages 6 to 9 the only sexual behaviors observed often enough to be considered normal were touching their own genitals when at home and trying to see others nude or undressing. The only sexual behavior displayed by a significant number of 10- to 12-year-olds was an interest in the opposite sex.

Childhood sexual behaviors must be seen in context. The frequency of a particular behavior, how often the child engages in it, is more important than the act itself. A child who exhibits an unusual behavior once or twice is probably not cause for concern. Conversely, if a child engages in one of the more common behaviors constantly, he or she might need help.

Polymorphous Perversity: the capacity to receive a form of sexual pleasure from stimulation of any part of the body

TABLE 9.1

Sexual Behaviors of Children

	Boys	Girls
Ages 2 to 5		
Touches private parts when at home	60.2%	43.8%
Touches or tries to touch mother or other women's breasts	42.4	43.7
Stands too close to people	29.3	25.8
Tries to look at people when they are nude or undressing	26.8	26.9
Ages 6 to 9		
Touches private parts when at home	39.8	20.7
Tries to look at people when they are nude or undressing	20.2	20.5
Ages 10 to 12		
Is very interested in the opposite sex	24.1	29.7

SOURCE: Friedrich et al., 1998, p. e9.

Friedrich et al., found that families with more relaxed attitudes about nudity or adult sexual privacy were more likely to report sexual behavior in their children. However, it is difficult to tell if this result was skewed by parental attitudes. Did the children of mothers with more education and with more open attitudes exhibit more sexual behavior, or were their mothers just more likely to report these behaviors?

Although very little research exists on children's sexual behaviors, it has been suggested that young children are expressing more sexual behavior and interest in sexual matters than they did in the past (Cavanaugh-Johnson, 1991). If true, it is unlikely that children have suddenly become innately more interested in sex; rather it is more likely that they have been exposed to more sexual information in today's society. Consequently, it is likely that some of this interest in sexuality will be behaviorally expressed. One study (Kaeser, DiSalvo, & Moglia, 2001) looked at sexual behavior of young children in a school setting and described the observations of kindergarten, first- and second-grade teachers toward the sexual behavior of their students. Behaviors were placed in one of four categories (see Table 9.2). Normal behaviors were considered no cause for alarm. "Yellow flag" behaviors should put caregivers on alert, require an adult response, or have the potential to be problematic. "Red flag" behaviors were problematic behaviors that definitely require an adult response and probably therapeutic follow-up. Behaviors labeled "No Questions" were those that require therapeutic follow-up and possibly should be reported to child protective services.

Of the 378 sexual behaviors that were observed, 162 were determined to be within the normative range of children's sexual behavior. A total of 184 behaviors were identified as problematic or potentially problematic requiring various levels of adult intervention or follow-up. Sexual behaviors of a communicative nature were the most frequently observed behaviors, followed by touching other students' genitals, buttocks, or breast area. There were 14 behaviors where students either forced other students to expose or touch their genitals, or used sexually explicit threats toward them. Only 8 of these incidents were reported to the school principal and none was reported to child protective services. If these behaviors are representative of what is occurring in other elementary schools, it can be presumed that a considerable amount of sexual behavior between students occurs in the kindergarten, first and second grades, some of which may be problematic and require adult intervention or response.

Children learn a great deal from parents' responses to their sexual activities. The best approach is to react calmly and communicate acceptance regarding sexuality. Acceptance does not mean that there are no limits on behavior, however. For example, a parent might tell the child that self-touching of the genitals is to be done in private. Parents who acknowledge rather than discourage or ignore sexuality can "strengthen a child's self-esteem, build a positive body image, and encourage competency and assertiveness" (Reinisch, 1990, p. 248).

FAQ:

What should you do if you find your child engaging in sexual behavior?

The ways in which parents respond to their children's sexual behavior has varied widely throughout history and across cultures. In 19th century America, parents attempted to discourage a child's masturbation by having them wear metal mittens or strapping them into "genital cages" resembling chastity belts. Boys' penises might be inserted into a spike-lined tube to inhibit erections. Some doctors advised parents to wrap their children in cold, wet sheets, tie their arms to the bedposts, or tie their legs together to prevent them from touching their genitals (Reinisch, 1990).

Although such harsh methods would today be considered child abuse, childhood sexuality continues to be widely discouraged or forbidden in our society. Some parents pull the child's hand away from his or her genitals, scold, or even spank a young child for touching "down there." Parents may send both clear messages and more subtle signals to their children that sexuality and sexual pleasuring are unacceptable.

TABLE 9.2

Normal, Yellow Flag, Red Flag and No Question Sexual Behaviors

Normal Behaviors
Genital or reproduction conversation with peers or similar age siblings
"Show me yours and I'll show you mine" behavior with peers or similar age siblings
Playing doctor
Occasional masturbation without penetration
Imitating seduction (for example, kissing, flirting)
Dirty words or jokes within cultural or peer group norms

Yellow Flags
Preoccupation with sexual themes
Sexually explicit conversation with peers
Preoccupation with masturbation
Mutual masturbation or group masturbation
Simulating foreplay with dolls or peers with clothing on
Single occurrences of peeping, exposing, obscenities, pornographic interests
Attempting to expose others' genitals
Sexual graffiti
Precocious sexual knowledge

Red Flags
Sexually explicit conversations with significant age difference
Repeatedly touching genitals of others
Degradation or humiliation of self/others' genitals
Forced exposure of others' genitals
Inducing fear or threats of force
Sexually explicit proposals or threats, including written notes
Repeated or chronic peeping, exposing, obscenities
Pornographic interest, sexually rubbing against another person
Compulsive masturbation, task interruption to masturbate
Masturbation that includes vaginal or anal penetration
Simulating intercourse with dolls, peers, animals

No Questions
Oral, vaginal, anal penetration of dolls, children, animals
Forced touching of genitals
Simulating intercourse with peers with clothing off
Any genital injury or bleeding not explained by accidental cause

SOURCE: Adapted from Kaeser, DiSalvo, & Moglia, 2001, p. 279.

Some children may be in a hurry to grow up and experience adult sexuality.

One study described four basic types of parental attitudes about childhood sexuality: sex repressive, sex avoidant, sex obsessive, and sex expressive (Ehrenberg & Ehrenberg, 1988) (Table 9.3). The essential message from sex-repressive parents is "don't think about it, don't talk about it, and don't do it." Repressive parents characterize sexuality as being dirty, evil, or dangerous. Sex-avoidant parents are likely to give their children the confusing message that "sex is healthy and natural, but I don't want to talk about it." Avoidant parents tend to intellectualize and lecture. While they may give their children information about the biology of sex, they omit the emotional aspects of sexuality. Sex-obsessive parents may overwhelm their children with exposure to sexual issues. In their desire to be open with their sexual attitudes, these parents may discuss their own sexual behavior with their children. Sex expressive parents are able to integrate sexuality into their family life in a balanced way. They accept sexuality as a natural and healthy part of life while setting limits on irresponsible and harmful behavior.

TABLE 9.3

Four Types of Parental Attitudes Toward Sexuality

	Sex Repressive	Sex Avoidant	Sex Obsessive	Sex Expressive
Premarital Sex	Forbidden	If you do it, I don't want to know about it	Encouraged	Responsible decision making emphasized
Nudity	Forbidden	Tolerated	Encouraged	Privacy valued but nudity is not shocking
Masturbation	Forbidden	Embarrassing	Encouraged	Privacy valued but masturbation is not shocking

(Adapted from Ehrenberg & Ehrenberg, 1988.)

ADOLESCENCE: THE TRANSITION TO ADULTHOOD

Puberty

The word *puberty* comes from the Latin *pubescere*, to be covered with hair. Indeed, one of the markers of puberty in both boys and girls is the appearance of pubic hair. When a child is between 8 and 14 years old the hypothalamus increases secretions that cause the pituitary to release larger amounts of gonadotropin hormones into the bloodstream. These hormones, which are chemically identical in males and females, stimulate testosterone production in boys' testicles and elevate estrogen levels in girls' ovaries. When pubertal changes begin at an unexpectedly early age, the condition is called **precocious puberty.**

As a result of higher levels of sex hormones during puberty, external characteristics of female and male sexual maturity develop. The secondary sex characteristics that were discussed in Chapter 2 begin to appear, such as a woman's breasts or a man's beard. The internal sex organs also undergo further development.

In girls, the vaginal walls begin to thicken, the uterus becomes larger, cervical secretions increase, vaginal pH changes from alkaline to acidic, and menstruation begins. Estrogen stimulates the growth of breast tissue as well as the growth of fatty and supporting tissue in the hips and buttocks. Along with estrogen, small amounts of androgens are produced by a female's adrenal glands; the androgens stimulate development of pubic and underarm hair. For a summary of the physical changes that girls undergo during puberty, see Table 9.4.

As a boy's testosterone levels increase, his testicles, scrotal sac, and penis enlarge. The prostate gland and seminal vesicles also increase in size, and semen production (and the ability to ejaculate) begins. Facial, body, and pubic hair appear. The voice begins to deepen in response to enlargement of the larynx. Erections become more frequent, sometimes spontaneously and at inopportune moments, in the locker room or when a student is requested to make a presentation in front of the class. For a summary of the physical changes that boys undergo during puberty, see Table 9.5.

Both males and females undergo a growth spurt during puberty. Girls usually shoot up in height before boys do, which is the source of some girls' dilemma of finding boys tall enough (and willing enough) to dance with at middle-school dances. Testosterone stimulates increased muscle mass in boys, resulting in weight gain, and increased shoulder circumference and chest width.

Some researchers believe that girls in the United States are reaching puberty earlier and earlier. A 1997 study of over 17,000 girls found that the average age at which girls begin to develop secondary sex characteristics was 8. The declining age of puberty raises the question of whether the increased incidence of chemicals, including certain

Adolescence: the period of physical and psychological development from the onset of puberty to maturity

Puberty: the stage of adolescence in which an individual becomes physiologically capable of sexual reproduction

Precocious puberty: the onset of pubertal changes at an unexpectedly early age

FAQ:

What's the difference between puberty and adolescence?

Many people confuse the terms adolescence and puberty. Although they may coincide, they are not the same. **Adolescence** is a culturally defined period between childhood and adulthood that is usually a time of rapid physical, social, emotional, spiritual, and cognitive development. **Puberty** refers to the time during which dramatic physical changes occur that mark the beginning of sexual maturity and the potential for sexual reproduction.

TABLE 9.4

Stages of Female Pubertal Development ♀	
Between ages 8 and 11	pituitary hormones stimulate ovaries to increase estrogen; internal reproductive organs begin to grow
Between ages 9 and 15	first the areola and then the breasts increase in size; the breasts may become more rounded; pubic hair becomes darker and coarser; normal vaginal discharge becomes noticeable; sweat and oil glands increase in activity; acne may appear; internal and external reproductive organs and genitals grow; height increases
Between ages 10 and 16	areola and nipples grow; pubic hair begins to grow in a triangular shape and cover the center of the mons veneris; underarm hair appears; menarche; internal reproductive organs continue to develop; ovaries may begin to release mature eggs capable of being fertilized; growth in height slows
Between ages 12 and 19	breasts near adult size and shape; pubic hair fully covers the mons veneris and spreads to the top of the thighs; voice may deepen slightly; menstrual cycle becomes more regular

Source: Adapted from Reinisch, 1991.

plastics and insecticides that mimic human estrogens, may be triggering an earlier onset of puberty (Herman-Giddens et al., 1997). This same study found that, while 15 percent of white girls began to develop by age 8, almost half of African American girls began to develop by this same age. African American girls were more advanced than white girls for the average age of breast development, the appearance of pubic hair, and the onset of menstruation (Table 9.6). The reasons for the ethnic disparity are unknown.

TABLE 9.5

Stages of Male Pubertal Development ♂	
Between ages 9 and 15	testicles and scrotum begin to grow; skin of scrotum becomes redder and coarser; a few straight pubic hairs appear at the base of the penis; muscle mass develops; areola grows darker and larger
Between ages 11 and 16	penis begins to grow larger; testicles and scrotum continue to grow; pubic hair becomes coarser, more curled, spreads to cover area between the legs; shoulders broaden; hips narrow; height increases; larynx (voice box or Adam's apple) enlarges resulting in deepening voice; sparse facial and underarm hair appears
Between ages 11 and 17	penis continues to increase in circumference and length; testicles continue to increase in size; texture of pubic hair more adultlike; growth of facial and underarm hair continues; shaving may begin; first ejaculation occurs; may develop acne; in nearly half of all boys breast enlargement occurs and then decreases
Between 14 and 18	body nears final adult height; genitals achieve adult size and shape; pubic hair spreads to the thighs and slightly upward toward the belly; chest hair appears; facial hair reaches full growth

Source: Adapted from Reinisch, 1990.

TABLE 9.6

Prevalence of Breast or Pubic Hair Development by Age and Ethnicity

Age	Whites	African Americans
3	1.0%	3.1%
4	0.9	7.6
5	1.9	5.7
6	3.7	14.3
7	6.7	27.2
8	14.7	48.3
9	38.2	77.4
10	67.9	94.6
11	88.0	98.4
12	96.6	100.0

SOURCE: Herman-Giddens et al., 1997.

Adolescence is a time of exploring sexuality and intimate relationships.

However, in 2001, two professional societies representing endocrinologists issued a statement saying that despite the conclusions of this study, it is not yet established that girls typically enter puberty earlier today. They questioned the study's conclusions that puberty was starting earlier, saying that the doctors and nurses who had evaluated girls might have mistaken fat tissue in overweight girls for breasts and that girls in the study had not been randomly selected. In addition, they noted that 12, the age of girls at the onset of first menstruation, the one incontrovertible sign of puberty, has been the same for decades. The groups urged that girls who appear to be starting sexual development at a young age see a specialist as soon as possible. The organizations, the Endocrine Society and the Lawson Wilkins Pediatric Endocrine Society, also urged that rigorous studies be undertaken to determine not just the average age when puberty begins, but how quickly it progresses.

Adolescence

Not all cultures recognize a period of adolescence. In some societies, one may go straight from being considered a child to being an adult, with no transition phase. Other groups, including most Americans, recognize but do not celebrate this transitional period from childhood to adulthood. Still others have elaborate rituals to mark this transition in life (Frayser, 1985).

As American as Apple Pie

CONSIDERATIONS

The 1999 movie *American Pie* and the 2001 sequel, *American Pie 2*, dealt with situations that are part of the adolescent experience—masturbation, premature ejaculation, losing one's virginity, drinking beer with a beer chaser! The film follows Jim, a compulsive masturbator, Kevin and his steady girlfriend who have yet to find the perfect moment to have intercourse, Oz who devotes his life to lacrosse, and the intellectual Finch who enjoys using Latin to make jokes; this group makes a pact to support one another so that by prom night they will no longer be sexual novices. Some critics thought the movie was nothing more than a vulgar gross-out contemporary youth comedy; others found it a light-hearted look at contemporary adolescent issues.

 What did you think the movie American Pie had to say to adolescents about sexual relationships?

—What other adolescent-oriented movies have been influential in shaping or reflecting adolescent sexuality?

—Which film that you've seen do you think most accurately portrays American adolescent sexuality?

FAQ:

Do teenagers who masturbate a lot have sex earlier than those who don't?

The frequency of masturbation typically increases during adolescence. Boys are more likely to report ever having masturbated than girls are (Coles & Stokes, 1985; Smith, Rosenthal, & Reichler, 1996). Boys also report having masturbated more frequently than girls (Hass, 1979; LoPresto et al., 1985; Smith, Rosenthal, & Reichler, 1996). There is wide variation among individuals: Some young people masturbate several times per day, while others never masturbate. In defiance of popular myths, no links have been found between adolescent masturbation and frequency of intercourse, number of different sex partners, or the age of first intercourse (see Chapter 12 for more on this topic) (Leitenberg et al., 1993; Smith, Rosenthal, & Reichler, 1996).

Adolescents may be bigger, stronger, and even smarter than their parents; they can reproduce and become parents themselves. At the same time that hormones are surging, society often gives adolescents mixed messages. The media inundate adolescents with sexual images, and teen sexuality permeates the culture. At the same time, we exhort teenagers to "just say no" to sex and warn them of the dangers of pregnancy and disease that can result from sexual behavior. It's no wonder that many adolescents are in conflict with their parents, society, and with themselves, about sexuality.

From an evolutionary perspective, adolescence commences the serious competition for mates. The transition of puberty means that a person is biologically ready to have sex and make children. According to evolutionary theory, this is the prime time in life for finding genes that will best combine with one's own to make the best gene pool. Adolescents are therefore programmed by nature to attend fiercely to the rules of competition. They learn what characteristics make them most able to attract highly desirable partners, size up their same-gender peers to see how they rank, and do whatever they can to improve their own sex appeal. Dieting among girls and fighting among boys may be related to the simple realities that in our culture (and others) slim girls and strong, dominating boys are seen as especially attractive romantic partners. Of course, culture plays an important role in dictating what criteria make one appealing to the opposite sex. In some cultures (see CROSS-CULTURAL PERSPECTIVES box) girls may seek to gain rather than lose weight in order to maximize their sex appeal, and boys may succumb to social pressure to engage in prestige-enhancing competitions and risk-taking behavior.

Sexual Behavior During Adolescence

Teenage sexuality is affected by the multitude of changes that occur during adolescence, and it often includes an exploration of sexual attitudes, beliefs, and behaviors. Increasing sexual interest during puberty presents numerous challenges and conflicts.

Noncoital Sexual Activity   Although much of the attention and research has focused on adolescent sexual intercourse, until recently, few studies have examined noncoital sexual activity in detail. However, a recent study (Woody et al., 2001) revealed that noncoital sex was common among both virgins and nonvirgins, and the rates (including those for oral sex) were similar for males and females. Among virgins, total abstainers

"Virtually any and all physical characteristics receive extraordinary attention and examination during this phase. [Adolescence] is a time when being different is to be avoided at almost any cost and when undesirable physical characteristics put the adolescent at risk for teasing, ridicule, or exclusion."

(SIEGEL, 1982, P. 538)

CROSS-CULTURAL PERSPECTIVES

Thin Isn't In

In some African countries women want to be fat. Fat symbolizes wealth, health, and prosperity and enhances a woman's marriage prospects. In southeastern Nigeria the Waririke and Efik communities send girls to the "fattening room" where they spend up to 6 months in a small ceremonial house doing nothing but eating. As soon as a girl begins to develop breasts she in confined in the traditional fattening room where she is required to eat bowl after bowl of rice, yams, plan- *tains, beans, and porridge. Everything she wants—beautiful wraps to wear, perfumes, moisturizing creams, and powders—is brought to her. Among Waririkes, a blacksmith fixes heavy copper leg bracelets called ikpala to the girls' legs, causing swelling and aching that prevent her from leaving the room or having sex. The ikpala make so much noise that if a girl is having sex everyone in the community will know.*

(from all sexual interaction) came from a lower socioeconomic status, had fewer social/dating opportunities, lacked viable relationships, and had lower grades. Two subgroups of virgins, those who came close to intercourse and those who did not, differed only on social/dating opportunities; of those who came close but did not have intercourse, nearly half continued with noncoital sexual activity. Compared to the "came close" group, the nonvirgin group reported greater use of alcohol, less religious involvement, fewer moral influences, and fewer traditional messages about sex from their parents. That group also noted poorer outcomes and a lower evaluation of their first intercourse decision. Females had a less positive emotional reaction to the experience, poorer outcomes, and lower evaluation of the decision than males.

Sexual Intercourse The motives and reasons for having first intercourse are varied. Some say it is raging hormones; for others it may be curiosity; and for some it may be love (Table 9.8). The sex hormones that are activated at puberty certainly play a role in increased sexual arousal. Like so many things related to sexuality, men and women report different motivations for first-time sexual intercourse. Over half the men say they did it out of curiosity, and most were not in love with their first partner. The women, in contrast, said that affection, if not love, was the primary reason for first intercourse (Michael et al., 1994).

Having had first sexual intercourse is not the same as having it often. Intercourse among adolescents is very episodic. Many younger adolescents do not have intercourse at all. Those who are sexually experienced are not necessarily constantly engaging in intercourse. A nationwide survey of sexually active adolescent males ages 15 to 19 found that they had not had any sexual intercourse in at least 6 of the previous 12 months (Leighton et al., 1992).

FAQ:

When do teenagers start having sex?

Although sexual experimentation continues to be a part of the teenage experience for many adolescents, the percentage of all high-school students (9th to 12th grades) who reported ever having had sexual intercourse has declined (see Table 9.7). In 1999, half of all 9th- to 12th-grade students had sexual intercourse; in 1991, 54 percent reported having had sexual intercourse. Males were slightly more likely than females to report having sex.

Most younger teens in the United States have not had sexual intercourse: In one study 8 in 10 girls and 7 in 10 boys had not experienced coitus by age 15 (Singh & Darroch, 1999). However, the likelihood of adolescents having intercourse increases steadily with age. More than half of 17-year-olds have had intercourse (Alan Guttmacher Institute, 1994), and only one in five have not had intercourse by age 19 (Singh & Darroch, 1999).

TABLE 9.7

Percentage of 9th to 12th Graders, by Gender, Who Have Had Sexual Intercourse

Year	Boys	Girls	Total
1991	57%	51%	54%
1993	56	50	53
1995	54	52	53
1997	49	48	48
1999	52	48	50

SOURCE: CDC Youth Risk Behavior Surveys 1991, 1993, 1994, 1997, and 1999.

TABLE 9.8

Reasons for Having First Consensual Sexual Intercourse

Attributed Reason	Men (%)	Women (%)
Affection for partner	25	48
Peer pressure	4	3
Curiosity/readiness for sex	51	24
Wanted to have a baby	0	1
Physical pleasure	12	3
Under the influence of alcohol/drugs	1	0
Wedding night	7	21

SOURCE: Adapted from Laumann et al., 1994, p. 329

The 1999 movie *Boys Don't Cry* is the true story of the life of Teena Brandon, a transgender youth who preferred her life in her male identity as Brandon Teena.

A study of adolescent sexual behavior of black and Hispanic families in Montgomery, Alabama, New York City, and San Juan, Puerto Rico found that neither adolescent gender, ethnicity, nor family structure variables (that is, income, parental education, and maternal marital status) appear to predict adolescent sexual behavior (Miller, Forehand, & Kotchick, 1999). So-called family process variables (maternal monitoring of behavior, mother-adolescent general communication, and sexual communication) have more influence; and place of residence does appear to be correlated with adolescent sexual behavior (ibid).

However, another study (Halprin et al., 2000) found that the frequency of adolescent sex is not solely due to neighborhood socioeconomic status and race, but rather that it is the social conditions that covary or proportionately move together. The study found that boys and girls who live with both parents have the lowest rates of sexual activity. Black and Hispanic boys had higher rates of sexual activity than white boys, and Hispanic girls exhibited a lower rate than white girls (Upchurch et al., 1999). Compared with adolescents of average intelligence, both the above-average and the below-average teenagers tend to put off having sex. The brighter students delayed not only sexual intercourse but also activities such as kissing and light petting. Although the reasons for the delays are unclear, it is suggested that perhaps the brighter students are more focused on their futures than on social relationships, and that parents of less intelligent adolescents may be more protective.

Although Western society tends to focus on the negative effects of early adolescent sexual involvement, there are positive effects as well. For example, one study (Billy et al., 1988) found that sex in early adolescence does not usually lead to pronounced changes in a teenager's social or psychological involvement. Early sexual relationships can also result in more positive sexual attitudes. On the other hand, sexually active teenagers are at greater risk for unintended pregnancies and for sexually transmitted infections, including HIV.

Sexual Orientation   Adolescents also are faced with the daunting task of sorting through socially prescribed gender roles and ideas about sexual orientation in the construction of their personal identities. During this period of experimentation and exploration some adolescents become aware of the possibility of a gay, lesbian, or bisexual orientation or being transgender (see Chapter 11 for more on these topics). In a large-scale study of Minnesota junior- and senior-high-school students, 88.2 percent described themselves as predominantly heterosexual, 1.1 percent said they were either bisexual or predominantly homosexual, and 10.7 percent were unsure of their sexual orientation. Uncertainty about sexual orientation declined with age; 25.9 percent of 12-year-old students said they were unsure, as compared to 5 percent of 17-year-olds (Remafedi et al., 1992).

For most teens, "fitting in" their local social environment is a primary concern. The struggle with their own sexual identity can result in a narrow, stereotypical view of sexual orientation and gender roles. Those who are "different" or suspected of being so may experience humiliating taunts, social rejection, and in some cases, bodily harm.

Each year nearly a million U.S. teens become pregnant.

Teen Pregnancy   Between 1995 and 1998 the national teen pregnancy rate fell 4 percent, from 101.1 to 97.3 pregnancies per 1,000 women ages 15 to 19 (Henshaw, 1999). Eight percent of the decline in the rate of teenage pregnancy is attributed to improved contraceptive use among sexually active adolescents and another 20 percent to increased abstinence (Saul, 1999). Although these statistics are encouraging, each year nearly a million U.S. teens become pregnant. Among sexually experienced adolescents, approximately 8 percent of 14-year-olds, 19 percent of 15- to 17-year-olds, and 22 percent of 18- to 19-year-olds become pregnant each year (Alan Guttmacher Institute, 1998). Thirteen percent of all births in the United States are to teenage mothers, making the U.S. teen pregnancy rate one of the highest in the developed world. About 78 percent of teenage pregnancies are unintended.

ADULTHOOD: THE TRANSITION TO MATURITY

Americans used to be fairly predictable. You dated in your teens, fell in love, sexually experimented with your partner, got married in your 20s, and then had 2.3 children and lived happily ever after. Although for some adults, this may still be the ideal, it is not the reality for many Americans. As in all stages of the life cycle, there are wide variations in sexual expression throughout the adult years. Some adults remain single by choice or circumstance. Some marry, while others choose to cohabit rather than formalize their commitment. Some form a lifetime monogamous-pair bond, and others explore their sexuality outside a committed relationship. Some learn to establish postmarital sexual relationships following divorce or death of a spouse, while others remain single. In the following sections we shall explore the effects of each of these options on sexual expression.

Singlehood

Whether it is for only a few years or for a lifetime, most men and women spend a portion of their adulthood without a permanent partner, a stage called **singlehood.** Some consider singlehood (or being a "singleton", as Bridget Jones writes in her diary) a temporary stage to mark time before or between marriages. Others may choose to remain single throughout their lives. Among men and women between the ages of 25 and 34, about 35 percent have never been married (Census Bureau Report, 1999).

Moreover, men and women in the United States are staying single longer. From 1970 to 1994 the number of never married adults more than doubled, from 21.4 million to 44.2 million. In 1994 the median age at first marriage in the United States was 24.5 for women and 26.7 for men, the oldest ever reported (Census Bureau Report, 1999). The portion of the population in their early 30s who have not married rose from 6 percent to 20 percent for women and 9 percent to 30 percent for men (Saluter, 1997). Census data indicate that there are more unmarried men than women in every age group until age 65. After age 65, men are more likely to be married than women are. This owes to the fact that women are likely to outlive their husbands. Single women in their 30s and 40s may have a harder time finding a husband, since male baby-boomers seem to prefer women who are 7 to 10 years younger than themselves. In support of this preference, one study reported that among 50-year-olds, 22 percent of women but only 8 percent of the men had no sexual partner in the past year. By ages 60 to 64, 45 percent of the women had no sexual partner in the past year, compared to 15 percent of the men (Michaels et al., 1994).

There appear to be a number of reasons why people are electing to delay marriage or to remain single. Students are staying in college longer or live together without marriage (Saluter, 1997). Some devote all of their energies to education and career goals (Barringer, 1991), some avoid commitment because of disappointment with past relationships, some enjoy the excitement of dating and meeting new people, and others simply haven't met "Mr. or Ms. Right"—or even "Mr. or Ms. O.K." Social pressure on couples to marry before having intercourse or even having children has declined. And many gays and lesbians feel increasingly less pressured to "fake" a marriage to appear straight (Barringer, 1991; Wolfe, 1993).

Single people, especially single women, must cope with a variety of negative social perceptions. Society is set up to favor couples, and people who remain single often feel that society discriminates against them. By their late 20s, more than 70 percent of men and more than 85 percent of women form long-term sexual and social partnerships, in the form of marriage or cohabitation (Laumann et al., 1994), so singles are definitely in the minority. Even in our modern, tolerant society, single people tend to be stereotyped as immature or unattractive (DePaulo, 2000).

The difference in the perception of single men and single women is reflected in the names we give them. While single men are referred to as *bachelors*, with positive implications of a free-living lifestyle, the derogatory term *spinster* is sometimes used to refer to single women, implying that they are unmarriageable.

Why is there so much concern about teens having babies?

Adolescent pregnancy has severe consequences for the teenage parents, for the child, and for society in general. Teenage mothers are more likely to drop out of high school and live in poverty. According to one study, more than 75 percent of all unmarried teen mothers began receiving welfare within 5 years of giving birth (Annie E. Casey Foundation, 1998). Children of teenage mothers have more health problems and developmental delays, and the infant mortality rate for children born to teen mothers is about 50 percent higher than for those born to women older than 20. Children born to adolescent mothers are more likely to be poor, abused, or neglected, and less likely to receive proper health care and nutrition. Teen fathers also experience negative consequences, although they are not as severe as those for the mothers and children. Teenage fathers are more likely to engage in delinquent behaviors, complete fewer years of schooling, and earn less money than childless peers or fathers of children born to mothers over age 20 (Annie E. Casey Foundation, 1998). ∎

Singlehood: the state of being unmarried

FAQ:

Are single people happier than married people?

Attitudes about singlehood vary widely, from satisfaction and comfort to frustration and desperation. Some singles choose not to date, while others date frequently. Finding dating partners may be more difficult without the social structure of school, and some single adults seek new social structures, such as singles bars, personal ads, or Internet chat rooms. Most of those who are single will eventually marry. Some may practice **serial monogamy;** as its name implies, this term refers to a pattern of involvement in a series of exclusive relationships. Being single, like being married, can be difficult. Although loneliness is the most frequently reported problem of those who are single (Kammeyer, Ritzer, & Yetman, 1990), most singles are content with their lives (Rollins, 1986), especially those who have a number of friends and a supportive social network (Austrom & Hanel, 1985).

Nearly all major surveys have found that married people are happier than single people, although the difference is not large. Moreover, happiness is reduced (in both groups) by having children. Childless married couples are the happiest; single parents are the least happy.

In the1940s, single men were regarded negatively; some companies even had policies against promoting single men. Marriage was seen not just as an option but a duty, and a man who remained single was suspected of being selfish, immoral, and childish if not homosexual (Ehrenreich, 1983). Part of the shift in this attitude came from the advocacy of single male life in *Playboy* magazine. This magazine initially appeared as little more than a way to sell photos of scantily clad women, but its early success encouraged the founder Hugh Hefner to develop the "Playboy philosophy" that it was acceptable, even cool and hip, to refuse marriage. Playboy began to depict a swinging bachelor lifestyle in a positive manner—to be unmarried did not mean to live without sex. *Playboy* depicted the single adult male as having a rich, exciting sex life, in which he could go to bed with different women without making a lasting commitment (Petersen, 1999).

Helen Gurley Brown tried to do the same for women. Her 1962 book *Sex and the Single Girl* suggested that an adult single woman could have a better sex life than most married ones. Her book rejected the traditional images of adult single women as sexless, undesirable spinsters and old maids and instead depicted a glamorous life of independence and sexual excitement. When she took over *Cosmopolitan* magazine, Gurley Brown transformed it into an advocate of that lifestyle (Petersen, 1999). Other mass media showed a shift in attitudes as well. A content analysis of women's magazines across several decades found that in the 1940s, women were expected to put marriage and family ahead of self-fulfillment, but by the 1960s the self was regarded as more important than marriage and family (Zube, 1972).

However, the success of mass media such as *Playboy* and *Cosmopolitan* may have been an effect rather than a cause. As the American economy boomed and job opportunities for everyone improved, more people had the means to live alone, so the traditional pattern of going from one's parents' house into marriage was no longer the only option. Plenty of people simply preferred to live alone instead of marrying, and once that lifestyle became possible, they seized it. In addition, it had long been risky for a single person to engage in sexual intercourse, because the risk of creating a pregnancy involved severe social stigma and lasting problems. When the birth control pill became widely available in the 1960s, people were better able to carry on an active sex life without the risk of conception. The success of magazines such as *Playboy* and *Cosmopolitan* may have resulted from the desire of more people for that lifestyle. In other words, the rising proportion of single people may have created the market for the magazines.

A 1985 study by Tucker and Mitchell-Kernan investigated the relationship between perceived marital opportunity and psychological well-being among African American, Hispanic, and white women in southern California. Findings of the study indicated that in some groups a perceived lack of available partners was strongly associated with greater depression, anxiety, loneliness, and less satisfaction with life. These effects were strong and pervasive for Latinas and white women but were either weak or nonexistent for African American women. It appears that when the perception of mate availability is viewed as individually rooted ("the reason I'm not married is because there's something wrong with me") as was the case for both Latinas and white women, the consequences of psychological well-being are negative. When mate availability is viewed as a feature of the environment over which she has little or no control ("the reason I'm not married is because there's something wrong with society"), as was the case for African American women, mental health is not affected. In addition, the study suggests that single African American women have a greater range of positive role models, which are less available to other groups of women.

A 2001 study found that 63 percent of the college women at least partly embrace the goal of finding a future husband while in college. However, the report also found that college women are confused about the dating-mating game. Basically college women feel that they have only two choices: "hooking up" briefly with a guy for casual sex, or being *joined at the hip* with a partner. The definition of "hooking up" varies, but 75 percent of the women in the study think it means anything from kissing to having sex without emotional involvement. Although the report finds that hooking up is common on campus, college women are ambivalent about hookups. Afterward some feel awkward and hurt if they had hoped for more from the relationship, while others report feeling strong, desirable, and sexy. The flip side of hooking up is a relationship that develops quickly and is very intense and exclusive. The study concludes that neither the undercommitted nor overcommitted relationship contributes much to finding a future husband while in college. The report decries the loss of courtship rituals and views the loss of older adults helping to influence younger people toward good marital choices as a major social problem (Marquardt et al., 2001).

The difference between single and married sex may represent a tradeoff of quality versus quantity. On average, married people have sex more frequently than single people (Laumann et al., 1993). In contrast, single people have more variety in their sexual partners, and the novelty of different partners may produce greater excitement. New sexual relationships are often characterized by periods of highly frequent and intensely satisfying sexual activity, so a person who remains single for many years will likely have such highly satisfying periods—punctuated by other periods with little or no opportunity for sexual activity.

Cohabitation

Cohabitation, or living together, may be used as an alternative to marriage or may represent an additional step in the transition from singlehood to marriage. Most college students no longer believe that living together is "living in sin" (Knox et al., 1999) and from Hollywood to Main Street there are many role models of long-term cohabiting relationships. If you're living together, the Census Bureau would describe you as a POSSLQ (Persons of Opposite Sex Sharing Living Quarters), a term that is not among the ten most common ways unmarried people introduce their partners (see Table 9.9).

In the United States, the number of cohabiting individuals has increased dramatically in recent years—from 3.2 million unmarried-partner households in 1990 to 5.5 million in 2000 (U.S. Census Bureau Report, 2001). That is an increase of 72 percent in 10 years. This includes both same-sex and opposite-sex couples; however, most are opposite-sex partners.

Although the stereotype is a young, heterosexual, never-married, childless couple, this is not true of all cohabitants. Some may have a nonsexual relationship and live together out of friendship or for convenience. About 40 percent of cohabiting couples have children. In one third of such families, the members of the cohabiting couple are the children's biological parents; in the other two thirds the children were born into a previous relationship of one member (Bumpass, Sweet, & Cherlin, 1991).

TABLE 9.9

"I'd Like You To Meet My . . . " The Ten Most Common Ways Unmarried People Introduce Their Partners

1. partner
2. boyfriend/girlfriend
3. significant other
4. the person's name without an explanation or descriptive word
5. friend
6. husband/wife
7. roommate or housemate
8. lover
9. spouse
10. sweetheart or sweetie

SOURCE: from www.unmarried.org.

Serial Monogamy: a form of monogamy (being married to only one person at a time) characterized by several successive, short-term marriages over the course of a lifetime

Cohabitation: act of living together; by implication a heterosexual couple

There has been a marked shift toward couples living together before marriage. In 1992, 5.8 percent of all couples in the United States were cohabiting (Smith, 1994). Ninety-three percent of women born between 1933 and 1942 married without ever living with their partner; 90 percent of these women were either virgins when they married or had premarital intercourse only with the man they married. However, just 36 percent of women born between 1963 and 1974 got married without living with their partner first (Laumann et al., 1994).

For both men and women, the younger they are when they form a partnership, the more likely they are to cohabit than marry. Those who had sexual intercourse before age 18 are more likely to cohabit than to marry. For women, the odds of cohabitation are nearly twice as high for those who have had one sex partner before age 18 as for those who have not had any (Laumann et al., 1994; Willis & Michael, 1994).

Ethnicity, religion, and family background also have an effect on our choices. Black women are more likely than white women to make the choice to live with their partners rather than marry (Laumann et al., 1994). Religious or spiritual beliefs as well as family background also influence the choice between cohabitation and marriage. Those who frequently attend religious services are far less likely to form cohabiting relationships than those who do not. Men and women who grew up in nonintact families are more likely to live together than those who grew up in the traditional two-parent household.

Economic and legal issues also contribute to this decision. Some couples that receive public assistance or Social Security benefits may cohabit rather than marry because they risk losing benefits if they get married (Steinhauer, 1995). Cohabitation can provide a consistent relationship without the legal entanglements or the formal commitment of marriage. For couples in an Australian study (Lindsay, 2000), moving in together was an ambiguous commitment rather than a trial marriage. It was a transition based on pragmatic rather than romantic premises. In contrast to marriage, moving in was played down in public and ritual was avoided. In Sweden, cohabitation is the norm before marriage and in many ways is equal to marriage.

By investigating the transition from cohabitation to marriage in Sweden, a 1999 study by Duvander sought to clarify how those who marry differ from those who do not. The results showed that the stage of life, potential economic gains in marriage, and family socialization predicted whether cohabiting women turn their unions into marriages.

A number of factors contribute to the decision to continue to cohabit or to dissolve the relationship. Cohabitors' economic circumstances, domestic contributions, gender attitudes, and feelings about domestic equity appear to affect whether they continue to cohabit, separate, or marry. Couples who favor traditional (sex-specialized) gender roles (women responsible for housework and men responsible for earning income) are more likely to get married than those who favor egalitarian or collaborative gender roles, where partners share both domestic and income-generating responsibilities more equally (Sanchez, Manning, & Smock, 1998).

Another factor that may influence whether a cohabiting couple remains together is "cheating." Virtually all couples, married or cohabiting, expect sexual exclusivity of one another. There is considerably more infidelity among cohabiting couples than among married couples. Blumstein and Schwartz (1983) found that women in cohabiting relationships were twice as likely as married women to have sex with someone else. This high rate of infidelity may be a reflection of a number of factors, including the lesser commitment of cohabitation and the greater interest in maintaining independence.

Although many couples believe that living together before marriage increases the likelihood that a future marriage will be successful, research studies show contradictory effects. Some studies indicate that cohabitation has no significant effect on marital stability, sexual satisfaction, or the likelihood of divorce (Newcomb & Bentler, 1980; Watson & DeMeo, 1987). However, other studies indicate that the likelihood of divorce within 10 years of marriage is nearly twice as great among married couples that lived together before marriage (Booth & Johnson, 1988; Bumpass & Sweet, 1989; Laumann, et al., 1994; Nock, 1995). The factors leading some couples to cohabit, rather than cohabitation itself, may explain the latter result, since those who cohabit tend to be more committed to personal independence, less traditional, and less religious than noncohabitors (Bumpass, 1995). The negative association between the length of a relationship and the satisfaction with that relationship also may be a factor; those who have lived together prior to marriage would have been together longer as a couple than other newlyweds and thus be more likely to grow weary of the relationship sooner (Sprecher & McKinney, 1993).

For some, cohabitation may be the only choice. Since same sex marriage is not legal in the United States, cohabitation is the only legal option for homosexual partners. In June 2000, a law that created a marriagelike civil union for same-sex couples came into effect in Vermont. Although this law gives same-sex couples many of the legal rights extended to heterosexual couples, it is unclear if these unions will be accepted nationwide. Because in most places there is no societal sanctioned event or ritual to mark a relationship, moving in together may take on special significance for gay and lesbian couples (Berger, 1990). A study of male homosexual couples found that almost 25 percent moved in together within a month of first meeting, with a median time of 4 months and a range of less than 1 week to 6 years. The quick transition from a dating relationship to a cohabiting relationship might be one explanation why some gay relationships don't endure (Berger, 1990).

Lesbians are more likely to form stable, monogamous, long-term partnerships. One study of the relationship quality of gay and lesbian couples found that all 47 of the lesbian couples in the study had sexually exclusive relationships (Kurdek, 1988). Surveys of gay men prior to the mid-1980s (and to the growing awareness of AIDS) found that monogamy was not the norm for male homosexual relationships (Bell & Weinberg, 1978; Harry, 1984; Jay & Young, 1979). However, the general population of gay men has significantly altered its sexual behavior in response to the AIDS crisis. One study of 83 couples found that 96.4 percent described their relationship as monogamous (Berger, 1990). Then again, another study of 65 gay couples found that 34 couples permitted sex outside the relationship; perhaps surprisingly, the nonexclusive gay couples lived together longer than the exclusive couples (Kurdeck, 1988).

There are several theories regarding the difference in stability of gay and lesbian relationships. It has been said that traditionally women are socialized to get married and to keep a marriage together, while men are socialized to explore their sexuality. These dynamics are intensified when you have two people who were socialized in the same way. Following this logic, you would expect the lesbian couples to be twice as committed as heterosexual couples, and the gay couples to be half as committed.

Data from 236 married couples, 66 gay cohabiting couples, and 51 lesbian cohabiting couples were used to assess whether members of married couples differed from gay and lesbian couples (Kurdeck, 1998). The study used five dimensions of relationship quality (intimacy, autonomy, equality, constructive problem-solving, and barriers to leaving), two relationship outcomes (the trajectory of change in relationship satisfaction, and relationship dissolution over 5 years), and the links between quality and outcome. Relative to married partners, gay partners reported more autonomy, fewer barriers to leaving, and more frequent relationship dissolution. Relative to married partners, lesbian partners reported more intimacy, more autonomy, more equality, fewer barriers to leaving, and more frequent relationship dissolution. Overall, the association of relationship quality and relationship outcome was the same for married partners as for gay and lesbian partners.

Marriage ceremony.

Marriage

For better or worse, most people in every known society get married at least once (Ember & Ember, 1990). Although increasing numbers of Americans believe that premarital sex and living together are acceptable, 90 percent of men and 93 percent of women in the United States choose to marry at least once by age 40 (Kammeyer, Ritzer, & Yetman, 1990) and married adults are still in the majority (U.S. Census Bureau Report, 1999). Marriage is a legally recognized relationship within which sexual intercourse and the birth of children are socially approved and encouraged (Frayser, 1985). As we noted in the previous chapter, marriage serves many societal functions and takes many different forms. However, most people in Western cultures are not thinking about society's needs when they marry; they are thinking about their own need for love, companionship, and support.

Unlike in previous eras, getting married today is more a choice than a necessity. Individuals can have sexual relationships and raise a family without the formality of marriage. The very meaning of marriage (and family) has changed fundamentally in recent history. A classic work by Burgess and Locke (1945) explained that throughout most of recorded history, the family essentially served as an economic unit. The various members worked together to produce the goods and services necessary for survival. Sometimes they produced more than they needed and would sell or trade the surplus. Because men and women did different jobs, a household needed both a man and a woman in order to survive. The person you married was primarily your lifetime economic partner; this choice was regarded as far too important to make on the basis of sexual attraction or romantic love. In many cases, of course, the decision was regarded as too important to leave to the young person at all, and parents would arrange marriages for their children (see Chapter 8). Even as the modern economy developed, the family unit remained essential for placing children into jobs and marriages. In essence, the family connected the individual to the broader society. A person without family connections was at a serious disadvantage.

Indeed, some historians have said that marriage was not even the main foundation of the family. MacFarlane (1986) concluded from historical and cross-cultural evidence that the bond between parent and child was the most important one, outside of the modern West (defined as Europe and North America since 1500). The parent-child bond was vital for survival in old age, for most societies in history have not had Social Security or old-age pensions; when people ceased being able to work the farm or hunt for themselves they relied on their children to feed and care for them. The bond between husband and wife has ascended to a comparable level of importance only during the last two or three centuries. Today fewer than a quarter of American households are traditional nuclear families—married couples living with their children (U.S. Census Bureau, 2000). Most people, then, are living in some arrangement outside the boundaries of the old social contract.

What changed was that the family lost most of its traditional economic functions. Hardly any families now work together to produce goods and services. Also, modern education, not family ties, is what places people into jobs; relying on family connections is a less common way of getting a start in life than it used to be. Today parents may help a child get a good education, which then may lead to an assortment of career opportunities. Most parents do not want to rely on their children to feed and house them in their retirement.

Shorn of its age-old function, the family underwent a dramatic transformation; it became a center of intimate companionship (Burgess & Locke, 1945). Marriage changed from an economic partnership to a relationship based on emotional factors. Young people began to marry for love rather than for economic reasons. In a modern marriage, people expect love and emotional support, as well as companionship and sex, from their partners. People today have children for the sake of their personal fulfillment and emotional bonds rather than as a necessary financial investment or for support in old age (Shorter, 1975).

Married people tend to be happier than singles. A worldwide study showed that in 16 of the 17 countries surveyed married people were happier than single people. Married people were also 3.4 times happier than cohabiting people. The same study found that marriage increases happiness equally among men and women. It is theorized that marriage increases happiness through multiple processes including the promotion of financial satisfaction and the improvement of health (Stack & Eshleman, 1998).

Some research indicates that men fare better in marriage than women in terms of both physical and mental health (Bernard, 1972; Knupfer, Clark, & Room, 1966; Morgan, 1980). However, a 1989 study (Wood, Rhodes, & Whelan) found that wives had higher scores on positive well-being than husbands, indicating that women benefit more from marriage than men. However, the researchers also reported more negative feelings and distress among married women than among married men. Women seem to get more of the highs of marriage, but men appear better able to avoid the lows.

The quality of marital life may be declining. One study found that couples married between 1981 and 1992 reported significantly lower levels of marital interaction and significantly higher levels of marital conflict and problems than couples married between 1969 and 1980. Changes in economic resources, work and family demands, wives' gender role attitudes, and cohabitation prior to marriage appear to each contribute to this decline (Rogers & Amato, 1997).

Of course not everyone in society has similar marriage opportunities or similar attitudes about marriage. For example, professional African American women who want to marry a successful, educated African American man of similar age have a particularly difficult time because fewer African American men than women finish high school and go on to college (Michaels et al., 1994). The result is that single white women are twice as likely to marry as single African American women. To add further to the shortage of available males, African American men marry interracially four times as often as African American women (D'Emilio & Freedman, 1988).

A 1999 study by King examined African American females' attitudes toward marriage, their perception of the impact of marriage on personal growth, and the relative importance of a successful marriage and a successful career. Results indicated that older, married black women expressed more positive attitudes toward marriage than younger, never-married black women. Highly educated and higher income subjects expressed more positive attitudes toward marriage than the less educated and lower income subjects. Those subjects who had never married indicated that a successful career was more important to them than a successful marriage.

Polygamy Many societies permit or encourage **polygamy,** having more than one spouse. In fact, 84 percent of all known societies are polygamous to some extent, with the overwhelming majority favoring men taking multiple wives, an arrangement known as **polygyny** (Fisher, 1992). Many women in Africa choose polygynous marriage rather than monogamous marriage, even in the absence of pressure from relatives. Western explanations of polygyny, also known as plural marriage, assume special qualities of the polygynous husband, usually identifying exceptional economic resources as the quality that makes women willing to share a spouse. However, a study conducted in and around Johannesburg and Pretoria South Africa from 1983 to 1986 found that other adult females were the most important resources. For these women the critical relationship was not with the man but with his female associates, including both family and cowives (Anderson, 2000).

Although it is outlawed in the United States, polygyny does occur. An estimated 20,000 to 60,000 polygynous Mormon families live in northern Arizona and Utah. While the Mormon Church officially banned polygyny in 1890, some Mormon fundamentalists share a belief in traditional gender roles, patriarchal authority, a large number of children, and plural marriage.

The two main fundamentalist Mormon churches in the United States today exist in a rural area on the Utah-Arizona border and in urban Salt Lake City County; there are a number of smaller groups and independent families as well. About two thirds of the plural marriages involve one husband and two wives. Frequently the wives are sisters. Ideally, the new wife's parents, the existing wife or wives, and relevant church leaders approve the addition of a new wife to the family. In some groups, however, marriages may be arranged by church leaders or initiated by women who want to become part of a particular family.

> **"Marriage is a relationship. When you make the sacrifice in marriage, you're sacrificing not to each other but to unity in a relationship. The Chinese image of Tao, with the dark and light interacting—that's the relationship of Yang and Yin, male and female, which is what marriage is. And that's what you have to become when you have married. You're no longer this one alone; your identity is in a relationship. Marriage is not a simple love affair; it's an ordeal, and the ordeal is the sacrifice of ego to a relationship in which two have become one."**
>
> (JOSEPH CAMPBELL, 1988, P. 7)

Polygamy: the practice of having more than one spouse at one time. Also called plural marriage

Polygyny: the practice of having more than one wife at one time

Tom Green, a husband of five and father of 29, was convicted of polygamy in May 2001.

Most polygynous families in the United States are in the middle to lower-middle socioeconomic level. The combination of large numbers of children and limited financial resources puts an obvious economic strain on these families. Most plural wives must work outside the home out of economic necessity. Although the husband is the nominal patriarch, many plural wives are described as being quite independent and self-reliant (Altman & Ginat, 1996).

Having multiple wives might sound like a perpetual sexual fantasy to some men, but be careful what you wish for. The picture of polygynous life that emerges from the research of Altman and Ginat (1996) is hardly that of a sexual idyll. The man is officially the head of his family, but in many respects his position is that of a permanent houseguest. Each woman has her own home with her children, and the husband spends a few nights each week there. In order to avoid showing favoritism, he cannot keep all his things in one place, so he ends up having different possessions scattered among the different apartments. He must keep anything he really needs every day in a suitcase in his car. If something unexpected comes up with one of the families, such as an illness, he must juggle his schedule without offending the others. When the wives disagree with one another, the man is caught in the middle.

Polyandry, women having more than one spouse, is preferred in only a few societies (Frayser, 1985). In 99.5 percent of cultures around the world, women marry only one man at a time. Among the Nyinba of northwestern Tibet, fraternal polyandry (marrying brothers) is the normative form of marriage and is highly valued culturally (Levine & Silk, 1997). The few societies in which polyandry does occur are generally those in which the cooperative labor of adult males is essential to the household economy. For example, in Tibet, Toda husbands must labor together to terrace fields and complete the physically strenuous demands of agricultural work necessitated by their harsh environment. Traditionally, polyandry also occurred among the families of chiefs in the Marquesas Islands; having multiple husbands allowed elite women to demonstrate their wealth.

Marriage and Sex   Although times are changing, as we discussed earlier, in American society sexual expression is *universally* approved and expected only in the context of marriage. However, the experience of sex by individuals and couples reflects personal reality. The frequency of sex can vary greatly among couples, and the sexual satisfaction of individuals invariably changes over the course of a relationship and throughout the stages of one's life.

The frequency with which married couples engage in coitus does not remain constant; it changes with age and the length of the relationship. While a newlywed couple may not be able to wait to get their hands on each other at the end of each day, the sexual pattern is apt to be much different in a couple married for decades. The data reported in the 1994 National Health and Social Life Survey (NHSLS) (Laumann et al., 1994) found that married couples in the United States engage in sexual relations an average of seven times a month. There is some evidence that cohabitors have more frequent sex than other types of couples (see Table 8.3). Blumstein and Schwartz (1983) found that people who were living together had sex more often than married couples. The reasons for this are not entirely clear. One may be that married people are more likely than cohabiting couples to have children, and the presence of children in the home may reduce opportunities for sexual (and other) intimacies. Marriage may impose a public quality or sense of contractual obligation that might diminish feelings of sexual passion. Or, it may simply be that if the sexual passion of cohabiting couples dries up, they break up, whereas married people are more likely to remain together, even if their desire diminishes. This would produce the statistical illusion that cohabitation produces more sex.

Polyandry: the practice of having more than one husband at one time

Sexual satisfaction is the most important factor in people's happiness with marriage. When nearly 800 couples were asked to rank the factors they most strongly associated with overall marital satisfaction, sexual satisfaction came first, followed by nonsexual aspects of the relationship, frequency of spouse orgasm per sexual encounter, frequency of sexual activity, and being sexually uninhibited (Young et al., 1998).

Not surprisingly, another study found a link between sexual satisfaction and the frequency of sexual intercourse. Blumstein and Schwartz (1983) found that for the 7,000 married respondents to their survey, the frequency of marital sexual interactions was strongly associated with ratings of sexual satisfaction. However, lots of sex is not the only factor in a good marriage. For most couples in long-term relationships and marriages, the quality of their sexual interactions reflects the more general quality of their relationship. If caring, respect, and enjoyment are present in the marriage, they probably will be present in the sexual relationship, also.

Parenthood   Most people who marry have children at some point in their lives. Considerable research has established that having a child leads to lower happiness in life and lower marital satisfaction (Anderson, Russell, & Schumm, 1983; Belsky, 1985; Belsky, Lang, & Rovine, 1985; Belsky, Spanier, & Rowvine, 1983; Campbell, 1981; Glenn & Weaver, 1978). In general, the "newlywed" phase is one of the happiest times in life, but happiness and marital satisfaction both go down significantly with the birth of the first child and do not recover until the last child has left home for college or career. Contrary to the stereotype, the "empty nest" stage of life, the time after the children have moved out and both spouses are alone together, is actually one of the happiest times of life for most people. People who marry but do not have children (for what-ever reason) tend to report high levels of happiness and marital satisfaction at all ages. The distinction between parents and childless adults reveals a diversity of experiences and attitudes. One study (Koropeckyj-Cox, 1999)

FAQ:

Are married people happy with their sex lives?

The NHSLS study (Laumann et al., 1994) asked participants to rate their physical and emotional satisfaction with their partner during the previous year (Table 9.11). Fifty-two percent of married men and 41 percent of married women reported being extremely physically satisfied with their primary partner. Forty-nine percent of married men and 42 percent of married women reported that they were extremely emotionally satisfied in their relationship. In general, then, one must give a tentative "Yes" answer to the question about whether married people are happy with their sex lives, even though some individuals occasionally wish for more or different patterns of sexual expression.

TABLE 9.10

Physical and Emotional Satisfaction Among Sexual Partners

	Percentage Extremely Physically Satisfied With Partner		Percentage Extremely Emotionally Satisfied With Partner	
	Men	Women	Men	Women
Age				
18–24	44	44	41	39
25–29	50	39	46	40
30–34	43	42	37	39
35–39	48	39	41	37
40–44	49	46	38	44
45–49	40	39	37	40
50–54	48	35	50	37
55–59	58	29	55	26
Marital Status				
Noncohabiting	39	40	32	31
Cohabiting	44	46	35	44
Married	52	41	49	42
Race/Ethnicity				
White	47	40	43	38
African American	43	44	40	40
Hispanic	51	39	43	39

SOURCE: Laumann et al., 1994, pp. 116–117.

Why does marital satisfaction go down when a couple has children?

Children demand energy and attention, and the care, attention, and support that were previously available may seem more limited (Anderson et al., 1983). Spouses may find that they have little opportunity to be together and to maintain the communication and rapport that brought them together in the first place. One research project observed married couples in shopping malls and other public locations; the couples with children present spent much less time talking to each other, touching each other, and smiling at each other than the couples not accompanied by children (Rosenblatt, 1974). Parents are also less likely than childless people to believe that their spouses understand them well (Bernard, 1982; Campbell, 1981). In addition, parents feel greater financial pressures, lack of sleep, and loss of opportunities to enjoy the fun and good times that they had when they were dating. Despite these clear findings, most parents believe that having children has made them happier and brought their relationship closer (Veroff, Douvan, & Kulka, 1981). Such responses may reflect self-deception, social pressures to say what is desirable, or efforts to rationalize the sacrifices that one has made. One way in which children strengthen a marriage is that some people are reluctant to divorce when children are involved, so parenthood makes people more willing to remain married and work out their problems.

Most people who marry have children at some point in their lives.

found no significant differences in loneliness and depression between parents and childless adults aged 50 to 84.

The effect of children on a married couple's sex life is generally regarded as negative, although different studies disagree. A large set of interviews by Blumstein and Schwartz (1983) found that the *quality* of sex declined, but not the *quantity*. That is, parents had sex as often as childless spouses, but the parents had to sneak in their sexual activity without letting the children know; these pressures for silence and stealth interfered with spontaneity and other factors. Parents of young children fail to get enough sleep, and physical exhaustion can also impair sexual enjoyment and response. Many fathers complained bitterly about the deterioration in their marital sex life after children were born, whereas mothers seemed to be bothered less by the decline in sex.

Extramarital Relationships Although attitudes toward many types of sexual behavior have changed substantially over the past decades, most Americans continue to disapprove of extramarital relationships. Referred to variously as adultery, cheating, infidelity, or having an affair, an extramarital relationship is engagement in sexual relations with someone other than a spouse. In the United States, roughly 90 percent believe that extramarital sexual relations are always or almost always wrong (Laumann et al., 1994). However, attitudes and beliefs tell only part of the story, and we also need to consider actual behavior (Table 9.12). Public figures from Bill Clinton to Bill Cosby have "cheated," and when the media report these actions, the stories stimulate widespread evaluation and discussion.

Most preliterate societies prohibit extramarital sexual relationships for one or both marriage partners. In one study, 74 percent of 58 societies examined forbid adultery either for the woman or for both sexes (Frayser, 1985). However, when examining cross-cultural data on extramarital sexual relations it is important to understand the culture's definition of adultery. A substantial majority of societies allow extramarital relations with individuals in certain kin relationships (Ford & Beach, 1951). If extramarital sex is permitted for only one of the two marital partners, in all cases it is male infidelity that is tolerated or even encouraged.

In Western culture, the mythology of adultery can be traced back through the medieval and early modern patterns of sexual activity at the royal courts. Peasants and middle-class people had fewer opportunities to engage in illicit sex. People in the centers of power surrounded themselves with attractive people and provided opportunities for engaging in such affairs. Architecture as well as economics can be considered contributing factors. After all, if you live in a one-room house with your spouse, parents, and children, and your intended lover does as well, there are fewer places to go to engage in sex than if you live in a palace or great house with many separate rooms and doors with locks.

The tradition of adultery at the royal courts was influenced in part by the patterns of arranged marriages. Parents chose their children's spouses with an eye to military, political, and financial advantages. Adulterous lovers, in contrast, are chosen based on personal preference and mutual attraction. When two people with little in common are married to each other by external forces, it is not surprising that each might be receptive to romance and sex on the side with a person of their own choosing.

Nationally representative survey data show a higher likelihood of sexual infidelity among those with strong sexual interests, more permissive sexual values, lower satisfaction with their relationship, weaker ties to their partner, and greater sexual opportunities (Treas & Giesen, 2000). Statistical tests show that overall men are more likely than women to report engaging in extramarital sex. However, there is no gender difference in lifetime incidence among those younger than 40 years of age. Those who have ever been divorced and those with more liberal attitudes toward extramarital sex have a higher incidence of extramarital sex compared to everyone else (Wiederman, 1997).

Extramarital emotional or sexual involvement may include brief sexual encounters, long-term romantic affairs, or consensual extramarital relationships. Brief sexual encounters with a prostitute or a close friend typically involve little or no emotional investment. Romantic affairs are likely to last longer and involve both sexual and emotional infidelity. In one study of 200 couples, men maintained their extramarital affairs for an average of 29 months; women sustained theirs for an average of 21 months (Hall, 1987). One research study that sought to identify reasons for a long-term partner's sexual and emotional infidelity found that sexual boredom was more closely related to a sexual infidelity such as a one-night stand, whereas relationship dissatisfaction was linked to an emotional infidelity such as a longer-term affair (Shackelford & Buss, 1997).

Consensual extramarital sex gained some popularity in the 1970s and early 1980s. So-called **open marriages** are those in which both partners regard their own relationship as primary but agree that each is permitted to have sexual relationships with others. George and Nena O'Neill popularized the concept of open marriages in the United States in a 1972 book entitled *Open Marriage*. The O'Neills (who later divorced) believed that emotionally and sexually intimate relationships with outside partners of either sex did not have to compromise the primary relationship. One motivation for open marriage is enhancement of the marital relationship; in a study of 35 couples in open marriages and 35 couples in sexually exclusive marital relationships, the open marriage couples reported greater marital satisfaction (Wheeler & Kilmann, 1983).

Swinging, also called comarital sex, is another form of consensual extramarital sex, in which a couple simultaneously participates in extramarital sex with one or more other couples. Unlike open marriage, in which mutual participation is not usual, swingers engage in sex in the same location at the same time. Swinging was most popular in the 1970s and early 1980s. Since then, available data suggest that fewer than 5 percent of men and women in the United States have experienced swinging (Duckworth & Levitt, 1985; Jenks, 1998).

Unlike those involved in open marriage or swinging, most people involved in an extramarital relationship invest a great deal of time and energy in keeping their infidelity a secret from their partner, believing "what my partner doesn't know won't hurt." Although presumably unknown to the spouse, "the affair nonetheless has enormous power to create feelings of shame, tension, distrust, fear, suspicion, and self-doubt in both partners" (Brown, 1993, p. 39).

In some cases, the theory is "what my partner doesn't know won't hurt *me*." One investigation that focused on the actions and attitudes of the guilty party after sexual infidelity found that as the partner's knowledge of the affair increased, the reactions of the one who strayed became more honest. Participants in an affair wanted to appear apologetic in case their partner knew of the affair, but they didn't want to give away too

> *[D]espite our attitude that philandering is immoral, regardless of our sense of guilt when we engage in trysts, in spite of the risks to family, friends, and livelihood that adultery inevitably entails, we indulge in extramarital affairs with avid regularity*
>
> (FISHER, 1992, P. 84).

TABLE 9.11		
Incidence of Extramarital Sexual Behavior		
Study	Married Men	Married Women
Kinsey (1948, 1953)	50%	26%
Hunt (1974)	41	18
Blumstein & Schwartz (1983)	26	21
Laumann et al. (1994)	25	15
Smith (1994)	21	13
Wiederman (1997)	24	12

Open Marriage: marital relationship in which spouses have sexual relationships with other people with their spouse's consent

Swinging: the sexual exchange of marital partners

Why do people have affairs?

People have extramarital relationships for many different reasons. Some may be seeking variety from the routine of marital sex (Lamanna & Riedmann, 1997). Others may have a nonsexual desire for emotional closeness. Men tend to justify affairs by citing a need for sexual excitement, while women are more likely to claim a need for emotional intimacy and communication (Townsend, 1995; Wright, 1992). In one study, 148 married men and 155 married women completed anonymous questionnaires rating the justification for an extramarital relationship. The researchers classified their responses into four categories: sexual excitement, romantic love, emotional intimacy, and extrinsic factors. The study found that women were less approving of having an affair for sexual excitement than for romance (Glass & Wright, 1992).

Most studies have concluded that there are some gender differences in motives and patterns for adultery (see Blumstein & Schwartz, 1983; Lawson, 1988). Men seem more likely to be content with a one-night stand offering nothing but sexual variety. Women tend to have affairs that bring emotional involvement. Men who stray tend to have more partners than women who stray. Men may engage in extramarital sex even if they are perfectly happy with their marriage, which again suggests that they simply want novelty and sexual adventure. Women, in contrast, tend to engage in extramarital sex only if they are in some way unhappy with their marriage.

much information in case they did not. Those interested in maintaining the relationship felt more guilty, accepted more blame for their actions, and presented kinder verbal responses (Mongeau & Schulz, 1997).

According to Lawson (1988), many people embark on an affair with the expectation that they can keep it under control and prevent it from affecting their marriage. It doesn't always turn out that way. Some people find that their feelings sweep them along and sensitize them to what they might be missing in their marriage. Others may maintain that their feelings for their primary partner have not changed, but if their partner discovers the affair, the partner's reaction may put a severe strain on the marriage.

The discovery of infidelity, regardless of whether it leads to dissolution of the marriage, tests the bonds of the marital relationship. The discovery of an affair can be devastating and the feelings of betrayal can do irreparable damage to a relationship. Some marriages, like that of Prince Charles and Princess Diana, don't survive; others, like that of Frank and Kathie Lee Gifford or Bill and Hillary Clinton, do. An examination of the effect of extramarital relationships on 62 Israeli marriages found that 34 percent ended in divorce, 43.5 percent were preserved but with a negative atmosphere, and 6 percent were intact but had a doubtful future. Only 14.5 percent were characterized by improvement and growth (Charny & Barnass, 1995).

Couples who stay together after infidelity is publicly or privately revealed do so for many, sometimes complicated, reasons. Some couples are motivated to maintain the marriage because of their children or a desire to preserve financial resources or social prestige. Others are able to repair the damage and make a new commitment to their relationship. Undoubtedly in some cases the partner's infidelity is not regarded as a major event. Attitudes toward a partner's infidelity are subject to wide cultural and individual variation. Certainly in some cases infidelity is a symptom of problems in the relationship rather than the sole cause for the dissolution of a marriage.

According to Kinsey's (1948, 1953) findings, people do not believe that their own infidelities contribute to relationship breakups or divorce—but they do believe that their partner's infidelity contributes to the breakup. Even those whose relationship falls apart tend to see *their* actions as *symptoms* of dissatisfaction, and *their partner's* actions as *causing* the dissatisfaction: "Your straying hurts the marriage, but my straying does not."

Supporting these findings, Blumstein and Schwartz (1983) found that couples who experienced infidelity were slightly (about 3 percent) more likely to break up than couples who remained monogamous. This was true even in "open marriages" or other explicit agreements in which the partners were permitted to have sex with other people. Couples who are more dissatisfied with each other are more likely to have extramarital sex and to break up later on, so the extramarital sex may be a signal rather than a cause. In other words, sometimes infidelity alone can cause a marriage to break up, whereas in other cases the infidelity is merely a sign of deeper problems that might well have led to a breakup even without the straying. Infidelity is considered a risk factor for divorce, which means that the odds of breaking up are higher if there is infidelity than if there is monogamy, but there is no proven causal relationship between the two.

Divorce

Some of those men who heeded Horace Greeley's 19th century call to "Go West, Young Man!" did so without taking their wives and children. Most of those adventurous young men just deserted or abandoned their families without bothering to go through the legalities of **divorce,** the legal dissolution of a marital relationship, which was uncommon in the United States until the 20th century. When economic or social reasons were the causes of a marriage, as was the case in many 19th century unions, those same factors could lead to its dissolution. Once love became the basis of most marriages in the 20th century, the loss of affection became an acceptable reason to justify the end of a marriage (D'Emilio & Freedman, 1988).

Although there is wide variation among cultures in attitudes toward divorce, it rarely has a positive value, so the cultural differences are simply a measure of the severity of the negative value judgment (Price & McKenry, 1988). A cross-cultural study that examined several variables in husband-wife relationships in 186 cultures found that a society's attitude toward marriage is generally consistent with their management of divorce. A society that is tolerant toward divorce generally requires no grounds, or reasons, for the divorce. This same study found no gender difference in the grounds for divorce in divorce-tolerant societies (Broude & Greene, 1993). The researchers concluded that tolerant attitudes towards divorce are associated with frequent divorce rates. An examination of attitudes toward divorce and the frequency of divorce in 85 societies (Table 9.12) found that most societies value marriage and use children and property considerations as pressures against divorce (Frayser, 1985).

Divorce: a legal or socially recognized dissolution of a marriage

In the United States, the number of marriages that end in divorce has increased dramatically. In 1950, one in four marriages ended in divorce. Today, half of all marriages don't last until death of a spouse. Higher rates of divorce do not necessarily reflect greater dissatisfaction with marriage. Until the 1960s, spousal misconduct had to be proved before a couple would be granted a divorce. The relaxation of legal restrictions, such as "no-fault" divorce laws, has made it easier to obtain a divorce. The ratio of divorces to marriages has shown a tendency to level off and has been relatively stable since 1977. After peaking at 5.2 divorces per 1,000 residents in 1980, the most recent U.S. Census data report that the divorce rate has declined to 4.3 divorces per 1,000 (Table 9.13). California has the most divorced people in the country (2.4 million) followed by Texas (1.6 million) and Florida (1.5 million). New Jersey has the lowest divorce rate (7.8 percent).

Although the divorce rate may seem high to us today, the respected historian Lawrence Stone (1977) calculated that 20th century marriages actually last longer than most marriages throughout history. Even though divorce was impossible in many times and places in history, many adults died in their 30s and 40s because of the low quality of medical care and public health. Stone concluded that in Early Modern England (1500–1800), the average marriage lasted between 17 and 20 years; by the middle of the 20th century the average was over 30 years. Stone suggested that the longest marriages in history, on average, occurred during the Victorian era (the late 1800s), because longevity had improved so that both spouses could expect to live until old age, but divorce was not yet widely available.

There is a correlation between divorce and economics. Divorce rates tend to be higher in times of economic prosperity than in times of recession or depression (Price

TABLE 9.12

Attitudes Toward and Frequency of Divorce in 67 Societies

	Percent
Expects, accepts, tolerates, does not disapprove of divorce	17.9
Mildly disapproves of divorce	25.4
Approves only if the reasons are considered justified	17.9
Expects, accepts, tolerates, does not disapprove of divorce during the first years of marriage or before children; otherwise disapproves	22.4
Strongly disapproves of divorce; stigma attached	16.4
Frequency of Divorce:	
Universal or almost universal divorce	8.5
Common, frequent, not uncommon to divorce	37.2
Moderate; a small minority of couples divorce	12.8
Divorce is frequent during the first years of marriage or before children are born; rare thereafter	11.7
Divorce is rare, occurs only in isolated instances or never occurs	29.8

SOURCE: Frayser, 1985.

FAQ:

Why do people divorce?

You might as well ask, "Why do people stay together?" The obvious answer is that people end a marriage when they are unhappy. But in fact, satisfaction is only one factor in the equation. Rusbult (1980, 1983) proposed that there are three factors that determine whether a couple stay together or breaks up. The first, sure enough, is the level of satisfaction. People who are happy with one an-other are more likely to stay together. The second factor is the quality of alternatives. People may remain in a less-than-ideal relationship if they think they will not be able to find someone better. People may be more willing to break off a relationship if they see many other eligible, desirable potential partners, or if they think they are highly attrac-tive and desirable themselves. The third factor is called "sunk costs." The more time and energy a person has sunk into a relationship, the more reluctant he or she is to break it off. In some cases, people may remain in trou-bled or abusive relationships because they feel they have put so much into the rela-tionship and suffered so much for it that they cannot bring themselves to toss it aside and start fresh with a new partner.

TABLE 9.13

Marriage and Divorce Rates in the United States, 1970–1997

	1970	1975	1980	1985	1990	1997
Number of marriages per 1,000 in the U.S.	10.6	10.0	10.6	10.2	9.8	10.3
Number of divorces per 1,000 in the U.S.	3.5	4.8	5.2	4.0	4.7	4.3

SOURCE: National Center for Health Statistics, 2000

& McKenry, 1988). A likely reason is that people put off getting a divorce until they are confident they can make it on their own financially. This conclusion was support-ed by studies of income support for poor families. Income support was introduced to provide more stable, reliable sources of income; it was thought that this would reduce divorce rates, but the results pointed in the opposite direction—providing more income to lower-class families led to a substantial *increase* in the divorce rate (see Price & McKenry, 1988).

There is a gender difference in the economics of divorce. If the level of economic development is low and female participation in the labor force is low, the economic status of women is low and men are more likely to divorce. If the level of economic de-velopment is high and female labor participation is high, women are less economically dependent on men and thus they are more likely to divorce (Trent & South, 1989).

Divorce can have severe social and personal consequences. Financial hardship is common after dissolution of a marriage. Results of the effects on men's incomes are mixed, but women's incomes drop dramatically, by about 24 percent (Bianchi & Spain 1997; Weitzman, 1985). The decline in economic status tends to be greater for women than for men for a number of reasons. First, there is the "marriage gradient" (e.g., Bernard, 1982; Guttentag & Secord, 1983). Women tend to marry men who earn more than they do, and men tend to marry women who earn less than they do; this causes hus-bands to have higher economic and educational status than their wives. When the cou-ple divorces and each person suddenly has to live on a single income, the man's is usually greater. Second, pervasive sex discrimination in the courts typically awards custody of the children to the wife rather than the husband. Although women regard getting the children as a benefit and a victory, it is also a financial burden (children are expensive!). The divorce courts do usually require the man to pay child support, but these amounts are not always enough to cover expenses, and not all men pay them reliably.

Most Americans now want tougher divorce laws—for other people. While a plu-rality of voters now believes that divorce is too easy, they are reluctant to restrict their own right to a no-fault divorce (*U.S. News*, 1996). Using data from the National Sur-vey of Families and Households, researchers examined how parental divorce is related to three types of family resources: economic resources, parental resources (that is, so-cialization practices), and community resources. Results support the negative economic consequences that we have already discussed. Marital disruption results in declines in effective parental practices, at least in the short term. There is some evidence that parental divorce results in gains in extra-household sources of community support, al-though in some areas such community resources decline after divorce as well (Hanson, McLanahan, & Thomson, 1998).

Virtually all divorced men (Stack & Gundlach, 1992) and most divorced women (Forest & Singh, 1990) return to having an active sex life after divorce. Divorced men have slightly more partners than divorced women do, but the typical pattern is having one or two sex partners a year. Divorced men and women who don't have children in the household and those under age 35 are more likely to be sexually active after a di-vorce (Stack & Gundlach, 1992).

Nearly all studies show that divorced men are more likely than divorced women to remarry, although many women remarry, too. So, do men like marriage more than

The Effect of Divorce on Children

Children raised by single parents fare worse than children who grow up with both their married parents—in terms of: school achievement, college attendance, criminality, even their own eventual marriage and divorce. Sociologist Sara McLanahan was herself a single parent and set out to show that single parents can do the job quite successfully. After many years of research, she concluded that they can—but on average they do not do as well as married parents (McLanahan & Sandefur, 1994).

These are broad averages. Many children of single parents do well in life, and married parents produce plenty of losers and criminals, even though on average the children of married parents do better. It is not even clear that parental divorce or absence is the causal factor. Some speculate that unreliable, impulsive tendencies may be genetic. Poverty, race, and ethnicity are confounding factors, because more poor minority children grow up without both parents than affluent white children. Moreover, divorce must be compared to what life is like for the child when the parents are together. Recent findings suggest that if the parents can get along to some degree, it is better for the child if they remain together, but if they are constantly in conflict the children may be better off if they divorce (Amato & Booth, 1998).

Generally, children are best off if their parents can manage to remain married and cooperate in raising the child. In your own sexual decision-making, you may want to consider the best interests of any children you may end up bringing into the world.

 Do you think the law should make it harder for parents than for childless couples to get a divorce?

---

women, or is it more difficult for divorced women to remarry? As already noted, children of divorce tend to remain with the mother, which can pose an obstacle to dating and remarriage. A majority of divorced men are typically not tied down to their children and therefore have more time and freedom to date new partners.

There is a marriage gradient in terms of age. The life expectancy for men is shorter than that for women, and husbands are usually several years older than their wives. Thus, as they get older, there are fewer potential partners for women and more for men. A woman looking for someone older than herself must beat ever-longer odds. The authors of the NHSLS (Laumann et al., 1994) summarized the effects of the marriage gradient as follows. By and large, most people get married in their 20s, and so the largest pool of potential spouses consists of people at that age. So the chances of remarriage are most strongly dependent on being able to appeal to people in their 20s. It is not unusual for a 40-year-old man to woo and marry a woman in her late 20s. It is more difficult for a 40-year-old woman to compete for a man in his 20s, and so divorcing at age 40 creates a more difficult situation for a woman than a man. To be sure, men in their 50s and 60s will generally find it harder to appeal to women in their 20s, and so the male advantage is limited, but to some extent this is offset by the availability of divorced women who are themselves out of their 20s. The changes in the odds of finding a partner as you get older bring us to the next section, which focuses on sexuality and aging.

AGING: THE FINAL TRANSITION

Our society tends to think of sex as youth-oriented. Lustful appetites and sexual passion that get cheers when you are in your 20s get jeers when you are 70. Sexuality for aging men and women often is characterized as being immoral, inappropriate, and an immature attempt to recapture lost vigor and youth. Aging bodies that are no longer trim and firm are thought of as shameful and revolting. As the percentage of the population over the age of 65 has tripled during the past century, the need to understand sexuality in older men and women has become essential.

When a group of college students were asked to answer questions about sexuality as they think they would at age 70, they were relatively optimistic about continued sexual enjoyment later in life. However, they also expected a considerable decrease in

"Like pair-bonding in foxes, robins, and many other species that mate only through a breeding season, human pair-bonds originally evolved to last only long enough to raise a single dependent child through infancy, the first four years, unless a second infant was conceived . . . [however] those first hominid forebears who remained together until their child was weaned survived disproportionately, selecting for serial monogamy. "

(FISHER, 1992, P. 154)

Longitudinal Study: a study in which individuals are followed, or in which a phenomenon is observed (continuously or intermittently), for a set period of time

sexual activity and an increase in sexual problems. In addition, their attitudes toward sexual activity in late life were more restrictive and conservative than their current attitudes (Floyd & Weiss, 2001).

Getting older is both a social and a physical process. As the body gets older, its sexual powers diminish. There is less energy and often less desire for sex. Because older people are widely seen as less sexually attractive than young people, many people may seek to minimize the physical evidence of aging by altering the appearance of their skin and hair and even resorting to cosmetic surgery. Without such efforts, or usually even in spite of them, the skin grows looser and wrinkled, hair loses its color and turns gray or white (or falls out), bones grow more brittle and vulnerable to breakage, and muscle is lost while fat is added (resulting in a gradual rise in body weight). Socially, aging brings a series of transitions, often including retirement from full-time work, reduced involvement in parenting (as children leave home), loss of some relationships as friends and others move away or die, and sometimes relocation to a new home. Early in the 20th century, elderly people were relatively poor financially and so aging involved a significant loss of financial status, but now the elderly are one of the wealthiest segments of the population. That change has made aging less traumatic than it once was.

The needs for intimacy, excitement, and pleasure continue throughout life. The aging process is characterized by complex physical, social, and psychological factors, all of which have effects on sexuality. However, there is nothing in the biology of aging to stop sexual activity for most people. While there are specific physiological changes in the sexual responses of postmenopausal females and declines in testosterone production in aging males, there is no biological reason for healthy adults to stop sexual activity. In fact, studies showing a decline in sexual activity by the elderly may actually be a measure of declining health (Table 9.14).

Cross-cultural data indicate that not all cultures share a negative view of sexuality among older people. In societies where sexual activity among the elderly is expected, 70 percent live up to this expectation (Winn & Newton, 1981). Women are expected to become more sexually uninhibited as they become older in 22 percent of the societies surveyed. Outdated myths about sex and aging persist in the United States because younger people do not want to face the inevitability of growing old (Hodson & Skeen, 1994).

While sexual activity may decline with age, a significant proportion of older people remain sexually active (Richardson, 1995). Continued sexual activity appears to be dependent on good physical and emotional health and the regularity of sexual expression, as it is at any age. One **longitudinal study** (a study that follows its subjects for many years) reported that patterns of sexual activity remain relatively stable during middle and late adulthood (George & Weiler, 1981). Similarly, Masters and Johnson (1966) found that the frequency of intercourse in early marriage and overall quality of sexual activity in early adulthood correlate significantly with the frequency of sexual activity in late adulthood.

While older people are sexual and often want and need sexual contact, they encounter many obstacles to the enjoyment of sexual pleasures. Some of these obstacles are physical, but most are social. Finding and enjoying sex in your 70s or later can present special problems. For example, many older people find themselves alone after the death of a long-time spouse or companion, decreasing the opportunities for sexual activity.

Another factor in the development of sexual relationships for older individuals is the imbalance between the number of males and females that we mentioned in the previous section. While longevity is increasing for all Americans, females still tend to live longer than males. The tendency for women to outlive their husbands is strengthened by the fact that women commonly marry older men. In such situations a woman is likely to survive her husband by many years. Forty-five percent of women 65 years old and over are widowed, and 7 in 10 of the elderly widows live alone (U.S. Census Bureau Report, 1999).

TABLE 9.14

Sexual Interest and Activity Among Older Adults

	Aged 50–59	Aged 60–69	Aged 70+
Women who remain sexually active	93%	81%	65%
Men who remain sexually active	98	91	79
Women sexually active having sex at least once a week	73	63	50
Men sexually active having sex at least once a week	90	73	58
Women sexually active reporting a high level of sexual enjoyment	71	65	61
Men sexually active reporting a high level of sexual enjoyment	90	86	75

SOURCE: Adapted from Brecher, 1984, pp. 314–316.

"[The elderly are able] . . . to enjoy themselves vivaciously and quite fully. This is one of the qualities it is thought adults are obligated to lose, or at least are likely to lose, with age. Why? First, what is wrong with age? It is a certificate of competence and implies a library of experience. Second, it is surely not inevitable that adults lose their fun."

(TIGER, 1992, P. 289)

The change in the sex ratio that occurs over the life course may necessitate changes in sexual behavior (Guttentag & Secord, 1983). According to social exchange theory (see Chapter 1), when there are more women than men (an increase in supply), men can obtain sex with less commitment or other investments. A single man in a retirement community may have many women who are interested in him. However, due to the shortage of men, a single woman in the same community may be unable to find a mate. The only solutions that seem plausible for this population are for older women to date younger men or to date each other, and neither of those options appears to have gained wide appeal. Many women simply give up and stop having sex as they grow older. The NHLHS survey confirmed the finding that increasing age brings a steep rise in the proportion of women who have no sex partner (Laumann et al., 1994).

Living arrangements affect opportunities for sexual activity at any age, and especially in the group living arrangements common among the elderly. For some, the opportunities for developing sexual relationships may be enhanced in retirement communities that offer a variety of social activities—from lawn bowling to bridge tournaments to dances. Such activities provide ample opportunities for meeting other people and developing relationships. On the other hand, the lack of privacy in nursing homes tends to discourage the sexual needs of their residents (Brown, 1989; Shell, 1994). Most nursing homes segregate men and women; few even make accommodations for married couples to share a room. The administrators and staff at some nursing homes aggressively discourage sexual relationships, apparently believing either that sex is inappropriate for the elderly or that sexual relationships would make their jobs more difficult. Moreover, there is a tendency to deal with "troublesome" sexual behavior by the quick administration of sedatives (Hodson, 1994).

The demographic reality is that Americans are living longer than they did even a generation ago and this trend will continue. A great number of individuals live into their 80s and beyond. There is no reason these people should not enjoy the gratification of pleasurable and fulfilling sexual relationships. Attitude is decisive when it comes to sexuality—if you believe that older people shouldn't have sexual feelings or if you expect that older people have diminished sexual capacity, then your own sexuality as an older person may be affected. If, in contrast, you have a positive attitude toward sexuality at any age, you are more likely to have a rewarding sex life.

The need for intimacy, excitement, and pleasure continues throughout life.

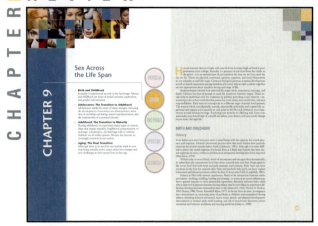

At any given age, your sexuality is a blend of your biologically developed needs and potentials and the social opportunities and constraints you experience. Rites of **1**_____ mark changes in social status and the **2**_____ and responsibilities of individuals in society. These rituals also may mark transitions in social definitions of sexuality. The four universal transitions or life crises which typically are marked by rites of passage are: **3**_____, _____, _____, and _____.

Even in utero **4**_____ have sexual responses. Infants frequently become sexually aroused and babies begin to stimulate themselves sexually at an early age. There is no evidence that early childhood sex play is harmful. On the other hand, there is research that indicates that a child deprived of physical closeness during infancy may be more likely to experience difficulties forming intimate relationships later in life.

5_____ refers to the time during which dramatic physical changes occur that mark the beginning of sexual maturity and the potential for sexual reproduction. Adolescence is defined as the period between **6**_____ and _____; it is a time of social and biological development. In North America there is no society-wide ritual to mark the transition from adolescence to **7**_____. It is during adolescence that most Americans begin to have sexual fantasies, enjoy masturbation, and begin to engage in sexual intercourse—although usually only sporadically.

Today, men and women in the United States are staying single longer than those of previous generations. **8**_____, or "living together," may be an alternative to marriage or represent an additional step in the transition from being single to getting married. In the

United States, there has been a marked shift toward couples living together before marriage. Since same-sex marriage is not legal in the United States, living together is the only legal option for homosexual partners.

9_____ is a legally recognized relationship within which sexual intercourse and the birth of children is socially approved and encouraged. In the United States, over **10**_____ percent of all individuals marry at least once before age 40. Some social scientists suggest that marriage in the United States has changed from an **11**_____ partnership to a relationship based on emotional factors and that the family has become a center of intimate companionship.

Overall, studies show that generally married people are happier, healthier, and live longer than the unmarried. Most societies prohibit extramarital sexual relationships, yet adultery occurs in every society.

Many societies permit **12**_____, that is, having more than one spouse. **13**_____ is the marriage of one man to two or more women at the same time. **14**_____ is the marriage of one woman to two or more men at the same time.

The frequency of sex can vary greatly among couples, and the sexual satisfaction of individuals invariably changes over the course of a relationship and throughout the stages of one's life. However, in general, married people are happy with their sex lives, even though some individuals occasionally wish for more or different patterns of sexual expression. For most couples in long-term relationships and marriages, the quality of their sexual interactions reflects the more general quality of their relationship. If caring, respect and enjoyment are present in the marriage, they probably will be present in the sexual relationship, also.

Most people who marry have children at some point in their lives. Typically, marital satisfaction goes **15**_____ when a couple has children.

Most studies have concluded that there are some gender differences in motives and patterns for adultery. Infidelity is considered a risk factor for divorce, which means that the odds of breaking up are higher if there is infidelity than if there is monogamy, but there is no proven causal relationship between the two.

In the United States, half of all marriages end in divorce. Younger people are more likely to divorce than older ones. Divorce peaks for individuals in their 20s. Children and financial concerns impact the likelihood of divorce. Divorces are most common in the early years of marriage. Divorced men are more likely than divorced women to remarry.

As we age our sexuality and our sexual behaviors tend to change. However, the need for intimacy, excitement, and pleasure continue throughout life, and there is nothing in the biology of aging to stop sexual function in older adults. What probably affects sex among older adults more than anything is the cultural stereotype that sex is inappropriate for elderly individuals. Attitude is everything; if you believe that older people shouldn't have sexual feelings or if you expect that older people have diminished sexual capacity, then your own sexuality as an older person may be affected.

While longevity is increasing for Americans, it remains true that females tend to live longer than males. Also, **16**_____ tend to marry individuals older than themselves. This creates an imbalance of opportunity for elderly females. Generally, the opportunities for sexual relationships are greater in retirement communities than in nursing homes.

SUGGESTED READINGS

Abrahms, J. & Spring, M. (1997). *After the Affair: Healing the Pain and Rebuilding Trust When a Partner Has Been Unfaithful.* New York: HarperCollins.

The authors offer practical solutions and strategies on how to move beyond blame to help both partners overcome the crisis of infidelity in a committed relationship.

Anderson, C. M., Steward, S., & Dimidiian, S. (1995). *Flying Solo: Single Women in Midlife.* New York: W.W. Norton & Co.

This book chronicles the lives of divorced, never married, or widowed women over 40 to demonstrate that being a single woman at midlife can be fulfilling.

Harris, R. H. (1994). *It's Perfectly Normal: A Book About Changing Bodies, Growing Up, Sex, and Sexual Health.* Cambridge, MA: Candlewick Press.

This book provides broad and detailed coverage that conveys the message that sex comprises many things, not just intercourse. Intended for children in grades 4 to 7 and their families, the text and illustrations may be too explicit for some.

James, J. W. & Friedman, R. (1998). *The Grief Recovery Handbook: The Action Program for Moving Beyond Death, Divorce, and Other Losses.* New York: HarperCollins.

James and Friedman explore the lifelong negative effects of unresolved grief and suggest specific actions to work through losses and regain energy and happiness.

Williamson, M. L. (2000). *Great Sex After 40: Strategies for Lifelong Fulfillment.* New York: John Wiley & Sons.

This book helps couples growing older together cope with normal side effects of aging and maintain, or even improve, their sexual relationship.

ANSWERS TO CHAPTER REVIEW

1. passage; **2.** roles; **3.** birth, maturation, marriage, death; **4.** fetuses; **5.** Puberty; **6.** childhood, adulthood; **7.** adulthood; **8.** Cohabitation; **9.** Marriage; **10.** 90; **11.** economic; **12.** polygamy; **13.** Polygyny; **14.** Polyandry; **15.** down; **16.** women.

CHAPTER 10

Sex and Gender

PHYSICAL

SOCIAL

EMOTIONAL

SPIRITUAL

COGNITIVE

■ **Males, Females, and Intersexuals**
An individual's sex can be categorized as male, female, or intersexual. Intersexuals include hermaphrodites, male pseudohermaphrodites, and female pseudo-hermaphrodites.

■ **Sexual Differentiation**
Prenatally, males and females develop homologous sex organs from undifferentiated tissue; differences in brain patterns between males and females also occur during embryonic development. Nevertheless, similarities between adult males and females—in terms of social, physical, cognitive, and personality traits—are great.

■ **Gender Roles**
Gender roles can vary from culture to culture. Trans-gender roles are socially approved gender roles that are neither male nor female. In cross-gender roles, a male or female assumes a social role normally reserved for the opposite sex.

■ **Gender Identity**
The psychological sense of being male or female is an important part of your self-concept. Gender identity disorders occur when there is a strong and persistent desire to identify as the opposite sex or discomfort with one's gender identity.

Your sex is (usually) what's between your legs. Gender is what's between your ears. In this context, *sex* refers to the biologically determined categories of male and female. *Gender*, on the other hand, is a socially constructed role that has emotional implications, cognitive aspects, and spiritual meaning.

Whether you think of yourself as male or female, you began life as a mass of undifferentiated cells that could produce a human female. The early embryo is described as undifferentiated because in the first month or so it is not possible to discern any differences between embryos that develop into females and those that develop into males. As the result of a complex series of events usually triggered by the absence or presence of a Y chromosome, some humans become males and others become females.

So typically a person's sex is relatively easy to understand. A person's gender, on the other hand, is not as straightforward. There are alternate genders, transgenders, and marginal genders. "No general categories can be induced, no taxonomy created, until after some significant amount of descriptive data are available" (Dickemann, 1993, p. 29). **Gender identity** (a person's inner sense of being male or female) and **gender roles** (the public image of being male or female that a person presents to others) are similarly complex and vary as widely as the people who assume them. Despite this complexity, there is enormous social pressure to force people into a limited array of categories.

Given the multitude of differences between men and women, it is not surprising that human sexuality also varies considerably. Many of the problems that individuals experience related to sex and gender can be attributed to cultural insistence on two categories of sex (homosexual or heterosexual) and two genders (female or male). Mildred Dickemann (1993, p. 29) has written, "There are as many kinds of alternate gender constructions as there are societies, and the variations within each kind are as various as the individuals who occupy, interpret and manifest them." In this chapter we shall examine the biological and social events that result in your gender identity and the gender role that you play in society.

MALES, FEMALES, AND INTERSEXUALS

Fill out any official form and you are almost always asked to identify your sex by checking one of two boxes: Male or Female. Most of us assume that these are the only two sexes. But two boxes aren't really enough to represent accurately the range of sexes of human beings (Figure 10.1). Hormonal variations during prenatal development may produce individuals with both ovarian and testicular tissue. Biologically speaking, the sexes also include a small number of **intersexuals,** those who are neither female nor male, but have both male and female traits (Fausto-Sterling, 1993). The frequency of intersexuality is estimated to be 1 or 2 in every 1,000 births (Blackless et al., 2000).

Chromosomes: small rod-shaped bodies in the nucleus of a cell at the time of cell division which contain, in the form of DNA, all the genetic information needed for the development of the cell and the whole organism

Transgender: appearing or attempting to be a member of the opposite sex

Gender Role: the public image of being male or female that a person presents to others

Intersexuals: persons having both male and female characteristics, including in varying degrees reproductive organs, secondary sexual characteristics, and sexual behavior

| Name: _____ |
| Date of Birth: _____ |
| Soc. Sec. # _____ _____ _____ |
| Age ☐ under 21 |
| ☐ 22 35 |
| ☐ 35 50 |
| ☐ over 50 |
| |
| Sex ☐ Male |
| ☐ Female |
| ☐ Intersexual |
| ☐ Transsexual |
| ☐ None of the Above |

FIGURE 10.1　**Check One.**

Broadly speaking, intersexuality constitutes a range of anatomical conditions in which key male and female anatomy are mixed. Intersexuals are sometimes referred to as **hermaphrodites,** after the Greek god Hermaphroditus. According to Greek mythology, Hermaphroditus was born male, but at age 15, became half female when his body fused with the body of a nymph with whom he had fallen in love. Since the end of the Middle Ages in Europe, hermaphrodites were forced to make a permanent choice between being male and being female, often under penalty of death. This choice made it easier to determine questions of inheritance, legitimacy, paternity, succession to title, and eligibility for certain professions. A carryover of this practice is the registration of babies as either female or male on their birth certificates.

There are three major intersex categories. However, there are many variations within each of these three categories.

Hermaphrodites: individuals in which reproductive organs of both males and females are present

X Chromosome: a sex chromosome of humans and most mammals that determines femaleness when paired with another X chromosome and that occurs singly in males

Y Chromosome: a sex chromosome of humans and most mammals that is present only in males and is paired with an X chromosome

Pseudohermaphrodite: person having the internal reproductive organs of one sex and external sexual characteristics of the other sex

Sexual Differentiation: the process by which males and females develop distinct anatomies

Wolffian Ducts: a pair of embryonic ducts which if allowed to develop become the male reproductive system

Müllerian Ducts: a pair of embryonic ducts which give rise to the genital passages in the female but disappear in the male

CROSS-CULTURAL PERSPECTIVES

"I Brought My Little Brother to the Infirmary and I Was Going Back Home With a Sister"

Despite heavy doses of traditional African medicine for his stomach cramps, Hamidou Dié, 18 years old, wasn't getting better so his older brother Modou took him to the infirmary in the next village. Modou was mystified when he was told that Hamidou had been transferred to the maternity ward and given birth to a baby boy. "I thought to myself," Modou said, "I brought my little brother to the infirmary and I was going back home with a sister and a nephew" (Onishi, 2001, p. A4).

As in most of rural Africa, the gender roles between men and women are rigidly drawn, and the story of Hamidou disrupted life in Sio, the small village in Burkina Faso in West Africa, where Hamidou had lived as a male for 18 years until he was transformed into Sita, a young woman. Born with ambiguous genitalia, she was named Sita at birth until her father decided the baby was a boy and renamed him Hamidou. Sita was born with two sexual organs, one of which—depending on the eye of the beholder—was more developed than the other. "My husband thought it was boy," said Sita's mother, "and what could I say against my husband?" (Onishi, p. A4)

Sita thought of himself as a boy until he began menstruating at age 14. Then, "I realized that I was not a boy but a girl" (Onishi, p. A4). Yet, Sita kept the change a secret and underwent the initiation rites into manhood with other boys.

Somehow one of her friends discovered the truth and a relationship began. Sita was able to keep her pregnancy hidden, perhaps because the villagers avoided the truth, perhaps because she continued her normal routine of harvesting millet and sorghum through the ninth month of her pregnancy. "I thought it was shameful to be pregnant because everyone thought I was a boy. But after the birth I was satisfied. Now I would be recognized as a woman." (Onishi, p. A4)

Unfortunately, Sita had no idea how to be a woman in Sio. She did not know how to care for a child, how to carry it strapped to her back; she did not know how to grind millet or prepare meals. She didn't even know how to tie the traditional female wrap around herself.

She has no role in Sio. Her male friends no longer visit; women shun her.

SOURCE: Adapted from Onishi, 2001.

1. *True hermaphrodites* possess one testis and one ovary. In some true hermaphrodites the testis and the ovary grow separately, one on each side of the body. In others they grow together within the same organ, forming an ovo-testis. Often at least one of the gonads functions effectively, producing sperm or ova, as well as functional levels of sex hormones. True hermaphrodites may have two X chromosomes or one X chromosome and one Y chromosome. (Recall from Chapter 5 that two X chromosomes signify a genetic female, and one X and one Y chromosome signify a genetic male.) Their external genitals are often a mixture of female and male structures.

2. Male *pseudohermaphrodites* have testes and some aspects of female genitalia (usually a vagina and a clitoris) but no ovaries. Male pseudohermaphrodites have one **X chromosome** and one **Y chromosome**. At puberty male pseudohermaphrodites often develop breasts, but they do not menstruate since they have no ovaries or uterus.

3. *Female pseudohermaphrodites* have ovaries (and sometimes a uterus), as well as some aspects of male genitalia, but they lack testes. Female pseudohermaphrodites have two X chromosomes.

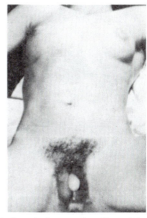

A female hermaphrodite with an enlarged clitoris and fused labia.

In our society few intersexuals maintain their natural sexuality. Because they do not fit into the traditional binary classification scheme, it is usually assumed that, left alone, they would be unhappy that they are not "like everyone else." At least since the 1940s, physicians have steered most intersexual infants into a program of hormonal and surgical management so that they can appear to be fully female or fully male.

SEXUAL DIFFERENTIATION

Prenatal Sexual Differentiation

The **sexual differentiation** of males and females begins at the moment of conception. The union of a sperm with an ovum can create either a male or a female. There are chromosomal, hormonal, gonadal, and internal and external reproductive differences between males and females. However, other than the difference in genetic coding in the spermatozoa, that is, whether the sperm carries an X or Y chromosome, the potential for maleness or femaleness is identical.

During the first weeks of development, embryos that will develop into males are indistinguishable from those that will develop into females (Figure 10.2). At this stage all embryos have primitive external genitals with no distinguishable maleness or femaleness, a pair of undifferentiated gonads, and two sets of primitive duct structures—the Müllerian and the Wolffian ducts.

It takes the presence of a particular chemical to effect a change from the basic female pattern of development. This chemical substance, called the H-Y antigen, must be present for maleness to develop. Not much is known about the H-Y antigen except that the Y chromosome controls its production. If the H-Y antigen is present, the primitive gonads develop into testes; otherwise the primitive gonads develop into ovaries.

The developing testes begin to produce androgens, including testosterone. In this case, the **Wolffian ducts** develop into the epididymis, vas deferens, seminal vesicles, and ejaculatory duct, while the **Müllerian ducts** shrink until they disappear. However, if no H-Y antigen has triggered the production of testes and testosterone, the Wolffian ducts degenerate and the Müllerian ducts develop into fallopian tubes, uterus, and the inner two thirds of the vagina (Figure 10.3).

Thus, for the first 6 or 7 weeks the tissues that will become the external genitalia are the same in all human embryos, female and male. If there is little testosterone present, an embryo

Human cells contain 22 pairs of matched chromosomes and one pair of sex chromosomes. Normally a female has two *X* chromosomes and a male has one *X* and one *Y* chromosome. This photograph shows the chromosomes of a genetic male.

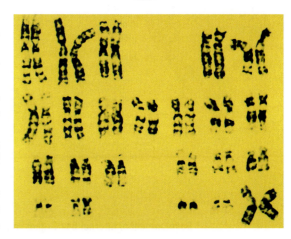

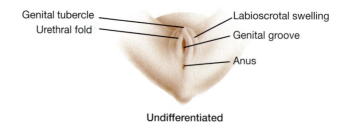

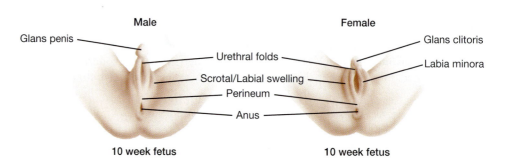

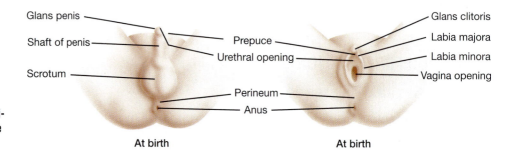

FIGURE 10.2 Undifferentiated External Sex Organs of the Human Embryo and Fetus.

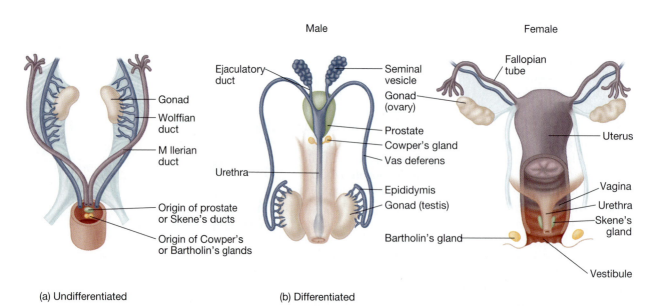

(a) Undifferentiated

(b) Differentiated

FIGURE 10.3 Development of Internal Sex Organs in a Human Embryo.

TABLE 10.1

Homologous Sex Organs

Female:	Male:
Clitoris	Glans of the penis
Hood of the clitoris	Foreskin of the penis
Labia minora	Shaft of the penis
Labia majora	Scrotal sac
Ovaries	Testes
Skene's ducts	Prostate gland
Bartholin's glands	Cowper's glands

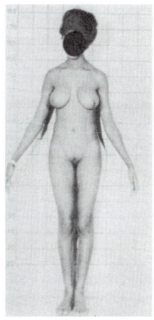

Androgen insensitivity syndrome in a genetic male.

develops into a female. In such an environment the embryo will develop a clitoris, vulva, and vagina in weeks 6 to 8. However, the presence of sufficient levels of testosterone stimulates the folds that would have developed into inner vaginal lips (labia minora) to grow together to form the shaft of a penis (see Figure 10.2). The tissue that would have developed into a clitoris is stimulated to form the glans of the penis. Likewise, the tissue that would have formed the outer vaginal lips of a female is stimulated to form a scrotum. Both ovaries and testes initially develop inside the abdominal region of an embryo. Only later do the ovaries move inside the pelvis and the testes move down into the scrotum. Because male and female sex organs derive from the same undifferentiated embryonic tissue, the organs compared above are said to be *homologous* (Table 10.1).

As the fetus develops, sexual differentiation occurs at three different levels: (1) the internal sex structures, (2) the external genitalia, and (3) the brain. These developmental processes are controlled by the interaction between the individual's genetic blueprint and the production of hormones. For example, even if the XY male chromosome pattern is present, without sufficient testosterone production at just the right time, anatomic development will tend toward the female rather than toward the male (Jost, 1953, 1972; Money & Ehrhardt, 1972; Wilson, George, & Griffin, 1981). It should be noted, however, that while female sex hormones are critical during puberty to provide girls with the characteristics typical of adult females, these hormones are not involved in prenatal sexual differentiations. In the absence of H-Y antigen and androgens, embryos will develop into females; no female sex hormones are required.

Abnormalities of Prenatal Differentiation

Chromosomal abnormalities can result in a child born with one or more extra or missing sex chromosomes, upsetting the delicate hormonal balance required to develop into a male or female. These abnormalities can result in 1 of over 70 identified conditions that affect internal and external reproductive organs and the ability to have children (Levitan & Montagu, 1977). Two of the most widely researched conditions are Klinefelter's syndrome and Turner's syndrome. **Turner's syndrome,** the absence of a second sex chromosome (XO), is relatively rare, estimated to occur in about 1 in every 2,000 live female births (Grayhold et al., 1998). **Klinefelter's syndrome,** the occurrence of an extra X chromosome (XXY) is much more common, occurring in an estimated 1 of every 500 live male births (Table 10.2) (Kruse et al., 1998).

Even embryos with the normal complement of sex chromosomes can experience hormonal abnormalities during prenatal development that can result in ambiguous sex organs or a combination of male and female sex organs. **Androgen insensitivity syndrome** is a rare genetic defect in which the body cells of a chromosomally male fetus are insensitive to the influence of androgens (Charnette et al., 1997). Because testosterone cannot exert its effects, prenatal development is feminized; the child is born with normal-looking female genitals and a shallow vagina and is usually raised as female.

Turner's Syndrome: a relatively rare condition characterized by the presence of one unmatched X chromosome resulting in affected individuals having normal female external genitals but their internal reproductive structures do not fully develop

Klinefelter's Syndrome: a condition characterized by the presence of two X chromosomes and one Y chromosome in which affected individuals have undersized external male genitals

Androgen Insensitivity Syndrome: a condition resulting from a genetic defect that causes chromosomally normal males to be insensitive to the action of testosterone and other androgens and to develop female external genitals

TABLE 10.2

Characteristics of Klinefelter's Syndrome and Turner's Syndrome

	Chromo-somal Sex	Gonadal Sex	External Genitals	Internal Reproductive Organs	Fertility	Secondary Sex Characteristics	Gender Identity
Klinefelter's Syndrome	XXY	Small testes	Small penis and testes	Normal male	Sterile	May have some breast development and rounded body contours	Usually male
Turner's Syndrome	XO	Streaks of ovarian tissue	Normal female	Underdeveloped uterus and fallopian tubes	Sterile	No breast enlargement	Usually female

Female Adrenogenital Syndrome: condition in which a chromosomally normal female who, as a result of excessive exposure to androgens during prenatal sex differentiation, develops external genitalia resembling those of a male

DHT-Deficiency: condition in which a chromosomally normal male develops external genitalia resembling those of a female as a result of a genetic defect that prevents the prenatal conversion of testosterone into DHT

Female adrenogenital syndrome occurs when a chromosomal female is masculinized prenatally by exposure to excessive androgens. The flood of androgens can be from a genetically induced malfunctioning of the fetus's own adrenal glands. In the 1950s some pregnant women were given androgenlike drugs to reduce the risk of miscarriage, however, these drugs sometimes caused female babies to be born with masculine-looking external genitals (Clarnette, Sugita, & Hutson, 1997).

DHT-deficiency is another genetic defect that prevents the conversion of testosterone into the hormone dihydrotestosterone (DHT), which is essential for normal development of external genitals in a male fetus. DHT-deficiency results in males with undescended testes and an underdeveloped penis and scrotum that resemble a clitoris and labia. Because their genitals appear more female than male, males with DHT-deficiency usually are identified as females and raised as girls. However, because their testes are functional, at puberty their testes descend and clitorislike organs enlarge into penises (see CONSIDERATIONS box). For a summary of ambiguous sex characteristics resulting from hormone abnormalities, see Table 10.3.

Males and Females: More Alike or Different?

Maybe because American men usually enjoy more power and prestige than women, it is sometimes assumed that men have every advantage over women. However, there is evidence that starting in the womb males have some very real disadvantages. While more boys than girls are conceived (perhaps because sperm carrying the male's Y chromosome swims faster than those carrying the larger X chromosome), when mothers experience stress, male embryos are more likely to perish. The male fetus is at greater risk of peril from almost all obstetric complications, including brain damage, cerebral palsy, and premature birth. By the time a baby boy enters the world, he is trailing the average girl developmentally by 6 weeks (Kraemer, 2001).

Social Differences Social pressures can compound biological vulnerability. Many experts are beginning to believe that the differences between men and women reflect a combination of innate basic tendencies and socialization into different roles (see Eagly & Wood, 1999). If that is true, a society can mold boys and girls into becoming more similar or more different. From that perspective, gender differences in North America today probably are at close to an all-time low, because significant changes in social organization have ended the age-old pattern of separate male and female social spheres.

All societies rely on **division of labor** to some extent, probably because assigning tasks to specialists gets better results than everyone trying to do everything. The

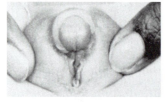

Female adrenogenital syndrome in a genetic female.

Nature or Nurture?

Researchers from Cornell University investigated 18 DHT-deficient males from the Dominican Republic who had been identified as and reared as female (Imperator-McGinley et al., 1979). At puberty their bodies began to change; their testes descended, their voices deepened, and what had been thought to be a clitoris expanded into a penis. When their bodies changed, 16 of the 18 assumed traditional male roles for their culture. One adopted a male gender identity but continued to maintain a female gender role and the other maintained a female gender identity and later sought gender-reassignment surgery.

 Does this case suggest that gender identity is predominantly based on environmental (nurture) or biological factors (nature)?

—Do you think that most of the children chose male gender identities because male roles are more positively valued in their culture?

separate spheres for men and women appear to have emerged prehistorically. Men did the hunting, made war, and tended the animals, while women gathered the plants and took care of the children. Even in Colonial America, men and women each performed separate but vital functions for the household. The Industrial Revolution evolved out of the scientific and technological work of men, but it took over many of the tasks that traditionally belonged to women. For example, the textile industry, regarded by some historians as the first wave of the Industrial Revolution, gradually put an end to the need for most individual women to make all of their family's clothes by hand. As their household burden was lifted, women began to clamor to be allowed into the men's sphere.

At present, the merger of the two spheres has progressed considerably, although it is still somewhat incomplete. Women are now found in nearly all occupational spheres that were once the exclusive province of men. They are not yet fully equal partners in

Nurture: the sum of environmental influences and conditions acting on an organism

Nature: the physical world not made by man; the forces that have formed it and control it

Division of Labor: the breakdown of work into its components and their distribution among different persons to increase productive efficiency

---

TABLE 10.3

Ambiguous Sex Characteristics Resulting From Hormone Abnormalities

	Chromosomal Sex	Gonadal Sex	External Genitals	Internal Reproductive Organs	Fertility	Secondary Sex Characteristics	Gender Identity
True Hermaphrodite	XX or XY	Testes and ovaries	Variable	Variable	Usually sterile	Variable	Variable
Androgen Insensitivity Syndrome	XY	Undescended testes	Normal female genitals and a shallow vagina	Neither male nor female internal structures	Sterile	Breast enlargement but no menstruation at puberty	Usually female
Female Adrenogenital Syndrome	XX	Ovaries	Typically more male than female	Normal female	Fertile	Normal female if treated with cortisone	Usually female
DHT-deficiency	XY	Undescended testes at birth, testes descend at puberty	Ambiguous at birth; at puberty genitals are masculinized	Vas deferens, seminal vesicles, and ejaculatory ducts but no prostate; partially formed vagina	Produce viable sperm but unable to inseminate	Become masculinized at puberty	Usually male

FAQ:

Are women really from Venus and men from Mars, as the author John Gray asserts?

Men and women may not be from different planets, but their differences transcend reproductive functions. Expert opinion about sex differences has evolved through several stages over the years. In the 1970s Maccoby and Jacklin (1974) compiled statistics from many different studies to confirm that in many ways males and females were significantly different from one another. By the 1980s, researchers began to examine the sizes of these "significant" differences. In the scientific sense, "significant" means "real" rather than "large and important." Indeed, the size of the effects, when they are present, is often not very large. For example, Eagly (1985) combined the results from several hundred published studies on two factors that are thought to differentiate men and women, helping and aggression. When all was said and done, men were both more helpful than women and more aggressive than women; this was consistent with what many researchers had thought, but in both cases the difference between males and females was small.

Overall, these differences between males and females are quite small, often depending on individual circumstances and perhaps cultural variation. ■

the men's sphere, as indicated by somewhat lower salaries and fewer women in the top ranks of power. At the same time, men have been encouraged to move into the women's sphere, and are spending more time performing housework and child-rearing tasks. However, men still spend far less time than women on such tasks. Men and women are today performing more of the same tasks in both traditional spheres than at almost any time in recorded history, and as a result men and women are probably more similar today than they have ever been.

The decreasing differences between men and women have a number of implications for sexuality (Bernard, 1983; Veroff, 1957). Society can either exaggerate or shrink the natural differences between men and women, resulting in a tradeoff between sexual excitement and intimate companionship. When men and women are confined to separate spheres, they develop into very different kinds of people. This makes mutual understanding and empathy between husband and wife more difficult and impairs the companionate aspect of marriage. On the other hand, the partner's differentness can be exciting, intensifying sexual relations. (This part of the argument resembles Bem's 1996 theory that "the exotic becomes erotic"—people are most aroused and excited by someone who is different. See Chapter 11 for more on Bem's theory). In contrast, when society merges the gender spheres, shrinking men and women's differences as in modern Western societies, they can understand each other better, which makes for better companionship. According to Bem's view, this may cause sexual excitement to be more short-lived, because there is less to make partners seem exotically different.

Physical Differences   On average, men's brains are about 15 percent, or 3 ounces, larger than women's brains. Previously it was assumed that men need a bigger brain to move their larger bodies. But, in fact, the parts of the brain that control large muscle movement are not enlarged in men and do not seem to account for the overall difference (Blum, 1997).

Like the sex organs, the brain undergoes prenatal sexual differentiation, and develops in the female pattern unless there is sufficient androgen stimulation to result in the male pattern (MacLusky & Naftolin, 1981; McEwen, 1981; Plapinger & McEwen, 1978). However, the precise nature and extent of this differentiation are as yet unclear. At a cellular level, distinct differences between male and female neural tissues are found. Male and female brains differ in the number and location of certain types of nerve cell connections (called **synapses**) in the hypothalamus (Carter & Greenough, 1979; Goldman, 1978). The hypothalamus, a multipurpose structure in the center of mammalian brains, serves as a relay station between the endocrine and nervous systems. It controls hunger, thirst, body temperature, ovulation in females, and libido. The patterns characteristic of females and males influence the function of the hypothalamus and the pituitary gland during and after puberty. For example, a group of neurons measuring 1 cubic millimeter in the hypothalamus is extremely sensitive to steroid hormones. This area is so different in males and females that it has been named the *sexually dimorphic nucleus (SDN)* (Hoffman & Swaab, 1989). This area causes females to have cyclic sex hormone production and menstrual cycles, resulting in cyclic female fertility. Activity of this same area in males results in a relatively constant level of sex hormone production and fertility.

The nerve fibers that connect the two hemispheres of the brain also differ in males and females. One narrow strip, called the **anterior commissure,** tends to be 10 to 12 percent larger in women. A larger web of nerve fibers that bridge the two hemispheres, the **corpus callosum,** is larger in adult women and shaped differently in women than in men (Durden-Smith & Desimone, 1983; Moir & Jessel, 1991). These differences have led one researcher to theorize that men are more "lateralized"; they rely on one hemisphere or the other in performing tasks while women generally can use both hemispheres at once (Gazzaniga, 1992). Results of a study that included detailed MRI imaging of the brains of subjects performing a rhyming task supported this thesis. As most of the men matched words with appropriate rhymes (for example, cake: bake), a small center called the *inferior frontal gyrus* (located behind the eyebrow) lit up only on the left side of the brain. In women the region lit in both left and right hemispheres (Shaywitz et al., 1995).

Newer research suggests that men listen with only half their brains. In a study of 20 men and 20 women, brain scans showed that men used mostly the left sides of their brains when listening (the left is the region associated with understanding language). Women in the study, however, used both sides (Lurito, 2000). These findings do not necessarily mean that women are better listeners. It could be that they have to use more of their brains than men to do the same task.

As you have already learned, traditional developmental models focus on the presence or absence of testosterone as the critical factor differentiating males from females. However, evidence suggests that ovarian hormones also play an important role in the development of the female brain. The existence of an active ovarian influence on female development changes assumptions and ideas about sexual differentiation. It also has theoretical and scientific implications for the study of similarities and differences in the behavior of men and women and the neural basis for these behaviors (Fitch et al., 1998).

Other physical differences between males and females are reasonably well known (see Figure 10.4). Men tend to be taller, heavier, and stronger than women. When one combines these physical traits with the most obvious behavioral differences, such as male aggressiveness and female nurturance, it is easy to conclude that males evolved to be fighters and females to be mothers. Recall from Chapter 1 that according to evolutionary theory reproductive success is the key to survival. The crucial factor in the female's reproductive success is her body's ability to bear children and nurture them. The male, on the other hand, will only be able to reproduce if he can fight his way to the top of the social hierarchy; the crucial factor in the male's reproductive success is his ability to fight and physically dominate other males (Dabbs, 2000).

Cognitive Differences According to conventional wisdom, girls have better verbal skills and boys excel at math-based tasks. One source of this assumption is that, on average, girls speak earlier than boys, and speak more fluently, with greater grammatical accuracy, and using better vocabularies. By age 10, girls excel at verbal reasoning, written prose, verbal memory, pronunciation and spelling, are better at foreign languages, stutter less, and are less often found to be dyslexic (Smith, 1984).

However, gender differences are not constant; there are more variations within each gender than between them (Lewin, 1988; Moller, 1988). Young girls may use words more easily than young boys, but in later years boys are likely to catch up. Although early research found that females are somewhat superior to males in verbal abilities (Maccoby & Jacklin, 1974), later studies have indicated that the only overall gender difference is that boys do not usually develop language skills as quickly as girls (Hyde & Linn, 1988).

Males generally do better than females in tests of visual-spatial abilities (Boyer et al., 1995) including the ability to follow a map in unfamiliar locations, construct a puzzle, or assemble a piece of equipment (Figure 10.5). There appears to be some relationship in females between the ability to do mental spatial rotation and math skills (Casey, 1996). Women tend to do better than men on tests of perceptual speed (Kimura, 1992) (see Figure 10.5). Females do better in computation in elementary school, though males do better in mathematical problem solving in high school and college (Hyde et al., 1990). Although boys outperform girls on the math portion of the SATs overall (Byrnes & Takahira, 1993), a recent study found that the difference was greater on items requiring spatial skills, shortcuts, or multiple solution paths than on problems requiring verbal skills or mastery of classroom-based content (Gallagher et al., 2000).

Studies of live brains using PET scanning techniques have shown that men and women seem to activate different parts of their brains while doing word or math/spatial tests. A comprehensive study analyzing 32 years of scores found that in the top 10 percent of math and science scorers, boys outnumbered girls three to one. In the top 1 percent, there were seven boys for every girl. In mechanical and vocational tests, such as electronics and auto repair, there were no girls in the top 10 percent—but it cannot be determined whether this finding reflects differences in intelligence or gender roles.

FAQ:

Do differences in the structures of men's and women's brains cause gender differences?

Where do gender differences originate? Transplant surgeons don't consider gender differences when recycling organs. Although there are numerous differences in the nonsexual anatomy of men and women (Figure 10.4), a human heart or kidney can function in the body of any transplant recipient, male or female. However, the brain is one vital organ exhibiting gender differences. Although scientists still argue whether sex differences in the brain cause sex differences in behavior, or if because the sexes behave very differently their brains become different, they do agree that male and female brains are visibly different.

Synapses: the junction across which a nerve impulse passes from an axon terminal to a neuron, muscle cell, or gland cell.

Anterior Commissure: an organized tract of fibers in the anterior part of the brain that connects corresponding parts of the right and left cerebral hemispheres

Corpus Callosum: the arched bridge of nervous tissue that connects the two cerebral hemispheres, allowing communication between the right and left sides of the brain

"If we set the two brains side by side . . . they look the same. We have to work hard to find what's different. The contrasts are too tiny, and still far too mysterious, to suggest that they [male and female brains] are profoundly different organs. They may do some things in different ways, but the brain repertoire is the same.

(BLUM, 1997, P. 63)

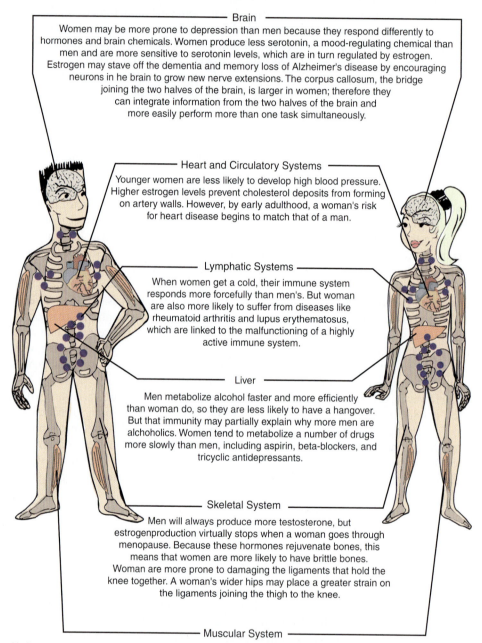

Body Size and Shape
The average man is 35 pounds heavier, has less body fat and is 5 inches taller than the average woman. Men tend to have broader shoulders, slimmer hips and slightly longer legs in proportion to their height.

Brain
Women may be more prone to depression than men because they respond differently to hormones and brain chemicals. Women produce less serotonin, a mood-regulating chemical than men and are more sensitive to serotonin levels, which are in turn regulated by estrogen. Estrogen may stave off the dementia and memory loss of Alzheimer's disease by encouraging neurons in he brain to grow new nerve extensions. The corpus callosum, the bridge joining the two halves of the brain, is larger in women; therefore they can integrate information from the two halves of the brain and more easily perform more than one task simultaneously.

Heart and Circulatory Systems
Younger women are less likely to develop high blood pressure. Higher estrogen levels prevent cholesterol deposits from forming on artery walls. However, by early adulthood, a woman's risk for heart disease begins to match that of a man.

Lymphatic Systems
When women get a cold, their immune system responds more forcefully than men's. But woman are also more likely to suffer from diseases like rheumatoid arthritis and lupus erythematosus, which are linked to the malfunctioning of a highly active immune system.

Liver
Men metabolize alcohol faster and more efficiently than woman do, so they are less likely to have a hangover. But that immunity may partially explain why more men are alchoholics. Women tend to metabolize a number of drugs more slowly than men, including aspirin, beta-blockers, and tricyclic antidepressants.

Skeletal System
Men will always produce more testosterone, but estrogenproduction virtually stops when a woman goes through menopause. Because these hormones rejuvenate bones, this means that women are more likely to have brittle bones. Woman are more prone to damaging the ligaments that hold the knee together. A woman's wider hips may place a greater strain on the ligaments joining the thigh to the knee.

Muscular System
Until puberty boys and girls are well matched in physical strength and ability, but once hormones kick in the average man has more muscle mass and greater upper body strength than the average woman.

FIGURE 10.4   Some Physical Differences Between Men and Women.

However, there were twice as many boys as girls at the very bottom of the test scores. Girls dominated reading comprehension tests and girls also did much better than boys in writing skills (Hedge & Nowell, 1995).

The small differences that exist in male and female cognitive abilities may be as much a reflection of environmental influences and cultural expectations as innate, genetically determined differences (Tobias, 1982). An examination of gender and motivation in high-school mathematics classes revealed that, for both males and females, endorsing the stereotype that math is a male domain was negatively related to reported effort (Greene et al., 1999). College students who performed two spatial tasks, a mental rotation test and a cognitive mapping test, revealed a gender difference in self-reported abilities and performance on the mental rotation test favoring men. No gender difference in the performance of the cognitive mapping task was found. However, although they did just as well as men on the cognitive mapping task, women reported less confidence in the accuracy of their skills (O'Laughlin & Brubaker, 1998).

Personality Differences Males and females exhibit a number of differences in personality. Females tend to be more extraverted, anxious, trusting, and nurturing than males. Males are more assertive, tough-minded, and have more self-esteem than females (Feingold, 1994). Are these personality traits biologically programmed, or shaped by the expectations of society?

Once again, viewed with a more critical eye, these differences tend to be small despite the attention given to them by society. Consider the highly politicized question of self-esteem, for example. The book *Reviving Ophelia*, which spent over 2 years on The *New York Times* Bestseller List, states that societal forces "cause girls to stifle their creative spirit and natural impulses, which ultimately destroys their self-esteem" (Piper, 1994, book jacket). A study by the American Association of University Women received considerable publicity for its conclusions that self-esteem among girls plummets as they reach adolescence and, as a result, teenage girls suffer from deep insecurities and self-doubts that do not afflict teenage boys. Inspired by these inflammatory statements, a team of researchers went through the laborious process of compiling data from over 200 different studies on levels of self-esteem in nearly 50,000 young Americans (Kling et al., 1999). They found that males do consistently have higher self-esteem than females. But the difference, though significant, was small. The effect was largest, although still small, in studies on older adolescents. It was smaller in the United States than in other countries, and white Americans showed a larger difference than African Americans. In short, there is a small but consistent difference between males and females in self-esteem.

The central personality differences between men and women, according to prevailing views in psychology, are groupings of traits that have been labeled communal and agentic (Bakan, 1966). **Communal traits,** those that facilitate forming and maintaining social relationships with others, include sensitivity to others, selflessness, desire to be united with others, emotional expressiveness (especially expressing affection and other tender feelings), kindness, sympathy, and warmth. These traits are regarded as more typical of women than men. **Agentic traits,** which focus on taking initiative and control in order to get things done, include independence, assertiveness, ambition, dominance, self-reliance, resilience (not giving up easily), being task-oriented, forcefulness, and willingness to make decisions. The agentic traits are seen as more typical among men than women. Indeed, many people regard the agentic traits as tantamount to masculinity and the communal traits as the essence of femininity (see Spence & Helmreich, 1978).

Communication Differences There are also gender-based differences in communication. Although girls tend to be more talkative than boys during early childhood, by the time they enter school, boys dominate classroom discussions (Sadker & Sadker, 1994). While women might not speak up as much in the classroom, they are more likely than men to disclose their feelings and to talk about their personal experiences (Dindia & Allen, 1992).

Linguistics professor Deborah Tannen (1990, 1995, 1998) has written several articles and books about the complexities of communication between men and women. She concludes that dialogue between the sexes often is difficult because men and women use language in essentially different ways. Although earlier studies proposed that communication broke down because men used it to attempt to dominate women, Tannen found that men's and women's conversational styles differ distinctly based upon gender

FAQ:

Are Men or Women Smarter?

Whether men or women are smarter overall has been a frequent focus of jokes and sexist comments—in both directions!—and a less frequent focus of serious inquiry. Girls mature somewhat faster than boys and therefore tend to be "smarter" during the school years. In adulthood, results based on millions of intelligence tests have made it quite clear that the average IQ scores of men and women are almost identical. However, the variance is higher among men's than women's IQ scores (Jensen, 1998; Lehrke, 1997; Roberts, 1945). In effect, this means that there are more men than women at both the mentally retarded and the genius levels. The difference is more conclusively established at the mentally retarded level, probably because there has been more research on retardation than on genius. Many experts are beginning to think that the IQ pattern is simply one reflection of a broad basic principle of greater male variability, i.e., men are more different from each other than are women.

Communal Traits: traits that facilitate forming and maintaining social relationships with others

Agentic Traits: traits that focus on taking initiative and control in order to get things done

and cultural conditioning, and it was these differences that caused misunderstandings. Women use conversation to indicate involvement and signal support; this style may make men feel that women are nags who never get to the point. Men tend to talk to preserve independence and negotiate status and position, which may lead women to feel that men just lecture and criticize.

Gender Gaps in Problem Solving

Tasks Favoring Men

Men tend to perform better than women on certain spatial task. They do well on tests that involve mentally rotating an object or manipulating it in some fashion, such as imagining turning this three-dimensional object:

or determining where the holes punched in a folded piece of paper will fall when the paper is unfolded:

Men also are more accurate than women in target-directed motor skills, such as guiding or intercepting projectiles:

They do better on disembedding tests, in which they have to find a simple shape, such as the one on the left, once it is hidden within a more complex figure:

And men tend to do better than women on tests of mathematical reasoning:

1,100	If only 60 percent of seedlings will survive, how many must be planted to obtain 660 trees?

Tasks Favoring Women

Women tend to perform better than men on tests of perceptual speed, in which subjects must rapidly identify matching items—for example, pairing the house on the far left with its twin:

In addition, women remember whether an object, or a series of objects, has been displaced.

On some tests of ideational fluency, for example, those in which subjects must list objects that are the same color, and on tests of verbal fluency, in which participants must list words that begin with the same letter, women also outperform men:

L _ _ _	Limp, Livery, Love, Laser Liquid, Low, Like, Lag, Live, Lug, Light, Lift, Liver, Lime Leg, Load, Lap, Lucid...

Women do better on precision manual tasks—that is, those involving fine-motor coordination—such as placing the pegs in holes on a board.

And women do better than men on mathematical calculation tests:

77	$14 \times 3 - 17 + 52$
43	$2(15 + 3) + 12 - \dfrac{15}{3}$

D. Kimura, "Sex Differences in the Brain", *Scientific American*, Vol. 267 (3). September 1992.

FIGURE 10.5 **Gender Gaps in Problem Solving.**
SOURCE: Kimura, 1992, pp. 120–121

Gender Stereotypes: images or beliefs about the so-called typical man or woman

www

EXPLORING SEXUALITY ONLINE

Gender Identity Online

A benefit, and a problem, of the Internet is that it allows people to experiment and switch genders when communicating via computer. Online gender swapping may be a fairly common practice. How can you tell if the person you're cyberchatting with is a biological male or a female? It has been speculated that because of differential language cues, men and women can be identified in text-based messages (Herring, 1993). In one study, 20 messages from previous research were sorted into gender groups and into high and low communication style categories. Participants were asked their perception of the probable gender of the message author and their certainty of that judgment. Accuracy and certainty of judgments of gender showed significant differences between gender communication style conditions. However, overall accuracy and certainty of judgments were not related. Neither was there a difference in accuracy or certainty of judgments between male and female judges. Messages sent by men were accurately judged for **gender stereotypes,** but messages sent by women were not (i.e., they showed more variation) (Savick et al., 1999).

GENDER ROLES

Gender roles are the ways males and females are expected to behave within their society. Cultures around the world assign roles that direct activities and govern behavior for men, women, girls, and boys. These gender roles exert various degrees of constraint, but in general the more rigid the gender role in a society, the sharper the gender division of labor and the lower the status accorded to women (World Health Organization, 1998).

There are several viewpoints as to why gender roles developed and why they are so firmly fixed. According to the biological perspective, gender differences in abilities such as spatial-relations and a predisposition to aggression can be explained by hormonal influences on the organization, growth, and activation of brain hemispheres. The result is a sexually dimorphic brain that has different patterns of plasticity, adaptive responses, vulnerability to various insults, and cognitive abilities (Pogun, 1997).

A number of psychological perspectives attempt to explain how children acquire and adopt stereotypical gender behavior patterns. Freud's psychodynamic theory explained gender roles in terms of identification with the parent of the same biological sex—boys identify with their fathers, and girls with their mothers. Social-learning theory holds that children learn what is deemed to be masculine or feminine from watching adult role models and from the ways their parents and other adults treat them. The psychodynamic and social learning views differ as to the inner processes that produce these consequences, with social learning theorists relying on the simple concept of learning by observing, while psychodynamic processes emphasize unconscious motivations to internalize the identity of the same-sex parent. Consciously or unconsciously, parents and other members of society foster gender-typed behavior by rewarding or approving behavior that is gender typical and by punishing gender atypical behavior patterns.

Gender atypical children, "tomboys" and "sissies," are often targets of harassment and abuse from peers, as well as being a cause of concern for parents. In one study (Sannabba & Ahlberg, 1999), 224 parents of 5-year-old children were asked about their attitudes toward cross-gender behavior in

More and more women are doing jobs that were once almost exclusively performed by men.

Children learn gender roles from observing and modeling after their parents.

"We may never know which early people first began to do separate tasks. But someone carted chunks of meat into the reeds and stripped these bones two million years ago. And I do not think that females with small children were the hunters or the butchers. At the same time, there is no reason to think that either sex had rigid, formal roles. Probably females without children joined and even led scavenging and hunting parties. Certainly men often gathered plants and nuts and berries. Probably some couples beat the grass together to catch small animals."

(Fisher, 1992, pp. 207–208)

children and their expectations of future adult behavior. The results revealed that boys exhibiting cross-gender behavior (playing with dolls, dressing up) were more negatively regarded than girls who crossed over ("tomboys," "jocks"). Men perceived more societal acceptance of cross-gender boys than women did. Children who exhibited cross-gender behavior were predicted to continue this behavior in adulthood and to be less psychologically well adjusted as adults than "typical" boys and girls. Boys exhibiting cross-gender behavior were expected to be less psychologically well adjusted than their female counterparts.

According to the cognitive developmental perspective, children themselves play a role in gender typing. A **gender schema** is a cluster of mental representations about male and female physical qualities, behaviors, and personality traits. Children form these schemas in stages (Kohlberg, 1966). Once they have acquired a gender schema, children begin to judge themselves according to those characteristics that are consistent with their gender and blend their developing self-concepts with the prominent gender schema of their culture. In effect, children use gender schemas to organize their perceptions of the world (Bem, 1981, 1985).

Developing a gender schema, also called cognitive gender typing, has three different aspects: gender identity, gender stability, and gender constancy (Kohlberg, 1966). Gender identity (discussed earlier), the psychosocial sense that one is a boy or a girl, is usually acquired by age 3. An understanding of the concept of **gender stability,** that people retain their genders for a lifetime, typically develops around age 5. While a 2-year-old boy might know that he is male, he might think that when he grows up he can be a mommy. At about age 7 or 8 children generally develop the concept of **gender constancy**—the idea that even if appearances or behavior change, gender remains constant. Even though a girl cuts her hair short and wears blue jeans, she is still a girl.

Gender roles may have evolved and survived because they increase the likelihood that we will reproduce and have viable offspring (Bjorklund & Kipp, 1996). According to this evolutionary view, the traditional male role as hunters and warriors and the female role as gatherers and caregivers are part of our genetic makeup. So men are genetically predisposed for aggression because of their greater upper body strength and other physical attributes. Women are predisposed to nurturing because these traits enable women to stay close to home and respond to children's needs.

Gender stereotypes (Table 10.4), fixed ideas about how men and women are expected to behave, have been studied extensively. Although they have a bad reputation as the foundation of prejudice, false opinion, and self-fulfilling prophecy, research has shown that stereotypes often have a kernel of truth to them, and that some stereotypes are quite accurate. One of the most dramatic illustrations of the accuracy of stereotypes was a landmark study by Janet Swim (1994). She gave male and female college students a list of traits and asked them to rate each one as more typical of men or women; if both men and women shared the trait, she also asked if there was any difference between the sexes, and the magnitude of the difference. Then she compared the students' ratings against the results of published studies of those same traits. She found that the students were correct (in the sense that the students' ratings closely matched what research had found about actual differences) in listing what traits went with which gender, and in estimating the size of the differences. In other words, the stereotypes were quite accurate.

Obviously stereotypes don't reflect the traits of all individual men and women. It is doubtful that anyone would describe Oprah Winfrey as being dependent, foolish, or unambitious, or use the terms cruel, disorderly, loud, and unscrupulous to describe Tom Hanks. The statement that stereotypes are accurate means that they correspond fairly well to broad, average differences between men and women as groups. It is tempting but unfair to apply stereotypes to individuals. Yes, on average men think about sex more than women (Michael et al., 1994), and the stereotype accurately reflects that men are more often occupied with erotic thoughts—but there are also plenty of women

TABLE 10.5

Gender Role Stereotyping in 30 Countries

Stereotypes of Males		Stereotypes of Females	
Active	Pleasure seeking	Affectionate	Modest
Adventurous	Precise	Appreciative	Nervous
Aggressive	Quick	Cautious	Patient
Arrogant	Rational	Changeable	Pleasant
Autocratic	Realistic	Charming	Prudish
Capable	Reckless	Complaining	Self-pitying
Coarse	Resourceful	Complicated	Sensitive
Conceited	Rigid	Confused	Sentimental
Confident	Robust	Dependent	Sexy
Courageous	Sharp witted	Dreamy	Shy
Cruel	Show off	Emotional	Softhearted
Determined	Steady	Excitable	Sophisticated
Disorderly	Stern	Fault finding	Submissive
Enterprising	Stingy	Fearful	Suggestible
Hardheaded	Stolid	Fickle	Superstitious
Individualistic	Tough	Foolish	Talkative
Inventive	Unscrupulous	Forgiving	Timid
Loud		Frivolous	Touchy
Obnoxious		Fussy	Unambitious
Opinionated		Gentle	Understanding
		Imaginative	Unstable
		Kind	Warm
		Mild	

SOURCE: Williams & Best, 1994.

who think about sex a lot and men who hardly think about sex at all. If you assume that a woman will always think about sex less often than a man, you will end up being right more often than you are wrong, but you will still be wrong quite often.

Attitudes toward and satisfaction with gender roles have remained relatively stable over the past few decades. Studies conducted in 1983 and 1999 asked women if they would prefer to be reborn as a male or female and the reasons for their choice. In both studies a large majority of women said they would want to come back as a female. In both studies those who wished to be reborn as male cited the societal advantages of male power and freedom as the reason for this choice. There was one notable difference in the results of the two studies; unlike the 1983 study, in the 1999 study the wish to be reborn male was not connected to overall negative feelings about being female (Minton et al., 1999).

The Effects of Gender on Sexual Behavior

Heterosexual sex acts other than masturbation involve one man and one woman, so each must appeal to the other and accommodate the other to some degree. If there are differences in how men and women approach sex, a successful sexual relationship will depend on resolving those differences or rendering them complementary rather than antagonistic.

Oliver and Hyde (1993) combined the results of 177 different studies for one of the most important summaries of gender differences in sexuality. There were a few large differences; the largest was that men were consistently found to be more likely to masturbate than women. Another large difference was in attitudes toward *casual sex* (sex outside a committed relationship); men were much more favorable toward casual sex than women. There were no consistent differences in attitudes toward homosexuality or in sexual satisfaction. Small to moderate differences were found on many

Gender Schema: a cluster of mental representations about male and female physical qualities, behaviors, and personality traits

Gender Stability: the concept that people retain their genders for a lifetime

Gender Constancy: the concept that even if appearances or behavior change, gender remains constant

dimensions. For example, men were moderately more favorable than women toward having sexual intercourse within a committed relationship or when engaged to be married, and men were more permissive with respect to infidelity. Males reported an earlier age of first intercourse, more sexual partners, more homosexual activity, and a higher frequency of intercourse, although these were all small differences. Women reported more negative feelings (for example, anxiety, guilt, and fear) about sex and expressed more support for the "double standard" that regards certain sex acts as acceptable for men but not for women.

Oliver and Hyde (1993) also compared older versus newer studies. From the 1960s to the 1980s, they found that many of the gender differences had become smaller. These shifts probably reflect continuing social change since the Sexual Revolution of the 1960s and 1970s. Most of the gender differences they found indicate that as female sexuality was liberated, women came to resemble men more closely with regard to sexual permissiveness. The differences did not disappear, however.

Gender Differences in Sex Drive

Traditionally, many people have simply noted that men tend to pursue sex while women resist and set limits, leading to the conclusion that men have the stronger urge for sex. Others have proposed that these patterns simply reflect social norms and roles. The view that women have the stronger sex drive is based on the fact that women can have multiple orgasms and are in principle insatiable, unlike men who generally have a refractory period after each orgasm.

However, the *sex drive* is defined as motivation to engage in sexual activity. It is not the same as capacity for sex. For example, the ability to have multiple orgasms is not the same as the desire to have them. Sex drive also does not include enjoyment of sex, for people may enjoy something immensely when it happens but not crave it all the time.

To approach this problem as a researcher would, imagine two people—two women, for example—who differ in the strengths of their sex drives. How would this difference show up in their thoughts, feelings, and behavior? The woman with the greater sex drive would probably think about sex more, want sex more, have more sexual fantasies, desire more partners, masturbate more, and so forth, than the woman with the milder sex drive.

By all of these measures, men have a higher sex drive than women. Most men think about sex every day, but most women do not think about it that often (Laumann et al., 1994; also Eysenck, 1971). Most young men feel sexually aroused every day, even several times a day, but most young women feel aroused a couple times a week (Knoth, Boyd, & Singer, 1988). Men have more frequent sexual fantasies than women, and men's fantasies involve more different partners and more different activities than women's (Leitenberg & Henning, 1995).

Men want sex more often than women. This starts early in a relationship. Men are typically ready and eager for sex before their female partners are (McCabe, 1987). Even after 20 years of marriage, husbands want sex more often than their wives (Ard, 1977). Data on same-sex couples confirm the differences. Gay men have sex more frequently than lesbian women, both at the start of the relationship and after many years together (Blumstein & Schwartz, 1983). Men desire more sex partners than women (Buss & Schmitt, 1993; Miller & Fishkin, 1997). Men are more likely to engage in extramarital sex, and when they do stray they seek out more partners than women (Cotton, 1975; Lawson, 1988; Spanier & Margolis, 1983; Thompson, 1983).

Masturbation is one good indicator of sex drive, because masturbation does not depend as much on the external constraint of finding a willing partner. In fact, Abramson (1973) found that frequency of masturbation correlates with strength of sex drive, such that within each gender, the people with the higher sex drive were more likely to masturbate. Many studies have found consistently that men are more likely to masturbate than women (see Oliver & Hyde, 1993). Even if we leave out the people (mostly women) who *never* masturbate, it is clear that men do it more often than women (Laumann et al., 1994).

Men find it more difficult than women to live without sex (including masturbation). Leigh (1989) studied men and women who avoid sex, and the women were more likely to cite lack of interest and desire as a reason. (The men tended to avoid sex because they were afraid of rejection.) Even when both men and women subscribe to a single standard of sexual purity, the men fail more often than the women. A study of Catholic priests and nuns by Murphy (1992) found that the nuns were better than the priests at refraining from all sexual activity. Many priests refrain from interpersonal sex but compromise by masturbating, but the nuns often do not require even this compromise.

Based on these and similar findings, it seems fair to conclude that the desire for sex typically is stronger for males than for females (Baumeister, Catanese, & Vohs, 2001). Several qualifications need to be pointed out. Some of the difference is probably due to socialization, learning, and social pressure, and so it is not safe to leap to the conclusion that women inevitably or innately have less sexual desire than men, although there is probably some difference. Also, there are wide variations among males and among females, and certainly there are many women who have a higher sex drive than many men. These findings also are merely descriptive, not prescriptive. That is, these findings should not be taken to mean that women should not desire sex, or should feel guilty about wanting it, or shouldn't enjoy it.

Too much sexual desire can be just as harmful (and potentially far more disruptive) than too little. The optimal level of sexual desire is probably somewhere in the middle, and the average man and the average woman are probably both in that middle, optimal range, even if the average man is somewhat higher than the average woman.

Erotic Plasticity The discussion of sex drive begs the broader question of whether sexual desire is more shaped by nature or by culture. This is one of the most bitterly debated topics in all of sexuality theory. As Hyde and DeLamater (1999) have contended, the field of sexuality has been torn between two poles of thought. One pole, the *constructionism*, emphasizes the role of culture and socialization in determining the nature of sexual responses. The other view, known as *essentialism*, holds that people are born a certain way and emphasizes the role of innate, biological determinants of sexuality. More male experts take essentialist positions, while the female and especially feminist experts have favored constructionism.

The term *erotic plasticity* has been used to refer to the degree to which innate sexual responses are shaped and altered by social, cultural, and situational factors (Baumeister, 2000). There is some reason to believe that men and women differ in the degree to which their sexuality is shaped by nature versus culture. Women's sexuality may be more influenced by cultural factors than men's.

Three broad signs of plasticity can be observed. The first is that a woman's sexual feelings will change more than a man's as she moves through her adult life and goes from one situation to another. The Kinsey (1948, 1953) reports, for example, found that women report greater discontinuities in total sexual activity than men. A woman might have an active sexual relationship for several years, but then break up with her partner and have no sex of any sort for a while, and then resume an active sex life with a new partner. In contrast, if a man loses his partner, he is likely to maintain his frequency of orgasms by masturbating or going to prostitutes. Another pattern of change over time is found with regard to homosexual activity. Women who have sex with other women are more prone to switch back and forth between male and female partners than are men. For example, Savin-Williams (1990; see also Rosario et al., 1996) found that 80 percent of lesbians have had sex with men, whereas only about half of gay men have ever had sex with women.

The second sign of plasticity is that particular social and cultural factors have a bigger impact on female sexuality than on male sexuality. Education and religion, in particular, have been shown to affect women more than men. The Sex in America (1994) survey found that the most educated women were sexually quite different from the least educated women, such as in performing oral sex or anal sex, having had a same-sex sexual experience, enjoying different sexual activities, and using contraception with secondary sex partners. In contrast, the most educated men were not much different from the least educated men in their sexual habits. The same was found for religion. The most religious and least religious women had quite different sex lives, but the sex lives of the most religious and least religious men were more similar (Laumann et al., 1994). Women's sexuality appears to differ from one culture to another more than men's, suggesting that cultural influences have a greater impact on women (for example, Barry & Schlegel, 1984). Also, peer groups influence and parenting patterns seem to influence the sexual behavior of teenage girls more than that of teenage boys (Billy & Udry, 1985; Miller & Moore, 1990; Mirande, 1968; Sack, Keller, & Hinkle, 1984; Thornton & Camburn, 1987).

A third indication of erotic plasticity is the greater gap between general attitudes and actual behaviors among women than among men. Studies have repeatedly found that women are more likely to engage in behaviors that are at odds with their broad attitudes. For example, most people advocate using condoms in casual sexual encounters, and many people fail to use them when they do actually have such experiences, but the gap between attitude and behavior is bigger for women than men (Herold & Mewhinney, 1993). Men's attitudes about infidelity predict their own behavior with a reasonable degree of accuracy, but women show less of a match. For example, a woman might engage in necking and petting with someone other than her boyfriend even though in principle she is opposed to such activity (Hansen, 1987). Many women say that in the abstract they would like to have a sexual experience with another woman but never actually do so, whereas nearly all men who want to have sex with other men usually do so (Laumann et al., 1994).

There are important implications of women's greater erotic plasticity. Female sexuality continues to develop and change throughout a woman's life. This makes it harder for women to be confident that they understand their own sexuality. Hence women will be less likely than men to feel sure about what they want sexually and how to get it (Vanwesenbeeck, Bekker, & van Lenning, 1998). Women will however be able to adapt to new circumstances more readily and easily than men.

What does this mean in practice? Women's sexual responses depend heavily on what sex means: what it signifies about the relationship, what the context is, and what the norms and expectations are. Male sexuality, in contrast, depends more on physical processes controlled by genes and hormones, which do not depend as much on meanings.

Are there any exceptions? Some signs point to a period of erotic plasticity during childhood for boys (see Baumeister, 2000). For example, men are more likely than women to exhibit sexual paraphilias, and currently the most likely explanation for these unusual sexual preferences is that they originate with some experiences during childhood and then become "stamped in" to remain there throughout life. Research with other species suggests that sexual imprinting tends to be strong and irreversible with males but not with females (Kendrick et al., 1998)—that is, a male's lifelong sexual preferences are firmly established early in childhood, whereas a female's remain open to change throughout adulthood. At present, the childhood influence pattern has not received enough study to permit a strong conclusion, but what little evidence is available suggests that boys may be more affected by childhood experiences than girls. After puberty, however, social and environmental influences have a consistently stronger effect on female than on male sexuality.

Promiscuity   A particular focus of research on gender differences in sexuality has been the desire for multiple partners. Men tend to desire a greater number of partners than women. In a study by Miller and Fishkin (1996), for example, college students were asked how many sex partners they would like to have over the rest of their lives. The average response by the women was 2.7, whereas for the men it was 64. Other research on infidelity and adultery suggests that unfaithful husbands seek out more sexual partners than unfaithful wives (Lawson, 1988), and indeed the simple desire for sexual novelty— someone new in your bed—is much more deeply appealing to men than to women. Many women are puzzled by men's apparent interest in sexual novelty, for they think women's bodies do not really differ from each other all that much, and they do not understand what enjoyment a man could get from simply seeing and touching an unfamiliar one.

Evolutionary theory emphasizes the difference in promiscuity as one of the most important and basic differences between men and women (Buss, 1994; Symons, 1979). The explanation lies in the different reproductive systems and their implications for passing on genes. As we discussed in Chapter 1, having many sex partners allows a man to have many offspring. The same strategy does not work so well for a woman. A woman can usually have only about one baby a year, by one man, regardless of whether she has sex with that same man all the time or with a hundred different men. In contrast, a man who has sex with a hundred different women can make far more babies than he could by having sex with the same woman a hundred times.

To understand the evolutionary process, imagine a distant past in which half the men and half the women were all monogamous, which means they desired only to have a single sex partner for life. Imagine the other half were promiscuous in the sense of wanting and having many different partners. The men who were promiscuous would have more children than the men who remained monogamous, and so after many generations there would be more men descended from the promiscuous ancestors than from the monogamous ones. However, the same logic does not apply to women. The promiscuous women would not generally produce more babies than the monogamous ones, so after many generations there would probably be the same number of monogamous and promiscuous women.

In fact, among women monogamy might be superior to promiscuity for passing along their genes. Remember, the key to evolutionary success is not just creating a baby—it requires that baby to grow up and reproduce, too. Surviving childhood requires care, protection, and feeding. Having a father who is there to provide those things might be a great advantage to a small child. The monogamous woman will therefore have a better chance of seeing her children grow into adults than the promiscuous woman.

Doesn't it make sense, then, that the monogamous men would make better fathers than the promiscuous ones? In fact, both monogamy and promiscuity may be viable strategies for men, and that may explain why modern society contains both types. If we take a closer look at the responses by those college students in the Miller and Fishkin (1996) study, we do see the monogamous men as well, even though the average response of desiring 64 lifetime partners suggests high promiscuity. Half the men in Miller and Fishkin's sample actually said they wanted only one sex partner for the rest of their lives, just like half the women. Both promiscuity and monogamy are viable reproductive strategies for men, and each has advantages and disadvantages. For women, however, monogamy seems generally the more effective strategy.

To be sure, individual men may do best by pursuing both strategies. That is, they may marry and provide for their wife's children while still occasionally having sex with women other than their wife (and thereby creating more babies). According to Betzig (1986), this has been how powerful men have usually acted throughout history. The great kings and emperors would typically have one primary wife but also find ways to have sex with other women, whether through informal affairs or through formal arrangements such as concubines.

In Chapter 3, we saw that the hormone testosterone tends to be high in single men, to drop slightly with marriage, and to drop more when a man becomes a father. Testosterone promotes sexual interest and restlessness and contributes to promiscuity, and so high levels of it may keep single men on the prowl for diverse sexual experiences, whereas low levels of it may make for a more stable, monogamous relationship. One way to look at this pattern is to suggest that biology keeps single men oriented toward promiscuity, whereas it shifts fathers toward more monogamous inclinations. Although such an interpretation is speculative, it would fit with the evolutionary reasoning, because it would allow individual men to pursue a mixture of both reproductive strategies.

These findings do not mean that men and women are trying to pass along their genes whenever they have sex. In fact, a woman who has an affair with a rich and powerful man, or a man who goes to bed with several different women in the same month,

FAQ:

Are there really no benefits to promiscuity for women?

Some evolutionary theorists might argue that it may be advantageous to a woman to have an occasional fling with a man other than her mate. In particular, having a discreet sexual affair with a highly powerful and successful man might be a way for a woman to get better genes than her everyday mate might have. Not every woman can marry the most desirable man, and so many women have to "settle" for a man who is less than ideal. To be ruthlessly pragmatic, the best strategy for such a woman would be to get pregnant by the man with the best possible genes and then convince her actual, less spectacular mate that her children are his so that he will provide for them. Still, this strategy calls for only occasional and very selective instances of infidelity. For the man, in contrast, having sex with someone other than his mate is nearly always a positive opportunity to pass along more of his genetic material.

may take precautions to avoid pregnancy. The evolutionary view is simply that patterns of sexual desire have been determined by what succeeded in making the most and best offspring over millions of years. People will feel desire based on those inherited patterns, even if they themselves do not want to have children.

An important point is that patterns of sexual desire do not automatically justify behaviors. A man who seeks to excuse his infidelity or promiscuity by saying "I can't help it, it's human nature" is stretching the point. Human beings are able to control their behavior. A man may not be able to stop himself from feeling desire or interest when he sees a pretty woman on the beach, and that is likely to remain true even if he is in a committed relationship. He is however able to stop himself from acting on that desire. People are responsible for their choices and actions, even if they cannot regulate their feelings.

Limitations on Sexual Activity   One aspect of the female role in sex that appears to be quite consistent across most times and places is that women are responsible for limiting sexual activity. Some believe that if men had their way, people would frequently have sex with many different partners, even without relationships or other considerations. When male sexuality occurs without the restraining influence of women, it sometimes evolves toward that pattern. The social and sexual lives of many gay men during the 1970s and early 1980s (after the initial success of gay liberation, but before the spread of AIDS) involved men going to clubs and bathhouses and having intercourse with many different partners in a single evening, often without even knowing their names (Shilts, 1987).

Studies of relationships reveal that it is usually up to the woman to decide whether and when the couple has sex. For example, McCabe (1987) examined couples at many different stages of relationship development. She coined the term *reluctant virgins* to refer to people who wanted to be having sex but were nonetheless virgins, a category that consisted almost entirely of men. McCabe found that when a woman wanted to start having sex, her partner almost always obliged. In contrast, the woman did not always go along when the man wanted to start having sex.

Women expect there to be more time spent together, such as more dates, before starting to have sex, as compared with men's expectations (Cohen & Shotland, 1996). Even if two people are both unattached and attracted to each other, women often say that they would not consent to sex if they had known the person only for a short time, whereas men have no such objections (Buss, 1994). Such findings suggest that many men are ready for sex from a very early point in the relationship, whereas most women are not, and so the onset of sexual activity will depend mainly on the woman's decision.

In the evolutionary view, it makes sense for a woman to be very careful and choosy about her sex partners. The cost of making a sexual mistake is much greater for a woman than for a man, and so she will have a greater incentive to be cautious in order to avoid making such a mistake. Apart from the relatively modern danger of being sued for child support, men do not have much to lose by copulating with a nonoptimal partner.

Cultural roles and influences may have contributed to the woman's role in limiting sexual activity. As you learned in Chapter 8, cultures tend to suppress female sexuality to restrict and control sex. Perhaps it is the greater erotic plasticity of women that is responsible for the sexual double standard (which we discussed in more detail in Chapter 8).

Transgender Roles

Not every society limits itself to two standard gender roles. In some cultures a third gender exists that is neither male nor female, but a blend of both masculine and feminine traits. These genders can be created surgically, or as a product of social institutionalization.

Transgender roles have been created in the Byzantine Empire (the eastern portion of the Roman Empire) and in India. In the fifth century A.D., the Byzantine

Transgender Roles: a blend of both masculine and feminine traits and traditional roles

civilization created a third gender called eunuchs through surgical removal or destruction of the testicles before puberty (Ringrose, 1994). There were great prestige and financial rewards associated with being a eunuch. This practice fell out of favor with the fall of the Byzantine Empire. Today, among the *hijras* of Gujarat, India, some adult males deliberately cut off both penis and testicles in order to become ritual performers dedicated to the Mother Goddess *Bahuchara Mata* (Nanda, 1994). Although this may sound extreme, it may be that becoming a *hijra* offers the prestige and economic rewards historically accorded the eunuchs as well as social support and psychological relief for transsexual males unable to access sex reassignment surgery (discussed later in this chapter).

In other instances, transgender roles have nothing to do with sex organs (no surgery is required). The Balkan sworn virgin was an institutionalized transgender role that occurred in the rural mountain areas of the Balkans (that is, Serbia, Montenegro, Albania, and Macedonia) in the 18th, 19th, and early 20th centuries. These women took an oath of lifelong virginity before a jury of elders, and they adopted the dress and lifestyle of males. The punishment for violating the oath was death.

At that time, the poverty-stricken Balkans had rigid gender roles, and the status of men was much higher than that of women. Sworn virgins could smoke and drink with men and carry guns. Unlike women, they might be victims of the blood feuds common to the region. Sworn virgins assumed male labor and social roles, often took male names and kinship titles, and had all the rights of men. In addition to elevated social status, there were a number of motivations for a girl to foreswear sex. Sworn virgins were freed of any betrothal commitments and thus could escape a forced marriage. Moreover, becoming a sworn virgin could provide economic advantages to the woman and her parents. **Gender dysphoria,** or discomfort with their sexual identity, also could have played a part for some individuals. One sworn virgin is quoted as saying, "Most of all I detest being a female . . . nature is mistaken" (Grémaux, 1989, p. 155).

The social masculinization of the sworn virgins was so complete that they might uphold the superior position of men and make deprecating remarks about women, as well as sexual overtures to women. Sexual relationships by sworn virgins, whether with males or females, were rare. Such female-to-male gender role changes can exist only in classless societies in which labor role and gender are absolutely equal (Dickemann, 1993). In such a society, to adopt the labor role of a male, a female must also adopt the gender role.

Perhaps the most famous case of a socially engineered transgender role was that of the North American **berdache,** or **two-spirit,** people of one gender who assumed the dress, occupations, and behaviors of the other gender to effect a change in gender status. Two-spirits did not shift from one gender role to the other but assumed an intermediate status with some male and some female social attributes. Berdache was fairly common among Native American societies. Male berdache has been described in almost 150 indigenous North American societies, and female berdache in perhaps 70.

There were three key features of male or female berdache roles. The first was productive specialization; male berdaches did crafts and domestic work, and female berdaches engaged in warfare, hunting, and leadership roles. Secondly, there was some type of supernatural sanction, authorization, or bestowal of powers from a source outside the society. Berdaches were often viewed as having supernatural powers or qualities; and status as a berdache might have been revealed through a vision of a supernatural entity. Third, gender variation commonly, but not always, was marked by cross-dressing (Roscoe, 1994). Some societies allowed individual berdache choice of dress and others insisted that berdaches dress in other gender clothing all of the time or on some occasions (Callender & Kochems, 1987).

Berdaches were accepted and respected members of their communities. Their economic and religious pursuits seem to have been more significant than their sexual practices. Among the Cheyenne, berdaches accompanied the warriors to care for the wounded and were awarded the scalps of the enemy. After returning to camp, the Cheyenne berdaches were in charge of the scalp dance and victory dance.

We'wha, a 19th century Zuni two-spirit (or berdache), a transgender role in many Native American cultures.

Gender Dysphoria: discomfort with one's gender identity

Berdache/ Two-Spirit: among certain Native American peoples, a person, usually a male, who assumes the gender identity and is granted the social status of the opposite sex

GENDER IDENTITY

Are you male or female? How do you know? While your attitudes and behaviors determine your gender role, your **gender identity** is the psychological awareness or self-concept of being male or female. It involves both how you see yourself and how others see you. Gender identity plays a major role in how you behave, how you think, and how you feel. Most children begin to develop an understanding of anatomic gender around age 2, and by the time they are 3 years old they usually have a strong sense of their gender identity (Marcus & Corsini, 1978; McConaghy et al., 1979; Money, 1977).

What determines gender identity? The answer is a source of continuous debate and controversy. Some believe that our brains are biologically programmed by prenatal sex hormones to be either male or female. That is, gender identity is largely a result of the specific mix of hormones that are present during development in utero. Others theorize that gender identity is a result of postnatal environmental factors or learning experiences; according to this view, gender is a cultural construct with no biological basis. A third position is that gender identity results from an integration of nature (our biology) and nurture (our environment). According to this model, your genetic blueprint strongly influences how you will react to environmental situations but it is not the sole influence on your construction of gender identity.

Gender identity is almost always consistent with an individual's genetic (that is, chromosomal) and anatomic gender. Biological females almost always have a female gender identity, and biological males almost always see themselves as being male. And, most often we are reared, and thus socialized, as males or females based on the appearance of our anatomic gender.

Perhaps the most famous case in gender identity research is that of a Canadian who at various times in his life has been called Bruce, Brenda, and David Reimer. In 1966 7-month-old identical twin infants, Bruce and Brian Reimer, were taken to the hospital for circumcisions. The physician botched the procedure and destroyed Bruce's penis.

When Bruce was 22 months old his parents decided to take the advice of Johns Hopkins University's world-famous psychologist John Money and raise him as a girl. Bruce's testicles were surgically removed and cosmetic surgery to construct an artificial vagina was planned. Bruce became Brenda. He was dressed in girl's clothing and raised as Brian's sister. At adolescence Brenda began to take female hormones.

Brenda/Bruce and Brian were brought to Johns Hopkins for annual examinations and were heralded as an unprecedented success in gender identity reassignment. The case became a model for treating infants born with ambiguous genitalia. The case, called "John-Joan" in the medical literature, was touted as convincing evidence that gender identity is determined exclusively by how a child is raised. In other words, gender is made, not born.

However, despite the attempts of "her" parents and psychologists, Brenda never accepted the designation as female and never felt, looked, or acted like a girl. Brenda insisted on standing up when urinating, wanted to have a mustache someday, and liked playing with cars and guns. "She" was ridiculed by peers and did poorly in school. When the truth finally came out, when Brenda was 14, he reclaimed his male identity and renamed himself David. He began taking steps to reverse the effects of hormone treatments, including a double mastectomy and construction of an artificial penis. David is now a married father of three adopted daughters. He has a good relationship with his parents and understands the choices they made, but he remains angry with the doctors who interfered with nature and caused his childhood to be so traumatic (Colapinto, 2000).

Gender Identity and Pseudohermaphrodites

Researchers have attempted to solve the nature versus nurture debate about gender identity by studying pseudohermaphrodites, which as you learned earlier in the chapter are individuals who possess the gonads and genes of one sex but external genitalia

Gender Identity: the psychological sense of being male or female

that are either ambiguous or typical of the other. Because of this ambiguity, pseudo-hermaphrodites are sometimes reared as members of the gender they resemble, not the one represented by their chromosomes. Like the case of Bruce/Brenda/David Reimer, studying the gender identity of pseudohermaphrodites can help determine the relative importance of nature and nurture.

Some research has focused on a rural area of the Dominican Republic with a prevalence of individuals with pseudohermaphroditism resulting from DHT-deficiency (see the CONSIDERATIONS box on page 299). Owing to their ambiguous genitalia as infants, many of these individuals are reared as females. During puberty, however, normal male testosterone production causes rapid masculinization. Of those individuals studied in the Dominican Republic, 17 of 18 who were raised as girls changed to a male gender identity, and 16 shifted to male gender roles after puberty (Imperato-McGinley et al., 1974).

Herdt and Davidson (1988) studied DHT-deficiency male pseudohermaphrodites among the Sambia of Papua New Guinea and found that those individuals who are raised as females from birth grow up in a normative female gender role. They have no special problems in psychosocial adaptation until puberty, when the expected female secondary sex traits fail to emerge. All of the Sambian subjects studied then assumed a male gender role, but only under severe external public pressure; they were not allowed the option of remaining females. As in the Dominican Republic, it is better to be male than female in Sambian society. However, the Sambian case differs from the Dominican case in at least one important respect—the Sambians recognize a third gender.

The three Sambian gender categories are male, female, and an ambiguous intersex called *kwolu-aatmwol*. Sex roles are rigidly typed and organized around polarized behavior and economic routines. Sambian men are traditionally hunters and warriors; Sambian women are gardeners and mothers. The *kwolu-aatmwol* gender leans more in the direction of masculinity.

All young Sambian women marry, derive status from marriage and children, and are economically supported by their husbands. Thus there is no place for an unmarried femalelike individual who will never bear children. It is understandable that such individuals would switch to the male role for better social adaptation. It may be that when three gender categories are present, the outcomes of any gender change are likely to be dependent upon the cultural expectations governing a person's adult identity (see CONSIDERATIONS box).

Gender Identity and Society

CONSIDERATIONS

- A true hermaphrodite who was pronounced a girl at birth and reared as female later reassigned herself as a male at age 28 (Diamond, 1997).

- A long-term study of the psychological well-being of 59 intersex children found that despite sex assignment, genital organ correction soon after birth, psychological counseling of parents, and intensive psychotherapy for the intersex children, general psychopathology was found in 39 percent of the subjects. Although 87 percent of the development of girls with a physical intersex condition was consistent with the assigned sex, 13 percent developed a gender identity disorder (see page 316) attributed to both biological and social factors (Slipper et al., 1998).

 If you had a child with ambiguous sexual organs, what would you do?

—*Do you think society has the right to assign the sex of a child?*

—*Should the individual decide? If so, at what age?*

—*Is there a place in society for individuals who are neither male nor female?*

CAMPUS CONFIDENTIAL

"When my parents told me and my sisters that they wanted to discuss something important with us I could tell by their expressions that it was something serious. I was sure they were going to tell us that they were getting a divorce or one of them was dying of some fatal disease. So, although I was prepared for something big, I sure didn't expect them to tell us that dad is a transsexual.

"It's been a rough year. I know my dad did his best to try and live a 'normal' life. He treated my mom well, had a good job, and was a great father. I guess kids are pretty oblivious to their parents' personal lives, 'cause I never had a clue that he was so unhappy. My sisters seemed to accept the news pretty well, so I tried to act like it was no big deal, but inside I was a wreck. I didn't know how to relate to my dad as a woman, what to call him, or how to feel about him. The pronoun confusion was enough to drive me nuts.

"I still get confused, but things have gotten easier. My folks divorced and they're both dating now. Dad's taking hormones and living as a woman full time while he's waiting for his surgery next month. Even though he could win an Ivana Trump look-alike contest, I still call him dad and we still hang out together. Do I wish my dad wasn't the way he is? Well, I guess I would be happier—but he would still be miserable, so I guess it wouldn't be worth it." •

GENDER IDENTITY DISORDERS

The American Psychiatric Association defines a **gender identity disorder** as a "strong and persistent cross-gender identification—not merely a desire for any perceived cultural advantages of being the other sex" (APA, 1994, p. 537). For an individual to be diagnosed with a gender identity disorder, two of the following four conditions must exist: (1) there must be strong and persistent evidence of cross-gender identification—the desire or insistence that one is of the other sex; (2) this cross-gender identification must not merely be a desire for the perceived cultural advantages of the other sex; (3) the person must not have a physical intersex condition; and (4) there must be evidence of significant distress or impairment in social, occupational, or other important areas of functioning (APA, 1994).

Boys with a gender identity disorder may be preoccupied with traditionally feminine activities and may have a preference for dressing in female attire. Girls with gender identity disorder generally manifest intense negative reactions to expectations that they wear feminine clothing, and they prefer boys as playmates. Adults with this disorder usually are preoccupied with their desire to live as a member of the other sex, which may be evidenced by adopting the social role of the other sex or acquiring the physical appearance of the other sex through hormone treatment or surgery.

There is some question as to whether gender identity disorder is truly a psychiatric condition or a manifestation of normal homosexual orientation. Particularly in the case of children, it would be incorrect and unethical to diagnose psychiatric illness in individuals who may be homosexual (Menvielle, 1998).

Some of those with *gender dysphoria*, a general term for persons who have confusion or discomfort about their birth gender, may come to accept their given gender role through psychological treatment. They may find it sufficient to express their preference through activities such as cross-dressing (Carroll, 1999). Others choose to undergo expensive, time-consuming, and irreversible gender reassignment surgery (discussed in the next section).

Transsexuals: When Sex and Gender Identity Don't Match

A **transsexual** is a person with a gender identity disorder who feels that he or she is trapped in a body of the wrong sex. Such individuals often have a deep and long-standing sense of discomfort about their sexual anatomy. Born with the anatomic genitals of one gender, many transsexuals desire the physical and social characteristics of the other gender. Transsexualism is considered by some researchers to be the extreme end of the spectrum of gender identity disorders (Cohen-Kettenis & Gooren, 1999).

Transsexuals are sometimes confused with transvestites. We discuss the latter in Chapter 12. **Transvestites,** sometimes called cross-dressers, are people who dress in clothing of the other gender for the purpose of obtaining sexual excitement. While transsexuals may cross-dress, they do so to transform their appearance to match their gender identity, not to become sexually aroused. Transvestites may display gender discordant behavior, but they usually maintain a gender identity that is consistent with their sexual anatomy. Thus transvestites do not seek to change their anatomical sex, and they are not necessarily homosexuals.

The prevalence of transsexuals is estimated to be 1 in 100,000 males and 1 in 130,000 females (Selvin, 1993). The reasons that some individuals are convinced that they are a man in a woman's body or a woman in a man's body are unknown. Most of the early psychiatric literature emphasized the psychoanalytic explanation for transsexualism: an inadequately formed sense of self. Others theorize that social-learning experiences contribute to transsexualism. According to this view, a child who identifies closely with and behaves like the parent of the opposite gender receives positive reinforcement from the parent's reaction; this type of conditioning supports behaviors traditionally associated with the opposite gender (Green, 1974). In one study of 17 male-to-female transsexuals, all had been treated inappropriately or ambiguously with regard to

CONSIDERATIONS

And You Think You've Had An Interesting Life: Dawn Langley Simmons (1922–2000)

Dawn Langley Simmons, the adopted daughter of the English actress Margaret Rutherford, was the author of more than 20 books, including novels, biographies and children's books. Named Gordon Langley Hall when she was born at the estate of the writer Vita Sackville-West (one of Virginia Woolf's lovers) in Sussex, England, Gordon was the illegitimate child of Sackville-West's chauffeur (a descendant of Rudyard Kipling's gardener) and a "high society" mother.

In his late teens Gordon emigrated to Canada where he worked as a missionary, teacher, and midwife among the Ojibwa Indians and became an editor for the *Winnipeg Free Press*. He moved to the United States and in the early 1950s was society editor of the *Nevada Daily Mail* in Missouri. In his 20s, Gordon met Margaret Rutherford and her husband, who adopted him; at this time he also befriended the painter Isabel Whitney, who left him $2 million when she died in 1962. Gordon moved from Missouri to a home in Charleston, South Carolina, that was once owned by Robert E. Lee.

In 1968 Gordon underwent a sex change operation at Johns Hopkins Hospital and became Dawn Pepita Langley Hall. Dawn said she was born with an adrenal abnormality that caused her female genitalia to resemble a man's and thus was raised as a boy, but she maintained that she was always female.

The following year Dawn married her 22-year-old African American butler, John-Paul Simmons. A bomb threat forced the couple to move their wedding from a Baptist church to the bride's home. On learning of Dawn's marriage, Margaret Rutherford declared, "I am delighted that Gordon has become a woman, and I am delighted that Dawn is to marry a man of another race, and I am delighted that Dawn is to marry a man of lower station, but I understand the man is a Baptist!"

Soon after the marriage Dawn appeared to be pregnant, and in 1972 she introduced her daughter Natasha. In 1974, after accusing her husband of beating her and selling her belongings to buy whiskey, she moved her family to Catskill, New York. Some time later, Mr. Simmons was confined to a mental institution where he continues to live. Mrs. Simmons spent most of her later years living in Hudson, New York, where she was an active member of the Episcopal Church and a leader of its youth group.

 Do you think Dawn Langley Simmons led such an interesting life because of, or in spite of, being a transsexual?

SOURCE: Adapted from Smith, 2000.

---

gender from infancy to puberty (Driscoll, 1971). However, other male-to-female transsexuals report that they were not dressed in girls' clothing, rewarded for feminine behavior, or treated like a girl by their families.

Biological theories suggest that brain differentiation may result in transsexuality (Pauly, 1974; Zhou et al., 1995). The stria terminalis (BSTc), a tiny structure deep within a part of the brain that controls sexual function, differs in structure and number of neurons among men and women. Dutch researchers found that in male-to-female transsexuals a part of the BSTc appears to be more like the type found in women than that found in men (Swaab et al., 1995). Another study found that male-to-female transsexuals have female neuron numbers in the BSTc. Prenatal exposure to hormones is thought to cause the change in brain differentiation. In animal studies, prenatal exposure to the anticonvulsant drugs phenobarbital and phenytoin has been shown to alter hormonal levels leading to sexual differentiation. A follow-up study carried out on 147 human male and female subjects prenatally exposed to these drugs found a remarkably high number of transsexuals compared to the general population (Dessens et al., 1999). Hormone treatment or sex hormone level fluctuations in adulthood do not seem to influence BSTc neuron numbers, supporting the theory that in transsexuals sexual differentiation of the brain and genitals may go in opposite directions—in other words, you might end up with a male brain in a female body or vice versa (Krujiver et al., 2000).

Gender Identity Disorder: a strong and persistent desire or insistence that one is of the other sex

Transsexual: a person who is predisposed to identify with the opposite sex, sometimes strongly enough to undergo hormone treatment and surgery to effect a change of sex

Transvestite: a person who dresses and acts in a style or manner traditionally associated with the opposite sex, especially for purposes of emotional or sexual gratification

Gender Reassignment

In 1951, George Jorgensen went to Denmark and returned to the United States as Christine Jorgensen and the "sex-change operation" made headlines across the country. Until recently, those seeking gender reassignment

BEFORE   AFTER   TODAY

Christine Jorgensen, a former U.S. soldier who underwent a sex change operation in Denmark in 1951.

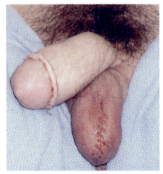

Female to Male Transsexual Surgery. A penile shaft is formed from abdominal tissue (or from forearm tissue and skin) or by routing the urethra through clitoral tissue in a meatidoplasty. The labia majora are surgically removed and the tissue closed to form a scrotum. Silicone testicles are inserted. To allow sexual intercourse, a temporary silicone rod can be inserted into the hollow center of the penile shaft or an inflatable penile prosthesis can be surgically attached to the pubic bone.

surgery had to travel long distances to places like Denmark or Morocco, and finding a skilled surgeon was difficult. It is estimated that of the approximately 25,000 transsexuals in the United States, about 6,000 to 11,000 have undergone gender reassignment surgery (Selvin, 1993). Advances in technology and changes in societal attitudes have eased, though not eliminated, the treatment obstacles transsexuals must overcome.

Gender reassignment surgery is a long and complex process. Those considering a sex change must first undergo counseling and a psychiatric evaluation. An important part of this screening is assessment of the patient's motives. If the patient is considered an eligible candidate for surgery, hormone therapy to accentuate the secondary sex characteristics of the desired gender is begun, and it must continue throughout the person's life. Males wishing to be female are given estrogen and drugs to inhibit testosterone production. The hormone treatment promotes some breast growth, softens the skin, reduces facial and body hair, diminishes muscle strength, and helps feminize body shape. Female to male transsexuals are treated with testosterone, which helps increase growth of body and facial hair, deepens the voice, suppresses menstruation, and slightly reduces breast tissue. Next comes the "real life test," a requirement to live for one year or more in the gender role they plan to assume after surgery.

Gender reassignment surgery for male-to-female transsexuals involves the removal of the penis and scrotum, followed by construction of a vagina out of pelvic tissues. Skin tissue of the penis, with its concentration of sensory nerves, is relocated inside the newly fashioned vagina. As a result of the surgery, vaginal intercourse is possible, although the use of a lubricant may be necessary. Many male-to-female transsexuals report postsurgical capacity to experience sexual arousal and orgasm (Blanchard et al., 1985; Carroll, 1999). Hormones alone may produce sufficient breast development, but implants are another option. Body and facial hair will be reduced by hormone treatments, but electrolysis may be elected.

Surgery for female-to-male transsexuals involves the removal of breasts, uterus, and ovaries. The vagina is surgically closed. A phalloplasty, in which a penis can be fashioned from abdominal skin or from tissue from the labia and perineum, can be performed. An alternative is a *meatidoplasty*, in which the urethra is routed through the clitoral tissue that will have enlarged as a result of hormone treatment. Either option will allow the postoperative transsexual to urinate at a public urinal. However, no method is available to construct a penis capable of natural erection in response to sexual arousal. In order to have vaginal intercourse with a woman, it is necessary to use an artificial device to make the constructed penis rigid. Silicone rods can be inserted into a skin tube on the underside of the penile shaft or a permanent inflatable device can be surgically inserted. If erotically sensitive tissue from the clitoris is left embedded at the base of the new penis, erotic feelings and orgasm are sometimes possible.

The large body of research on the outcome of gender reassignment surgery indicates that for the majority of those who undergo the surgery, the outcome is positive (Carroll, 1999). In 1984, a review of the international literature reported that about 90 percent of those who had gender reassignment surgery reported positive results (Lundstrom et al., 1984). A follow-up study of 28 male-to-female transsexuals found that physical and functional results of surgery were judged to be good, with few subjects needing additional corrective surgery. There was satisfaction with the appearance of the genitals and the ability to experience orgasm. Most reported they were able to return to their jobs and live more fulfilling social and personal lives (Rehman et al., 1999). Results of a follow-up study of 17 postoperative male-to-female transsexuals found that 94 percent rated the surgery as successful (Schroder & Carroll, 1999).

Predictors of a good postoperative outcome include good pre-reassignment psychological adjustment, family support, psychological treatment, and good surgical outcomes. Postoperative adjustment apparently is more positive for female-to-male transsexuals. In one study, less than 5 percent of female-to-male transsexuals had negative outcomes; negative outcomes in 10 percent of male-to-female transsexuals included severe psychological disorders, hospitalizations, requests for reversal surgery, and suicide (Abramowitz, 1986). However, female-to-male transsexuals may do better after surgery because they tend to have better social adjustment than male-to-female transsexuals before surgery (Kockott & Fahrner, 1987; Pauly, 1974).

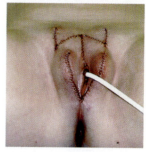

Male to Female Transsexual Surgery. After surgically removing the penis and testes, a vulva and vagina are constructed out of sensitive pelvic and penile tissue.

REVIEW

When it comes to sexual categories, things are not as simple as male or female; nor are gender identities and roles easy to categorize. **1**_____ occurs when an individual has some male and some female primary sexual characteristics, or ambiguous sexual characteristics.

So-called true **2**_____ possess one testis and one ovary. **3**_____ have an X and a Y chromosome, testes, and some aspects of female genitalia, but no ovaries. **4**_____ have two X chromosomes, ovaries, and some aspects of male genitalia, but no testes.

Prenatal sexual differentiation is a complex process that usually causes embryos to become male or female. The presence of **5**_____ causes testes to develop; in this case, Müllerian ducts shrink and **6**_____ develop into the epididymis, vas deferens, seminal vesicles, and ejaculatory ducts. However, if no H-Y antigen is present, the Wolffian ducts shrink and the **7**_____ develop into fallopian tubes, uterus, and the inner two-thirds of the vagina.

Usually in embryos with an X and a Y chromosome, androgens lead to the development of a penis, scrotum, and prostate gland. However, the development of ovaries will occur without the presence of any hormones. If there is little androgen present in the embryo, it will develop **8**_____ external genitalia, but the presence of sufficient androgens will result in the development of **9**_____ external genitalia.

The homologous sex organs for males and females include: clitoris/penile **10**_____; clitoral hood/penile **11**_____; labia minora/penile **12**_____; labia majora/**13**_____; and ovaries/**14**_____.

Chromosomal abnormalities can result in a child born with one or more extra or missing sex chromosomes. **15**_____, the absence of a second sex chromosome (XO), is relatively rare. **16**_____, the occurrence of an extra X chromosome (XXY) is much more common, occurring in an estimated 1 of every 500 live male births. Even embryos with the normal complement of sex chromosomes can experience hormonal abnormalities during prenatal development that can result in ambiguous sex organs or a combination of male and female sex organs.

Differences between men and women transcend reproductive functions. These differences may reflect a combination of innate basic tendencies and socialization into different roles. Significant social, physical, cognitive, personality, and communication differences between males and females have been measured.

17_____ are the ways males and females are expected to behave in a society. Researchers have reported differences in sexual behavior for males and females, though there is no agreement on how much such differences owe to cultural factors. It appears that the desire for sex typically is stronger for males than for females.

The Balkan sworn virgin and the North American **18**_____ are examples of institutionalized transgender roles.

19_____ is the awareness or self-concept of being male or female, and is almost always consistent with an individual's genetic and anatomic gender.

20_____ is a gender disorder in which the individual feels trapped in a body of the wrong sex. Some people with this condition undergo gender reassignment surgery.

SUGGESTED READINGS

Blum, D. (1997). *Sex and the Brain: Biological Differences Between Men and Women.* New York: Penguin Putnam Company.

Blum, a science writer, synthesizes research about gender differences from evolutionary biology, anthropology, animal behavior, neuroscience, and psychology.

Colapinto, J. (2000). *As Nature Made Him: The Boy Who Was Raised as a Girl.* New York: HarperCollins.

The story of Bruce/Brenda/David Reimer, who was born male but after a botched circumcision was raised as a girl until age 14.

Dreger, A. D. (1999). *Hermaphrodites and the Medical Invention of Sex.* Cambridge, MA: Harvard University Press.

Dreger chronicles the medical diagnosis and treatment of hermaphrodites from the perspective of both the subject and the medical community during the late 19th and early 20th centuries.

Fausto-Sterling, A. (2000). *Sexing the Body: Gender Politics and the Construction of Sexuality.* New York: Basic Books.

Fausto-Sterling, a biologist, examines the cultural biases underlying current scientific thought on gender.

Herdt, G., (Ed.). (1996). *Third Sex, Third Gender: Beyond Sexual Dimorphism in Culture and History.* Cambridge, MA: Zone Books.

This book presents 11 essays in history and anthropology that examine gender and sex; a new role for the study of alternative sex and gender systems is proposed.

McCloskey, D. N. (1999). *Crossing.* Chicago: University of Chicago Press.

This is a memoir of Deirdre McCloskey's transformation at age 52 from Donald, an economist at the University of Iowa and married of father of two, into the woman he wanted to be.

Yelland, N., (Ed.). (1998). *Gender in Early Childhood.* New York: Routledge.

Yelland explores the ways in which young children perceive and are perceived as gendered individuals.

ANSWERS TO CHAPTER REVIEW

1. Intersexuality; **2.** hermaphrodites; **3.** Male pseudo-hermaphrodites; **4.** Female pseudohermaphrodites; **5.** H-Y antigen; **6.** Wolffian ducts; **7.** Müllerian ducts; **8.** female; **9.** male; **10.** glans; **11.** foreskin; **12.** shaft; **13.** scrotal sac; **14.** testes; **15.** Turner's syndrome; **16.** Klinefelter's syndrome; **17.** Gender roles; **18.** berdache; **19.** Gender identity; **20.** Transsexual

CHAPTER 11

Sexual Orientation

PHYSICAL

SOCIAL

EMOTIONAL

SPIRITUAL

COGNITIVE

- **A continuum of sexual orientation**
  Sexual orientation, the erotic, romantic, and emotional attachment to individuals of the same sex, the opposite sex, or both, may be best understood as a continuum or range.

- **The basis of sexual orientation**
  Psychosocial, biological, and evolutionary theories have been offered to explain the existence and variability of sexual orientation.

- **Dating, sex, and relationships**
  Relationships are similar, regardless of whether they are heterosexual, homosexual, or bisexual. However, the social lives of homosexuals and bisexuals differ in certain respects from those of the heterosexual majority.

- **Homophobia**
  Homophobia is an obsessive, irrational hatred and fear of persons of homosexual orientation.

- **Coming out of the closet**
  The decision to come out, or openly identify oneself as having a less-accepted sexual orientation, remains a difficult one. However, increasing numbers of individuals now feel sufficiently secure to live openly as gays or lesbians.

Sexual orientation is the erotic, romantic, and emotional attachment to individuals of the same sex (**homosexuality**), the opposite sex (**heterosexuality**), or both (**bisexuality**). It is not simply a matter of sexual behavior, but a multidimensional phenomenon involving love, sex, and identity, with both subjective and behavioral dimensions. "The subjective aspect is comprised of private thoughts, fantasies, attractions, dreams and identity labels. The behavioral aspect involves the objectifiable, more public features, such as partner-seeking behaviors, [and] sexual acts. The subjective and behavioral aspects of this orientation do not invariably correspond" (Levine, 1992, p. 164). In this chapter we shall explore the various sexual orientations, including heterosexuality, homosexuality, and bisexuality, and discuss some related issues. In the process you may find challenges to some of your basic assumptions. Popular stereotypes of homosexuals and bisexuals are as erroneous and misleading as any heterosexual stereotype. Homosexuality and bisexuality cut across ethnic, racial, class, socioeconomic, occupational, and religious boundaries.

Sexual orientation should not be confused with gender identity. As you learned in Chapter 10, gender identity is your inner conviction of your maleness or femaleness. Your gender identity usually matches your biological sex. Sexual orientation is something completely different. For example, despite popular stereotypes, most homosexual men do not want to be women. They are, and want to continue to be, men. Similarly, most **lesbians** are, and want to remain, women.

Attraction to one sex does not preclude an attraction to the other. Individuals may participate in homosexual behavior without defining themselves as homosexual. Similarly, individuals may be predominantly attracted to members of their own sex yet never have a physical homosexual relationship. Many are uncomfortable with the idea that sexuality is fluid and dynamic.

Categorizing people as either heterosexual or homosexual may serve the social function of reducing anxiety (Ross et al., 1988); it enables people to feel secure in identifying with a single sexual orientation and prevents them from recognizing or examining the full range of their sexual feelings.

Homosexual behavior has existed throughout human history and in most, if not all, human cultures (Blackwood, 1986; Duberman et al., 1989; Greenberg, 1988). At different times and in different places it has been condoned, ignored, or condemned. The ancient Greeks idealized homosexual relations and believed they created particularly fulfilling, long-lasting bonds. While heterosexuality was the dominant orientation in Greek society, homosexuality was widely accepted in the Greek military and among the aristocrats who controlled political power. A survey of 190 cultures found that two thirds of them considered homosexuality to be socially acceptable for certain individuals or in specific circumstances (Ford & Beach, 1951).

Sexual Orientation: The direction of one's sexual interest toward members of the same, opposite, or both sexes

Homosexuality: sexual attraction, desire or behavior directed toward a person or persons of one's own sex

Heterosexuality: sexual attraction, feeling, or behavior directed toward a person or persons of the opposite sex

Bisexuality: sexual attraction, feeling, or behavior directed toward person or persons of both one's own and the opposite sex

Lesbians: female homosexuals

Historically, the focus has been on the *acts*, not on the *actors*. That is, those who had sexual relations with those of the same sex were not seen as a different type of people (Boswell, 1980). You could have a sexual relationship with someone of the same sex and not be considered a homosexual.

Categorizing individuals by their sexual orientation is a rather recent concept. The terms *heterosexuality* and *homosexuality* were not in widespread use until the late 19th century (SIECUS, 1993). David Halperin (1990) states that the term *homosexuality* first appeared in a German pamphlet in 1869; it did not appear in English until two decades later. Yet today we spend a lot of our individual and community resources, time, and energy dealing with the implications of these terms.

In the late 19th century, those in the emerging specialization of psychiatry and other medical professionals began to view homosexuality as a form of mental illness. "Treatments" eventually included lobotomies, aversion therapy, the castration of **gay** men, and hysterectomies for lesbians.

Until 1973 the American Psychiatric Association included homosexuality in its *Diagnostic and Statistical Manual* as a disease associated with psychopathic and paranoid personality disorders. Although homosexuality was never proven to be a pathology, the illusion was sustained for decades by entrenched prejudices among therapists as well as attitudes of their homosexual patients. Some homosexuals went to their therapists hoping to be "cured" of their homosexuality; these cases helped sustain the status of homosexuality as a disease. Despite the claims of a few therapists, there is no evidence that any treatment ever "cured" a homosexual. (It is considered more likely that these therapists were working with bisexual clients who for various reasons decided not to engage in homosexual behaviors.) In 1990 the American Psychological Association confirmed this, stating that so-called conversion therapy has not been proven to work and in fact can do more harm than good. The American Counseling Association passed a resolution in 1998 expressing concerns about the ethics and efficacy of conversion therapy.

CROSS-CULTURAL PERSPECTIVES

The Sambia of New Guinea

The Sambia of New Guinea, as described by anthropologist Gilbert H. Herdt (1984), are horticulturists who define male/male sexual contacts as normal during adolescence. The ritualized sexual interaction between Sambian males is viewed as necessary for individual health and the continuation of society. In their view, the ingestion of semen is required for growth and the development of strength. If a boy does not consume semen, he cannot grow into a strong adult—he will not become a man.

From the moment boys begin the initiation into manhood until the day they marry, adolescent males engage in regular sexual interaction with other adolescent males. Over a period of years,

adolescent boys regularly perform fellatio on older adolescent males, considered young bachelors. When the boys have completed their initiations into bachelorhood, younger boys will then perform fellatio on them. After marriage, heterosexual intercourse with one's wife replaces sex with other males. Similar practices are found in a number of other cultures, especially in Melanesia.

The Sambia challenge our traditional views of sexual orientation. Since all males engage in male/male sex, do you think all Sambian males are homosexual? Does the shift from a decade of exclusively male/male sex to exclusively male/female sex after marriage represent a change in sexual orientation?

| 0 | 1 | 2 | 3 | 4 | 5 | 6 |

| Exclusively heterosexual | Predominantly heterosexual, incidentally homosexual | Predominantly heterosexual, more than incidentally homosexual | Equally homosexual and heterosexual | Predominantly homosexual and more than incidentally heterosexual | Predominantly homosexual incidentally heterosexual | Exclusively homosexual |

FIGURE 11.1 Kinsey's Continuum of Sexual Orientation.
SOURCE: Adapted from Kinsey et al., 1948, p. 638.

A CONTINUUM OF SEXUAL ORIENTATION

We have already used the three categories that traditionally designate an individual's sexual orientation: heterosexual, homosexual, and bisexual. We tend to categorize people as being **gay** (homosexual) or **straight** (heterosexual); a person who is not exclusively heterosexual or homosexual is considered bisexual. Given the diversity of human sexual responsiveness, this three-category system may be misleading.

We introduced you to Alfred Kinsey in Chapter 1. Kinsey was the first scientist to reject the view of sexual orientation as a series of categories. He proposed that sexual orientation is a bipolar, one-dimensional continuum. The Kinsey scale of sexual attraction and behavior (Figure 11.1) consists of seven ratings, from entirely heterosexual to entirely homosexual. It is based on both overt sexual experiences and more internal, psychological reactions such as erotic fantasies.

According to Kinsey's continuum, a bisexual, someone who has both heterosexual and homosexual attraction and behavior, scores in the middle, around a 3. Kinsey's perspective on bisexuality has been questioned because of the implication that bisexuality is a compromise between heterosexual and homosexual extremes.

Some researchers believe that Kinsey's polarization of homosexuality and heterosexuality on either end of the continuum leads to the misunderstanding that they are opposites (Katz, 1995). An alternative model (Figure 11.2) suggests separate dimensions of responsiveness to male-female stimulation (**heteroeroticism**) and sexual stimulation that involves someone of the same sex (**homoeroticism**). According to this model, created by Michael D. Storms (1980), bisexuals are high in both heteroeroticism and homoeroticism, whereas those who are low in both dimensions are essentially **asexual**.

Fritz Klein (1990) has expanded on Kinsey's research and developed the Klein Sexual Orientation Grid (Table 11.1). The Klein grid takes into consideration the fact that many people's sexual orientations change over time. Klein views sexual orientation as a dynamic process. The grid breaks down sexual orientation into seven component variables (A through G). The columns of the grid represent the person's past feelings and experiences, those he or she is experiencing at present, and his or her future ideal. A rating of 1 to 7 (see key in Table 11.1) is assigned for each variable in each of the three time periods.

Research shows that a majority of adult lesbian and bisexual women have had heterosexual intercourse at some point in their lives (Johnson et al., 1987). There are a number of possible explanations for this. One of these is that childhood sexual abuse, incest, and rape are more prevalent among lesbian and bisexual young women than their heterosexual peers (Simari & Baskin, 1982). Others may have heterosexual relationships before they identify themselves as being a lesbian. Some adolescents who are confused about their sexual orientation may attempt to "cure" their homosexuality or "prove" they aren't gay by having heterosexual relationships, a strategy called "heterosexual immersion" (Rosair et al., 1996; Troiden, 1988). Many homosexual men also have had heterosexual experiences.

Gay: male homosexuals

Straight: heterosexual

Heteroeroticism: sexual stimulation that involves someone of the opposite sex

Homoeroticism: sexual stimulation that involves someone of the same sex

Asexual: free from or unaffected by sexuality

FIGURE 11.2 Storms's Model of Sexual Orientation.
SOURCE: Adapted from Storms, 1980.

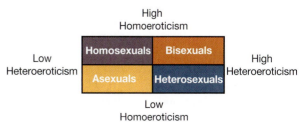

TABLE 11.1			

Klein Sexual Orientation Grid

KEY

For variable A to E:	**For variables F and G:**
1=other sex only	1=heterosexual only
2=other sex mostly	2=heterosexual mostly
3=other sex somewhat more	3=heterosexual somewhat more
4=both sexes equally	4=hetero/gay-lesbian equally
5=same sex somewhat more	5=gay/lesbian somewhat more
6=same sex mostly	6=gay/lesbian mostly
7=same sex only	7=gay/lesbian only

Variable	Past	Present	Ideal
A. Sexual attraction			
B. Sexual behavior			
C. Sexual fantasies			
D. Emotional preference			
E. Social preference			
F. Heterosexual/homosexual lifestyle			
G. Self-identification			

SOURCE: Adapted from Klein, 1990.

According to one study, about half of homosexual males have had sex with a woman at some point in their lives (Savin-Williams, 1990). Similar factors—confusion, coercion, experimentation, and attempts to prove oneself to be heterosexual—account for gay males' experiences with heterosexual sex.

Some studies estimate that as many as 80 percent of lesbians have had heterosexual experiences (Rosario et al., 1996; Savin-Williams, 1990; Whisman, 1996). Could this difference be attributed to females going through a longer heterosexual stage before realizing they might be gay? This does not appear to be the case, because the difference persists in heterosexual experiences after identifying oneself as gay (Bell & Weinberg, 1978; Whisman, 1996). Lesbians are far more likely than gay men to have heterosexual dreams or meaningful heterosexual relationships after being openly gay for years.

Sexual orientation appears to be more changeable among women than among men. Men tend to engage in exclusively heterosexual or homosexual behavior; they rarely fall into the middle categories of Kinsey's scale. In contrast, more women fall into the middle categories and are more likely to move back and forth along the continuum. This fits the general pattern of female erotic plasticity that we described in Chapter 10.

Bisexuality

There is a tendency to group together everyone who has had both heterosexual and homosexual relationships as being bisexual. As previously noted, bisexuality is the sexual, emotional, and social attraction to members of both sexes, though not necessarily at the same time or to the same degree. While bisexuals may have a preference for one sex over the other, this preference may change over time. A majority of bisexuals first establish heterosexual relationships and later experience homosexuality. Most do not consider themselves to be bisexual until several years after they have engaged in sexual relations with both men and women (Weinberger et al., 1994). Many bisexuals feel their primary attraction is to an individual, regardless of that individual's sex.

There are several different ways to look at bisexuality. Some see bisexuality as a distinct sexual orientation. Others believe that we all have the potential for attraction to both men and women; in other words, everyone is, or has the capacity of being,

Androgyny: having both masculine and feminine traits, as in dress, appearance, or behavior bisexual. Still others view bisexuality as a period of experimentation or transition from one sexual orientation to another. Another theory is that bisexuality is a denial of one's true sexual orientation; the belief persists that bisexual men have sex with women in an attempt to deny their homosexuality.

Bisexuals are sometimes pressured to "choose sides" or identify themselves as either homosexual or heterosexual (Fox, 1991). If an adult male who was homosexually active in his youth later marries and has children, it is often said that he was "really" straight all along or, conversely, that he is attempting to deny his homosexuality. If a woman leaves her husband and children for a relationship with another woman, it may be alleged that she was "really" a lesbian all along, or that if a lesbian leaves her partner for a man that she was "really" a heterosexual. These views all share the widely held prejudice that a person who has sex with both males and females must be truly attracted to only one of them.

Some gays and lesbians contend that bisexuals are really homosexuals who don't have the courage to affirm their true sexual orientation. Some in the gay community criticizes bisexuals for "passing" as heterosexuals and enjoying the "heterosexual privileges" of

Having It Both Ways

Bisexuals are often characterized as living in the shadows between the gay and the straight worlds, breaking all the rules by "going both ways." But more and more bisexuals are emerging in all forms of the media. In the 1970s bisexuality seemed to be synonymous with **androgyny** (having the characteristics of both male and female). Artists such as Mick Jagger and David Bowie (who have openly discussed having sexual relationships with both men and woman) blurred the lines of masculine and feminine in their dress and behavior. In the 1980s, when a female attorney on the television show *L.A. Law* kissed another woman, it was considered shocking. But by the time Roseanne tried an experimental kiss with a woman on her show bisexuality had moved into the mainstream. "Many of the men who taught us to be men—Cary Grant, James Dean—and the women who taught us to be women—Billie Holiday, Marlene Dietrich—enjoyed sex with both men and women" (Leland, 1995, p. 444). Marjorie Garber notes in her

Artists such as (a) Marlene Dietrich and (b) David Bowie publicly explore and celebrate androgyny.

book, *Vice Versa: Bisexuality and the Eroticism of Everyday Life* (1995), that celebrities such as Madonna constantly reinvent themselves by reconfiguring their clothes, their bodies, and their hair, but also their sexuality.

 Do you think that androgynous celebrities are truly bisexual or are they just trying to get more publicity?

—Does their behavior promote or encourage bisexuality?

the straight world (see CONSIDERATIONS box). When these critics become most bitter and hostile, they may take the route of revealing someone's sexual orientation to the world, a tactic called "outing." This is an unjustifiable invasion of privacy.

Perhaps because they have more partners to choose from, bisexuals are often viewed as being inherently nonmonogamous. However, many bisexuals do choose to relate monogamously. This does not mean that a bisexual has "chosen" to be gay or lesbian if the partner is of the same sex or to be straight if the partner is of the opposite sex. It means that they have committed to an individual and to a specific relationship. Just as a heterosexual partner may continue to be sexually attracted to members of the opposite sex but choose not to act on that attraction, a bisexual individual may be sexually active with a particular male or female but continues to be attracted to members of both sexes.

Incidence of the Various Sexual Orientations

Measuring the percentage of homosexuals in a population is more complex than it might appear. Many people are reluctant to disclose personal information about their private sexual behavior and feelings, particularly about their sexual orientation. In addition, many people are unsure of their own sexual orientation. And, how do you decide who is homosexual and who is heterosexual? As we have already discussed, an individual may have sexual feelings toward someone of the same sex but never act on these feelings. For those who have acted on their impulses, is a homosexual anyone who has had a single same-sex experience or only those who have had exclusively homosexual experiences? In addition, different definitions of homosexuality can dramatically alter the estimates of its prevalence.

One study found that around 40 percent of men and an even higher proportion of women have been erotically attracted to members of the same sex at some time (McConaghy, 1979). Comparing this figure to the range above, you can see that homosexual *attraction* appears to be much more common than homosexual *behavior*. Kinsey and his colleagues (1948) labeled people who had sex with opposite-sex partners more frequently than with same-sex partners as predominantly heterosexual with incidental homosexuality. However, few people are likely to think of themselves as being "incidentally homosexual."

The 1994 National Health and Social Life Survey (Laumann et al., 1994) focused on two different aspects of homosexuality: (1) being sexually attracted or having sex with persons of the same sex and, (2) identifying oneself as homosexual or bisexual. The survey found that far more people fit into the first category than into the second. In other words, most people who have been attracted to or acted on their attraction to a same-sex partner identify themselves as heterosexual. However, as Figure 11.3 shows, men are more likely to act upon their desire for other men. Men who desire other men and have had sex with men also are more likely than women in that situation to identify themselves as homosexuals.

Relatively few people identify themselves as bisexual. Among those who do, if one controls for the higher rate of same-sex activity among males, bisexuality is more common among women. In other words, among people who have ever had any same-sex sexual relations, a higher proportion of females than males might be defined as bisexual (Laumann et al., 1994). This is related to our earlier point that men tend to be either gay or straight, whereas women tend to fill up all seven points of Kinsey's continuum.

THE BASIS OF SEXUAL ORIENTATION

Psychosocial Theories

Sociological and psychological theories attempt to explain sexual orientation in terms of parenting patterns, the influence of life experiences, and personal adjustment. Domineering mothers, passive fathers, traumatic early childhood sexual experience, emotional

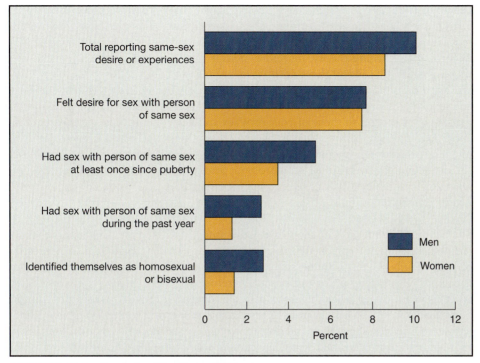

FIGURE 11.3 **Same-Sex Attraction and Behaviors.**
SOURCE: Adapted from Michael et at., 1994, p. 176.

disturbance, and the failure to attract heterosexual partners have all been theorized at various times to cause an individual to develop a homosexual orientation. These theories generally are based on an assumption that heterosexuality is the normal condition and that homosexuality is somehow a less permanent condition than heterosexuality.

Freudian Theory   Sigmund Freud (1915), the founder of modern psychoanalysis, believed childhood experiences, especially the relationship with parents, to be crucial in the development of sexual orientation. Freud believed we are innately polymorphically perverse but that with "normal" developmental experiences an individual would establish a heterosexual orientation. However, if a male had a poor relationship with his father and an overly close relationship with his mother, he might become fixated at the homosexual stage of development. Although there has never been any data offered in support of Freud's theories, they are historically significant since they were the first to attempt to explain what we now call sexual orientation.

The Theory of the "Homo-Seductive" Mother   Psychoanalyst Irving Bieber (1962, 1976) claimed he found a pattern among gay males of a dominant, overprotective, seductive, "smothering" mother and a passive, aloof, unaffectionate, detached father, suggesting that family relationships determine sexual orientation. Bieber and others thought that this familial pattern caused a boy to develop an unconscious fear of sexual contact with women, represented by his mother, and fear of retaliation by his father. Other researchers found that gay males described themselves as more distant from their fathers during childhood than did either heterosexual controls or the gay men's own heterosexual brothers. These men also reported greater closeness to their mothers. However, this pattern of gay men's parental relationships may be an effect of sexual orientation, not a cause. These relationships might have reflected the *son's* alienation from the *father* and not the reverse. That is, the son might have been so attached to his mother or so uninterested in typically masculine activities that he rebuffed paternal attempts to engage him in conventional father-son activities (Pillard, 1990; Pillard & Weinrich, 1986).

FAQ:

How does a person develop a particular sexual orientation?

Many explanations of sexual orientation have been offered over the years. The social and cultural assumptions of the researchers and prevailing beliefs of the time influence research findings; it is difficult to make breakthroughs once such assumptions are accepted (Bullough & Bullough, 1998). Until recently, much of the research into sexual orientation has been based on the assumption that heterosexuality is "normal," and homosexuality and bisexuality are somehow "abnormal." Historically, physicians who subscribed to the theory presented earlier in this chapter that homosexuality was a disease that could somehow be cured dominated research.

Many people continue to believe that homosexuality is a choice that is freely made, or a disease or an addiction. Mistakenly, these individuals think that people could, and should, be cured of this behavior. It is now widely accepted that sexual orientation is determined early in life. Sexual orientation is not something you "catch," like the flu, or learn, like arithmetic. However, as yet there is no definitive proof concerning the cause or causes of sexual orientation. The nature or nurture controversy continues: Is sexual orientation a product of genes or environment? Various studies that have tried to determine the genetic, hormonal, or environmental factors shaping sexual orientation have thus far been inconclusive. No single scientific theory about what causes sexual orientation has been thoroughly substantiated.

"Of all the odd misperceptions current about homosexuality, perhaps the oddest is that it is a choice, that people choose to be homosexual. That strikes me as so patently silly. Did any of us who are straight choose to be heterosexual? When? Did we wake up one morning when we were fifteen and say, 'Gosh, I think I'll be a heterosexual'? For heaven's sakes, how can anyone believe that people choose to be homosexual? 'I think it would be a lot of fun to be called queer and sissy for the rest of my life, so I think I'll be gay.'"

(MOLLY IVINS, 1993, P. 230.)

Learning theory emphasizes the role of early childhood experiences in determining sexual orientation.

Learning Theory   Learning theory emphasizes the role of reinforcement of early patterns of sexual behavior in determining sexual orientation. The idea behind reinforcement is that human beings tend to repeat pleasurable activities and avoid painful ones. According to learning theory, therefore, if your early experiences are primarily with those of the same sex and these encounters are pleasurable, you might develop a homosexual orientation (Gagnon & Simon, 1973). Conversely, if you associate anxiety and parental disapproval with early same-sex sexual contact, you would learn to inhibit feelings of attraction to those of your own sex and develop a firmer heterosexual orientation. However, learning theorists have not identified specific experiences that lead to a particular sexual orientation. In addition, most adolescent or childhood same-sex sexual encounters, even if pleasurable, do not lead to an adult homosexual orientation. Despite pleasurable early same-sex sexual experiences, many people develop a strong heterosexual orientation.

Sociological Theory   The most exhaustive study of the sociological factors that affect sexual orientation dispelled many common, firmly entrenched myths. The research of Bell, Weinberg, and Hammersmith (1981) disputed the theory that homosexuality is caused by a scarcity of, or unpleasant, heterosexual experiences. They found that adult lesbians neither lacked heterosexual experiences nor found those relationships to be particularly unhappy. They just preferred to be sexual with women. The high-school dating experiences of gay men and lesbian women were not found to be different than those of heterosexuals. The researchers concluded that: (1) male homosexuality is not the result of a dominant mother and a weak father; (2) female homosexuality is not the result of girls choosing their fathers as role models; (3) homosexuality is not caused by being seduced by an older person of the same sex; (4) sexual orientation is established before adolescence; (5) as youths, homosexuals have as many heterosexual experiences as their heterosexual counterparts but they do not find these encounters gratifying. While sociological research has dispelled many traditional hypotheses about the causes of homosexuality, it has not been any more successful than psychological theories at identifying causal differences between homosexuality and heterosexuality.

Interactional Theory   Psychologist Daryl Bem (1996) proposed a theory to explain a developmental path by which biological correlates might lead to a particular sexual orientation. Bem's exotic-becomes-erotic theory suggests how biological variables might interact with experiential and sociocultural factors to influence an individual's sexual orientation. According to Bem, genetic and hormonal variables influence two aspects of childhood temperament that show reliable gender differences: aggression and activity level. Boys are typically more aggressive and more active than girls, and most girls prefer quieter play activities. Because children primarily associate with others who enjoy the same activities, most children will associate with those of the same sex. Boys who are not particularly active or aggressive and girls who are more aggressive than their peers develop gender-nonconforming play patterns and have more opposite-sex playmates.

These childhood experiences create a feeling that the children with whom they have less contact and who are different from them are exotic. According to Bem's theory, at some point in life the presence of exotic others cause feelings of generalized arousal. These nonspecific, automatic arousal patterns are transformed into sexual and romantic attraction. For heterosexuals, the exotic opposite sex becomes erotic, while for homosexuals the exotic same sex becomes eroticized.

For the most part, Bem's theory fits what is currently known about homosexuality. It finds evidence of genetic influence but avoids saying that there exists a specific "gay gene" that directly causes homosexuality. In Bem's view, genes determine temperament, and temperament leads to certain patterns of childhood experience, which lays the foundation for sexual orientation. It is not known whether the arousal that comes from encountering the different, "exotic" sex does become transformed into sexual arousal.

Critics state that Bem's theory is not supported by facts (Peplau et al., 1998). A core proposition of Bem's theory is that gays' and lesbians' childhood playmates were primarily of the other sex. However, most children, whether gay or straight, had close same-sex friends, a significant proportion of friends of the same-sex, and considerable contact with other-sex peers. In addition, Bem's claim that his theory applies equally to both sexes is questioned and it is argued that it neglects and misrepresents women's experiences. Bem's critics assert that lesbians in general are particularly likely to form an erotic attraction rising out of an emotional attachment based on connectedness and familiarity.

Biological Theories

Some researchers have approached sexual orientation from a biological perspective. Biological research into the cause of sexual orientation has focused on three main areas: brain structure, the role of genetics, and hormonal and other prenatal factors.

Brain Structure   Simon LeVay (1991), a neuroanatomist at the Salk Institute, theorizes that sexual orientation is linked to sexual differentiation in the brain. In a 1991 study of the dissected brains of deceased men, LeVay reported significant differences in certain cells in the anterior portion of the hypothalamus of gay and straight men. The hypothalamus is a tiny structure in the brain believed to influence sexual activity (see page 81). The hypothalamic cells were reported to be twice as large in heterosexual men as in homosexual men. In a later study, LeVay (1996) concluded that about 50 percent of a male's sexual orientation is genetic. He theorized that part of the other half can be attributed to a nongenetic biological factor or random processes in prenatal environmental development and the rest is determined by environmental and postnatal factors.

Serious questions about LeVay's findings have been raised, including the fact that LeVay had only 19 gay men and 16 straight men in his sample. The study included no women—lesbian or straight. Records identified the homosexual men in the study at the time of their death; the heterosexual men were just "presumed" to be straight. Most of the homosexual men in his samples had died of AIDS. The size of the hypothalamus in these men could have been influenced either by the progress of the disease or by drug treatments.

Genetic Factors   Several researchers have attempted to locate a "gay gene" that influences the development of homosexuality. Psychologists Michael Bailey and Richard Pillard (1991a) found that genetically identical male twins are more likely to have the same sexual orientation than nontwin brothers. If one identical twin is gay, the other has more than a 50 percent likelihood of being gay also. This rate is almost three times higher than if the twins are fraternal (recall that fraternal twins are only as close genetically as nontwin siblings). A similar study conducted by Bailey and Pillard (1993) on lesbians and their twin or adoptive sisters found that 48 percent of identical twins of lesbians were homosexual compared with 16 percent of nonidentical twins. Only 6 percent of the adoptive sisters and 5 percent of the women's brothers were gay. These findings support the theory that sexual orientation has a strong genetic basis. But genetics does not tell the whole story. After all, the 50 percent finding means that half the time that one twin is gay, the other will be *not* gay even though they have identical genes. Genes and heredity play a significant role, but experiences apparently play an important role too.

Researchers have been looking for just where in the family tree a "gay gene" might reside. In 1993, researchers led by Dean Hamer at the National Cancer Institute found that male homosexuality seems to run in families, specifically on the mother's side. After studying the **DNA** of pairs of homosexual brothers, they concluded that a region on the X chromosome (which male children inherit from their mothers), contributes to homosexuality in males. This same effect was not found in women, suggesting that a different mechanism influences female sexual orientation.

> *Someone has said that if this sexual orientation were indeed a matter of personal choice, the homosexual persons must be the craziest coots around to choose a way of life that exposes them to so much hostility, discrimination, loss and suffering.*
>
> (ARCHBISHOP DESMOND TUTU FROM THE FORWARD OF *WE WERE BAPTIZED TOO*)

DNA: deoxyribonucleic acid; the main component of chromosomes and the material that transfers genetic characteristics in all life forms

Bailey, Pillard, and their associates (1999) attempted to replicate their previous findings and confirm Hamer's conclusions in a study examining the possibility of an X-linked gene for homosexuality. They found that the percentage of siblings of gays rated as either homosexual or bisexual ranged from 7 to 10 percent for brothers and 3 to 4 percent for sisters. The researchers state that these estimates are higher than recent population-based estimates of homosexuality, supporting the importance of familial factors for male homosexuality. In another study (Dawood et al., 2000), researchers found that, gay brothers were similar in their degree of childhood gender nonconformity, suggesting that this variable may be genetically based. The large majority of gay men with homosexual brothers knew about their own homosexual feelings before they learned about their brothers' homosexuality, suggesting that discovery of a brother's homosexuality is not an important cause of male homosexuality.

While some research supports the conclusions of Hamer and Bailey et al. (Turner, 1995), other researchers have failed to replicate these findings (Ebers, 1999). Note that the failure to replicate results does not necessarily invalidate the notion that genes influence sexual orientation, nor does it rule out the possibility that such genes are on the X chromosome. Further research is needed before any firm conclusions regarding the role of genetics in determining sexual orientation can be reached.

Hormonal and Other Prenatal Factors   Some biological theories of sexual orientation emphasize the role of early androgens in sexual differentiation of partner preference. As you learned in Chapter 5, testosterone is essential to sexual differentiation in the male fetus. Because of this fact, many researchers have attempted to determine whether the testosterone levels of homosexual men are different from those of heterosexual men. So far, these studies have not found any hormonal differences between gay and straight men (Banks & Gantrell, 1995; Friedman & Downey, 1994; Gooren et al., 1990).

The effect of prenatal hormone levels on female sexual orientation also has been examined. Groups of women who had been exposed prenatally to DES, a synthetic

The Fickle Finger of Fate?

Researchers at Berkeley asked 720 adults about their sexual orientations and then measured their fingers. The fingers of lesbians were closer to the typical male configuration—a shorter index finger than ring finger—than the fingers of heterosexual women. These findings suggest that lesbians are exposed to higher levels of testosterone early in life than heterosexual women (Williams et al., 2000).

Other researchers have examined the role of handedness in sexual orientation. A meta-analysis of 20 studies of nearly 7,000 homosexuals and more than 16,000 heterosexuals found that homosexual subjects had 39 percent greater odds of being left-handed, supporting the notion that sexual orientation in some men and women has an early neurodevelopmental basis (Lalumiere, Blanchard, & Zucker, 2000).

 How do you think the researchers came up with the idea of linking finger length and handedness to sexual orientation?

—If true, what are some implications of these studies?

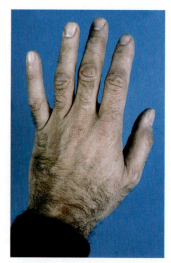

One research study reported the fingers of lesbians were closer to the typical male configuration—a shorter index finger than ring fingers—than the fingers of heterosexual women.

CONSIDERATIONS

Nature or Nurture?

A study (Schmalz, 1993) asked 1,154 adults if their attitudes about homosexuality were affected by their belief that homosexuals are born or made. The results are shown in Table 11.2.

Would proof of a biological causality assure homosexuals protection under the same civil rights laws designed to prevent discrimination on the basis of race or sex? As Kevin Cathcart of the Lambda Legal Defense and Education Fund points out, "Race and gender are clearly biologically determined, and yet that hasn't eliminated racism and misogyny" (Angier, 1993b, p. 000). If sexual orientation is shown to be biological in origin, some might be tempted to find a "cure." For example, gene therapy could be used to change sexual orientation. Another possibility is that women who have prenatal genetic testing done might choose to abort a fetus with an undesirable sexual orientation.

 Do you think that homosexuality is a choice? That it is completely preprogrammed? Or is it a mixture of the two?

—*If biology were found to be the determining factor in sexual orientation, would your view of homosexuals change?*
—*What role should society play in regulating research and protecting homosexuals from discrimination?*

estrogen given to women to prevent miscarriage from the 1940s to the 1960s, were found to be more likely to be lesbian or bisexual than women who were not exposed to DES (Meyer-Bahlburg et al., 1995).

Other prenatal factors may play a role in the development of sexual orientation. One study found that sexual orientation in men correlates with the number of older brothers a man has. Each additional older brother increases the odds of homosexuality by approximately 33 percent. Fraternal birth order also reflects the progressive immunization of some mothers to H-Y antigen by each succeeding male fetus and the increasing effects of H-Y antibodies on the sexual differentiation of the brain in each succeeding male fetus (Blanchard & Klassen, 1997).

Herdt and McClintock (2000) considered the hypothesis that sexual orientation follows the onset of puberty (see Chapter 9), precipitated by the development of stable and memorable attraction toward others approximately by the age of 10. If homosexuals have been subject to atypical androgenzing influences, such influences also may affect other sexual traits such as pubertal timing. Based on this rationale, a study by Tenhula and Bailey (1998) examined the onset of puberty in lesbians. The authors hypothesized

TABLE 11.2

Attitudes Toward Homosexuality		
	Those who say homosexuality is a choice	**Those who say homosexuality can't be changed**
Homosexuals should have equal rights for job opportunities	69%	90%
Object to having a homosexual as a child's elementary-school teacher	71	39
Homosexual relations between consenting adults should be legal	32	62
Would permit their child to play at the home of a friend who lives with a homosexual parent	21	50
Have a close friend or family member who is gay or lesbian	16	29

SOURCE: Schmalz, 1993, p. A17.

that lesbians would have a later age of pubertal onset compared to heterosexual women. However, the researchers found no significant difference in pubertal onset between homosexual and heterosexual women.

Evolutionary Theories

As you learned in Chapter 1, the theory of natural selection proposes that reproductive success is what shapes species. However, homosexual individuals do not reproduce. For evolutionary theorists then, the pressing questions are these: If homosexuality is not adaptive for human reproductive success, how did it develop, why is it so widespread, and why does it continue to exist?

At this point there is no dominant evolutionary theory to explain sexual orientation, but several hypotheses have been suggested. The concept of *balanced polymorphism* suggests that homosexual behavior is retained because it co-occurs with some other trait, possibly rates of development (Hutchinson, 1959). In other words, it is not sexual orientation that is the selected trait but some other trait that occurs along with sexual orientation.

According to the *kin-selection theory*, homosexuals altruistically forgo reproduction to assist the offspring of a relative (Weinrich, 1987; Wilson, 1975). Thus, they are indirectly ensuring the reproductive success of someone else who shares many of the same genes. Another theory, called *parental manipulation*, suggests that parents manipulate some of their children to forgo reproduction and become homosexual in order to assist other offspring (Ruse, 1988; Trivers, 1974).

Bagemihl's (1999) theory of *biological exuberance* is based on the concept of *biodiversity*—that the vitality of a biological system is a direct consequence of the diversity it contains. As diversity increases, so do stability and resilience; thus diverse sexuality, including homosexuality, should be expected throughout the animal kingdom. In fact, homosexual behavior, pair bonding, and coparenting are found in more than 400 different species.

Another hypothesis is that homosexual behavior comes from individuals selected for *reciprocal altruism* (any altruistic behavior occurring between individuals who are not related) based on the principle that help offered in one instance will be returned when the need for help is reversed. According to this view, same-sex alliances have reproductive advantages, and sexual behavior at times helps to maintain these alliances. Nonhuman primates, including apes, use homosexual behavior in same-sex alliances. Such alliances appear to have been key in expanding the geographic distribution of some species by providing evolutionary advantages that allow expansion into new territories. According to Kirkpatrick (2000), homosexual emotion and behavior are strongly influenced by social and historical factors.

Muscarella (2000) emphasized homoerotic behavior itself irrespective of sexual orientation. His evolutionary model was drawn from cross-species and cross-cultural evidence. He proposed that humans evolved a disposition for homoerotic behavior because it increased same-sex affiliation and indirectly influenced rates of survival and reproductive success.

A more recent biological approach to homosexuality is proposed by Rahman and Wilson (2001). They note that biological explanations for homosexuality are necessary because the evidence from many different studies suggests that between 40 percent and 70 percent of the cause of male homosexuality is genetic. However, the existing biological theories have not fared well against the evidence. For example, gay adults do not seem to devote their resources and efforts to caring for the offspring of their siblings, as the parental manipulation theory suggests. (The same-sex alliance theory, however, does seem plausible to Rahman and Wilson.)

Rahman and Wilson (2001) also suggest that male homosexuality may simply be a result of an excess of feminine traits in males. The crucial point is that some degree of feminine traits in a man may be appealing to women because women appreciate men who are tender, sensitive, and empathetic. Thus, it would confer a reproductive advantage on a man to have some of these feminine traits. When those traits exist to a high degree, however, they cause the man to become homosexual. This theory has the advantage of being able to explain why genetic homosexuality continues to exist despite the fact that homosexual sex does not lead to reproduction. An ultra-masculine male may not appeal to many women, whereas a man with some feminine traits will appeal to more women. And, owing to this appeal, some degree of femininity in a man will increase the odds of his being able to pass along his genes. However, these same genes may increase a man's feminine traits so much that they make him homosexual.

DATING, SEX, AND RELATIONSHIPS

Heterosexuals tend to think that gay people live a different kind of life. In most respects, homosexuals face the same problems and issues as everyone else. Having a crush on someone, avoiding rejection, finding a suitable partner for a relationship, communicating about sexual desires, and keeping love alive are inherent to the nature of romance, whether heterosexual or homosexual.

There are, however, some issues that are specific to homosexuality. The social lives of gays and lesbians are different in certain respects from those of the heterosexual majority. First and foremost is the problem of statistics. A gay male will only be able to establish a sexual relationship with another gay male, and there are far fewer gay males than heterosexual ones. Most of the men he meets are therefore not potential romantic partners. A lesbian encounters a similar problem; she may meet many women, but most of them will not be interested in her as a potential sex partner. If you are a heterosexual, you can perhaps get some idea by considering how difficult it is for you to find a romantic partner who is right for you—and then consider that the first 20 partners who you thought were perfect for you turned out not to be interested in you.

Most large cities have a greater proportion of homosexuals than the population rates of homosexuality would suggest. Think about it: if you were the only lesbian living in a small town, you would have almost no chance of experiencing a sexual or romantic relationship. You would have more luck finding a loving partner (and perhaps be more accepted) in a big city. Certain places such as New York City, San Francisco, and Key West have acquired reputations as centers of gay activity.

The problem of having relatively few potential partners is compounded by the difficulty of knowing who they are. A heterosexual man may meet a dozen women in a day and can reasonably hope that many of them would potentially be willing to date him, assuming he were somewhat personable and attractive and they were unattached. Perhaps one of those women might be a lesbian, but the odds are definitely on his side. In contrast, if a lesbian met the same dozen women, perhaps only one of them might be receptive to her interest—and she probably cannot tell which one. Asking all 12 women for a date in order to find out which one (if any) is willing may not be practical and can certainly be disheartening.

Indeed, it can even be dangerous for a gay person to approach a heterosexual. The next section of this chapter explains how angry and even violent behavior can be directed toward homosexuals; in many cases the most negative and harmful acts come in direct response to unwanted homosexual advances. Nearly all adolescents have "crushes," or romantic attractions, to other individuals, but homosexuals must be more careful of revealing their feelings to avoid violent responses.

Homosexuals cope with the difficulty of identifying partners in various ways. Some attempt to communicate their interest by means of subtle signs, such as by dressing

Gay Bars are a popular meeting place for some homosexuals—just as some straight men and women sometimes meet one another at bars or clubs.

or acting in a particular way. These patterns have in the past given rise to homosexual stereotypes. This is a delicate matter; if a person is too obviously gay, he or she may attract hostility from homophobic heterosexuals. Then on the other hand, if the signals are too subtle he or she may either appear heterosexual or make errors and end up approaching heterosexuals. In bars or other places that are known to cater to homosexuals, a gay person can feel reasonably safe about approaching an attractive person and initiating a flirtation.

Adolescents who first recognize themselves as homosexuals are often too young to go to gay bars or other places where homosexuals meet. Just like everybody else, they are likely to begin recognizing their own sexual nature by having romantic attractions to classmates in school. Of course, it is far more difficult and dangerous for adolescent homosexuals to act on these attractions. For some gay youth, the only viable option is to seek out older partners who are overtly gay—but that means that one's first sexual experiences come with people who are quite a bit older and, possibly for that reason, less likely to be relationship partners (see Diamond, Savin-Williams, & Dube, 1999). The result can be a separation of sex and intimacy. The young person forms platonic (intimate but nonsexual) friendships with the same-age peers and explores sex with older people.

Ultimately, many gay adolescents do not have the opportunity to date someone toward whom they feel both sexual and emotional attraction. Herdt and Boxer (1993; see also Diamond et al., 1999) found that less than one out of five gay and lesbian adolescents had their first sexual experience in the context of a relationship. In contrast, according to one study, half of male heterosexual adolescents and three quarters of the females have their first sex in a relationship context (Jessor & Jessor, 1997). Starting sex with a steady dating partner improves the experience of losing one's virginity and is something that many people prefer. It is fair to assume that homosexual adolescents would prefer to have sex with a committed partner, but it is far more difficult for them to accomplish this (Savin-Williams, 1990).

Another difference in the social lives of homosexuals and heterosexuals is the number of sex partners. The stereotypes of the promiscuous gay male and the stable lesbian relationship are both subject to question. The Sex in America survey by Laumann et al. (1994) found that both male and female homosexuals reported more sex partners than heterosexuals, and this held true whether one asked about lifetime partners or recent experiences. Both gay males and lesbians averaged three to four times as many partners as heterosexuals.

Why this difference? There is no clear answer. It could be that because homosexuals learn to separate sex from intimacy during adolescence, they are more willing to engage in casual sex throughout life. Alternatively, because society does not allow homosexuals to marry, perhaps they are less likely to settle down with one person for a long period of time. Still another reason may be that the generally negative attitude of society toward homosexuals puts greater stress on relationships; even when monogamous partnerships are formed, they may be more likely to break up. (Indeed, the longitudinal study of relationships by Blumstein and Schwartz [1983] found that lesbian couples had the highest rate of ending relationships of all types of couples.) The greater statistical difficulty of finding the perfect partner could mean that people spend more time unattached and hence have more casual sexual experiences with other unattached homosexuals. It is also plausible that people who desire a higher number of sex partners are more likely to engage in homosexual activity. It will remain for future research to establish the correct explanation.

Other special aspects of the social lives of homosexuals have been reported by individuals and noted in informal observations, but they have not yet received systematic study and documentation. One is the notion of *overinvestment*. Because it is so difficult to find a good match, a gay man or a lesbian may have a greater fear of losing a good relationship partner. Many people, both homosexual and heterosexual, idealize their partners and relationships, and extreme emotional reactions, including suicide, are sometimes linked to breaking up. These patterns may be

Homophobia: unreasoning fear of or antipathy toward homosexuals and homosexuality

intensified among homosexuals (Hendin, 1982). That is, the homosexual may be especially despondent when a relationship breaks up and especially likely to feel that he or she will never find another.

Infidelity takes on special meanings among homosexuals. Many people, gay or straight, experience a loss of self-esteem when they discover that their partners are having affairs, because of the possible implication that the partner preferred someone else. This blow to pride is doubled among homosexuals. A heterosexual man who discovers his wife is having an affair with the repairman does not usually pause to agonize over why the repairman didn't want to have sex with him instead of with his wife. In a gay love triangle, however, both of those engaged in the affair would be potential partners, so the person may end up feeling rejected by both the lover and the interloper.

Until recently homosexual relationships have been hidden and gays and lesbians had few relationship role models. Heterosexual couples have usually been raised with ample exposure to the roles of "husband" and "wife." In contrast, homosexual couples do not have prescribed roles to fill. Even in dating there may be uncertainties. Who opens the door for whom? The lack of preset roles may appear liberating, but ambiguity may also be a stressful burden.

Lesbians and gays may have a greater fear of losing a good relationship partner.

HOMOPHOBIA

Homophobia is an obsessive, irrational hatred and fear of lesbian and gay people. George Weinberg first used the term in 1967 after he surveyed people about their anxiety and dread of people who engage in sexual acts that are not intrinsically harmful to anyone. He concluded that such feelings were the result of a phobia, an obsessive and irrational fear. The term is really a misnomer since it is not truly a phobia in any clinical sense.

For example, studies suggest that heterosexuals who are hostile to gays and lesbians typically do not manifest the same physiological reactions to homosexuality associated with other phobias, such as fainting or rapid heart rate (Shields & Harriman, 1984). An antihomosexual attitude is more of a prejudice than a phobia (Logan, 1996). Using the term *homophobia* implies that this prejudice is an individual psychological problem rather than a widespread social phenomenon that operates on both the individual and the cultural levels. Recently the term *heterosexism* has increasingly been used as an alternative to homophobia. This term emphasizes the similarities between antigay sentiment and other forms of prejudice such as racism and sexism. Other alternative terms, such as *homoaggression*, *homoanxiety*, *homorevulsion* (White, 1999), *homonegativism*, and *sexual prejudice* (Herek, 2000), have been proposed and may be more accurate in describing negative attitudes toward an individual because of his or her sexual orientation.

Whatever term you use, negative attitudes and institutionalized biases toward lesbians and gays pervade our society (Katz, 1995) (see CONSIDERATIONS box). However, attitudes toward homosexuality have generally become more accepting over the past quarter century in the United States (Table 11.3). Those with antigay attitudes are more likely to be strongly religious, to support traditional gender roles, to believe that sexual orientation is a matter of personal choice, and to be older and less well educated than those with tolerant attitudes toward gays (Johnson et al., 1997). A 1996 study investigated the role of homosexual arousal in exclusively heterosexual men who professed antigay attitudes. The study measured changes in penile circumference of men exposed to sexually explicit erotic stimuli of heterosexuals, gays, and lesbians. The homophobic men reported that they disliked the gay male videos, but they exhibited the highest levels of arousal while watching these. The contrast between the self-reported

Homophobia is really more a prejudice than a phobia.

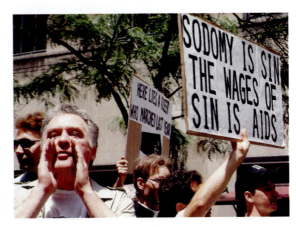

The Sound of Music

Society's attitudes are reflected in the popular media. Grammy-award-winning rap artist Eminem reveals some of the more extreme attitudes toward gays and lesbians in the following lyrics: "My words are like a dagger with a jagged edge/That'll stab you in the head/Whether you're a fag or a lez/Or the homsex, hermaph or a trans-a-vest/Pants or dress/Hate fags? The Answer's 'yes.'"

? *Can homophobic songs influence an audience and perhaps incite some individuals to acts of violence?*

—*Should Eminem's lyrics be protected as free speech?*

—*If someone leaves a concert where this song has been performed and then engages in gay bashing, should Eminem be held accountable for the harm to the victim?*

reaction and the bodily response led the researchers to conclude that homophobia is associated with homosexual arousal that the person is either unaware of or denies (Adams et al., 1996).

This finding harks back to Sigmund Freud's theory of **defense mechanisms** (see Chapter 1). Freud held that when a person cannot accept a personal characteristic, he or she denies having the trait and projects it onto other people—he or she might even condemn others for it. Freud proposed that people who hate gays might actually be struggling with their own homosexual tendencies. Because they do not want to accept their own homosexual feelings, they strongly deny having any such feelings and in fact may exhibit intensely negative reactions to homosexuality. The homosexual participants in the Adams et al. (1996) study claimed to have negative feelings toward homosexuals even though their responses indicated that gay sex was arousing to them.

Men appear to view gay men more negatively than they do lesbians. The process of internalizing homophobia seems to be different for women. "Girls are not taught to shun boyishness with nearly such ferocity. The dread of being homosexual is not impressed upon girls as it is upon boys" (Weinberg, 1972, p. 77). As a result, women tend to endorse fewer antigay attitudes, beliefs, and behaviors than men. Herek (2000) also explored the question of whether and how heterosexuals' attitudes toward lesbians differ from their attitudes toward gay men. Herek found that heterosexual women generally hold similar attitudes toward gay men and lesbians, whereas heterosexual men are more likely to make distinctions according to gender. According to Herek, these findings suggest that heterosexuals' attitudes toward gays are organized both in terms of minority group politics and personal sexual and gender identity.

A meta-analysis combining results from many different studies found that among younger people, men were more negative toward homosexuality overall, but older men

Defense Mechanism: an unconscious process that protects an individual from unacceptable or painful ideas or impulses.

TABLE 11.3

Changes in Attitudes Toward Homosexuality, 1973–1994

	1973	1994
Are sexual relations between adults of the same sex:		
Always wrong	74	63
Almost always wrong	7	4
Only wrong sometimes	8	6
Not wrong at all	11	22
Should an openly homosexual man be allowed to teach at a college or university?		
Yes	49	71

SOURCE: NORC, 1994.

and women showed little or no difference (Oliver & Hyde, 1993). This conclusion seems consistent with the view that negativity toward homosexuals is correlated with a fear of having to fend off homosexual advances, probably a more worrisome and reasonable fear for young people than older people.

Homophobic attitudes appear to be more common among males who identify with a traditional male gender role and those who hold a fundamentalist religious orientation and a conservative ideology (Heaven & Oxman, 1999; Kerns & Fine, 1994). The religious aspects of homosexual prejudice will be discussed more fully in Chapter 17.

Gender-role reversal can be perceived as a threat to some individuals. There are those who believe that homosexual men are "defective" because they share characteristics with women, the "inferior" sex (Lewes, 1988). In Latin American and Asian societies, gender role often is more important than the sex of the partner. A distinction may be made between the insertive and receptive partners in male-male oral or anal sex. The partner who penetrates (the insertive partner) maintains his manhood and is considered heterosexual, while the one who is penetrated (the receptive partner) is viewed as homosexual (Matteson, 1997). Black and Latino men also follow this pattern (Peterson & Marin, 1988). Lesbianism is a direct threat to ethnic groups, such as many Hispanic and Asian cultures, that place high or exclusive importance on a woman's childbearing role and subservience to men (Chan, 1995; Guerro-Pavich, 1986).

African Americans have been found to be significantly more homophobic than whites or Hispanics (Poussaint, 1990; Waldner, Sikka, & Baig, 1999). In a study by Ernst and associates in 1991, African Americans were significantly more likely to agree with the statement "AIDS will help society reduce the number of homosexuals (gay people)" than other racial or ethnic groups. Black women were especially negative about homosexuals as compared with white women (Ernst et al., 1991). The researchers suggest that black women's more negative attitudes toward homosexuals may be due to the perception that homosexuality is one of many forces diminishing the pool of eligible black men.

You might assume that societal attitudes toward bisexuals would be identical to those towards gays and lesbians. One study did find that there is a degree of correlation between the two. However, negative attitudes toward bisexual men were more prevalent than negative attitudes about lesbians or gay men. Therefore, antigay prejudice and antibisexual prejudice are related, but distinct, attitudes (Eliason, 1997).

There has been an increase in reports of antigay bias since the beginning of the AIDS crisis. Rather than creating new hostility, researchers have found the disease has given bigots an excuse to act out their hatred. In one study, college students were given eight stories that described a person who had just received a positive HIV test. The stories were identical except for the sex of the person described and identification of his or her high-risk group (for example, hemophiliacs, homosexuals, or injection-drug users). After reading the stories, the students were asked to assess responsibility, blame, and characteristics of the person described in the story, as well as their own homophobia

Self Hatred

Prejudice against homosexuals of your own sex seems somewhat paradoxical. Heterosexuals should be *happy* when members of their own sex turn gay, because that reduces the potential competition for attractive mates. Imagine if you were the only heterosexual member of your sex left on your campus or in your city. You would have your pick of the most desirable people to date! Yet instead of following this seemingly rational pattern, many heterosexuals are hostile toward gay members of

their own sex. Some heterosexual men eroticize lesbianism (Whitley et al., 1999). Again, this does not appear to make sense as lesbians increase the competition for a potential mate.

Why do you think heterosexuals would feel threatened by same-sex homosexuals?

—Why might some heterosexual men find lesbianism erotic?

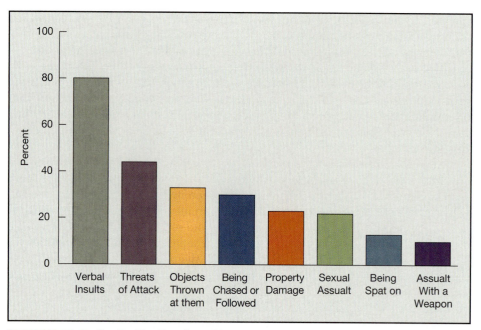

FIGURE 11.4 **Gay Bashing Experienced by 15- to 21-year-old Gay, Lesbian, and Bisexual Youth.** SOURCE: Adapted from Hershberger & D'Augelli, 1995.

and knowledge about AIDS. Results revealed that homophobia was a significant factor affecting the students' perceptions of the HIV-infected person in the story. Hemophiliacs were judged least harshly by the students, followed by heterosexuals; homosexuals were second only to injection-drug users in this blame game (Johnson & Baer, 1996).

One of the most disturbing and extreme displays of homophobia is the physical violence involved in **"gay bashing"** (Figure 11.4). These attacks against gays and suspected gays are more prevalent among adolescents and young adult males who may be less secure in their own sexual identities than are older adult males. The rationalization for such violence often is to "teach them a lesson." Lesbians are also the object of homophobia and **hate crimes,** including rape. The victims of hate crimes appear to show more psychological distress than victims of random crimes, apparently because they have an increased sense of personal danger and link this vulnerability to their homosexual identity (Herek, 1992). The 1993 murder of transgender teenager Brandon Teena (the subject of the 1999 movie *Boys Don't Cry*), the slaying of two lesbian activists in Oregon in 1995, the 1998 murder of University of Wyoming student Matthew Shepard, and the 1999 beating death of a gay soldier at Fort Campbell, Kentucky, are just a few cases of hate crimes towards gays and lesbians.

Heterosexual youth who grow up in a biased social environment may find it difficult to accept homosexuals as equals or even be tolerant of gays and lesbians. A hostile social environment also may create self-doubt in homosexual youth and make it even more difficult for them to express their sexuality (Figure 11.5). The verbal and physical abuse that threatens gay, lesbian, and bisexual youth is often associated with school-related problems, running away from home, conflict with the law, substance abuse, prostitution, and suicide (Savin-Williams, 1994). According to some reports, homosexual youth account for 30 percent of youth suicides; there is a particularly strong association between suicidal ideation and bisexuality and homosexuality in males (Remafedi, 1996).

Homophobia has an impact on heterosexuals as well as on gays and lesbians. Straight men and women may restrict their lives by avoiding any behavior that might be perceived as homosexual. For example, a heterosexual male might be reluctant to explore his interest in fashion design out of fear of being labeled a "queer" or a heterosexual woman might restrict her athletic interests in order not to be thought of as

Gay Bashing: a threat, assault or act of violence directed toward a homosexual or homosexuals

Hate Crime: a crime (such as assault or defacement of property) that is motivated by hostility to the victim as a member of a group (as one based on color, creed, gender, or sexual orientation)

Coming Out of the Closet: the acknowledgment by gays, lesbians, or bisexuals of their sexual orientation, first to themselves and then to others

a "dyke." Men's fear of same-sex attraction may keep them from allowing themselves the emotional vulnerability required for deep friendships, thus limiting their relationships with other men (Nelson,1985).

There has been very little research about the attitudes of homosexuals toward heterosexuals. In order to compare the attitudes of both groups, one study reworded a questionnaire to create a "heterophobia" questionnaire. Sixty straight and 60 gay and lesbian students were matched on the basis of demographic and social criteria and each group was given its respective "phobia" questionnaire. The homosexual participants in the study reported less phobia than heterosexuals, and lesbians reported more phobia than gay men (White & Franzini, 1999).

COMING OUT OF THE CLOSET

The closet has become a metaphor for those things we wish to keep hidden away. To **come out of the closet,** sometimes referred to simply as coming out, has come to mean that gays, lesbians, or bisexuals acknowledge their sexual orientation, first to themselves and then to others. Because some individuals try to suppress or deny their sexual orientation from themselves as well as from others, the first step in the coming out process is recognizing one's own sexual feelings. Some people report that they have "always" known that they were gay or lesbian while others come to that realization later in life (Figure 11.6).

After acknowledging sexual orientation, the important next step is self-acceptance. It is difficult to be part of a sexual minority in a society that assumes that everyone is heterosexual. Lesbian, gay, and bisexual youth have few role models and few places where they can go for guidance and support (Rotello, 1995). Typically they endorse the erroneous negative stereotypes about homosexuality and may develop feelings of self-hatred (Telliohann et al., 1995).

Reasons for coming out range from the personal (self-identity and emotional well-being), to the political (the desire to challenge society's assumptions about homosexuals). Lying, avoiding questions about marriage, and sidestepping friendly attempts to be fixed up with members of the other sex can all take their toll on those who stay in the closet.

Hate crimes such as the 1998 murder of University of Wyoming student Matthew Shepard outrage many Americans.

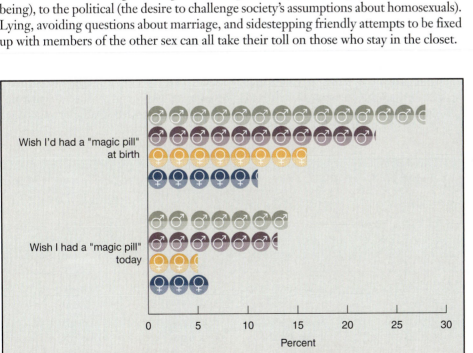

FIGURE 11.5   **Percentage of Gays and Lesbians Who Wish They Had Been Given a "Magic Heterosexuality Pill" at Birth or Wish They Could Receive One Today.**

SOURCE: Adapted from Bell & Weinberg, 1978.

CAMPUS CONFIDENTIAL

"I just found out that this guy I've been friends with since junior high school is gay. Believe me, Matt is the last guy you would suspect. He seems so normal. You know what I mean . . . he seems like a regular guy.

"When he first told me, I tried to be cool about it and not freak out too much. But it was really weird. I started to think about all the times we've been in the locker room together and wondered if he was getting turned on when we were in the showers. I've never thought of myself as being uptight about anything having to do with sex . . . whatever floats your boat is okay with me. But it seems different when it's someone you've known forever.

"I've never known any gays before. Well, I guess that's not true anymore. Maybe I have more gay friends, or even relatives and just didn't know it. Now I'm starting to think about all the times I've called someone a "fag" and all the "queer" jokes I've told or laughed at. I wonder what that was like for Matt.

"I guess I'm glad Matt trusted me enough to tell me, but in a way I also wish he hadn't. I don't want to feel differently about our friendship. This is going to take some getting used to." ●

FIGURE 11.6 **When Did You Become Aware of Your Sexual Orientation?**

SOURCE: Adapted from Elliott & Brantley, 1997.

Coming out of the closet can be risky. Most people take baby steps, privately revealing their sexuality first to selected friends or family members. Some may find their job in jeopardy, their career at a dead end; they may lose custody of their children or be rejected by friends and family. Many gays and lesbians have heard the "jokes" and comments made by their friends or associates and don't want to become the focus of snickers and stares. There are also those who feel that their sexual orientation is private and thus no one else's business.

Some gays may resist coming out of the closet because they do not want their entire identity to be colored by their sexuality. It may be awkward and undignified to have people you have just met quickly learn intimate things about your sex life. For example, if you were a heterosexual woman who happened to enjoy being spanked before sex, or a man who loved to perform cunnilingus, you would not necessarily want to disclose this right away to everyone you knew. Perhaps you would reveal this to trusted friends, but it would hardly be the first thing you would want a business acquaintance to know about you! You certainly would not want all your acquaintances to imagine you performing such acts. Once they have identified themselves publicly, homosexuals may find that other people use homosexuality to define their whole identity. It is hardly surprising that many prefer to wait to disclose their homosexuality, even if they are completely comfortable with their sexual orientation.

Lesbian, gay, and bisexual students often choose to come out at college, but studies have demonstrated that the university setting is often hostile to homosexuals. Lesbian, gay, and bisexual students often have a more negative experience in the university environment than heterosexual students (Waldo, 1998). Research shows that when they have a choice, gays and lesbians are more likely to disclose their sexual orientation to members of groups that are generally more tolerant of homosexuality. These groups include women, liberals, and the college educated (Herek & Capitanio, 1996).

For many gays, lesbians, and bisexuals, coming out to their parents is the most difficult step out of the closet. Even as adults, the emotional relationship with parents can be particularly complicated. Because telling family members about their sexual orientation can be so difficult, many gays and lesbians choose not to do so. They may follow the military's "don't ask, don't tell" policy and neither confirm nor deny their homosexuality. Even heterosexual adults have problems discussing any aspect of their sexuality with their parents. Being rejected by a sibling or parent can hurt far more than the anonymous taunts of strangers or the unkind remarks of acquaintances. To their surprise, many find that their sexual orientation is not an issue with their parents and that unconditional love and acceptance are readily forthcoming. However, some parents have

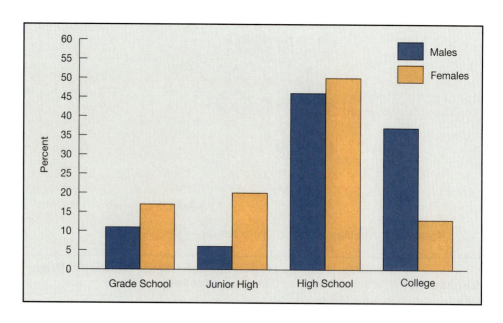

CONSIDERATIONS

Coming Out in Public

Those who are already in the public eye find that coming out is a very public act, or maybe even a media event. Few individuals have had as public a coming out as comedian Ellen DeGeneres. In April 1997 it was big news when DeGeneres publicly revealed that she was a lesbian only 2 weeks before the character she plays on television came out on prime time across the country. In doing so she became the first openly gay leading character on a television series. Topics presented in the episode included denial, discrimination, fear of exposure, fear of contagion, and the emotional impact of the coming out process (Ryan & Boxer, 1998). Today, television shows such as *Will and Grace* deal with sexual orientation in a far more matter-of-fact manner.

 Why do you think the "coming out" episode was such a huge media event?

—*Was it "about time" for television to reflect our society more accurately, or do you consider open portrayal and discussion of homosexuality to be offensive or inappropriate?*

—*Do you agree with the network's decision to put a parental warning on the episode?*

---

been known to throw their gay and lesbian children out of the house or stop providing financial support (Warren, 1997). Parents also may react with anger or guilt about what they "did wrong" (Woog, 1997). After a period of adjustment, many of these families turn around and become increasingly open to learning more about their child's sexual orientation. Local and national organizations such as PFLAG (Parents, Family and Friends of Lesbians and Gays) can be an invaluable source of information and support for some families of gays and lesbians.

Not surprisingly, adolescents who have a closer relationship with their parents tend to come out at a younger age and to experience more positive sexual identities than do those who have a poor relationship with their families (Beaty, 1999). A study of 194 lesbian, gay, and bisexual youth aged 14 to 21 who were living at home found that three quarters had told at least one parent, more often the mother, about their sexual orientation. Those who had disclosed their orientation reported more verbal and physical abuse by family members and acknowledged more suicidal tendencies than those who had not "come out" to their families. Few of those who chose not to disclose expected parental acceptance (D'Augelli, Hershberger, & Pilkington, 1998).

Although the practice of "outing" is controversial (see CONSIDERATIONS box), disclosure of a homosexual orientation has been shown to decrease negative attitudes about homosexuals. If you found out that your sister, cousin, teacher, or coworker is lesbian or gay, it might be more difficult to hold on to a prejudice about homosexuals as a group. One study found that when lesbian, gay, or bisexual educators come out to their students, there was a positive effect on their students' attitudes (Waldo & Kemp, 1997). Heterosexuals who have two or more close friends or family members who are gays or lesbians tend to hold favorable attitudes toward homosexuals (Herek & Capitanio, 1996). Direct, open discussion of homosexuality appears to play an important role in changing attitudes.

Outing: publicly identifying the sexual orientation of gays and lesbians who previously have chosen not to acknowledge their sexual orientation publicly

Outing

CONSIDERATIONS

Some gay and lesbian activists believe that they cannot achieve acceptance and equal rights as long as so many heterosexuals continue to believe the negative stereotypes about homosexuals. They argue that homosexuals need to be honest about their sexual orientation so that heterosexuals can discover that people they already know, love, and respect are gay or lesbian. Some groups and individuals believe so strongly in this view that they have publicly identified gays and lesbians who previously had not chosen to come out and publicly reveal their sexual orientation, an action commonly referred to as **outing.** However, most people feel that the decision to come out of the closet should be made by the individual and that those who choose to keep their homosexuality private have every right to do so.

 Do you think that anyone has a right to "out" anyone else?

—*Would you think differently about a close friend or relative if you discovered he or she was gay?*

WWW EXPLORING SEXUALITY ONLINE

Connecting Online

A connection to the Internet can be a connection to a homosexual virtual community. Youth Resource (www.youth-resource.com) an Internet site for gay, lesbian, and bisexual high-school and college students, has campus links, news, chat rooms and online communities that offer support for the specific needs of Hispanic and African-American gay, lesbian, and bisexual youth. Internet chat groups allow people to interact with others in a relatively anonymous fashion. Chat groups can provide individuals access to resources and a place to belong that might otherwise not be available. Members of these online communities expect their identities to remain private, and in fact the 1986 Electronic Privacy Act (EPA) ensures that not even government agencies can obtain private information without a warrant.

However, Internet privacy is not a sure thing. In January 1998, a Senior Chief Officer in the U.S. Navy was discharged after 17 years of service for homosexual conduct because his America Online (AOL) profile identified him as gay (we will discuss the military's policies on homosexuality in Chapter 18). The Navy would not have been able legally to link him with his profile if an AOL employee had not provided a naval investigator with a name. In doing so AOL violated not only its own explicitly stated privacy policies but also the EPA. It appears that both the Navy and AOL may have violated the EPA, since no subpoena was ever issued. A federal judge ordered the Navy to reinstate the officer stating that "Suggestions of sexual orientation in a private, anonymous e-mail account did not give the Navy sufficient reason to investigate to determine whether to commence with discharge proceedings" (Graham, 1998, p. 2).

CHAPTER 11 REVIEW

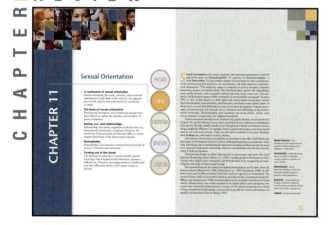

1_____, the erotic, romantic, and emotional attraction to individuals of the same sex, to the opposite sex, or to both men and women, is a multidimensional phenomenon involving love, sex, and identity.

2_____ was the first scientist to view sexual orientation as a continuum ranging from the exclusively heterosexual orientation to the exclusively homosexual orientation. This perspective assumes that both of the extremes, as well as the gradations between them, are natural. A **3**_____ is someone who has both heterosexual and homosexual attractions. Research indicates that genetic inheritance and experience work together to shape sexual orientation.

It is impossible to verify the percentage of homosexuals in a population because of variations in perceptions of what constitutes homosexuality. For example, the National Health and Social Life Survery found that far more people find others of the same sex sexually attractive and have experimented with homosexual behavior than identify themselves as being homosexual or bisexual.

A number of theories have been offered to explain sexual orientation. **4**_____, the founder of modern psychoanalysis, thought that the relationship you had with your parents was crucial to the development of sexual orientation. Recent research has shown that this was an incorrect assumption. Bem's **5**_____ theory suggests how biological variables might interact with experiential and sociocultural factors to influence an individual's sexual orientation. A possible link between brain structure and sexual orientation was first suggested by **6**_____ . Research by Michael Bailey and Richard Pillard indicates that genetically identical twins are more likely to share the same sexual orientation than other siblings.

7_____ is the obsessive, irrational hatred and fear of lesbian and gay people, which is often influenced by institutionalized biases in a society. One of the more extreme displays is the physical violence involved in "gay bashing." However, attitudes toward homosexuality have generally become more accepting over the past quarter century in the United States.

8_____ is a term used to refer to the process of self-disclosure that one is a gay or lesbian. **9**_____ refers to the forced disclosure of another's homosexuality.

SUGGESTED READINGS

Clausen, J. & Duberman, M. B. (1996). *Beyond Gay and Straight: Understanding Sexual Orientation.* New York: Chelsea House Publications.

This book is an examination of various theories, historical and contemporary, that have been proposed to explain sexual orientation.

DeCecco, J. P. & Parker, D. A. (Eds.). (1995). *Sex, Cells, and Same Sex Desire: The Biology of Sexual Preference.* New York: Haworth Press.

This volume contains 20 papers by scientists and scholars in the social sciences and humanities regarding biological research on sexual orientation.

Herdt, G. (1997). *Same Sex, Different Cultures: Gays and Lesbians Across Cultures.* Boulder, CO: Westview Press.

Drawing on research into sexual initiation rites and sexuality from Africa to the American Southwest, this book explores how sexual orientation is explained and dealt with in different societies.

Hogan, S. & Hudson, L. (1998). *Completely Queer: The Gay and Lesbian Encyclopedia.* New York: Henry Holt.

This volume contains approximately 600 articles arranged in alphabetical order that focus on the accomplishments of Western gays and lesbians over the past few decades.

Katz, J. N. (1992). *Gay American History: Lesbian and Gay Men in the U.S.A.* New York: Meridian Press.

Katz offers a comprehensive collection of documents on American gay life from the early days of European settlement to the emergence of modern American gay culture.

Sears, J. T. & Williams, W. L. (Eds.). (1997). *Overcoming Heterosexism and Homophobia: Strategies That Work.* New York: Columbia University Press.

This book consists of essays that provide ideas and strategies for affirming diversity and overcoming sexual prejudice in a variety of settings.

Sherrill, J.-M. & Hardesty, C. A. (1994). *The Gay, Lesbian, and Bisexual Students' Guide to Colleges, Universities, and Graduate Schools.* New York: New York University Press.

This guide is based on information provided by students about the climate toward gay and lesbians students on college campuses.

Signorille, M. (1996). *Outing Yourself: How to Come Out as Lesbian or Gay to Your Family, Friends, and Coworkers.* New York: Fireside Publishers.

This is a step-by-step no-nonsense guide to coming out of the closet by an editor of *Out* magazine.

ANSWERS TO CHAPTER REVIEW

1. Sexual orientation; **2.** Alfred Kinsey; **3.** bisexual; **4.** Sigmund Freud; **5.** exotic-becomes-erotic; **6.** Simon LeVay; **7.** Homophobia; **8.** Coming out (of the closet); **9.** Outing

CHAPTER 12

Consensual Sexual Behavior

PHYSICAL

SOCIAL

EMOTIONAL

SPIRITUAL

COGNITIVE

- **Celibacy**
  Celibacy, the decision not to engage in sex, is a viable choice.

- **Sexual Arousal During Sleep**
  While it is not a voluntary activity, and thus not a conscious sexual behavior like sexual fantasy or masturbation, sexual arousal during sleep occurs with great regularity.

- **Autoerotic Sexual Activity**
  Sexual fantasy and masturbation are two types of autoeroticism, sexual pleasure that does not require the direct participation of another person.

- **Sex With a Partner**
  Partner sex, which involves intimate communication and, ideally, mutual pleasuring, may involve reproductive (coital) or nonreproductive (noncoital) sexual activities.

- **Atypical Sexual Behaviors**
  Uncommon sexual practices may be performed alone or involve consenting adult partners.

exuality can be expressed in many different ways. Whether it is intended to meet the physical need of reproduction or not, whether alone or with others, sexual behavior is an important way for people to meet their needs. It makes a social statement that communicates something about who you are to others. When you engage in sexual behaviors with a partner, you may be seeking to meet emotional or spiritual needs for companionship and intimacy. At the same time you may sense how social institutions, societal norms, and cultural expectations influence your behavioral choices. You may decide to engage in a certain behavior because "everyone does it." On the other hand, you may avoid a certain behavior because you sense that others might find it silly or repugnant.

Like most people, you probably associate sex with being intimate with another person. However, partners aren't always available or even necessary for sexual pleasure. Even couples in long-term relationships may find solitary sexual behavior rewarding. It may take two to tango, but you can dance alone and still enjoy the music.

You may engage in solitary sexual behavior when you have erotic dreams and become sexually aroused during sleep, when you have sexual fantasies, and when you masturbate. Or you may express your sexuality by being celibate. The number of possible sexual behaviors is increased when you engage in sex with a partner. Oral-genital stimulation, anal intercourse, and a diversity of coital positions can provide nearly limitless possibilities of pleasure. While many individuals find a few of the more typical sexual behaviors to be sufficient for their sexual repertoire, others seek a wider variety to gratify their needs. There are also those who express their sexuality in atypical ways, such as sadomasochistic behaviors or fetishes.

While the sexual behaviors discussed in this chapter include the usual and the unusual, they all involve consensual sexual activity, that is, sexual behavior between consenting adults. Nonconsensual sexual behaviors, also called coercive sexual behaviors, are those involving the use of force, children, or nonconsenting adults. These will be discussed in Chapter 13.

As you consider the many alternatives for meeting your sexual needs, ask yourself the following questions: Why do you select one option over another? To what extent are your decisions influenced by the expectations of other people? What is the relationship between your personal needs and those of society?

CELIBACY

Celibacy is the conscious decision not to engage in sexual behavior. While technically celibacy may be more of a sexual "nonbehavior," the decision itself is an expression of sexuality. It is certainly possible to be both celibate and retain your sexuality. People may choose celibacy for religious, health, or personal reasons. The decision to be celibate may be a lifetime commitment or a temporary choice (see CAMPUS CONFIDENTIAL box).

Celibacy: abstention from sexual intercourse

The decision to be celibate may be a lifetime commitment, as chosen by the individuals shown here, or a temporary choice for personal renewal.

Some who are celibate abstain from all sexual activity, while others may masturbate but not participate in any sexual interaction with a partner. Still others consider celibacy to mean they are not having coitus. A study of high-school students who had never had vaginal intercourse found that 29 percent had engaged in heterosexual masturbation of a partner and 31 percent in masturbation by a partner. About 10 percent had engaged in oral-genital sex and 1 percent in anal sex (Schuster et al., 1996). Many people deliberately choose to regard oral sex as "not sex" in order to avoid the guilt they might feel when engaging in sexual intercourse (Sanders & Reinisch, 1999). According to this very limited definition of sex, even people with considerable sexual experience can consider themselves celibate.

Men and women of all ages and backgrounds choose to be celibate. In her book, *Women, Passion, and Celibacy*, author Sally Cline (1993) interviewed women in the United States, Canada, and England who gave up sex to improve their psychological well-being. Reasons for celibacy included the desire to grow spiritually or emotionally, escape from male violence, adjustment to widowhood or the end of a relationship, fear of AIDS, and boredom with sex. The women Cline surveyed believed that celibacy helped them learn to control their own lives, take risks, make decisions, and value friendships. Many said they felt very sensual. Celibacy is not for everyone, but for some people it can be a positive choice.

In some cultures, such as in ancient India, Tibet, and parts of New Guinea, it was believed that sexual activity drained away vital energies, weakening the participant, particularly the man. This also was a widespread belief among North American athletes through much of the 20th century. In such cultures it is believed that semen contains vital chemicals or magical or spiritual powers that leave a man's body when he ejaculates.

The long history of opposition to masturbation was based in part on the belief that the loss of bodily fluids through ejaculation would weaken or damage the body, causing both physical and psychological illness. Sigmund Freud's theory of sublimation held that the sex drive contains energy that can be diverted to higher purposes such as art, learning, and scholarship. Indeed, he was fond of remarking that students who had too much sex ceased to be able to learn and perform well in school. (Don't worry—these beliefs appear to be unfounded.) To retain this vital fluid, some men practice a form of sexual intercourse without ejaculation. The man simply exerts self-control, possibly including ceasing the motion of intercourse whenever he gets too close to orgasm.

According to what we know today, sexual abstinence does not produce any medical, psychological, or physical benefits. It is true that sex carries some risks of sexually transmitted infections (see Chapter 7), so abstaining from sex may help prevent them and their complications. It is also true that some people put an inordinate amount of time, energy, and other resources into the pursuit of sex, so celibacy may actually help conserve some of those resources.

❝ [O]ur erotic daydreams are the true X-rays of our sexual soul. . . . We should value our erotic reveries because they are the complex expressions of what we consciously desire and unconsciously fear. To know them is to know ourselves better. ❞

(FRIDAY, 1991, P. 6)

SEXUAL AROUSAL DURING SLEEP

While it is not a voluntary activity, and thus not a conscious sexual behavior like sexual fantasy or masturbation (discussed in the next section), sexual arousal during sleep occurs with great regularity. Over the course of a typical 8 hours of sleep, most people have episodes of arousal (including vaginal swelling and lubrication or penile erection) approximately every 90 minutes; these usually occur during periods of **rapid eye movement (REM) sleep.** Neither men nor women have direct control over these responses. According to one theory, these responses are the body's way of checking to make sure that a person's brain, nervous system, and genitals are functioning properly.

Men have two to five erections a night during REM sleep (Reinisch, 1991). The morning erection that many men experience results from abrupt awakening during the last cycle of REM sleep. The fact that some men have their highest testosterone levels in the early morning hours may also contribute to morning erections. One of the few studies to measure physiological response patterns of sexual arousal in women during sleep (Rogers et al., 1985) found that the highest levels of vaginal pulse amplitude (blood flow to the vagina indicating sexual arousal) also occurred during REM sleep. Both men and women may experience orgasm involuntarily during sleep. When males experience nocturnal orgasm, they usually ejaculate; if this happens, it is called a **nocturnal emission** or "wet dream." It is estimated that 80 percent of men and 40 percent of women have had at least one nocturnal orgasm, with peak rates for men when they are in their 20s and for women in their 40s (Reinisch, 1991).

While dreams almost always accompany a nocturnal orgasm, some sexual responses, such as the aforementioned erections and vaginal responses, occur regularly during sleep and may or may not involve sexual dreams. However, nearly all men and approximately 70 percent of women are thought to have sexual dreams (Ware et al., 1997). The content of sexual dreams, as with any dream, can vary from the mundane to the bizarre. Just because you have a dream about something does not necessarily mean that it is something you want to do or even would consider actually doing.

AUTOEROTIC SEXUAL ACITIVITY

Autoeroticism is sexual desire or gratification experienced by an individual that does not require the direct participation of another person. The absence of a specific sexual partner during masturbation or sexual fantasy "does not mean that autoerotic activities are without social content or social origins" (Laumann et al., 1994, p. 134). Sexual fantasies often incorporate the imagined or real presence of others. Masturbation can be performed whether alone, in the presence of a partner, or in the case of mutual masturbation, with a partner.

Sexual Fantasies

Sexual fantasies, erotic thoughts and daydreams about sexual activities, are both normal and common. According to the National Health and Social Life Survey (NHSLS), more than 50 percent of men have erotic thoughts at least once every day, and only 4 percent think about sex less than once a month. About two thirds of women in this same study reported that they think about sex a few times a week or a few times a month (Michael et al., 1994). A 1990 survey found that 84 percent of men and 67 percent of women had sexual fantasies (Reinisch, 1990).

Sexual fantasies can be erotic, exotic, amusing, or unsettling. Fantasies can be unconscious—a thought that seems to come from nowhere. Alternatively, you can control the content of the fantasy with deliberate scripting, editing and casting. Some fantasies may be rerun more often than episodes of *I Love Lucy*, while others may have a single showing.

While sexual fantasy is a private mental activity that may be experienced without sexual behavior, fantasies also can be used to enhance sexual relations with a partner. Some couples find it arousing to share their fantasies, to act them out, or to use their erotic thoughts or images to heighten sexual response. A study of college students found that 60 percent fantasized during intercourse (Sue, 1979), for a variety of reasons (Figure 12.1). Across many different studies, the percentages of men and women who fantasize during sexual intercourse have been about equal (Leitenberg & Henning, 1995). When not engaged in sex, men have generally been found to have more frequent sexual fantasies than women. Women enjoy their fantasies as much as men and are neither more nor less likely to report feeling guilt (or other unpleasant emotions) about their fantasies.

Fantasy is a safe way to experience a sexual activity that a person might not morally, safely, legally, or maybe physically, be able to do in real life. The only limit is your imagination. Some people relieve the monotony of waiting in line, listening to a

CAMPUS CONFIDENTIAL

"I know that many of my friends think that there's something wrong with me because I have made the decision to be celibate. I think that in all respects I'm a perfectly normal guy who happens to believe that I need to put my energies into other areas of my life right now. For me it's about balance. For a while all I did was party and I neglected most other parts of my life. I've taken a long hard look at myself and decided that I wasn't the kind of person that I want to be and that I needed to make some important changes if I was to achieve my goals.

"I'm not judging anyone else's choice. But I have to feel whole within myself before I have anything to offer anyone else." ●

Rapid Eye Movement (REM) Sleep: a stage in the normal sleep cycle during which dreams occur and the body undergoes marked changes, including rapid eye movement, loss of reflexes, and increased pulse rate and brain activity

Nocturnal Emission: the release of semen during sleep, often during a sexual dream; also called a "wet dream"

Autoeroticism: self-satisfaction of sexual desire, as by masturbation or the arousal of sexual feeling without an external stimulus

Sexual Fantasies: pleasant sexual thoughts or daydreams, often about something longed-for but unlikely to happen

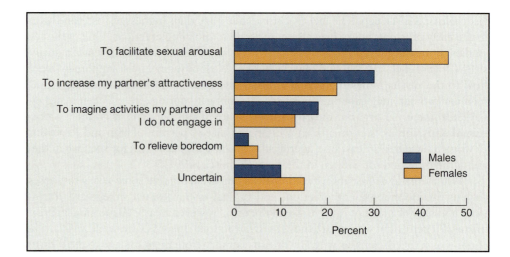

FIGURE 12.1 **Stated Purpose of Fantasies During Intercourse.**
SOURCE: Adapted from Sue, 1979.

boring lecture, or performing routine chores by having a sexual fantasy. Sexual fantasies also can be helpful in overcoming sexual anxiety (Coen, 1978). Sexual fantasies can be used therapeutically to increase arousal before or during masturbation or partner sex (Lunde et al., 1991).

Psychoanalytic theory proposed that fantasies are important as substitutes for reality. Whether the topic is revenge, success, adventure, or sex, people resort to their imaginations when the reality is out of reach. Although plausible, research on sexual fantasy does not support the psychoanalytic view of sexual fantasy. Findings across many studies confirm that people who have more sex also have more sexual fantasies—precisely the opposite of what would be predicted if fantasy were a substitute for experience (Leitenberg & Henning, 1995). Instead, the data seem to suggest that both sexual activity and sexual fantasy follow from the person's overall interest in sex and sexual motivation.

You name it; someone has had a fantasy about it. Every known and unknown person, place, and position has been part of someone's fantasy. Some fantasies may relive or enliven past incidents that actually have been experienced. Others may be based on a movie or book with fictitious or famous characters in leading and supporting roles. Some fantasies have elaborate, detailed story lines, while others are more basic. Some people may continue a certain fantasy theme, such as group sex, and just change the characters and settings. Others' fantasies may generally involve the same cast of characters, but with variations in plot, setting, and dialogue.

There are some gender differences in the content of sexual fantasies (Table 12.1). In an early study, Hunt (1975) found that men reported fantasies of intercourse with strangers twice as often as women did; women reported more frequent masturbatory fantasies of being forced to have sex and of homosexual activities. In contrast, the 1994 National Health and Social Life Survey reported that nearly all women report fantasies that are "soft, hazy, romantic, that veer far from explicit sex" (Michael et al., 1994, p. 150). Men's sexual fantasies tend to have greater sexual variety. Four times as many men as women report that they have already imagined having sex with more than a thousand sexual partners, while women were twice as likely as men to be emotionally involved with their fantasy partners (Ellis & Symons, 1990). An exploration of gender differences in the proportion of sexual fantasies involving someone other than a current partner (*extradyadic fantasies*) found that 98 percent of men and 80 percent of women reported having extradyadic fantasies in the past 2 months (Hicks & Leitenberg, 2001).

The results of several studies combined in a review article by Leitenberg and Henning (1995) found that men's fantasies had more vivid visual details and explicit physical details, whereas women's fantasies emphasized feelings and story line. Consistently,

TABLE 12.1

The Sexual Fantasy Top Ten Lists

Most Frequent Sexual Fantasies of College Men and Women

Men	Women
1. touching/kissing sensuously	1. touching/kissing sensuously
2. being sensuously touched	2. being sensuously touched
3. oral-genital sex	3. naked caressing
4. naked caressing	4. walking hand in hand
5. watching partner undress	5. oral-genital sex
6. seducing partner	6. seducing partner
7. intercourse in unusual positions	7. watching partner undress
8. masturbating your partner	8. intercourse in unusual positions
9. walking hand in hand	9. sex in unusual locations
10. sex that lasts for hours	10. getting married

Least Frequent Sexual Fantasies of College Men and Women

Men	Women
1. sexual relations with animals	1. sexual relations with animals
2. dressing in clothes of opposite sex	2. torturing sex partner
3. being attracted to someone with a physical abnormality	3. degrading sex partner
4. sex with a close relative	4. being whipped/beaten by partner
5. watching someone else make love to your partner	5. being attracted to someone with a physical abnormality
6. being whipped/beaten by a partner	6. whipping/beating partner
7. being a prostitute	7. mate swapping
8. being sexually degraded	8. being tortured by sex partner
9. degrading sex partner	9. watching someone else make love to your partner
10. torturing sex partner	10. sex with a close relative

SOURCE: Adapted from Hsu et al., 1994.

FAQ:

If a woman has a sexual fantasy about being forced to have sex, does it mean she wants to be raped?

As indicated earlier, some people worry that having a fantasy may be a warning they actually may act out the behavior in real life. However, most people are able to keep their imaginary lives and reality separate. There is a difference between a sexual fantasy (thinking about something) and a sexual urge (wanting to *do* something). Just because a woman may fantasize about being forced to have sex, it does not imply that she wants to be raped. If a man has erotic thoughts of group sex, it does not mean that he really wants to participate in an orgy. Researchers who examined women's sexual fantasies found that more than half the women in the study reported having engaged in a force fantasy (Strasber & Lockerd, 1998). The women who reported this type of fantasy also had less sexual guilt, more sexual experience, and engaged in more fantasizing than those who did not. Any history of exposure to sexual coercion was unrelated to the report of force fantasies. Rather than being an attempt to deal with sexual guilt, the research suggests that these fantasies represent a relatively open, unrestricted, and varied approach to sexuality.

men have been found to have fantasies involving more different sexual acts than women. Another consistent pattern found by Leitenberg and Henning (1995) was that men fantasize about *doing* something sexual *to* someone, whereas women tend to fantasize about *having something done* to them. This pattern of active men and passive women is similar to real sexual behavior; as you learned in Chapter 10, men tend to initiate sexual activity more often than women. Along the same lines, men are more likely than women to fantasize about dominating their partners and forcing them to have sex, whereas women are more likely to have fantasies about being overpowered and forced to have sex. These so-called "submission" or "rape" fantasies do not resemble actual rapes (see Chapter 13). Rather, in a typical scenario someone the woman is attracted to overpowers her token resistance and they engage in mutually satisfying sex. In another version of this type of fantasy, she imagines being a willing sexual slave to her lover or some other man for whom she has affection. However, there are plenty of men who like to imagine being the sex slave to a dominating woman, and plenty of women who fantasize about the dominant role. Overall, there appear to be more similarities than differences in fantasy patterns of males and females (Masters, Johnson, & Kolodny, 1992).

Because they allow us to indulge our impulses without social constraints or conventions, sexual fantasies provide an interesting window to our evolutionary instincts. In one study (Wilson, 1997) men and women were asked a number of

> **Sexual fantasies are probably the best aphrodisiacs around—and they don't cost anything, either**
>
> (MASTERS, JOHNSON, & KOLODNY, 1994, P. 99).

questions about their fantasies, including whether or not they fantasize about sex with strangers, group sex, and sex with a famous person. Of the four categories, group sex was the favorite of men (42 percent) and least often mentioned by women (10 percent). In the evolutionary view, men, who have copious amounts of sperm and can spread their genes by impregnating many women, would be expected to fantasize more often about group sex and anonymous partners. Evolutionary theory would also argue that because women have a limited number of eggs and fewer opportunities to pass on their genetic material, heterosexual sex fantasies about a famous person might reflect their desire to align themselves with males with good genes who will provide for and protect their offspring (Wilson, 1997). So women should be more likely to fantasize about having sex with a famous partner. However, in Wilson's study sex with a famous person was only slightly more prevalent in women (17 percent) than men (16 percent). Others believe that the differences in male and female fantasy content are likely to be cultural, "reflecting what we tell boys and girls and men and women about what is a masculine vision of sexiness and what is a feminine vision" (Michael et al., 1994, p. 150).

As with any other sexual activity, physical or mental, sexual fantasies can be healthy or unhealthy. Many therapists encourage clients who may have difficulty with sexual desire or arousal to use erotic fantasy to enrich and increase sexual interest (Meuwissen & Over, 1991).

There are no reliable statistics on how many people may act out their sexual fantasies. Acting out a fantasy can be a pleasurable way for an individual or couple to increase their sexual repertoire. Others may be disappointed to find out that the fantasy is better than the reality. Acting out a fantasy is only cause for concern if it involves pressuring or coercing an unwilling partner, goes against your value system, or puts you or a partner at physical or emotional risk. One way some people explore a sexual fantasy is through the Internet (see EXPLORING SEXUALITY ONLINE box).

EXPLORING SEXUALITY ONLINE

Online Fantasy

Are you curious about just what a transvestite dominatrix does, but not curious enough to visit your local S&M parlor? If daydreaming about a sexual fantasy isn't satisfying enough, but acting it out in reality is a bit too much, a commercial interactive sex-fantasy Web site may be the answer. Customers can "chat" with performers who type their responses or start a show using remote-controlled cameras. Some users jump right into a sexual fantasy or request performance of a fetish act, while others just want to talk. These sites can provide the opportunity for more interaction than strip clubs, erotic magazines, and videos, as well as the advantage of privacy—who's to know if you're really obeying the dominatrix's commands to drip hot wax on your nipples? You can't get a disease, become pregnant, or be physically hurt fulfilling a sexual fantasy online, but it can become a financially and emotionally expensive habit. Many online sexual sites charge a fee, and using your computer at work to explore your erotic fantasies can get you fired. As we discussed in Chapter 4, compulsive cybersex can be damaging to relationships. In Chapter 7 we noted that those seeking sex partners on the Internet appear to be at greater risk for STIs than those who do not (McFarlane et al., 2000).

Masturbation

Masturbation is the stimulation of one's own or another's genital organs, usually to orgasm, by manual contact or means other than coitus. It can be either a solitary sexual behavior or part of a couple's sexual repertoire. Although often defined as sexual self-stimulation, masturbation can involve touching your own sex organs or your partner's, for sexual pleasure. Some couples masturbate themselves or one another to orgasm as part of their sexual interaction, including intercourse, or as a pleasurable sexual activity separate from intercourse. People masturbate for pleasure, to release tension or anxiety, or to explore their sexuality. In contrast to numerous popular beliefs, masturbation does NOT cause pimples or warts, affect fertility, cause insanity, enlarge or shrink genitalia, cause disease, or decrease sexual responsiveness with a partner. It is not physically, mentally, or emotionally harmful. As an added bonus, masturbating is definitely safe sex.

In a 1994 study, Kolata described the history of the condemnation of masturbation in Western societies. Strong feelings about masturbation have existed in Western cultures for centuries. In 1741 "Onanism, or a Treatise on the Disorders of Masturbation," was published by a Swiss doctor (Kolata, 1994). The widely popular pamphlet warned that masturbation drained the body of vital fluids, causing wasting illnesses like tuberculosis, and that too much sexual excitement and masturbation caused neuroses and could damage the nervous system. Benjamin Rush, a signer of the Declaration of Independence and a physician, wrote that masturbation caused poor eyesight, epilepsy, memory loss, and tuberculosis (Kolata, 1994). Rush stated that masturbaters were easy to spot because they appeared sickly. In 1888 J. H. Kellogg wrote a book informing parents of the 39 signs of masturbation including acne, bashfulness, boldness, nail-biting, use of tobacco, and bed wetting (Kolata, 1994). He advised parents to bandage their child's genitals, to enclose the genitals in a cage, or to tie the child's hands. Today, Kellogg is better remembered as the inventor of corn flakes than as the author of advice to parents on preventing masturbation. The two are related, however. In the late 1800s, many people believed that sexual thoughts and vices were stimulated by tasty and spicy foods; people who believed in sexual restraint sought out foods that would be sexually nonstimulating. Kellogg's Corn Flakes were originally invented as a breakfast food that would help avoid masturbation. Graham crackers, invented by Sylvester Graham, became popular as another ostensible antidote to masturbation (Money, 1985). As you may have already guessed, there is no scientific evidence that eating corn flakes or graham crackers will actually reduce or prevent masturbation. While modern science is far less worried about the medical consequences of masturbation than it was back in the 1800s, the topic is still rather controversial (see CONSIDERATIONS box).

Masturbation, or as *Seinfeld* called it, being "master of your own domain," is one of the most widely practiced but least talked about sexual behaviors. It isn't just "beginner's sex" that kids do until they're ready for the "real thing." People of all

Masturbation: the stimulation of one's own or another's genital organs, usually by manual contact or means other than coitus

---

 ### Listen to Our Elders

CONSIDERATIONS

In 1994, Dr. Jocelyn Elders, U.S. Surgeon General under President Clinton, resigned under pressure over comments she made about masturbation. Elders suggested that, instead of preaching abstinence in sex education classes, we accept the reality that students are already exploring their bodies and their sexuality. She believed that we should teach them about how their bodies work. It wasn't educating students about intercourse, pregnancy, or STIs that was so controversial, it was the suggestion to include masturbation in sex education classes that cost Dr. Elders her job.

 Do you think that masturbation is a viable form of sexual expression that should be taught in high-school sex education classes?

—Do you think it was right to force Elders from her position for advocating the teaching of masturbation?

Do single adults or members of couples masturbate more frequently?

While some may believe that single adults are more likely to masturbate, the 1994 Sex in America survey found that adults with a partner were more likely to masturbate than those who did not have partners. The researchers concluded that masturbation is "not an outlet so much as a component of a sexually active lifestyle" (Michael et al., 1994, p. 159). It is interesting to note that while couples may masturbate with or without their partner, most partners attempt to keep their solitary masturbatory activity a secret from each other (Grosskopf, 1983; Hessellund, 1976; Reinisch, 1991).

❝Masturbation neither pollutes the environment nor requires scarce natural resource. . . . it needn't cost any money and usually requires no costly artifacts . . . With masturbation, there are not even the issues of social responsibility, sexual diseases, or differences of opinion about sex styles and frequency. ❞

(TIGER, 1992)

ethnic backgrounds, ages, and orientations masturbate—men and women, boys and girls, couples and singles, heterosexuals and homosexuals. Among Americans aged 18 to 59, approximately 60 percent of the men and 40 percent of the women reported that they had masturbated in the past year. In one study, about 25 percent of the men and 10 percent of the women reported masturbating at least once a week (Michaels et al., 1994).

There are gender differences in the frequency of masturbation. Research consistently indicates that males masturbate more frequently than females (Kinsey, 1948, 1953; Laumann et al., 1994). This discrepancy appears to exist not only in the United States, but also throughout the world. A study of Japanese high-school and university students found that 98 percent of the boys, but only 39 percent of the girls, had masturbated (Hatano, 1991). According to a study in Turkey, 11 percent of the female subjects and 87 percent of the males masturbated (Erker et al., 1990). A Colombian study reported masturbation by 70 percent of the females and 99 percent of the males (Alzate, 1989). These differences may have several causes, including cultural beliefs about male pleasure and sexuality. In addition, there is the anatomical reality that male genitalia are more accessible and available to touch. Boys are taught to hold their penis while they urinate, thus giving them early experience in sanctioned genital holding. Of course, the difference in masturbation can also be explained as one sign of a generally higher sex drive. Abramson (1973) found that masturbation correlated with self-rated sex drive within each gender; that is, both men and women with higher sex drives were more likely to masturbate. Throughout Western history, society has made more consistent and dramatic efforts to stamp out masturbation among males than females. Boys have been warned that masturbation would cause them to go blind or insane. The Young Men's Christian Association (YMCA) was formed to offer physically tiring exercise in a religious setting to drain off time and energy that might otherwise be used for sexual sins. As you can see from the studies cited here, there is little sign that these efforts have had a great deal of success.

Some recent studies (for example, Sharma & Sharma, 1998) indicate that the gap in the rates of male and female masturbation may be narrowing. Two reasons for this may be increased awareness and acceptance of female sexuality and greater understanding of female orgasm. When it was widely believed that female orgasm was primarily a function of intercourse, women who masturbated by simulating intercourse manually or using objects probably met with little orgasmic success. For many, manual stimulation of the clitoris is the most reliable technique for regular orgasm.

Some people may worry that if their partner masturbates there must be something wrong with the relationship. However, there appears to be no significant correlation between frequency of masturbation and frequency of partner sex (Abramson, 1973). Masturbation may actually have positive effects on a couple's sexual relationship. One study found greater marital and sexual satisfaction among married women who masturbated than among those who did not (Hurlbert & Whitaker, 1991). Masturbation appears to be not a substitute for those who are sexually deprived, but an activity that stimulates and is stimulated by other sexual behaviors.

Female Masturbation Techniques There is wide variation in how women masturbate. Masters and Johnson (1966) reported never observing any two women masturbate in exactly the same way. Women may use one or several fingers to stroke the clitoral region, or rub it against a pillow. Because of its extreme sensitivity, the clitoral glans is rarely stroked directly for any length of time. Rubbing or putting pressure on the clitoral shaft or by tugging on the labia minora to stimulate the clitoris indirectly instead achieves clitoral stimulation. Some women stimulate their breasts or anus while masturbating to increase pleasure. Masturbation rarely mimics the stimulation experienced during sexual intercourse; very few women insert anything into their vagina. The uses of a vibrator or flowing water from a bathtub tap or handheld showerhead are other options. Shere Hite (1976) described six basic types of female masturbation, outlined in Figure 12.2.

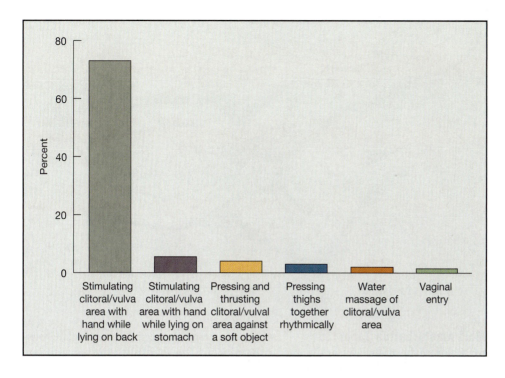

FIGURE 12.2 **Female Masturbation.**
Source: Hite, 1976.

The vibrator was developed to perfect and automate a function that doctors had historically performed. For centuries women diagnosed with hysteria were thought to suffer from a lack of sexual satisfaction. Treatment of hysteria was genital massage, a job that some male physicians considered a drudgery (Maines, 1999). Today, vibrators are used primarily to enhance sexual responsiveness and sexual pleasure, most commonly in autoerotic activity. However, in one study more than two thirds of the women reported using vibrators in partnered activity (Davis et al., 1996). A majority of the women indicated that orgasms triggered by vibrator stimulation were more intense than other orgasms. Nearly half experienced multiple orgasms when using a vibrator. The clitoris is the preferred site of vibrator stimulation, but there is great diversity in both preferred location and technique (Davis et al., 1996).

Female masturbatory techniques vary widely. However, most women indirectly stimulate the clitoris and few simulate penile intercourse.

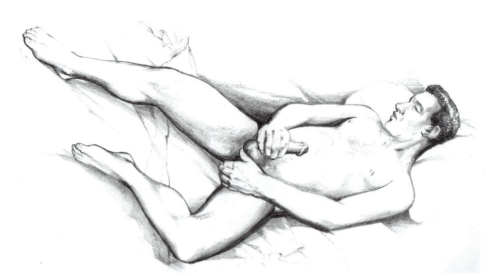

There is usually less variation in male masturbation techniques. Most men rub or stroke the shaft of the penis with one hand.

Male Masturbation Techniques There is less variation in male than female masturbation techniques. Generally, men rub or stroke the shaft of the penis with one hand. Some also stimulate the head of the penis, scrotum, frenulum, or anal area with the other hand (Hite, 1981; Kinsey et al., 1948; Masters & Johnson, 1979). Most frequently, a man will stroke the shaft and glans of his penis with one hand until he has an erection. Once erect, he will increase the speed and pressure of the stroking pattern, with his grip tightening and motions speeding up as orgasm nears. At orgasm, the penile shaft may be tightly gripped, but generally the glans is too sensitive for direct contact. Hite (1981) found that the majority of the men in her survey usually had their strongest orgasms during masturbation. As with women, masturbation techniques for men typically do not mimic the activities of sexual intercourse. Male masturbation rarely involves thrusting behavior, however, some men do stimulate themselves by moving against a pillow or mattress, or by using a sex toy. While some laughed and others cringed when Ben Stiller's penis caught in his zipper while masturbating in the 1998 movie *There's Something About Mary* or at Jason Bigg's dilemma when mistaking Super Glue for a lubricant in 2001's *American Pie 2*, one form of masturbation can have far more serious consequences (see CONSIDERATIONS box).

CONSIDERATIONS

Fatal Masturbation: A Case of Asphyxophilia

In February 1994, Stephen Milligan, age 45, a member of the British Parliament, died alone with a plastic bag over his head, an orange in his mouth, and an electrical cord around his neck. It appeared that Milligan's death resulted from **autoerotic asphyxiation.** This extremely dangerous practice involves a person (almost always a male) placing a noose of some sort around his neck in order to cut off the air supply while masturbating to orgasm, in the belief that oxygen deprivation enhances orgasm (Money, 1986). Most asphyxophiliacs construct what they think is a self-rescue device such as a slipknot on the noose. Milligan was found with a piece of orange in his mouth, apparently believing that

it would allow air to pass freely so he could breathe if he accidentally blacked out. It is estimated that there may be as many as 1,000 autoerotic deaths each year in the United States (Bechtel, Westerfield, & Eddy, 1990). This may be a conservative estimate, as many of these deaths may not be reported or may be mislabeled as suicides. (Reinisch, 1991)

 Using what you learned about the physiology of orgasm in Chapter 3, come up with an explanation of why oxygen deprivation might enhance pleasure. Why might someone risk death for the sake of orgasm?

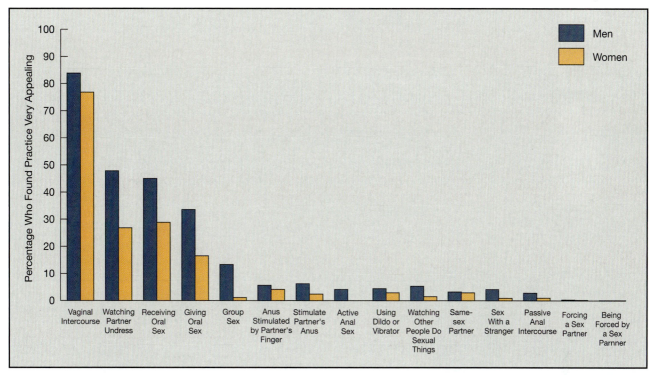

FIGURE 12.3   Sex Appeal.   The numbers reflect the percentage of subjects who found the practice "very appealing."   SOURCE: Adapted from Laumann et al., 1994, pp. 152–154.

SEX WITH A PARTNER

Sexual expression involving another person is a type of communication. Great sex requires clear communication. Experience only goes so far. What is pleasurable with one partner may not work with another. It is difficult to know what your partner likes if he or she doesn't tell you or show you. You need to make your own needs and desires known as well. (See Figure 12.3 for preferences expressed in a national survey.)

Individual feelings and attitudes strongly influence choices about sexual behavior. For most couples, sexual techniques may not be as important as other aspects of a relationship. Sex with the most experienced and accomplished sexual acrobat may not be as satisfying as sex with a partner who may be more sexually awkward, but with whom you share emotional intimacy, trust, and respect. There is a lot more to good sex than "technique." Communicating your needs and expressing your emotions will be discussed more fully in Chapters 15 and 16.

Noncoital Sexual Behavior

The term **foreplay,** sexual activity that precedes intercourse, implies that it is something that occurs before the "big event"—intercourse. Calling all sexual behavior that does not involve a penis penetrating a vagina "foreplay" diminishes its importance and meaning and totally negates most homosexual behavior. Touching, hugging, kissing, and stroking are pleasurable activities in themselves without being a prelude to intercourse. In addition, these behaviors may be pleasurable and satisfying following intercourse as "afterplay." For these reasons, we prefer to use the term **noncoital behavior** to refer to sexual behavior among partners that does not involve intercourse.

Kissing and Hugging   While there are wide variations in noncoital behavior (see CROSS-CULTURAL PERSPECTIVES box), heterosexual couples typically begin lovemaking with shared touching, such as kissing, stroking the body, and manually or

Autoerotic Asphyxiation: practice in which an individual cuts off the air supply while masturbating to orgasm with the belief that oxygen deprivation enhances orgasm

Foreplay: sexual stimulation, usually as a prelude to sexual intercourse

Noncoital Behavior: sexual behavior that does not involve intercourse

CROSS-CULTURAL PERSPECTIVES

Take Your Time

There is widespread cultural variation regarding the frequency and duration of noncoital sexual activity. For example, according to Ford and Beach (1951), foreplay among the Lepcha people of the Himalayas is minimal, whereas noncoital behavior may continue for hours among the people of the Pacific Island of Ponape.

Goldstein (1976) identified several methods of sexual stimulation and ranked them according to frequency of *use in human societies: (1) general body contact (hugging, body caresses); (2) simple kissing; (3) tongue kissing; (4) manual manipulation of female breasts; (5) manual manipulation of female genitalia; (6) oral stimulation of female breasts; (7) manual stimulation of male genitalia; (8) oral stimulation of male genitalia (fellatio); (9) oral stimulation of female genitalia (cunnilingus); (10) oral stimulation of anal area (anilingus).*

For many people, touching is the significant method of sexual stimulation.

Kissing is found in almost every culture and is a nearly universal behavior.

orally stimulating the breasts and genitals prior to intercourse. Homosexual couples, especially lesbians, tend to spend more time engaging in these behaviors (Blumstein & Schwartz, 1983). One study of college students found that males preferred coitus while females preferred foreplay and afterplay (Denny, Field, & Quadagno, 1984). Since most women do not achieve orgasm through vaginal intercourse alone, it is not surprising that they do not necessarily consider coitus the "main event."

Touching is not only usually the first method of stimulation used in a sexual encounter; for many people it is the most significant. Our skin contains nearly a million sensory receptors, making it a primary mechanism for experiencing pleasure. Skin to skin contact can be a sensual experience that increases feelings of closeness. Touching can be periodic or continuous, focused on a particular body area or exploratory, arousing or relaxing.

Touch need not be directly to the genitals or breasts to be erotic. For couples who are sexually aroused, holding hands or a gentle caress to the face can be as sexually stimulating as stroking the clitoris or penis.

Kissing is a nearly universal behavior. In over 90 percent of all cultures people kiss (Fisher, 1992). However, kissing was reportedly unknown among many societies including the Somali, the Lepcha of the Himalayas, and the Sirionó of South America until they had contact with Westerners. The Thonga of Mozambique and a few other peoples traditionally found kissing to be disgusting (Ford & Beach, 1951). However, even in these cultures, lovers would lick, rub, suck, nip, or blow in each other's faces prior to copulation. And, it is not just the human species that kiss; many mammals engage in similar behavior (Geer, Heiman, & Leitenberg, 1984).

Not all kissing is sexual. Kissing can be an affectionate rather than a passionate gesture. However, Blumstein and Schwartz (1983) found that 95 percent of lesbian couples, 80 percent of heterosexual couples, and 71 percent of gay couples kiss every time they have sexual relations. Kissing can be on the lips with the mouth closed (simple kissing), or with lips parted and tongues inserted in one another's mouth (deep kissing, French kissing, or soul kissing). Kissing is not limited to the mouth, either. Other body parts, including other areas of the face, the neck, hands, feet, legs, and genitals also are often kissed.

While the breasts, especially the nipples, of both men and women are erotically sensitive, men are more likely to stimulate women's breasts than to have their breasts fondled. Masters and Johnson (1979) found that gay men frequently stroke their partner's nipples before stimulating the penis. Breast size bears no relationship to a woman's capacity for pleasure from breast stimulation. Either the hands or the mouth may be used to stimulate the breast. Some women are able to achieve orgasm through breast stimulation alone (Masters & Johnson, 1966). Men and women may have been socially conditioned to associate breast stimulation with female sexual pleasure, but men's breasts have equal erotic potential.

Manual stimulation of the genitals is a frequent noncoital activity. A man's partner may use one or two hands to stimulate his genitals. One hand may be used to caress the scrotum, perineum, or nipples while the other hand strokes the penile shaft and glans. Some men prefer that their partner grip the penis between fingertip and thumb, just behind the coronal ridge, and stroke it up and down. While many men find that direct manual stimulation of the penile glans may be uncomfortable, they do enjoy having the frenulum stimulated. As arousal increases, many men prefer a more vigorous stroke similar to the one they use while masturbating. In fact, some couples find that watching a partner masturbate is an ideal way to learn about his or her preferences. Many men enjoy having lotion or oil applied as a lubricant during penile stimulation. However, if manual stimulation leads to intercourse, be sure to use a water-soluble product. As we discussed in Chapter 6, oil-based lubricants will cause a condom to deteriorate and break.

As with men, there is great individual variation in the kind of genital touch that women find to be arousing. Some women are highly sensitive to any direct pressure to the clitoral glans and prefer touching to the side of the clitoral shaft or the labia with a single finger, several fingers, or the flat of the hand. Insertion of a finger into the vagina to stroke the vaginal walls also may be pleasurable. Since the clitoris and vaginal lips have no lubrication of their own, either bringing lubrication from the vagina or using saliva, lotion, oil, or water-soluble lubricants can reduce friction and irritation when manually stimulating female genitals.

Oral-Genital Stimulation   The popularity of *oral-genital stimulation*, often referred to simply as *oral sex*, has increased dramatically since Kinsey's study (1948, 1953), which found that 60 percent of married college-educated couples, 20 percent of those with a high-school education, and 10 percent of those with a grade-school education had experienced oral-genital contact. Oral sex performed on a male is referred to as **fellatio.** Oral sex performed on a female is referred to as **cunnilingus.**

By 1994 the Sex in America survey reported that 68 percent of women and 77 percent of men between the ages 18 and 59 had engaged in active oral sex (that is, had performed oral sex) at some time in their lives (Table 12.2). Nineteen percent of the women and 27 percent of the men had active oral sex the last time they had sex. Seventy-three percent of the women and 79 percent of the men had engaged in passive oral sex (that is, they had received oral sex) sometime in their lives, and 20 percent of the women and 28 percent of men engaged in passive oral sex the last time they had sex (Michael et al., 1994). Ethnicity and education also influence sexual behavior. The study also showed that African Americans and Hispanics are less likely than whites to engage in

FAQ:

Is oral sex considered "safe sex"?

It is possible for sexually transmitted infections, including HIV, to be contracted during oral-genital sex, particularly if the active partner has bleeding gums, or cuts or sores in the mouth or in the throat. Safe sex precautions are well advised. A condom can be used for fellatio or a rubber square used by dentists, called a dental dam, can be used for protection during cunnilingus.

TABLE 12.2

Oral-Genital Sex				
	Active Oral Sex		**Passive Oral Sex**	
	Lifetime	**Last Event**	**Lifetime**	**Last Event**
Men				
White	81%	28%	81%	29%
Black	51	17	66	18
Hispanic	66	25	67	15
Women				
White	75	21	78	22
Black	34	10	49	13
Hispanic	56	11	62	15

SOURCE: Adapted from Michael et al., 1994, p. 141.

Fellatio: oral stimulation of the penis

Cunnilingus: oral stimulation of the clitoris or vulva

FIGURE 12.4 Oral-genital stimulation may be done simultaneously.

oral sex and both men and women with some college education were more likely to have performed oral sex on a partner and have had oral sex performed on them than those with less than a high-school education.

Oral-genital stimulation may be done individually or simultaneously. The latter is sometimes referred to as "69" because of the similarity of the body positions to that number. Some prefer simultaneous arousal, while others feel that it detracts from their enjoyment of their partner's pleasure. Blumstein and Schwartz (1983) found that 50 percent of gay couples, 39 percent of lesbian couples, and 30 percent of heterosexual couples usually or always have oral sex. Male participation in oral sex seems related to opportunity, lowered inhibition, and emotional commitment, while female participation is more closely linked to features of the ongoing relationship (Gagnon & Simon, 1987).

Hite (1976) found that 42 percent of the women in her survey reported that they regularly had an orgasm during oral-genital stimulation. Moreover, other studies (for example, Rubin, 1991) have reported that cunnilingus is the only way other than masturbation that some women can achieve orgasm. Because the tongue is able to apply less pressure than a finger, the highly sensitive clitoris may be more receptive to the intense stimulation of direct oral contact. Variations in oral stimulation include kissing and licking the vulva, gentle tugging or sucking of the labia, licking or gently sucking the clitoris itself, or thrusting the tongue in and out of the vaginal opening.

Many men report that the up-and-down movements of the penis in the partner's mouth or the licking of the penis during fellatio is highly arousing. Fellatio often includes licking the shaft, glans, frenulum and the scrotum. Some men enjoy combined oral stimulation of the glans and manual stroking of the penile shaft or testicles. Some partners may take all or most of the penis into their mouth, while others have a gagging sensation that is triggered by pressure at the back of the tongue or in the throat. This gag reflex is a very real physiological reaction and not a sign of rejection or disgust. Couples often have a prior agreement as to whether or not a man will ejaculate into the partner's mouth, as well as personal preferences regarding swallowing of the ejaculate. Approximately one tablespoon of semen is ejaculated (and it contains only about five calories!).

Anal Sex Anal sex is penile penetration or oral or manual stimulation of the anus. Because the anus is composed of delicate tissues; special care needs to be taken during anal sex. The lining of the rectum can tear easily, allowing passage of many sexually transmitted infections, including HIV, into the recipient's bloodstream. Since there is no natural lubrication of the anal area, it can be damaged easily by dry or abrasive objects. Therefore, a nonirritating lubricant should be used with a condom to avoid discomfort or injury. Neither the penis nor any other object should be forced into the anus. The anus should be gradually dilated with a finger prior to insertion of the penis. The upper parts of the rectum are insensitive to pain and the colonic wall can be perforated without the individual being aware of the injury at the time. Perforation can result in peritonitis, a potentially fatal infection caused by the release of normal colonic organisms into the abdominal cavity (Agnew, 1986).

Some individuals insert a foreign object into the anus to provide sexual stimulation; while this can be pleasurable, it is easy to lose control of an object that is inserted into the anus, especially if the object is well lubricated and the person is highly aroused. Emergency room physicians have removed turnips, cucumbers, toothbrush holders, broom handles, salamis, and water glasses from rectums across the country (Agnew, 1986). Fisting, the insertion of a hand, usually up to the wrist, into the rectum of a sexual partner, can rupture the rectum walls or cause severe damage to the anus (Sohn, Weinstein, & Gonchar, 1977).

Anal Sex: penile penetration or other stimulation of the rectum

TABLE 12.3

Anal Sex			
	Lifetime	**Past 12 Months**	**Last Sex Event**
Men			
White	26%	8%	2%
Black	23	8	3
Hispanic	38	15	2
Women			
White	23	8	1
Black	10	6	2
Hispanic	19	3	1

SOURCE: Michael et al., 1994, p. 141.

Bacteria that are normally present within the anus can cause vaginal as well as urethral infection in both males and females. Anything—whether it is a dildo or a penis—that has been inserted into the anus can cause infection unless it is thoroughly washed prior to insertion into the vagina. Condoms should always be changed after any type of anal penetration before engaging in vaginal sex.

As with the rear entry position (discussed in the next section) anal sex is highly erotic for some men who are stimulated by looking at and touching their partner's buttocks. This position allows the man to caress his partner's breast and clitoris; she in turn may stroke his testicles or her clitoris. The anal area contains numerous nerve endings and is thus particularly sensitive. Many heterosexual and homosexual couples enjoy **anilingus,** orally stimulating the anus, or manual stimulation or penetration of the anus. Although this activity is traditionally associated with male homosexuality, a review of several recent studies on sexuality concluded that approximately 10 percent of heterosexual couples in the United States regularly engage in anal sex (Table 12.3).

Coital Sex

Coital sex, also called sexual intercourse or coitus, involves penetration of a woman's vagina by a man's penis. Coitus can be performed in numerous ways or sexual positions. One commentator on the *Kama Sutra* identified 529 possible coital positions (cited in Gregersen, 1994, p. 62). Variations include every possible combination of arm and leg positions that agile bodies and creative minds can imagine. The ancient Chinese had elegant, poetic names for many of these positions: Bamboo by the Altar (a couple standing and facing each other), Bunny Licking Its Fur (the couple lying with the woman on top facing the man's feet), Seagulls Soaring (the woman lying on the edge of the bed with her legs in the air and the man standing up between them), and Old Man Pushing the Wheelbarrow (the woman standing on her hands). These 529 positions all boil down to who's on top, side-by-side, sitting, standing, or kneeling (Tarcher, 1993).

Despite what some authors promise in sex manuals, magazine articles, and on talk shows, there is no one coital position that is best for everyone, everywhere, all the time. Mastery of the greatest number of positions doesn't necessarily make someone a better lover, nor do the most physically challenging positions ensure greater sexual pleasure. Different positions may work better for different partners, or even for the same couple at different times.

Man-on-Top Position Kinsey (1948, 1953) reported that the most frequently used heterosexual position for intercourse is the man-on-top position, also called the **missionary position,** in which the woman lies on her back and the man lies on top of her

Anilingus: oral stimulation of the anus

Coital Sex: activities associated with sexual intercourse

Missionary Position: sexual intercourse in the man-on-top position

A Thousand Times More Complicated

No group of animals rivals insects in the intricate designs of their genitalia or the acrobatics required to fit them together. For millipedes, the arrangement of bodies is crucial. A male initiates sex by running up the back of his partner and gripping her with the pads on his numerous legs and then entwining his body so that they come to rest head to head. Female genitalia open just behind her head, on the second segment of her body, while males' genitalia are further back on the seventh segment. When millipedes are properly aligned, the male inflates his mating organs and works them into the female's open receptacles where they remain for up to 2 hours. During this time the male passes sperm, which are stored in the female's body until the female needs them.

The male millipede's sex organ bears no resemblance to the mammalian penis. Normally withdrawn into the body, it consists of three parts, including a pair of wings; the organ is fashioned from a pair of the insect's legs. During copulation, the base of the organ is rhythmically retracted and released, causing the rest of the organ to twist and turn like a trowel inside the female's vulvalike receptacle (Sparks, 1999).

 Why do you think such different adaptations evolved for different species?

—*If human genitalia resembled the millipede, what changes in cultural and social customs might we have today? (For example, if a woman's vulva were on the back of her neck, would long hair and broad-brimmed hats be more common?)*

---

or props himself up on his elbows (Figure 12.4). In Kinsey's time, 70 percent of couples he surveyed reportedly used this position exclusively. Human females have a downward-tilted vagina rather than the backward-oriented vulva of other primates. Because of this tipped vulva, face-to-face coitus is both comfortable and provides the best chance for conception since the semen is deposited close to the mouth of the cervix (Fisher, 1992). In addition, the couple is able to look into one another's face, engage in kissing, and caress the breasts and other parts of the body.

Few sexual positions provide direct stimulation of the clitoris. However, it can be stimulated indirectly. For example, some women find the rubbing of the man's pelvic bone against the clitoris in face-to-face coitus extremely stimulating (Fisher, 1992). Other women find that the missionary position provides inefficient clitoral stimulation. (Women or their partners may stimulate the clitoris manually as they engage in intercourse.) In addition, some women may feel pinned down beneath the weight of their partner and find it difficult to move freely, control the depth of penetration, or stimulate the clitoris manually. Some men also find this position uncomfortable since they have to support their weight on their elbows and knees. As we discussed in Chapter 4 (see Treatment for Female Orgasmic Disorder), many women find that the rocking, vibrating movement of the coital alignment technique may stimulate female orgasm.

FIGURE 12.5   Man-on-Top Position of Coitus.

Woman-on-Top Position   In the woman-on-top, face-to-face position, the woman straddles her partner in a squatting or seated position or lies against him with legs together or apart (Figure 12.5). This position provides the woman with greater freedom of movement than the man-on-top position. In this position the woman is better able to control the depth of penetration, thrusting, and tempo of intercourse and her hands are free to caress her partner's body. This position can be helpful for men who have difficulty with premature ejaculation, since the female can slow down the rhythm to prevent the male from becoming aroused too quickly. This position also can facilitate orgasm for a woman. She can position herself so that her clitoris is stroked externally by her partner's penis, adjust her position so that her partner's pubic bone rubs against her clitoris, or have her clitoris stimulated directly by herself or her partner.

Rear-Entry Position   The rear-entry, sometimes referred to as "doggy style" for obvious reasons, is the position that most mammals use. In this position the man faces the woman's rear (Figure 12.6). She can be lying face down with her hips propped up by a pillow, on her hands and knees, or the couple can lie on their sides in the "spoon position." Rear-entry can also be performed in a sitting or standing position.

This position is highly erotic for some men who are stimulated by viewing and having contact with their partner's buttocks. This position enables the man to reach around to caress his partner's breast and clitoris; she in turn may reach behind her or between her legs and stroke his testicles or her clitoris. The deeper penetration made possible by this position may be pleasurable for some women and uncomfortable for others. This is the position that many women find to be most comfortable during the late stages of pregnancy. However, other couples may find the rear-entry position less satisfying because of the lack of visual and oral contact.

Side-to-Side Position   In the side-to-side position, partners face each other lying on their sides (Figure 12.7). It can be difficult to insert the penis in the vagina and easy for the penis to slip out. It also is difficult to achieve vigorous pelvic thrusting in this

"Perhaps the so-called missionary position . . . derived its ironic slang name because it interfered with more entertaining sexual positions in conflict with a Christian ethic that viewed sex mainly as a reproductive duty, not an opportunity for real pleasure"

(TIGER, 1992)

(a)

(b)

FIGURE 12.6 Woman-on-Top Positions. (a) lying down; (b) seated.

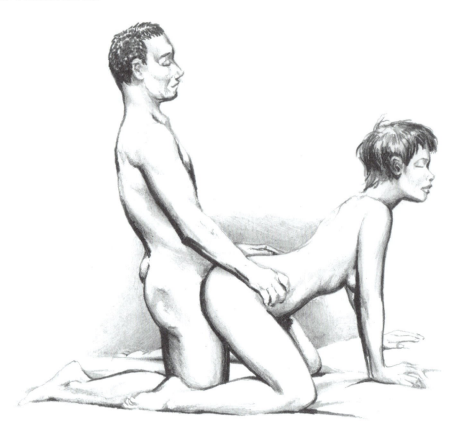

FIGURE 12.7 **Rear-Entry Position.**

position, which can either be less stimulating or more restful. The side-to-side position also may allow for greater ejaculatory control. Depth of penetration is easily controlled and this position allows for visual contact, kissing, breast fondling, and stroking of one another's bodies.

ATYPICAL SEXUAL BEHAVIORS

The sexual behaviors described to this point in the chapter are considered typical because large percentages of people engage in them. Less typical and uncommon variations of sexual behaviors abound, with varying degrees of social acceptance and approval. Some individuals, and some cultures, might find any sexual behavior other than "heterosexual-intercourse-in-the-missionary-position-with-the-lights-out-once-a-week" to be abnormal. Atypical sexual behaviors such as fetishes, transvestism, and sadomasochistic behavior

FIGURE 12.8 **Side-to-Side Position.**

may seem shocking, disgusting, or just plain silly to some. The primary similarity among these behaviors and the more typical behaviors described earlier in this chapter is that, unlike the behaviors described in Chapter 13, none involve forcible sexual behavior and, if partners are involved, they are consenting adult partners.

What constitutes socially acceptable sexual contact varies not only from culture to culture, but even within a culture from time period to time period. For example, historical sources rarely mention cunnilingus, yet fellatio is mentioned frequently. In the United States today, however, cunnilingus is quite common and few people regard it as a deviant behavior (Bullough, 1988). There are several possible reasons for changes in attitudes toward sexual expression. Before you condemn our ancestors for their narrow-mindedness, recall that for many centuries people hardly ever took baths, toilet paper was not invented until the 19th century, and the rags used for menstrual pads did not approach the effectiveness of what is available today. Undoubtedly those factors would have made cunnilingus quite different and possibly less appealing than it is today. It may be no coincidence that the British (and others) often labeled oral sex as a French practice, because toilet paper came into use in France much earlier than in Britain.

There are many different words used to label atypical sexual behaviors. Most are misleading, judgmental, or stigmatizing. These behaviors or those who practice them are often referred to as "deviant," "perverted," "unhealthy," "kinky," "sick," or "crazy." Even the more scientific and relatively neutral term *paraphilia*, derived from the Greek roots meaning "alongside of" (*para*) and "love" (*philia*), does not differentiate between coercive and noncoercive sexual behaviors. Thus we have chosen to use the nonjudgmental terms *typical* and *atypical* for noncoercive behaviors, and *coercive* for those where force or threat of force is used, or when sex is exploitative, or when sexual gratification is obtained at another's expense without permission. In the following paragraphs we consider some atypical sexual behaviors. Coercive sex is the subject of Chapter 13.

Fetishism

Fetishism is sexual arousal by an inanimate article. A person with a fetish for articles such as high heel shoes, or a specific material such as leather or rubber, is called a fetishist. However, fetishism is not limited to inanimate objects; it can also include arousal by a specific part of the body (Sargent, 1988), such as the "waddle," or soft underside of the chin, preferred by a popular character on the television series *Ally McBeal*. Depending on what it is and on the fetishist's preference, the fetish object may be worn by the person or partner, or looked at or touched while masturbating (Money, 1980).

Fetishism may develop when an individual incorporates the object or body part through fantasy in a masturbation sequence where the reinforcement of orgasm strengthens the fetishistic association (Bachman, 1966; Langevin & Martin, 1975; Rachman & Hodgon, 1968). Another possible explanation is that some children may learn to associate sexual arousal with a particular object that belongs to an emotionally significant person, such as a mother or older sister (Freund & Blanchard, 1993). In a process called *symbolic transformation*, the object of the fetish becomes endowed with the essence of its owner so that the child responds to the object as he might react to the actual person.

In most cases, a person with a fetish is no danger to others and pursues the use of the fetish object in private. If the fetish involves another person, it is a consensual arrangement. Fetishists sometimes collect objects that are arousing to them and may spend a great deal of money or go to great lengths to add to their collection of fetish objects. Others may steal fetish items, either to add to their excitement or, more commonly, because of the fear that the fetish will be revealed.

Transvestism

From Shakespeare to Milton Berle, from *Tootsie* to *Mrs. Doubtfire*, there has been a public fascination with men dressing in women's clothing. **Transvestism,** sometimes referred to as cross-dressing, is characterized by dressing in the clothing of the

Fetishism: sexual arousal by a material object or a nonsexual part of the body

Transvestism: the practice of adopting the clothes or the manner or the sexual role of the opposite sex

Take It or Leave It?

Thomas Sargent (1988), who describes himself as "a rubber fetishist and professional therapist, in that order" relates an incident when he consulted a psychiatrist regarding his love of rubber. Sargent states that the psychiatrist told him that if he felt guilty, he could either eliminate the guilt or eliminate the rubber. Sargent decided to get rid of the guilt and keep the rubber.

 What about you?

—Would you have eliminated the guilt or the rubber?

---

opposite sex to obtain sexual pleasure. Someone who cross-dresses is referred to as a *transvestite*. Transvestism has been described as a fetish (Freund et al., 1996). However, not all cross-dressing has sexual motive. Cross-dressing is an integral part of certain rites of passage. For example, in the U.S. Navy male sailors used to be required to don women's clothing when they crossed the equator for the first time. Few of the participants in these rituals considered themselves to be transvestites and most would deny experiencing any sexual gratification. Transvestites should not be confused with female impersonators who cross-dress to entertain. Homosexual "drag queens" may cross-dress on occasion but don't experience sexual arousal or psychological dependence as a result of that behavior.

Most transvestites are male and begin cross-dressing early in life, often wearing their mother's or a sister's clothes while masturbating. A survey of 372 cross-dressing males found that they began secretly cross-dressing as children at a median age of 8.5 years old (Bullough & Bullough, 1997). The childhood experiences and family dynamics reported in another sample of cross-dressing males indicate a higher percentage of only children and eldest children, and much closer relationships with their mothers than with their fathers (Schott, 1995). The majority of transvestites are married heterosexuals (Buhrich, 1976; Talamini, 1982; Wise & Meyer, 1980). Although a majority of cross-dressers are heterosexual, a significant portion (more than 30 percent) identify themselves as bisexual, homosexual, or not sexually involved with another person (Bullough & Bullough, 1997).

New Jersey Governor Edward Hyde (1661–1723) chose to have his official portrait painted "in drag."

Although many women dress in what may be considered traditional male clothing, there appear to be fewer women who derive sexual excitement from cross-dressing. It may be that because women have so many more socially sanctioned opportunities to wear male clothing it is more difficult to detect female transvestites. Then again, the difference may simply conform to the broad pattern that males engage in almost all sexual practices (unusual as well as typical) more frequently than women. However, it is unlikely that wearing jeans and a flannel shirt sexually arouses many women.

There is a wide range of transvestite behaviors. A specific female garment arouses some transvestites while others prefer to wear a complete female outfit including wig and makeup. Some male cross-dressers may wear women's underpants beneath their suit and tie when they go to work every day. Others may don full female regalia in the privacy of their own home on an occasional basis.

As we discussed in Chapter 10, transsexualism and transvestism are often confused. Recall that male-female transsexuals are genetic males who desire to become females. Most transvestites have masculine gender identities and do not want to change their anatomy. A study of more than 1,000 cross-dressers found that 87 percent described themselves as heterosexual and 83 percent were married (Docter & Prince, 1997).

Most married men who cross-dress do not tell their wives about their transvestism prior to marriage because they believe that the urge to cross-dress will disappear after they are married (Weinberg & Bullough, 1986, 1988). While some wives know and are understanding about their husband's cross-dressing, others are confused or angry when they discover their husband's secret. One study found that more than half of the men who disclosed their cross-dressing to their spouse reported that it became a major problem in their marriage (Brown & Collier, 1989). A 6-year study of more than 100 female partners of male transvestites found two variables associated with acceptance of their mate's cross-dressing. Those who discovered the cross-dressing after marriage were less likely to accept their partner's transvestism than those who knew about it before they said "I do." Those women who reported at least occasionally becoming sexually aroused by their mate's cross-dressing (approximately 25 percent) were more likely to accept their relationship with a transvestite partner (Brown, 1994).

Paraphilias

The essential feature of a **paraphilia** as defined by the American Psychiatric Association (1994) is a recurrent, intense sexual urge and sexually arousing fantasies involving nonhuman objects, the suffering or humiliation of oneself or one's partner, or children or other nonconsenting persons. When paraphiliac behaviors become a compulsion they may interfere with relationships and intimacy. Paraphilias as compulsive behavior were discussed in Chapter 4. Coercive paraphilias, including pedophilia, will be covered in Chapter 13.

Zoophilia, also called bestiality, is a sexual attraction to animals and is not uncommon as a transitory experience among young people with limited access to human sexual partners and easy access to animals (Money, 1981). Most adolescents who experiment with zoophilia make a transition to sexual relations with human partners. Males are more likely to be involved with farm animals and to have penile-vaginal intercourse or to have their genitals orally stimulated by a farm animal (Hunt, 1975; Kinsey et al., 1948). Women are more likely to have their genitals licked by a domestic animal, although there are some adult women who train a dog to mount them and engage in intercourse (Gendel & Bonner, 1988).

Necrophilia, obtaining sexual gratification by viewing or having intercourse with a corpse, is extremely rare. While some employees of morgues or funeral homes may choose their profession because of the accessibility of corpses for their sexual arousal (Tollison & Adams, 1979), most people who work in these settings have no necrophilic tendencies. Since it is difficult to obtain a corpse, those with a necrophilic preference may have their partner simulate death with cosmetics, props, and by lying completely still during intercourse. For a summary of the various types of paraphilias, see Table 12.4.

Sadomasochism

Sadism and *masochism* are forms of sex play that involve pain, bondage (or other loss of control), and humiliation. The *sadist* derives pleasure from inflicting these on other people, whereas the *masochist* wants to be dominated by other people in these ways. These practices, collectively referred to as **sadomasochism (S&M),** are performed by a broad range of people, including heterosexuals and homosexuals. In general, they are most popular among successful upper-middle-class and upper-class individuals in the contemporary Western world, and by people with lots of imagination and sexual energy.

Many people who participate in S&M activities play both roles, but the clear majority have a preference for the masochistic (submissive) role. In fact, many clubs that cater to S&M find that they are frequently lacking in people who want to play the dominant role. By most estimates, masochists outnumber sadists by about three or four to one. This means that even if a person who likes S&M finds a partner willing to join in those games, the partner is also likely to want to play the submissive role, and in many cases the couple will have to take turns (Baumeister, 1989; Scott, 1983). There is also evidence that most sadists started out as masochists and then "graduated" to the other role, but even they often get a kind of masochistic pleasure out of dominating someone, because they enjoy imagining what the other person is experiencing.

RuPaul took cross-dressing into mainstream pop culture.

Paraphilia: any of a group of psychosexual disorders characterized by sexual fantasies, feelings, or activities involving a nonhuman object, a nonconsenting partner such as a child, or pain or humiliation of oneself or one's partner

Zoophilia: erotic attraction to or sexual contact with animals

Necrophilia: erotic attraction to or sexual contact with corpses

Sadomasochism (S&M): deriving of pleasure, especially sexual gratification, from inflicting or submitting to physical or emotional abuse

TABLE 12.4

Types of Paraphilias

Autopedophilia: sexual arousal by imagining oneself as a child or being treated as a child
Autoscopophilia: sexual gratification from looking at one's own body, particularly the genitals
Avoniepiphilia: sexually arousal by wearing diapers
Coprophilia: the use of feces for sexual arousal
Formicophilia: becoming sexually aroused by bugs or other crawling creatures
Klismaphilia: sexual pleasure resulting from the use of enemas
Mysophilia: sexual excitement from filthy or soiled objects
Narratophilia: sexual arousal from listening to erotic stories
Necrophilia: sexual gratification by viewing or having intercourse with a corpse
Pictophilia: the need for sexual pictures for sexual response
Urophilia: the use of urine for sexual arousal
Zoophilia: sexual attraction to animals

The idea of sadomasochistic activity is disturbing to many people, who confuse it with rape or other violent (and nonconsensual) activity. In reality, the people who practice S&M do so by consent and often have various safeguards to make sure that no one is hurt or has an unpleasant experience. For example, the couple may agree in advance on a code word that the submissive person can use to call an immediate halt to the activity. S&M manuals also explain carefully how to dominate someone in a safe manner. For example, one should never leave a partner alone while he or she is tied up, nor should someone be bound for a long period of time. Spanking or whipping is usually aimed at the lower half of the buttocks and the top of the thighs, which can absorb the sensations but do not involve much risk of injury.

Much (but not all) sadomasochistic activity involves *pain*. The idea that pain is magically transformed into pleasure does not appear correct. The pain does really hurt, although pain thresholds do rise during sexual arousal. Spanking is the most common form of inflicting pain, although there are various other activities, such as using a paddle or whip (which must be done very carefully), or putting clamps on the nipples. The most severe form of painful sex play (other than a hard whipping) involves holding a lit candle over the submissive person's body, so that the candle wax drips down onto the skin, which creates a startling and painful burning sensation but does not burn the skin. The accompanying photograph shows some of the "tools" used in S&M encounters.

The second aspect of sadomasochism is *bondage* or *loss of control*. This is probably the most common practice; many couples will experiment with having sexual activity while one of them is blindfolded, because it creates a feeling of helplessness and anticipation and may intensify sensory awareness of touch. Some S&M couples engage in bondage without either pain or humiliation. Tying a partner to the bed or putting him or her in handcuffs creates a similar sense of helplessness. Bondage is relatively safe, if common sense is used. It is also important to make sure that the bound position is reasonably comfortable and does not cut off blood circulation. If a gag is used, the person applying it must ensure that his or her partner can breathe and swallow. As already noted, a bound person should never be left alone; think about it—if you fell while bound you wouldn't be able to protect your head, and if there were a fire or other emergency you might not be able to escape.

The third category of sadomasochistic practices involves *humiliation* or *embarrassment*. These behaviors take a variety of forms, and many masochists have very specific preferences. They may wish to be insulted verbally, to be

A wide variety of S & M paraphernalia is available in specialty shops around the world.

required to kneel, or to be referred to as a slave. The mouth is the focus of many humiliations; the masochist may be instructed to kiss the partner's feet or buttocks, perform oral sex on the partner, or have panties stuffed into his or her mouth. Some masochists like to be treated like a dog (for example, put on a leash and required to walk on "all fours") or a baby (for example, dressed in a diaper). Being naked when others are present is embarrassing to many people, and some masochists like to be displayed naked (for example, tied up with legs spread), or forced to masturbate or receive a spanking in front of an audience. Other scenarios include having to perform housework while naked, being lent out to perform sexual services for people other than the dominant partner, being urinated upon, being required to perform homosexual acts (embarrassing for people who identify themselves as heterosexual), and (for male masochists) being dressed up in women's clothing.

It might seem easy to understand why a sadist might like to have a sex slave, but the appeal of masochism is harder to understand. Psychoanalytic theory has offered some speculations about masochism, although these have generally been discredited. For example, Freud believed that the urge to dominate others is common, but because people feel guilty about hurting someone, they may transform this wish to dominate into a desire to be dominated by someone else. The view that masochism is a secondary phenomenon is difficult to reconcile with the data showing that masochism is far more common than sadism and that people who play both roles generally start out as masochists.

Another psychoanalytic view is that people who feel guilty about sex desire to be punished so that they may enjoy sex more fully; however, there is no evidence that masochists suffer from sexual guilt. Indeed, when masochists seek therapy, they usually feel guilty or troubled about the masochistic activity but not about normal sex, and they want the therapist to make them content with normal sex—precisely the opposite of what you would expect if the masochist felt guilty about normal sex. All in all, it is rather clear that people who feel guilty or inhibited about sex do not progress to engaging in these unusual forms of sex play.

One psychoanalytic hypothesis about masochism is that it is a "female" preference (for example, Deutsch, 1944) in the sense that women are inherently inclined toward masochism. According to this view, women are biologically destined to learn to submit to being invaded during sex, including the "injury" of having the hymen ripped when losing their virginity, and this pattern paves the way for female masochism. Yet as Reik (1944) and others have pointed out, more men than women engage in masochism, so masochism should perhaps be regarded as a masculine trait. Women do outnumber men in occurrence of masochistic or submissive *fantasies* (Leitenberg & Henning, 1985); trying to link masochism to either gender depends on whether you count actual behavior or mere fantasy. In short, masochism is not particular to either gender and is only practiced by a minority of each, and in that sense it is neither male nor female.

Men and women do appear to practice masochism somewhat differently, however. Based on a content analysis of masochistic fantasies, Baumeister (1988a, 1989) concluded that male masochists tend to emphasize more intense experiences, whereas females use more fantasy and imagination. Female masochists prefer a mild spanking; males seek out more stern whippings. Female masochists prefer embarrassing experiences, such as being displayed naked; males emphasize the degrading experiences such as being insulted, having to kiss someone's toes or anus, or being treated like a dog. Male masochists like to be dressed in women's clothing, but female masochists do not normally get dressed in men's clothing. Female masochists often have genital intercourse with their partners, but males do so much less often. This last difference may reflect the attitude that a man possesses a woman in genital intercourse, so it is acceptable for a dominant male to have intercourse with a submissive female. However, it would be inappropriate for a submissive male, often called a "slave," to possess his dominant mistress, often referred to as a *dominatrix*.

One study investigated three different explanations for gender differences in sadomasochistic arousal among college students (Donnelly & Fraser, 1998). The *male-arousal hypothesis* theorizes that because of socialization, which emphasizes sexual

FAQ:

Who engages in masochism?

Perhaps surprisingly, people who are successful and powerful in their ordinary lives seem most drawn to masochism (for example, Janus, Bess, & Saltus, 1977; Scott, 1983). Masochists are not typically mentally ill and in many respects are better adjusted than average (Cowen, 1982). Masochists tend to be white, middle- and upper-class individuals with an active imagination and a high sex drive (but possibly a slow response pattern, so that the elaborate games of S&M are helpful to bring them to a peak of sexual excitement). Being uninhibited is also conducive to trying S&M, contrary to the view that inhibited people want to be spanked and dominated in order to escape from guilt.

Masochism is more culturally relative than almost any other form of sexual activity. That is, masochism is unequally distributed across cultures. Tannahill (1980) noted that the ancient Chinese sex manuals from thousands of years ago contained almost all the same practices that one finds today, with the conspicuous exception of masochism. Likewise, reviews of medieval Christian writings about sex covered all the variations and deviations known in the modern world, except for masochism (Bullough & Brundage, 1982). Masochism appears to be limited to modern Western societies, plus Japan (see Baumeister, 1989, for review).

aggression and experimentation, men will be more aroused by both sadism and masochism than women. The *female-arousal hypothesis* argues that because women are socialized to be passive, they will be more aroused by masochistic activities than males, but not by sadistic activities. The *convergence hypothesis* suggests that male and female socialization have converged in recent years, resulting in similar responses to S&M behavior among both men and women. The study found no evidence for the female masochism hypothesis and only weak evidence for the convergence theory. The strongest evidence was for the male arousal hypothesis, with males scoring significantly higher than females on 7 of 12 measures of sadomasochistic arousal (Donnelly & Fraser, 1998). However, this may again simply fit the usual pattern that men are more aroused by and interested in almost any form of sexual behavior.

Another theory of masochism has viewed it as a way of escaping from one's identity and losing oneself (Baumeister, 1988b, 1989). According to this view, masochists desire to forget who they are, as a way of escaping from the stress of self-awareness. The central features of masochism are directly opposite to most of what psychologists have learned about the ordinary operation of the self. The self normally seeks to be in control, but masochists desire bondage and helplessness. The self normally seeks to maintain high self-esteem, but masochists seek out humiliation and embarrassment. The self seeks to avoid pain, whereas masochists seek out pain.

Research has fairly little to say about the cause of masochism. It is thought that these behavior patterns begin early in childhood, although a few may be related to hormonal or developmental factors that influence brain development prior to birth (Reinisch, 1991). However, many people do not discover their enjoyment of these activities until adulthood.

Even less is known about the cause of sadism. It is possible that there are more mentally ill or simply dangerous people among sadists, who are attracted to the idea of harming others. This would not presumably apply to the people who started out as masochists and then "graduated" into sadism; someone who wanted to dominate others from the start is more of a cause for concern. The smaller number of sadists (than masochists) renders it even harder to study them scientifically. Undoubtedly, however, some creative researchers will find ways to shed more light on these unusual and theoretically rich patterns of sexual behavior.

CHAPTER REVIEW

Our sexuality can be expressed in many ways including celibacy, involuntary arousal, autoeroticism, and sex with a partner.

Approximately every 90 minutes during sleep a person will have episodes of arousal (including vaginal swelling and lubrication in females or erection in males); these usually occur during periods of **1**_____ (REM) sleep. Both males and females may experience orgasm involuntarily during sleep. When males experience nocturnal orgasm, they usually ejaculate, which is called **2**_____ or a "wet dream."

Nearly all men and most women have sexual dreams. Similarly, most men and women have sexual fantasies. Typically, sexual fantasies are used to increase arousal before or during masturbation or sex with a partner. Sexual fantasies are only problematic for those few individuals for whom the fantasy becomes sufficiently powerful to control or affect their behavior.

Autoeroticism, more commonly known as **3**_____, is not physically, mentally, or emotionally harmful. People stimulate themselves sexually for pleasure, to relieve tension or anxiety, or to explore their sexuality. Males are more likely to masturbate than females, and adults with a partner are more likely to masturbate than those without a partner.

Noncoital sex may be pleasurable and satisfying independent of coitus. Since few women achieve orgasm through coitus alone, noncoital sex play should not be viewed simply as a precursor to intercourse. **4**_____ is oral stimulation of male genitalia. **5**_____ is oral stimulation of female genitalia. **6**_____ is oral stimulation of the anal area. Since it is possible for HIV and other STIs to be contracted during oral-genital sex and anal sex, safe sex precautions, such as use of a condom, are highly recommended—just as they are for coitus.

No one coital position is best for everyone, everywhere, all the time. The most frequently used heterosexual position is face-to-face with the **7**_____ on

top. The face-to-face position with the woman on top offers some advantages to the woman and is helpful for men who tend to have premature ejaculation. A **8**_____ position provides the best chances for conception, since the semen is deposited close to the mouth of the **9**_____ .

10_____ is sexual arousal caused by an inanimate object or material, or by a specific body part. **11**_____ is characterized by eroticized dressing in the clothing of the opposite sex. A **12**_____ is a recurrent, intense sexual urge and sexually arousing fantasies involving nonhuman objects, the suffering or humiliation of oneself or one's partner, or nonconsenting persons. For example, **13**_____ is the use of feces for sexual arousal; and **14**_____ or bestiality involves sexual attraction to animals. **15**_____ is the intentional infliction of pain on another person to obtain sexual excitement. **16**_____ is the need to experience pain or humiliation in order to achieve sexual gratification.

SUGGESTED READINGS

Comfort, A. (1997). *Sexual Positions.* New York: Crown Publishers.

One of the *Joy of Sex* series, this book describes a range of sexual postures from the exotic to the relatively simple.

Dodson, B. (1996). *Sex for One: The Joy of Selfloving.* New York: Crown Publishers.

The author, dedicated to taking the shame out of masturbation, discusses it as a healthy form of sexual expression.

Friday, N. (1973). *My Secret Garden: Women's Sexual Fantasies.* New York: Pocket Books, and (1980). *His Secret Life: Male Sexual Fantasies: The Triumph of Love over Rage.* New York: Dell.

Using direct quotes about their fantasies, Friday's books challenge myths about female and male sexuality.

Love, B. (1992). *The Encyclopedia of Unusual Sex Practices.* Fort Lee, NJ: Barricade Books.

A study of neurological cycles, imprinting, and primal needs, this book describes how people form their own unique sexual preferences.

MacKendrick, K. (1999). *Counterpleasure.* Albany: State University of New York Press.

MacKendrick describes a series of literary and physical acts that intuitively might not appear to be pleasurable, ranging from saintly asceticism to Sadean narrative to leather sex. Each is placed in its cultural context to unfold its history and argue for the value and power of pleasure.

ANSWERS TO CHAPTER REVIEW

1. rapid eye movement; **2.** nocturnal emission; **3.** masturbation; **4.** Fellatio; **5.** Cunnilingus; **6.** Anilingus; **7.** man; **8.** face-to-face; **9.** cervix; **10.** Fetishism; **11.** Transvestism; **12.** paraphilia; **13.** coprophilia; **14.** zoophilia; **15.** Sadism; **16.** Masochism.

CHAPTER 13

Sexual Coercion

PHYSICAL

SOCIAL

EMOTIONAL

SPIRITUAL

COGNITIVE

■ **Nonconsenting Sexual Behaviors**
Nonconsensual sexual behaviors that do not involve physical contact or verbal coercion include frotteurism, voyeurism, and obscene telephone calls.

■ **Verbal Sexual Coercion**
Verbal sexual coercion includes sexual harassment and verbal pressure; persistent messages intended to manipulate another person into a sexual behavior.

■ **Forcible Sex**
Forcible sex includes rape, that is, the use or threat of force to obtain sex, and sexual abuse of children, that is, any sexual contact between an adult and a child.

Sexual coercion involves a range of nonconsenting, abusive, forcible sexual behaviors, most of which are illegal. Unlike some of the atypical sexual behaviors discussed in Chapter 12, these are not solo sexual activities and don't involve the participation of consenting adults. It is exploitive and harmful for an individual to be deprived of free choice and to be used unwillingly for someone else's sexual excitement.

The physical aspects of sexual coercion include possible biological explanations for forcible sexual behaviors, as well as the physical harm that the victim may experience. From a social perspective, it is important to consider why sex is the weapon of choice in these criminal acts. Some victims of sexual crimes experience long-lasting emotional repercussions and spiritual crises. Contemporary sexual politics continues to focus on this issue; the legality of the various nonconsensual sexual behaviors has changed throughout history.

NONCONSENTING SEXUAL BEHAVIORS

Nonconsenting sexual behaviors include **frotteurism,** obtaining sexual pleasure by pressing or rubbing against a fully clothed nonconsenting person in a public place; **exhibitionism,** exposing of one's genitals to unsuspecting strangers; **voyeurism,** observing unsuspecting persons who are naked, undressing, or engaged in sexual relations; and **obscene phone calling.**

While these behaviors are sometimes minimized and called "nuisance" offenses, they can have a profound emotional impact on the victims. In addition, there is some evidence that the occurrence of a nonconsenting sexual behavior increases the probability that others will occur, and that some offenders progress to more violent sexual crimes (Bradford et al., 1992; Fedorea et al., 1992). Victims may feel violated, frightened that the perpetrator will commit increasingly more violent sexual acts, have recurring nightmares, or feel misplaced guilt that they are to blame for the behavior. The emotional impact of receiving an obscene telephone call, being rubbed against in a crowded subway, or of seeing a "flasher" may range from annoyance to more severe psychological trauma (Cox, 1988; Marshall, Eccles, & Barbaree, 1991).

Frotteurism

Although you might not know the term *frotteurism*, if you live in an urban area with crowded public transportation, you are probably aware of this sexual behavior. Frotteurism, also known as mashing or frottage, often occurs in places such as an elevator, subway, sporting event, or concert where the initial rubbing might not be immediately noticed. The most frequent form of contact occurs when a man covertly rubs or

Sexual Coercion: to forcibly persuade someone to do something that she or he may not want to do

Frotteurism: a sexual disorder in which an individual deliberately and persistently seeks sexual excitement by touching and rubbing against nonconsenting people

Exhibitionism: the compulsive public exposure of the genitals to a stranger

Voyeurism: observing unsuspecting individuals, usually strangers, who are naked, in the process of disrobing, or engaging in sexual activity

Obscene Phone Calling: a sexual disorder in which an individual seeks sexual excitement by telephoning nonconsenting people and making sexual remarks

A crowded subway is an ideal place for a frotteurist to rub against an unsuspecting victim.

presses his penis against a woman's buttocks or legs. While rubbing against his victim, the frotteurist might fantasize a consensual relationship with her and incorporates these images into masturbatory fantasies.

Frotteurism may be more common than indicated by statistics, as it often goes unreported. One study of a sample of "typical" college men found that 21 percent of the respondents had engaged in one or more acts of frotteurism (Templeman & Stinnett, 1991). The behavior is so fleeting and furtive that it may go unnoticed by bystanders. Even the victim may assume that the touching is accidental. Frotteurism is an exclusively male behavior (Spitzer et al., 1989), and most perpetrators are relatively young, 15 to 25 years old (American Psychiatric Association, 1994).

Exhibitionism

Exhibitionism, or "flashing," involves the urge to expose or the actual exposing of one's genitals to unsuspecting strangers for the purpose of achieving sexual arousal or gratification. The prevalence of exhibitionism is not known, but a study of more than 800 college women in nine randomly selected U.S. universities found that one third reported they had been "flashed"; only 15 of these 270 or so students reported the incident to the police (Cox, 1988).

The typical exhibitionist, or "flasher," is a male who exposes his genitals to an unsuspecting adult woman or female child (Freund, 1990; Marshall, Eccles, & Barbaree, 1991). While a few cases of female exhibitionism have been reported (Grob, 1985; Hollender, Brown, & Roback, 1977), most exhibitionists are married white males, in their 20s or 30s, of above-average intelligence, who have no evidence of a serious psychological problem (Amberson, Dwyer, & Tenley, 1986; Smukler & Schiebel, 1975; Stoller, 1977). Some exhibitionists may fantasize about exposing themselves or have an orgasm triggered by the act of exposure, and a few may masturbate during exposure (American Psychiatric Association, 1994). Typically, exposure occurs in a location that allows for easy escape, for example, on a deserted street, in a park, or in a car.

Two issues, consent and intent, may explain why women who expose themselves may not be perceived as exhibitionists. Generally, socially approved exhibitionist behavior, such as stripping or wearing revealing swimwear, involves a consenting audience. The exhibitionist or flasher, however, generally wants involuntary observers in order to elicit a reaction of disgust, shock, or fear. There is also a difference between an adolescent act of "mooning" or "streaking" and repeated exhibitionist behavior.

Some exhibitionists may have powerful feelings of inadequacy and fear of rejection (Goldstein, 1986). Exhibitionists tend to have issues of trust, shame, and the desire for immediate gratification (Miner & Dwyer, 1997). Exposing themselves may be an attempt to somehow involve others in their sexual expression, while limiting the contact to such a brief period of time that the chance for rejection is minimized. Others may simply be seeking attention. Still others use exhibitionist behavior as an act of hostility (Geer, Heiman, & Leitenberg, 1984). In these cases, exposure may be a form of reprisal against a person or persons whom the exhibitionist believes caused him emotional pain.

Exhibitionists may need to risk being caught to experience a heightened erotic response (Stoller, 1977). Some exhibitionists may progress to more serious offenses, such as physical assault of their victims. About 1 in 10 exhibitionists has considered or attempted rape (Gebhard et al., 1965; Meyer, Landis, & Hays, 1988).

Voyeurism

Voyeurs (sometimes called "peepers" or "peeping Toms") have a strong, repetitive urge to observe unsuspecting persons who are naked, undressing, or engaged in sexual relations (American Psychiatric Association, 1994). The term *peeping Tom* is said to date back to the 11th century when Lady Godiva took a nude horseback ride to protest the oppressive tax that her husband had imposed on his tenants. According to legend, Lady Godiva asked the townspeople not to look at her during her nude ride. A tailor, Tom of Coventry, was the only townsperson not to grant her request. He peeped and went blind.

Typically, the voyeur becomes sexually aroused by the act of watching but does not seek to have sexual relations with the observed person. While most voyeurs are nonviolent, some do commit violent crimes such as assault and rape (Langevin et al., 1985). Those voyeurs who break into and enter a home or building or tap on a window to get the attention of their victims are among the more dangerous.

Voyeurism is not the same thing as the enjoyment of looking at attractive people, whether on the beach, the sidewalk, or at a topless bar. You are not a voyeur if you enjoy watching your partner undress or sometimes like to watch erotic films. Voyeurism, like exhibitionism, involves *unsuspecting* victims. It is the victim's attitude that distinguishes voyeurism from the common pleasure of looking at nude or scantily clad bodies.

The voyeur may masturbate while "peeping" or may mentally relive and fantasize about the experience while masturbating later. Most voyeurs spend a great deal of time planning their observations and may risk physical injury, discovery, and apprehension while waiting hour after hour to view their targets. Often the voyeur is most sexually aroused by situations in which the risk of discovery is high, which may explain why most voyeurs are not particularly attracted to nude beaches, topless bars, or other places where nudity is accepted (Tollison & Adams, 1979).

A relatively new form of voyeurism is the video voyeur, who uses technology to gain access into private places via hidden camera. Bathrooms and locker rooms are two popular targets of the video voyeur. Unfortunately, even if a victim discovers the videotaping, today's criminal sanctions are often insufficient. While both federal and state laws forbid unauthorized covert audiotaping, legislation regarding videotaping is vague and inconsistent (Simon, 1997).

Voyeurism is found almost exclusively among males, and it usually begins before age 15 (American Psychiatric Association, 1994). Voyeurs tend to be less sexually experienced than other sex offenders and are less likely to be married (Gebhard et al., 1965). Voyeurs tend to have feelings of inadequacy, poor self-esteem, and lack social and sexual skills (Dwyer, 1988). Looking without participation may protect the voyeur against possible failure in a sexual activity; viewing the victim in secret also may give him a sense of superiority. A voyeur may enjoy thinking about the victim's helplessness and the feeling of humiliation that might be experienced if he or she discovered the voyeur's presence (American Psychiatric Association, 1994).

Obscene Telephone Calling

"Is your refrigerator running?" "You'd better go catch it." Making "phony" telephone calls is a common childhood prank. Early adolescents who experiment with such phone calls, which may or may not be obscene, are different from the habitual obscene caller. Adolescents with poor social skills are more likely to use obscene telephone calls as an interim way to make sexual contact (Matek, 1988). Habitual obscene telephone callers seek to become sexually aroused by shocking victims with a verbal barrage of sexual obscenities.

Obscene telephone calling, sometimes referred to as *telephone scatology*, differs from calling a telephone sex line for sexual arousal or gratification. The two differ on the issue of consent. The recipient of a call to a telephone sex line is a willing participant; the recipient of an obscene telephone call is not. Once again, the attitude of the victim becomes the dividing line between normal, permissible behavior and objectionable, coercive behavior. Obscene telephone calls are illegal but very common. In one college study, 75 percent of female undergraduates reported they had received

What should I do if I receive an obscene telephone call?

Obscene callers typically experience sexual arousal when their victims vocalize their horror or disgust. If you receive an obscene call, the best thing to do is quietly and quickly hang up. Banging down the receiver, screaming, or confronting the caller only plays into the caller's wishes. If the phone rings again immediately, don't answer. If the phone calls persist or are threatening, report them to the authorities. In such a situation you might want to consider adding caller identification to your service, changing your number, getting an unlisted phone number, or using an answering machine to screen your calls.

an obscene phone call (Murray & Beran, 1968); other studies have shown that virtually all women have received such calls at one time or another (Adams & Chiodo, 1983). Have you?

Some callers repeatedly contact the same victim. More often, unless the victim shows a willingness to stay on the phone, the caller dials different numbers. In the past, it was difficult to catch an obscene phone caller unless the line was being monitored and the caller could be kept on it long enough for the call to be traced. Today, with the wide availability of various services including caller identification and return call service (for example, *69, which provides phone number of last call received), obscene callers have a more difficult time avoiding detection unless they use public telephones.

Telephone scatology has long been associated with exhibitionism and also frequently occurs in association with other paraphilic disorders (Price et al., 2001). The obscene phone caller is almost always male and typically has difficulties with interpersonal relationships. The behavior patterns of obscene callers vary greatly. Most do not select a specific victim but choose phone numbers at random. Some masturbate during the phone call, while others fantasize and masturbate later. Some callers are silent or emit sounds such as heavy breathing, while others use threats or sexual language. It appears that imagery plays an important part in building the offender's sexual excitement. The physical appearance of the victim is irrelevant; the caller is free to imagine the appearance and dress of his victim. The ability to impose himself on someone while not exposing himself or having to negotiate a relationship provides a sense of control (Matek, 1988).

Mead (1975) identified three major groupings of obscene callers. One group proceeds almost immediately to use profanity and to make lewd propositions. Ingratiating seducers, another group, tell the victim a somewhat believable story, for example, that they have a mutual friend or have met previously. A third group, the tricksters, falsely present themselves as having a legitimate reason for talking to the victim about sexual matters. Some obscene callers will pretend they are physicians or researchers in order to elicit sexual information or conversation.

Theoretical Perspectives on Nonconsenting Sexual Behaviors

Many of us might find it difficult to understand how and why some people feel compelled to engage in these nonconsenting sexual behaviors. Different theoretical perspectives can suggest possible insights into the reasons for these behaviors.

Classical psychoanalytic theory suggests that these behaviors are psychological defenses against unresolved castration anxiety (Fenichel, 1945). For example, by exposing his genitals, the exhibitionist unconsciously seeks reassurance that his penis is still there. Similarly, psychoanalytic theory suggests that the voyeur identifies with the man in the observed couple as he identified with his own father during childhood observations of the primal scene, a child's first real or imagined observation of parental sexual intercourse.

Learning theory holds that these behaviors are learned and acquired through experience. Children may become conditioned to respond to a particular stimulus associated with pleasurable experiences. An early study that supports this theory (McGuire et al., 1965) describes two young boys who were surprised by an attractive woman while urinating. Although they were embarrassed at the time, the boys' memories of the incident were sexually stimulating and they masturbated repeatedly while fantasizing about the event. Reinforced by frequent orgasms, the fantasies persisted and after a while they purposely began to expose themselves, seeking the same high level of sexual excitement.

Another theory of the origins of these nonconsenting sexual behaviors is courtship disorder theory (Freund, 1983; Freund & Blanchard, 1986). This theory identifies four phases of *normal* human male courtship behavior: location and initial appraisal of a potential partner; pretactile interaction (smiling at or talking with a prospective partner); tactile interaction (embracing or touching); and effecting genital union, or coitus. According to this theory, frotteurism, exhibitionism, voyeurism, and obscene phone calling may be viewed as distortions of one or more of these distinct phases. For example, voyeurism is seen as a distortion of the first phase. Exhibitionism and obscene telephoning are distortions of pretactile interactions, and frotteurism is a distortion of the third phase, tactile interaction. Rape is theorized to be a distortion of coitus, the fourth courtship phase (Freund, 1983; Freund & Blanchard, 1986).

Evolutionary theory suggests that both men and women want their bodies to be admired and desired by members of the opposite sex. Recall that, according to evolutionary theory (see Chapter 1), women do not generally desire sexual contact with strangers. Behaviors such as exhibitionism are aimed at relative strangers, so women would not wish to attract such attention. Evolutionarily speaking, men are more likely to desire sex with strangers to "spread the wealth," and so would be more prone to expose themselves as a way of getting strangers to become interested in them. The relative caution that characterizes the female selection of sex partners would suggest that a woman would not want to display her sexual parts to a man unless she had already evaluated that person and decided that he would be a good partner. This argument might explain why some female "groupies" remove their clothes or underwear in the presence of musicians and other celebrities, even if they are not personally acquainted—they have already identified the celebrities as desirable mates and wish to attract their sexual interest.

Social exchange theory emphasizes the asymmetry of sexual exchange; as you learned in Chapter 1, according to this view sex is something that women give to men in exchange for protection and security. A woman would be unlikely to expose herself to a man because this would be giving up something without getting anything in return. The social exchange also involves consent; as we have already discussed, if a woman were to expose herself to a man, the man would probably be grateful and happy rather than upset. According to this theory, women who pursue careers such as strippers (and perhaps some actresses and models) appear to receive pleasure from being looked at and desired by men, even men they do not know. No one considers these acts to be perverse or criminal, however, because the men enjoy looking and are therefore not victimized. For a man to force an unknown woman to look at his penis is a form of sexual interaction that the woman typically would not desire; thus, it violates the basic rule of sexual exchange, in which the man must offer the woman something she wants in order for a sexual interaction to occur.

Other theories offer explanations about why some are more likely to develop these atypical sexual behaviors. A biological perspective holds that a genetic predisposition, hormonal factors, brain abnormalities, or a combination of these and other factors might play a role in developing one's vulnerability to these behaviors (Brody, 1990). Another perspective is that childhood sexual experiences etch patterns in the brain called a *lovemap* that determines the types of stimuli and activities that become sexually arousing to the individual (Money & Lamacz, 1989).

Feminist theory suggests that these nonconsenting sexual behaviors are a tactic that men use to intimidate women. According to this view these behaviors help men sustain their power over women. Some women feel that crimes such as exhibitionism are trivialized by the police and by men in general (Riordan, 1999).

VERBAL SEXUAL COERCION

Verbal sexual coercion, the use of words to influence or force an individual into unwanted sexual attention or behavior can be of two types. **Sexual harassment** is the use of deliberate and repeated verbal comments, gestures, or physical contact of a sexual nature that is considered unwelcome by the recipient (U.S. Merit Systems Protection Boards, 1981). **Verbal sexual pressure** involves manipulation or deceit to influence the recipient into unwanted sexual behavior.

Verbal Sexual Coercion: verbally influencing or forcing an individual into unwanted sexual attention or behavior

Sexual Harassment: unwanted and offensive sexual advances or sexually offensive remarks or acts, especially by one in a superior or supervisory position or when acquiescence to such behavior is a condition of continued employment, promotion, or satisfactory evaluation

Verbal Sexual Pressure: the use of manipulation or deceit to influence the recipient into unwanted sexual behavior

Sexual Harassment

Flirting feels good to both parties involved. Joking is funny to both parties involved. Sexual harassment is neither flattering nor funny to the person on the receiving end. Such harassment may include unwanted sexual attention, gender harassment, or sexual coercion (O'Donohue et al., 1990). In 1986 the U.S. Supreme Court recognized sexual harassment as a form of sex discrimination under Title VII of the Civil Rights Act of 1964. In the past many courts narrowly interpreted Title VII as prohibiting sexual harassment only between males and females. However, in 1998 a case was brought before the U.S. Supreme Court involving an offshore oil rig worker's claim that male coworkers taunted and touched him sexually. The Court ruled that workplace sexual harassment involving an offender and victim of the same sex is also prohibited by Title VII.

As we have discussed, sexual behavior has a cultural context. Sexual harassment research has been primarily limited to the United States. Sexual attention including leering, touching (patting or pinching), and brushing against a person's body may be viewed differently in other societies. For example, in some Latin American countries, *priopo* is a traditional form of street flirtation. Comments such as *"¡Qué piedras!"* (What legs!) likely would be perceived as flattery by both the speaker and the recipient.

Obvious forms of sexual coercion can be demands for sexual favors with implied or actual threats to one's job or student status, as well as physical assault (Powell, 1991). However, sexual harassment may be subtler and include such behaviors as an unwelcome sexual joke, a suggestive comment, or sexual innuendo. These remarks, gestures, or behaviors are *unwelcome*, *unsolicited*, and *unappreciated*. Many critics believe that sexual harassment legislation has spiraled out of control and feel that the laws are so broad that no one is quite sure what constitutes sexual harassment (Rosen, 1998).

One problem is that the exact same behavior may be perceived as harassment by one person and not by another, simply because the two recipients have different attitudes about the behavior or the person behaving. Sometimes honest misunderstandings

CROSS-CULTURAL PERSPECTIVES

Taking on the Man

In a society where male power and privilege are deeply embedded, confronting sexual harassment takes real courage. In 1999 Moeko Tanaka, a 23-year-old university student, successfully sued the governor of Osaka, Japan's second largest prefecture, for sexually molesting her during his election campaign. When Ms. Tanaka complained after being groped by the governor for 30 minutes in a van in the presence of several other campaign workers, the workers who witnessed the ordeal told her to cheer up and not take it so hard. Her divorced mother begged her not to take the matter to court. She separated from her boyfriend and lost many friends who questioned her decision to sue. Even her lawyers advised her to remain anonymous, saying that she must think about her future.

Although Ms. Tanaka faced the governor in court and in 2001 wrote a book, A Governor's Sexual Harassment, My Struggle, *about her ordeal, her true identity has never been publicly revealed. (Moeko Tanaka is a pen name.) She was awarded nearly $89,000 in a civil suit, and the governor, who resigned from office in disgrace, was given an 18-month suspended sentence for indecent assault, but she remains anonymous. Ms. Tanaka's fears (that if she revealed her identity she would never be able to get a job) seemed valid in a country where women are largely confined to clerical or ceremonial work in the corporate world. Maymi Hareno, the first woman to bring a sexual harassment case in Japan, agreed that even when a woman is the victim, the Japanese culture holds women responsible.*

arise; for example, a man might think that a woman will enjoy a sexual joke or suggestive comment that in fact makes her seriously uncomfortable. Interviews exploring gender differences in perceptions of sexual harassment found that more women than men reported that telling dirty/sexual jokes was nonharassing behavior, qualified these same behaviors as harassing when they happened in the workplace, and considered behaviors as nonharassing when the man's intentions were not harmful. More men than women reported that requesting a date was a nonharassing behavior, qualified the request as harassing when the woman did not welcome the behavior, and considered it as nonharassing when they did not violate workplace norms (Hurt et al., 1999). Although it is not possible to prevent all misunderstandings, if a person makes a simple and direct statement that such talk is inappropriate, a repeated pattern can be prevented. If the behavior persists beyond that point, it is more likely to be motivated by malicious intent. True sexual harassment is often intended to exploit someone or make daily life unpleasant.

Both men and women can commit sexual harassment or be sexually harassed. However, a study by the Equal Employment Opportunity Commission (EEOC, 2001) reports that for 2000 of the 15,836 sexual harassment complaints filed in the United States, only 13.6 percent were filed by males. However, this is up from 9.9 percent in 1995. The EEOC also reports that approximately 9 percent of complaints involve same-sex harassment. Only 1 percent of complaints involved a woman harassing a man.

Just Kidding?

These are actual cases that have occurred throughout the United States over the past few years.

Case: A six-year-old girl complains that boys on her school bus made lewd remarks and sexually taunted her.
Ruling: The Minnesota Department of Human Rights ruled that the school district had not correctly handled the girl's complaints as a violation of the school's sexual harassment policy.

Case: A workplace displays nude and pornographic pictures.
Ruling: Federal District Judge in Jacksonville, Florida, ruled that displaying nude calendars, pinups, or photos could be a form of sexual harassment.

Case: A male manager at a spa manufacturing plant said his former female supervisor sexually harassed him on the job for 6 years.
Ruling: A jury in a California Superior Court awarded the man $1 million in damages for sexual harassment.

Case: A woman charged that the president of the company where she was employed made inappropriate sexual innuendoes and would do such things as ask female employees to put their hands in his pants pocket to retrieve change.
Ruling: A lower court ruled that while the employer's behavior was "annoying and insensitive," it was not harassment because the employee did not prove that she had suffered psychological injury. The decision was appealed to the U.S. Supreme Court. In a unanimous opinion the justices ruled that workers suing employers for sexual harassment need not show they suffered psychological injury.

Case: A mother was keeping her 6-year-old boy home from school for a physician's appointment and had him in the bathtub so he wouldn't see the school bus. His sister told him that the school bus was coming, however, and the boy jumped from the tub and ran to the window to shout to the driver to wait for him.
Ruling: Because the boy was nude, the school in Canton, Ohio, ruled that he had sexually harassed the other pupils on the bus. He was suspended and required to sign a statement that he understood the charges against him.

Case: In March 1993 Jerold Mackenzie, a manager at Miller Brewing Company in Milwaukee, asked coworker Patricia Best if she had seen the previous night's *Seinfeld* in which Jerry forgets the name of a woman he is dating. In the episode Jerry knows that her name rhymes with a female body part and finally remembers that her name is Dolores. When his coworker didn't get the joke, Mackenzie claims that he showed her a dictionary definition of clitoris. Best reported the incident to her boss, and Miller Brewery fired Mackenzie for "unacceptable managerial performance."
Ruling: In 1997 a jury awarded Mackenzie $26.6 million for wrongful termination. Reportedly none of the jurors, 10 of whom were women, were offended by the *Seinfeld* story and wanted to make the point that sexual harassment is more important than this type of behavior.

 Do you think these incidents represent sexual harassment?

In 1991, law professor Anita Hill's testimony at the confirmation hearings of Supreme Court Justice nominee Clarence Thomas focused national attention on sexual harassment.

Sexual Harassment in the Workplace   Sexual harassment in the workplace falls into two categories. One category is *quid pro quo* or "I'll do something for you if you do something for me." For example, a superior lets it be known that an employee's job future is dependent on submitting to sexual advances. A second category involves the creation of a hostile, intimidating, or offensive environment that violates an individual's civil rights (Clark, 1993). Harassers in the workplace may be employers, supervisors, coworkers, or clients.

Employers can be held responsible if such behavior is deemed to create a hostile or abusive work environment or to interfere with an employee's work performance. Employers can be held responsible not only for their own personal actions but also for sexual harassment by their employees in cases when they either know or should know that harassment is taking place and fail to eliminate it promptly.

In the past some men and women accepted and expected behaviors that are today considered sexual harassment. High-profile cases such as Anita Hills' allegation that Supreme Court nominee Clarence Thomas sexually harassed her when she worked in his office, the allegations of more than 25 women against former Senator Robert Packwood, and Paula Jones's charges against President Clinton have heightened awareness and increased reports of sexual harassment. Since Anita Hill's testimony during the Thomas confirmation hearings, sexual harassment claims in the United States rose by more than 50 percent but have since leveled off (Equal Employment Opportunity Commission, 2000). Anita Hill may have sensitized the American public to the fact of sexual harassment, but it was Rena Weeks, a secretary at the law firm of Baker & McKenzie, who sensitized corporate America to the consequences of this problem; she won a $3.5 million judgment against the firm. But not all victims are compensated as well as Weeks; the average $38,500 claim paid on a sexual harassment case is far lower than the six-figure awards in sexual and racial discrimination cases (Armour, 1998).

Sexual Harassment in the Military   Sexual harassment in the U.S. military has been the focus of national attention for the past several years. The 1991 Tailhook scandal, in which 26 women accused Navy aviators of sexual assault during a convention in Las Vegas, brought public attention to this problem. In 1996 several women trainees at the Army's Aberdeen Proving Ground in Maryland accused male drill instructors of sexual harassment. By spring 1997, more than 50 women recruits had filed official complaints ranging from sexual harassment to rape against male officers at Aberdeen.

An Army survey conducted in conjunction with an investigation into the Aberdeen allegations revealed that 47 percent of women soldiers reported experiencing unwanted sexual attention, 15 percent had been subjected to sexual coercion, and 7 percent had been victimized by sexual assault. About half of the male troops also reported experiencing sexual harassment; 30 percent reported being the targets of unwanted sexual attention and 9 percent indicated sexual coercion. Only 12 percent of the male or female soldiers had filed a formal complaint (Shenon, 1997). One soldier who did file a complaint was Lieutenant General Claudia Kennedy who accused Major General Larry Smith of attempting to kiss and fondle her in 1996. In 2000 after Kennedy's accusations were substantiated, Major General Smith, who had been poised to be promoted to deputy inspector general, was allowed to retire with a reprimand.

Results of a study of the impact of sexual harassment on military personnel found that while military men and women experienced similar psychological, health, and job-related outcomes, some differences did emerge. Women were more likely to have been sexually harassed than men, women experienced sexual harassment at higher frequencies than did men, and the negative impact on women was greater. Moreover, women almost always experience sexual harassment from men whereas men were somewhat more likely to experience such behaviors from men than from women (Magley et al., 1999).

Sexual Harassment in Education   A study (Barringer, 1993) commissioned by the American Association of University Women Educational Foundation surveyed 1,600 American students in grades 8 through 11. Eighty-five percent of the girls and

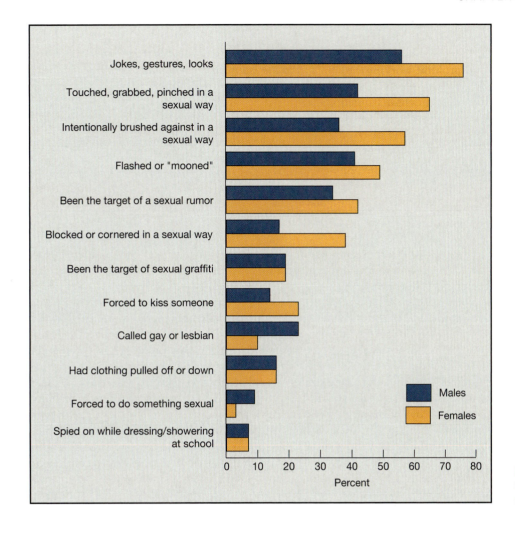

FIGURE 13.1   **Types of Sexual Harassment.**
SOURCE: Barringer, 1993, p. B9.

76 percent of the boys stated they had experienced some type of objectionable sexual comment, gesture, or physical contact. Two thirds of the boys and over half the girls said that they had harassed other students. More than one third of those harassed said that they thought the behavior was a normal part of school life, and 25 percent of the harassers thought the target of harassment enjoyed the attention. Eighteen percent identified their harasser as being an adult. Harassing behaviors experienced by the students are shown in Figure 13.1.

Estimates of the frequency of sexual harassment by instructors on college campuses vary, depending on the definition of sexual harassment. In one survey, from 7 to 27 percent of undergraduate and graduate men and from 12 to 65 percent of women on campuses reported they had been sexually harassed (McKinney & Maroules, 1991). Although some acts of sexual harassment on campus involve the *quid pro quo* of exchanging sex for grades, most incidents of harassment are not linked to any promise of a higher grade. They involve suggestive looks, sexual comments, propositions, and light touching (McKinney & Maroules, 1991; see the CONSIDERATIONS box for more on this). Peer harassment, sexual harassment among students or colleagues, is similar to that of coworker harassment in the workplace. Like employers, academic institutions can be found liable for such behavior.

In some cases it may be the professor, not the student, who is being sexually harassed. Women faculty members may be harassed by male students or by colleagues. Male faculty and staff members also may be subject to harassment. Of the 235 male faculty surveyed at the University of California at Berkeley, 6 percent reported being sexually harassed by a student (Grauerholz, 1989). A more recent study found that while

An 'A' for a Lay?

Most universities have developed policies that sanction unwanted sexual attention and prohibit working and learning environments that are hostile to women. In addition to these sanctions, some universities have banned any intimate relationships between students and faculty. Some feel that this taboo has been fueled by cases of elementary and high-school teachers sexually abusing students with the result that student-faculty romances are viewed as being pornographic.

 Do you think that universities are overreacting to the issue of sexual harassment by banning student-faculty relationships?

—Why or why not?

—Do you think that a faculty member can be objective about the academic performance of a student he or she is sexually involved with?

—Have you heard of a case of a faculty member offering to trade grades for sex on your campus?

the frequency of harassment did not differ significantly between male and female faculty, female faculty were significantly more bothered by it than male faculty members (Matchen & DeSouza, 2000).

Dealing With Sexual Harassment   "I felt insulted, demeaned, and intimidated by that remark." "Jeez, I was just kidding, can't you take a joke?" As we have already discussed, the perceptions of the alleged harasser and the person being harassed are likely to be quite different. What may be considered a harmless remark by some can have serious emotional consequences. One study found that 75 percent of females who have been sexually harassed reported physical or emotional reactions such as anxiety, irritability, and anger (Loy & Stewart, 1985). One reason that sexual harassment can be so stressful is that the person being harassed is often blamed for encouraging or exaggerating the harassing behavior (Powell, 1991).

Despite the increased awareness about sexual harassment, most cases continue to go unreported. The most common response to sexual harassment is to avoid the person doing the harassing. Maypole (1991) found that women choose to delay or diffuse the conflict as their primary response. Of the students in grades 8 through 11 surveyed, only 7 percent told a teacher and 23 percent told a family member (Barringer, 1993); of the clients who reported being abused by a therapist, only 8 percent reported the incident to authorities. In a survey of sexual harassment in the workplace, only 3 percent filed a formal complaint (Loy & Stewart, 1985). The financial and emotional consequences to those reporting sexual harassment can be devastating.

How do adult women respond to sexual harassment? A careful, systematic study by Woodzicka and LaFrance (2001) involved a hypothetical job interview in which a male interviewer asked a female candidate several questions that involved mild sexual harassment, such as "Do you have a boyfriend?" and "Do you think a woman should wear a bra to work?" The researchers examined the responses of the candidates in two ways. In one, they merely described the situation to women and asked them what they would do. The most common responses were to tell the interviewer that these questions were inappropriate, to walk out of the interview, and to report the episode to someone in authority. Thus, women commonly said they would not stand for the harassment but would object in some clear, overt manner. When the researchers hired a confederate and actually conducted the interviews (after advertising for an actual job) with those same questions, the live, real-life responses were not at all similar to the hypothetical ones. The women in the live interviews almost never expressed any objection, nor did they leave the interview or make a formal complaint. Instead, they tried to conceal their discomfort by avoiding the question or by making a joke.

Another aspect of the Woodzicka and LaFrance study is revealing. The first attempt to run the live-interview part of the study was a failure. The confederate they hired to conduct the interviews was a charming young man with a British accent; many of the women seemed to respond favorably to his suggestive questions. For example, when he asked a woman if she had a boyfriend, she would reply, "No, do you have a girlfriend?" Clearly the research could not proceed if the questions were not perceived as sexual harassment, so the researchers fired the charming young man and hired another confederate, who was more successful at conducting the harassment procedure, possibly because he did not appeal as much to the women and therefore his advances were less appealing. This incident highlights an important fact—the victim's attitude is a defining criterion for harassment. The essence of sexual harassment is that the comments are unwelcome to the victim, and her reaction depends on many factors. The two men worked from the same script and made the same exact comments, but for some reason the women felt more harassed by the one than by the other.

Theoretical Perspectives on Sexual Harassment   From a feminist perspective, sexual harassment is seen as a male abuse of power rather than as sexual behaviors (Goleman, 1991). The harasser usually is in a dominant position in relation to the victim. He abuses that position, using sexual harassment to keep a subordinate "in her place." Since men are more frequently in positions of power in the workplace and academia, it probably is not surprising that harassers are more likely to be men.

In contrast, the evolutionary perspective regards sexual harassment as being about sex. Thus, even when women gain power, they may be less likely than men to engage in harassment because of evolved differences in sexuality. Evolutionary theory emphasizes that gaining power has always been a crucial means by which men obtained sex. In many species, animals live in small groups and the males form a power structure, and only the top-ranked male (called the alpha male) gets to have sex with the females. (In reality, sometimes the other males manage to sneak in an occasional copulation when the alpha male isn't watching.) Power has been a way to gain sexual access to women throughout human history as well; a historical study by Betzig (1986) showed that kings and rulers have generally produced many more offspring than ordinary men. Their reproductive success confirms that power confers sexual advantages to men.

Even today, many ambitious men seek power because they believe that it will enhance their sex appeal. According to evolutionary psychologists, women find powerful men to be sexually more attractive (for example, Buss, 1994). A woman who marries a powerful man is likely to find that she and her children are well cared for. Even having an affair with a powerful man may obtain genes that would make a woman's baby more fit than the genes she might get from a more low-status partner. According to this view, powerful men are successful because of their genetic advantages.

Bargh et al. (1995) examined whether thinking about power automatically makes someone think about sex. They found that power and sex are most closely linked in the minds of men who are prone to engage in sexual harassment. Among men who were not prone to engage in sexual harassment, power and sex did not have the same mental links. These findings, and the evolutionary theories cited previously, suggest that some men consider sex to be a reward of power. They may believe that power will make them more attractive to women and increase their chances for sex. Because modern life does not resemble the conditions under which our species evolved, their expectations may not be met, and they may begin to put inappropriate sexual pressure on women.

None of these findings or considerations justifies sexual harassment. It is fair for a person to express his or her sexual or romantic interest in another, but if it is made clear that interest is unwanted, such expression should stop. Putting pressure on someone or making advances that are clearly unwanted is improper and, in many situations, illegal. Even if a person cannot refrain from *desiring* sex with someone, he or she can refrain from *acting* on those desires, and in many situations has both a moral and a legal obligation to do so.

Verbal Sexual Pressure

"I know you really want to do it." "You're just so sexy, I can't control myself around you." Seduction "lines" like these (see also the CONSIDERATIONS box) are so common and pervasive that they often are not recognized as a form of sexual coercion. In one study

---

FAQ:

What should you do if you experience sexual harassment?

Sometimes harassment can be stopped by a professional, businesslike, task-oriented response. It may be uncomfortable, but, if possible, either verbally or in writing, inform the harasser that the behavior is objectionable. Maintain written documentation of the harassment that includes the date and time, where the harassment took place, what happened, how you felt, and the names of any witnesses or persons you informed of the events. Seek support from those you trust, both for emotional support as well as to secure possible witnesses. If you are not satisfied with the harasser's response, or if the harassment continues, file a complaint with the appropriate official; companies and organizations are required by law to respond to complaints of sexual harassment. The Equal Employment Opportunity Commission and your state's Human Rights Commission may offer advice on how to protect your legal rights and proceed with a formal complaint. If you are fired for reasons arising from sexual harassment, consult an attorney; you may be entitled to back pay, reinstatement, and punitive damages (Powell, 1991).

Power is the ultimate aphrodisiac.

HENRY KISSINGER

What Part of "NO" Don't You Understand?

NO. Please. NO. What's wrong? NO. Come on. NO. It'll be great. NO. I know you want to. NO. Yeah, you want to. NO. I just want to make you happy. NO. I just want to show you how much I love you. NO. Come on, just this once. NO. But I need it. NO. Are you seeing someone else? I bet you're doing it with him. NO. Then come on, let's do it. NO. What are you, frigid or something? NO. You've got to loosen up and relax. NO. It's not like you're a virgin or anything, is it? What's the big deal? NO. Come on, I'll make you feel so good you won't want to stop. NO. I promise, I'll make you feel so good. NO. I'm tired of fooling around here, just shut up and do it. NO.

 Have you ever used any of these lines?

—Have any of them ever been used on you?

---

of 194 male undergraduates, 43 percent admitted to verbally coercing a woman into sex (Craig et al., 1989); another survey of 325 undergraduates men found that about one in five reported attempting to have sexual intercourse by saying things to women they didn't mean (Lane & Gwartney-Gibbs, 1984). A survey of adolescent males and females found that adolescents had fewer strategies to promote sexual encounters than adults. However, a higher percentage of adolescent males engaged in coercive strategies such as pressuring, lying, and getting a partner drunk or high (Eyre et al., 1997).

One theory is that males are more likely to use sexually coercive tactics if they are unable to access desirable mates. This hypothesis was refuted by a study involving a sample of 156 heterosexual university men. Men who identified themselves as sexually coercive tended to have higher self-perceived mating success, had significantly more extensive sexual histories, and did not report lower relative earning potential. Coercive men also reported a greater preference for partner variety and casual sex (Lalumiere et al., 1996).

Sexually permissive attitudes are found to be significant predictors of men's use of verbal coercion (Tyler et al., 1998). However, not all unwanted sexual contact involves males as perpetrators and females as victims. Although women are more likely to be victims of physical force, one study reported that men were as likely to be the recipients of sexual coercion as women (Larimer et al., 1999). A study of more than 200 predominantly heterosexual college men found that 34 percent indicated they had been the recipients of coercive sexual contact: 24 percent from women, 4 percent from men, and 6 percent from both sexes. In 88 percent of the cases, sexual contact was the result of persuasion, intoxication, threat of love withdrawal, or bribery (Struckman-Johnson & Struckman-Johnson, 1994).

He Said, She Said

Line: Everybody's doing it.
Response: Well, I'm not everybody. I'm me. Besides, I know it's not true that everybody's doing it.

Line: If you love me, you'll have sex with me.
Response: If you love me, you'll respect my feelings and not push me into something I'm not ready for.

Line: I know you want to do it too. You're just afraid of what people will say.
Response: You can't read my mind. Besides, if I wanted to do it, I wouldn't be arguing with you.

Line: We've had sex before, so what's the big deal?
Response: I have a right to change my mind. I've decided to wait until I'm older to have sex again.

Line: If you won't have sex with me, I won't see you anymore.
Response: Too bad, I'll miss you.

Line: Don't you want to try it to see what it's like?
Response: That's a stupid reason to have sex.

Line: But I have to have it.
Response: No you don't. If I can wait, you can wait.

Line: Come on, have a drink. It'll get you in the mood.
Response: No thanks. I don't want to get drunk and not know what I'm doing.

SOURCE: *www.girlsinc.org*, 2000

FORCIBLE SEX

Rape

Most people would agree that a man breaking into a house, holding a knife to a woman's throat, threatening to kill her if she doesn't cooperate, and proceeding to have intercourse with her is rape. But consider the following scenario: A couple has been drinking and making out at a party; he wants to have sex, she doesn't, and while she never really says "no" she doesn't say "yes" either. In a variation of this scene, the woman of a couple who have previously had intercourse doesn't want to have sex that evening, so he tells her that if she won't have sex with him, he'll find someone who will; she doesn't want to risk losing him so, against her better judgment, she acquiesces. Is it rape if a sexually inexperienced man is taunted by his date that a "real man" would have gotten her into bed by now, and he gives in after she threatens to tell all his friends what a wimp he is? What is the difference between a bad sexual experience and rape? What is the line between miscommunication or insensitivity and rape?

Traditionally, legal definitions of rape were based on common-law statutes that valued women as property. In this context, rape was seen as lowering the marketability of that property (Loh, 1981). By such definitions, it was not possible for a man to be raped, nor could a husband rape his wife because he "owned" her sexuality already by virtue of marriage. The legal concept has since shifted toward the issue of consent, but principle and practice are not always the same thing. There are often wide gaps between what society considers rape and what the individual may experience. The legal definition of rape varies from state to state and nation to nation, but generally **rape** is defined as the use of force, or the threat of force, to obtain sex. Culture and context heavily influence the occurrence of rape. Broude and Greene (1987) found that rape was present in 76 percent of societies they surveyed. Rozee-Koker (1987) found rape in 100 percent of the societies in her sample.

Some social scientists view rape as primarily a crime of violence, not sex. Others believe that the sexual element is a critical distinction between rape and other violent crimes. Sometimes rape primarily is about sex, and sometimes it is about violence. In some rapes, the sexual element is relatively low and the need to punish, humiliate, and retaliate is high. Even when the sexual element is relatively weak, the expression of dominance and power in a sexual form may be significant. Groth (1979) asked convicted rapists to rate their degree of sexual pleasure from the rape on a scale from 1 (minimal) to 10 (very high), and most gave a rating of 3 or less. He also reported that none of the rapists said rape was more sexually gratifying than consensual intercourse. Warren et al. (1989) collected similar data from a sample of convicted serial rapists, and they too rated the degree of sexual pleasure at around 3 on a similar scale. These findings seem consistent with the view that rape is not primarily about sex, although it appears that in some cases the men expected the rape to provide more sexual pleasure and were quite disappointed in the outcome. It is also important to remember that these data are based on stranger rapes; date rapes may be experienced as offering greater pleasure, although evidence is lacking. In any case, it does not appear that committing rape is in fact a promising way for men to obtain sexual pleasure.

Anthropologist Keith Otterbein (1979) conducted an earlier cross-cultural study of rape. He found that the level of rape was higher in societies where there were powerful groups of related males that resort to aggression to defend members' interests; such groups are known as fraternal interest groups (FIGs). On the other hand, Otterbein also found that rape is deterred by the potential for punishment. He concluded that the best predictor for the level of rape in a society was a combination of both factors. As is discussed later, the United States has both FIGs (for example, men's sports teams, college fraternities, and gangs) and relatively impotent deterrence for rapists (for example, conviction is uncertain and punishment often is less than severe).

Prevalence of Rape   It is difficult to obtain accurate estimates of the prevalence of rape because so many rapes are not reported to authorities. Probably the most

> ❝*If a woman chooses not to have intercourse and the man chooses to proceed against her will, that is . . . rape.*❞
>
> SUSAN BROWNMILLER

> ❝*If there is no force and no threat of force and she consented, that is not rape.*❞
>
> LINDA FAIRSTEIN

Rape: the crime of forcing another person to submit to sex acts, especially sexual intercourse

CONSIDERATIONS

Rape-Prone Societies

Anthropologist Peggy Reeves Sanday (1981) categorized societies as being either *rape-prone* or *rape-free*. According to her model, in rape-free societies, rape is either infrequent or does not occur at all. Rape-prone societies are defined as those in which rape is a ceremonial act, or where rape may be used as a threat to control women or an act to punish women. In such societies, sexual assault of women by men is either culturally allowable or largely overlooked. The factors that distinguished the two were the existing level of violence, child-rearing practices (especially the attitude of fathers), and the presence of an ideology of male dominance. Sanday found that 47 percent of the 95 societies in her study were rape-free. These societies were characterized by sexual equality and placed high value on women's contribu-

tions to social continuity. In rape-free societies, men and women share power and authority, and children are taught to value nurturing and to avoid aggression. Eighteen percent of the societies Sanday sampled were categorized as rape-prone. Men in these societies often have special gathering spots; women generally have less economic and political power; women's judgments are frequently demeaned by men; fathers are generally aloof, cold, and stern; and women's tasks such as child-rearing and household duties are not highly valued.

 Sanday identified our own country as a rape-prone society. Are you surprised by this result?

—Why or why not?

FAQ:

Where do most rapes occur? Who is most likely to be a rape victim?

About two thirds of rapes occur at night; they most frequently occur in the victims' home, on the street, or in or near a friend's home. Unmarried women are statistically more likely to be raped, as are women who live alone. The rapist and victim are likely to be of the same race (Harlow, 1991).

underreported are those that occur in married couples, heterosexual dating relationships, or homosexual relationships. These victims may be less likely to report a crime because they do not define the incident as rape, fear revenge from the offender, or think that they will not be believed (Hart, 1986; Kanen, 1984; Koss et al., 1988; Russell, 1990). Hundreds of thousands of rapes occur in the context of war—from ancient times to Vietnam and Bosnia (see Wartime Rape later in this section)—yet these assaults are rarely counted in rape statistics.

Using a definition of rape that included forced vaginal, oral, and anal intercourse, a 1998 National Violence Against Women (NVAW) Survey conducted by the U.S. Department of Justice found that 18 percent of U.S. women and 3 percent of U.S. men have experienced an attempted or completed rape at some time in their life (Tiaden & Thoennes, 1998). Similarly, the National Health and Social Life Survey found that 22.8 percent of women reported they had been forced by men to do something sexually that they did not want to do, usually by someone they knew well, whom they loved, or to whom they were married. The researchers acknowledged, however, that there was an error in their survey, and a slightly lower figure may be correct. Only 2.8 percent of the men participating in the survey said that they had ever forced a woman into a sexual act. The wide gulf between these numbers may be due to underreporting, or it may be that many men do not recognize how coercive women perceived their behavior to be (Michael et al., 1994).

In 1997 the U.S. government more than doubled its estimate of rapes or attempted rapes per year to 310,000 (Bureau of Justice Statistics, 1997). The actual rate of assaults did not increase; rather, after years of controversy, the Justice Department changed the questions it asked in the National Crime Victimization Survey, used to interview 100,000 Americans ages 12 and older. Before 1992 the interviewers only asked about attacks of any kind; they did not mention rape or sexual assault specifically. Previously the Bureau of Justice Statistics estimated that there were 133,000 total rapes and attempted rapes each year; they had no data at all on other types of sexual assault. The revised data estimated that there are 500,000 sexual assaults on women in the United States annually, including 170,000 rapes and 140,000 attempted rapes.

An examination of more than 1,000 sexual assault victims treated at an urban trauma center from 1992 to 1995 found that 96 percent of the victims were females (Houry, 2000) and that younger females were more likely to be raped than older women (Tiaden & Thoennes, 1998). Women age 16 to 24 are three times more likely to be raped than older women. Convicted rape and sexual assault offenders serving time in state prisons report that two thirds of their victims were under the age of 18; 58 percent said their victims were aged 12 or younger (Bureau of Justice Statistics, 1997). One study of 100 college women found that low self-esteem, low assertiveness, and a large number of sex-related alcohol experiences were associated with verbal sexual coercion but not with rape or attempted rape. Higher levels of casual sexual activity combined with alcohol consumption were associated with both sexual coercion and rape (Testa & Derman, 1999).

There has been relatively little research regarding sexual coercion in homosexual relationships. One study of gay men and lesbians from several colleges found that 12 percent of the men and 31 percent of the women reported that they had been forced to engage in sexual activity by their most recent partner (Waterman, Dawson, & Bologna, 1989). Another study found that 36 percent of lesbians surveyed had experienced physical or sexual violence in a lesbian relationship (Schilit, Lie, & Montagne, 1990). In a more recent study of nearly 4,000 ethnically diverse gay men, lesbians, bisexuals, and transgendered people, only 1 percent reported that they had experienced forced sex in their current relationship; 9 percent had experienced forced sex in a past relationship. In the same study, physical violence was reported in 9 percent of current relationships and 32 percent of past relationships, and emotional abuse was reported by 83 percent of the participants (Turell, 2000).

Heterosexual rape of men has received much less research attention than heterosexual rape of women. It is only recently that sexual coercion by women has been examined. A survey of men who have experienced sexual coercion by women found that 43 percent of the men reported having had at least one coercive sexual experience with a woman since the age of 16. Thirty-six percent of the men had had at least one incident of sexual touch, and 27 percent of the men reported at least one incident involving intercourse (Struckman-Johnson & Struckman-Johnson, 1998).

Very few women are arrested for rape. Men may be reluctant to press charges, or they may feel that what they suffered was relatively unimportant. One study of college men's reactions to a vignette in which they were to imagine receiving a physically forceful sexual advance from a casual female acquaintance found that men with more restricted sexual standards had significantly more negative reactions to the advance than did men with more permissive standards. Men who were instructed to assume that they had a girlfriend in the scenario situation had more negative reactions to the advance than did men who assumed that they did not have a girlfriend. Evidence also was found for a beauty bias: men who read that the initiator was average looking had less positive reactions than did men who read that the initiator was very attractive (Struckman-Johnson & Struckman-Johnson, 1997).

The social exchange theory of sex suggests one reason for the asymmetry. If sex is something women give to men, then it is considered wrong for men to "steal" sex by means of rape. If a woman forces a man into sex, he has not lost something in the same sense that a female rape victim has. A feminist analysis would also suggest that rape would occur mainly by men, because rape reflects the power differences in society, which is dominated by men. Evolutionary analyses would explain the gender difference in rape

Sisterhood

CONSIDERATIONS

A study on college campuses found that sorority women were significantly more likely than nonsorority women to have been raped. In addition, there was a significantly higher rate of rape among sorority women while under the influence of alcohol or drugs (Kalof, 1993).

 Why do you think that sorority women are more likely than nonsorority women to have been raped?

by suggesting that women do not generally need to obtain sex by force, because their reproductive goals can be easily served. Men, in contrast, may want many partners and sometimes cannot get what they want by legitimate methods.

Attitudes and Beliefs About Rape "You can't thread a moving needle—if a woman really wanted to she could resist a rape." "When a woman says 'no' she really means 'yes.'" "Dressed like that she was just asking for it." And, on the victim's side, "It could never happen to me." These are only a few of the widely held misconceptions and false beliefs about rape, rapists, and rape victims. Those with strong beliefs in such myths are more tolerant of the rapists and less tolerant of the victims than those with weaker beliefs in such myths (Varelas & Foley, 1998). These beliefs also can affect law enforcement. A study of police officers' perceptions of rape found that 51 percent of the officers provided definitions of rape that mixed outdated legal definitions with some victim blaming (Campbell & Johnson, 1997).

To understand why some social scientists and feminists classify the United States as a rape-prone society (see CONSIDERATIONS box on page 386), it is helpful to consider attitudes and beliefs that may be conducive to rape. Commonly held beliefs help to create a social climate that legitimizes rape and blames the victims. These include traditional gender roles, the perception that sex is adversarial, and the acceptance of violence in interpersonal relations. Both gender and professional status appear to affect attitudes toward rape victims. In one study, male undergraduates had the most negative attitudes toward rape victims, and female professionals had the most favorable attitudes. All males in the study held more negative attitudes of rape victims than did their female counterparts, regardless of the subject's professional status (White et al., 1999).

Those holding less traditional gender-role stereotypes appear to perceive rape scenarios overall as more serious and are less likely to blame the victim (Simonson & Subich, 1999). Some men ascribe to the belief that "real" men are expected to be sexually aggressive and overcome a woman's resistance (Stocks, 1991). One study found that college men who believed strictly in traditional gender roles expressed a greater likelihood of committing rape, were more accepting of violence against women, were more likely to blame rape survivors, and were more aroused by depictions of rape (Check & Malamuth, 1983). A sample of 477 male university students found that fraternity men reported significantly greater agreement with five statements supportive of rape and adversarial gender beliefs than a control group. This same study found that athletes reported significantly greater agreement with 14 rape-supportive statements than the control group (Boeringer, 1999). Kanin (1985) found that the majority of date rapists believed that rape could be justified under some conditions, for example, if the woman encouraged the man's sexual interest and advances, and allowed him to spend money on her but then refused to have sex. Only 19 percent of other men held this same view.

Beliefs about the victim as well as the perpetrator contribute to the common pattern of blaming the victim for the attack. An attractive woman in a low-cut blouse or short skirt is seen as "asking for it." Subjects who viewed a photograph of a victim wearing a short skirt attributed more responsibility to the victim than subjects not shown a photograph (Workman & Freeburg, 1999). Subjects in two studies were shown portraits of 32 young women who varied widely in physical attractiveness; they were told that half of these women had been victims of a crime and half had not and were asked to guess what type of crime they had experienced. In both studies, attractive women were more often categorized as victims of rape (DeJong, 1999). However, this finding may simply reflect the assumption that men would prefer to have sex—whether by force or consent—with an attractive woman than with a less attractive one.

It is of course unfair that people would blame innocent victims for crimes committed against them. Why might people do this? One answer is that it is personally reassuring to believe that innocent people are not victimized. The "just world" belief (Lerner, 1980) is a general belief that the world is fair, including the view that people get what they deserve and deserve what they get. By concluding that "she must have

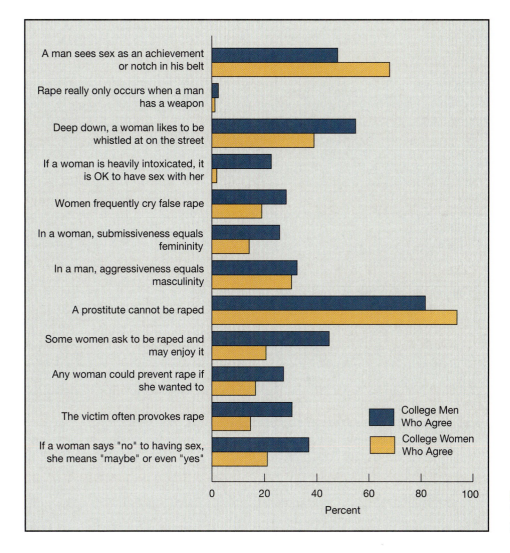

A man sees sex as an achievement or notch in his belt

Rape really only occurs when a man has a weapon

Deep down, a woman likes to be whistled at on the street

If a woman is heavily intoxicated, it is OK to have sex with her

Women frequently cry false rape

In a woman, submissiveness equals femininity

In a man, aggressiveness equals masculinity

A prostitute cannot be raped

Some women ask to be raped and may enjoy it

Any woman could prevent rape if she wanted to

The victim often provokes rape

If a woman says "no" to having sex, she means "maybe" or even "yes"

College Men Who Agree
College Women Who Agree

0   20   40   60   80   100
Percent

FIGURE 13.2 **Attitudes Toward Rape.** SOURCE: Holcomb et al., 1991.

asked for it," people can reassure themselves that the world is basically fair. This helps them believe that they themselves (or the women they love) will not become victims of rape. To believe otherwise can be threatening. After all, if the victim acted in a totally reasonable, rational, appropriate manner and still got raped, then anyone else who behaves properly could become a victim too. Many people want so desperately to hang on to the myth of a just world that they cannot bring themselves to believe this.

In one study a group of college students were given a scenario of a rape in which the sex and sexual orientation of the victim were varied; they were then asked questions designed to measure their perceptions of the rape and evaluation of the responsibility of the perpetrator and victim. Women were perceived to be more at fault for the incident if they were heterosexual, and men were perceived to be more at fault if they were homosexual (Ford et al., 1998). In a separate study, more responsibility, more pleasure, and fewer traumas were attributed to a homosexual victim than a heterosexual rape victim; male respondents attributed more responsibility and pleasure to the homosexual victim than female respondents (Mitchell et al., 1999).

Rape attitudes can affect the judicial system as well. When allegations of rape are reported to the police, the police investigate and report their findings to the district attorney. If the victim is blamed, the case may be less likely to be prosecuted. Unfounded cases of rape do not necessarily mean that a rape did not occur, only that there was not enough evidence to indict or prosecute the accused rapist. However, false allegations of rape do occur. These false allegations appear to reflect impulsive and desperate efforts by the accuser to cope with personal and social stress and serve

Sadistic Rape: preplanned ritualistic, brutal, and violent sexual assault

Anger Rape: sexual assault motivated by hatred and resentment toward women

Power Rape: sexual assault motivated by the desire to control and dominate the victim

Acquaintance Rape: forced sexual intercourse after an initial social encounter

Date Rape: forced sexual intercourse perpetrated by the victim's social escort

three major functions: providing an alibi, seeking revenge, and obtaining sympathy and attention (Kanin, 1994). The rate of false accusation of rape is similar to that for any other violent crime.

Motivations for Rape   No single motive or characteristic describes all rapes or rapists; as a result, rape has been divided into several categories (see Table 13.1). Although some characteristics of one type of rape may predominate within a specific act of rape, these categories are not necessarily mutually exclusive.

Sadistic Rape.   **Sadistic rapes** are preplanned ritualistic, brutal, and violent attacks "involving bondage, torture, and sexual abuse, in which aggression and sexuality become inseparable" (Groth & Hobson, 1983, pp. 167–168). The sadistic rapist wants his victim to suffer and gets pleasure from degrading or hurting her. This is the least common type of rape.

Anger Rape.   The **anger rape** is "an unpremeditated, savage, physical attack prompted by feelings of hatred and resentment" (Groth & Hobson, 1983, p. 163). Motivated by anger and resentment toward women, sexual gratification has little or nothing to do with anger rape. Anger rapes usually involve physical force against a total stranger. Many rapists believe women have wronged them, and they regard rape as a way of gaining revenge for this mistreatment (Lisak & Roth, 1988).

Power Rape.   **Power rape** is motivated by the desire to control and dominate the victim. Overwhelmed with an increasing sense of failure, sexual assault may be used in an attempt "to combat deep-seated feelings of insecurity and vulnerability" (Groth & Hobson, 1983, p. 165). Since the intent is not to physically injure the victim but to achieve control, power rapists usually use only enough force to cause the victim to cooperate in a submissive fashion.

Rape as a Means of Sexual Gratification.   Most **acquaintance rapes** and **date rapes** (rapes by a perpetrator known to the victim), as well as many others, may be categorized as motivated primarily by the desire for sexual gratification. Typically, no more

TABLE 13.1				
Categories of Rape				
	Motivation	**Use of Force**	**Relationship to Victim**	**Premeditation**
Sadistic	Complex motives involved	Ritualized, savage assault; may include bondage, mutilation, and murder	Stranger	Carefully planned
Anger	Revenge, anger, and resentment	Use of physical force and violence	Stranger	Unplanned, immediate
Power	To control and dominate	Only enough to make the victim cooperate	Stranger	Premeditated
Sexual Gratification	Sexual arousal	Likely to use no more force than necessary	Acquaintance or date	Unplanned, immediate

EXPLORING SEXUALITY ONLINE

Cyber-Rape

Computer networks are the high-tech place for people to meet and even have cybersex on the super-information highway. There are some people, however, who turn cybersex into cyber-rape. One online group had been playing a virtual reality consensual sex game when one user had his character forcibly take the female characters into an imaginary room and violently assault them. The Web-master kicked the offender off the network.

In another case, a California computer engineer pleaded no contest to having sadomasochistic sex with a 14-year-old boy he met through a computer bulletin board. Prosecutors are receiving special training in computer technology to help them keep up with the technology of online sex criminals (Armstrong, 1994).

---

force is used than the amount necessary to gain cooperation of the victim. If it becomes evident that an excessive amount of force or violence is necessary, the sexual gratification rapist may terminate the sexual assault. Sexual gratification rapes seem to far outnumber most other categories (Laumann et al., 1994).

Types of Rape

Gang Rape.   **Gang rape** is sexual assault of a victim by a group of assailants. As we have already discussed, male peer groups may support sexual coercion by socializing men to accept aggression as an acceptable way to obtain sex (Copenhaver & Grauerholz, 1991; Martin & Hummer, 1989). When there are pre-existing male bonds, such as those that link members of athletic teams, fraternities, or military units, it appears that rape does occur with greater frequency (Eskenazi, 1990, Frintner & Rubinson, 1993). In one study, almost 60 percent of sexual assaults on a college campus occurred at a fraternity house or involved a fraternity member (Copenhaver & Grauerholz, 1991). McCall (1995) wrote a memoir of his life as a young criminal, and in it he provided vivid descriptions of how he and his friends learned to lure girls from their school and from the community into gang hangouts, where all the young men would rape them. McCall said that these activities helped form bonds of loyalty and trust among the male group, which gradually evolved into a violent youth gang.

A study comparing a group of fraternity men with a group of independents found that fraternity men are more likely to know men who had engaged in coercive sex, to receive reinforcement from friends for sexually coercive activities, to participate in nonphysical sexual coercion, and to ply dates with drugs and alcohol as a tactic for obtaining sex (Boeringer, Shehan, & Akers, 1991). An analysis of individual offender and gang rape incidents reported to the Chicago police found that victims and offenders in gang rape incidents were younger and more likely to be unemployed than men who raped individually, but they were similar in marital status and race. This study found that gang rapes involved more alcohol and drug use, fewer weapons, more night attacks, less victim resistance, and more severe sexual assault outcomes than individual rapes (Ullman, 1999).

Acquaintance Rape.   Acquaintance rape, also called *date rape*, occurs when the rapist is someone known to the victim. In most crimes the relationship of the offender to the victim is irrelevant, but a distinction is made in the case of rape (see CONSIDERATIONS box). Most rape victims know their rapists (Harney & Muehlenhard, 1990; Koss, 1992; Parrott & Bechhofer, 1991). Date rape is most likely to occur in the early stage of dating; it is more likely to occur in the first month of a relationship than on the first date (Copenhaver & Grauerholz, 1991).

Gang Rape: rape of a victim by several attackers in rapid succession

Alcohol and Responsibility

Alcohol has long enjoyed a prominent place in seduction, and both men and women have tried to get someone drunk when they want to persuade that person to have sex. Alcohol does weaken inhibitions and self-control, and so its popularity as a tool of seduction is well founded. Still, in recent years some legal changes have been instigated to reduce this practice and protect women.

Many states now have laws that invalidate a woman's consent to sex if she is drunk at the time. This means that if a man has sex with a woman who is drunk, he is guilty of rape even if she consented (indeed, even if she initiated and controlled the sexual activity). In particular, if the next day she decides she wishes she had not had sex with him she can file a rape complaint and have him punished.

These laws are designed to protect women, but they create an interesting double standard that some women (and men) find offensive. If a man and a woman both consume alcohol during a date and then have sex, the woman is legally not responsible for her actions, but the man is legally responsible for his. In other words, sex between intoxicated adults constitutes rape by the man of the woman, and the man's drunkenness does not excuse his behavior, even though the woman's intoxication renders her consent legally invalid. If you consume alcohol on a date that may involve sex, you should be aware of these laws.

 Do you think these laws are degrading to women, because they assume that women but not men cannot be responsible for their actions when intoxicated?

Earlier in the chapter we discussed miscommunication and misinterpretation of consent; mixed signals between the members of a dating couple are often given as an excuse for date rape. Some argue that relatively few men engage in sexual coercion without realizing or being able to realize that what they are doing is rape (McCaw & Senn, 1998).

Although it is the most widely feared type of rape, stranger rape makes up only a small percentage of rapes (Figure 13.3). If stranger rapes were entirely eliminated, the total incidence of sexual coercion in the United States would decrease only slightly. In fact, many rapes occur between people who have had sexual relationships. A survey by O'Sullivan, Byers, and Finkelman (1998) found that the majority of rape victims had previously had consensual sex with the rapist. Nearly half said they had engaged in some consensual activity with the rapist on the same day as the rape. In a similar finding, most men who admitted to date rape said the rape followed some degree of consenting sexual activity (usually heavy petting or oral sex). Apparently, these instances occurred during a date or on an occasion in which the couple both felt attracted to each other and engaged in some sexual activity. The woman then wanted to stop short of intercourse, and the man refused to honor her wishes and forced himself upon her (Kanin, 1985).

Relationships that break up seem to constitute a special risk factor for rape. Felson and Krohn (1990) found that former husbands and boyfriends commit rape of their former partners at a far higher rate than would occur by chance. This pattern indicates that many men resent losing the option of having sex with a particular woman once they have had it, a reaction relevant to *narcissistic reactance theory* (discussed later in this chapter). Felson and Krohn also found that an elevated risk of physical injury to the victim accompanies rapes of former relationship partners. Anger over the breakup, over the relationship problems that led to the breakup, or over the

FIGURE 13.3 Women's Relationships With Men Who Forced Them to Do Something Sexual That They Did Not Want to Do.
SOURCE: Laumann et al., 1994.

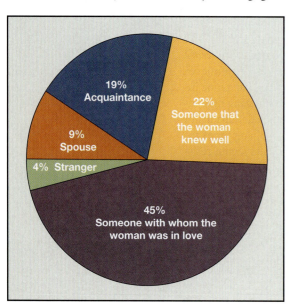

19% Acquaintance

22% Someone that the woman knew well

9% Spouse

4% Stranger

45% Someone with whom the woman was in love

loss of sexual partnership may cause these men to be especially violent toward their victims.

Because by definition the rapist and victim know one another in a date rape situation, the issue of consent takes on special significance. According to Muehlenhard et al. (1992), there are two ways in which consent and nonconsent can be defined: (1) nonconsent is assumed unless explicit consent is given; or (2) consent is assumed unless explicit nonconsent is given. College sexual offense policies often assume the first definition of nonconsent and state that consent for sexual behavior must be verbal, mutual, and reiterated for every new level of sexual behavior. Though the intent of such policies is good, practical application may be difficult if not impossible (Barrow et al., 1998).

Some men may misinterpret a woman's agreement to engage in holding and kissing as a desire to engage in intercourse (Goodchilds & Zellman, 1984; Muehlenhard, 1988; Muehlenhard & Linton, 1987). Others conclude that a woman's token resistance to intercourse is a pretense so that she does not appear too "easy." One study of 610 undergraduate women found that almost 40 percent had engaged in token resistance to sex at least once for this reason, or because of uncertainty about a partner's feelings or a desire to be in control (Muehlenhard & Hollabaugh, 1989). So in some cases the men were right; according to these findings, two out of every five women had said no to sex when they meant yes. This study also found that two out of every three women had said no when they meant maybe. A number of studies have found that some men regard rape as justifiable if a woman leads a man on by such actions as dressing provocatively or agreeing to go to his apartment (Goodchild & Zellman, 1984; Kanin, 1969, 1985; Muehlenhard & Linton, 1987; Muehlenhard & McCoy, 1991). Krahe (1998) found that women who used token resistance were more likely than other women to be the victims of sexual aggression and coercion. This finding suggests that clear and direct communication of your sexual wishes may be an important way to deter unwanted sexual aggression.

Hall (1998) examined how heterosexuals give consent for several types of sexual behavior. Participants in Hall's study were asked to describe how consent was given to engage in intercourse or other intimate sexual behavior. Hall found that participants gave permission for some sexual behaviors but not for every behavior in a sexual interaction. Permission giving was most strongly associated with initial sexual behaviors, oral sex, and intercourse; most permission giving for sexual behavior other than intercourse (for example, kissing, touching) was nonverbal. About 90 percent of male and female participants reported giving permission for penile/vaginal intercourse by either verbal or nonverbal means. About half the time both males and females use some nonverbal behavior, such as smiling or moving closer to their partner, to indicate that they want to engage in intercourse. Men report using more indirect nonverbal behaviors (for example, touching and kissing) to indicate sexual consent; women reported using indirect verbal behaviors more often to indicate their sexual consent (Hickman, 1998). It is obviously easier to misinterpret nonverbal behavior; reliance on such cues may lead to unwanted sexual activity (Burrow et al., 1998).

The Morning After

In her book *The Morning After: Sex, Fear, and Feminism on Campus* 25-year-old author Katie Roiphe (1993) accuses those she calls "rape-crisis feminists" of embracing the same sexist stereotypes women have long sought to dispel. Roiphe argues that the line between rape and regret has become blurred. She believes that rape occurs only when an explicit "No" is overridden by violence or the threat of violence and that including

behaviors such as getting a date drunk or verbally pressuring her to have sex drain the word *rape* of its meaning. The idea that women can't withstand verbal or emotional pressure infantilizes them and denies female sexuality.

 Do you agree with Roiphe's view?

—*Why or why not?*

Verbal statements produce clearer perceptions of consent than nonverbal actions. Contextual cues such as body language or facial expression rarely override linguistic cues (Lim & Roloff, 1999). An investigation into women's response strategies found that the more direct responses were less likely to be interpreted as token resistance by both men and women (Garcia, 1998). Direct responses also resulted in less positive feelings and more negative feelings being attributed to the woman in the situation. Men who held beliefs consistent with rape myths were more likely to interpret a woman's response as token resistance. Another study found that men with a stronger belief in token resistance are relatively more sensitive to situational cues; these same men were less likely to judge that rape had occurred unless the verbal refusal was strong and there were few cues of availability. Men with weaker beliefs in token resistance were more sensitive to verbal refusal (Osman & Davis, 1997).

Alcohol, marijuana, and other drugs are important risk factors in acquaintance rape (Slaughter, 2000). Drug or alcohol use by the victim, offender, or both occurs in the majority of incidents of sexual assault in close relationships (Copenhaver & Grauerholz, 1991; Harney & Muehlenhard, 1991; Koss, 1988). The use of alcohol may be a strategy used in combination with other tactics to influence a partner to have sex (Christopher & Frandsen, 1990). The psychological and pharmacological effects of alcohol impact the ability of sexually coercive and noncoercive men to discriminate when a female wants a partner to stop sexual advances (Marx et al., 1999). Alcohol also increases the likelihood that a male will misperceive a female companion's sexual intentions and that this misperception will lead to sexual assault (Abbey et al., 1998).

In the past few years, drug-facilitated sexual assaults have received media attention. In addition to alcohol, among the most popular drugs used in date rape are flunitrazepam (Rohypnol), a fast-acting benzodiazepine, and gamma-hydroxybutyrate (GHB). These drugs are widely available and act rapidly to produce disinhibition, relaxation of voluntary muscles, and lasting loss of memory for events that occur under the influence of the drug (Schwartz et al., 2000). If you experience the following symptoms, your drink may have been spiked with a date-rape drug: euphoria, slurred speech, nausea, dizziness, or loss of reflexes. Symptoms can appear within minutes of ingesting the drug. Some individuals experience seizures or fall into a coma. Most symptoms wear off in hours, but you should immediately ask someone to help you seek medical attention.

Marital Rape. There appears to be a strong association between marital violence and spousal or **marital rape.** Wives who are raped by their husbands are frequently the victims of verbal and physical abuse as well. In a study of 137 women who had reported beatings from their husbands, 34 percent also reported marital rape (Frieze, 1973). Marital rape often goes unrecognized by the victim. In this same study, 43 percent of the women said that sex was unpleasant because their husbands forced them to have sex. You do the math—9 percent of these women did not consider it marital rape when their husbands forced them to have sex.

In 1992 a man went on trial in South Carolina for the rape of his estranged wife; the jury was shown a videotape of the incident, in which the woman's hands and legs were tied with rope, and her mouth and eyes were covered with duct tape. The man's attorney argued that the woman enjoyed it when her husband slapped her and that her screams were part of a sex game. A jury of eight women and four men acquitted him. Prosecutors felt that denial played a role in the jury's verdict. "If we can say, 'She did something wrong, and that's why she was raped,' then somehow this won't happen to us" (Soto, 1992, p. A12).

In a study of women in San Francisco, 14 percent of married women claimed to have been sexually assaulted by their husbands (Russell, 1990). Most wives are extremely reluctant to press charges because of fear of reprisals, fear that they won't be believed, or self-blame. Thus, it is difficult to estimate accurately the number of marital rapes.

A minority of marriages include physical violence; wives are slightly more likely to attack their spouse physically (Archer, 2000). DeMaris (1997) found that couples in

Marital Rape: forced sexual intercourse perpetrated by the victim's spouse

violent marriages actually had sex more frequently than nonviolent couples. When he analyzed the data more closely, DeMaris found that the rate of sexual intercourse goes up when the husband is violent but not when the wife is violent. The explanation appeared to be that female victims of spousal abuse try to keep their husbands happy (and thereby prevent the violent abuse) by giving them more sex, in keeping with the social exchange model. Sex is a gift that a woman can give a man in return for his refraining from violence, but it is not something that a man can offer his wife in exchange for her refraining from violence. The increase in sexual activity as a result of marital violence is not clearly a case of rape, but it is, as DeMaris termed it, "sexual extortion," illicit, unfair pressure on the unfortunate victims.

Prison Rape.   Many male-on-male rapes occur in prison. Rape is considered to be a way for prisoners to assert dominance, to "prove their manhood," to satisfy sexual needs, and to exert power over other inmates (Donaldson, 1993). The exact number of sexual assaults that occur in prisons is unknown since few prison rapes are reported to authorities; fewer still are prosecuted. One conservative estimate is that more than 290,000 men are sexually assaulted behind bars each year (Donaldson, 1993). The term *homosexual rape* is misleading when applied to prison rapes, since the assailants and victims almost always consider themselves to be heterosexual. There is very little information available regarding sexual attacks on women prisoners by other female inmates or by guards.

Wartime Rape.   Since the time of ancient Greece there have been reports of mass rapes of women during wartime. Wartime rape is used as a means to dominate, humiliate, and control the enemy. Rapes of Belgian women by German soldiers were reported during World War I. In 1937 Japanese troops carried out the infamous "Rape of Nanking" on Chinese women in the city of Nanking. During World War II between 100,000 and 200,000 mostly Korean women were abducted as sexual conscripts for the Japanese army (Swiss & Giller, 1993). Court-martial records of U.S. soldiers reveal that rape of Vietnamese women by American GIs occurred numerous times during the Vietnam War. In 1994 the Hutu majority in the central African nation of Rwanda implemented the mass slaughter of the Tutsi minority. In just 100 days, estimates of the number of women and girls raped in Rwanda ran as high as 250,000 to 500,000 (Flanders, 1998).

There have been extensive reports of mass rapes perpetrated by Serbian soldiers on an estimated 30,000 to 50,000 Muslim and Croatian women and girls and an unknown number of rapes of men in the former Yugoslavia. It is nearly impossible to estimate the number of men raped during the war in the Balkans, primarily because the stigma attached to male rape is similar to that in the United States—many men would rather not report that they were raped. In 1996 the United Nations International Criminal Tribunal ruled that wartime rape is a punishable crime, marking the first time that sexual assault has been treated separately as a war crime.

Theoretical Perspectives on Rape   There are many theories about the reasons for rape; no one model is likely to apply to all cases. Moreover, the scientific research on rape tends to be scattered and based on a variety of imperfect research methods. Hence there are several different theories about the reason(s) for rape. No single theory stands out as the right one, but some of them are beginning to be ruled out, as you will see shortly. Most focus on rape by men; rape and coercion by women have just begun to be studied.

Poor Social Skills.   One theory is that men rape because they cannot obtain sex any other way. In particular, it has been suggested that rapists lack social skills that might persuade women to have sexual relationships. They turn to rape because they cannot relate to women in an appropriate, normal manner. This theory has been largely abandoned. Several studies have found that rapists do not lack social skills, as compared to other men (Koralewski & Conger, 1992; Muehlenhard & Falcon, 1990;

Segal & Marshall, 1985; Ward, McCormack, & Hudson, 1997). Even more to the point, rapists do not seem to lack for other sexual partners. Many rapists have wives and girlfriends (for example, Brownmiller, 1975). Kanin (1985) found that sexually coercive men reported a higher rate of sexual activity, including about twice as many orgasms per week, than the average man. Several studies have found that rapists have had more sex partners (not counting the rape victims) than other men (Lalumiere et al., 1996; Mahoney, Shively, & Traw, 1986). Thus, rape does not appear to be a desperate last resort by men who cannot get sex any other way.

Feminism and Power.   The feminist approach emphasizes that rape is about power rather than sex. This view has been articulated in many feminist writings, but Susan Brownmiller's (1975) book *Against Our Will* was the most famous statement of this perspective, as well as the most forceful. Brownmiller asserted that rape is one of the many strategies men use to dominate women: Men are socialized to become rapists and to support rape by other men because all men benefit from rape. Brownmiller has been widely quoted for her powerful statement that rape "is nothing more or less than a conscious process of intimidation by which all men keep all women in a state of fear"—a statement that was printed on the cover of the paperback edition of her book.

Two assertions are central to the feminist position. The first is that rape is not centrally or primarily about sex. That is, the rapist is not primarily motivated by the quest for sexual gratification. Instead, women are raped to keep them in an inferior position in society. To support this view, Brownmiller pointed out that many rapists already have sex partners and that victims of rape are not just the most desirable sex partners but also include homely, elderly, and very young women.

Others dispute the claim that rape is not about sex. After reviewing the evidence, Palmer (1988) said the fact that many rapists already have wives or other sex partners proves nothing. For example, he pointed out that most customers of prostitutes and consumers of pornography likewise have wives or girlfriends, but that doesn't prove that sex is irrelevant to prostitution and pornography. Indeed, by the same logic, even adultery would have to be classified as not relevant to sex, because by definition adulterers are married and thus already have a sex partner. Although some victims of rape are elderly women, these are a distinct minority. Most rape victims are young women in their prime; according to national crime statistics fewer than 8 percent of victims are past the age of 40 (Felson & Krohn, 1990). Palmer (1988) proposed that rape victims are chosen for a combination of their sex appeal and vulnerability; in some cases an older woman may be chosen because she is less able to fight back than a young, vigorous woman. Generally, though, rapists choose women around the age of peak sex appeal.

The second point in the feminist theory is that rape involves a conspiracy by all men against all women. That is, all men benefit from rape and thus provide some degree of support for rape. Even women who are not victimized by being raped are affected because the possibility of rape keeps them in an inferior position. Women may become afraid to go out at night or do other things that would enable them to compete against men for power in society. Arguing against this theory, Roiphe (1993) points out that it is an empirical fact that men are victimized by all violent crimes far more often than women (rape is an exception); if anyone is kept indoors out of fear of crime, it should be men. More generally, there is no evidence to suggest that the majority of men support rape or seek to benefit by it.

More broadly, the feminist approach treats rape as reflecting the power struggles between men and women. A feminist perspective on rape, with a focus on sexual socialization, claims that rape myth beliefs deny or justify male sexual aggression against women. Ellis and Beattie (1983) sought to test this by comparing 26 American cities on various indices of gender equality and rape rates. Few correlations were significant. In fact, the study found that the incidence of rape was higher in cities where gender equality was higher. In another test performed by Korman and Leslie (1982), they predicted that women who paid their way on dates would be less likely to be victims of sexual coercion because paying one's way promotes equality. These researchers found that the women who paid their own way were *more* likely to be subjected to sexual aggression by their male dates. Although no one of these findings should be considered decisive, they do suggest that rape does not have a direct relationship with gender equality.

Most feminist theorists are women and thus approach rape from a women's perspective. The theory that rape is not about sex may not be a correct assessment of the perpetrator's motivations, but it is likely to be a very valid and accurate summary of the experiences of the victim. Rape victims do not regard what they have suffered as a sex act. Instead, they typically feel themselves to be victims of violent crime.

Evolutionary Strategy.   According to evolutionary theorists Randy Thornhill and Craig Palmer (2000), rape is best viewed in a larger theoretical framework of natural selection. In their book *A Natural History of Rape: Biological Bases of Sexual Coercion*, they argue that since the majority of rape victims are women of childbearing age, rape is not an act of pathology but a strategy for procreation. Critics of this position argue that rapists generally operate on a "hit-and-run" basis—which may be all right for stocking sperm banks, but not as effective if the goal is to produce offspring who will survive in a challenging environment (Ehrenreich, 2000).

The evolutionary approach of Thornhill and Palmer does not necessarily mean that today's rapists are trying to make babies. Rather, they claim that over the thousands of years during which the human race evolved, some genetic predispositions to obtain sex by force were passed along because they succeeded in creating offspring. Evolutionary approaches emphasize that forcible sex is not the best strategy for passing on one's genes (consistent with Ehrenreich's criticism) but may be the only option in some cases. Highly powerful and successful males do not need to rape, because they can often find willing partners. But men who cannot attract women—especially young men with relatively low social status—may find that rape is the only way they can obtain sex. Low-status men who meekly accept their lack of sex appeal did not produce offspring, but low-status men who raped may have had some success at passing on their genes.

Evolutionists emphasize that males tend to desire sex with many partners but females are highly selective and hence not receptive to many different males. This produces a conflict between men and women. Most men will respond to this conflict by simply trying to persuade the women they desire, but some men may resort to force. The inclination toward promiscuity offers one explanation of why some men who have wives or girlfriends might still commit rape.

These arguments are largely speculations, and Thornhill and Palmer (2000) acknowledge that the current state of scientific knowledge does not permit many firm conclusions about whether there are genetic or evolutionary factors in rape. Moreover, some evidence does not fit a simple evolutionary analysis. Many rapists are not simply "losers" at the bottom of the social status hierarchy. Hale (1997) found that incarcerated rapists had a mean educational level of 12.7 years, ranging from seventh grade to college graduates, which does not fit the view that they have uniformly low educational attainment.

Evolutionary approaches to explaining rape may have some validity, but most evolutionary psychologists agree that biology alone is not sufficient to explain its cause or excuse its occurrence. Yes, rape is one way to pass along genes, so some men may have inherited a biological tendency to be willing to use force to obtain sex. However, rape will only occur if that tendency is nurtured by other experiences.

Social Learning Theory.   Ellis (1989) theorizes that while evolution has instilled in men the greater desire for multiple sexual partners, social learning also is relevant. Social experiences teach men various strategies for obtaining sex, one being the use of force or coercion. This is consistent with evidence that rapists tend to use a variety of legal and marginally legal techniques for getting sex in addition to rape. For example, Craig et al. (1989) found that sexually coercive men were more likely than other men to say they had tried to obtain sex by making false promises or false declarations of love. Likewise, Kanin (1985) found that date rapists were more likely than other men to report having tried to get sex by getting a woman drunk, falsely promising marriage, threatening to end the relationship, or threatening to leave the woman stranded far from home at the end of a date.

Narcissistic Reactance.   Based on a review of research findings, a recent theory of rape has been put forward by Baumeister, Catanese, and Wallace (2002) that combines two concepts from social and personality psychology. The first involves the concept of *reactance*, a person's psychological response to being deprived of the freedom to act the way he or she wants (Brehm, 1966). When people are told they may not do something, they typically have at least one of three reactions: (1) They want the forbidden activity all the more; (2) they try to do what they were told not to do; or (3) they may attack the person who told them not to do it. Hence, when a man wants or expects to have sex with a woman, and she refuses, he may experience reactance. As a result, he may: (1) desire her more; (2) try to have sex with her; or (3) attack her for saying no.

While women refuse men's sexual advances fairly often, rape is relatively rare. Baumeister et al. (2002) link reactance to a second concept, narcissism. **Narcissism** is defined as excessive self-love; narcissists think of themselves as superior to other people, want to be admired, believe that they deserve special treatment and are entitled to things that others cannot have, exploit other people, have low empathy, envy others, enjoy being envied, and are generally arrogant or conceited (American Psychiatric Association, 1994). Baumeister et al. propose that the self-centered men who exhibit these patterns are less willing than other men to take no for an answer when they approach a woman for sex. They are more likely than other men to believe that they are entitled to have sex with a particular woman, to assume that she will want to have sex, and to use exploitative or coercive methods to get what they want. Narcissists are also less likely to feel empathic concern over her feelings if she is forced into sex against her will.

The narcissistic reactance theory treats the goal of rape as both sexual and egotistical. The rapist desires sex for its own sake but also because having a "conquest" gives him an ego trip. This would explain why most rapists tend to deny that they used force—they prefer to think that the woman consented, because her consent would be more flattering to the man's ego. Rapists (especially date rapists) tend to have peer groups that talk about sex and put pressure on their members to report sexual conquests (Craig et al., 1989; Kanin, 1985; Krahe, 1998). These men feel pressure to live up to the expectations of their peer group, so they feel they need to have sexual adventures to boast about. If a narcissistic man tells his friends he is going out on a date with an attractive woman, he might be reluctant to report that she rejected his advances; he may be willing to use force to get his way so he can brag about it to his friends.

The narcissistic reactance theory seems to fit well with what is known about some categories of rape, such as date rape and marital rape. It does not apply as well to violent and sadistic rapes, in which the rapist derives pleasure from making the woman suffer. Such rapes are a small minority of rapes, however (Groth, 1979).

Characteristics of Rapists   Although most rapists are men, most men are certainly not rapists. While men who commit rape exhibit a wide range of backgrounds, personality traits, and motivations, some common characteristics have been identified. Many rapists have self-centered personalities that may render them insensitive to other's feelings (Dean & Malamuth, 1997; Marshall, 1993; Pithers, 1993). You may recognize this characteristic from the description of the narcissist previously. In fact, Scully (1990) found that many rapists in prison described themselves as highly talented and successful individuals who were much loved by everyone (even, in some cases, their victims—an absurdly false belief!). In general rapists are no less intelligent or more mentally ill than other people (Renzetti & Curran, 1989), and many have no evidence of a psychological illness (Dean & de Bruyn-Kops, 1982).

Men with a high tendency to rape have more rape supportive attitudes, are more likely to consider victims to be responsible for rape, and are less knowledgeable about

Narcissism: excessive love or admiration of oneself

the negative impact on the victims. These men tend to misperceive cues in social interactions with women, fail to generate inhibitory self-verbalizations to suppress association of sex and aggression, and have more coercive sexual fantasies (Drieschner & Lange, 1999).

Although most studies find that rapists and sexually coercive men respond more positively to rape depictions than other men, it would be misleading to say that they actually prefer rape. In fact, the usual finding is that the coercive men respond positively to both rape and consensual sex, whereas noncoercive men only enjoy the consensual sex and find depictions of rape to be a severe turnoff (Abel et al., 1977; Baxter, Barbaree, & Marshall, 1986; Freund et al., 1986). One study found that rapists had a slight preference for consensual sex (Baxter et al., 1986). The point is simply that rapists do not seem to care very much whether the woman consents or not. Low empathy, rather than an actual preference for forcible sex, seems the most fitting explanation of this pattern.

A national research study of a representative sample of male college students found that four factors predispose males to be sexually coercive with women: a hostile home environment; a history of delinquent behavior; a heavy emphasis on sexual conquests to gain self-esteem and status with the peer group; and deep-seated hostility toward women, together with negatively defined exaggerated masculinity (Malamuth et al., 1991). Several studies have shown that men who commit stranger rapes frequently have difficulty establishing interpersonal relationships, have low self-esteem, and feel socially and personally inadequate (Baxter et al., 1984; Groth & Burgess, 1977; Levin & Stava, 1987; Marshall & Barbaree, 1984). However, other studies have found social competence to be unrelated to rape behavior (Muehlenhard & Falcon, 1990).

One study asked a group of men to imagine the possibility of forcing sex on a woman against her will in which there was no risk of being caught, no one would find out, there was no risk of disease, and their reputations would not be damaged. Thirty-five percent of the men indicated that there was some likelihood, although in most cases only a slight likelihood, that under these conditions they would force sex on the woman (Malamuth, 1981). A later study using a similar method found 27 percent of the men indicated some likelihood if there was no chance of getting caught (Young & Thiessen, 1992). Such findings have been used to support the feminist position that many men are potential rapists, but they may be misleading. Evidence suggests that responses to the question about hypothetical rape willingness have little or no relation to actually engaging in rape or sexual coercion (Greenlinger & Byrne, 1987). The reason for the high numbers is that the question is usually embedded in a series of questions about sexual fantasies and sexual desires. Martin and Kerwin (1991) asked a similar question in two contexts: the first was within a series of questions about sexual activities, and the second in questions about violent crimes. Far fewer men said yes when the question was presented in the context of violent crime. Recall that many women have fantasies about being forced into sex (Leitenberg & Henning, 1995). Both scenarios are abstract fantasies that have little or no relationship to actual behavior or intentions. In other words, most men do not want to rape, and most women do not want to be raped, even if they might occasionally enjoy the fantasy.

Many men fail to have orgasms during rape. Groth and Burgess (1977) found that a third of rapists experienced some form of sexual dysfunction during the rape, most commonly lack of erection or difficulty in ejaculating (and sometimes ejaculation without any sensation of pleasure). Groth (1979) pointed out that erectile dysfunction among rapists appears to be limited to those situations, for generally these men report good sexual response and performance with consenting partners. Some rapists resort to masturbating themselves in order to get an erection, and others demand that their victims stimulate them orally in the hope of becoming erect. Groth also noted that premature ejaculation was the least frequent sexual dysfunction reported by rapists, even though it is the most common sexual dysfunction reported by men of comparable age. The discrepancy between the high rate of impotence and the low rate of premature ejaculation among rapists suggests that the rape situation makes normal sexual response difficult, due perhaps to fear of getting caught, anxiety, guilt, shame, or negative emotions of the victim. These data suggest that the rape situation is not generally conducive to men's sexual pleasure and indeed often causes a poor penile response. These findings pertain mainly to stranger rapes, however, and it is possible that the more common patterns (especially date rape) do not elicit sexual dysfunction at the same rates.

Rape Resistance Strategies to resist or avoid rape depend on the situation and the individual. Screaming, hitting, kicking, and biting may discourage or deter a rapist, or they may frighten or anger him and increase the likelihood of injury.

A Bureau of Justice Statistics (1986) study found that over 80 percent of women used one or more forms of resistance against a rapist, including physical resistance, screaming, running away, or verbally pleading and attempting to persuade the rapist not to attack. About 19 percent of those who resisted reported that resistance worsened the situation in some way. Other studies have found that resistance of any kind was associated with an incomplete attack (Bart & O'Brien, 1985; Quinsey & Upfold, 1985). Yet another study found that forceful physical resistance by the victim was unrelated to the use of physical force by the offender during or after the rape. It was the offender's use of physical force prior to rape that was significantly related to force during and after the rape (Ullman, 1998).

The problem of whether to resist was aptly summed up by Ghiglieri (2000). Putting up a physical resistance to attempted rape has both a benefit and a cost. The benefit is that it reduces the risk of being raped, insofar as resistance sometimes succeeds in preventing the rape. The cost is that it also increases the risk of being physically injured during the rape, if the rapist decides to fight to get what he wants. Ghiglieri proposed that the benefits of resistance outweigh the costs, because the reduction in completed rapes is larger than the increase in physical injury. It must be emphasized that these are statistical averages, and that no single answer is optimal for all cases.

Some experts say that a woman's reaction when she is first approached by an assailant can determine the outcome. If possible, at the first encounter with a potential rapist, act with firmness and self-assurance. If you believe that you or your loved ones may be seriously hurt if you try to defend yourself, then don't. If the rapist has a gun to your head, screaming or fighting with him might be dangerous. Strategies that have been used successfully include pretending that a male is about to arrive or is waiting, pretending to faint, acting insane, and urinating. If he tries to force you into a car, scream "no" and run. If the attacker is in your car, attempt to drive erratically or do something to attract attention. If you feel it is safe to attack and you are able to do so, aim for the man's eyes, ears, nose, mouth, Adam's apple, or groin (Brody, 1992).

One other response has been noted to be remarkably effective—vomiting. Although we do not have systematic data, a growing body of anecdotal evidence suggests that when a rape victim vomits during an attack, the would-be rapist often stops and flees. This pattern makes the most sense if the rapist considers rape a sexual act. Being vomited on is almost universally a source of a powerful disgust reaction. Many rapists have difficulty maintaining an erection during rape, and vomiting is likely to make that even more difficult.

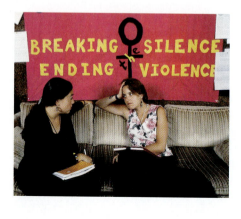

Rape crisis centers provide medical, legal, and psychological services to rape survivors.

Rape Survivors In a recent study, medical personnel found that 68 percent of female victims of sexual assault experience genital trauma at one or more sites of injury (Slaughter et al., 1996). However severe the physical injury, the psychological trauma of rape often inflicts far more long-term damage. Rape victims are faced with a number of crises immediately after surviving a rape. They may be confronted with the possibility of contracting one or more sexually transmitted infections, including HIV, or becoming pregnant. Sexually transmitted infections have been found in up to 40 percent of rape victims and pregnancy in up to 5 percent (Holmes et al., 1997). Again, these numbers apply to stranger rapes; and date rapes may be different.

TABLE 13.2

Ten Things *NOT* to Say to a Rape Survivor

1. Why didn't you stop him?
2. If rape is inevitable, why not just lie back and enjoy it?
3. I've taken self-defense and I'm too smart ever to let that happen to me.
4. Maybe God is punishing you for sleeping around.
5. It must have been God's will.
6. You should never have gone out with that guy. Couldn't you tell he was a creep?
7. You must have said or done something to provoke him.
8. You've had sex before, what's the big deal?
9. Don't tell anyone; they'll never believe you and it will just give you a bad name.
10. I just can't believe you. He can get any girl he wants, why would he have to rape you?

Rape Trauma Syndrome: two-phase response patterns of rape survivors

Rape survivors must also consider the implications of reporting the rape to the police and the responses of friends, family members, and others who become aware of the assault. Rape can be very difficult for the victims' partners. They may feel guilt, anger, and rage toward the assailant, and confusion about how to help. Unsupportive family members can have a severely negative impact on a rape survivor's adjustment (Davis et al., 1991). Rape survivors need to be believed and supported, not have their judgment questioned. They need to regain control of their lives, and perhaps most of all, they need to be listened to (Castleman, 1980). If you don't know what to say, see Table 13.2 for a list of things *not* to say to a survivor of rape.

Unlike most crimes, it is often a difficult decision whether to report a rape. The rape victim must consider the reactions of those around her, repercussions from the perpetrator, possible media exposure, and the difficulties involved in testifying in court (Table 13.3).

The psychological impact of rape can be profound. Some of the common response patterns of rape survivors have been collectively identified as **rape trauma syndrome** (Burgess & Homstrom, 1974). Rape trauma syndrome occurs in two phases: the acute

TABLE 13.3

Rape Reporting Rationales

Reasons *For* Reporting a Rape to the Police		Reasons *For Not* Reporting a Rape to the Police	
To keep the incident from happening again	60%	Private or personal matter or took care of it herself	26%
To punish the offender	47	Afraid of reprisal by the offender or his family	17
To stop the incident from happening again	31	Police would be inefficient, ineffective, or insensitive	16
To fulfill a duty	18	Lack of proof or no way to find the offender	12
To get help after the incident	15	Reported it to someone else	10
Because there was evidence or proof	8	Police wouldn't think it important enough	7
Because it was a crime	5	Did not think it was important enough	5
Other	20	Offender was unsuccessful	5
		Other: (embarrassed, feeling of being partly responsible, wanting to get event over with, fear of questions, fear of publicity)	33

SOURCE: Harlow, 1991, p. 6.

phase and the reorganization phase. The acute phase of rape trauma syndrome occurs immediately after the rape and may last for several weeks. In the first hours after a rape, the survivor's responses are characterized by either an expressive reaction of obvious emotion or a calm, controlled, matter-of-fact appearance. The feelings that accompany the acute phase include depression, anxiety, anger, distrust, guilt, and a sense of powerlessness (Finkelhor & Yllo, 1985; Koss et al., 1988; Muehlenhard & McCoy, 1991; Murnen, Perot, & Byrne, 1989). Physical symptoms, including nausea, headaches, and sleep disorders, also are commonly experienced (Lesserman & Drossman, 1995; Walker, 1994). A woman is more likely to experience guilt and blame herself for a rape that did not involve physical coercion (Murnen, Perot, & Byrne, 1989). She may feel that she was somehow responsible for the rape, or that there was something she should have known or done that would have prevented the assault. Such self-blame leads to higher rates of depression (Frazier, 1991).

The emotional turmoil often continues during the long-term reorganization phase of rape trauma syndrome, which may last for many years. Long-term depression is especially likely for women who continue to have contact with the offender, as may be the case in marital or acquaintance rapes (Koss et al., 1988). Many rape survivors find that their sexuality is severely affected. One study found that 40 percent of rape survivors refrained from sexual contact for 6 months to a year after the assault; almost 75 percent reported that the frequency of their sexual activity remained below preassault levels for as long as 4 to 6 years (Burgess & Holstrom, 1979). In another study, although only a small number of rape survivors reported physiological orgasmic difficulties, they did report fear of sex and a lack of arousal and desire (Becker et al., 1984).

Rape victims may develop **posttraumatic stress disorder (PTSD),** a long-term anxiety disorder characterized by flashbacks, sleep disturbances, nightmares, depression, and anxiety (American Psychiatric Association, 1994). Fears of situations associated with the trauma may severely curtail a rape survivor's activities. For example, if the rape occurred in the victim's home, she may need to change residence. If the rape occurred outdoors, she may experience *agoraphobia*, a fear of being outside her home.

Women who receive help soon after a sexual assault experience less severe emotional repercussions than those who delay treatment (Duddle, 1991). The first phase of treatment of rape survivors typically involves crisis intervention to provide support and information; this helps the victim express her feelings and develop strategies to cope with the trauma (Resick & Schicke, 1990). Often rape survivors have a need to talk about the assault and its impact on their lives. Group or individual counseling can help survivors cope with the emotional consequences of rape and regain a sense of control over their lives.

Statistics on the incidence of emotional and physical trauma of rape should be combined with recognition of what sort of rape is involved. Being raped by a gang of violent strangers may have effects that differ from being forced by a boyfriend to have intercourse, although of course both are genuine instances of criminal victimization and the sense of betrayal of being assaulted by someone you trusted can be profound. Murnen, Perot, and Byrne (1989) found that many female victims of sexual coercion seemed to dismiss the event as unimportant. In their sample, about half the victims had no further contact with the rapist, but over 25 percent still considered him to be a friend, and 11 percent said the rapist was now their current boyfriend. Probably most of these instances involved acquaintance or date rape. If the man apologized, the woman was more likely to forgive him and remain friends with him. In a different sample, the authors (Koss et al., 1988) concluded that 40 percent of date rape victims would go on to have consensual sex with the rapist on a subsequent occasion.

Just as there is no single answer to the question of why rape occurs, there is no right answer to the question of how rape affects people. Some victims will suffer for years, while others seem to dismiss the incident as unimportant and even carry on a romantic relationship with the man who raped them. The national sample studied by Laumann et al. (1994, 1999) contained similar variability. Some victims of rape suffered health problems, sexual problems, and lowered happiness in life for many years—but many others seemed to recover completely and go on with their lives.

Posttraumatic Stress Disorder (PTSD): characteristic symptoms following exposure to an extreme traumatic stressor involving direct personal experience of an event that involves actual or threatened death or serious injury

Are there any factors that predict who will suffer long-term problems and who will not? A sample of rape victims, mostly involving stranger rape, studied by Meyer and Taylor (1986) attempted to predict who would cope best. Victims who blamed themselves suffered more problems than others. Women who engaged in stress reduction practices such as meditation and positive thinking recovered better, as did women who received social support from counselors, friends, and family. In contrast, women who withdrew from social interaction (such as by staying home more and more) fared worse. These differences may reflect aspects of the women's personalities that preceded the rape, so the causative relationship between the strategies and recovery is unclear. The different strategies do, however, seem to predict the long-term outcomes.

WWW SEXUAL HEALTH AND YOU

What to Do If You've Been Raped

Making decisions after a sexual assault can be extremely difficult. There are no right answers, only what is right for you. However, here are some suggestions on what to do if you have been sexually assaulted.

1. Go to a safe place and call someone you trust for help and support.

2. Help preserve evidence. Don't change your clothing, wash any part of your body, comb your hair, or change anything about the scene where the assault occurred.

3. Get medical attention even if you do not have any obvious physical injuries. Medical attention can help preserve evidence as well as provide preventive treatment for sexually transmitted infections or pregnancy.

4. Report the assault to the police. This keeps your options open but does not mean that you have decided to seek prosecution. To receive compensation for medical costs or losses incurred as a result of rape, the assault must be reported.

5. Get counseling as soon as possible even if you aren't experiencing any severe psychological symptoms.

IT IS NOT YOUR FAULT. Rape is a crime and it is the rapist, not the victim, who is responsible for criminal behavior.

Rape Prevention Rape prevention efforts may reduce, but certainly will not eliminate, rape. Changing cultural attitudes that support rape is neither a quick nor an easy solution. However, victim empathy programs that educate men about the trauma caused by rape may make it less likely that these men would commit rape (Hamilton & Yee, 1990). Many colleges and universities offer or require lectures or workshops on date rape and some provide women students campus escorts after dark. Men Against Rape or Men Can Stop Rape groups have formed on several college campuses and in conjunction with rape crisis centers to stop perpetuating rape myths and to work with women in preventing rape.

Victims cannot necessarily prevent rape, and it is important to avoid victim blaming when discussing rape prevention. However, until cultural attitudes about rape change, women may want to reduce the risk of being raped by avoiding high-risk situations, learning self-defense strategies, never admitting that you are home alone, locking windows and using deadlock bolts on doors, not allowing strangers into your home without proper identification, and screaming loudly to attract attention if you feel threatened.

Sexual Abuse of Children

Sexual abuse of children is any form of sexual contact between an adult and a child, with or without the use of force or physical threat. Even if he or she cooperates with the behavior, a child does not have the experience, knowledge, or emotional maturity to provide informed consent to sexual involvement. Young children are not capable of understanding the impact and consequences of sexual behavior.

A wide range of behaviors can be considered abusive, including the following: fondling; kissing; oral-genital stimulation; oral, anal, or vaginal penetration; exhibition of nudity; observing the child nude; taking nude photos of a child; and showing sexually explicit photos to a child. Some behaviors are abusive in any context. Other behaviors, such as bathing, cuddling, and kissing a young child can be nurturing and caring or can be abusive if the motivation is to provide sexual gratification for the adult. Touching of the genitals is by far the most frequent sexually abusive behavior; it occurs in over 80 percent of the cases of sexual abuse of boys and over 90 percent of the cases of sexual abuse of girls. Vaginal intercourse is more common when boys are sexually abused by older girls or by women, occurring in 42 percent of the reported cases of women abusing boys. Vaginal penetration occurs in only 14 percent of the cases of girls abused by men (Laumann et al., 1994).

Prevalence of Child Sexual Abuse   No one knows how many children are sexually abused every year. As with other sex crimes, child sexual abuse often goes unreported. Statistics vary widely depending on the population surveyed and the definition of sexual abuse. A 1985 report by the U.S. Department of Health and Human Services estimated that one in every four or five girls and one in every nine or ten boys is sexually abused before age 18. Kohn (1987) estimates that at least 10 percent of boys and 25 percent of girls in the United States have been sexually abused as children. A 1990 survey by psychologist David Finkelhor and colleagues found that 16 percent of men and 27 percent of women disclosed a history of being sexually touched or of penetration during their childhood. According to the Janus Report (1992), 11 percent of men and 23 percent of women reported childhood sexual molestation. The National Health and Social Life Survey found that about 12 percent of the men and about 17 percent of the women report that adults had touched them sexually when they were children (Laumann et al., 1994).

An examination of the prevalence of child sexual abuse among blacks and whites living in Los Angeles in 1994 found that 34 percent of the total sample reported at least one incident of sexual abuse prior to age 18 (Wyatt et al., 1999). Results show that whites had a higher prevalence of abuse, reported being abused more in public environments, and reported more incidents of attempted or completed rape than did blacks. While comparisons with 1984 data revealed no significant differences in prevalence rates over the 10-year period, changes in the location of abuse, severity of incidents, and length of time during which abuse occurred were noted. Perhaps the most comprehensive estimate of the prevalence of child sexual abuse analyzed data from 16 separate studies in the United States and Canada. A summary of these studies found that approximately 22 percent of women and 9 percent of men indicated that they were sexually abused as children (Gorey & Leslie, 1997).

Incest   **Incest** is sexual contact between family members, one of whom may be a child (see Figure 13.4). Family members are typically defined as blood relatives, but some researchers and therapists have broadened the definition to include sexual contact with a child by any person in a position of trust and authority, including stepparents, stepbrothers, stepsisters, and others who have a family relationship with the child. It is felt that the presence or the absence of a blood relationship between incest participants is of far less significance than the kinship roles they play (Sgroi, 1982). Incest usually occurs within the context of family disruption and dysfunction. Spousal abuse, marital problems, and alcohol abuse are common factors in incestuous families (Alter-Reid et

Sexual Abuse of Children: sexual activity between an adult and a minor

Incest: sexual relations between persons who are so closely related that their marriage is illegal or forbidden by custom or law

al., 1986, Sirles & Franke, 1989). Incest often repeats from generation to generation. A study of 154 cases of children who were sexually abused by a family member found that more than one third of the male offenders and about half of the female offenders either had been abused themselves or were exposed to abuse as children (Faller, 1989).

The incest taboo is the first sexual rule that a child implicitly learns and the only sexual restriction that is in effect throughout a person's lifetime (Frayser, 1985). There is no known society that does not have a rule that prohibits sexual relations between a father and his daughter, a mother and her son, and a brother and his sister (Frayser, 1985). The only exceptions are a few societies (for example, ancient Egypt, Hawaii, and the Incas) that permitted brother-sister marriages among the deified royalty; because they were considered gods, they could not marry commoners. In many societies, the taboo extends only to the parent from whom inheritance or descent is determined, your *matrilineal* or *patrilineal* relatives. In most of the United States, first cousins, regardless of whether they are maternal or paternal cousins, are forbidden to marry. However, in other cultures, first cousins are preferred marriage partners.

Most of the identified cases of incest involved father-daughter incest for which the father was eventually arrested. One study found sexual abuse by fathers or stepfathers in 4.5 percent of women surveyed (Russell, 1984). Stepfathers were more likely to be abusers than biological fathers. Seventeen percent of the women reported being abused by their stepfathers; only 2 percent identified their biological father as the abuser. Another study found that of those women who reported being sexually abused, fathers were the perpetrators in 14 percent of the cases and stepfathers in 21 percent (Boyer, Fine, & Killpack, 1991). The abuse often starts as a "playful" activity involving wrestling, tickling, kissing, and touching; over time, the activity gradually moves to include genital touching followed by oral or manual stimulation of the genitals and, in some cases, intercourse. In most cases, a father is more likely to use persuasion than physical force. He may convince his daughter that it is his responsibility to teach her about sex, may offer her rewards for her participation and silence or may exploit her need for affection and attention.

There are far fewer reports of mothers sexually abusing their children (Marvasti, 1986). This may be due at least partially to the fact that society permits women to touch children in ways that can be rationalized as being nonsexual and harmless. For example, a mother may bathe a child long after the child is able to bathe alone, may sleep

Cleopatra (69BC–30BC) ruled Egypt with her younger brother, Ptolemy XIII, who was also her husband.

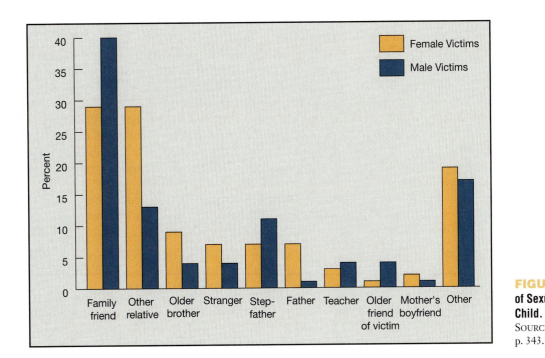

FIGURE 13.4 **Relationship of Sexual Abuser to Abused Child.**
SOURCE: Laumann et al., 1994, p. 343.

CAMPUS CONFIDENTIAL

"I thought I was the only one.

"It's only since I've been in therapy that I've learned that other men were sexually abused, and that it's not all that unusual for a child to be sexually abused by more than one molester. A female babysitter sexually abused me when I was 6 years old. It went on for about 2 years. I never told anyone. I don't exactly remember why I didn't tell my mother, except that maybe that I would get into trouble.

"Talking about being abused by the babysitter was hard, but it was only after months and months of therapy that I could tell my counselor that my uncle also abused me when I was 10. I was much more ashamed of having been molested by a man. And the hardest thing to admit to myself was that sometimes it felt good. I'm learning to understand what happened to me and to go on with my life." ●

Pedophile: an adult who is sexually attracted to a child or children

with and cuddle with a child, or may stroke a child's body in ways that are not permitted for adult males in our society. Although maternal sexual abuse may not be widely recognized or reported, it does occur. In one nonclinical sample of 25 adult male survivors of childhood sexual abuse, 13 of the men reported being abused by a female; in 7 of these cases it was the mothers who abused them (Etherington, 1997).

Perhaps the most common, and least reported, form of incest occurs between siblings (Finkelhor, 1980). Consensual incidents may result from curiosity; nonconsensual incidents may be exploitive and traumatic. The most harmful incidents are those that are recurrent, involve threats and coercion, consist of more intrusive sexual acts (such as coitus), and trigger harsh parental responses (Laviola, 1989). One study found that prolonged sibling separation during early childhood was associated with sibling sexual intercourse but was not associated with other types of sexual activity (Reyc & Silverman, 2000).

Characteristics of Child Sex Offenders Pedophiles are adults who have persistent or recurrent sexual attraction to children. In 1886 Kraft-Ebbing first introduced the concept of pedophilia as a disorder and differentiated between pedophilic and nonpedophilic sex offenses against children. All sexual abusers of children are not pedophiles, and all pedophiles are not sexual abusers of children. A pedophile may have the desire to have sex with a child but never act on those desires, while others repeatedly sexually abuse children. Some molesters may only seek sexual contact with a child when under unusual stress. Incest offenders may or may not be pedophiles.

There is some research that suggests that sexual attraction to children may be more common than is generally believed. One study administered an anonymous survey to a sample of 193 college men and found that 21 percent admitted to having been sexually attracted to a small child. Nine percent reported sexual fantasies involving young children and 5 percent reported masturbating to such fantasies. Seven percent said that there was some likelihood that they would have sex with a young child if they knew they could avoid detection and punishment (Briere & Runtz, 1989).

Abused/abuser theories purport that sexual abuse in childhood makes adults prone to commit sexual acts against children. A larger proportion of pedophiles and other sex offenders claim they were sexually abused in childhood than men who have not committed a sex offense (Freund et al., 1990). A study of pedophilic and nonpedophilic sex offenders found that the self-report of having been sexually abused in childhood is connected mainly with pedophilia; a status as a sex offender was not related to childhood abuse (Freund et al., 1994). It is important to note that most adults who were sexually abused as children do not go on to molest children.

Finkelhor and Williams (1988) studied 118 incestuous fathers and stepfathers and identified fives types of incestuous fathers. Twenty-six percent were categorized as *sexually preoccupied*, men who obsessed about sex and who tended to sexualize almost every relationship. *Adolescent regressives*, who had adolescentlike yearnings for young girls, composed 33 percent of the sample. Twenty percent were categorized as *instrumental self-gratifiers*, who molested a child while fantasizing about someone else. Only 10 percent were classified as *emotionally dependent* men who turned to children for the emotional support they lacked from others. Another 10 percent were described as *angry retaliators*. This group assaulted children out of rage at the victim or someone else; these men were the most likely to be violent.

A four-factor model of child sex offenders that applies to pedophilic, nonpedophilic, incestuous, and nonincestuous sexual abuse was developed to identify the preconditions that need to be met by an offender for sexual abuse to occur (Araji & Finkelhor, 1985):

1. *Sexual arousal.* In order for an adult to be aroused by a child there has to have been a cultural or familial conditioning to sexual activity with children, victimization as a child, or early fantasy that is reinforced by masturbation.

2. *Emotional congruence.* The adult feels a level of comfort and satisfaction and fit of emotional need lacking in contact with other adults; frequently this is due to the adult's immaturity and low self-esteem.

3. *Blockage.* Adult sexual opportunities may be blocked by traumatic experience with adult sexuality, sexual dysfunction, inadequate social skills, or marital disturbance.

4. *Disinhibition.* The adult may lack inhibition and lose control due to an impulse disorder, alcohol or drug use, situational stress, or mental illness.

Although pedophiles and other child sexual abusers are mostly male, it is likely that cases involving female sex offenders are vastly underreported. Matthews's (1987) study of 100 women sex offenders found that female abusers tended to be more violent with their female victims while treating boys more like substitute lovers. A small percentage of female sex offenders were psychotic and almost all had an adult sex partner living with them. Matthews identified four major categories of female sex offenders:

At age 35, Mary Kay Letourneau, admitted having sexual relations with a thirteen-year-old boy who had been her student when he was in the second grade.

1. *The Teacher-Lover.* Usually an older woman who preys on a young adolescent. This situation is often unnoticed by society, socially sanctioned, or even glorified (for example, in the movies *The Last Picture Show*, *Summer of '42*, and *Ramblin' Rose*).

2. *The Experimenter-Exploiters.* These are often women from sexually repressed families who may take jobs as baby sitters or do other child-care work in order to exploit small children.

3. *The Predisposed Offender.* A woman with a history of severe physical or sexual abuse reenacts her abuse with a child.

4. *The Male-Coerced Offender.* Some women are pressured or forced into sexually abusing a child by a husband or lover.

Perhaps the best-known female sex offender in the United States is Mary Kay Letourneau (see accompanying photo). At age 35, the former Washington state teacher admitted having sexual relations since the summer of 1996 with a 13-year-old boy who had been a student of hers in the second grade. Letourneau pleaded guilty to two counts of second-degree child rape in August 1997. Sentenced to 6 months in jail, she was then given probation under the condition that she have no further contact with the boy. However, shortly after her release Letourneau was found in a car with the boy and sent to serve out her 7½-year prison sentence. Letourneau professed her love for the boy with whom she had two children (being cared for by his mother) and her belief that their love transcended traditional societal boundaries. Like many child sex offenders, Letourneau is not a pedophile but does have a personality disorder that resulted in her offending behavior.

Adults who sexually abuse children come from all races, religions, occupations, educational levels, and economic backgrounds. In 1996 a Nobel Prize winner was charged with child sex abuse; other offenders include clergymen, teachers, and community

EXPLORING SEXUALITY ONLINE

The Pedophile Playground

The Internet has become the pedophile's 21st century playground. FBI agents across the country are posing as preteen bait for Internet child molesters. A survey by the National Coalition for Missing and Exploited Children (2000) of more than 1,000 children ages 10 to 17 who regularly use the Internet found that one in four had been exposed to unwanted sexual material. One in five had been approached or solicited for sex over the Internet. One in 33 had been telephoned, sent letters, money, or gifts, or asked to meet a person for sex. One in 17 had been threatened or harassed. Only 17 percent of those who had been sexually approached online knew which agency handled complaints of this nature.

408

FAQ:

What happens when the older person in a sexual relationship turns 18?

Childhood sexual abuse and statutory rape are defined as any contact between an adult and a child. Legally, the 18th birthday marks the boundary. Hence any sex between a person over 18 and one under 18 is forbidden in most states.

This creates some curious dilemmas. Suppose a 17-year-old and a 16-year-old fall in love and begin having sex. Society will not formally object to what they are doing at first. However, the couple's problems begin when the older one reaches his or her 18th birthday. The next time they have sex, and from then on, the older one is guilty of child sexual abuse and may be prosecuted for statutory rape. Only when the second one reaches the age of 18 does sex between them become legal again.

leaders. Profiles of sex offenders suggest that they tend to be shy, lonely, poorly informed about sexuality, and very moralistic or religious (Bauman et al., 1984). They have poor interpersonal social and sexual relationships with other adults and feel socially isolated and inadequate (McKibben et al., 1994; Mino & Dwyer, 1997). However, these characteristics may reflect only the majority of the child sex offenders who are caught, and not those who escape prosecution. Sex offenders, including pedophiles, may victimize children of their same gender, opposite gender, or both. It is important to remember that homosexuality does not make someone more likely to sexually abuse children. The problem is not the gender of the victim, but his or her age.

The Effects of Child Sexual Abuse Regardless of the perpetrator, children who are sexually abused frequently have an array of short- and long-term psychological and emotional problems. Physical problems also can be inflicted on a child; these include injuries to the child's mouth, urethra, vagina, penis, or anus, and the contraction of sexually transmitted infections. Sexually abused children may exhibit sexualized behavior including masturbating in public, initiating sexual behaviors with other children, or sexualized talk. Adults who were abused as children often develop a pattern of failure to enjoy sex or are highly sexually active. They may have low self-esteem and a poor body image. Other victims may suffer symptoms of posttraumatic stress disorder, including amnesia, dissociation, and flashbacks (Riggs, 1997). Negative attitudes about sex as well as many types of sexual dysfunction are common aftereffects of child sexual abuse and incest (Courtois, 2000).

One thing that a child may learn from being abused is how to be abused again. Childhood victimization increases the risk of adolescent victimization, which in turn significantly affects the likelihood of revictimization among women (Humphrey & White 2000). They learn that there is no protection and there is nothing or no one that can help them when they are in trouble. This is one reason why abuse survivors may be more likely to be adult rape victims or have abusive adult relationships.

Abuse survivors are less likely to use birth control, have more unplanned pregnancies and abortions, and are at higher risk for sexually transmitted infections (Gold, 1986; Grant, 1999; Wyatt et al., 1992). Both men and women who suffered childhood sexual abuse are far more likely as adults to report pain during sex, anxiety about sexual performance, and emotional problems that interfere with their sex lives. They are consistently more sexual in adulthood than those who have not been abused, have a higher number of sex partners, are more likely to participate in oral, anal, and group sex, and think about sex more often (Laumann et al., 1994).

Not all survivors of childhood sexual abuse suffer severe adverse effects. The intensity or inevitability of negative consequences for children or adolescents who experience sex with adults should not be exaggerated (Browne & Finkelhor, 1986; Okami, 1990; Willis et al., 1991). Overstating the effects of childhood sexual abuse affects victims and their families who "may be further victimized by exaggerated claims about the effects of sexual abuse. It is not possible to maintain two sets of conclusions about the effects of sexual abuse: a dire one for political purposes and a hopeful one for family members" (Browne & Finkelhor, 1986, p. 178).

A highly controversial study on the long-term effects of child sexual abuse by Rind, Tromovitch, and Bauserman (1998) used the technique of meta-analysis, which as you will recall is the statistical combination of the results of many different studies. Most researchers believe that meta-analysis, if used properly, gives the most valid conclusions that are currently possible, because it transcends the limitations of any one study such as statistical accidents or peculiarities of a single method or sample. Rind and his colleagues combined results from 59 different research studies surveying college students about childhood sexual abuse. The researchers used the same definition of childhood sexual abuse offered earlier: any sexual contact between adults and children (those under the age of 18). They also included sexual contact between two people who were both under the age of 18, provided that force was used. On average, they found that

14 percent of college men and 27 percent of college women reported having childhood experiences that fit the definition of abuse. Of course, because of the broadness of that definition, some of those experiences involved consenting experiences between a teenager and someone past the age of 18.

The conclusions from this large investigation challenged traditional assumptions. The relationship between childhood sexual abuse and psychological adjustment in adulthood was significant but very small, amounting to less than 1 percent of the variance in adult adjustment. In other words, the victims were about 1 percent less well adjusted than nonvictims. Furthermore, there was reason to doubt that even that small drop in adjustment was actually caused by the childhood sexual abuse. As Rind et al. pointed out, many victims of childhood sexual abuse come from problem-filled family environments that would affect adult psychological adjustment even if the abuse did not occur. When the researchers statistically controlled for family environment, there was no significant relationship between childhood sexual abuse and adult adjustment. Put another way, the victims of childhood sexual abuse were (slightly) worse off as adults because of their bad family environments rather than because of the sexual abuse per se.

The findings of any research study can in no way minimize or negate the pain of any individual experience. While the consequences of abuse can be severe, they may not be inevitable and there is effective treatment available. It is essential that the responsibility for the abuse be directed where it belongs, to the adult abuser, in order to relieve the survivor of the shame and guilt so often associated with sexual abuse. Survivors have choices as adults that they did not have as children, and they can go on with their lives and establish loving, healthy relationships.

Prevention of Child Sexual Abuse

"Don't talk to strangers; don't accept gifts from strangers; don't get in a car with a stranger." These are some of the warning parents give children in an attempt to prevent childhood sexual abuse. However, these warnings will not help prevent sexual abuse in which the offender is a family member, a teacher, a scout leader, or a clergyman. Prevention programs often are school-based and generally of two types: single presentations and curriculum-based programs integrated into the school's regular instruction.

In addition to being wary of strangers, several concepts are commonly found in most child sexual abuse prevention programs: (1) body ownership (the children's bodies belong to them and they have the right to control access to their body); (2) touch continuum (there is "good" touch and "bad" touch); (3) secrecy (some secrets you are instructed not to tell anyone should be told); (4) intuition (children have a good sense of what is appropriate and inappropriate behavior and should trust their feelings); (5) saying no (children should respond to abuse by saying no and running away); and (6) support systems (there are many different people the child can turn to for help) (Conte et al., 1985). The concept that the child is not to blame for the abuse is also emphasized frequently in these programs.

Child sexual abuse prevention programs have grown dramatically in the United States, but do they work? One study found that children who participate in sexual abuse prevention training are more likely to use strategies such as running away, yelling, or saying no when they are threatened by an abuser and are more likely to report the incident to an adult (Goleman, 1993). However, others question if children really can be expected to understand concepts such as body ownership or if evidence supports the notion that children have an intuitive sense of good and bad touch (Krivacska, 1989). A child intimidated by an abusive adult or emotionally bound to an incest abuser might be unable to say no, even though he or she wants to and know that it is the right thing to do (Waterman et al., 1986). Just as adult rape victims cannot always prevent an assault, victims of childhood sexual abuse cannot be expected to prevent the abuse and should *never* be made to feel guilty about not doing something to stop it.

Sexual coercion involves a range of nonconsenting, abusive, forcible sexual behaviors, most of which are illegal.

1_____involves obtaining sexual pleasure by pressing or rubbing against a fully clothed, nonconsenting person. **2**_____ is the exposure of one's genitals to an unsuspecting person. Since exhibitionists usually want to frighten, surprise, or humiliate their victims, the best advice is to remain calm, continue on your way, and report the act to the police as soon as possible.

3_____ have a strong, repetitive urge to observe unsuspecting persons who are naked, undressing, or engaged in sexual relations. **4**_____ typically experience sexual arousal when their victims react with horror or disgust to their telephone calls. If you receive such a call, the best advice is to hang up the phone quietly.

5_____ involves the use of deliberate and repeated verbal comments, gestures, or physical contact of a sexual nature that is unwelcome by the recipient. This includes sexual remarks, gestures, or behaviors that are unwelcome, unsolicited, and unappreciated. If you are harassed in school or the workplace, maintain written documentation, confront the harasser, seek support, and file a complaint with the appropriate official. **6**_____ involves manipulation or deceit to influence the recipient into unwanted sexual behavior.

7_____ is the use of force or the threat of force to obtain sex. Males in our society often learn that using power and aggression to get their way is the male prerogative and that their role as a male is to seek sex successfully. This may explain why ours is a rape-prone society, but it is no excuse for irresponsible behavior. Most social scientists view rape as primarily a crime of **8**_____, not of passion or sexual desire. Sex is used as an instrument to express the rapist's anger, aggression, and power. However, the fact that the act took a sexual form of expressing dominance and power may be significant.

While no single motive or characteristic describes all rapes or rapists, the four motivations for rape identified in the text are: **9**_____ rape, _____ rape, _____ rape, and rape for sexual gratification.

10_____ rape is when a group of males sexually assault a victim. It usually occurs when there are preexisting male bonds, such as those that link members of athletic teams, fraternities, or military units. The only difference between **11**_____ rape and _____ rape is whether the victim knows the rapist. Drug or alcohol use is a contributing factor in many incidents of sexual assault among acquaintances. **12**_____ rape occurs when a husband forces his wife to have sex against her will. There is a strong association between marital violence and marital rape.

Resisting a rapist may decrease the risk of being raped but **13**_____ the risk of being injured.

14_____ is any sexual contact between an adult and a child. Most frequently the abuser is a family friend or a relative outside the immediate family.

15_____ is sexual contact between family members, one of whom may be a child. All human societies have taboos against such activity, though the specific definitions may vary considerably. In our society, probably the most common and least reported form involves **16**_____. **17**_____ are more likely to commit incest than biological fathers.

18_____ describes a behavioral pattern in which an adult, primarily or exclusively, is sexually attracted to and sexually aroused by children.

SUGGESTED READINGS

Herman, J. (1997). *Trauma and Recovery.* New York: Basic Books.

A Harvard Medical School psychiatrist presents her own and other leading research on trauma in an individual and social context.

Lefkowitz, B. (1998). *Our Guys: The Glen Ridge Rape and the Secret Life of the Perfect Suburb.* New York: Vintage Books.

The true story of a developmentally delayed teenager who was sexually assaulted with a baseball bat and a broomstick by a group of high-school football stars.

Paludi, M. A. (Ed.). (1996). *Sexual Harassment on College Campuses: Abusing the Ivory Power.* Albany: State University of New York Press.

Thirteen studies covering legal, methodological, and conceptual issues related to sexual harassment and academia.

Sanday, P. R. (1997). *A Woman Scorned: Acquaintance Rape on Trial.* Berkeley: University of California Press.

An anthropologist charts America's attitudes toward sex and rape from the time of the Puritans to the present.

Van Der Kold, B., McFarlane, A. C., & Weissaeth, L. (Eds.). (1996). *Traumatic Stress: The Effects of Overwhelming Experiences on Mind, Body, and Society.* New York: Guilford Press.

The authors present the current state of research and clinical knowledge on traumatic stress and treatment.

ANSWERS TO CHAPTER REVIEW

1. Frotteurism; **2.** Exhibitionism; **3.** Voyeurs; **4.** Obscene callers; **5.** Sexual harassment; **6.** Verbal sexual pressure; **7.** Rape; **8.** Violence; **9.** sadistic, anger, power; **10.** Gang; **11.** date or acquaintance, stranger; **12.** Marital; **13.** increase; **14.** Sexual abuse of children; **15.** Incest; **16.** siblings; **17.** Stepfathers; **18.** Pedophilia.

CHAPTER 14

The Business of Sex

- **Why Sex Sells**
  Several theoretical positions offer some explanation for the economic value associated with sex.

- **Prostitution**
  Prostitution, the sale of sexual services, flourishes, even though it is illegal in most of the United States. It is a means of employment for many women, men, and children.

- **Pornography**
  Pornography, defined as sexually arousing or erotic art, is legal. Obscenity, that which is offensive to morality and decency, is not.

- **Sex and Profits**
  Sex is big money in the advertising and entertainment industries. Consideration of social consequences or corporate morality sometimes seems to lose to the pursuit of profits.

PHYSICAL

SOCIAL

EMOTIONAL

SPIRITUAL

COGNITIVE

Sex sells. Whether it is the illusion of sex used in advertising to increase sales or the reality of sex in prostitution, sex is big business. If you go to the movies, watch music videos, or look at the advertisements in a magazine, it is nearly impossible not to be influenced by the buying and selling of sex. Sex lotions, potions, toys, and devices are marketed with the promise of increasing sexual response and desire. Advertisers use sexual imagery to encourage us to buy products we fervently hope will enhance our sex appeal. What was once considered to be pornographic and furtively viewed behind closed doors is now plastered on billboards up and down Main Street. And, despite the threat of sexually transmitted infections, prostitution thrives throughout the world.

WHY SEX SELLS

The sex industry shows the processes of social exchange theory at work. Recall that, according to this theory, sex is a female resource and men will trade other resources to obtain it. These resources include money. The vast majority of the money that is spent on sex comes from men. To the male customer, the woman is the principal appeal, whether this involves paying to have intercourse with her (as in prostitution) or simply paying to see an image of her (as in pornography). Although the money flows from men to women, the women do not always keep the profits, because in many circumstances men perform the managerial and administrative roles in the sex industry and hence retain much of the profits. Still, the scarce and crucial resource is female sexuality, and money flows from various men to whoever can provide it.

The marketplace has periodically tried to reach out to female customers, too. After all, if women could be induced to spend as much on sex as men do, twice as much money would flow to the smart entrepreneurs. *Playgirl* was founded in the early 1970s as a female version of *Playboy*, but the novelty quickly wore off and the magazine gradually downplayed pictures of naked men as its crucial selling point. *Viva*, introduced in 1973, was the only glossy magazine to feature explicit photographs of male genitals. Although this advantage should have enabled it to capture the market, the demand was not large enough, and the magazine folded after 3 years (Abramson & Pinkerton, 1995).

Since its inception, the sex industry has inspired controversy, and it continues to do so. Opposition comes from an unlikely pair—the religious right and the feminist left. Religious conservatives oppose the sex industry just as they oppose sexual permissiveness in general. Many feminists believe that the sex industry exploits women. To be sure, these positions are not unanimous; some feminists speak out in support of prostitutes and treat prostitution as a freedom of choice issue, and certainly some conservatives do tolerate (and even patronize) prostitutes.

On average, women are more opposed to the sex industry than men (Justice Bureau Statistics, 1987; Klassen, Williams, & Levitt, 1989; Lottes, Weinberg, & Weller, 1993). Women involved in the sex industry are generally more positive about it than other women. According to social exchange theory, women's greater objection to the sex industry may arise because it offers men sexual gratification in ways other than marriage, thereby weakening men's dependency on women (Cott, 1977). In essence, prostitution and pornography undermine female control of sex.

Although some feminists support the sex industry for providing opportunities for women to express their sexuality, from a feminist perspective the sale of sex is a way that men exploit and degrade women. Some feminists believe that pornography is a crucial part of male domination and the male conspiracy to commit rape. In a famous summary statement, Robin Morgan (1974) said, "Pornography is the theory, and rape is the practice". According to the feminist view, when they watch pornography, men acquire the attitudes and intentions that the male patriarchy wants them to have in order to facilitate their ability to commit rape; this keeps women in an oppressed position. Many feminists also believe that the prostitution industry is part of men's efforts to keep women in an inferior position. For example, Campbell (1998) wrote, "the motivations of men who pay for sex . . . can be understood . . . as the shaping of a persistently hegemonic discourse of male sexuality that impacts on male sexual identity" (p. 170); in simpler terms, men go to prostitutes to prove that they are superior to women.

Hugh Gene Loebner (1998), a self-appointed activist who has campaigned in support of both prostitutes and clients, proposed an interesting contrast to these views. Loebner has written, "I pay for food. I pay for clothing. I pay for shelter. Why should I not also pay for sex?" (p. 221). His explanation for using prostitutes was simply that he could not obtain sex any other way. He rejected the view that men exploit women in prostitution. "I pay sex workers more for a one-hour session than I pay the men I employ in my business for a week's work. Who is being exploited?" (p. 223). He also observed that one of his favorite prostitutes has sex with her boyfriend, who does not pay, but Loebner must pay, even though his desires and sexual activities are the same as the boyfriend's. If anyone was exploited, Loebner felt, it was he. And since he freely consented and desired it, it could hardly be classified as oppressive exploitation.

Evolutionary theory sees prostitution as simply an extension of the more general pattern in which men offer women resources in exchange for sex (see any connection to social exchange theory?). Some biologists have claimed that prostitution exists in other species. For example, de Waal (1995) observed bonobo males giving females food in exchange for sex, including cases in which the female initiated the exchange and set the "price" (see Chapter 3). Human males' ancient and traditional interest in hunting may have been shaped by the fact that successful hunters could obtain more sex.

The degree of choice that a woman enjoys is crucial to many moral and legal arguments about the sex industry. In some circumstances, women are forced to be prostitutes against their will; women have been kidnapped or kept in brothels by physical violence and intimidation. These women are certainly victims of criminal oppression. However, other women turn freely to sexual work as a promising way to make money. A woman who finances her education by dancing in a strip club once or twice a week may consider this profitable work that is better than her alternatives. Campaigns against such clubs would deprive the woman of a choice of employment. Some argue that strip clubs actually benefit women and exploit men: (1) the money comes from the men, and (2) the option of making good money by taking off one's clothes is much more widely available to women than to men. A man who wants to pay off his debts, support his children, or finance his drug addiction by having women pay him to have sex will likely find his opportunities much more limited than a woman in a similar position.

Prostitution: the act or practice of engaging in sex for money

Johns: colloquial term for prostitution customers

CONSIDERATIONS

Sex Licensing

Two alternatives to the criminal status of prostitution are legalization and decriminalization. With legalization, prostitution is regulated, licensed, and taxed by the government. With decriminalization, criminal penalties for engaging in prostitution are removed although the act would remain illegal. With either alternative, prostitutes may be required to register and undergo mandatory health checks. Prostitution is illegal in the United States except in some counties in Nevada, where it is restricted to state-licensed brothels. Several countries, including France, Italy, Britain, Japan, Denmark, Singapore, and the Netherlands, have decriminalized prostitution.

Some advocates believe that decriminalizing prostitution would protect prostitutes from exploitation and shield both the public and the prostitutes from sexually transmitted infections. Others believe that it would be morally wrong to legitimize paying for sex.

 Do you think that prostitution should be decriminalized?

—Legalized?
—Neither?
—Explain your position.

PROSTITUTION

Prostitution, the exchange of sexual services for money or other resources, is often referred to (though arguably erroneously) as the world's oldest profession. In ancient agrarian societies, women could choose "one of two quite different sexual careers, becoming cloistered housewives or courtesans, concubines or prostitutes" (Bullough & Bullough, 1977, p. 93). Ancient civilizations in Greece, Rome, Palestine, and China required prostitutes to live in separate areas or to wear distinctive clothing. Prostitution was part of the religious rituals of some ancient cultures; relations between prostitutes and their customers were sometimes seen as sacred acts. Some traditional Navajo women chose to live alone and trade sex for a fee rather than marry (Reichard, 1950). Among the Mehinaku of the Amazon, some women received fish, meat, or trinkets in payment for sex (Gregor, 1977). Throughout history, prostitution often has been viewed as a necessary outlet for man's "uncontrollable" sexual urges and a preferable alternative to rape, adultery, celibacy, or masturbation. For women, prostitution may be either a choice or her only means of survival.

The National Health and Social Life Survey (NHSLS) found that 16 percent of men reported paying for sex at some time (Laumann et al., 1994). Although there are no accurate data on the number of prostitutes in the United States, according to one estimate, over 1 million women in the United States earn all or part of their living as prostitutes (Boston Women's Book Collective, 1992). While publicly condemned by most modern societies, prostitution is often ignored or tacitly tolerated (see CONSIDERATIONS box). Technically the laws regarding prostitution apply to both the seller of sex (the prostitute) and to the purchaser of sex (the client, or **john**). However,

CONSIDERATIONS

"We Are Merely Haggling About the Price!"

In a widely quoted story attributed to Winston Churchill, he asked a woman at a party (hypothetically) whether she would accept a rich man's offer of a vast sum of money for sex. When the woman said yes, Churchill asked her whether she would do it for the equivalent of a few dollars. She replied indignantly, "No, of course not! What do you think I am?" His response was, "We've already established what you are; we are merely haggling about the price!"

The implication of the story is that exchanging money for sex is not something that is totally unaccept-able to some women. Possibly what is seen as most objectionable about the prostitute is not that she takes money for sex, but that she takes so little money for sex.

 Do you think that the amount of money a woman accepts for sex matters?

—Is there any amount of money that you would consider taking for having sex with a stranger?
—Why or why not?

Customers at this Nevada brothel select a sex partner from among a group of women.

it is more often the prostitute than the customer who is charged with a crime (Atchison, Fraser, & Lowman, 1998).

How do the prostitutes perceive the unequal arrests? McElroy (1998) talked with dozens of prostitutes about some recent police efforts to prosecute male clients more aggressively, and she found the women to be "appalled" by this trend. In their view, the threat of arrest and public humiliation (such as when the names of men are published in the newspaper) would be enough to deter many respectable, decent men from using prostitutes. The loss of business would be bad enough, but even worse was the fact that dangerous and criminally violent men would not likely be discouraged, so the prostitutes would be at increased risk. "Thus, police/feminist policy keeps peaceful johns off the streets and leaves women to compete more vigorously for johns and screen less rigorously those who approach them" (McElroy, 1998, p. 338). Arresting clients of prostitutes may serve the interests of feminists and others who seek to stamp out prostitution, but prostitutes themselves are against that trend and may suffer both reduced income and increased violence because of it.

Female Prostitutes

Call Girl: a female prostitute with whom an appointment can be made by telephone, usually to meet at the client's address

Madam: a woman who manages a brothel

Brothel: a house where men can go to have sexual intercourse with prostitutes for money

Streetwalker: a prostitute who solicits customers on the street

Pimp: a procurer; a person, usually a man, who solicits customers for a prostitute, usually in return for a share of the earnings

Female prostitutes are classified by the location where they conduct their work. The three major categories are call girls, brothel workers, and streetwalkers. There are additional differences in the amount of money they charge for their services, their degree of visibility, and their method of acquiring customers (Table 14.1).

Call girls are usually the most highly paid prostitutes, the least visible to the public, and the least at risk for arrest. Clients are usually by referral only; many call girls have regular customers with standing appointments. Call girls may provide social companionship along with sex. Some call girls work with a **madam** who schedules clients in exchange for a percentage of the fee. Although Heidi Fleiss ("The Hollywood Madam") never made her client list public, reportedly her clients included a number of celebrities including actor Charlie Sheen. The Mayflower Madam, Sidney Biddle Barrows, was an elite socialite. Other call girls work independently. Customers may be seen at the call girl's residence or special place of business (*incalls*), or the call girl may meet the customer at a specified location (*outcalls*). Many escort services are fronts for prostitution.

Before World War II, prostitutes traditionally worked in **brothels,** locations where a group of prostitutes ply their trade; these were variously called "houses of ill repute," "whore houses," or "bordellos," and were often located in the "red light district." While there are fewer bordellos in the United States today, some massage parlors, nude photo studios, and escort services serve a similar function; brothels continue to be the primary location for prostitution in some foreign countries. The prostitutes' fees are split with the management who supply customers as well as a location. Prostitutes working in a brothel are moderately visible to the public and sometimes are provided a degree of protection by their employer.

Streetwalkers solicit customers who walk or drive by them.

As the name implies, **streetwalkers** are prostitutes who generally solicit their customers by either standing or walking in a particular public location; they may also frequent a bar or other place where potential clients congregate. Customers may be serviced on the street, in their cars, or in a hotel known to provide rooms for such activities. Many streetwalkers work under the direction of a **pimp**, almost always a man, who may serve as a business manager, companion, protector, or drug supplier. Streetwalkers have the lowest status among prostitutes. They receive the lowest fees, have the highest visibility, have the least protection against violence and other mistreatment by dangerous clients, and they incur the highest risk of arrest and of violence. In one study 62 percent of prostitutes reported having been raped and 73 percent reported having experienced physical assault (Farley et al., 1998).

TABLE 14.1

Characteristics of Female Prostitutes

	Employment	Typical Work Location	Risk of Arrest	Degree of Public Visibility	Method of Acquiring Customers	Fees
Call Girls	May work for an escort service or work independently	Private residence of client or prostitute	Low	Least visible	Referral	Most highly paid
Brothel Workers	Employer who functions as a madam or pimp	Massage parlors	Moderate	Moderate	Advertising	Moderate
Street-walkers	Almost always have a pimp	Public streets, bars	High	High	Public solicitation	Low

Male Prostitutes

Among homosexuals as well as heterosexuals, far more men than women employ other people for sexual services (Tiger, 1992). Heterosexual male prostitutes, sometimes referred to as **gigolos,** are the male equivalent of call girls (Table 14.2). They are relatively highly paid, nearly invisible, and often provide social companionship in addition to sexual services.

Male prostitutes who perform homosexual acts with paying customers may consider themselves to be heterosexual in their private lives. Unlike female prostitutes, few male prostitutes are attached to pimps. Some sex workers are transgendered, genetic males who present themselves as females. Like female prostitutes, homosexual male prostitutes may work much like call girls and work independently seeing regular customers and providing companionship as well as sex. Much more visible are **hustlers,** the homosexual male equivalent of streetwalkers. Other categories of male prostitutes include **kept boys,** who are either partially or fully supported by an older man (Coleman, 1989), **peer-delinquent prostitutes,** who often work in small groups and use homosexual prostitution as a vehicle for assault and robbery (Allen, 1980), and *call boys,* homosexual male prostitutes who operate out of their homes or offices rather than on the street. Men who seek out pubescent male prostitutes are sometimes referred to as **chickenhawks.**

Gigolo: a man who provides sexual services or social companionship to a woman in exchange for money or gifts

Hustler: homosexual male prostitute who solicits customers on the street

Kept Boy: a man who has a continuing sexual relationship with and receives financial support from an older man

Peer-Delinquent Prostitute: males who often work in small groups and use homosexual prostitution as a vehicle for assault and robbery

Chickenhawk: an adult male who seeks out pubescent male prostitutes

TABLE 14.2

Characteristics of Male Prostitutes

	Employment	Typical Work Location	Risk of Arrest	Degree of Public Visibility	Method of Acquiring Customers	Fees
Male-Male Prostitutes or Hustlers	May have a pimp or work independently	Public places, the street, bars, restrooms	Moderate to High	High	Solicitation, referral, or advertising	Moderate to low
Male-Female Prostitutes or Gigolos	Most work independently but may be employed by escort service	Private residence	Low	Low	Referral	Moderate to high

Motives for Becoming a Prostitute

In the past, many researchers assumed that all prostitutes must have deep-rooted psychological problems and "overlooked not only the social and economic factors affecting these women, but also the general place of prostitution in the way society structures sexuality" (Schur, 1988, p. 112). There appear to be four pathways to prostitution: poverty, childhood sexual abuse, running away from home, and drug use. Pimps target girls or women who seem naive, lonely, homeless, and rebellious. At first, the pimp's attention and affection may convince her to "turn out." Later, verbal abuse and physical coercion keep her working the streets, according to antiprostitution activist Kathleen Barry (1995).

A very different picture emerges from other studies. McElroy (1998) noted that antiprostitution feminists generally seek out the most victimized prostitutes from among the streetwalkers, who form the most vulnerable and lowest rung on the ladder of prostitution. For example, Farley and Hotaling (1995) found that nearly their entire sample of prostitutes had been victims of physical violence while working as prostitutes, most wanted to leave prostitution, and three quarters had drug problems. In contrast, an intensive survey of a prostitutes' organization by McElroy (1998) found that only about one in four had experienced violence (and usually from police or coworkers rather than customers), none had a drug problem, and only 17 percent wanted to quit prostitution (a lower figure than for many other jobs!). The difference between the two sets of findings, according to McElroy, is that she surveyed call girls rather than streetwalkers, and the call girls have much better lives and working conditions.

In many countries, including the United States, poverty is the main reason that men and women become sex workers. Unskilled, desperate women and men may see prostitution as their only means of survival. In one study, 60 percent of male prostitutes cited money as their principal motivation (Fisher et al., 1982).

Some prostitutes are part of an underground economy in which sex is exchanged for drugs or money to buy drugs. A study of female crack users indicated that both those who reported exchanging sex for drugs and money and those who did not had frequent unprotected sex. However, women who exchanged sex for drugs or money to buy drugs had a greater number of sexual partners, had sex more often, used drugs before and during sex more often, and had a higher rate of sexually transmitted infections than those who did not exchange sex for money (Logan & Leukenfeld, 2000).

In addition to earning a living or supporting an existing or acquired drug habit, many prostitutes have been victims of childhood sexual abuse or rape. Perhaps 80 percent of male and female streetwalkers were victims of incest, sexual abuse, or rape (Boyer, 1989; Gordon & Snyder, 1989). Interviews with nearly 500 American, European, African, and Asian prostitutes found that nearly two thirds could be diagnosed with posttraumatic stress disorder (PTSD) resulting from sexual abuse (Farley et al., 1998).

A comparison of the early family environment of a sample of 16- to 47-year-old sex workers with women of similar ages and backgrounds in New Zealand found that the sex workers were significantly more likely to report childhood sexual abuse, to have left home early, to have become pregnant before the age of 19, and to have dropped out of school. The sex workers in the study came from families with more interpersonal difficulties during childhood and adolescence than the control sample (Potter et al., 1999).

Not all sexually abused children or runaways become prostitutes. In a study of females ages 16 to 18 who had been sexually abused, only 12 percent became involved with prostitution (Seng, 1989). However, abused children who run away from home are much more likely to become involved in prostitution, probably because it is difficult for youth to find full-time legal employment to support themselves. Data on 142 female prostitutes found that running away had a dramatic effect on entry into prostitution in early adolescence. Childhood sexual victimization nearly doubled the odds of entry into prostitution throughout the lives of the women in the study. Although the prevalence of drug use was significantly higher among the prostitutes than among nonprostitutes, there was no correlation between drug abuse and entry into prostitution (McClanahan et al., 1999).

Prostitution is a job that may appeal to people who want to make money without severe external controls (such as bosses and time cards) and who lack the skills and credentials that would enable them to work as professors, consultants, and other professionals without such controls. Walkowitz (1980) described the efforts of the women's movements in 19th century Britain and America to "reform" prostitutes. Organizations of middle-class women undertook to approach these women, rescue them from their brothels, and get them paid employment elsewhere. Because prostitutes had few skills apart from sex, the main options for employment were working in factories or as a maid in someone's home. These efforts failed repeatedly, as Walkowitz described, often because the prostitutes did not find those jobs appealing. Such jobs also tended to pay a great deal less than prostitution. The Victorian ladies were surprised that many women preferred prostitution to "honest labor."

In short, prostitution, though hardly an ideal job, is one way for women without skills or education to earn substantial amounts of money in a relatively short time. The average prostitute in Amsterdam (where prostitution is legal) can earn about $400 in an 8-hour shift, from which she must pay the rental for the room (which may be $50 or more, depending on the location) as well as some other expenses. Still, a net profit of even $200 to $300 per night is better than most people can expect from unskilled labor (although some prostitutes consider themselves highly skilled at what they do!). An added benefit is flexibility; the prostitute may be able to support herself by working just a couple of nights a week.

Are the motives of male and female prostitutes similar or different? Boles and Elifson (1994) found that male-male prostitutes could be sorted into two categories, heterosexual male prostitutes and homosexual male prostitutes. The heterosexuals found the work (which involved having sex with men) distasteful and did it simply for the money, lacking the skills to earn it through other means. Some of them even said that they found the work disgusting. In contrast, the homosexuals tended to enjoy their jobs as male prostitutes and reported that getting paid for having sex was a good situation, even if they did not find all their clients to be sexually desirable. West (1998) found that male street prostitutes tended to be poor and desperate, sometimes not even having a place of their own to sleep (so they would sleep with clients). They tended to have been forced into prostitution because of circumstances, including the need to earn a living and the lack of other options. Some gay male prostitutes had literally been thrown out of their homes because their families could not accept their sexual orientation (Kruks, 1991). In one study, three fourths of the male prostitutes had run away from home by an average age of 15 (Weisberg, 1985). In contrast, call boys, who operated out of their homes or offices rather than on the street, were better organized and lived reasonably well. They had generally chosen this line of work rather freely; one of the reasons they cited for this line of work was their homosexual orientation.

What Do Prostitutes Actually Do?

Freund, Leonard, and Lee (1989) studied the behavior of female prostitutes in a New Jersey city and found that the average streetwalker serviced four clients a day, 4 or 5 days each week. This comes out to about 7,500 transactions over the average 8-year career, but that does not mean that each woman had sex with over 7,000 different men. In fact, the researchers found that about half the contacts were with regular customers, men who visited the same prostitute at least once per month.

This same study found that the most common service provided by the street prostitutes was fellatio (Freund et al., 1989). All of the prostitutes surveyed reported performing oral sex. Fellatio may be especially popular with prostitutes and their clients for several reasons: (1) it is fairly easy to do; (2) it can be performed in many places with low risk of detection (genital intercourse usually requires a bed if not a room); (3) married clients often regard fellatio as less of a betrayal than vaginal intercourse; (4) many of the men who desire oral sex find that their wives or girlfriends refuse to perform it. Most prostitutes also reported vaginal intercourse as a common activity; anal sex was relatively rare.

FAQ:

Do prostitutes kiss clients?

In the movie *Pretty Woman*, the streetwalker (played by Julia Roberts) is advised by her friend never to kiss a client, because kissing can lead to emotional intimacy. Is this true for real life prostitutes? Freund et al. (1989) found that most prostitutes do refuse to kiss their clients, and indeed 60 percent of the ones they interviewed said they never kissed. Overall, 6 percent of the contacts between prostitutes and clients included kissing on the mouth.

Another stereotype is that the prostitute never has an orgasm with a client and usually derives no pleasure at all from her work. However, Savitz and Rosen (1988) found that most streetwalkers sometimes did get sexual enjoyment out of their work, although certainly not with all clients. Some did have orgasms. The prostitutes reported that the greatest enjoyment accompanied cunnilingus. Because streetwalkers are the lowest rung on the ladder of prostitution, it may be assumed that call girls would derive even more pleasure from their interactions. Savitz and Rosen also found that the prostitutes who had the most enjoyment of sex in their private lives reported more pleasure with their customers.

Some prostitutes provide more elaborate services, such as sadomasochistic activities. These are typically more expensive than fellatio or intercourse. In a survey of expensive call girls in Washington, D.C., Janus, Bess, and Saltus (1977) were surprised to find a relatively high rate of requests for sexual domination. The researchers found that rich and powerful men were far more likely to want to be dominated than to dominate the women themselves, and in fact the call girls reported that the men's requests to be spanked outnumbered requests to deliver a spanking by about eight to one.

Motives for Using Prostitutes

The reasons why customers, sometimes known as "johns" or "tricks," seek prostitutes are as varied as the reasons why others become prostitutes. Six primary reasons have been identified as common motives: (1) loneliness; (2) not having to risk rejection; (3) feelings of inferiority, anxiety, or shame regarding sex; (4) seeking sexual variety or sexual acts a regular partner won't perform; (5) avoiding emotional involvement and commitment; and (6) the desire to degrade and to humiliate women.

There has been a long-standing stereotype of men who go to prostitutes as being pathetic, neurotic losers, but recent data have not provided much evidence to support that view. From the first systematic studies (for example, Winick, 1962; see Atchison et al., 1998), men who pay for sex have been found to be quite similar to other men in most respects. Only the vaguest hints of pathology or even pathological experiences have been found. For example, Atchison et al. (1998) found that men who used prostitutes were more likely than other men to report having been victims of child sexual abuse, and in this respect the clients of prostitutes may resemble the prostitutes themselves.

The strongest single factor that predicts the use of prostitutes is simply being male. In all studies, men are far more likely than women to pay for sex. One large recent study used the Internet in the deliberate attempt to find both male and female customers of prostitution (Atchison, Fraser, & Lowman, 1998). The researchers found plenty of men, but they were only able to find two women who reported paying for sex. In both of those cases, the woman had accompanied a male partner to pay a female prostitute to engage in a threesome with the couple. There were no cases of women paying for one-on-one lesbian sex or, most relevant, of women paying men for sex.

The obvious reason that men go to prostitutes is that they want to have sex. More precisely, some men cannot find as many women willing to go to bed with them as they would like. Even men who have a regular sex partner may find that a prostitute is the main option for novelty of either partner or act.

Laumann et al. (1994) found that 7 percent of American men who came of age before 1950 had their first sex with prostitutes, whereas only 1.5 percent of men in later generations did so—a dramatic decrease. The difference is probably a result of the Sexual Revolution of the 1960s; the liberalized attitudes of women greatly increased men's opportunities to have sex with a willing partner. In fact, prostitutes complained bitterly about the Sexual Revolution, accusing other women of being "charity girls" who gave men sex at no cost, thereby undermining the prostitutes' ability to profit from their work (Reuben, 1969). So if women cooperated much more widely with men's sexual wishes and fantasies, including being willing to have casual sex frequently with many partners, could prostitution be radically reduced or perhaps

Come and Go

CONSIDERATIONS

Why would attractive, rich, successful, and powerful men such as Hugh Grant and Charlie Sheen pay for sex? One possible explanation is that they don't want to be bothered with romance; they would rather have sex without obligation. "Men don't pay for sex; they pay to leave" (Bachrach, 1993, p. 164).

? *What other explanations can you think of for why attractive, powerful men would pay for sex?*

Although he was romantically involved with model and actress Elizabeth Hurley at the time, actor Hugh Grant was arrested after soliciting sex from Hollywood prostitute Divine Brown.

eliminated? That is a possibility, judging by the great decline in prostitution following the Sexual Revolution. Likewise, prostitution is relatively rare on college campuses, where there are many young, sexually active single women.

Men who use female prostitutes come from all ethnic groups, socioeconomic levels, and religions; many, if not most, are married. In the United States, most customers are white, middle-aged, middle-class, and married (Adams, 1987). A study of the personality characteristics of male clients of female prostitutes in Australia found two distinct subgroups of men. Men in one subgroup had low social sexual effectiveness and appeared motivated to visit sex workers because of an interpersonal need for intimacy. A second group was characterized by high sensation seeking and appeared motivated to visit sex workers because of a need for novelty and variety in sexual encounters (Xantidis & McCabe, 2000).

Motives for using male prostitutes may be similar to those for patronizing a female prostitute: sex without commitment, eroticism and variety, sex without negotiation, and a need for social interaction. In addition, men confused about their sexual orientation, curious about homosexuality, or those who are afraid or ashamed of being gay might occasionally or regularly seek male prostitutes for sex. As West (1998) has pointed out, gay males have more reason than other men to resort to prostitutes. The minority status of homosexuals makes it much more difficult for a homosexual than for a heterosexual to find a willing sex partner, so for many gay men the choice is celibacy or a prostitute.

An important study by Sullivan and Simon (1998) examined a variety of factors that differentiated men who had used a female prostitute, using the data from the NHSLS. Age was one factor. Older men were more likely to have used prostitutes, which may reflect the simple fact that, being older, they have had more time in which to do so, or (more likely) it reflects the generational changes involving the Sexual Revolution. Another important factor was military service. Men who had served in the armed forces were three times as likely as other men to have visited a prostitute. Military service tends to put men among other men in unfamiliar places, where their chances of finding a willing female sex partner are lower than usual.

Men with a greater number of sex partners, especially those who had had more than 10 partners, were more likely to have used prostitutes. Furthermore, men who had more interest in a variety of sexual experiences, including group sex, watching a partner undress, and watching other people have sex, were more likely to use a prostitute. Other signs of high libido were also correlated with paying for sex, including watching nude dancers, liking pornography, and liking oral and anal intercourse (Sullivan & Simon, 1998). A study of clients by Atchison et al. (1998) found that men who paid for sex had begun sexual activity earlier in life than other men. Taken together, these factors suggest that men who use prostitutes have a higher and broader sex drive than other men; for these men going to prostitutes may simply reflect a quest for a variety of sexual experiences. In simple terms, paying for sex is one indication of wide-ranging sexual behavior or "hypersexuality" (see Chapter 4 and Sullivan & Simon, 1998, p. 151).

Sullivan and Simon (1998) also called attention to the similarities between users of prostitution and other men. Those who had paid for sex were no more likely than others to be Republican or Democrat, to be religious, to be rich or poor, or to have generally permissive versus conservative attitudes about sexual behavior. In many respects, clients of prostitutes are much like other men.

Another recent investigation of clients of prostitution confirmed that they are not deviant or sexually inadequate but rather extremely ordinary, typical men in most respects (Campbell, 1998). The reasons men gave for going to prostitutes involved seeking out sexual thrills, including specific acts that their regular sex partner (if they had one) would not perform, the chance to experience sex with a variety of different women, and the chance to have sex with a woman with particular physical characteristics (for example, large breasts). "My wife's not interested in sex any more, so that's why I go to prostitutes," said one man (Campbell, 1998, p. 163); another responded, "My wife won't try anything different, so I go to prostitutes" (Campbell, 1998, p. 163). A few gave other reasons, however; one man said he was so ugly that no woman would date or have sex with him unless he paid her.

Child Prostitution

While some may consider adult prostitution to be a career choice or a way for unskilled laborers to earn a living, child prostitution throughout the world is not a choice but a necessity forced upon them by poverty or abuse. Many youth trying to make it on their own—whether runaways or "throwaways"—often resort to prostitution in an effort to earn a living.

In brothels in Manila, Bangkok, and Frankfurt, children ages 8 to 13 are in great demand for sex, perhaps because clients think they are safer than adult prostitutes. It is assumed that children are free of disease, particularly AIDS. However, children's tissues tear easily in sex with adults, making them highly susceptible to infection and at *greater* risk for contracting HIV.

Although there are no reliable statistics as to how widespread child prostitution might be, the United Nations estimates that there are as many 60,000 child prostitutes in the United States. A study of adolescent prostitution found that the majority of prostitutes under age 18 were younger than 16 when they first began to turn tricks. The average age for the first act of prostitution was 14 (Weisberg, 1985).

Many of the children have backgrounds similar to that of a 9-year-old in Manila whose aunt "rented" her to foreign men for 3 years and then sold her to a visiting German pedophile (Satchell, 2000). Mounting third world poverty, the rise of organized crime in Eastern Europe and Russia, the spread of "sex tourism" (discussed next), fear of AIDS, and the spread of child pornography on the Internet are some of the factors believed to be responsible for the rising number of children being forced into prostitution (Satchell, 2000). According to Agnes Fournier de Saint Maur, who tracks global child sex trends, the demand comes not only from pedophiles but from men eager to "push the envelope" of sexual adventure.

Sex Tourism

Traditionally, the greatest use of prostitutes has been among men who are away from home, such as businessmen at conventions. Today, sex is often the purpose, not just a byproduct, of travel. Sex represents an important tourism attraction for many developing countries. Men from around the world are "vacationing" specifically to have sex with adult prostitutes and with children.

Sex tours, which initially concentrated in Southeast Asia, spread across the world as wealthy tourists from Europe, North America, Australia, and Japan made them a growth industry that rakes in an estimated $5.5 billion a year (Marks, 1999). Some tour promoters advertise their "pleasure" or "romance" tours in magazines, newspapers, and on the Internet. Some sex tourists do not view their activities as a form of deviance but fully consistent with the norms of tourism: satisfaction of needs of social companionship, fantasy fulfillment, the search for something new, and opportunities for relaxation (Ryan & Kinder, 1996). A study funded by the European Union found that while some of the sex tour clients of child prostitutes are pedophiles, a great many of them, probably the majority, are first and foremost prostitute users who become child sexual abusers through their prostitute use rather than the other way around (Watson, 1999).

Thailand and the Philippines are the traditional destinations for sex tourists. In the past few years, as these countries have enacted public awareness campaigns and stricter laws and enforcement against the sex trade, the sex tours have moved to Central America and Africa. An international women's rights group, Equality Now, has spearheaded a movement to attack the international sex trade by pressuring legislators for laws that would make sex tourism illegal. Several countries, including Canada, Great Britain, Germany, Sweden, and Australia, make having sex with minors abroad a crime that can be prosecuted at home when the individual returns. Others are trying to educate airlines, travel agents, and the public about the dangers of sex tourism. In 1999 several European airlines, including Lufthansa, Olympic Airways, and Air Europa began showing an in-flight video warning travelers to exotic destinations about the problems and dangers of sex tours.

Women can also be sex tourists, although as you may already have guessed their participation, like their solicitation of prostitutes in general, is much rarer. Herold (2000) conducted a study of Canadian women who engaged in sexual affairs with beach boys in the Dominican Republic. The men who work that trade know that women do not usually pay for sex, and to make a living they have to be extremely resourceful. Herold found that the successful ones would not bother approaching an attractive young woman, because she would already have plenty of men interested in having sex with her. Instead, they would regard as more promising an older, overweight woman. They also could not simply ask a woman to pay for sex the way a female prostitute would ask a male client. Instead, they had to take her out, form a relationship, begin having sex, and then tell the woman that they were having money problems, such as being unable to pay for an operation for a family member. The woman would then give money out of her affection and concern, rather than paying specifically for sex.

Thailand was a prime destination for sex tourists until the government enacted a public awareness campaign, stricter laws, and enforcement against sex trade.

The Cost of Prostitution

Although earnings from prostitution are illegal in most of the United States and therefore undeclared, untaxed income, prostitutes may have high expenses. Fees are often split with a pimp or madam who acts as the prostitute's "agent," and the costs of rent and payoffs for a business location may be high. Some bail bondsmen and attorneys make a large portion of their legitimate business income from prostitutes. Generally, fines paid by convicted prostitutes do not equal the court costs, which are paid by the taxpayers. High-profile prostitutes and madams like the Happy Hooker, the Mayflower Madam, and the Hollywood Madam are the exception not the rule. There are very few real life parallels to the *Pretty Woman* streetwalker who ends up living happily ever after with the millionaire.

Prostitution has been largely responsible for the spread of AIDS in some countries. It is believed that the AIDS epidemic in Thailand was mainly caused by the widespread patronage of prostitutes in that country. Sex with prostitutes is the most important factor in the male-to-female transmission of HIV in Africa. One study found that 85 percent of 1,000 prostitutes in Nairobi, Kenya, were infected with HIV (Lambert, 1988).

Although brothel owners in Nevada test their workers for HIV and require their customers to wear condoms, this is the exception rather than the rule. Despite the risks

FAQ:

Why is the price higher when prostitution is illegal?

You might think that the price for illegal prostitution would be lower. After all, legal industries must pay taxes, whereas illegal prostitutes do not. But illegality brings other costs that more than offset the difference in tax. If you operate a hardware store and a customer takes a drill without paying, you can call the police to have him arrested, and so you will get your money. But if you are a prostitute and a customer refuses to pay for services rendered, you cannot resort to the police, and so you need a criminal source of protection such as a pimp or organized crime group that is willing to use violence on your behalf. Such criminal services are expensive, and so they inflate the cost (for example, Gambetta, 1993). The cost of prostitution is also increased by the need to pay fines (when one is arrested) or bribes (to prevent being arrested).

Pornography: sexually explicit pictures, writing, or other material whose primary purpose is to cause sexual arousal

Erotica: literature or art with a sexual content

Obscenity: behavior or language that is considered offensive, lewd, or indecent according to accepted moral standards

of HIV infection, many prostitutes in the United States have not altered their sexual behavior. Streetwalkers and other prostitutes of lower socioeconomic status are much more likely to be infected with HIV than call girls. In one study of New York City streetwalkers, 35 percent were infected with HIV, and 50 percent never used condoms (Weiner, 1996). In general the length of time working as a prostitute and contact with a sex worker organization appear to increase the use of safer sex strategies (Marino et al., 2000).

The expense of visiting a prostitute varies widely. Based on detailed memoirs of a madam in Paris, Norberg (1998) concluded that the brothel had no fixed price nor even negotiated prices before sex. The customer merely paid the girl what he thought appropriate; if the madam regarded the amount as too low he would not be welcome to visit again. Today, the price of a visit to a prostitute may vary from as little as $10 or $20 (for example, for oral sex from a drug addict) to well over $1,000 (for a night with a high-class call girl, especially if unusual sexual acts are requested).

At the most basic level, prostitution is an economic exchange and depends on supply and demand. How much does the man want sex? How badly does the woman need the money? Many women prefer to earn money by other means than sex; as employment opportunities for women improve, the supply of prostitutes goes down, and the price goes up. Bullough and Bullough (1998) summarized a variety of studies indicating that in the 19th century, between 5 and 15 percent of young women worked as prostitutes at some point. Far fewer young women would do so today, and one likely cause of the difference is that there are a great many other ways for women to make money. It is hardly surprising that prostitutes tend to cost more in the United States than Southeast Asia and developing nations. Despite Cuba's geographical proximity to the North American mainland, its economy is in shambles, so prostitution is reportedly quite cheap. Cuba has become a convenient, attractive destination for North American sex tourists. The rich tourists can easily afford the low cost of sex with Cuban women; the Cuban women earn more in a single night of prostitution with a few Canadian customers than in an entire month of working at their normal jobs.

The legal status of prostitution is another important factor in determining the cost of prostitution. Like gambling, drugs, alcohol, and other industries, prostitution is more expensive when it is illegal than when it is legal. In Amsterdam, for example, prostitution is legal and openly practiced, and the girls offer men oral sex for 50 guilders (about $25 US); intercourse costs 100 guilders ($50 US). The higher cost of prostitution in North America is thus due partly to the availability of other jobs, and partly because it is illegal.

The growth of organized crime is one of the greatest social costs of illegal prostitution. Large amounts of money are involved in prostitution; the flow of these profits to organized crime attracts more criminals. In the United States, organized crime syndicates grew rapidly during the Prohibition era, because they ran the liquor industry when it was illegal. Making alcohol legal again was a huge setback for organized crime. Making prostitution legal would likewise reduce opportunities for criminal profits.

Opposition to legalized prostitution tends to come from two perspectives—conservatives, whose opposition often is based on moral grounds (for example, looking at sex as sin), and feminists who believe that prostitution exploits women. The economic factors have, however, begun to sway some conservative thinkers toward advocating legalized prostitution, just as some of them have advocated legalizing drugs and gambling. The argument is essentially that prostitution does not cease to exist simply because there is a law against it—rather, one effect of such laws is to shift the profits to criminals. Therefore, it is deemed better to make prostitution legal and let the government tax and regulate it. The contrary view is that making prostitution legal will cause it to become even more widespread; keeping it illegal keeps the number of prostitutes down.

There is little debate about what is better for the prostitutes. Prostitutes are much better off where prostitution is legal. Legal prostitutes can keep more of their earnings and avoid becoming dependent on organized crime figures and pimps. Legalizing prostitution would also reduce the stress of working in an illegal occupation. As one prostitute wrote, "I have been in the business now for twenty years. I am so tired of having to avoid being arrested all the time that sometimes I feel sort of crazed. . . ." (St. James et al., 1998, p. 123).

PORNOGRAPHY

Is James Joyce's novel *Ulysses* a literary masterpiece or filthy trash? Is *Playboy* a healthy expression of human sexuality or an excuse to look at dirty photos of naked women? Is the music of Eminem (see page 340) a realistic expression of how some men think or is it demeaning and degrading to women? If your partner rents an adult video, is it a thinly veiled criticism of your sex life together, does it mean that your partner is a sick pervert, or is it a stimulating form of entertainment? Do XXX-rated films promote sexual violence? Is censorship of sexually explicit materials the only way to control pornography? These are just a few of the questions posed in the debate about pornography and its effect, if any, on sexual attitudes and behavior.

Our perception of what is pornographic may vary according to our judgments about the role sexuality plays in human life, our sensitivity to the diversity of sexual expression, and our appreciation of sexuality in literary and artistic contexts. Many serious and important works of art are sexually explicit. We must look at artistic sexual representations in their larger context. "Just as it would be rash and ill-informed to take Tolstoy's *Anna Karenina* as an endorsement of suicide, or Twain's *Huckleberry Finn* as an endorsement of slavery, it would be equally rash and ill-informed to take the film *9½ Weeks* as an endorsement of profligate or indiscriminate sexual behavior" (Baird & Rosenbaum, 1991, p. 9).

Controversy about works of art portraying the human body is nothing new. Prehistoric cave drawings depict sexual activity. Ancient Grecian urns and cups are decorated with explicit heterosexual and homosexual paintings. Erotic art is depicted on many ancient Hindu temples. All of these examples, plus Goya's *Maya Desnuda* and Manet's *Le Dejeuner sur L'Herbe*, at one time or another have been considered obscene by some. Some observers make a distinction between **erotica,** works that are sexually explicit but nonviolent and nonsexist, and violent and nonviolent pornography. Others classify pornography as either hard-core or soft-core. *Hard-core pornography* typically includes graphic depictions or illustrations of sex organs and sexual acts; X-rated films and *Hustler* magazine are examples of hard-core pornography. *Soft-core pornography* is less explicit, leaving a bit more to the viewer or reader's imagination; some R-rated movies and *Playboy* might be considered soft-core.

Pornography and the Law

Obscenity laws address the right to create and disseminate written, visual, or spoken material of a sexual nature intended for the purpose of sexual arousal. Pornography is legal in the United States, but **obscenity,** something offensive to morality and decency, is not. As you have already seen, the boundary between the legal and illegal, the acceptable and unacceptable, the artistic and the offensive, is not easily defined. Individuals have vastly different opinions about what is obscene.

The Comstock Act of 1873 outlawed both the dissemination of information about birth control and the mailing of obscene literature. In the 1957 case *Roth v. United States,* the U.S. Supreme Court ruled that the portrayal of sexual activity was protected under the First Amendment of the Constitution unless its dominant theme was sex that appealed to prurient interest. In the 1973 case *Miller v. California,* the Supreme Court ruled that a determination of obscenity is based on the average person, applying contemporary community standards. In this ruling Justice William Brennan admitted that obscenity is incapable of definition with sufficient clarity to withstand attack

Michelangelo's statue "David"; is it art or is it pornography?

on vagueness grounds. Clarification was attempted in the case of *Pope v. Illinois*; the Supreme Court held that the proper inquiry is not whether an ordinary member of any given community would find serious literary artistic, political, or scientific value in allegedly obscene material, but whether a reasonable person would find such value in the material taken as a whole. As Justice Potter Stewart said, although he couldn't objectively define obscenity, he knew it when he saw it. Justice Stewart's lament indicates the need to understand the subjective experience of pornography, since it cannot be explained in purely objective terms.

In 1997 the U.S. Supreme Court ruled for the first time on government regulation of the Internet. The Court struck down the Communication Decency Act, a federal law that sought to shield children from indecent material online by drawing on the government's authority in regulating indecency on the radio and television (the government may not regulate indecent material in print). The Court declared that the Act was too broad, vague, and a violation of First Amendment rights. The Justices rejected arguments applying the same reasoning that justifies broadcast regulation to the Internet. In May 2000 the Supreme Court ruled that Congress went too far when it passed the Telecommunications Act of 1996, a law meant to shield children from sexually explicit cable television programming.

Three forms of pornography are often considered to be particularly obscene and offensive: violent pornography, degrading pornography, and child pornography. *Violent pornography* depicts sexual aggression in the form of rape, beating, mutilation, or even murder. *Degrading pornography* debases its subjects as sexual objects. *Child pornography*, the sexual exploitation of children, is especially harmful. However, there is little consensus regarding these categories. Some consider the entire genre of "slasher" films to be violent pornography, whereas others feel that all pornography is degrading, and Calvin Klein's advertisements have been repeatedly attacked as child pornography.

The Effects of Exposure to Sexually Explicit Materials

Just as the censors and legal experts can't tell us what is art and what is pornography, politicians and researchers aren't sure about the effects of exposure to sexually explicit material. In 1970 the U.S. Congress appointed the Commission on Obscenity and Pornography to study the effects of exposure to sexually explicit materials. Although the study found that some people were sexually aroused by pornography and increased the frequency of their usual sexual activity, they did not engage in more antisocial sexual behaviors. The Commission concluded that there were no significant long-lasting effects of pornography and that it might even have some educational benefits.

Adolescents are particularly active media users and there is a great deal of concern about how the media images and messages about sex affect their sexual attitudes and behaviors. "Because consensually accepted programs of sexual education are lacking, erotica have come to serve as the primary agent of sexual socialization" (Zillmann, 2000, p. 41). Most studies on the effects of exposure to pornography have been undertaken either with sex offenders or college students, not a representative sample of the population.

In Like Flynt

Hustler magazine publisher Larry Flynt has predicted that if the obscenity laws in the United States are rescinded, the amount of hard-core material sold would skyrocket—but not for long. Once the taboo is lifted and porn loses the aura of a forbidden vice, people will lose interest in it.

Do you think that people would lose interest in hard-core pornography if it were made legal?

—Why or why not?

CONSIDERATIONS

Artistic License

In the winter of 1994, a 45-year-old businessman with no previous criminal record was arrested on child endangerment charges after 110 nude photographs of his 6-year-old daughter were found. The father explained that the photographs were for an art class at the International Center of Photography. An art photography expert described the photos as hasty, affectionate, amused, playful glimpses of someone equally playful, while local detectives and prosecutors viewed them as smut.

An Ohio photo developer turned nude photos of an 8-year-old girl over to the police. The girl's mother was arrested for taking pictures of her daughter bathing. To avoid trial, the woman agreed to counseling and surrendered the photos, which were deemed offensive. Had she been convicted, the mother could have lost custody of her daughter and been sentenced to 15 years in prison.

In 2000, a 65-year-old New Jersey woman was arrested when she picked up her photographs from a film developer. The woman, who had taken a nude photography class in 1983, had taken nude pictures of her two granddaughters, ages 3 and 8, dancing around the bedroom. She was suspended from her job of 32 years as a school social worker and placed in a pretrial intervention program.

 Do you think that prosecution in these cases was justified?

—Why or why not?

Thematic Content   A fascinating study by Fisher and Byrne (1978) examined the mental and the physical responses to pornography. Male and female viewers saw either a soft-core or a hard-core sex film. The hard-core version depicted explicit sex and full nudity, whereas the soft-core film showed no more than people in their underwear kissing and fondling each other. The degree of explicitness of the film had no effect on arousal.

There was another variable that did make a big difference. The researchers gave people different synopses of the story line, with differing implications for what the characters in the film were thinking and feeling. Some participants were told that the scene involved a man and a prostitute, and others that it involved sex between newlyweds; still others were led to believe that it involved a man and a woman who had just met at a dance and were having sex for the first time. The researchers predicted that the newlywed theme would be most appealing to women viewers, but their data showed something quite different. Both men and women were most stimulated when they thought the scene involved a man and woman who had just met each other. As noted in an earlier chapter, the brain is a very important sex organ!

The importance of the story theme was also shown by Cowan and Dunn (1994). They showed male and female viewers a variety of different scenes, with different story lines. Their initial interest was in ascertaining which themes would be perceived as most degrading to women. In particular, they predicted that the theme of "submission," defined as a scene in which a woman initially rejected sexual advances but then changed her mind and became a willing participant, would be perceived as most degrading. Contrary to their prediction, neither male nor female viewers rated that theme—nor, indeed, any of the themes—as degrading to women. In fact, the "submission" theme was rated by the female viewers as most arousing, by a substantial margin. This same theme was also the most arousing to the male viewers, although the males had several favorite themes and the differences among those favorites were small. Garcia et al. (1984) found that women were more aroused when the stories they read depicted women initiating and controlling the sexual activity. Men in their study were more aroused in response to stories in which men initiated and controlled the sexual activity.

Anyone who has watched a bit of pornography knows that most films devote little effort to developing the plot, characterization, story line, and emotional attitudes of the characters. The research findings cited here suggest that viewers might find the products significantly more arousing if the producers paid more attention to these aspects of the films!

What are the effects on women of viewing violent pornography?

One study found that the degree to which women who have been exposed to sexually violent mass media hold female abuse victims accountable is dependent upon three factors: situational relevance, personal similarity, and emotional arousal. Among other findings was that subjects who were not desensitized by exposure to sexually violent movies perceived there was more psychological injury to rape victims (Dexter et al., 1997).

The Effects of Pornography on Sexual Violence   The Meese Commission reexamined the effects of pornography in 1985. Appointed by President Reagan, the findings of the panel, headed by Attorney General Edwin Meese, were in direct opposition to those of the 1970 commission report. The Meese Commission concluded that there is a causal relationship between exposure to violent pornography and sexual violence, and that pornography is harmful both to individuals and to society. Critics claim that the Meese Commission relied on overgeneralizations of laboratory findings (Wilcox, 1987) and failed to distinguish between the effects of sexually explicit and violent materials (Donnerstein & Linz, 1987).

There are those who believe that increases in the availability of even nonviolent pornography in the United States probably are correlated with increasing rates of sexually maladaptive behaviors (Mawhinney, 1998). Many critics of pornography believe that it depersonalizes sexuality and devalues women in our society by encouraging heterosexual males to associate sexual excitement with depictions of women as sex objects. Pornography occasionally represents women being dominated by men and men being dominated by women. Broscus, Weaver, and Staab (1993) have argued that contemporary pornography typically involves a narrow range of highly stylized content conventions, emphasizing the male orientation toward sexual behavior. However, depictions of healthy sexuality such as communication between partners, expressions of affection or emotion (except fear and lust), and concern about sanitation or the consequences of sexual activities are absent or minimized.

If pornography causes sexual violence, then there should be more rape in areas where pornography is more common. Results have been inconsistent, ever since Denmark first liberalized its laws on pornography and reported that sex offenses went down. Amsterdam, Holland, known as the porn capital of the world, has fewer crimes of assault against women than most other Western cities. Scott and Schwalm (1988) found a positive correlation between rape rates in the 50 American states and circulation rates of *Playboy* and other soft-core adult magazines. That is, the higher the circulation of *Playboy*, the more rapes. The circulation of these magazines did not correlate with other violent crimes. Interestingly, circulation of the more sexually explicit magazines (such as *Hustler*) did not show any correlation with crime rate. The correlation could simply mean that more permissive areas have higher circulation rates of soft-core magazines as well as better police procedures and hence more accurate reporting of rape.

The exposure of sex offenders to pornography is another area of research. Like 1970s serial rapist and murderer Ted Bundy, who was executed in 1989, many sex offenders implicate pornography in the commission of their offenses. In a study of 89 nonincarcerated sex offenders, slightly more than a third reported at least occasionally being incited to commit an offense by exposure to pornography. Of these, 33 percent of the rapists and 54 percent of the child molesters said they deliberately used pornography in preparation for committing their crimes (Feinsiedel, 1986). Another study of 80 convicted male sex offenders and 96 nonconvicted males ages 13 to 19 found that being a sex offender was significantly associated with the use of sexually explicit materials (Zgourides et al., 1997).

In 1999, a study was conducted in which some U.S. college students were randomly assigned to one of two groups; one group viewed a video portraying stereotyped sexual imagery, and the other was shown a video that excluded all sexual images. The researchers found some evidence of an interaction among subject's gender, exposure to traditional sexual imagery, and the acceptance of interpersonal violence (Kalof, 1999).

The relationship of sexual aggression and violent pornography has been widely studied. Some laboratory studies have shown that men exposed to violent pornography are more likely to become aggressive toward women and to show less sensitivity to women who have been sexually assaulted. In a classic 1980 study, 120 college men interacted with either a male or female partner (an accomplice in the experiment) who treated the subject in either a neutral or hostile manner. The subjects were then shown neutral, nonviolent pornographic or violent pornographic films and given the opportunity to deliver an electric shock to the accomplice, presumably to help the accomplice learn a new task.

The subjects didn't know that the accomplices were not actually shocked. Unprovoked subjects (those who had been treated neutrally) who viewed violent pornography showed greater aggression toward the female accomplices (as measured by the strength of the shock) than did unprovoked subjects who viewed nonviolent films. Provoked subjects (those who had been treated with hostility) who were shown violent pornography selected the highest shock levels of all (Donnerstein and Linz, 1987). Sapolsky and Zillman (1981) found that exposure to very arousing and somewhat disturbing pornography caused people to respond more aggressively later in response to a provocation—but that the pornography did not increase hostility or aggression toward an "innocent bystander" who had not insulted or provoked the person. Pornography thus did not have any effect by itself, but it did increase the degree of aggression in response to provocation.

In contrast to the results just cited, many other studies have found no discernible effects of pornography on violent behavior. Fisher and Grenier (1994) gave their article on violent pornography the subtitle "In Search of Reliable Effects," in order to indicate the haphazard and inconsistent pattern of findings. They reviewed many studies on how exposure to violent pornography may affect the way men think about women and treat women, and these studies were highly inconsistent. Fisher and Grenier then conducted a pair of laboratory studies of their own, both of which failed to find any increase in negative thoughts, attitudes, or actions toward women as a result of exposure to violent pornography.

Usually when different studies find different results, the proper conclusion is that the pattern depends on other factors. If that is true of violent pornography, then we might reasonably conclude that violent pornography can increase violence toward women under certain circumstances—but not others. Researchers should see the mixed results as a challenge to identify these other factors.

Probably the best conclusion is that watching films of people having sex does not cause aggressive behavior in the vast majority of viewers. Watching sex is certainly less likely to cause antisocial behavior than watching violence. Studies that do find effects of violent pornography generally find their subjects exhibiting them immediately after viewing the film, suggesting that such effects may be temporary. The possibility that a few dangerous individuals may be incited to perpetrate violent acts, while most viewers are unaffected, raises a difficult policy issue. At what point does significant harm to a few individuals justify restricting the freedom of many others? Our society grapples with this issue in many spheres, including recreational drugs (used by most with no problem, but with disastrous results for others), gambling, film violence, and even automobiles (convenient for many, but deadly for a few). The inconsistent evidence about violent pornography highlights the need for further research. At present, there appears to be very little cause for concern that nonviolent pornography causes violent behavior.

Pornography and Gender Attitudes

A study compared attitudes concerning the Equal Rights Amendment, a law against marital rape, and punishment for date and marital rape among 194 men who rented X-rated videos. No correlations were found between the number of videos a man had rented and his attitudes toward feminism and rape. These findings suggest that calloused attitudes toward women may not be generated by sexually explicit videos (Davies, 1997). Another study found that while exposure to interactive computer pornography resulted in sexual arousal, it did not affect attitudes or behaviors toward women (Barak & Fisher, 1997).

Other Effects of Pornography

In an ambitious experiment Mann et al. (1974) studied the effect of pornography on consenting sexual behavior. They recruited married couples and had them keep a diary of all their sexual activity for 4 weeks in order to establish a baseline. Then for 4 weeks they showed the couples pornographic films one night a week, as the couples continued to record their sex lives. Finally, the couples were asked to continue recording their sexual activities for another 4 weeks without exposure to pornography, so that any long-term consequences could be assessed.

FAQ:

Is there a link between pornography and oppression of females in general?

Several studies have attempted to examine the effect of pornography on attitudes. Male subjects in one study viewed one of three equally stimulating films determined by an independent set of viewers to be: (1) sexually explicit and degrading, (2) sexually explicit and non-degrading or (3) non-sexual. After viewing the films, the men interacted with women and evaluated their partners' intellectual competence, sexual interest, and dominance. The women involved in these interactions evaluated their own feelings. No effects for film exposure alone were found for any of these variables. Neither were there interaction effects between film and partners' sex-role orientation in the women's evaluations of their partners. However, men's sex-role orientation moderated film effects for men's evaluations of their female partner's intellectual competence and sexual interest (Jansma et al., 1997).

FAQ:

Do women like pornography?

Kinsey (1953) found that women expressed far less interest in and response to pornography than men. Most said that they did not like pornography and did not find it appealing. However, studies that actually expose women to pornography generally find that women respond to pornography by becoming sexually aroused. Moreover, women who report liking pornography the least often show the greatest sexual arousal in response to it (Morokoff, 1985), suggesting that a dislike of pornography is a defense mechanism by which they deny unacceptable responses. It also is possible that these women were most aroused because they had had the lowest prior exposure to such materials—more evidence of the importance of novelty in producing response to pornography.

If both men and women find pornography to be sexually arousing, why is it only men seek it out on a regular basis? Based on current knowledge, it is impossible to say whether this reflects the greater power of the male sex drive, greater male initiative in pursuing sexual activity, or cultural suppression of female interest in and enjoyment of pornography.

The study found no lasting consequences. The couples' sex lives were no different during the 4 weeks following the exposure to pornography than they had been during the initial, baseline period. In fact, there was hardly any sign that the effects of pornography lasted beyond the night the films were viewed.

On the nights the couples watched pornography, however, there was a dramatic increase in sexual behavior. During the baseline period, about 20 to 25 percent of the couples had sex on any given night, but on the first night that the couples watched pornography, two thirds of them had sex. Viewing pornography thus had a powerful aphrodisiac effect (that is, it influenced them to have sex).

However, that dramatic increase in sexual activity occurred only on the first night the couple watched pornography. The effect was still present but noticeably weaker the following week, when the couple was exposed to pornography for the second time, and by the fourth week there was no noticeable increase at all. The only exception was found among couples who initially saw simple pornography and later switched to seeing more unusual pornography, such as threesomes and whipping. These couples showed a significant increase in sexual activity after the change in subject matter. Thus, the effects of pornography may be dramatic at first, but they wear off quickly. Much of the impact of pornography appears to depend on novelty, and once the novelty is gone, pornography ceases to have its effect.

Mann and his colleagues were also able to address the common question of whether people who watch unusual sex acts in pornography are induced to engage in some of those activities themselves. From their study, the answer was no. Regardless of whether couples watched the conventional sex films or the unusual activities, they did not show any noticeable changes in the types of activities they performed. To put it simply, watching pornography made the couples sexually aroused, so they did what they usually did when aroused—have sex in their established, familiar manner. For example, watching a scene of a woman whipping a man before sex did not inspire the married viewers to try that for themselves. In psychological terms, the effects of pornography appeared to be mediated by arousal (getting turned on) rather than by modeling (copying what was seen).

Focusing on the effects on couples may be misleading. It seems likely that most pornography has always been used in solitary. In that context, its most consistent effect is probably masturbation; indeed, many people deliberately obtain pornography to use in connection with their masturbatory activities. Whether pornography causes an increase in masturbation, or merely makes it easier and more fun, has not been established conclusively, but the link between pornography and masturbation is difficult to deny. This link is probably also an important reason that previous generations attempted to suppress pornography—they believed that masturbation was harmful, so they tried to protect people from being exposed to materials associated with that activity.

SEX AND PROFITS

Yesterday's pornography is today's pop culture. In every way, shape, and form sex is big business. However, men are more likely than women to be consumers of sexually explicit products (see Figure 14.1). Moreover, the sexual content of American culture has changed greatly in recent decades. Consider the following examples of sex in popular media. Tracy Lord, once an adult video porn star, moved to prime time to appear on *Melrose Place*. Advertisements have moved from a 1980s Brooke Shields purring that "nothing comes between me and my Calvins" to Gucci ads depicting oral and lesbian sex. As lyricist and composer Cole Porter so aptly put it, "In golden days a glimpse of stocking was looked on as something shocking. Now heaven knows, anything goes."

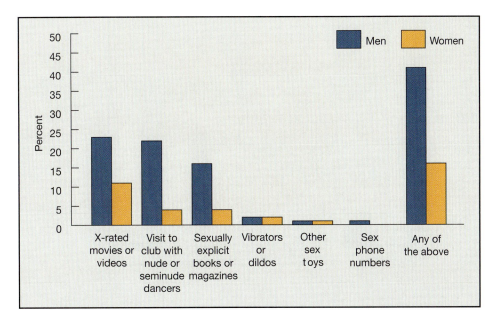

FIGURE 14.1   **Purchases of Autoerotic Materials During the Past Year**
SOURCE: Adapted from Michael et al., 1994, p. 157.

Advertising

"If I buy this product I will be sexy, desirable, and irresistibly attractive." Sound familiar? Cigarette, alcohol, automobile, clothing, and cosmetics companies spend millions of dollars every year hoping that we continue to associate their products with sex appeal. Sex in advertising may be subtle with the use of innuendo and double entendres, or may be more blatant by displaying unclothed or underclothed young, fit, attractive bodies to attract our attention, stimulate our hormones, and unleash our fantasies (see accompanying photograph). However, sexy ads can backfire if viewers pay so much attention to the sexy imagery that they forget what product is being advertised (Edgley, 1980; Severn et al., 1990).

Sexual imagery does help sell products. The advertising industry would have abandoned sexy images long ago if they failed to work. A thought-provoking study by Smith and Engel (1968) provided an experimental test of sexual content in advertising. Young men viewed various advertisements for cars. One of the cars was paired with an image of an attractive young woman wearing only a black sweater and black lace panties and holding a large spear (chosen for its ostensibly phallic symbolism). Different men saw different versions of the ads, so that the woman was paired with a different car each time. When asked to rate their preferences, the men showed a significantly enhanced preference for whichever car had been paired with the attractive model. They did not, however, say that they liked the car because of the woman. On the contrary, they gave various other reasons, such as gas mileage, safety rating, or some other features. The men did not realize that their preference had been shaped by the sexy image.

Movies

Sex in films is nothing new. As early as 1899 nudes appeared in motion pictures. Films containing scenes of sexual intercourse could be privately screened in the early 1900s. Sadomasochistic films were privately commissioned in the 1920s, as were nude films made for homosexual audiences. Early "stag" films usually had little plot, lots of nudity, and were crudely made (Brown &

Calvin Klein is as well known for his company's sexually provocative advertising as he is for his clothing and perfume.

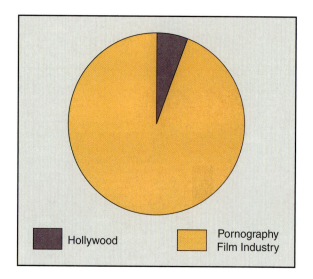

FIGURE 14.2 **New Video Releases in 1997.**
SOURCE: Lapham, 1997.

Bryant, 1989). In the 1970s, sexually explicit films such as *Deep Throat* and *I Am Curious Yellow* became socially acceptable; since the advent of the VCR in the 1980s, one in three video rentals is an X-rated movie. According to *Adult Video News*, an industry trade publication, the number of hard-core video rentals rose from 75 million in 1985 to 490 million in 1992 and to 665 million in 1996. Adult films, once a shady back street business, now churn out over 150 new titles each week (Figure 14.2) and make millions of dollars for major hotel chains (Schlosser, 1997).

Sharon Stone's flash of pubic hair in *Basic Instinct*, and the glimpse of Harvey Keitel's penis in *The Piano* are atypical for Hollywood movies. However, shots of female breasts and male and female buttocks are frequently displayed in today's cinema. In 1968 the Motion Picture Association created a rating system to ward off government intervention. A board screens films and votes for what most parents would consider being that film's appropriate rating. The familiar G, PG, PG-13, R, and NC-17 (which replaced the X rating in 1990) were intended to help parents decide what their children should see (see Table 14.3), although the rating system is confusing and inconsistent. The 1989 PG-13 film *Parenthood* shows Steve Martin's character crashing his car when his wife fellates him, while movies as diverse as *Shakespeare in Love* and *Eyes Wide Shut* received R ratings.

Would you rather see a PG-rated film or one with an R rating? Movie ratings apparently influence the movie choices of adult viewers also. When college students read

TABLE 14.3

Motion Picture Rating System	
G	General Audiences. No sex, nudity, bad language, or drug use. The film should be suitable for all audiences.
PG	Parental Guidance Suggested. The film may contain some material not suitable for children. The film may include brief nudity.
PG-13	Parents Strongly Cautioned. May not be appropriate for children under age 13. The film may contain bad language, brief nudity, sexual overtones, and drug usage.
R	Restricted, under 17 not admitted without a parent or adult guardian. The film will definitely contain adult material. It will probably contain bad language, violence, sex, and drug usage and have an adult theme.
NC-17	No one 17 and under will be admitted. Adult film with explicit sex scenes, sexually oriented language, or excessive violence.

one of two synopses of a movie, they preferred those that included the words *nudity* or *sexuality* (Bah, 1998). Are you surprised to learn that this was particularly true of female students?

Literature

Sometime between 206 B.C. and A.D. 24 highly detailed and explicit Chinese sex manuals were written (Tannahill, 1980). When the Indian book, the *Kama Sutra*, written around A.D. 400 to 500, first appeared in the West, it was denounced as being obscene. U.S. Courts have censored or sought to ban such works as James Joyce's *Ulysses*, *Lady Chatterley's Lover* by D. H. Lawrence, and Henry Miller's *Tropic of Cancer*. Public tolerance of sexually explicit writings has increased gradually. Phillip Roth's discussion about his penis in *Portnoy's Complaint* and Erica Jong's sexual methods of overcoming her *Fear of Flying* helped move literature with sexual themes into the mainstream. Today, books with sexual themes are far more likely to be bestsellers than to be banned.

Theater

Sex has been a part of live theater performances as far back as Aristophanes. Early burlesque shows often had sexual themes, bawdy humor, and stripteases (with the emphasis on the "tease"). The nudity contained in the shows *Hair* and *Oh! Calcutta!* shocked many theatergoers in the 1960s. The topless craze that began in the 1960s spread like wildfire across the United States; topless dancers and strippers are now common in cities throughout the 50 states (see CAMPUS CONFIDENTIAL box). Even the most explicit bottomless/topless club in the United States would probably seem quite tame to anyone who has attended performances such as those in Japan where customers are permitted not only to touch but also to have sexual relations with the performers (Bornoff, 1991).

Television

Television may be the medium with the most pervasive influence on our views and values. Since the 1970s, television programs have become increasingly sexually oriented. Daytime soap operas plot the constant coupling, uncoupling, and recoupling of their characters. Talk show guests openly discuss orgasms, fantasies, genitalia, and the how, when, where, and what of all their sexual partners. The separate beds on *I Love Lucy* and the virginity of *Happy Days* have given way to *Sex in the City* and *Temptation Island* and *Queer as Folk*. Some of the same television stations that once refused to air the show *NYPD Blue*, stating that it is nothing more than soft-core pornography because of the exposure of actor David Caruso's buttocks, have no such qualms about guests on Sally Jesse Raphael or Jerry Springer discussing their sex lives. Cable and satellite programming, which are not subject to the same federal regulations as network television, contain even more explicit language as well as graphic depictions of sexual activity.

Music

"Wine, women and song" have gone together since well before the first nervous date put Ravel's "Bolero" on the stereo to set a mood for seduction. Today, many people believe that popular music has an enormous and mostly detrimental effect on "the younger generation's" attitude toward sex. Those who swooned over Sinatra became those who were shocked at Elvis; those who screamed to The Rolling Stones became those who think rappers go too far. Lyrics that barely could be understood (people still debate the words to "Louie, Louie") are now vividly portrayed in music videos. Crotch grabbing, pelvis grinding, bisexuality, and sexual violence are incorporated into many musical performances and videos. In his 1990 ruling upholding prior restraint (a prohibition imposed on expression before the expression takes place) of 2 Live Crew's album "As

CAMPUS CONFIDENTIAL

"I'm working my way through college and it pays a lot better than slinging burgers. I love to dance. I make good money and I'm proud of my body. I've got no problems with what I do. Nobody is forced to come watch me perform. I just don't see this as some big moral issue; it's entertainment.

"To me it's just my job. I know that most people don't take off most of their clothes to go to work, but I just think of my birthday suit as my work outfit. Most of the customers are okay, but every now and then you get someone who wants to touch not just look. But I can handle that. There's probably more than a little bit of the exhibitionist in me, but that doesn't mean I have sex with the customers. I think a lot of the people who put down dancers are just jealous. Besides, men have been watching strippers for years. I think it's great that women can come to a club like ours and have some fun." ●

The fact that women think about, talk about, and like to have sex is fundamental to the widely popular HBO series, "Sex and the City."

Nasty as They Wanna Be," U.S. District Court Judge Jose Gonzalez stated that the album "is an appeal to dirty thoughts and the loins, not to the intellect. It cannot be reasonably argued that the violence, perversion, abuse of women, graphic descriptions of all kinds of sexual conduct, and microscopic descriptions of human genitalia contained on this recording are comedic art" (Curriden, 1990–91, pp. 13–14).

A study was conducted in which the subjects were exposed to the music and sexually explicit lyrics of 2 Live Crew, other rap music, and nonrap music. The students were asked to make judgments of offensiveness, prurient appeal, and artistic merit. Results indicated the music of 2 Live Crew that was high in sexual explicitness was rated as more offensive than other equally sexual materials. There was no significant gender difference among the subjects; women in this study did not find the music more offensive than men. Rebellious sexual attitudes, the belief that rap music causes societal degradation, and disaffection toward society helped predict subjects' responses to all materials on patent offensiveness and prurient appeal scales (Dixon & Linz, 1997).

Magazines

Since the 1950s copies of *Playboy* magazine have been the source of consternation for some and inspiration to others. *Playboy* is one of many magazines that contain photos of nudes and sexually related content. In numerous bathrooms the nude centerfold somehow sidetracks males who claim they purchased the magazine to read the articles. Some magazines have no editorial stance and little if any text, devoting every page to photographs that emphasize genitalia. In 1986, the Meese Commission identified more than 2,300 pornographic magazine titles. In 1999 *Hustler* publisher Larry Flynt opened his first of a planned chain of upscale pornography–coffee shop emporiums in Los Angeles.

Britney Spears publicly declares "I'm not so Innocent" in song and dress.

A 1986 study identified four categories of magazines based on their target audience: magazines for heterosexual upwardly mobile males such as *Playboy*, *Penthouse*, and *Oui*; *Gallery* and *Hustler*, which are geared toward working-class heterosexual males; *Blueboy* and *Mandate* for homosexual males; and *Playgirl* for heterosexual females (Brown & Bryant 1989). Erotic magazines for lesbians, such as *On Our Backs*, have also been introduced and enjoyed some success. However, such ventures face economic obstacles, most notably the small size of the market niche. There are relatively few lesbians in the United States compared to other categories of sexual orientations, and women spend less money than men on erotic and sexual materials in general (Laumann et al., 1994).

Telephone Sex

Although people have probably been talking about sex on the phone since its invention, commercial telephone sex began in 1982 when the Federal Communication Commission (FCC), in a deregulatory move, ruled that the phone company could no longer have a monopoly on recorded messages. That meant the phone company could no longer keep recorded messages clean, and once there were "dirty" messages recorded there was bound to be live telephone sex. The first live telephone sex service began in 1983 with Dial-a-Porn; phone sex continues to be popular, and various services are widely advertised.

It is estimated that every night between the peak hours of 9:00 P.M. and 1:00 A.M. 250,000 Americans push-button a connection to commercial phone sex. Customers are usually billed by credit card and listen either to a prerecorded message or a live performer who describes sexual activities or participates in the caller's verbal fantasy. With an average call lasting 6 to 8 minutes and with charges ranging from 89 cents to $4 a minute it is estimated that Americans spend nearly $1 billion a year on phone sex.

In 1991 the FCC banned "obscene communications for commercial purposes"; however, no such restrictions apply to overseas calls. Phone sex providers now make financial arrangements with foreign phone companies and route their business to phone sex operators in the Caribbean and Russia. Half of every dollar spent on an international sex call goes to the domestic phone company. Some phone sex providers have even started their own long-distance phone companies in order to cut costs and increase profits (Schlosser, 1997).

Sex Toys

Sex toys, devices reputed to enhance sexual pleasure, have been abundant for centuries. During the Ming dynasty in China, jade penis rings were used to increase the duration of an erection and Ben Wa balls were inserted in the vagina to provide sexual pleasure. Today, sex toys and props (see accompanying photograph) are widely available through mail-order catalogues, at private parties, or in specialty stores.

Sex toys can be used by couples or for solitary sexual pleasure. Vibrators are the most widely used sexual aid. Some vibrators are used with a dildo, a penis-shaped object, some buzz, some give a gentle massage. Other widely available devices and enhancers include inflatable rubber dolls with mouths, vaginas, and anuses. If you don't want to spend much money, blindfolds, scarves for bondage, and all kinds of foods (remember Kim Basinger and Mickey Rourke in the movie *9½ Weeks*?) can be used as sexual playthings.

Many adults enjoy playing with a variety of sex toys.

EXPLORING SEXUALITY ONLINE

The Business of Cyberporno

Every new technology since the printing press has been used for sexual commerce. In the early to mid-1990s, up to 80 percent of all Internet traffic was sex-related. While many e-commerce sites have yet to make a profit, Internet users spent $970 million on access to cybersex, online sex-content sites, in 1999 alone. According to the research firm Datamonitor, that figure could rise to more than $3 billion by 2003. Because online pornographers can digitize their product, which means that no live participants are required, their delivery cost is essentially zero (Lane, 2000).

With low advertising and labor costs, sex sites typically enjoy profit margins of 30 percent or more; compare this figure to the profit margins of online brokerages, just 0.2 percent in 2000 (Koerner, 2000). Internet sex is so profitable there are even "starter kits" available for cybersex entrepreneurs, prepackaged collections of photos and video clips that cost as little as $200. Perhaps profits will go down as competition increases; Webcams that cost as little as $100 allow any exhibitionist to become an Internet porn star.

Sex Toys: objects or devices used to enhance sexual pleasure

Here's to You, Mrs. Robinson

Most Internet sex cases that are prosecuted have involved child pornography. However, in 2000, charges of wholesale promotion of obscene materials were brought against Tammy and Herbert Robinson of Lakeland, Florida, after Mr. Robinson took photographs of his wife in their home and sold the photographs on a Web site. The Robinsons became crusaders for Internet freedom and took their case to national television talk shows. The charges were dropped in 2001.

Some people look to the Internet as a place where adults can make legal choices in relative liberty. Civil liberties groups and the American Library Association have filed suit to block the Children's Internet Protection Act, a federal law passed in December 2000 that would require schools and libraries to install Internet filters on computers to keep children from viewing pornography. These groups believe that the software does not block all the sex sites. The ability of filtering software to block only selected categories creates the potential for huge administrative problems. In addition, while the law threatens to deny schools and libraries significant federal funding if they do not filter Internet access, they do not make funds available to buy the software.

Do you think consenting adults should be allowed to use the Internet for sex-related businesses?

—What do you think about the federal Children's Internet Protection Act?

—Is the real problem with the Internet or in trying to control behavior instead of educating students?

CHAPTER REVIEW

Prostitution, pornography, and sex in advertising are examples of sex in the marketplace.

1_____ is the exchange of sexual services for money or other resources. In the United States more than 1 million women earn all or part of their living as prostitutes. The NHSLS found that 16 percent of men reported paying for sex at some time.

There are three main types of female prostitutes. **2**_____ have regular customers whom they see at a designated place of business; new customers are usually by referral only. **3**_____ or bordellos are business places that accept walk-in clients. **4**_____ solicit customers at a particular public location.

A **5**_____ may be a business manager, companion, protector, and/or drug supplier for prostitutes. A

6_____ refers and schedules clients for call girls for a percentage of the prostitute's fee.

7_____ are heterosexual male prostitutes whose work is similar to that of call girls.

8_____ are homosexual male prostitutes who operate similar to streetwalkers. Men who seek out young adolescent male prostitutes are called **9**_____.

There appear to be four pathways to prostitution: poverty, childhood sexual abuse, running away from home, and drug use. Primary reasons for the use of prostitutes include: loneliness; not having to risk rejection; feelings of inferiority, anxiety or shame regarding sex; seeking sexual variety or acts a regular partner won't perform; avoiding emotional involvement and commitment; and the desire to degrade and to humiliate women.

In general, the price and availability of prostitution depends on the female labor market.

10_____ is sexually arousing or erotic art, music, literature, film, or other media. **11**_____ is something offensive to morality and decency. Pornography is legal in the United States; obscenity is not. In our society there often is little agreement on the boundary between pornography and obscenity.

The **12**_____ Act of 1873 outlawed the dissemination of information about birth control and made it a felony to send obscene literature through the mail. In 1957 the U.S. Supreme Court ruled that the portrayal of sexual activity was protected under the First Amendment of the Constitution unless its dominant theme appealed to "prurient interest."

The 1970 Commission on Obscenity and Pornography concluded that there were no significant long-lasting effects of pornography and that it might even have some educational benefits. However, the 1985 **13**_____ Commission concluded that there is a causal relationship between exposure to violent pornography and sexual violence and that pornography is harmful to both individuals and to society. Research has produced inconsistent evidence, but the general conclusion is that there is little cause for concern that nonviolent pornography causes violent behavior, nor does it seem to affect men's attitudes toward women.

Sex in advertising and in popular media (for example, movies, books, television, and music) are ubiquitous in our society. Telephone sex and online sex are the most recent innovations in the business of sex.

SUGGESTED READINGS

Elias, J., Bullough, V., & Bullough, V. (Eds.). (1999). *Prostitution: On Whores, Hustlers and Johns.* Amherst, NY: Prometheus Books.

This comprehensive collection by scholars, therapists, and sex workers looks at prostitution in a historical context and explores questions including why customers pay for sex, if prostitutes can enjoy their work, and the future of prostitution.

Lane, F. S. (2000). *Obscene Profits: The Entrepreneurs of Pornography in the Cyber Age.* New York: Routledge Press.

A lawyer and computer consultant looks at how technology, including telephones, VCRs, and computers, has increased the business of pornography.

Stoller, R. J. & Levine, I. S. (1996). *Coming Attraction: The Making of an X-Rated Video.* New Haven, CT: Yale University Press.

A psychiatrist and a screenwriter interview adult video performers, writers, directors, producers, and technicians to examine the technical aspects of making an X-rated video and the motivations and backgrounds of those working in the industry.

Ullman, S. (1998). *Sex Seen: The Emergence of Modern Sexuality in America.* Berkeley: University of California Press.

Ullman charts the changes in sexual mores in the United States over the past century by focusing on the city of Sacramento. A blend of social history, media analysis, and court cases are used to explain how sexuality and desire became an essential part of personal identity in the 20th century.

Weitzer, R. (Ed.). (1999). *Sex for Sale: Prostitution, Pornography, and the Sex Industry.* New York: Routledge Press.

This is a collection of original essays on sex work, its risks, and its political implications, including studies of gay pornography, legal brothels, police vice squads, and strippers.

Williams, L. (1999). *Hard Core: Power, Pleasure, and the 'Frenzy of the Visible.'* Berkeley: University of California Press.

Williams explores the social function of "offensive" imagery from a wide range of theoretical perspectives, arguing against censorship and that we take pornography seriously, whether or not we like it or think it is art.

ANSWERS TO CHAPTER REVIEW:

1. Prostitution; **2.** Call girls; **3.** Brothels; **4.** Streetwalkers; **5.** pimp; **6.** madam; **7.** Gigolos; **8.** Hustlers; **9.** Chickenhawks; **10.** Pornography; **11.** Obscenity; **12.** Comstock; **13.** Meese.

Sex and Love

- **What Is Love?**
  The many types of love include passionate and companionate love. Sternberg's triangular theory of love, Lee's typology, and the evolutionary approach are a few of the many theories used to explain this universal human phenomenon.

- **Attraction: Looking for Love**
  Physical appearance is one of the many factors in attraction to another person. While different cultures have different ideals of beauty, evolutionary theorists suggest that a number of universally favored traits are indicators of good reproductive health.

- **Romance: Falling in Love**
  Romance depends on five criteria: proximity, familiarity, readiness, similarity, and reciprocity.

- **Sex: Making Love**
  While sex and love are closely linked, each can exist without the other. Even the physical pleasure of orgasm has a strong emotional component.

- **Attachment: Staying in Love**
  Attachment is one of many components of human love. Although attachment can exist without love, it is doubtful that love can exist in the absence of attachment. Committed relationships offer many benefits, but there is no single basis for long-term relationships.

- **Intimacy, Love, and Sexual Communication**
  Intimacy, love, and sexual communication are essential to healthy, long-term sexual relationships. There are gender differences as well as individual differences in communication styles.

PHYSICAL

SOCIAL

EMOTIONAL

SPIRITUAL

COGNITIVE

Love conquers all. You can't be in love with two people at the same time. You will know when you have met your one true love. Love means never having to say you're sorry. These are just a few of the romantic myths that many of us have heard so often that we assume they must be true. "We all have talked to friends, read magazine articles and survey results, we remember what our mothers told us, and by the time we're adults in long-term committed relationships (or looking for one), we've absorbed this 'wisdom' to the point that it's virtually unconscious" (Schwartz, 2000, p. 2). Accepting these myths as fact can keep us from forming or maintaining healthy relationships. For example, if you believe that there is only one person in the universe who is your perfect mate, you may spend your whole life looking for a romantic ideal and miss out on a real-life relationship with a flawed, but wonderful, life partner.

In previous chapters we have explored how sex meets our physical need for reproduction and pleasure and our social need to form close relationships. We now look at sexuality and our emotional need for **intimacy,** a relationship marked by a warm friendship developing through long association. Although some people oppose research on love, saying that the emotions of love are beyond the scope of scientific research and should be left to the poets and philosophers, clinical experience and research studies have a lot to tell us about how we conduct our sexual and emotional lives.

WHAT IS LOVE?

Does any definition of **love**—to like something very much, to have a great affection for someone or something, to get pleasure from another—really do justice to the intensity of the emotion? Artists try to capture its force in painting and poetry, while researchers examine the brain in an attempt to understand its neurological and physiological bases. Throughout history, poets and scientists alike have been inspired to explore the mysteries of love—**attraction, romance** and **passion,** intimacy and **commitment**—and seek answers to the questions of what love is and how and why we fall in love with the people we do.

Love is so powerful that it has toppled kingdoms, started wars, inspired great works of art, and turned otherwise strong, articulate adults into masses of quivering mush. It can be the source of the greatest joy in life, as well as its deepest despair. Love is a complex mixture of emotions, including passion, intimacy, caring, and commitment. The darker side of love, including the emotions of grief and jealousy, is discussed in Chapter 16.

Certainly you can have love without sex or sex without love, but love and sex are as closely connected as mind and body. Researchers continue to explore the many questions we have about the relationship of these two important concepts. Some social scientists argue that we can understand love only in terms of cultural conceptions of the beloved, the feelings and thoughts that accompany love, and the actions or relations the lover has with the beloved (Beall & Sternberg, 1995). Other scientists believe that,

"How on earth are you ever going to explain in terms of chemistry and physics so important a biological phenomenon as love?"

ALBERT EINSTEIN

Intimacy: mutual understanding and caring for each other

Love: a deep, tender feeling of affection and solicitude toward a person, such as that arising from kinship, recognition of attractive qualities, or a sense of underlying oneness.

Attraction: the relationship existing between things or persons that are naturally or involuntarily drawn together

Romance: an interpersonal relationship marked by admiration, sensitivity, passion, and intensity

Passion: intense feelings of emotional excitement (arousal), absorption in the other, and sexual desire

Commitment: a pledge or promise; the state of being bound emotionally or intellectually to a course of action or to another person

while the emotions associated with love may be beyond the scope of experimental science, scientists can analyze the behavior prompted by love and the body's responses in an attempt to understand love's effects. For example, researchers have found that oxytocin, a chemical that fosters the bond between mothers and children, probably helps fuel romantic love as well (Insel & Hulihan, 1995). **Endorphins,** the morphinelike brain chemicals that blunt pain and induce feelings of euphoria, also may make you feel good when you're with someone you love (Carter, 1998).

While certain other mammals share many of the same neural and chemical pathways involved in human love, no one knows if those other animals feel a similar surge of wild and tender feelings. Though rare among animals, the social bonds formed by pairs during courtship and mating function to facilitate reproduction. Studies of **pair bonding** and maternal attachment in other mammals provide clues to the mechanisms underlying close social bonds (Carter, 1998). There appears to be an association between high levels of activity in the hypothalamic-pituitary-adrenal (HPA) axis of the brain (see Figure 3.1) and the subsequent expression of social behaviors and attachments. Positive social behaviors, including social bonds, may reduce brain activity in the HPA axis, while in some cases negative social interactions may increase HPA activity (Carter, 1998).

Types of Love

There are all kinds of love. You can love your parents, your dog, ice cream, or basketball—but probably not in the exact same way. There are infatuation, caring, lust, and romantic, passionate love. In one study, people listed 93 different types of love (Fehr & Russell, 1991). One of the problems in studying love is that there is no clear and consistent consensus on what love is or the relationship among loving thoughts, emotions, and behavior (Jankowiak, 1992).

Some Western scholars have argued that to develop romantic love a culture needs to have enough leisure time away from work to have the energy to pursue romance (Aries, 1956). Others believe that a certain level of artistic refinement is necessary to properly express these romantic feelings (Stone, 1986). However, love is not the recent invention of Western civilization. A 1992 study of cross-cultural perspectives on romantic love contradicted this Eurocentric view. People in all cultures experience love; there are words for it in every language. Jankowiak and Fischer (1992) found evidence of romantic love in 147 of the 166 different cultures that they studied, and they concluded that romantic love is a universal phenomenon.

Romantic love is probably as old as humankind. Our craving for romance, the desire to make a sexual attachment, the restlessness during long relationships, our optimism about a new sweetheart—"these emotions must come from our ancestry" (Fisher, 1992, p. 163). There is something intrinsic to the human condition that results in the desire to seek loving relationships.

Two phases of love have been identified: passionate love and companionate love (Hatfield & Rapson, 1987). **Passionate love,** also known as *romantic love* or *infatuation,* thrives on excitement and is characterized by intense feelings of emotional excitement (arousal), absorption in the other, and sexual desire. Less positively, this condition is also known as love sickness or obsessive love. Typically, intense passionate love occurs early in a relationship. We're more likely to avoid conflicts and to overlook our lover's faults when infatuated. It makes people want to spend as much time as possible together, to touch each other, and to engage in other physical intimacies (often including sex), to think about each other and feel joy merely upon seeing each other. Complete the Passionate Love Scale (Figure 15.1) to see how highly you rate passionate love.

Although most cultures have recognized the existence of passionate love, different cultures have held very different attitudes about it. According to the historian Lawrence Stone (1965), in bygone centuries in Europe, for example, people regarded passionate love as a form of mental imbalance that made people feel and act in strange, even

Endorphins: any of a group of peptide hormones that bind to opiate receptors and are found mainly in the brain; endorphins reduce the sensation of pain and affect emotions

Pair Bonding: the selective social attachment formed between monogamous males and females during courtship and mating

Passionate Love: also known as romantic love, is characterized by intense feelings of emotional excitement (arousal), absorption in the other, and sexual desire

This questionnaire asks you to describe how you feel when you are passionately in love. Some common terms for this feeling are passionate love, infatuation, love sickness, or obsessive love.

Please think of the person whom you love most passionately right now. If you are not in love right now, think of the last person you loved passionately. If you have never been in love, think of the person whom you came closest to caring for in that way. Keep this person in mind as you complete this questionnaire. (The person you choose should be of the opposite sex if you are heterosexual or of the same sex if you are homosexual.) Try to tell us how you felt at the time when your feelings were the most intense.

Answer each item in terms of this scale:

① ② ③ ④ ⑤ ⑥ ⑦ ⑧ ⑨

not at   moderately   definitely
all true   true   true

1. I would feel deep despair if _____ left me.
2. Sometimes I feel I can't control my thoughts; they are obsessively on _____.
3. I feel happy when I am doing something to make _____ happy.
4. I would rather be with _____ than anyone.
5. I'd get jealous if I thought _____ were falling in love with someone else.
6. I yearn to know all about _____.
7. I want _____ physically, emotionally, mentally.
8. I have an endless appetite for affection from _____.
9. For me, _____ is the perfect romantic partner.
10. I sense my body responding when _____ touches me.
11. _____ always seems to be on my mind.
12. I want _____ to know me — my thoughts, my fears, my hopes.
13. I eagerly look for signs indicating _____'s desire for me.
14. I possess a powerful attraction for _____.
15. I get extremely depressed when things don't go right in my relationship with _____.

Scoring: A higher score on the PLS indicates greater passionate love.

FIGURE 15.1 **Passionate Love Scale (PLS).** SOURCE: Hatfield & Rapson, 1996, p. 63.

crazy ways. They did not think that passionate love was a good reason for marrying someone—indeed, proposing marriage while in love would strike them as similar to making any major life decision while drunk or on drugs! They certainly didn't think that passionate love made a good basis for marriage.

One reason for the skepticism about passionate love is that it tends to be temporary. This is hard for most people to appreciate, especially young people who may not yet have spent many years in a romantic relationship and think that their passionate feelings are sure to be permanent. But most people experience passionate love for a relatively brief period in a relationship—a year, perhaps, or two or three at most. As the relationship continues, it tends to rely more on companionate love.

Companionate love is based on familiarity, and it involves feelings of affection and deep attachment. Less intense than passionate love, it usually is more realistic; we appreciate our lover's strengths and tolerate his or her weaknesses. Companionate love means perceiving the other person as your soul mate or special partner. It signifies a high level of mutual understanding and caring and, in many cases, commitment to making the relationship succeed. As the term implies, companionate love makes people want to remain each other's good companions. Someone high in companionate love is likely to say things like, "My wife is my best friend." Obviously, that kind of love is not the same as the feelings that motivate people to start new sexual relationships. A successful long-term relationship depends on making an effective transition from one kind of love (passionate) to another (companionate).

Companionate Love: feelings based on familiarity, affection, and deep attachment

Theories of Love

There are many different theories about love. Some of these are based on the observation that sexual attraction is found in all species, and that human love is derived from this universal phenomenon. According to Freud's psychoanalytic theory, when sexual attraction is put through the complexities of the human psyche, it is combined with affection and other emotions to produce love. In particular, Freud thought that many human beings were unable to acknowledge that they had sexual feelings for others, so they used "love" as a defense mechanism to disguise these sexual feelings.

Maslow's B-Love and D-Love   Social scientists make distinctions between different kinds of loving relationships. Abraham Maslow viewed love as a basic human need. In order for individuals to realize their full potential as human beings, Maslow believed it was necessary not only to love, but also to be loved in return. Maslow (1968) identified two types of love: *B-love* (Being-love) and *D-love* (Deficiency love). Maslow's B-love is unselfish, nurturing, and unpossessive. D-love is characterized by a high level of dependency, jealousy, and selfishness. In one study, college students were asked to assess which of Maslow's levels is most important to happiness. Falling or staying in love (B-love) was chosen significantly more often than D-love by both male and female undergraduates (Pettijohn, 1996).

Sternberg's Triangular Theory of Love   Robert Sternberg (1986) proposed a more elaborate theory of the nature of love. As its name implies, Sternberg's *triangular theory of love* suggests that love is composed of three different ingredients (Figure 15.2). The first of these is passion, which he explained in terms of feelings of physical attraction, romantic attraction, and sexual interest. The physical element of passion is characterized by high bodily arousal: When you feel passion, your heart beats more rapidly than usual, you become excited and alert, and you may also feel sexual arousal. The elements of romantic attraction and sexual interest make people want to be together and in many cases make them want to kiss, hold hands, and perhaps have sex.

Intimacy is the second ingredient in Sternberg's scheme. Intimacy, the "common core" of all love relationships, refers to feeling close to the other person. *Empathy*, the ability to share someone else's feelings or experience, is important to intimacy; indeed, intimacy includes a sense of understanding the partner and being understood by him or her. Intimacy also entails a mutual concern for each other's welfare and happiness. Two people with a high degree of intimacy have basic feelings of caring and concern

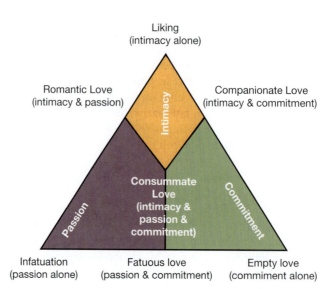

FIGURE 15.2 Sternberg's Triangular Theory of Love.
SOURCE: Sternberg, 1988, p. 122.

about one another, want each other to be happy and healthy, and often seek to do things that will benefit the other. Intimate partners try to take care of each other, and they emphasize communication about their lives, feelings, and problems.

The third ingredient in Sternberg's triangle is commitment. Sternberg observed that when many people speak of love, they refer more to a conscious decision than to a feeling state. Emotions come and go, but commitments based on such decisions remain constant unless they are deliberately revoked. For example, if you ask a woman whether she loves her husband or her children, she may say "Of course!" without having to think about it. If love referred only to passion or intimacy, she would have to stop and examine her emotions at that moment. But if love means commitment, and she has made that commitment, then she does not need to survey her current inner feelings.

According to Sternberg, passion, intimacy, and commitment are not three different "kinds" of love. Rather, any given love relationship is some mixture of these three ingredients (Table 15.1). Some love relationships may be high in intimacy and commitment, but low in passion. Others might have passion and commitment but little intimacy. An ideal love might contain substantial measures of all three. In his research, Sternberg concluded that intimacy is the most common ingredient; relatively few relationships utterly lack intimacy. However, the feeling commonly called "love at first sight" consists primarily of passion, because you hardly know the person yet; this is one example of a low intimacy relationship.

We can use Sternberg's theory to account for the shift from passionate love to companionate love described earlier. Companionate love emphasizes intimacy, whereas passionate love consists mainly of passion (obviously). Commitment may help solidify the trust and mutual concern that contributes to companionate love. Thus, in his model, a typical long-term sexual relationship might start out consisting mainly of passion, but over time the intimacy grows stronger as passion grows weaker, and at some point a decision is made to solidify a long-range commitment. Commitment can help sustain a relationship during periods of conflict or dissatisfaction, which many couples experience sooner or later. If the commitment is not made, or if intimacy does not grow, then the relationship is likely to break up after the passion dies down; because there is little to replace it, there is little to keep the couple together.

According to Sternberg's theory, well-matched couples have similar levels of intimacy, passion, and commitment. Problems occur when the partners' triangles don't match. For example, one person may have intimacy but no passion or commitment while the other person may have all three.

Lee's Styles of Loving   Instead of defining different types of love, sociologist John Allan Lee (1974, 1988) identified six *styles* of love in human relationships. Lee's styles of loving suggests that loving relationships often fail to thrive over time because their

TABLE 15.1

Different Combinations of the Three Elements Produce Different Types of Love Relationships

	Intimacy	Passion	Commitment
Nonlove	No	No	No
Liking	Yes	No	No
Infatuation	No	Yes	No
Empty love	No	No	Yes
Romantic love	Yes	Yes	No
Companionate love	Yes	No	Yes
Fatuous love	No	Yes	Yes
Consummate love	Yes	Yes	Yes

SOURCE: Adapted from Sternberg, 1986.

efforts to build a lasting relationship may be undermined by a losing struggle to integrate incompatible loving styles. According to Lee's theory, satisfaction and success in loving relationships often depend on finding someone who "shares the same approach to loving, the same definition of love" (Lee, 1974, p. 44).

1. Eros: a romantic style of love with emphasis on physical passion and beauty.

2. Ludus: a game-playing love style with little commitment and a number of different partners.

3. Storge: a friendly, affectionate love style that develops over time.

4. Pragma: a thoughtful, rational style of love that is based on practical criteria such as similar background and shared interests.

5. Mania: an obsessive love style characterized by jealousy.

6. Agape: a selfless love style with a caring desire to give to another without expectation of receiving anything in return.

Rubin's Love Scale Psychologist Zick Rubin developed a 13-item Love Scale that identified characteristics of people who said they were in love. Rubin's Love Scale distinguished between affectionate relationships that were primarily "liking" and those that were "loving." Loving relationships had three components: attachment, caring, and intimacy. Attachment is the desire to be with and provide emotional support to the other person. Caring is concern for the other person's well-being, and intimacy refers to the desire for close, personal communication with the other person (Rubin, 1973).

Tennov's Theory of Limerence Dorothy Tennov (1979) coined the term **limerence** to describe the feeling of "being in love." The basic components of limerence include intrusive thoughts about the object of passionate desire, an acute longing for the feeling to be reciprocated, and the dependence of your mood on your perception of your loved one's actions. Limerence also includes the fear of rejection and unsettling shyness in the loved one's presence, especially in the beginning of a relationship. At least up to a point, limerence intensifies through adversity; weathering problems together only strengthens the bond. There is an acute sensitivity to any activity, from a look in the eye to a telephone call made—or missed. You know you're "in limerence" when your heart aches, all other concerns and problems are left in the background, and you think that the object of your affection is wonderful, despite all faults and weaknesses.

Other Theories of Love A more recent theory considers love to be a product of sexual attraction. According to Shaver, Hazan, and Bradshaw (1988), the capacity for love evolved as a way to forge a lasting attachment between sex partners. That is, people will have sex, just as animals in most other species, and afterward they may or may not stay together. Sex can produce children, however, and children have a better chance of survival if their parents remain together. Evolution thus favored couples who developed an emotional attachment to each other, because it kept them together and thus benefited their children.

Anthropologist Helen Fisher (2000) defines three different types of love—lust, romantic love, and long-term attachment. Lust, according to Fisher, is related to bursts of testosterone; romantic love is related to abnormalities in the neurotransmitters serotonin, dopamine, and norepinephrine, making it biochemically similar to obsessive-compulsive disorder (Marazziti et al., 2001). Then, as excitement and novelty subside, the brain kicks in endorphins which calm the mind and provide the basis for long-term attachment.

Biologists similarly theorize that love has a primitive basis as nature's way of getting people to mate efficiently (Buss, 1994; Crews, 1998; Fisher, 1992). It's much

Limerence: Tennov's term for being in love

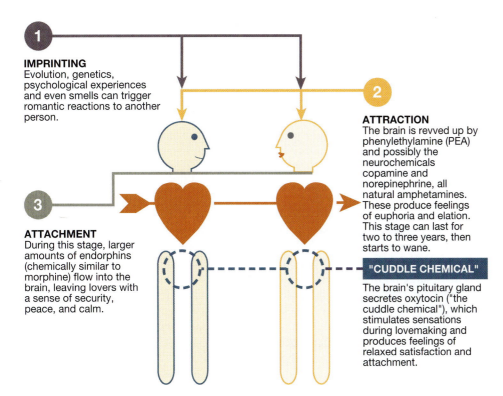

1 IMPRINTING
Evolution, genetics, psychological experiences and even smells can trigger romantic reactions to another person.

2 ATTRACTION
The brain is revved up by phenylethylamine (PEA) and possibly the neurochemicals copamine and norepinephrine, all natural amphetamines. These produce feelings of euphoria and elation. This stage can last for two to three years, then starts to wane.

3 ATTACHMENT
During this stage, larger amounts of endorphins (chemically similar to morphine) flow into the brain, leaving lovers with a sense of security, peace, and calm.

"CUDDLE CHEMICAL"
The brain's pituitary gland secretes oxytocin ("the cuddle chemical"), which stimulates sensations during lovemaking and produces feelings of relaxed satisfaction and attachment.

FIGURE 15.3   The Chemistry of Love.   Source: Holmes, 1993.

more romantic to describe your heart pounding with ecstasy than attribute your heart rate to supernormal levels of norepinephrine, the chemical that causes your pupils to dilate, your blood pressure to climb, and your artery walls to relax (see Figure 15.3). These visceral sensations are the work of the vagus nerve, which coordinates the activities of internal organs and ferries signals between these organs and our brains. Without the vagus, love would be impossible (Porges, 1997). Part of the nerve controls primitive functions such as sex, hunger, and fear in response to oxytocin, another brain chemical. The vagus also serves as the pathway between sexual organs and the brain; without it we would feel neither arousal nor emotional satiation. Only in humans do branches of the vagus connect emotional brain centers with the heart, face, and voice, helping to coordinate feeling with facial and verbal expression. This connection also helps slow the heart and keep our bodies calm enough for the brain to pay attention to such signals from other people, enabling us to read others' emotions.

People who feel passionately in love experience emotional churning and the sense of being in an altered state (sometimes compared to being high on drugs). This is very likely linked to some chemical in the body, and **phenylethylamine (PEA)** is a leading candidate (Figure 15.3). People in love have high levels of PEA, a neurotransmitter that enables information to travel from one brain cell to another (Liebowitz, 1983). This chemical produces strong emotional feelings, including those "tingling" sensations of excitement and euphoria that you get when the person you love walks into the room or holds your hand. It also helps produce high intensity and frequency of sexual desire. Companionate love does not seem to be characterized by these elevated levels of PEA. Hector Sabelli, a researcher at the Chicago Center for Creative Development, believes that PEA may be the hormone of libido. Sabelli's research shows that high PEA levels help explain increased sex drive and activity in the manic phase of bipolar disorder, while low PEA levels reflect loss of libido in depression (Sabelli & Javaid, 1995).

Phenylethylamine (PEA): a substance that occurs naturally as a neurotransmitter in the brain and has pharmacological properties similar to those of amphetamine, and may produce amphetamine-like effects of euphoria and elation associated with passionate love

CAMPUS CONFIDENTIAL

"I admit it, I'm really a shallow person. The first thing that attracted me to my boyfriend was the way he looks in tight jeans, not his intelligence or his personality. The man is a hunk and a half. This probably isn't a 'forever after' kind of love. And, I guess if he was a total jerk I wouldn't stay with him. But for right now we're having a lot of fun." ●

ATTRACTION: LOOKING FOR LOVE

Physical Appearance

Is Lyle Lovett your type, or are you more attracted to Taye Diggs, Jason Scott Lee, Ricky Martin, Greg Louganis, or Sean Connery? Do you dream about Naomi Campbell, Susan Sarandon, Lucy Liu, k.d. lang, or Jennifer Lopez?

We may not agree on who is the sexiest man or woman alive, but there is no doubt that physical appearance is a major component of sexual attraction (Hatfield & Sprecher, 1986). Many first dates have been the last because of bad first impressions or imperfect chemistry. Be honest: Across a crowded room, is it sensitivity or intelligence that sparks your interest, or are you drawn to someone with a great body and bedroom eyes? Is this love at first sight or is it lust (see CAMPUS CONFIDENTIAL)?

Songwriters ask the question "Do you love me because I'm beautiful, or am I beautiful because you love me?" Scientists are not sure. One study investigated determinants of five factors of physical attractiveness in college students: masculinity (strength, large body and chest, and broader chin), femininity (longer hair, makeup, and larger and rounder eyes), self-care (overall grooming, shapely figure, flat stomach, erect posture, and fitted clothes), pleasantness (friendly, happy, and babyish face), and ethnicity. Self-care, masculinity/femininity, and pleasantness were found to be positive correlates of male/female attractiveness. Attractiveness was described in terms of emotions. That is, more attractiveness elicited more pleasure, more arousal, and less dominance. The researchers concluded that these emotional reactions mediated the relations of physical features to judgments of attractiveness (Mehrabian & Blum, 1997).

Beauty may be in the eye of the beholder, but the beholder's vision is not always 20/20. University students were asked to rate the attractiveness of opposite-sex patrons at a popular college club (Madey et al., 1996). Whether or not the subject was already in a relationship affected the perceived attractiveness of others at the bar. At closing time, those not in a relationship rated opposite-sex patrons as significantly more attractive than did those in a relationship. In addition, significant differences were found at each of three time periods during the evening, 10:00 P.M., midnight, and 1:30 A.M. Those not in a relationship found other patrons got more and more attractive with each passing hour, while those in a relationship rated attractiveness the same at each time period (Madey et al., 1996).

Who do you think is sexy?

TABLE 15.2

The Top Ten Traits Most Effective in Attracting Opposite-Sex Partners

Most Effective Male Traits	Most Effective Female Traits
1. good sense of humor	1. good sense of humor
2. sympathetic to troubles	2. well groomed
3. good manners	3. sympathetic to troubles
4. well groomed	4. good manners
5. effort to spend time together	5. showered daily
6. offered to help	6. physically fit
7. showered daily	7. made jokes
8. physically fit	8. effort to spend time together
9. exercised	9. stylish, fashionable clothing
10. wore attractive clothing	10. offered to help

SOURCE: Adapted from Buss, 1989.

FAQ:

Is there really such a thing as beauty bias?

When we first meet someone, we usually have a more positive response toward a person who is physically attractive. There also seems to be a beauty bias; we tend to overgeneralize from appearance, assuming that people who are physically attractive are nicer and have better future prospects (Dion, 1986; Warner & Sugarman, 1986). Beauty bias can affect behavior. If you believe someone is good as well as beautiful, you have doubled your perception of the potential rewards of being with that person (Brehm, 1985). But there can be a downside to looking too good. Attractive men and women are sometimes stereotyped as being vain, egotistical, unfriendly, and unintelligent (Brehm, 1985).

Research indicates that both men and women rate personal qualities as more important than physical traits in long-term, meaningful relationships (see Table 15.2). However, physical traits may be more important in short-term sexual relationships, especially to men (Nevid, 1984; Regan & Berscheid, 1997). The importance of physical attributes differs between short-term relationships, which may be as brief as a one-night stand, and committed, long-term partnerships. In one study, some men who found their sex partner highly attractive before orgasm viewed him or her as less attractive, even homely, moments later (Buss, 1994). On the other hand, long-term relationships allow for more emotional attachment, which then may positively affect the perception of attractiveness.

Hollywood is particularly fond of the beauty-and-goodness stereotype. Attractive characters in movies are often portrayed more favorably than unattractive characters. A random sample taken from five decades of top-grossing films found that the link between beauty and positive characteristics was stable across time periods, character gender, and the character's centrality to the plot. In addition, the researchers found that exposure to highly stereotyped films can elicit stronger beauty-and-goodness stereotyping. Subjects watching a highly biased film subsequently showed greater favoritism toward attractive individuals than those who viewed a less biased film (Bazzini et al., 1997).

CROSS-CULTURAL PERSPECTIVES

The Eye of the Beholder

The meaning of beauty varies cross-culturally. Consider the following examples provided by Fisher (1992):

When Europeans first immigrated to Africa, their blond hair and white skin reminded some Africans of albinos, and their looks were regarded as hideous and horrifying. Traditionally, the Namba of southern Africa preferred women with *dangling vulvar lips, so mothers massaged the genitals of their infant daughters to make the vulva hang more enticingly. In an effort to achieve cultural ideals, women in Tonga traditionally diet to stay slim, while Siriono women of Bolivia eat continuously to stay appealingly fat.*

Culture dictates that her lip plate enhances this Ethiopian woman's beauty.

Physically attractive people are more likely to have a history of positive social interactions; they may have developed especially good social skills that allow them to continue to elicit positive responses from others (Brehm, 1985). Your positive response to beauty may also enable someone to develop the positive personal characteristics you expect (Langlois, 1986). There is a clear interactive effect between love and the perception of attractiveness. In a sense, loving someone and believing he or she is beautiful create reactions that confirm your expectations. It becomes a self-fulfilling prophecy. If you think someone is attractive, you are more likely to act in a friendly manner; and in response that person is more likely to behave in ways that are more attractive (Snyder, Tanke, & Berscheid, 1977).

The Beauty Evolution

Fashion may change, but certain physical characteristics are almost universally found to be sexually attractive. Men and women around the world are attracted to clean people with good complexions, and in most places men prefer plump, wide-hipped women to slim ones (Ford & Beach, 1951; Frayser, 1985). Across cultures, men and women have devised a variety of strategies to trigger attraction: stretched necks, molded heads, filed teeth, pierced noses, tattoos, scarred breasts, scorched or tanned skin, dyed hair, and even purple beards (Fisher, 1992) (see accompanying photograph). We primp, paint, pad, pierce, and rearrange our bodies to try to attract a sexual partner (Etcoff, 1999).

Evolutionary theorists suggest that those traits that are universally found attractive are ones that indicate good reproductive health. From this perspective it is to a male's genetic advantage to fall in love with a woman who will produce viable offspring. Because ovulation in human females is concealed, men are forced to rely on external cues of childbearing ability (Buss, 1987; Kendrick et al., 1990; Symons, 1979). The best natural indicators are youth, clear skin, bright eyes, vibrant hair, white teeth, supple body, and a vivacious personality.

A cross-cultural study of 33 societies found that men were attracted to young, good-looking, "spunky" women (Buss, 1989). Men in most countries rated good looks in a mate more important than women did. In a study, Singh (1993) found that facial features do not indicate reproductive capabilities and seem secondary in the consideration of a potential mate. However, another study (Kalick et al., 1998) reported that attractive people are rated as healthier than their peers. They found that the correlation between perceived health and medically assessed health increased when attractiveness was statistically controlled, which implies that attractiveness suppressed the accurate recognition of health.

Gender and Sex Appeal

What makes someone attractive to a member of the opposite sex? There is no single answer to this question, and in fact the set of answers is somewhat different depending on whether we are talking about a man or a woman.

Looking Young   One feature of attraction is youth. Both men and women are regarded as more attractive if they are young, but the importance of looking young appears to be greater for women than for men.

Human beings differ from other species in the proportion of life spent in a childhood state. Along with a longer period of childhood comes an attraction to young-looking features. Many adults try to look young by imitating childlike features. For example, children's eyes tend to seem disproportionately large, which makes them stand out in comparison with the full body. When adult women try to look attractive, they will often apply makeup to highlight their eyes and make them stand out, which gives the impression of larger eyes and hence a more youthful appearance. Likewise, children hardly ever have hair on their faces or bodies, and women seek to look attractive by eliminating facial and body hair.

In contrast, some men do cultivate beards and other signs of maturity. But even men may trim their eyebrows to look younger, because a bushy eyebrow is a powerful cue for age in males, especially for men past the age of 40 (when looking younger is often more important). It is apparent that the desire to look young is more prevalent in adult women than in adult men and starts much earlier in life for women than men. Men in their 30s often have ample sex appeal, but many women begin to lose their desirability before that age. One way to summarize the data is that women seem to strive to look like they are in their teens and 20s, whereas men strive to look like they are in their 20s and 30s.

The attraction to young-looking women is plausibly based on biological factors, given how widespread it is. (Researchers have not found much evidence of other cultures in which women gain sex appeal by looking older, and so the view that cultural influences alone shaped the preference for young-looking women seems unlikely.) From the standpoint of evolutionary psychology, sexual attraction is based on looking good by whatever patterns caused our ancestors to pass along their genes, because patterns of attraction that failed to lead to reproduction were removed from future generations. Suppose, for example, that when human beings first evolved, the men were equally divided between those who were attracted to young-looking women and those who were attracted to old-looking women. Suppose that each group of men was relatively successful in courting and mating the women of the sort they desired. Because of menopause and short life spans, older women cannot have babies or at least not many, and so the men who married them would not have had any children. Meanwhile, the men who liked young-looking women would have found mates who would reproduce for many years. As a result, we who are alive today are all descended from the men who were attracted to younger rather than older women.

While there has been increasing evidence that attractiveness in humans is an indicator of health, it has been unclear whether this applies both to facial and bodily characteristics. In a recent study, Thornhill and Grammer (1999) had Viennese and American men (aged 19–55) rate the attractiveness of photographs of 92 nude women. Independent ratings of photographs of faces, fronts with faces covered, and backs of the same women were significantly and positively correlated. The researchers concluded that this implies that women's faces and external bodies comprise a single image of attractiveness for males, signaling hormonal and perhaps developmental health.

The Importance of Symmetry   One important key to attractiveness is *symmetry*. People whose facial and bodily features are symmetrical are generally seen as more attractive than others (Gangestad & Thornhill, 1999; Thornhill & Gangestad, 1993). There is even some evidence that this is true for nonhuman animals if all aspects of bodily symmetry are considered (such as equal size fins, feathers, etc.). Higher symmetry is associated with greater sex appeal, a greater number of sex partners, and more desirable sex partners.

One study manipulated the symmetry of individual faces and had college students rate the attractiveness of each photo (see accompanying photographs). Perceived attractiveness increased when symmetry was increased, and decreased when it was reduced (Rhodes et al., 1998). Similar results have been found by other researchers (Watson & Thornhill, 1994; Zaidel, Chen, & German, 1995), suggesting that facial symmetry is a preferred characteristic and evidence of good health.

Asymmetric animals are less successful at mating, across many different studies (see Møller & Thornhill, 1998, for meta-analysis and review). The biological explanation is that when the basic plan of the body is to have both sides be the same (such as having the same size ears), any deviation from this is the result of some abnormality. Genetic abnormalities are generally bad, in the sense that one would prefer one's offspring to be normal rather than abnormal, and so people (and animals) who mate with symmetrical partners will be obtaining better genes to mix with their own for the offspring. Over millions of years, animals that preferred symmetrical sex partners produced more successful offspring. Thus, part of our genetic heritage is a preference for a symmetrical partner.

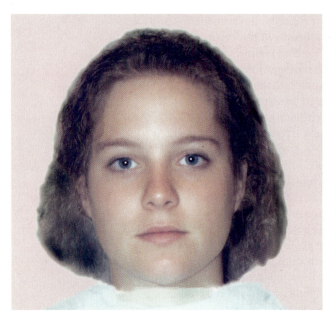 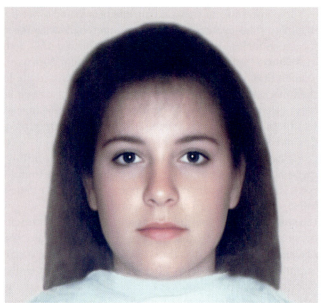

Studies have shown that symmetrical body features, especially in the face, are viewed as being more attractive. The photograph on the right shows a face with the features averaged by computer to make it more symmetrical.

The advantages of symmetry apply especially to people seeking short-term mating partners and those who are more selective. Gangestad and Simpson (2000) proposed that women are much more selective than men are about sex partners, and so symmetry should count for more in men. Consistent with this, they found that men who were more symmetrical on various body features (for example, width of foot, size of hand, length of ear) had more sex partners over their lifetime than did men who were asymmetrical. Among women, however, there was no effect, probably because men are far less choosy about sex partners. Symmetrical and asymmetrical women did not differ in their total number of sex partners. The preference for symmetrical men was most pronounced among women who were interested in having multiple partners and short-term affairs. Gangestad and Simpson have summarized many findings showing that women who are open to having affairs prefer symmetrical men.

In another study, it was found that women have more orgasms when having sex with a symmetrical man than with an asymmetrical man (Thornhill, Gangestad, & Comer, 1995). Thus, not only do the symmetrical men get more women, they also satisfy them better—probably because the women get more turned on by the symmetrical partner. In a fascinating study, Gangestad and Thornhill (1998) measured men's bodily symmetry and then instructed each man to wear a particular t-shirt for sleeping for two nights. Then a sample of women were permitted to sniff each shirt and rate how appealing it was. (The researchers wanted to look at how fertile women might respond, so women taking the pill were excluded from the analysis.) Women in the fertile phase of the menstrual cycle gave the most favorable ratings to the t-shirts worn by the most symmetrical men. At other points in the menstrual cycle, there was no difference in how the women rated the t-shirts' smell.

Evolutionary theory gives one explanation for these preferences. Not every woman can marry the most desirable man, and so many women will have to compromise and marry someone less than perfect. Indeed, the most desirable men (that is, the most symmetrical) may be less willing to be faithful and committed, so women may actually prefer to marry someone else. But the optimal evolutionary strategy for a woman is to marry a man who will remain committed to her but then to have an occasional sexual fling with the genetically most perfect man. If she can get pregnant with the best genes while having another man provide for her, her offspring get the best chance to succeed in life. This explains the attraction to symmetrical men of both women interested in casual sex or affairs, and those at the most fertile point in their menstrual cycle. The higher rate of orgasm may help those extramarital couplings to have the best chance of resulting in pregnancy.

What Makes a Pretty Face?   OK, so far we have young and symmetrical. What else makes a face beautiful? Research has identified several features. The German philosopher Immanuel Kant proposed an intriguing theory of facial beauty in his classic work on aesthetic theory, *Critique of Judgment* (1790/1924). Kant suggested that the mind could retrieve from memory all the faces it has seen and superimpose them on each other, so that the composite "average" face is seen as the ideal standard of beauty. This view received little attention for many decades after Kant proposed it, but modern computer technology has enabled researchers to morph multiple faces together and construct a genuinely "average" face—which was in fact rated as supremely beautiful by research subjects (Langlois & Roggman, 1990). The more faces that had been combined by the computer into the composite face, the more attractive it was rated as being. Thus, having facial features that are precisely normal and average for one's group cause one to be seen as handsome or beautiful.

Michael Cunningham (1990) identified a combination of men's facial features that portray dominance and are therefore thought of as attractive by women. These features include thick eyebrows, small eyes, thin lips, and a square jaw. However, others found that women are most attracted by an optimal combination of large eyes, small nose, full lips, prominent cheekbones, a large chin, and good grooming. Clear, unblemished skin also is seen as beautiful; clear skin and symmetry are both signs of good health. In our evolutionary past, many people suffered from serious diseases, and even if they survived, their ability to bear healthy children was impaired. Some of these diseases left marks on the face and other areas of the body. The people who were most attracted to healthy partners probably passed along their genes more effectively than others did. Therefore today's human beings are descendants of people who found healthy-looking faces to be sexually attractive.

Tall, Light, and Handsome?   One of the peculiarities of human sex appeal is the gender difference in coloring preference. Dark skin and hair are attractive in a man ("tall, dark, and handsome"), whereas fair skin and light-colored (blond) hair are more appreciated in females. Many dark-haired women dye their hair blond, but very few natural blondes dye their hair dark. The difference is difficult to explain. Even among African Americans, relatively light skin sometimes is seen as more attractive than the relatively darker hues (see CONSIDERATIONS box).

The issue of coloring has complex ramifications in a heterogeneous society. For example, consider the implications of media images. Social psychologist Julia Hare (reported in Carpenter, 1998, p. E1), director of the Black Think Tank research organization, said that when she hears black girls talk about the celebrities they find attractive, she often picks up on an unspoken message in their words. "They'll say something like they think Halle Berry's pretty and Whoopi Goldberg's not. They may not say it, but I think they're also looking at skin color and hair". The media do not often portray an accurate picture of a society's diversity. Mok (1998) suggests that the paucity of Asian images in the media greatly affects Asian American perceptions of both their own racial group and of the larger society.

In a study of stereotyping based on physical appearance, three different photographs of the same female—as a blonde, as a brunette, and as a redhead—were shown to a group of male and female students. The students rated the photographs with a standard set of photographs of other females on a number of dimensions that included intelligence and temperament. True to the stereotypes of "dumb blondes" and "fiery redheads," male students attributed significantly lower intelligence to blondes than to brunettes, and females rated redheads as more temperamental than blondes or brunettes (Weir, & Fine-Davis, 1989).

Black is Beautiful

As a color, black is as neutral as white, but black is often used as a synonym for negative, bad, evil, or repugnant traits. In American western movies, the bad guys always wore black hats, and the good guys always wore white ones. The phrase "black is beautiful" was coined in the 1960s by Black Power and pan-African movements in the U.S. to increase the self-image and pride of people of color.

Since before the Civil War, when lighter skinned slaves were treated better than those with darker skin, status among blacks has been connected to skin tone (Russell, Wilson, & Hall, 1992). A 1998 study of 200 African American college freshmen indicated a statistically significant relationship between lighter skin color and a perception of physical beauty (R. E. Hall, 1998).

Some researchers believe that this color hierarchy continues to affect the way some people feel about their African features. In her article "Mammy-ism: A Diagnosis of Psychological Misorientation for Women of African Descent," psychologist Afi Samella Abdullah (1998) explores the feeling of self-hatred that African American women can experience when they evaluate and then devalue their physical characteristics (facial features, skin color, hair texture), in comparison to beauty standards set by European Americans.

Other theorists are skeptical of the patronizing view that today's African American citizens still embrace values merely because their ancestors learned them during slavery. Symons (1995) has proposed a provocative theory; he argues that light coloring is attractive in women because it is a signal of youth and fertility. In every race,

according to Symons, lighter-colored women are preferred. As women grow older and have children, their skin becomes darker. The seemingly inexplicable but culturally widespread preference for blond women may reflect the same cue, because as women grow older and bear children their blond hair tends to become darker. Symons speculated that this preference for light skin within races is also applicable *between* races. When the Japanese first encountered the outside world in the late 1800s, they thought European and American women were beautiful and African women were unattractive, even though in most respects they looked down on all foreigners.

There is growing evidence that white teenage girls dislike their bodies, but black girls are proud of theirs. One study found that while 90 percent of white junior-high and high-school girls studied voiced dissatisfaction with their weight, 70 percent of the African American teens were satisfied with their bodies (Parker et al., 1995). Even significantly overweight black teens described themselves as happy with their bodies. When asked to describe women as they age, two thirds of the black teens said they get more beautiful as they age (Parker et al., 1995).

? ***What do you think about these views of African American perceptions of beauty?***

—*What are some possible explanations for why African American teens are more satisfied with their bodies than white teens?*

Thinness Men are generally attracted to women with the curves that come from full breasts and a moderately low waist-to-hip ratio (which produces something like the "hourglass" figure), as opposed to the straighter lines of a very thin woman. Fallon and Rozin (1985) highlighted the irony of the pursuit of female thinness. They asked women how thin they wanted to be and how thin their boyfriends wanted them to be. The researchers also asked the boyfriends what they preferred. Although women often feel that the pressure to be thin is based on the need to appeal to men, the women's views of what men wanted differed from what the men actually wanted. The men wanted a fuller, more curvaceous figure than the women thought; the women overestimated how thin their boyfriends wanted them to be. (The men's average preferences actually resembled the average actual woman, which is perhaps another sign of how averaging produces criteria of beauty.) Even more important, the women's own personal ideals were thinner yet. The recent emphasis on female slimness has encouraged many women to strive for the severely thin look of today's fashion models, even though stressful and constant dieting is required to achieve that look and many women simply cannot maintain that degree of thinness.

Research indicates men judge a woman's figure by the ratio of waist to hips. The ideal proportion suggested by a number of studies is that the hips be roughly one third larger than the waist. There is evidence that body fat distribution as measured by this ratio may be related to potential reproductive success (Furnham, Tan, & McManus, 1997; Singh, 1993).

Men prefer women who are plumper than women want to be (Polivy, Garner, & Garfinkel, 1986). Nigel Barber (1998) studied the changes in standards of bodily attractiveness in American females and the different masculine and feminine ideals. The female's ideal body according to women is that of a slender *Vogue* model, while the curvaceous body men idealize can be found in *Playboy*. An interesting aspect of this gender gap is that when ideal sizes change over time, women's changed ideals precede the men's, and the women's changes are greater in magnitude. This implies that women may determine the standard. This slim standard is associated with occupational success; however, it is not consistent with men's preferences or childbearing readiness.

At the height of her celebrity in the 1960s, Marilyn Monroe was a voluptuous size 12. To show how times have changed, in one study, mean body mass indices of North Americans ages 18 to 24 years collected from 11 national health surveys from the 1950s to the 1990s were compared to *Playboy* centerfold models, Miss America beauty pageant winners, and male *Playgirl* models. While the body sizes of Miss America winners decreased significantly and the body sizes of *Playboy* centerfolds remained well below normal body weight, the body sizes of *Playgirl* models and young adult North American women and men increased significantly. The increase in body size of *Playgirl* models appears to be due to an increase in muscularity, whereas the increase in body size of the more typical young adult is more likely due to an increase in body fat. Today's models weigh approximately 23 percent less than the average woman (Mullen, 1996). In one study, after viewing fashion magazines of models who represent a thin ideal, female university students were less satisfied with their own bodies, more depressed, and angrier (Pinhas et al., 1999).

The woman representing California in one of the first Miss America contests probably would be considered too large to compete in a beauty pageant today.

Unlike women, more men want to gain rather than lose weight (Drewnowski, Kurkth, & Krahn, 1995). As we discussed in Chapter 3, some men use steroids to accomplish this goal of a larger body. Women, however, tend to find men of average size to be most attractive. However, women prefer men with moderately broad shoulders who are of medium height and have a chest slightly larger than average, but not as large and powerful as a traditional body builder's chest (Cunningham, 1990). Men found in the typical size range were judged as more attractive, healthy, and possessing many positive personal qualities (Singh, 1995).

It is evident that a clear gender gap exists with respect to physical attractiveness preferences. Women desire average size men, while wanting a smaller, thinner physique for themselves. Men, on the other hand, want larger than average bodies for themselves and prefer their female mates to be a bit larger than the women would actually like to be. With these differences in preferences, it is no wonder why finding one's ideal mate can be so difficult!

Whether the preference for female thinness is rooted in biological preferences, cultural constructs, or (more likely) some mixture of both is not known at present. There are some cultures and some ethnic groups that do not hold the thin female to be ideal, but these are certainly in a relatively small minority. In the United States, African American women have not generally embraced the ideal of being thin, whereas white American women generally do want to be thin. Such differences point to the importance of culture.

The costs of the wish to be thin are considerable. Many women develop eating disorders in the quest to become thin. Many others hold negative views of their physical attractiveness because they are not thin enough in their own eyes; these negative self-views contribute to lower self-esteem (Kling et al., 1999). Martin Seligman (1993) has even proposed that the ideal of female slimness contributes to a major mental health problem among women—the relatively high rate of female depression. Women suffer from clinical and subclinical depression at much higher rates than men do. According to Seligman, cross-cultural comparisons show that those few cultures that reject the ideal of the thin female do not have elevated rates of female depression. Seligman's theory is that trying to live up to an unrealistic ideal of slimness (and starving oneself in the process) causes women to become depressed.

Barbie's periodic body changes are meant to reflect current standards of physical attractiveness. Mattel overhauled Barbie in 1998, giving her slimmer hips, a wider waist, and smaller breasts.

Slim Waist or Fat Wallet? There is a difference in the qualities women and men notice first when looking at persons of the opposite sex. In a study by David Buss (1988), the tendency for women to focus on their physical features when pursuing romantic relationships was evident. Buss asked newlyweds what they did to be more appealing when they first met their spouse. While men emphasized material resources such as gifts, money, possessions, and bragging about their importance at work, females tended to make physical changes such as dieting, buying new clothes, and getting a haircut or tan (see Table 15.3).

The appearance of human males is important as well. According to evolutionary theorists, competition for sex is the overriding evolutionary pressure responsible for the appearance of adult males. "When choosing sexual partners, females are often judging males for various strengths, and what they find 'sexy' depends upon the species to which they belong and the nature of their breeding arrangement" (Sparks, 1999, p. 47). Males of many species attempt to display their superior qualities through their appearance. Human plumage can't compete with the peacock's flashy feathers, so women depend on other cues that a potential mate has good genes. A man's physical appearance is a factor when it communicates **social dominance,** the superiority of relationship and rank of an individual in relation to associates. Social dominance has the combined effects of intimidating reproductive rivals and attracting mates (Barber, 1998).

Researchers in Scotland and Japan concluded that a woman's fertility status determines whether she is more interested in a man's looks or his personality (Penton-Voak et al., 1999). Japanese women shown composite photos of men during the one week of their menstrual cycle when they could conceive preferred men with rugged, stereo-typical masculine features. During the other three weeks of the month, when the chances of getting pregnant are lower, the women were more interested in rounder, more feminine faces. The explanation suggested by the researchers is that men who are more masculine looking advertise good health and thus good genes for having children. A woman who cannot get pregnant, however, wants a relationship with a man who appears to be a good provider and more stable (Penton-Voak et al., 1999).

However, good looks are only one trait that females look for in a mate. It is to a woman's evolutionary advantage to be with a mate who can protect and provide for her offspring. "(W)hether they be chest-thumping gorillas or heavily veiled fighting fish . . . weapons and large body size have been overwhelmingly advantageous, enabling hefty, well-armed males to win more mates" (Sparks, 1999, p. 12).

Females may need practical proof that a male would be a worthy mate. For example, a lack of food may restrict a female's capacity to manufacture eggs, so in the animal kingdom a male who brings edible gifts may have an advantage. In our species, some women place great value on a man's education and professional degrees, since these characteristics are strongly linked with social status (Buss, 1994).

Social Dominance: superiority of relationship and rank of an individual in relation to his or her associates

TABLE 15.3	
Tactics of Attraction for Undergraduate Males and Females	
Tactics Used Significantly More by Males	**Tactics Used Significantly More by Females**
Display resources	Wear makeup
Brag about resources	Keep clean and groomed
Display strength	Alter general appearance
Display athleticism	Wear stylish clothes
Show off	Wear jewelry
Act promiscuous	Act nice

SOURCE: Adapted from Buss, 1988.

Men also strive to be thin, although these strivings tend to be more common among men who are beginning to pass their physical prime and wish to prolong their young-adult appearance. An intriguing study by Singh (1995) showed that waist-to-hip ratios are important for male sex appeal, not just female. They showed female research subjects a variety of body silhouettes and had them rate these for appeal. How much would you like to date, or marry, someone who looked like this? Sure enough, the lower waist-to-hip ratios (but not too low) increased men's attractiveness.

In the final phase of the Singh study, the researchers included a second variable. Along with showing the man's body shape, the researchers told the female subjects how much money the man earned. The effects of male salary made the body shape effects seem puny by comparison. At least according to this study, the size of a man's wallet is far more important than the size of his waist.

There is a stronger link between male sex appeal and height than between sex appeal and weight. Women tend to prefer tall men, although again this preference is probably far down the list of important traits, and most short men have ample ways to attract women. Still, all else being equal, women prefer taller men. In personal advertisements, for example, men who indicate that they are tall get more responses from interested women than other men get (Buss, 1994). The advantage of male height presents a contrast to the ideal of female thinness. A woman can control her weight to some degree, whereas there is almost nothing a man can do to make himself taller.

The Apparel Appeal   Bodies are most often seen when covered by clothes, of course, and clothes also contribute to sex appeal. In some Middle Eastern cultures, women wear formless clothes (and even veils) so that their bodies are not visible. Such outfits would seemingly relieve women from the pressure to diet and from worries about being sex objects, and so one might think that many women would favor them. However, in fact when women gain the choice they tend to prefer the sexier, revealing outfits that predominate in the Western world. Short skirts and tight blouses or sweaters call attention to the features of the body that men prefer, and, at least in some parts of the world, they also indicate that a woman chooses to identify with modern Western cultures.

Men's clothing can have an effect too, although as usual the emphasis is more on display of resources than of the body itself. Townsend and Levy (1990) had men pose for photographs wearing different sets of clothes. One outfit was a Burger King uniform with a baseball cap; another was a white shirt, navy blue blazer, tie, and expensive watch. Women who saw those photographs said they had no interest in dating, having sex with, or marrying the men in the Burger King clothes, but the same men in the expensive clothes were rated as much more desirable. In sum, women use clothes to show off their bodies; men use clothes to show off their money.

The Marriage Gradient   Thus far we have seen that male sex appeal tends to emphasize money, power, and status, whereas female sex appeal depends more on looking young and pretty. This gender difference in mating routines is evident across the globe as well. Men around the world are more interested in women who are youthful and physically attractive. However, what men find physically attractive varies from culture to culture. Some cultures value female fatness when courting a women. Anderson et al. (1992) researched the socioecological factors that determine attitudes toward fatness in women. Important factors included food security, climate, value placed on female work, relative social dominance of women, and adaptive reproductive suppression of females in the society.

The "trophy mate" pattern reflects an extreme form of this pattern. Trophy mating involves obtaining a partner who seems quite superior to yourself in some aspect of sex appeal. Most commonly, it consists of rich, powerful, but older and less physically appealing men marrying young, beautiful, but relatively unaccomplished women. Although the two may seem mismatched in age, physical attractiveness, wealth, and status, in fact they may have matched up well overall. The woman is at the peak of her physical appeal, and the man is at the peak of his status and wealth. The opposite pattern, matching a handsome young man with a rich, elderly woman, is far less common, though there may be natural attraction between an older wealthy woman and a younger male "hunk."

The trophy mate pattern conforms to a broader pattern in which the mates that men and women choose do not match them precisely. In fact, there are systematic differences between spouses on many measures of social status. Put simply, women usually seem to marry up and men marry down. The average husband is about 4 years older, commands a somewhat higher salary, and has a year or two more education than his wife (Bernard, 1982). The broad tendency of husbands to outrank their wives on these (and similar) dimensions of status has been termed the "marriage gradient."

An early version of this gradient can often be seen in dating patterns among high-school and college students. In most universities, the older students have higher status than the younger ones, which probably reflects simply the progress through the educational establishment. Although many people date partners their own age, the unequal patterns consistently conform to the pattern of higher status among males. Sophomore women will date senior men, but sophomore men are much less likely to date senior women. Hence the loneliest year in college is likely to be the first (freshman) year for the man and the last (senior) year for the woman, and many people in those situations find themselves trying to preserve a long-distance relationship with their partner from the previous year rather than finding someone new.

Outside of college life, the marriage gradient affects who will have the hardest time finding mates. Men at the bottom of the socioeconomic scale find it difficult to attract women. Conversely, women at the top levels also find it difficult. A woman who makes several hundred thousand dollars a year will find only a small group of men who seem eligible to her, assuming she follows the standard pattern of expecting her husband to earn even more than she does. Another effect of the marriage gradient is that it tends to preserve male supremacy within each couple. Because the man is a little older, better educated, and better paid than the woman, both husband and wife may expect the husband to take a leadership role.

The marriage gradient theory proposes that for men income level is positively related to the probability of getting married. The proportion of married men increases as income level increases. The marriage gradient suggests that men marry women who are slightly lower down the social class continuum (younger, a little poorer, less educated). The pool of eligible mates decreases for women as they get older, richer, and more educated. The pool of eligible mates increases for men as they get older, richer, and more educated.

The marriage gradient is found quite consistently, but no one is entirely sure why people regularly match up along those lines. One view, favored by constructionist theories, is that societies train men to want to dominate their relationships, and so they seek out younger women for partners because the men's superior age, education, and wealth enable them to be the boss. Another explanation could be attempted on evolutionary grounds, which would point to the fact that men reach their peak attractiveness at a somewhat later age than women do, so if people mate during their period of peak attractiveness the men would naturally be older than the women. A social exchange view would explain the marriage gradient on the basis that sex constitutes the woman's contribution to the relationship, and so to achieve equity overall the man has to put in more in the way of other resources.

The Effect of Sexual Orientation on Sexual Attraction   Recent studies offer evidence that today's college students perceive sexual attraction in much the same way that our ancestors did. Men still prefer potential partners to be physically attractive, while women emphasize nonphysical characteristics such as ambition, status, and dominance in a potential mate (Townsend & Wasserman, 1998). However, another study suggests that despite the importance of our genetic predisposition to prefer mates with reproductive value, both men and women report that they place greater weight on personal characteristics than on physical features when judging prospective mates (Buss, 1994).

Few researchers have examined the traits that gays and lesbians find attractive and look for in a romantic partner. However, there is some evidence that homosexuals are subject to many of the same social and psychological factors that influence heterosexual relationships (Engel & Saracino, 1986; Howard, Blumstein, & Schwartz, 1987).

ROMANCE: FALLING IN LOVE

Theories of love attempt to explain how and why we love, but what are the factors that determine with whom you fall in love and how long your love will last? Five elements are important in the development of a loving relationship: proximity, familiarity, readiness, similarity, and reciprocity.

Proximity

Friendship and love can grow out of frequent interactions. To meet someone is not necessarily to love someone, but to love someone you must first meet, whether online (see EXPLORING SEXUALITY ONLINE box) or in real life. Thus, **proximity,** or being close to someone, is necessary for familiarity to develop. Being near someone doesn't guarantee positive interactions (Brehm, 1985), but repeated contact with someone does increase the chances of having a positive interaction. Research has shown that a series of brief (no more than 35 seconds) face-to-face contacts without talking increased positive responses (Saegert, Swap, & Zajonc, 1973). Even this limited exposure was sufficient to increase attraction. The research subjects found they liked people they saw often more than those seen less frequently.

Looking into someone's eyes may be a particularly potent way to increase attraction. In one study, opposite-sex pairs of college students were instructed to spend 2 minutes gazing into each other's eyes (Kellerman, Lewis, & Laird, 1989). These people reported significant increases in feelings of romantic love, attraction, interest, and warmth. These feelings increased more in the gazing couples than in couples who spent the same amount of time doing other things together.

Proximity: the state, quality, sense, or fact of being near or next to; closeness

EXPLORING SEXUALITY ONLINE

Clicking Online

Of course it worked beautifully for Tom Hanks and Meg Ryan in the 1998 movie *You've Got Mail*, but online love can be a risky business. Some people are just cyberflirting, others may be cyberstalking, while there are those who are genuinely looking for romance online.

At a time when many people are staying single longer, busy professionals may find the Internet a fast and efficient way to meet people. IRL (that's cyberese for In Real Life) you see someone and then decide whether to talk to him or her, but online you chat with people first, getting to know them before you decide if you want to see what they look like. You can meet your online date at midnight in your pajamas without worrying if you're having a bad hair day.

Falling in love with someone you've never met isn't anything new. Cyberdating takes us back to the days of courtship by letter writing. Writing (or typing) changes the way we get to know each other and forces us to think and reflect in ways that talking doesn't.

But it might not be Meg or Tom at the other end of the modem. It's important to practice safe sex online, too. Don't give your full name, phone number, employer, or address until you feel comfortable. And if you decide to meet IRL, be sure to follow the same rules you would for any blind date: meet in a public place, tell a friend where and when you're meeting, and call him or her after the date to let your friend know you're home safe.

In Chapter 8, we presented data from the National Health and Social Life Survey showing that most people meet their sex partners in places like work or school where they see the same people over and over. It is far more unusual to find sex partners in places where strangers intermingle and may see each other only once, such as singles bars. We also reported that less than 2 percent of relationships that lead to marriage started out with the individuals having sex within 2 days after they first met. One reason for these patterns is the tendency to gradually grow fond of the people we see over and over again, a concept called familiarity (see following section). Most people are not quick enough to connect with someone during a first meeting. Many people are reluctant to ask someone for a date until they know that person reasonably well and can feel somewhat confident that their request will not be rejected. The repeated and frequent interactions that come with proximity can help overcome those obstacles.

Familiarity

The second element in the development of a loving relationship is **familiarity,** having close knowledge and shared experiences with another person. Although a degree of unfamiliarity is essential to promote infatuation, and a minimal sense of mystery is critical to romantic love (Fisher, 1992), feelings of affection and deep attachment develop over time. However, familiarity in itself is not sufficient for love. If you strongly dislike someone, repeated exposure can increase hostility (Perlman & Oskamp, 1971). As you may recall from Chapter 11 (see "Interactional Theory"), familiarity played a crucial role in Bem's (1996) theory about the development of sexual orientation, in which the "exotic becomes erotic." The familiar is the opposite of the exotic. According to Bem, when boys grow up surrounded by boys, they regard boys as familiar but girls as exotic, and so the erotic attraction is to girls. To support his theory, Bem summarized a variety of studies indicating that familiarity undermines eroticism for both heterosexuals and homosexuals. For example, although your brother or sister may be quite similar to you in many respects, and you may even date people who are similar to your brother or sister, you probably feel little or no sexual attraction to a brother or sister—possibly because, having grown up together, the familiarity makes the sexual attraction impossible. You might dispute that interpretation by saying there are special (perhaps biological) reasons that people are not sexually attracted to their siblings. But Bem described research showing that people lack sexual attraction to their childhood playmates even when they are not biologically related. In Israel, unrelated boys and girls may be raised together on a kibbutz (commune). When these children grow up, they hardly ever date or marry one another.

Familiarity may also help explain the gradual decline in sexual passion and sexual activity over the course of a long-term relationship. There is some evidence that excessive familiarity can decrease attraction (Harrison, 1977); most individuals report a decrease in sexual desire for people they see on a regular basis. As we have seen, nearly all couples shift toward less frequent sex as the years go by, even if they remain happy with the relationship. The fact that people may have less energy and fewer sex hormones as they get older may contribute something to this, but it is not a full explanation, because when a long-term couple breaks up and the people find new partners, they start having sex much more frequently again (Call, Sprecher, & Schwartz, 1995). There seems to be something to the increase in familiarity that produces a decrease in sexual excitement.

Familiarity can help account for the difference between heterosexual and homosexual relationships in sexual behavior across time. Various studies, including the careful and thorough investigation by Blumstein and Schwartz (1983), have found that the decline in frequency of sex is more extreme in homosexual couples than in heterosexual couples. That is, sex decreases over time in all couples, but it decreases more sharply in homosexual couples. Gay male couples start off having sex more frequently than

Gazing into someone's eyes may significantly increase feelings of romantic love, attraction, interest, and warmth.

Familiarity: the state or quality of having personal knowledge, exposure, or information about someone or something

heterosexual (married or cohabiting) couples, but after 10 years they are having sex less frequently than comparable heterosexual couples. Many lesbian couples find that their sex lives diminish to nearly zero. There is no obvious theoretical reason why sex should decrease more in homosexual than in heterosexual couples, but one possible reason is that familiarity develops more rapidly when the partners have similar bodies.

As a relationship develops you might find that a trait that initially attracted you to a lover or potential lover becomes a source of annoyance. As you get to know someone better you might find that you like that person more—or less. Just as a negative first impression can later reverse, a positive first impression can turn sour. What seems positive in the short term may not be in the long run (Table 15.4).

Readiness

Timing, or **readiness,** also plays an important role in the development of love relationships. You need to be ready to fall in love; a person who might be Mr. Right in 5 years could be Mr. Wrong today. Or you might meet someone who is perfect for you, except for the fact that you are involved in a committed relationship at the time. You are more likely to fall in love when you are looking for adventure, craving to leave home, lonely, displaced, in a foreign country, passing into a new stage in life, or financially and psychologically ready to share yourself or to start a family (Fisher, 1992). You are more likely to be attracted to someone if you are not in a relationship or if you desire to begin a new one (Berscheid et al., 1976).

Similarity

Similarity is a key to long-term love. Research shows that people who form relationships appear similar on almost every objective variable—physical health, family background, age, ethnicity, religion, and level of education; moreover, this finding doesn't seem to have changed over time (Burgess & Wallin, 1953; Hendrick, 1981; Michael et al., 1994). In part this occurs because we tend to be around those similar to us. Usually, we live in neighborhoods and go to schools with people much like ourselves. However, even in a new environment, people who have similar backgrounds like each other more than those who come from different backgrounds (Newcomb, 1961).

Believing that self-expansion is a basic motivation for human behavior, Aron and Aron (1986) state that people are attracted to others in whom they see the opportunity for personal growth. They also believe that their theory can clarify some

Readiness: the state of being ready or prepared

Similarity: the state or quality of being alike or having a close resemblance to something; being of the same kind, but not identical

TABLE 15.4

Initial Attraction

Initial Attractions for Women	Turned into this Negative Trait
Funny and fun	Embarrasses me in public
Spontaneous	Irresponsible
Relaxed	Constantly late
Successful and focused	Workaholic
Strong willed	Macho and stubborn

Initial Attractions for Men	Turned into this Negative Trait
Nurturing	Smothering
Intense interest in me	Jealous and possessive
Offbeat personality	Too unconventional
Strong	Domineering
Willing to have sex	Always wants sex

SOURCE: Adapted from Felmlee, Sprecher, & Bassin, 1990.

The 2001 marriage of Andre Agassi and Steffi Graf is a love match between two tennis stars who have much in common.

controversial issues related to attraction. For example, how do you explain the controversy between the idea that "birds of a feather flock together" and the notion that "opposites attract"?

According to Aron and Aron, the seeming contradictions merely reflect the roles similarity plays in different phases of a relationship. In the beginning, similarity serves as a "precondition variable" (that is, if a relationship is even possible). After the perceived possibility, however, it is the opposite of this precondition variable that determines the development of the relationship. At this later point, dissimilarity rather than similarity makes a person believe that the relationship offers an opportunity for self-expansion.

We are attracted to people with similar backgrounds and to those who have similar attitudes, values (Byrne, 1971; Byrne, Ervin, & Lamberth, 1970; Newcomb, 1961; Sachs, 1976), and personalities (Barry, 1970; Boyden, Carroll, & Maier, 1984). Individuals also are attracted to people who have similar levels of physical attractiveness (Feingold, 1988; Folkes, 1982). Similarity may be attractive because we expect to be accepted by people who are like us (Sprecher & McKinney, 1993). Moreover, there may be an even greater fear of rejection if you think someone is much more attractive than you (Bernstein et al., 1983).

Similarity in physical attractiveness also may serve as a screening device in the early stages of a relationship. In first encounters it may foster attraction; later it could strengthen attachment. However, among committed couples where a match already has been made, similarity in physical attractiveness has not been shown to influence the progress of the relationship (Murstein & Christy, 1976; White, 1980). Researchers say that partners with similar ethnic, racial, and religious backgrounds are more likely to be sexually compatible and are more likely to agree on how to bring up children (Michael et al., 1994).

There is little evidence to support the old saying that opposites attract (Barry, 1970; Fishbein & Thelm, 1981; Nias, 1977). In fact, dissimilarity may lead to repulsion and the desire to avoid. We may react to new people by avoiding those who are dissimilar and approaching those who are similar (Byrne, Clove, & Smeaten, 1986; Byrne & Murnen, 1988; Rosenbaum, 1986). This doesn't mean that couples with different backgrounds can't be happy, just that it might take more effort to make the relationship work.

Reciprocity

Most people like people who like them (Condon & Crano, 1988; Curtis & Miller, 1986). We especially like people who say nice things about us (Byrne & Rhamey, 1965; Sachs, 1976). You are likely to react positively to flattery or compliments (Byrne & Murnen, 1988). At the very least, people tend to like people who agree with them (Jellison & Oliver, 1983) and to assume that people they find attractive share their attitudes (Marks, Miller, & Maruyama, 1981).

Liking people who like us is an example of **reciprocity.** A relationship marked by reciprocity is one with mutual give and take; where both individuals give something and get something in return. You may exchange emotional rewards, physical pleasure, or anything you value. Stable, long-lasting relationships are likely to have a balance of exchanges between the couple. If one partner does most of the giving, it creates an inequity that almost inevitably contributes to the end of the relationship.

SEX: MAKING LOVE

Many people believe that sex without love is less fulfilling to the body, the mind, the heart, and the soul. On the other hand, many people believe that love without sex can be frustrating and unfulfilling. The physical pleasures of sex can't be denied. In fact, some researchers believe that sexual pleasure is the primary motivational force behind human sexuality and that reproduction is simply a byproduct (Abramson & Pinkerton, 2001). In other words, people engage in sex because it brings them pleasure, and reproduction happens as a result.

Reciprocity: a relation of mutual dependence. Two people give to each other equally

The emotional pleasures of sex may be equally important. In fact, there are those who feel that even the physical pleasure of orgasm has a strong emotional component. Orgasm is more than a series of muscular contractions; it has many of the features of an altered state of consciousness since "it requires an ability to let go of inhibitions and involves changed perceptions of time, space and motion" (Konner, 1990, p. 190). In other words, orgasm occurs in the mind as well as in the body.

Love and Lust

While most of us probably believe that sex and love are closely linked, we are also aware that each can exist without the other (Table 15.5). There can be **lust,** intense sexual desire, without love, and there can be feelings of love without any sexual relationship. However, the ideal relationship for most people is one that is both loving and sexual. A group of college students was given information about a hypothetical heterosexual dating couple's sexual desire, sexual behavior, and romantic feelings for each other, and were then asked to make inferences about the couple's relationship. Results suggested that both male and female students viewed sexual desire as an important feature of romantic love and that its presence or absence in a dating relationship is believed to have implications for the emotional character and interpersonal dynamics of that relationship (Regan, 1998).

There may be some evidence that sex is emotionally, if not always physically, better with the person you love. The 1994 National Health and Social Life Survey found that 29 percent of women and 75 percent of men reported always having orgasms during sex with their primary partner. However, the number of women and men who reported feeling emotionally satisfied by sex with their partners was nearly equal (Laumann et al., 1994).

Women are sometimes accused of confusing sex with love, while men are maligned for wanting sexual conquests devoid of emotion. Research supports this stereotype, suggesting that the primary motive for men having sexual intercourse is physical pleasure while women's motivation is affection and closeness (Sprague & Quadagno, 1989). However, a subsequent study found that as women age, physical pleasure becomes a more important motivation (Murstein & Tuerkheim, 1998).

Can men separate sex from love more easily than women? The answer is yes and no. Casual sex, defined as sex without love performed merely for the temporary pleasure, is far more appealing to men than to women (Oliver & Hyde, 1993a). On the other hand, love without sex is more appealing to women than to men. Surveys that ask whether love and sex are different things find that women can separate the two more than men (Janus & Janus, 1993).

Lust: to want, crave, covet, or sexually desire someone or something

TABLE 15.5		
The Relationship of Sex and Love		
	Women (% who agree)	**Men (% who agree)**
I have been sexually attracted without feeling the slightest trace of love.	53	79
There are more important things in life than love.	28	37
Sometimes I tell my friends about my sexual experiences, but not about being in love.	8	30
I have enjoyed sex more when it was with someone I was not in love with.	4	11

SOURCE: Adapted from Tennov, 1979, p. 223.

FAQ:

Do men lust and women love?

Do women have sex in order to be loved? Do men give love in order to have sex? In her report on women, Shere Hite (1976) states, "Women liked sex more for the feelings involved than for the purely physical sensations of intercourse per se . . . it is the emotional warmth shared at this time, and the feeling of being wanted and needed . . . which are the chief pleasures of sex and intercourse" (p. 431). Men undeniably enjoy the physical aspects of sex and are given greater latitude in our culture to separate physical pleasure from emotional feelings. However, Hite found that the most important pleasures men said they get from intercourse are psychological, "a giving and a getting of acceptance and warmth, validation . . . [and] that only during 'sex' are they allowed to be totally out of control, to release the pent up emotions they are taught they 'should' repress at all other times" (p. 339).

It is probably true for both men and women that love makes for better sex. Having intercourse with someone who does not love you can feel cheap and empty, or it can be a mild source of fun like playing a game. It generally falls far short of the intensely positive experiences of two people who care deeply about each other and make love as a way of expressing their passionate feelings and commitment.

The separation of love and lust may reflect an adaptive mechanism. Psychodynamic and evolutionary theorists argue that commitment, intimacy, and security are most important to women, while for men physical appearance and sexual appeal are paramount. On the other hand, social constructionists argue that the similarities in romantic attraction between men and women are greater than the differences.

Age and experience may impact our romantic love beliefs (Knox, Schact, & Zusman, 1999), but nearly everyone has had the experience of falling in love at least once. However, adult women more often believe that their partners have fallen in love at a relatively early stage; men believe that their partners have fallen in love later in the relationship (Riehl-Emde, 1997).

Although many studies show that there is a difference between how males and females experience love (see Table 15.6), most of this research has been with heterosexual college-age students and may not apply to all groups of people. The most extensive study on gender differences in the way we love was done by Hendrick and Hendrick (1986) utilizing Lee's model of six love styles. It was found that women scored higher than men on storge, mania, and pragma while men had higher scores on ludus. There was no gender difference on agape, and the results for eros were inconsistent.

Speed of Falling in Love

Kanin and Davidson (1972) surveyed several hundred young people about their most recent dating experiences and relationships. Their study had a near-zero refusal rate (that is, almost everyone answered the questions), which makes it especially strong methodologically. In general, the men fell in love more quickly than the women. The researchers asked people how they felt after four dates and after 20 dates with the same person (the most recent dating partner). Within the first four dates, 27 percent of the men but only 15 percent of the women said they had feelings of love for the other person. At the other end of the spectrum, nearly half the women but less than a third of the men reported that they still did not feel love for the partner after 20 dates.

A pair of studies by Huston et al. (1981) confirmed that love blooms more rapidly in male than female hearts. Before a pair was recognized as being a couple, the men had feelings of love but the women usually did not. Men were ready to move from the "dating" stage to the "couple" stage several months earlier than women (on average, 2.6 versus 5.5 months). Men were more likely than women to believe that the relationship was headed for a stable, long-term commitment such as marriage.

These studies focus on mutual relationships, but research on failed relationships (to which we shall turn in Chapter 16) provides the same picture. The phenomenon of unrequited love involves one person being in love and the other refusing that love. Hill,

TABLE 15.6

The Importance of Love

How Important is Love to You?	Men	Women
Very important	72%	85%
Important	24	13
Not sure	3	1
Unimportant	0	1
Very unimportant	1	0

SOURCE: Janus & Janus, 1993, p. 65

TABLE 15.7

Important Traits in Selecting a Mate

Men's Ratings	Women's Ratings
1. mutual attraction/love	1. mutual attraction/love
2. dependable character	2. dependable character
3. emotional stability and maturity	3. emotional stability and maturity
4. pleasing disposition	4. pleasing disposition
5. good health	5. education and intelligence
6. education	6. sociability
7. sociability	7. good health
8. desire for home and children	8. desire for home and children
9. refinement, neatness	9. ambition and industry
10. good looks	10. refinement, neatness
11. ambition and industry	11. similar education
12. good cook and housekeeper	12. good financial prospect
13. good financial prospect	13. good looks
14. similar education	14. favorable social status or rating
15. favorable social status or rating	15. good cook and housekeeper
16. chastity	16. similar religious background
17. similar religious background	17. similar political background
18. similar political background	18. chastity

SOURCE: Buss et al., 1990, p. 19.

FAQ:

Who is more romantic, men or women?

To answer this question, Hobart (1958) developed a questionnaire measure of romanticism and actually found that, on average, men scored as more romantic than women. Other studies have found little or no difference in romanticism between the sexes. One test of being romantic is falling in love, so wouldn't it make sense that those who fall in love more quickly are more romantic? If this is so, the men win again, because the data consistently show that men fall in love more rapidly than women.

Rubin, and Peplau (1976) conducted a well-known survey of relationship breakups. Their findings conformed to the broad formulation that men fall in love more readily than women; women also fall out of love more easily than men. They concluded that woman's criteria for falling in love and staying in love are higher than men's criteria. The reverse (woman in love, man not in love) does certainly happen, but less frequently.

Another important finding from the Hill et al. (1976) study was that men suffered more than women from the breakup of a relationship. They found that women were more willing than men to break off the relationship; even independent of this fact, the breakups caused greater suffering among men than women. Similar findings were reported by Albrecht, Bahr, and Goodman (1983), who showed that women are more likely than men to initiate divorce and that men are more likely to remarry and to do so quickly. Thus, it appears that men fall in love more rapidly than women, and men fall out of love more reluctantly (and painfully) than women.

The gender differences in speed of falling in love may help explain some other patterns. We have noted that men are ready for sex earlier in a relationship than women. Part of this is attributable to men being more interested than women in casual sex, defined as sex without love. But if men actually fall in love sooner than women, they will probably want to express this love sexually sooner as well. This is especially true because men find it harder than women to accept love without sex.

ATTACHMENT: STAYING IN LOVE

Attachment, a connection or feeling of being emotionally close to someone, is a component of most definitions of human love (Bartholomew & Perlman, 1994; Sternberg & Barnes, 1988). Although attachment can exist without love, it is doubtful that love can exist in the absence of attachment. Attachment is a selective social or emotional bond (Ainsworth, 1989). Although the emotional bonds of love cannot be measured directly, scientists can investigate the behavioral or physiological processes associated with attachment. For example, researchers can observe how physically close a person stays to the object of attachment, or the number of times they are in contact, and compare these to responses toward an unfamiliar individual.

Attachment: a strong feeling of being emotionally connected or close to someone or something

Attachment Styles

It appears that attachment has its roots in infancy and that romantic love and the infant/caregiver relationship have a lot in common. Mary Ainsworth and her colleagues (Ainsworth, 1989; Ainsworth et al., 1978) observed mothers and infants and identified three different attachment styles: secure, anxious/ambivalent, and avoidant. In *secure attachments*, the infant feels safe even when the mother is out of sight, confident that she will return to provide care and protection. In *anxious/ambivalent attachments*, the infant shows separation anxiety when the mother leaves. In *avoidant attachment*, the infant wants close bodily contact with the mother but senses her detachment. In Ainsworth et al.'s study (1978), 65–70 percent of infants were secure, less than 10 percent anxious/ambivalent, and 20–25 percent were avoidant. The type of attachment developed during infancy seems to continue throughout our lives, influencing how we relate to others (Table 15.8).

Psychologists Hatfield and Rapson (1996) expanded on Ainsworth's attachment theory and identified six variations in attachment styles: secure, clingy, skittish, fickle, casual, and uninterested. *Secure* adults seem to do better than others in terms of negotiating stable, companionate, intimate relationships. *Clingy* types obsess about their partner's feelings and have trouble finding committed, companionate relationships, as their insatiable demands seem to drive others away. The *skittish* types seem to fear romantic intimacy. Pessimistic about love, they avoid intimate social contact. *Fickle* lovers are drawn to the challenge of the unavailable. Sometimes the fickle fall passionately in

TABLE 15.8

Attachment Styles

Secure Adults	Anxious/Ambivalent Adults	Avoidant Adults
About 56%	About 20%	About 24%
Find it relatively easy to get close to others.	Feel that others don't get as close as they would like.	Feel uncomfortable being close to others.
Have few worries about being left by a partner.	Worry that their partner doesn't really love them and will leave.	Believe that love doesn't last and inevitably one day their partner will leave.
Aren't concerned about a partner getting too close. Comfortable with depending on others and being depended upon.	Want to merge completely with their partner.	Are distrustful and fearful of getting too close and becoming dependent.
Are less likely to believe in media images of love. Their love experiences tend to be happy, friendly, and trusting. They accept and support their partners.	Feel that it's easy to fall in love. Love relationships are often obsessive and marked by a high degree of sexual attraction, jealousy, and emotional highs and lows.	Want less closeness than their partner does. They fear intimacy and experience emotional highs, lows, and jealousy.
Relationships last an average of 10 years.	Relationships average about 5 years.	Relationships last an average of 6 years.

SOURCE: Adapted from Ainsworth, 1989; Ainsworth et al., 1978.

love but are less likely than any other group to have ever been involved in a long-term committed, intimate relationship. The *casual* types just want to have a good time. The more casual they are about relationships, the less likely they were to have experienced either passionate or companionate love. Those who are *uninterested* in relationships are extremely unlikely to have experienced much passionate or companionate love.

Doherty et al. (1994) at the University of Hawaii examined the influence of culture and ethnicity on love and attachment. Students from Chinese-, European-, and Japanese-American, and Pacific Islander ethnic backgrounds were asked if they were currently in love and how passionately and companionately in love they were. The study found that there were no significant differences among ethnic groups in the likelihood of being in love, nor in the intensity of the passionate and companionate love they felt. Men's and women's adult attachment styles rather than cultural or ethnic differences predicted romantic feelings and experiences.

Because of the absence of longitudinal research or of studies of attempts by people to change their attachment styles, we do not know the extent to which individuals can alter attachment styles developed during infancy. However, evidence is accumulating in support of the basic tenets of attachment theory. Nonetheless, further research is needed on the possibility of altering attachment style in adulthood.

Time and Passion

As we have already discussed, and perhaps as you have learned from experience, the high of passionate love doesn't last forever. The body builds up a tolerance to the natural chemicals in the brain associated with being in love; more and more are needed to feel the same level of euphoria. Some people interpret the corresponding decrease in sexual energy to mean they are no longer in love, and indeed for some it does mark the end of a relationship. However, rather than an end to love, it may be a transition into the longer-lasting companionate love.

It appears that the brain cannot tolerate the continually revved-up state of passionate love (Fisher, 1992). As the newness of passion fades, "the brain kicks in new chemicals, the endorphins, natural morphine-like substances that calm the mind" (Fisher 1992, p. 163). The excitement may diminish, but the security of companionate love can provide a different, not necessarily a lesser, pleasure.

Successful relationships must eventually negotiate the shift from passionate love to companionate love; one reason for this is that the time courses of passion and intimacy are quite different (Sternberg, 1986). Passion tends to rise sharply early in the relationship but then drops off, as indicated by the decrease in frequency of sex (among other signs). Intimacy rises more slowly. Hence a couple that has been together for 10 or 15 years may have a very high degree of intimacy but a relatively low amount of passion. In other words, they understand each other very well, feel deeply committed to each other, and care a great deal about each other's welfare—but they are not frequently overcome with eagerness to rip each other's clothes off and leap into bed.

One possible explanation of the relationship between passion and intimacy is that passion is a function of *change* in intimacy (Baumeister & Bratslavsky, 1999). That is, passion is high when intimacy is rising rapidly, such as when a couple is first getting to know each other, first expressing feelings for each other, and first disclosing deeply personal things to each other. This occurs relatively early in the relationship. Later on, a high degree of intimacy may be reached, but it remains stable, and so passion will be low. (Of course, if the couple starts to break up, intimacy will be experienced as diminishing, and that will set off a different set of passionate feelings!) An interruption in intimacy followed by a return to the high level will, however, be experienced as a rise in intimacy, so even couples who have been together for a long time may experience moments of passionate love on certain occasions—such as when they make up after a fight, or when they are reunited after a period of separation. See Figure 15.4 to evaluate the current level of intimacy with your partner.

> *"... as infatuation wanes, a new sensation saturates the mind—attachment. Perhaps this is the most elegant of human feelings, that sense of contentment of sharing of oneself with another human being."*
>
> **(FISHER, 1992, P. 162)**

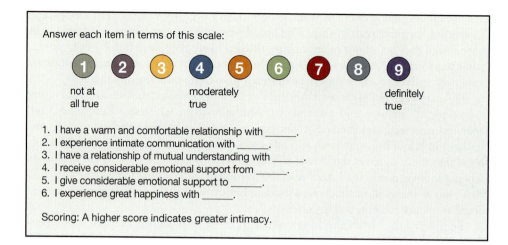

FIGURE 15.4   The Intimacy Love Scale.   SOURCE: Hatfield & Rapson, 1996, p. 64.

Committed Relationships

Being in a committed relationship has innumerable benefits. Our ancestors derived many benefits if they remained in committed relationships; for example, the efficiency of complementary skills and "a division of labor, a sharing of resources, a unified front against mutual enemies, a stable home environment for rearing children, and a more extended kinship network" (Buss, 1989, p. 23). While survival and reproduction may depend on our brains being genetically wired for attachment, it is the mind that makes the decision to be in a long-term committed relationship (see Figure 15.5). Most experts agree that a committed relationship benefits modern couples, too.

Research studies show that in most areas of life, married men and women do better than those who are not married (Myers, 1997). For 25 years the National Opinion Research Center's General Social Survey has regularly asked married people in the United States whether they are very happy, pretty happy, or not too happy with their marriages. In no year have even 5 percent of married people described their marriage as not too happy, and the split between men's and women's perceptions of wedded bliss is generally small. However, some researchers believe that in terms of their physical and mental health, men seem to have an edge. It appears that marriage may disproportionately benefit men in marital satisfaction, life satisfaction, and rates of physical and mental health (Gottman, 1996). However, other researchers have found that marriage brings considerable health benefits to both women and men (Waite & Gallagher, 2000) and that married women are slightly happier than married men (Wood, Rhodes, & Wheland, 1989).

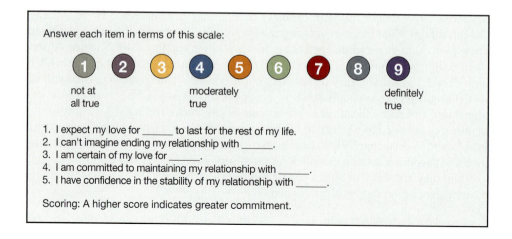

FIGURE 15.5   A Commitment Love Scale.   SOURCE: Hatfield & Rapson, 1996, p. 64.

You certainly don't have to be married to be happy. Many couples choose to live together rather than marry, while many gay and lesbian couples, who are not legally able to marry in the United States, are certainly happy. A study of married, engaged, and cohabiting couples found a huge happiness factor. At least 90 percent of both men and women polled in every category of years together reported themselves happy (Stanley & Markman, 1992).

INTIMACY, LOVE, AND SEXUAL COMMUNICATION

Commitment allows you to feel safe and secure in a relationship; intimacy allows you to feel understood and accepted (Hatfield & Rapson, 1996). If we can believe what they say in the film *Love Story*, love means never having to say you're sorry. However, mindreading doesn't automatically accompany love. Effective communication skills do not magically appear when you fall in love, but they can be learned. Self-communication and partner communication are significant predictors of relationship satisfaction (Meeks, Hendrick, & Hendrick, 1998). And, as we discussed in Chapter 13, sexual *mis*communication may sometimes result in sexual harassment and date rape. Even when communication problems don't reach this extreme, many couples have problems for years because of an unwillingness to discuss their sexual needs; or, they may misinterpret their partner's sexual responses. For example, your partner might interpret your groans and grimaces as pain when you are really expressing pleasure (Levy & Davis, 1988).

Opening Lines

Peacocks strut, dogs sniff, and humans flirt. Getting attention is the opening move in the courtship dance. Scientists are finding that we humans have some striking similarities to other species in our methods of attracting potential romantic partners. In the first phase of courtship we broadcast our desire for attention with nonverbal messages, such as the way we move, our manner of dress, and gestures. The first message is "Notice me" and the second is "I am harmless." Harmlessness is conveyed in gestures like a palm-up placement of the hand on a table or a knee, the shrug of a shoulder, or playfulness (Givens, 1995).

Anthropologist Helen Fisher (1992) describes a universal pattern of female **flirting.** Whether human or baboon, the female first smiles at her admirer, then lifts her eyebrows in a rapid, jerky motion as her eyes open wide to gaze at the object of her affection. She then drops her eyelids, tilts her head down and to the side as she coyly looks away. Sometimes she covers her face with her hands, giggling nervously. Both animals and human females frequently toss their heads to solicit attention. Male courting tactics also are similar to those of other species. Chest thrusts and standing tall are posture messages sent throughout the animal kingdom.

Several types of opening lines, or "grooming talk" (Morris, 1971) have been identified (Kleinke, Meeker, & Staneski, 1986). These include: cute, flippant remarks ("Has anyone ever told you that you look just like Julia Roberts?"); innocuous statements ("It sure is cold out"); or more direct approaches ("I'd like to get to know you"). Honest or "quality" courtship may require different tactics than exploitative or "quantity" courtship. A study of male courtship tactics found that tactics of quality courtship involved honest advertisement through mutual assessment, resource expenditure, and a delay in sexual relations, while quantity courtship tactics involve indirect or direct threat, psychological pressure, and talking about sex (Hirsch & Paul, 1996).

Men tend to be more active in the beginning stages of developing a relationship and to be more interested than women in the goal of sexual intimacy. Men are more likely to take direct steps, such as asking for a phone number, when approaching a potential date. Women are more likely to use indirect strategies such as hinting (Clark, Shaver, & Abrahams, 1999). In Western society, men are traditionally expected to initiate a date, decide what to do, pay for the date, initiate any physical contact, and ask for another date. However, it is the woman who usually starts the courtship sequence, with

Flirting: playful behavior intended to arouse sexual interest

subtle, nonverbal cues that she is open to being approached. In this sense the woman is the one who "chooses" a potential date, but if he fails to respond the courtship proceeds no further (Perper, 1985).

Talking About Sex

You've gotten past the opening lines, first date, first kiss, and first sexual encounter. Now how do you talk about sex? Sexual behavior is a form of communication. Among animals this communication operates at three levels: signals used to increase the likelihood of sexual interaction; signals that inhibit inbreeding (mating with closely related individuals) or facilitate outbreeding (mating with unrelated individuals); and signals that allow selection among potential mates (Bernstein et al., 1993). But animals have it easy. They don't have to worry about embarrassment, rejection, or guilt.

Even those who communicate well at work, with close friends, or in other areas of their lives can have difficulty discussing their sexual relationships with their partners. A couple can spend countless hours discussing jobs, friends, family, finances, or popular television shows, yet never discuss their sexual relationship.

How could you expect your lover to know your favorite food unless you shared this information with him or her? Maybe there are days when a salad would please you more than a hamburger. How can your partner know your sexual preferences unless you communicate? No one can instinctively know what his or her partner most enjoys. It is your responsibility to communicate your sexual preferences; it is not your partner's responsibility to read your mind.

It may be easier to discuss sex with your partner by talking about talking. You might tell your partner it is uncomfortable to discuss your sexual needs, and explain what fears or concerns you have. Express your embarrassment, fear of hurting your partner's feelings, or concern about your partner's reaction. Before you begin the conversation, carefully consider what it is you really want. It might be useful to think about those sexual experiences that you enjoyed the most and what made that particular experience so pleasurable. Was it the setting? Was a particular technique or position used? What time of day was it? What had you been doing beforehand? Work with your partner to include as many of these favorable factors as possible.

An Australian study (Ferroni & Taffe, 1997) reported that women who enjoy good communication with their partners about sexual needs are less depressed and have higher self-esteem. Similarly, those who communicate well in the bedroom are more likely to be happy with their relationships and engage in sexual interactions with their partners more frequently. These results should be interpreted with caution; it may be that women who are less depressed and have higher self-esteem are more likely to communicate their needs.

Talking About Love

"My partner wants to discuss and dissect every aspect of our relationship. It doesn't do any good; why do we have to talk about it all the time?" Do you think a man or a woman asked this question? If you are like most people, you probably would answer that this is a typical male perspective: "It has become the stuff of stereotypes and greeting cards that . . . women talk about their feelings, men change the subject to basketball scores" (Blum, 1997, p. 66).

Sociolinguist Deborah Tannen (1990, 1994) found that gender differences in communication are apparent from early childhood. Women value agreeable, congenial behavior and therefore tend to be complimentary and apologetic when communicating. Men generally take verbal rejection personally and resist doing what they are told because they don't want to feel submissive in a relationship. According to Tannen, a typical area of conflict for couples is the expression of needs. A woman who says what she wants may be focusing on intimacy and connection, but the man may hear only that she is making demands of him. If she says she wants to know when he will be home so she won't worry or can make plans, he may hear this as a challenge to his freedom and resist what he perceives to be controlling behavior.

John Gottman (1994, 1998, 1999), a psychologist who studies couples whose marriages work, claims that he can predict with more than 90 percent accuracy which couples are likely to stay together by the way couples communicate and resolve conflicts. Happily married couples have such a deep understanding of their partner's dreams and fears that they can negotiate problems without creating emotional turmoil; they tend to use the constructive communication tactics shown in Table 15.9. Couples headed for divorce use criticism, contempt, defensiveness, and stonewalling, the destructive communication tactics shown in Table 15.10.

Although it might be clear why the tactics listed in Table 15.10 have a negative impact on a relationship, you may be surprised by some of the techniques in Table 15.9 that Gottman found to be constructive in a relationship. Contrary to popular belief, the volatile style (loud, heated arguing) and the conflict avoidant style (agreeing to disagree and avoiding head-on conflicts) were not found to be detrimental to a relationship. Although these methods of problem solving might not lead to as rapid a solution as the validating method, at least they don't make the problem worse; criticizing, attacking, blaming, and shaming your partner create a whole new set of problems to solve.

TABLE 15.9

Constructive Communication Tactics

Type of Comment	Explanation	Example
Validating	Compromise, calm working out of problems together	"Let's sit down and talk about this and see what we can agree on."
Volatile	Resolving conflict with passionate dialogue	"OK, let's get it all out on the table and deal with this once and for all."
Conflict Avoidant	Agreeing to disagree, avoiding head-on conflict	"We're never going to agree about this so let's just forget it."

SOURCE: Adapted from Gottman, 1994.

TABLE 15.10

Destructive Communication Tactics

Type of Comment	Explanation	Example
Criticism	Personal attacks, blaming, not giving specifics when discussing problems	"You never do anything right."
Contempt	Abuse, insults, name-calling, sarcasm	"It's really hard to believe that anyone could be so stupid."
Defensive	Feeling victimized, denial of responsibility, making excuses, cross (angry), complaining	"I did not"; "you did too."
Stonewalling	Withdrawal, not responding, shutting out the other person	The silent treatment

SOURCE: Adapted from Gottman, 1994.

How words are said also is important. Your tone of voice may convey a message that is far clearer than your words. Imagine the different meaning of the words "OK, let's just forget about it" if they are loudly yelled, dripping with sarcasm, meekly whispered, or matter-of-factly stated. The meaning of a sentence can differ vastly according to the emphasis placed on one word or the gestures that accompany what is said. The meaning of the words, "I don't want to talk about that now" is very different when accompanied by a soft stroke of your partner's cheek than said with a clenched fist.

Good communication involves listening as well as talking. Some people are passive listeners, while others listen actively. How do you feel when you're talking to someone who is passively staring into space with barely a flicker of discernible interest in what you're saying? Is the person bored, indifferent, or not interested in you? Without any cues to encourage you, you might give up trying to communicate with someone who doesn't seem to be emotionally present.

Being an active listener involves verbal and nonverbal confirmation that you're not just listening but interested in what your partner is saying. Maintaining eye contact with your partner may be an important way of communicating your interest, but this varies from culture to culture (see CROSS-CULTURAL PERSPECTIVES box in the next section). Give feedback, ask questions, and share your own thoughts and feelings.

Paraphrasing what you've heard your partner say is one way to let your partner know that you are listening. In addition, it gives your partner the opportunity to agree or disagree with your understanding of what was said and, if needed, to try to express the message again in a different way. Another technique many therapists encourage couples to use is "I" messages. "I'd really like to try oral sex the next time we make love" is quite different from saying, "How come you never want to have oral sex?"

Children in toy stores and adults in love learn that just because they ask nicely for something doesn't mean that they're going to get it. But it is important that you accept responsibility for getting your needs met. Intimate relationships thrive on genuine, open, honest communication.

Communicating Without Words

Good communication doesn't have to be verbal. Even when you are silent, you are communicating something by the expression on your face, your body posture, and the physical distance, or space, between you and your partner. One problem with nonverbal messages is that they easily can be misinterpreted. Is the person frowning, or about to cry? Is that a smile or a sneer? The ability to interpret nonverbal communication correctly may be as important to a relationship as understanding spoken words.

CROSS-CULTURAL PERSPECTIVES

The Look of Love

Just as words have a cultural context, so does nonverbal communication. In Western cultures, looking someone directly in the eye is usually perceived as a positive gesture. In some Asian cultures, direct eye contact may be perceived as aggressive. In some Native American cultures it is uncommon to reveal feelings with facial expression. Arab and Hispanic societies are generally "contact" cultures in which people tend to stand close together and touch *frequently. An Anglo may interpret the establishment of a neutral or comfortable distance by a person of Hispanic descent as a move toward seduction, since the "neutral zone" is much wider in Anglo culture than in Hispanic culture. It is important to be aware of these cultural differences to avoid miscommunication, but it is equally important not to stereotype someone on the basis of cultural preferences.*

Touch is a powerful form of communication. Obviously how you touch is important. A slap conveys a very different message than a caress. But the where, when, and how often are just as important. A vigorous rubdown from a massage therapist may feel good in a different way than the touch of a lover stroking your back. Touching can communicate a desire for closeness, symbolize togetherness or "ownership," or be a means of diffusing anger or anxiety.

James Prescott (1975) examined the relationship between the treatment of infants and the level of adult violence in 49 cultures. Those cultures in which infants are reared with a great deal of physical affection tend to display little physical violence; conversely, those cultures in which infants are deprived of physical affection display high levels of physical violence among adults. On the basis of these observations, Prescott suggested that affection and aggression are, to some extent, mutually exclusive. That is, children reared with physical affection are likely to be affectionate and nonviolent as adults.

If you can't take your eyes off someone, it certainly says that you're very interested. As indicated earlier, eye contact can provide a great deal of information. Looking your partner (or potential partner) directly in the eye conveys a very different message than looking down at your feet or off in the distance. As we've said, observing facial expressions is also important. Words said with a genuine smile may have a different meaning than those said with a grimace. If a person's words and facial expression do not match, there is the potential for mixed messages that may be misinterpreted.

SEXUAL HEALTH AND YOU

Working on Relationships

Author John Gottman (1999) indicates that working briefly on your relationship every day will do more for your health and longevity than working out at a health club! He offers the following daily suggestions for creating a successful relationship:

- Before you say goodbye in the morning, be sure to learn about one thing that is happening that day with your partner.

- Be sure to engage in stress-reducing conversations at the end of each workday.

- Each day, find some way to communicate genuine affection and appreciation toward your partner.

- Kiss, hold, and touch each other during the time you are together.

- Give at least one genuine compliment to your partner each day.

CHAPTER 15

REVIEW

It seems reasonable to think of loving relationships as having two phases. **1**_____ or romantic love thrives on excitement characterized by intense arousal, absorption, and sexual desire. Chemicals released in the emotional centers of the brain may produce the passionate high of romance. Such a high cannot last indefinitely since the brain builds up a tolerance to these natural chemicals and more are needed to feel the same level of euphoria. The period of romance lasts a year or two or three.

2_____ love is based on familiarity, with feelings of affection and deep attachment. It is possible that the emotions of this type of love are triggered by the release in the brain of endorphins, natural morphinelike substances that calm the mind.

Love is a complex phenomenon that is easier to categorize than to define. We do know that romantic love is not just a uniquely Western experience. Psychologist Abraham Maslow, who viewed love as a basic human need, distinguished **3**_____ (unselfish, nurturing, and not possessive) from **4**_____ (with dependency, jealousy, and selfishness). Robert Sternberg has proposed a **5**_____ theory of love based on passion, intimacy, and commitment. Zick Rubin developed a scale to measure love. He identified three components in loving relationships: **6**_____, _____, and _____. Dorothy Tennov coined the term **7**_____ to describe the feeling of "being in love." This feeling may well have a chemical basis. Sociologist John Allan Lee has identified six styles of love in human relationships; of these **8**_____ is a

romantic style of love with emphasis on physical passion and beauty.

Physical attractiveness is a major determinant of sexual attraction, especially for **9**_____. Moreover, your perception of another's physical attractiveness can affect your behavior toward them and their response to your behavior. In addition, loving someone and believing he or she is beautiful tend to produce the reality.

Our perceptions of beauty are culturally influenced. Cross-culturally men tend to rate good looks in a mate as more important than women, however, both males and females rate kindness, understanding, and intelligence above earning power and attractiveness.

The marriage **10**_____ reflects the tendency of men to outrank their wives on several dimensions of social status (for example, age, income, education).

There are five elements in the development of a loving relationship. **11**_____ entails being close enough for **12**_____ to develop. **13**_____ is critical since you are more likely to fall in love at certain points in your life and less likely at others. **14**_____ is a key to long-term relationships since we are likely to form such relationships with others who are like us in almost every way. Finally, if a relationship is to last, it must be marked by **15**_____, that is, mutual give and take or the exchange of equivalent benefits for both partners.

Initial infatuation may not last, since the traits that you find attractive at first may not prove to be sufficient or even correct. The **16**_____ traits that may bring couples together initially are less important than personal qualities in the formation of long-term relationships.

17_____ is key to the development of loving relationships, and the type developed during infancy seems to continue throughout our lives. **18**_____ allows one to feel safe and secure in a relationship. Being in a committed relationship benefits one's emotional and physical well-being.

While men and women tend to communicate differently, both men and women have difficulty discussing their sexual needs and desires. Good communication involves effective **19**_____ as well as talking.

SUGGESTED READINGS

Booth, R. & Jung, M. (1996). *Romancing the Net: A "Tell-All" Guide to Love Online.* Rocklin, CA: Prima Publishers.

This book offers advice by people who have experienced the highs and lows of cyber romance.

Etcoff, N. (1999). *Survival of the Prettiest: The Science of Beauty.* New York: Doubleday.

Written by a Harvard Medical School psychologist, this book synthesizes much of the recent evolutionary research about physical attractiveness. Etcoff takes the position that sensitivity to beauty is a biological adaptation governed by brain circuits shaped by natural selection.

Fromm, E. (1989). *The Art of Loving.* New York: Harper-Collins.

This classic explores all aspects of the emotion from romantic and parental love to love of God.

Jankowiak, W. (Ed.) (1997). *Romantic Passion: A Universal Experience.* New York: Columbia University Press.

Contributors to this volume explore expressions of love in various cultures.

Schnarch, D. (1998). *Passionate Marriage: Love, Sex, and Intimacy in Emotionally Committed Relationships.* New York: Henry Holt.

The author, a clinical psychologist and sex therapist, believes that sex is the barometer of a love relationship. He uses anecdotes mixed with explanation to describe how differentiation, the process of defining yourself as separate from your partner, inevitably draws you closer together.

Schwartz, P. (2000). *Everything You Know About Love and Sex Is Wrong.* New York: Putnam.

A sociologist looks at 25 myths about love and sexual relationships.

ANSWERS TO CHAPTER REVIEW

1. Passionate; **2.** Companionate; **3.** Being in love (or B-love); **4.** Deficiency love (or D-love); **5.** triangular; **6.** attachment, caring, intimacy; **7.** limerence; **8.** eros; **9.** men; **10.** gradient; **11.** Proximity; **12.** familiarity; **13.** Readiness; **14.** Similarity; **15.** reciprocity; **16.** physical; **17.** Attachment; **18.** Commitment; **19.** listening.

CHAPTER 16

Sex and Heartache

- **Relationships Can Make You Sad**
  Sex can leave you feeling depressed and lonely. Breaking up with a loved one or dealing with rejection is a difficult experience for most people. Some people associate sex with feelings of guilt or shame.

- **Relationships Can Make You Mad**
  There are sociological, psychological, and evolutionary theories to explain jealousy, an emotion often associated with sexual relationships that can erode relationships and even lead to violence.

- **Relationships Can Make You Scared**
  Sexual performance anxiety, normalcy anxiety, and fears of intimacy and commitment are problems for many couples. Shyness makes it difficult for some individuals to engage in the self-disclosure necessary to develop committed relationships.

PHYSICAL

SOCIAL

EMOTIONAL

SPIRITUAL

COGNITIVE

While sex can provide pleasure and enjoyment, it can also produce painful and frightening emotions. Sex might not be the focus of so much of our art, literature, and music if it was only associated with reproduction or recreation, or if there were only happy endings to our sexual stories. We probably wouldn't spend so much time thinking about sex, talking about it, dreaming about it, or crying over it. We wouldn't live for it, or die for it. Romantic attraction at its best can be the beginning of a lifetime partnership. At its worst, it can serve as the basis for depression, stalking, homicide, or suicide. Sexual feelings can and should be pleasurable and enjoyable; however, the darker emotions it provokes cannot be ignored.

The emotional aspect of sexuality is intertwined with its physical, social, spiritual, and cognitive aspects. To reduce the frequency, duration, and intensity of unpleasant emotions, it can be helpful to distinguish between what you are thinking, how you are behaving, and what you are feeling. Your actions may not accurately reflect your thoughts or your emotions. For example, a soldier may behave aggressively while feeling extremely anxious and having thoughts of being elsewhere. A rejected lover may scream and yell and throw things, yet the underlying feeling may not be anger but fear of being alone or sadness related to feelings of low self-worth or loss.

Some evidence suggests that the best way to avoid the unpleasant emotions that can accompany a sexual relationship is to have sex with only one partner, preferably a spouse or a cohabiting partner. An exclusive primary sex partner is associated with the lowest rates of negative feelings, as well as the highest rates of positive feelings (Laumann et al., 1994) (Table 16.1). There is, to be sure, the usual chicken-and-egg question. Does monogamy make people happier, or are happy people more likely to be monogamous? Cause and effect aside, it does appear that sexual monogamy and happiness are linked.

Certainly most of us would rather feel pleasure than pain; it is natural to want to avoid disagreeable feelings. Anger, sadness, and anxiety are usually red flags that something is wrong and needs your attention. By identifying and exploring your emotions, you will be better able to make decisions about how, why, when, and with whom you want to express your sexuality. This chapter is designed to help you understand and identify possible sources of the painful feelings that can accompany sex, and to suggest ways to minimize or avoid those feelings.

The human craving for romance, our perennial optimism about our new sweetheart—these passions drag us like a kite upon the wind as we soar and plunge unpredictably from one feeling to another.

(FISHER, 1992, P. 163)

'Tis better to have loved and lost / Than never to have loved at all.

—ALFRED TENNYSON,
IN MEMORIAM A.H.H.

TABLE 16.1				
How Did Sex Make You Feel?				
Sexual Partners over the Past 12 Months	**Sad**	**Worried**	**Scared**	**Guilty**
One Partner Only				
Spouse	3.5%	8.2%	2.6%	2.8%
Cohabitant	5.6	14.8	5.6	5.8
Other	5.5	19.3	9.2	12.6
At Least Two Partners: Primary Partner				
Spouse	16.4	16.4	9.0	10.5
Cohabitant	11.6	15.8	12.6	9.5
Other	7.2	20.7	11.0	13.8

SOURCE: Laumann et al., 1994, p. 368.

RELATIONSHIPS CAN MAKE YOU SAD

Is it really better to have loved someone and then lost that person than never to have been in love? Sex can be the source of some of life's greatest joys—and some of life's deepest sorrows. Loneliness, the loss of love, rejection, and feelings of guilt and shame in a sexual relationship can be emotionally debilitating. In an attempt to avoid the pain of loss, there may be a temptation to avoid all future intimacy. (Have you ever heard the expression "Once burned, twice shy"?) It *is* risky to take a chance on loving someone. Love and sex, of course, don't come with a guarantee of happiness. But without the risk of being hurt there is no possibility of experiencing the satisfaction and pleasure that intimate sexual relationships can bring.

It is important to distinguish negative feelings related to relationship problems from those related to **clinical depression.** An absence of sexual desire, one of the many reasons for problems in a relationship, is one of the signs of depression. In such cases, sexual desire may be restored by one of the many treatments for depression, which include psychotherapy and medication. Then again, many antidepressant drugs have the side effect of reducing sexual desire.

There also may be a chemical basis for the sadness that often accompanies the loss of love. When a relationship ends, endorphin levels drop, and you may suffer without the accustomed daily dose of these natural morphinelike substances that produce a sense of calm and security (Liebowitz, 1983). When the body's attachment system is threatened, powerful emotional reactions may follow.

The sadness experienced upon the breakup of a romantic relationship varies in intensity, like all other emotions. The large number of terms for such feelings reflects the variations; you can feel "blue", unhappy, "down in the dumps," or severely depressed. Your background as well as your attachment to your partner can affect the intensity of these feelings; the sadness you feel may be linked to painful experiences or other losses in your past. "One person may be suffering from the other effects of having been sexually abused in childhood, another may have a predisposition to respond to any stress with melancholy, a third may have a pessimistic personality style that fosters depressive interpretation of facts" (Tavris, 1989, p. 111).

In some African languages there is a single word for both anger and sadness. English has many words to describe different emotions, reflecting the importance and complexity of feelings in our culture (Tavris, 1989). Although some people believe that sadness is anger turned inward, there is a great deal of research that disputes this theory. The "mistake does justice to neither emotion. Sometimes depression is anger turned inward, but sometimes it is only depression, which is enough" (Tavris,

Clinical Depression: a state of depression so severe as to be considered abnormal and require clinical intervention

Loneliness: feelings of sadness at being abandoned or alone

1989, p. 108). Anger and depression may be felt simultaneously, or they may be completely unrelated. As unpleasant as angry feelings may be, they may be preferable to feeling sad. Consciously or unconsciously, we may focus on angry responses (see "Relationships Can Make You Mad" later in this chapter) to avoid the pain of helpless despair.

Loneliness

The "need to belong" is one of the most fundamental and powerful motives that drive human beings. According to a review of hundreds of research findings, the need to belong shapes how people think, act, and feel in myriad ways (Baumeister & Leary, 1995). The need to belong appears to have two parts. First, people want frequent interactions with others, and these can be either affectively pleasant or neutral (but not negative, as in arguing). Second, people desire a long-term context of mutual caring and understanding. One part without the other is less than satisfying. Forming new social bonds (such as by getting married, having a baby, making a new friend, getting a job, joining a club) is usually associated with positive feelings, while strong negative emotions accompany the breaking of social bonds. In fact, many studies have found that lonely people actually have as many interpersonal interactions as other people, so loneliness is not necessarily the absence of human contact (Wheeler, Reis, & Nezlek, 1983).

One crucial factor in avoiding loneliness is having some ongoing close relationships. Consistent with this view, Reis (1990) found that "having lots of friends" ranks relatively low among most people's goals, whereas having a few close friends ranks quite high. Caldwell and Peplau (1982) also found that most men and women express a clear preference for having a few close relationships rather than a large number of less intimate friendships. On a university campus, there are so many people that one could conceivably interact with new and different people all the time; perhaps surprisingly, hardly anyone does this. Wheeler and Nezlek (1977) found that the vast majority of students have most of their meaningful interactions with only a handful of people. From the review cited earlier, Baumeister and Leary (1995) concluded that the average person wants four to six close relationships. People who have fewer than that feel deprived and want to form more bonds. Once a person reaches about six close relationships, he or she generally shows little interest in forming additional ones; if these do form, they add much less to the person's happiness and other benefits than the previous relationships. Put another way, people with three close relationships may be better off than people with one, but the difference between having seven and nine may be negligible.

There is some evidence that suggests that there are two distinct types of loneliness: *social loneliness*, a lack of companionships, and *emotional loneliness*, a lack of intimacy (Weiss, 1973). Emotional loneliness can be broken down further into *romantic emotional loneliness* and *family emotional loneliness* (DiTommaso & Spineer, 1997). Chronic feelings of loneliness appear to have roots in childhood and early attachment processes. Chronically lonely individuals are more likely to have negative feelings, act in a socially withdrawn fashion, lack trust in self and others, feel little control over success or failure, and be generally dissatisfied with their relationships (Ernst & Cacioppo, 1999).

Loneliness has been found to be particularly prevalent among college students; social isolation seems to be most strongly related to feelings of loneliness reported in college samples (Damsteegt, 1992). Again, it may seem ironic that students would feel lonely; as previously indicated, a college campus is a people-rich environment that constantly throws together people of presumably similar interests in a variety of settings. However, college is also an environment in which people come and go at regular intervals, which makes many relationships transient. As a result, many students will periodically find themselves with less than the four to six close relationships that seem essential to satisfy the need to belong.

Social isolation has been shown to have a negative long-term influence on feelings of loneliness. However, the subjective experience of loneliness is influenced by

FAQ:

I have lots of friends, and a really fun boyfriend; why am I so lonely?

Loneliness is the feeling of being alone and alienated or disconnected from positive persons, places, or things (Woodward & Kalvan-Masih, 1990). It is important to remember that solitude and loneliness are not the same thing. Human beings are born with the need to be alone as well as the need to be connected with others (Buchholz & Catton, 1999). You can be perfectly content being alone, and you can feel desperately lonely in a large crowd. Some people who don't have many friends may feel sad and lonely because they are physically, socially, and emotionally isolated. Others may be part of a large social network yet continue to feel lonely because of the lack of close relationships and intimacy in their lives.

Loneliness and being alone are not necessarily the same thing.

personality, situational variables, and perhaps gender. One study found a significant difference in male and female loneliness; males appear more reluctant to admit social deficits such as loneliness (Cramer & Nevedley, 1998). However, another study found that while loneliness was lower for androgynous than for masculine, feminine, and undifferentiated women, androgynous and masculine men were not less lonely than men with other gender role orientations (Rotenberg, 1997).

Data taken from studies in 17 nations indicate that marriage is associated with substantially less loneliness than being single. In addition, the study found that marriage is considerably more predictive of reduced loneliness than cohabitation, that both marriage and parental status are associated with lower levels of loneliness among men than women, that the association of marriage and decreased loneliness is independent of health and financial satisfaction, and that the strength of the marriage-loneliness relationship is constant across 16 of the 17 nations studied (Stack, 1998).

Individuals find many different ways of coping with loneliness. Some people isolate themselves, while others actively seek new relationships. Some try to distract themselves by keeping busy or attempt to soothe themselves with alcohol or drugs. Pessimistic avoidance strategies such as isolation or substance abuse have been associated with subsequent feelings of increased loneliness (Nurmi et al., 1997). Correlational studies suggest that one close friend or romantic partner may be sufficient to buffer those at risk for loneliness (Ernst & Cacioppo, 1999). The coping strategies identified as most helpful in reducing the pain of loneliness are accepting and reflecting on what you are experiencing, increasing social contacts, and increasing your activity level. Attempting to distance yourself from what you are feeling by ignoring or denying your condition tends to be less effective (Rokach, 1996; Rokach & Brock, 1998).

Breaking Up

Think back to the start of your current relationship; was it fate? A match made in heaven? Now think back to the start of your last *failed* relationship; do you perceive it differently? When preparing to break up, people rewrite the story of their relationship. Most happy couples have a somewhat idealized version of how they got together; they were meant for each other, they discovered each other in some magical fashion, they conducted a delightful romance, and so forth. These stories accentuate the positive and help justify the relationship as ideal. Needless to say, these stories tend to be somewhat distorted versions of reality. When people prepare for breakup or divorce, they distort things in the opposite direction. They may depict the start of their relationship as a mere accident or a reflection that both were

Princess Diana said that "there were three of us" in her marriage to Prince Charles, and held Camilla Parker Bowles responsible for her divorce.

desperate for companionship or not thinking clearly. These revised stories emphasize the negative aspects of the relationship and downplay the positive (Vaughan, 1987).

Most relationships start out with such high hopes that perhaps the only direction they can go is down. Long-term relationships dissolve for a variety of reasons; one person in the relationship may leave in order to be with someone else, or to be alone. Anthropologist Laura Betzig (1989) analyzed information from 160 societies and found that infidelity, particularly by the wife, is the most commonly offered reason for seeking to dissolve marriage. Sterility is next on the list, followed by cruelty (particularly by the husband), then a variety of dissatisfactions about a spouse's personality or behavior including a bad temper, jealousy, talkativeness, nagging, disrespect, laziness (of the wife), nonsupport (by the husband), sexual neglect, long absences, or running off with a lover.

Some people judge their current relationship in terms of the possibilities that they might be missing: "Maybe I'm wasting my time with Mr. or Ms. Just-OK and missing out on meeting Mr. or Ms. Perfect." Who knows—there just might be someone better looking, wealthier, smarter, or more fun just around the corner, if only you weren't tied down with your

Absence Makes the Heart Grow Fonder
or Out of Sight, Out of Mind?

People who have long-distance romantic relationships typically value the connection but are also frustrated by the inability to spend time together (Gerstel & Gross, 1982, 1985). Other studies have found that while absence really could make a man's heart grow fonder, it doesn't appear to affect women in the same way. In a study of people on and around college campuses, researchers found that the more time spent apart after sex, the more eager men were to copulate with their lovers again. However, women were generally unaffected by separation; their eagerness was unaffected by the amount of time since their last sexual encounter. The evolutionary explanation for this gender difference is that a man's urge for sex after separation is the thought that another man might have gotten there first and beat out his sperm in the race to fertilize his partner's egg.

However, research by Ward, LeBlanc, and Shackelford (1999) did not support two other hypotheses based on sperm competition theory. The research found that time apart was not related to how much a man figured his partner was sexually interested in other men, nor how distressed he was if his partner refused to have sex.

 Have you or has anyone you know ever been involved in a long-distance relationship?

—*If so, did you find that you idealized your partner (absence makes the heart grow fonder) or thought about him or her less when you were apart (out of sight, out of mind)?*
—*What role does sex play in the challenges of maintaining a long-distance relationship?*

current partner. According to interdependence theory, individuals assess their existing comparison level and their comparison level for alternatives when deciding between staying in or leaving a relationship (Kelley & Thibaut, 1978). The comparison level is the individual's subjective expectation regarding what he or she wants and feels he or she deserves from a relationship. The comparison levels for alternatives, all other available alternatives to the current relationship, are assessed in terms of their rewards and costs relative to the rewards and costs of the existing relationship. When it is determined that the existing comparison level is greater than the comparison level for alternatives, the couple usually remains together, but when the comparison level for alternatives is greater, typically the relationship dissolves. The interdependence theory fits the social exchange model; that is, relationships end when the costs for staying in the relationship outweigh the rewards for continuing the relationship (Kelley & Thibaut, 1978; Levinger, 1999).

Another model describes four phases of dissolving a relationship: intrapsychic, dyadic, social, and grave-dressing (Duck, 1982) (Figure 16.1). During the *intrapsychic phase*, each partner privately assesses the relationship in terms of its equity, satisfaction, and possible alternatives. When these private thoughts become public, the couple enters the *dyadic phase*, in which they alternate between attempts to repair the relationship and attempts to end it. Once the couple decides to end the relationship, the *social phase* of dissolution begins. During the social phase the couple must accept the societal repercussions for separating. They then move to the final *grave-dressing phase*, in which they begin to come to terms with the breakup and look for reasons why the relationship died.

The **cascade model** of dissolving a close relationship (Gottman, 1994; Gottman & Levenson, 1992) posits that there are four phases of relationship dissolution: complain/criticize, contempt, defensiveness, and stonewalling (Figure 16.2). It is called the cascade model because it is arranged or occurs in a series or in a succession of stages so that each

Cascade Model: a four-phase model of dissolving a close relationship: complain/criticize, contempt, defensiveness, and stonewalling

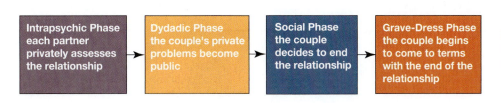

FIGURE 16.1 Duck's Phases of Dissolving a Relationship.
SOURCE: The Alan Guttmacher Institute, 1998.

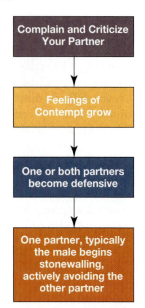

FIGURE 16.2 **The Cascade Model of Dissolving a Close Relationship.** SOURCE: The Alan Guttmacher Institute, 1998.

stage derives from or acts upon the product of the preceding. One partner begins the cascade by *complaining* about and *criticizing* the other partner. As feelings of *contempt* for one another grow from these complaints and criticisms, one or both partners become *defensive*. This defensive posturing continues until one of the partners, typically the male, begins *stonewalling*, actively avoiding interactions with the other partner.

Some people blame themselves when breaking up—"I don't know what's wrong with me"—while others put all the responsibility on their partner. Ending a relationship generally requires some justification by both partners. The person leaving and the person being left both want to know "why isn't the relationship working?" The answer for the person being left is almost never satisfying. Would it really help reach closure to be handed an itemized list of "Reasons Why This Relationship Is Over" when a relationship ends? Is it any better to have a relationship end because your ex has found a new love than because she or he thinks you have a lousy sense of humor, are too self-absorbed, or too boring? The explanations for ending the relationship may be valid or they may be rationalizations to protect one's own or one's partner's feelings.

Whatever the stated reason for the end of the relationship, it's not likely to make you feel good about being dumped. In one study, researchers attempted to identify a script for ending a relationship by asking male and female undergraduates to list the steps that typically occur when a couple breaks up (Battaglia et al., 1998). Analysis of the data indicated a 16-step ordered script for relationship dissolution (Table 16.2). According to the script, the breakup process begins at the point when one person loses interest in either the partner or the relationship and other people begin to become attractive alternatives as possible dating partners. The less-interested partner then begins to withdraw emotionally from the relationship. Next, the couple talks about the issues that make them feel dissatisfied with the relationship and they agree to try to work things out. Although they agree to work on the relationship, the lack of interest resurfaces and the possibility of breaking up becomes a serious consideration. The cycle continues as the couple notice alternative dating partners, which eventually leads to dating others while still dating one another. The couple decides to get back together one last time before considering breaking up again. Before officially breaking up, couples tend to experience a sense of having moved on. That is, they have already emotionally detached themselves from their current partners and the relationship.

TABLE 16.2

An Ordered Script for Relationship Dissolution?

1. Lack of interest
2. Notice other people
3. Act distant
4. Try to work things out
5. Physical distance/avoidance
6. Lack of interest
7. Consider breakup
8. Communicate feelings
9. Try to work things out
10. Notice other people
11. Act distant
12. Date other people
13. Get back together
14. Consider breakup
15. Move on/recover
16. Break up

SOURCE: Battaglia et al., 1998, p. 840.

TABLE 16.3

How College Students Ended Their Last Relationship

	Men	Women
Face to Face	75%	68%
Telephone	9	19
Faded away	16	10
Letter	0	3
E-mail	0	1

SOURCE: Adapted from Knox, Zusman, & Nieves, 1998.

Breaking Up Is Hard to Do   Based on long interviews with people about their romantic breakups, Diane Vaughan (1986) found that there were important differences between the person who initiates the breakup (the "initiator") and the person who is dropped. One person usually becomes dissatisfied first but is typically reluctant to face this reality. Still, this person may begin privately to question the relationship and to think about what life would be like after the breakup. The person may even start looking at new romantic prospects and enlist a close friend to confide in about his or her dissatisfaction. The initiator also will begin to develop justifications and rationalizations for leaving the relationship and then make up his or her mind to do so. All this happens while the other person is unaware of it or at most may see minor conflicts and problems. When the initiator finally tells the partner about being unhappy in the relationship, the partner recognizes the problems and may be willing and even eager to try to fix them—which is unfortunate because by this time the initiator has already started to give up on the relationship and is making preparations to leave (see Table 16.3).

When Vaughan asked her research subjects when they first recognized the problems that would lead to the dissolution of the relationship, they typically divided their answer into two parts. The first part of the answer involved awareness of a series of conflicts or difficulties, which at first were seen as isolated incidents, none serious enough to jeopardize the relationship. The second part of the answer involved recognizing these conflicts and problems as part of a broad pattern of dissatisfaction. Thus, the process of breaking up begins in earnest when the person stops seeing individual, unrelated conflicts and starts seeing a broad, interconnected pattern of problems.

While there may be a script that tells us how relationships end, unfortunately there is no foolproof way to say goodbye that guarantees that no one will be hurt. However, there are ways of ending a relationship that may result in less pain or hostility. Be as certain as you can be about your motivation and your feelings about ending the relationship. Are you reacting to pressures or stresses outside the relationship? Are the problems in the relationship irreparable? Do you no longer want to be involved with this specific person? Or, do you not want to be involved with anyone

TABLE 16.4

What We Say Versus What We Mean

The Breakup Words	The Breakup Meaning?
You deserve someone better than me.	I want someone better than you.
I wouldn't mind if you dated other people.	I want to date other people.
I just need some space.	I need to get away from you.
I hope we can still be friends.	I hope you won't kill me.
There's nobody else.	There's somebody else.
The problem isn't you, it's me.	It's you.

FAQ:

What is the best way to break up with my partner?

When saying, "it's over," it is probably useful to remember the Golden Rule: "Do unto others as you would have others do unto you." How would you want to be told that a relationship is over? While most people appreciate honesty, there is a difference between being honest and being cruel. You can honestly express your feelings without giving a critical assessment of the other person's perceived character flaws. It is one thing to say, "My feelings have changed and I won't be seeing you anymore." It is another thing to declare, "You're so arrogant and obnoxious that I can't imagine what I ever saw in you." Focus on the other person's feelings and reactions rather than on complaints or personal attacks. When the decision to leave is yours, you have a responsibility to choose your language carefully (Table 16.4).

While you are not responsible for your ex-partner's response to the end of the relationship, you are responsible for your own actions. If you treat a person with disrespect and a lack of consideration, you might expect a negative reaction. It is understandable to want to end the break up scene as quickly as possible. At best, it is an awkward and embarrassing situation; and it can be overwhelmingly painful. It hurts to witness another person's despair or to be the target of his or her anger. However, as with all communication, it is important to listen as well as to talk. You may not like what you hear, but you can listen with empathy and respect.

CAMPUS CONFIDENTIAL

"I can't believe she dumped me. I never saw it coming. I thought everything was great. We always seemed to have fun together. We liked the same things, talked a lot, laughed a lot, and things were great in bed. I don't understand what happened.

"When she first told me that she wanted to date other guys, I was really pissed. I started calling her names and said a lot of stuff I really didn't mean. Then I started feeling bad about myself. I felt like such a loser. I kept trying to figure out what I'd done wrong. I thought if she would just tell me what was wrong with me then I could fix it and we'd get back together.

"I think I've finally accepted that it's over. I don't like it, but there's nothing I can do about it. I know that sooner or later I'll meet someone else. I just hope it's sooner. . . ." ●

Rejection: the act or process of spurning, refusing, or dismissing someone

Cognitive-Affective Processing: the way we think about how we feel

Dependent Love: love that relies on or is subordinate to someone or something else

right now? Is the problem external, something about the other person, or is the problem internal, something about you? Is the only consistency in your relationships the pattern of you leaving? The psychiatrist Peter Kramer (1998) suggests that it makes sense to stay and confront your fears and disappointments in a relationship, especially if you and your partner are well matched emotionally.

Being Dumped Is Even Harder Sticking pins in a voodoo doll and devising elaborate revenge fantasies may work temporarily, but holding on to your anger or hurt keeps you stuck in the past. According to Vaughan (1986), one of the biggest differences between the person who initiates the breakup and the abandoned partner is preparation. The initiator has typically had ample time to prepare for life after the relationship. This person may have made new friends, begun flirting with potential new partners, or even found someone, dealt with the emotional pain of separation, made crucial decisions about where to live and work, and in other ways prepared for the transition. The abandoned partner is typically unaware that any of this is going on and so has no opportunity to prepare. Moreover, as we have already discussed, when the initiator finally does express the extent of his or her dissatisfaction, the other person may respond by trying to fix the relationship rather than preparing for the breakup. Hence, when the breakup does come, the abandoned person is neither practically nor emotionally ready for it.

Most people survive the loss of a love, go on with their lives, and develop new relationships. However, ending a relationship is usually painful for at least one of the partners, and sometimes it can be traumatic, or even dangerous. The incidence of depression, and the rates of successful suicides, suicide attempts, and accidents resulting from suicidal carelessness are all high among those in the midst of a breakup or who have recently broken off a romantic relationship. It is theorized that the attempt to avoid the agony of acute unhappiness associated with the end of a romantic relationship is not uncommon, nor is it limited to persons considered psychologically unbalanced. For example, a study of Australian adolescents who attempted suicide found that 76 percent reported an attempted suicide in the context of a dispute or relationship breakup (Vajda & Steinbeck, 2000).

Three primary motives for attempted or completed suicide have been identified (Menninger, 1938): (1) anger or revenge: "I'll show you; now you'll be sorry"; (2) absolution of self-blame by seeking self-punishment: "Everything that goes wrong is my fault; everyone would be better off if I were dead"; (3) escape from unbearable suffering: "I can't take this pain anymore." There appears to be no difference in the frequency of the three motives (Lester, Lester, & Yang, 1992), and the motives apply to suicides associated with the ending of a romantic relationship, as well as other causes of depression.

Some people are more sensitive to **rejection** than others. Those who are especially sensitive anxiously tend to expect, to perceive, and to overreact to social rejection. One study found that our **cognitive-affective processing,** the way we think about how we feel, can undermine intimate relationships. People who enter romantic relationships with anxious expectations of rejection readily perceive unintentional rejection in the insensitive behavior of their new partners. Rejection-sensitive individuals and their partners tend to be dissatisfied with their relationships. Rejection-sensitive men's jealousy and rejection-sensitive women's hostility and diminished supportiveness may help explain their partner's dissatisfaction (Downey & Feldman, 1996). The relationships of people with high rejection-sensitivity are more likely to break up than those of low rejection-sensitive people.

Rejection can be a self-fulfilling prophecy. In one study following naturally occurring relationship conflicts, the partners of high rejection-sensitive women were more rejecting than the partners of low rejection-sensitive women. A laboratory study showed that negative behavior during conflictual discussions helped explain their partners' rejecting responses after a fight (Downey et al., 1998).

Dependent love is the basis of much of our popular culture. Music, literature, and the movies often glorify and romanticize "I can't live without you" and "If you leave me I'll die" relationships. Making your own life and happiness dependent on how someone else feels about you almost guarantees disappointment and heartache. Many problematic relationships are based on excessive dependency: "To feel good about me, I need you to love and desire me." The unrealistic expectation that anyone will meet all your needs inevitably leads to feelings of disappointment or a sense of betrayal. Any help that is given can and might be used against the well-meaning caregiver. It is equally difficult to be the one who is depended upon. The initial satisfaction and pleasure of taking care of someone you love can quickly become a burden and lead to resentment.

The quality of the relationship is not always a good indicator of how you will feel if it ends. It is possible to think you are madly in love, and then, when the relationship ends, to realize that you don't really miss it. Or, you may think the relationship is boring and going no place but feel regret and longing when it's over (Brehm, 1993). According to social exchange theory, your emotional response to breaking up reflects the amount of benefit lost rather the perceived emotional quality of the relationship.

Unrequited Love

You don't have to break up to be sad over love. Some relationships never get off the ground. Not everyone is a suitable mate for everyone else; incompatibilities cannot all be recognized before a first date, so some of these failures are inevitable. At best, they can be handled with a bit of humor and mutual understanding. Often, however, the two people may come to different conclusions about the potential for the relationship. One person may feel love and sexual attraction while the other doesn't. These cases of mismatched feelings are awkward, unpleasant, and can even be painful for both parties.

Unrequited love is a situation in which one person loves another, who fails to return that love. Most of us will fall in love with someone who doesn't return our feelings. Conversely, someone to whom we are not attracted will at some time pursue most of us. One sample of upper-level college students found that on average they had experienced one serious and powerful episode of unrequited love, two additional moderate attractions (also not reciprocated), and three or four additional passing attractions or "crushes" that were not returned—all in the past five years! (Baumeister, Wotman, & Stillwell, 1993). Over 90 percent of the sample reported having had at least one serious heartbreak from unrequited love during that same period. Naturally, the rate of these romantic woes diminishes later in life, especially as people settle down into long-term relationships, but being single and unattached is associated with an almost annual exposure to some disappointment or heartbreak.

Some degree of unrequited love is probably an inevitable part of the process of searching for a mate. People do end up with partners who are roughly equal to them in overall desirability. In a typical marriage, husband and wife are usually fairly equal in intelligence, socioeconomic status (Macfarlane, 1986), and physical attractiveness (Murstein & Christy, 1976). White (1980) found that romantic couples who were most evenly matched in attractiveness were more likely to progress from casual dating to more serious and committed involvements than less well-matched couples. However, people don't fall in love only with people who are equal to themselves, though life might be much easier if they did.

An ambitious study by Walster and others (1966) set up a college dating service that actually (secretly) just matched men and women at random. The researchers wanted to see how well people would enjoy their dates. They had elaborate theories about matching. Their hypothesis was that people would be most attracted to the partners who were most similar to them, not only in opinions and education, but also in sex appeal, intelligence, and other factors. Unfortunately, those elaborate theories were not supported by the data. Instead, a simple pattern emerged. People liked the most desirable partners best. In other words, you didn't have the best time with the person who was the most equitable match for you—rather, you had the best time with the most gorgeous and charming partner.

FAQ:

I've been dumped—now what do I do?

There are healthier ways of mending a broken heart than eating a gallon of Ben and Jerry's ice cream, chugging a case of beer, or acting out those revenge fantasies. First, recognize that you are grieving a loss. Even if you know that ending the relationship is for the best, and that sooner or later you would have broken up, still you have lost something that was important to you. It will take time to adjust. In the meantime, you might want to do some of those things that your "ex" didn't want to do. If your ex hated action films and Chinese food, this might be a good time to indulge in a night of Bruce Willis videos while eating chow mein. Call a friend and ask for emotional support if you need it, do something interesting, and don't isolate yourself. Remember that the end of one relationship opens the door to the possibilities of the next one (see CAMPUS CONFIDENTIAL).

Unrequited Love: love that is not returned or reciprocated

Can we still be friends?

Maybe. But not every couple can —or should— remain friends after the breakup. In most cases it is probably best not to try to be friends until you have had some time to decide if it is really in your best interest to remain connected to a former lover. Be honest about your motivation for wanting to continue as friends. Are you really just hanging around hoping that your ex's feelings will change and you'll get back together? Will an agreement to be "just friends" prolong the pain and cause further disappointment and hurt? Or can you overlook the feelings of rejection and have a true friendship? Couples are more likely to remain friends when the man rather than the woman is the one to initiate the breakup (Hill, Rubin, & Peplau, 1976).

Putting those findings together, we can see a recipe for trouble. People are attracted to highly desirable partners, but they end up with partners about equal to themselves. Before you find the equal partner, therefore, you are likely to have several disappointments, because you may become attracted to people who are more desirable than you (or think they are). In some cases, the partners may truly be mismatched. In other cases, the match may have been equal, but the partner may feel that someone more desirable is a better match. It is fairly well established that many people overestimate their good qualities (Taylor & Brown, 1988), so they are likely to make optimistic errors in assessing who would be a good match. So if a potential partner rejects your advances on this basis, he or she is probably headed for disappointment.

There are plenty of other reasons for unrequited love. Don't assume that a person is (or believes himself or herself to be) too good for you just because your romantic interest is rejected. Some people reject romantic advances because they already have someone, or because they are not ready for a close relationship, or because they have an inner image of the person they want and that image does not fit you. And in some cases the person may really enjoy being just friends and not want to change the relationship into a romance.

Regardless of the reasons behind it, unrequited love tends to be quite painful and unpleasant. People whose love is rejected tend to suffer considerable emotional distress, which can last for a short time or drag on for months or even years. Many suffer a blow to their self-esteem, because they think they were rejected because something was wrong with them. Recovery of self-esteem is often the most difficult part of getting over a broken heart, after the initial anguish wears off (Baumeister & Wotman, 1992). During the most painful period of unrequited love, a person may be willing to sacrifice his or her dignity in pursuing the other, even begging or pleading for the other's love. Although at the time dignity may seem like a trivial consideration compared with the craving for love, these humiliating moments are often among the most painful memories, and in retrospect the person may wish that he or she had maintained more pride.

Perhaps surprisingly, an episode of unrequited love is often quite unpleasant for the person who does the rejecting, too. Rejecters often find it difficult to turn down someone's love and break that person's heart. Many rejecters struggle with feelings of guilt, particularly if they think they might have encouraged the other's romantic interest in some way (Baumeister, Wotman, & Stillwell, 1993). Rejecters also indicate that they do not know how they are supposed to act, and they may be genuinely sad or embarrassed to cause pain to someone. All in all, people seem to find it quite hard and unpleasant to reject someone's love.

Although both sides of unrequited love contain unpleasant emotions, there are some important differences. The rejecter tends to have the more thoroughly negative view of the episode, whereas the aspiring (and then disappointed) lover tends to look back on it with a bittersweet mixture of both positive and negative feelings. For the would-be lover, the story has the character of an emotional roller coaster, with alternating periods of euphoria ("He smiled at me today!") and despair ("I saw him dancing with someone else"). Another difference is that the would-be lover tends to suffer the most intense distress, even if it is (in retrospect) partly offset by the mixture of good feelings. When people were asked to rate how extreme their emotions became, the rejected persons reported more severe and extreme distress than the ones who rejected them (Baumeister, Wotman, & Stillwell, 1993).

Poor communication often prolongs these painful situations of unrequited love. For one thing, people are reluctant to reveal the true reasons for their lack of romantic interest, so they make excuses instead; these excuses leave the door open for the person to ask again (Folkes, 1982). For example, if a woman is asked to go out on a date by a man she is not interested in, she may say something like, "I'm sorry, but I have a term paper due on Monday" or "My parents are coming to visit this weekend"— but then of course the man feels free to ask her out again next week, when the paper is done or the parents are gone. If she said, "I don't want to go out with you because I find you rather dull and stupid, and you are too fat for me, and you don't have enough money, and you smell bad" (all quite plausible reasons), he probably would not call her back the following week. Of course, after that experience, he might not get the nerve to ask *anyone* out again for a very long time.

Even if the rejecter does manage to express the rejection in seemingly clear and firm terms, the aspiring lover may not get the message. People who are in love often jump at any sign of encouragement and may ignore any negative or discouraging words. They want desperately to believe there is a chance, so they will cling to any hope.

In short, romantic rejection is hard to communicate. One person doesn't want to say it, and the other doesn't want to hear it. No wonder that people sometimes find it hard to rid themselves of unwanted romantic attentions! In fact, one of the biggest differences between rejecters and aspiring lovers in unrequited love is the degree of persistence shown by the aspiring lover. Rejecters often complain that the person who loved them refused to take no for an answer and persisted excessively and unreasonably. The aspiring lovers are often hardly aware that what they are doing is excessive; they are so caught up in their own passions and hopes that they lose perspective.

Many decades ago, the sociologist Willard Waller articulated the principle of least interest to describe what happens in cases of unequal love. The principle of least interest holds that whoever is less in love has more power (Waller & Hill, 1938/1951). The person who is more in love is more vulnerable to being hurt and to being taken advantage of in other ways, because of his or her greater emotional involvement. Indeed, this may be one factor that helps account for the gender difference in the speed of falling in love that we discussed in Chapter 15 (see pages 462–463). Because women are already vulnerable in many ways, including typically having less money, less power in society, and less physical strength than men, they may be reluctant to take on the added vulnerability of being more deeply in love. Additionally, women may become vulnerable to sexual exploitation if they fall in love with a man who does not return their love, because a man may want to have sex even if he does not feel love. The risk of sexual exploitation is less severe and less troubling to men, and so they may be more willing to fall in love rapidly as a result. Indeed, the data show that young men experience unrequited love more often than young women, whereas young women are more likely to find themselves in the role of rejecting unwanted attentions (Baumeister, Wotman, & Stillwell, 1993).

Unrequited love is not the same as having a "crush" on someone or believing in a nonexistent romance. With unrequited love, you actually know the person who does not return your feelings. With a **crush,** a strong but temporary attraction, you may or may not know the person you yearn for, but you have no illusions about a relationship with this person. People who do believe in a nonexistent relationship with another are said to suffer from **erotomania,** the irrational belief that someone, often a public figure, has passionate feelings for you but that because of some obstacle— a spouse, differences in social class, shyness—those feelings cannot be revealed. The object of the erotomanic's fantasy is someone unattainable. Like most people suffering from delusional disorders, erotomanics cannot be persuaded that a relationship exists only in their imagination. Erotomanics may maintain their delusions for years and can devise such detailed and elaborate fantasies that they convince themselves as well as others that they are having a sexual relationship with the object of their delusions.

Typically erotomanics are lonely people who have had few sexual partners and view their lives as a series of disappointments. Most erotomanics have no history of mental illness and are able to contain their delusion to the extent that they can hold jobs and appear perfectly normal. Unlike sexual addiction, erotomania has little to do with sex. What is desired is an idealized romantic love. Although erotomanics rarely resort to violence, statistics show that 1 in 20, most of them men, will commit an assault. One study of 14 patients with erotomania reported that all the subjects studied engaged in stalking behaviors that included loitering in the victim's vicinity,

Crush: infatuation; a strong but temporary attraction for someone

Erotomania: a delusional, romantic preoccupation with a stranger, often a public figure

Erotomania is the delusional belief that someone, often a celebrity, has a romantic interest. David Letterman obtained a court injunction to keep Margaret Mary Ray, who falsely claimed to be his wife, out of his Connecticut home. Ms. Ray, who had a lengthy history of mental illness, committed suicide in 1998.

approaching, telephoning, and sending letters. In five cases victims were violently assaulted; in seven instances, sexual attacks occurred. Those believed to stand in the way of their delusional love also were occasional victims of violence (Mullen & Pathe, 1994).

Guilt

When we violate the sexual values that we have established for ourselves or that are established for us by others (such as our parents), we are likely to experience guilt. **Guilt** is anxiety or unhappiness resulting from the feeling that we have done something wrong, such as caused harm to another person. Sexual guilt can interfere with pleasure and intimacy and block a person from taking precautions, such as the use of condoms to avoid unwanted pregnancy or exposure to a sexually transmitted infection. However, guilty feelings can serve a more constructive purpose as well; guilt can help us to make choices that are consistent with our values.

Feeling guilty about sex or a particular sexual activity can be related to a belief that sex is immoral, sinful, or dirty. Freud maintained that libido is one of the core drives in human behavior and personality formation. According to Freud, beginning at birth a child receives parental messages about sexual attitudes and sexual expression. If adults condemn a behavior, there is the potential for guilt among those who have engaged in that behavior. For example, if adults view common activities among preadolescents such as masturbation and sexual play with peers as morally wrong, children who participate in such play may experience feelings of guilt.

TABLE 16.5

How Guilty Would You Feel?

Scoring: 1=No Guilt; 2=Little Guilt; 3=Moderate Guilt; 4=Considerable Guilt

	Average score
1. You have intercourse with someone 18 years older than you. Both of you are unmarried.	2.04
2. You decide not to tell the person you are about to marry any information concerning a previous relationship because you believe it will have no bearing on your marriage.	2.18
3. The person you are about to marry learns of your previous sexual affair with another person you did not particularly care for prior to your present relationship.	2.20
4. You reveal to an associate that a person who had invited you to dinner was gay and there were to be no other guests.	2.48
5. Your mother discovers that you, at age 16, are having intercourse with a member of the other sex.	2.76
6. You conceal from the person you are about to marry that you had earlier contracted and been cured of gonorrhea.	2.88
7. Your parents learn of your sexual relationship with someone of another race, and you know they disapprove.	3.02
8. As a student, you are in love with a teacher who is fired because your sexual relationship has been brought to the attention of the instructor's dean.	3.51
9. You are in a committed relationship with a person, yet you had intercourse with someone else.	3.52
10. Your fiancé learns that you had a sexual encounter with your fiancé's best friend while your fiancé was away visiting a grandparent.	3.66

SOURCE: Adapted from Know et al., 1991.

Guilt: a feeling of remorse resulting from a sense of having done wrong

When asked about their emotional responses to their first coital experience, women were significantly more likely than men to report that they felt sadness, nervousness, tension, embarrassment, fear, and guilt (Guggino & Ponzetti, 1997). Uncommunicative mother and father figures, an overly strict father figure, discomfort with sexuality, physiological and psychological dissatisfaction with first intercourse, and guilt feelings about current intercourse are significant variables correlated with guilt at first intercourse among college women (Moore & Davidson, 1997) (Table 16.5).

RELATIONSHIPS CAN MAKE YOU MAD

Sexual intimacy renders us physically and emotionally vulnerable. As you bare your body and your soul, you begin to trust your lover. Trust betrayed can lead to angry feelings and dangerous behaviors. The perception of a threat to a relationship leads to actions designed to reduce or eliminate that threat (Daly & Watson, 1988).

Jealousy

Jealousy is any aversive emotional reaction that occurs as a result of a partner's outside relationship, whether real, imagined, or considered likely to occur (Bringle & Buunk, 1991). Jealousy and envy are two distinct emotions that can occur together or separately. While jealousy involves a perceived threat to an existing relationship, **envy** is the desire to obtain something that someone else already possesses. The intensity of envious feelings depends on the value we place on the other person's possessions or accomplishments and the closeness of our relationship with the other person (Tesser, 1988) (Table 16.6).

Jealousy is more likely to arise in a romantic relationship than between friends. It usually occurs when, correctly or not, we imagine our partner is involved in another sexual relationship. Perceptions of sexual threats may have an especially low threshold. All we may need to become jealous is the barest hint that our partner is sexually interested in someone else (Brehm, 1992).

According to one study (White & Mullen, 1989), two situations are likely to activate jealousy. One is a threat to your self-esteem; for example, your partner flirts with someone you think is more attractive than you are. The second situation is a threat to the relationship; for example, your partner is going away for the weekend with some work colleagues, and you're not invited. Once the switch is flipped, we go through several stages of jealousy, often very quickly. The first is a cognitive response, in which we make initial appraisals of the situation and find a threat to self-esteem or to the relationship. Next we experience a two-phase emotional response: a rapid stress response (a "jealous flash") and reappraisal of the situation and decision about how to cope with it. The intense initial emotions quiet down and may be replaced by feelings of moodiness (Figure 16.3).

"Heav'n hath no rage like love to hatred turn'd. / Nor Hell a fury, like a woman scorn'd."
—WILLIAM CONGREVE, *THE MOURNING BRIDE*

Jealousy: mental uneasiness from suspicion or fear of rivalry or unfaithfulness perceived as a threat to an existing relationship

Envy: a feeling of resentment of or desire to obtain another person's qualities, better fortune, or success

TABLE 16.6

Jealousy and Envy

Jealousy	Envy
Fear of loss	Feelings of insecurity
Anxiety	Longing
Suspicion of betrayal	Resentment of circumstances
Low self-esteem, sadness	Ill-will toward envied person
Uncertainty, loneliness	Motivation to improve
Distrust	Disapproval of feelings

SOURCE: Adapted from Parrott & Smith, 1993.

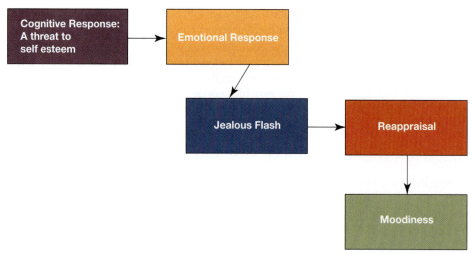

FIGURE 16.3 Jealousy. The first phase is the cognitive response; initial appraisals of the situation find a threat to self-esteem or to the relationship. This is followed by a two-stage emotional response: (1) the rapid stress response ("jealous flash") and (2) reappraising the situation and deciding how to cope with it. Then, the intense initial emotions quiet down and may be replaced by feelings of moodiness. SOURCE: Knox et al., 1998.

Sociologists view jealousy as a boundary setting mechanism established by the group or society to preserve important relationships (Reiss, 1986). According to attachment theory, introduced in Chapter 15 and mentioned earlier in this chapter, the attachment system is activated to manage thoughts, feelings, and behaviors that stem from potential separation and relationship threat. Of course, jealousy can serve these individual and social functions simultaneously.

Jealousy appears to be a nearly universal human experience (Buss, 1994) (see CROSS-CULTURAL PERSPECTIVES box). Some researchers believe that jealousy may have served an evolutionary purpose. According to the evolutionary view, sexual jealousy may have developed in response to "paternity uncertainty." Having sexual intercourse with a woman does not guarantee a man that a child she bears will be his biological offspring. However, by jealously guarding his mate, a male may ensure that his genetic material, and not that of his rivals, will be passed down to his

CROSS-CULTURAL PERSPECTIVES

The Green-Eyed Monster

A study of more than 2,000 individuals from the United States, Hungary, Ireland, Mexico, the Netherlands, the Soviet Union, and Yugoslavia found that in all seven countries men and women expressed identically negative emotional reactions to thoughts of their partner's flirting or having sexual relations with someone else (Buunk & Hupka, 1987). However, while jealousy apparently exists in all cultures, the specific events that trigger jealousy and how people respond to jealousy differ across and within

cultures (Gordon & Snyder, 1989). For example, traditionally, a proper Ammassalik Eskimo would, as a good host, invite a male guest to have sex with his wife, signaling the invitation by putting out a lamp. However, the same husband would undoubtedly be angry if he found his wife having sex with a man in other circumstances (Hupka, 1982); a classic study found male sexual jealousy to be the leading cause of spousal homicide among the Eskimos (Rasmussen, 1931).

children. Evolutionary theorists point to the fact that men are especially distressed by evidence of their partner's sexual infidelity, whereas women are troubled more by a partner's emotional infidelity (Buss, 1994), suggesting an innate difference arising from the male's need to be assured of paternity and the female's need for male investment in their offspring.

As noted earlier, there is a gender difference in sexual jealousy, but the reasons for it are unclear. When college students were asked to compare two distressing events—sexual intercourse between their partner and someone else, and formation of a deep emotional attachment between their partner and someone else—83 percent of the women found their partner's emotional infidelity more upsetting, whereas only 40 percent of the men did (Buss et al., 1992). This means that 60 percent of the men and 17 percent of the women experienced their partner's sexual infidelity as more upsetting. A more recent study with Swedish college students confirmed this finding; a majority of the men found the sexual infidelity scenarios more upsetting whereas a majority of the women were more disturbed by emotional infidelity scenarios (Widerman & Kendall, 1999).

Expanding on this research, another study examined college students' ratings of unfaithfulness and expected reactions of jealousy to a wider range of unfaithful behaviors including sexual behavior, sexual fantasies, romantic attachments, flirting, and group social activities including one or more members of the other gender. This study found that men and women rated all the behaviors as jealousy-provoking except group social activities. Women reported greater jealousy than men in response to a hypothetical partner's sexual fantasies, romantic attachments, and flirting behavior (Yarab, Allgeir, & Sensibaugh, 1999). Another study concluded that while men found male-female infidelity most upsetting, women were more disturbed by male-male infidelity. Female-female sexual infidelity was rated the least likely to arouse jealousy in both men and women (Widerman & LaMar, 1998).

There is some controversy regarding the physiological manifestation of male-female differences in jealousy. In one study, after they were fitted with electrodes to measure frowning, sweating, and pulse rate, 60 men and women were asked to imagine both sexual and emotional infidelity. The men became more physiologically distressed by the sexual infidelity. Their heart rates accelerated by nearly five beats per minute, and their skin conductance (sweating) and frowning increased more with thoughts of sexual infidelity than with responses to emotional infidelity. Women tended to show the opposite pattern, with increased frowning, sweating, and heart rates in response to emotional infidelity (Buss et al., 1992). However, attempts to replicate these results have not been successful (Grice & Seely, 2000; Harris, 2000).

Some researchers believe that sexual jealousy is related to the individuals' beliefs concerning the connection between sexual cheating and emotional infidelity (DeSteno & Salovey, 1996). In other words, if you believe that passionate sex results in a deep emotional commitment, you are more likely to experience jealousy (Harris & Christenfeld, 1996).

Attempts to cope with jealousy lead to a variety of behaviors, most of them problematic. Despite the reputed fury of a woman scorned, it is male, not female, jealousy that is the leading cause of spousal homicide in the United States (Daly & Wilson, 1988; Milroy 1995). While men are responsible for the majority of killings and serious injury resulting from jealousy, this may reflect less a quality of male jealousy and more the qualities of male aggression. Men not only tend to be bigger and stronger than women, they also are more likely to use fists, guns, and knives when they become violent, while women are more likely to slap, punch, or throw things (Tavris, 1989).

Men typically blame their partner or the third party (Daly et al., 1982). Men whose real or imagined jealousy is aroused by a third party are more likely than women to confront their rival or their own partner with demands, ultimatums, anger, and even violence (Barker, 1987). As recently as 1974,

"Jealousy can be emotional acid that corrodes marriages, undermines self-esteem, triggers battering, and leads to the ultimate crime of murder."

(BUSS, 2000, P. 2)

Dorothy Stratten, 1980 Playboy Playmate of the Year, was murdered by her estranged husband, Paul Snider, who reportedly was jealous of Stratten's relationship with director Peter Bogdanovich. Stratten's murder was the subject of the 1983 film, "Star 80."

An atypical response to jealousy took place in 1989 when Betty Broderick, a San Diego housewife, shot and killed her ex-husband and his new wife while they slept. Broderick claimed the murders were committed under emotional stress caused by a cold and manipulative ex-spouse who had discarded her for a younger and slimmer woman. Broderick was sentenced to 32 years to life.

murder committed by a husband who caught his wife with another man still fell under the "reasonable man" standard in the Texas penal code and went unpunished. The frequency of men killing their partners is even higher in some other countries. Spousal homicide rates in Russia indicate that Russian women are 2.5 times more likely to be killed by their spouses or lovers than their counterparts in the United States (Gonndolf & Shestakov, 1997). In some instances, after murdering a partner, the perpetrator will then commit suicide. Psychological studies of perpetrators have found a variety of problems in addition to jealousy, including depression, psychosis, alcohol abuse, and paranoia (Felthous & Hempel, 1995).

Women typically blame themselves when there is a conflict over jealousy, and avoid confrontations when jealous (Barker, 1987). They tend to respond to jealousy by increasing their efforts to be attractive to their partners rather than by seeking revenge or retribution (Wiederman & Allgeier, 1993). Some studies have shown that women are more inclined than men to provoke jealousy in their partners deliberately (White, 1981; White & Helbick, 1988). However, a study of college students found that a majority of men and women had previously attempted to evoke jealousy in a romantic partner and that arousing jealousy did not produce immediate relationship benefits (Sheets et al., 1997).

Intense feelings of jealousy do not prove that it is "true love." Instead, those feelings may reflect your own insecurities and sensitivities. When confronted with your own feelings of jealousy, it is wise first to determine if there is a rational basis for your distress. Your partner's sexual fantasies, friendships, and attractions do not necessarily mean that your relationship is over. Even if your partner does decide to be with someone else, it does not mean that you are less worthwhile, less deserving, or less lovable.

Conflict

Conflict about sex can make you angry, sad, or anxious and can develop at any stage in a relationship. At the beginning of a relationship, partners may have different expectations about how quickly they should become sexually involved. For example, on their first date, a man and a woman have a pleasant evening and enjoy each other's company. He invites her back to his place for a drink. She's thinking, "He's really a nice guy. I'd like to spend more time getting to know him better, so I'll go." He's thinking, "If she agrees to come, it means she expects to have sex." He makes his move; she turns him down. He persists and she resists more emphatically. Now he's angry because he thinks she's a tease, and she's mad because he won't take "no" for an answer. The date ends with two angry people who may be compatible, but who in all likelihood will never go out again. Or, consider the example of a couple that has been together for several years. She quietly seethes because he's much too rough when he tries to stimulate her clitoris. He gets upset because she doesn't like fellatio.

Sex can be the source of unacknowledged tension in a relationship; disagreements about sex also may be the most frequent source of open conflict. One study found that at least once a month 47 percent of heterosexual couples disagree with their partner about sex (Byers & Lewis, 1988). This study found that the disagreements stemmed from the man's desire to engage in a particular sexual behavior that his partner was not interested in. Another study of married couples found that the strongest predictor of a husband's sexual dissatisfaction was the wife's refusal to have sex. For women, the strongest predictor of sexual dissatisfaction was the husband's sexual aggression (Buss, 1989).

Disagreement about sex may reflect other problems in the relationship. Problems in any aspect of a couple's relationship can create conflict in other areas. And, sometimes, problems may relate more to communication than to sex. We have a lot invested in our intimate relationships, and if we don't get what we need, we can feel angry and resentful. Whether it is conflict about leaving the dishes unwashed or socks on the floor, or the frequency of sex, most people "rarely feel angry with others who are of no consequence to them. The opposite of love, after all, is not anger, but indifference" (Tavris, 1989, p. 248). In Western culture the individual is considered more important than the relationship, so it is acceptable to express anger and it would be considered hypocritical not to do so. In contrast, throughout much of Asia, people are expected to control their emotions because the relationship comes first. Open expression of negative feelings might jeopardize a relationship and is therefore considered inappropriate.

Despite the popular belief that if we don't vent our feelings and "blow off steam" we'll erupt like volcanoes, study after study shows that expressing anger almost always makes people feel even angrier (Tavris, 1989). While it is true that sometimes you can let go of your anger by talking about it, it is also true that talking about your anger may intensify your feelings and lead you to justify staying angry. As you repeat your list of grievances to sympathetic friends, arousal builds up all over again and you end up feeling as angry as you did when the provoking incident occurred. People who vent their anger by yelling are likely just to become angrier. Once angry words are spoken, you can't take them back. Thus, it is important to consider the social consequences of expressing your anger before acting.

That is not to say that you should sit and sulk. Neither silently holding on to your resentments nor yelling and screaming do much to resolve a problem. It is one thing to acknowledge your anger, and another to act out your anger or deny your feelings. It can be helpful to say, "I am angry because you didn't call to let me know you would be late; I was worried." There is little benefit to screaming, "You are so inconsiderate and selfish; you never think of anyone but yourself."

There is a lot of wisdom in the advice to count to 10 when you're angry. You may find that whatever provoked your anger is not very important; as advised by a popular author, "Don't sweat the small stuff" (Carlson & Carlson, 2000). Taking a few minutes to reflect on the problem may help you realize that you are dumping your anger onto the wrong person. You may be yelling at your partner because you've had a bad day at work or at school, or screaming at your children when you are really angry with your partner. Often we hold other people responsible for our feelings and blame others for our emotional responses (for example, "You make me so angry"). Certainly what others say and do affects us. However, we are responsible for our own feelings and have choices about how to communicate those feelings to others. A time-out or cool-down period gives you the opportunity to distinguish between minor irritations and major problems and to determine the most effective way of dealing with the issue at hand.

Some people consider anger to be a negative emotion because they confuse angry feelings with aggressive behavior. Although anger and aggression can coexist, they are not the same thing. Anger is an emotion whereas aggression is a behavior. You can be very angry and choose not to act aggressively. And you do not *have* to get angry or aggressive just because you do not get what you wanted, someone treats you badly, or life doesn't turn out the way you wanted it to. You are not required to respond with any particular emotion. To say that you "had to get angry" when someone wrongs you is irrational. You no more have to be angry than you have to be afraid of the dark or have to love kittens.

RELATIONSHIPS CAN MAKE YOU SCARED

Your heart is racing, your palms sweat, goosebumps prickle your arms; you feel breathless, and you're sick to your stomach. Either you're scared to death or you're in love. From a physiological perspective, anxiety and love are very much the same (Gottshalk et al., 2001).

You might be concerned about the possibility of pregnancy or afraid of contracting a sexually transmitted disease. You might be uncertain of your partner's commitment to the relationship—"Will she or he still love me tomorrow?" You might be concerned about satisfying your lover or whether your lover can meet your needs (see Table 16.7). Your anxiety may be related to ethical or moral issues about sexual activity.

FAQ:

Isn't it flattering to have a jealous lover?

It can be flattering to know that your lover cares enough about your relationship that he or she is jealous of anything or anyone that poses a threat. You might think your partner didn't care if there was no reaction to your going out with someone else. A little jealousy might keep a relationship fresh; but the stalker, control-freak, "If I can't have you no one else can" type of jealousy is a different, and very dangerous, ballgame.

News stories about a murder or murder-suicide when a jilted lover kills an ex-partner and then commits suicide are common. The following are cues that the person you are with might be dangerous: phone calls in the middle of the night to check on your whereabouts; grilling your friends about every detail of your life; extreme hostility towards your old lovers; constantly going through your things and snooping on you; and/or threatening to harm you or to commit suicide if you leave (Schwartz, 2000).

TABLE 16.7

Anxieties Associated with Nonmarital Sexual Intercourse

Females	Males
1. Can I satisfy him?	1. Can I satisfy her?
2. Will he like my body?	2. Is my penis the right size?
3. Will he respect me after we have sex?	3. Will I have a good erection?
4. Does he love/care for me?	4. Will she want a commitment?
5. Will I have an orgasm?	5. Will I perform well?
6. Are my breasts large enough?	

SOURCE: Adapted from Snegroff, 1986.

A certain amount of sexual anxiety might be helpful to some relationships. For some couples, feeling completely secure in a relationship leads to complacency and taking each other for granted. If the relationship has a certain element of uncertainty, arousal levels are constantly recharged and romantic love thrives. Just the right level of tension might keep a relationship interesting, but unstable.

Sometimes anxious feelings may be a warning that there is something wrong. It is important to pay attention to your intuition. Suppose your partner suggests you experiment with group sex. Your head may tell you that it would be fun to experiment and you don't want your partner to think you're a prude, but your "gut" may tell you that you really don't want to participate. In another scenario, you start to feel uncomfortable during a casual conversation with someone you just met. You might regret it if you ignore your uncomfortable feelings.

Each of us develops **coping mechanisms,** adaptations to stress based on conscious or unconscious choice that enhance control over behavior or give psychological comfort, to help us take care of ourselves during stressful times. Usually when our anxiety level is raised, we react in characteristic ways but with greater intensity. If you tend to withdraw when faced with a problem, under great stress you might totally isolate yourself. Conversely, if your tendency is to seek social companionship, when tension rises you might compulsively pursue company and seek constant social support. Behaviors that in the short run may relax us and reduce anxiety may carry a high price tag over time (Lerner, 1997).

The painful feelings that can be associated with sexual relationships can't always be avoided. It requires effective interpersonal skills to communicate successfully with a partner. To take care of yourself, your personal awareness must be well-developed.

Performance Anxiety

Sex is not an Olympic event. A panel of expert judges is not scoring your "performance." You won't receive a grade, and there are no established standards for sexual excellence. You and your partner are the only ones whose opinions matter. It is considerate to want to please your partner, but pressuring yourself or your partner to "perform" can be destructive. Nevertheless, some people experience **performance anxiety,** feelings of dread that they will be judged inadequate in their sexual activities.

As we discussed in Chapter 4, sexual anxieties can play a role in many types of sexual problems. Sexual function is dependent on a complex physical and emotional process that may be disrupted by a number of factors including fear. When we are anxious, our palms sweat and our hands become cold. These symptoms are caused by vasoconstriction, a narrowing of the blood vessels that supply blood for circulation. This same process can affect vaginal lubrication and male erection. For example, if blood vessels constrict, the blood doesn't flow, and the penis cannot become erect (Tiger, 1992).

Coping Mechanisms: adaptations to environmental stress that are based on conscious or unconscious choice and that enhance control over behavior or give psychological comfort

Performance Anxiety: feelings of dread and foreboding of being judged in connection with sexual activity

Most of us don't like feeling that we have failed, and we'll take all kinds of defensive measures to protect ourselves from embarrassment. Anxiety about sex can become a vicious circle—the more you worry about past or future sexual problems, the more likely it is that you will be unable to relax enough to experience pleasure. Sexual problems lead to increased anxiety, which leads to continued problems, which cause more anxiety. Anxiety distracts our attention from the erotic sensations and thoughts that are an essential part of sexual arousal (Beck & Barlow, 1986).

Normalcy Anxiety

"Am I normal?" This question may be the root of most of our anxieties and concerns about sexuality. **Normalcy anxiety** is the fear associated with being unlike other people. Maybe you worry that you started having sex too young, or that you waited too long before becoming sexually active. You may worry that you think about sex too often, or not often enough. You may worry that you're too sexually inexperienced to please your lover, or so experienced your partner might think you're promiscuous. You may worry that your penis or breasts are too small, that you're too fat or too thin, or just not attractive enough. You may worry that you masturbate too much. Or you worry about what your partner might think if you asked to be tied up the next time you have sex. We read books and magazines, take sex surveys, watch television and movies, and talk to our friends in an attempt to discover if other people feel, think, and behave the same way we do. We may attempt to determine if our desires, interests, or behaviors are normal by comparing ourselves to other people. However, in "the realm of sexuality . . . social comparisons become difficult because people have no way to know what other people are doing . . . and are forced to rely on depictions and discussions through books and other media" (Tiefer, 1995, p. 15).

What is normal? There are many ways to define normalcy. Normalcy may be totally subjective: "I am normal. Therefore anyone who is like me is normal." Statistics may be more objective, but the frequency of a behavior in the sample population can only reveal so much. Statistically, the most frequent sexual behavior is vaginal intercourse; does that mean that any other sexual act is abnormal? In addition, there are cultural norms to worry about. Among some groups in south central Borneo, nearly every man wears a pin inserted in his penis, so this is considered normal. However, even with the increasing popularity of body piercing in the United States, an American male who sticks a pin through his penis is most likely to be considered abnormal. Psychiatry defines normalcy primarily by the absence of a mental illness, but the criteria used to diagnose mental illnesses change over time. Remember, until 1973 homosexuality was considered a psychiatric disorder.

The following five steps may help relieve normalcy anxiety: identify your fears, understand the source of your anxiety, recognize your usual methods of dealing with stress, explore other options, and then take action. Sometimes all that is needed is some support and reassurance that you are "normal." Perhaps you are holding yourself to impossible standards of perfection. Your ideas about sexual normalcy may be based on what you see in the media. Remember, actors and actresses have a script, director, and body double to rely on. Other fears may be more deeply rooted; resolution might require the assistance of a therapist.

Fear of Commitment and Intimacy

Not all emotionally intimate relationships are sexual, and not every sexually intimate relationship involves emotional intimacy. You can touch someone sexually but remain unconnected emotionally, or you can be emotionally close to someone you have never physically touched. "That's close enough" may be the verbal or nonverbal message that first indicates a fear of intimacy. These messages can be very confusing. One day your partner is madly pursuing you and urging you to make a

Normalcy Anxiety: feelings of dread and foreboding in connection with conforming with, adhering to, or behaving in a typical, usual, or standard pattern in connection with sexual activity

TABLE 16.8	
Intimacy and Commitment	
Six Ways of Experiencing Intimacy	**Five Ways of Experiencing Commitment**
Openness	Supportiveness
Sex	Expressions of love
Affection	Fidelity
Supportiveness	Expressions of commitment
Togetherness	Consideration and devotion
Quiet company	

SOURCE: Adapted from Marston et al., 1998.

commitment to an exclusive relationship. The next day the rules have changed and your partner tells you, "I need more space," picks a fight with you, works overtime, or finds other ways to keep distance between the two of you.

In a study of the links between attention to relationship alternatives and relational outcomes, subjects were asked to describe their relationships, inspect slides of attractive opposite-sex targets, and 2 months later to report whether their relationships had ended. Those who were highly satisfied with their investment in, commitment to, and adjustment in a dating relationship showed less interest in the slides than those who were not as satisfied with their current relationship. No better predictor of relationship failure was found than high attentiveness to romantic alternatives. "Even if the grass is greener on the other side of the fence, happy gardeners will be less likely to notice" (Miller, 1997, p. 758).

Fear of intimacy appears to be gender-related. A study of 243 heterosexual college-aged dating couples, found that males reported higher fear of intimacy than females. Fear of intimacy for both sexes was significantly correlated with actual and desired intimacy. However, for women, the correlation between fear of intimacy and desired intimacy was significantly lower than the correlation with actual intimacy. In a 6-month follow-up, the researchers found that females who were no longer in the same relationship had higher fear of intimacy than those who were continuing in their relationships (Thelen et al., 2000).

Mutual caring, acceptance, and trust characterize successful intimate relationships. Neither partner "silences, sacrifices, or betrays the self, and each party expresses strength and vulnerability, weakness, and competence in a balanced way" (Lerner, 1997, p. 3). If you do not trust yourself enough to allow yourself to be vulnerable, it's hard to allow anyone to get close enough to you to build an intimate relationship. If you believe that your partner has the power to make you happy, you may fear that power could be used to make you unhappy—even to hurt you. Thus you may protect yourself by not allowing anyone to have that power over you, and you miss out on one of the most wonderful experiences life has to offer.

For ways of experiencing intimacy and commitment, see Table 16.8.

Shyness

Social avoidance or social anxiety may be interpreted as disinterest, conceit, or snobbery. However, it may be that the individual is avoiding relationships because of shyness. **Shyness** is a feeling of nervousness, embarrassment, or discomfort around other people. Shy people may be paralyzed by fears of ridicule, rejection, or inadequacy. Observations suggest that shy females may be more committed to making a relationship work, whereas shy males may be more willing to abandon a problematic relationship (Johnson et al., 1995).

Shy people may have low interpersonal skills and thus they may hesitate to engage in the self-disclosure necessary to develop a committed relationship (Matsushima et

Shyness: the state or quality of being nervous, uncomfortable, bashful, or timid with others

TABLE 16.9

Sexual Phobias	
haptephobia	fear of being touched
eurotophobia	fear of female genitals
gamophobia	fear of marriage
aichmophobia	fear of pointed objects, including penises
gymnophobia	fear of naked bodies
hedonophobia	fear of pleasure
genophobia	fear of sex in general
coitophobia	fear of sexual intercourse
cypriphobia	fear of sexually transmitted infection

al., 2000). **Cognitive interference,** for example, from thoughts about yourself or the situation, also has been found to interfere with subsequent sexual arousal. There appears to be a relationship between interacting socially and reduced sexual arousal among shy people (Karafa & Cozzarelli, 1997). While interpersonal competence and fear of rejection appear to be central to shyness, the shy do not necessarily hold unrealistically high standards for themselves or view others as expecting perfection from them (Jackson et al., 1997).

"I'll go if you will" is a strategy that many shy people utilize to engage in or facilitate anxiety-provoking social interactions (Bradshaw, 1998). Extremely shy people actively cope with their anxiety by recruiting others into their social networks. This appears to help them enter into situations they would otherwise avoid. However, unless you're into group sex, this strategy will not be helpful in sexual interactions.

Sexual Phobias

While sexual anxieties can be problematic (as we discussed in Chapter 4), some people develop such intense sexual fear that their erotic responses are severely impaired. Some of these fears develop into **sexual phobias,** extreme irrational fears that are out of proportion to any actual danger. Table 16.9 lists a number of sexual phobias.

Cognitive Interference: task-irrelevant thoughts

Sexual Phobia: anxiety provoked by exposure to a specific feared object or situation, often leading to avoidance behavior

■ R E V I E W

CHAPTER

Sex is not just a reproductive process. Sexual relationships evoke intense emotional responses. Thus, it is important to explore the emotional aspects of your sexuality.

Sexual monogamy appears to be the approach of people who end up happy; that is, an exclusive primary sex partner is associated with the lowest rates of negative feelings, as well as the highest rates of positive feelings.

There appear to be two types of loneliness; **1**_____ loneliness is a lack of companions, while **2**_____ loneliness is a lack of intimacy. Chronic feelings of loneliness appear to have roots in childhood and early attachment processes. Constructive ways to deal with the loneliness that can accompany the end of a relationship are accepting and reflecting on your experience, increasing social contacts, and increasing your activity level.

Relationships end for many different reasons. When a relationship ends, try to assess whether there are recurring patterns in your experiences with intimate partners.

Don't allow your entire sense of self-worth to be dependent on the approval of a romantic partner. You will not be attracted to everyone you meet, nor will everyone be attracted to you.

A social **3**_____ model of relationship dissolution posits that relationships end when the costs for staying together outweigh the rewards for continuing the relationship. While a breakup can precipitate emotional problems, most people survive the loss of a love, go on with their lives, and develop new relationships.

Dependent love, making your own life and happiness dependent on how someone else feels about you, almost guarantees disappointment and heartache.

Unrequited love consists of one person loving someone else who fails to return that love; it can be quite painful for both parties. In cases of unequal love, the principle of least interest holds that whoever is less in love has more power in the relationship.

4_____ is a feeling of anxiety or unhappiness because we have done something wrong, such as caused harm to another person. Sexual guilt can interfere with pleasure and intimacy and block a person from taking precautions, such as the use of condoms to avoid unwanted pregnancy or exposure to a sexually transmitted infection. However, guilty feelings can serve a more constructive purpose as well; guilt can help us to make choices that are consistent with our values.

5_____ is the fear of losing an important person to someone else. An evolutionary explanation for the male response to his partner being sexually involved with another man is the uncertainty of **6**_____. Jealousy may serve both an individual and a social function. Males are more likely to be upset by sexual infidelity, while females are more concerned with emotional infidelity. Male jealousy is the leading cause of spousal homicide in the United States.

There are social consequences to expressing anger; people who vent their anger by yelling are likely to become angrier. Although they are often linked, anger is an emotion whereas **7**_____ is a behavior.

Many people are anxious about their sexuality; some even develop a **8**_____, an irrational fear out of proportion to any real danger. **9**_____ anxiety can accompany a fear that you are not able to give or receive sexual pleasure. Comparing yourself to others and judging yourself to be inadequate can result in **10**_____ anxiety. These anxieties can become self-fulfilling prophecies that result in problems of sexual response and satisfaction.

Mutual caring, acceptance, and trust characterize successful intimate relationships. To be truly intimate with another person you must first know, like, and trust yourself.

A lover is not a mind reader. It is important to communicate your sexual needs and desires to minimize the sadness, anger, or fear that can occur with sexual relationships.

SUGGESTED READINGS

Baumeister, R. F. & Wotman, S. (1992). *Breaking Hearts: The Two Sides of Unrequited Love.* New York: Guilford Press.
This exploration of unrequited love from the viewpoints of the aspiring and eventually brokenhearted lover and that of the unwilling beloved shows how radically different and often contradictory the two experiences actually are.

Buss, D. M. (2000). *The Dangerous Passion: Why Jealousy Is As Necessary As Love and Sex.* New York: Free Press.
Using examples from insect, primate, and human populations, Buss asserts that jealousy is an adaptive behavior that helped our human ancestors cope with reproductive threats.

Dowrick, S. (1996). *Intimacy and Solitude.* New York: W.W. Norton.

A psychotherapist looks at the links between intimacy and solitude, explaining how to move from an enjoyment of being alone to true intimacy.

Fillion, K. & Ladowsky, E. (1998). *How to Dump a Guy: (A Coward's Manual).* New York: Workman Publishing.
The authors offer advice about dumping dos and don'ts from the first sign that it's over to the final breakup.

Firestone, R. & Catlett, J. (1999). *Fear of Intimacy.* Washington, DC: American Psychological Association.
The authors show how therapists can help couples identify and overcome internal messages that foster distortions of the self and loved ones.

Lerner, H. (1989). *The Dance of Intimacy.* New York: Perennial Library.
Lerner looks at those relationships where intimacy is most challenged by too much distance, too much

intensity, or too much pain and suggests how we can achieve a more solid sense of self and a more intimate connectedness with others.

Salovey, P. (Ed.). (1991). *The Psychology of Jealousy and Envy.* New York: Guilford Press.
This volume contains chapters from many of the major contributors to the psychological literature on jealousy and envy.

Schneier, F. & Welkowitz, L. (1996). *The Hidden Face of Shyness: Understanding and Overcoming Social Anxiety.* New York: Avon Books.
The authors suggest ways to measure and to manage social anxiety and shyness, and offer explanations of scientific research on shyness.

ANSWERS TO CHAPTER REVIEW

1. social; **2.** emotional; **3.** exchange; **4.** Guilt; **5.** Jealousy; **6.** paternity; **7.** aggression; **8.** sexual phobia; **9.** Performance; **10.** normalcy.

Sexuality, Spirituality, and Religious Traditions

CHAPTER 17

- **Spirituality and Sexuality**
  Spirituality and sexuality connect body, mind, and emotions. In addition, for some, sexuality may be a path to personal and spiritual fulfillment.

- **Sexuality and Religion**
  The emphasis in most traditional religions is on the potential impact of sex on reproduction, not on interpersonal issues.

- **Sexuality and Religious Traditions**
  Sexuality and religious traditions are closely linked. Judaism, Christianity, Islam, Taoism, Hinduism, Buddhism, and Tantric practices all have different approaches to sexuality.

PHYSICAL

SOCIAL

EMOTIONAL

SPIRITUAL

COGNITIVE

Religion and sex have multiple connections. Our physical bodies join us in social relationships that create emotional responses that feed our souls. Many people want more from sex than physical, social, emotional, or cognitive satisfaction and, for many people, sexuality is intricately related to personal and spiritual fulfillment.

Spirituality is concerned with the spirit or soul rather than the body or physical things. **Religion** is a personal or institutionalized system grounded in a belief in a supernatural power or powers regarded as creator and governor of the universe. Religion and spirituality are very personal, but they are also part of group dynamics and the larger culture. Even if you do not consider yourself to be religious, the dominant religious traditions of the culture you live in are likely to influence you. Many individuals and societies look to organized religion for guidance, structure, and answers about important life issues, including sexuality. In this chapter we examine several of the major religious traditions, focusing on each religion's tenets regarding sexuality and the effects of these beliefs on sexual behavior.

SPIRITUALITY AND SEXUALITY

Spirituality is about consciousness, meaning, and hope—about our connections to one another and with something beyond ourselves. It is a means of bringing about human transformation and deepening our awareness of the human experience. Our spirituality is manifested in our behavior, especially our behavior toward others. Spirituality helps to define our human potential. Your spiritual needs are defined by what you believe is right (your **morals**), what you believe is desirable (your **values**), and how you believe people should behave (your **ethics**). Each of these also is a critical element of your sexuality.

Hamilton and Jackson (1998) explored how spirituality becomes a conscious component of life by asking the following questions: What does spirituality mean to you? How did you become aware of your spirituality? How did others in your life react to your emerging spirituality? And what in your life prohibits or blocks you from experiencing or getting in touch with your spirituality? The researchers found that spirituality was both a way of being and a way of doing. The process of becoming self-aware appeared to be the primary vehicle for acquiring knowledge of one's spirituality. Adversity was the most frequently cited catalyst in the process of self-awareness. The spirituality of most of the subjects in the study was influenced by others and was influential in improving the quality of their relationships.

Spirituality is integral to the therapy process. An investigation concerning spirituality in therapy found that most counselors recognize the importance of being aware of their own spiritual beliefs. Spirituality was viewed as a universal phenomenon that can act as a powerful psychological change agent (Hickson, Housley, & Wages, 2000).

Spirituality: concerned with or affecting the spirit or soul rather than the body or physical things

Religion: a personal or institutionalized system grounded in a belief in and reverence for a supernatural power or powers regarded as creator and governor of the universe

Morals: judgment of the goodness or badness of human action and character; what you believe is right

Values: principles, standards, or qualities considered worthwhile or desirable; what you believe is desirable

Ethics: a set of principles of right conduct; how you believe people should behave

Eros, the Greek god of love.

For thousands of years, sexuality has been used as a spiritual path. The desire to be connected with a greater wholeness was personified by the ancient Greeks in Eros, their god of desire and relationships. While sex was seen as just one manifestation of desire, according to the Greeks, it was the strongest. The erotic was seen as the basis for creativity, sensory experiences, all human relationships, and the meaning of life.

It is interesting that some people use spiritual morality as a means of limiting sexual expression, while others believe that if we paid more attention to beauty, sensuality, and pleasure we might actually enhance our spirituality, by giving life more meaning (Moore, 1994). Both spirituality and sexuality touch the human essence. Sex with a partner involves a unique and profound form of self-disclosure. In an intimate relationship, you bare your soul as well as your body. Moore (1994) has suggested that in a sexual relationship you may discover who you are in ways otherwise unavailable; at the same time you allow your partner to see and know the new you.

SEXUALITY AND RELIGION

The word *religion* denotes both observance of ritual obligations and an inward spirit of reverence, and it covers a wide spectrum of meanings that reflect the enormous variety of ways the term can be interpreted. A religion's spiritual power may be in the form of gods, spirits, ancestors, or another type of sacred reality with which believers interact either directly or symbolically. Some recognize only their own traditions and practices as true religious faith, while others acknowledge many paths to spiritual understanding.

Religion is a universal phenomenon that plays a part in all human cultures. Many religions encourage spiritual discipline and insight as avenues for the total understanding of life's meaning and purpose (Richards, 1992). Although religions differ in the sexual attitudes and behaviors they promote or prohibit, the moral systems of all religions address sexuality through mythology, rituals, or specific laws sanctioned by a supernatural being or "higher power."

For thousands of years, religion has offered explanations of the origin of the world, life after death, the mysteries of nature (for example, fire, weather, the behavior of animals, fertility, and vegetative cycles), as well as rudimentary moral ideas of right and wrong. Radical changes occurred in the religions of major agrarian societies within the few hundred years before and after the birth of Jesus (the year 1 in most Western calendars). All over the world, religions began to offer concepts of **salvation,** the transformation and improvement of individuals to an ideal of perfection (embodied in different religions as heaven, divine rebirth, nirvana, and enlightenment), along with explanations of how to achieve it. To achieve salvation, it is necessary to perform right actions and avoid wrong ones (among other qualifications). During this time the moral rules of the salvation-oriented religions became much more elaborate, including rules about sex. Serious seekers of spiritual progress (including Christian and Buddhist monks and Islamic Sufis) were forbidden to engage in sex of any kind, including masturbation. Ordinary believers were permitted to engage in sex under proper circumstances, but sexual sins were believed to be spiritually harmful to them as well.

While most religions have promoted sexual virtue among their believers, at the same time some of them sought to associate sexual vice and perversity with their spiritual rivals. Within Christianity, sexual misbehavior has long been used to blacken certain views that the official church wished to reject as heresy and to stifle targeted individuals or groups. For example, the term *bugger,* which refers to anal sex, is derived from *Bulgar,* referring to people who lived in Bulgaria, home to a religious movement that was ruthlessly and cruelly suppressed by the authorities. Accusations of homosexuality also figured prominently in the destruction of the Knights of the Temple, a Christian order that had been a powerful force during the Crusades but later fell out of favor with the Christian elite who ruled from the Vatican.

Salvation: deliverance from the power or penalty of sin; redemption

Like other elements of culture, the religions of the world have become truly global as their adherents have scattered across the Earth. As a result, these traditions have come to impact and influence one another's followers in new ways, some intentional and some unintentional. Because of their proselytizing traditions (the conversion of nonbelievers), Christianity and Islam were expected to spread globally from the places of their inception; however, even without such traditions, Buddhism and Hinduism are serious influences in the West today. After the Holocaust and the establishment of a Jewish state in Israel, global acceptance has accompanied the new worldwide attention focused on Judaism. "Many of these religions had come in contact before and even grown up side by side, but a truly global presence of each and the accompanying growth of understanding leading to a deeper appreciation of alternate traditions" is a more recent phenomenon (Runzo & Martin, 2000, p. 1).

Religion can play a significant role in promoting an understanding of healthy sexuality as an expression of respect, caring, equality, and love. Religion also can provide justification for sexual guilt, intolerance, and oppression. What all religions seem to have in common is an effort to control sexuality (see Table 17.1). Most traditional religions have little to say about the interpersonal effects of sex; the emphasis is on the potential impact on reproduction. The nearly exclusive emphasis on reproductive sexuality, especially in Western religions, may have affected the strength of religious morality for some individuals in an era when reproduction is easily controlled by the technology of condoms and birth control pills.

An investigation of the attitudes toward sexuality and sexual behaviors of over 800 urban middle school students revealed that "very religious" students and their less religious peers differed on only two attitudes. The less religious students felt that intercourse was a normal part of teenage dating and that intercourse was all right if the two people were in love (Donnelly et al., 1999), while the more religious students felt that premarital sex was unacceptable. A survey of over 600 college students found that religious affiliation and student perceptions of the influence of religion on their sexual behaviors were significantly related to a student's probability of engaging in sexual intercourse. **Religiosity** (strength of beliefs and religious service attendance) and religious affiliation also were significant in distinguishing between contraceptive methods used by sexually active students (Pluhar et al., 1998).

Religiosity: the quality of being religious; excessive or affected piety

---

TABLE 17.1

Religious Positions on Some Sex Issues

Key: ↑ = blessed   √ = morally acceptable in most cases   ↔ = neutral or no clear position
   × = morally unacceptable in most cases   ↓ = condemned

	Baptist	**Methodist**	**Catholic**	**Mormon**	**Jewish**	**Muslim**	**Buddhist**
Premarital Sex	↓	×	↓	↓	√	↓	√
Extramarital Sex	↓	×	↓	↓	↓	↓	×
Masturbation	↔	↔	×	×	↔	√	↑
Abortion	↓	↔	↓	×	×*	↔	↔
Contraceptives	↔	↑	↓	√	√	√	√
Married Clergy	↑	↑	↓	↑	↑	√	↔
Female Clergy	×	↑	↓	×	↑	×	↔
Homosexual Orientation	×	√	↔	×	√	↓	√
Homosexual Behavior	↓	↓	↓	↓	↓	↓	√
Same-Sex Marriage	↓	×	↓	↓	×	↓	√
Ordination of Homosexuals	×	×	↔	↓	×	↓	√

SOURCE: Adapted from *San Francisco Chronicle*, 1994, at www.acme.com/~jef/religion_sex.
*Orthodox Judaism

Because religion is such a sensitive and emotional subject, research has been subject to bias and political pressure not unlike that affecting sexuality research (see Chapter 1). Also similar to the difficulties experienced by sexuality researchers, even coming to agreement on the definitions of basic terms has been a problem (recall the problems in defining *rape* that we discussed in Chapter 13). How exactly do you determine whether someone is religious or not? One way is simply asking whether a person is religious, or whether he or she believes in God. By that measure, most people report being religious. If only those people who attend services once a week or pray every day are considered religious, far fewer people fit the profile. Stark and Bainbridge (1985) reported from national surveys that 96 percent of Americans pray sometimes and 94 percent believe in God, but only half say they pray every day. Some studies have sought to classify people based on whether they claim to be Catholic, Protestant, Jewish, Islamic, Buddhist, atheist, agnostic, or "other," but these categories do not prove very helpful because each contains a wide range of religious involvement.

The National Health and Social Life Survey (NHSLS) (Laumann et al., 1994) divided respondents into three categories based on their attitudes toward sexual issues. About one third of those surveyed said that their religious beliefs always guide their sexual behavior, a group the researchers categorized as "traditional." This group believed that homosexuality is always wrong, that there should be restrictions on legal abortions, and that premarital and extramarital sex are wrong. About half of the respondents believed that sex should be part of a loving, although not necessarily married, relationship, the "relational" category. A little more than a quarter of those surveyed fell into the "recreational" category, believing that sex need not have anything to do with love (Table 17.2).

The findings from the NHSLS confirmed the link between religion and sexual restraint. The effects of religion on sex seem to be more consistent and powerful among women. The sex lives of the most religious women (defined as conservative Protestant Christians) were quite different from the sex lives of the least religious women (those who listed "none" as their religious preference), whereas the sex lives of the most religious and least religious men were more similar. This is consistent with the view presented in Chapter 10 that women have higher erotic plasticity than men.

Highly religious people (especially women) were less likely than the nonreligious to give or receive oral sex, to perform anal sex, or to be homosexual or bisexual. Religious people were more likely to report that they never masturbated and, if they did masturbate, were less likely to report that they usually or always had an orgasm when they

TABLE 17.2

Religion and Sexual Attitudes in the United States

	Recreational	Traditional	Relational
Men			
No religion	11.7%	39.1%	49.2%
Mainline Protestant*	24.2	43.8	32.0
Conservative Protestant**	44.5	30.1	25.3
Catholic	17.8	49.6	32.6
Women			
No religion	10.4	44.4	45.2
Mainline Protestant*	30.9	51.4	17.7
Conservative Protestant**	50.5	38.4	11.2
Catholic	22.2	58.0	19.8

NOTE: Percentages in rows total 100 percent.

*Mainline Protestants include Methodists, Lutherans, Presbyterians, Episcopalians, and United Church of Christ.

**Conservative Protestants include Baptists, Pentecostals, Churches of Christ, and Assemblies of God.

SOURCE: Laumann et al., 1994, p. 237.

did. Despite these seeming restrictions on sexual activity, the religious people reported higher rates of physical and emotional satisfaction with their sex lives. This could mean that restricting one's sexuality based on religious values is ultimately beneficial to the individual. However, it could mean simply that people with lower sex drives are more likely to become and remain religious, so that they are more satisfied with less sex.

Other studies have confirmed that religious people (especially women) are more restrained in their sexual attitudes, and sometimes in their behaviors, compared with less religious people. Reiss (1967) found that people who attended church regularly had less permissive attitudes toward sex than people who rarely attended church. Adams and Turner (1985) found that 83 percent of elderly women who did not go to church masturbated, while only 19 percent of elderly women who regularly attended church engaged in sexual self-stimulation. (There was no corresponding difference among men, however.) Among students at a religious college, Earle and Perricone (1986) found that the more religious the students were, the less permissive their attitudes toward sex.

Many religions promote sexual virtue and restraint, so the effects on the attitudes of their adherents are hardly surprising. Sometimes, however, there is a gap between what people say and what they do. Blumstein and Schwartz (1983) found that religious couples who attended religious services regularly did indeed report more conservative sexual values than nonreligious people. But their sexual behavior was no different. Religious people were just as likely to commit adultery as nonreligious people, despite stating stronger opposition to it. This suggests that religion shapes people's *attitudes* more easily than their *behavior*. In recent decades the pious reputations of many religious figures and preachers (including Jim Bakker, Jimmy Swaggert, and Jesse Jackson) have been damaged by sexual scandals. Research on Catholic priests by Sipe (1995) has concluded that only about 10 percent of them manage to live up to their vows of celibacy. Such incidents illustrate that many people may hold religious ideals of sexual virtue but fail to live up to them.

Restrictions are not the only effect religion has on sexuality. In some religious cults, female devotees are permitted and even encouraged to have sex with male leaders. The women may regard intimacy with a spiritual authority as an honor and a spiritual benefit at the time, and they may even be told that the sexual connection will help advance their spiritual progress. Later, however, such women may come to look back on these sexual trysts as a form of exploitation. Women who leave religious groups after such sexual activities often look back on them with bitterness (Jacobs, 1984). Sexual harassment and similar abuses are thus not limited to business, political, educational, military, and other organizations. Of course, in religious as in other kinds of organizations, only a small minority of adherents commit such abuses.

SEXUALITY AND RELIGIOUS TRADITIONS

In the following discussion, we offer brief overviews of seven religious traditions. The focus is on their sexual beliefs and behaviors to illustrate how different religions view sexuality and sexually related issues.

Judaism

Judaism is based on the belief in an omnipotent, omniscient, and omnipresent God who is just and merciful. The teachings of Judaism are based on the **Old Testament,** the **Torah** (the first five books of the Bible), and the **Talmud** (a collection of postbiblical teachings). The Old Testament and ancient Hebrew tradition viewed sexuality as fundamentally positive and marital sex as a gift of God. Although Genesis warns about the destructive potential of sex, the Old Testament is not antisex. Sexuality is seen as a deep and intimate part of a relationship. The use of the verb *to know* (as in "Adam knew Eve and she conceived a child") demonstrates the biblical connection of sexual intercourse and sexual intimacy.

> *Love is as powerful as death; passion is as strong as death itself. It bursts into flame and burns like a raging fire. Water cannot put it out; no flood can drown it.*
>
> (SONG OF SOL. 8:6B–7A, TODAY'S ENGLISH VERSION)

Judaism: a religion developed among the ancient Hebrews and characterized by belief in one transcendent God and by a religious life in accordance with Scriptures and rabbinic traditions

Old Testament: Christian designation for the Holy Scriptures of Judaism, referring to the covenant of God with Israel, as distinguished in Christianity from the dispensation of Jesus constituting the New Testament

Torah: the first five books of the Hebrew Scriptures

Talmud: the collection of Jewish laws and traditions relating to religious and social matters

The creation stories of the Old Testament explain biological sex and the reasons why there are two genders.

❝If brothers dwell together, and one of them dies and has no son, the wife of the dead shall not be married outside the family to a stranger; her husband's brother shall go in to her, and take her as his wife, and perform the duty of a husband's brother to her. And the first son whom she bears shall succeed to the name of his brother who is dead, that his name may not be blotted out of Israel. ❞

(DEUT. 25:5–6, RSV)

The creation stories in Genesis explain biological sex and the reasons for two sexes. Eve was created from Adam's rib because God recognized that "it is not good that the man should be alone" (Gen. 2:18, Revised Standard Version) and that he needed not only a companion but a lover: "Be fruitful and multiply" (Gen. 1:28, RSV). The goal of union is sexual pleasure, not just procreation: "Therefore a man leaves his father and his mother and cleaves to his wife and they become one flesh" (Gen. 2:24, RSV). The importance of sexual intercourse and the role of desire appear numerous times in Genesis. For example, Sarah describes sexual intercourse as "pleasure" (Gen. 18:12, RSV), Isaac is said to be "fondling his wife Rebekah" (Gen. 26:8, NRSV), Leah and Rachel negotiate for Jacob's sexual favors (Gen. 30:13–16), and Potiphar's wife wants Joseph to sleep with her (Gen. 39:7).

Ambivalence about sex can also be found early in the Bible. When Adam and Eve ate from the tree of the knowledge of good and evil in the Garden of Eden, the main knowledge they seemed to gain was that of sexual morality, for they realized they were naked and sewed clothes to cover themselves (Gen. 2:9 and 3:6–7). It was those clothes that enabled God to realize that they had eaten the forbidden fruit, and he expelled them from paradise. This can be interpreted to mean that the original sin (causing the fall of humankind from Paradise) was a sexual transgression, making sex responsible for all of mankind's suffering. It can also be interpreted to mean that the acquisition of sexual morality and sexual shame was the cause of the fall—so that sex was acceptable in paradise, but guilt and shame over sex were not.

A passage in Deuteronomy underscores the importance of sexuality in the first year of marriage. "When a man is newly married, he shall not go out with the army or be charged with any business; he shall be free at home one year, to be happy with his wife whom he has taken" (Deut. 24:5, RSV). The Talmud specified minimum marital sexual obligations according to the man's profession and the amount of time that he spent at home with his wife. Gentlemen of leisure, with no occupation, were expected to have sex daily. Laborers working outside their city of residence were expected to have sexual relations twice a week. Weekly sex was expected of scholars, donkey drivers, and laborers working in the city in which they resided, while camel drivers were scheduled for monthly sex, and sailors every 6 months.

While Judaism recognized sex as being pleasurable, the emphasis was on procreation; the tribes of Israel were to "be fruitful and multiply, and fill the earth" (Gen. 1:28). Israel began as a small group of tribes whose survival demanded that there be enough children, especially males, to feed and protect them. Nonprocreative sex, therefore, was frowned upon. The positive attitude toward procreative sex is typical and useful for a small community that feels itself under siege by external forces and that needs to produce many children in order to survive.

Adultery is clearly condemned by the Old Testament, not only as a sexual sin, but also as a violation of property rights. The Bible defines adultery not as sex outside of marriage but as sex with another man's wife or concubine without his permission. Proverbs (6:26) urges men to seek prostitutes rather than be tempted by the wife of another. The Old Testament permitted polygyny but monogamy was preferred, and most Hebrews, following the biblical example of Adam and Eve, were monogamous.

In Judaism, marriage is considered to be the natural state for men and women. Widows and widowers are encouraged to remarry as soon as possible. Married couples are expected to have children; historically, childlessness was grounds for divorce. If a man died without having a son by his wife, it was his brother's duty to marry and impregnate the deceased brother's wife. (Anthropologists call this practice the **levirate**, after Levi, namesake of the Levites.)

Onanism is another term for masturbation. However, many biblical scholars interpret the sin of Onan not as masturbation but as Onan's refusal to honor the Levite law to procreate with his dead brother's wife. Onan did not masturbate to avoid procreation, he engaged in *coitus interruptus* because he "knew that the offspring would not be his; so when he went in to his brother's wife he spilled the semen on the ground, lest he should give offspring to his brother" (Gen. 38:9, RSV).

Pregnant, nursing, and postmenopausal women are all encouraged to continue sexual relations. However, menstruating women are considered to be "unclean." Historically sexual relations were prohibited during the 7-day menses period, followed by a ritual bath, the **mikvah,** still required for Orthodox Jewish women today. Prohibiting sexual activity during the woman's least fertile time (that is, during the menses) also serves the purpose of increasing the likelihood of couples engaging in coitus when a woman is most fertile, thus increasing the chances of conception—and increasing the Hebrew population.

Jewish wives are encouraged to take an active role and to initiate sex if they wish. They are also permitted to reject their husband's sexual advances. Both the husband and the wife are expected to derive pleasure from sexual contact. According to the Talmud, "the best way a man could be certain of begetting a son was to bring his wife to orgasm before he himself achieved it" (Bullough, 1976, p. 76). Despite this acknowledgement of women's sexuality, Judaism traditionally viewed a woman's role as assisting and serving her husband and she was considered to be her husband's property.

The different sects or denominations of Judaism are usually referred to as movements. There are basically three major movements in the United States today: Orthodox, Conservative, and Reform. Some also include a fourth, smaller movement, the Reconstructionist. Orthodox and sometimes Conservative movements are described as "traditional" movements. The Reformist and Reconstuctionist (and sometimes Conservative) are described as "liberal" or "modern" movements. Orthodox Jews, who live strictly by the rabbinic interpretation of the Hebrew scriptures, continue to follow traditional Jewish dietary practices and intermarriage laws. One Orthodox group, the Chasidim, live separately and dress distinctively. Orthodox men thank God for not creating them women because the legal category of person in Jewish law is a male, and women are conceived as incomplete males (Fishbane, 1987). However, many Conservative and Reform Jews have interpreted these laws more liberally and have an egalitarian approach to religious life and liturgy.

FAQ:

Does the Old Testament forbid homosexuality?

The Old Testament contains only two verses about same-sex sexual relations: "You shall not lie with a male as with a woman; it is an abomination" (Lev. 18:22, RSV) and "If a man lies with a male as with a woman, both of them have committed an abomination; they shall be put to death; their blood is upon them" (Lev. 20:13, RSV). The same scripture says that cursing your mother and father (Lev. 20:9) or sex with the wife of a neighbor (Lev. 20:10) also is punishable by death. Some argue that "abominable" does not mean unnatural, only forbidden. Nowhere does the Torah suggest that one ought not have homosexual inclinations or desires, only that one may not engage in homosexual behavior (Cohen, 1990).

In Orthodox Judaism, men and women are separated for religious ceremonies.

Levirate: the practice of marrying the widow of one's childless brother to maintain his line, as required by ancient Hebrew law

Onanism: masturbation or coitus interruptus, withdrawal of the penis in sexual intercourse so that ejaculation takes place outside the vagina

Mikvah: a ritual purification bath taken by Jews on certain occasions, as before the Sabbath or after menstruation or ejaculation

It is tragic that so many within the Christian faith have dwelt on a few scriptural references and force-fit them into their own concepts of sexual morality rather than on the central core of Jesus' message of love and compassion.

(STAYTON, 1992, P. 9)

The mystical school of Judaism came to be known as Kabbalah, from the Hebrew root *Oof-Bet-Lamed*, meaning "to receive, to accept." Kabbalah is a body of mystical teachings of rabbinic origin, which involves use of hidden knowledge to affect the world in ways that could be described as magic achieved through the power of God. Within the Jewish kabbalistic traditions, God is seen as the locus of sexuality. For example, through God there is a union of the active and the passive, procreation and conception, from which all mundane life and bliss are derived (Scholem, 1954).

Christianity

Christianity is the religion based on traditions of the Old Testament outlined previously and the teachings of Jesus, believed to be the Son of God, that compose the portion of the Bible referred to as the **New Testament.** Although Judaism and Christianity base much of their theology on the same scriptures, their adherents interpret them very differently. Within Christianity, the many different Christian denominations all believe in Jesus Christ but also have varying interpretations of the Bible. There are two primary divisions in Christianity, Catholicism and Protestantism. Catholics, the largest Christian group in the United States, are distinguished by their belief in the infallibility of the Pope, the spiritual head of the Church. Protestantism, the second division, separated from the Catholic Church in the 16th century. The many different Protestant denominations include Baptist, Methodist, Lutheran, Presbyterian, and Episcopalian. Subdivisions within these denominations differ in their interpretation of church doctrine. For example, Baptist churches include those affiliated with the Southern Baptist Convention; the National Baptist Convention, USA; and the Progressive National Baptist Convention.

While we know very little about Jesus' views on sexuality, the teachings of Jesus focused on love and tolerance. Christianity is rooted in a belief in a God of love, or to use the Greek word, a God of **agape.** God's love becomes the basis for other forms of love and all moral human relationships. Indeed, Christianity is sometimes referred to as "the love religion" because of the central importance it places on love. It preaches that God's love is the basis for salvation and it urges Christians to practice loving each other, although not primarily in a sexual sense.

Historically, Christianity has had a difficult time integrating sexuality with spiritual growth. Perhaps in response to the excesses of the Roman Empire, early Christian expression and interpretation of the New Testament emphasized the control and restriction of sexuality. According to sexual historian Reay Tannahill (1980), Christianity burst on the ancient Roman scene with a much more negative and restrictive view of sex than any of the other religions that were popular at that time. Other religions sometimes permitted homosexuality, masturbation, contraception, sex with animals, and even abortion and adultery, but the new church condemned all of them. As the worship of Jesus gradually developed, Christianity emphasized the view that neither Jesus nor his earthly parents, Mary and Joseph, had ever had sex. According to some, only the celibate could hope to gain entrance to heaven—in other words, sex ruined your soul for eternity. Later, sex within marriage became accepted as compatible with eventual salvation, but even then the prevailing wisdom was that marriage was merely a concession to the sinful desires of humankind and that celibacy was spiritually superior. Today, Catholic clergy, both male (priests) and female (nuns), are expected to renounce all forms of sexual pleasure.

The Christian ideal of rising above the sins of the flesh and abstaining from all sexual activity has presented a difficult struggle for many individuals throughout church history. Origen, one of the great early Christian thinkers, could only achieve celibacy by castrating himself. As more and more churchmen adopted this extreme practice, the official church found it necessary to pass a law making self-castration a sin.

On the other hand, at some times and places the Christian doctrines of clerical celibacy were treated as mere polite fictions. Many clergy and even a few popes have had mistresses and illegitimate children (Chamberlin, 1969). Because sexual

Christianity: a religion that includes the Catholic, Protestant, and Eastern Orthodox churches and is founded on the life and teachings of Jesus

New Testament: the collection of the books of the Bible that were produced by the early Christian church, comprising the Gospels, Acts of the Apostles, the Epistles, and the Revelation of St. John the Divine

Agape: the love of Christians for other persons, corresponding to the love of God for humankind

misdeeds by clergymen have often contributed to loss of public respect for the church, movements for reform have often emphasized sexual purity. Even today, the Catholic Church has struggled to maintain its status and legitimacy in the face of periodic scandals involving sexual activity by clergy.

Sexual celibacy is required for Catholic clergy.

The ideal of sexual abstinence has consistently presented greater problems for Christian men than for women. Murphy (1992) surveyed several hundred modern Catholic clergy, and by all measures the women were more successful than the men in resisting sexual temptations. Priests were more likely than nuns to engage in sex, and among those who did engage in it, the men did it more often and with more partners than the women. If a nun ever did commit a sexual sin, she would in many cases do it only once, whereas the men more commonly became repeat offenders. Sipe (1995) has devoted his career to studying celibacy among Catholic priests, and by his estimates only about 10 percent of the men can come close to achieving it. Even among those who do not engage in sex, the majority masturbate occasionally, and Sipe says that the practice is so common that it has gained a measure of tacit acceptance, though it is technically a violation of Catholic law.

Some theologians believe that it was one of Jesus' disciples, the Apostle Paul, who almost single-handedly transformed a fringe movement of Messianic Jews into a vibrant new faith that within a few generations would sweep the Greco-Roman world and alter the course of Western history (Sheler, 1999). Like many religious leaders, the life and works of Paul have been surrounded by controversy. Paul's writings on sexuality have been particularly controversial. In 1 Corinthians, Paul recognizes the sacredness of the body and sexual relationships, reinforces that sexual desire is part of life, and respects the importance of mutual and egalitarian pleasure and responsibility in intimate relationships.

On the other hand, Paul emphasized the importance of overcoming "desires of the flesh" and associated spirituality with sexual abstinence. In approximately A.D. 50 Paul expressed the view that celibacy was the preferred state for man and was spiritually superior to marriage.

Of all Paul's teachings, those related to homosexuality and the role of women in the church may be the most controversial. Writing to Timothy, Paul declared that a woman is not permitted "to teach or to have authority over men; she is to keep silent"(1 Tim. 2:12, RSV). In the letter to the Ephesians he urges, "Wives, be subject to your husbands as to the Lord. For the husband is the head of the wife" (Eph. 5:22–23, RSV). Writing to Christians in Rome, Paul denounced those he said had forsaken God's ways. "God gave them up to dishonorable passions. Their women exchanged natural relations for unnatural, and the men likewise gave up natural relations with women and were consumed with passion for one another, men committing shameless acts with men and receiving in their own persons the due penalty for their error" (Rom. 1:26–27, RSV).

Paul's writings reflect the complex and ambivalent attitudes of Christianity toward women. The church leader Clement of Alexandria, who lived about A.D. 150 to A.D. 215, furnished an apt brief summary, saying that women were men's equals in everything, but men were always better than women at everything (Tannahill, 1980). Given such ambivalence, different writers have come up with wildly different characterizations, depending on whether they focus on the negative or the positive. The feminist writer Mary Daly wrote in *The Church and the Second Sex* (1985) that "a woman's asking for equality in the church would be comparable to a black person's demanding equality in the Ku Klux Klan" (p. 6). More generally, she treated the history of Christianity as a protracted effort by the Christian establishment to justify keeping women in an inferior, exploited position.

In contrast, the Church has itself long claimed to have benefited women, such as by offering women a theoretically equal opportunity to achieve salvation (unlike many

"It is good for a man not to touch a woman. . . . I say therefore to the unmarried and widows, it is good for them if they abide even as I. But if they cannot contain, let them marry: for it is better to marry than to burn."

(1 COR. 7:1B, 8–9, KING JAMES VERSION)

Today many Protestant denominations have female ministers.

other religions). Christianity was created and run by bachelor males for most of its history, and even today the Catholic Church refuses to allow women to become priests, let alone cardinals or popes. It does, however, permit women to become saints, and in many places the Virgin Mary has been the most admired and most worshiped human in world history. Despite the mixed messages, Christianity has always appealed strongly to women.

Stark's (1996) history of the rise of Christianity provides convincing data that women were more strongly attracted to the upstart church than were men. Women outnumbered men in the church membership lists, and when the men did join it was often because their wives brought them in. This suggests that even if early Christianity did have some negative views about women, it offered them more than other religions. Although men dominated the religious hierarchy, as members they drifted away from church by the end of the Middle Ages. In early modern Europe and America women outnumbered men in church on a regular basis, often by a wide margin (Cott, 1977); this gender imbalance persists today.

Later church leaders expanded on the view that sex was sinful. As a young man, St. Augustine (A.D. 354–430) had a concubine and fathered an illegitimate son. He is famous for one of his early prayers, which can be loosely translated as: "Dear God, please help me to achieve chastity, but not just yet." He later proclaimed that only celibacy would open the heavenly gates. His reversal is evident in his proclamation in A.D. 375 that even within marriage sex was contaminated by original sin and all sexual desires were therefore sinful. These early Christian views of sexuality continued to be influential throughout the Middles Ages. Thomas Aquinas (A.D. 1225–1274) maintained that human sexual organs were designed for procreation and that any other use was against God's will. Aquinas detailed rules about sexual behavior and condemned sexual acts done only for pleasure.

Although since Aquinas's time homosexuality has been condemned as sin in much of the Western World, there was no explicit prohibition against homosexuality until the writings of St. Augustine in the fourth century. Medieval historian John Boswell (1995) located 80 versions of an early Catholic ritual for same-sex marriages dating from the eighth through the 16th centuries. Boswell contends that this is proof that homosexual relationships were once tolerated and even blessed by the church. Liturgies uncovered by Boswell resemble rituals the early church used for heterosexual marriages including joined right hands, a veil placed over the spouses, a kiss, and a feast. Critics of Boswell's work believe that what Boswell translates from the Greek as "same-sex unions" are meant to celebrate fraternity or brotherhood, not homosexual relationships.

The Church's opposition to homosexuality focused mainly on the so-called sins of men. The historian Judith Brown (1986) found that the medieval and early modern Christian Church courts tried hundreds, even thousands of cases of homosexuality, but almost none involved sex between women. The penalties meted out in the few documented trials of lesbians were far more lenient than those for male homosexuals (Brown, 1986).

Over the centuries, a greater understanding of the importance of joyous sexuality has evolved. However, the traditional Roman Catholic viewpoint has been that genital sexuality is good and moral only within a heterosexual, monogamous union that is at least potentially biologically procreative, based on mutual love and fidelity, and sanctioned by some kind of covenanted marriage commitment (Nugent & Gramick, 1989). Abortion, contraceptive devices, masturbation, homosexuality, and technologically-assisted means of reproduction are all still prohibited by the Roman Catholic Church.

A separate branch of Christianity began in the 16th century during a period that became known as the Protestant Reformation. Protestantism rejected some premises of the Catholic Church but retained many of its sexual ethics. Martin

Luther (1483–1546), one of the driving forces behind the Protestant Reformation, celebrated marriage as a positive force and not inferior to celibacy, even for the clergy. John Calvin (1509–1564), a leading Protestant reformer, also expressed a belief that sex within marriage was holy and honorable. He believed that sex could be harnessed and set to constructive uses, whereas Luther simply sought to confine its "raging" within marriage (Cole, 1966). Sex and sexual desires were seen as natural drives, although premarital sex, adultery, masturbation, and homosexuality continued to be seen as sinful.

The Protestant Reformation also gave rise to Puritanism. The Puritans followed the teachings of St. Augustine that emphasized original sin. This led to the use of civil law to regulate behavior in an attempt to suppress immorality. Although H. L. Mencken (1920) jokingly characterized Puritanism as "the lurking fear that someone, somewhere may be happy," the Puritans had an appreciation of sexual expression within marriage.

While the examples we have cited are historical, even today some Christians support a literal interpretation of the Bible and strict rules of sexual behavior. In 1997 the Southern Baptist Convention, the largest Protestant denomination in the United States, included a declaration that "A wife is to submit graciously to the servant leadership of her husband" (Southern Baptist Convention, 1998). According to one study, evangelical Christian women have sex more frequently and experience orgasms more often than American women in general because of a desire by evangelical Christian women to please their mates (Taylor, Hart, & Hart Weber, 2000).

EXPLORING SEXUALITY ONLINE

Cyberreligion

Religious groups are now using technology to spread their message and communicate with the faithful. Although sex sites still may get more hits, a religious revival has hit the Internet and almost every religion is now online. The Gospel Communications Network, launched in 1995, hosts over a hundred Christian ministries and gets more than 2 million visitors to its searchable Bible and personal testimonials. A computer network connects the 285 parishes of the Catholic diocese of Los Angeles. The Internet also attracts groups that may feel rejected by their religion, such as gay Christians or feminist Muslims, who also may search for and find a spiritual community online.

Islam

In the seventh century A.D., the prophet Muhammad founded **Islam,** which comes from the Arabic root word meaning "peace" and "submission." His teachings are recorded in the **Koran,** the Holy Scriptures and basic code of Islam. Islam was founded in the Middle East, but like Christianity and Judaism, its followers have spread beyond the Arabic nations and today live throughout the world. Islam teaches that one can only find peace in life by submitting to **Allah,** the Almighty God.

There are five formal acts of worship, called the Five Pillars of Islam, which help strengthen a Muslim's faith and obedience. Testimony of faith (*shahada* or *kalima*) is simply the declaration "I bear witness that there is no deity but Allah, and I bear witness that Muhammad is His servant and messenger." The Second Pillar of Islam is prayer (*salat*) as the connection to Allah through which one gathers strength, guidance, and peace of mind. Islam prescribes five formal prayers daily, during which Muslims repeat and refresh their beliefs. Every Muslim whose financial conditions are above a certain minimum must pay alms (*zakat*, the Third Pillar) of at least 2 percent

Islam: the religious faith of Muslims, based on the words and religious system founded by the prophet Muhammad

Koran: the sacred text of Islam revered as the word of God and accepted as the foundation of Islamic law, religion, culture, and politics

Allah: God, especially in Islam

Muslim women are instructed to keep their bodies covered, even while enjoying a day at the beach.

annually to a deserving needy person. Fasting *(saem),* the Fourth Pillar, is done in the month of **Ramadan,** the ninth month of the Muslim year. During this month, from dawn to dusk, Muslims do not eat or drink anything in order to suppress desires and remember Allah alone. The Fifth Pillar, a pilgrimage to Mecca *(Hajj)* in the 12th month of the lunar year, must be made at least once in a lifetime by all Muslims who are financially and physically able to do so. All pilgrims wear white and are required to suppress passion, refrain from any bloodshed, and be pure in word and deed during *Hajj.*

The Islamic tradition highly values marriage and sexual fulfillment in marriage. Muhammad decreed that marriage was the only road to virtue and regarded sex as one of the great joys of life (Minai, 1981). The Koran depicts sexual intercourse as a good, religious deed and regards sexuality as a gift from Allah (Bullough, 1976). Celibacy is frowned upon and marriage is proposed to be the highest good in the Muslim tradition (Ahmed, 1991).

Polygyny is permissible for Muslims; a man is allowed to have up to four wives. However, a woman may have only one husband. Factors that determine whether monogamy or polygyny prevail in a particular Islamic country or period "has been a matter, not so much of faith or morals, as of social, sexual, or economic convenience" (Bullough, 1976, p. 217). Thus, even where it is allowed, most Muslim men have only one wife. In marriage, the wife's primary responsibility is to provide children for her husband. Despite the emphasis on procreation, a study of Islamic religious leaders in Jordan found that 90 percent believe that family planning is in keeping with the tenets of Islam (Underwood, 2000).

Although Islam celebrates sexuality, and pious Muslims praise Allah for having created woman, Islam is a male-dominated religion that teaches that Allah created men to be superior to women and that women are "erotic creatures continually giving trouble to man" (Bullough, 1976, p. 213). Women are seen as inherently sexual, and in order to contain female sexuality, traditional Islamic women are subject to many restrictions that do not apply to Islamic men. Women are regarded as the property of men and are under the control of their nearest male relative. They are not to be seen nor discussed openly by males other than close relatives and must be veiled when out in public. All Islamic social activity is strictly segregated by sex.

The Koran recognizes that the clitoris is the source of female passion and Muhammad encouraged husbands to be "slow and delaying" during sex. All forms of heterosexual intercourse between unmarried persons are prohibited, but within marriage, anal intercourse and oral-genital sex are permissible with the consent of both partners. Masturbation is not generally condemned, transvestism among males was historically common, and bestiality was tolerated. Homosexual activity between men, although officially condemned, has been tolerated and seen as "a natural outgrowth of a sex-positive, sexually segregating religion" (Bullough, 1976, p. 238).

Sex outside of marriage is a serious offense for traditional Muslims. "Honor killings" of adulterous wives who dishonor their husbands or promiscuous daughters who dishonor their family, still occur in some regions. According to Islamic law, the penalty for premarital and extramarital intercourse is a public whipping and stoning to death. Anything that leads to "illegal" sex also is prohibited. This includes dating, free mixing of the sexes, provocative dress, nudity, obscenity, and pornography.

Although some Westerners view Islam as a sexually oppressive religion, as shown here traditional Islam accepts sensuality and sexuality as being of high value. Fundamentalist Muslims tend to have more rigid views about sexuality and more stringent sanctions for those who deviate from accepted sexual behaviors than their more liberal counterparts.

Ramadan: the ninth month of the Muslim calendar, a period of fasting from sunrise to sunset

Taoism: a principal philosophy and system of religion of China, based on the teachings of Lao-tzu and on subsequent revelations; characterized by a pantheon of many gods and by the practice of alchemy, divination, and magic

Yin: the passive, female cosmic principle in Chinese philosophy

Yang: the active, male cosmic principle in Chinese philosophy

Taoism

Taoism (also known as Daoism), which originated in the sixth century B.C., is based on the teachings of the Chinese philosopher Lao-tzu (640–531 B.C.), which emphasize the importance of harmony with all of nature. Lao-tzu, an old man when the Chinese philosopher Confucius was born, was seeking a Tao (a way or path) that would avoid the constant feudal warfare and other conflicts of that time. The essential Taoist philosophical beliefs can be found in Lao-tzu's book *Tao Te Ching*. Taoism, along with *Buddhism* (discussed later) and *Confucianism*, became the three great religions of China. While Confucianism urged the individual to conform to the standards of an ideal social system, Taoism maintained that the individual should ignore the dictates of society and seek only to conform to the underlying pattern of the universe. With the end of the Ch'ing dynasty in 1912, state support for Taoism ended. The 1949 Communist victory and subsequent Cultural Revolution restricted religious freedom, destroying much of the Chinese Taoist heritage.

"I do not know its name," Lao-tzu said, "so I call it Tao. If you insist on a description I may call it vast, active, moving in great cycles" (abodetao.com, 2000). The goal of each Taoist believer is to become one with Tao, the first-cause of the universe and the force that flows through all life. This Supreme State of Being is not seen as something unattainable or far removed from humankind, but something of which we are integrally a part. The concept of a personified deity is not part of the Taoist religion. Taoist priests view their many gods as manifestations of the one Tao "which could not be represented as an image or a particular thing." Development of virtue is the chief task of life and is attained through the Three Jewels: compassion, moderation, and humility.

In Taoism, time is cyclical, not linear as in Western thinking. Life is made up of cycles and the only constant is change. People have no control over change but can control their responses to the changes that life has to offer. For a Taoist, attempts to resist change are a waste of time and energy and without honor. Lao-tzu speaks of the principle of the soft overcoming the hard, the weak overcoming the strong, that resistance only makes that which you are resisting stronger. Those who follow the Tao are said to be strong of body, clear of mind, and sharp of sight and hearing. They are flexible and do not fill their minds with anxieties as they see simplicity in the complicated and learn to achieve greatness in little things.

The earliest and most detailed sex manuals can be traced to China around 2500 B.C. (Simons, 1985). These manuals were intended for women as well as for men and included information regarding sex play, sexual techniques, and intercourse positions. Sexual behavior is viewed as a means of promoting spiritual growth, not just a means of producing offspring. In the teachings of Taoism, sex is a sacred duty, a form of worship leading to immortality. "Harmony in one's sexual desires, passions, and joys is a natural and important aspect of health. Sexuality is considered part of nature and is not associated with any kind of sin or moral guilt. In fact, lovers joined in ecstasy can experience a transcendent union with the cosmos." (Francoeur, 1992, p. 3)

A key concept in Taoism is that of the polar energies of **Yin** and **Yang**. In Taoism, the vital energies of Yin (earth, dark, receptive, female) and Yang (heaven, light, penetrating, male) are complementary rather than opposing aspects of nature, like the body/mind dualism of Western thought. The challenge of life is to achieve a healthy, dynamic balance between these two energies that coexist in everyone in varying proportions. Yin and Yang are aroused through sexual activity and can be channeled to the heart and the head (Francoeur, 1992).

According to Taoist thought, the Great Mother (female) has an inexhaustible life force that she gives to the male in union. Thus the purpose of Taoist sexual techniques is to prolong intercourse and increase the amount of female essence or **yin** a man can absorb from her. The man's semen, his **yang,** is in limited supply and not to be squandered. If a male's yang force were continually fed by the female's yin, it would

In managing affairs there is no better advice than to be sparing

To be sparing is to forestall

To forestall is to be prepared and strengthened

To be strengthened is to be ever successful

To be successful is to have infinite capacity.

(FROM TAO TE CHING, CHAPTER 59, IN CHANG, 1991, P. 15)

FIGURE 17.1 Yin and Yang.

The Kama Sutra contains illustrations of many different sexual techniques and practices.

result in increased health and longevity. It is essential that the woman reach orgasm during intercourse. The more of a woman's essence a man can receive without giving out his precious male substance, the greater his strength will grow (Bullough, 1976). Taoist tradition generally emphasizes the importance of nongenital touch and sexual enjoyment for both men and women. Sexual exercises, similar to modern sex therapy techniques discussed in Chapter 4, are utilized to prolong male ejaculation as well as female pleasure.

Hinduism

Hinduism, also known to followers as Sanatana Dharma, which means everlasting or eternal religion/truth/rule, is better thought of as a way of life or philosophy rather than a religion. Hinduism is based on the teachings of ancient sages and scriptures like the **Veda**, the four ancient scriptures of Hindu philosophy, and the Upanishads, philosophic texts characterized by mystical speculation on the nature of the self and ultimate reality.

Hinduism includes a highly varied complex of practices and beliefs. It recognizes that the individual differences among humans cause them to follow different paths toward their ultimate goals in life. It teaches that sexual fulfillment is a form of spiritual energy and is one way to become reincarnated at a higher level of existence. Sex is considered a duty that can lead to spiritual union with the Infinite. In the ideal life, a Hindu male can pursue four goals: *kama* (sexual love), *artha* (power and material gain), *dharma* (spiritual duty), and *moksha* (liberation). Those choosing the path of *kama* emphasize sexual pleasure. Those taking the paths of *dharma* and *moksha* might be celibate, although Hindu priests may marry. Most Hindus, "even the ascetics and monks, view sex as something natural, to be enjoyed in moderation without repression or overindulgence" (Francoeur, 1992, p. 2). However, the paths of sexual pleasure and power traditionally were considerations only for males. While Hindus celebrate sexual pleasure and the religious power of sexual unions, children, particularly sons, are the primary goal of sexual intercourse. At the same time, however, it is a common Hindu belief that women enjoy sex much more than men (Bullough, 1976).

Only three of the many Hindu scriptures on the art of eroticism have been translated into English. The most famous of these, the *Kama Sutra*, was written some time between the third and fifth century B.C. by a Hindu priest. The *Kama Sutra* includes detailed illustrations and descriptions of sexual positions and techniques as well as discussion of the spiritual aspects of sexuality. Eighty-four different sexual positions are described in the *Kama Sutra*, but one commentator listed 529 variations. Not all these variations could be performed by all couples. Some positions are highly dependent on physical peculiarities of the individual (Bullough, 1976). Consider, for example, the "Two Palms" position in which the couple makes love with the man leaning back against a wall with his lover clinging to his neck with her feet placed in his palms; or the "Wrestler" in which the woman lies on her front, grasping her ankles in her hands and pulling them up behind her.

Many Westerners prefer to focus their study of Hinduism on the sexual acrobatics depicted in the *Kama Sutra* rather than on the connectedness of sexuality and spirituality that is essential to Hindu belief. Unlike the art of Western religions that traditionally represents historical events, Hindu artists depict eternal moments of Brahma, the eternal essence of the universe, including the playfulness of love (Runzo, 2000). The exterior walls of the Kandariya Mahadeva temple in India depict entwined human sexual couplings rising up, level upon level, toward the sky and the pinnacles of the gods.

Buddhism

Buddha was born Siddhartha Gautama in the sixth century B.C. in what is now Nepal. His father was a ruler, and Siddartha grew up living an extravagant life while looking for happiness that was not subject to change and decay. He sought answers wandering

Hinduism: a diverse body of religion, philosophy, and cultural practice native to and predominant in India, characterized by a belief in reincarnation and a supreme being of many forms and natures, and by the view that opposing theories are aspects of one eternal truth, and by a desire for liberation from earthly evils

Veda: any of four ancient and most authoritative Hindu sacred texts, composed in Sanskrit; or, these books collectively

the wilderness, studying with different religious teachers, and submitting himself to rigorous physical austerities. Ultimately he found a state of calm mental absorption and realized that only through such a state of meditation could liberation be found.

For some, **Buddhism** is a religion, while for others it is a philosophy or a way of life. Founded in India in the fifth century B.C., Buddhism evolved from Hinduism. Buddha's ideas were deeply influenced by Hinduism. Over a period of about a thousand years, Buddhism spread north into Tibet, south into Sri Lanka, southeast into Lao, Cambodia, and Vietnam, and east into Burma, China, Korea, and Japan. As Buddhism spread and adapted to the different cultures, it developed and changed. As with other major religions, different forms of Buddhism have evolved and been reinterpreted over the centuries. Today there is no single Buddhist theology but a vast array of traditions. While this diversity of view might be confusing to some, the lack of doctrinal rigidity is its source of appeal to others.

The core teachings of the historical Buddha, Shakyamuni, create a collective source for Buddhism in its many forms. Buddha's first teachings, the Four Noble Truths of Buddhism, are that suffering exists, suffering arises from attachment to desires, suffering ceases when attachment to desire ceases, and freedom from suffering is possible by practicing the Eightfold Path of virtue, concentration, and discernment (Right View, Right Thought, Right Speech, Right Action, Right Livelihood, Right Effort, Right Mindfulness, and Right Contemplation). The recognition and understanding developed in meditation is central to Buddhism. Through meditation we remain in the present moment by dropping past memories and fantasies about the future.

Buddhism is more united in its goal than in its doctrines about the nature of the world. Many scholars even regard Buddhism as atheistic at its core. Salvation is regarded as something that one pursues and, occasionally, achieves in this life on earth, unlike many other religions, which postpone salvation until after death. The Buddha is reputed to have achieved enlightenment or **nirvana,** a dimension transcending time and space, during his lifetime, based on his ethical practices and his meditations. Some Buddhist traditions believe that in your present life you should merely try to make some progress toward salvation, which may not come until many future lifetimes have passed. Other Buddhist traditions, notably the *Zen Buddhism* developed in Japan, emphasize making an all-out effort to reach enlightenment during the present lifetime. Many Japanese as well as many Westerners have claimed to reach these enlightened states by following strict procedures of living in a monastery and meditating frequently every day under the guidance of a learned teacher; this process typically takes at least 5 years.

"It must be karma." The Buddhist term **karma** has become part of the English language. Karma is a **Sanskrit** word that basically translates into "action." In context, Buddhism divides human individuality into five *skandhas* (heaps) of Form, Feelings, Perceptions, Intentionality, and Consciousness. Karma is a part of the Fourth Skandha, Intentionality; your intentions are the basis for your priorities. More generally, karma refers to conscious physical, mental, or verbal actions and the natural reactions that occur as a result of these actions. In other words, whatever we say, or do, or think, has an impact; for every cause, there is an effect. In Buddhist tradition karma is not individualized; we are subject to family and group, national and human karma as well as our own personal karma. The collective activities of any group can create karma for the entire group.

As Buddhist tradition developed, celibacy for priests was mandatory and encouraged for monks and nuns. However, other followers of Buddha are instructed to enjoy sexual activity. Premarital sex, masturbation, contraception, and homosexual orientation and behavior are morally acceptable in most cases, or even promoted in others. Sexual intercourse is seen "not just as a satisfaction of instinct but the repetition of the primal copulation of the divine couple, the eternal principle of all things, and a means of ascending the spatial-temporal plane of life" (Bullough, 1976, p. 272).

A 17th century Tibetan statue depicting the supreme Buddha Kalacakra uniting with Visyamata, mother of all.

Buddhism: a spiritual tradition originating in India, based on the teaching of Buddha that life is permeated with suffering caused by desire, that suffering ceases when desire ceases, and that enlightenment obtained through right conduct, wisdom, and meditation releases one from desire, suffering, and rebirth

Nirvana: enlightenment in the Buddhist tradition, a dimension transcending time and space, marked by disinterested wisdom and compassion

Karma: the total effect of a person's actions and conduct during the successive phases of the person's existence, regarded as determining the person's destiny

Sanskrit: an Indo-European, Indic language, in use since about 1200 B.C. as the religious and classical literary language of India

Tantra

While many religions relegate the pleasure of orgasm to a baser level of human behavior, **Tantra** is "based on an experientially founded tenet that the most profound, subtle and powerful level of consciousness, the mind of clear light, manifests in intense orgasm" (Hopkins, 2000, p. 271). Tantra, from the Sanskrit word meaning "web," "warp," "thread," or "continuity," is based on Hindu and Buddhist texts that provide practical methods of developing awareness of physical potential and acceptance of all emotions, sensations, and desires. Tantra has come to be accepted as a historical religion, though some argue that Tantrism is largely a product of 19th century British colonialism and Orientalist discourse that came to be defended, rationalized, and sanitized by some 20th century scholars (Urban, 1999). Today the term *Tantra* is often applied to any religious or spiritual practices in which slow nonorgasmic sexual union or masturbation forms a path to the experience of spiritual ecstasy.

In the Tantric belief system, consciousness is divided into three parts: the gross, which consists of the five senses; the subtle, our emotions, feelings, and drives; and the very subtle, which is reached through meditative focus on sensitive parts of the body, through orgasm, or through dying (Hopkins, 2000). Present day Tantra directly employs the imagery and practice of erotic love as a skillful means toward enlightenment. Tantric philosophy is a way of life "that includes the conscious and creative utilization of sexual energy to achieve liberation from the limits of the individual self" (Aldred, 1996, p. 12).

More than the practice of specific sexual acts or rituals, Tantric sexual systems emphasize cosmology and celebrate heightened awareness of sex and all of life. By embracing Tantra, followers believe that they become more complete. By recognizing and stimulating their inherent sensual spirituality, practitioners release energy that can be used to achieve both worldly and spiritual goals and allow them to enjoy life to its

Tantra: any of a comparatively recent class of Hindu or Buddhist religious literature written in Sanskrit and concerned with techniques and rituals including meditative and sexual practices

CONSIDERATIONS

Religious Declaration on Sexuality, Morality, Justice, and Healing

In January 2000 more than 850 American religious leaders endorsed the Religious Declaration on Sexual Morality, Justice, and Healing, a statement that affirms that sexuality is one of God's most fulfilling gifts and outlines a new nondiscriminatory paradigm of sexual morality. Endorsers of the declaration represented a broad range of faith traditions and included two denomination presidents, 15 seminary presidents and academic deans, and theologians from more than 43 seminaries, as well as 14 bishops.

The declaration states:

> Sexuality is God's life-fulfilling gift. We come from diverse religious communities to recognize sexuality as central to our humanity and as integral to our spirituality. We are speaking out against the pain, brokenness, oppression, and loss of meaning that many experience about their sexuality.
>
> Our faith traditions celebrate the goodness of creation, including our bodies and our sexuality. We sin when this sacred gift is abused or exploited. However, the great promise of our traditions is love, healing, and restored relationships.

Our culture needs a sexuality ethic focused on personal relationships and social justice rather than particular sexual acts. All persons have the right and the responsibility to lead sexual lives that express love, justice, mutuality, commitment, consent, and pleasure. Grounded in respect for the body and for the vulnerability that intimacy brings, this ethic fosters physical, emotional, and spiritual health. It accepts no double standards and applies to all persons, without regard to sex, gender, age, bodily condition, marital status, or sexual orientation.

God hears the cries of those who suffer from the failure of religious communities to address sexuality. We are called today to see, hear, and respond to the suffering caused by violence against women and sexual minorities, the HIV pandemic, unsustainable population growth and overconsumption, and the commercial exploitation of sexuality.

 What do you think of this declaration?

—Do you think your religious leaders would endorse this declaration?

fullest. Followers of Tantra learn from a guru, or teacher, how to raise their psychosexual energy, the curled serpent power (Kundalini) that lies at the base of the spine through successive focal points, chakras, until it reaches the highest chakra at the top of the skull. Tantra techniques include the repetition of mantra, special sounds and words, and the use of yantras, symbolic geometric forms that represent the different forces of energy. It also includes ritual practices such as yoga, movement, breath control, and meditation techniques. "It is the use of such techniques that can lead to living experience with the Divine" (Mumford, 1993, p. xiv).

To reach sexual ecstasy, you need to be aware of your own body and your partner's body. Knowledge of sexual anatomy and the body's response to sexual stimulation are important. Tantric sexology believes that one of the most important sexual skills a man can develop is ejaculation control and semen retention. These skills help him achieve orgasm without ejaculation and enable him to prolong intercourse and ensure that his partner also reaches orgasm.

Because some people view Tantra as erotic orgiastic cults, followers of Tantra have been attacked and the practice of Tantric traditions has been outlawed in some countries. According to Francoeur (1992) Tantric rituals are highly secret and require severe discipline as well as extreme physical, sexual, mental, and moral effort. Ultimate bliss is achieved when you push your enjoyment to its highest power and then use it for spiritual elevation (Rawson, 1973).

REVIEW

Your spiritual needs can be defined by what you believe is right, what you believe is desirable, and how you believe people should behave. This holds for sexual and nonsexual needs alike. Religion is one way to address such needs.

The moral systems of all religions address sexuality through mythology, rituals, or specific laws with supernatural sanctions. However, religions differ in the sexual attitudes and behaviors they attempt to promote or prohibit. What all religions seem to have in common is an effort to control sexuality and hence **1**_____ and population growth. This becomes obvious when you consider that the discourses offered in most traditional

religions have little to say about the interpersonal effects of sex.

In our society, there is little consensus among the major religious organizations on such sexual issues as homosexuality, masturbation, abortion, and premarital and extramarital sex.

Traditional Judaism permitted polygyny but **2**_____ was preferred. Any sexual act not involving marriage and procreation, for example, adultery and incest, was forbidden. The levirate required a man to marry his brother's widow, if his brother had no sons.

Both the husband and the wife were expected to derive pleasure from sexual contact. Nevertheless, a woman's role was to assist and serve her husband and she was considered to be her husband's property.

Christianity has emphasized that sexuality is something to be controlled and restricted. Traditionally, **3**_____ was the preferred state, and spiritually superior to marriage.

St. **4**_____ (A.D. 354–430) had a concubine and fathered an illegitimate son. However, he later proclaimed that only celibacy would open the heavenly gates. Thomas **5**_____ in the 13th century maintained that human sexual organs were designed for procreation and that any other use was against God's will.

Christianity has evolved over the past 2,000 years. For example, during the **6**_____ Reformation of the 16th century **7**_____ celebrated marriage as a positive force, even for clergy. Today various Protestant denominations may have views of sexuality that differ considerably from each other and with the Roman Catholic Church.

Islam was founded in the seventh century A.D. by the prophet **8**_____ whose teachings are recorded in the **9**_____, the holy scriptures and basic code of the religion. Islam has accepted sensuality and sexuality as being of high value and provides a moral code based on avoiding excess. However, women, who are regarded as the property of men, are subject to many restrictions that do not apply to Islamic men.

The Koran recognizes that the **10**_____ is the source of female passion. However, sex outside of marriage is a serious offense.

Taoism, which originated in the sixth century B.C., is based on the teachings of the Chinese philosopher **11**_____ and emphasizes the importance of harmony with all of nature. Traditionally, sexual behavior was viewed as a means of promoting spiritual growth, not just a means of producing offspring. In the teachings of Taoism, sex is a sacred duty, a form of worship leading to immortality.

The earliest and most detailed sex manuals were a product of **12**_____. The purpose of Taoist sexual techniques was to prolong intercourse and increase the amount of female essence or **13**_____ a man could absorb, and it was essential that the woman reach orgasm during intercourse. According to Taoism, men have a limited supply of **14**_____, which is restored by sexual intercourse. Sexual exercises, similar to modern sex therapy techniques, were utilized to prolong male ejaculation as well as female pleasure.

15_____, the dominant spiritual tradition in India, explicitly recognizes that individuals may achieve their ultimate goals in life by following different paths because humans differ. Sex is considered to be a religious duty that may lead to spiritual union with the Infinite. While Hindus celebrate sexual pleasure and the religious power of sexual unions, traditionally women were limited to childrearing and household duties. The **16**_____ is an ancient Hindu text that discusses the spiritual aspects of sexuality.

17_____ evolved from Hinduism in the fifth century B.C. Buddhist tradition requires celibacy for priests, but other believers are to enjoy sex as a transcendent repetition of the primal copulation of the divine couple.

18_____ sexual traditions are based on Hindu and Buddhist texts. An important tantric precept is the belief that one of the most important sexual skills a man can develop is ejaculation control and semen retention. However, more than the practice of specific sexual acts or rituals is the emphasis on cosmology and the celebration of heightened awareness of sex and all of life.

SUGGESTED READINGS

Cleary, T. (Translator). (1999). *Sex, Health and Long Life: Manuals of Taoist Practice.* New York: Shambhala Publications.
> This volume contains five traditional Taoist texts that offer the Taoist approach to a healthy sex life.

Danielou, A. (Translator). (1994). *The Complete Kama Sutra: The First Unabridged Modern Translation of the Classic Indian Text.* Rochester, VT: Inner Traditions International.
> This version of the *Kama Sutra* includes commentaries on the text of this traditional Indian guide to sexuality as a pathway to spiritual bliss.

Fox, T. C. (2000). *Sexuality and Catholicism.* New York: George Braziller Press.
> The editor of the *National Catholic Reporter* discusses the history of the church's views of sexuality and papal encyclicals analyzing issues of abortion, homosexuality, priest pedophilia, birth control, and the role of women in the church.

Gomes, P. J. (1998). *The Good Book: Reading the Bible with Mind and Heart.* New York: Morrow.
> Gomes, pastor of Memorial Church and Professor of Theology at Harvard University, is an African American gay man. His book not only reviews biblical passages on sexuality and race, but it examines the roots of homophobia, sexism, anti-Semitism, and racism.

Ignacio Cabezon, J. (Ed.) (1992). *Buddhism, Sexuality and Gender.* Ithaca: State University of New York Press.
> This volume is an exploration of Buddhist history and contemporary culture, with discussions of gender and homosexuality within different historical contexts.

Shaw, M. (1994). *Passionate Enlightenment.* Princeton, NJ: Princeton University Press.

A well-researched historical look at sacred sexuality and the role of women in Tantric Buddhism.

Westheimer, R. K. & Marks, J. (1996). *Heavenly Sex: Sexuality in the Jewish Tradition.* New York: New York University Press.

In this book the popular Dr. Ruth looks at the role of sexuality in the context of Jewish religion and culture.

Wiesner-Hanks, M. F. (2000). *Christianity and Sexuality in the Early Modern World: Regulating Desire, Reforming Practice.* New York: Routledge.

Wiesner-Hanks surveys the ways in which Christian ideas and institutions shaped sexual norms and conduct from the time of Martin Luther and Columbus to that of Thomas Jefferson.

ANSWERS TO CHAPTER REVIEW:

1. reproduction; **2.** monogamy; **3.** celibacy; **4.** Augustine; **5.** Aquinas; **6.** Protestant; **7.** Martin Luther; **8.** Muhammad; **9.** Koran; **10.** clitoris; **11.** Lao-tzu; **12.** Taoism; **13.** yin; **14.** yang; **15.** Hinduism; **16.** *Kama Sutra*; **17.** Buddhism; **18.** Tantric.

CHAPTER 18

Sexual Politics and Legal Issues

PHYSICAL

SOCIAL

EMOTIONAL

SPIRITUAL

COGNITIVE

- **Sexual Politics**
  The politics of sexuality are evident within particular groups or constituencies, as well as in the ways those groups try to influence attitudes and decisions at all levels of society.

- **The Politics of Sex Research**
  Politics, especially at the federal level, can influence which areas are investigated and how research findings are received.

- **Gay and Lesbian Rights**
  The political battle over gay and lesbian rights has engaged many segments of society in questions such as family and relationship rights, gays in the military, and other areas of discrimination.

- **The Politics of AIDS**
  The politics of AIDS has evolved from discussions about what was perceived as a gay male disease to a global pandemic involving scientists, politicians, and drug manufacturers.

- **Reproductive Rights**
  Reproductive rights have long been a major political issue that is now framed as one between antiabortion and pro-choice differences.

- **Regulating the Sexual Behavior of Consenting Adults**
  Regulating the sexual behavior of consenting adults is an issue of concern in many states, as well as in the U.S. military.

- **Some Unintended Effects of Legislation**
  Laws, including those affecting sexuality, are generally passed to solve a specific problem; however, they may have unintended consequences.

Sexual politics and legal issues involve the cognitive decision-making processes of drafting and promoting legislation and voting on it. Laws formalize a society's moral values, ethical principles, and judgments about behavior, and they are the ultimate example of social control. Legislation pertaining to sexuality also has strong emotional and spiritual components, as evidenced by the continuing heated debate about the abortion issue.

When there is a conflict between what society feels is moral or immoral and what is legal, people push for change. A positive example of this force is the repeal over the past decades of **miscegenation** laws, laws outlawing marriages between persons of different races. As more and more people came to see such laws as being more immoral than the acts that the laws sought to ban, these laws were abolished as discriminatory and unconstitutional. As society's views concerning sexual issues change, eventually that consensus will be reflected in legislation.

The United States today criminalizes a wider range of sexual conduct than other developed countries. The United States also punishes sexual conduct more severely than it does nonsex crimes (Posner, 1992). An already strained American legal system is overloaded with legal battles on sexual issues including those centering on AIDS, gay and lesbian rights, federal funding of erotic art, pornography, prostitution, marital and date rape, sexual harassment, sexual abuse, surrogate motherhood, artificial insemination, and abortion rights.

SEXUAL POLITICS

Sexual politics gives new meaning to the phrase "the body politic." The activities of our bodies are subject to political discussions that beget legislation (among other things). Laws about sexual behavior reflect a society's attempts to encourage acceptable behavior, discourage unacceptable behavior, and define what a society considers to be moral and immoral (Figure 18.1). Most laws about sexual behavior in Western nations are rooted in Judeo-Christian tradition. In many Islamic countries criminal law is drawn directly from religious law. The economic and political climate of a nation also influences laws regulating sexual behavior.

The earliest known laws regulating sexuality date from the time of ancient Mesopotamia, about 1100 B.C. In the United States, from colonial times to the Victorian era to today, society's changing views concerning sexual issues have been reflected in legislation.

In the United States, issues of sexuality permeate the political arena and campaign rhetoric. Sex has become an integral part of political life. It is increasingly difficult for any politician to avoid taking a stand on some aspect of human sexuality. From Pat Buchanan, the Republican Party candidate for president in 1992, proclaiming at the National Convention that gay rights have no place "in a nation we still call God's country," to Bill Clinton's impeachment trial for lying under oath about his sexual

> *"... the enjoyment of sex has forever—at least since Eden, Mother Eve, and the apple-of-knowledge pie—been a political question."*
>
> (TIGER, 1992, P. 173)

Miscegenation: marriage, cohabitation, or reproduction by parents of different races (especially by white and nonwhite persons)

519

Although Bill Clinton publicly proclaimed, "I never had sex with that woman" he later admitted to a sexual relationship with White House intern Monica Lewinsky.

relationship with White House intern Monica Lewinsky, to California congressman Gary Condit's affair with Chandra Levy, sex has become as much a part of political reality as shaking hands and kissing babies. Politicians' private sexual behavior has become as important, if not more important, than their public stance on sexual issues. While Franklin Roosevelt's mistress never became a political issue and John Kennedy's sexual liaisons were not public knowledge until years after his death, Bill Clinton's legacy will always be linked to his affair with Monica Lewinsky.

Some laws affect sexuality in wide-ranging, and sometimes unintended, ways. The 1873 **Comstock Laws** that outlawed the importation and circulation of pornography also was used to justify the confiscation of any contraceptive information or devices sent through the mail on the grounds that this information was obscene. It wasn't until the 1930s that a panel of federal judges ruled that this prohibition did not apply to contraceptives used by physicians in their medical practices. The **Mann Act,** passed in 1910, forbid the transportation of women across state lines for "immoral purposes"; it was supposed to prevent the illicit transportation of women for purposes of forced prostitution. However, the Supreme Court interpreted this statute to mean that a man could be prosecuted for taking any woman who was not his wife across state lines for purposes of sex. Selective enforcement of this law was used to convict Jack Johnson, who in 1908 was the first black heavyweight-boxing champion, for having sexual relationships with white women. Incredibly, it was not until 1986 that Congress overhauled the Mann Act and retitled it the Transportation for Illegal Sexual Activity and Related Crimes Act.

The sexual atmosphere of the 1960s that was so liberating to some and repellent to others became a political platform for many candidates seeking elected office. During this post–birth control pill and pre-AIDS era, reproduction and sex were permanently separated and sexual activity was no longer publicly confined to marriage-oriented relationships. The "Make Love Not War" anti–Vietnam War rallies and protests taught a generation how to use the political system, fueled the fears of those already bewildered by rapid social change, and revitalized the latest in a long line of political purity movements. Advocates of so-called purity politics seek to restore sexuality exclusively to marriage; they must contend with "the permeation of the erotic throughout American culture, the expansive and varied roles available to American women, and a contraceptive technology that sustained the nonprocreative meanings of sexual behavior" (D'Emilio & Freedman, 1988, p. 358).

Politicians reflect the nation's concerns and are quick to recognize that sexual issues garner newspaper headlines, sound bites on the evening news, and Election Day votes. Homosexual rights, abortion, and AIDS are examples of sexual issues that have become hot items on the political agenda. Because they highlight the differences between men and women, the issues of women's rights can also be considered sexual politics. Among these issues are the discrepancy between the salaries of men and women; the relatively few numbers of women in high-status positions, such as judges and corporate managers; and the imbalance in the performance of household duties (even women employed full-time in the work force still perform most domestic chores). Worldwide, the legal and social status of women is far from equivalent to that of men.

Americans continue to perform illegal sexual acts every day. While the definition, enforcement, and penalties for sex-related crimes vary from one state to the next and change from year to year due to new judicial decisions and legislation, in many jurisdictions, adultery, homosexuality, oral, and anal sex are punishable by fines or even prison terms.

Comstock Laws: 1873 federal laws that outlawed the importation and circulation of pornography, also used to justify the confiscation of any contraceptive information or devices sent through the mail

Mann Act: 1910 law making the transportation of women across state lines for "immoral purposes" illegal

THE POLITICS OF SEX RESEARCH

A great deal of scientific research is dependent on public funding, and public funding is strongly influenced by politics. As we discussed in Chapter 1, the National Health and Social Life Survey (NHSLS) was originally funded by the federal government, but in

	Supportive ✓	Unsupportive ⊘	Neutral/No law ▬			
	Contraceptive Services[1]	Abortion Services[2]	HIV/Aids[3]	Sexual Orientation[4]	Sexual Behaviors[5]	Sexual Exploitation[6]
Alabama	✓	⊘	⊘	⊘	⊘	✓
Alaska	✓	✓	✓	⊘	✓	✓
Arizona	⊘	⊘	▬	⊘	⊘	✓
Arkansas	✓	⊘	▬	⊘	⊘	✓
California	✓	✓	✓	▬	✓	✓
Colorado	✓	✓	▬	⊘	✓	✓
Connecticut	✓	✓	▬	✓	✓	✓
Delaware	✓	⊘	✓	⊘	✓	✓
District of Columbia	▬	✓	✓	▬	✓	⊘
Florida	✓	▬	▬	⊘	⊘	✓
Georgia	▬	⊘	✓	⊘	⊘	✓
Hawaii	✓	✓	✓	▬	✓	✓
Idaho	⊘	⊘	⊘	⊘	⊘	✓
Illinois	✓	⊘	✓	⊘	✓	✓
Indiana	⊘	⊘	▬	⊘	✓	✓
Iowa	⊘	⊘	✓	⊘	✓	✓
Kansas	✓	⊘	✓	⊘	⊘	✓
Kentucky	✓	⊘	✓	⊘	✓	✓
Louisiana	✓	⊘	▬	⊘	⊘	✓
Maine	✓	▬	✓	⊘	✓	✓
Maryland	✓	▬	▬	⊘	⊘	✓
Massachusetts	✓	✓	✓	▬	⊘	✓
Michigan	✓	⊘	▬	⊘	⊘	✓
Minnesota	✓	✓	▬	✓	⊘	✓
Mississippi	✓	⊘	⊘	⊘	⊘	✓
Missouri	✓	⊘	▬	⊘	⊘	⊘
Montana	✓	✓	✓	⊘	✓	✓
Nebraska	⊘	⊘	▬	⊘	✓	✓
Nevada	⊘	✓	⊘	⊘	✓	✓
New Hampshire	✓	✓	✓	▬	✓	✓
New Jersey	✓	✓	▬	▬	✓	✓
New Mexico	✓	✓	▬	⊘	✓	✓
New York	✓	✓	✓	⊘	✓	✓
North Carolina	✓	⊘	⊘	⊘	⊘	✓
North Dakota	▬	⊘	⊘	⊘	✓	✓
Ohio	✓	⊘	▬	⊘	✓	✓
Oklahoma	✓	▬	▬	⊘	⊘	✓
Oregon	✓	✓	▬	⊘	✓	✓
Pennsylvania	⊘	⊘	✓	⊘	✓	✓
Rhode Island	✓	⊘	✓	▬	⊘	✓
South Carolina	✓	⊘	⊘	⊘	⊘	✓
South Dakota	▬	⊘	⊘	⊘	✓	✓
Tennessee	✓	✓	⊘	⊘	✓	✓
Texas	⊘	✓	▬	⊘	⊘	✓
Utah	⊘	⊘	▬	⊘	✓	✓
Vermont	✓	✓	✓	▬	✓	✓
Virginia	✓	⊘	▬	⊘	⊘	✓
Washington	✓	✓	▬	⊘	✓	✓
West Virginia	✓	✓	▬	⊘	✓	✓
Wisconsin	✓	⊘	▬	✓	✓	✓
Wyoming	⊘	⊘	⊘	⊘	✓	⊘

[1] Contraceptive services incline public funding, insurance coverage and parental consent/notice.

[2] Abortion services include public funding, mandate insurance for abortion service, parental consent waiting period, procedure bans and anti violence laws.

[3] HIV infection surveillance by public health authorities and HIV testing options.

[4] Workplace discrimination, public school discrimination and family formation discriminating against gays and lesbians.

[5] There are laws in the state criminalizing sodomy.

[6] There are laws in the stated criminalizing sexual exploitation that include prostitution, computer crimes and sexual harassment in school setting,

FIGURE 18.1 **General Position on Some Sexual Issues by States.** Source: Adapted from SIECUS, 2000.

At their meeting in July 2001, Pope John Paul II urged President George W. Bush to bar the creation of human embryos for stem cell research, saying that America has a moral responsibility to reject actions that "devalue and violate human life."

1991 the U.S. Senate passed an amendment prohibiting the government from funding the study due to the concerns of a number of very vocal public officials. Private foundations stepped in and provided the necessary financial support to complete much of the research, although the full plan was never carried out.

Stem Cell Research

Stem cell research is another example of the dependence of research on the political climate. Research on the transplantation of undifferentiated fetal tissue, called stem cells, shows great promise for saving human lives. This tissue is available from miscarried as well as aborted embryos and fetuses. This research has been affected dramatically by the changing political climate. As advances in medical research using fetal cells have increased, so has the controversy. In 1974 the National Commission for the Protection of Human Subjects of Biomedical and Behavioral Research was established with federal funds to examine the study of fetuses. The Commission issued regulations that research involving fetal tissue be permitted in accordance with state law (Coutts, 1993). Medical research with fetal tissue proceeded to increase from the mid-1970s until 1987, when the *New England Journal of Medicine* reported the successful transplantation of fetal neural tissue into the brains of two young patients with Parkinson's disease. The successful procedure led to requests for government funding of similar procedures as well as a heated outcry from antiabortion activists. The latter led to the Reagan administration's moratorium on all federally funded research involving the transplantation of tissue from induced abortions. Despite the conclusions of the 1988 National Institutes of Health Fetal Tissue Transplantation Research Panel, which stated that such research was acceptable public policy, the moratorium was extended under the Bush administration and was not lifted until Clinton took office in 1993 (see NIH, 1993).

The continuing tension between politics and scientific research was illustrated by the response to a single issue of *Science* magazine in April 2001. The issue contained two reports on stem cell research in mice, which were heralded as major advances with significant potential for health care. In the first of the two studies, researchers at the National Institutes of Health had used embryonic stem cells to produce insulin that could be used to treat Type I diabetes (Vogel, 2001). In the second study, conducted at Rockefeller University, skin cells from a mouse were converted into an embryo; the embryo's stem cells were then used to produce cells to treat Parkinson's disease (McKay & Isacson, 2001). To move from research on mice to human trials, human embryo stem cells would need to be used.

In August 2001 President George W. Bush announced that he would allow federal funding for a limited amount of research on embryonic stem cells. Bush said he would allow funding for research on 64 existing stem cell lines. A human embryonic stem cell line is a colony of cells derived from a days-old embryo. However, Bush would not sanction the creation of any new stem cell lines from existing or future embryos because extracting the cells involves the destruction of human embryos. This compromise pleased some, angered others, and raised questions of whether the Bush plan is adequate to support research.

The Effects of Childhood Sexual Abuse

In Chapter 13, we discussed an article by Rind, Tromovitch, and Bauserman (1998) that challenged traditional assumptions about the effects of childhood sexual abuse (see Sexual Abuse of Children in Chapter 13). The study also found that experiences of childhood sexual abuse were more negative for girls than for boys both at the time and in terms of lasting consequences. This article went through the scientific review process and was published without fanfare in one of the most prestigious and competitive journals in psychology. Soon after its publication, however, controversy erupted. Radio moralist "Dr. Laura" Schlessinger attacked the article during her call-in talk show, decrying the technique of meta-analysis as "junk science" and exhorting her listeners to send angry letters or faxes to Congress. The tremendous response to her show caused Congress to pass a resolution condemning the article and its conclusions. Pressure was put on the American Psychological Association to retract the article and fire the journal editor who had allowed the work to be published, although there was no finding that the article had been methodologically or scientifically invalid.

Eugenics

On the political level, **eugenics,** the study of methods of improving humans by allowing only carefully chosen people to reproduce, has influenced all sorts of public policy debates on issues such as gay rights, sex crimes, and sexual dysfunction. Eugenic racial theories proclaiming that people of Eastern European ancestry were genetically inferior to Anglo-Saxons led to a 1924 law to restrict immigration. By 1940 more than 30 states had laws permitting forced sterilization of people suffering from conditions ranging from poverty to mental illness. At the time, eugenics was not a marginal, bigoted movement but a mainstream, progressive program designed to harness science in the reduction of suffering and misfortune (Allen, 1997). Idealists hoped that the eugenic program of sterilization would reduce the number of babies born with birth defects, mental retardation, and other handicaps. Although a 1997 poll showed that less than one American in five believes that genes play a major role in controlling behavior, there is some concern that eugenics will make a comeback (Herbert, 1997).

The emerging view in the nature versus nurture debate is that many complicated behaviors probably have some measure of genetic loading that gives some people susceptibility, but the development of the behavior requires what National Institute of Mental Health Director Stephen Hyman calls an "environmental second hit." This second hit operates through the genes themselves to create chemical changes in the brain. Nature or nurture? Psychologist William Greenough says, "To ask what's more important . . . is like asking what's more important to a rectangle, its length or its width" (quoted in Herbert, 1997, USNews.com).

GAY AND LESBIAN RIGHTS

There have always been homosexual voters and homosexual politicians, but it is only within the past few decades that gays and lesbians have been recognized as a political force and homosexual rights have become part of the political agenda. Gays and lesbians are not a cohesive, unified political entity any more than are African Americans, Hispanics, labor unions, women, or southerners. There is a wide range of political views among homosexuals concerning issues related to sexual orientation as well as broader economic and social policy. Like the population at large, some gays and lesbians are apolitical, some favor dramatic confrontational political action (see Chapter 11), and others prefer to work within the existing political structure to accomplish their goals.

In Colonial America, homosexuality was considered a serious crime. Homosexuals could be condemned to death by drowning or burning. In the late 1770s, Thomas Jefferson was among the political leaders who suggested that the punishment for homosexuality be reduced from death to castration, a liberal view for his time (Katz, 1976). While many groups have organized to change laws regarding sexuality, homosexuals have had a particularly difficult challenge. The laws that prohibit gays and lesbians from expressing their sexuality have a long-standing basis in Western tradition. Not only are the physical expressions of homosexuality illegal in many states, but homosexual discrimination, unlike discrimination against other subgroups of the population, is entirely legal.

Eugenics: the study of hereditary improvement of the human race by controlled, selective breeding

FAQ:

When did the gay and lesbian rights movement originate?

Many people date the modern gay and lesbian liberation movement to the June 1969 riot that followed a routine police raid at the Stonewall Inn, a gay bar in New York City's Greenwich Village. This event sparked the gay and lesbian rights movement and the formation of many gay and lesbian rights groups throughout the United States (Marcus, 1992). Beginning in the 1970s, these groups sought to extend civil rights statutes to prohibit discrimination on the basis of sexual orientation. National attention was focused on these concerns in 1977 when legislators in Dade County, Florida, passed legislation ensuring civil rights for homosexuals. Anita Bryant, a singer and spokesperson for the Florida orange juice industry, and former Miss Oklahoma, formed the Save Our Children organization to combat what she viewed to be an endorsement of the homosexual lifestyle. The powerful political organization the Moral Majority soon joined Bryant's campaign to repeal the Dade County ordinance. Bryant's claims that homosexuals "can only recruit children, and this is what they want to do" combined with evangelist Jerry Falwell's allegations that "so-called gay folks just as soon kill you as look at you" helped to defeat gay rights ordinances across the country (quoted in D'Emilio & Freedman, 1988, p. 347).

TABLE 18.1

Do You Think Homosexuals Should or Should Not Be Hired for Each of the Following Occupations?			
	Percent Responding "Should"	Percent Responding "Should Not"	Percent No Opinion/ Missing Data
Salesperson	91	6	3
Doctor	78	18	4
Member of the president's cabinet	75	21	4
Member of the armed forces	72	23	5
High-school teacher	63	33	4
Elementary-school teacher	56	40	4
Clergy	54	39	7

SOURCE: Gallup, 2001

Family and Relationship Rights

Marriage is a contract between a couple and the state. It is a powerful legal and social bond that protects and supports intimate family relationships by providing a unique set of rights, privileges, and benefits. In April 2000 Vermont became the first state legally to recognize relationships between gay and lesbian couples. Although the Vermont legislation does not provide for gay or lesbian marriages, it does enable same-sex couples to form "civil unions" and entitles them to all of the rights and benefits enjoyed by married couples under state law.

Other states have banned same-sex marriage to block residents from forming a civil union in Vermont and suing for home-state recognition and benefits. As of 2000, anti-same-sex marriage legislation was pending in Colorado, Massachusetts, Nebraska, Nevada, New Jersey, New York, Ohio, and Wisconsin; was adopted in California, South Dakota, and West Virginia; and was blocked in Missouri, New Hampshire, New Mexico, and Rhode Island. Pro-same-sex marriage legislation also was introduced in Hawaii, Maryland, Rhode Island, Vermont, and Wisconsin (Figure 18.2).

For many couples, being a family includes having and raising children. Some children of gays and lesbians were born to one of the partners in a previous relationship, others are born during the couple's relationship, and still others are adopted. Many states have moved to safeguard the interests of children with gay or lesbian parents. Twenty-one states have granted second-parent adoptions (in which both members of the couple are granted adoption) to lesbian and gay couples, ensuring that their children can have the benefits of having two legal parents. A majority of the states no longer deny custody or visitation rights to a person based on sexual orientation. However, despite the research that consistently concludes that the children of gay and lesbian parents grow up as successfully as the children of heterosexual parents (Bailey et al., 1995; Gottman, 1990; Patterson, 1992), a few states do continue to use a parent's sexual orientation to deny custody, adoption, visitation rights, and

For many couples, having and raising children is an important part of being a family.

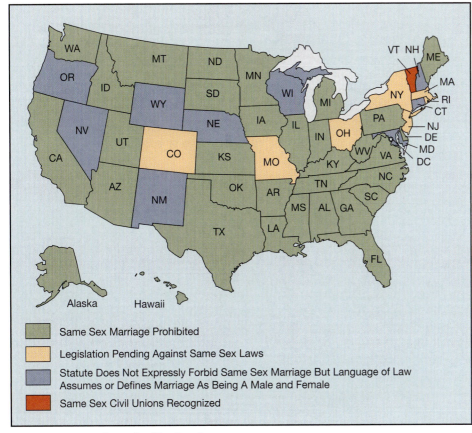

FIGURE 18.2 **Same-Sex Marriage Laws.** SOURCE: CNN Interactive, 2000.

Legend:
- Same Sex Marriage Prohibited
- Legislation Pending Against Same Sex Laws
- Statute Does Not Expressly Forbid Same Sex Marriage But Language of Law Assumes or Defines Marriage As Being A Male and Female
- Same Sex Civil Unions Recognized

foster care. Florida is the only remaining state that expressly bars lesbians and gays from adopting children. In contrast, Connecticut law allows gays and other unmarried people to adopt their partners' children.

Gays in the Military

Because the military is a highly visible, federally funded, traditionally male institution, it has always received a great deal of political attention. Homosexuals have served in the U.S. military, some openly, since Valley Forge (Shilts, 1993); yet since 1943 it has been the official policy of the U.S. military to exclude homosexuals from serving our country. The Defense Department contends that the purpose of excluding gays and lesbians from the military is to preserve the order, discipline, and morale of the military, because some heterosexual soldiers would not want to serve with and take orders from homosexuals (Shilts, 1993).

While gays and lesbians legally serve in the armed forces in many countries, including Italy, Japan, Sweden, Holland, Denmark, Norway, Germany, Israel, and Australia, the U.S. military has continued to support the view that allowing homosexuals in the armed services would be detrimental. In the 1980s the Defense Department spent an estimated $500 million to eject 17,000 gays and lesbians from the armed services (Easton, 1993). One argument of those opposed to allowing gays to serve in the military is that the close quarters of the military, from the barracks to the foxhole, would make heterosexual soldiers vulnerable to the advances of supposedly predatory homosexual soldiers. Heterosexual males have expressed concerns that the public showers and general lack of privacy in the military would mean that gays would look upon them as sex objects. Perhaps men accustomed to viewing their own sexual partners as objects assume that a gay man would do the same toward them (Angier, 1993b).

FAQ:

Do those who support gay and lesbian rights seek special treatment, or equal consideration?

Many of those opposed to homosexual rights care deeply about their families and communities and seek to ensure that their vision of a moral America prevails. Some believe that their efforts to bar civil rights legislation for homosexuals is not "antigay" but a stand against giving homosexuals "special" rights. They see the push for gay and lesbian rights as another instance of a minority group seeking special protections. Groups who believe that homosexuality is a sin have pressured local and state governments to prevent granting "special rights to sodomites." Their view is that if homosexuals receive these rights then the door is open to pedophiles, polygamists, pornographers, and prostitutes asking for the same protection.

Others argue that gay and lesbian rights advocates do not want special treatment, just equal consideration under the law. Homosexuals are seeking the same rights that heterosexual Americans enjoy: to marry, adopt children, have insurance benefits, serve in the military, and have freedom from discrimination in housing and employment. As stated earlier, there is no single "gay agenda." However, gay activists have focused on two main areas: family and relationship issues, including marriage, adoption, and other parenting rights; and discrimination issues involving gays in the military, employment, and hate crimes legislation.

Two-Parent Families

In September 2001, a federal district court judge up-held a 1977 Florida law that bans adoptions by gays and lesbians. The judge's ruling stated that placing children in the homes of married couples is in the best interests of children. Yet in Florida a quarter of all the children adopted every year go to single hetero-sexual adults.

? **What do you think about gays and lesbians adopting children?**

—Do you think all adopted children should be placed in two-parent homes, or only if the parents are heterosexual?

—Is it in the best interests of a child to be in foster care or with gay or lesbian parents?

FAQ:

What benefits are same-sex partners entitled to receive?

Without the benefit of marriage or civil union, gays and lesbians have no right to many benefits that other couples take for granted. Same-sex couples have no right to spousal income tax deductions, public assistance, the disposition of property after the dissolution of marriage, spousal nonsupport, payment of workers' compensation benefits after a partner's death, health insurance, the ability to enter into family trusts, or spousal privilege when testifying in court, and the confidentiality of marital communication. Gay and les-bian partners do not have legal status with their part-ner's children, cannot make medical decisions or burial arrangements, and have no right to spousal support or to inherit property if a partner dies without leaving a will. Even passage of the civil union legislation in Vermont does not entitle same-sex couples to *federal* benefits available to married couples, such as tax benefits and Social Security.

Sexual Discrimination

In January 1991 the Cracker Barrel restaurant chain fired dozens of gays and lesbians and announced that it would no longer employ people who lack "normal heterosexual values"; and they did this *without violating any laws*. In 1992 Colorado voters adopted a ballot measure that prohibited local governments from enacting laws to protect gays and lesbians from job and housing discrimination. (In 1994, the Colorado Supreme Court ruled the ballot measure unconstitutional, but similar measures appeared in other states.) In 1998 the U.S. Supreme Court declined to hear the appeal of a lawyer who had a job offer with the Georgia Attorney General withdrawn after he learned that she had par-ticipated in a symbolic religious marriage ceremony with her female partner. In June 2000 the U.S. Supreme Court ruled that it is unconstitutional for the state to require a Boy Scout troop to admit a gay scoutmaster. A major goal of many gay and lesbian advocates is legislation to amend the 1964 Civil Rights Act to add "affectional or sex-ual orientation" to its ban of discrimination on the basis of race, creed, color, and sex. This amendment would make it illegal to discriminate on the basis of sexual orienta-tion in housing, public accommodations, insurance, or employment.

TABLE 18.2

Breakdown by Service of Those Who Said They Heard Offensive Antigay Comments at Least Once in the Past Year	
Marine Corps:	45%
Army:	37
Navy:	32
Air Force:	23

SOURCE: U.S. Department of Defense, 2000.

TABLE 18.3

Responses to the Question: "In General, Do You Think Homosexuals Should or Should Not Have Equal Rights in Terms of Job Opportunities?"		
	Have equal rights (%)	Not have equal rights (%)
June 1977	56	33
October 1989	71	18
November 1996	84	12
February 1999	83	13

SOURCE: Gallup, 2002.

Hate Crimes

He was pistol-whipped, tortured, then lashed to a fence and left to die. The death of University of Wyoming student Matthew Shepard in 1998 became a symbol of growing violence against gays and the need to include sexual orientation as part of hate crimes legislation. As we discussed in Chapter 11, hate crimes are acts designed to intimidate or harm that are motivated by bias. At present, criminal acts performed because of bias motivated by race, religious, and national origin are designated as hate crimes. Hate crimes include crimes against property (vandalism and arson) as well as crimes against persons (assault and murder). There are three key elements to hate crime laws: bias motivation, criminal conduct, and penalty enhancement with longer sentences.

As of 2001, 22 states and the District of Columbia punish hate crimes motivated by sexual orientation, and four states plus the District of Columbia included punishment for crimes based on gender identity as well as sexual orientation. The United States now grants political asylum for persecution based on sexual orientation. Some of those who have been granted asylum are a Russian lesbian who was repeatedly arrested, fired from jobs, and threatened with psychiatric hospitalization, an Iranian lesbian activist facing the death penalty, and a gay Brazilian who was raped at gunpoint by police.

Every day in the United States, three homosexuals become victims of a hate crime (Southern Poverty Law Center, 1999). In 1997, 14 percent of hate crimes reported to the Federal Bureau of Investigation (FBI) were motivated by bias against sexual orientation; 66 percent of these were specifically antimale homosexual bias and 17 percent specifically antifemale homosexual bias (FBI, 1998b). Although incidents of antigay violence decreased in 1998 and 1999, substantial increases occurred in several areas including Cleveland (up 64 percent), Colorado (up 107 percent), Orlando (up 100 percent) and Providence (up 40 percent) (FBI, 1998a, 1998b). In response to the seriousness of these crimes, President Clinton called on Congress to pass strong hate crimes legislation and the evangelist Jerry Falwell, often accused of gay-bashing, said that he never again would make statements that can be construed as sanctioning hate or antagonism against homosexuals.

THE POLITICS OF AIDS

Since the early years of the HIV/AIDS epidemic, researchers and activists have pointed out the political and governmental factors that play a role in AIDS prevention and treatment. Ethical considerations, constitutional issues, government bureaucracies, medical research, and economic resources each play a role in influencing policy responses to HIV/AIDS. In September 2000 the Institute of Medicine of the National Academy of Sciences, the nation's leading science organization, sharply criticized the Clinton administration for what it said was a failure to develop a comprehensive and effective plan to combat AIDS. At the same time, the Institute called for the abolition of federal, state, and local laws and policies that hinder proven prevention strategies.

Because the first recognized victims of AIDS in the United States were gay men, some of those already hostile to the gay community used this devastating illness as "a vehicle to whip up hysteria and move its political agenda forward" (D'Emilio & Freedman, 1988, p. 354). Some antigay groups proselytized that AIDS was God's punishment for the "sin" of homosexuality and that gays bring AIDS upon themselves with their "sinful" behavior, thus justifying discrimination of gays. AIDS even gave groups not considered antigay the excuse for open discrimination. Some insurance carriers sought to deny coverage to all gay men, considering them all members of a group at high risk for infection with HIV and the resulting expensive treatments (Marcus, 1992).

AIDS also galvanized gay and lesbian political involvement. Many formerly apolitical homosexuals were incensed at the policies of funding for AIDS research. Many people, both gay and straight, accused the government of moving too slowly and

---

FAQ:

What is the "don't ask, don't tell" policy?

In 1993 Congress passed the National Defense Authorization Act barring gays and lesbians from openly serving in the military. The "don't ask, don't tell, don't pursue" policy of the Clinton administration permitted gays and lesbians to serve in the military as long as they did not openly reveal their sexual orientation. However, the military discharged 67 percent more gay and lesbian troops after "don't ask, don't tell" than when the policy was first adopted. A total of 997 military personnel were discharged for homosexuality in 1997, compared with 597 in 1994 (U.S. Department of Defense Report, 1998). A 1997 U.S. District Court ruling struck down the ban as unconstitutional for violating the First and Fifth Amendments.

In 2000 the Pentagon acknowledged that its "don't ask, don't tell" policy wasn't working. A Pentagon report found that 85 percent of the servicemen and women surveyed believed that anti-gay comments were tolerated (Table 18.2). Thirty-seven percent had personally witnessed or been the target of harassment because of perceived homosexuality, and 9 percent had witnessed physical assaults of gays. Seventy-three percent said nothing was done to stop harassment witnessed by a senior officer. In response to the survey the Secretary of Defense expanded the description of the "don't ask, don't tell" policy to include "don't harass." A subsequent report released by the Servicemembers Legal Defense Network in 2001 said that anti-gay harassment in the military had not decreased.

"Individual risk of HIV/AIDS is influenced by cognitive, attitudinal and behavioral factors—what people know and how they understand it, what people feel about situations and about others and what people do. Societal vulnerability to HIV/AIDS stems from socio-cultural, economic and political factors that limit individuals' options to reduce their risk. "

(UNAIDS/WORLD HEALTH ORGANIZATION, 1999, P. 3)

expending too few resources to combat what was viewed as a "gay disease." In 1987, ACT UP, the AIDS Coalition To Unleash Power, organized to fight discrimination against people with HIV infection and to exert pressure on the government to deal vigorously with this worldwide health crisis. While the United States and Europe spend more than $3 billion a year on drugs to treat HIV infection, the whole world spends just $350 million a year on AIDS vaccine research. However, some believe that too much money is being spent on a disease that affects a relatively small portion of the population.

AIDS has changed how we think about sex, how we teach our children about sex, and how we have sex. As the incidence of AIDS has increased among heterosexuals, many sexual issues have been highlighted including adolescent sexual behavior, sexuality education, the presentation of sex in the media, contraceptive devices, and sexual fidelity. This has caused some groups to take a new look at these issues and modify their positions. Some conservatives, who generally have less permissive views about sexual issues, have recognized the need for disseminating accurate information about how AIDS spreads and about the preventative use of condoms. On the flip side, some liberals have rethought their views of sexual freedom to include a greater emphasis on personal responsibility.

An increasing number of countries now require an HIV test as part of a medical exam for long-term visitors (Figure 18.3, page 530). Because of these restrictions, it is recommended that travelers who are HIV-positive check with the embassy of the country to be visited to learn about the entry requirements and if United States test results are acceptable.

Between 1991 and 1996 over 300 cases involving HIV/AIDS were litigated in the courts. Many of these cases dealt with the confidentiality of a person's HIV status and mandatory HIV testing (see CONSIDERATIONS box). Several court cases have upheld state confidentiality statutes that prohibit disclosing a person's HIV status to anyone other than a health-care provider. However, a number of courts and state legislatures allow exceptions to strict confidentiality rules and permit disclosure of a person's HIV status to those who have a "need to know." Even when disclosure is permitted, it is not mandated. Generally, the responsibility for decisions regarding disclosure is left to the treating health-care provider and the patient.

Several hundred people have been charged with battery, assault, or attempted murder and criminally prosecuted for knowingly and deliberately infecting another person with HIV. For example, an Ohio man who knew that he was HIV-positive attempted to rape an 8-year-old boy; he was convicted of attempted murder as well as attempted rape. A Maryland man who knew he had full-blown AIDS was charged with first-degree assault and reckless endangerment after infecting several women, including an estranged partner, with HIV. In another case, an HIV-infected man accused of infecting more than a dozen young women in upstate New York pleaded guilty to rape and reckless endangerment for having unprotected sex with a 13-year-old girl who didn't know his HIV status. Sexual deception laws provide the basis for civil action if, either through failure to disclose or by engaging in outright deception, a person is not informed that a sex partner is HIV-positive.

The high cost of drugs to treat HIV has become an international political issue. The average HIV/AIDS patient spends $300 to $600 a month (per prescription) on medications, or $900 to $1,800 a month for the combination therapy that has proven beneficial to many of those living with HIV. This doesn't include the cost of doctor visits or outpatient therapies. Forty-six percent of those who are HIV-infected have incomes of less than $10,000 per year, 68 percent had public health insurance or no insurance. The estimated direct expenditures for the care of patients with HIV comes to about $20,000 per patient, per year (Bozzette et al., 1999). Even with the discounts offered by a number of pharmaceutical companies, the high costs of AIDS therapies are out of reach for most of those in developing countries. To add to the problem, ineffective medical infrastructures in developing countries make it difficult to deliver the treatments.

The Dilemma of Mandatory HIV Testing

If testing were mandatory, everyone would be aware of his or her HIV status and would not be able unknowingly to spread the virus. Those who tested positive for HIV would be able to receive treatment as quickly as possible, to keep themselves as healthy as possible for as long as possible.

Both the U.S. Centers for Disease Control (CDC) and the Public Health Service oppose compulsory testing. In their view, mandatory testing is an invasion of privacy, and people who initially test negative might have a false sense of security and engage in high-risk behaviors. As AIDS continues to spread, demands for mandatory testing and involuntary quarantining are likely to increase. Officials at the CDC are concerned that if these sanctions are enacted, infected people will be driven underground, be further denied insurance benefits, face even greater discrimination, and not receive needed treatment.

Those opposed to mandatory partner notification argue that even though the identity of the infected person is not revealed, it is usually easy for the notified person to figure out and therefore it is yet another violation of privacy. There is also concern that some people would be less likely to get tested and notify partners on their own if they knew their partners would be contacted by an agency.

Do you think that the right to privacy is outweighed by the rights of those who might be at risk for past, present, or future infection?

—*Would you want to be informed if your partner tested positive for HIV?*

REPRODUCTIVE RIGHTS

The question central to the issue of reproductive rights is "When does life begin?" There is no single answer to this question. A woman in ancient Assyria who attempted an abortion was impaled on a stake, and, if she died during an abortion, her corpse was given the same punishment (Tannahill, 1982). However, abortion early in pregnancy was legal in ancient China, Greece, and Rome. In the 13th century, Thomas Aquinas proposed that a male fetus does not acquire a human soul until 40 days after conception, while a female fetus does not acquire a soul until after 80 days (Rodman, Sarvis, & Bonar, 1987).

Early American law, based on English common law, permitted abortions performed in the early months of pregnancy since it was the accepted belief that life did not begin until a woman felt fetal movement (D'Emilio & Freedman, 1988). By the 1860s, the high mortality rate due to crude abortion methods and the belief that population growth was important to the nation contributed to the move to criminalize abortion in the United States (Sheeran, 1987). The Roman Catholic Church continues to support Pope Pius IX's declaration of 1869 that human life begins at conception; therefore, most forms of contraception are prohibited and abortion is considered immoral under any circumstances. In traditional Catholic thought, abortion is considered to be worse than infanticide because it condemns the fetus to purgatory, barring its access to heaven. Evangelical and fundamentalist Protestants and Orthodox Jewish traditions also hold that life begins at the moment of conception and disapprove of any abortion not required to save the mother's life (Posner, 1992).

Legislation outlawing abortion did not stop women desperate to terminate a pregnancy from finding ways to do so. Women who could afford it traveled to countries where abortion was legal; others were able to find licensed physicians willing to perform abortions. Most, however, were forced to choose between illegal abortions, often in unsafe and unsanitary conditions, or attempting to abort the fetus themselves (Stubblefield & Grimes, 1994). Estimates of the annual number of illegal abortions in the 1950s and 1960s in the United States range from 200,000 to 1.2 million (Tietze & Henshaw, 1986). In 1969, complications from illegal abortions accounted for 23 percent of all pregnancy-related municipal hospital admissions in New York City (Institute of Medicine, 1975). In 1965, 17 percent of all deaths due to pregnancy and childbirth were the result of illegal abortion.

As we discussed in the beginning of the chapter, the 1873 Comstock Laws outlawed the importation and circulation of pornography, and the law was used to justify the

FAQ:

If someone is diagnosed with AIDS, is his or her partner notified?

Partner notification, also called contact tracing, is standard practice with cases of gonorrhea and syphilis infection. An infected person is asked to identify any sexual partners, and without revealing the patient's name, those partners are notified that they may be infected and should be tested. Currently, there is no mandatory partner notification for HIV. More than half the states require that the names of HIV-infected people be reported to confidential registries. However, New York and California, the two states with the most cases, do not have this requirement. It is not required that any previous partners, or even the person's spouse, be notified.

COUNTRY	TEST REQUIRED FOR	COUNTRY	TEST REQUIRED FOR
Aruba	Intending immigrants	Jordan	Anyone staying more than 3 months
Australia	All applicants for permanent residence over age 15	Korea	Foreigners working as entertainers staying over 90 days
Belize	All persons applying for residency permits	Kuwait	Those seeking to obtain a residency permit
Brunei	All persons applying for work permits	Lebanon	Those seeking residency or work
Bulgaria	All intending immigrants (and may be required for foreigners staying longer than one month for purposes of study or work)	Lithuania	Applicants for permanent residency permits
Canada	Any foreigners suspected of being HIV positive	Panama	Women intending to work in prostitution and anyone who adjusts visa status once in Panama
China	Foreigners applying for residence permits	Papua New Guinea	Applicants seeking work or residency visas and their dependents
Colombia	Anyone suspected of being HIV positive	Paraguay	Applicants seeking temporary or permanent residency status
Cuba	Anyone staying over 90 days excluding diplomats	Russia	All foreign visitors staying longer than 3 months
Cyprus	All foreigners working or studying after entry	Saudi Arabia	Applicants for residency or work permits
Dominican Republic	Foreigners seeking residence	Singapore	Workers who earn less than $1250 per month and applicants for permanent resident status
Egypt	Foreigners applying for study, training, or work permits	South Africa	All mine workers
El Salvador	All applicants for multiple-entry tourist visas, temporary and permanent residency between the ages of 12 and 86	Spain	Anyone seeking residence, work, and student permits
Hungary	Anyone staying over 1 year and all intending immigrants	Syria	All foreigners ages 15 to 60 staying more than 15 days
India	All students over 18, anyone between the ages of 18 and 70 with a visa valid for 1 year or more, and anyone extending a stay to a year or more	Taiwan	Applicants for residency and work permits or staying more than 90 days
		Ukraine	Anyone staying longer than 3 months
Iraq	All foreigners (except diplomats, Muslim pilgrims, children under 14 who do not have hemophilia, men over 60 and women over 50) will be tested upon entry unless they have a current medical certificate confirming they are not HIV positive	United Kingdom	Anyone who does not appear to be in good health may be required to undergo a medial exam, including an HIV test

FIGURE 18.3 **HIV Testing Requirements for Foreign Travel.** SOURCE: Lambda Legal Defense and Education Fund, 1997.

Roe v. Wade: 1973 Supreme Court case that legalized abortion during the first trimester of pregnancy

confiscation of any contraceptive information or devices sent through the mail. Margaret Sanger (1883–1966) challenged the Comstock Act and was a leader in the struggle for free access to birth control. Sanger believed that birth control was fundamental to securing freedom and independence for working women and that it fulfilled a critical psychological need by enabling women to enjoy sex fully, free from the fear of pregnancy.

Shocked by the inability of women to obtain effective birth control, Sanger published *The Woman Rebel*, a newspaper advocating birth control. When indicted for sending "obscene" materials through the mail in 1914, Sanger fled to Europe. Sanger returned to New York in 1916 and opened a clinic in Brooklyn. She was arrested and served 30 days in jail for distributing information about contraceptives. In 1929 Sanger formed the National Committee on Federal Legislation for Birth Control to lobby for birth control legislation that granted physicians the right to legally disseminate contraceptives. Although her efforts to secure government support for birth control failed, in 1936 the U.S. Court of Appeals ruled that physicians were exempt from the Comstock Law's ban on the importation of birth control materials. Although the ban on importing contraceptive devices for personal use was not lifted until 1971, this decision in effect gave doctors the right to prescribe or distribute contraceptives. The introduction of the birth control pill in 1964 was one factor credited with improving the status of women in the United States (the other was the introduction of women into the workforce during World War II).

Some scientists mark the beginning of life at about the 30th week of pregnancy, when the fetus develops the brain wave activity needed to produce thought (Sagan & Druyan, 1992). Many individuals believe that abortion is a medical procedure and that the individual woman, not the government, should be allowed to make decisions that affect her life. Pro-choice advocates, who believe that women should have the right to decide whether to have an abortion and generally oppose legislative restrictions on the availability of abortions, propose that a woman's ability to control her fertility has implications not only for herself and her family, but globally as well. It can be argued that since each of us depletes the earth's available resources, there is a decreasing supply of fuel, clean air, water, and food that must be balanced against the needs of an increasing population. Increased population carries high financial and social costs, and abortion is seen as a social necessity to control population, since birth control methods are imperfect. Advocates of the antiabortion position, sometimes referred to as the **pro-life** position, believe that life begins with conception and therefore abortion is tantamount to murder.

In 1973 the U.S. Supreme Court held in ***Roe v. Wade*** that during the first trimester of pregnancy, the decision to have an abortion might be made free of state interference except for a requirement that a licensed physician perform the abortion. After the first trimester, the Court ruled, the state has a compelling interest in protecting the woman's health and may regulate abortion to promote that interest. At the point of fetal viability (capacity for sustained survival outside the uterus), the Court held that the state has a compelling interest in protecting potential life and may ban abortion except when necessary to preserve the woman's life or health. This carefully crafted decision brought the state's interest and the woman's right to choose into careful balance. *Roe v. Wade* does not provide for abortion on demand. A woman has the right to choose abortion until fetal viability, but the state's interest outweighs the woman's right after that point. After viability, states may ban any abortions as they see fit, as long as exceptions are made to protect the life and health of the woman. Forty-one states and the District of Columbia have laws that specifically address abortion after viability; and in 1977 the Hyde Amendment was passed, prohibiting federal Medicaid funds for abortions. In 1993 the Hyde Amendment was modified to require states to fund abortions for rape and incest victims, although some states refused to comply with this ruling. (See Table 18.4 for a summary of major U.S. Supreme Court rulings on reproductive health.)

Judicial bypass proceedings can pose an obstacle for young women who find the legal process intimidating, cannot attend hearings scheduled during school hours, or fear that the proceedings are not confidential. Furthermore, many young women do not want to reveal intimate details of their lives to strangers. Some young women may have a good relationship with their parents but want to avoid doing anything that might disappoint or hurt their parents, and therefore may not want to seek judicial permission. One such case involved 17-year-old Becky Bell of Indiana, a state that requires minors to get permission from a parent or judge before obtaining an abortion. Not wanting to hurt her parents, in September 1988, Becky obtained an

FAQ:

If a minor wants an abortion, must her parents be notified?

Forty-two states mandate the involvement of at least one parent in the abortion decision of a minor (Figure 18.4). Recognizing that some minors cannot or will not speak with their parents about their pregnancy (for example, if the pregnancy is the result of incest, or because of fears it would trigger parental violence), the U.S. Supreme Court has stated that in order to be constitutional, a state statute requiring parental involvement must offer an alternative such as a judicial bypass, petitioning a judge for permission to obtain an abortion. Three criteria for a judicial bypass procedure are stipulated: the statute must allow the minor to show that she is mature enough to make her own decision regarding abortion or that the abortion is in her best interests; the bypass procedure must ensure the minor's anonymity and confidentiality; and the bypass procedure must be conducted expeditiously.

Margaret Sanger, a pioneer in the fight for women to have access to birth control.

TABLE 18.4

Timeline of Major U.S. Supreme Court Rulings on Reproductive Health, 1973–2000

Year	Case	Nature of Case	Holding
1973	*Roe v. Wade*	Challenge to a Texas law prohibiting abortions except to save the woman's life.	The law is ruled to be unconstitutional. The right to privacy extends to a woman, in consultation with her physician, to terminate her pregnancy.
1976	*Planned Parenthood of Central Missouri v. Danforth*	Challenge to a Missouri law requiring parental consent to a minor's abortion; a husband's consent to a married woman's abortion; the woman's written informed consent; that no second trimester abortion be done by saline amniocentesis; and that abortion providers do certain record keeping and reporting.	Parental and spousal consent requirements are held unconstitutional because they delegate to third parties an absolute veto power over a woman's abortion decision. The requirement that the woman certify that her consent is informed and freely given is constitutional as are the record keeping and reporting requirements. The ban on saline amniocentesis is struck down; the choice of methods must be left to the physician.
1979	*Bellotti v. Baird*	Challenge to a Massachusetts law that a minor first attempt to obtain parental consent for an abortion before approaching a court for permission for her abortion; that parents be notified when a minor files a petition for judicial waiver; and that the judge hearing the minor's petition may deny the petition if the judge finds that an abortion would be against the minor's best interests.	The law is ruled unconstitutional. All minors must have an opportunity to approach a judge without first consulting their parents and the proceeding must be confidential. A mature minor must be given permission for an abortion, regardless of the judge's view as to her best interests.
1980	*Harris v. McRae*	Challenge to the Hyde Amendment, banning federal Medicaid funds for abortion, except those necessary to save the woman's life.	The Hyde Amendment is ruled constitutional. The government has no obligation to provide funds for the exercise of the right to choose abortion even if it pays for the cost of childbirth.
1983	*City of Akron v. Akron Center for Reproductive Rights*	Challenge to an Akron, Ohio, ordinance requiring that a woman wait 24 hours between consenting to and receiving an abortion; all abortions after the first trimester be performed in full-service hospitals; minors under 15 have parental or judicial consent for an abortion; the attending physician personally gives the woman information relevant to informed consent; specific information be given to a woman prior to an abortion including details of fetal anatomy, a list of risks and consequences of procedure, and a statement "that the child is a human life from the moment of conception"; and fetal remains be "humanely" disposed of.	All challenged portions of the ordinance are ruled unconstitutional.
1983	*Planned Parenthood of Kansas City v. Ashcroft*	Challenge to a Missouri law requiring that all post-first-trimester abortions be performed in hospitals; minors under 18 have parental consent or judicial authorization for their abortions; two doctors be present at the abortions of a viable fetus; and a pathologist's report be obtained for every abortion.	The hospitalization requirement is ruled unconstitutional. The parental consent requirement is upheld; the presence of two doctors at late-term abortions is constitutional as it serves the state's compelling interest in protecting potential life after viability; the requirement of a pathologist report is constitutional because it poses only a small financial burden to the woman and protects her health.
1986	*Thornburgh v. American College of Obstetricians and*	Challenge to Pennsylvania's 1982 Abortion Control Act requiring that a woman be given specific information before she has an abortion including state-produced printed materials describing the fetus; that physicians	The informed consent provision is ruled invalid because it interferes with the physician's discretion and requires a woman be given information designed to dissuade her from having an abortion; the provision restricting

TABLE 18.4 con't

Timeline of Major U.S. Supreme Court Rulings on Reproductive Health, 1973–2000, con't

Year	Case	Nature of Case	Holding
(cont'd)	*Gynecologists, Pennsylvania Section*	performing post-viability abortions use the method most likely to result in fetal survival unless it would cause significantly greater risk to a woman's life or health; the presence of a second physician at post-viability abortions; detailed reports to the state by providers on each abortion; and one parent's consent or a court order for minor's abortions.	post-viability abortion methods is ruled invalid because it requires the woman to bear an increased risk to her health; the second physician requirement is struck down because it does not make an exception for emergencies; the reporting requirement is ruled unconstitutional because it could lead to disclosure of the woman's identity; and the parental consent issue is remanded to the lower court for consideration.
1989	*Webster v. Reproductive Health Services*	Challenge to Missouri's 1986 act declaring that life begins at conception; forbidding the use of public funds for the purpose of counseling a woman to have an abortion not necessary to save her life; forbidding the use of public facilities for abortions not necessary to save a woman's life; and requiring physicians to perform tests to determine viability of fetuses after 20 weeks gestational age.	The Court allowed the declaration of when life begins to go into effect because five justices agreed that there was insufficient evidence that it would be used to restrict protected activities. In addition, the Court upheld restrictions barring public employees from performing or assisting in abortions not necessary to save the pregnant woman's life; public buildings cannot be used for performing abortions; and doctors must perform tests to determine whether the fetus is viable if they believe the woman may be at least 20 weeks pregnant.
1990	*Hodgson v. Minnesota*	Challenge to a 1981 Minnesota statute that required notification of both biological parents, followed by a wait of at least 48 hours, prior to a minor's abortion. A second section provided for a judicial bypass if the two-parent notification provision were judicially enjoined without a waiver procedure.	The Court held that two-parent notification with no judicial bypass alternative poses an unconstitutional burden on a minor's right to abortion. The Court allowed the second section of the law to stand, because of the addition of a judicial alternative. In addition, the Court upheld the validity of the 48-hour waiting period.
1991	*Sullivan v. Rust*	Challenge to 1988 regulations that forbid providing information about abortion in federally funded family planning clinics.	The Court upheld legislation barring federally funded clinics from discussing the option of abortion with patients.
1992	*Planned Parenthood v. Southeastern Pennsylvania v. Casey*	Challenge to Pennsylvania's 1989 Abortion Control Act, which required that except in narrowly defined medical emergencies a woman wait 24 hours between consenting to and receiving an abortion; the woman be given state-mandated information about abortion and offered state-authorized materials on fetal development; a married woman inform her husband of her intent to have an abortion; and minors' abortions be conditioned upon the consent provided in person at the clinic of one parent or guardian or upon a judicial waiver.	The Court upheld that all restrictions, except for the husband notification requirement, are constitutional. In upholding the Pennsylvania abortion restrictions, the Court overturned portions of two of its previous rulings: *City of Akron v. Akron Center for Reproductive Rights* (1983) and *Thornburgh v. American College of Obstetricians and Gynecologists* (1986).
1994	*Madsen v. Women's Health Center*	Appeal by three antiabortion protesters of a Florida Supreme Court ruling that upheld an injunction establishing a "buffer zone" around an abortion clinic to protect access to the facility.	The Court upheld the 36-foot buffer zone does not infringe on the First Amendment rights of abortion opponents.
1997	*Shenck v. Pro-Choice Network of Western New York*	Challenge on First Amendment ground to injunction aimed at protecting access to reproductive health-care clinics.	The government interests in ensuring public safety and protecting a woman's freedom to seek pregnancy-related services justify properly tailored injunctions to secure unimpeded physical access to clinics.

TABLE 18.4 con't

Timeline of Major U.S. Supreme Court Rulings on Reproductive Health, 1973–2000, con't

Year	Case	Nature of Case	Holding
2000	*Stenberg v. Carhart*	Challenge of a Nebraska ban on late-term or so-called "partial birth abortions"	Court affirmed that restrictions against abortion in the first half of pregnancy violate *Roe v. Wade* and other precedents by failing to include an exception to preserve the health of women and by imposing an undue burden on women's ability to choose an abortion. Moreover, the Court found the state ban so broad and vague that it potentially criminalized all abortions.
2000	*Hill v. Colorado*	Challenge of buffer zones around those entering or leaving clinics that perform abortions	The Court found it unlawful to knowingly approach within 8 feet of another person without that person's consent for the purpose of passing a leaflet or handbill to, displaying a sign to, or engaging in oral protest, education, or counseling with that person.

SOURCE: Adapted from NARAL, 2001.

FAQ:

What abortion rights do fathers have?

Although men are held to share legal and financial responsibility for a pregnancy, men do not legally have any say in pregnancy termination. If the father wants the baby and the mother wants to abort, her wishes have legal precedence over his, and she can have the abortion regardless of what he says. Conversely, if the father wants to abort and the mother wants to have the baby, her wishes take precedence again.

illegal abortion; a week later she died of a massive infection. In other instances pro-life judges have routinely denied minors' petitions for abortions. For example, a judge in Toledo, Ohio denied permission to a 17-year-old woman who was an A- student who planned on attending college and testified that she was not financially or emotionally prepared to be a mother. In 1999 a Massachusetts judge told a minor seeking judicial permission for an abortion "to keep her legs crossed and tell her boyfriend to keep his pants on" (Center for Reproductive Law and Policy, 1999). In addition, by-pass procedures and appeals can delay abortions, increasing the risk of any subsequent abortion procedure.

The George W. Bush Administration is expected to seek legislation to further restrict access to abortion. Bush administration Secretary of Health and Human Services Tommy Thompson announced at his confirmation hearings that he would call for a review of the FDA's approval of RU-486, and antiabortion Attorney General John Ashcroft will play a key role in judicial appointments to lower federal courts, which have an enormous impact on abortion rulings. The Unborn Victims of Violence Act, passed by the House of Representatives in April 2001, makes it a federal crime to injure or kill the fetus of a pregnant woman. Although the act specifically exempts abortion, the act is viewed by some as a crucial first step in a campaign by abortion opponents to secure the status of "personhood" for the fetus.

There are personal as well as social implications of abortion. A study of children born before Sweden modified its abortion law in 1975 found that children born after their mother was denied permission for an abortion had a higher than average incidence of alcoholism, were more likely to have a criminal record, and were generally less well adjusted (Adams & Winston, 1980). A study comparing African American teenagers who had an abortion with those who carried their babies to term found that 2 years later those who opted for abortion were more likely to have graduated high school, were better off financially, and less likely to have had a subsequent pregnancy (Zabin, Hirsch, & Emerson, 1989). Women who have abortions typically experience some anxiety or depression, but these feelings decrease over time and most women are relieved once the abortion is over (Rodman, Sarvis, & Bonar, 1987). C. Everett Koop, the U.S. Surgeon General in the Reagan administration, personally opposed abortion. Nevertheless, he concluded that studies failed to show that women who had abortions suffered serious psychological aftereffects (Koop, 1987). The American Psychological Association organized a panel to review studies on the psychological responses of

	One Parent	Two Parents	Consent	Notice	Judicial Bypass
Alabama	✓		✓		✓
Alaska	✓		✓		✓
Arizona	✓		✓		✓
Arkansas		✓		✓	✓
California	✓		✓		✓
Colorado	✓			✓	
Connecticut					
Delaware	✓			✓	✓
District of Columbia					
Florida	✓			✓	✓
Georgia	✓			✓	✓
Hawaii					
Idaho	✓		✓		✓
Illinois	✓			✓	✓
Indiana	✓		✓		✓
Iowa	✓			✓	✓
Kansas	✓			✓	✓
Kentucky	✓		✓		✓
Louisiana	✓		✓		✓
Maine	✓		✓		✓
Maryland	✓			✓	
Massachusetts	✓		✓		✓
Michigan	✓		✓		✓
Minnesota		✓		✓	✓
Mississippi		✓	✓		✓
Missouri	✓		✓		✓
Montana	✓			✓	✓
Nebraska	✓			✓	✓
Nevada	✓			✓	✓
New Hampshire					
New Jersey	✓			✓	✓
New Mexico	✓		✓		
New York					
North Carolina	✓		✓		✓
North Dakota		✓	✓		✓
Ohio	✓			✓	✓
Oklahoma					
Oregon					
Pennsylvania	✓		✓		✓
Rhode Island	✓		✓		✓
South Carolina	✓		✓		✓
South Dakota	✓			✓	✓
Tennessee	✓		✓		✓
Texas	✓			✓	
Utah		✓		✓	✓
Vermont					
Virginia	✓			✓	✓
Washington					
West Virginia	✓			✓	✓
Wisconsin	✓		✓		✓
Wyoming	✓		✓		✓

FIGURE 18.4 Restrictions on Minors' Access to Abortion. SOURCE: NARAL, 2000.

women having legal abortions and found that legal abortion of an unwanted pregnancy in the first trimester does not pose a psychological hazard for most women (Adler et al., 1990). There have been few studies of men's emotional reactions to their partners' abortions. One study of 1,000 men who accompanied partners undergoing abortions at clinics suggests that men may experience feelings of anxiety, hurt, guilt, and anger (Shostak, McLouth, & Seng, 1984).

Universal Life

Cross-cultural evidence reveals no universal consensus about "who or what constitutes a person, for personhood is evaluated and bestowed on the basis of moral criteria which vary tremendously among and within different sociocultural contexts" (Morgan, 1994, p. 30). While Western societies do not recognize biological and social birth as separate events, in other cultures a fetus is not recognized as "human" until biological birth, and newborns may not be labeled as "persons" until social birth rites are performed, often several days or months after biological birth.

Among the Arunta of Central Australia, a premature birth is not considered to be an undeveloped human being. "[I]t is nothing like a Kuruna (spirit) or a tappa (newborn); they are perfectly convinced that it is the young of some other animal, such as a kangaroo, which

has by mistake got inside the woman" (Montagu, 1974, p. 31). On the island of Truk (in the Pacific Caroline Islands) deformed infants were considered to be ghosts and were burned or thrown into the sea. The Trukese do not consider this infanticide; in their view a ghost is not a person and cannot be killed (Gladwin & Sarason, 1953).

Chinese population control policies dictating that couples only be allowed one child have led to an increased number of abortions. It has been reported that China will begin using abortions to "avoid new births of inferior quality and heighten standards of the whole population." Pregnant women diagnosed with certain infectious diseases or abnormal fetuses "will be advised to halt the pregnancy," thus preventing the birth of some 10 million Chinese with possible birth defects.

Impassioned debate regarding abortion continues in the United States today, but American attitudes about abortion are hard to survey using tools as crude as the average opinion poll. That's because polls typically don't offer enough choices to express people's complex feelings about this emotional and much-discussed subject. For example, a *Los Angeles Times* poll in June 2000 found more than half of those surveyed agreeing with the statement that abortion is murder. Yet two out of three also agreed that the decision to have an abortion should be up to a woman and her doctor (Rubin, 2000).

When the Supreme Court appeared on the verge of overturning the constitutional right to abortion in 1989, the political struggle on the issue was renewed. Abortion rights groups mobilized their supporters and were able to garner increased political support. Most politicians are compelled to take a stand on abortion. Every ruling by a potential Supreme Court nominee is closely scrutinized to determine what it may reveal about the nominee's position on abortion issues. Whether to include abortion as a part of a national health-care plan is another issue embroiled in controversy.

Antiabortion groups actively support candidates opposed to abortion, legislation making abortion illegal, and a constitutional amendment prohibiting abortion. The majority of those opposed to abortion use persuasion, information, and political pressure to influence legislators. Many mainstream antiabortion groups agree with Gail Quinn, the director of the National Conference of Catholic Bishops, who believes that violence is not part of the pro-life message. However, a few antiabortion groups protest in front of the homes of physicians known to perform

It is expected that the abortion issue will continue to be the subject of heated debate and protests for many years to come.

Who Has Abortions?

CONSIDERATIONS

Forty-nine percent of pregnancies among American women are unintended; half of these are terminated by abortion.

Each year an estimated 50 million abortions occur worldwide. Of these, 20 million procedures are obtained illegally.

In 1996, 1.37 million abortions took place in the United States, down from an estimated 1.61 million in 1990.

Each year, 2 out of every 100 women aged 15 to 44 have an abortion; 47 percent of them have had at least one previous abortion, and 55 percent have had a previous birth.

Fifty-two percent of U.S. women obtaining abortions are younger than 25.

Black women are more than three times as likely as white women to have an abortion; Hispanic women are roughly two times as likely as white women to end a pregnancy voluntarily.

Catholic women are 39 percent more likely than Protestants to have an abortion, but they are about as likely as all women nationally to do so.

Two-thirds of abortions are among never-married women.

About three fourths of those having an abortion say their reason for doing so is that a baby would interfere with work, school, or other responsibilities; about two thirds say they cannot afford a child; and half say they do not want to be a single parent or are having problems with their husband or partner.

About 14,000 women a year have an abortion because of rape or incest.

Eighty-eight percent of abortions occur in the first 12 weeks of pregnancy

Fifty-eight percent of women having abortions in 1995 had used a contraceptive method during the month they became pregnant.

 What preconceptions did you have about women who have abortions? Do these statistics change these preconceptions?

SOURCE: Alan Guttmacher Institute, 2000.

abortions, block abortion clinic entrances and harass patients and staff, or bomb and burn abortion clinics. A leading antiabortion group Operation Rescue takes down license plate numbers, obtains addresses from the Department of Transportation, and then mails out letters such as the following received by an Iowa woman in 1993, 6 days after suffering a miscarriage: "God's curses for the shedding of innocent blood include barrenness and disease, as well as economic and family hardships and even death." The woman had sought treatment from her gynecologist (who also performed abortions) to save her troubled pregnancy. The Iowa communications director of Operation Rescue offered no apology for their error.

Life Advocate, a publication of Advocates for Life Ministries, an Oregon-based militant antiabortion group, has published several articles defending the idea of killing doctors who perform abortions. His bishop censured the Rev. David Trosch, a Roman Catholic priest, after Trosch tried to place a newspaper advertisement that described the killing of abortion providers as justifiable homicide. Some have criticized the mainstream pro-life leadership, including the National Right to Life Committee, the nation's largest antiabortion organization, for not doing more to try to stop extremist violence (Figure 18.5).

In May 1994, a Houston jury awarded Planned Parenthood of Southeast Texas $1.01 million in punitive damages from abortion opponents, including Operation Rescue and Rescue America, who were found to have conspired illegally to close clinics by protests during the 1992 Republican National Convention. That same month President Clinton signed into law the Freedom of Access to Clinic Entrances Act, making it a federal crime to attack abortion clinics and to assault, threaten, or obstruct the people who use them. However, the violent actions of some antiabortionists have had an impact. The number of abortion providers declined 14 percent between 1992 and 1995 (Alan Guttmacher Institute, 2000). Fewer doctors are willing to perform abortions due to the harassment, hate mail, and death threats they receive. Although the Accreditation Council for Graduate Medical Education (ACGME, 1999) published a set of guidelines that recommends

1993:	An abortion opponent killed Dr. David Gunn, a physician who provided abortions in Pensacola, Florida.
1993:	Dr. George Tiller, an abortion provider, was shot in both arms outside an abortion clinic in Wichita, Kansas. The woman charged with the shooting has been arrested in cities across the country for trespassing and blockading clinic entrances.
1994:	Rev. Paul Hill, the well-known director of the anti choice group Defensive Action, murdered Dr. John Britton and his security escort, James Barrett outside a reproductive health clinic in Pensacola, Florida.
1994:	A gunman in Massachusetts shot and killed abortion clinic receptionists Shannon Lowney and Leanne Nichols and wounded seven others.
1994:	Dr. Gary Romalis was gravely wounded as he was eating breakfast in his home in Vancouver, British Columbia.
1996:	Outside a women's clinic in New Orleans, Dr. Calvin Jackson, an abortion provider, was stabbed so severely that he lost four pints of blood and one ear was almost severed. The assailant was apprehended a few hours later after illegally entering another clinic carrying a knife.
1998:	A homemade bomb exploded in a health care clinic in Birmingham, Alabama, killing a security guard and seriously injuring a nurse.
1998:	A known antiabortion activist shot and killed Dr. Barnett Slepian, an abstetrician-gynecologist who performed abortions, with a single bullet fired through his kitchen window in Amherst, New York.
1999:	A bomb exploded at an Asheville, North Carolina, abortion clinic a half hour before the clinic was scheduled to open.
2000:	Two bombs were discovered at Cincinnati Women's Services and Planned Parenthood of Southwestern Ohio and Northern Kentucky.

FIGURE 18-5 **The History of Abortion Violence.** SOURCE: Adapted from NARAL, 2000.

that all residents receive abortion training, only 12 percent of all medical school residency programs in the country offer routine training to physicians in performing first trimester abortions, and only 17 percent of county facilities in the United States perform abortions (MacKay & MacKay, 1995). Although a more recent study found 81 percent of medical school programs offer first-trimester abortion training (Almeling, Tews, & Dudley, 2000), the findings have been questioned because of two major handicaps: a low response rate and a lack of definition of routine versus elective training (Steinauer & Ryan, 2001).

Pro-choice advocates believe that the approval of RU-486, the so-called abortion pill (see Chapter 6), would make it nearly impossible for such harassment to continue since highly visible clinics could be replaced by the privacy of the doctor's office. However, Randall Terry, founder of Operation Rescue, has stated that "every chemical assassin" would be "hunted down and tried for genocide" (Geiman, 1995).

Some antiabortion groups are changing tactics and attempting to persuade, not blame, women considering an abortion to continue the pregnancy. An example is the book, *Making Abortion Rare: A Healing Strategy for a Divided Nation* (Reardon, 1996). The author, David Reardon, along with other advocates, is pushing for a "kinder, gentler" pro-life movement that places concern for protecting women on an equal level with concern for preventing abortions.

ASK YOURSELF

Abortion Questionnaire

Are you pro-choice, antiabortion, or somewhere in between? To find out, indicate your level of agreement or disagreement with each of the following items by entering the number that most closely represents your feelings.

1 = Strongly Agree   2 = Agree   3 = Mixed Feelings   4 = Disagree
5 = Strongly Disagree

_____ **1.** Abortion is a matter of personal choice.

_____ **2.** Abortion is a threat to our society.

_____ **3.** A woman should have control over what is happening to her own body by having the option to choose abortion.

_____ **4.** Only God can decide if a fetus should live.

_____ **5.** Even if there are some cases in which it is justified, abortion is still basically wrong.

_____ **6.** Abortion violates an unborn person's fundamental right to life.

_____ **7.** A woman should be able to exercise her rights to self-determination by choosing to have an abortion.

_____ **8.** Outlawing abortion could take away a woman's sense of self and personal autonomy.

_____ **9.** Outlawing abortion violates a woman's civil rights.

_____ **10.** Abortion is morally unacceptable and unjustified.

_____ **11.** The notion that an unborn fetus may be a human life is not a deciding issue in considering abortion.

_____ **12.** Abortion can be described as taking a life unjustly.

_____ **13.** A woman should have the right to decide to have an abortion based on her own life circumstances.

_____ **14.** If a woman feels that having a child might ruin her life, she should consider an abortion.

_____ **15.** Abortion could destroy the sanctity of motherhood.

_____ **16.** An unborn fetus is a viable human being with rights.

_____ **17.** If a woman feels she can't care for a baby, she should have an abortion.

_____ **18.** Abortion is destruction of one life for the convenience of another.

_____ **19.** Abortion is murder.

_____ **20.** Even if one believes that there are times when abortion is immoral, it is still basically the woman's own choice.

Scoring: First add your scores for items 1, 3, 7, 8, 9, 11, 13, 14, 17 and 20. This score represents your pro-choice point of view. Then add your scores for items 2, 4, 5, 6, 10, 12, 15, 16, 18, and 19. This score represents your support for an antiabortion (pro-life) point of view. Now subtract your pro-choice score from your pro-life score. A positive score indicates agreement with a pro-life philosophy, and a negative score indicates agreement with a pro-choice philosophy. Scores can range from -40 to +40. The closer your score is to 40 or -40, the more strongly you agree with the philosophy you endorsed.

SOURCE: Parsons, Richards, & Kanter, 1990.

REGULATING THE SEXUAL BEHAVIOR OF CONSENTING ADULTS

Have you ever committed a sex crime? Your immediate response probably is "No, of course not!" Here's another question: have you ever had premarital, oral, or anal sex? If your answer was yes, depending on which state you were in at the time, these activities are considered illegal and subject to prosecution.

While most adults might agree that rape and child sexual abuse should be illegal, general agreement about the status of other sexual behaviors is not easily achieved. We continue to struggle to balance laws that ensure the private rights of individuals with legislation to enforce social morality. Most people agree that behavior that harms or victimizes another person is rightly declared to be illegal. However, it has been more difficult to achieve consensus regarding the legality of sexual behavior between consenting adults.

We have many laws controlling the sexual behavior of consenting adults. These laws are often said to regulate "victimless" crimes, though defining "victim" can be difficult and not everyone agrees on what "victimless" means. Prostitution is one example of a victimless crime. However, as we saw in Chapter 14, some see prostitutes as victims of their pimps, their customers, and of society in general. In addition, many communities feel victimized when prostitutes bring drugs and other criminal activity into their neighborhoods.

WWW EXPLORING SEXUALITY ONLINE

Free (Cyber) Speech

A federal law enacted in 1996, the Communications Decency Act, intended to eliminate smut from cyberspace, made it a crime to send or display "indecent" material online in a way available to minors. In June 1997 the U.S. Supreme Court declared the Act to be unconstitutional. This decision marked the first time the court extended the principles of the First Amendment into cyberspace. The court's opinion held that communication via the Internet is entitled to the highest level of First Amendment free speech protection, similar to the protection given to books and newspapers.

In May 2001 the Court agreed to hear an appeal of another restrictive law, the Child Online Protection Act (COPA), which already has been struck down twice by lower courts. The idea behind COPA was that Web sites would have to use some kind of identifier, such as a credit card, to verify the age of the user. The problem is that information on the Web that may be interesting or important to adults also can be somewhat embarrassing and identifiers eliminate anonymity, which makes researching sensitive topics less appealing for some people.

Gender Differences in Sex Laws and Sex Law Enforcement

Laws against sex are mainly targeted at men, which may seem ironic in view of the fact that men have constituted the majority of legislators throughout history. The FBI classifies sex crimes into three categories (Federal Bureau of Investigation, 1998). The first involves rape and other forms of sexual coercion. Even though there is research that suggests many women coerce men into sex (Struckman-Johnson, 1988), women are hardly ever prosecuted for this; 99 percent of the arrests are of men. The second category involves commercial sex, especially prostitution, and in this category

60 percent of the arrests are of women and 40 percent of their clients or pimps. The third category involves all other sex crimes, from child pornography to exhibitionism; here 92 percent of the arrests are of men.

Male homosexuality has been persecuted much more thoroughly and systematically than female homosexuality. The medieval and early modern Christian authorities persecuted male homosexuals zealously but paid little or no attention to lesbianism (Tannahill, 1982). Even in the late 1800s, when the British Parliament passed laws against homosexuality, only male homosexuality was specified. This was probably not because the legislators supported lesbianism (rather, it is said that Queen Victoria insisted that a ban on lesbianism was unnecessary, because women would never do such things). Clearly, laws about sex are mainly made and enforced with the aim of restricting the behavior of men, although infidelity by wives has generally been punished more severely than infidelity committed by husbands.

Obsenity Laws

In most jurisdictions in the United States it is a crime to sell or present material that is obscene. The problem has been, is currently, and probably will continue to be what exactly is obscene and how that will be determined without violating the First Amendment's guarantee of freedom of expression. As we discussed earlier, the Comstock Laws of 1873 prohibited the mailing of obscene or lewd material in the United States; the Act left the definition of what was obscene to the U.S. Postal Service. In 1957 the Supreme Court attempted to clarify the issue by ruling that sexually related material and obscene material were not one and the same. Sexual material was ruled obscene, and therefore outside the protection of the First Amendment, only when presented in a lewd and lascivious manner as judged by the "average" person.

Fifty-five separate legal opinions in 13 obscenity cases between 1957 and 1968 attempted to define obscenity more explicitly. As a result, the phrase "utterly without redeeming social value" was added to the definition. Then in 1973 the court rejected its own "utterly without redeeming social value" criterion and came up with the definition of obscenity that is currently in effect: work that, taken as a whole, the average person applying contemporary community standards would find appealing to prurient interests; work that depicts or describes in a patently offensive way, sexual conduct specified by state law; and work that, taken as a whole, lacks serious literary, artistic, political, or scientific value (FindLaw, 2001).

Laws Against Fornication and Adultery

Until 1967, 25 states had laws against miscegenation, sex between married or unmarried persons of different races, when the Supreme Court overturned them in the case of *Loving v. Virginia*. However, it was not until November 2000 that Alabama voters removed a 1901 state law banning marriage between "a Negro and Caucasian," the last such state law in the nation. Many states continue to have **fornication laws** prohibiting sexual intercourse between unmarried adults, and **adultery laws** forbidding extramarital sex. Although these "Scarlet Letter" laws are rarely enforced, adultery is frequently considered legal grounds for divorce and can have severe legal consequences.

Several of the most publicized cases involving fornication and adultery laws have involved members of the U.S. military. Air Force Captain Jerry Coles spent 159 days in jail in 1995 before being court-martialed and sentenced to 5 months in prison for having an affair with the wife of another military man. In 1996 Colonel Karen Tew pled guilty to an affair with an enlisted man. Tew, who was married, was dismissed from the service a year shy of retirement and committed suicide 5 days later. In 1997 Air Force officer Kelly Flinn was prosecuted for significant breaches of official conduct after having an adulterous affair. And, in 1997 Air Force First Lieutenant Crista Davis was charged with conduct unbecoming an officer for allegedly sending sexually explicit letters to the wife of an Air Force Academy professor with whom she has a son.

"When your 10-year-old comes home singing 'Bitch I'm a kill you' . . . you don't care if you once adored Richard Pryor and William Burroughs."

(LACAYO, 2000)

Fornication laws: legislation prohibiting sexual intercourse between unmarried adults

Adultery laws: legislation forbidding extramarital sex

FAQ:

Is anal sex illegal in this state?

Until recently, nearly every state had laws prohibiting sodomy (Table 18.5). Four states (Kansas, Missouri, Oklahoma, and Texas) currently have laws against sodomy between people of the same sex. Twelve states (Alabama, Arizona, Florida, Idaho, Louisiana, Massachusetts, Michigan, Mississippi, North Carolina, South Carolina, Utah, and Virginia) prohibit sodomy between both same-sex and opposite-sex partners. Sentences for sodomy range from fines to jail terms of up to 20 years.

Technically, although there have been rules against adultery for more than 200 years, mere infidelity is not illegal in the military. But Article 134 of the Uniform Code of Military Justice prohibits adultery when it is prejudicial to "good order and discipline" or will "bring discredit upon the armed forces." The military also has fraternization rules prohibiting extracurricular association of officers with enlisted personnel. Complicating the matter is that adultery and fraternization issues are handled by the commander, who can issue an informal warning, fine, reprimand, demotion, or court-martial at his or her discretion.

Sodomy Laws

Sodomy laws were first initiated by religious institutions to prevent "crimes against nature" and were later enforced by English common laws in the sixteenth century. Originally intended to forbid anal intercourse, the definition of **sodomy** has broadened to include oral-genital sex. Sodomy laws are most frequently used to prosecute and persecute homosexuals. In 1986 the U.S. Supreme Court ruled in *Bowers v. Hardwick* that prosecuting a Georgia gay couple for engaging in consensual sex in their own bedroom did not violate the federal right to privacy. The decision was widely criticized, and in *Powell v. State* (1998) the state's highest court overturned the Georgia sodomy law.

SOME UNINTENDED EFFECTS OF LEGISLATION

Legislative bodies generally pass laws to solve specific problems; this does not guarantee that laws have the desired effects. Many have unintended consequences. Given that American governments have been passing laws for over two centuries, you might think that all the necessary laws may have already been created (and then some!), but each year many new laws are enacted. One reason is that a law passed to solve one problem may create another, necessitating a new law to address the new problem. And the new law . . . well, you get the picture!

Although the laws against adultery, fornication, and sodomy you just read about are infrequently enforced, the very fact that these laws continue to exist means that millions of Americans engage in criminal behavior every day. Many people are not even aware that these laws exist, and many of those who are ignore them. If all the current laws regulating sexual behavior were strictly enforced, the already overloaded courts and prison system would be doing nothing but dealing with sexual "criminals."

Even those laws that are largely ignored have an impact. For example, the existence of laws against sodomy can be used to strengthen the arguments of those who want to restrict the acceptance of homosexuals as equal members of society. In Florida and Texas, sodomy statutes have been used to deny employment to homosexual job applicants, as was done in Georgia before its statute was repealed in 1998. In North Carolina and Virginia, these laws have provided a basis for denying child custody and visitation rights to lesbian mothers or gay fathers. Having laws on the books that are not enforced also trivializes our legal system and encourages disrespect for the law.

For example, in the 1990s the Ohio legislature was disturbed by reports of babies born in prison, so a law was passed permitting early release of pregnant women from prison. This was intended to affect only a very few cases in which a woman found herself in prison and pregnant, but the effect of the law was to make pregnancy a virtual "Get out of jail free" pass. Many female convicts began looking for ways to get pregnant, such as by having sex with prison guards or lawyers. A furlough from prison to attend some family event such as a funeral or even just to return to court for legal proceedings (for example, a court appeal), loomed as a major opportunity to get pregnant; some women treated these trips as sexual marathons and did everything they could to become pregnant.

Divorce laws have likewise had effects beyond what was probably intended. Many people supported the liberalization of divorce laws in the 1960s and 1970s, and in

Sodomy Laws: legislation forbidding anal or oral copulation

TABLE 18.5

Status of U.S. Sodomy Laws

Alabama	Existing same-sex and opposite-sex laws
Alaska	Repealed 1980
Arkansas	Existing same-sex laws
Arizona	Existing same-sex and opposite-sex laws
California	Repealed 1976
Colorado	Repealed 1982
Connecticut	Repealed 1971
Delaware	Repealed 1971
District of Columbia	Repealed 1993
Florida	Existing same-sex and opposite-sex laws
Georgia	Invalidated by court 1998
Hawaii	Repealed 1973
Idaho	Existing same-sex and opposite-sex laws
Illinois	Repealed 1962
Indiana	Repealed 1977
Iowa	Repealed 1978
Kansas	Existing same-sex law
Kentucky	Invalidated by court 1992
Louisiana	Existing same-sex and opposite-sex laws
Maryland	Invalidated by court 1999
Maine	Repealed 1976
Massachusetts	Existing same-sex and opposite-sex laws
Michigan	Existing same-sex and opposite-sex laws
Minnesota	Invalidated by court 2001
Mississippi	Existing same-sex and opposite-sex laws
Missouri	Existing same-sex law
Montana	Invalidated by court 1997
Nebraska	Repealed 1978
Nevada	Repealed 1993
New Hampshire	Repealed 1975
New Jersey	Repealed 1979
New Mexico	Repealed 1975
New York	Invalidated by court 1980
North Carolina	Existing same-sex and opposite-sex laws
North Dakota	Repealed 1973
Ohio	Repealed 1974
Oklahoma	Existing same-sex law
Oregon	Repealed 1972
Pennsylvania	Invalidated by court 1980
Rhode Island	Repealed 1998
South Carolina	Existing same-sex and opposite-sex laws
South Dakota	Repealed 1977
Tennessee	Invalidated by court 1996
Texas	Existing same-sex law
Utah	Existing same-sex and opposite-sex laws
Vermont	Repealed 1977
Virginia	Existing same-sex and opposite-sex laws
Washington	Repealed 1976
West Virginia	Repealed 1976
Wisconsin	Repealed 1983
Wyoming	Repealed 1977

SOURCE: Adapted from NARAL, 2001.

particular the feminist movement championed them as a way to enable women to escape bad marriages and abusive husbands. However, these liberal laws have made it relatively easy for many people to discard their mates without the need to establish abuse or any other substantial reason.

NAMBLA

NAMBLA, the North American Man/Boy Love Association is a self-proclaimed civil rights organization opposed to age of consent laws. Members of NAMBLA claim that children need to be liberated from a "sexaphobic" society and that adults should be permitted to have sexual relations with children. Founded in 1978, NAMBLA claims a membership of around 1,500. It has a national hot line and a monthly newsletter illustrated with photographs of pubescent boys. Peter Melzer, a teacher at the Bronx High School of Science, was suspended from his job when it became known that he was a NAMBLA member, although Mr. Melzer said he had never broken any law.

 Do you think that NAMBLA'S goal is a reasonable one? Why or why not?

—Do you think the teacher should have been suspended from his job?

Many states have passed laws to protect women from male desertion; these laws have also been abused. If a man abandons his wife, she gains the right to refuse him re-entry, even to retrieve his personal possessions. There have been cases in which a man has left his home, and his wife or girlfriend has used this law to confiscate it and prevent him from returning (see CONSIDERATIONS box).

As you have already learned, laws regarding sexuality vary from state to state. Entering into a sexual relationship with someone creates immense legal vulnerabilities for both men and women. Even when the laws themselves are written to be fair, they are hardly perfectly suited for every case. Moreover, the way in which juries and judges apply them can make a huge difference. In principle, a woman has a right to go to a man's apartment and engage in necking and petting but refuse to have sex, so if the man forces her to have intercourse it is rape. However, a persuasive defense attorney who asserts that she really did want to have sex and had regrets afterward may sway a jury. (A man, of course, would find it even harder to persuade a jury that a woman raped him in the aftermath of consensual petting.) Along with the joy and pleasure that sex can provide comes the responsibility to be aware of your rights as well as the laws of your community and how they are enforced.

When Dave Met Cheryl

Dave and Cheryl met at a party where they were drinking. They had sex that night, and Cheryl became pregnant. Dave did not consider her an ideal partner but he tried to make the best of things by moving in with Cheryl and helping to raise their son. Their life together was not very happy, and they had many arguments. Cheryl also began having an affair with her drug dealer. One day, after an argument with Dave, Cheryl asked him nicely if he would leave her alone for a couple days so she could have some time for herself. He accommodated her and spent a couple nights at his mother's apartment. When he returned, Cheryl's new boyfriend had moved in, and they refused to allow Dave to enter, even to get his clothes and personal possessions. By law, he had no right to enter the home until a court settlement determined what his possessions were, and by the time the court had done so, many of his things had become lost or damaged. In the end Dave was able to persuade Cheryl to give him custody of the boy.

 Does the law seem fair in this case? Why or why not?

CHAPTER 18

■ R E V I E W

The earliest known laws regulating sexuality date from the time of ancient **1**_____ about 1100 B.C. Today issues concerning sexuality can be found in many political arenas, including gay and lesbian rights, reproductive rights, and local, state, and federal laws and policies.

From colonial times to the Victorian era to today, society's changing views concerning sexual issues have been reflected in legislation.

In 1873, the U.S. Congress passed the **2**_____ Law that outlawed the importation and circulation of contraceptive information and devices through the mail. This law was used to restrict the use of contraceptives until the 1930s when a panel of federal judges ruled that his prohibition did not apply to contraceptives used by physicians in their medical practice.

The **3**_____ Act, passed in 1910, forbids the transportation of women for purposes of forced prostitution. The Supreme Court interpreted this statute to mean that a man could be prosecuted for taking any woman who was not his wife across state lines for the purposes of sex.

Americans continue to perform illegal sexual acts every day. While the definition, enforcement, and penalties for sex-related crimes vary from one state to the next and change from year to year due to new judicial decisions and legislation, in many jurisdictions, adultery, homosexuality, oral, and anal sex are punishable by fines or even prison terms.

The influence of politics on sex research can be seen in the current debate on funding **4**_____ research, research involving undifferentiated fetal tissue. Even survey research has been impacted. For example, in 1991, the U.S. Senate passed an amendment prohibiting federal funding of the National Health and Social Life Survey. Private foundations subsequently funded a scaled-down version.

Since the 1970s there has been an organized movement to extend civil rights statutes to include provisions prohibiting discrimination on the basis of sexual orientation. There also have been organized efforts to combat such attempts.

Family and relationship rights are a major issue in gay and lesbian politics. In 2000, **5**_____ became the first state legally to recognize "civil unions," entitling gays and lesbians to all of the rights and benefits extended to married couples under state law.

Homosexuals have served in the military, some openly, since Valley Forge, yet it is only recently that the presence of gays and lesbians in the armed forces has become a political issue. In 1993, Congress passed the **6**_____ Act barring gays and lesbians from openly serving in the military. While the "don't ask, don't tell" policy of the Clinton administration permitted gays and lesbians to serve in the military as long as they did not openly reveal their sexual orientation, the military subsequently discharged **7**_____ percent more gay and lesbian troops than they had previously.

AIDS significantly increased the visibility of gays and lesbians in politics. While the AIDS epidemic has galvanized gay and lesbian political involvement, it has also given some individuals and organizations the excuse to discriminate openly against gays. Moreover, AIDS has affected heterosexual political issues. Some conservatives with more rigid views about sexual issues now recognize the need for disseminating accurate information about how AIDS spreads and about the preventative use of condoms, while some liberals have rethought their views of sexual freedom.

Women entering the workforce during World War II and the introduction of the birth control pill in **8**_____ are two factors credited with fostering changes in the traditional status of women.

9_____ challenged the Comstock Act and was a leader in the struggle for full access to birth control. She believed that birth control was fundamental to securing freedom and independence for working women, and that it fulfilled a critical psychological need by enabling women fully to enjoy sex free from the fear of pregnancy.

It is safe to assume that women everywhere since ancient times have sought abortions. Even now, laws outlawing abortion or making it difficult to obtain do not stop women desperate to terminate a pregnancy from finding ways to do so.

In 1973, the U.S. Supreme Court held in **10**_____ that during the first trimester of pregnancy, the decision to have an abortion might be made free of state interference. This gave women the right to choose abortion until fetal viability, but after that the state's interest would outweigh the woman's interest. Forty-one states and the District of Columbia have laws that specifically address abortion after viability. In 1977, the **11**_____ Amendment was passed prohibiting federal Medicaid funds for abortions.

Although men are held to share legal and financial responsibility for a pregnancy, men do not legally have any say in pregnancy termination.

Laws against sex are mainly targeted at men. However, throughout history, infidelity by wives has been punished more severely than infidelity by husbands, though male homosexuality has been persecuted much more thoroughly than female homosexuality.

There were laws against miscegenation in 25 states until 1967 when the U.S. Supreme Court invalidated them. However, it was not until 2000 that the state of **12**_____ removed a 1901 state law banning marriage between "a Negro and Caucasian."

The U.S. military has laws against fornication and adultery. And, many states still have laws prohibiting premarital, oral, or anal sex—even between consenting adults.

SUGGESTED READINGS

Boehmer, U. (2000). *The Personal and the Political: Women's Activism in Response to the Breast Cancer and AIDS Epidemics.* Albany: State University of New York Press.

This book provides an in-depth look at the social and political dimensions of AIDS and breast cancer within the context of social movement and feminist theories.

Brandt, E. (Ed.). (1999). *Dangerous Liaisons: Blacks, Gays, and the Struggle for Equality.* New York: New Press.

This collection of essays explores the mutual suffering of blacks and homosexuals in America, why it has not led to mutual sympathy and collaboration, and how this division is counterproductive in combating both racism and homophobia.

D'Emilio, J., Urvashi, V., & Turner, W.B. (2000). *Creating Change: Sexuality, Public Policy, and Civil Rights.* New York: St. Martin's Press.

The authors trace the impact of the gay and lesbian movements since Stonewall.

Feldman, E., & Bayer, R. (Eds.). (1999). *Blood Feuds: AIDS, Blood, and the Politics of Medical Disaster.* New York: Oxford University Press.

Contributors from law, political science, public health, and the medical sciences look at the legal and political dimensions of the AIDS epidemic

Gorney, C. (1998). *Articles of Faith: A Frontline History of the Abortion Wars.* New York: Simon & Schuster.

Gorney personalizes the abortion conflict by following the careers of two advocates—one pro-choice, the other a dedicated antiabortionist.

Gurstein, R. (1998). *The Repeal of Reticence: A History of America's Cultural and Legal Struggles Over Free Speech, Obscenity, Sexual Liberation, and Modern Art.* New York: Hill & Wang.

This is a history of the struggle between the public and private needs and rights framed as a battle between the party of exposure and the party of reticence.

Jacobs, J. B., & Potter, K. (1998). *Hate Crimes: Criminal Law and Identity Politics.* New York: Oxford University Press.

The authors argue that the definition of *hate crime* is often too vague to be meaningful and that the development of hate crime legislation arises from the identity politics movements, which have gained strength since the passage of the Civil Rights Act.

O'Leary, A., & Jemmott, L. S. (Eds.). (1997). *Women and AIDS: Coping and Care.* New York: Plenum Publishing.

This volume brings together current research results to offer an in-depth look at the medical, psychological, and policy dilemmas of HIV-positive women.

Posner, R. A. (Ed.). (1996). *A Guide to America's Sex Laws.* Chicago: University of Chicago Press.

Posner provides a compendium of the nation's sex laws. Seventeen chapters summarize American laws on topics such as rape, age of consent, incest, and voyeurism.

Shilts, R. (1998). *Conduct Unbecoming: Gays and Lesbians in the U.S. Military.* New York: World Publications.

Over 1,000 interviews provide the foundation for this investigation into the presence and treatment of homosexuals in the military.

ANSWERS TO CHAPTER REVIEW:

1. Mesopotamia; **2.** Comstock; **3.** Mann; **4.** stem cell; **5.** Vermont; **6.** National Defense Authorization; **7.** 67; **8.** 1964; **9.** Margaret Sanger; **10.** *Roe v. Wade*; **11.** Hyde; **12.** Alabama.

Sexuality Education

- **Who Decides What Gets Taught?**
  Federal policy regarding sexuality education is weak; state and local policies vary greatly. Only 19 states require schools to provide sexuality education.

- **Where Should Sexuality Education Be Taught?**
  Everyone seems to agree that parents would be the best instructors, but parents think schools should do more.

- **What Should Sexuality Education Courses Teach?**
  National surveys indicate that parents want more topics (birth control, abortion, and sexual orientation) covered in school-based courses than are currently offered nationally.

- **Does Sexuality Education Make a Difference?**
  There is no proof that sexuality education leads to experimentation; but there is evidence that it may help to postpone first sexual intercourse and prevent pregnancy and disease.

- **Do Parents Talk About Sexuality? Do Children Listen?**
  Parents and children agree that parents and caregivers should be the primary sexuality educators of their children. But even when parents talk to their children about sex, their sons and daughters may not always be listening.

CHAPTER 19

PHYSICAL

SOCIAL

EMOTIONAL

SPIRITUAL

COGNITIVE

earning about sex is a lifelong physical, social, emotional, spiritual, and cognitive process. Although the term *sex education* is widely associated with school-based instruction, as you learned in Chapter 9, we begin learning about sexuality long before we set foot in a classroom. Whether it is the study of arithmetic or sexuality, we learn the basics as young children and build on these fundamentals in adolescence. Unfortunately, many adults think that they know everything—or at least enough—and cease attempts to further their knowledge once they are no longer in the classroom. However, just as knowing how to add does not mean that you understand mathematics, knowing that the joining of sperm and egg can make a baby does not mean that you understand human sexuality. Moreover, education about any subject involves much more than the accumulation of facts.

As in so many areas, we need to update, revise, and sort out the barrage of information on sexual issues. AIDS, for example, was not part of the curriculum of sex education courses 20 years ago; we are constantly learning more about contracting, preventing, and treating HIV.

Marriage manuals, self-help books, sex videos, sex therapy, and Internet research are some of the ways that adults can update and increase their understanding of sexuality. Many adults find that they need education in the same sexual topics and issues as adolescents: sexually transmitted infections, relationship issues, and contraception. Adults in long-term relationships may find that their sexual relationships have changed. Physical changes related to menopause or prostate problems that seemed so far in the future to a 20-year-old may now be very real.

There is a great deal of controversy about the who, what, where, when, and how of sexuality education. Programs run the gamut from the **comprehensive** approach, in which abstinence is taught as one possible option for adolescents, to **abstinence-only** programs, in which abstinence is the only method of birth control taught and discussion of contraception is prohibited, unless to emphasize its shortcomings. Somewhere in between falls the **abstinence-plus** program, which teaches abstinence as the preferred option but allows for contraception to be discussed as effective in protecting against unintended pregnancy and disease. Although a majority of educators say that they provide a comprehensive approach to sex education, one third deliver the abstinence-only message (Kaiser Family Foundation, 2000a). As you will learn in this chapter, sex education is an issue that inspires almost as much heated debate as abortion.

Comprehensive Sex Education: programs that teach both contraception and abstinence as options

Abstinence-Only Sex Education: programs that teach abstinence as the only method of birth control; discussion of contraception is prohibited, unless to emphasize its shortcomings

Abstinence-Plus Sex Education: programs that teach abstinence as the preferred option but allow for contraception to be discussed

WHO DECIDES WHAT GETS TAUGHT?

Federal Policies

There is no national law or policy on sexuality education. State and local policies primarily guide sexuality education in the United States; traditionally, the involvement of the federal government has been fairly limited. The first substantial federal action on sex education came in 1981 when Congress passed the **Adolescent Family Life Act (AFLA),** Title XX of the Public Health Service Act, which provides funding for the teaching of abstinence as the only option for teenagers.

The primary stated goal of AFLA is to prevent premarital teen pregnancy by establishing "family-centered" programs to "promote chastity and self-discipline" (Saul, 1998). Secondary goals include promoting adoption as the preferred option for pregnant teens and providing support services for pregnant and parenting teens. Many of AFLA's early grants went to groups to develop curricula that teach abstinence as the only option for adolescents. Because many of these curricula promoted religious values, the American Civil Liberties Union filed a federal lawsuit in 1983 asserting that parts of AFLA were a violation of the First Amendment's requirement of separation of church and state. The plaintiffs in the lawsuit (*Kendrick v. Sullivan*) claimed that the program constituted a federal endorsement of a particular religious point of view. Although the Supreme Court ruled that the statute was constitutional, litigation continued concerning the way in which the program was administered.

In 1993 a settlement was reached prohibiting AFLA-funded sex education programs from including religious references or from taking place in churches or parochial schools. In response to findings that some programs distorted information about the effectiveness of contraception, perhaps to make abstinence a more appealing option, the settlement also specified that sex education must be medically accurate. When the settlement expired in 2000, the Office of Adolescent Pregnancy Prevention, which administers AFLA, maintained that it would continue to follow the settlement guidelines.

In 1996, through an abstinence-only education provision in welfare reform legislation entitled **Temporary Assistance to Needy Families (TANF) Act,** the federal government again addressed sex education. Some $250 million was made available to states over a 5-year period to support programs that promoted abstinence. Administered under the Maternal and Child Health Service Block Grant, the funds may be used for community-based as well as in-school programs and must adhere to specific criteria (see Table 19.1), including the provision that sex should be confined to

Adolescent Family Life Act (AFLA): 1981 act of Congress that provided funding for sex education programs teaching abstinence as the only option for teenagers

Temporary Assistance to Needy Families (TANF) Act: 1996 welfare reform legislation that made federal funds available to states over a 5-year period to support programs that promoted abstinence

TABLE 19.1

Objectives of Abstinence in the 1996 TANF Act

- Abstinence has social, psychological, and health benefits.
- Unmarried, school-age children must abstain from sex.
- Abstinence is the only certain way to prevent out-of-wedlock pregnancy and sexually transmitted infections.
- A mutually faithful and monogamous married relationship is the standard for sexual activity.
- Sexual activity outside marriage is likely to have harmful psychological and physical effects.
- Out-of-wedlock childbearing is likely to harm a child, the parents, and society.
- There are many ways to reject sexual advances.
- Alcohol and drug use increases vulnerability to sexual advances.
- It is important to attain self-sufficiency before engaging in sex.

SOURCE: Abstinence Education. Social Security Act, Title V, Section 510, 42, U.S.C. 71D

married couples and that abstinence education is the "exclusive purpose" of sex education. Funding for the program was upgraded to entitlement status, meaning that Congress would automatically fund abstinence-only education each year during the appropriations process. As long as the specific curriculum and teaching of sex education do not violate the abstinence until marriage standard, the project qualifies for federal funds. Programs that discuss contraception and other protective behaviors are not eligible for funds. Funds also are not available to support the teaching of abstinence as one component of a more comprehensive program (see CONSIDERATIONS box).

In 1999 all 50 states plus Puerto Rico and the Virgin Islands applied for and received TANF funds, although California and New Hampshire subsequently chose not to use the money. Preliminary reviews of how states have used the funds indicate a wide array of abstinence programs, both within and outside schools. Thirty-eight states funded grants to community-based organizations, 27 states funded media campaigns, and 25 states funded education agencies (SIECUS, 1999). Many states have interpreted the TANF guidelines to mean that contraceptive failure rates are the only information about birth control allowed to be disseminated in programs that receive this funding. In 1997 Congress approved $6 million for a national evaluation of abstinence programs funded by TANF. Additionally, at least 39 states have indicated that they are conducting some form of evaluation, using a portion of their federal funds.

While the law makes it clear that abstinence-only classes must teach that sex should be confined to married couples, the legislation does not define many crucial concepts. For example, the legislation does not define "sexual activity" or what sexual behaviors these programs are supposed to address. Abstinence from penetrative sex? From masturbation? From kissing, hugging, and petting? This lack of definition is problematic for a statute responsible for millions of dollars of federal funding.

In addition to these federal initiatives, the Centers for Disease Control and Prevention (CDC) have funded HIV education since 1988. In 1999 the CDC budgeted approximately $47 million for in-school HIV education. Some opponents to this grant money objected to language and materials in the proposed curriculum that they felt were too explicit. In March 2000, Ohio purposely missed the deadline to apply for a health education grant (about 10 percent of which would have been earmarked for sex education), becoming the first state to reject this funding.

State Policies

Different states have different policies regarding the teaching of sexuality education, and policies may vary within a state as well, with the potential for a great deal of confusion. A state may have no specific policy on sex education, but still "recommend" particular

Just Say No

CONSIDERATIONS

Assume that All-American High, a public high school, has conducted a sex education class for ninth graders. The class curriculum calls for providing information about contraception and instruction in the use of various birth control devices. Now assume that school officials decide that they would like to revise the course to include a unit that follows exactly the definition of the abstinence education outlined in TANF. However, the language of TANF clearly states that the "exclusive purpose" of abstinence education is teaching the principles outlined in the statute. If the abstinence unit is part of a course that teaches the use of birth control, then it violates the "exclusive purpose" criterion. The school will not be able to receive much-needed federal funding for sexuality education if it does not adhere to the statute guidelines.

 What would you do if you were a school official at All-American High?

—Would you eliminate the portion of the class dealing with birth control?

courses of action or even specify that a school district adhere to a particular curriculum. Other states may give no guidelines at all and leave local officials to make decisions regarding whether to teach about sexuality or what curriculum to select (see "Local Policies" section). Within an individual state there may be differing policies affecting mandates for contraception or abstinence education. It is also common for states to have different requirements for students in different grade levels. For example, if in a particular state there is local control of sexuality education, one school district may teach abstinence-only to its students from elementary through high school, while in the next town over, complete instruction on birth control methods may be given to high-school students (but not elementary students), and in another nearby town there may be no instruction at all. (As young people frequently cross local, county, and even state boundaries to socialize, you can see where confusion and misunderstandings might arise.)

In fact, more states require schools to offer specific HIV or STI education than general sex education. As of 2000, only 18 states plus the District of Columbia required schools to provide sex education (Figure 19.1). Thirty-two do not. Of those states that require schools to provide sexuality education, three (Illinois, Kentucky, and Utah) require that sex education teach abstinence but do not require information about contraception. In contrast, 34 states plus the District of Columbia require schools to provide STI, HIV, or AIDS education. Of these states, two (Indiana and Ohio) require that their programs teach abstinence until marriage and prohibit information about other preventative behaviors or methods of prevention (Kaiser Family Foundation, 2000b).

Local Policies

Even where state policy on sex education exists, oversight is left to the local school districts. A national survey of school superintendents conducted in 1999 found that two thirds of U.S. school districts have a district-wide policy to teach sex education (Landry, Kaeser, & Richards, 1999). The remaining districts leave the decision to individual schools. In large school districts with multiple schools, students who live less than a mile apart could learn different things about sexuality. Among districts that have a local policy to teach sex education, 14 percent report that their policy takes the comprehensive approach outlined earlier, teaching abstinence as one of a number of options for adolescents. Fifty-one percent promote abstinence-plus. The remaining 35 percent have an abstinence-only policy.

In a Kaiser Family Foundation study, 88 percent of public secondary school principals reported that school districts and local governments have at least some influence on their schools' sex education curricula. For example, the leading reason given by principals for not covering abortion and sexual orientation was a school or district policy, followed closely by actual or perceived pressure from the community. Forty-eight percent of principals say there have been recent discussions or debates at the

TABLE 19.2

Controversial Issues in Sexuality Education Reported by Principals

Percent of principals reporting discussion or debate in recent years	
Teaching abstinence-only	31
How parents give permission for sex education	26
What topics to teach in sex education	26
Whether to teach abstinence-only	17
Whether sex education classes should be single-sex or coed	16

Source: Adapted from Kaiser Family Foundation, 2000a.

	Sexual Education Mandate	STD,HIV/AIDS Education Mandate	Must Teach Abstinence*	Must Teach Abstinence Until Marriage*	Must Teach Contraceptive Options*
Alabama	No	Yes	Yes	Yes	No
Alaska	No	No	No	No	No
Arizona	No	No	Yes	No	No
Arkansas	No	No	Yes	No	Yes
California	No	Yes	Yes	Yes	Yes
Colorado	No	Yes	No	No	No
Connecticut	No	Yes	No	No	Yes
Delaware	Yes	Yes	Yes	No	Yes
District of Columbia	Yes	Yes	Yes	No	No
Florida	No	Yes	Yes	Yes	Yes
Georgia	Yes	Yes	Yes	Yes	Yes
Hawaii	No	No	Yes	No	Yes
Idaho	No	No	No	No	No
Illinois	Yes	Yes	Yes	Yes	No
Indiana	No	Yes	Yes	Yes	No
Iowa	Yes	Yes	Yes	No	Yes
Kansas	Yes	Yes	No	No	No
Kentucky	Yes	Yes	Yes	No	No
Louisiana	No	No	Yes	Yes	No
Maine	No	No	No	No	No
Maryland	Yes	Yes	No	No	No
Massachusetts	No	No	No	No	No
Michigan	No	Yes	Yes	No	No
Minnesota	Yes	Yes	No	No	No
Mississippi	No	No	Yes	Yes	Yes
Missouri	No	Yes	Yes	Yes	Yes
Montana	No	No	No	No	No
Nebraska	No	No	No	No	No
Nevada	Yes	Yes	No	No	No
New Hampshire	No	Yes	No	No	No
New Jersey	Yes	Yes	Yes	No	Yes
New Mexico	Yes	Yes	Yes	No	Yes
New York	No	Yes	No	No	No
North Carolina	Yes	Yes	Yes	Yes	Yes
North Dakota	No	Yes	No	No	No
Ohio	No	Yes	No	No	No
Oklahoma	No	Yes	Yes	No	No
Oregon	No	Yes	Yes	No	Yes
Pennsylvania	Yes	Yes	No	No	Yes
Rhode Island	Yes	Yes	Yes	No	Yes
South Carolina	Yes	Yes	Yes	Yes	No
South Dakota	No	No	No	No	No
Tennessee	Yes	Yes	Yes	Yes	Yes
Texas	No	No	Yes	Yes	No
Utah	Yes	Yes	Yes	Yes	No
Vermont	Yes	Yes	Yes	No	Yes
Virginia	No	No	Yes	Yes	Yes
Washington	No	Yes	No	No	No
West Virginia	Yes	Yes	Yes	No	Yes
Wisconsin	No	Yes	No	No	No
Wyoming	No	No	No	No	No

*If sex education is taught; not required in all states.

FIGURE 19.1 Sexuality Education Map. SOURCE: Adapted from SIECUS, 2000, and NARAL, 2000.

PTA, school board, or other public meetings on some aspect of sex education, from what to teach to how parents give permission (Table 19.2). However, most (58 percent) report no change in the curriculum as a result of these discussions (Kaiser Family Foundation, 2000a).

WHERE SHOULD SEXUALITY EDUCATION BE TAUGHT?

At Home

Discussions about sexuality education often raise questions about where it should be taught. Many parents believe that sexuality education is a parent's job, not that of schools or government. Many educators and community leaders would agree with this position *if* children received better sex education in the home. However, not all parents are willing or able to provide accurate information about sex or to provide their children an opportunity to discuss sexuality. Parents may have as much difficulty acknowledging the sexual nature of their children as their children do in seeing their parents as sexual beings. There also is the problem that many parents simply do not know much about sexuality. Many parents received little or no formal sex education and have an incomplete or even erroneous understanding of many aspects of sex. For example, how many of your parents learned about AIDS in their sex education classes at school?

A child's education about sexuality begins not with a discussion of the birds and the bees, but with parental attitudes from birth about their bodies, their children's bodies, and their sexuality. The attitudes and values of the home environment directly affect a child's developing sexuality. As we discussed in Chapter 9, children learn as much about sex from a parent's tone of voice or facial expression as from the words they use to explain the birds and the bees; observations of parental behavior also teach them a great deal.

A recent study of college women asked whether parents, teachers, or peers, were the first source of information regarding sexuality. Data suggested that those girls whose parents first taught them practiced a number of safer sex behaviors and exhibited more positive sexual attitudes. There was no measurable effect on safer sexual decisions among those whose teachers educated them first. Peers had the most negative effect (for example, encouraging risky behaviors such as drug and alcohol use) on safer sexual decisions (Moore & Davidson, 1999).

One study asked university students to rate 34 potential sources of sexuality information and identified in rank order the five sources of information that had most influenced their knowledge of human sexuality. Female students considered parents more influential than did males, and students reported more sexuality discussions with mothers than with fathers.

While overwhelmingly students reported more discussions about sexuality with same-sex sources (Ballard & Morris, 1998), getting fathers and sons to talk about sexuality is especially difficult. There is a long-standing bias toward women's reproductive education and treating males as irresponsible and the cause of most sexual problems (Melby, 2000). In addition, parents tend to be more involved with an adolescent daughter's education than with a son's. Carter and Wojtkiewicz (2000) analyzed several types of parental involvement for gender differences. Generally daughters experienced more parental involvement with their education than did sons.

High-school students who completed surveys describing the frequency and importance of communication about 20 different sex topics rated parental communication about sexuality as unimportant. The less frequent the parental communication, the less importance it held for the student (Rosenthal, Feldman, & Edwards, 1998). In other words, if parents want to impact their child's sexuality education, they need to talk early and talk often.

Although it may be uncomfortable for some parents—and children—it is important that they discuss sexuality issues with one another.

At School

In spite of the confusing array of regulations about and requirements for sexuality education, a large majority of public school students, 89 percent, take sex education sometime between 7th and 12th grades. Typically these classes are taught within another course, such as health, and they usually cover just a few class periods. Forty-four percent of 13- to 18-year-olds cite this brief exposure as one of their most important resources for sexuality information (Kaiser Family Foundation, 2000).

Revolutionary Sex Ed

Controversy over sex education is hardly limited to North America. In Russia, the controversies have had a different focus, as attitudes toward the role of sexuality in modern life evolved under Soviet Communism and in the post-Soviet era. After the Russian Revolution, Communist leaders changed their minds about sex and sex education repeatedly. First they sought to liberate people from the sexual inhibitions that they associated with capitalism, but then they decided that liberation had gone too far and insisted that movements toward free love should be stifled. As one sign of these changes, abortion was legalized in 1920 but criminalized again in 1936 (when Stalin wanted more workers and soldiers), then decriminalized in 1955 (when Khrushchev's government wanted to reduce the harmful effects of underground abortions).

Sex education played an important role in attempts to advance the regime's wishes regarding sexual behavior (Rivkin-Fish, 1999). The decriminalization of abortion in 1955 was accompanied by efforts to teach young people that abortion was a betrayal of women's true maternal nature. Masturbation among young men was condemned as wasting energies that could be used for productive work in society; however, masturbation among young women was not recognized as an issue.

In 1984, the Communist leaders required a sex education course on "Ethics and Psychology of Family Life" for all ninth- and tenth-grade students. This course sought to teach Communist sexual values to young people. These values included sexual restraint and the importance of a stable family life (Rivkin-Fish, 1999). Because the declining population was seen as a danger to the state, this course emphasized that everyone should want to have at least three children. The earlier hostility toward masturbation was downplayed, and the new course stated

that masturbation was physically harmless if done in moderation. Teachers were cautioned not to condemn masturbation, because their negative attitudes could be traumatic to schoolchildren, potentially even causing neurosis and impotence. There was still no discussion of female masturbation. In fact, Rivkin-Fish concluded that no writings for sex education or health ever mentioned female sexual desire or pleasure until after the fall of Communism.

The abrupt change away from a Communist society in 1989 led to many changes, and a sexual revolution was one of them (Rivkin-Fish, 1999). The society was not accustomed to any public discussion of sex, but the new freedom led to much greater sexual openness. Conservative forces still maintained their attitudes of sexual reticence and restraint from the Communist era, and many people opposed sex education as likely to foster what Russians perceived as Western civilization's problems, including homosexuality, birth control, and casual sex. Meanwhile, sexuality educators presented themselves as fighting to eliminate the problems of sexual ignorance that developed during the Soviet era. They sought to provide information about topics such as sexual behavior and contraception. Unlike sex education in the United States, it was still considered important to emphasize messages of sexual morality and restraint. Primarily, sex was considered a proper way to make a family, and birth control and abortion were discussed in somewhat negative terms. Masturbation, however, was covered in the new sex education classes as acceptable for both males and females as a way to learn about one's body and prepare for adult sexuality. Sexual intercourse outside the context of family life was condemned to varying degrees, and sex educators would often rely on instilling fear by depicting the dangers associated with sexual indulgence.

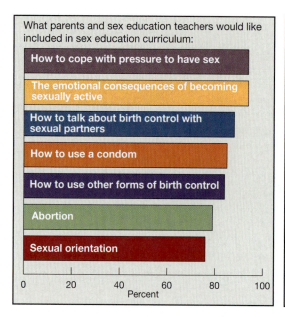

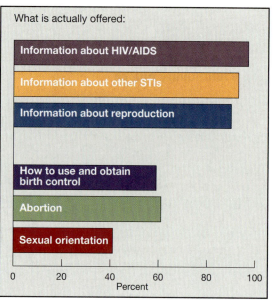

FIGURE 19.2 **The Preferences of Parents and Teachers Versus What Is Actually Taught in Sexuality Education Courses.** SOURCE: Adapted from Kaiser Family Foundation, 2000.

Overall, students who receive sex education instruction in the classroom, regardless of the curriculum, know more and feel better prepared to handle different situations and decisions than those who do not (Kaiser Family Foundation, 2000a). Still, not all students' information needs are being met through sex education courses. Challenging the conventional wisdom that Americans are reluctant to have sexuality education taught in schools, the most recent Kaiser Family Foundation survey showed that most parents, educators, and students would expand sex education courses and curriculum (Kaiser Family Foundation, 2000). Eighty-seven percent of adults in the United States approve of giving courses in sex education in the schools but disagree on the grades in which these courses should begin (Figure 19.2).

A pioneer in sexuality education, Dr. Mary Calderone (1904–1998), the daughter of the photographer Edward Steichen, was a woman of many talents. After graduating from Vassar College with a major in chemistry, she decided to go on the stage before going to medical school at age 30. She received an M.D. in 1939 and a master's degree in public health in 1942. In 1953 she became director of the Planned Parenthood Federation of America, where she carried forward Margaret Sanger's mission for family planning. In 1961 Dr. Calderone took part in the first American Conference on Church and Family run by the National Council of Churches. With five colleagues at the conference, Dr. Calderone set up an informal committee to study human sexuality. Out of the committee, the Sex Information and Education Council of the United States (SIECUS) was created in 1964. Dr. Calderone believed that sex education in the schools should start in kindergarten; under her leadership SIECUS became the moving force for education about human sexuality in the schools as well as in the community.

Ideally, formal sex education programs in the schools complement rather than replace what parents are teaching their children at home. However, as indicated earlier, not all parents are willing or able to assume the role of teacher in this area. Some children are more willing to accept information about sex and to speak more openly about sexual issues with someone other than a parent. Moreover, an informed teacher may be in a much better position to teach children accurate and current information about "new" diseases such as HIV and AIDS. On the other hand, teachers who are unprepared, do not have accurate information about sex, have their own personal problems with sexuality, or allow their own biases to influence their teaching could have a negative effect on their students.

The emphasis of most school programs has been on prevention of disease and pregnancy. Unfortunately, many sex education programs ignore the equally important issues of sexual communication and decision making. Most sex educators are more comfortable telling people what *not* to do; just as important is teaching what to do to have healthy, meaningful, responsible, pleasurable sexual relationships. As we have already discussed, approaches to sex education vary widely; at some schools, sex education includes condom distribution, while at others it is essentially summed up by telling kids to "Just say, 'No.'"

A large majority of students receive some type of school based sexuality education program.

WHAT SHOULD SEXUALITY EDUCATION COURSES TEACH?

Traditionally, sexuality education programs in the United States have been largely limited to how the basic plumbing works, lectures with endless diagrams of fallopian tubes and seminal vesicles, and lectures on abstinence aimed mainly at the female student. In their attempts not to offend anyone, these watered-down courses may do an adequate job of rehashing what most students are already learning in biology classes, but they avoid teaching the sexual topics that students want and need to learn. Many parents and educators have shied away from values-based sexuality education out of fear of some very vocal opponents. Because some parents will protest, "We don't want you to impose your values on our children," most schools teach no values or ethics at all (Gordon, 1992).

The first national model for comprehensive sexuality education in the United States was developed by SIECUS in 1990 and up-dated in 1995. According to *The SIECUS Guidelines for Comprehensive Sexuality Education: K–12*, the primary goal of sexuality education is the promotion of sexual health. Sexuality education should provide accurate information; an opportunity for young people to question, explore, and assess their sexual attitudes; and help students develop interpersonal skills, including communication, decision making, assertiveness, and peer refusal skills, as well as the ability to create satisfying relationships. In addition, the *SIECUS Guidelines* emphasize the need to help students exercise responsibility regarding sexual relationships. Key concepts and topics included in the *SIECUS Guidelines* include human development, relationships, personal skills, sexual behavior, sexual health, and society and culture.

There are many organizations that support only those sexuality education programs that promote abstinence until marriage, or oppose all school-based sexuality

CONSIDERATIONS

Valuing Sex

The *SIECUS Guidelines* (1990) were developed to be consistent with certain values. Values inherent in the *Guidelines* include the following:

- Sexuality is a natural and healthy part of living.
- All persons are sexual.
- Sexuality includes physical, ethical, social, spiritual, psychological, and emotional dimensions.
- Every person has dignity and self-worth.
- Individuals express their sexuality in varied ways.
- Parents should be the primary sexuality educators of their children.
- In a pluralistic society people should respect and accept the diversity of values and beliefs about sexuality that exist in a community.

- Sexual relationships should never be coercive or exploitative.
- All sexual decisions have effects or consequences.
- Abstaining from sexual intercourse is the most effective method of preventing pregnancy and STIs, including HIV.
- Young people who are involved in sexual relationships need access to information about health-care services.
- All persons have the rights and the obligation to make responsible sexual choices.

? *Are these values consistent with your personal values?*

   —With those of your family?
   —With those of your community?

education programs entirely. For example, the American Life League, a Christian pro-life, antiabortion group "supports only educational programs that teach sexual morality in the context of leading children toward the practice of virtue and that avoid examining the subject of sex in any concrete, detailed, or descriptive way in the classroom or other public setting" (American Life League, 2001). The Eagle Forum is an organization that supports major cuts in federal spending, supports American sovereignty and independence, and opposes all currently proposed treaties, including with the United Nations. Its position is that, "School should not deprive children of their free-exercise-of-religion rights, or impose on children courses in explicit sex or alternate lifestyles, profane and immoral fiction or videos, New Age practices, anti-Biblical materials, or 'Politically Correct' liberal attitudes about social and economic issues" (Eagle Forum, 2001). The Best Friends Foundation is an organization that sponsors a youth development program with a character-building in-school curriculum for girls in grades 5 to 12 (it plans to start a program for boys, Best Men, in the near future). The Best Friends curriculum operates from the premise that adolescents "want to hear the abstinence message and will respond when it is offered in a developmentally sound program in an educational setting that provides fun, companionship and caring, and builds connectedness to school" (Best Friends Foundation, 2001).

The very vocal opposition to sexuality education represents the minority view. The overwhelming majority of parents want schools to go farther than they currently do on the topics of reproduction and abstinence, HIV/AIDS, and other STIs, and to address issues often labeled as controversial, like abortion and sexual orientation, as well as to teach safer sex and negotiation skills (Kaiser Family Foundation, 2000).

Sexual abuse is another sticky topic. Teaching children awareness of potentially hazardous situations, how to handle such situations, and how to get help if they need it is an important part of any sex education curriculum. However, in warning children about sexual abuse and other negative aspects of sexuality, including rape, sexually transmitted infections, and AIDS, it is possible inadvertently to give the message that sex is a dangerous activity. It is important to present a balanced, complete education about human sexuality. An integrated sexuality education process can help explore attitudes, enhance self-esteem, further understanding of relationships, and develop decision-making skills. Sex education often focuses on the mechanics of sex; comprehensive sexuality education includes values and meaningful connections to specific behaviors.

DOES SEXUALITY EDUCATION MAKE A DIFFERENCE?

Sexuality education has probably been the most controversial subject in the curriculum since it first entered the school system. Margaret Sanger (see Chapter 18) championed some of the first sex education programs in the United States at the beginning of the 20th century. Although Sanger was an advocate of promoting contraceptive information, the early sex education movement in the United States was characterized by an emphasis on the dangers of sex and the need for self-control not birth control. In the 1940s, the focus of sex education changed to include the prevention of venereal diseases. By the 1960s, the prevention of unwanted teenage pregnancy as well as sexually transmitted infections became the subject of most sex education programs (Strouse & Fabes, 1983). Today, HIV and AIDS concerns are often the focus of school-based sexuality programs.

Despite the fears of some, researchers have not been able to demonstrate any connection between sexuality education and early sexual experimentation among children and adolescents (Eisen & Zellman, 1987). College students who reported experiencing meaningful sex education in middle school or high school before losing their virginity were significantly more likely to delay sexual debut than were those students who had not received sex education (Sawyer & Smith, 1996). However, other studies have found no relationship between exposure to sexuality education and subsequent sexual activity (Gray & Saracino, 1989; Kirby, 1989; Stout & Rivara, 1989).

www E XPLORING SEXUALITY ONLINE

Searching for Sex

The Internet provides sexual health educators with unique and unprecedented opportunities, and difficult challenges, to speak directly to millions of Americans about these issues. Because there is no centralized and continuously updated master index of sexuality resources on the World Wide Web, most users employ commercial search engines when looking for sexuality education information resources. However, due to the nature of these search engines, you are as likely to have hits on triple X pornography sites as information on how to prevent sexually transmitted infections. It may be helpful to go to a trusted Web site such as those listed on the Web site for this textbook (*www.prenhall.com/miracle*) and follow the links to other sites.

There is disagreement as to how effective school sexuality programs are in promoting responsible sexual behavior. While evaluations of many programs have failed to demonstrate positive effects, others have. One study of four inner-city schools in Baltimore found that in the two schools without condom distribution programs the pregnancy rates rose 57.6 percent over a 3-year period; pregnancy rates dropped 30.1 percent in the two schools with condom distribution programs (Zabin, Hirsch, & Emerson, 1986). A New York program that combined sexuality education with health services, self-esteem enhancement, a sports program, tutoring, and job training decreased pregnancy rates and increased employment and college enrollment (Carrera & Dempsey, 1988). A California program led to significant decreases in unprotected intercourse; students who took the course before they were sexually active either delayed the onset of sexual intercourse or increased their use of contraceptives (Kirby, Waszak, & Ziegler, 1991).

Those who assume that teenagers are going to have sex whether adults like it or not have criticized programs that emphasize abstinence. However, teenage pregnancy rates in Maryland dropped more than 10 percent in 2 years following a $5 million campaign that included such slogans as "Abstinence Makes the Heart Grow Fonder" and "Virginity Is Not a Dirty Word" (Gross, 1994). Some high-school-level abstinence classes have had success delivering the message that the students can always have sex, but this may be their only opportunity to get an education. The most effective sexuality education programs intended to curb adolescent sexual behavior combine contraceptive education with lessons on how to resist social and peer pressure (Gross, 1994).

DO PARENTS TALK ABOUT SEXUALITY? DO CHILDREN LISTEN?

Almost everyone agrees that parents and caregivers should be the primary sexuality educators of their children—even children agree. Research shows that the extent to which parents are involved and the manner in which they are involved in their children's lives are critical factors in the prevention of high-risk sexual activity (Blake et al., 2001). However, studies show that many parents abdicate this responsibility and allow peers and the media to be the primary sources of sexuality information (King & Lorusso, 1997). Some parents feel that it is inappropriate to involve young children in what, to them, is an adult issue. They want to protect the innocence of young children, and they may argue that ignorance is bliss. "These arguments present the narrow view that sex education is solely about reproduction, and that as this information is better given on a need-to-know basis, it does not concern young children" (Hayes, 1995). There is also the fear,

CAMPUS CONFIDENTIAL

"In a million years I could never talk to either of my parents about anything even remotely related to sex. While my mother says that she wants me to be able to talk about sex openly, her attitude makes it evident that she finds the subject awkward, embarrassing, and distasteful. And my father . . . forget it. He changes the channel if there's a commercial for feminine hygiene products, and he squirms at every sexual reference in a movie. Without saying a word he makes it very clear that I am expected to remain a virgin—even after I get married. Essentially, my parents' message is 'don't talk about it,' 'don't do it,' and 'if you do it, we don't want to know about it.'" ●

discussed earlier, that sex education encourages children to experiment in activities inappropriate to their age and development. However, as we have discussed throughout this book, sexuality is part of our entire being; it is not just what we do with our genitals.

Determining the appropriate age for discussions about sexuality can be problematic for many parents. One study found that when asked about the age at which children should learn about sexual topics, parents of young children inevitably suggest an age later than their own child's present age (Gagnon & Roberts, 1983). In other words, when it comes to sex, whatever age their child is, it's not old enough. Those parents who wait until their child reaches puberty to have the "big talk" about sex will probably find that they are repeating information that their child already knows.

Research in primary schools in England used draw-and-write techniques to find out what students know about the sex differences between females and males and how people use their bodies to show people they love them. For the differences between boys and girls of the same age as themselves, 7- and 8-year-old children drew girls with long hair and boys with short hair, almost without exception. Only 24 percent indicated a difference of genitalia, boys being more likely to mention this than girls. When asked to draw 15-year-olds, there was only one major difference—15 percent, most of them girls, indicated that girls' breasts develop. Only one in four 7- and 8-year-olds were able to name the sexual parts of the body and the differences between the two sexes accurately (Brown, 1995).

What effect does the parental "talk" have on children? The results of one survey indicated that 9 in 10 mothers had talked to their teenage sons or daughters about sex but only two thirds of their children reported having such a discussion. Perhaps the parents' idea of talking about sex is different from that of their children, or perhaps their children were not listening. Another study found that just half of adolescents feel they had one "good talk" about sexuality during the past year with their mothers—and only a third had one with their fathers (Raffaelli, Bogenschneider, & Flood, 2000). The likelihood that a teenager would report having had such a discussion was reduced if the mother had reservations about talking to her children about sex, particularly if she was concerned that her child would think she was prying or would not want to hear what she had to say (Jaccard, Dittus, & Gordon, 2000).

Direct and indirect communication between mothers and adolescents about premarital sex and its influence on the formation of adolescent beliefs about sexual behavior was studied by Dittus, Jaccard, and Gordon in 1999. Results of the study indicate that adolescent motivations were related to their sexual behavior and that maternal beliefs about sex were predictive of those motivations, independent of reports of the amount of communication that had taken place. Children whose parents talk with them about sexual matters or provide sexuality education or contraceptive information at home are more likely than others to postpone sexual activity. And when these adolescents become sexually active, they have fewer sexual partners and are more likely to use contraceptives than those who do not discuss sexual matters with their parents (Blake et al., 2001).

The Talk

? **How did your parents talk to you about sex?**

—At what age or ages did they talk with you about sex?

—What topics did they discuss with you and which ones did they avoid?

—Did they seem to be embarrassed? Judgmental? Unemotional?

—What sexual values did you implicitly or explicitly learn from your parents?

—Were pleasure and healthy sexual relationships discussed?

—What would you do differently?

Straight Talk

The news and entertainment media make it nearly impossible for a child in the United States not to have heard of HIV and AIDS. Another topic that children are exposed to is erectile dysfunction. Commercials for Viagra are frequently seen during prime time television.

 How would you explain HIV to a young child?

—*How would you answer a young child's question, "What is anal sex?"*
—*How would you explain erectile dysfunction to a young child?*
—*How would you expect your child's second-grade teacher to answer those same questions?*

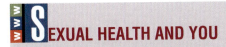

SEXUAL HEALTH AND YOU

How to Talk to Your Children About Sex

We all want to protect our children's sexual health. We don't want them to get pregnant or get someone pregnant, contract an STI, or get hurt by a bad sexual experience. But just as important is conveying to our children what is involved in a healthy sexual relationship and how to develop healthy sexual values and behaviors.

Don't wait for your children to ask questions. Many never ask and some important topics never get discussed. As a parent, you need to decide what is important for them to know and then tell them before a crisis occurs. Telling your daughter about menstruation or your son about nocturnal ejaculation after these events have occurred is too late.

Find "teachable moments." Make use of books, magazine articles, advertisements, song lyrics, music videos, movies, and TV shows, even if you believe they send the wrong message. Ask your child what he or she thinks about the message being conveyed and also express your own opinion.

Relax and be "ask-able." It's okay to feel uncomfortable. Some aspects of sexuality are easier to talk about than others. If your child asks you a question about contraception, instead of responding, "You're too young to be worrying about such things," reward the question with a positive response, such as "I'm glad you came to me." He or she will be more likely to come to you with other questions if the initial response is a positive one.

Share your feelings, values, and beliefs. Tell your children why you feel the way you do about sexuality.

Know your facts. When factual information is called for, be sure you have the correct information. If you don't know the answer to a child's question, it's okay to say so. Research the topic and be sure to get back to your child with the requested information.

Listen, listen, listen. There's an old saying that we have two ears and only one mouth so we can listen twice as much as we talk. In response to a question, ask why they want to know and what they already know. That may help you prepare your answer. Be sensitive to the "questions behind the questions." For example, is a child who asks, "Where did I come from?" asking about conception or place of birth? The unspoken question "Am I normal?" is often hiding behind questions about sexual development, sexual thoughts, and sexual feelings. Reassure your child as often as possible.

The joys are just as important to teach as the dangers. Teach your children that loving relationships are the best part of life and that intimacy is a wonderful part of adult life. Remember that what they hear from you now will affect their happiness and well-being throughout their lives.

In their discomfort, some parents try to avoid or delay answering questions. Others, who believe that "good" children would not have sexual thoughts or ask sexual questions, scold their children for their curiosity about sex. Parents who tell a child that babies are delivered by the stork, found in the cabbage patch, or come from the hospital do so not because their children cannot handle the truth, but because the parents cannot. Parents who tell themselves and their child that they aren't old enough yet, and they'll talk about it later, should not be surprised if the right time never comes. If parents wait for their children to ask questions, the responsibility for sexuality education becomes the child's instead of the parents'. Ideally, sexuality education should be a process, not just one talk; parents should discuss sex with their children whenever the subject arises naturally. Sexuality education should be integrated into the other activities of child-rearing that parents engage in to raise happy, healthy, responsible adults (see SEXUAL HEALTH AND YOU).

■ R E V I E W

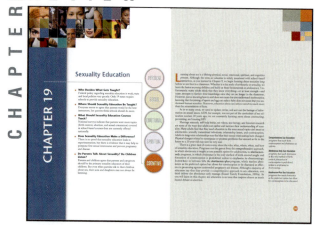

Although the term is widely associated with school-based instruction, *sexuality education* is a lifelong process. There are three broad categories of sexuality education: the comprehensive approach, **1**_____-only programs, and abstinence-plus programs. There is no national law or policy on sexuality education, and in the United States, the role of the federal government has been limited; school-based programs are guided primarily by state and local policies. The first substantial federal action on sexuality education came in 1981 when Congress passed the **2**_____ Act, which provides funding for the teaching of abstinence as the only option for teenagers.

As of 2000, only **3**_____ states and the District of Columbia require schools to provide sex education. However, **4**_____ states and the District of Columbia require schools to provide STI, HIV, or AIDS education. **5**_____ percent of public school students take some form of sexuality education between the 7th and 12th grades. Typically, sexuality education classes are taught within another course, such as health, and usually cover just a few class periods. However, 44 percent of 13- to 18-year-olds cite this brief exposure as one of their most important resources for sexuality information.

Children learn a great deal about sex at home, as much from a parent's tone of voice or facial expression as from the information discussed; parents also teach by example. Mothers are more likely than fathers to discuss sexual matters with their children.

Overall, students who take sexuality education classes at school know more and feel better prepared than those who have not had such courses. Ideally, formal sexuality education programs in the schools complement rather than replace what parents are teaching their children at home. However, most parents want schools to teach more about reproduction, HIV/AIDS, STIs, abortion, and sexual orientation. **6**_____ percent of parents say sex education should be taught by grade 5 or 6.

Almost everyone agrees that parents should be the primary sexuality educators of their children, but many parents are ill-prepared and others abdicate their responsibility for this task. A committee set up by **7**_____ founded the Sex Information and Education Council of the United States (SIECUS) in 1964. SIECUS remains a primary force for education about human sexuality in schools and communities.

Research has not been able to demonstrate any connection between sexuality education and early sexual experimentation. On the other hand, some research shows that effective sexuality education helps to postpone first sexual intercourse, and prevents pregnancy and disease.

SUGGESTED READINGS

Bell, R. et al. (1998). *Changing Bodies, Changing Lives: A Book for Teens on Sex and Relationships* (3rd ed.). New York: Times Books.

This is a popular book intended for youth and parents.

Bruess, C. E. & Greenberg, J. S. (1994). *Sexuality Education: Theory and Practice.* Madison, WI: Brown & Benchmark.

The authors provide content information and instructional strategies for those wanting to teach sexuality education to students of all ages. The book emphasizes that sex education is an integral part of a comprehensive health education program.

McKay, A. (1999). *Sexual Ideology and Schooling: Towards Democratic Sexuality Education.* Albany: State University of New York Press.

McKay offers a structured argument for sexuality education.

ANSWERS TO CHAPTER REVIEW

1. abstinence; **2.** Adolescent Family Life; **3.** 18; **4.** 34; **5.** Eighty-nine; **6.** Sixty-seven; **7.** Dr. Mary Calderone.

CHAPTER 20

Defining Responsibility in a Changing World

- **Values and Sexuality**
  Values, your concepts of the desirable that serve as criteria for meaning and understanding, and for evaluating behavior, are closely related to your concepts of right and wrong. Your sexual values provide a framework for understanding and evaluating sexual behavior.

- **Sexual Ethics**
  Your sexual ethics, the set of moral principles you use to determine your sexual behavior, are dependent on your values and the assumptions you make in determining right behavior. Different assumptions lead to different conclusions about whether a particular behavior is ethical or unethical.

- **Sexual Decision Making**
  Your sexual decisions may be influenced by a number of factors. You can decide what is the right action for you in a particular situation, but there are ways to steer toward good decision making and away from bad choices.

PHYSICAL

SOCIAL

EMOTIONAL

SPIRITUAL

COGNITIVE

Your sexuality can be considered a journey, with many bumps and forks in the road. The complexity of sexuality makes it difficult to find a single path that meets all of your needs and then to stay on it. For example, if at some point in your journey you focus solely on your emotional need for intimacy, you may ignore your physical need for good health by not using a condom.

As an individual, you are responsible for the consequences of the choices you make in order to satisfy your needs. But remember that your actions affect others—those close to you, and perhaps those in your community or even the larger society. If you have a sexually transmitted infection, become pregnant or impregnate someone, or if your sexual behavior hurts others, you are responsible for the consequences of your actions as well as their effects on other people. Although you are not responsible for what others do, because of the social nature of sexual interaction, at some point you will undoubtedly have to deal with the consequences of other people's behavior. For example, you may become a victim of sexual harassment or may unwittingly contract a sexually transmitted infection from a dishonest partner. Alternately, you may benefit from a potential partner's decision to forego intercourse because neither of you has a condom.

Sex is so important that almost everyone has something to say about it. As you explore your sexuality you must negotiate a path through society's contradictory messages about sex. Do it. Don't do it. Everybody else does it. Only a fool does that. It's cool. It's stupid. What are you waiting for? Why not wait? It's your body. Your body is a temple. If it feels good, do it. It can kill you. These various messages represent the many different perceptions and interests that exist in our diverse society. Commercial interests use sexual images to promote their products, hoping to increase sales; and health-care interests promote safer sex in an effort to decrease the costs of suffering.

With sexuality comes a tremendous responsibility for making choices that fit your needs, the needs of others around you, and the needs of society. The following examination of sexual values and sexual ethics will help you to clarify your own beliefs and to make responsible choices.

VALUES AND SEXUALITY

Values are our concepts of what is desirable. They serve as criteria for meaning and understanding, and they help us to evaluate behavior. A classic philosophical notion holds that values are a set of guidelines for making choices resulting in genuine happiness or emotional well-being. Our systems of values both connect us to and separate us from the external world, other people, and other communities or cultures.

Morals

Our values are closely related to our **morals,** our concept of what is right and wrong. The idea that happiness is the goal of moral principles is well rooted in both science and religion. Pioneers in behavioral sciences believed that morality was central to a scientific theory of human nature. Freud considered moral principles so significant that they

Values: concepts of the desirable that serve as criteria for meaning and understanding, and as a guide for evaluating behavior

Morals: concept of what is right and wrong

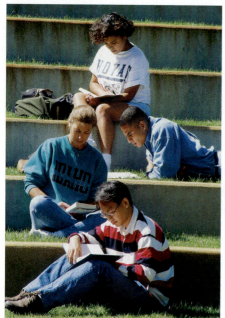

Although we may come from different racial, ethnic or religious backgrounds, as Americans we share some common values.

occupied a fundamental position in his structural model of the mind. More recently, Ramm (1996) has identified seven types of dysfunctional behavior that lead to a threat to or loss of happiness. Alternatively, rational, industrious, self-respecting, honest behaviors, and appropriately considered interpersonal interactions, can serve as values that are likely to contribute to a sense of well-being (Ramm, 1996). Thus, moral behavior may be its own reward.

However, we often face contradictory moral claims, such as expecting both justice and forgiveness. Given certain social constraints, individuals may choose whether to demand "an eye for an eye" or to "turn the other cheek." Moreover, few individuals consider their values rationally prior to determining their behavioral options. Thus, a person can state a value, illustrate its application in making judgments, identify its boundaries, and then choose to ignore it behaviorally (Williams, 1979). For example, a parent who tells a child that honesty is always the best policy is unlikely to say to his or her boss, "Honestly, I believe you truly are stupid," even though the parent believes that to be the case.

It is for this reason that when describing the relationship between values and behavior it is preferable to talk about a person's **value orientation,** a rational and sensible approach to decision making that will maximize one's potential to thrive. Although people may not always be perfectly consistent in acting on their values, they adhere closely enough to a general orientation that their behavior is usually predictable. Predictability is essential for stable social relations within a society.

Your value orientation is determined by your life experiences. Basic value orientations are acquired early in life and are well established by adolescence. On rare occasions, subsequent life events, especially personal crises, may significantly change your values. You may refine your individual values as you go through life, but your basic value orientation remains much the same.

Who has the biggest influence on your value orientation? Most of us get our values from the previous generation. Parents have learned what they believe to be important, practical, necessary, and desirable, and they pass these beliefs along to their children—intentionally or otherwise. This happens generation after generation, with a cumulative effect that becomes part of a society's traditions or culture. Since in any society, at any given point in time, many life experiences may be shared, it is to be expected that many individuals born about the same time will tend to share some values. As a result, these individuals may share some common understandings of what is desirable.

However, it should not be supposed that all members of a society are alike. Indeed no two individuals, even twins, have identical life experiences. We each have different opportunities to experience life and to learn from those experiences. Those differences might not be as significant for identical twins, but men and women, the rich and the poor, city folk and those growing up in rural areas, those in the majority and ethnic minorities experience significant differences in life experiences that impact the development of values. Value orientation is also subject to reinforcement. In other words, if people see you as a "good" person, they will interpret your behavior as ethical; this in turn reinforces your tendency to act like a good person.

Sexual Values

Value Orientation: a rational and sensible approach to decision-making that will maximize one's potential to thrive

Your values about sex are integrated with other values that may, on the surface, seem to have little to do with sexuality. The anthropologists Florence Kluckhohn and Fred Strodtbeck (1961) have suggested that there are a limited number of universal categories of primary values. Those they identified include human nature, nature and the use of technology, time, human activity, and human relationships. In the following examples we shall use their categories to illustrate how your values about sexuality are embedded within other values.

Human Nature. Do you believe that people are basically evil, basically good, or some mixture of the two? Do you believe that human nature can be changed, or that it is fixed? Since the time of the Puritans, the traditional American orientation has been that human nature is basically evil but perfectible. According to this view, constant control and self-discipline are required if any real goodness is to be achieved. However, an American trend began in the 20th century to view human nature as neutral or a mixture of good and evil. If you believe that human nature is basically evil, you are more likely to distrust the intentions of others—including your boyfriend or girlfriend. And, when a relationship dissolves, you may attribute it to the lack of goodness in your partner or yourself. If, on the other hand, you believe that human nature is basically good, you may be more likely to develop trust, an essential element of a long-lasting relationship.

Some cultural groups, such as the Bolivian Aymara, are more oriented toward the past than the present or the future.

Nature and the Use of Technology. Kluckhohn and Strodtbeck (1961) found three value orientations with regard to nature and the use of technology. Some people value subjugation to nature, some value living in harmony with nature, and others value mastery over nature. The third view, mastery over nature, has been the dominant orientation of most Americans; we use any necessary technology to overcome natural forces for the benefit of humans. This view also can be expanded to explain an individual's duty to overcome any obstacle, not just the natural ones.

If you lean toward the mastery over nature view, you will not hesitate to use birth control pills or other contraceptive devices; similarly, you will have no qualms about employing technology for the purposes of reproduction (for example, in vitro fertilization) or examination of a fetus (for example, amniocentesis). Those with the mastery over nature orientation are also less likely to question abortion in the case of known genetic defects. On the other hand, if you are more oriented toward harmony with nature or subjugation to nature, you may view the use of such technology as intrusive or even morally questionable.

Time. Your attitude toward time also may affect your sexuality. All individuals in all societies must deal with past, present, and future dimensions of time. However, there are clear differences in orientation toward these dimensions. While most middle-class Americans are future-oriented, members of some cultural groups may be more oriented to the present (for example, Mexican Americans) or even the past (for example, the Aymara who live in the Andean region of South America). Do you postpone immediate gratification for long-term goals **(future-dominant),** or do you focus on the present because the future seems vague and unpredictable **(present-dominant)?** Or, do you focus on events and relationships from your past **(past-dominant)?**

If you live for the present, immediate sexual pleasure and gratification may seem reasonable. If you are future-oriented, the desire to finish college or establish your financial independence may affect your decisions about having sex, using birth control, or having an abortion. If you are oriented toward the past, your sexual history will strongly influence current and future relationships.

Future-Dominant: decisions based primarily upon the time to come

Present-Dominant: decisions based primarily upon the here and now

Past-Dominant: decisions based primarily upon what has already occurred

Being Orientation: self-focus on spontaneous human expression

Being-in-Becoming Orientation: self-focus on the development of the human essence

Doing Orientation: self-focus on measurable accomplishments

Human Activity. Kluckhohn and Strodtbeck (1961) also identify self-expression in human activity as a universal value orientation. They suggest three variations for this conception: being, being-in-becoming, and doing. In the **being orientation,** the preference is for spontaneous expression of the individual human essence or personality, and of its impulses and desires. Personal self-expression is primary for a person with this orientation. The **being-in-becoming orientation** also emphasizes the human being but focuses on the development of the human essence or personality. A person with this orientation doesn't focus on the current status of one's self, but the potential of what one might become. "The being-in-becoming orientation emphasizes that kind of activity which has as its goal the development of all aspects of the self as an integrated whole" (Kluckhohn & Strodtbeck, 1961, p. 17). Traditionally, the **doing orientation**

Buddhism is an example of the being-in-becoming orientation.

has been the characteristic one for most Americans; this orientation demands the type of activity that results in accomplishments measurable by external standards. Whereas personal recognition might be sufficient for the being orientation, and personal fulfillment might be an accomplishment from the being-in-becoming orientation, the doing orientation demands measurable accomplishments such as a high number of sexual conquests or the birth of a child.

Human Relationships. Kluckhohn and Strodtbeck's final category is the value placed on human relationships. There are three general ways humans relate to each other; these can be simplified as family, group, and individualistic. It should be noted that these are simply useful analytic concepts because, in reality, all humans relate to others in all three ways.

Those with a strong sense of lineality—that individuals are biologically and culturally related to each other through time—may be said to have primarily a **family orientation.** For such individuals, family goals are dominant, especially continuity of the family through time.

Those with a strong **group orientation** usually give primacy to peer relationships, such as those found in voluntary associations (for example, clubs and churches). (Note that many voluntary associations are constructed around the model of the family and may use fictive kin terms to define ideal relationships, such as *lodge brother* or *sorority sister*.) **Individual orientation** or individuality is the third relational category. While no society exists where individuals are without autonomy, in many societies it is limited. Although individualism is dominant in America, it is commonly integrated with the other variations of relational orientation.

If your orientation includes a strong sense of family, you may more easily follow your parents' recommendations about sex. If you have a strong sense of group orientation, you may more readily be influenced by the teachings of your church or the expectations of your fraternity brothers. However, if your primary orientation is individualistic, you will probably chart your own sexual course after determining what seems to be in your personal best interests.

How strong is your sense of your own autonomy? How heavily do you rely on the wishes of your family? And, how much are you influenced by the groups to which you belong (for example, peer, church, or school groups)? While individualism is strong in America, it is commonly integrated with the other variations of the relational orientation.

The following is a more direct test of your sexual values. Take this test, which was composed by Susan Hendrick and Clyde Hendrick (1987). After you have completed the test and scoring, compare your results to the norms reported in Table 20.1 to see how you compare.

The norms shown in Table 20.1 are based on college students. The higher your score for Permissiveness, the more likely you are to have had more sexual relationships, to have engaged in a greater variety of sexual practices, and to believe that love isn't a

What Are Your Value Orientations?

Human Nature: evil, neutral or mixed, or good? fixed or changeable?

Nature and Technology: subjugation to nature, harmony with nature, or mastery over nature?

Time: past-dominant, present-dominant, or future-dominant?

Human Activity: being, being-in-becoming, or doing?

Human Relationships: family-oriented, group-oriented, or individual-oriented?

 How do your value orientations compare to those identified by Kluckhohn and Strodtbeck?

—*Do you think your personal values on these scales impact your sexual behaviors?*

ASK YOURSELF

What Are Your Sexual Attitudes and Values?

For each statement that follows, fill in the response that indicates how much you agree or disagree. Whenever possible, answer the question with your current partner in mind. If you are not currently in a relationship, answer the questions with your most recent partner in mind. If you have never had a sexual relationship, answer in terms of what you think your response would most likely be.

1=strongly disagree 2=moderately disagree 3=neutral—neither agree nor disagree 4=moderately agree 5=strongly agree

1. I do not need to be committed to a person to have sex with him or her.
2. Casual sex is acceptable.
3. I would like to have sex with many partners.
4. One-night stands are sometimes very enjoyable.
5. It is OK to have ongoing sexual relationships with more than one person at a time.
6. It is OK to manipulate someone into having sex as long as no future promises are made.
7. Sex as a simple exchange of favors is OK if both people agree to it.
8. The best sex is with no strings attached.
9. Life would have fewer problems if people could have sex more freely.
10. It is possible to enjoy sex with a person and not like that person very much.
11. Sex is more fun with someone you don't love.
12. It is all right to pressure someone into having sex.
13. Extensive premarital sexual experience is fine.
14. Extramarital affairs are all right as long as one's partner doesn't know about them.
15. Sex for its own sake is perfectly all right.
16. I would feel comfortable having intercourse with my partner in the presence of other people.
17. Prostitution is acceptable.
18. It is OK for sex to be just good physical release.
19. Sex without love is meaningless.
20. People should at least be friends before they have sex together.
21. In order for sex to be good, it must also be meaningful.
22. Birth control is part of responsible sexuality.
23. A woman should share responsibility for birth control.
24. A man should share responsibility for birth control.
25. Sex education is important for young people.
26. Using "sex toys" during lovemaking is acceptable.
27. Masturbation is all right.
28. Masturbating one's partner during intercourse can increase the pleasure of sex.
29. Sex gets better as a relationship progresses.
30. Sex is the closest form of communication between two people.
31. A sexual encounter between two people deeply in love is the ultimate human interaction.
32. Orgasm is the greatest experience in the world.
33. At its best, sex seems to be the merging of two souls.

Family Orientation: value of relationships influenced by and centered on one's family

Group Orientation: value of relationships is influenced by and centered on peer relations

Individual Orientation: value of relationships is influenced by and centered on the individual

34. Sex is a very important part of life.

35. Sex is usually an intensive, almost overwhelming experience.

36. During sexual intercourse, intense awareness of the partner is the best frame of mind.

37. Sex is fundamentally good.

38. Sex is best when you let yourself go and focus on your own pleasure.

39. Sex is primarily the taking of pleasure from another person.

40. The main purpose of sex is to enjoy oneself.

41. Sex is primarily physical.

42. Sex is primarily a bodily function like eating.

43. Sex is mostly a game between males and females.

SCORING: Add your scores for items 1–21 to get your Permissiveness score (items 19, 20, and 21 are reverse scored, so subtract your score from the number 6 for each of those items). Add your scores for Items 22–28 to get your Sexual Practices score. Add your scores for items 29–37 to get your Communion score. Add your scores for items 38–43 to get your Instrumentality score.

SOURCE: Hendrick & Hendrick, 1987.

necessary prerequisite for sex. If you scored high in the Sexual Practices dimension, you tend to accept your sexuality, value this aspect of your life, and place high value on sexually responsible behavior. High scores in this area indicate that you value new sexual experiences but believe that it is important to conform to society's norms when you engage in novel behavior; you also tend to have more intimate verbal interactions

TABLE 20.1

Norms for the Sexual Attitudes and Values Scale

	Score Men	Women	Percentile
Permissiveness	34	21	15
	47	25	30
	60	38	50
	73	51	70
	86	64	85
Sexual practices	18	18	15
	22	22	30
	28	28	50
	32	32	70
	35	35	85
Communion	26	26	15
	31	31	30
	36	36	50
	41	41	70
	45	45	85
Instrumentality	9	6	15
	13	10	30
	17	14	50
	21	18	70
	24	22	85

SOURCE: Bonder, Martin & Miracle, 2001.

Reflections on the Sexual Values Scale

Did taking this test cause you to consider your personal sexual values in a new light?

—Did any of your answers surprise you?

—Do you think that any questionnaire can ever illustrate the complexity of an individual's value system?

—What might be the relationship between answers on a values scale and a person's actual behavior?

—What questions would you ask to discover someone's sexual values?

---

with your partner. If you scored high in the Communion sub-scale, you tend to have a very emotional, idealistic approach to sex and consider the spiritual elements of sex more important than the physical act. The Instrumentality dimension reflects a somewhat selfish, egocentric view of sexual relationships. High scorers tend to be "game-players" who believe it is all right to deceive and manipulate potential partners in order to get what they want (Hendrick & Hendrick, 1987).

SEXUAL ETHICS

Ethics is a set of moral principles for determining behavior. Some ethical choices seem relatively simple: It is wrong to kill another person; it is right to take care of your family. But what if these two are in conflict? If an intruder threatens your loved ones, is it all right to kill that person? It seems that all too often we are confronted with decisions that don't neatly fit into the box that says, "absolutely, positively, beyond a shadow of a doubt, totally and completely right"—or wrong. While ethics may seem an abstract concept, whether you realize it or not you participate in ethical decision making every day. The practical question with regard to the study of ethics is how cognitively aware you are of those decisions. Reflection (that is, weighing the options) is central to deciding a right course of behavior.

I am the Lord thy God,.... Thou shalt have no other gods before me.

Thou shalt not make unto thee any graven images.

Thou shalt not take the name of the Lord thy God in vain.

Remember the sabbath day, to keep it holy.

Honor thy father and thy mother: that thy days may be long.

Thou shalt not kill.

Thou shalt not commit adultery.

Thou shalt not steal.

Thou shalt not bear false witness against thy neighbor.

Thou shalt not covet thy neighbor's house.

FIGURE 20.1   The Ten Commandments.

The Role of Authority in Ethical Decision Making

The role of authority in ethical decision making is basic to determining right actions. To illustrate this we offer the examples of two contrasting positions: the authoritarian and situational approaches. The **authoritarian approach** assumes that when we make choices about what to do we can rely on a normative standard derived from an authority higher than the individual. The normative standard may be a list of specific rules such as the Ten Commandments (Figure 20.1), or a set of general laws and principles such as a professional code of ethics. Generally, authoritarians believe that there is a single right behavior for any situation, which can be determined from that normative standard.

The **situational approach** assumes no such outside authority; while situationalists may take into account traditional wisdom collected over the generations, in this view the responsibility for making ethically sound decisions rests squarely with the individual. Situationalists accept the burden of not always being able to know with certainty the right course. Indeed, they would argue that acceptance of uncertainty is an essential ingredient for responsible behavior (Fletcher, 1966). For a comparison of the authoritarian and situationalist views, see Table 20.2.

Ethics: a set of moral principles for determining behavior

Authoritarian Approach: belief that assumes we make choices based on a normative standard within society

Situational Approach: belief that assumes we make choices based on the individual responsibility

TABLE 20.2

The Role of Authority in Decision Making

Authoritarian	Situationalist
Ethics must be grounded in collective wisdom.	An individual should consider collective wisdom as a source for ethical decision making.
Most individuals are not sufficiently wise to make ethical determinations.	While all individuals are not equally wise, each must assume responsibility for his or her actions.
Most individuals are not sufficiently strong to do what is right, therefore they must submit to social sanctions to guide them down the straight and narrow.	Social sanctions are useful to provide for social order, but an ethical individual may choose to violate these guides.
There is one right way; when two principles seem to conflict, the conflict is only apparent since the law also orders these principles.	If principles conflict, individuals must decide the right course and then accept responsibility for their own actions.
It is true that these things must be decided through interpretation (usually by a deliberative body).	Frequently principles are in conflict and decisions must be made in situ not a priori.

SOURCE: Adapted from Bonder, Martin, & Miracle, 2001.

ETHICS AND SEXUAL ISSUES

Sexual ethics is about right behavior pertaining to sex and sexual issues. Sexual ethics pertain to all aspects of sexuality, not just the "should I or shouldn't I" debate. As you have already learned, there are ethical decisions to be made concerning birth control, sexually transmitted infections, the use of technology to reverse infertility, the commercialization of sex, sexual research, sexuality education, and attempts to control sex through legislation. New dimensions of science and technology such as genetic engineering and the cloning of human beings require ethical consideration as well. For example, it is expected that in the next few years cloning technology will make it possible to grow partial human fetuses to harvest organs for transplants. What are the ethical implications of this biomedical technology?

Doing what is right can create special problems in pluralistic societies marked by a diversity of religious and moral traditions. This becomes apparent when the right behavior of one group is in conflict with the right behavior of another. Earlier we stated our belief in the golden rule of civil society, that you must give others individual freedom if you would have them allow you freedom. Of course, this rule assumes the presence of sufficient agreement among society's constituencies on how the society generally ought to work in order to maintain minimal social structures and contracts. The fact that those with great power or those with the support of a majority of all voters decide on a course of action or a particular law does not mean that the action or the law is morally right. For example, the right of women to vote began as a minority movement attacking the position of the majority. While it took decades to change the existing statutes, few today would question that denying women the right to vote would be an immoral position.

When political power is equated with moral right there is the danger of tyranny. This may be especially true for sexual issues such as women's rights, gender equity, and gay and lesbian rights. The inherent relationships between sexuality and reproduction and the control of production render sexuality intensely emotional, religiously charged, and innately political.

Sexual Ethics: a set of moral principles pertaining to sex and sexual issues

Procreationist: view that reproduction is the primary purpose of sexuality

Recreationist: view that anything that gives a person pleasure is inherently good

Naturalist: belief that the individual must make his or her own decisions based on circumstances

Doing the Right Thing

In 1999 a California woman gave birth to a child using sperm retrieved from her dead husband. The sperm were retrieved 30 hours after the man's death and then frozen for 15 months. Some ethicists have stated that this procedure raises questions about reproductive freedom and men giving their consent to be fathers. Others question whether it is right to consciously bring a child into the world with a dead father and if it is appropriate to perform a medical procedure to assuage the grief of a surviving spouse.

A husband and wife are both dwarfs, each carrying one flawed copy of the gene responsible for a condition called achondroplasia. The couple learns that if their child inherits two flawed genes, it probably will die in infancy. A child with one flawed gene will be a dwarf while a child with two normal genes will be of more average height. The couple states that knowing the child would die in infancy, they plan to abort any fetus that carries two flawed genes. They also plan to abort the fetus if is has two normal genes because they want a baby like themselves.

The parents of a 17-year-old developmentally disabled woman want to have her surgically sterilized because they believe that her limited intellectual capacity and immaturity would not permit her to make responsible contraceptive choices or to be an adequate parent if she became pregnant.

 These are hypothetical cases, but they could occur. How would you respond to each of these situations?

SOURCE: Adapted from Fackelmann, 1994.

The Ethical Permissibility of Sex Acts: Three Contrasting Arguments

If individuals begin with different assumptions about what is right, they may reach different conclusions, even though the logic of their arguments may be sound. Consider the following arguments for three illustrative positions we have labeled procreationist, recreationist, and naturalist. These positions are summarized in Table 20.3.

As the term implies, the **procreationist** assumes that procreation is the primary function of sexuality and that human reproduction is the primary basis for ethical sexuality. For the procreationist, sex may yield pleasure, but pleasure is not a sufficient reason to engage in sex since pleasure may mask the potential emotional, physical, or material harm that may be caused by nonreproductive sex. In other words, the procreationist believes that the only ethical reason for having a sexual relationship is to conceive a baby.

The **recreationist** assumes that anything that gives a person pleasure is inherently good. If a sexual act has the potential to be both pleasurable and harmful, the individual must weigh the pros and cons in order to choose a right course of action. The Epicureans of ancient Greece believed that seeking pleasure is the highest good. Following the teachings of Epicurus (341–270 B.C.), Epicureans made personal pleasure primary in determining a right course of action.

The **naturalist** assumes that procreation, pleasure, love, and intimacy are all valid reasons for engaging in sex. Thus, each individual must determine the right course of action for a particular set of circumstances, since no standard or criterion is primary.

Belliotti's Five Tiers of Sexual Morality

Raymond A. Belliotti (1993) has provided another way to evaluate sexual behavior in his book *Good Sex: Perspectives on Sexual Ethics*. Belliotti composed a five-step method for evaluating the morality of sexual behavior. The steps or tiers are arranged in a specific order. For example, only if the act passes evaluation at Tier 1 do you need to consider subsequent tiers (Figure 20.2).

FIGURE 20.2   The Five Tiers of Ethical Decision Making. SOURCE: Adapted from Belliotti, 1993.

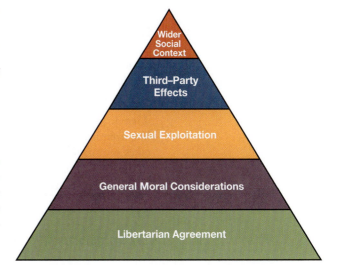

TABLE 20.3

The Ethical Permissibility of Different Sex Acts

Act	Procreationist	Recreationist	Naturalist
Masturbation	No, procreation is not possible	Yes, if it is pleasurable	Yes; there is little chance of harm
Birth Control	No, procreation is not intended	Yes, if it increases pleasure by reducing anxiety	Yes, it gives individuals more control
Bestiality	No, procreation is not possible	Yes, if it gives pleasure to the person and does not harm the animal	Yes, if no harm results to person or animal
Prostitution	No, procreation is not intended	Yes, if it is pleasurable and responsible	Yes, but only if it can be demonstrated that no harm accrues to either person
Teen Sex	Only in marriage for procreation	Yes, if it is pleasurable and responsible	Yes, if they are old enough to be responsible
Homosexual Sex	No, procreation is not possible	Yes, if it is pleasurable and responsible	Ethics are the same as for heterosexual sex
Outside Marriage	Not unless procreation is intended	Yes, if it is pleasurable and responsible	Only if it can be demonstrated that no harm will accrue to anyone

Tier 1: Libertarian Agreement. The parties, possessing the basic capacities necessary for autonomous choice, must agree to a particular sexual interaction without force, fraud, or explicit duress. (Children, the mentally incompetent, and the mentally incapacitated are excluded from ethical sexual interactions since they do not possess the capacities for autonomous choice.) For example, two capable (not under the influence of drugs or alcohol) adults agree to have intercourse—and neither has used force, fraud, or social pressure.

Tier 2: General Moral Considerations. Some basic principles, including the consideration of motives and intentions, apply to sexual decision making. The general moral principles acknowledged in our society include the following: keep promises; tell the truth; return favors; aid others in distress; make reparation for harm to others that is one's own fault; oppose injustices; promote just institutions; assume one's fair share of societal burdens; avoid causing pain or suffering to others; avoid inexcusable killing of others; and avoid stealing or otherwise depriving others of their property. For example, an individual cannot withhold knowledge that he or she has an STI—even though there is a libertarian agreement to engage in intercourse.

Tier 3: Sexual Exploitation. Any exploitative or coercive sex is morally impermissible, even if the exploitation or coercion is subtle. Exploitation occurs when one party takes advantage of another party's attributes or situation to exact personal gain or gain for the exploiter's compatriots. For example, one cannot imply—even subtly—that having sexual relations may result in a job promotion or a better course grade and remain ethical.

Tier 4: Third-Party Effects. When the considered sexual activity meets the previous ethical considerations, it may still be morally impermissible if anyone not directly involved in the act will nevertheless be harmed as a result. For example, children might suffer indirectly as a result of their parents' sexual actions.

CONSIDERATIONS

Reflections on Belliotti's Five Tiers

 Do you think Belliotti's approach to sexual morality can be applied to every type of sexual behavior?

—Would your own intuition generally lead you to the same decisions as Belliotti's logic?

—In what case(s) would your decision making likely produce different results?

Tier 5: Wider Social Context.   Even if a sex act meets all other criteria it might be morally impermissible if it reinforces oppressive social roles, contributes to continued social inequality, gives rise to new forms of gender oppression, or otherwise adds to the contamination of the wider social and political context surrounding sexual activity.

SEXUAL DECISION MAKING

Should I let him touch my breasts? Should we use a condom? Do I love her enough to have sex with her? If she said no last week, should I ask her again? Should I ask if she is on the pill? Is it safe to accept a ride in his car, or to go up to his room for a drink? Should I have sex with this person?

Sex is an interpersonal act that can have profound personal, social, romantic, professional, and legal consequences. Having sex is generally subject to conscious, voluntary decisions. Every day millions of people decide whether to engage in sexual activity; usually these decisions affect not just them but their partners or potential partners. Some of these decisions turn out well; others turn out badly and cause regret. In order to help you make good decisions about sex, in this section we examine the sexual decision-making process.

Why are decisions sometimes so difficult? It is not simply a matter of confusion about values. Even people who have firm values may have trouble knowing the right course of action in some situations, because many decisions must be made in uncertain circumstances. If you do not know all the facts, you may have to make a decision based on a level of knowledge that is insufficient to make clear the best course of action. For example, you are trying to decide whether to have sex with a new partner. According to your value orientation people should both love each other before having intercourse, but your partner's feelings are not clear to you. So you must make your decision with incomplete information.

Male/Female Differences in Decision Making

According to most major theories, men and women typically face somewhat different decisions with regard to sex. Feminist theories have emphasized how women are often in positions of lesser power—politically, economically, and even physically. Some men may abuse this power to coerce women into unwanted sexual activity, and women often must make decisions that carry some risk of such victimization. Social exchange theory points out that in sex in particular, women are often in the position of greater power, insofar as the man wants sex more and the final decision about whether to have sex generally depends on the woman.

As discussed throughout this text, evolutionary theory emphasizes that the costs of sexual mistakes are much greater for women than for men, because the minimum investment in a pregnancy is only a few minutes for a man but close to a year for a woman. One theory about how evolutionary differences produce gender differences in decision-making styles is called **error management theory** (Haselton & Buss,

Error Management Theory: theory that people make decisions in ways that will minimize whatever kind of error has been most costly in the evolutionary past

2000). According to this approach, people make decisions in ways that will minimize whatever kind of error has been most costly in the evolutionary past. In simplest form, the men's worst error has been to miss an opportunity for sex, because males will be most successful at passing on their genes if they take every opportunity to copulate with every willing partner. The biggest mistake among women has been to engage in sex with the wrong person, as women will be most successful at giving their genes (and their children) the best chance to thrive if they only copulate with the highest quality partners.

Consistent with error management theory, Haselton and Buss (2000) found that men tended to overestimate women's sexual intent. In other words, when women act in a friendly manner, men tend to think that they are interested in having sex. Haselton and Buss found that men could be quite accurate in estimating the sexual intentions of their sisters, who were not potential sex partners. They only overestimated the intent of potential partners. Having this type of bias helps men avoid missing out on a sexual opportunity (Haselton & Buss, 2000). For example, suppose a man has two conversations with women, and in both cases the women stand fairly close and smile at him and seem very interested in what he says. Suppose also that one of the women really is sexually interested in him, while the other is just being friendly and has no sexual or romantic interest. Crucially, he cannot tell the difference. If he decides to be cautious and assume that neither of them is interested in him, he would miss out on the sexual opportunity actually there. Hence it is in an important way more rational for him to act as if both of them might be sexually interested.

Conversely, women tend to make errors that underestimate the degree of commitment of a potential sexual partner (Haselton & Buss, 2000). As you learned in Chapter 15, women tend to think that men are generally afraid of commitment, but evidence suggests that men fall in love faster than women and are ready to move a relationship forward (even to marriage) before the women are ready (for example, Huston et al., 1981; Kanin, Davidson, & Scheck, 1970). Haselton and Buss (2000) point out it is adaptive for women to underestimate a man's commitment because the cost of overestimating commitment could be high. If a woman believed a man to be highly committed to her when in fact he was not, she might have sex with him and become pregnant, only to have him leave her. In that case she would be left to raise the child by herself without a male provider, as well as suffering some damage to her reputation and reducing her appeal to other, possibly more desirable (and more willing to commit) partners. The opposite error would tend to have only a minor cost. Although there is the risk that the potential partner would move on, in many cases the man just tries harder to prove his love for her.

Women's sexual behavior is more often contrary to their general values and attitudes than is men's. Men's sexual behavior tends to conform to their attitudes, whereas women are far more likely to report doing things they do not approve of and failing to do things that they say they would like (see Baumeister, 2000, for review). The gap between attitudes and behaviors is larger for women than for men in such areas as using condoms, engaging in premarital or extramarital sex, engaging in homosexual acts, and acting out submissive fantasies (for example, Bell & Weinberg, 1978; Croake & James, 1973; Hansen, 1987; Herold & Mewhinney, 1993; Laumann et al., 1994; for review, see Baumeister, 2000). Because a woman's sexual response depends heavily on the immediate situation and context, her attitudes and personal standards may more likely be set aside when a particular situation appears to be an exception. For example, sometimes a woman will express strong disapproval of engaging in sexual activity with someone other than her boyfriend, but in the complexity of actual circumstances she might actually do it. Suppose, for example, that she and her boyfriend have had a fight, she has been approached by someone she always liked and found out that he has been secretly in love with her for months, and she thinks no one will ever find out. Hansen (1987) found that a woman's attitudes toward infidelity were much less predictive of her actual behavior than was the case for a man.

How to Make Good Decisions

A variety of psychological processes influences how we make decisions; sometimes this results in doing things you later regret. In this section we discuss some of these personal biases. If you know what the common mistakes are, perhaps you can avoid some of them!

One of the most common patterns of bad decisions involves misjudging the trade-off between short-term gains and long-term costs. For example, most college students would be better off financially in the short run if they dropped out of college (where they are typically earning very little money and often running up substantial debts) and got a job. In the long run, however, college graduates end up making far more money on average than people who do not have a degree. Hence it is rational to sacrifice the short-term gain to pursue the long-term one, although some people do make the tempting (but eventually costly) opposite choice.

Sexual decision making presents many such tradeoffs. Decisions are often difficult precisely because there is an appealing promise of short-term pleasure that must be weighed against more distant risks and costs. It is often tempting to go ahead and have sex with someone you desire, and perhaps to do so without using a condom or other protection. Having impulsive, unprotected sex will likely bring substantial pleasure and satisfaction, as well as other rewards such as the ego boost of feeling desired and the sense of adventure that comes from new sexual experiences. These short-term gains must be balanced against the risks of pregnancy, sexually transmitted infections, guilt, heartbreak, and the like—all of which will not be seen until well after the night is over.

It Can't Happen to Me   There is a broad tendency of people to subscribe to favorable, optimistic views about themselves and their lives (Taylor & Brown, 1988), including unrealistic optimism. Research has shown that people believe they are more likely than their peers to have something good happen, such as having a gifted child or earning a high salary. By the same token, they believe they are less likely than other people to experience bad outcomes, such as being unemployed, being a crime victim, or having a severe automobile accident (for example, Weinstein, 1980).

Such overconfidence also exists in the sexual sphere. Burger and Burns (1988) found that sexually active college women systematically underestimated their chances of getting pregnant, relative to various comparison groups. For example, the women rated the chances that they would get pregnant in the next 12 months as under 10 on a scale running from 0 (no chance at all) to 100 (guaranteed to become pregnant). They rated one another's chances at 27, and rated American women overall at about 40. Clearly they thought that unwanted pregnancy was something that would happen to other people and not to themselves. If the women were objective, they ought to have rated their own chances as higher than those of women on average, because the participants in the study were sexually active whereas many other women were not, and obviously having sex is a major risk factor for pregnancy. The researchers Perloff and Fetzer (1986) used the term **illusion of unique invulnerability** to describe this pattern: risks that pertain to other people do not pertain to me, and I will be exempt from the bad outcomes that afflict others.

The illusion of unique invulnerability was linked to taking risks. Burger and Burns (1988) asked the women whether they had used contraception in their most recent sexual experiences, and their responses correlated with their illusions. The more a woman believed that she would not get pregnant, the less likely she was to report using contraception. Logically, using contraception should be more, not less, likely to make a woman confident that she will be safe from pregnancy. However, it appears that some women simply think that they are exempt from the danger of pregnancy, an attitude likely to bring them to grief. In fact, Burger and Burns found that almost one out of every four women in their sample did become pregnant.

Illusion of Unique Invulnerability: belief that you are exempt from the consequences that apply to others

"Lechery, sir, it [alcohol] provokes, and unprovokes: it provokes the desire, but it takes away the performance: therefore, much drink may be said to be an equivocator with lechery: it makes him, and it mars him; it sets him on, and it takes him off; it persuades him, and disheartens him; makes him stand to, and not stand to; in conclusion, equivocates him in a sleep, and, giving him the lie, leaves him."

MACBETH,
BY WILLIAM SHAKESPEARE,
ACT 2, SCENE 3

AIDS and other sexually transmitted infections are another group of bad outcomes affected by the illusion of unique invulnerability. In one study researchers asked men to estimate their chances of getting AIDS. The men rated their risk as very low, regardless of whether they were engaging in sexually risky behaviors or not. Some men had not had sex with anyone for a long time and had not engaged in any high-risk behavior, and they (appropriately enough) said they were quite unlikely to get AIDS. Other men had been engaging in risky sex, without condoms, with multiple different partners on numerous occasions—but they gave themselves essentially the same risk-free rating as the celibate men (Hansen, Hahn, & Wolkenstein, 1990)!

Another study explored how gay men rationalize taking sexual risks (Offir et al., 1993). Some men said their partners had not penetrated them, so they felt safe. Some had been penetrated but said they felt safe because their partner had not had an orgasm inside them. Some felt safe because they had not let the partner have an orgasm in their mouth. Others said they were safe, even though their partner had had an orgasm during fellatio, because they had not swallowed the semen. (Recall from Chapter 7 that the AIDS virus can be absorbed through any cuts or sores in the mouth as well as the anus, whereas it is rapidly killed in the stomach, so swallowing semen is essentially irrelevant to any danger of getting AIDS from fellatio.) Some simply said that they engaged in unsafe practices but had not done so as frequently as other men, so their risk was relatively low.

One personality trait that seems to influence such illusions and errors in judgment is self-esteem. High self-esteem is in general associated with a style of thinking that distorts perceptions in a favorable manner that pleases and flatters the self. When Smith, Gerrard, and Gibbons (1997) asked women to estimate their chances of becoming pregnant from unprotected sex, women with high self-esteem were the most likely to underestimate their risk. In that study, the women were asked to list their sexual activities and rate their risk of pregnancy. The self-reported behaviors of women with high self-esteem were essentially the same as those of women with low self-esteem. But the women with high self-esteem rated their behaviors as less risky than people with low self-esteem.

Alcohol and Sexual Choices   Alcohol has long played a role in sexual behavior, and it is widely regarded as an aphrodisiac. Careful research has questioned that view, however. It may be simply that alcohol undermines inhibitions and restraints without changing the desire itself—so that the same desires that were there all along are more likely to lead to action. A well-known paper by Steele and Southwick (1985) compiled results from dozens of studies to test the hypothesis that alcohol produces wild, extreme behavior of all kinds ("Drunken Excess," in the title of their article). They concluded that alcohol only increased that sort of behavior when the person had already desired it. Specifically, they said that alcohol's effects were mainly found when the person had an inner response conflict, such as both wanting to do something and not wanting to do it. Getting drunk did not increase the desire to do it, but it reduced the factors that normally held the person back. As they put it, alcohol inhibits the inhibitors. For example, alcohol does not create any new or increased level of aggressive impulses, but it undermines the inner restraints that normally stop people from acting on their violent impulses.

So alcohol will not produce any new sexual desires (such as making you want to do something you have never desired before, or making you want to have sex with someone you have never been attracted to)—but it can remove the inhibitions that have prevented you from acting on existing desires.

There are several theories about how alcohol manages to weaken inhibitions. One line of thinking emphasizes **self-awareness** (defined as focusing your conscious attention on yourself), which is typically a matter of thinking about what

Drinking alcohol is no excuse for irresponsible sexual behavior.

you are doing and comparing yourself to ideals, norms, moral rules, personal goals, and other standards. Hull (1981) showed that alcohol reduces people's self-awareness. The desire to escape from self-awareness is probably one of the main reasons people like to drink (Hull, 1981). After a personal misfortune or setback, it is unpleasant to think about yourself when some rejection or failure has put you in a bad light. Likewise, when you want to celebrate, it helps to forget yourself and enter into the fun without worrying "Will people think I'm foolish?" or "Do I look undignified wearing a lampshade on my head?" Anything that reduces self-awareness is likely to sweep away some sexual inhibitions.

Another theory focuses on the narrowing of attention caused by alcohol intoxication. *Myopia* is the medical term for near-sightedness, or the ability to see only those things that are close to one's eyes. Josephs and Steele (1990) coined the term **alcohol myopia** to refer to alcohol's role in reducing the ability to think about many different things and process different levels of meaning, leading to an intense focus on one thing. For example, people may succeed in escaping from a bad mood by drinking, but only if they do so with a distraction (such as watching a ball game while drinking beer) that will take their mind off their problems. If they drink and continue thinking about their problems, they may end up feeling worse than ever, because the alcohol myopia will make them all the more absorbed in their troubles.

Although the alcohol myopia pattern has not been tested in sex research studies, it does suggest another pathway toward sexual mistakes. Alcohol intoxication can narrow a person's focus so that a potential partner seems more sexually appealing. (Some people use the term "beer goggles" to describe how intoxication can seem to enhance the perceived attractiveness of a potential sex partner.) The urge for physical contact then may consume the thoughts of an intoxicated person, leaving little room for thoughts about long-range consequences.

Loss of Self-Control   The psychology of self-control offers another perspective on decision making. **Self-control** is the ability to control and regulate one's own behavior. People have an assortment of sexual desires and impulses, but they can choose whether to act on them or restrain them. Restraining impulses requires self-control, so any factor that weakens self-control will make people more likely to engage in sex acts that self-control would normally prohibit.

One crucial aspect of self-control is the ability to monitor your behavior. Most people find that successful self-control depends heavily on careful monitoring of their actions. For example, successful dieters keep track of what they eat and weigh themselves regularly.

Alcohol appears to undermine nearly all forms of self-control (Baumeister, Heatherton, & Tice, 1994); this pattern is due at least in part to the fact that people stop monitoring their behavior when they become intoxicated. Drunken people eat more, spend more, boast more, and get into fights more than sober people. In fact, some careful studies suggest that drinking even causes people to drink more, because they lose track of how much they are drinking (see Lansky, Nathan, & Lawson, 1978). Hence it is not surprising that alcohol makes people more willing to perform sex acts they would normally avoid, because they stop thinking about what they are doing.

Strong emotional arousal also interferes with self-control. This pattern is well established, although there are a number of competing theories about how emotion produces this effect (Baumeister, Heatherton, & Tice, 1994). Much more research needs to be done to determine which of them are correct. Strong arousal is of course especially relevant to sexual decisions, given the context in which many of them are actually made. Sex researchers have long noted large gaps between what people say they would or should do (especially what they say when they are not aroused and are quietly filling out a questionnaire in a research study) and what they actually do (for example, Hansen, 1987; Herold & Mewhinney, 1993). Why the difference? People may have all sorts of good intentions and sensible guidelines, but the actual decisions may be made in the heat of the moment when the person is flushed with arousal and

Self-Awareness: focusing your conscious attention on yourself

Alcohol Myopia: the role of alcohol in reducing the ability to think about many different things and process different levels of meaning, leading to an intense focus on one thing

Self-Control: the ability to control and regulate one's own behavior

desire. The combination of alcohol intoxication and passionate arousal (as in sexual desire) is thus a double blow to self-control—yet it is also a combination that is quite common when it comes to making sexual decisions.

Further, self-control seems to operate like a muscle, in that it becomes "tired" from exercise and is then less able to function until it is restored by rest (for example, Baumeister et al., 1998). Hardly anyone gets up from a good night's sleep and immediately breaks a diet with an eating binge or launches on an alcoholic bender. As the day wears on, people's ability to control themselves grows progressively weaker. Diets are broken late in the day, when people are tired, and that is also when the largest number of impulsive crimes are committed (see Baumeister, Heatherton, & Tice, 1994), when drug or alcohol relapses occur, and so forth. Times of stress (imminent work deadlines, or examination periods at universities) are also likely to undermine self-control, because people are using all their self-control in the effort to cope with the stress, and they do not have enough left over to deal with other issues.

People may be most vulnerable to making bad sexual decisions when they are tired or under stress. (To be sure, stress may detract from someone's sexual motivation, and so the person may be less likely to desire sex—which may partly offset the reduced self-control.) A dating couple may be more likely to have unwise sex at 3:00 A.M. than at 10:00 P.M. Keeping a potential sexual partner up until very late may be one (very unethical) strategy for overcoming that person's resistance.

Choosing the Wrong Mate

Selecting a partner is another domain in which people make bad decisions and come to grief. Most young people are confident that they will never marry the wrong person or face divorce, but the numbers are hard to dispute. Roughly half the couples who start out with deep love and promises to cherish each other "till death do us part" end up divorcing.

In modern society, most people marry for love. Most people want very much to persuade themselves that the person they love would be a good person to marry. It may seem contrary to the spirit of love to objectively analyze a potential mate. Then again, many people do pause to contemplate whether the person they love would in fact make a good spouse and co-parent. These ruminations are, however, subject to considerable bias. As generally happens when mental processes are subject to strong, biasing motivations, people tend to search for reasons that help them reach the conclusion they want, and to ignore or rationalize signs to the contrary.

As you learned in Chapter 15, passionate love is an altered state of consciousness, which in some respects resembles the effects of a very strong drug. Deciding to get married during that state is therefore a somewhat delicate business, not unlike making a binding career decision or financial investment while seriously intoxicated. In some cultures, parents arrange marriages for their children, and the children usually have fairly little input into the process (although often they are permitted to veto an unacceptable prospect). There may be several reasons for this. For example, marriage may be regarded as a financial or political transaction between families rather than an expression of individual romantic love. The practice of arranged marriage has also been defended on the basis that young people cannot be trusted to make a sensible choice for themselves, especially when they are deranged by passionate love. So are people in arranged marriages deeply unhappy with each other, mismatched, and disappointed? There are little data to suggest that arranged marriages are less happy or less successful than modern American marriages based on love. In other words, people do not choose all that wisely for themselves even when they are free to follow their heart.

Strictly speaking, there are three possible ways that romantic, passionate love can impair a person's choice of partner. One is that being wildly in love makes people see their partners in an idealized, unrealistic manner. Your partner may seem like sheer perfection to you, even though your friends are asking themselves what on earth you see in that person. In short, your ability to make an objective assessment of your partner is impaired when you are passionately in love. This might not matter if you could sustain that inflated, idealized image of your partner forever, but because passionate love tends to subside after a period of months or sometimes a few years (see Chapter 15), at some point you will be able to see your partner more accurately again, and you may wonder why you were so quick to marry someone with such obvious flaws.

Second, passionate love may also change your partner (this is assuming that your partner is in love with you at the same time). Passionate love produces psychological and biochemical changes in the body, and these can produce substantial alterations in behavior. Try to imagine how differently an unhappily married couple must have acted toward each other when they were dating. Love has great power to transform an ordinary person into a witty, charming, passionate, devoted partner, but when the love wears off the person may go back to being his or her dull and grumpy old self. Thus, the person you marry may not be the person you end up living with for many years thereafter.

Third, passionate love is itself such a compelling, addictive experience that some people marry in order to preserve that feeling. People may even notice that at some level their partner is not a good match and has several potentially troublesome faults—but who cares about a few bad habits when simply being in that person's presence brings a rush of excitement and ecstasy? Again, because of the temporary nature of passionate love, marrying in order to perpetuate that feeling is a mistake.

Instead, the success of a marriage will depend on whether the people can make the transition from passionate to companionate love (see Chapter 15). The phase of passionate love can be a wonderful time to lay the foundations for a deep intimacy that will produce a lasting companionate love. The ideal partner will make the transition with you from passionate lovers to best friends.

Ending a Relationship   The decision to end a relationship is another difficult one. Passionate love makes it hard to decide against continuing a relationship, especially because being in love makes the person seem unique and irreplaceable. A common feature of heartbreak (see Chapter 16) is the sense that one will never find anyone else this good and hence never be this happy again (for example, Baumeister & Wotman, 1992; Hendin, 1982). Most people experience the feeling that they are losing the one and only person who is right for them—but then as the months go by they find someone else and are just as happy (if not more so) with the new partner. When you are preparing to end a relationship, it is difficult but important to recognize as an illusion the feeling that this is the only person with whom you could live happily ever after.

Self-Esteem, Narcissism, and Depression   What traits would you look for in a spouse? In modern America self-esteem is considered an important, desirable trait, especially because some people believe that loving yourself is a first step toward being able to love others. Some research suggests that high self-esteem may help relationships last. High self-esteem is associated with greater fidelity in relationships (Sheppard, Nelson, & Andreoli-Mathie, 1995), although it is not clear whether the high self-esteem is the cause or the consequence of being faithful. People with high self-esteem may be more willing to work on solving at least some problems in the relationship before turning to another partner (Thoits, 1994).

However, research on self-esteem and relationships offers little reason to think that high self-esteem actually produces better relationships. Dion and Dion (1975) found that people with low self-esteem had more intense experiences of love than individuals with high self-esteem. Hendrick and Hendrick (1986) found that low self-esteem was associated with a certain kind of wild, all-consuming, slightly crazy love (called manic love) whereas high self-esteem was linked to passionate love. These findings suggest that people with low self-esteem get very wrapped up in relationships. Contrary to popular belief, they do not indicate that loving yourself leads to loving others. (If anything, they suggest the opposite.)

In addition, some research shows that people with high self-esteem tend to respond to conflict by taking steps to end the relationship and find someone else (Rusbult,

Johnson, & Morrow, 1987). Similarly, Sommer et al. (in press) found that people with high self-esteem were quicker to think about breaking up in response to receiving the silent treatment from their relationship partners. In other words, people with high self-esteem are more willing to do things that might end the relationship, whereas people with low self-esteem tend to hang on. People who think well of themselves tend to believe that they can find someone else relatively easily. When relationships run into trouble, they think, "I don't need to put up with this," and they start looking around for someone new. A person with low self-esteem is less confident about being able to find a new partner, giving him or her more reason to try to make the relationship succeed.

These findings are magnified in cases of narcissism, a personality type based on extreme levels of self-esteem. The term *narcissism* comes from Greek mythology. Narcissus was a young man who fell in love with his own reflection in the water. Modern narcissists tend to have grandly favorable views of how brilliant and talented they are. They believe they are special and can only be understood by other high-status, talented people. They consider themselves to be entitled to special treatment, and become angry and hostile when other people criticize them or fail to give them what they want. They are also willing to exploit others for their own advantage. They can be very charming, especially to people they admire or those who help them reach their goals, but they can also become quite unpleasant to people who do not cooperate (see, for example, American Psychiatric Association, 1994). They can empathize with others, but often they do not bother doing so, and as a result they tend to be more concerned with their own needs and feelings than with those of other people. On average, men are slightly more narcissistic than women, but both sexes include plenty of narcissists (as well as plenty of people who are not narcissistic).

Narcissists have high self-esteem and self-love, but these qualities do not make for good relationships; indeed, negative qualities such as selfishness may harm relationships. They approach relationships in a game-playing spirit of having fun or as a pragmatic way of getting what they want (including sex) (Campbell, Foster, & Finkel, 2001). They seek out successful, beautiful, admired people to date, because they think they are like them, and the narcissist feels it is important to be seen with such star-quality people (Sedikides et al., 1998).

Narcissists tend to take the credit when a relationship is going well but blame their partners when things go badly (Sedikides et al., 1998; Farwell & Wohlwend-Lloyd, 1998; Morf & Rhodewalt, 1993); this can obviously put a strain on any relationship. Schütz (2001) conducted an observational study in which couples discussed problems that threatened their self-esteem; narcissists (identified by standard tests and measures) had fewer positive interactions with their spouses.

Ultimately, narcissists tend to be less committed to love relationships than other people (Campbell & Foster, in press). They tend to keep one eye on the relationship but another eye out to see whether a better partner might be available. A narcissist may love you for the time being, but he or she will dump you as soon as someone better comes along.

If self-love leads to loving others, narcissists should be the best lovers, because they love themselves the most. The evidence presented thus far in this section suggests the opposite, however. Among narcissists, at least, loving yourself detracts from loving others. Although narcissism is one extreme, it is necessary to acknowledge that some forms of self-love and self-esteem may be helpful. A milder form of self-love is called **self-acceptance,** which means simply regarding yourself as being a reasonably good person. The same study that found narcissism to be linked to low positive interactions with the spouse found that self-acceptance was linked to *more* positive interactions (Schütz, 2001). These findings suggest that having a very negative, critical attitude toward yourself can interfere with the capacity to love as much as an overly positive attitude.

Self-Acceptance: regarding yourself as being a reasonably good person

Guilt and Shame   Guilt and shame tend to be correlated, but they are quite different emotions, and they will lead a romantic partner to behave in very different ways. Both guilt and shame involve feeling bad in connection with something one has done.

Shame is a global negative feeling about the self ("I'm a bad person"). **Guilt** is a negative feeling about a particular action ("I did a bad thing") (for example, Tangney, 1991, 1992).

Shame is a destructive emotion, because it causes the person to feel wholly bad. It does not produce many constructive responses, and it can make people withdraw from their partners. Research shows that shame also tends to foster anger, which can lead to lashing out at others, which is also harmful to a relationship (Tangney et al., 1992). People may respond to feelings of shame by thinking "No, I'm not a bad person, and you must be bad for making me feel this way."

Guilt, on the other hand, is a constructive emotion. A person who experiences guilty feelings believes that he or she is basically a good person who has done something bad. This is a much more solvable problem than believing you are a bad person. Guilt motivates people to apologize for wrong actions, to make amends, to learn a lesson and resolve never to repeat what they did wrong, and to reaffirm their positive feelings toward the person they may have hurt (Baumeister, Stillwell, & Heatherton, 1994). These are all positive responses that can help strengthen and sustain a good relationship. In other words, love *can* mean having to say you're sorry.

Naturally there are extremes. You do not want to marry someone who is wracked with guilt all the time. Then again, you certainly do not want to marry someone who is immune to guilt. The clinical name for people who are incapable of experiencing guilt is **psychopath** (Hare, 1993). Psychopaths tend to be quite selfish and exploitative. They may treat you nicely as long as you do what they want, but they will not hesitate to do something that may hurt you deeply if it benefits them. In short, you want a partner who is guilt-prone but not shame-prone. No one can behave perfectly forever, and so the ideal is the person who will feel guilty about misbehaving and will, as a result of this guilt, try to make it up to you and try to avoid repeating his or her mistake.

I Love You Just the Way You Are

One of the many clichés about marriage is "The woman thinks the man will change, and the man thinks the woman won't change." In reality, the attitudes of men and women are not that different, but the cliché may have some validity.

Personality tends to be fairly stable, although the degree of stability is still fiercely debated among researchers (for example, Caspi & Roberts, 2001; Lewis, 2001). Still, during courtship you probably see your partner at his or her best; marrying that person with the expectation of further improvements is unrealistic. Someone who is immature, impulsive, unreliable, lazy, prone to drunkenness, or lacking in ambition is not likely to change simply as a result of marriage. One of the most popular themes in Western literature is that of a flawed man who is transformed into a better person through the love of a good woman (Fiedler, 1982). For example, Samuel Richardson (the very first modern novelist, according to Fiedler) developed those themes in his novels *Pamela* and *Clarissa*. Still, people should not be swayed by the popularity of this myth in novels and movies. By and large, flawed men remain flawed after they get married.

It is no accident that courtship and marriage tend to occur at the times when women are at their peak in attractiveness. Some men will disregard personality flaws or other drawbacks in a woman simply because they find her physically attractive. Although having a beautiful wife is undoubtedly a pleasure, it is not safe to assume that a woman who is pretty and sexy in her early 20s will still be that way in her 40s or 50s. Marrying for looks is thus also questionable as a long-term strategy.

Testosterone and Commitment

A poorly understood aspect of mating is women's attraction to dangerous men. It appears that some women find it exciting to be linked with powerful, aggressive, unpredictable men. In some cases women become involved repeatedly with men who end up mistreating and abusing them (for example, Gondolf, 1985).

Some theories propose that women seek out dangerous men because they have masochistic or self-destructive impulses (see Caplan, 1984; Shainess, 1984). However,

> ❝*Love means never having to say you're sorry.*❞
>
> (ERICH SEGAL, *LOVE STORY*)

Shame: a global negative feeling about the self ("I'm a bad person")

Guilt: a negative feeling about a particular action ("I did a bad thing")

Psychopath: a person with an antisocial personality disorder, manifested in aggressive, criminal, or amoral behavior without conscience, empathy, or remorse

subsequent research has failed to support that view. When self-defeating behavior occurs, the reason is usually that the risks and costs are outweighed by positive experiences (see Baumeister & Scher, 1988; Shainess, 1984). It is likely, therefore, that dangerous men have some positive appeal that makes women willing to accept the bad.

Research on testosterone suggests one class of tradeoffs. Dabbs (2000) has nicely explained both the costs and benefits of testosterone in his aptly named book *Heroes, Rogues, and Lovers*—a title that sums up both the appeal and the drawbacks of men high in that hormone. According to Dabbs, high levels of testosterone confer on men traits that are likely to make them both an appealing, exciting, sexy partner and a poor prospect for a long-term mate. Men with high levels of testosterone have a higher sex drive than other men, and they are also more aggressive (and even violent). A man high in testosterone will often be on the prowl and seeking adventure. Women may find his sexual and aggressive feelings exciting. His appeal may also benefit from testosterone-induced restlessness, which makes him constantly curious and seeking new experiences. (The high testosterone men in Dabbs's studies were so restless that many of them wandered into different laboratory rooms if they were left alone for a few minutes.) Men high in testosterone are also more ambitious, which as you learned in Chapter 15 is a trait that figures prominently in male sex appeal throughout the world (Buss, 1994).

Yet the very testosterone-loaded traits that make a man sexy can also render him less suitable as a husband and father. It is exciting to date a man who is adventurous and sexually driven—but in a husband, those traits may lead him to seek out sexual entanglements on the side. His willingness to fight may also be charming in a date, especially to a woman who likes to feel that her man will be able to defend her—but a physically aggressive husband may endanger himself in fights with other men or turn on his wife or child. Husbands are expected to settle down and stay home, but the adventurous restlessness may make the high-testosterone man less willing to tolerate the long-term commitment of marriage. High ambition and leadership tendencies could help him be a better provider, but it could also mean that he loves his work more than his family or that he is bossy and tyrannical at home.

Thus, sex appeal in the short run may run counter to what makes for the best spouse in the long run. A rebellious, aggressive, adventurous man may be extremely sexy and exciting, but he is unlikely to change easily into a devoted husband who is content to snuggle with his wife and share diaper-changing and dishwashing duties.

Weighing Good Versus Bad Part of the process of deciding whether to commit to someone in a long-term relationship is to add up the person's good and bad points, and then decide whether the good ones outweigh the bad. When making such calculations, it is important to keep one principle in mind: bad is stronger than good. In close relationships, as in many other spheres of psychology and human life, bad qualities end up carrying more weight than good qualities. When researchers make careful, independent measurements of the good and the bad things that happen in a long-term relationship, they consistently find that the bad things have a bigger impact on the relationship. For example, the number of constructive, positive responses made by a dating couple is less important than the number of destructive, hurtful ones (Rusbult, Johnson, & Morrow, 1986). Similarly, in predicting whether a newly married couple will stay together or divorce, the amount of love and affection is less relevant than the amount of conflict, negativity, and bad feelings (Huston et al., 2001). Gottman (1994) has even produced a formula for predicting whether a relationship will succeed. The pleasant, good interactions have to outnumber the bad, conflictual interactions by at least five to one. To reach the five-to-one threshold, the relationship has to be good 83 percent of the time. To put it another way, if on average you are unhappy with your relationship more than one day per week, it is not likely to last. In assessing a possible mate, it is therefore useful to pay more attention to the person's drawbacks than to the good qualities that brought you together. Ask yourself, what would be the worst things about being married to this person? If you can live with those things, then the person may be a serious prospect.

What's Right for You?

In addition to the information we have provided so far, sexual decision making involves deciding what sex means to you. Consider the following four questions:

Is sex for fun, or does it have a special meaning beyond pleasure and physical gratification? The potential for an exciting, enjoyable sex life that honestly separates lust from love has its advantages. As long as both partners are honest with themselves and each other, no one has to feign everlasting love in order to have a sexual relationship. This choice can lower the possibility of ending up in a long-term relationship with someone who's not right for you. While some people may be able to have healthy sexual relationships that are primarily based on physical pleasure, others might find sex without love and emotional intimacy to be less satisfying.

Is sex a way of saying "I like you and enjoy being with you" or a commitment to future involvement? For some people, the meaning of the message "I want to have sex with you" is "I find you attractive and would enjoy having sex with you." For others it means "I want to have a relationship with you." Misunderstandings can be avoided if the issue of future intentions is made clear. Casual sex can be a way of finding out more about a person. However, having casual sex with a friend can be stressful to the friendship.

Does sex mean "I love you and want to be with you right now" or "I want to be with you forever"? The security and comfort of a committed relationship is more rewarding to some, while others think it is premature to insist that you must commit to someone before having sex. There can be as many unhealthy reasons for linking sex and commitment as there are for engaging in casual sex. Making a commitment because of a need to be taken care of or protected, a bad home situation, the desire to "hook a good catch," or because all your friends are in a relationship can lead to many problems later in a relationship.

Is sex a sacred act that means lifelong commitment, regardless of the difficulties that arise? If your answer is "yes," you are among those for whom sex is spiritual unity in an everlasting relationship such as marriage. This option is almost always socially acceptable and therefore guilt-free. It can symbolize the special nature of a permanent commitment to another person. However, it can also lead to overly high expectations, disappointment, and feelings of being trapped.

You must decide what is right for you. If you are more cognitive in your decision making you may weigh each piece of information we have provided and think through each and every action. More intuitive individuals may rely more on instinct when making choices. All of us use both cognition and intuition to some degree. Whether you think you are being rational or emotional, you are undoubtedly acting in response to the value orientations and accumulated past experiences that you have acquired through education and socialization.

Postponing your decision until the passion of the moment has subsided does not relieve you of the responsibility of your choices. Nor does accepting the suggestions of another or giving in to pressure relieve you of liability. Moreover, when it comes to ethics, doing "nothing" is doing something. There simply is no way to avoid responsibility for your behavior.

By now it should be apparent that defining sexual responsibility is not always easy. Your physical, social, emotional, and spiritual needs may confound cognitive decision-making attempts. Sexual desire, sexual problems, the wish to get pregnant or avoid pregnancy or disease may weigh heavily on anyone attempting to determine responsible behavior. Similarly, the lessons you have learned through social interaction, your age, life situation, gender, sexual orientation, and previous sexual experiences will impact the context of your decision making. Your emotional needs will also play a large part in the decision-making process. Your religious beliefs as well as your values and perspective on ethics clearly affect your understanding. The sexuality education you have received as well as your opinions on sexual issues and politics also have an impact.

FAQ:

"Should I have sex or not?"

This seemingly simple question is more complex than it appears. It actually consists of two parts, along with some unstated considerations. First, is sex a right action for you at this point in your life? If you decide that sex is morally permissible for you then you must ask yourself the second part of the question. Namely, with which person or persons would sex be morally permissible, and is the specific person in question included among them?

If the answer to the second part of this question is also "yes," there are a few other things to consider before you can proceed. What kind of sex is permissible? Under what conditions is sex permissible? In reaching your decision, you will have to consider a number of issues we have raised in this text, such as mutual agreement, love and intimacy, safety and birth control, sexual orientation, and marital status.

Ethical Considerations

Ethicists seldom agree on absolutes. However, the following basic considerations can provide an ethical foundation for your sexual decisions.

1. Do nothing to harm another, physically or psychologically. This includes third-party and indirect effects your behavior will have on others. It also includes potential others such as future offspring.

2. Never use psychological or physical force or coercion. Don't exploit the weakness or subordinate status of others, and don't try to persuade someone to do something he or she doesn't want to do.

3. Take responsibility for your actions. Use no deception and break no promises. Make it clear what you want to do sexually.

? *Are there other ethical questions that you take into consideration when making sexual decisions?*

Being responsible for your actions, however, is not an undue burden. In fact, acting responsibly can enhance sexual pleasure and life satisfaction, as well as protect your health and general well-being. Certain potential benefits of responsible sexual behavior are easily seen. For example, the benefits of protecting yourself against diseases and unwanted pregnancy are self-evident. The potential benefits of not using force or other illegal behaviors also should be clear. Less obvious may be the potential benefits of not endangering the health or welfare of a partner or potential partner, not taking advantage of status differences or manipulating someone who is impaired—whether developmentally or temporarily with drugs or alcohol. Seeking competent, willing sexual partners is almost certain to lead to greater pleasure and better relationships. In fact, many individuals find that concentrating on providing maximum pleasure to their partners results in an increase in their own pleasure. It is our shared belief that human sexuality should be a wonderful, as well as wondrous, part of life, and that knowledge about sexuality will enhance your potential to find the maximum satisfaction in your life.

CHAPTER REVIEW

1_____ are an individual's concepts of what is desirable, which serve as criteria for meaning and understanding, as well as criteria for evaluating behavior.
2_____ are our concepts of what is right and wrong. **3**_____ is a set of moral principles for determining behavior.

Sexual **4**_____ is about right behavior pertaining to sex and sexual issues. The role of authority in ethical decision making is basic; two contrasting approaches are the authoritarian and situational approaches. Of course, different assumptions about what is right also affect ethical conclusions.

There are special considerations for ethics in a diverse society. Doing what is right can create special problems in pluralistic societies marked by a diversity of religious and moral traditions. This becomes apparent when the right behavior of one group is in conflict with the right behavior of another.

5_____ in ancient Greece believed that seeking pleasure is the highest good.

According to Belliotti's framework for sexual ethics, the parties, possessing the basic capacities necessary for autonomous choice, must agree to a particular sexual interaction without force, fraud, or explicit duress. This constitutes the **6**_____ agreement.

7_____occurs when one person takes advantage of another person's attributes or situation to exact personal sexual gain or sexual gain for the exploiter's compatriots. Behavior may be considered exploitive when one person views another as a mere instrument for the advancement of one's own purposes and profits.

Most major theories agree that men and women face decisions with regard to sex somewhat differently. In particular, evolutionary theory emphasizes that the costs of sexual mistakes have been much greater for women than for men. **8**_____ theory suggests that people make decisions in ways that will minimize whatever kind of error has been most costly in the evolutionary past.

Several factors can promote bad sexual decisions. One of the most common patterns of bad decisions is the failure to evaluate short-term gains and long-term costs.

Another source of costly mistakes is the belief that bad things are unlikely to happen to the self; this is the illusion of **9**_____.

Alcohol can remove the inhibitions that have prevented you from acting on sexual desires; clearly, this can lead to bad decisions. The combination of alcohol intoxication and passionate arousal (as in sexual desire) is thus a double blow to self-control. People are also vulnerable to making bad sexual decisions when they are tired or under stress.

In making decisions, we suggest three absolutes with regard to ethical sexual behavior. Do nothing to harm another. Never use force or coercion. Assume responsibility for your actions.

Human sexuality should be a wonderful, as well as wondrous, part of life, and knowledge about sexuality may enhance your potential to find the maximum satisfaction in your life.

SUGGESTED READINGS

Francoeru, R. T. & Taverner, W. J. (Eds.). (2000). *Taking Sides: Clashing Views on Controversial Issues in Human Sexuality.* Guilford, CT: Dushkin Publishing Group.
This volume provides a balance of considerations for controversial sexuality issues.

Gerken, J. D. (1995). *An American Ethic: A Philosophy of Freedom Applied to Contemporary Issues.* Middletown, NJ: Caslon.
Gerken, a philosopher, considers a number of issues including sexual morality, homosexuality, and abortion.

Lebacqz, K. with Sinacore-Guinn, D. (Eds.). (1999). *Sexuality: A Reader.* Cleveland, OH: Pilgrim Press.
This collection of articles, most with a religious or ethical slant, offers a variety of views on a number of

sexual issues. Authors' perspectives include Jewish, Christian, Islamic, Buddhist, and secular, as well as gay, lesbian, and feminist.

Reiss, I. L. with Reiss, H. M. (1997) *Solving America's Sexual Crises.* Amherst, NY: Prometheus Press.
The authors challenge traditional thought on a number of sexual issues including teenage sex, pornography, and the role of religion.

Williams, M. E. (Ed.). (2000). *Sex: Opposing Viewpoints.* San Diego: Greenhaven Press.
This volume is one of a continuing series of point/counterpoint collections on sexual issues.

ANSWERS TO CHAPTER REVIEW:

1. Values; **2.** Morals; **3.** Ethics; **4.** ethics; **5.** Epicureans; **6.** libertarian; **7.** Sexual exploitation; **8.** Error management; **9.** unique invulnerability.

Glossary

"K" Strategy a biological strategy for successful reproduction that emphasizes producing fewer offspring and investing a great deal of care in each offspring

"r" Strategy a biological strategy for successful reproduction that emphasizes producing as many offspring as possible

Abortifacient a drug or device used to cause abortion

Abortion induced expulsion of a human embryo or fetus

Abstinence-Only Sex Education programs that teach abstinence as the only method of birth control; discussion of contraception is prohibited, unless to emphasize its shortcomings

Abstinence-Plus Sex Education programs that teach abstinence as the preferred option but allow for contraception to be discussed

Acquaintance Rape forced sexual intercourse after an initial social encounter

Acquired Immunodeficiency Syndrome (AIDS) a disease caused by infection with the human immunodeficiency virus (HIV-1, HIV-2), a retrovirus that causes immune system failure and debilitation

Adolescence the period of physical and psychological development from the onset of puberty to maturity

Adolescent Family Life Act (AFLA) 1981 act of Congress that provided funding for sex education programs teaching abstinence as the only option for teenagers

Adoption the process of taking a child into one's family through legal means and raising the child as one's own

Adultery laws legislation forbidding extramarital sex

Adultery extramarital relationship; sexual intercourse between a married person and a partner other than the lawful spouse

Agape: the love of Christians for other persons, corresponding to the love of God for humankind

Agentic Traits traits that focus on taking initiative and control in order to get things done

Alcohol Myopia the role of alcohol in reducing the ability to think about many different things and process different levels of meaning, leading to an intense focus on one thing

Allah God, especially in Islam

Amenorrhea the absence of menstruation for more than 6 months

Amniocentesis test performed during the 16th to 18th week of pregnancy in order to determine the presence of birth defects in the developing fetus

Amniotic Fluid fluid within the amniotic sac that suspends and protects the fetus

Amniotic Sac the sac containing the developing fetus

Anabolic Steroids synthetic derivative of testosterone

Anal Sex penile penetration or other stimulation of the rectum

Anatomy the form and structure of an organism

Androgen Insensitivity Syndrome a condition resulting from a genetic defect that causes chromosomally normal males to be insensitive to the action of testosterone and other androgens and to develop female external genitals

Androgens hormones that promote the development of male sex characteristics

Androgyny having both masculine and feminine traits, as in dress, appearance, or behavior

Anger Rape sexual assault motivated by hatred and resentment toward women

Anilingus oral stimulation of the anus

Anonymous information in which the party involved is not named or identified

Anorgasmia failure to experience orgasm

Anovulation the absence of ovulation

Anovulatory Cycles cycles without ovulation

Anterior Commissure an organized tract of fibers in the anterior part of the brain that connects corresponding parts of the right and left cerebral hemispheres

Antibodies any of a large variety of immunoglobulins normally present in the body or produced in response to an antigen that it neutralizes, thus producing an immune response

Antigens a substance that when introduced into the body stimulates the production of an antibody

Anus the opening through which solid waste is eliminated from the body

Aphrodisiac a substance that increases or is believed to increase sexual desire or capability

Areola area of dark-colored skin on the breast that surrounds the nipple

Aromatase an enzyme that converts androgen to estrogen

Arranged Marriage any marriage in which the selection of a spouse is outside the control of the bride and groom

Artificial Insemination the process of depositing specially prepared sperm inside the woman's reproductive tract

Asexual Reproduction the production of offspring by a single organism or parent

Asexual free from or unaffected by sexuality

Assisted Reproductive Technology (ART) a term used to describe medical procedures that enhance the opportunity for egg fertilization and pregnancy

Attachment a strong feeling of being emotionally connected or close to someone or something

Attraction the relationship existing between things or persons that are naturally or involuntarily drawn together

Authoritarian Approach belief that assumes we make choices based on a normative standard within society

Autoerotic Asphyxiation practice in which an individual cuts off the air

supply while masturbating to orgasm with the belief that oxygen deprivation enhances orgasm

Autoeroticism self-satisfaction of sexual desire, as by masturbation or the arousal of sexual feeling without an external stimulus

Bacteria plural of bacterium; a large group of single-cell micro-organisms; some cause infections and disease in animals and humans

Bacterial Vaginosis (BV) vaginal infection resulting from a change in the balance of naturally occurring bacteria, allowing disease-causing bacteria, especially *Gardnerella vaginalis*, to predominate

Bartholin's Glands small glands inside the vaginal opening that secrete a few drops of fluid during sexual arousal

Basal Body Temperature (BBT) a fertility awareness method of birth control in which a woman takes her temperature when she first wakes in the morning and records it on a chart each day of her menstrual cycle to retrospectively identify when she may have ovulated in order to abstain from sexual intercourse when ovulation is most likely

Behavior Therapy therapy that seeks to modify undesirable behaviors using learning techniques

Being Orientation self-focus on spontaneous human expression

Being-in-Becoming Orientation self-focus on the development of the human essence

Benign noncancerous; does not invade nearby tissue or spread to other parts of the body

Berdache/ Two-Spirit among certain Native American peoples, a person, usually a male, who assumes the gender identity and is granted the social status of the opposite sex

Biased Sample a sample that is not representative of the larger group

Binary Fission a method of asexual reproduction that involves the splitting of a parent cell into two approximately equal parts

Birth Control Implants rubber capsules containing progestin inserted under the skin in a woman's upper arm, which prevents ovulation and pregnancy

Birth the act or process of bearing children

Bisexuality sexual attraction, feeling, or behavior directed toward person or persons of both one's own and the opposite sex

Blastocyst an embryo composed of two groups of cells. One group will develop into the fetus and the other will become the placenta

Blastula the early developmental stage of an animal, following the morula stage and consisting of a single, spherical layer of cells enclosing a hollow, central cavity

Braxton-Hicks Contractions "false labor"; intermittent, painless contractions that may occur every 10 to 20 minutes after the first trimester of pregnancy.

Brothel a house where men can go to have sexual intercourse with prostitutes for money

Buddhism a spiritual tradition originating in India, based on the teaching of Buddha that life is permeated with suffering caused by desire, that suffering ceases when desire ceases, and that enlightenment obtained through right conduct, wisdom, and meditation releases one from desire, suffering, and rebirth

Calendar Method/ Rhythm Method a method of birth control in which the couple abstains from sexual intercourse during the period when ovulation is most likely to occur

Call Girl a female prostitute with whom an appointment can be made by telephone, usually to meet at the client's address

Cancer disease in which cells in body grow without control

Capacitation the changes that a sperm goes through to be capable of penetrating the layers covering the egg

Cascade Model a four-phase model of dissolving a close relationship: complain/criticize, contempt, defensiveness, and stonewalling

Case Study an in-depth study of an individual or a small group of individuals

Causation the act or agency that produces an effect

Celibacy abstention from sexual intercourse

Cerebral Cortex thin outer layer of the brain's cerebrum that is responsible for higher mental processes including perception, thought, and memory

Cervical Cap a small, rubber, cup-shaped device that fits over the cervix to prevent the entry of sperm

Cervical Factor Infertility condition in which the cervical mucus of some women contains antibodies that attack the male's sperm

Cervical Mucus Monitoring Method a fertility awareness method of birth control in which women become alert to changes in the amount and texture of their cervical secretions and abstain from sexual intercourse during the period when ovulation is most likely to occur

Cervix small, lower end of the uterus that protrudes into the vagina

Cesarean Section method of childbirth in which the fetus is delivered through a surgical incision in the abdomen; C-section

Chancroid a sexually transmitted disease caused by the bacteria *Hemophilus ducreyi* that causes multiple painful ulcers on the penis and the vulva

Chickenhawk an adult male who seeks out pubescent male prostitutes

Chlamydia the most common sexually transmitted bacterium (*Chlamydia trachomatis*) that infects the reproductive system

Chorionic Villus Sampling (CVS) a test that is done early during pregnancy to check for the presence of genetic disorders. It involves obtaining a biopsy of the placenta, usually between the 10th and 13th weeks of pregnancy

Christianity a religion that includes the Catholic, Protestant, and Eastern Orthodox churches and is founded on the life and teachings of Jesus

Chromosomes small rod-shaped bodies in the nucleus of a cell at the time of cell division which contain, in the form of DNA, all the genetic information needed for the development of the cell and the whole organism

Circumcision surgical removal of the foreskin

Clinical Depression: a state of depression so severe as to be considered abnormal and require clinical intervention

Clitoral Glans the head of the clitoris, which has a large number of nerve endings

Clitoridectomy surgical removal of the clitoris

Clitoris highly sensitive female organ located above the urethral opening that's only known function is sexual pleasure

Cognitive Interference task-irrelevant thoughts

Cognitive-Affective Processing the way we think about how we feel

Cohabitation act of living together; by implication a heterosexual couple

Cohabitation to live together in a sexual relationship, especially when not legally married

Coital Sex activities associated with sexual intercourse

Coitus Interruptus sexual intercourse deliberately interrupted by withdrawal of the penis from the vagina prior to ejaculation

Coitus sexual intercourse

Colostrum a thin fluid secreted by the breasts at the termination of pregnancy before milk production begins; it is high in proteins and rich in antibodies that confer temporary immunity to the newborn

Colostrum thin yellowish fluid secreted by the mammary glands at the time of parturition that is rich in antibodies and minerals. It precedes the production of true milk

Coming Out of the Closet the acknowledgment by gays, lesbians, or bisexuals of their sexual orientation, first to themselves and then to others

Commitment a pledge or promise; the state of being bound emotionally or intellectually to a course of action or to another person

Communal Traits traits that facilitate forming and maintaining social relationships with others

Companionate Love feelings based on familiarity, affection, and deep attachment

Comprehensive Sex Education: programs that teach both contraception and abstinence as options

Compulsive Sexual Behavior excessive sexual desire and behavior

Comstock Laws 1873 federal laws that outlawed the importation and circulation of pornography, also used to justify the confiscation of any contraceptive information or devices sent through the mail

Conception fertilization of an ovum by a sperm to form a viable zygote

Conception the union of sperm and ovum

Confidential information that is communicated in confidence and cannot be disclosed without permission

Confidentiality keeping the identity and responses of a research study private

Contraception the deliberate prevention of conception or impregnation through the use of various devices, agents, drugs, sexual practices, or surgical procedures

Coping Mechanisms adaptations to environmental stress that are based on conscious or unconscious choice and that enhance control over behavior or give psychological comfort

Corpora Cavernosa structures in the shaft of the penis that engorge with blood during sexual arousal

Corpus Callosum the arched bridge of nervous tissue that connects the two cerebral hemispheres, allowing communication between the right and left sides of the brain

Corpus Luteum the mass of cells left in the ovary by the ruptured follicle during ovulation, releasing an egg; subsequently it produces progesterone and estrogen

Corpus Spongiosum structure at the base of the penis that extends up into the shaft and forms the penile glans

Correlation a statistical measure of the linkage or relationship between two or more variables

Couvade Syndrome males having "sympathetic pregnancies" in which they experience a number of pregnancy symptoms

Cowper's Glands glands located beneath the prostate that produce a clear, colorless liquid before ejaculation that neutralizes acid to prevent damage to the sperm

Crura two trunks of the clitoris that separate and join at the pubic arch and attach the clitoris to the pubic bone

Crush infatuation; a strong but temporary attraction for someone

Cunnilingus oral stimulation of the clitoris or vulva

Cyst membranous sac containing a gaseous, liquid, or semisolid substance

Date Rape forced sexual intercourse perpetrated by the victim's social escort

Defense Mechanism an unconscious process that protects an individual from unacceptable or painful ideas or impulses.

Dependent Love: love that relies on or is subordinate to someone or something else

Descriptive Statistics numbers used to present a collection of data in a brief yet meaningful form

DHT-Deficiency condition in which a chromosomally normal male develops external genitalia resembling those of a female as a result of a genetic defect that prevents the prenatal conversion of testosterone into DHT

Diaphragm device consisting of a thin flexible disk, usually made of rubber, that is designed to cover the cervix to prevent the entry of sperm during sexual intercourse

Dilate to open or grow wider; expand

Dilation and Curettage (D&C) a surgical procedure in which the cervix is expanded using a dilator and the uterine lining scraped with a curette

Dilation and Evacuation (D&E) a surgical procedure in which the cervix is expanded using a dilator and then surgical instruments and suction curettage are used to remove the contents of the uterus

Division of Labor the breakdown of work into its components and their distribution among different persons to increase productive efficiency

Divorce a legal or socially recognized dissolution of a marriage

DNA deoxyribonucleic acid; the main component of chromosomes and the material that transfers genetic characteristics in all life forms

Doing Orientation self-focus on measurable accomplishments

Double Standard set of principles permitting greater opportunity or liberty to one group than to another, especially the granting of greater sexual freedom to men than to women

Douching injecting a stream of water, often containing medicinal or cleansing agents, into the vagina for hygienic or therapeutic purposes

Doula a woman who assists women during labor and after childbirth

Down Syndrome a genetic disorder, associated with the presence of an extra chromosome 21, characterized by mild to severe mental retardation, a low nasal bridge, and epicanthic folds at the eyelids

Dysmenorrhea pain or discomfort before or during menstruation

Dyspareunia sexual dysfunction in which there is a persistent or recurrent pain or discomfort during coitus

Ectoparasite a parasite that lives on the exterior of the host organism

Ectopic Pregnancy pregnancy in which the fertilized ovum become implanted some place other than the uterus

Edema excessive accumulation of fluid resulting in swelling

Effacement the thinning of the cervix, which occurs before and while it dilates

Ejaculate semen

ELISA (Enzyme-Linked Immunoabsorbent Assay) a type of enzyme immunoassay to determine the presence of antibodies to HIV in the blood or oral fluids

Embryo transplant the process of depositing fertilized eggs (or embryos) inside the uterus

Embryonic Stage the stage of prenatal development that lasts from implantation through the first 8 weeks and is characterized by the differentiation of the major organ systems

Emergency Contraceptives methods of preventing pregnancy after unwanted or unprotected sexual intercourse

Endocrine System the body system of ductless glands that produce and secrete hormones directly into the bloodstream

Endogamy marriage within one's own group in accordance with custom or law

Endometriosis condition in which endometrial tissue grows in pelvic regions outside the uterus

Endometrium tissue that lines the inside of the uterine walls

Endoparasite a parasite that lives within the host organism

Endorphins any of a group of peptide hormones that bind to opiate receptors and are found mainly in the brain; endorphins reduce the sensation of pain and affect emotions

Engagement process prior to childbirth during which the fetus turns so that the widest part of its head is positioned firmly against the woman's pelvic bones

Envy: a feeling of resentment of or desire to obtain another person's qualities, better fortune, or success

Epididymis tightly coiled thin-walled tube where sperm maturation is completed

Epidural Anesthesia an injection through a catheter of a local anesthetic to relieve pain during labor, usually done at the lumbar level of the spine

Episiotomy a surgical incision in the perineum that widens the birth canal to prevent tearing during childbirth

Erectile Dysfunction the inability to have or maintain an erection firm enough for coitus

Erection firm and enlarged condition of a body organ or part when surrounding erectile tissue becomes engorged with blood; especially such a condition of the penis or clitoris

Erogenous Zones parts of the body that are especially sensitive to stimulation

Erotica literature or art with a sexual content

Erotomania: a delusional, romantic preoccupation with a stranger, often a public figure

Error Management Theory: theory that people make decisions in ways that will minimize whatever kind of error has been most costly in the evolutionary past

Estradiol principal estrogen produced by the ovary during a woman's reproductive years

Estriol an estrogen hormone found in the urine during pregnancy

Estrogen a hormone secreted by the ovary and responsible for typical female sex characteristics

Estrone a weaker estrogen found in urine and placental tissues during pregnancy

Estrous the cycle of most female non-primate mammals when they are most sexually receptive to males

Ethics a set of moral principles for determining behavior

Ethics: a set of principles of right conduct; how you believe people should behave

Eugenics the study of hereditary improvement of the human race by controlled selective breeding

Evolutionary Theory theory that emphasizes the gradual process of development of species through biological adaptation

Excitement Phase first stage of Masters and Johnson's sexual response cycle; characterized by erection in the male and vaginal lubrication in the female

Exhibitionism the compulsive public exposure of the genitals to a stranger

Experimental Research a method in which researchers restrict, change, or

manipulate a subject's experience and assess the effects on the subject

Extramarital Relationship a sexual relationship with someone other than one's spouse

Fallopian Tubes ducts that connect the ovaries to the uterus; oviducts

Familiarity the state or quality of having personal knowledge, exposure, or information about someone or something

Family Orientation: value of relationships influenced by and centered on one's family

Fellatio oral stimulation of the penis

Female Adrenogenital Syndrome condition in which a chromosomally normal female who, as a result of excessive exposure to androgens during prenatal sex differentiation, develops external genitalia resembling those of a male

Female Circumcision surgical removal of the prepuce, with or without excision of part or the entire clitoris

Female Condom a device consisting of a loose-fitting polyurethane sheath closed at one end, which is inserted intravaginally before sexual intercourse

Female Genital Mutilation surgical procedures in which all or a portion of the external female genitalia is removed for cultural, religious, or other nontherapeutic reasons

Female Orgasmic Disorder sexual dysfunction in which a woman is unable to achieve orgasm during sexual activity

Female Sexual Arousal Disorder sexual dysfunction in which there is persistent or recurrent inadequate vaginal lubrication for coitus

Feminist Theory theoretical views that emphasize the need to include the female experience and perspective in research

Fertility Awareness birth control methods that depend on detailed knowledge and tracking of the female partner's menstrual cycle to identify when intercourse is most likely to result in a pregnancy

Fertilization conception

Fertilize to join male and female cells, sperm and ova, so that offspring develop

Fetal Alcohol Syndrome (FAS) cluster of symptoms caused by maternal alcohol use in which a child has developmental delays and characteristic facial features

Fetishism sexual arousal by a material object or a nonsexual part of the body

Fetus in humans the product of conception from the beginning of the ninth week until birth

Fetus the developing human organism from about 8 weeks after conception until birth

Fibroids benign smooth muscle tumors of the uterus that may cause pain, irregular bleeding, and an enlarged uterus

Fimbriae the fingerlike projections at the end of the fallopian tube nearest the ovary that capture the egg and deliver it into the tube

First Trimester first 3 months of pregnancy

Flirting playful behavior intended to arouse sexual interest

Follicle-Stimulating Hormone (FSH) pituitary hormone that stimulates the development of the ovarian follicles (eggs) and the release of estrogen in women

Follicle small sac in the ovary that contains a developing egg

Forceps an instrument resembling a pair of pincers or tongs, used for grasping, manipulating, or extracting the fetus from the uterus or vagina

Foreplay sexual stimulation, usually as a prelude to sexual intercourse

Foreskin covering of skin over the penile glans; prepuce

Fornication laws legislation prohibiting sexual intercourse between unmarried adults

Frotteurism a sexual disorder in which an individual deliberately and persistently seeks sexual excitement by touching and rubbing against nonconsenting people

Fundus the uppermost part of the uterus

Fungi plural of fungus; any organism that superficially resembles a plant but does not have leaves and roots, and lacks chlorophyll

Future-Dominant decisions based primarily upon the time to come

Gamete Intrafallopian Transfer (GIFT) a procedure where eggs are retrieved from the woman, placed together with sperm in a catheter, and transferred back into the woman's fallopian tubes to allow fertilization inside the woman's body

Gang Rape rape of a victim by several attackers in rapid succession

Gay Bashing a threat, assault or act of violence directed toward a homosexual or homosexuals

Gay male homosexuals

Gender Constancy the concept that even if appearances or behavior change, gender remains constant

Gender Dysphoria discomfort with one's gender identity

Gender Identity Disorder a strong and persistent desire or insistence that one is of the other sex

Gender Identity the psychological sense of being male or female

Gender Role the public image of being male or female that a person presents to others

Gender Schema a cluster of mental representations about male and female physical qualities, behaviors, and personality traits

Gender Stability the concept that people retain their genders for a lifetime

Gender Stereotypes images or beliefs about the so-called typical man or woman

Genes the basic units of heredity that carry information about traits passed on from parent to offspring

Genital Herpes a sexually transmitted infection caused by a herpes virus that results in the episodic outbreak of a painful skin eruption on the genitalia

Genitals male and female sexual organs

Germ cell an ovum or sperm cell or one of its developmental precursors

Gigolo a man who provides sexual services or social companionship to a woman in exchange for money or gifts

Gonadotropin-Releasing Hormone (Gn-RH) hormone produced and released in a pulsating manner by the hypothalamus; controls the pituitary gland's production and release of gonadotropins

Gonadotropins hormones that stimulate the activity of the function of the gonads (ovaries and testicles)

Gonads organs that produce the sex cells and sex hormones; testicles in males and ovaries in females

Gonorrhea a sexually transmitted infection caused by *Neisseria gonorrhoeae* bacteria that affects the mucous membrane chiefly of the genital and urinary tracts and is characterized by an acute purulent discharge and painful or difficult urination, though women often have no symptoms

Gräfenberg Spot a mass of tissue in the front wall of the vagina, claimed by some women to produce sexual arousal, orgasm, and an ejaculation of fluids when stimulated; also called **G spot**

Group Orientation value of relationships is influenced by and centered on peer relations

Guilt a feeling of remorse resulting from a sense of having done wrong

Guilt a negative feeling about a particular action ("I did a bad thing")

Gynecology branch of medicine that deals with women's health, especially the diagnosis and treatment of disorders affecting the reproductive organs

Hate Crime a crime (such as assault or defacement of property) that is motivated by hostility to the victim as a member of a group (as one based on color, creed, gender, or sexual orientation)

Hegar's Sign changes in the size, shape, and consistency of the uterus (uterus becomes softened or "doughy") between the uterine body and the cervix

Hepatitis A inflammation of the liver caused by infection with the hepatitis A virus, which is spread by fecal-oral contact, including that of sex partners

Hepatitis B inflammation of the liver caused by infection with the hepatitis B virus, which is most commonly passed on to a partner during intercourse, especially during anal sex, as well as through sharing of drug needles

Hermaphrodites individuals in which reproductive organs of both males and females are present

Heteroeroticism sexual stimulation that involves someone of the opposite sex

Heterosexual Activity sexual relations with the opposite sex

Heterosexuality sexual attraction, feeling, or behavior directed toward a person or persons of the opposite sex

Hinduism a diverse body of religion, philosophy, and cultural practice native to and predominant in India, characterized by a belief in reincarnation and a supreme being of many forms and natures, and by the view that opposing theories are aspects of one eternal truth, and by a desire for liberation from earthly evils

HIV-2 a virus closely related to HIV-1 that has also been found to cause AIDS. It was first isolated in West Africa. Although HIV-1 and HIV-2 are similar in their viral structure, modes of transmission, and resulting opportunistic infections, they have differed in their geographic patterns of infection.

Homo sapiens the species of primates to which modern humans belong

Homoeroticism sexual stimulation that involves someone of the same sex

Homologous having the same basic structure

Homophobia unreasoning fear of or antipathy toward homosexuals and homosexuality

Homosexual Activity sexual relations with the same sex

Homosexuality sexual attraction, desire or behavior directed toward a person or persons of one's own sex

Hormone Replacement Therapy (HRT) use of synthetic hormones to replace estrogen no longer produced by the ovaries in postmenopausal years

Hormones chemicals produced by one tissue and conveyed by the bloodstream to another to effect physiological activity

Host a plant or animal harboring another organism

Human Immunodeficiency Virus (HIV) the virus that causes acquired immunodeficiency syndrome (AIDS)

Human Papilloma Virus (HPV) a sexually transmitted infection that causes genital warts

Human Papilloma Virus (HPV) genital warts; a sexually transmitted disease characterized by a soft wartlike growth on the genitalia

Hustler homosexual male prostitute who solicits customers on the street

Hyaluronidase enzyme found in the testes that degrades hyaluronic acid in the body thereby increasing tissue penetrability to fluids

Hydrotherapy hot whirlpool baths used in birthing centers

Hymen membrane that partially covers the vaginal opening

Hypoactive Sexual Desire having little or no interest in sex

Hypothalamus brain structure that plays a major role in controlling the production of sex hormones and regulates many sexual responses

Hysterectomy surgical removal of the uterus

Hysterotomy surgical removal of the fetus and uterine contents through an incision in the abdomen and uterus

Illusion of Unique Invulnerability belief that you are exempt from the consequences that apply to others

Immune System/Lymphatic System the body's complicated natural defense against disruption caused by invading foreign agents

Implantation attachment of the fertilized egg to the uterine lining

In Vitro Fertilization (IVF) fertilization outside of the body in a laboratory

Incest: sexual relations between persons who are so closely related that their marriage is illegal or forbidden by custom or law

Incestuous Relationship a sexual relationship between persons so closely related that law forbids them to marry

Incubator an apparatus for maintaining an infant, especially a premature infant,

in an environment of controlled temperature, humidity, and oxygen concentration

Individual Orientation: value of relationships is influenced by and centered on the individual

Inferential Statistics a set of procedures for determining what conclusions can be legitimately inferred from a set of data

Infertility inability to conceive a child

Infibulation surgical removal of part or all of the external genitalia and stitching or narrowing of the vaginal opening

Informed Consent agreement of participants in a research study that they understand the purpose, risks, and benefits of the study

Injectable Contraceptive injection of progestin to inhibit ovulation and prevent pregnancy

Interfemoral Coitus sexual activity in which the male rubs his erect penis between the thighs of a woman without insertion into the vagina

Intersexuals persons having both male and female characteristics, including in varying degrees reproductive organs, secondary sexual characteristics, and sexual behavior

Interview a research method in which subjects are asked questions by an interviewer

Intimacy a close, affectionate, usually loving relationship

Intimacy the state of having or being likely to cause a very close friendship or personal or sexual relationship

Intrauterine Device (IUD) a plastic or metal loop, ring, or spiral that is inserted into the uterus to prevent implantation

Introitus the opening of the vagina

Islam the religious faith of Muslims, based on the words and religious system founded by the prophet Muhammad

Jaundice a condition that turns the skin and the whites of the eyes a yellowish color, resulting from an excess of bilirubin in the blood, and often a symptom of liver disease.

Jealousy: mental uneasiness from suspicion or fear of rivalry or unfaithfulness

perceived as a threat to an existing relationship

Johns colloquial term for prostitution customers

Judaism a religion developed among the ancient Hebrews and characterized by belief in one transcendent God and by a religious life in accordance with Scriptures and rabbinic traditions

Karma the total effect of a person's actions and conduct during the successive phases of the person's existence, regarded as determining the person's destiny

Kept Boy a man who has a continuing sexual relationship with and receives financial support from an older man

Klinefelter's Syndrome a condition characterized by the presence of two X chromosomes and one Y chromosome in which affected individuals have undersized external male genitals

Koran the sacred text of Islam revered as the word of God and accepted as the foundation of Islamic law, religion, culture, and politics

Labia Majora large folds of skin that form the outer lips of the vulva

Labia Minora folds of skin located within the labia majora that form the inner lips of the vulva

Labor process by which childbirth occurs, beginning with contractions of the uterus and ending with the expulsion of the fetus or infant and the placenta

Lactation production of milk by the mammary glands

Lamaze Method method in which a woman and her coach (often the baby's father) learn about childbirth and how to relax and breathe in patterns that conserve energy and decrease pain

Lesbians female homosexuals

Levirate the practice of marrying the widow of one's childless brother to maintain his line, as required by ancient Hebrew law

Libido sexual desire

Limbic System a group of interconnected deep brain structures that especially influence motivation and emotion

Limerence Tennov's term for being in love

Loneliness feelings of sadness at being abandoned or alone

Longitudinal Study a study in which individuals are followed, or in which a phenomenon is observed (continuously or intermittently), for a set period of time

Love a deep, tender feeling of affection and solicitude toward a person, such as that arising from kinship, recognition of attractive qualities, or a sense of underlying oneness.

Lumpectomy surgery to remove a breast tumor and a small amount of tissue surrounding the tumor

Lust to want, crave, covet, or sexually desire someone or something

Luteal Phase phase of the menstrual cycle in which the corpus luteum is formed and the uterus is prepared to nourish a fertilized egg

Luteinizing Hormone (LH) hormone secreted by the pituitary gland that triggers ovulation and helps prepare the uterine lining for implantation

Madam a woman who manages a brothel

Male Condom a flexible sheath, usually made of thin rubber or latex, designed to cover the penis during sexual intercourse for contraceptive purposes or as a means of preventing sexually transmitted diseases

Male Orgasmic Disorder sexual dysfunction in which a male is unable to ejaculate during coitus

Malignant cancerous; a growth that invades nearby tissue or spreads to other parts of the body

Mammary Glands glands found in female mammals that produce milk

Mammogram X-ray exam of the breast to detect cancerous tumors

Mann Act 1910 law making the transportation of women across state lines for "immoral purposes" illegal

Marital Rape: forced sexual intercourse perpetrated by the victim's spouse

Marriage the legal union of a man and woman as husband and wife

Mastectomy surgical removal of the breast

Masturbation stimulation of the genitals for sexual pleasure by manual contact or means other than sexual intercourse

Masturbation the stimulation of one's own or another's genital organs, usually by manual contact or means other than coitus

Meiosis cell division that produces reproductive cells in sexually reproducing organisms in which the nucleus divides into four nuclei each containing half the chromosome number

Menarche the initial onset of menstruation in life

Menopause the cessation of menstruation in life

Menorrhagia excessive menstrual discharge

Menstrual Cycle the time from the beginning of one menstrual period to the beginning of the next; typically 28 days

Menstrual Phase the phase of the menstrual cycle during which the lining of the uterus is shed

Menstrual Synchrony the development of congruent menstrual cycles that sometimes occur among women who live together

Menstruation the sloughing off of built-up uterine lining that recurs in nonpregnant women from menarche to menopause

Meta-analysis the process or technique of synthesizing research results by using various statistical methods to retrieve, select, and combine results from previous separate but similar studies

Midwife a person, usually a woman, who is trained to assist women in childbirth

Mifepristone an abortion procedure, also known as RU-486, in which an antiprogesterone drug blocks receptors of progesterone and prevents the fertilized egg from attaching to the uterine wall

Mikvah: a ritual purification bath taken by Jews on certain occasions, as before the Sabbath or after menstruation or ejaculation

Miscarriage spontaneous abortion; spontaneous expulsion of a human fetus before it is viable and especially during the first 20 weeks of gestation

Miscegenation marriage, cohabitation, or reproduction by parents of different races (especially by white and nonwhite persons)

Missionary Position sexual intercourse in the man-on-top position

Mitosis cell division in which the nucleus divides into nuclei containing the same number of chromosomes

Mons Veneris mound of fatty tissue over the pubic bone above the vagina

Morals concept of what is right and wrong

Morals judgment of the goodness or badness of human action and character; what you believe is right

Morning Sickness symptoms of pregnancy including nausea, vomiting, and food aversions experienced by some women

Morula the mass of cells resulting from the cleavage of the ovum before the formation of a blastula.

Motility spontaneous movement

Müllerian Ducts a pair of embryonic ducts which give rise to the genital passages in the female but disappear in the male

Multiple Orgasms experiencing one or more additional orgasms within a short time following the first

Myometrium the smooth muscle layer of the uterine wall

Myotonia muscle tension

Narcissism: excessive love or admiration of oneself

Natural Selection the process by which forms of life having traits that better enable them to adapt to specific environmental pressures will tend to survive and reproduce in greater numbers

Naturalist belief that the individual must make his or her own decisions based on circumstances

Nature the physical world not made by man; the forces that have formed it and control it

Necrophilia erotic attraction to or sexual contact with corpses

New Testament the collection of the books of the Bible that were produced by the early Christian church, comprising the Gospels, Acts of the Apostles, the Epistles, and the Revelation of St. John the Divine

Nipple protuberance through which milk is drawn from the breast

Nirvana enlightenment in the Buddhist tradition, a dimension transcending time and space, marked by disinterested wisdom and compassion

Nocturnal Emission the release of semen during sleep, often during a sexual dream; also called a "wet dream"

Noncoital Behavior sexual behavior that does not involve intercourse

Nonmarital Relationship a sexual relationship between nonmarried individuals

Normalcy Anxiety: feelings of dread and foreboding in connection with conforming with, adhering to, or behaving in a typical, usual, or standard pattern in connection with sexual activity

Nurture the sum of environmental influences and conditions acting on an organism

Obscene Phone Calling a sexual disorder in which an individual seeks sexual excitement by telephoning nonconsenting people and making sexual remarks

Obscenity behavior or language that is considered offensive, lewd, or indecent according to accepted moral standards

Observational Research a method of research in which subjects are watched and studied in a laboratory or natural setting

Obstetrician a physician who specializes in pregnancy and childbirth

Old Testament Christian designation for the Holy Scriptures of Judaism, referring to the covenant of God with Israel, as distinguished in Christianity from the dispensation of Jesus constituting the New Testament

Onanism masturbation or coitus interruptus, withdrawal of the penis in sexual intercourse so that ejaculation takes place outside the vagina

Open Marriage marital relationship in which spouses have sexual relationships with other people with their spouse's consent

Opportunistic Infections illnesses caused by various organisms, some of which usually do not cause disease in persons with normal immune systems

Oral Contraceptives/ Birth Control Pills pills, typically containing synthetic hormones, that inhibit ovulation and thereby prevent conception

Orgasm the peak state of sexual excitement; it is marked by rhythmic contractions of the pelvic floor muscles

Orgasmic Disorders Sexual dysfunctions in which despite sufficient sexual stimulation an individual is persistently or recurrently unable to reach orgasm

Orgasmic Phase the third phase of Masters and Johnson's sexual response cycle in which orgasm occurs

Orgasmic Platform the thickening of the walls of the outer third of the vagina that occurs during the plateau phase due to vasocongestion

Os opening in the middle of the cervix that leads to the interior of the uterus

Outing publicly identifying the sexual orientation of gays and lesbians who previously have chosen not to acknowledge their sexual orientation publicly

Ova egg cells

Ovaries female gonads that produce ova and sex hormones

Overpopulation having too many people for the amount of food, materials, and space available

Oviducts fallopian tubes

Ovulation the discharge of a mature ovum from the ovary

Oxytocin pituitary hormone that stimulates uterine contractions during labor and facilitates the secretion of milk during nursing

Pair Bonding the selective social attachment formed between monogamous males and females during courtship and mating

Paraphilia any of a group of psychosexual disorders characterized by sexual fantasies, feelings, or activities involving a nonhuman object, a nonconsenting partner such as a child, or pain or humiliation of oneself or one's partner

Parasite a plant or animal that for all or part of its life obtains food and physical protection from a living organism of another species (the host), which is usually damaged by and never benefits from its presence

Passion intense feelings of emotional excitement (arousal), absorption in the other, and sexual desire

Passionate Love also known as romantic love, is characterized by intense feelings of emotional excitement (arousal), absorption in the other, and sexual desire

Past-Dominant decisions based primarily upon what has already occurred

Pedophile an adult who is sexually attracted to a child or children

Peer-Delinquent Prostitute males who often work in small groups and use homosexual prostitution as a vehicle for assault and robbery

Pelvic Inflammatory Disease (PID) an inflammation of the female pelvic organs, most commonly the fallopian tubes, usually as a result of bacterial infection

Penis Sheath object or material that is tied around the foreskin to prevent the glans from showing should a man have an erection

Penis the male sexual organ

Peptide Hormones group of hormones such as oxytocin and vasopressin that are produced in the hypothalamus

Performance Anxiety: feelings of dread and foreboding of being judged in connection with sexual activity

Perimenopause period before menstruation completely stops at menopause

Perimetrium the thin membrane covering the outside of the uterus

Perinatal phase surrounding the time of birth, from the 20th week of gestation to the 28th day of newborn life.

Phenylethylamine (PEA) a substance that occurs naturally as a neurotransmitter in the brain and has pharmacological properties similar to those of amphetamine, Symmetry

Pheromones airborne chemical substances secreted externally by some animals that convey information or produce specific responses in other members of the same species

Physiology the vital processes or normal functions in a living organism

Pimp a procurer; a person, usually a man, who solicits customers for a prostitute, usually in return for a share of the earnings

Pituitary Gland small gland in the base of the brain that receives instructions from the hypothalamus and secretes hormones

Placebo an inactive substance or preparation given to reinforce a patient's expectation to get well, as a control in an experiment, or to test the effectiveness of a medicine

Placenta the organ in most mammals, formed in the lining of the uterus by the union of the uterine mucous membrane with the membranes of the fetus, that provides for the nourishment of the fetus and the elimination of its waste products.

Plateau Phase the second phase of Masters and Johnson's sexual response cycle in which muscle tension, heart rate, and vasocongestion increase

Polar Body the smaller of two cells produced during meiotic division

Polyandry the practice of having more than one husband at one time

Polygamy the practice of having more than one spouse at one time. Also called plural marriage

Polygyny the practice of having more than one wife at one time

Polymorphous Perversity the capacity to receive a form of sexual pleasure from stimulation of any part of the body

Pornography sexually explicit pictures, writing, or other material whose primary purpose is to cause sexual arousal

Post Partum Taboo cultural belief that forbids sexual intercourse for a specified period of time after the birth of a child

Postpartum period following child-birth

Posttraumatic Stress Disorder (PTSD) characteristic symptoms following exposure to an extreme traumatic stressor involving direct personal experience of an event that involves actual or threatened death or serious injury

Power Rape sexual assault motivated by the desire to control and dominate the victim

Precocious puberty the onset of pubertal changes at an unexpectedly early age

Preeclampsia symptoms that are a precursor of eclampsia, a serious condition affecting pregnant women in which the entire body is affected by convulsions and the patient eventually passes into a coma

Pregnancy the period between conception and birth during which offspring develop in the womb

Premarital Relationship a sexual relationship that takes place prior to marriage

Premature Birth/Preterm Birth child born prior to 37 weeks gestation, though often defined in terms of birth weight rather than gestation

Premature Ejaculation sexual dysfunction in which ejaculation occurs so rapidly as to interfere with the couple's sexual satisfaction

Premenstrual Syndrome (PMS) physical and emotional symptoms of discomfort that occur in some women prior to menstruation

Prenatal existing or occurring before birth

Prepuce a covering fold of skin

Prepuce foreskin

Present-Dominant: decisions based primarily upon the here and now

Priapism a condition characterized by persistent erection of the penis

Primary Oocyte the enlarging ovum before maturity is reached

Primary Spermatocyte early stage in the development of sperm cells before maturity is reached

Procreation the act of reproduction

Procreationist view that reproduction is the primary purpose of sexuality

Progesterone a hormone produced in the ovary that prepares and maintains the uterus for pregnancy

Progesterone an antiestrogenic steroid produced by the corpus luteum and placenta or prepared synthetically that stimulates proliferation of the endometrium and is involved in the regulation of the menstrual cycle

Progestin generic term for any substance, natural or synthetic, that effects some or all of the biological changes produced by progesterone

Progestin hormone of the corpus luteum from which progesterone can be isolated in pure form

Prolactin pituitary hormone that stimulates production of milk

Proliferative Phase the phase of the menstrual cycle in which the ovarian follicles mature

Prostate Gland gland, which lies just below the bladder and surrounds the urethra, that produces about 30 percent of the seminal fluid released during ejaculation

Prostitution the act or practice of engaging in sex for money

Protease Inhibitors antiviral drugs that act by inhibiting the virus protease enzyme, thereby preventing viral replication

Protozoa a family of unicellular organisms that are the simplest form of animal life

Proximity: the state, quality, sense, or fact of being near or next to; closeness

Pseudohermaphrodite person having the internal reproductive organs of one sex and external sexual characteristics of the other sex

Psychoanalytic Theory theory of personality originated by Sigmund Freud that is based on the belief that unconscious conflict can result in psychological or physical symptoms

Psychopath: a person with an antisocial personality disorder, manifested in aggressive, criminal, or amoral behavior without conscience, empathy, or remorse

Psychosexual Therapy treatment approach developed by Helen Singer Kaplan that combines behavioral and psychoanalytic techniques

Psychotherapy treatment of emotional problems primarily through verbal and nonverbal communication and interventions rather than other treatments such as medications

Puberty the stage of adolescence in which an individual becomes physiologically capable of sexual reproduction

Pubic Lice/ Pediculosis infestation with lice of the family *Pediculidae pediculus*

Questionnaire a method of research in which subjects are asked to respond to a list of written questions

Ramadan the ninth month of the Muslim calendar, a period of fasting from sunrise to sunset

Random Sample a sample drawn without bias from a population so that each individual has an equal chance of being selected

Rape Trauma Syndrome two-phase response patterns of rape survivors

Rape the crime of forcing another person to submit to sex acts, especially sexual intercourse

Rapid Eye Movement (REM) Sleep a stage in the normal sleep cycle during which dreams occur and the body undergoes marked changes, including rapid eye movement, loss of reflexes, and increased pulse rate and brain activity

Readiness the state of being ready or prepared

Reciprocity a relation of mutual dependence. Ideas, feelings or action or influence

Recreationist: view that anything that gives a person pleasure is inherently good

Refractory Period period of time following orgasm during which a male is no longer responsive to stimulation

Rejection: the act or process of spurning, refusing, or dismissing someone

Reliability the consistency or accuracy of a research measure

Religion a personal or institutionalized system grounded in a belief in and reverence for a supernatural power or powers regarded as creator and governor of the universe

Religiosity the quality of being religious; excessive or affected piety

Reproduction/Production Relationship the link between sex and a community having enough food and resources for their present and future members

Reproductive Relationship a relationship in which reproduction is both expected and socially approved

Resolution Phase the fourth phase of Masters and Johnson's sexual response cycle during which the body gradually returns to its prearoused state

Retrovirus a type of virus that, when not infecting a cell, stores its genetic information on a single-stranded RNA molecule instead of the more usual double-stranded DNA

Reverse Transcriptase Inhibitors enzymes that convert the single-stranded viral RNA into DNA, the form in which the cell carries its genes

Rh Incompatibility a condition in which antibodies produced by a pregnant woman are transmitted to the fetus and may cause brain damage or death

Roe v. Wade 1973 Supreme Court case that legalized abortion during the first trimester of pregnancy

Romance: an interpersonal relationship marked by admiration, sensitivity, passion and intensity

Sadistic Rape preplanned ritualistic, brutal, and violent sexual assault

Sadomasochism (S&M) deriving of pleasure, especially sexual gratification, from inflicting or submitting to physical or emotional abuse

Salvation deliverance from the power or penalty of sin; redemption

Sample the portion of a population selected for a study and from which research results may be generalized

Sanskrit an Indo-European, Indic language, in use since about 1200 B.C. as the religious and classical literary language of India

Scabies a contagious skin disease caused by a parasitic mite

Scientific Method a set of rules and procedures on how to study, observe, or conduct experiments

Scrotum the external pouch of skin beneath the penis that contains the testicles

Second Trimester the fourth, fifth and sixth months of pregnancy

Secondary Oocyte an oocyte that arises from the primary oocyte after it completes the first meiotic division

Secondary Sex Characteristics physical characteristics, other than the genitals, that indicate sexual maturity and distinguish males from females

Secondary Spermatocyte a spermatocyte that arises from the primary oocyte after it completes the first meiotic division

Self-Acceptance: regarding yourself as being a reasonably good person.

Self-Awareness: focusing your conscious attention on yourself

Self-Control: the ability to control and regulate one's own behavior

Semen fluid containing sperm and secretions from the testicles, prostate, and seminal vesicles that is expelled from the penis during ejaculation; ejaculate

Seminal Fluid fluid from the prostate and other sex glands that helps transport semen out of a man's body during ejaculation

Seminal Vesicles small glands that lie behind the bladder and secrete fluid that combines with sperm in the ejaculatory ducts

Seminiferous Tubules thin coiled tubes located in the testicles in which sperm are produced

Sensate Focus Exercises form of therapy designed by Masters and Johnson to treat a variety of sexual problems without the pressure to "perform"

Serial Monogamy a form of monogamy (being married to only one person at a time) characterized by several successive, short-term marriages over the course of a lifetime

Seronegative showing no significant level of serum antibodies, or other immunologic marker in the serum, that would indicate previous exposure to the infectious agent being tested

Seropositive showing a significant level of serum antibodies, or other immunologic marker in the serum, indicating previous exposure to the infectious agent being tested

Sex Flush rash that appears on the chest or breasts of some individuals during the sexual response cycle

Sex Skin reddening of the labia minora that occurs during the plateau phase

Sex Toys objects or devices used to enhance sexual pleasure

Sexologist sex researcher

Sexual Abuse of Children sexual activity between an adult and a minor

Sexual Arousal Disorder sexual dysfunctions in which there is a persistent or recurrent failure to become adequately sexually aroused to engage in or sustain sexual intercourse

Sexual Arousal heightened state of sexual interest and excitement

Sexual Aversion an extreme and irrational fear of sex

Sexual Coercion to forcibly persuade someone to do something that she or he may not want to do

Sexual Desire Disorders sexual dysfunctions in which people have a persistent or recurrent lack of desire for sex

Sexual Differentiation the process by which males and females develop distinct anatomies.

Sexual Dysfunction a persistent sexual disorder or impairment that interferes with sexual desire, arousal, or satisfaction

Sexual ethics a set of moral principles pertaining to sex and sexual issues

Sexual Fantasies pleasant sexual thoughts or daydreams, often about something longed-for but unlikely to happen

Sexual Harassment: unwanted and offensive sexual advances or sexually offensive remarks or acts, especially by one in a superior or supervisory position or when acquiescence to such behavior is a condition of continued employment, promotion, or satisfactory evaluation

Sexual Orientation The direction of one's sexual interest toward members of the same, opposite, or both sexes

Sexual Pain Disorders Sexual dysfunctions in which persistent or recurrent pain is experienced during sexual intercourse

Sexual Phobia anxiety provoked by exposure to a specific feared object or situation, often leading to avoidance behavior

Sexual Relationship a relationship in which reproduction is neither expected nor socially approved

Sexual Reproduction the production of offspring from the union of two different organisms or parents

Sexual reproduction the process in which two cells fuse to form one fertilized cell with a new genome that is different than that of either parent

Sexual Response Cycle physiological processes and events that occur during sexual activity

Sexually Transmitted Infections (STIs) infections whose usual means of transmission is by sexual contact

Shame: a global negative feeling about the self ("I'm a bad person")

Shyness the state or quality of being nervous, uncomfortable, bashful, or timid with others

Similarity the state or quality of being alike or having a close resemblance to something; being of the same kind, but not identical

Simultaneous Orgasm partners experience orgasm at the same time

Singlehood the state of being unmarried

Situational Approach belief that assumes we make choices based on the individual responsibility

Social Constructionism theory that emphasizes the importance of social learning on how we evaluate and apply socialization and information to our lives

Social Dominance Theory complex societies are group-based hierarchies in which the dominant group is characterized by possession and control over a disproportionately large share of the material and symbolic goods people desire; most forms of group conflict and oppression are manifestations of humans' predisposition toward these social hierarchies

Social Dominance superiority of relationship and rank of an individual in relation to his or her associates

Social Exchange Theory theory in which social interactions are analyzed in terms of costs and rewards

Socialization the process of learning how to think, act, and feel the way other members of a particular culture or society do

Sodomy laws legislation forbidding anal or oral copulation

Sonogram the visual pattern or picture resulting from an ultrasound examination

Sperm Cells mature male reproductive cells

Sperm Donor male who gives his sperm for artificial insemination

Sperm male reproductive cell

Spermatic Cord cord that suspends the testes within the scrotum

Spermatids cells produced through meiosis in males that mature into sperm cells

Spermatogenesis the production of sperm cells

Spermatozoa sperm cells; spermatozoon, sing.

Spirituality concerned with or affecting the spirit or soul rather than the body or physical things

Sterilization the process of making a man or woman infertile

Steroid Hormones group of hormones that include estrogen and testosterone

Straight heterosexual

Stratified Sample a sample drawn to ensure that specific subgroups of a population are adequately represented

Streetwalker a prostitute who solicits customers on the street

Superovulation stimulation of multiple ovulation with fertility drugs

Surrogate Mother a women who agrees to be impregnated through artificial insemination and then give the child to another woman who is incapable of becoming pregnant

Survey a research method in which subjects are interviewed or complete a questionnaire

Swinging the sexual exchange of marital partners

Synapses the junction across which a nerve impulse passes from an axon terminal to a neuron, muscle cell, or gland cell.

Syphilis a sexually transmitted disease caused by the spirochete *Treponema pallidum* that may progress through several stages of development

T-4 cells antibody-triggered immune cells that seek and attack invading organisms; also called CD4+ or helper T-cells

T-Cells white blood cells, derived from the thymus gland, that participate in a variety of cell-mediated immune reactions

Talmud the collection of Jewish laws and traditions relating to religious and social matters

Tantra any of a comparatively recent class of Hindu or Buddhist religious literature written in Sanskrit and concerned with techniques and rituals including meditative and sexual practices

Taoism a principal philosophy and system of religion of China, based on the teachings of Lao-tzu and on subsequent revelations; characterized by a pantheon of many gods and by the practice of alchemy, divination, and magic

Target Population the larger population being studied, which the sample should represent

Temporary Assistance to Needy Families (TANF) Act 1996 welfare reform legislation that made federal funds available to states over a 5-year period to support programs that promoted abstinence

Teratogen a drug or other substance capable of interfering with the development of a fetus, causing birth defects

Testes the male reproductive organs within the scrotum that produce sperm and are the primary source of testosterone; testicles

Testicles testes

Third Trimester the last 3 months of pregnancy

Torah the first five books of the Hebrew Scriptures

Toxemia an abnormal condition associated with the presence of toxic substances in the blood

Toxic Shock Syndrome disease that occurs most often in menstruating females using tampons in which an overgrowth of bacteria may cause fever, vomiting, diarrhea, and often shock

Transference the projection of feelings, thoughts, and wishes onto the therapist, such as feelings of attachment or attraction to a therapist

Transgender Roles a blend of both masculine and feminine traits and traditional roles

Transgender appearing or attempting to be a member of the opposite sex

Transsexual a person who is predisposed to identify with the opposite sex, sometimes strongly enough to undergo hormone treatment and surgery to effect a change of sex

Transvestism the practice of adopting the clothes or the manner or the sexual role of the opposite sex

Transvestite a person who dresses and acts in a style or manner traditionally associated with the opposite sex, especially for purposes of emotional or sexual gratification

Trichomoniasis an infection caused by a trichomonad (*Trichomonas vaginalis*) that results in vaginal discharge and itching and may also invade the male urethra and bladder

Tubal Ligation surgical sterilization of a woman by obstructing or "tying" the fallopian tubes

Tumor an abnormal mass of tissue

Turner's Syndrome a relatively rare condition characterized by the presence of one unmatched X chromosome resulting in affected individuals having normal female external genitals but their internal reproductive structures do not fully develop

Ultrasound Examination the use of high frequency sound waves to locate body tissue and form a picture of the fetus in utero

Umbilical cord tube that connects the fetus to the placenta

Underpopulation having too few people to provide protection and other resources for a community

Unrequited Love love that is not returned or reciprocated

Urethra the tube through which urine from the bladder is expelled

Urethral Opening the duct through which urine is discharged from the bladder

Uterine body the central region of the uterus in which a fetus may develop

Uterus hollow, muscular internal female organ in which the fertilized egg develops until birth

Vacuum Aspiration/ Suction Curettage abortion procedures performed during the first trimester of pregnancy, in which the contents of the uterus are withdrawn through a narrow tube

Vacuum Extraction removal of the fetus from the uterus or vagina at or near the end of pregnancy with a metal traction cup that is attached to the fetus's head. Negative pressure is applied and traction is made on a chain passed through the suction tube

Vagina the stretchable canal that extends from the external genital opening to the cervix

Vaginal Spermicides chemical agents that kill spermatozoa

Vaginal Sponge a soft, disposable, synthetic sponge containing spermicide inserted into the vagina, which helps prevent sperm from entering the uterus and kills or makes sperm inactive

Vaginismus a sexual dysfunction characterized by involuntary spasmodic contractions of the vaginal muscles that prevent penetration or make coitus painful

Vaginitis inflammation of the vagina, typically caused by bacteria or yeast infection

Validity the extent to which research measures what the researcher intends

Value Orientation: a rational and sensible approach to decision-making that will maximize one's potential to thrive

Values concepts of the desirable that serve as criteria for meaning and understanding, and as a guide for evaluating behavior

Values principles, standards, or qualities considered worthwhile or desirable; what you believe is desirable

Vas Deferens tubes that convey sperm from the testes to the ejaculatory duct of the penis

Vasectomy surgical sterilization of a man by cutting or blocking the vas deferens

Vasocongestin engorgement of blood vessels in response to sexual arousal

Vasopressin a pituitary hormone that causes blood vessels and smooth muscles to contract

Veda any of four ancient and most authoritative Hindu sacred texts, composed in Sanskrit; or, these books collectively

Verbal Sexual Coercion verbally influencing or forcing an individual into unwanted sexual attention or behavior

Verbal Sexual Pressure the use of manipulation or deceit to influence the recipient into unwanted sexual behavior

Vestibular Bulbs structures on each side of the vaginal opening that engorge with blood and swell during sexual arousal

Vestibule the area of the vulva inside the labia minora

Vibrator a mechanical device that shakes slightly and quickly, which is held against the body to achieve sexual pleasure

Viropause/ Andropause male menopause; period when testosterone levels may decrease

Viruses a microscopic infectious organism that reproduces inside living cells

Voyeurism observing unsuspecting individuals, usually strangers, who are naked, in the process of disrobing, or engaging in sexual activity

Vulva the external female genitals

Western Blot a laboratory test for specific antibodies to confirm repeatedly reactive results on the ELISA test

Wolffian Ducts a pair of embryonic ducts which if allowed to develop become the male reproductive system

Womb the uterus

X Chromosome a sex chromosome of humans and most mammals that determines femaleness when paired with another X chromosome and that occurs singly in males

Y Chromosome a sex chromosome of humans and most mammals that is present only in males and is paired with an X chromosome

Yang the active, male cosmic principle in Chinese philosophy

Yin the passive, female cosmic principle in Chinese philosophy

Zona Pellucida A translucent, elastic, noncellular layer surrounding the ovum of many mammals.

Zoophilia erotic attraction to or sexual contact with animals

Zygote Intrafallopian Transfer (ZIFT) fertilizing eggs and sperm outside of the body and immediately placing them in the fallopian tubes to enhance the chances of pregnancy

Zygote an egg that has been fertilized but not yet divided

References

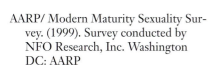

AARP/ Modern Maturity Sexuality Survey. (1999). Survey conducted by NFO Research, Inc. Washington DC: AARP

Abbey, A., Auslan, P., & Ross, L. (1998). Sexual assault perpetration by college men: The role of alcohol misperception of sexual intent and sexual beliefs and experience. *Journal of Social Clinical Psychology, 172,* 167–195.

Abdullah, A. S. (1998). Mammy-ism: A diagnosis of psychological misorientation for women of African descent. *Journal of Black Psychology, 24,* 196–210.

Abel, G., Barlow, D., Blanchard, E., & Guild, D. (1977). The components of rapists' sexual arousal. *Archives of General Psychiatry, 34,* 895–903.

Able et al. v. USA, U. S. Court of Appeals for the Second Circuit, 95–9111(L).

Abramowitz, S. I. (1986). Psychosocial outcomes of sex reassignment surgery. *Journal of Consulting and Clinical Psychology, 54,* 183–189.

Abramson, P. R. (1973). The relationship of the frequency of masturbation to several aspects of behavior. *Journal of Sex Research, 5,* 133–144.

Abramson, P. R. (1990). Sexual science: Emerging discipline or oxymoron? *Journal of Sex Research, 26,* 147–165.

Abramson, P., & Pinkerton, A. (1995). *Sexual nature, sexual culture.* Chicago: University of Chicago Press.

Abramson, P. R., & Pinkerton, S. D. (2001). *With pleasure: Thoughts on the nature of human sexuality.* New York: Oxford University Press.

Abstinence Education. Social Security Act, Title V, Section 510, 42 U. S. C. 710.

Accreditation Council for Graduate Medical Education. (1999). Program requirements for residency education in obstetrics and gynecology. From http://www.acgme.org

Adams, C. G., & Turner, B. F. (1985). Reported change in sexuality from young adulthood to old age. *Journal of Sex Research, 21,* 126–141.

Adams, C. T., & Winston, K. T. (1980). Mothers at work: Public policy in the United States, Sweden, and China. New York: Longman.

Adams, F. (1987). The role of prostitution in AIDS and other STDs. *Medical Aspects of Human Sexuality, 21,* 27–33.

Adams, H. E., & Chiado, J. (1984). Sexual deviations. In H. E. Adams & P. B. Sutker (Eds.), *Comprehensive handbook of psychopathology* (pp. 777–806). New York: Plenum.

Adams, H. E., Wright, J. W., & Lohr, B. A. (1996). Is homophobia associated with homosexual arousal? *Journal of Abnormal Psychology, 105,* 440–445.

Adams, V. (1980, August). Sex therapists in perspective. *Psychology Today,* 35–36.

Adler, N. R., David, H. P., Major, B. N., Roth, S. H., Russo, N. F., & Wyatt, G. E. (1990). Psychological responses after abortion. *Science, 246,* 41–44.

Agnew, J. (1986). Hazards associated with anal erotic activity. *Archives of Sexual Behavior, 15,* 307–314.

Ahmed, R. (1991). Women in Egypt and the Sudan. In L. L. Adler (Ed.), *Women in Cross-Cultural Perspective.* New York: Praeger.

Ainsworth, M. (1962). The effects of maternal deprivation: A review of findings and controversy of maternal care: A reassessment of its effects. Public Health Papers (No. 14). Geneva: World Health Organization.

Ainsworth, M. D. (1989). Attachments beyond infancy. *American Psychologist, 44,* 709–715.

Ainsworth, M. D., Blehar, M. C., Waters, E., & Wall, S. (1978). *Patterns of attachment: A psychological study of the strange situation.* Hillsdale, NJ: Erlbaum.

Alan Guttmacher Institute. (1993). *Sexually transmitted disease and the public health response.* New York: Author.

Alan Guttmacher Institute. (1994). *Sex and America's teenagers.* New York: Author.

Alan Guttmacher Institute. (1998). *Into a new world: Young women's sexual and reproductive lives.* New York: Author.

Alan Guttmacher Institute (2000). *Facts in brief: Induced abortion.* New York: Author.

Albert, A. E., Warner, D. L., Hatcher, R. A., Trussell, J., & Bennett, C. (1995). Condom use among female commercial sex workers in Nevada's legal brothels. *American Journal of Public Health, 85,* 1485–1488.

Albrecht, S. L., Bahr, H. M., & Goodman, K. L. (1983). *Divorce and remarriage: Problems, adaptations, and adjustments.* Westport, CT: Greenwood Press.

Aldred, C. (1996). *Divine sex: Tantric and Taoist acts of conscious loving.* San Francisco: Harper.

Allen, D. (1980). Young male prostitutes: A psychosocial study. *Archives of Sexual Behavior, 9,* 399–426.

Allen, G. E. (1997). The social and economic origins: A case study of the American eugenics movement, 1900–1940, and its lessons for today. *Genetica, 99,* 77–88.

Almeling, R., Tews, L., & Dudley, S. (2000). Abortion training in U.S. obstetrics and gynecology residency programs, 1998. *Family Planning Perspectives, 32,* 268–271, 320.

Alter-Reid, K. et al. (1986). Sexual abuse of children: A review of the empirical findings. *Clinical Psychology Review, 6,* 249–266.

Altman, I., & Ginat, J. (1995). *Polygamous families in contemporary society.* New York: Cambridge University Press.

Altman, L. K. (2000, June 25). A new AIDS mystery: Prostitutes who have remained immune. *The New York Times,* from http://www.nytimes.com/library/national/science/aids/020300sci-aids-infection.html.

Alzate, H. (1989). Sexual behavior of unmarried Colombian university students: A follow-up. *Archives of Sexual Behavior, 18,* 239–250.

Alzate, H., & Lodano, M. L. (1984). Vaginal erotic sensitivity. *Journal of Sex and Marital Therapy, 10,* 499–500.

Amato, P. R., & Booth, A. (1998). *A generation at risk: Growing up in an era of family upheaval.* Cambridge, MA: Harvard University Press.

American Academy of Pediatrics. (1997). Policy statement: Breastfeeding and the use of human milk. *Pediatrics, 100,* 1035–1039.

American Academy of Pediatrics. (1999). Circumcision policy statement. *Pediatrics, 103,* 686–693.

American Cancer Society. (1999). *Penile cancer: Prevention and risk factors* from http://www3.cancer.org/cancerinfo/load_cont.asp?st=pr&ct=35&language=english

American Cancer Society. (2000a). *Breast cancer: Prevention and risk factors* from http://www3.cancer.org/cancerinfo/load_cont.asp?st=pr&ct=5&language=english

American Cancer Society, (2000b). *Cervical cancer: Prevention and risk factors* from http://www3.cancerinfo/load_cont.asp?ct=8&st=pr

American Cancer Society. (2000c). *Ovary cancer: Overview* from http://www3.cancer.org/cancerinfo/load_cont.asp?ct=33&doc=37

American Cancer Society. (2000d). *Prostate cancer: Overview* from http://www3.cancer.org/cancerinfo/load_cont.asp?ct=36&doc=38&language=english

American Cancer Society. (2000e). *Testicular cancer: Prevention and risk factors* from http://www3.cancer.org/cancerinfo/load_cont.asp?ct=41&st=pr

American Cancer Society. (2000f). *Vulvar cancer: What is it?* from http://www3.cancer.org/cancerinfo/load_cont.asp?ct=45&st=wi

American Cancer Society. (2001). *Endometrial cancer: Detection and symptoms* from http://www3.cancerinfo/load_cont.asp?st=ds&ct=11&language=english

American Civil Liberties Union. (2001). "Crime" and punishment in America.

from http://www.aclu.org/issues/gay/sodomy.html.

American Life League (2001). from http://www.all.org

American Psychiatric Association. (1994). *Diagnostic and statistical manual of mental disorders, (4th ed).* Washington, DC: Author.

American Society for Reproductive Medicine. (1999). *Patient's fact sheet: Multiple gestation and multifetal pregnancy reduction* from http://www.asrm.com

Anderson, J. L., Crawford, C. B., Nadeau, J., & Lindberg, J. (1992). Was the Duchess of Windsor right? A cross-cultural review of the sociobiology of ideas of female body shape. *Ethology and Sociobiology, 13,* 197–227.

Anderson, J. K., & Rybo, G. (1990). Levonorgestrel-releasing intrauterine device in the treatment of menorrhagia. *British Journal of Gynecology, 97,* 690–694.

Anderson, S. A., Russell, C. S., & Schumm, W. R. (1983). Perceived marital quality and family life-cycle categories: A further analysis. *Journal of Marriage and the Family, 45,* 127–139.

Anderson-Hunt, M., & Dennerstein, L. (1994). Increased female sexual response after oxytocin. *British Medical Journal, 309,* 929.

Angell, M. (1997). The ethics of clinical research in the third world. *New England Journal of Medicine, 337,* 847–849.

Angier, N. (1993a, December 26). Bias against gay people: Hatred of a special kind. *The New York Times,* p. 4E.

Angier, N. (1993b). Reports suggest homosexuality is linked to genes. *The New York Times,* pp. A12, D21.

Angier, N. (1999). *Women: An intimate geography.* New York: Anchor Books.

Annie E. Casey Foundation. (1998). *When teens have sex: Issues and trends.* Baltimore, MD: Author.

Annon, J. (1974). The behavioral treatment of sexual problems (Vol. 1). Honolulu, HI: Enabling Systems

Anson, O. (1999). Exploring the bio-psycho-social approach to premenstrual experiences. *Social Science and Medicine, 49,* 67–80.

Araji, S., & Finkelhor, D. (1985a). A review of research. In D. Finklehor (Ed.), *Sourcebook on child sexual abuse.* Beverly Hills, CA: Sage Publications.

Araji, S., & Finkelhor, D. (1985b). Explanations of pedophilia: Review of empirical research. *Bulletin of the American Academy of Psychiatry and the Law, 13,* 17–37.

Archer, J. (2000). Sex differences in aggression between heterosexual partners: A meta-analytic review. *Psychological Bulletin, 126,* 697–702.

Archer, J., Birring, S. S., & Wu, F. C. W. (1998). The association between testosterone and aggression in young men: Empirical findings and a meta-analysis. *Aggressive Behavior, 24,* 411–420.

Ard, B. N. (1977). Sex in lasting marriages: A longitudinal study. *Journal of Sex Research, 13,* 274–285.

Arenttewicz, B., & Schmidtt, G. (Eds.). (1983). *The treatment of sexual disorders.* New York: Basic Books.

Aries, P. (1956). *Centuries of childhood.* New York: Random House.

Armour, S. (1998, May 25). Prevention slows sex harassment. *USA Today,* from http://www.usatoday.com/news/nds22.htm

Aron, A., & Aron, E. N. (1986). *Love and the expansion of self: Understanding attraction and satisfaction.* New York: Hemisphere.

Arora, R. R., & Melilli, L. (1999). Acute myocardial infarction after the use of sildenafil. *New England Journal of Medicine, 341,* 9.

Atchison, C., Fraser, L., & Lowman, J. (1998). Men who buy sex: Preliminary findings of an exploratory study. In J. E. Elias, V. L. Bullough, V. Elias, & G. Brewer (Eds.), *Prostitution: On whores, hustlers and johns* (pp. 172–203). New York: Prometheus Books.

Austrom, D., & Hanel, K. (1985). Psychological issues of single life in Canada: An exploratory study. *Inter-*

national Journal of Women's Studies, 8, 12–23.

Austoni, E. G, & Guarneri, G. A. (1999). Penile elongation and thickening—a myth? Is there a cosmetic or medical indication? *Andrologia, 31* (Supp.l), 45–51.

Bagemihl, B. (1999). *Biological exuberance: Animal homosexuality and natural diversity.* New York: St. Martin's Press.

Bahrke, M. S., Yesalis, C. E., & Wright, J. E. (1996). Psychological and behavioral effects of endogenous testosterone and anabolic-androgenic steroids. An update. *Sports Medicine, 22,* 367–390.

Bailey, J. M., Bobrow, D., Wolfe, M., & Mikach, S. (1995). Sexual orientation of adult sons of gay fathers. *Developmental Psychology, 31,* 124–139.

Bailey, J. M., & Pillard, R. C. (1991, December 16). Are some people born gay? *The New York Times,* p. A15.

Bailey, J. M., Pillard, R. C., Dawood, K., Miller, M. B., Farrer, L. A., Trivedi, S., & Murphy, R. L. (1999). A family history study of male sexual orientation using three independent samples. *Behavior Genetics, 29,* 79–86.

Bailey, J. M., Pillard, R. C, Neale, M. C., & Aguel, Y. (1993). Heritable factors influence sexual orientation in women. *Archives of Gender Psychiatry, 40,* 217–223.

Bailey, R. C., & Aunger, R. (1995). Sexuality, infertility, and sexually transmitted disease among farmers and foragers in Central Africa. In P. R. Abramson & S. D. Pinkerton (Eds.), *Sexual nature/sexual culture* (pp. 195–222). Chicago: University of Chicago Press.

Baird, R. M., & Rosenbaum, S. E. (1991). *Pornography: Private rights or public menace?* Buffalo, NY: Prometheus Press.

Bakan, D. (1966). Behaviorism and American urbanization. *Journal of the History of the Behavioral Sciences. 2,* 5–28.

Bakwin, H. (1974). Erotic feelings in infants and young children. *Medical Aspect of Human Sexuality, 8,* 200.

Ballard, S. M., & Morris, M. L. (1998). Sources of sexuality information for university students. *Journal of Sex Education and Therapy, 23,* 278–287.

Banks, A., & Gartrell, N. K. (1995). Hormones and sexual orientation: A questionable link. *Journal of Homosexuality, 28,* 247–268

Bannion, J. (2000). Afterword. In J. R. Llewellyn, *Murder of a prophet: Dark side of Utah polygamy.* Salt Lake City, UT: Agreka Books.

Barak, A., & Fisher, W. A. (1997). Effects of interactive computer erotica on men's attitudes and behavior toward women: An experimental study. *Computers in Human Behavior, 13,* 353–369.

Barbach, L. G. (1975). *For yourself: The fulfillment of female sexuality.* New York: Doubleday.

Barber, N. (1998). Secular changes in standards of bodily attractiveness in American women. *The Journal of Psychology, 132,* 87–94.

Barber, N. (1999). Women's dress fashions as a function of reproductive strategy. *Sex Roles: A Journal of Research, 40,* 459–471.

Bargh, J. A., Raymond, P., Pryor, J. B., & Strack, F. (1995). Attractiveness of the underling: An automatic power–sex association and its consequences for sexual harassment and aggression. *Journal of Personality & Social Psychology, 68,* 768–781.

Barker, R. L. (1987). *The green-eyed marriage: Surviving jealous relationships.* New York: Free Press.

Barnhart, K., Furman, I., & Devoto, L. (1995). Attitudes and practice of couples regarding sexual relations during the menses and spotting. *Contraception, 51,* 93–98.

Baron, L. (1990). Pornography and gender equality: An empirical analysis. *Journal of Sex Research, 27,* 363–380.

Barrett, G., Pendry, E., Peacock, J., Victor, C., Thakar, R., & Manyonda, I. (1999). Women's sexuality after childbirth: A pilot study. *Archives of Sexual Behavior, 28,* 179–191.

Barringer, F. (1991, June 7). Changes in family patterns: Solitude and single parents. *The New York Times,* pp. A1–A18.

Barringer, F. (1993, April 1). Report finds 1 in 5 infected by virus spread sexually. *The New York Times,* p. A1.

Barry, H., & Schlegel, A. (1984). *Crosscultural samples and codes.* Pittsburgh, PA: University of Pittsburgh Press.

Barry, H., & Schlegel, A. (1986). Cultural customs that influence sexual freedom in adolescence. *Ethnology, 25,* 151–162.

Barry, K. (1985). *The prostitution of sexuality.* New York: New York University Press.

Barry, W. A. (1970). Marriage research and conflict: An integrative review. *Psychological Bulletin, 73,* 41–54.

Bart, P., & O'Brien, P. (1985). Stopping rape: Successful survival strategies. Elmsford, NY: Pergamon Press.

Bartholomew, K., & Perlman, D. (1994). *Advances in personal relationships.* London: Jessica Kingsley.

Basow, S. A., & Johnson, K. (2000). Predictors of homophobia in female college students. *Sex Roles, 42,* 391–404.

Bastien, L. A., Nanda, K., Hasselblad, V., & Simel, D. L. (1998). Diagnostic efficiency of home pregnancy test kits: A meta-analysis. *Archives of Family Medicine, 7,* 465–469.

Battaglia, D. M., Richard, F. D., Datteri, D. L., & Lord, C. G. (1998). Breaking up is (relatively) easy to do: A script for dissolution of close relationships. *Journal of Social and Personal Relationships, 15,* 829–845.

Bauman, R., Kasper, C., & Alford, J. (1984). The child sex abusers. *Corrective and Social Psychiatry, 30,* 76–81.

Baumeister, R. F. (2000). Gender differences in erotic plasticity: The female sex drive as socially flexible and responsive. *Psychological Bulletin, 126,* 347–374.

Baumeister, R. F., & Bratslavsky, E. (1999). Passion, intimacy and time: Passionate love as a function of a change in intimacy. *Personality and Social Psychology Review, 3,* 49–67.

Baumeister, R. F., Bratslavsky, E., Muraven, M., & Tice, D. M. (1998). Ego depletion: Is the active self a limited resource? *Journal of Personality and Social Psychology, 7,* 1252–1265.

Baumeister, R. F., Catanese, K. R., & Vohs, K. D. (2001). Is there a gender difference in strength of sex drive? Theoretical views, conceptual distinctions, and a review of relevant evidence. *Personality and Social Psychology Review, 5,* 242.

Baumeister, R. F., Catanese, K. R., & Wallace, H. M. (in press). Conquest by force: A narcissistic reactance theory of rape and sexual coercion. *Review of General Psychology.*

Baumeister, R. F., Heatherton, D. F., & Tice, D. M. (1994). *Losing control: How and why people fail at self-regulation.* San Diego, CA: Academic Press.

Baumeister, R. F., & Leary, M.R. (1995). The need to belong: Desire for interpersonal attachments as a fundamental human motivation. *Psychological Bulletin, 117,* 497–529.

Baumeister, R. F., & Scher, S. J. (1988). Self-defeating behavior patterns among normal individuals: Review and analysis of common self-destructive tendencies. *Psychological Bulletin, 104,* 3–22.

Baumeister, R. F., Sommer, K. L., & Cicora, K. F. (1996). Inequity and equity in marriage. *Justice Research, 9,* 199–212.

Baumeister, R. F., Stillwell, A. M., & Heatherton, T. F. (1994). Guilt: An interpersonal approach. *Psychological Bulletin, 115,* 243–267.

Baumeister, R. F., & Tice, D. (2001). *The social dimension of sex.* Boston: Allyn & Bacon.

Baumeister, R. F., & Wotman, S. R. (1992). *Breaking hearts: The two sides of unrequited love.* New York: Guilford Press.

Baumeister, R. F., Wotman, S. R., & Stillwell, A. M. (1993). Unrequited love: On heartbreak, anger, guilt, scriptlessness, and humiliation. *Journal of Personality and Social Psychology, 64,* 377–394.

Baxter, D., Marshall, W., Barabee, H., Davidson, P., & Malcolm, P. (1986). Deviant sexual behavior: Differentiating sex offenders' criminal and personal history, psychometric measures, and sexual response. *Criminal Justice and Behavior, 11,* 477–501.

Bazzini, D. G., McIntosh, W. D., Smith, S. M., & Cook, S. (1997). The aging women in popular film: Underrepresented, unattractive, unfriendly, and unintelligent. *Sex Roles, 36,* 531–543.

Beall, A. E., & Sternberg, R. J. (1995). *The psychology of gender.* New York: Guilford Press.

Beaty, L. A. (1999). Identity development of homosexual youth and parental influences on the coming out process. *Adolescence, 34,* 597–601.

Bechtel, L. S., Westerfield, C., & Eddy, J. M. (1990). Autoerotic fatalities: Implications for health educators. *Health Education, 21,* 38–40.

Beck, M. (1992, May 25). Menopause. *Newsweek,* 71–79

Beck, J. G., & Barlow, D. H. (1986). The effects of anxiety and attentional focus on sexual responding: II. Cognitive and affective patterns in erectile dysfunction. *Behaviour Research & Therapy 24,* 19–26.

Becker, J., Skinner, L., Abel, G., Axelrod, R., & Cichon, J. (1984). Sexual problems of sexual assault survivors. *Women and Health, 9,* 5–20.

Beckwith, B. E., Petros, T. V., Couk, D. I., & Tinius, T. P. (1990). The effects of vasopressin on memory in healthy young adult volunteers. Theoretical and methodological issues. *Annals of New York Academic Science, 579,* 215–226.

Bell, A. P., & Weinberg, M. S. (1978). *Homosexualities: A study of diversity among men & women.* New York: Simon and Schuster.

Bell, A. P., Weinberg, M. S., & Hammersmith, S. K. (1981). *Sexual preference: Its development in men and women.* Bloomington: Indiana University Press.

Belliotti, R. A. (1993). *Good sex: Perspectives on sexual ethics.* Lawrence, KS: University of Kansas Press.

Belsey, E. M., & Pinol, A. P. (1997). Menstrual bleeding patterns in untreated women. Task force on long-acting systemic agents for fertility regulation. *Contraception, 55,* 57–65.

Belsky, J., Lang, M., & Rovine, M. (1985). Stability and change in marriage across the transition to parenthood: A second study. *Journal of Marriage and the Family, 47,* 855–866.

Bem, D. (1996). Exotic becomes erotic: A developmental theory of sexual orientation. *Psychological Review, 103,* 320–335.

Bem, S. (1985). Androgyny and gender schema theory: A conceptual and empirical integration. In T. B. Sondeeregger (Ed.), *Nebraska symposium on motivation, 1984, Psychology and gender.* Lincoln: University of Nebraska Press.

Bem, S. (1981). Gender schema theory: A cognitive account of sex typing. *Psychological Review, 88,* 354–364.

Berger, G., Goldstein, M., & Fuerst, M. (1989). *The couple's guide to fertility.* New York: Doubleday.

Berger, P. C., & Luckmann, T. (1967). *The social construction of reality: A treatise in the sociology of knowledge.* New York: Anchor Press.

Berger, R. M. (1990). Men together: Understanding the gay couple. *Journal of Homosexuality, 19,* 31–47.

Berman, J. B., & Berman, L. (2001). *For women only: A revolutionary guide to overcoming sexual dysfunction and reclaiming your sex life.* New York: Henry Holt.

Bernard, J. (1982). *The future of marriage.* New Haven: Yale University Press.

Bernard, J. (1983). *The future of marriage.* New Haven: Yale University Press.

Bernat, A., Wilson, A. E., & Calhoun, K. S. (1999). Sexual coercion history, calloused sexual beliefs and judgments of sexual coercion in a date rape analogue. *Violence Victimology, 14,* 147–160.

Bernstein, I. S., Judge, P. G., & Ruehlmann, T. E. (1993). Kinship, association, and social relationships in rhesus monkeys. *American Journal of Primatology, 31,* 41–53.

Bernstein, J., Sugarman, R., Bernstein, D., & Bernstein, I. L. (1997). Prevalence of human seminal plasma hypersensitivity among symptomatic

women. *Annals of Allergy, Asthma and Immunology, 78,* 54–58.

Bernstein, W. M., Stephenson, B. O., Snyder, M. L., & Wicklund, R. A. (1983). Causal ambiguity and heterosexual affiliation. *Journal of Experimental Social Psychology, 19,* 78–92.

Best Friends Foundation. (2001). From http://www.bestfriendsfoundation. org

Betzig, L. (1986). *Despotism and differential reproduction: A Darwinian view of history.* New York: Aldine.

Bevc, I., & Silverman, I. (2000) Early separation and sibling incest: A test of the revised Westermarck theory. *Evolution and Human Behavior, 21,* 151–161.

Bianchi, S., & Spain, D. (1996). Women, work and family in America. *Population Bulletin, 51,* 1–48.

Bieber, I. (1976). A discussion of "Homosexuality: The ethical challenge." *Journal of Consulting and Clinical Psychology, 44,* 163–166.

Bieber, I., Dain, H., Dince, P., Drellich, M., Grand, H., Gundlach, R., Kremer, M., Rifkin, A., Wilbur, C., & Bierber, T. (1962). *Homosexuality.* New York: Vintage Books.

Billy, J. O. G., & Udry, R. (1985). Patterns of adolescent friendship and effects on sexual behavior. *Social Psychology Quarterly, 48,* 27–41.

Billy, J. O. G. et al. (1988). Effects of sexual activity on adolescent social and psychological development. *Social Psychology Quarterly, 51,* 190–212.

Bjorklund, D. F., & Kipp, K. (1996). Parental investment theory and gender differences in the evolution of inhibition mechanisms. *Psychological Bulletin, 120,* 163–188.

Blackless, M., Charuvastra, A., Derryck, A., Fausto-Sterling, A., Lauzanne, K., & Lee, E. (2000). How sexually dimorphic are we? *American Journal of Human Biology, 12,* 151–166.

Blackwood, E. (1985). Breaking the mirror: The construction of lesbianism and the anthropological discourse on homosexuality. *Journal of Homosexuality, 11,* 1–17.

Blake, S. M., Simkin, L., Ledsky, R., Perkins, C., & Calabrese, J. M. (2001). Effects of a parent-child communications intervention on young adolescents' risk for early onset of sexual intercourse. *Family Planning Perspectives, 33,* 52–61.

Blakeslee, S. (1993, June 2). New therapies are helping men to overcome impotence. *The New York Times,* p. B8.

Blanchard, R., & Klassen, K. (1997). H-Y antigen and homosexuality in men. *Journal of Theoretical Biology, 185,* 373–378.

Blanchard, R., Steiner, B., & Clemmensen, L. (1985). Gender dysphoria, gender reorientation, and the clinical management of transsexualism. *Journal of Counseling & Clinical Psychology, 53,* 295–304.

Blau, P. N. (1964). *Exchange and power in social life.* New York: Wiley.

Blount, R. (1995, Feb.). Sex, lies and media myths. *Men's Journal,* 15–16.

Blum, D. (1997). *Sex on the brain: The biological differences between men and women.* New York: Penguin.

Blumenthal, R. S., Heldman, A. W., Brinker, J. A., Resar, J. R., Coombs, V. J., Gloth, S. T., Gerstenblith, G., & Reis, S. E. (1997). Acute effects of conjugated estrogen on coronary blood flow response to acetylcholine in men. *American Journal of Cardiology, 158,* 1021–1024.

Blumstein, R., & Schwartz, P. (1983). *American couples.* New York: Morrow.

Boddy, J. (1989). Womb as oasis: The symbolic context of pharaonic circumcision in rural northern Sudan. *American Ethnologist, 9,* 1989.

Boddy, J. (1995). *Wombs and alien spirits: Women, men and the zar cult in northern Sudan.* Madison: University of Wisconsin Press.

Boeringer, S., Shehan, C., & Akers, R. (1991). Social contexts and social learning sexual coercion and aggression: Assessing the contribution of fraternity membership. *Family Relation, 40,* 58–64.

Boles, J., & Elifson, K. (1994). Sexual identity and HIV: The male prostitute. *Journal of Sex Research, 31,* 39–46.

Bonder, B. R., Martin, L., & Miracle, A. W. (2001). *Culture in clinical care.* Thorofare, NJ: Slack.

Booth, A., & Dabbs, J. M. (1993). Testosterone and men's marriages. *Social Forces, 72,* 463–477.

Booth, A., & Johnson, D. (1988). Premarital cohabitation and marital success. *Journal of Family Issues, 9,* 255–272.

Booth, A., Shelly, G., Mazur, A., Tharp, G., & Kittok, R. (1989). Testosterone, and winning and losing in human competition. *Hormonal Behavior, 23,* 556–571.

Bornoff, N. (1991). *Pink samurai: Love and marriage and sex in contemporary Japan.* New York: Pocket Books.

Boston Women's Health Book Collective (1992). *Our bodies, ourselves.* New York: Simon & Schuster.

Boswell, J. (1981). *Christianity, social tolerance, and homosexuality.* Chicago: University of Chicago Press.

Boswell, J. (1995). *Same sex unions in Premodern Europe.* New York: Vintage Books.

Bowers v. Hardwick, 478 U.S. 186 (1986).

Bowie, W., Hammerschlag, M., & Martin, D. (1994). STDs in 1994: The new CDC guidelines. *Patient Care, 28,* 29–53.

Boyden, T., Carroll, J. S., & Maier, R. A. (1984). Similarity and attraction in homosexual males: The effect of age and masculinity-femininity. *Sex Roles, 10,* 939–948.

Boyer, C. B., Shafer, M. A., Teitle, E., Wibbelsman, C. J., Seeberg, F., & Schnachter, J. (1999). Sexually transmitted diseases in a health maintenance organization teen clinic. *Archives of Pediatrics and Adolescent Medicine, 153,* 838–844.

Boyer, D. (1989). Male prostitution and homosexual identity. *Journal of Homosexuality, 17,* 151–184.

Boyer, D., Fine, D., Killpack, S., Jacobs, S. E., and Thompson, E. (1992).

Final Report: Victimization and other risk factors for child maltreatment among school age parents: A longitudinal study. Washington, DC: Washington Alliance Concerned with School Aged Parents (WACSAP).

Boyer, R. W., & Charleston, D. E. (1985). Auditory memory-search. *Perceptual & Motor Skills, 60,* 927–939.

Bozzette, S. A., Berry, S. H., Duan, N., Frank, M. R., Leibowitz, A. A., Lefkowitz, D., Emmons, C. A., Senterfitt, J. W., Berk, M. L., Morton, S. C., & Shapiro, M. F. (1999). The care of HIV-infected adults in the United States: HIV cost and services utilization study consortium. *New England Journal of Medicine, 340,* 512–513.

Bradford, J. M., Boulet, J., & Pawlak, A. (1992). The paraphilias: A multiplicity of deviant behaviours. *Canadian Journal of Psychiatry, 37,* 104–108.

Bradshaw, S. D. (1998). I'll go if you will: Do shy persons utilize social surrogates? *Journal of Social and Personal Relationships 15,* 651-669.

Breached, E., Grazing, W., Monson, T., & Dormer, M. (1976). Outcome dependency: attention, attribution and attraction. *Journal of Personality and Social Psychology, 33,* 709–718.

Brecher, E. M. (1984). *Love, sex and aging.* Boston: Little Brown.

Brehm, S. S. (1985). *Intimate relationships.* New York: McGraw Hill.

Breslow, N., Evans, L., & Langley, J. (1985). On the prevalence and roles of females in the sadomasochistic subculture. *Archives of Sexual Behavior, 14,* 303–317.

Breslow, N., Evans, L., & Langley, J. (1986). Comparisons among heterosexual, bisexual and homosexual male sadomasochists. *Journal of Homosexuality, 13,* 83–107.

Briere, J., & Runtz, M. (1989). University males' sexual interest in children; Predicting potential indices of "pedophilia" in a nonforensic sample. *Child Abuse and Neglect, 13,* 65–75.

Brinton, L., Reeves, M., Herrero, R., Gaitan, E., Tenoria, E., de Briton, R.,

Garcia, M., & Rawls, W. (1989). The male factor in the etiology of cervical cancer among sexually monogamous women. *International Journal of Cancer, 44,* 199–203.

Brody, J. E. (1992, April 1). Personal health. *The New York Times,* p. B7.

Broscus, H. B., Weaver, J. B., & Staab, J. F. (1993). Exploring the social land sexual "reality" of contemporary pornography. *Journal of Sex Research, 30,* 161–170.

Broude, G. J., & Greene, S. J. (1976). Cross-cultural codes on twenty sexual attitudes and practices. *Ethnology, 15,* 409–429.

Brown, D., & Bryant, J. (1989). The manifest content of pornography. In D. Zillmann & J. Bryant (Eds.), *Pornography: Research advances and policy consideration.* Hillsdale, NJ: Erlbaum.

Brown, E. M. (1993, May/June). The open secret. *The Family Networker,* 39–45.

Brown, G. R., & Collier, L. (1989). Transvestites' women revisited: A nonpatient sample. *Archives of Sexual Behavior 18,* 73–83.

Brown, J. (1986). *Immodest acts: The life of a lesbian nun in Renaissance Italy.* Oxford University Press.

Brown, T. (1995). Girls have long hair. *Health Education, 2,* 23–29.

Brownmiller, S. (1975). *Against our will: Men, women and rape.* New York: Simon and Schuster.

Buchholz, E. S., & Catton, R. (1999). Adolescents' perceptions of aloneness and loneliness. *Adolescence 34,* 203–213.

Buckley, T., & Gottlieb, A. (1988). A critical appraisal of theories of menstrual symbolism. In T. Buckley & A. Gottlieb (Eds.), *Blood magic: The anthropology of menstruation.* Berkeley: University of California Press.

Bullough, B., & Bullough, V. (1987). *Women and prostitution: A social history.* Buffalo, NY: Prometheus.

Bullough, V. (Ed.). (1976). Sexual variance in society and history. New York: John Wiley.

Bullough, V. (1988). Historical perspectives. In D. M. Dailey (Ed.), *The sexually unusual,* (pp. 15–24). New York: Haworth Press.

Bullough, V., & Bullough, B. (1993). *Cross dressing, sex, and gender.* Philadelphia: University of Pennsylvania Press.

Bullough, V., & Bullough, B. (1997). Are transvestites necessarily heterosexual? *Archives of Sexual Behavior, 26,* 1–12.

Bullough, V. L., & Weinberg, T. S. (1988). Women married to transvestites: Problems and adjustments. *Journal of Psychology and Human Sexuality, 1:* 83–104.

Bumpass, L. L. (1995). The declining significance of marriage: Changing family life in the United States. National Survey of Families and Households, Center for Demography and Ecology. Madison: University of Wisconsin.

Bumpass, L., Sweet, J., & Castro Martin, T. (1990). Changing patterns of remarriage. *Journal of Marriage and the Family, 52,* 747–756.

Bumpass, L. L., Sweet, J. A., & Cherlin, J. (1991). National estimates of cohabitation. *Demography, 26,* 615–625.

Bureau of Justice Statistics (1985). United States Department of Justice. Summary findings. From http://www.ojp.usdoj.gov

Bureau of Justice Statistics (1997). United States Department of Justice. Summary findings. From http://www.ojp.usdoj.gov

Burger, J. M., & Burns, L. (1988). The illusion of unique invulnerability and use of contraception. *Personality and Social Psychology Bulletin, 14,* 267–270.

Burgess, E. W., & Homstrom, L. L. (1974). Rape trauma syndrome. *American Journal of Psychiatry, 131,* 981–986.

Burgess, E. W., & Locke, H. J. (1945). The family from institution to companionship.

Burgess, E., & Wallin, P. (1953). *Engagement and marriage.* Philadelphia: Lippincott.

Burns, A., & Dunlop, R. (1999). "How did you feel about it?" Children's

feelings about their parents' divorce at the time and three and ten years later. *Journal of Divorce and Remarriage, 31,* 19–35.

Buss, D. M. (1987). Selection, evocation, and manipulation. *Journal of Personality and Social Psychology, 53,* 1214–1221.

Buss, D. M. (1988). The evolution of human intrasexual competition: Tactics of mate attraction. *Journal of Personality and Social Psychology, 54,* 616–628.

Buss, D. M. (1989). Sex differences in human mate preferences: Evolutionary hypotheses tested in 37 cultures. *Behavioral and Brain Science, 12,* 1–49

Buss, D. (1994). *The evolution of desire: Strategies for human mating.* New York: Basic Books.

Buss, D. M. (2000). *The dangerous passion: Why jealousy is as necessary as love and sex.* New York: The Free Press.

Buss, D. M., Abbott, M., Angleitner, A., Asherian, A., Biaggio, A., Blanco-Villasenor, A., Bruchon-Schweitzer, M., Ch'u, H., et al. (1990). International preferences in selecting mates: A study of 37 cultures. *Journal of Cross Cultural Psychology, 21,* 5–47.

Buss, D. M., & Schmitt, D. P. (1993). Sexual strategies theory: An evolutionary perspective on human mating. *Psychological Review, 100,* 204–232.

Buunk, B. P., & Hupka, R. B. (1987). Cross cultural differences in the elicitation of sexual jealousy. *Journal of Sex Research, 23,* 1,12–22.

Byer, C. O., & Shainberg, L. W. (1991). *Dimensions of human sexuality.* Dubuque, IA: Wm C. Brown Publishers.

Byers, E. S., & Lewis, K. (1988). Dating couples' disagreements over the desired level of sexual intimacy. *Journal of Sex Research, 24,* 15–29.

Byrne, D. (1971). *The attraction paradigm.* New York: Academic Press.

Byrne, D. (1997). An overview (and underview) of research and theory within the attraction paradigm. *Journal of Social and Personal Relationships, 14,* 417–431.

Byrne, D., & Fisher, W. A. (1983). *Adolescents, sex and contraception.* Hillsdale, NJ: Erlbaum.

Byrne, D., Clove, G., & Smeaten, G. (1986). The attraction hypothesis: Do similar attitudes affect anything? *Journal of Personality and Social Psychology, 51,* 1167–1170.

Byrne, D., Ervin, C., & Lamberth, J. (1970). Continuity between the experimental study of attraction and "real life" computer dating. *Journal of Personality and Social Psychology, 16,* 157–165.

Byrne, D., & Murnen, S. K. (1988). Maintaining loving relationships. In R. J. Sternberg & M. L. Barnes (Eds.), *The psychology of love.* New Haven, CT: Yale University Press.

Byrne, D., & Rhamey, R. (1965). Magnitude of positive and negative reinforcements as a determinant of attraction. *Journal of Personality and Social Psychology, 2,* 884–889.

Byrne, J., & Takahira, S. (1993). Explaining gender differences in SAT-math items. *Developmental Psychology, 29,* 805–810.

Caldwell, J. D., Prange, A. J., & Pedersen, C. A. (1986). Oxytocin facilitates the sexual receptivity of estrogen treated female rats. *Neuropeptides 7,* 175–189.

Call, V. R., Sprecher, S., & Schwartz, P. (1995). The frequency of marital sex. *Journal of Marriage and the Family, 57,* 639–652.

Callender, C., & Kochems, L. M. (1983). The North American berdache. *Current Anthropology, 24,* 443–459.

Campbell, A. (1981). *The sense of well being in America: Patterns and trends.* New York: McGraw-Hill.

Campbell, R. (1998). Invisible men: Making visible male clients of female prostitutes in Merseyside. In J. Elias, V. Bullough, V. Elias, & G. Brewer (Eds.), *Prostitution: On whores, hustlers, and johns* (pp. 155–171). Amherst, NY: Prometheus.

Campbell, R., & Johnson, C. R. (1997). Police officer perceptions of rape: Is there consistency between state law and individual beliefs? *Journal of Interpersonal Violence, 12,* 255–274.

Campbell, W. K., & Foster, C. A. (in press). Narcissism and commitment in romantic relationships: An investment model analysis. *Personality and Social Psychology Bulletin.*

Campbell, W. K., Foster, C. A., & Finkel, E. J. (2001). Does self-love lead to love for others?: A story of narcissistic game-playing. Unpublished manuscript, University of Georgia at Athens.

Cannistra, S. A., & Niloff, J. M. (1996). Cancer of the uterine cervix. *New England Journal of Medicine, 334,* 1030–1038.

Caplan, P. (1984). The myth of women's masochism. *American Psychologist, 39,* 130–139.

Capuzzo, M. (2001). *Close to Shore: A True Story of Terror in an Age of Innocence.* NY: Broadway Books.

Carlin, G. (1999). 1971–77: Little David Years. Disc 3. Atlantic Records. Also from http://staff.dstc.edu.au/bill/carlin.html

Carlson, R. J., & Carlson, K. (2000). *Don't Sweat The Small Stuff in Love.* Disney Press.

Carnes, P. (1983). *Out of the shadows: Understanding sexual addiction.* Minneapolis, MN: CompCare Publishers.

Carns, D. E. (1969). *Religiosity, premarital sexuality and the American college student: An empirical study.* Bloomington: University of Indiana Press.

Carpenter, S. (1998, March 24). Social psychologist explores how black people see themselves. *The Times-Picayune,* p. E1.

Carrera, H. A., & Dempsey, P. (1988, Jan./Feb.). Restructuring public policy priorities on teen pregnancy: A holistic approach to teen development and teen services. *SIECUS Reports, 18.*

Carroll, R. A. (1999). Outcomes of treatment for gender dysphoria. *Journal of Sex Education and Therapy, 24,* 128–136.

Carter, R. S., & Wojtkiewicz, R. A. (2000). Parental involvement with adolescents' education: Do daughters or sons get more help? *Adolescence, 35,* 29–44.

Carter, S. C. (1998). Neuroendocrine perspectives on social attachment and love. *Psychoneurology and Endocrinology, 23,* 779–818.

Casey, M. B. (1996). Understating individual differences in spatial ability within females: A nature nurture interactionist framework. *Developmental Review, 16* , 241–260.

Caspi, A., & Roberts, B. W. (2001). Personality continuity and change across the life course. In L. A. Pervin & O. P. John (Eds.), *Handbook of personality theory and research* (2nd ed.). New York: Guilford.

Castleman, M. (1980). *Sexual solutions.* New York: Simon & Schuster.

Cates, W. (1999). Chlamydial infections and the risk of ectopic pregnancy. *Journal of the American Medical Association, 281,* 117–118.

Center for Reproductive Law and Policy. (1999, Sept.) "Tell it to the judge: Teens fall on hard times. *Reproductive Freedom News, 8.* From http://www.crlp.org/fnviii08.html

Centers for Disease Control (1993, Jan.). AIDS case watch. *Clinical Care, 5,* 1.

Centers for Disease Control (1997, July). The human immunodeficiency virus and its transmission. *HIV/AIDS Prevention,* 1–4.

Centers for Disease Control. (1998). Guidelines for treatment of sexually transmitted disease: Diseases characterized by vaginal discharge. Atlanta, GA: Department of Health and Human Services.

Centers for Disease Control. (1999). HIV/AIDS surveillance report. Atlanta, GA: Department of Health and Human Services.

Centers for Disease Control. (2001a). African Americans disproportionately affected by STDs. Atlanta, GA: Department of Health and Human Services.

Centers for Disease Control (2001b). Fact sheet. Chlamydia in the United States. Atlanta, GA: Department of Health and Human Services.

Centers for Disease Control (2001c). Tracking the hidden epidemic: Trends in STDs in the United States (2000). Atlanta, GA: Department of Health and Human Services.

Chagnon, N. (1968). *Yanormano: The fierce people.* New York: Holt, Rinehart and Winston.

Chamberlin, E. R. (1969). *The Bad Popes.* New York: Barnes & Noble Books.

Chan, C. (1995). Issues of sexual identity in an ethnic minority: The case of Chinese American lesbians, gay men and bisexual people. In A. D'Augelli & C. Patterson (Eds.), *Lesbian, gay and bisexual identities over the lifespan.* New York: Oxford University Press.

Chan, M., Giovannucci, E., Andersson, S. O., Yuen, J., Adami, H. O., & Wolk, A. (1998). Dairy products, calcium, phosphorous, vitamin D, and risk of prostate cancer. *Cancer Causes Control, 9,* 559–566.

Chang, P. (1986). *The inner teachings of Taoism.* Translated by T. Leary. Boston: Shambala Press.

Charny, I. W., & Barnass, S. (1995). The impact of extramarital relationships on the continuation of marriage. *Journal of Sex & Marital Therapy, 21,* 100–115.

Chasnoff, I. J., Landress, H. J., & Barrett, M. E. (1990). The prevalence of illicit-drug or alcohol use during pregnancies in mandatory reporting in Pinellas County, Florida. *New England Journal of Medicine, 323,* 1202–1206.

Check, J., & Malamuth, N. (1983). An empirical assessment of some feminist hypotheses about rape. *International Journal of Women's Studies, 8,* 414–423.

Chessare, J. (1992, Feb.) Circumcision: Is the risk of urinary tract infection really the pivotal issue? *Clinical Pediatrics,* 100–104.

Cheung, M. (1999). Children's language of sexuality in child sexual abuse investigations. *Journal of Child Sexual Abuse, 8,* 65–83.

Choi, P. Y. (1992). The psychological benefits of physical exercise: Implications for women and the menstrual cycle. Special issues: The menstrual cycle. *Journal of Reproductive and Infant Psychology, 10,* 111–115.

Chowdbury, A. N. (1994). Koro following cannabis smoking: Two case reports. *Urology, 43,* 883–885.

Chowdbury, A. N. (1996, Mar.). The definition and classification of koro. *Culture and Medical Psychiatry, 20,* 41–65.

Christopher, I. S., & Frandsen, M. M. (1990). Strategies of influence in sex and dating. *Journal of Social and Personal Relationships, 7,* 89–105.

Clark, C. L., Shaver, P. R., & Abrahams, M. F. (1999). Strategic behaviors in romantic relationship initiation. *Personality and Social Psychology Bulletin, 25,* 707–720.

Clark, J. K. (1993, Aug./Sept.). Complications in academia: Sexual harassment and the law. *SIECUS Report,* 6–10.

Clark, K. (1956). *The Nude.* Princeton, NJ: Princeton University Press.

Clarnette, T. D., Sugita, Y., & Hutson, J. M. (1997). Genital anomalies in human and animal models reveal the mechanisms and hormones governing testicular descent. *British Journal of Urology, 79,* 99–112.

Clarren, S. K., & Smith, D. W. (1978). The fetal alcohol syndrome. *New England Journal of Medicine, 298,* 1063–1067.

Clement, S. (1990). Survey of heterosexual behavior. *Annual Review of Sex Research, 1,* 45–74.

Cline, R. W., Johnson, S. J., & Freeman, K. E. (1992). Talk among sexual partners about AIDS: Interpersonal communication for risk reduction or risk enhancement. *Health Communication, 4,* 39–56.

Cline, S. (1993). *Women, passion and celibacy.* London: Optima.

Clutton-Brock, T. H., & Parker, G. A. (1995). Sexual coercion in animal societies. *Animal Behavior, 49,* 1345–1365.

CNN Interactive. (2000). Same sex marriage laws. From http://www.

cnn.com/2000/LAW/o5/25/samesexmarriage.

Coen, S. (1978). Sexual interviewing, evaluation, and therapy: Psychoanalytic emphasis on the use of sexual fantasy. *Archives of Sexual Behavior, 7,* 299–305.

Cohen, F., Kennedy, M. E., Kearney, K. A., Zegans, L. S., Nurhaus, J. M., & Conant, M. A. (1999). Persistent stress as a predictor of genital herpes recurrence. *Archives of Internal Medicine, 159,* 2430–2436.

Cohen, L. L., & Shotland, R. L. (1996). Timing of first sexual intercourse in a relationship: Expectation, experiences and perceptions of others. *Journal of Sex Research 33,* 291–299.

Cohen, M. S. (1990). The biological prohibition of homosexual intercourse. *Journal of Homosexuality, 19,* 3–20.

Cohen-Kettenis, P. T., & van Goozen, S. H. M. (1999). Sex reassignment or adolescent transsexuals: A follow-up study. *Journal of the American Academy of Child and Adolescent Psychiatry, 36,* 263–271.

Colapinto, J. (2000). *As nature made him: The boy who was raised as a girl.* New York: Harper Collins.

Cole, W. G. (1966). *Sex in Christianity and psychoanalysis.* New York: Oxford University Press.

Coleman, E. (1989). The development of male prostitution activity among gay and bisexual adolescents. *Journal of Homosexuality, 17,* 131–149.

Coleman, J. S. (1961). *The adolescent society.* New York: Free Press.

Coles, B., & Stokes, F. S. (1985). *Sex and the American teenager.* New York: Harper and Row.

Coles, C. D., Platzman, K. A., Raskind-Hood, C. L., Brown, R. T., Falek, A., & Smith, D. (1997). A comparison of children affected by prenatal alcohol exposure and attention deficit hyperactivity disorder. *Alcohol and Clinical Experimental Research 21,* 150–161.

Collins, E., & Turner, C. (1975). Maternal effects of regular salicylate ingestion on pregnancy. *Lancet, 2,* 335–339.

Comfort, A. (1972). *The new joy of sex: A gourmet guide to lovemaking.* New York: Crown.

Condon, J. W., & Crano, N. D. (1988). Inferred evaluation and the relation between attitude similarity and interpersonal attraction. *Journal of Personality and Social Psychology, 54,* 787–797.

Conte, R., Rosen, C., Saperstein, L., & Shermack, R. (1985). An Evaluation of a program to prevent the sexual victimization of young children. *Child Abuse and Neglect, 9,* 319-328.

Cooper, A., Putnam, D. E., Planchon, L. A., & Boies, S. C. (1999). Online sexual compulsivity: Getting tangled in the net. *Sexual Addiction & Compulsivity, 6,* 79–104.

Corbet, J., & Kapsalis, T. (1996). Aural sex: The female orgasm in popular sound. *The Drama Review, 40,* 102–111.

Coperhaver, S., & Gauerholz, E. (1991). Sexual victimization among sorority women: Exploring the link between sexual violence and institutional practices. *Sex Roles, 24,* 31–41.

Cott, N. F. (1977). *The bonds of womanhood: Women's sphere in New England, 1780–1835.* New Haven, CT: Yale University Press.

Cotten-Huston, A. L., & Wheeler, K. A. (1983). Preorgasmic group treatment: Assertiveness, marital adjustment and sexual function in women. *Journal of Sex and Marital Therapy, 9,* 296–302.

Courtois, Christine, A. (2000). *Healing the incest wound.* New York: WW Norton & Company.

Coutts, M. C. (1993). Fetal tissue research. *Kennedy Institute of Ethics Journal 3,* 81–101.

Cowan, G., & Dunn, K. (1994). What themes in pornography lead to perceptions of the degradation of women? *Journal of Sex Research, 31,* 1–21.

Cowan, L. (1982). *Masochism: A Jungian view.* Dallas, TX: Spring Publications.

Cowley, G. (1993, March 22). The future of AIDS. *Newsweek,* 47–52.

Cox, P. (1988). Incidence and nature of male genital exposure behavior as reported by college women. *Journal of Sex Research, 24,* 227–234.

Craig, M. E., Kalichman, S. C., & Follingstad, D. R. (1989). Verbal coercive sexual behavior among college students. *Archives of Sexual Behavior, 19,* 421–434.

Crane, D. (2000). *Fashion and its social agendas: Class, gender, and identity in clothing.* Chicago: University of Chicago Press.

Craner, K. M., & Nevedley, K. A. (1998). Sex differences in loneliness: The role of masculinity and femininity. *Sex Roles 38,* 645–653.

Crenshaw, T. (1996). *The alchemy of love and lust.* New York: Putman.

Crews, D. (1998). The evolutionary antecedents to love. *Psychoneuroendocrinology, 23,* 751–764.

Croake, J. W., & James, B. (1973). A four-year comparison of premarital sexual attitudes. *Journal of Sex Research, 9,* 91–96.

Crockett, A. T., Takihara, H., & Cosentino, M. J. (1984). The varicocele. *Fertility and Sterility, 41,* 5–11.

Crooks, R., & Baur, K. (1996). *Our sexuality.* (6th ed). Pacific Grove, CA: Brooks/Cole.

Crossette, B. (1998, June 13). An old scourge of war becomes its latest crime. *The New York Times,* Sect. 4, p. wk 1.

Cunningham, M. (1990). What do women want. *Journal of Personality and Social Psychology, 59,* 61–72.

Curriden, M. (1990–91). But is it art? *Barrister, 17,* 13–14.

Curtis, R., & Miller, K. (1986). Believing another likes or dislikes you: Behavior making the beliefs come true. *Journal of Personality and Social Psychology, 51,* 284–290.

Cutler, W. B., Friedman, E., & McCoy, N. L. (1998). Pheromonal influences on sociosexual behavior in men. *Archives of Sexual Behavior, 27,* 1–13.

Dabbs, J. M. (1998). Trial lawyers and testosterone: Blue-collar talent in a

white-collar world. *Journal of Applied Social Psychology, 28*, 84–94.

Dabbs, J. M. (2000). *Heroes, rogues, and lovers.* New York: McGraw-Hill.

Dabbs, J. M., Carr, T. S., Frady, R. L., & Bird, J. K. (1995). Testosterone, crime and misbehavior among 692 male prison inmates. *Journal of Personal and Individual Differences, 18*, 627–633.

Daly, M. (1965). *The church and the second sex.* Boston: Beacon Press.

Daly, M., & Wilson, M. (1988). Evolutionary social psychology and family homicide. *Science, 242*, 519–524.

Damsteegt, D. (1992). Loneliness, social provisions and attitude. *College Student Journal 26*, 135–139.

Dank, B. M., & Fulda, J. S. (1997). Forbidden love: student-professor romance. *Sexuality and Culture, 1*, 107–130.

Dann, T. C. (1996). Teenage sex: Trend toward earlier menarche stopped 30 years ago. *British Medical Journal, 312*, 1419.

Dannenbring, D., Stevens, M. J., & House, A. E. (1997). Predictors of childbirth pain and maternal satisfaction. *Journal of Behavioral Medicine, 20*, 127–142.

Daring, D. S., Stevens, M. J., & House, A. E. (1997). Predictors of childbirth pain and maternal satisfaction. *Journal of Behavioral Medicine, 20*, 127–142.

Darling, C., & Davidson, J. (1986). Enhancing relationships: Understanding the feminine mystique of pretending orgasm. *Journal of Sex and Marital Therapy, 12*, 182–196.

Darling, C., Davidson, J., & Conway-Welch, C. (1990). Female ejaculation: Perceived origins, the Gräfenberg spot/area, and sexual responsiveness. *Archives of Sexual Behavior, 19*, 29–47.

Darroch, J. E., Landry, D. J., & Singh, S. (2000). Changing emphases in sexuality education in U.S. public secondary schools, 1988–1999. *Family Planning Perspectives, 32*, 204–211, 265.

Darwin, C. (1936). *The origin of species and the descent of man.* New York: The

Modern Library. [Original: *The descent of man* published 1871.]

D'Augelli, A. R., Hershberger, S. L., & Pilkington, N. W. (1998). Lesbian, gay and bisexual youth and their families: Disclosure of sexual orientation and its consequences. *American Journal of Orthopsychiatry, 68*, 261–371.

Davey-Smith, G., Frankel, S., & Yarnell, J. (1997). Sex and death: Are they related? Findings from the Caerphilly Cohort Study. *British Medical Journal. 315*, 1641–1644.

Davies, K. A. (1997). Voluntary exposure to pornography and men's attitudes toward feminism and rape. *Journal of Sex Research, 34*, 131–137.

Davis, C. M., Blank, J., Lin, H., & Bonillas, C. (1996). Characteristics of vibrator use among women. *Journal of Sex Research, 33*, 313–320.

Davis, R. C., Brickman, E., & Baker, T. (1991). Supportive and unsupportive responses of others to rape victims: Effects on concurrent victim adjustment. *American Journal of Community Psychology, 19*, 443–451.

Davis, S. R. (1998). The clinical use of androgens in female sexual disorders. *Journal of Sex and Marital Therapy, 24*, 153–163.

Dawood, K., Pillard, R. C., Horvath, C., Revelle, W., & Bailey, J. M. (2000). Familial aspects of male homosexuality. *Archives of Sexual Behavior, 29*, 155–163.

DeAlbuquerque, K. (1999). Sex, beach boys, and female tourists in the Caribbean. In B. M. Dank & R. Refinetti [Eds.], *Sexwork and sex workers: Sexuality and culture* (pp. 87–111). New Brunswick, NJ: Transaction Publishers.

Dean, C. W., & deBruyn-Kops, E. (1982). *The crime and consequences of rape.* Springfield, IL: Charles C. Thomas.

Dean, K., & Malamuth, N. M. (1997). Characteristics of men who aggress sexually and of men who imagine aggressing: Risk and moderating variables. *Journal of Personality and Social Psychology, 72*, 449–455.

DeJong, W. (1999). Rape and physical attractiveness: Judgments concerning likelihood of victimization. *Psychological Reports, 85*, 32–34.

DeMaris, A. (1997). Elevated sexual activity in violent marriages: Hypersexuality or sexual extortion? *Journal of Sex Research, 34*, 361–373.

De Martino, M. (1990, Oct.). How women want men to make love. *Sexology*, 4–7.

D'Emilio, J., & Freedman, E. (1988). *Intimate matters: A history of sexuality in America.* New York: Harper and Row.

Dennerstein, L., Gotts, G., Brown, J., Morse, C., Farley, T., & Pinol, A. (1994). The relationship between the menstrual cycle and female sexual interest in women with PMS complaints and volunteers. *Psychoneuroendocrinology, 19*, 295–304.

Denney, N., Field, J., & Quadagno, D. (1984). Sex differences in sexual needs and desires. *Archives of Sexual Behavior, 13*, 233–245.

DePaulo, B., & Morris, W. (2000). *Stereotypes about singles.* The DePaulo Lab, from http://www. people.virginia.edu/~bmd/ research.html

Dessens, A. B., Cohen-Kettenis, P. T., Mellenbergh, G. J., Poll, N., Kopper, J. G., & Boer, K. (1999). Prenatal exposure to anticonvulsants and psychosexual development. *Archives of Sexual Behavior, 28*, 31–44.

DeSteno, D. A., & Salovery, P. (1996). Evolutionary origins of sex differences in jealousy? Questioning the "fitness" of the model. *Psychological Science 7*, 367–372.

Deutch, H. (1944). *The psychology of women : A psychoanalytic interpretation. Volume 1*, New York: Grune and Stratton.

De Waal, F. (1995). Sex as an alternative to aggression in the bonobo. In P. Abramson & S. Pinkerton (Eds.). *Sexual nature, sexual culture* (pp. 37–56). Chicago: University of Chicago Press.

De Waal, F. (1997). *Bonobos: The forgotten ape.* Berkeley, CA: University of California Press.

de Wied, D., Gaffori, O., van Ree, J. M., & deJong, W. (1989). Central target for the behavioral effects of vasopressin neuropeptides. *Nature, 309,* 276–278.

Dexter, H. R., Penrod, S., Lind, D., & Saunders, D. (1997). Attributing responsibility to female victims after exposure to sexually violent films. *Journal of Applied Social Psychology, 27,* 2149–2171.

Diamant, A. L., Schuster, M. A., McGuinan, K., & Lever, J. (1999). Lesbian sexual history with men: Implications for taking a sexual history. *Archives of Internal Medicine, 15a,* 2730–2736.

Diamond, L. M., Savin-Williams, R. C., & Dube, E. M. (1999). Sex, dating, passionate friendships, and romance: Intimate peer relations among lesbian, gay, and bisexual adolescents. In W. Furman, B. B. Brown, & C. Feiring (Eds.), *The development of romantic relationships during adolescence,* (pp. 175–210). New York: Cambridge University Press.

Diamond, M. (1997). Sexual identity and sexual orientation in children with traumatized or ambiguous genitalia. *Journal of Sex Research, 34,* 199–211.

Dickermann, M. (1993). *The Balkan sworn virgin: A European cross-gendered female role.* Manuscript in preparation.

Dindia, K., & Allen, M. (1992). Sex differences in self-disclosure: A meta-analysis. *Psychological Bulletin, 112,* 106–124.

Dion, K. K. (1986). Stereotyping based on physical attractiveness: Issues and conceptual perspectives. In C. P. Herman, M. P. Zanna, & E. T. Higgins (Eds.), *The Ontario Symposium: Vol. 3, Physical Appearance, Stigma and Social Behavior.* Hillsdale, NJ: Erlbaum.

Dion, K. K., & Dion, K. L. (1975). Self-esteem and romantic love. *Journal of Personality, 43,* 39–57.

DiTommaso, E., & Spinner, B. (1997). Social and emotional loneliness: A re-examination of Weiss' typology of loneliness. *Personality and Individual Differences 22,* 417–427.

Dittus, P. J., Jaccard, J., & Gordon, V. V. (1999). Direct and nondirect communication of maternal beliefs to adolescents: Adolescent motivation for premarital sexual activity. *Journal of Applied Social Psychology, 29,* 1927–1963.

Dixon, T. L., & Linz, D. (1997). Obscenity law and rap music: Understanding the effects of sex, attitudes and beliefs. *Journal of Applied Communication Research, 25,* 217–241.

Docter, R. F., & Prince, V. (1997). Transvestism: A survey of 1032 cross-dressers. *Archives of Sexual Behavior 26,* 589–605.

Doherty, R. W., Hatfield, E., Thompson, K., & Choo, P. (1994). Cultural and ethnic influences on love and attachment. *Personal Relationships, 1,* 391–398.

Donahey, K. M., & Miller, S. D. (2001). Applying a common factors perspective to sex therapy. *Journal of Sex Education and Therapy, 25,* 221–239.

Donaldson, S. (1993, Dec. 29). The rape crisis behind bars. *The New York Times.*

Donnelly, D., & Fraser, J. (1998). Gender differences in sadomasochistic arousal among college students. *Sex Roles, 37,* 391–407.

Donnelly, J., Duncan, D. F., Goldfarb, E., & Eadie, C. (1999). Sexuality attitudes and behaviors of self-described very religious urban students in middle school. *Psychological Reports, 85,* 607–610.

Donnerstein, E., & Linz, D. (1987). *The question of pornography.* New York: Free Press.

Donnerstein, E., & Linz, D. (1998). Mass media, sexual violence, and male viewers. In Mary E. Odem, Jody Clay-Warner (Eds.). *Confronting rape and sexual assault.* (Worlds of women, No. 3, pp. 181–198). Wilmington, DE: SR Books/Scholarly Resources.

Dorris, R. L. (1989). Interactions of nicotinamide with dopamine receptors in vivo. *Pharmacological and Biochemical Behavior, 33,* 915–917.

Downey, G., & Feldman, S. I. (1996). Implications of rejection sensitivity for intimate relationships. *Journal of Personality and Social Psychology 70,* 1327–1343.

Drewnowski, A., Kurkth, C. L., & Krahn, D. D. (1995). Effects of body image on dieting, exercise, and anabolic steroid use in adolescent males. *International Journal of Eating Disorders, 17,* 381–386.

Drieschner, K., & Lange, A. (1999). A review of cognitive factors in the etiology of rape. *Clinical Psychology Review, 19,* 37–77.

Driscoll, J. P. (1971, Mar.-Apr.). Transsexuals. *Transaction, 28–37,* 66–68.

Duberman, M. B., Vicinus, M., & Chauncey, G. (Eds.). (1989). *Hidden from history: Reclaiming the gay and lesbian past.* New York: Penguin Books.

Du Bois-Reymond, M., & Ravesloot, J. (1994). The role of parents and peers in the sexual and relational socialization of adolescents. In F. Nestmann & K. Hurrelmann (Eds.), *Social networks and social support in childhood and adolescence* (pp. 217–239). Berlin/New York: Walter de Gruyter.

Duckworth, J., & Levitt, E. (1985). Personality analysis of swingers' club. *Lifestyles: A Journal of Changing Patterns, 8,* 35–45.

Duddle, M. (1991). Emotional sequelae of sexual assault. *Journal of the Royal Society of Medicine, 84,* 26–28.

Dunn, K. M., Croft, P. R., & Hackett, G. I. (1999). Association of sexual problems with social, psychological, and physical problems in men and women: A cross sectional population survey. *Journal of Epidemiology and Community Health, 53,* 144–148.

Dunn, M. E., & Trost, J. E. (1989). Male multiple orgasms: A descriptive study. *Archives of Sexual Behavior, 18,* 377–387.

Durden-Smith, J., & Sesimone, D. (1983). *Sex and the brain.* New York: Arbor House.

Dwyer, S. M., & Amberson, I. J. (1985). Sex offender treatment program: A follow-up study. *American Journal of Social Psychiatry, 4,* 56–60.

Eagle Forum. (2001). From http://www.eagleforum.com

Eagly, A. H. (1995). The science and practice of comparing men and women. *American Psychologist, 50,* 145–158.

Eagly, A. H., & Wood, W. (1999). The origins of sex differences in human behavior: Evolved dispositions versus social roles. *American Psychologist, 54,* 408–423.

Earle, J. R., & Perricone, P. J. (1986). Premarital sexuality: A ten-year study of attitudes and behavior on a small university campus. *Journal of Sex Research, 22,* 304–310.

Easton, S. C. (1993, Nov.). A matter of pride: Being a gay woman in the nineties. *Cosmopolitan,* 226–229.

Eby, M. (2000, Feb. 7). Cited in A. J. S. Rayl, Music stars spotlight artificial insemination. *U.S.A. Today,* from http://www.usatoday.com/life/health/doctor/lhdoc085.htm

Edgley, C., & Turner, R. (1979). Subliminal Seduction: Popular Vocabularies of Motive and the Myth of the Mental Masseuse. *Free Inquiry, 7,* May.

Ehrenberg, M., & Ehrenberg, O. (1988). *The intimate circle: The sexual dynamics of family life.* New York: Simon & Schuster.

Ehrenreich, B. (1983). *The hearts of men: American dreams and the flight from commitment.* New York: Anchor Press/Doubleday.

Ehrenreich, B. (2000, Jan. 31). How "natural" is rape? Despite a daffy new theory, it's not just a guy in touch with his inner caveman. *Time,* 88.

Eisen, M., & Zellman, G. L. (1987). Changes in incidence of sexual intercourse of unmarried teenagers following a community-based sex education program. *Journal of Sex Research, 23,* 527–533.

Eliason, M. J. (1997). The prevalence and nature of biphobia in heterosexual undergraduate students. *Archives of Sexual Behavior, 26,* 17–26.

Elliott, L., & Brantley, C. (1997). *Sex on campus.* New York: Random House.

Ellis, B., & Symons, D. (1990). Sex differences in sexual fantasy: An evolutionary psychological approach. *Journal of Sex Research, 27,* 527–555.

Ellis, L. (1989). *Theories of rape: Inquiries into the causes of sexual aggression.* New York: Hemisphere.

Ellis, L., & Beattie, C. (1983). The feminist explanation for rape: An empirical test. *Journal of Sex Research, 19,* 74–93.

Ember, M., & Ember, C. (1996). Cultural anthropology. (8th ed.). Upper Saddle River, NJ: Prentice Hall.

Eng, T. R., & Butler, W. T. (1997). *The hidden epidemic: Confronting sexually transmitted diseases.* Washington, DC: National Academy Press.

Engel, J. W., & Saracino, M. (1986). Love preferences and ideals: A comparison of homosexual, bisexual and heterosexual groups. *Contemporary Family Therapy, 8,* 241–250.

Erker, H., Dilbaz, N., Serber, G., Kaptanoglu, C., & Tekin, D. (1990). Sexual attitudes of Turkish university students. *Journal of Sex Education and Therapy, 16,* 251–261.

Ernst, J. M., & Cacioppo, J. T. (1999). Lonely hearts: Psychological perspectives on loneliness. *Applied and Preventive Psychology 8,* 1–22.

Ernst, T. M. (1991). Onabasulu male homosexuality: Cosmology affect and prescribed male homosexual activity among the Onabasulu of the Great Papuan plateau. *Oceania, 62,* 1–11.

Eskenazi, G. (1990, June 3). The male athlete and sexual assault. *The New York Times,* p. L1

Espinos, J. J., Rodriguez-Espininosa, J., Senosiain, R., Aura, M., & Vanrell, C. (1999). The role of matching menstrual data with hormonal measurements in evaluating effectiveness of postcoital contraception. *Contraception, 60,* 243–247.

Estes, R. J., & Weiner, N. A. (2001). *The commercial exploitation of children in the U. S., Canada and Mexico.* Philadelphia: University of Pennsylvania, School of Social Work, Center for the Study of Youth Policy.

Etcoff, N. (1999). *The science of beauty.* New York: Doubleday.

Etherington, K. (1997). Maternal sex abuse of males. *Child Abuse Review, 17,* 107–117.

Eugster, A., & Vingerhoets, A. (1999). Psychological aspects of in-vitro fertilization: A review. *Social Science and Medicine, 58,* 575–589.

Evans, C., & Thornton, M. (1989). *Immigrant women in the land of dollars: Life and culture on the Lower East Side, 1890–1925.* New York: Monthly Review Press.

Everitt, J. (1990). Sexual motivation: A neural and behavioral analysis of mechanisms underlying appetitive and copulatory responses of male rats. *Neuroscience and Biobehavioral Review, 14,* 217–232.

Eyre, S. L., Read, N. W., & Millstein, S. G. (1997). Adolescent sexual strategies. *Journal of Adolescent Health, 20,* 286–293.

Fackelmann, K. (1994, Nov. 5). Beyond the genome: The ethics of DNA testing (identification of disease-causing genes). *Science News, 146,* p. 298.

Fair, W., Fuks, Z., & Scher, H. (1993). Cancer of the urethra and penis. In V. De Vito, S. Hellman, & S. Rosenberg (Eds.) *Cancer principles and practice of oncology* (pp. 1052–1072). Philadelphia: Lippincott.

Fairstein, L. (1993). *Sexual violence: Our war against rape.* New York: William Morrow.

Faller, K. C. (1989). Why sexual abuse? An exploration of the intergenerational hypothesis. *Child Abuse and Neglect, 13,* 543–548.

Fallon, A. E., & Rozin, P. (1985). Sex differences in perceptions of desirable body shape. *Journal of Abnormal Psychology, 94,* 102–104.

Fang, C. Y., Sidaniys, J., & Pratto, F. (1998). Romance across the social status continuum: Interracial marriage and the ideological asymmetry effect. *Journal of Cross-Cultural Psychology 29,* 290–305.

Farb, P., & Armelagos, G. (1980). *Consuming Passions: The Anthropology of Eating.* Boston: Houghton Mifflin Co.

Farley, E., Loup, D., Nelson, M., Mitchell, A., Esplund, G., Macri, C., Harrison, C., & Gray, K. (1997). Neoplastic transformation of the endocervix associated with down regulation of lactoferrin expression. *Molecular Carcinography, 20,* 240–250.

Farley, M., Baral, I., Kiremire, M., & Sezgin, U. (1998). Prostitution in five countries: Violence and posttraumatic stress disorder. *Feminism and Psychology, 9,* 405–426.

Farley, M., & Barkan, H. (1998). Prostitution, violence, rape and post-traumatic stress disorder. *Women and Health, 27,* 37–48.

Farley, T. M., Rosenberg, M. J., Rowe, P. J., Chen, J. H., & Meirik, O. (1992). Intrauterine devices and pelvic inflammatory disease: An international perspective. *Lancet, 339,* 785–788.

Farwell, L., & Wohlwend-Lloyd, R. (1998). Narcissistic processes: Optimistic expectations, favorable self-evaluations, and self-enhancing attributions. *Journal of Personality, 66,* 65–83.

Fausto-Sterling, A. (1993, Mar. 12). How many sexes are there? *The New York Times,* pp. A15–16.

Federal Bureau of Investigation (1998a, Nov. 22). *Crime in the United States.* U.S. Department of Justice, Washington, DC Press Release.

Federal Bureau of Investigation (1998b). *Hate crime statistics.* Washington, DC: U.S. Department of Justice.

Fedora, O., Reddon, J. R., Morrison, J. W., & Fedora, S. K. (1992). Sadism and other paraphilias in normal controls and aggressive and nonaggressive sex offenders. *Archives of Sexual Behavior, 21,* 1–15

Fehr, B., & Russell, J. A. (1991). The concept of love viewed from a prototype perspective. *Journal of Personality and Social Psychology, 3,* 425–438.

Feingold, A. (1988). Matching for attractiveness in romantic partners and same-sex friends: A meta-analysis and theoretical critique. *Psychological Bulletin, 104,* 226–235.

Feingold, D. A. (1994). Gender differences in variability in intellectual abilities: A cross-cultural perspective. *Sex Roles, 30,* 81–92.

Felmlee, D., Sprecher, S., & Bassin, E. (1990). The dissolution of intimate relationships: A hazard model. *Social Psychology Quarterly, 53,* 13–30.

Felson, R. B., & Krohn, M. (1990). Motives for rape. *Journal of Research in Crime and Delinquency, 27,* 222–242.

Felthous, A. M., & Hempel, A. (1995). Combined homicide-suicides: A review. *Journal of Forensic Sciences 40,* 846–857.

Fensterheim, H., & Kantor, J. S. (1980). Behavioral approach to sexual disorders. In B. B. Wolman & J. Money (Eds.), *Handbook of Human Sexuality* (pp. 314–324). Englewood Cliffs, NJ: Prentice Hall.

Fergusson, D., Lawton, T., & Shannon, E. (1988). Neonatal circumcision and penile problems: An 8-year longitudinal study. *Pediatrics, 81,* 537–540.

Ferraro, G. (1995). *Cultural anthropology: An applied perspective* 2nd ed. St. Paul, MN: West Publishing.

Ferroni, P., & Taffe, J. (1997). Women's emotional well-being: The importance of communicating sexual needs. *Sexual and Marital Therapy, 12,* 122–138.

Fiedler, L. A. (1982). *Love and death in the American novel.* New York: Scarborough.

FindLaw. (2001). Selected U.S. Supreme Court obscenity decisions. From http://guide.biz.findlaw.com/01topics/06constitutional/cases.html

Finkelhor, D. (1980). Sex among siblings. In L. L. Constantine & E. M. Martinson (Eds.), *Children and sex: New findings, new perspectives.* Boston: Little-Brown.

Finkelhor, D., & Williams, L. M. (1988). *Nursery crimes.* Beverly Hills, CA: Sage Publications.

Finkelhor, D., & Yllo, K. (1985). *License to rape: Sexual abuse of wives.* New York: Free Press.

Fishbane, M. (1987). *Judaism: Religious traditions of the world.* San Francisco: Harper & Row.

Fishbein, M. D., & Thelm, M. H. (1981). Psychological factors in mate selection and marital satisfaction in young married couples. *Journal of Personality and Social Psychology, 35,* 331–342.

Fisher, B., Weisberg, D. K., & Marotta, T. (1982). Report on adolescent male prostitution. San Francisco: Urban and Rural Systems Associates.

Fisher, H. (1992). *Anatomy of love: A natural history of monogamy, adultery and divorce.* New York: W. W. Norton.

Fisher, H. (2000). Lust, attraction, attachment: Biology and evolution of the three primary emotion systems for mating, reproduction and parenting. *Journal of Sex Education and Therapy, 25,* 96–104.

Fisher, W. A., & Byrne, D. (1978). Sex differences in response to erotica: Love versus lust. *Journal of Personality and Social Psychology, 36,* 117–125.

Fisher, W. A., & Grenier, G. (1994). Violent pornography, antiwoman thoughts, and antiwoman acts: In search of reliable effects. *Journal of Sex Research, 31:* 23–38.

Fitch, R. H., Cowell, P. E., & Denenberg, V. H. (1998). The female phenotype: Nature's default? *Developmental Neuropsychology, 14,* 213–231.

Flanders, L. (1998, Mar.-Apr.). Rwanda's living casualties. *Ms. Magazine,* 27–30.

Fletcher, J. (1966). *Situation Ethics.* Philadelphia: Westminster Press.

Foa, E. B., & Riggs, D. S. (1997). Posttraumatic stress disorder and rape. In R. S. Pynoos (Ed.), *Posttraumatic stress disorder: A clinical review* (pp. 133–163). Lutherville, MD: Sidran Press.

Folkes, V. S. (1982). Forming relationships and the matching hypothesis. *Personality and Social Psychology Bulletin, 9,* 631–636.

Ford, C. S., & Beach, F. A. (1951). *Patterns of sexual behavior.* New York: Harper and Row.

Ford, T. M., Liwag-McLamb, M. G., & Foley, L. A. (1998). Perception of rape based on sex and sexual

orientation of victim. *Journal of Social Behavior and Personality, 12*, 253–262.

Forrest, J. D., & Singh, S. (1990). Public sector savings resulting from expenditures for contraceptive services. *Family Planning Perspectives, 222*, 6–15.

Fox, R. (1972). Sexual selection and human kinship systems. In B. Campbell (Ed.), *Sexual selection and the descent of man 1871–1971* (pp. 282–331). Chicago: Aldine Press.

Foxman, B. (1990). Recurring urinary tract infection: Incidence and risk factors. *American Journal of Public Health, 80*, 331–333.

Frackiewicz, E. J., & Shiovitz, T. M. (2001). Evaluation and management of premenstrual syndrome and premenstrual dysphoric disorder. *Journal of American Pharmacology Association, 41*, 437–447.

Francoeur, R. T. (1992). Sexuality and spirituality: The role of Eastern traditions. *SIECUS Reports, 20*, 1–8.

Franzini, L. R., & White, S. (1999). Heteronegativism? The attitudes of gay men and lesbians toward heterosexuals. *Journal of Homosexuality 37*, 65–79.

Frayser S. G. (1985). *Varieties of sexual experience: An anthropological perspective on human sexuality.* New Haven, CT: HRAF Press.

Frazier, P. A. (1991). Self-blame as a mediator of postrape depressive symptoms. *Journal of Social and Clinical Psychology 10*, 47–57.

Freeman, D. (1998). *The fateful hoaxing of Margaret Mead: A historical analysis of her Samoan research.* Boulder, CO: Westview Press.

Freud, S. (1975). *Three essays on the theory of sexuality.* New York: Basic Books. (Original work published in 1905).

Freund, K., & Blanchard, R. (1986). The concept of courtship disorders. *Journal of Sex and Marital Therapy, 12*, 79–92.

Freund, K., & Kuban, C. (1994). The basis of the abused abuser theory of pedophilia: A further elaboration on

an earlier study. *Archives of Sexual Behavior, 34*, 553–563.

Freund, K., & Seto, M. C. (1998). Preferential rape in the theory of courtship disorder. *Archives of Sexual Behavior, 27*, 433–443.

Freund, K., Watson, R., & Rienzo, D. (1988). The value of self-reports in the study of voyeurism and exhibitionism. *Annals of Sex Research, 1*, 243–262.

Freund, M., Lee, N., & Leonard, T. L. (1991). Sexual behavior of clients with street prostitutes in Camden, New Jersey. *Journal of Sex Research, 28*, 579–591.

Freund, M., Leonard, T. L., & Lee, N. (1989). Sexual behavior of resident street prostitutes with their clients in Camden, New Jersey. *Journal of Sex Research, 26*, 460–478.

Friday, Nancy. (1991). *Women on Top: How Real Life has Changed Women's Sexual Fantasies.* New York: Simon & Schuster.

Friedman R. C., & Downey, J. (1989). Neurobiology and Sexual Orientation: Current Relationships" *Journal of Neuropsychiatry 5*, 149.

Friedrich, M. J. (1999). Ovarian cancer investigators aim at cell signaling pathways. *Journal of the American Medical Association, 281*, 973–975.

Friedrich, W. N., Fisher, J., Broughton, D., Houston, M., & Shafran, C. R. (1998). Normative sexual behavior in children: A contemporary sample. *Pediatrics, 101*, E9.

Frieze, I. J. (1983). Investigating the cause and consequences of marital rape. *Sign, 8*, 532–533.

Frintner, M. P., & Rubinson, L. (1993). Acquaintance rape: The influence of alcohol, fraternity membership, and sports team membership. *Journal of Sex Education & Therapy 19*, 272–284.

Fu, H., Daroch, J. E., Taylor, H., & Ranjit, N. (1999). Contraceptive failure rates: New estimates from the 1995 national survey of family growth. *Family Planning Perspectives, 31*, 56–63.

Furrnham, A., Tan, T., & McManus, C. (1997). Waist-to-hip ratio and prefer-

ences for body shape: A replication and extension. *Personality and Individual Differences, 22*, 539–549.

Gagnon, J. H., & Roberts, E. J. (1983). Content and process in parental verbal communication about sexuality to pre-adolescent children. Unpublished manuscript. State University of New York, Stony Brook.

Gagnon, J. H., & Simon, W. (1973). *Sexal conduct: The social origins of human sexuality.* Chicago: Aldine Press.

Gagnon, J., & Simon, W. (1987). The sexual scripting of oral-genital contacts. *Archives of Sexual Behavior, 16*, 1–25.

Gaith, G. A., & Plaud, J. J. (1999). *The effects of secondary stimulus characteristics of men's sexual arousal.* Washington, DC: ADA/PsychInfo.

Gallagher, A. M., DeLisi, R., Holst, P. C., McGillicuddy-DeLisi, R., Marley, M., & Cohalan, C. (2000). Gender differences in advanced mathematical problem solving. *Journal of Experimental Child Psychology, 75*, 165–190.

Gallup Organization. (2001, June 4). Poll analyses. American attitudes toward homosexuality continue to become more tolerant. Gallup News Service.

Gangestad, S. W., & Simpson, J. A. (2000). The evolution of human mating: Trade-offs and strategic pluralism. *Behavioral and Brain Science, 23*, from http://www.cogsci.soton.ac.uk/bbs/Archive/bbs.gangestad.html

Gangestad, S. W., & Thornhill, R. (1998). The analysis of fluctuating asymmetry redux: The robustness of parametic statistics. *Animal Behaviour 55*, 497–501.

Gangestad, S. W., & Thornhill, R. (1999). Individual differences in developmental precision and fluctuating asymmetry: A model and its implications. *Journal of Evolutionary Biology, 12*, 402–416.

Garber, M. (1995). *Vice versa: Bisexuality and the eroticism of everyday life.* New York: Simon & Schuster.

Garcia, L. T. (1998). Perceptions of resistance to unwanted sexual advances. *Journal of Psychology of Human Sexuality, 10*, 43–52.

Garcia, L., Brennan, K., DeCarlo, M., McGlennon, R., & Tait, S. (1984). Sex differences in sexual arousal to different erotic stories. *Journal of Sex Research, 20,* 391–402.

Gartrell, N., Herman, J. L., Olarte, S., & Feldstein, M. (1986). Psychiatrist-patient sexual contact: Results of a national survey: I. Prevalence. *American Journal of Psychiatry, 143,* 1126–1131.

Gartrell, N., Herman, J. L., Olarte, S., & Feldstein, M. (1987). Psychiatrist-patient sexual contact: Results of a national survey: II. Psychiatrist's Attitudes. *American Journal of Psychiatry, 144,* 164–169.

Gazzaniga, M. (1992). *Nature's mind: The biological roots of thinking, emotions, sexuality, language and intelligence.* New York: Basic Books.

Gebhard, P. H., Gagnon, J., Pomeroy, W. B., & Christensen, C. (1965). *Sex offenders: An analysis of types.* New York: Harper and Row.

Geer, J., Heiman, J., & Leitenberg, H. (1984). *Human sexuality.* Englewood Cliffs, NJ: Prentice Hall.

Geimann, S. (1995). Anti-abortion group threatens journal. *Albion Monitor,* Sept. 2. From http://www.monitor.net/monitor/9-2-95/threat.html

Gendel, E., & Bonner, E. (1988). Gender identity disorders and paraphilias. In H. Goldman (Ed.), *Review of general psychiatry.* Norwalk, CT: Appleton & Lange.

Genet, J. (2001). Quoted from http://www.boutcider.com/01_outcoming/qotes.html

George, L. K., & Weiler, S. J. (1981). Sexuality in middle age and late life: The effects of age cohort and gender. *Archives of General Psychiatry, 38,* 919–923.

Gerstel, N., & Gross, H.E. (1982). Commuter marriages: A review. *Marriage and Family Review Sum 5,* 71–93.

Ghiglieri, M. P. (1999). *The dark side of man: Tracing the origins of violence.* New York: Perseus Press.

Gibson, W. (1994). *Necromancer.* New York: Ace Books.

Gil, E., & Cavanaugh-Johnson, T. (1993). *Sexualized children.* Rockville, MD: Launch Press.

Gilbert, S. (1998, Sept. 22). Doctors report rise in elective caesareans. *The New York Times,* p. F7.

Gilliland, F. D., Berhane, K., McConnell, R., Gauderman, W. L., Vora, H., Rap, E. B., Avol, E., & Peters, J. M. (2000). Maternal smoking during pregnancy, environmental tobacco smoke exposure and childhood lung function. *Thorax, 55,* 271–276.

Gilman, M. A. (1988). Assessment of the effects of analgesic concentrations of nitrous oxide on human sexual response. *International Journal of Neuroscience, 4,* 27–33.

Girls, Inc. (2000). From http://www.girlsinc.com

Gissmann, L. (2001). Possibilities of vaccination against HPV infection in cervical carcinoma. Zentralbl. *Gynakologyica, 123,* 299–301.

Givens, D. B. (1995). *Love signals: How to attract a mate.* New York: Crown.

Gladwin, T., & Sarason, S. B. (1953). *Truk: Man in paradise.* Viking Fund Publications in Anthropology, No. 20. New York: Wenner-Gren Foundation.

Glasier, A., & Baird, D. (1998). The effects of self-administering emergency contraception. *New England Journal of Medicine, 339,* 1–4.

Glass, S. P., & Wright, T. L. (1992). Justifications for extramarital relationships: The association between attitudes, behaviors, and gender. *Journal of Sex Research I 29,* 361–387.

Glenn, N., Marquardt, E. et al. (2001). Hooking up, hanging out and hoping for Mr. Right: College women on mating and dating today. Austin, TX: An Institute for American Values Report to the Independent Women's Forum.

Glynn, P. (1982). *Skin to skin: Eroticism in dress.* New York: Oxford University Press.

Gold, E. (1986). Long term effects of sexual victimization in childhood: An attributional approach. *Journal of Counseling and Clinical Psychology, 54,* 471–475.

Gold, S. N., & Heffner, C. L. (1998). Sexual addiction: Many conceptions, minimal data. *Clinical Psychology Review, 18(3),* 367–381.

Goldberg, D. C. et al. (1982). The Gräfenberg spot and female ejaculation: A review of initial hypotheses. *Journal of Sex and Marital Therapy, 9,* 27–37.

Goldman, P. S. (1978). Neuronal plasticity in primate telencephalon: Anomalous projections induced by prenatal removal of frontal cortex. *Science, 2,* 768–770.

Goldstein, B. (1976). *Human sexuality.* New York: McGraw-Hill.

Goldstein, I., Lue, T. E., Padmap, H. H., Rosen, C., Steers, W. D., & Wicker, P. A. (1998). Oral sildenafil in the treatment of erectile dysfunction: Sildenafil study group. *New England Journal of Medicine, 338,* 1394–1404.

Goleman, D. (1991, Oct. 22). Sexual harassment: It's about power not lust. *The New York Times,* p. C1.

Gondolf, E. W. (1985). *Men who batter.* Holmes Beach, FL: Learning Publications.

Gondolf, E., & Shestakov, D. (1997). Spousal Homicide in Russia: Gender Inequality in a Multi-factor Model. *Violence Against Women 3,* 533–546.

Goodchild, J. D., & Zellman, G. L. (1984). Sexual signaling and sexual aggression in adolescent relationships. In N. M. Malamuth & E. Donnerstein (Eds.), *Pornography & sexual aggression.* New York: Academic Press.

Gooren, L., Fliers, E., & Courtney, K. (1990). Biological determinants of sexual orientation. *Annual Review of Sex Research, 1,* 175–196.

Gordon, C. S., Smith, M. F. S., Smith, M. B., & McNay, J. E. (1998). First trimester growth and the risk of low birth weight. *New England Journal of Medicine, 339,* 1817–1822.

Gordon, S. (1992, Aug./Sept.). Values based sexuality education. *SIECUS Report, 20,* 1–14.

Gordon, S., & Snyder, C. W. (1989). *Personal issues in human sexuality: A guidebook for better sexual health* (2nd ed). Boston: Allyn & Bacon.

Gorey, K. M., & Leslie, D. R. (1997). The prevalence of child sexual abuse: Integrative review adjustment for potential response and measurement biases. *Child Abuse & Neglect, 21,* 391–398.

Gottman, J. M. (1991). *The marriage clinic: A scientifically-based marital therapy.* New York: W. W. Norton.

Gottman, J. (1994b). *Why marriages succeed or fail.* New York: Simon & Schuster.

Gottman, J. M. (Ed.). (1994b). *What predicts divorce: The measures.* New York: Erlbaum.

Gottman, J. M., Coan, J., Carrere, S., & Swanson, C. (1998). Predicting marital happiness and stability from newlywed interaction. *Journal of Marriage and the Family, 60,* 5–22.

Gottman, J. M. (1999). *The seven principles of making marriage work.* New York: Crown Publishers.

Gottman, J. M., and Levenson, R. W. (1992). Marital processes predictive of later dissolution: Behavior, physiology, and health. *Journal of Personality and Social Psychology 63,* 221–233.

Gottman, J. S. (1990). Children of gay and lesbian parents. In E. W. Bozett & M. B. Sussman (Eds.), *Homosexuality and family relations* (pp. 177–196). New York: Harrington Park Press.

Gould, J. L., & Gould, C. F. (1997). *Sexual selection: Mate choice and courtship in nature.* New York: Freeman/Scientific American.

Gould, S. J. (1987, Feb.). Freudian slip. *Natural History,* 15–21.

Gräfenberg, E. (1950). The role of urethra in female orgasm. *International Journal of Sexology, 3,* 145–148.

Graham, B. (1998, Jan. 30). The judge tells Navy not to dismiss sailor with "gay" online identity: Ruling reinforces electronic confidentiality rights. *The Washington Post,* A02.

Graham, C. A., Rasmos, R., Bancroft, J., Maglaya, & Farley, T. M. (1995). The effects of steroidal contraceptives on the well-being and sexuality of women: A double-blind, placebo-controlled, two center study of combined and progestogen-only methods. *Contraception, 52,* 363–369.

Grant, S. M. (2000). Incidence and risk factors of sexual harassment among working women: Implications for counseling psychology and the workplace. *Dissertation Abstracts International, 60 (07A),* 2384. (University Microfilms No. AAG9939059)

Grauerholz, E. (1989). Sexual harassment of women professors by students: Exploiting the dynamics of power, authority and gender in a university setting. *Sex Roles, 21,* 789–801.

Gray, L. A., & Saracino, M. (1989). AIDS on campus: A preliminary study of college students' knowledge and behaviors. *Journal of Counseling and Development, 68,* 199–202.

Grayhold, C., Juul, S., Naeraa, R., & Hansen, J. (1998). Morbidity in Turner syndrome. *Journal of Clinical Epidemiology, 51,* 147–158.

Graziottin, A. (1998). Hormones and libido. *Maturitas, 27,* 1–11.

Green, R. (1974). *Sexual identity conflict in children and adults.* New York: Basic Books.

Greenberg, D. F. (1988). *The construction of homosexuality.* Chicago: University of Chicago Press.

Greene, B. A., DeBacker, T. K., Ravindran, B., & Krows, A. J. (1999). Goals, values and beliefs as predictors of achievement and effort in high-school mathematics classes. *Sex Roles, 40,* 421–458.

Greenlinger, V., & Byrne, D. (1987). Coercive sexual fantasies of college men as predictors of self-reported likelihood to rape and overt sexual aggression. *Journal of Sex Research, 23,* 1–11.

Greenough, W. T., Carter, C. S., & Steerman, C. (1977). Sex differences in dendritic patterns in hamster preoptic area. *Brain Research, 126,* 63–72.

Gregersen, E. (1994). *The world of human sexuality: Behaviors, customs, and beliefs.* New York: Irvington Publishers.

Gregor, T. (1977). *Mehinaku: The drama of life in a Brazilian Indian village.* Chicago: University of Chicago Press.

Gremaux, R. (1989). Mannish women of the Balkan mountains: Preliminary notes of the "sworn virgin" in male disguise, with special reference to their sexuality and gender identity. In J. Bremmer (Ed.), *From Sappho to Sade* (pp. 143–172). London: Routledge.

Grice, J. W., & Seely, E. (2000). The evolution of sex differences in jealousy: Failure to replicate previous results. *Journal of Research in Personality, 34,* 348–356.

Grmek, M. D. (1990). *History of AIDS: Emergence and origin of a modern pandemic.* Princeton, NJ: Princeton University Press.

Grob, C. S. (1985). Female exhibitionism. *Journal of Nervous and Mental Disease, 73,* 253.

Grodstein, F., Stamefer, M., Coloditz, G., Willett, W., Manson, J., Joffee, M., Rosner, B., Fuchs, C., & Hunkinson, S. (1997). Postmenopausal hormone therapy and mortality. *New England Journal of Medicine, 336,* 1769–1779.

Gross, J. (1994, Jan. 16). Sex educators for young see new virtue in chastity. *The New York Times,* p. A1.

Grosskopf, D. (1983). *Sex and the married woman.* New York: Simon and Schuster.

Groth, A. N. (1979). *Men who rape.* New York: Plenum Press.

Groth, A. N., & Burgess, A. W. (1977). Sexual dysfunction during rape. *New England Journal of Medicine, 298,* 764–766.

Groth, A. N., & Hobson, W. (1983). The dynamics of sexual assault. In L. Schlesinger & E. Revitch (Eds.), *Sexual dynamics of anti-social behavior* (pp. 158–170). Springfield, IL: Thomas.

Guerrero-Pavich, E. (1986). A Chicana perspective on Mexican culture and sexuality. In L. Lister (Ed.), *Human sexuality, ethnoculture, and social work* (pp. 47–65). New York: Haworth Press.

Guggino, J. M., & Ponzetti, J. J., (1997). Gender differences in affective reactions to first coitus. *Journal of Adolescence, 20,* 189-200.

Guttentag, M., & Secord, P. F. (1983). *Too many women: The sex ratio question.* Beverly Hills, CA: Sage Publications.

Guttman, N., & Zimmerman, D. R. (2000). Low income mothers' views on breastfeeding. *Social Science and Medicine, 40,* 457–472.

Guzick, D. S., Carson, S. A., Courifaris, C., Overstreet, J., Wolitvak, P., Steinkampf, M. P., Hill, J. A., Mastroianni, L., Buster, J., Nakaiima, S. T., Bogel, D. L., & Canfield, R. E. (1999). Efficacy of superovulation and intrauterine insemination treatment of infertility. *New England Journal of Medicine, 340,* 177–183.

Haig, D. (1993). Genetic conflicts in human pregnancy. *Quarterly Review of Biology, 68,* 495–532.

Hale, R. (1997). Motives of reward among men who rape. *American Journal of Criminal Justice, 22,* 101–119.

Hall, J. A. (1998). How big are nonverbal sex differences? The case of smiling and sensitivity to nonverbal cues. In D. J. Canary, K. Dindia (Eds.). *Sex differences and similarities in communication: Critical essays and empirical investigations of sex and gender in interaction.* (pp. 155–179). Mahwah, NJ: Erlbaum.

Hall, R. E. (1998). Skin color bias: A new perspective on an old social problem. *Journal of Psychology, 132,* 238–240.

Hall, T. (1987, June 1). Infidelity and women: Shifting patterns. *The New York Times,* p. B8.

Halperin, D. (1990). *One hundred years of homosexuality and other essays on Greek love.* New York: Routledge.

Halperin, D. (1999). Heterosexual anal intercourse: Prevalence, cultural factors, and HIV infection and other health risks. Part I. *AIDS Patient Care STDs, 13,* 717–730.

Halperin, D. T., & Bailey, R. C. (1999). Male circumcision and HIV infection: 10 years and counting. *Lancet, 354,* 1813–1815.

Hamer, D., Hu, H. S., Magnuson, V. L., Hu, N., & Pattatucci, M. L. (1993). A linkage between DNA markers on the X-chromosome and male sexual orientation. *Science, 261,* 321–327.

Hamilton, D. M., & Jackson, M. H. (1998). Spiritual development: Pats and processes. *Journal of Instructional Psychology, 25,* 262–270.

Hamilton, M., & Yee, J. (1990). Rape knowledge and propensity to rape. *Journal of Research in Personality, 24,* 111–122.

Handy, B. (1998, May 4). The Viagra craze. *Time, 151,* 50–57.

Hansen, G. L. (1987). Extradyadic relations during courtship. *Journal of Sex Research, 23,* 382–390

Hansen, W. B., Hahn, G. L., & Wolkenstein, B. H. (1990). Perceived personal immunity: Beliefs about susceptibility to AIDS. *Journal of Sex Research 27,* 622–628.

Hanson, T. L., McLanahan, S. S., & Thomson, E. (1998). Windows on divorce: Before and after. *Social Science Research, 27,* 329–349.

Haraphap, M., & Siregar, A. (1988). Circumcision: A review and a new technique. *Journal of Dermatology and Surgical Oncology, 14,* 283–286.

Hardy, L. M., Haynes, B. F., & Voberding, P. A. (1994). From the institute of medicine. *Journal of the American Medical Association, 272,* 423.

Hare, R. D. (1993). *Without conscience: The disturbing world of the psychopaths among us.* New York: Simon & Schuster/Pocket.

Hare, R. D., & McPherson, L. M. (1984). Violent and aggressive behavior by criminal psychopaths. *International Journal of Law & Psychiatry, 7,* 35–50.

Harker, L., & Thorpe, K. (1992). "The last egg in the basket?" Elderly primiparity: A review of findings. *Birth, 19,* 23–30.

Harlow, C. (1991). *Female victims of violent crime.* Washington, DC: U.S. Department of Justice, Bureau of Justice Statistics, NCJ-126826.

Harlow, H. F., & Harlow, M. K. (1962). *Social deprivation in monkeys. Psychology in progress: Readings from Scientific American.* San Francisco: W.H. Freeman. 223–231.

Harney, D., & Muehlenhard, C. (1990). Rape. In E. Graverhold & M. Korlewski (Eds.), *Sexual coercion: A sourcebook on its nature, causes and prevention.* Lexington, MS: Lexington Books.

Harrell, B. (1981). Lactation and menstruation in cultural perspective. *American Anthropologist, 83,* 797–823.

Harris, C. R., & Christenfeld, N. (1996). Gender, jealousy, and reason. *Psychological Science 7,* 364–366.

Harris, M. (1975). *Cows, pigs, wars and witches.* New York: Vintage

Harris, M., & Ross, E. B. (1987). *Sex, death and fertility: Population regulation in preindustrial and developing societies.* New York: Columbia University Press.

Harrison, A. A. (1977). Mere exposure. In L. Berkowitz (Ed.), *Advances in experimental social psychology: Vol 10.* New York: Academic Press.

Harry, J. (1982). Decision making and age differences among gay male couples. *Journal of Homosexuality 8,* 9–21.

Hart, B. L. (1986). Medical preoptic anterior hypothalamic lesions and sociosexual behavior of male goats. *Physiology and Behavior, 35,* 301–305.

Hartman, W. E., & Fithian, M. A. (1984). *Any man can: The multiple orgasm techniques for every loving man.* New York: St. Martin's Press.

Haselton, M. G., & Buss, D. M. (2000). Error management theory: A new perspective on biases in cross-sex mind reading. *Journal of Personality and Social Psychology, 78,* 81–91.

Hatano, Y. (1991). Changes in sexual activities of Japanese youth. *Journal of Sex Education and Therapy, 17,* 1–14.

Hatcher, R., Guest, F., Stewart, G., Trussell, G., Trussell, J., & Frank, E. (1990). *Contraceptive technology 1990–1991* (15th ed.). New York: Irvington.

Hatcher, R., Trussell, J., Stewart, F., Stewart, G., Kowal, D., Guest, E., Cates, W., & Policar, M. (1994). *Contraceptive technology* (16th ed.). New York: Irvington.

Hatfield, E., & Rapson, R. L. (1987). Passionate love: New directions in research. In W. J. Jones & D. Perlamn (Eds.), *Advances in personal relationships: Vol 2.* Greenwich, CT: JAJ Press

Hatfield, E., & Rapson, R. L. (1996). *Love and sex: Cross-cultural perspective.* Boston: Allyn & Bacon.

Hatfield, E., & Sprecher, S. (1986). Measuring passionate love in intimate relationships. *Journal Adolescence, 9,* 383–410.

Havemann, E., & Lehtinen, M. (1990). *Marriage and families: New problems, new opportunities.* Englewood Cliffs, NJ: Prentice Hall.

Hayes, J. (1995). Sex education in the early years. *Health Education, 1,* 22–27.

Hawton, K., Catalan, J., & Fagg, J. (1991). Low sexual desire: Sex therapy results and prognostic factors. *Behavior Research, 29,* 217–224.

Heath, D. (1984). An investigation into the origins of a copious vaginal discharge during intercourse "enough to wet the bed" that is not urine. *Journal of Sex Research, 20,* 194–215.

Heaven, P. C., & Oxman, L. N. (1999). Human values, conservatism and stereotypes of homosexuals. *Personality and Individual Differences, 27,* 109–118.

Hedge, L. V., & Nowell, A. (1995). Sex differences in central tendency variability and numbers of high scoring individuals. *Science, 269,* 4045.

Heinonin, O. P. (1977). Cardiovascular birth defects and antenatal exposure to female sex hormones. *New England Journal of Medicine, 296,* 67–70.

Held, V. (1973). Marx, sex and the transformation of society. *Philosophical Forum, 5,* 172–173.

Hendin, H. (1982). Psychotherapy and suicide. In *Suicide in America.* New York: Norton.

Hendin, H. (1996). *Suicide in America.* New York: W. W. Norton and Co.

Hendrick, C., & Hendrick, S. (1986). The theory and method of love. *Journal of Personality and Social Psychology, 50,* 392–402.

Hendrick, S. S. (1981). Self-disclosure and marital satisfaction. *Journal of Personality and Social Psychology, 50,* 1150–1159.

Hendrick, S., & Hendrick, C. (1987). Multidimensionality of sexual attitudes. *Journal of Sex Research, 23,* 502–526.

Henshaw, S. K. (1999). *Special report: U.S. teen pregnancy statistics: With comparative statistics for women aged 20–24.* New York: Alan Guttmacher Institute.

Henslin, J. M., & Biggs, M. A. (1978). Dramaturigal desexualization: The sociology of the vaginal examination. In J. M. Henslin & F. Sagarin (Eds.), *The sociology of sex: An introductory reader.* New York: Schocken Books.

Herbert, W. (1997, Apr. 21). Politics of biology. *U.S. News & World Report, 122,* 72–74.

Herdt, G., & Boxer, B. (1993). *Children of horizons: How gay and lesbian teens are leading the way out of the closet.* Boston: Beacon Press.

Herdt, G., & McClintock, M. (2000). The magical age of 10. *Archives of Sexual Behavior, 29,* 587–606.

Herdt, G. H., & Davidson, J. (1988). The Sambia "Turnim Man": Sociocultural and clinical aspects of gender formation in male pseudohermaphrodites with 5-alpha reductase deficiency in Papua, New Guinea. *Archives of Sexual Behavior, 17,* 33–55.

Herek, G. M., & Capitanio, J. P. (1996). Some of my best friends: Intergroup contact, stigma, and heterosexuals' attitudes toward gay men and lesbians. *Personality and Social Psychology Bulletin, 22,* 412–424.

Herek, G. M. (2000). The psychology of sexual prejudice. *Current Dimensions in Psychological Science, 9,* 19–27.

Herman-Giddens, M., Slora, E., Wasserman, R., Bourdony, C., Bhapka, M., Koch, C., & Hesemeier, C. (1997). Secondary sexual characteristics and menses from the pediatric research office settings network. *Pediatrics, 99,* 505–512.

Herold, E. S., & Mewhinney, D. K. (1993). Gender differences in casual sex and AIDS prevention: A survey of dating bars. *Journal of Sex Research, 30,* 36–42.

Herring, Susan. (1993). Gender and democracy in computer-mediated communication. In T. Benson (Ed.) [special issue], *Electronic Journal of Communication, 3.*

Hershberger, S., & D'Augelli, A. (1995). The impact of victimization on the mental health and suicidality of lesbian, gay, and bisexual youths. *Developmental Psychology, 31,* 65–74.

Herz, R. S., & Cahill, E. D. (1999). Differential use of sensory information in sexual behavior as a function of gender. Washington, DC: AP/PsychINFO.

Herzog, L. (1989). Urinary tract infections and circumcision. *American Journal of Diseases of Children, 154,* 348–350.

Hessellund, H. (1976). Masturbation and sexual fantasies in married couples. *Archives of Sexual Behavior, 5,* 133–147.

Hickman, S. E. (1998). Young women's and men's perceptions of sexual consent in heterosexual situations. *Dissertation Abstracts International: Section B: The Sciences and Engineering Univ. Microfilms International, 59,* 1368.

Hicks, E. K. (1996). *Female mutilations in Islamic Northeastern Africa.* New York: Transaction Publishers.

Hickson, J., Housley, W., & Wages, D. (2000). Counselors' perceptions of spirituality in the therapeutic process. *Counseling and Values, 45,* 58–66.

Hill, C. T., Rubin, Z., & Peplau, L. A. (1976). Breakups before marriage: The end of 103 affairs. *Journal of Social Issues, 32,* 147–168.

Hillier, L., Harrison, L., & Warr, D. (1998). When you carry condoms all the boys think you want it: Negotiating competing discourses about safe sex. *Journal of Adolescence, 21,* 15–29.

Hines, P. (1999). Early pregnancy prenatal diagnostic testing: Risks associated with chorionic villus sampling and early amniocentesis and screening options. *Journal of Perinatal Neonatology, 13,* 1–3.

Hirsch, L. R., & Paul, L. (1996). Human male mating strategies: Courtship tactics of the "quality" and "quantity" alternatives. *Ethology and Sociobiology, 12,* 55–76.

Hirsch, M. S. et al. (1998). Antiretroviral drug resistance testing in adults with HIV infection. *Journal of the American Medical Association, 279,* 1984–1991.

Hite, S. (1976). *The Hite report: A nationwide study of female sexuality.* New York: Dell.

Hite, S. (1981). *The Hite report on male sexuality.* New York: Ballantine Books.

Ho, D. (1998). Paper presented at the Fifth Conference on Retroviruses and Opportunistic Infections. Chicago.

Hobart, C. W. (1958). Incidence of romanticism during courtship. *Social Forces, 36,* 363–367.

Hodson, D. S., & Skeen, P. (1994). Sexuality and aging: The hammerlock of myths. *Journal of Applied Gerontology, 13,* 219–235.

Hoebel, E. A. (1978). *The Cheyenne: Indians of the Great Plains* (2nd ed.). New York: Holt, Rinehart & Winston.

Hofman, M. A., & Swaab, D. F. (1989). The sexual dimorphic nucleus of the preoptic area in the human brain: A comparative morphology. *Journal of Anatomy, 164,* 55–72.

Holcomb, D. R., Holcomb, L. C., Sondag, K. A., & Williams, N. (1991). Attitudes about date rape: Gender differences among college students. *College Student Journal, 25,* 434–439.

Holditch-Davis, D., Sandelowski, M., & Harris, B. G. (1999). Effect on infertility on mothers' and fathers' interactions with young infants. *Journal of Reproductive and Infant Psychology, 17,* 159–173.

Hollender, M. J., Brown, C. W., & Roback, H. B. (1977). Genital exhibitionism in women. *American Journal of Psychiatry, 132,* 436–438.

Holliday, M. A., Pincert, T. L., Kiernan, S. C., Kunos, I. I., Angelus, P., & Keszler, M. (1999). Dorsal penile nerve block vs. topical placebo for circumcision in low-birth weight neonatals. *Archives of Pediatric and Adolescent Medicine, 153,* 476–480.

Holmes, M. M., Resnick, H. S., Kilpatrick, D. G., & Best, C. L. (1997). Rape-related pregnancy. *ACOG Clinical Review, 2,* 10.

Homans, G. (1950). *The human group.* New York: Harcourt Brace.

Hook, E. B., Cross, P. K., & Schreinemacher, D. M. (1983). Chromosomal abnormality rates at amniocentesis and in live-born infants. *Journal of the American Medical Association, 249,* 2034–2038.

Hooten, T. M., Hillier, S., Johnson, C., et al. (1991). Escherichia coli bacteriuria and contraceptive method. *Journal of the American Medical Association, 265,* 64–69.

Hopkins, J. (2000). *The Meaning of Life: Buddhist Perspectives on Cause and Effect.* Boston: Wisdom Publishing.

Horgan, E. (1992). *The Shaker Holy Land: A community portrait.* Cambridge, MA: The Harvard Common Press.

Houry, D., Feldman, K. M., & Abbott, J. (2000). Mandatory Reporting Laws. Annals of Emergency Medicine, 35, 404.

Howard, J. A., Blumstein, P., & Schwartz, P. (1987). Social or evolutionary theories? Some observations on preferences in human mate selection. *Journal of Personality and Social Psychology, 51,* 102–109.

Howell, M. R., Kassler, W. J., & Haddix, A. (1997). Partner notification to prevent pelvic inflammatory disease in women: Cost effectiveness of two strategies. *Sexually Transmitted Diseases, 24,* 287–292.

Hrdy, S. B. (1996). The evolution of female orgasm: Logic please but no atavism. *Animal Behavior, 52,* 851–852.

Hrdy, S. B. (2000). *Mother Nature: A history of mothers, infants, and natural selection.* New York: Pantheon Books

Hsu, R. (1994). Gender differences in sexual fantasy and behavior in a college population: A ten-year replication. *Journal of Sex and Marital Therapy, 20,* 103–118.

Hubble, M. A., Duncan, B. L., & Miller, S. D. (1999). *The heart and soul of change: What works in therapy.* Washington, DC: American Psychological Association.

Huber, S. C. (1985). The marketing of vasectomy: An analysis of the case studies. In S. C. Huber (Ed.), *The social marketing of vasectomy services: An international review.* The Social Marketing International Association. Queretaro, Mexico.

Hueston, W. J., & Kasik-Miller, S. (1999). Changes in functional health status during normal pregnancy. *Journal of Family Practice, 43,* 209–212.

Hull, J. G. (1981). A self-awareness model of the causes and effects of alcohol consumption. *Journal of Abnormal Psychology, 90,* 586–600.

Hunt, M. (1974). *Sexual behavior in the 1970s.* Chicago: Playboy Press.

Hunter, M. S., Swann, C., & Ussher, J. M. (1995). Seeking help for premenstrual syndrome: Women's self-reports and treatment preferences. *Sexual & Marital Therapy, 10,* 254–262.

Hurd, W. W., Kelly, M. S., Ohl, D. A., Gauvin, J. M., Smith, A. J., & Cummins, C. A. (1992). The effect of cocaine on sperm motility characteristics and bovine cervical mucus penetration. *Fertility and Sterility, 57,* 178–182.

Hurlbert, D., & Whitaker, K. (1991). The role of masturbation in marital and sexual satisfaction: A comparative study of female masturbators and nonmasturbators. *Journal of Sex Education and Therapy, 17,* 272–282.

Huston, T. L., Caughlin, J. P., Houts, R. M., Smith, S. E., & George, L. J. (2001). The connubial crucible: Newlywed marital delight, distress, and divorce. *Journal of Personality and Social Psychology, 80,* 281–293.

Huston, T. L., Surra, C. A., Cate, R. M., & Fitzgerald, N. M. (1981). From courtship to marriage: Mate selection as an interpersonal process. In S. Duck & R. Gilmour (Eds.), *Personal relationships:* Vol. 2 (pp. 53–88). London: Academic Press.

Hutchinson, G. E. (1959). A speculative consideration of certain possible forms of sexual selection in men. *American Naturalist, 93,* 81–91.

Hyde, J. S., & DeLamater, J. (1999). *Understanding human sexuality.* New York: McGraw Hill.

Hyde, J., Fenneman, E., & Lamon, S. (1990). Gender differences in mathematics performance: A meta-analysis. *Psychological Bulletin, 107,* 139–155.

Hyde, J. S., & Linn, M. C. (1988). Gender differences in verbal ability: A meta-analysis. *Psychological Bulletin, 104,* 53–69.

Iams, J. D., Goldenberg, R. L., Mercer, B. M., Moawad, A., Thom, E., Meis, P. J., McNellis, D., Caritis, S. N., Miodovnik, M., Menard, M. K., Thurnau, G. R., Bottoms, S. E., Roberts, J. M. (1998). The preterm prediction study: Recurrence risk of spontaneous preterm birth. National Institute of Child Health and Human Development Maternal-Fetal Medicine Units Network. *American Journal of Obstetrics & Gynecology, 178,* 1035–1040.

Ikonomido, C., Bosch, F., Miksa, M., Bittigau, P., Vöckler, Dikranian, K., Tenkova, T., Stefovska, V., Turski, L., & Olney, J. W. (1999). Blockade of NMDA receptors and apoptotic neurodegeneration in the developing brain. *Science, 293,* 70–74.

Immerman, R. S., & Mackey, W. C. (1999). The societal dilemma of multiple sexual partners: The costs of the loss of pair-bonding. *Marriage and Family Review, 29,* 3–19.

Imperato-Mcginley, J., Peterson, R., Gautier, T., & Sturla, E. (1979). Androgens and the evolution of male gender identity among male pseudohermaphrodites with 5-alpha reductase deficiency. *New England Journal of Medicine, 300,* 1233–1237.

Insel, T. R., & Hulihan, T. J. (1995). A gender-specific mechanism for pair bonding: Oxytocin and partner preference formation in monogamous voles. *Behavioral Neurosciences, 109(4),* 782–789.

Institute of Medicine. (1975). *Legalized abortion and the public health.* Washington, DC: National Academy of Sciences.

Ivins, M. (1993). *Nothing but good times ahead.* New York: Macmillan Library.

Iwasawa, A., Nieminen, P., Lehtinen, M., & Paavonen, J. (1997). Human papillomavirus in squamous cell carcinoma of the vulva by polymerase chain reaction. *Obstetrics and Gynecology, 89,* 81–84.

Jaccard, J., Dittus, P. J., & Gordon, V. V. (2000). Parent-teen communication about premarital sex: Factors associated with the extent of communication. *Journal of Adolescent Research, 15,* 187–208.

Jackson, T., Towson, S., & Narduzzi, K. (1997). Predictors of shyness: A test of variables associated with self-presentational models. *Social Behavior and Personality, 25,* 149–154.

Jacobs, J. (1984). The economy of love in religious commitment: The deconversion of women from nontraditional religious movements. *Journal for the Scientific Study of Religion, 23,* 155–171.

Jamison, P. L., & Gebhard, P. H. (1988). Penis size increase between flaccid and erect states: An analysis of the Kinsey data. *Journal of Sex Research, 24,* 177–183.

Jankowiak, W. R. (1992). *Sex, death, and hierarchy, in a Chinese city: An anthropological account.* New York: Columbia University Press.

Jankowiak, W., & Fischer, E. F. (1992). A cross-cultural perspective on romantic love. *Ethnology, 31,* 149–155.

Jansma, L. L., Linz, D. G., Mulac, A., Imprich, D. J. (1997). Men's interactions with women after viewing sexually explicit films: Does degradation make a difference? *Communication Monographs, 64,* 1–24.

Janus, S., Bess, B., & Saltus, C. (1977). *A sexual profile of men in power.* Englewood Cliffs, NJ: Prentice Hall.

Janus, S. S., & Janus, C. L. (1993). *The Janus report on sexual behavior.* New York: John Wiley.

Jay, K., & Young, A. (1979). *The gay report.* New York: Summit.

Jellison, J. M., & Oliver, D. F. (1983). Attitude similarity and attraction: An impression management approach. *Personality and Social Psychology Bulletin, 9,* 111–115.

Jenks, R. J. (1998). Swinging: A review of the literature. *Archives of Sexual Behavior, 27,* 507–521.

Jensen, A. R. (1998). *The g factor: The science of mental ability.* Westport, CT: Praeger.

Jessor, R., & Jessor, S. (1977). *Problem behaviour and psychosocial development: A longitudinal study of youth.* New York: Academic Press.

Johnson, D. E. (2000). Long-term medical issues in international adoptees. *Pediatric Annals, 29,* 234–241.

Johnson, M. E., & Baer, A. J. (1998). College students' judgments and perceptions of persons with AIDS from different risk groups. *Journal of Psychology, 130,* 527–536.

Johnson, M. E., Brems, C., & Alford-Keating, P. (1987). Personality correlates of homophobia. *Journal of Homosexuality, 34,* 57–69.

Johnson, N. P., Caughlin, J. P., & Huston, T. L. (1999). The tripartite nature of marital commitment: Personal, moral, and structural reasons to stay married. *Journal of Marriage & the Family, 61,* 160–177.

Jolly, A. (1972). *The evolution of primate behavior.* New York: Macmillan.

Jones, J. H. (1997). *Alfred C. Kinsey: A public/private life.* New York: W.W. Norton.

Jordan, C., & Revenson, T. A. (1999). Gender differences in coping with infertility: A meta-analysis. *Journal of Bahavior Medicine, 22,* 341–358.

Josephs, R. A., & Steele, C. M. (1990). The two faces of alcohol myopia: Attentional mediation of psychological stress. *Journal of Abnormal Psychology, 99,* 115–126.

Jost, A. (1966) Problems of foetal endocrinology. *Progress in hormonal research, 22,* 541–574.

Jost, A. (1972). A new look at the mechanism controlling sex differentiation

in mammals. *Johns Hopkins Medical Journal, 130,* 38–53.

Judge Advocates General. Uniform Code of Military Justice, 934. Art. 134 general article. From http://jaglink.jag.af.mil/ucmj.htm

Kaeser, F., DiSalvo, C., & Moglia, R. (2001). Sexual behaviors of young children that occur in schools. *Journal of Sex Education and Therapy, 25,* 277–285.

Karafa, J. A., & Cozzarelli, C. (1997). Shyness and reduced sexual arousal in males: The transference of cognitive interference. *Basic and Applied Social Psychology 19,* 329–344.

Kaiser Family Foundation (1998). *Sexually transmitted diseases in America: How many and at what cost?* Menlo Park, CA: Author.

Kaiser Family Foundation (2000a). Sex Education in America: A View from Inside the Nation's Classrooms. Summary of findings. Menlo Park, CA: Author

Kaiser Family Foundation. (2000b, September). Sex education in America: Policy and politics. (Update) From http://www.kff.org

Kalick, S. M., Zebrouwitz, L. A., Langlois, J. H., & Johnson, R. M. (1998). Does human facial attractiveness honestly advertise health? Longitudinal data on an evolutionary question. *Psychological Science, 9,* 8–13.

Kalof, L. (1993). Rape supportive attitudes and sexual victimization experiences of sorority and on sorority women. *Sex Roles, 20,* 767–777.

Kalof, L. (1999). The effects of gender and music video imagery on sexual attitudes. *Journal of Social Psychology, 39,* 378–385.

Kambic, R. T., & Lamprecht, V. (1996). Calendar rhythm efficacy: A review. *Contraception, 12,* 123–128.

Kammeyer, K. C. W., Ritzer, G., & Yetman, N. R. (1990). *Sociology: Experiencing changing societies.* Boston: Allyn & Bacon.

Kanin, E. J. (1969). Selected aspects of male sex aggression. *Journal of Sex Research, 4,* 12–28.

Kanin, E. J. (1985). Date rapists: Differential sexual socialization and relative deprivation. *Archives of Sexual Behavior, 13,* 219–231.

Kanin, E. J. (1994). False rape allegations. *Archives of Sexual Behavior, 23,* 81.

Kanin, E. J., Davidson, K. D., & Scheck, S. R. (1970). A research note on male-female differentials in the experience of heterosexual love. *Journal of Sex Research, 6,* 64–72.

Kanin, E., & Davidson, K. R. (1972). Some evidence bearing on the aim-inhibition hypothesis of love. *Sociological Quarterly, 13,* 210–217.

Kant, I. (1924). *Critique of judgment.* Hamburg, Germany: Felix Meiner Verlag. (Originally published in 1790.)

Kaplan, H. S. (1974). *The new sex therapy: Active treatment of sexual dysfunction.* New York: Brunner/Mazel.

Kaplan, H. S. (1979). *Disorders of sexual desire.* New York: Brunner/Mazel.

Kaplan, H. S. (1987). *The illustrated manual of sex therapy.* New York: Brunner/Mazel.

Kaplan, H. S. (1995). *The sexual desire disorders: Dysfunctional regulation of sexual motivation.* New York: Brunner/Mazel.

Katchadourian, H. A., & Lunde, D. T. (1975). *Fundamentals of human sexuality.* New York: Holt, Rinehart & Winston.

Katz, J. (1976). *Gay American history.* New York: Avon Books.

Katz, J. (1995). *The invention of heterosexuality.* New York: Dutton.

Kaunitz, A. M. (1997). The role of androgens in menopausal hormonal replacement. *Endocrinology and Metabolism Clinics of North America, 26(2),* 391–397.

Kellerman, J., Lewis, J., & Laird, J. D. (1989). Looking and loving: The effects of mutual gaze on feelings of romantic love. *Journal of Research in Personality, 23,* 145–161.

Kelley, H. H., & Thibaut, J. W. (1978). *Interpersonal relations: A theory of interdependence.* New York: Wiley.

Kelly, G. F. (1995). *Sexuality today: The human perspective.* (5th ed.) Dubuque, IA: Brown & Benchmark.

Kendrick, D. T., Sadalla, E. K., Groth, G., & Trost, M. R. (1990). Evolution, traits, and the stages of human courtship: Qualifying the parental investment model. *Journal of Personality, 58,* 97–118.

Kendrick, K. M., Hinton, K., Atkins, M. A., Haupt, R., & Skinner, J. D. (1998). Mothers determine sexual preferences. *Nature, 395,* 229–230.

Kendrick, K. M., Keverne, E. B., & Baldwin, B. A. (1987). Intracerebroventricular oxytocin stimulates maternal behavior. *Neuroendocrinology, 46,* 56–61.

Kern, C. (1992, Apr. 18). Cited in Acquittal of husband spurs anger; Wife accused him of raping her. *The Houston Chronicle,* p. A3.

Kerns, J. G., & Fine, M. A. (1994). The relation between gender and negative attitudes toward gay men and lesbians: Do gender role attitudes mediate this relation? *Sex Roles, 31,* 297–307.

Khattak, S., Moghtader, G., McMartin, K., Barrera, M., & Kennedy, D. (1999). Pregnancy outcome following gestational exposure to organic solvents: A prospective controlled study. *Journal of the American Medical Association, 282,* 1033.

Kilmann, P. R. et al. (1987). The treatment of secondary orgasmic dysfunction, II. *Journal of Sex and Marital Therapy, 13,* 93–104.

Kimura, D. (1992). Sex differences in the brain. *Scientific American, 9,* 119–125.

King, A. E. O., (1999). African American females' attitudes toward marriage: An exploratory study. *Journal of Black Studies, 29,* 416–437.

King, B. M., & Lorusso, J. (1997). Discussions in the home about sex: Different recollections by parents and children. *Journal of Sex and Marital Therapy, 23,* 52–60.

Kinsella, G. H., & Duffy, E. D. (1979). Psychosocial readjustment in the spouse of aphasic patients: A comparative study of 79 subjects. *Scandina-*

vian *Journal of Rehabilitation Medicine, 11*, 120–131.

Kinsey, A., Pomeroy, W., & Martin, C. (1948). *Sexual behavior in the human male.* Philadelphia: Saunders.

Kinsey, A., Pomeroy, W., Martin, C., & Gebhard, P. (1953). *Sexual behavior in the human female.* Philadelphia: Saunders.

Kirby, D. (1989). Research effectiveness of sex education programs. *Theory Into Practice, 29*, 165–171.

Kirby, D., Waszak, C., & Ziegler, T. (1991). Six school based clinics: Their reproductive health services and impact on sexual behavior. *Family Planning Perspectives, 23*, 6–16.

Kirkpatrick, R. C. (2000). The evolution of human homosexual behavior. *Current Anthropology, 41*, 385–413.

Kissinger, Henry. Quoted from http://www.quotemeonit.com/kissinger.

Klassen, A. D., Williams, C. J., & Levitt, E. E.; edited by O'Gorman, H. J. (1989). Sex and morality in the U.S.: An empirical enquiry under the auspices of the Kinsey Institute. Middletown, CT: Wesleyan University Press.

Klebanoff, M. A., Lewine, R. J., Der-Simonian, R., Clemens, J. D., & Wilkins, D. G. (1999). Maternal serum paraxanthine, a caffeine metabolite, and the risk of spontaneous abortion. *New England Journal of Medicine, 341*, 1639–1644.

Klein, F. (1990). *The bisexual option.* New York: Harrington Park Press.

Kleinke, C. L., Meeker, F. B., & Stanaeski, R. A., (1986). Preferences for opening lines: Comparing ratings by men and women. *Sex Roles, 15*, 585–600.

Kleinsmith, L. J., & Kish, V. M. (1995). *Principles of cell and molecular biology* (2nd ed.). New York: Harper Collins.

Kling, K. C., Hyde, J. S., Showers, C., & Buswell, B. (1999). Gender differences in self-esteem: A meta-analysis. *Psychological Bulletin, 125*, 470–500.

Kluckhohn, F. R., & Strodtbeck, F. L. (1961). *Variations in value orientations.* Evanston, IL: Row, Peterson.

Kluver, H., & Buey, P. C. (1939). Preliminary analysis of functions of the temporal lobes in monkeys. *Archives of Neurology and Psychiatry, 42*, 979.

Knopf, J., & Seiler, M. (1990). *Inhibited sexual desire.* New York: Warner Books.

Knoth, R., Boyd, K., & Singer, B. (1988). Empirical tests of sexual selection theory: Predictions of sex differences in onset, intensity and time course of sexual arousal. *Journal of Sex Research 24*, 73–89.

Knox, D., Schact, C., & Zusman, M. E. (1999). Love relationships among college students. *College Student Journal, 33*, 149–151.

Knox, D., Walters, L. H., & Walters, J. (1991). Sexual guilt among college students. *College Student Journal, 25*, 432–433.

Knox, D., Zusman, M. E., & Nieves, W. (1998). Breaking away: How college students end love relationships. *College Student Journal, 32*, 482–484.

Knox, D., Zusman, M. E., Snell, S., & Cooer, C. (1999). Characteristics of college students who cohabit. *College Student Journal, 33*, 510–512.

Knupfer, F., Clark, W., & Room, R. (1966). The mental health of the unmarried American. *Journal of Psychiatry, 122*, 841–851.

Kockott, G., & Fahrner, E. M. (1987). Male-to-female and female-to-male transsexuals: A comparison. *Archives of Sexual Behavior, 17*, 539–545.

Koerner, Brendan I. "A lust for profits." U.S. News Online. Retrieved March 27, 2000 from http://www.usnew.com/usnews/issue/000327/eporn.htm

Kohlberg, L. (1966). A cognitive developmental analysis of children's sex-role concepts and attitudes. In E. Maccoby (Ed.), *The development of sex differences.* Stanford, CA: Stanford University Press.

Kohn, A. (1987, Feb.). Shattered innocence. *Psychology Today*, 54–58.

Kolata, G. (1980). NIH panel urges fewer cesarean births. *Science, 210*, 176–177.

Kolata, G. (1993, Feb. 25). Studies say mammograms fail to help many women. *The New York Times*, pp. A1, A15.

Konner, M. (1990). *Why the reckless survive . . . and other secrets of human nature.* New York: Penguin Books.

Koop, C. E. (1987). *The Surgeon General's report on the public health effects of abortion.*

Koralewski, M. A., & Conger, J. C. (1992). The assessment of social skills among sexually coercive college males. *Journal of Sex Research, 29*, 169–188.

Korber, B., Muldoon, M., Theiler, J., Gao, F., Gupta, R., Lapedes, A., Hahn, B. S., Wolinsky, S., & Bhattacharya, T. (1999). Timing the ancestor of the HIV-a pandemic strains *Science, 288*, 1789–1796.

Korman, S. K., & Leslie, G. R. (1982). The relationship of feminist ideology and date expense sharing to perceptions of sexual aggression in dating. *Journal of Sex Research, 18*, 114–129.

Koropeckyj-Cox, T. (1998). Loneliness and depression in middle and old age: Are the childless more vulnerable? *Journal of Gerontology: Social Sciences, 6*, 303–316.

Korzekwa, M., & Steiner, M. (1999). Assessment and treatment of premenstrual syndrome. *Primary Care Update for OB/GYNs, 6*, 153–162.

Koss, M. P. (1992). The under detection of rape: Methodological choices influence incidence estimates. *Journal of Social Issues, 48*, 61–75.

Koss, M. P., Dinero, T., Siebel, C., & Cox, S. (1988). Stranger and acquaintance rape: Are there differences in the victim experience? *Psychology of Women Quarterly, 12*, 1–24.

Koutsky, L. A., Holmes, K. K., Critchlow, C. W., Stevens, C. E., Paayonnen, J., Beckmann, A. M., DeRouen, T. A., Galloway, D. A., Vernon, D., & Kijviat, N. B. (1992). A cohort study of the risk of cervical intraepithelial neoclassic grade 2 or 3 in relation to papillomavirus infection. *New England Journal of Medicine, 327*, 1272–1278.

Kraemer, S. (2000). The fragile male. *British Medical Journal, 321,* 1609–1612.

Krahe, B. (1998). Sexual aggression among adolescents: Prevalence and predictors in a German sample. *Psychology of Women Quarterly, 22,* 537–554.

Kramer, P. D. (1997). *Should you leave?* New York: Simon & Schuster.

Krivacska, J. J. (1989). Child sexual abuse prevention programs: What school boards should know. American School Board *Journal, 176,* 35–37.

Krujiver, F. P., Zhou, J. N., Pool, C. W., Hofman, M. A., Gooren, L., & Swaab, D. E. (2000). Male-to-female transsexuals have female neuron numbers in a limbic nucleus. *Journal of Clinical Endocrinology, 85,* 2034–2040.

Kruks, G. (1991). Gay and lesbian homeless/street youth: Special issues and concerns. [Special issue]: *Journal of Adolescent Health, 12,* 515–518.

Kruse, R., Guttenbach, M., Schartman, B., Schubert, R., van der Ven, H., Schmid, M., & Propping, P. (1998). Genetic counseling in a patient with XXY/XXXY/XY mosak Klinefelter's syndrome: Estimates of sex chromosome aberration in sperm before intracutoplasmic sperm injection. *Fertility and Sterility, 69,* 482–485.

Ku, L. et al., (1998). Understanding changes in sexual activity among young metropolitan men: 1979–1995, *Family Planning Perspectives, 30(6),* 256–262.

Ku, L. C., Sonestein, F. L., & Pleck, J. H. (1994). The dynamics of young men's condom use during and across relationships. *Family Planning Perspectives, 26,* 246–251.

Kurdeck, L. A. (1988). Relationship quality of gay and lesbian cohabiting couples. *Journal of Homosexuality, 15,* 93–118.

Lacayo, R. (2000, Sept. 18). Washington to Hollywood: Oh, Behave. Movies, CDs and video games are already playing rough with kids. Should government elbow in? *Time Magazine,* from http://www.cnn.com/ALLPOLITICS/time/2000/09/25/hollywood.

Lalumiere, M. L., Blanchard, R., & Zucker, K. J. (2000). Sexual orientation and handedness in men and women: A meta-analysis. *Psychological Bulletin, 126,* 575–592.

Lalumiere, M. L., Chalmers, L. J., Quincey, V. L., & Seto, M. C. (1996). A test of mate deprivation hypothesis of sexual coercion. *Ethnology and Sociobiology, 17,* 299–318.

Lamanna, M. A., & Riedmann, A. (1997). *Marriages and families: Making choices in a diverse society* (6th ed.). Belmont, CA: Wadsworth.

Lambert, B. (1988, Sept. 20). AIDS among prostitutes not as prevalent as believed, studies show. *The New York Times,* p. B1.

Lammer, E., Chen, D., Hoar, R., Agnish, M., Benke, P., Curry, C., Fernhoff, P., Grix, A., Lott, L., Richard, J., & Sun, S. (1985). Retinoic acidembryopathy. *New England Journal of Medicine, 313,* 837–841.

Landry, D. J., Kaeser, L., & Richards, C. L. (1999). Abstinence promotion and the provision of information about contraception in public school district sexuality education policies, *Family Planning Perspectives, 31,* 280–286.

Landry, S., & Kennell, J. H. (1998). Support during labor improves mother-child interaction. Paper presented at the American Academy of Pediatrics, New Orleans.

Lane, F. S. (2000). *Obscene profits: The entrepreneurs of pornography in the cyber age.* New York: Routledge.

Lane, K. E. and Gwartney-Gibbs, P. A. (1985). Violence in the context of dating and sex. *Journal of Family Issues, 6,* 45–59.

Langevin, R., & Lang, R. A. (1987). The courtship disorders. In G. D. Wilson (Ed.), *Variant sexuality: Research and theory* (pp. 202–208). Baltimore, MD: The Johns Hopkins University Press.

Langevin, R., & Martin, M. (1975). Can erotic responses be classically conditioned? *Behavior Therapy, 6,* 350–355.

Langfeldt, T. (1982). Childhood masturbation. In L. L. Constantine & E. M. Martinson (Eds.), *Children and sex* (pp. 63–74). Boston: Little Brown.

Langlois, J. H., & Roggman, L. A. (1990). Attractive faces are only average. *Psychological Science, 1,* 115–121.

Langlois, J. J. (1986). From the eye of the beholder to behavioral reality: Development of social behaviors and social relations as a function of physical attractiveness. In C. P. Herman, M. P. Zanna & E. T. Higgins (Eds.), *Physical appearance, stigma and social behavior: The third Ontario symposium in personality and social psychology.* Hillsdale NJ: Erlbaum.

Lansky, D., Nathan, P. E., & Lawson, D. M. (1978). Blood alcohol discrimination by alcoholics: The role of internal and external cues. *Journal of Consulting and Clinical Psychology, 46,* 953–960.

Lapham, L. (1997, Aug.). In the garden of tabloid delight. *Harper's Magazine,* 35–39, 42–43.

Larimer, M. E., Lydun, A. R., Anderson, B. K., & Anderson, A. P. (1999). Male and female recipients of unwanted sexual contact in a college student sample: Prevalence rates, alcohol use, and depression symptoms. *Sex Roles, 40,* 295–308.

Laumann, E. O., Gagnon, J. H., Michael, R. T., & Michaels, S. (1994). *The social organization of sexuality: Sexual practices in the United States.* Chicago: University of Chicago Press.

Laumann, E. O., Masi, C. N., & Zuckerman, E. W. (1997). Circumcision in the United States: Prevalence, prophylactic effects and sexual practice. *Journal of the American Medical Association, 277,* 1052–1057.

Laumann, E. O., Paik, A., & Rosen, R. C. (1999). Sexual dysfunctions in the United States. *Journal of the American Medical Association, 281,* 537–544.

Lauresen, N., & Graves, Z. (1994). Pretended orgasm. *Medical Aspects of Human Sexuality, 19,* 74–81.

Laviola, M. (1989). Effects of older brother-younger sister incest: A review of four cases. *Journal of Family Violence, 4,* 259–274.

Lawson, A. (1988). *Adultery: An analysis of love and betrayal.* New York: Basic Books.

Lawson, A., & Samson, C. (1988). Age, gender and adultery. *British Journal of Sociology, 39,* 409–440.

Leary, W. (1990, Sept. 13). New focus on sperm brings fertility success. *The New York Times,* p. B11.

Lee, J. A. (1974). The style of loving. *Psychology Today, 8,* 43–51.

Lee, J. A. (1976). *The colors of love.* Englewood Cliffs, NJ: Prentice Hall.

Lee, J. A. (1988). Love-Styles. In R. Sternberg & M. Barnes (Eds.) *The psychology of love.* New Haven, CT: Yale University Press.

Lee, N. C., Ribin, G. L., & Borucki, R. (1988). The intrauterine device and pelvic inflammatory disease revisited: New results from the Women's Health Study. *Obstetrics and Gynecology, 72,* 1–6.

Leiblum, S., Bachman, G., Kemmann, E., Coburn, D., & Swartzman, L. (1983). Vaginal atrophy in the post-menopausal woman: The importance of sexual activity and hormones. *Journal of the American Medical Association, 249,* 2195–2198.

Leigh, B. (1989). Reasons for having and avoiding sex: Gender sexual orientation, and relationship to sexual behavior. *Journal of Sex Research, 26,* 199–208.

Leitenberg, H., & Henning, K. (1995). Sexual fantasy. *Psychological Bulletin, 117,* 469–496.

Leland, J. (1995, July 17). Bisexuality. *Newsweek,* 44–50.

Lennon, S. J., Johnson, K. K. P., & Schulz, T. L. (1999). Forging linkages between dress and the law, part I: Rape and sexual harassment. *Clothing and Textiles Research Journal, 17,* 144–156.

Lerner, H. (1997). *The dance of anger: A woman's guide to changing the patterns of intimate relationships.* New York: HarperCollins.

Lerner, M. J. (1980). *The belief in a just world: A fundamental delusion.* New York: Plenum Press.

Leroy, V., Newell, M. L., Dabis, F., Peckham, C., van de Perre, P., Bulterys, M., Kind, C., Simonds, R. J., Wiktor, S., & Msellati, P. (1998). International multicentre pooled analysis of late postnatal mother-to-child transmission of HIV-1 infection. Ghent International Working Group on Mother-to-Child Transmission of HIV. *Lancet, 352,* 597–600.

Lesserman, J., & Drossman, D. A. (1995). Sexual and physical abuse history and medical practice. *General Hospital Psychiatry, 17,* 71–74.

Lester, D., Leenaara, A., & Yang, C. (1992). Menninger's motives for suicide in the notes of completed and attempted suicides, *Psychological Reports, 70,* 369–370.

LeVay, S. (1991). A difference in hypothalamic structure between heterosexual and homosexual men. *Science, 253,* 1034–1037.

LeVay, S. (1993). *The sexual brain.* Cambridge, MA: MIT Press.

Levin, S., & Stava, L. (1987). Personality characteristics of sex offenders. *Archives of Sexual Behavior, 16,* 57–79.

Levine, N. E., & Silk, J. B.(1997). Why polyandry fails: Sources of instability in polyandrous marriages. *Current Anthropology, 38,* 375–398.

Levine, S. B. (1992). *Sexual life: A clinician's guide.* New York: Plenum.

Levinger, G. (1999). Duty toward whom? Reconsidering attractions and barriers as determinants of commitment in a relationship. In Adam, J. M., & Jones, W. H. (Eds.) *Handbook Of Interpersonal Commitment And Relationship Stability.* New York: Kluwer Academic Publishers.

Levitan, M., & Montagu, A. (1977). *A textbook of human genetics.* New York: Oxford University Press.

Levy, M. B., & Davis, K. E. (1988). Lovestyles and attachment styles compared: Their relations to each other and to various relationship characteristics. *Journal of Social and Personal Relationships, 5,* 439–471.

Lewes, K. (1988). *The psychoanalytic theory of male homosexuality.* New York: Simon & Schuster.

Lewin, R. (1988). *Bones of contention: Controversies in the search for human origins.* New York: Simon and Schuster.

Lewin, T. (1994, Oct. 6). Sex in America: Faithfulness in marriage thrives after all. *The New York Times,* pp. A1, A11.

Lewis, M. (1999). On the development of personality. In L. A. Pervin & O. P. John (Eds.), *Handbook of personality theory and research* (2nd ed., pp. 327–346). New York: Guilford.

Libby, R. W., Gray, L., & White, M. (1978). A test and reformulation of reference group and role correlates of premarital sexual permissiveness theory. *Journal of Marriage and the Family, 40,* 79–92.

Libman, E., Fitchen, C. S., & Brender, W. (1985). The role of therapeutic format in the treatment of sexual dysfunction: A review. *Clinical Psychology Review, 5,* 103–117.

Liebowitz, M. (1983). *The Chemistry of Love.* Boston: Little, Brown.

Lightfoot-Klein, H. (1989). *Prisoners of ritual: An odyssey into female genital circumcision in Africa.* Binghamton, NY: Haworth Press.

Lim, G., & Roloff, M. E. (1999). Attributing sexual consent. *Journal of Applied Communication Research, 27,* 1–23.

Lindegren, M. I., Byers, R. H., Thomas, P., Davis, S. F., Caldwell, B., Rogers, M., Swin, M., Ward, J. W., & Fleming, P. L. (1999). Trends in perinatal transmission of HIV/AIDS in the United States. *Journal of the American Medical Association, 282,* 531–538.

Lindsay, J. M. (2000). An ambiguous commitment: Moving in to a cohabiting relationship. *Journal of Family Studies, 6,* 120–134.

Linz, D. G., Donnerstein, E., & Penrod, S. (1988). Effects of long-term exposure to violent and sexually degrading depictions of women. *Journal of Personality and Social Psychology, 55,* 758–768.

Lipkin, M., & Lamb, G. (1982). The couvade syndrome: An epidemiological study. *Annals of Internal Medicine, 96,* 509–511.

Lisak, D., & Roth, S. (1988). Motivational factors in nonincarcerated sexually aggressive men. *Journal of Personality & Social Psychology, 55:* 795–802.

Litwin, M. S., Flanders, S. C., Pasta, D. J., Stoddard, M. L., Lubeck, D. P., & Henning, J. M. (1999). Sexual function and bother after radical prostatectomy or radiation for prostate cancer: Multivariate quality-of-life analysis from CaPSURE. Cancer of the Prostate Strategic Urologic Research Endeavor. *Urology, 54,* 503–508.

Logan, C. R. (1996). Homophobia? No, homoprejudice. *Journal of Homosexuality, 31,* 31–53.

Logan, T., & Leukenfeld, C. (2000). Sexual and drug use behavior among female crack users: A multi-site sample. *Drug and Alcohol Dependence, 58,* 237–245.

Loh, W. D. (1991). What has reform of rape legislation wrought? *Journal of Social Issues, 37,* 28–52.

LoPiccolo, J. (1980). Low sexual desire. In S. R. Leiblum & A. Pervin (Eds.), *Principles and practice of sex therapy.* (pp. 29–64). New York: Guilford Press.

LoPiccolo, J., & Friedman, J. (1988). Broad-spectrum treatment of low sexual desire: Integration of cognitive, behavioral, and systemic therapy. In S. Lieblum & R. Rosen (Eds.), *Sexual desire disorders.* New York: Guilford Press.

LoPiccolo, J., & Stock, W. E. (1986). Treatment of sexual dysfunction. *Journal of Consulting and Clinical Psychology, 54,* 158–167.

LoPresto, C. T., Sherman, M. F., & Sherman, N. C. (1985). The effects of a masturbation seminar on high school males' masturbation guilt, false beliefs, and behavior. *The Journal of Sex Research, 21:* 142–156.

Lottes, I., Weinberg, M., & Weller, I. (1993). Reactions to pornography on a college campus: For or against? *Sex Roles: A Journal of Research, 29,* 69–90.

Louderback, L. A., & Whitely, B. E. (1997). Perceived erotic value of homosexuality and sex-role attitudes as mediators of sex differences in heterosexual college students' attitudes toward lesbians and gay men. *Journal of Sex Research, 34,* 175–182.

Love, S. (1998). *Dr. Susan Love's hormone book: Making informed choices about menopause.* New York: Random House.

Loy, P., & Stewart, L. (1985). The extent of effects of sexual harassment on working women. *Sociological Focus, 17,* 31–43.

Lunde, J., Larsen, G. K., Fog, E., & Garde, K. (1991). Sexual desire, orgasm, and sexual fantasies: A study of 625 Danish women born in 1910, 1936, and 1958. *Journal of Sex Education and Therapy, 17,* 111–115.

Lundstrom, B., Pauly, J., & Walinder, J. (1984). Outcome of sex reassignment surgery. *Acta Psychiatric Scandinavica, 70,* 289–294.

Lupe, P. J., & Gross, T. L. (1986). Maternal upright posture and mobility in labor—A review. *Journal of Obstetrics and Gynecology, 67,* 727–734.

Lurito, J. T., Lowe, M. J., Sartorius, C., Mathews, V. P. (2000). Comparison of fMRI and intraoperative direct cortical stimulation in localization of receptive language areas. *Journal of Computer Assisted Tomography, 24:* 99–105.

Maccoby, E., & Jacklin, C. (1974). *The psychology of sex differences.* Palo Alto, CA: Stanford University Press.

Macfarlane, A. (1986). *Marriage and love in England: Modes of reproduction, 1300–1840.* New York: Oxford University Press.

MacFarlane, K., & Waterman, J. et. al.. (1986). *Sexual Abuse of Young Children: Evaluation and Treatment.* New York: Guilford Press.

MacKay, H. T., & MacKay, A.P. (1995). Abortion training in obstetrics and gynecology residency programs, *Family Planning Perspectives, 27,* 112–115.

MacLusky, N. J., & Naftolin, F. (1981). Sexual differentiation of the central nervous system. *Science, 211,* 1294–1303.

Madey, S. F., Simo, M., Dillworth, D., & Kemper, D., et al. (1996). They do get more attractive at closing time, but only when you are not in a relationship. *Basic & Applied Social Psychology, 18,* 387–393.

Magley, V. J., & Hulin, C. L. et al. (1999). "Outcomes of self-labeling sexual harassment." *Journal of Applied Psychology 84,* 390–402.

Mahoney, F., Shivley, M., & Traw, M. (1986). Sexual coercion and assault: Male socialization and female risk. *Sexual Coercion and Assault, 1,* 2–8.

Maines, R. P. (2000). *The technology of orgasm: "Hysteria," the vibrator and women's sexual satisfaction.* Baltimore: Johns Hopkins University Press.

Maier, J. S., & Malony, J. A. (1997). Nurse advocacy for selective versus routine episiotomy. *Journal of Obstetrical, Gynecological and Neonatal Nurses, 26,* 155–161.

Malamuth, N. (1981). Rape proclivity among males. *Journal of Social Issues, 37,* 138–157.

Malamuth, N. M., Sockloskie, R. J., Koss, M. P., & Tanaka, J. S. (1991). Characteristics of aggressors against women: Testing a model using a national sample of college students. *Journal of Consulting and Clinical Psychology, 59,* 670–681.

Malinowski, B. (1927). *Sex and repression in savage society.* Chicago: Meridian Books, New American Library.

Malinowski, B. (1929). *The sexual life of savages in northwestern Melanesia.* London: Routledge.

Mann, J., Sidman, J., & Starr, S. (1973). Evaluating social consequences of erotic films: An experimental approach. *Journal of Social Issues, 29,* 113–131.

Mann, K., Klingler, T., Roeschke, J., & Benkert, O. (1996). Therapeutic effect of yohimbine in organic and nonorganic erectile dysfunction. *European Neuropsychopharmacology, 6,* 14.

Manning, A. (1993, Dec. 23). Impotence common, increases with age. *USA Today*, p. 3D.

Manson, J. E., & Martin, K. A. (2001). Clinical practice: Postmenopausal hormone-replacement therapy. *New England Journal of Medicine, 345*, 34–40.

Marazziti, D., Dell'Osso, L., Gemignani, A., Ciapparelli, A., Presta, S., Nasso, E. D., Pfanner, C., & Cassano, G. B. (2001). Citalopram in refractory obsessive-compulsive disorders: An open study. *International Clinical Psychopharmacology, 6*, 215–219.

Marcus, E. (1992). *Making history: The struggle for gay and lesbian equal rights, 1945–1990.* New York: HarperCollins.

Marecek, J. (1987). Counseling adolescents with problem pregnancies. *American Psychologist, 42*, 89–93.

Marino, R., Browner, J., & Minichiello, V. (2000). An instrument to measure safer sex strategies used by male sex workers. *Archives of Sexual Behavior, 29*, 217–228.

Marks, A. (1999, Jan. 15). Activists unleash campaign to shut down sex tours. *The Christian Science Monitor*, p. 2.

Marks, G., Miller, N., & Maruyama, G. (1981). Effects of targets' physical attractiveness on assumption of similarity. *Journal of Personality and Social Psychology, 41*, 198–204.

Marshall, D. (1971). Sexual behavior on Mangaia. In D. Marshall & R. Suggs (Eds.), *Human sexual behavior: Variations in the ethnographic spectrum.* Englewood Cliffs, NJ: Prentice Hall.

Marshall, W. L. (1993). A revised approach to the treatment of men who sexually assault adult females. In G. Hall & C. Nagayama (Eds.), *Sexual aggression: Issues in etiology, assessment, and treatment* (pp. 143–165). Philadelphia: Taylor & Francis.

Marshall, W., & Barbaree, H. (1984). A behavioral view of rape. *International Journal of Law and Psychiatry, 7*, 51–77.

Marshall, W., Eccles, A., & Barbaree, H. (1991). The treatment of exhibitionists: A focus on sexual deviance versus cognitive and relationship features.

Behavior Research and Theory, 201, 129–135.

Marston, P. J., Hecht, M. L., Manke, M. L., McDaniel, S., & Reeder, H. (1998). The subjective experience of intimacy, passion, and commitment in heterosexual loving relationships. *Personal Relationships, 5*, 15–30.

Martin, L., & Kerwin, J. (1991). Self-reported rape proclivity is influenced by question context. Presented at the convention of the American Psychological Society, Washington, DC.

Martin, P., & Hummer, R. (1989). Fraternities and rape on campus. *Gender and Society, 3*, 457–473.

Martini (2001). *Fundamentals of Anatomy and Physiology* (5th ed.). Upper Saddle River, NJ: Prentice Hall.

Martinson, F. M. (1981). Eroticism in infancy and childhood. In L. L. Constantine & F. M. Martinson (Eds.), *Children and sex: New findings, new perspectives* (pp. 23–35). Boston: Little-Brown.

Marvasti, J. (1986). Incestuous mothers. *American Journal of Forensic Psychiatry, 8*, 63–69.

Marx, B. P., Gross, A. M., & Juergens, J. P. (1999). The effects of alcohol consumption and expectancies in an experimental date rape analogue. *Journal of Psychopathology and Behavioral Assessment, 19*, 281–302.

Marx, G. (2001). Quoted from http://www.quotegarden.com/sex.html

Maslow, A. (1968). *Toward a psychology of love.* Princeton, NJ: Van Nostrand.

Masters, W. H., & Johnson, V. E. (1966). *Human sexual response.* Boston: Little Brown.

Masters, W. H., & Johnson, V. E. (1979). *Homosexuality in perspective.* Boston: Little Brown.

Masters, W. H., Johnson, V. E., & Kolodny, R. C. (1992). *Human sexuality* (4th ed.). New York: HarperCollins.

Masters, W. H., Johnson, V. E., & Kolodny, R. C. (1994). *Heterosexuality.* New York: HarperCollins.

Matasushima, R., Shiomi, K., & Kuhlman, D. (2000). Shyness in self-

disclosure mediated by social skill. *Psychological Reports, 86*, 333–338.

Matchen, J., & DeSouza, E. (2000). The sexual harassment of faculty members by students. *Sex Roles, 19*, 281–302.

Matek, O. (1988). Obscene phone callers. *Journal of Social Work and Human Sexuality, 7*, 113–130.

Matteson, D. (1997). Bisexual and homosexual behavior and HIV risk among Chinese-, Filipino-, and Korean-American men. *Journal of Sex Research, 34*, 93–104.

Matthews, R. (1987). Preliminary typology of female sex offenders. Minneapolis, MN: PHASE and Genesis for Women.

Mawhinney, V. T. (1998). Behavioral sexual maladaption contagion in America: An applied theoretical analysis. *Behavior & Social Issues, 8*, 59–193.

Maxwell, K. (1997). Sex in the future: Virtuous and virtual? *The Futurists, 4*, 29.

Maypole, D. (1987). Sexual harassment at work: A review of research and theory, *Affilia, 2*, 24–38.

McAninch, J. (1990). Editorial comment on the report of the task force on circumcision. *Pediatrics, 84*, 667.

McCabe, M. (1987). Desired and experienced levels of premarital affection and sexual intercourse during dating. *Journal of Sex Research, 23*, 23–33.

McCabe, M. B. (1998). Childhood, adolescents and current psychological factors associated with sexual dysfunction. *Sexual and Marital Therapy, 9*, 267–276.

McCall, N. (1995). *Makes me wanna holler: A young black man in America.* New York: Vintage Books.

McCauley, C., & Swann, C. (1978). Male-female differences in sexual fantasy. *Journal of Research in Personality, 12*, 76–86.

McCaw, J. M., & Senn, C. (1998). Perception of cues in conflictual dating situations: A test of the miscommunication hypothesis. *Violence Against Women, 4*, 609–624.

McClanahan, S. F., McClelland, G. M., Abraham, K. M., & Teplin, L. A. (1999). Pathways into prostitution

among female jail detainees and their implications for mental health service. *Psychiatric Services, 50,* 606–613.

McConaghy, M. J. (1979). Gender performance and the genital basis of gender: Stages in the development of constancy of gender. *Child Development, 50,* 1223–1226.

McConaghy, N. (1997). Sexual and gender identity disorders. In S. M. Turner & M. Hersen (Eds.), *Adult psychopathology and diagnosis* (3rd ed., pp. 409–464). New York: John Wiley.

McElroy, W. (1998). Prostitutes, Anti-Pro Feminists and The Economic Associates of Whores, in James E. Elias, Vern L. Bullough, Veronica Elias, Gwen Brewer (eds.), *Prostitution: On whores, hustlers, and johns.* New York: Prometheus Books, pp. 333–344.

McEwen, B. S. (1981). Sexual differentiation of the brain. *Nature, 291,* 610.

McFarlane, J., & Williams, T. (1994). Placing premenstrual syndrome in perspective. *Psychology of Women Quarterly, 18,* 339–373.

McFarlane, M., Bull, S. S., & Rietmeijer, C. A. (2000). The Internet as a newly emerging risk environment for sexually transmitted diseases. *Journal of the American Medical Association, 284,* 443–446.

McGreal, C. (2001, Apr. 5). Mbeki's AIDS experts split over link to HIV: Report spares South African president from embarrassment. *The Guardian,* Foreign Pages, 14.

McKay, R., & Isacson, O. (2001, Feb. 16). *Reconstructing animals with stem cells.* Paper presented at the meeting of the American Association for the Advancement of Science. San Francisco.

McKibben, A., Proulx, J., & Lusignan, R. (1994). Relationships between conflict, affect and deviant sexual behaviors in rapists and pedophiles. *Behaviour Research & Therapy, 32,* 571–575.

McKinney, K., & Maroules, N. (1991). Sexual harassment. In E. Graverhold & M. Koralewski (Eds.), *Sexual coercion: A sourcebook on nature, causes and prevention.* Lexington, MA: Lexington Books.

McLahahan, S., & Sandefur, G. (1994). *Growing up with a single parent: What hurts, what helps.* Cambridge, MA: Harvard University Press.

McMahon, M. J., Luther, E. R., Bowes, W. A., & Olshan, A. F. (1996). Comparison of a trial of labor with an elective second cesarean section. *New England Journal of Medicine, 335,* 689–695.

Mead, M. (1928). *Coming of age in Samoa: A psychological study of primitive youth for western civilization.* New York: William Morrow.

Mead, M. (1935). *Sex and temperament in three primitive societies.* New York: William Morrow.

Mead, T. (1975). Coping with obscene phone calls. *Medical Aspects of Human Sexuality, 9,* 127–128.

Meana, M., Binik, Y. M., Khalife, S., & Cohen, D. (1997). Dyspareunia: Sexual dysfunction or pain syndrome? *Pain, 71*(3), 211–212.

Meeks, B. S., Hendrick, S. S., & Hendrick, C. (1998). Communication, love and relationship satisfaction. *Journal of Social and Personal Relationships, 15,* 755–773.

Meggitt, M. J. (1965). In P. Lawrence & M. J. Meggitt (Eds.), *Gods, ghosts and men in Melanesia.* New York: Oxford University Press.

Mehrabian, A., & Blum, J. S. (1997). Physical appearance, attractiveness, and the mediating role of emotions. *Current Psychology, 6,* 20–42.

Meigs, A. (1973). A Papuan perspective on pollution. *Man, 13,* 304–318.

Meissner, W. W. (1980). Psychoanalysis and sexual disorders. In B. E. Wolman & J. Money (Eds.), *Handbook of human sexuality.* Englewood Cliffs, NJ: Prentice Hall.

Melby, T. (2000). Two to tango: Why boys still don't know much about sex and new efforts to teach them. *Contemporary Sexuality, 34,* 1–4.

Mencken, H. L. (1920). A Book of Burlesques. Quoted from the Columbia Dictionary of Quotations, R. Andrews (Ed.). New York: Columbia University Press.

Menninger, K. (1938). *Man against himself.* New York: Harcourt Brace & World.

Menvielle, E. J. (1998). Gender identity disorder. *Journal of the American Academy of Child & Adolescent Psychiatry, 37,* 243–244.

Mercharnt, J. S., Oh, K., & Klerman, L. V. (1999). Douching: A problem for adolescent girls and young women. *Archives of Pediatric and Adolescent Medicine, 1530,* 834–837.

Merton, R. K. (1957). *Social theory and social structure* (rev. ed.). New York: Free Press of Glencoe.

Messenger, J. (1971). Sex and repression in an Irish folk community. In D. Marshall & R. Suggs (Eds.), *Human sexual behavior: Variations in the ethnographic spectrum.* Englewood Cliffs, NJ: Prentice Hall.

Meuwissen, I., & Over, R. (1991). Multidimensionality of the content of female sexual fantasy. *Behavior Research and Therapy, 29,* 179–189.

Meuwissen, I., & Over, R. (1992). Sexual arousal, across phases of the human menstrual cycle. *Archives of Sexual Behavior, 21,* 101–119.

Meyer, C. B., & Taylor, S. E. (1986). Adjustment to rape. *Journal of Personality & Social Psychology, 50,* 1226–1234.

Meyer, R. G., Landis, E. R., & Hays, J. R. (1988). *Law for psychotherapists.* London: W. W. Norton.

Meyer-Bahlburg, H., Ehrhardt, A., Rosen, L., Gruen, R., Veridiano, N., Vann, F., & Neuwalder, H. (1995). Prenatal estrogen and the development of homosexual orientation. *Developmental Psychology, 31,* 12–21.

Michael, R. T., Gagnon, E. O., & Kolata, G. (1994). *Sex in America.* Boston: Little Brown.

Michener, W., Rozin, P., Freeman, E., & Gale, L. (1999). The role of low progesterone and tension as triggers of premenstrual chocolate and sweet cravings: Some negative experimental evidence. *Physiology and Behavior, 67,* 417–420.

Milhausen, R. R., & Herold, E. S. (1999). Does the sexual double standard still

exist? Perceptions of university students. *Journal of Sex Research, 36,* 361–368.

Miller, B. A., Kolonel, L. N., Bernstein, L., Young, Jr., J. L., Swanson, G. N., West, D., Key, C. R., Liff, J. M., Glover, C. S., Alexander, G. A. et al. (Eds.). (1996). Racial/ethnic patterns of cancer in the United States 1988–1992 (NIH Publication No. 96-4104). Bethesda, MD: National Cancer Institute.

Miller, B. C., & Moore, K. A. (1990). Adolescent sexual behavior, pregnancy, and parenting: Research through the 1980s. *Journal of Marriage and the Family, 52,* 1025–1044.

Miller, K. S., Forehand, R., & Kotchick, B. A. (1999). Adolescent sexual behavior in two ethnic minority samples: The role of family variables. *Journal of Marriage and the Family, 61,* 85–98.

Miller, L. C., & Fishkin, S. A. (1997). On the dynamics of human bonding and reproductive success: Seeking windows on the adapted-for-human-environmental interface. In J. A. Simpson, D. T. Kenrick (Eds.), *Evolutionary social psychology* (pp. 197–236). Hillsdale, NJ: Erlbaum.

Miller, L. J. (Ed.). (1999) *Postpartum mood disorders.* Washington, DC: Americn Psychiatric Press.

Miller, N. S., & Gold, M. S. (1988). The human sexual response and alcohol and drugs. *Journal of Substance Abuse Treatment 5,* 171–177.

Mills, J. L., & England, L. (2001). Food fortification to prevent neural tube defects. *Journal of the American Medical Association, 285,* 3022.

Milroy C. (1995), The epidemiology of homicide-suicide (dyadic death). *Forensic Science International 71,* 117–122.

Minai, N. (1981). Women in Islam: Tradition, transition in the Middle East. New York: Seaview Books.

Miner, M. H., & Dwyer, S. M. (1997). The psychosocial development of sex offenders: Differences between exhibitionists, child molesters and incest offenders. *International Journal of Of-* *fender Theory and Comparative Criminology, 41,* 36–41.

Minton, J., Solomon, L. Z., Stokes, M., Charash, M., & Kendzior, J. (1999). Attitudes toward being female viewed over time. *Journal of Social Behavior and Personality, 14,* 207–220.

Minturn, L., Grosse, M., & Haider, S. (1969). Cultural patterning of sexual beliefs and behaviors. *Ethnology, 8,* 301–318.

Miotti, P. G., Taha, E., Taha, T., Kumwenda, R., Broodhead, L., Mtimavalve, L., van der Hoeven, J., Chiphangwi, G., Liomba, R. (1999). HIV transmission through breastfeeding. *Journal of the American Medical Association, 282,* 744–749.

Miracle, A. W., & Miracle, T. S. (2001). Sexuality in late adulthood. In B. R. Bonder & M. B. Wagner (Eds.), *Functional performance in older adults* (2nd ed., pp. 218–233). Philadelphia: F. A. Davis.

Mirande, A. (1968). Reference group theory in adolescent sexual behavior. *Journal of Marriage and the Family, 30,* 572–577.

Mishell, D. (1991). Long-acting contraceptive steroids: Postcoital contraceptives and antiprogestins. In D. R. Misell, V. Davaian, & R. Lobo, (Eds.), *Infertility, contraception and reproductive endocrinology,* (3rd ed., pp. 872–894). Boston: Blackwell Scientific Publication.

Mishell, D. (1996). Pharmacokinetics of depot medroxyprogesterone acetate contraception. *Reproductive Medicine, 41,* 381–390.

Mishell, D. R., Stenchever, M. A., Herbst, A. L., Droegermueller, W., Gunter, A. (Eds.). (1997). *Comprehensive gynecology.* St. Louis: Mosby/Year Book.

Mitchell, D., Hirschman, R., & Hall, G. C. (1999). Attribution of victim responsibility, pleasure and trauma in male rape. *Journal of Sex Research, 36,* 369–372.

Mohr, D., & Beutler, L. (1990). Erectile dysfunction: A review of diagnostic and treatment procedures. *Clinical Psychology Review, 10,* 123–150.

Moir, A., & Jessel, D. (1991). *Brain Sex.* New York: Carol Publishing Group.

Mok, T. (1998). Getting the message: Media imagers and stereotypes and their effect on Asian Americans. *Cultural Diversity and Ethnic Minority Psychology, 4,* 185–202.

Møller, A., & Thornhill, R. (1998). Developmental stability and sexual selection: A meta-analysis. *American Naturalist, 151,* 174–192.

Møller, A. P. (1988). Female choice selects for male sexual ornaments in the monogamous swallow. *Nature, 332,* 640–642.

Moller, L. C., & Serbin, L. A. (1996). Antecedents of toddler sex segregation: Cognitive consonance, gender typed toy preferences and behavioral compatibility. *Sex Roles, 35,* 445–460.

Money, J. (1975). Ablatiopenis: Normal male infant sex–reassignment as a girl. *Archives of Sexual Behavior, 4,* 65–72.

Money, J. (1980). *Love and love sickness: The science of sex, gender differences and pair-bonding.* Baltimore: Johns Hopkins University Press.

Money, J. (1981). Paraphilias: Phyletic origins of erotosexual dysfunction. *International Journal of Mental Health, 10,* 75–109.

Money, J. (1982). *Still more lovemaps to keep loving.* Baltimore: Johns Hopkins University Press.

Money, J. (1986). *Lovemaps: Clinical concepts of sexual/erotic health and pathology, paraphilias and gender transposition in childhood, adolescence, and maturity.* New York: Irvington Press.

Money, J., & Ehrhardt, A. (1968). Prenatal hormonal exposure: Possible effects on behavior in man. In R. P. Michael (Ed.), *Endocrinology and human behaviour* (pp. 32–48). London: Oxford University Press.

Money, J., & Lamacz, M. (1989). *Outcome of seven cases in pediatric sexology.* Amherst, NY: Prometheus Books.

Monga, T. N. (1993). Sexuality post stroke. In R. Teasell (Ed.)., *Long term consequences of stroke* (pp. 225–236). Philadelphia: Hanley & Belfus.

Monga, T. N., & Osterman, H. J. (1995). Sexuality and sexual adjustment in stroke patients. In T. N. Monga (Ed.), *Sexuality and disability* (pp. 345–360). Philadelphia: Hanley & Belfus.

Mongeau, D. A., & Schulz, B. E. (1997). "What he doesn't know won't hurt him" (or me): Verbal responses and attributions following sexual infidelities. *Communications Reports, 10,* 143–152.

Montagu, A. (1974). *Coming into being among the Australian Aborigines: A study of the procreative beliefs of the Australian Aborigines.* New York: Routledge.

Moore, N. B., & Davidson, K. (1999). Parents as first information sources: Do they make a difference in daughters' sexual attitudes and behavior? *Journal of Sex Education and Therapy, 24,* 155–163.

Moore, T. (1994). *Soul mates: Honoring the mysteries of love and relationships.* New York: HarperCollins.

Morf, C. C., & Rhodewalt, F. (1993). Narcissism and self-evaluation maintenance: Explorations in object relations. *Personality and Social Psychology Bulletin, 19,* 668–676.

Morgan, C. S. (1980). Female and male attitudes toward life: Implications for theories of mental health. *Sex Roles, 6,* 367–389.

Morgan, R. (Ed.). (1974). *Sisterhood is powerful.* New York: Random House.

Morgan, R. (1994). *The anatomy of freedom: Feminism in four dimensions.* New York: W. W. Norton.

Morokoff, P. J. (1985). Effects of sex guilt, repression, sexual "arousability," and sexual experience on female sexual arousal during erotica and fantasy. *Journal of Personality & Social Psychology, 49,* 177–187.

Morokoff, P. J. (1993). Female sexual arousal disorder. In W. Donohue & J. H. Greer (Eds.), *Handbook of sexual dysfunction assessment and treatment* (pp. 157–199). Boston: Allyn & Bacon.

Morrell, M., Dixen, J., Carter, C., & Davidson, J. (1984). The influence of age and cycling status on sexual arousality in women. *American Journal of Obstetrics and Gynecology, 148,* 66–67.

Morrell, V. (1995). Zeroing in on how hormones affect the immune system. *Science, 269,* 773–775.

Morris, D. (1971). *Intimate Behavior.* New York: Random House.

Mortola, J. F. (1998). Premenstrual syndrome: Pathophysiologic considerations. *New England Journal of Medicine, 338,* 256–257.

Moser, C. (1988). Sadomasochism. *Journal of Social World and Human Sexuality, 7,* 43–56.

Muehlenhard, C. (1988). Misinterpreting dating behaviors and the risk of date rape. *Journal of Social and Clinical Psychology, 6,* 20–37.

Muehlenhard, C., & Falcon, P. (1990). Men's heterosexual skill and attitude towards women as predictors of verbal coercion and forcible rape. *Sex Roles, 23,* 241–259.

Muehlenhard, C., & Hollenbaugh, L. (1989). Do women sometimes say no when they mean yes? The prevalence and correlates of women's token resistance to sex. *Journal of Personality and Social Psychology, 54,* 872–879.

Muehlenhard, C., & Linton, M. (1987). Date rape and sexual aggression in dating situations: Incidence and risk factors. *Journal of Consulting Psychology, 34,* 186–196.

Muehlenhard, C., & McCoy, M. L. (1991). Double standard/double bind: The sexual double standard and women's communication about sex. *Psychology of Women Quarterly, 15,* 447–461.

Muehlenhard, C., Powch, I., Phelps, J., & Giusti, L. (1992). Definitions of rape: Scientific and political implications. *Journal of Social Issues, 48,* 23–44.

Mullen, P. E., & Pathe, M. (1994). The pathological extensions of love. *British Journal of Psychiatry, 165,* 614–623.

Mumford, J. (1993). *Ecstasy through Tantra.* St. Paul, MN: Llewellyn Publications.

Munjack, D. J., & Kanno, P. H. (1979). Retarded ejaculation: A review. *Archives of Sexual Behavior, 8,* 139–150.

Murphy, S. (1992). *A delicate dance.* New York: Crossroad.

Murray, F. S., & Beran, L. C. (1958). A survey of nuisance calls received by males and females. *Psychological Records, 18,* 107–109.

Murren, S. K., Perot, A., & Byrne, D. (1989). Coping with unwanted sexual activity: Normative responses, situational determinants, and individual differences. *Journal of Sex Research, 26:* 85–106.

Murstein, B. I., & Tuerkheim, A. (1998). Gender differences in love, sex and motivation for sex. *Psychological Reports, 82,* 425–450.

Murstein, B. J., & Christy, P. (1976). Physical attractiveness and marital adjustment in middle aged couples. *Journal of Personality and Social Psychology, 34,* 537–542.

Muscarella, F. (2000). The evolution of homoerotic behavior in humans. *Journal of Homosexuality, 40,* 51–77.

Myers, S. M. (1997). Marital uncertainty and childbearing. *Social Forces, 75,* 1271–1289.

Nachtigall, R. (1991, Mar.). Assessing fecundity after age forty. *Contemporary OB/GYN,* 11–33.

Nadler, S. (1997). Arthritis and other connective tissue diseases. In M. L. Sipski & C. J. Alexander (Eds.), *Sexual function in people with disability and chronic illness* (pp. 261–278). Gaithersburg, MD: Aspen Books.

Nanda, S. (1994). Hijras: An alternative sex and gender role in India. In G. Herdt (Ed.), *Third sex, third gender: Beyond sexual dimorphism in culture and history* (pp. 373–417). New York: Zone Books.

National Abortion and Reproductive Rights Action League (NARAL). (1999). From http://www.naral.org/publications/facts/clinic.html.

National Abortion and Reproductive Rights Action League (NARAL), (2000a). From http://www.NARAL.org

National Abortion and Reproductive Rights Action League (NARAL), (2000b). From http://www.NARAL.org

National Abortion Rights Action League. (2001). Supreme court decisions concerning reproductive rights. From http://www.naral.org/mediaresources/fact/supremecourt.html

National Abortion Rights Action League. (2001). Who decides? A state-by-state review of abortion and reproductive rights (10th ed.). From http://www.naral.org/mediaresources/publications/2001/whod.html

National Cancer Institute. (2001). Cancer facts: Lifetime probability of breast cancer in American women. From http://cis.nci.nih.gov/fact/5-6.html

National Center for Health Statistics (1997). *Multiple births multiply during past two decades.* Centers for Disease Control. From http://www.cdc.gov/nchswww/releases/97facts/97/sheets

National Center for Health Statistics (2000). Fertility/infertility. (Vital and Health Statistics, Series 23, No. 19). From http://www.cdc.gov/nchs.fastats/fertile.

National Institute of Allergy and Infectious Diseases (1999). *Fact sheet: HIV/AIDS statistics.* Bethesda, MD: National Institutes of Health.

National Institute of Allergy and Infectious Diseases (2000a). *Fact sheet: Chlamydial infection.* Bethesda, MD: National Institutes of Health.

National Institute of Allergy and Infectious Diseases. (2000b). *Fact sheet: Human Papilloma virus and genital warts.* Bethesda, MD: National Institutes of Health.

National Institute of Allergy and Infectious Diseases (2000c). *Fact sheet: Pelvic inflammatory disease.* Bethesda, MD: National Institutes of Health.

National Institute of Allergy and Infectious Diseases (2000d). *Fact sheet: Vaginitis due to vaginal infections.* Bethesda, MD: National Institutes of Health.

National Institute of Allergy and Infectious Diseases. (2000e). General Information: HIV-Perinatal transmission. Bethesda, MD: National Institutes of Health.

National Institutes of Health. (1993, March 19). NIH guidelines for the support and conduct of therapeutic human fetal tissue transplantation. NIH Guide, 22.

National Opinion Research Center (1994). Queer counts: the sociological construction of homosexuality via survey research. Chicago: National Opinion Research Center.

Nersessian, E. (1998). A cat as fetish: A contribution to the theory of fetishism. *International Journal of Psychoanalysis, 79,* 713–725.

Nevid, J. (1984). Sex differences in factors of romantic attraction. *Sex Roles, 11,* 401–411.

Newcomb, M. D., & Bentler, P. M. (1980). Assessment of personality and demographic aspects of cohabitation. *Journal of Personality Assessment, 44,* 11–24.

Newcomb, T. M. (1961). *The acquaintance process.* New York: Holt, Rinehart & Winston.

Newcomer, S., & Udry, J. (1985). Oral sex in an adolescent population. *Archives of Sexual Behavior, 14,* 41–46.

New Mexico AIDS InfoNet (1999). T-cell tests fact sheet no. 412. From http://aegis.org/pubs/nmap/1999/412

Newton, N. (1978). The role of the oxytocin reflexes in three interpersonal reproductive acts: Coitus, birth and breast-feeding. In L. Carenza, P. Pancheri, & L. Zichella (Eds.), *Clinical psychoneuroendocrinology in reproduction* (pp. 411–418). New York: Academic Press.

Ng, M. (1999). Vaginismus: A disease, symptom or culture-bound syndrome? *Sexual & Marital Therapy, 14*(1), 9–13.

Nias, D. K. B. (1977). Martial choice: Matching of complementation. In M. Cook & G. Wilson (Eds.), *Love and Attraction.* Oxford: Pergamon Press.

Nock, S. (1995). A comparison of marriage and cohabiting relationships. *Journal of Family Issues, 16,* 53–76.

Norberg, K. (1993). The Libertine whore: Prostitution in French pornography from Margot to Juliette. In L. Hunt (Ed.), *The invention of pornography* (pp. 225–252). New York.

Norcross, J. C., & Newman, C. F. (1992). Psychotherapy integration: Setting the context. In J. C. Norcross (Ed.), *Handbook of psychotherapy integration.* New York: Basic Books.

Notzon, F. S., Placek, P. J., & Taffel, S. M. (1987). Comparison of national cesarean section rates. *New England Journal of Medicine, 316,* 386–389.

Nugent, R., & Gramick, T. (1989). Homosexuality: Protestant, Catholic and Jewish issues: A fishbone tale. *Journal of Homosexuality, 18,* 200–218.

Nurmi, J. E., Toivonen, S., Salmela-Aro, K., & Aronen, S. (1997). Social strategies and loneliness. *Journal of Social Psychology, 137,* 764–777.

Nurnberg, H. G., Lauriello, J., Hensley, P. L., Parker, L. M., & Keith, S. J. (1999). Sildenafil for iatrogenic serotonergic antidepressant medication-induced sexual dysfunction in 4 patients. *Journal of Clinical Psychiatry, 60,* 792.

O'Donohue, W., Dopke, C. A., & Swingen, D. N. (1997). Psychotherapy for female sexual dysfunction: A review. *Clinical Psychology Review, 17*(5), 537–566.

O'Donohue, W. T., Swingen, D. N., Dopke, C. A., & Regev., L. B. (1999, Aug.). Psychotherapy for male sexual dysfunction: A review. *Clinical Psychology Review, 19,* 591–630.

Office of Technology Assessment (1988). *Infertility: Medical and social choices.* Washington, DC: Government Printing Office.

Offir, J. T., Fisher, J. D., Williams, S. S., & Fisher, W. A. (1993). Reasons for inconsistent: AIDS-preventive behaviors among gay men. *The Journal of Sex Research, 30,* 62.

Okami, P., Olmstead, R., & Abramson, P. (1990). Sexual experiences in early

childhood: 18-year longitudinal data from the UCLA Family Lifestyles Project. *Journal of Sex Research, 34,* 339–347.

Oktay, K., & Karlikaya, G. (2000). Ovarian function after transplantation of frozen, banked autologous ovarian tissue. *New England Journal of Medicine, 342,* 1919.

Olasov, B., & Jackson, J. (1987). Effects of expectancies on women's reports of mood during the menstrual cycle. *Psychosomatic Medicine, 49,* 65–78.

O'Laughlin, E. M., & Brubaker, B. S. (1998). Use of landmarks in cognitive mapping: Gender differences in self report versus performance. *Personality and Individual Differences, 24,* 595–601.

Oliver, M. B., & Hyde, J. S. (1993). Gender differences in sexuality: A meta-analysis. *Psychological Bulletin, 114,* 29–51.

O'Neill, N., & O'Neill, G. (1972). *Open marriage: A new lifestyle for couples.* New York: M. Evans.

Onishi, N. (2001, May 3). Sio journal: Oh no! My little brother has just had a baby! *The New York Times,* p. A4.

Osman, S. L., & Davis, C. M. (1997). Predicting perceptions of date rape based on individual beliefs and female alcohol consumption. *Journal of College Student Development, 40,* 701–709.

O'Sullivan, L. F., Byers, E. S., Finkelman, L. (1998). A comparison of male and female gender differences in rape reporting. *Sex Roles, 40,* 11–12.

Ouellette, E. M., Rossett, H. L., Rosman, N. P., & Weiner, L. (1977). Adverse effects on offspring of maternal alcohol abuse during pregnancy. *New England Journal of Medicine, 297,* 529–530.

Padgett, V. R., Brislin-Slutz, J. A., & Neal, J. A. (1989). Pornography, erotica, and attitudes toward women: The effects of repeated exposure. *Journal of Sex Research, 26,* 479–491.

Palmer, C. T. (1988). Twelve reasons why rape is not sexually motivated: A skeptical examination. *Journal of Sex Research, 25,* 512–530.

Parker, S., Nichter, M., Nuckovic, N., Sims, C., & Ritenbaugh, C. (1995). Body image and weight concerns among African American and white adolescent females: Differences that make a difference. *Human Organization, 54,* 103–114.

Parrott, A., & Bechhofer, L. (1991). *Acquaintance rape: The hidden crime.* New York: Wiley and Sons.

Parrott, W. G., & Smith, R. H. (1993). Distinguishing the experiences of envy and jealousy. *Journal of Personality & Social Psychology, 64,* 906–920.

Parsons, N. K., Richards, R. C., & Kanter, G. D. (1990). Validation of a scale to measure reasoning about abortion. *Journal of Counseling Psychology, 37,* 107–112.

Partnership for Women's Health. (1999, May 18). Cited in K. Painter. How to get back to good sex if Viagra lets you down. *USA Today,* p. A4.

Patterson, C. J. (1992). Children of lesbian and gay parents. *Child Development, 63,* 1025–1042.

Pauker, S. P., & Pauker, S. G. (1994). Prenatal diagnosis: Why is 35 a magic number? *New England Journal of Medicine, 330,* 1151–1157.

Paul, M. (1999). *A Clinician's Guide to Medical and Surgical Abortion.* New York: Churchill Livingstone.

Pauly, J. (1974). Female transsexualism: Part II. *Archives of Sexual Behavior, 3,* 509–526.

Pedersen, C. A. et al. (1992). *Oxytocin in maternal, sexual, and social behaviors.* New York: New York Academy of Science.

Penton-Voak, I. S., Perrett, D. I., Castles, D. L., Kobayashi, T., Burth, D. M., Murray, L. K., & Minamisawa, R. (1999). Menstrual cycle alters face preference. *Nature, 399,* 741–742.

Peplau, L., Garnets, L., Spalding, L., Conley, T., & Veniegas, R. (1998). A critique of Bem's "exotic becomes erotic" theory of sexual orientation. *Psychological Review, 128,* 140–156.

Perlman, D., & Oskamp, S. (1971). The effects of picture context and exposure frequency on evaluations of Negroes and whites. *Journal of Experimental Social Psychology, 7,* 503–514.

Perloff, L. S., & Fetzer, B. K. (1986). Self-other judgments and perceived vulnerability to victimization. *Journal of Personality and Social Psychology, 50,* 502–510.

Perper, T. (1985). *Sex signals: The biology of love.* Philadelphia: ISI Press.

Petersen, J. R. (1999). *The century of sex: Playboy's history of the sexual revolution, 1900–1999.* New York: Grove/Atlantic.

Peterson, J., & Marin, G. (1988). Issues in the prevention of AIDS among black and hispanic gay men. *American Psychologist, 43,* 871–877.

Petit, C. (1994, May 17). Treatment found for premature ejaculation. *The San Francisco Chronicle,* p. A4.

Pettijohn, T. F. (1996). Perceived happiness of college students measured by Maslow's hierarchy of needs. *Psychological Reports, 79,* 759–762.

Pierson, E. C., & D'Antonio, W. V. (1976). *Female and male: Dimensions of human sexuality.* Philadelphia: Lippincott.

Pillard, R. C., & Weinrich, J. D. (1986). Evidence of familial nature of male homosexuality. *Archives of Sexual Behavior, 43,* 808–812.

Pinhas, L., Toner, B. B., Ali, A., Garfinkel, D. E., & Stuckless, M. (1999). The effects of the ideal of female beauty on mood and body satisfaction. *International Journal of Eating Disorder, 25,* 223–225.

Pipher, M. (1994). *Reviving Ophelia: Saving the selves of adolescent girls.* New York: Putnam.

Pithers, W. D. (1993). Treatment of rapists: Reinterpretation of early outcome data and exploratory constructs to enhance therapeutic efficacy. In G. Hall & C. Nagayama (Eds.), *Sexual aggression: Issues in etiology, assessment, and treatment* (pp. 167–196). Philadelphia: Taylor & Francis.

Piver, M. S., Goldberg, J. M., Tsukada, Y., Mettling, C. J., Jishi, M. F., & Nataraian, N. (1996). Characteristics of familial ovarian cancer: A report of

the first 1,000 families in the Gilda Radner Familial Ovarian Cancer Registry. *European Journal of Gynaecological Oncology, 17,* 169–176.

Platzke, A. C., Lew C. D., & Steward, D. (1980). Drug "administration" via breast milk. *Hospital Practice,* Sept., 111–122.

Pluhar, E., Frongillo, E. A., Stycos, J. M., & Dempster-McClain, D. (1998). Understanding the relationship between religion and the sexual attitudes and behaviors of college students. *Journal of Sex Education and Therapy, 23,* 288–296.

Pogun, S. (1997). Sex differences in cognition and addiction. *International Journal of Psychophysiology, 25,* 60.

Polivy, J., Garner, D. M., & Garfinkel, P. E. (1986). Causes and consequences of the current preference for thin female physiques. In C. P. Herman, M. P. Zanna, & E. T. Higgins (Eds.), *Physical appearances, stigma, and social behavior: The Third Ontario Symposium in personality and social psychology.* (pp. 89–112). Hillsdale, NJ: Erlbaum.

Pollak, M., Beamer, W., & Zhany, J. C. (1998–1999). Insulin-like growth factors and prostate cancers. *Cancer Metastasis Review, 17,* 383–390.

Pook, M., Roehrle, B., & Krause, W. (1999). Individual prognosis for changes in sperm quality on the basis of perceived stress. *Psychotherapy and Psychosomatics, 68,* 95–101.

Porges, S. W. (1997). Love: An emergent property of the mammalian automatic nervous system. *Psychoneuroendocrinology, 23,* 837–861.

Posner, R. A. (1992). *Sex and reason.* Cambridge, MA: Harvard University Press.

Potter, K., Martin, J., & Romans, S. (1999). Early developmental experiences of female sex workers: A comparative study. *Australian & New Zealand Journal of Psychiatry, 33,* 935–940.

Poussaint, A. (1990, Sept.). An honest look at black gays and lesbians. *Ebony,* 124–126, 130–131.

Powell v. State of Georgia 510 S. E. 2d 18 (1998).

Powell, E. (1991). *Talking back to sexual pressure.* Minneapolis: CompCare Publishers.

Prescott, J. (1975). Relationship between the treatment of infants and the level of adult violence in 49 cultures. *The Bulletin of the Atomic Scientist,* Nov., 10–20.

Price, S. J., & Mckenry, P. C. (1988). *Divorce* (Family Studies Text Series, Vol 9.). Thousand Oaks, CA: Sage Publications.

Prior, J., & Vigna, Y. (1991). Ovulation disturbances and exercise training. *Clinical Obstetrics and Gynecology, 24,* 180–190.

Pritchard, J. A., MacDonald, P. C., & Grant, N. E. (1985). *Williams obstetrics* (17th ed.). Norwalk, CT: Appleton Century-Crofts.

Proctor, E. B., Wagner, N. N., & Butler, J. C. (1974). The differentiation of male and female orgasm: An experimental study. In N. N. Wagner (Ed.), *Perspectives of Human Sexuality* (pp. 115–132). New York: Behavioral Publications.

Quinsey, V., & Upfold, D. (1985). Rape completion and victim injury as a function of female resistance strategy. *Canadian Journal of Behavior Science, 17,* 40–50.

Rachman, S., & Hodgon, R. J. (1968). Experimentally-Induced "Sexual Fetishism": Replication And Development. *Psychological Record, 18,* 25–27.

Raffaelli, M., Bogenschneider, K., & Flood, M. F. (1998). Parent-teacher communication about sexual topics. *Journal of Family Issues, 19,* 315–333.

Rafjer, J., Aronson, W., Bush, P., Dorey, F., & Ignarro, L. (1992). Nitric oxide as a mediator of relaxation of the corpus cavernosum in response to nonadrenergic, noncholinergic neurotransmission. *The New England Journal of Medicine, 326,* 90–94.

Rahman, Q., & Wilson, G. D. (2001). The psychobiology of sexual orientation. Manuscript submitted for publication. Institute of Psychiatry, London.

Ramm, D. R. (1996). Clinically formulated principles of morality. *New Ideas in Psychology, 14,* 237–256.

Rawson, P. (1973). *Tantra: The Indian cult of ecstasy.* New York: Avon Books.

Reardon, D. C. (1996). *Making abortion rare: A healing strategy for a divided nation.* San Francisco: Acorn books.

Reed, D. (1998). In J. S. Greenberg, C. E. Bruess, & D. W. Haffner (Eds.), *Exploring the dimensions of human sexuality.* Sudbury, MA: Jones and Bartlett.

Reeve, C. (1998). *Still me.* New York: Random House.

Regan, P. C. (1996). Rhythms of desire: The association between menstrual cycle phase and female sexual drive. *The Canadian Journal of Human Sexuality, 5,* 145–156.

Regan, P. (1998). Of lust and love: Beliefs about the role of sexual desire in romantic relationships. *Personal Relationships, 5,* 139–157.

Regan, P., & Berscheid, E. (1997). Characteristics desired in potential sexual and marital partners. *Journal of Psychology and Human Sexuality, 9,* 25–37.

Rehman, J., Lazer, S., Benet, A. E., Schaefer, L. C., & Meiman, A. (1999). The reported sex and surgery satisfaction of 28 postoperative male-to-female transsexual patients. *Archives of Sexual Behavior, 28,* 71–89.

Reichard, G. A. (1950). *Navaho religion: A study of symbolism* (Bollingen Series XVIII). Princeton, NJ: Princeton University Press.

Reik, T. (1944). *A Psychoanalyst Looks at Love.* New York: Farrar & Rinehart.

Reinisch, J. M. (1991). *The Kinsey Institute new report on sex: What you must know to be sexually literate.* New York: St. Martin's Press.

Reinisch, J. M., Beasley, R., & Kent, D. (Eds.). (1990). *The Kinsey Institute new report on sex.* New York: St. Martin's Press.

Reiss, I. (1967). *The social context of sexual permissiveness.* New York: Holt, Rinehart, & Winston.

Reiss, I. (1986). *Journey into sexuality: An exploratory voyage.* Englewood Cliffs, NJ: Prentice Hall.

Reissing, E. D., Binik, Y. M., & Khalife, S. (1999). Does vaginismus exist? A critical review of the literature. *Jour-*

nal of Nervous & Mental Disease, 187(5), 261–274.

Remafedi, G. (1996). The relationship between suicide risk and sexual orientation: Results of a population-based study. Journal of Adolescent Health, 18, 123.

Remafedi, G., Resnick, M., Blum, R., & Harris, L. (1992). Demography of sexual orientation in adolescents. Pediatrics, 89, 714–721.

Renzetti, C. M., & Curran, D. J. (1989). Women, men, and society: The sociology of gender. Boston: Allyn & Bacon.

Resick, P. A., & Schicke, M. K. (1990). Treating symptoms in adult victims of sexual assault. Journal of Interpersonal Violence, 5, 488–506.

Resnick, M. (1999). Cited in L. Fraser. Why more men are going under the knife. The Ottawa Citizen. Sept. 6, A10.

Rhodes, G., Proffitt, F., Grady, J. M., & Sumich, A. (1998). Facial symmetry and the perception of beauty. Psychonomic Bulletin & Review, 5, 659–669.

Rice, G., Anderson, C., Risch, N., & Ebers, G. (1999). Male homosexuality: Absence of linkage to microsatellite markers at Xq28. Science, 284, 665–667.

Richards, D. E. (1992). Sexuality and study commissions in churches and synagogues. SIECUS Reports, April/May, 16–17.

Richardson, J. P., & Lazur, A. (1995). Sexuality and aging. Urologic Clinics of North America, 22, 711–726.

Riddle, J. M. (1997). Eve's herbs: A History of contraception and abortion in the west. Cambridge: Harvard University Press.

Ridley, M. (1994). The red queen. New York: MacMillan Publishing.

Riehl-Emde, A. (1997). Is his marriage also her marriage?—An old question in a new light. System Familie, 12, 132–138.

Rind, B., Tromovitch, P., & Bauseman, R. (1998). A meta-analytic examination of assumed properties of child sexual abuse using college samples. Psychological Bulletin, 124, 22–53.

Rinehart, N. J., & McCabe, M. P. (1998). An empirical investigation of hypersexuality. Sexual and Marital Therapy, 13, 369–384.

Ringrose, K. M. (1994). Living in the shadows: Eunuchs and gender in Byzantium. In G. Herdt (Ed.), Third sex, third gender: Beyond sexual dimorphism in culture and history. New York: Zone Books.

Riordan, S. (1999). Indecent exposure: The impact upon the victim's fear of sexual crime. Journal of Forensic Psychiatry, 10, 309–316.

Rivkin-Fish, M. (1999). Sexuality education in Russia: Defining pleasure and danger for a fledgling democratic society. Social Science & Medicine 49. 801–814.

Robbins, M., & Jensen, G. (1978). Multiple orgasm in males. Journal of Sex Research, 14, 21–26.

Roberto, L. (1983). Issues in diagnosis and treatment of transsexualism. Archives of Sexual Behavior, 12, 445–472.

Roberts, J. (1990). Is routine circumcision indicated in the newborn? An affirmative view. The Journal of Family Practice, 311, 185–196.

Roberts, R. O., Lieber, M. M., Bostwick, D. G., & Jacobsen, S. J. (1997). A review of clinical and pathological prostatitis syndromes. Urology, 49, 809–821.

Robinson, D., & Rock, J. (1967). Intrascrotal hyperthalmia induced scrotal insulation: Effects on spermatogenesis. Obstetrics and Gynecology, 29, 217–223.

Robinson, G. (1989). Premenstrual syndrome: Current knowledge and management. Canadian Medical Association Journal, 140, 605–611.

Robinson, J. E., & Short, R. V. (1977). Changes in breast sensitivity at puberty, during the menstrual cycle and at maturation. British Medical Journal, 1, 1188–1191.

Rodgers, J. L., & Rowe, D.C. (1990). Adolescent sexual activity and mildly deviant behavior: Sibling and friendship effects. Journal of Family Issues, 11, 274–293.

Rodman, H., Sarvis, G., & Bonar, J. (1987). The abortion question. New York: Columbia University Press.

Rogers, G. S., Van de Castle, R. L., Evans, W. S., & Critelli, J. W. (1985). Vaginal pulse amplitude response patterns during erotic conditions and sleep. Archives of Sexual Behavior, 14, 327–342.

Rogers, S. J., & Amato, P. R. (1997). Is marital quality declining? The evidence from two generations. Social Forces, 75, 1089–1100.

Rokach, A. (1996). The subjectivity of loneliness and coping with it. Psychological Reports, 79, 475–481.

Rollins, J. (1986). Single men and women: Differences and similarities. Family Perspectives, 20, 117–124.

Rosario, M., Meyey-Bahlurg, H. F. L., Hunter, J., & Exner, T. M. (1996). The psychosexual development of urban lesbian, gay, and bisexual youths. Journal of Sex Research, 33, 113–126.

Roscoe, W. (1994). Beyond sexual dimorphism in culture and history. In G. Herdt (Ed.), Third sex, third gender. New York: Zone Books.

Rosen, L., & Martin, L. (1998). Incidence and perceptions of sexual harassment among male and female U.S. Army soldiers. Military Psychology, 10, 239–257.

Rosen, R., Lane, R. M., & Menza, M. (1999). Effects of SSRIs on sexual function: A critical review. Journal of Clinical Psychopharmacology 19, 67–85.

Rosen, R. C., & Leiblum, S. R. (1995). Treatment of sexual disorders in the 1990s: An integrative approach. Journal of Consulting and Clinical Psychology, 63, 877–890.

Rosenbaum, M. E. (1986). The repulsion hypothesis: On the nondevelopment of relationships. Journal of Personality and Social Psychology, 51, 1156–1166.

Rosenthal, D. A., Feldman, S., & Edwards, D. (1998). Mom's the word: Mothers' perspectives on communication about sexuality with adolescents. Journal of Adolescence, 21, 727–743.

Ross, M. W., Paulsen, J. A., & Stalstrom, O. W. (1988). Homosexuality and mental health: A cross-cultural review. *Journal of Homosexuality, 14,* 131–152.

Rosser, B. R., Gobby, J. M., & Carr, W. P. (1999). The unsafe sexual behavior of persons living with HIV/AIDS: An empirical approach to developing new HIV prevention interventions. *Journal of Sex Education and Therapy, 24,* 18–28.

Rosser, B. R.S., Short, B. J., Thurmes, P. J., & Coleman, E. (1998). Anodyspareunia, the unacknowledged sexual dysfunction: A validation study of painful receptive anal intercourse and its psychosexual concomitants in homosexual men. *Journal of Sex and Marital Therapy, 24*(4), 281–292.

Rotello, G. (1995, Apr. 18). The inning of outing. *The Advocate,* p. 80.

Rotenberg, K. J. (1997). Loneliness and the perception of the exchange of disclosures. *Journal of Social and Clinical Psychology, 16,* 259–276.

Rotolo, J. E., & Lynch, J. H. (1991). Penile cancer: Curable with early detection. *Hospital Practice, 26,* 131–138.

Rozee-Koker, P. D. (1987). Cross-cultural codes on seven types of rape. *Behavior Science Research, 21,* 101–117.

Rubin, A. (2000, June 18). Americans narrowing support for abortion: Nation: Results reveal a conflicted stance—they think it's murder yet lean toward leaving the choice to women. Still, support increases for limiting the procedure's availability. *The Los Angeles Times.*

Rubin, L. B. (1991). *Erotic wars: Whatever happened to the sexual revolution.* New York: Harper Perennial.

Rubin, Z. (1973). *Liking and loving.* New York: Holt, Rinehart & Winston.

Runzo, J., & Martin, N. (Eds.) (1999). *The meaning of life in the world religions.* Oxford, England: Oneworld Publications.

Runzo, J., & Martin, N. (Eds.) (2000). *Love, sex and gender in the world's religions.* Oxford, England: Oneworld Publications.

Rusbult, C. E. (1980). Commitment and satisfaction in romantic association: A test of the investment model. *Journal of Experimental Social Psychology, 16,* 172–186.

Rusbult, C. E., Johnson, D. J., & Morrow, D. G. (1986). Predicting satisfaction and commitment in adult romantic involvements: An assessment of the generalizability of the investment model. *Social Psychology Quarterly, 49,* 81–89.

Ruse, M. (1988). *Homosexuality: A philosophical inquiry.* New York: Basil Blackwell.

Russell, D. E. (1984). *Sexual exploitation.* Beverly Hills, CA: Sage Publications.

Russell, D. E. (1990). *Rape in marriage.* Bloomington: University of Indiana Press.

Russell, K. Y., Wilson, M., & Hall, R. E. (1992). *The color complex: The politics of skin color among African Americans.* New York: Anchor Books.

Ryan, C., & Kinder, R. (1996). Sex, tourism and sex tourism: Fulfilling similar needs? *Tour Magazine, 17,* 507–518.

Ryan, C. C., & Boxer, A. M. (1998). Coming out in primetime: The mental health impact of Ellen's "debut." *Cultural Diversity and Mental Health 4,* 135–142.

Sabelli, H. C. L., Carlson-Sabelli, L., & Javaid, J. J. (1990). The thermodynamics of bipolarity: A bifurcation model of bipolar illness and bipolar character and its psychotherapeutic applications. *Psychiatry, 53,* 346–368.

Sabelli, H. C., & Javaid, J. I. (1995). Phenylethylamine modulation of affect: Therapeutic and diagnostic implication. *Journal of Neuropsychiatry and Clinical Neuroscience, 7,* 6–14.

Sachs, D. (1976). The effects of similarity evaluation and self-esteem on interpersonal attraction. *Representative Research in Social Psychology, 7,* 44–50.

Sack, A. R., Keller, J. F., & Hinkle, D. E. (1984). Premarital sexual intercourse: A test of the effects of peer group, religiosity, and sexual guilt. *Journal of Sex Research, 20,* 168–185.

Sadker, M., & Sadker, D. (1994). *Failing at fairness: How America's schools cheat girls.* New York: Scribner.

Saegert, S. C., Swap, W., & Zajonc, R., (1973). Exposure context and interpersonal attraction. *Journal of Personality and Social Psychology, 25,* 234–252.

Sagan, C., & Druyan, A. (1990, April 12), Is it possible to be Pro-Life and Pro-Choice? *Parade Magazine.*

Sagan, C., & Druyan, A. (1992). *Shadows of forgotten ancestors: A search for who we are.* New York: Ballantine.

St. James, M. (1980). What a girl like you . . .? In C. Jaget (Ed.), *Prostitutes, our life.* Bristol, UK: Falling Wall Press.

Saluter, A. F. (1997). Household and family characteristics: March (1996). U.S. Bureau of the Census. Current Population Reports, Series P20–495.

San Francisco Chronicle. (1994). Cited from http://www.acme.com/~jef/religion_sex

Sanchez, L., Manning, W. D., & Smock, P. J. (1998). Sex-specialized or collaborative mate selecting? Union transitions among cohabitors. *Social Science Research, 27,* 280–304.

Sanday, P. (1981). The socio-cultural context of rape: A cross-cultural study. *Journal of Social Issues, 37,* 5–27.

Sanders, S. A., & Reinisch, J. M. (1999). Would you say you "had sex" if . . . ? *Journal of the American Medical Association, 281,* 275–277.

Sandnabba, N. K., & Ahlberg, C. (1999). Parents' attitudes and expectations about children's cross-gender behavior. *Sex Roles, 40,* 249–263.

Santelli, J. S., Lindberg, J. D., Abma, J., McNeely, C. S., & Resnick, M. (2000). Adolescent sexual behavior: Estimates and trends from four nationally representative surveys. *Family Planning Perspectives, 32,* 156–165, 194.

Sapolsky, B. S., & Zillmann, D. (1981). The effect of soft-core and hard-core erotica on provoked and unprovoked hostile behavior. *Journal of Sex Research, 17,* 319–343.

Saragin, E. (1971). Sex research and sociology: Retrospective and prospective. In J. Henslin & M. Saragin (Eds.), *Studies in the Sociology of Sex* (pp. 249–277). New York: Appleton-Crofts.

Sargent, T. O. (1988). Fetishism. *Journal of Social Work and Human Sexuality*, 7, 27–42.

Satchell, M. (2000, May 8). Fighting the child sex trade: One priest's battle to protect exploited kids. *U.S. News and World Report*.

Saul, R. (1998, Apr.). Whatever happened to the adolescent family life act? *The Guttmacher Report on Public Policy*, 1,7.

Saul, R. (1999). Teen pregnancy: Progress meets politics. The Guttmacher Report on Public Policy. New York: The Alan Guttmacher Society. From http://www.agi-usa.org/pubs/journals/gr010203

Savicki, V., Kelly, M., & Oesterreich, E. (1999). Judgments of gender in computer mediated communication. *Computers in Human Behavior*, 15, 185–194.

Savin-Williams, R. C. (1994). Dating those you can't love and loving those you can't date. In R. Montemayor, G. R. Adams et al. (Eds.), *Personal relationships during adolescence: Advances in adolescent development* (Vol. 6, pp. 196–215). Thousand Oaks, CA: Sage Publications.

Savin-Williams, R. C. (1996). Dating and romantic relationships among gay, lesbian, and bisexual youths. In Savin-Williams, R. C., Cohen, K. M. (Eds.), *The lives of lesbians, gays, and bisexuals: Children to adults* (pp. 166–180). Orlando, FL: College Publishers.

Savin-Williams, R. C., & Lenhart, R. E. (1990). AIDS prevention among gay and lesbian youth: Psychosocial stress and health care intervention guidelines. In D. G. Ostrow, (Ed.), *Behavioral aspects of AIDS* (pp. 75–99). New York: Plenum.

Savitz, L., & Rosen, L. (1988). The sexuality of prostitutes: Sexual enjoyment reported by "streetwalkers". *Journal of Sex Research*, 24, 200–208.

Sawyer, R. G., & Smith, N. G. (1996). A survey of situational factors at first intercourse among college students. *American Journal of Health Behavior*, 20, 208–217.

Scheib, J. E., Gangestad, S. W., & Thornhill, R. (1999). Facial attractiveness, symmetry and cues of good genes. *Proceedings of the Royal Society of London, B*, 266, 1913–1918.

Schieve, L. A., Peterson, H. B., Meikle, S. F., Jena, G., Daniel, I., Burnette, N. M., & Willcox, L. (1999). Live-birth rates and multiple-birth risk using in-vitro fertilization. *Journal of the American Medical Association*, 282, 1832–1838.

Schiffman, M., Herrero, R., Hildesheim, A., Sherman, M., Bratti, M., Wacholder, S., Alfaro, M., Hutchinson, M., Morales, J., Greenberg, M., & Lorincz, L. (2000). HP DNA testing in cervical cancer screening. *Journal of the American Medical Association*, 283, 87–93.

Schilit, R., Lie, G. L., & Montagne, M. (1990). Substance abuse as a correlate of violence in intimate lesbian relationships. *Journal of Homosexuality*, 19, 51–65.

Schiltz, M. A., & Sandford, T. G. (2000). HIV positive people risk and sexual behavior. *Social Science and Medicine*, 40, 1571–1588.

Schlegel, P. (1991, June). New treatment options for the infertile male. *Medical Aspects of Human Sexuality*, 22–31.

Schlosser, E. (1997, Feb 10). The business of pornography. *U.S. News & World Report Archive*.

Schmalz, J. (1993) Survey finds U.S. divided over gays. *The Oregonian*, p. A17.

Schmidt, P., Nieman, L., Danaceau, M., Adams, L., & Rubinow, D. (1998). Differential behavior effects on gonadal steroids in women with and in those without premenstrual syndrome. *New England Journal of Medicine*, 238, 209–216.

Schnarch, D. (1991). *Constructing the sexual crucible*. New York: Norton.

Schnur, P. (2000, Feb.). Cited in D. Hudepohl, I had cosmetic surgery on my genitals. *Marie Claire*, 169–170.

Scholem, G. G. (1954). *Major trends in Jewish mysticism*. New York: Schocken Books.

Schott, R. L. (1995). The childhood and family dynamics of transvestites. *Archives of Sexual Behavior*, 24: 309–327.

Schover, L. R., Evans, R. B., & von Eschenbach, A. C. (1987). Sexual rehabilitation in a cancer center: Diagnosis and outcome in 384 consultations. *Archives of Sexual Behavior*, 16, 445–461.

Schover, L. R., & Leiblum, S. R. (1994). Commentary: The stagnation of sex therapy. *Journal of Psychology & Human Sexuality*, 6, 5–29.

Schroder, M., & Carroll, R. A. (1999). New women: Sexological outcomes of male-to-female gender reassignment surgery. *Journal of Sex Education and Therapy*, 24, 137–146.

Schur, E. M. (1988). *The Americanization of sex*. PA: Temple University Press.

Schuster, M. A., Bell, R. M., & Knouse, D. E. (1996). The sexual practices of adolescent virgins: Genital sexual activities of high school students who have never had sexual intercourse. *American Journal of Public Health*, 86, 1570–1576.

Schütz, A. (2001). Self-esteem and interpersonal strategies. In J. P. Forgas, K. D. Williams, & L. Wheeler (Eds.), *The social mind: Cognitive and motivational aspects of interpersonal behavior* (pp. 157–176). New York: Cambridge University Press.

Schwartz, P. (2000). *Everything you know about love and sex is wrong?: Twenty-five relationship myths redefined to achieve happiness and fulfillment in your intimate life*. New York: Putnam Publishing Group.

Schwartz, P., & Rutter, V. (1998). *The gender of sexuality*. Thousand Oaks, CA: Pine Forge Press.

Schwartz, R. J., Milteer, R., & LeBeau, M. (2000). Drug facilitated sexual assault. *Southern Medical Journal*, 93, 558–561.

Schweiger, U. (1991). Menstrual function and luteal–phase deficiency in

relation to weight changes and dieting. *Clinical Obstetrics and Gynecology, 34,* 191, 197.

Scott, G. G. (1983). *Dominant women—submissive men: An exploration in erotic dominance and submission.* New York: Praeger Publishers.

Scott, J., & Schwalm, H. (1988). Attitude strength and social action in the abortion dispute. *American Sociological Review, 53,* 785–793.

Scully, D., & Porter, S. (2000). HIV topic update: Oro-genital transmission of HIV. *Oral Disease, 6,* 92–98.

Sedikides, C., Campbell, W. K., Reeder, G. D., & Elliott, A. J. (1998). The self-serving bias in relational context. *Journal of Personality & Social Psychology 74,* 378–386.

Segal, E. (1971). *Love story.* New York: Harper & Row.

Segal, Z. V., & Marshall, W. L. (1985). Heterosexual social skills in a population of rapists and child molesters. *Journal of Consulting and Clinical Psychology, 53,* 55–63.

Segraves, R. T., & Segraves, K. B. (1993). Medical aspects of orgasm disorders. In W. O'Donohue & J. H. Green (Eds.), *Handbook of sexual dysfunction: Assessment and treatment* (pp. 225–252). Boston: Allyn & Bacon.

Seligman, M. E. P. (1993). *What you can change and what you can't.* New York: Knopf.

Seligmann, J. (1991). Condoms in the classroom. *Newsweek, 118,* p. 61.

Selvin, B. W. (1993, June 1). Transsexuals are coming to terms with themselves and society. *New York Newsday,* pp. 55, 58, 59.

Semans, J. (1956). Premature ejaculation, a new approach. *Southern Medical Journal, 49,* 353–358.

Sgori, S. M. (1982). *Handbook of clinical intervention in child sexual abuse.* Lexington, MA: D.C. Heath.

Seng, M. J. (1989). Child sexual abuse and adolescent prostitution: A comparative analysis. *Adolescence, 24,* 665–675.

Servicemembers Legal Defense Network. (2001, March 15). Watchdog group reports continued high rate of anti-gay harassment in military while pentagon sits on anti-harassment action plan. Press Room. From http://www.sldn.org/templates/press/record.html?record=255

Severn, J., Belch, G. E., & Belch, M. A. (1990). The effects of sexual and non-sexual advertising appeals and information level on cognitive processing and communication effectiveness. *Journal of Advertising, 19,* 14–22.

Shackelford, T. K., & Buss, D. M. (1997). Anticipation of marital dissolution as a consequence of spousal infidelity. *Journal of Social and Personal Relationships, 14,* 793–808.

Shainess, N. (1984). *Sweet suffering: Woman as victim.* New York: Bobbs-Merrill.

Shandall, A. A. (1967). Circumcision and infibulation of females: A general consideration of the problem and a clinical study of the complications in Sudanese women. *Sudan Medical Journal, 5,* 178–212.

Shangold, M. (1984). Causes, evaluation and management of athletic oligomenorrhea. *Medical Clinics of North America, 69,* 83–95.

Sharma, V., & Sharma, A. (1998). The guilt and pleasure of masturbation: A study of college girls in Gujarat, India. *Sexual and Marital Therapy, 13,* 63–70.

Sharp, M., & Collins, D. (1998). Exploring the "inevitability" of the relationship between anabolic-androgenic steroid use and aggression in human males. *Journal of Sport and Exercise Psychology, 20,* 379–394.

Sharpe, R., & Skakkebaeck, N. S. (1993). Are oestrogens involved in falling sperm counts and disorders of the male reproductive tract? *Lance, 341,* 1392–1395.

Sharts-Hopco, N. (1997). STDs in women: What you need to know. *American Journal of Nursing, 97,* 46–54.

Shaver, P., Hazan, C., & Bradshaw, D. (1988). Love as attachment: The integration of three behavioral systems. In R. J. Sternberg & M. L. Barnes (Eds.), *The Psychology of Love,* New Haven, CT: Yale University Press, pp. 68–99.

Shaywitz, S. F., Pugh, R., Constable, R. T., Skudlarski, P., Fulbright, R. K., Bronen, R. A., Fletcher, J. M., Shakweiler, D. P., Katz, L., & Gore, J. C. (1995). Sex differences in the functional organization of the brain for language. *Nature, 373,* 607–608.

Sheehy, G. (1992). *The silent passage.* New York: Random House.

Sheeran, P. J. (1987). *Women, society, the state, and abortion: A structuralist analysis.* New York: Praeger.

Sheets, V. L., Frededall, L. L., & Claypool, H. M. (1997). Jealousy evocation, partner reassurance and relationship stability: An exploration of the potential benefits of jealousy. *Evolution and Human Behavior, 18:* 387–402.

Sheler, J. (1999). *Is the Bible true?* San Francisco: Harper Collins.

Shenon, P. (1998, Jan. 20). New finding on mixing sexes in military. *The New York Times,* p. A12.

Sheppard, V. J., Nelson, E. S., Andreoli-Mathie, V. (1995). Dating relationships and infidelity: Attitudes and behaviors. *Journal of Sex and Marital Therapy, 21*(3), 205.

Sherman, S. M., & Flaxman, P. W. (2000). Morning sickness: A mechanism for protecting mother and embryo. *Quarterly Review of Biology, 75,* 113–148.

Sherwin, B. B. (1997). The use of androgens in the postmenopause—evidence from clinical studies. *Maturitas, 27,* 100.

Sheung-Tak, C. (1996, Mar.). A critical review of Chinese Koro. *Culture, Medicine and Psychiatry, 20,* 67–82.

Shields, S. A., & Harriman, R. E. (1984). Fear of male homosexuality: Cardiac responses of low and high homonegative males. *Journal of Homosexuality, 10,* 53–67.

Shilts, R. (1987). *And the band played on: Politics, people and the AIDS epidemic.* New York: St. Martin's Press.

Shilts, R. (1993). *Conduct unbecoming: Gays and lesbians in the U.S. military.* New York: St. Martin's Press.

Shorter, E. (1975). *The making of the modern family.* New York: Basic Books.

Shostak, A., McLouth, G., & Seng, L. (1984). *Men and women: Lessons, losses and love.* New York: Praeger.

Shute, N. (1997, Nov. 10). No more hard labor. *U.S. News & World Report.*

SIECUS (Sexuality Information and Education Council of the United States) National Guidelines Task Force. (1990). The SIECUS guidelines for comprehensive sexuality education: K-12. (2nd ed.) New York: SIECUS. From http://www.siecus.org/pubs/guidlines

SIECUS (Sexuality Information and Education Council of the United States) (1993, Feb./Mar.). Fact sheet on comprehensive sexuality education: Sexual orientation and identity, *SIECUS Report,* 19–20.

SIECUS (Sexuality Information and Education Council of the United States) (1996). Guidelines for comprehensive sexuality education: K-12, New York: Author.

SIECUS (Sexuality Information and Education Council of the United States) (1999). Between the lines: States' implementation of the federal government's section 510(b) abstinence education program in fiscal year 1998. New York: Author.

SIECUS (Sexuality Information and Education Council of the United States). (2000). State sexuality education and/or HIV/AIDS/STD education mandates. From http://www.siecus.org/school/sex_ed/mand0000.html

Siegel, O. (1982). Personality development in adolescence. In B. B. Wolman et al. (Eds.). *Handbook of developmental psychology.* Englewood Cliffs, NJ: Prentice Hall.

Silverman S. (1989). Interaction of drug-abusing mother, fetus, types of drugs examined in numerous studies. *Journal of the American Medical Association,* 261, 1689–1693.

Simari, C. G., & Baskin, D. (1982). Incestuous experiences within homosexual populations: A preliminary study. *Archives of Sexual Behavior,* 11, 329–344.

Simon, R. J. (1997). Video voyeurs and the covert videotaping of unsuspecting victims: Psychological and legal consequences. *Journal of Forensic Science,* 42, 884–889.

Simons, G. L. (1985). *The illustrated book of sexual records.* (2nd ed.) London: Virgin Books.

Simons, J. W., Mikhak, B., Chang, J. F., Dearzo, A. M., et al. (2000). Induction of immunity to prostate cancer antigens: Results of a clinical trial of vaccination with irradiated autologous prostate tumor cells engineered to secrete granulocyte-macrophage colony-stimulating factor using ex vivo gene transfer. *Cancer Research,* 59, 160–168.

Simonson, K., & Subich, L. M. (1997). Rape perceptions as a function of gender-role traditionality and victim-perpetrator association. *Sex Roles,* 40, 617–634.

Sinding, S. W., & Segal, S. J. (1991, Dec. 19). Birth-rate news. *The New York Times,* p. A31.

Singer, D. B. (1995). Human embryogenesis. In D. B. Coustan, B. V. Haning Jr., & D. B. Singer (Eds.), *Human reproduction: Growth and development.* Boston: Little-Brown.

Singer, J., & Singer, J. (1972). Types of female orgasm. *Journal of Sex Research,* 8, 255–267.

Singh, D. (1993). Adaptive significance of waist-to-hip ratio and female psychical attractiveness. *Journal of Personality and Social Psychology,* 65, 293–307.

Singh, D. (1995). Female judgment of male attractiveness and desirability for relationships: Role of waist-to-hip ratio and financial status. *Journal of Personality and Social Psychology,* 69, 1089–1101.

Singh, S., & Darroch, J. E. (1999). Trends in sexual activity among adolescent American women: 1982–1995. *Family Planning Perspectives,* 31, 211–219.

Singh, S., Wulf, D., Samara, R., & Cuca, Y. P. (2000). Gender differences in the timing of first intercourse: Data from 14 countries. *Family Planning Perspectives,* 26, 21–28, 43.

Sipski, M. L. (1997). Spinal cord injury and sexual function: An educational model. In M. L. Sipski & C. J. Alexander (Eds.), *Sexual function in people with disability and chronic illness* (pp. 303–335). Gaithersburg, MD: Aspen.

Sipe, R. (1995). Sex, priests and power: Anatomy of a crisis. Philadelphia: Bruner/Mazel.

Sirles, E. A., & Franke, P. J. (1989). Factors influencing mothers' reactions to intrafamily sexual abuse. *Child Abuse and Neglect,* 13, 131–139.

Slade P., Escott, D., Spiby, H., Henderson, B., & Fraser, R. B. (2000). Antenatal predictors and use of coping strategies in labour. *Psychology and Health,* 15, 555–569.

Slaughter, L. (2000). Involvement of drugs in sexual assault. *Journal of Reproductive Medicine,* 45, 425–430.

Slaughter, L., Brown, C., Crowley, S., & Peck, R. (1997). Patterns of genital injury in female sexual assault victims. *American Journal of Obstetrics and Gynecology,* 176, 609–616.

Slijper, F. M. E., Drop, S. L.S., Molenaar, J. C., deMuinck Keizer-Schrama, S. M. P. F. (1998). Long-term psychological evaluation of intersex children. *Archives of Sexual Behavior,* 27, 125–144.

Small, M. (1995). *What's love got to do with it?* New York: Anchor Books.

Smith, A. M., Rosenthal, D. A., & Reichler, H. (1996). High schoolers masturbatory practices: Their relationship to sexual intercourse and personal characteristics. *Psychological Reports,* 79, 499–509.

Smith, D. (2000, Sept. 24). Dawn Langley Simmons, flamboyant writer dies at 77. *The New York Times,* p. 53.

Smith, G. E., Gerrard, M., & Gibbons, F. X. (1997). Self-esteem and the relation between risk behavior and perceptions of vulnerability to unplanned pregnancy in college women. *Health Psychology,* 16, 137–146.

Smith, G. H., & Engel, R. (1968). Influence of a female model on perceived characteristics of an automobile. *Proceedings of the Annual Convention of the American Psychological Association, 3,* 681–682.

Smith, L. (1984). A content analysis of gender differences in children's advertising. *Journal of Broadcasting & Electronic Media, 38,* 333–337.

Smith, T. W. (1994). *The demography of sexual behavior.* Menlo Park, CA: Kaiser Family Foundation.

Smukler, A. J., & Schiebel, D. (1975). Personality characteristics of exhibitionists. *Diseases of the Nervous System, 36,* 600–603.

Snegroff, S. (1986). The stressors of non-marital sexual intercourse. *Health Education, 17,* 21–23.

Snyder, H. (1991). To circumcise or not. *Hospital Practice,* January 15: 201–207.

Snyder, M., Tanke, E. D., & Berscheid, E. (1977). Social perception and interpersonal behavior: On the self-fulfilling nature of social stereotypes. *Journal of Personality and Social Psychology, 35,* 356–366.

Sobel, J. D. (1997). Current concepts: Vaginitis. *New England Journal of Medicine, 337,* 1896.

Sohn, N., Weinstein, M. A., & Gonchar, J. (1977). Social injuries of the rectum. *American Journal of Surgery, 134,* 611.

Sostek, A. J., & Wyatt, R. J. (1981, Oct.). The chemistry of crankiness. *Psychology Today,* p. 120.

Southern Baptist Convention. (1998, June 9). Report of the Baptist faith and message study committee. From http://www.sbc.net

Southern Poverty Law Center. (1999). Ten ways to fight hate: A community response guide. Montgomery, AL: SPLC.

Spanier, G. B., & Margolis, R. L. (1983). Marital separation and extramarital sexual behavior. *Journal of Sex Research, 19,* 23–48.

Spark, R. F. (2000). *Sexual health for men: The complete guide.* Cambridge, MA: Perseus.

Sparks, J. (1999). *Battle of the sexes: The natural history of sex.* New York: TV Books.

Spector, I., & Carey, M. (1990). Incidence and prevalence of the sexual dysfunctions: A "critical" review of the empirical literature. *Archives of Sexual Behavior, 19,* 389–408.

Spence, J. T., & Helmreich, R. L. (1980). Masculine instrumentality and feminine expressiveness: Their relationships with sex role attitudes and behaviors. *Psychology of Women Quarterly, 5,* 147–163.

Spengler, A. (1977). Manifest sadomasochism of males: Results of an empirical study. *Archives of Sexual Behavior, 6,* 441–456.

Spitz, I. M., Bardin, C. W., Benton, L., & Robbins, A. (1998). Early pregnancy termination with mifepristone and misoprostol in the United States. *New England Journal of Medicine, 338,* 1241–1247.

Spitzer, R. L. et al. (1989). *DSM-III-R casebook.* Washington DC: American Psychiatric Press.

Sprague, J., & Quadagno, D. (1989). Gender and sexual motivation: An exploration of two assumptions. *Journal of Psychology and Human Sexuality, 2,* 57–76.

Sprecher, S., & McKinney, K. (1993). *Sexuality.* Newbury Park, CA: Sage.

Sprecher, S., McKinney, K., & Orbuch, T. J. (1991). The effect of current sexual behavior on friendship, dating, and marriage desirability. *Journal of Sex Research, 28,* 387–408.

Sprecher, S., Regan, P. C., McKinney, K., Maxwell, K., & Wazienski, R. (1997). Preferred level of sexual experience in a date or mate: The merger of two methodologies. *Journal of Sex Research, 34,* pp. 327–337.

Stack, S., & Eshleman, J. R. (1998). Marital status and happiness: A 17-nation study. *Journal of Marriage and the Family, 60,* 527–531.

Stack, S., & Gundlach, J. (1992). Divorce and sex , *Archives of Sexual Behavior, 21,* 359–367.

Stanford, J. L., Feng, Z., Hamilton, A. S., Gilliland, F. D., Stephenson, R. A., Eley, W., Albersten, P. C., Harlan, L. C., & Potosky, A. L. (2000). Urinary and sexual function after radical prostatectomy for clinically localized prostate cancer. *Journal of the American Medical Association, 283,* 354–360.

Stanley, S. M., & Markman, H. J. (1992). Assessing commitment in personal relationships. *Journal of Marriage and the Family, 54,* 595–608.

Stanislaw, H., & Rice, E. J. (1988). Correlation between sexual desire and menstrual cycle characteristics. *Archives of Sexual Behavior, 17,* 499.

Stark, R. (1996). *The rise of Christianity: A sociologist reconsiders history.* Princeton, NJ: Princeton University Press.

Stark, R., & Bainbridge, W.S. (1985). *The future of religion: Secularization, revival and cult formation.* Berkeley: University of California Press.

Stayton, W. (1992). A theology of sexual pleasure. SIECUS Report, 20.

Steele, C. M., & Southwick, L. (1985). Alcohol and social behavior I: The mediating role of inhibitory conflict. *Journal of Personality and Social Psychology, 48,* 18–34.

Steele, V. (1985). *Fashion and eroticism: Ideals of feminine beauty from the Victorian to the Jazz Age.* Fairlawn, NH: Oxford University Press.

Steinauer, J. E., & Ryan, K. J. (2001). How available is abortion training? *Family Planning Perspectives, 33.*

Stern, K. N., & McClintock, M. K. (1996). Individual variation in biological rhythms: Accurate measurement of preovulatory LH surge and menstrual cycle phase. In *Psychopharmacology and women: Sex, gender and hormones* (pp. 393–413). Washington, DC: American Psychiatric Press.

Sternberg, R. (1986). A triangular theory of love. *Psychological Review, 93,* 119–135.

Sternberg, R. J. (1988) Triangular love. In R. J. Sternberg & M. L. Barnes (Eds.), *The psychology of love* (p. 122). New Haven, CT: Yale University Press.

Sternberg, R. J., & Barnes, M. L. (1988). *The psychology of love.* New Haven, CT: Yale University Press.

Stewart, G. K. (1998). Intrauterine devices. In R. A. Hatcher et al., *Contraceptive technology* (17th ed.) (pp. 511–544). New York: Ardent Media.

Stewart, M., & Tooley, S. (1992). Premenstrual syndrome: Is there a basis for a holistic approach? *Maternal and Child Health,* March, 86–88.

Stitik, T. P., & Benevento, B. T. (1997). Cardiac and Pulmonary Disease. In M. L. Sipsku & C. J. Alexander (Eds.), *Sexual function in people with disability and chronic illness* (pp. 303–335). Gaithersburg, MD: Aspen.

Stoller, R. (1977). Sexual deviations. In E. Reach (Ed.), *Human sexuality in four perspectives.* Baltimore: Johns Hopkins University Press.

Stone, L. (1965). *Crisis of the aristocracy, 1558–1641.* New York: Oxford University Press.

Stone, L. (1986). *Family, sex and marriage in England, 1500–1800.* New York: HarperCollins.

Storey, A. E., Walsh, C. L., Quinton, R. L., & Wynne-Edward, K. E. (2000). Hormonal correlates of paternal responsiveness in new and expectant fathers. *Evolution and Human Behavior, 21,* 79–95.

Storms, M. (1980). Theories of sexual orientation. *Journal of Personality and Social Psychology, 38,* 783–792.

Stout, J. W., & Rivara, F. P. (1989). Schools and sex education: Does it work? *Pediatrics,* March 375–379.

Strassberg, D. S., de Gouveia Brazao, C. A., Rowland, D. L., Tan, P., & Slob, A. K. (1999). Clomipramine in the treatment of rapid (premature) ejaculations. *Journal of Sex and Marital Therapy, 252,* 89–101.

Strassberg, D. S., & Lockerd, L. K. (1998). Force in women's sexual fantasies. *Archives of Sexual Behavior, 27,* 403–411.

Streissguth, A. P., Sampson, P. D., & Barr, H. M. (1989). Neurobehavioral dose-response effects of prenatal alcohol exposure in humans from infancy to adulthood. *Annals of New York Academy of Science, 562,* 145–158.

Strouse, J., & Fabes, R. A. (1983). Formal vs. informal sources of sex education: Competing forces in the sexual socialization of adolescents. *Adolescence, 20,* 251–262.

Struckman-Johnson, C., & Struckman-Johnson, D. (1997). Men's reactions to hypothetical forced sexual advances from women: The role of sexual standards, relationship availability, and the beauty bias. *Sex Roles, 37,* 319–333.

Struckman-Johnson, C., & Struckman-Johnson, D. (1998). The dynamics and impact of sexual coercion of men by women. In P. B. Anderson (Ed.) *Sexually aggressive women: Current perspectives and controversies.* New York: The Guilford Press.

Stubblefield, P. G., & Grimes, D. A. (1994). Septic abortion. *New England Journal of Medicine, 331,* 310–314.

Sue, D. (1979). Erotic fantasies of college students during coitus. *Journal of Sex Research, 15,* 299–305.

Suggs, D. N. (1987). Female status and role transition in the Tswana life cycle. *Ethnology, xxvi,* 2.

Sullivan, E., & Simon, W. (1998). The client: A social, psychological, and behavioral look at the unseen patron of prostitution. In J. Elias, V. Bullough, V. Elias, & G. Brewer (Eds.), *Prostitution: On whores, hustlers, and johns* (pp. 134–154). Amherst, NY: Prometheus.

Sun, C., Skaletsky, H., Birren, B., Devon, K., Tang, Z., Silber, S., Oates, R., Page, D. C. (1999). An azoospermic man with a de novo point mutation in the Y-chromosome gene USP9Y. *Nature Genetics, 23,* 429–432.

Sung, J. C., Kabalin, J. N., & Terris, M. K. (2000). Prostate cancer detection, characterization, and clinical outcomes in men aged 70 years and older referred for transrectal ultrasound and prostate biopsies. *Urology, 56,* 295–301.

Sussman, N. (1999). The role of antidepressants in sexual dysfunction. *Journal of Clinical Psychiatry Monograph Series, 17,* 9–14.

Swan, S. H., Elkin, E. R., & Fenster, L. (1997). Have sperm densities declined? A reanalysis of global trend data. *Environmental Health Perspective, 1051,* 1228–1232.

Swim, J. K. (1994). Perceived versus meta-analytic effect sizes: An assessment of the accuracy of gender stereotypes. *Journal of Personality & Social Psychology, 66,* 21–36.

Symons, D. (1979). *The evolution of human sexuality.* New York: Oxford University Press.

Symons, D. (1990). *The evolution of human sexuality.* Oxford: Oxford University Press.

Symons, D. (1995). Beauty is in the adaptations of the beholder: The evolutionary psychology of human female sexual attractiveness. In P. R. Abramson, & S. D. Pinder (Eds.), *Sexual nature/sexual culture,* pp. 80–118. Chicago: University of Chicago Press.

Talamini, J. (1982). *Boys will be girls: The hidden world of the heterosexual male transvestite.* Lanham, MD; University Press of America.

Tangney, J. P. (1991). Moral affect: The good, the bad, and the ugly, *Journal of Personality and Social Psychology, 61,* 598–607.

Tangney, J. P. (1992). Situational determinants of shame and guilt in young adulthood. *Personality and Social Psychology Bulletin, 18,* 199–206.

Tangney, J. P., Wagner, P. E., Fletcher, C., & Gramzow, R. (1992). Shamed into anger? The relation of shame and guilt to anger and self-reported aggression. *Journal of Personality and Social Psychology, 62,* 669–675.

Tannahill, R. (1982). *Sex in history.* New York: Stein and Day.

Tannen, D. (1990). *You just don't understand.* New York: William Morrow.

Tannen, D. (1994). *Gender and discourse.* New York: Oxford University Press.

Tannen, D. (1998). *The argument culture: Moving from debate to dialogue.* New York: Random House.

Tarcher, J. P. (1993). *The yin-yang butterfly: Ancient Chinese sexual secrets for western lovers.* New York: Putnam.

Tavris, C. (1989). *Anger: The misunderstood emotion.* New York: Touchstone Books.

Taylor, D., Hart, A., & Hart Weber, C. (2000). The national survey on Christian female sexuality. *Contemporary Sexuality, 34,* 1.

Taylor, S., & Brown, J. (1988). Illusion and well-being: A social psychological perspective on mental health. *Psychological Bulletin, 103,* 193–210.

Tedeschi, J. T., & Falcon, R. B. (1994). *Violence, aggression, and coercive actions.* Washington, DC: American Psychological Association.

Telliohann, S., Price, J., Pouresslami, M., & Easton, A. (1995). Teaching about sexual orientation by secondary health teachers. *Journal of School Health, 65,* 18–22.

Templeman, T. L., & Stinnett, R. D. (1991). Patterns of sexual arousal and history in a "normal" sample of young men. *Archives of Sexual Behavior, 20,* 137–150.

Tenhula, W., & Bailey, J. M. (1998). Female sexual orientation and pubertal onset. *Developmental Neuropsychology, 14,* 369–384.

Tennov, D. (1979). *Love and limerence.* New York: Stein & Day.

Teresi, D. (1994, Nov. 27). How to get a man pregnant. *The New York Times Magazine,* pp. 54–55.

Tesser, A., & Collins, J. E. (1988). Emotion in social reflection and comparison situations: Intuitive, systematic, and exploratory approaches. *Journal of Personality and Social Psychology, 55:* 695–709.

Testa, M., & Derman, K. H. (1999). The differential correlates of sexual coercion and rape. *Journal of Interpersonal Violence, 14,* 548–561.

Thelen, M. H., Vander Wal, J. S., Muir, J. A., & Harmon, R. (2000). Fear of intimacy among dating couples. *Behavior Modification, 24:* 223–240.

Thoits, P. A. (1994). Stressors and problem-solving: The individual as psychological activist. *Journal of Health and Social Behavior, 35,* 143–159.

Thompson, A. P. (1983). Extramarital sex: A review of the research literature. *Journal of Sex Research, 19,* 1–22.

Thompson, R. (1990). Is routine circumcision indicated in the newborn? An opposing view. *Journal of Family Practice, 31,* 189–196.

Thornhill, R., & Gangestad, S. W. (1993). Human facial beauty: Averageness, symmetry and parasite resistance. *Human Nature, 4,* 237–269.

Thornhill, R., & Gangestad, S. W. (1996). Human female copulatory orgasm: A human adaptation or phylogenetic holdover? *Animal Behaviour, 52,* 853–855.

Thornhill, R., Gangestad, S. W., & Comer, R. (1995). Human female orgasm and mate fluctuating asymmetry. *Animal Behaviour, 50,* 1601–1615.

Thornhill, R., & Palmer, C. (2000). *A natural history of rape.* Cambridge, MA: MIT Press.

Thornton, A., & Camburn, D. (1987). The influence of the family on premarital sexual attitudes and behavior. *Demography, 24,* 323–340.

Tiaden, P., & Thoennes, N. (1998). Prevalence, incidence and consequences of violence against women, Findings from the National Violence Against Women study. Research in Brief, U.S. Dept. of Justice, NCJRS, 17283.

Tiefer, L. (1995). *Sex is not a natural act and other essays.* Boulder, CO: Westview Press.

Tierney, J. (1998, Nov. 9). The big city; monkey business: Strippers, testosterone and the Dow. *The New York Times,* p. B1.

Tietze, C., & Henshaw, S. K. (1986). *Induced abortion: A world review.* New York: Alan Guttmacher Institute.

Tiger, L. (1992). *The pursuit of pleasure.* Boston: Little, Brown.

Tobias, S. (1982). Sexist equation. *Psychology Today, 16,* 14–17.

Todd, T. (1986). Anabolic steroids: The gremlins of sports. *Journal of Sport History, 14,* 87–107.

Toivonen, J., Luukkainen, T., & Allonen, H. (1991). Protective effect of intrauterine release of levonorgestrel on pelvic infection: Three years' comparative experience of levonorgestrel and copper-releasing intrauterine devices. *Obstetrics and Gynecology, 77,* 261–264.

Tollison, C. D., & Adams, H. E. (1979). *Sexual disorders: Treatment, theory and research.* New York: Gardner Press.

Toppo, G. (1996, Nov. 29). Circumcision reversal gains popularity. *The New Mexican,* p. C1.

Towner, D., Castro, M. A., Eby-Wilkens, E., & Gilbert, W. M. (1999). Effect of mode of delivery in nulliparous women on neonatal intracranial injury. *New England Journal of Medicine, 341,* 709–714.

Townsend, J. M., & Levy, G. D. (1990). Effects of potential partners' costume and physical attractiveness on sexuality and partner selection. *Journal of Psychology, 124,* 371–389.

Townsend, J. M., & Levy, G. D. (1995). Effects of potential partners' physical attractiveness and socioeconomic status on sexual and partner selection. *Archives of Sexual Behavior, 371,* 149–164.

Townsend, J. M., & Wasserman, T. (1998). Sexual attractiveness: Sex difference in assessment and criteria. *Evolution and Human Behavior, 19,* 171–191.

Trachtenberg, P. (1988). *The Casanova complex.* New York: Poseidon Press. Treiman, K., Lisking, L., Kols, A., & Rinehart, W. (1995). IUDs—an update. Population Reports, Series B., No. 6, December.

Trause, M. A., Kennell, J., & Klaus, M. (1977). Parental attachment behavior. In J. Money & H. Musaph (Eds.), *Handbook of Sexology.* New York: Elseview/North Holland.

Treas, J., & Giesen, D. (2000). Sexual infidelity among married and cohabiting Americans. *Journal of Marriage and the Family, 62,* 48–60.

Trent, K., & South, S. (1989). Structural determinants of the divorce rate: A cross-societal analysis. *Journal of Marriage and the Family, 67,* 391–404.

Trivers, R. (1974). Parent-offspring conflict. *American Zoologist, 14*, 249–264.

Troiden, R. (1988). *Gay and lesbian identity: A sociological analysis.* New York: General Hall.

Trussell, J., Ellertson, C., & Stewart, F. (1996). The effectiveness of the Yuzpe regimen of emergency contraception. *Family Planning Perspectives, 29*, 60.

Trussell, J., & Grummer-Strawn, L. (1990). Contraception failure of the ovulation method of periodic abstinence. *Family Planning Perspectives, 22*, 65–75.

Trussell, J., & Kowal, D, (1998). The essentials of contraception: Efficacy, safety and personal considerations. In R. A. Hatcher et al. (Eds.), *Contraceptive technology* (17th ed.). Irvington, NY: Ardent Media.

Trussell, J., Leveque, J. A., Koenig, J. D., London, R., Borden, S., Henneberry, J., LaGuardia, K. D., Stewart, F., Wilson, T. G., Wysocki, S. et al. (1995). The economic value of contraception: A comparison of 15 methods. *American Journal of Public Health, 85*, 494–503.

Trussell, J., Vaughn, B., & Stanford, J. (1999). Contraceptive failure, method-related discontinuation, and resumption of use: Results from the 1995 National Survey of Family Growth. *Family Planning Perspectives, 31*, 64–72, 93.

Tucker, M. B., & Mitchell-Kernan, C. (1995). Marital behavior and expectations: Ethnic comparisons of altitudinal and structural correlates. In M. B. Tucker & C. Mitchell-Kernan (Eds.) *The decline in marriage among African Americans: Causes, consequences, and policy implication* (pp. 145–171). New York: Russell Sage Foundation.

Turnbull, C. (1968). The Importance of flux in two hunting societies. In R. B. Lee and I. DeVore, eds, *Man the Hunter*, 132–137. Chicago: Aldine.

Turner, W. J. (1995). Homosexuality, Type I: An Xg28 phenomenon. *Archives of Sexual Behavior, 24*, 109–123.

Turrell, S. C. (2000). A descriptive analysis of same-sex relationship violence for a diverse sample. *Journal of Family Violence, 15*, 281–293.

Tyler, K. A., Hoyt, D. R., & Whitbeck, L. B. (1998). Coercive sexual strategies. *Violence and Victims, 13*, 47–61.

Ullman, S. E. (1998). Does offender violence escalate when rape victims fight back? *Journal of Interpersonal Violence, 12*, 179–192.

Ullman, S. E. (1999). A comparison of gang and individual rape incidents. *Violence and Victims, 14*, 123–133.

UNAIDS/World Health Organization (1999). Report on the global HIV/AIDS epidemic. Geneva: World Health Organization.

Underwood, C. (2000). Islamic precepts and family planning: The perceptions of Jordanian religious leaders and their constituents. *International Family Planning Perspectives, 26*, 110–117.

UNICEF. (2000). *The state of the world's children 2000.* New York: United Nations.

Upchurch, D. M., Aneshensel, C. S., Sucoff, C. A., & Levy-Storm, L. (1999). Neighborhood and family contexts of adolescent sexual activity. *Journal of Marriage and the Family, 61*, 920–933.

Urdy, J. R., Morris, N. M., & Kovonock, J. (1995). Androgen effects on women's gendered behavior. *Journal of Biosocial Science, 27*, 359–368.

U.S. Bureau of the Census. (1999). Marital status.

U.S. Department of Defense. (1998). Report to the Secretary of Defense: Review of the effectiveness of the application and enforcement of the department's policy on homosexual conduct in the military. Washington, DC: Office of the Undersecretary of Defense (Personnel and Readiness.)

U.S. Department of Defense. (2000, Mar. 16). Office of the Inspector General, Report on the military environment with respect to the homosexual conduct policy.

Vaida, J., & Steinbeck, J. (2000). Factors associated with repeat suicide attempts among adolescents. *Australian and New Zealand Journal of Psychiatry, 34*: 437.

Vance, E. B., & Wagner, N. N. (1976). Written descriptions of orgasm: A study of sex differences. *Archives of Sexual Behavior, 5*, 87.

Vanwesenbeeck, I., Bekker, M., & Van Lenning, A. (1998). Gender attitudes, sexual meanings, and interactional patterns in heterosexual encounters among college students in the Netherlands. *Journal of Sex Research, 35*, 317–327.

Varelas, N., & Foley, L. A. (1998). Blacks' and whites' perceptions of interracial date rape. *Journal of Social Psychology, 138*, 392–400.

Velde, E. R., & Cohlen, B. J. (1999). The management of infertility, *New England Journal of Medicine, 340*, 224–226.

Verkauf, B. S., von Thron, J., & O'Brien, W. F. (1991). Clitoral size in normal women. *Obstetrics & Gynecology, 80*, 41–44.

Vernon, S. D., Unger, E. R., Miller, D. L., Lee, D. R., & Reeves, W. C. (1997). Association of human papillomavirus type 16 integration in the E2 gene with poor disease-free survival from cervical cancer. *International Journal of Cancer, 74*, 50–56.

Veroff, J., Douvan, E., & Kulka, R. A. (1981). *The inner American: A self portrait from 1957 to 1976.* New York: Basic Books.

Vogel, G. (2001). Stem cells are coaxed to produce insulin. *Science, 292*, 615–617.

Waggoner, R. W. (1980). A brief description of the Masters and Johnson treatment for sexual dysfunction. In B. B. Wolman (Ed.), *Handbook of human sexuality* (pp. 325–328). Englewood Cliffs, NJ: Prentice Hall.

Wagley, C. (1977). *Welcome of tears: The Tapirapé Indians of central Brazil.* New York: Oxford University Press.

Waite, L. J., & Gallagher, M. (2000). *The case for marriage: Why married people are happier.* New York: Doubleday.

Wald, A., Langenberg, A. G., Link, K., Izu, A. E., Ashley, R., Warren, T., Tyring, S., Douglas, J. M., & Corey, L. (2001). Effect of condoms on reducing the transmission of herpes simplex virus type 2 from men to women. *Journal of the American Medical Association, 285,* 3100–3106.

Waldinger, M. D., Berendsen, H. H. G., Blok, B. F. M., Olivier, B., & Holstege, G. (1998). Premature ejaculation and serotonergic antidepressants-induced delayed ejaculation: The involvement of the serotonergic system. *Behavioral Brain Research, 92,* 111–118.

Waldner, L. K., Sikka, A., & Baig, S. (1999). Ethnic and sex differences in university students' knowledge of AIDS, fear of AIDS, and homophobia. *Journal of Homosexuality, 37(3),* 117–133.

Waldo, C. R., Hesson–McInnis, M. S., & D'Augelli, A. R. (1998). Antecedents and consequences of victimization of lesbian, gay, and bisexual young people: A structural model comparing rural university and urban samples. *American Journal of Community Psychology, 26,* 307–334.

Waldo, C. R., & Kemp, J. L. (1997). Should I come out to my students? An empirical investigation. *Journal of Homosexuality, 34,* 79–94.

Walensky, L. D., Roskams, A. J., Lefkowitz, R. J., Snyder, S. H., & Ronnett, G. V. (1995). Odorant receptors and desensitization proteins localize in mammalian sperm. *Molecular Medicine, 1,* 130–141.

Walker, A., & Pratibha, P. (1993) *Warrior marks: Female genital mutilation and the sexual binding of women.* New York: Harcourt Brace.

Walker, B. D., & Goulder, P. J. R. (2000). AIDS: Escape from the immune system. *Nature, 407,* 313–314.

Walker, L. (1993). PTSD and child sexual abuse: Commentary. *Journal of Child Sexual Abuse 2,* 129–132.

Walkowitz, J. R. (1983). *Prostitution and Victorian society.* Cambridge, England: Cambridge University Press.

Wallace, R. A., Sander, G. P., & Ferl, R. J. (1999). *Biology: The Science of Life,* (4th ed.). NY: Harper Collins.

Wallen, K., Maestripieri, D., & Mann, D. R. (1995). Effects of neonatal testicular suppression with a GnRH antagonist on social behavior in group-living juvenile rhesus monkey. *Hormonal Behavior, 29,* 322–337.

Waller, W., & Hill, R. (1951). *The family: A dynamic interpretation.* New York: Dryden. (Original work published 1938)

Wallerstein, E. (1980). *Circumcision.* New York: Springer

Walster, E., Aronson, V., Abrahams, D., and Rottmann, L. Importance of physical attractiveness in dating behavior. *Journal of Personality and Social Psychology, 4, 1966,* 508–516.

Ward D., LeBlanc G., Shackelford T. (2000, June 7–11). *Preventing, correcting, and anticipating female infidelity: Three adaptive problems of sperm.* Paper presented at the meeting of The Human Behavior And Evolution Society.

Ward, T., McCormack, J., & Hudson, J. (1997). The assessment of rapists. *Behaviour Change, 14,* 34–54.

Ware, J. C., Hirshkowitz, M., Thornby, J., & Salis, P. (1997). Sleep-related erections: Absence of change following pre-sleep sexual arousal. *Journal of Psychosomatic Research, 42,* 547–553.

Warner, D. L., & Hatcher, R. A. (1954). Male condoms. In R. A. Hatcher et al. *Contraceptive technology,* (17th ed.), pp. 325–355. New York: Ardent Media.

Warner, D. L., & Hatcher, R. A. (1994). A meta-analysis of condom effectiveness in reducing sexually transmitted HIV. *Social Science Medicine, 38,* 1169–1170.

Warner, R. M., & Sugarman, D. B. (1986). Attributions of personality based on physical appearance, speech, and handwriting. *Journal of Personality and Social Psychology, 50,* 792–799.

Warnock, J. K., Bundren, J. C., & Morris, D. W. (1997). Female hypoactive sexual desire disorder due to androgen deficiency: Clinical and psychometric issues. *Psychopharmacology Bulletin, 33,* 761–766.

Warren, J. L., Reboussin, R., Hazelwood, R., & Wright, J. (1991). Prediction of rapist type and violence from verbal, physical, and sexual scales. *Journal of Interpersonal Violence, 6,* 55–67.

Warren, P. (1997, Aug.). Down and out. *The Advocate,* p, 5.

Waterman, C. K., Dawson, L. J., & Bologna, M. J. (1989). Sexual coercion in gay male and lesbian relationships: Prediction and implications for support services. *Journal of Sex Research, 26,* 118–124.

Watkin, N.A., Beiger, N.A., & Moisey, C.U. (1996). Is the conservative management of the acute scrotum justified on clinical grounds? *British Journal of Urology, 78,* 623–627.

Watson, P., & Thornhill, R. (1994). Fluctuating asymmetry and sexual selection. *Trends in Ecology and Evolution, 9,* 21–24.

Watson, R. (1999, May 27). In-flight video bid to combat sex tourism. *The [Glasgow] Herald,* p. 6.

Watson, R. E., & Dunlop, R. E. (1997). Premarital cohabitation vs. traditional courtship and subsequent marital adjustment: A replication and follow-up. *Family Relations: Journal of Applied Family and Child Studies 36,* 193–197.

Weinberg, G. (1973). *Society and the healthy homosexual.* New York: Anchor Press.

Weinberg, M. S., Williams, C. J., & Pryor, D. W. (1994). *Dual attraction: Understanding bisexuality* (pp. 26–38). New York: Oxford University Press.

Weiner, A. (1996). Understanding the social needs of streetwalking prostitutes. *Social Work, 41,* 97–106.

Weiner, D. M., & Lowe, F. C. (1998). Psychotropic drug-induced priapism: Incidence, mechanism and management. *CNS Drugs 9(5),* 371–379.

Weinrich, J. D. (1987). A new sociobiological theory of homosexuality applicable to societies with universal marriage. *Ethnology and Sociobiology, 8,* 37–47.

Weinstein, N. D. (1980). Unrealistic optimism about future life events. *Journal of Personality and Social Psychology, 39,* 806–820.

Weir, S., & Fine-Davis, M. (1989). "Dumb blonde" and "temperamental redhead": The effect of hair colour on some attributed personality characteristics of women. *Irish Journal of Psychology, 10,* 11–19.

Weisberg, D. K. (1985). *Children of the night.* Toronto, Ont.: Lexington Books.

Weiss, R. S. (1973). *Loneliness: The experience of emotional and social isolation.* Cambridge, Massachusetts: MIT Press

Weiss, R. S. (1987). How dare we? Scientists seek the sources of risk-taking behavior. *Science News, 132,* 57–59.

Weitz, C. M. (1985). Vaginal birth after cesarean section. *Postgraduate Obstetrics and Gynecology, 5,* 1–4.

Weitzman, L. (1983). *The divorce revolution.* NY: Free Press / Macmillan.

Welch, L. (1992). *The complete book of sexual trivia.* New York: Citadel Press.

Welch, M. R., & Kartub, P. (1978). Socio-cultural correlates of incidence of impotence: A cross-cultural study. *Journal of Sex Research, 14,* 218–230.

Weller, A., & Weller, L. (1993). Human menstrual synchrony: A crucial assessment. *Neuroscience and Biobehavioral Reviews, 16,* 427–439.

Weller, A., & Weller, L. (1998). Prolonged and very intensive contact may not be conductive to menstrual synchrony. *Psychoneuroendocrinology, 23,* 19–32.

Werner-Wilson, R. J. (1998). Gender differences in adolescent sexual attitudes: The influence of individual and family factors. *Adolescence, 33,* 519–531.

West, D. J. (1998). Boys and sexual abuse: An English opinion. *Archives of Sexual Behavior, 27,* 539–559.

Weston, L. (1980). Incidence, prevalence, and trends of acute pelvic inflammatory disease and its consequences in industrialized countries. *American*

Journal of Obstetrics & Gynecology, 13, 880–892.

Wheeler, J., & Kilmann, K. (1983). Communal sexual behavior: Individual and relationship variables. *Archives of Sexual Behavior, 12,* 295–306.

Wheeler, L., Reis, H., & Nezlek, J. B. (1983). Loneliness, social interaction, and sex roles. *Journal of Personality and Social Psychology, 45:* 943–953.

Wheeler, M. (1999). Home and laboratory pregnancy-testing kits. *Professional Nurse, 14,* 571–576.

Whipple, B., & Komisaruk, B. R. (1997). Sexuality and women with complete spinal cord injury. *Spinal Cord, 35,* 136–138.

Whipple, B., Myers, B. R., & Komisaruk, H. R. (1998). Male multiple ejaculatory orgasm: A case study. *Journal of Sex Education and Therapy, 23,* 157.

Whitbourne, S. K. (1988). Sexuality and aging. *Generations, 12,* 28–30.

White, B. H., & Kurpius, S. E. (1999). Attitudes toward rape victims. *Journal of Interpersonal Violence, 14,* 989–995.

White, G. (1980). Physical attractiveness and courtship process. *Journal of Personality and Social Psychology, 39,* 660–668.

White, G. L. (1980). Physical attractiveness and courtship progress. *Journal of Personality and Social Psychology, 39:* 660–668.

White, G. L. (1999). Attitudes toward victims of rape among university populations. *Dissertation Abstracts International Section A: Humanities and Social Sciences University Microfilms International 58:* 3435.

White, G. L., & Helbick, T. R. M. (1988). Understanding and treating jealousy. In R. A. Brown & J. R. Field (Eds.), *Treatment of sexual problems in individual and couples therapy* (pp. 245–265). Costa Mesa, CA: PMA Publishing Corp.

White, T. (1999). Homophobia: A misnomer. *Transactional Journal, 29,* 77–83.

Whitman, D. (1997, May 19) Was it good for us? *U.S. News & World Report* Archive.

Wiedeman, M. W. (1997). Extramarital sex: Prevalence and correlates in a national survey. *Journal of Sex Research, 24,* 167–174.

Wiederman, M. W., & Allgeier, E. R. (1993). Gender differences in sexual jealousy: adaptionist or social learning explanations? *Ethology and Sociobiology, 14:* 115–140.

Wiederman, M. W., & Kendall, E. (1999). Evolution, sex, and jealousy: Investigation with a sample from Sweden. *Evolution and Human Behavior, 20,* 121–128.

Wiederman, M. W., & LaMar, L. (1998). "Not with him you don't!": Gender and emotional reactions to sexual infidelity during courtship. *Journal of Sex Research, 35,* 288–297.

Wiest, W. (1977). Semantic differential profiles of orgasm and other experiences among men and women. *Sex Roles, 3,* 399–403.

Wikander, B., & Theorell, T. (1997). Fathers' experience of childbirth and its relation to crying in his infant. *Scandinavian Journal of Caring and Science, 11,* 151–158.

Wilcox, A., Weinberg, C., & Baird, D. (1995). Timing of sexual intercourse in relation to ovulation: Effects on the probability of conception, survival of the pregnancy and sex of the baby. *New England Journal of Medicine, 333,* 1517–1521.

Wilcox, B. L. (1987). Pornography, social science, and politics: When research and ideology collide. *American Psychologist, 42,* 941–943.

Wiles, R., & Cambell, C. (1993). Testimony before the subcommittee on health and the environment. House Committee on Energy and Commerce. Environmental working group. Washington, D.C.

Willett, W. C., Colditz, G., & Stampfer, M. (2000). Postmenopausal estrogen—opposed, unopposed, or none of the above. *Journal of the American Medical Association, 283,* 4.

Williams, J. E., & Best, D. L. (1994). Cross-cultural views of women and men. In W. J. Lonner & R. S.

Malpass (Eds.), *Psychology and culture* (pp. 191–196). Boston: Allyn & Bacon.

Williams, K., & Umberton, D. (1999). Medical technology and childbirth: Experiences of expectant mothers and fathers. *Sex Roles, 41,* 147–168.

Williams, L., & Sobieszczyk, T. (1997). Attitudes surrounding the continuation of female circumcision in the Sudan: Passing the tradition to the next generation. *Journal of Marriage and the Family, 59,* 966–981.

Williams, R. H. (1979). The ability of a simulation game to change attitudes when structured to conform to either the cognitive dissonance or incentive models of attitude change. *Dissertation Abstracts, 40,* 659–660.

Williams, T. (1980, c 1947). *A streetcar named desire.* New York: New Directions.

Williams, T. J., Pepitone, M. E., Christensen, S. E., Cooke, B. M., Huberman, A. D., Breedlove, N. J., Breedlove, T. J., Jordan, C. L., & Breedlove, S. M. (2000). Fingerlength ratios and sexual orientation. *Nature, 404,* 455–456.

Williamson, M. (1997). Circumcision anesthesia: A study of nursing implications for dorsal penile nerve block. *Pediatric Nursing, 23,* 59–63.

Willis, R. J., & Michael, R. T. (1994). Innovation in family formation: Evidence on cohabitation in the United States. In J. Ermisch & N. Ogawa (Eds.), *The family, the market, and the state in aging societies* (pp. 119–145). London: Oxford.

Willis, S. E., & Horner, R. D. (1987). Attitudes, experience, and knowledge of family physicians regarding child sexual abuse. *Journal of Family Practice, 25,* 516–519.

Wilson, E. O. (1975). *Sociobiology: The new synthesis.* Cambridge: Harvard University Press.

Wilson, G. D. (1997). Gender differences in sexual fantasy: An evolutionary analysis. *Personality and Individual Differences, 22,* 27–31.

Wilson, J. D., George, F., & Griffin, J. (1981). The hormonal control of

sexual development. *Science, 211,* 1278–1284.

Wincze, J. P., Bansal, D., Malbotra, A., Balka, J. G., Susset, J. G., & Malmud, M. (1988). A comparison of nocturnal penile tumescence and penile response to erotic stimulation during waking states in comprehensively diagnosed groups of males experiencing erectile dysfunction. *Archives of Sexual Behavior, 17,* 333–348.

Winick, C. (1962). Prostitutes clients' perception of the prostitutes and themselves. *International Journal of Social Psychology, 8,* 2889ff.

Winn, R. L., & Newton, N. (1982). Sexuality in aging: A study of 106 cultures. *Archives of Sexual Behavior, 11,* 283–298.

Winton, M. A. (2001). The medicalization of male sexual dysfunctions: An analysis of sex therapy journals. *Journal of Sex Education and Therapy, 25,* 231–239.

Wise, T. N., & Meyer, J. K. (1980). The border area between transvestism and gender dysphoria: Transvestitic applicants for sex reassignment. *Archives of Sexual Behavior, 9:* 327–342.

Wiswell, T. E. (1997). Circumcision-circumspection. *New England Journal of Medicine, 336,* 1244–1245.

Woldorff, M. G., Gallen, C. C., Hampson, S. A., Hillyard, S. A., Pantev, C., Sobel, D., & Bloom, F. E. (1993). Modulation of early sensory processing in human auditory cortex during auditory selective attention. *Proc Natl Acad Sci U S A 90,* 8722–8726.

Wolfe, L. (1993). *Women who never marry: The reasons, realities and opportunities.* Atlanta: Longstreet Press.

Wood, W., Rhodes, N., & Wheland, M. (1989). Sex differences in positive well-being: A consideration of emotional style and marital status. *Psychological Bulletin, 106,* 249–264.

Woodward, J. C., & Kalvan-Masih, V. (1990). Loneliness, coping strategies and cognitive styles of the gifted rural adolescent. *Adolescence, 25,* 977–988.

Woods, N., Lentz, M., Mitchell, E., Lee, K., Taylor, D., & Allen-Barash,

N. (1987). Women's health: The menstrual cycle/premenstrual symptoms: Another look. *Public Health Reports, 102,* 106–112.

Woody, J. D., Russel, R., D'Souza, H. J., & Woody, J. K. (2000). Non-coital sex among adolescent virgins and non-virgins. *Journal of Sex Education and Therapy, 25,* 4, 261–268.

Woodzicka, J. A., & LaFrance, M. (2001). Real versus imagined gender harassment. *Journal of Social Issues, 57,* 15–30.

Workman, J. E., & Freeburg, E. W. (1999). An examination of date rape, victim dress, and perceiver variables within the context of attribution theory. *Sex Roles 41,* 261–277.

World Health Organization. (1996). *Global prevalence and incidence of selected curable sexually transmitted diseases: Overview and estimates.* Geneva, Switzerland: Author.

World Health Organization. (1998a, Apr. 8). Cited in *Medical Industry Today* from http://www.medicaldata.com/MIT/default.asp

World Health Organization. (1998b). *Facts and figures about STDs.* Geneva, Switzerland: Author.

World Health Organization. (1998c). *Gender and health.* Geneva, Switzerland: Author.

World Health Organization. (2000a, June). *Female genital mutilation. WHO fact sheet No. 241.* Geneva, Switzerland: WHO Press Release.

World Health Organization. (2000b), HIV/AIDS STI surveillance: Report on the global HIV/AIDS epidemic. Geneva, Switzerland: Author.

World Health Organization. (2000c, April 10). In Strategies for safer blood, *The New York Times,* p. A18.

Worthman, C. M. (1999). Faster, farther, higher: Biology and the discourses on human sexuality. In D. N. Suggs & A. W. Miracle (Eds.), *Culture, biology, and sexuality* (pp. 64–75). Athens: University of Georgia Press.

Worthman, C. M., Beall, C. M., & Stallings, J. F (1997). Population variation in reproductive function in

men. *American Journal of Physical Anthropology*, suppl. 24, 246.

Wortley, D. M., Hammond, T. A, & Fleming, P. L. (1998). Donor insemination and human immunodeficiency virus transmission. *Obstetrics and Gynecology*, 91, 515–518.

Wright, T. C., Denny, L., Kuh, L., Pollack, A., & Lorincz, A. (2000). HPV DNA testing of self-collected vaginal samples compared with cytologic screening to detect cervical cancer. *Journal of the American Medical Association*, 283, 81–86.

Wyatt, G. E., Loeb, T. B., Solis, B., Carmona, J. V., & Romero, G. (1999). The prevalence and circumstances of child sexual abuse: Changes across a decade. *Child Abuse and Neglect*, 23, 45–60.

Xantidis, L., & McCabe, M. P. (2000). Personality characteristics of male clients of female commercial sex workers in Australia. *Archives of Sexual Behavior*, 29, 165–176.

Xu, Y., Shen, Z. S., Wiper, D. W., Minzhi, W., Morton, R. E., Elson, P., Kennedy, A. W., Belinson, J., Markman, M., & Casey, G. (1998). Lysophosphatidic acid as a potential biomarker for ovarian and other cancers. *Journal of the American Medical Association*, 280, 719–723.

Yarab, P. E., Allgeir, E. R., & Sensibaugh, C. C. (1999). Looking deeper: Extradydadic behaviors, jealousy and perceived unfaithfulness in hypothetical dating relationships. *Personal Relationships*, 5, 305–316.

Yesalis, C. E., Barsukiewicz, D. K., Kopstein, A. N., & Bahrke, M. S. (1997, Dec.). Trends in anabolic-androgenic steroid use among adolescents. *Archives of Pediatric & Adolescent Medicine*, 151, 1197–1206.

Yesalis, C. E., Wright, J. E., & Bahrke, M. S. (1989, Sept.). Epidemiological and policy issues in the measurement of the long term health effects of anabolic-androgenic steroids. *Sports Medicine*, 8, 129–138.

Young, R. K., & Thiessen, D. (1992). The Texas rape scale. *Ethnology and Sociobiology*, 13, 19–33.

Zaviacic, M., & Whipple, B. (1993). Update on the female prostate and the phenomenon of female ejaculation. *Journal of Sex Research*, 30, 148–151.

Zabin, L. S., Hirsch, M. B., & Emerson, M. R. (1989). When urban adolescents choose abortion: Effects on education, psychological status and subsequent pregnancy. *Family Planning Perspectives*, 21, 248–255.

Zaidel, D. W., Chen, A. C., & German, C. (1995). She is not a beauty even when she smiles: Possible evolutionary basis for a relationship between facial attractiveness and hemispheric specialization. *Neuropsychologia*, 33, 649–655.

Zax, M., Sameroff, A. J., Farnum, J. E. (1975, Sept. 15). Childbirth education, maternal attitudes, and delivery. *American Journal of Obstetrics & Gynecology*, 123, 185–190.

Zgourides, G., Monto, M., & Harris, R. (1997). Correlates of adolescent male sexual offense: Prior adult sexual contact, sexual attitudes, and use of sexually explicit materials. *International Journal of Offender Therapy & Comparative Criminology*, 41, 272–283.

Zhou, J., Hoffman, M., Gooren, L., & Swaab, D. (1995). A sex difference in the human brain and its relation to transsexuality. *Nature*, 378, 68–70.

Zilbergeld, B., & Evans, M. (1980). The inadequacy of Masters and Johnson. *Psychology Today*, 14, 29–43.

Zillmann, D. (2000). *Media entertainment: The psychology of its appeal*. Mahwah, NJ: Erlbaum.

Credits

CHAPTER 8 PHOTOS **242** CORBIS **243** CORBIS **245** CORBIS **246** (left) The Image Works **246** (right) CORBIS **258** CORBIS TEXT **238** T8.1 from "Sexual Rules" from http://www.discovery.com/area/history/courtship. Used with permission from Discovery.com. **240** T8.2 from "Cultural Codes on 20 Sexual Attitudes and Practices" by G. J. Broude and S. J. Green, *Ethnology*, 15, 1976. Copyright © 1976. Reprinted by permission of *Ethnology*, Department of Anthropology, University of Pittsburgh. **243** T8.3 Table, p. 116 from *Sex in America: A Definitive Survey* by Robert T. Michael, John H. Gagnor, Edward O. Laumann and Gina Kolata. Copyright © 1992. Reprinted by permission of Little, Brown, & Company. **257** T8.4 from "Cultural Codes on 20 Sexual Attitudes & Practices" by G. J. Broude and S. J. Green, *Ethnology*, 15, 1976. Copyright © 1976. Reprinted by permission of *Ethniology*, Department of Anthropology, University of Pittsburgh.

CHAPTER 9 PHOTOS **264** The Image Works **266** Photo Researchers, Inc. **269** Photo Researchers, Inc. **272** (top) *Boys Don't Cry* © 1999 Fox Searchlight Pictures, Inc. All rights reserved **272** (bottom) Stock Boston **277** Stock Boston **280** CORBIS **282** Photo Researchers, Inc. **289** Visuals Unlimited TEXT **265** T9.1 From Table 5, p.e9 from "Normative Sexual Behavior in Children: A Contemporary Sample" by W. N. Friedrich, J. Fisher, D. Broughton, M. Houston, and C. R. Shafran, *Pediatrics*, 101, 1998. Copyright © 1998 by American Academy of Pediatrics. Reprinted with permission. **266** T9.2 from "Sexual Behaviors of Young Children that Occur in Schools" by F. Kaeser, D. DiSalvo, and R. Maglia in *Journal of Sex Education and Therapy*, 25, 2001. Copyright © 2001. Reprinted by permission of Guilford Press. **268** T9.4 from *The Kinsey Institute New Report on Sex: What You Must Know to be Sexually Literate* by J. Reinisch. Copyright © 1991. Reprinted by permission of St. Martin's Press. **268** T9.5 From *The Kinsey Institute New Report on Sex: What You Must Know to be Sexually Literate* by J. Reinisch. Copyright © 1991. Reprinted by permission of St. Martin's Press. **269** T9.6 Figure 4 from "Secondary Sexual Characteristics and Menses from the Pediatric Research Office Settings Network" by Herman-Giddens, et al, *Pediatrics*, 99, 1997. Copyright © 1997 by American Academy of Pediatrics. Reprinted with permission. **270** Quote from "Personality Development in Adolescence" by O. Siegel, *Handbook of Developmental Psychology* ed. by B. B. Wolman, et al. Copyright © 1982. Reprinted by permission of Pearson Education. **271** T9.8 From *Sex in America: A Definitive Survey* by Robert T. Michael, John H. Gagnor, Edward O. Laumann and Gina Kolata. Copyright © 1992. Reprinted by permission of Little, Brown & Company. **275** T9.9 from http://www.unmarried.org. Alternatives to Marriage Project. Used with permission. **281** T2.10 Table from pp. 116-117 from *The Social Organization of Sexuality: Sexual Practive in the* US by Edward O. Laumann, et al. Copyright © 1994.k Reprinted with permission of The University of Chicago Press. **283** Quote from *Anatomy of Love: A Natural History of Monogamy, Adultery, and Divorce* by H. Fisher. Copyright © 1992. Reprinted by permission of W. W. Norton & Com-

pany. **285** T9.13 from *Varieties of Sexual Experience: An Anthropological Perspective on Human Sexuality* by Frayser. Copyright © 1985. Reprinted by permission of HRAP from Human Relations Area Files. **288** Quote from *Anatomy of Love: A Natural History of Monogamy, Adultery, and Divorce* by H. Fisher. Copyright © 1992. Reprinted by permission of W. W. Norton & Company. **289** Quote from *The Pursuit of Pleasure* by L. Tiger. Copyright ©1992. Reprinted by permission of Little, Brown & Company. **289** T9.14 Table from pp.313-316 in *Love, Sex, and Aging* by Brecher. Copyright © 1984. Reprinted by permission of Little, Brown, and Company.

CHAPTER 10 PHOTOS **295** (top) National Library of Medicine **295** (bottom) Visuals Unlimited **297** National Library of Medicine **298** National Library of Medicine **305** Stock Boston **306** Pearson Education/PH College **313** Smithsonian Institution/Office of Imaging, Printing, and Photographic Services **318** (top) CORBIS **318** (bottom) Photo Courtesy of Daniel P. Greenwald, M.D. FACS, Bayshore Plastic Surgery **319** Photos Courtesy of Daniel P. Greenwald, M.D. FACS, Bayshore Plastic Surgery TEXT **294** Box from "Sio Journal: Oh No! My Little Brother Has Just Had a Baby!" by N. Onishi in *The New York Times*, May 3, 2001. Copyright © 2001 by The New York Times Company. Reprinted by permission. **302** Quote from *Sex on the Brain* by Deborah Blum. Copyright © 1997 by Deborah Blum. Used by permission of Viking Penguin, a division of Penguin Putnam, Inc. **302** F10.4 Figure from "Sex Differences in the Brain" by D. Kimura in *Scientific American*, Vol. 267, (3), September 1992. Copyright © 1992. Reprinted by permission of Scientific American. **306** Quote from *Anatomy of Love: A Natural History of Monogamy, Adultery, and Divorce* by H. Fisher. Copyright © 1992. Reprinted by permission of W. W. Norton & Company. **307** T10.5 Table 1 from "Cross-Cultural Views of Women and Men" by J. E. Williams and D. L. Best in *Psychology and Culture* ed. by W. J. Lonner and R. Malpass. Copyright © 1994. Reprinted by permission of Allyn and Bacon.

CHAPTER 11 PHOTOS **327** (left) CORBIS **327** (right) Photofest **330** Jeroboam, Inc. **332** The Image Works **335** Stock Boston **337** (top) Visuals Unlimited **337** (bottom) Stock Boston **341** AP/Wide World Photos TEXT **325** F11.1 Figure from *Sexual Behavior in the Human Male* by A. Kinsey, et al. Copyright 1948. Reproduced by permission of Indiana University Press. **326** T11.1 From *The Bisexual Option* by Klein. Copyright © 1990 by The Harrington Park Press. Reprinted by permission of Haworth Press, Inc. **330** Quote from p. 230 in *Nothin' But Good Times Ahead* by Molly Ivins. Copyright © 1993. Reprinted by permission of Random House. **331** Quote from Foreword by Archbishop Desmond Tutu from *We Were Baptized Too: Claiming God's Grace for Lesbians and Gays* by Marilyn B. Alexander and James Preston. Copyright © 1996. Reprinted by permission of Westminster John Knox Press. **333** T11.2 from "Survey Finds US Divided Over Gays" by J. Schmalz in *The Oregonian*, March 5, 1993, p. A17. Copyright © 1993. Reprinted by permission of the publisher. **338** T11.3 from *Queer*

Counts: The Sociological Construction of Homosexuality via Survey Research, NORC, 1994. Reprinted by permission of NORC, Chicago, IL.

CHAPTER 12 PHOTOS **348** The Image Works **358** (top) Photo Researchers, Inc. **358** (bottom) Woodfin Camp & Associates **367** CORBIS **368** Joel Gordon Photography **402** Unidentified Woman (Formerly Edward Hyde, Lord (Viscount) Cornbury) by Unidentified artist, early 18th Century, oil on canvas, 49 1/4" x 38 7/8", accession number 1952.80, negative number 4260. © Collection of The New-York Historical Society TEXT **348** Quote from *Women on Top: How Real Life Has Changed Women's Fantasies* by Nancy Friday. Copyright © 1991. Reprinted by permission of Simon & Schuster. **351** T12.1 From "Gender Differences in Sexual Fantasy and Behavior in a College Population: A Ten-Year Replication" by R. Hsu in *Journal of Sex and Marital Therapy*, 20, 1994. Copyright © 1994. Reproduced by permission of Taylor & Francis, Inc., http://www.routledge-ny.com. **352** Quote from p. 99 in *Heterosexuality* by Masters, Johnson, and Kolodny. Copyright © 1994. Reprinted by permission of HarperCollins Publishers, Inc. **354** Quote from *The Pursuit of Pleasure* by L. Tiger. Copyright © 1992. Reprinted by permission of Little, Brown & Company. **355** F12.2 from *The Hite Report: A Nationwide Study of Female Sexuality* by S. Hite, Copyright © 1976. Reprinted by permission of Simon & Schuster. **359** T12.2 from p. 141 in *Sex in America: A Definitive Survey* by Robert T. Michael, John H. Gagnor, Edward O. Laumann & Gina Kolata. Copyright © 1992. Reprinted by permission of Little, Brown & Company. **361** T12.3 from p. 141 in *Sex in America: A Definitive Survey* by Robert T. Michael, John H. Gagnor, Edward O. Laumann and Gina Kolata. Copyright © 1992. Reprinted by permission of Little, Brown & Company. **363** Quote from *The Pursuit of Pleasure* by L. Tiger. Copyright © 1992. Reprinted by permission of Little, Brown & Company.

CHAPTER 13 PHOTOS **374** Photo Researchers, Inc. **380** CORBIS **400** The Image Works **405** The Image Works **407** AP/Wide World Photos TEXT **381** F13.1 from "Report Finds 1 in 5 Infected by Virus Spread Sexually" by Barringer in *The New York Times*, April 1, 1993. Copyright © 1993 by The New York Times Company. Reprinted by permission of The New York Times Company. **384** Considerations Box from http://www.girlsinc.org, 2000. By permission of Girls, Inc. **385** Quote from *Against Out Will* by Susan Brownmiller. Copyright © 1975 by Linda Brownmiller. Reprinted with permission of Simon & Schuster. **385** Quote from *Sexual Violence* by Linda Fairstein. Copyright © 1993 by Linda A. Fairstein. Reprinted by permission of HarperCollins Publishers, Inc. **389** F13.2 From "Attitudes About Date Rape: Gender Differences Among College Students" by D. R. Holcomb, L. C. Holcomb, K. A. Sondag, and N. Williams from *College Student Journal*, 25, 1991. Copyright © 1991. Published by permission of Project Innovation, Inc., P. O. Box 8508, Spring Hill Station, Mobile, AL, 36689-0508. **392** F13.3 from *The Social Organization of Sexuality: Sexual Practice in the US* by Edward Laumann, et al. Copyright © 1994. Reprinted by permission of The University of Chicago Press. **405** F13.4 from *The*

Social Organization of Sexuality: Sexual Practice in the US by Edward Laumann, et al. Copyright © 1994. Reprinted by permission of The University of Chicago Press.

CHAPTER 14 PHOTOS **416** (top) Woodfin Camp & Associates **416** (bottom) Joel Gordon Photography **421** Retna Ltd. USA **423** Woodfin Camp & Associates **425** Woodfin Camp & Associates **431** Joel Gordon Photography **434** (top) PhotoEdit **434** (bottom) AP/Wide World Photos **435** Joel Gordon Photography TEXT **431** F14.1 from p. 157 in *Sex in America: A Definitive Survey* by Robert T. Michael, John H. Gagnor, Edward O. Laumann and Gina Kolata. Copyright © 1992. Reprinted by permission of Little, Brown & Company. **432** F14.2 from "In the Garden of Tabloid Delight" by L. Lapham in *Harper's Magazine*, August 1997. Copyright © 1997 by *Harper's Magazine*. All rights reserved. Reproduced by special permission.

CHAPTER 15 PHOTOS **446** (left) CORBIS **446** (center) © Mitchell Gerber/CORBIS **446** (right) © Rufus F. Folkks/CORBIS **448** Photo Researchers, Inc. **450** Dr. Judith Langlois **453** (top) CORBIS **453** (bottom) The Image Works **458** CORBIS **460** CORBIS TEXT **441** F15.1 from *Love and Sex: Cross-Cultural Perspectives* by Elaine Hatfield and Richard L. Rapson. Copyright © 1996. Reprinted by permission of Allyn and Bacon. **442** F15.2 from p. 122 in "The Triangle of Love" by R. J. Sternberg in *The Psychology of Love* ed. by D. J. Sternberg and M. L. Barnes. Copyright © 1988. Reprinted by permission of Yale University Press. **443** T15.1 from "A triangular Theory of Love" by R. Sternberg in *Psychological Review*, 93, 1986. Copyright © 1986 by the American Psychological Association. Adapted with permission. **445** F15.3 "The Chemistry of Love" from "How Do Fools Fall in Love?" by Nigel Holmes, *Time*, February 15, 1993. Copyright © 1993 by Time, Inc. Reprinted by permission. **447** Quote from *Anatomy of Love: A Natural History of Monogamy, Adultery, and Divorce* by H. Fisher. Copyright © 1992. Reprinted by permission of W. W. Norton & Company. **459** T15.4 from "Sex Differences in Human Mate Preferences: Evolutionary Hypotheses Tested in 37 Cultures" by D. M. Buss in *Behavioral & Brain Sciences*, Vol. 12, 1989. Copyright © 1989. Reprinted by permission of Cambridge University Press. **461** T15.5 from *Love and Limerance* by Dorothy Tennov. Copyright © 1979. Reprinted by permission of Madison Books, Inc. **462** T15.6 from *The Janus Report on Sexual Behavior* by S. S. Janus and C. L. Janus. Copyright © 1993. Reprinted by permission of John Wiley and Sons, Inc. **463** T15.7 from "International Preferences in Selecting Mates: A Story of 37 Cultures" by D. M. Buss, et al in *Journal of Cross-Cultural Psychology*, 21, 1990. Copyright © 1990. Reprinted by permission of Sage Publications, Inc. **466** F15.4 from *Love and Sex: Cross-Cultural Perspectives* by Elaine Hatfield and Richard L. Rapson. Copyright © 1996. Reprinted by permission of Allyn and Bacon. **468** Quote from p. 66 in *Sex on the Brain* by Deborah Blum. Copyright © 1997 by Deborah Blum. Used by permission of Viking Penguin, a division of Penguin Putnam, Inc. **469** Quote from *Anatomy of Love: A Natural History of Monogamy, Adultery, and Divorce* by H. Fisher. Copy-

right © 1992. Reprinted by permission of W. W. Norton & Company. **469** T15.9 from *Why Marriages Succeed or Fail* by John Gottman. Copyright © 1994. Reprinted by permission of Simon & Schuster, Inc. **469** T15.10 from *Why Marriages Succeed or Fail* by John Gottman. Copyright © 1994. Reprinted by permission of Simon & Schuster, Inc.

CHAPTER 16 PHOTOS **477** Custom Medical Stock Photo, Inc. **478** The Image Works **485** Retna Ltd. USA **489** Photofest **490** AP/Wide World Photos TEXT **475** Quote from *Anatomy of Love: A Natural History of Monogamy, Adultery, and Divorce* by H. Fisher. Copyright © 1992. Reprinted by permission of W. W. Norton & Company. **476** T16.1 from p. 368 in *The Social Organization of Sexuality: Sexual Practice in the US* by Edward Laumann, et al. Copyright © 1994. Reprinted by permission of The University of Chicago Press. **479** F16.1 from The Alan Guttmacher Institute, *Into a New World: Young Women's Sexual and Reproductive Lives*, New York: The Alan Guttmacher Institute, 1998. Used with permission. **480** T16.2 from "Breaking Up Is (Relatively) Easy To Do: A Script for Dissolution of Close Relationships" by D. M. Battaglia, et al, in *Journal of Social and Personal Relationships*, 15, 1998. Copyright © 1998. Reprinted by permission of Sage Publications, UK. **480** F16.2 from The Alan Guttmacher Institute, *Into a New World: Young Women's Sexual and Reproductive Lives*, New York: The Alan Guttmacher Institute, 1998. Used with permission. **487** T16.6 From "Distinguishing the Experiences of Envy and Jealousy" by W. G. Parrott and R. H. Smith in *Journal of Personality & Social Psychology*, 64, 1993. Copyright © 1993 by the American Psychological Association. Adapted with permission. **488** F16.3 from "Breaking Away: How College Students End Love Relationships" by D. Knox, L. H. Walters, and J. Walters, *College Student Journal*, 32, 1998. Copyright © 1998. **489** Quote reprinted with the permission of The Free Press, a Division of Simon & Schuster, Inc. from *The Dangerous Passion: Why Jealousy Is As Necessary As Love and Sex* by David M. Buss. Copyright © 2000 by David M. Buss. **494** T16.8 from "The Subjective Experience of Intimacy: Passion and Commitment in Heterosexual Loving" by P. J. Marston, M. L. Hecht, M. L. Manke, S. McDaniel, and H. Reeder in *Personal Relationships*, Vol. 5, 1998. Copyright © 1998. Reprinted by permission of Cambridge University Press.

CHAPTER 17 PHOTOS **500** Scala/Art Resource, NY **504** CORBIS **505** Stock Boston **507** Aurora & Quanta Productions **508** Photo Researchers, Inc. **510** PhotoEdit **512** The Granger Collection **513** Philip Goldman Collection, London TEXT **502** T17.2 from p. 237 in *The Social Organization of Sexuality: Sexual Practice in the US* by Edward Laumann, et al. Copyright © 1994. Reprinted by permission of The University of Chicago Press. **506** Quote from p. 9 in "A Theology of Sexual Pleasure" by W. Stayton, *SIECUS Report*, Vol. 20, 1992. Copyright © 1992. Reprinted by permission of SIECUS. **511** Quote by Tao Te Ching, p. 15 in *The Inner Teaching of Taoism* by Chang, trans. by T. Leary. Copyright © 1991. Reprinted by permission of Shambhala Publications, Inc.

CHAPTER 18 PHOTOS **520** Retna Ltd. USA **522** AP/Wide World Photos **524** AP/Wide World Photos **531** AP/Wide World Photos **536** Photo Researchers, Inc. TEXT **519** Quote from *The Pursuit of Pleasure* by L. Tiger. Copyright © 1992. Reprinted by permission of Little, Brown & Company. **521** F18.1 From SIECUS, 2000. Used with permission. **524** T18.1 from The Gallup Organization, 2001. Used with permission. **525** F18.2 Map as reported on http://www.aclu.issues/gay/haymar.html, American Civil Liberties Union, 1998. Copyright © 1998 by American Civil Liberties Union. Reprinted with permission of the American Civil Liberties Union. **526** T18.3 from The Gallup Organization, 2002. Used with permission. **528** Quote from *Report on the Global HIV/AIDS Epidemic*, UNAIDS, 1999, p. 3. Reproduced by kind permission of the Joint United Nations Programme on HIV/AIDS (UNAIDS). **530** F18.3 Figure from Lambda Legal Defense and Education Fund, June 1997. Used with permission. **535** F18.4 From NARAL, 2000. Used with permission. **537** Considerations Box from The Alan Guttmacher Institute, *Into a New World: Young Women's Sexual and Reproductive Lives*, New York: The Alan Guttmacher Institute, 1998. Used with permission. **538** F18.5 from NARAL, 2000. Used with permission. **539** Ask Yourself Box from "Validation of a Scale to Measure Reasoning About Abortion" by N. K. Parsons, R. C. Richards, G. D. Kanter in Journal of Counseling Psychology, 37, 1990. Copyright © 1990 by the American Psychological Association. Adapted with permission. **541** Quote from "Washington to Hollywood: Oh, Behave. Movies, CDs and Videogames are Already Playing Rough with Kids. Should Government Elbow In?" by R. Lacayo, *Time*, September 18, 2000. Copyright © 2000 by Time, Inc. Reprinted with permission.

CHAPTER 19 PHOTOS **554** Getty Images, Inc. **557** Photo Researchers, Inc. TEXT **552** T19.2 from The Alan Guttmacher Institute, *Into a New World: Young Women's Sexual and Reproductive Lives*, New York: The Alan Guttmacher Institute, 1998. Used with permission. **556** F19.2 from The Alan Guttmacher Institute, *Into a New World: Young Women's Sexual and Reproductive Lives*, New York: The Alan Guttmacher Institute, 1998. Used with permission. **557** Considerations Box from *SIECUS Guidelines* 1990. Used with permission.

CHAPTER 20 PHOTOS **566** Photo Researchers, Inc. **567** Andrew W. Miracle **568** Joel Gordon Photography **578** Woodfin Camp & Associates TEXT **569** Ask Yourself Box from "Multidimensionality of Sexual Attitudes" by Hendrick & Hendrick, *Journal of Sex Research*, 23, 1987. Copyright © 1987. Reprinted by permission of Copyright Clearance Center. **570** T20.1 From p. 159 in *Culture in Clinical Care* by Bonder, Martin, & Miracle. Copyright © 2001. Used by permission of SLACK Incorporated. **583** Quote from *Love Story* by Erich Segal. Reprinted by permission of HarperCollins Publishers, Inc. **584** Quote from p. 175 in "Marx, Sex, and the Transformation of Society" by V. Held, *Philosophical Forum*, 5, 1993. Copyright © 1993. Reprinted by permission.

Name Index

Subject Index